From the Authors

So . . . why write another textbook on Strategic Management? After all, isn't this an already crowded market? Is there really something missing in the current books—something so important that a new book must be written?

We think "yes". But here is the irony—the thing missing in most other textbooks is that *nothing* is missing. Most of these books incorporate virtually every idea, every concept, and every theory that has been mentioned in strategic management literature in the last 20 years. First editions are inclusive. Later editions are more inclusive as authors compare their texts with other texts to make sure that everything "is covered".

Our view in writing this text is different. We believe that because most strategic management texts are missing nothing, they are missing the most important thing—a point of view, a consistent perspective, an integrating framework broad enough to be applied in analyzing a wide variety of cases and business settings, but simple enough to understand and share with others. This text introduces such an integrative framework—The VRIO framework. Many of you already know this framework and its relationship to the resource-based theory of strategy. This is the first undergraduate text that uses such a theory-based, multi-chapter organizing framework to introduce additional structure to the field of strategic management.

Now, don't worry. That much of the text is organized around a single framework doesn't mean that critical ideas and theories are ignored. It's all here—the five forces framework, competitive dynamics, the value chain, generic strategies, corporate strategy, and so forth. In fact, because the VRIO framework provides a simple integrative structure, we are actually able to address issues in this book that are largely ignored elsewhere—including discussions of vertical integration, outsourcing, real options logic, and mergers and acquisitions, to name just a few. In the end, every concept had to pass a simple test to be included in the book: **"Does this concept help students analyze cases and real business situations?"** If "yes," the concept was in. If "no," it was out.

This "less is more" strategy has some obvious implications. First, this book is shorter than the competition (we include fewer, but far more selective cases and tightly integrate them within the parts of the book). Second, instead of buying a huge book and using less than half of it, students using this book will use more of it—both the text and the cases that are closely linked to the text. Third, and most importantly we have included fewer topics albeit more tightly connected through an integrative framework—VRIO. This promotes real understanding versus rote memorization. The result of real understanding is that this book provides students with the tools they need to do strategic analysis. Nothing more. Nothing less.

Other Benefits

Element	Description	Benefit	Example
Chapter Opening Cases	We have chosen firms that are familiar to most students. Opening cases focus on competing strategies in the music download industry; TiVO's challenges in changing the way we watch TV; how Electronic Arts dominates the video game industry; whether or not Wal-Mart can continue its remarkable success; the secret of Victoria's Secret's success; and how HBO is able to produce such successful series as *Sex in the City*, *The Sopranos*, etc. Cases are integrated throughout the chapters.	By having cases tightly linked to the material, students can develop strategic analysis skills by studying firms familiar to them.	3-4
Full Length Cases	This book contains selective, part-ending cases that underscore the concepts in each part. This provides a tight link to the chapter concepts to reinforce understanding of recent research. These are 1) decision oriented, 2) recent, 3) student-recognized companies and 4) cases where the data are only partly analyzed.	Provides a tight link to chapter concepts, facilitating students' ability to apply text ideas to case analysis.	1-56–1-64 (*Concepts and Cases* only)
Strategy in Depth	For professors and students interested in understanding the full intellectual underpinnings of the field (knowledge in strategic management, continuous to evolve rapidly, some beyond what is normally included in an introductory text), we have included an optional *Strategy in Depth* feature in every chapter.	Customize your course as desired to provide enrichment material for advanced students.	282-283
Research Made Relevant	The *Research Made Relevant* feature highlights very current research findings related to some of the strategic topics discussed in that chapter.	Shows students the evolving nature of strategy.	250-251
Challenge Questions	These might be of an ethical or moral nature, forcing students to apply concepts across chapters, apply concepts to themselves, or extend chapter ideas in creative ways.	Requires students to think critically.	110
Problem Set	*Problem Set* asks students to apply theories and tools from the chapter. These often require calculations. They can be thought of as homework assignments. If students struggle with these they might have more trouble with the more complex cases. These problem sets are largely diagnostic in character.	Sharpens quantitative skills, and provides a bridge between chapter material and case analysis.	142-143
Ethics and Strategy	Highlights some of the most important dilemmas faced by firms when creating and implementing strategies.	Helps students make better ethical decisions as managers.	229
Global Perspectives	Most firms, most of the time, need to be concerned about global issues. Thus, we have integrated a global perspective into each chapter in two ways 1) Each chapter has a section that discusses the issues raised in that chapter in a global context; 2) Each chapter includes a *Global Perspectives* feature that provides an extended example of a strategic issue in a global context.	Gets students to think about the global implications of strategic decision making.	193
Strategy in the Emerging Enterprise	Growing number of graduates work for small and medium-sized firms. This feature presents an extended example, in each chapter, of the unique strategic problems facing those employed in small and medium-sized firms.	This feature highlights the unique challenges of doing strategic analysis in emerging enterprises, and small and medium-sized firms.	132-133
Tools for the Professors	We have provided a suite of tools to help support you, the professor. They include: ■ Instructor's Manual ■ Case Teaching Notes ■ Computerized Test Bank ■ Test Bank ■ Companion Web site		

V R I O

"VALUE. RARITY. IMITABILITY. ORGANIZATION."

What Is It?

This book is not just a list of concepts, models and theories. It is the first undergraduate textbook to introduce a **theory-based, multi-chapter organizing framework** to add additional structure to the field of strategic management.

"VRIO" is a mechanism that integrates two existing theoretical frameworks: the positioning perspective and the resource-based view. It is the primary tool for accomplishing internal analysis. It stands for four questions one must ask about a resource or capability to determine its competitive potential:

1. **The Question of Value:** Does a resource enable a firm to exploit an environmental opportunity, and/or neutralize an environmental threat?
2. **The Question of Rarity:** Is a resource currently controlled by only a small number of competing firms?
3. **The Question of Imitability:** Do firms without a resource face a cost disadvantage in obtaining or developing it?
4. **The Question of Organization:** Are a firm's other policies and procedures organized to support the exploitation of its valuable, rare, and costly-to-imitate resources?

What's the Benefit of the VRIO Framework?

The VRIO framework is the organizational foundation of the text. **It creates a decision-making framework for students** to use in analyzing case and business situations.

Students tend to view concepts, models, and theories (in all of their coursework) as fragmented and disconnected. Strategy is no exception. This view encourages rote memorization, not real understanding. VRIO, by serving as a consistent framework, connects ideas together. This encourages real understanding, not memorization.

This understanding enables students to better analyze business cases and situations—the goal of the course.

The VRIO framework makes it possible to discuss the formulation and implementation of a strategy simultaneously, within each chapter.

Because the VRIO framework provides a simple integrative structure, we are actually able to address issues in this book that are largely ignored elsewhere— including discussions of vertical integration, outsourcing, real options logic, and mergers and acquisitions, to name just a few.

Author Biographies

JAY B. BARNEY

Jay B. Barney is a Professor of Management and holder of the Bank One Chair in Strategic Management at the Fisher College of Business, The Ohio State University. He received his undergraduate degree from Brigham Young University, and his master's and Ph.D. from Yale University. After graduation, he served on the faculties at UCLA and at Texas A&M University. Professor Barney moved to Ohio State in 1994 where he teaches business policy and strategy.

He has also taught in a variety of executive programs at Ohio State, Texas A&M, UCLA, Southern Methodist University, Texas Christian University, the University of Michigan, Bocconi University (in Milan, Italy), and for the consulting firm McKinsey and Company. He has received teaching awards at UCLA (1983), Texas A&M (1992), and Ohio State (1995, 1996, 1999, 2000, and 2001).

Professor Barney's research focuses on the relationship between firm resources and capabilities and sustained competitive advantage. He has published over 75 articles in a variety of books and journals. Some of his published work is among the most cited research in the fields of strategic management and entrepreneurship. Professor Barney has also delivered scholarly papers at over 50 universities around the world, won the College of Business Distinguished Research Award at Texas A&M in 1992, received an honorary doctorate degree from Lund University in 1997; and was appointed an Honorary Visiting Professor at Waikato University in Hamilton, New Zealand in 2001. In 2001 he was elected as a Fellow in the Academy of Management and in 2005 was awarded the Irwin Outstanding Educator Award for the Business Policy and Strategy Division of the Academy of Management.

Professor Barney has consulted with a wide variety of public and private organizations, including Hewlett Packard, Texas Instruments, Tenneco, Arco, McKinsey and Company, Nationwide, and the Columbus Public Schools.

WILLIAM S. HESTERLY

William S. Hesterly is the Zeke Dumke Professor of Management in the David Eccles School of Business, the University of Utah. He has twice been selected as the outstanding teacher in the MBA program (1992 and 1997) and also received the Student's Choice Award in 1994. He received the Western Academy of Management Ascendant Scholar Award in 1999. Dr. Hesterly has also received best paper awards from the Western Academy of Management and the Academy of Management.

His research on organizational economics, vertical integration, organizational forms, and entrepreneurial networks has appeared in leading journals including the *Academy of Management Review*, *Organization Science*, *Strategic Management Journal*, the *Journal of Management*, and the *Journal of Economic Behavior and Organization*. Currently, he is studying the sources of value creation in firms and also what determines who capture the value from a firm's competitive advantage. His research on the history of innovation in Major League Baseball recently appeared in the journal *Business History*.

Dr. Hesterly serves on the editorial board of *Strategic Organization* and has previously served on the boards of *Organization Science* and the *Journal of Management*. He has served as Department Chair and also Vice-President and President of the faculty at the David Eccles School of Business at the University of Utah. Professor Hesterly has served as a consultant to *Fortune* 500 firms in the electronic, office equipment, paper, telecommunications, energy, aerospace, and medical equipment industries. He has also consulted with smaller firms in several other industries. After studying at Louisiana State University, he received bachelors and masters degrees from Brigham Young University and a Ph.D. from the University of California, Los Angeles.

Strategic Management and Competitive Advantage

Concepts and Cases

Strategic Management and Competitive Advantage

Concepts and Cases

Jay B. Barney
The Ohio State University

William S. Hesterly
The University of Utah

PEARSON

Prentice
Hall

Upper Saddle River, New Jersey 07458

Library of Congress Cataloging-in-Publication Data

Barney, Jay B.
Strategic management and competitive advantage: concepts and cases / Jay B. Barney, William S. Hesterly.
   p. cm.
Includes bibliographical references and index.
ISBN 0-13-154274-5
1. Strategic planning.   2. Business planning.   3. Industrial management.
4. Competition.   I.   Hesterly, William S.   II.   Title.
HD30.28.B36834 2006
658.4′ 012—dc22   2005045936

Senior Acquisitions Editor: Michael Ablassmeir
VP/Editorial Director: Jeff Shelstad
Associate Editor: Melissa Yu
Editorial Assistant: Richard Gomes
Developmental Editor: Erika Rusnak
Media Project Manager: Ashley Santora
VP/Director, Market Development: Annie Todd
Marketing Manager: Anke Braun
Marketing Assistant: Patrick Danzuso
Associate Director Production Editorial: Judy Leale
Production Editor: Mary Ellen Morrell
Permissions Supervisor: Charles Morris
Associate Director, Manufacturing: Vincent Scelta
Production Manager: Arnold Vila
Manufacturing Buyer: Diane Peirano

Design Manager: Maria Lange
Art Director: Janet Slowik
Interior Design: Raven Design
Cover Design: Maria Lange
Cover Illustration: Gary Hovland
Illustrator (Interior): P.J. Loughran, Gary Hovland
Illustrator (Figure Art): ElectraGraphics, Inc.
Director, Image Resource Center: Melinda Reo
Manager, Rights and Permissions: Zina Arabia
Manager, Visual Research: Beth Brenzel
Manager, Cover Visual Research & Permissions: Karen Sanatar
Image Permission Coordinator: Craig A. Jones
Manager, Print Production: Christy Mahon
Composition/Full-Service Project Management: Preparé, Inc.
Printer/Binder: Courier-Kendallville

Credits and acknowledgments borrowed from other sources and reproduced, with permission, in this textbook appear on appropriate page within text.

Pearson Education LTD.
Pearson Education Singapore, Pte. Ltd
Pearson Education, Canada, Ltd
Pearson Education–Japan

Pearson Education Australia PTY, Limited
Pearson Education North Asia Ltd
Pearson Educatión de Mexico, S.A. de C.V.
Pearson Education Malaysia, Pte. Ltd

1 0 9 8 7 6 5 4 3 2
ISBN 0-13-154274-5

This book is dedicated to my expanding family: my wife, Kim; our children, Lindsay, Kristian, and Erin; their spouses, Ryan, Amy, and Dave; and most of all, our four grandchildren, Isaac, Dylanie, Audrey, and Chloe. They all help me remember that no success could compensate for failure in the home.

Jay B. Barney
Columbus, Ohio

This book is for my family who has taught me life's greatest lessons about what matters most. To my wife, Denise; my sons, Drew, Ian, Austin, and Alex; my daughters, Lindsay and Jessica (and their husbands, Matt and John); and grandchildren, Ellie and Owen.

William Hesterly
Salt Lake City, Utah

Brief Contents

Contents

Part 1: THE TOOLS OF STRATEGIC ANALYSIS

Chapter 3: Evaluating a Firm's Internal Capabilities   74

Part 2: BUSINESS LEVEL STRATEGIES

Chapter 4: Cost Leadership   114

Chapter 5: Product Differentiation   144

Part 3: CORPORATE STRATEGIES

Acknowledgments

Obviously, a book like this is not written in isolation. We owe a debt of gratitude to all those at Prentice Hall who have supported its development. In particular, we want to thank Jeff Shelstad, VP/Editorial Director; Eric Frank, Director of Marketing; Michael Ablassmeir, Senior Acquisitions Editor; Annie Todd, VP/Director of Market Development; Kathleen McLellan, Market Development Manager; Mary Ellen Morrell, Production Editor; Janet Slowik, Art Director; Judy Leale, Associate Director Production Editorial; Melissa Yu, Associate Editor and Erika Rusnak, Development Editor. We are also grateful to our friend and colleague, Mark Hansen, for his important work on the Instructor's Manual and PowerPoints. Louis Marino helped with the test bank, and Deborah Gilliard has helped with the development of the web site. All these people were instrumental in creating this new approach to teaching strategic management.

Many people were involved in reviewing early drafts of this manuscript. Their efforts undoubtedly improved the manuscript dramatically. Their efforts are largely unsung, but very much appreciated.

Thank you to these professors who participated in early manuscript reviews:

Mainuddin Afza—*Bloomsburg University*

Peter Antoniou—*California State University-San Marcos*

Kendall Artz—*Baylor University*

Susan Barnes—*Washington State University*

Steven Congden—*University of Hartford*

Jim Davis—*University Notre Dame*

David Deeds—*Case Western Reserve University*

Tom Douglas—*Clemson University*

Jon Down—*Oregon State University*

Alan Ellstrand—*University of Arkansas*

James Fiet—*University of Louisville*

Jeff Furman—*Boston University*

Carole Jacobson—*Purdue University*

Joseph Mahoney—*University of Illinois*

Rick Martinez—*Baylor University*

Sharon Matusik—*University of Colorado at Boulder*

Gerry McNamara—*University of California-Riverside*

Elaine Mosakowski—*University of Colorado at Boulder*

Jeffrey Parker—*Jacksonville State University*

Pamela Pommerenke—*Michigan State University*

Peter Ring—*Loyola Marymount University*

Jiten Ruparel—*Otterbein College*

Rhetta Standifer—*University of Missouri*

Edward Ward—*Saint Cloud State University*

Thank you to the following professors who participated in multiple review activities:

Todd Alessandri—*Syracuse University*

Vikas Anand—*University of Arkansas*

Barry Dean Baysinger—*University of Kansas*

James Bloodgood—*Kansas State University*

Brian Boyd—*Arizona State University*

Trevis Certo—*Texas A&M University*

Rebecca Guidice—*University of Nevada-Las Vegas*

Mark Hansen—*Brigham Young University*

Andrew Inkpen—*Thunderbird University*

Constance James—*Pepperdine University*

Janice Joplin—*University of Texas at El Paso*

Franz Kellermanns—*Mississippi State University*

Laura Poppo Lockwood—*Virginia Polytechnic Institute and State University*

Denise Luethge—*University of Michigan-Flint*

Ram Mudambi—*Temple University*

Michael Pitts—*Virginia Commonwealth University*

David Sirmon—*Clemson University*

Jim Thurman—*George Washington University*

Marta White—*Georgia State University*

Thank you to these professors who participated in the Strategic Management Society Focus Groups in 2003 and 2004:

Todd Alessandri—*Syracuse University*

Brian Boyd—*Arizona State University*

Clay Dibrell—*Oregon State University*

Michael Fern—*University of North Carolina*

Marta Geletkanycz—*Boston College*

Amy Hillman—*Arizona State University*

Constance James—*Pepperdine University*

Franz Kellermanns—*Mississippi State*

Ram Mudambi—*Temple University*

Laura Poppo Lockwood—*Virginia Polytechnic Institute and State University*

David Sirmon—*Clemson University*

Jim Thurman—*George Washington University*

1

THE TOOLS
OF STRATEGIC ANALYSIS

What Is Strategy and the Strategic Management Process?

The music business is a mess. U.S. music sales were down 8.2 percent in 2002. Most major record labels have seen their profit margins fall from 15 to 20 percent in the late 1980s to below 5 percent currently. In 2003, many of these labels—including BMG, EMI, and Sony Music—laid off thousands of employees. Even artists like Metallica and Dr. Dre have complained that the structure of the music industry is fundamentally flawed and needs to be redesigned.

Singer-songwriter Sheryl Crow recently observed: "This industry

What Has Napster Wrought?

has been in such a funk. It really needs something . . . to get it going again." In fact, everyone associated with the music business is unhappy—except consumers. Consumers have never been happier.

Of course, it all began with Napster. A Web site where consumers could trade digital music

with each other, Napster opened up the possibility that people could download an entire music library to their hard drive and burn CDs, all for free. Not surprisingly, Napster's founder, Shawn Fanning, got a louder reception than any of the bands when he was introduced at the MTV Music Video Awards.

And while the original Napster was found to violate U.S. copyright laws and was forced out of business, free online downloading continues. Indeed, some researchers suggest that there was a

Learning Objectives

After reading this chapter, you should be able to:

1. Define the concept of strategy.

2. Describe the strategic management process.

3. Define competitive advantage and its relationship to economic value creation.

4. Describe two different measures of competitive advantage.

5. Explain the difference between emergent and intended strategies.

6. Discuss the importance of understanding a firm's strategy even if you are not a senior manager in a firm.

7. Describe how the strategic management process can be extended to include international business activities.

35 percent increase in free downloaded music from 2002 to 2003, despite several well-publicized prosecutions of individual file swappers.

Current free music download Web sites—like KaZaA, eDonkey, and Bit Torrent—operate on the margin of the law. However, since these Web sites do not reside on a single server, their proprietors are difficult to identify and prosecute.

The great irony is that, historically, the creation of new music formats has always enhanced the profitability of record labels. From the 78-rpm single of the 1930s and 1940s, to the 33-rpm long-playing record of the 1950s and 1960s, to the cassette tapes of the 1970s and 1980s, and the compact discs of the 1990s, every time a new recording format has been introduced, record company profits have soared. This has been the case even though some of these formats—including cassette tapes and burnable CDs—were not copy protected. But, so far, no record company has figured out how to make a profit from downloading music off the Internet.

Now, iTunes, Rhapsody, Sony Connect, and Wal-Mart Music Downloads have all recently entered the fee-based Internet music download market. These companies contract with various record companies to make music available to consumers over the Web for a fee. That way, record companies (and artists) are compensated for producing music, these Web sites earn a profit, and consumers have the opportunity to legally download music—albeit for a fee.

These and other fee-based music download firms have adopted two distinct strategies.

Some of them—including Apple iTunes, Sony Connect, and Wal-Mart Music Downloads—have no monthly subscription fee and charge relatively low per-song downloading fees (99 cents per song at Apple iTunes and Sony Connect and 88 cents per song at Wal-Mart Music Downloads), but they require users to purchase a particular brand of hardware to play downloaded songs. Apple iTunes requires users to purchase an Apple iPod; Sony Connect requires users to purchase a Sony player; and Wal-Mart Music Downloads requires users to purchase players that run Microsoft software. Apparently, Apple, Sony, and Wal-Mart are willing to forego some of the revenues associated with monthly subscriptions in the expectation that users will purchase hardware they either manufacture or sell.

Other firms—including Rhapsody—do not lock users into a particular type of portable player: You can actually burn CDs directly from the Rhapsody Web site. However, they charge a $10-per-month subscription fee, in addition to 79 cents for every song that you burn.

It is too early to tell which, if either, of these strategies may ultimately solve the "free Internet downloading" problem of record companies. Currently, Apple's iTunes Web site has about 70 percent of this fee-based market. However, Sony has a major marketing campaign with McDonald's—every time you buy a Big Mac, you get a free Sony Connect download—so Apple's market share advantage may begin to shrink. Also, it is difficult to rule out a firm as large and powerful as Wal-Mart. Moreover, the whole strategy of linking music downloads to particular technology standards is inconsistent with the initial vision of music downloading—to make it easy to gain access to music. Thus, Rhapsody's open architecture strategy also has merit. And, despite the efforts of these firms to grow the download-for-a-fee market, consumers currently pay for less than three percent of the music they download from the Web—and record company profits continue to fall.

Sources: D. Bank (2003). "RealNetworks is launching its own online-music network." *Wall Street Journal*, Wednesday, May 28, p. B7; P. Boutin (2004). "It's all groovy, baby." *Wired*, July, p. 91; B. Hindo (2004). "Music pirates: Still on board." *BusinessWeek*, January 26, p. 13; D. Leonard (2003). "Songs in the key of Steve." *Fortune*, May 12, pp. 52 +; W. Mossberg (2004). "The music man." *Wall Street Journal*, Monday, June 14, pp. B1 +.

The problems of the music industry—and the efforts of various firms to profitably solve these problems—exemplify the kinds of strategic management problems that all firms face. "What is happening in our industry?" "What is our competition going to do next?" "How should we respond?" "What can we do to make money in our business?" are among the central questions that all strategic managers—whether they work at Raytheon (one of the largest defense contractors in the United States) or Rhapsody, Sears or Sony Connect, IBM or iTunes Music Store—must address if they are going to survive and prosper. The process by which these questions are answered is the strategic management process. And the answer a firm develops for these questions is a firm's strategy.

Strategy and the Strategic Management Process

While most can agree that a firm's ability to survive and prosper depends critically on choosing and implementing a *good strategy*, there is less agreement about what a *strategy* is, and even less agreement about what constitutes a *good* strategy.

Indeed, there are almost as many different definitions of these concepts as there are books written about them.

Defining Strategy

In this book, a firm's **strategy** is defined as its theory about how to gain competitive advantages.[1] A *good strategy* is a strategy that actually generates such advantages. Apple's, Sony's, and Wal-Mart's *theory* of how to gain a competitive advantage in the music download-for-a-fee business is to use the music download business to help drive sales of their portable digital listening devices. Rhapsody's *theory* is that users will want to download music to a highly flexible format—the burned CD—and will be willing to pay a subscription fee for that opportunity.

Each of these theories of how to gain competitive advantages in the music download-for-a-fee business—like all theories—is based on a set of assumptions and hypotheses about the way competition in this industry is likely to evolve, and how that evolution can be exploited to earn a profit. The greater the extent to which these assumptions and hypotheses accurately reflect how competition in this industry actually evolves, the more likely it is that a firm will gain a competitive advantage from implementing its strategies. If these assumptions and hypotheses turn out not to be accurate, then a firm's strategies are not likely to be a source of competitive advantage.

But here is the challenge. It is usually very difficult to predict precisely how competition in an industry will evolve, and so it is rarely possible to know for sure that a firm is choosing the right strategy. This is why a firm's strategy is almost always a theory—it's a firm's best bet about how competition is going to evolve, and how that evolution can be exploited for competitive advantage.

The Strategic Management Process

While it is usually difficult to know—for sure—that a firm is pursuing the best strategy, it is possible to reduce the likelihood that mistakes are being made. The best way to do this is to choose a firm's strategy carefully and systematically, and to follow the strategic management process. The **strategic management process** is a sequential set of analyses and choices that can increase the likelihood that a firm will choose a *good strategy*, that is, a strategy that generates competitive advantages. An example of the strategic management process is presented in Figure 1.1. Not surprisingly, this book is organized around this strategic management process.

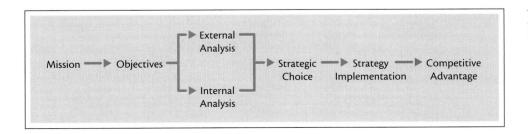

Figure 1.1   The Strategic Management Process

A Firm's Mission

The strategic management process begins when a firm defines its mission. A firm's **mission** is its long- term purpose. Missions define both what a firm aspires to be in the long run and what it wants to avoid in the meantime. Missions are often written down in the form of **mission statements**. Table 1.1 contains examples of several mission statements taken from well-known firms.

Some Missions May Not Affect Firm Performance. As shown in Table 1.1, most mission statements incorporate many common elements. For example, many define the businesses within which a firm will operate—automobiles for Ford; computer hardware, software, and services for IBM. Some define how a firm will compete in those businesses—doing everything direct at Dell, and just winning at the Oakland Raiders. Many even define the core values that a firm espouses—the "soul of Dell" and Anheuser-Busch's values.

Indeed, mission statements often contain so many common elements that some have questioned whether or not having a mission statement actually creates value for a firm.[2] Moreover, even if a mission statement does say something unique about a company, if that mission statement does not influence behavior throughout an organization, it is unlikely to have much impact on a firm's actions. After all, Enron's 1999 annual report includes the following statement of values:

> *Integrity: We work with customers and prospects openly, honestly and sincerely. When we say we will do something, we will do it; when we say we cannot or will not do something, then we won't do it.*[3]

This statement was published at exactly the same time that senior management at Enron was engaging in activities that ultimately defrauded investors, partners, and Enron's own employees—and has landed some Enron executives in jail.[4]

Table 1.1   **Examples of Mission Statements Taken from Several Well-Known Firms**

Anheuser-Busch

Our vision

Through all our products, services, and relationships, we will add to life's enjoyment.

Our mission

Be the world's beer company.
Enrich and entertain a global audience.
Deliver superior returns to our shareholders.

Our values we believe in

Quality in everything we do.
Exceeding customer expectations.
Trust, respect, and integrity in all our relationships.
Continuous improvement, innovation, and embracing change.
Teamwork and open, honest communication.
Each employee's responsibility for contributing to the company's success.
Creating a safe, productive, and rewarding work environment.
Building a high-performing, diverse workforce.
Promoting the responsible consumption of our products.
Preserving and protecting the environment and supporting communities where we
   do business.

Dell

Dell is building its technology, its business, and its communities through direct relationships with our customers, our employees, and our neighbors. Through this process, we are committed to bringing value to customers and adding value to our company, our neighborhoods, our communities, and our world through diversity, environmental and global citizenship initiatives.

The core elements of the "soul of Dell"

Customers: We believe in creating loyal customers by providing a superior experience at a great value.

The Dell Team: We believe our continued success lies in teamwork and in the opportunity each team member has to learn, develop, and grow.

Direct Relationships: We believe in being direct in all we do.

Global Citizenship: We believe in participating responsibly in the global marketplace.

Winning: We have a passion for winning in everything we do.

Ford Motor Company

Our vision

To become the world's leading consumer company for automotive products and services.

Our mission

We are a global family with a proud heritage passionately committed to providing personal mobility for people around the world.

We anticipate consumer need and deliver outstanding products and services that improve people's lives.

Our values

Our business is driven by our consumer focus, creativity, resourcefulness, and entrepreneurial spirit.

We are an inspired, diverse team. We respect everyone's contribution. The health and safety of our people are paramount.

We are a leader in environmental responsibility. Our integrity is never compromised and we make a positive contribution to society.

We constantly strive to improve in everything we do. Guided by these values, we provide superior returns to our shareholders.

IBM

At IBM, we strive to lead in the invention, development, and manufacture of the industry's most advanced information technologies, including computer systems, software, storage systems, and microelectronics. We translate these advanced technologies into value for our customers through our professional solutions, services, and consulting businesses worldwide.

The Oakland Raiders

Just Win—Baby!

Sources: www.anheuser-busch.com; www.dell.com, used with permission of Dell Computer Corporation; www.ford.com, used with permission of Ford Motor Company; www.ibm.com, used with permission of IBM; www.oaklandraiders.com.

Table 1.2   **A Sample of Visionary Firms**

3M	Marriott
American Express	Merck
Boeing	Motorola
Citicorp	Nordstrom
Ford	Philip Morris
General Electric	Procter & Gamble
Hewlett-Packard	Sony
IBM	Wal-Mart
Johnson & Johnson	Walt Disney

Source: J. C. Collins and J. I. Porras. *Built to last: successful habits of visionary companies.* New York: Harper Collins Publishers Inc. ©1994 James C. Collins and Jerry I. Porras. Reprinted by permission.

Some Missions Can Improve Firm Performance. Despite these caveats, research has identified some firms whose sense of purpose and mission permeates all that they do. Some of these **visionary firms**, or firms whose mission is central to all they do, are presented in Table 1.2.[5] One interesting thing to note about visionary firms is their long-term profitability. From 1926 through 1995, an investment of $1 in one of these firms would have increased in value to $6,536. That same dollar invested in an average firm over this same time period would have been worth $415 in 1995.

These visionary firms earned substantially higher returns than average firms even though many of their mission statements suggest that profit maximizing, while an important corporate objective, is not their primary reason for existence. Consider what Jim Burke, a former CEO at Johnson & Johnson (one of the visionary firms identified in Table 1.2), says about the relationship between profits and his firm's mission and mission statement:

All our management is geared to profit on a day-to-day basis. That's part of the business of being in business. But too often, in this and other businesses, people are inclined to think, "We'd better do this because if we don't, it's going to show up on the figures over the short-term." [Our mission] allows them to say, "Wait a minute. I don't have to do that." The management has told me that they're . . . interested in me operating under this set of principles.[6]

Some Missions Can Hurt Firm Performance. Although some firms have used their missions to develop strategies that create significant competitive advantages, missions can hurt a firm's performance as well. For example, sometimes a firm's mission will be very inwardly focused and defined only with reference to the personal values and priorities of its founders or top managers, independent of whether or not those values and priorities are consistent with the economic realities facing a firm. Strategies derived from such missions or visions are not likely to be a source of competitive advantage.

For example, Ben & Jerry's Ice Cream was founded in 1977 by Ben Cohen and Jerry Greenfield, both as a way to produce super-premium ice cream and as a way to create an organization based on the values of the 1960s counterculture. This strong sense of mission led Ben & Jerry's to adopt some very unusual human resource and other policies. Among these policies, the company adopted a compensation system whereby the highest paid firm employee could earn no more than five times the income of the lowest paid firm employee. Later this ratio was adjusted to seven to one. However, even at this level, such a compensation policy made it very difficult to acquire the senior management talent needed to ensure the growth and profitability of the firm without grossly overpaying the lowest paid employees in the firm. When a new CEO was appointed to the firm in 1995, his $250,000 salary violated this compensation policy.

Indeed, though the frozen dessert market rapidly consolidated through the late 1990s, Ben & Jerry's Ice Cream remained an independent firm, partly because of Cohen's and Greenfield's commitment to maintaining the social values that their firm embodied. Lacking access to the broad distribution network and managerial talent that would have been available if Ben & Jerry's had merged with another firm, the company's growth and profitability lagged. Finally, in April of 2000, Ben & Jerry's Ice Cream was acquired by Unilever. However, the 66 percent premium finally earned by Ben & Jerry's stockholders in April 2000 had been delayed for several years. In this sense, Cohen's and Greenfield's commitment to a set of personal values and priorities was at least partly inconsistent with the economic realities of the frozen dessert market in the United States.[7]

Obviously, since a firm's mission can help, hurt, or have no impact on its performance, missions by themselves do not necessarily lead a firm to choose and implement strategies that generate competitive advantages. Indeed, as suggested in Figure 1.1, while defining a firm's mission is an important step in the strategic management process, it is only the first step in that process.

Objectives

Where a firm's mission is a broad statement of its purpose and values, its **objectives** are specific measurable targets a firm can use to evaluate the extent to which it is realizing its mission. Consider, for example, 3M's mission statement in Table 1.3. This statement emphasizes the importance of finding innovative products and producing high returns for shareholders. However, 3M also lists some objectives associated with its mission: growth in earnings per share averaging 10 percent or better per year, a return on employed capital of 27 percent or better, at least 30 percent of sales from products that are no more than four years old, and so forth.

High-quality objectives are tightly connected to elements of a firm's mission and are relatively easy to measure and track over time. Low-quality objectives either do not exist or are not connected to elements of a firm's mission, are not quantitative, and are difficult to measure or difficult to track over time. Obviously, low-quality objectives cannot be used by management to evaluate how well a mission is being realized. Indeed, one indication that a firm is not that serious about realizing part of its mission statement is when there are no objectives, or only low quality objectives, associated with that part of the mission.

External and Internal Analysis

The next two phases of the strategic management process—external analysis and internal analysis—occur more or less simultaneously. By conducting an **external analysis**, a firm identifies the critical threats and opportunities in its competitive environment. It also examines how competition in this environment is likely to evolve and what implications that evolution has for the threats and opportunities

Table 1.3   **3M's Mission Statement**

We are committed to

Satisfying our **customers** with superior quality and value.

Providing **investors** with an attractive return through sustained, high-quality growth.

Respecting our **social and physical environment**.

Being a company that **employees** are proud to be a part of.

Satisfying our customers with superior quality and value

- Providing the highest quality products and services consistent with our customers' requirements and preferences.
- Making every aspect of every transaction a satisfying experience for our customers.
- Finding innovative ways to make life easier and better for our customers.

Providing investors with an attractive return through sustained, high-quality growth

Our goals are:

- Growth in earnings per share averaging 10 percent a year or better.
- A return on capital employed of 27 percent or better.
- A return on stockholders' equity of between 20 and 25 percent.
- At least 30 percent of our sales each year from products new in the last four years.

Respecting our social and physical environment

- Complying with all laws and meeting or exceeding regulations.
- Keeping customers, employees, investors, and the public informed about our operations.
- Developing products and processes that have a minimal impact on the environment.
- Staying attuned to the changing needs and preferences of our customers, employees, and society.
- Uncompromising honesty and integrity in every aspect of our operations.

Being a company that employees are proud to be a part of

- Respecting the dignity and worth of individuals.
- Encouraging individual initiative and innovation in an atmosphere characterized by flexibility, cooperation, and trust.
- Challenging individual capabilities.
- Valuing human diversity and providing equal opportunity for development.

Source: J. Abrahams (1995). *The mission statement book.* Berkeley, CA: Ten Speed Press, pp. 400–402. Courtesy of 3M Company.

a firm is facing. A considerable literature on techniques for and approaches to conducting external analysis has evolved over the last several years. This literature is the primary subject matter of Chapter 2 of this book.

Where external analysis focuses on the environmental threats and opportunities facing a firm, **internal analysis** helps a firm identify its organizational strengths and weaknesses. It also helps a firm understand which of its resources and capabilities are likely to be sources of competitive advantage and which are less likely to be sources of such advantages. Finally, internal analysis can be used by firms to identify those areas of its organization that require improvement and change. Just as is the case with external analysis, a considerable literature on techniques for and approaches to conducting internal analysis has evolved over the past several years. This literature is the primary subject matter of Chapter 3 of this book.

Strategic Choice

Armed with a mission, objectives, and completed external and internal analyses, a firm is ready to make its strategic choices. That is, a firm is ready to choose its "theory of how to gain competitive advantage."

The strategic choices available to firms fall into two large categories: business-level strategies and corporate-level strategies. **Business-level strategies** are actions firms take to gain competitive advantages in a single market or industry, and are the topic of Part Two of this book. The two most common business-level strategies are cost leadership (Chapter 4) and product differentiation (Chapter 5).

Corporate-level strategies are actions firms take to gain competitive advantages by operating in multiple markets or industries simultaneously and are the topic of Part 3 of this book. Common corporate-level strategies include vertical integration strategies (Chapter 6), diversification strategies (Chapters 7 and 8), strategic alliance strategies (Chapter 9), and merger and acquisition strategies (Chapter 10).

Obviously, the details of choosing specific strategies can be quite complex, and a discussion of these details will be delayed until later in the book. However, the underlying logic of strategic choice is not complex. Based on the strategic management process, the objective when making a strategic choice is to choose a strategy that (1) supports the firm's mission, (2) is consistent with a firm's objectives, (3) exploits opportunities in a firm's environment with a firm's strengths, and (4) neutralizes threats in a firm's environment while avoiding a firm's weaknesses. Assuming this strategy is implemented—the last step of the strategic management process—a strategy that meets these four criteria is very likely to be a source of competitive advantage for a firm.

Strategy Implementation

Of course, simply choosing a strategy means nothing if that strategy is not implemented. **Strategy implementation** occurs when a firm adopts organizational policies and practices that are consistent with its strategy. Three specific organizational policies and practices are particularly important in implementing a strategy: a firm's formal organizational structure, its formal and informal management control systems, and its employee compensation policies. A firm that adopts an organizational structure, management controls, and employee compensation that are consistent with and reinforce its strategies is more likely to be able to implement those strategies than a firm that adopts an organizational structure, management controls, and compensation policies that are inconsistent with its strategies. Specific organizational structures, management controls, and compensation policies used to implement the business-level strategies of cost leadership and product differentiation are discussed in Chapters 4 and 5. How organizational structure, management controls, and compensation can be used to implement corporate-level strategies, including vertical integration, strategic alliance, and merger and acquisition strategies, is discussed in Chapters 6, 9, and 10, respectively. However, there is so much information about implementing diversification strategies that an entire chapter, Chapter 8, is dedicated to the discussion of how this corporate-level strategy is implemented.

What Is Competitive Advantage?

Of course, the ultimate objective of the strategic management process is to enable a firm to choose and implement a strategy that generates a competitive advantage. But what is a competitive advantage? In general, a firm has a **competitive advantage** when it is able to create more economic value than rival firms. **Economic value** is simply the difference between the perceived benefits gained by a customer that purchases a firm's products or services and the full economic cost of these products or services. Thus, the size of a firm's competitive advantage is the difference between the economic value a firm is able to create and the economic value its rivals are able to create.[8]

Consider the two firms presented in Figure 1.2. Both these firms compete in the same market for the same customers. However, Firm I generates $180 of economic value each time it sells a product or service, while Firm II generates $150 of economic value each time it sells a product or service. Since Firm I generates more economic value each time it sells a product or service, it has a com-

Figure 1.2   The Sources of a Firm's Competitive Advantage

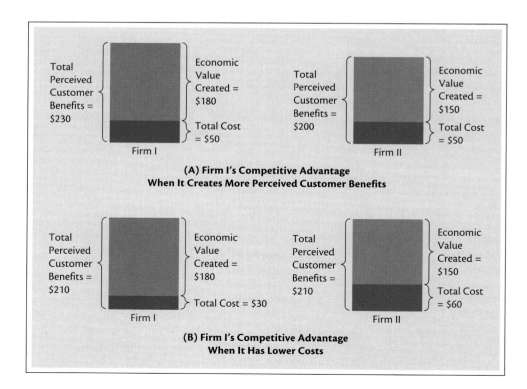

(A) Firm I's Competitive Advantage
When It Creates More Perceived Customer Benefits

(B) Firm I's Competitive Advantage
When It Has Lower Costs

petitive advantage over Firm II. The size of this competitive advantage is equal to the difference in the economic value these two firms create, in this case, $30 ($180 − $150 = $30).

However, as shown in the figure, Firm I's advantage may come from different sources. For example, it might be the case that Firm I creates greater perceived benefits for its customers than Firm II. In panel A of the figure, Firm I creates perceived customer benefits worth $230, while Firm II creates perceived customer benefits worth only $200. Thus, even though both firms' costs are the same (equal to $50 per unit sold), Firm I creates more economic value ($230 − $50 = $180) than Firm II ($200 − $50 = $150). Indeed, it is possible for Firm I, in this situation, to have higher costs than Firm II and still create more economic value than Firm II if these higher costs are offset by Firm I's ability to create greater perceived benefits for its customers.

Alternatively, as shown in panel B of the figure, these two firms may create the same level of perceived customer benefit (equal to $210 in this example), but have different costs. If Firm I's costs per unit are only $30, it will generate $180 worth of economic value ($210 − $30 = $180). If Firm II's costs are $60, it will generate only $150 of economic value ($210 − $60 = $150). Indeed, it might be possible for Firm I to create a lower level of perceived benefits for its customers than Firm II and still create more economic value than Firm II as long as its disadvantage in perceived customer benefits was more than offset by its cost advantage.

A firm's competitive advantage can be temporary or sustained. As summarized in Figure 1.3, a **temporary competitive advantage** is a competitive advantage that lasts for a very short period of time. A **sustained competitive advantage**, on the other hand, can last much longer. How long sustained competitive advantages can last is discussed in the Research Made Relevant feature. Firms that create the same economic value as their rivals experience **competitive parity**. Finally, firms that generate less economic value than their rivals have a **competitive disadvantage**. Not surprisingly, competitive disadvantages can be either temporary or sustained, depending on how long they last.

Figure 1.3 Types of Competitive Advantage

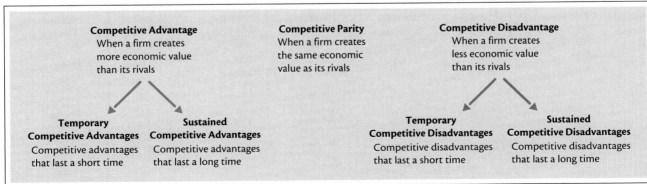

Research Made Relevant

For some time, economists have been interested in how long firms are able to sustain competitive advantages. Traditional economic theory predicts that such advantages should be short-lived in highly competitive markets. This theory suggests that any competitive advantages gained by a particular firm will quickly be identified and imitated by other firms, ensuring competitive parity in the long run. However, in real life, competitive advantages often last longer than what traditional economic theory predicts.

One of the first scholars to examine this issue was Dennis Mueller. In his article, Mueller divided a sample of 472 firms into eight categories, depending on their level of performance in 1949. He then examined the impact of a firm's initial performance on its subsequent performance. The traditional economic hypothesis was that all firms in the sample would converge on an average level of performance. This did not occur. Indeed, firms that were performing well in an earlier time period tended to perform well in later time periods and firms that performed poorly in an earlier time period tended to perform poorly in later time periods as well.

How Sustainable Are Competitive Advantages?

Geoffrey Waring followed up on Mueller's work by explaining why competitive advantages seem to persist longer in some industries than in others. Waring found that, among other factors, firms that operate in industries that (1) are informationally complex; (2) require customers to know a great deal in order to use an industry's products; (3) require a great deal of research and development; and (4) have significant economies of scale are more likely to have sustained competitive advantages compared to firms that operate in industries without these attributes.

Peter Roberts studied the persistence of profitability in one particular industry—the U.S. pharmaceutical industry. Roberts found that not only can firms sustain competitive advantages in this industry, but that the ability to do so is almost entirely attributable to the firms' capacity to innovate by bringing out new and powerful drugs.

In many ways, the difference between traditional economics research and strategic management research is that the former attempts to explain why competitive advantages should not persist while the latter attempts to explain when they can. Thus far, most empirical research suggests that firms, in at least some settings, can sustain competitive advantages.

Sources: D. C. Mueller (1977). "The persistence of profits above the norm." *Economica*, 44, pp. 369–380; P. W. Roberts (1999). "Product innovation, product-market competition, and persistent profitability in the U.S. pharmaceutical industry." *Strategic Management Journal*, 20, pp. 655–670; G. F. Waring (1996). "Industry differences in the persistence of firm-specific returns." *The American Economic Review*, 86, pp. 1253–1265.

The Strategic Management Process, Revisited

With this description of the strategic management process now complete, it is possible to redraw this process, as depicted in Figure 1.1, to incorporate the various options a firm faces as it chooses and implements its strategy. This is done in Figure 1.4. Figure 1.4 is the organizing framework that will be used throughout this book.

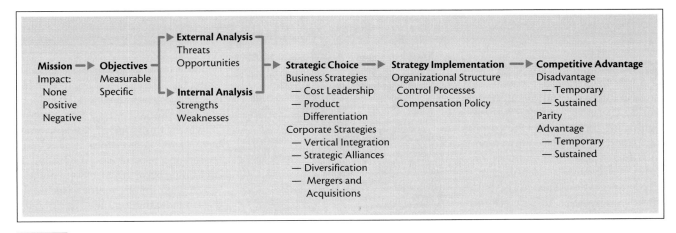

Figure 1.4   Organizing Framework

Measuring Competitive Advantage

A firm has a competitive advantage when it creates more economic value than its rivals, and economic value is the difference between the perceived customer benefits associated with buying a firm's products or services and the cost of producing and selling these products or services. These are deceptively simple definitions. However, these concepts are not always easy to measure directly. For example, the benefits of a firm's products or services are always a matter of customer perception, and perceptions are not easy to measure. Also, the total costs associated with producing a particular product or service may not always be easy to identify or associate with a particular product or service. Despite the very real challenges associated with measuring a firm's competitive advantage, two approaches have emerged. The first estimates a firm's competitive advantage by examining its accounting performance; the second by examining its economic performance. Each of these approaches is discussed below.

Accounting Measures of Competitive Advantage

A firm's **accounting performance** is a measure of its competitive advantage calculated by using information from a firm's published profit and loss and balance sheet statements. A firm's profit and loss and balance sheet statements, in turn, are typically created using widely accepted accounting standards and principles. The application of these standards and principles makes it possible to compare the accounting performance of one firm to the accounting performance of other firms, even if those firms are not in the same industry. However, to the extent that these standards and principles are not applied in generating a firm's accounting statements, or to the extent that different firms use different accounting standards and principles in generating their statements, it can be difficult to compare the accounting performance of firms.

Global Perspectives

*H*istorically, there have been important differences in accounting standards in different countries around the world. These differences can have a significant impact on the profits, losses, and capital stock a firm reports, and thus a significant impact on a firm's performance as measured by its accounting ratios. This suggests that those interested in determining whether, say, Matsushita (a Japanese consumer electronics firm) is outperforming Philips (a Dutch consumer electronics firm) must take into consideration the accounting standards and practices of these two firms.

One of the most important of these accounting differences has to do with how a firm values its current assets. Many countries, including the United States and Japan, require firms to carry assets on their books according to their historical cost, minus depreciation.

**Accounting Around
the World**

However, this approach sometimes understates the true market value of these assets. For example, it may have cost a firm $100 million to construct a building on a particular piece of land. Using the historical cost approach, this building will be valued at $100 million, minus depreciation, on a firm's books. However, the value of the land may have skyrocketed since it was purchased and used to erect a building. It could now be worth $1 billion, not just $100 million. Some countries—including the United Kingdom, the Netherlands, and Australia—let firms restate the value of their assets on their books to reflect current market values. This can have a significant impact on a firm's balance sheet which, in turn, can affect a firm's accounting ratios.

Another way accounting practices vary around the world is how firms are allowed to value their inventories. Two general approaches to valuing inventories exist: LIFO (last in, first out) and FIFO (first in, first out). When inflation is high, LIFO approaches to valuing inven-

---

As described in the Global Perspective feature, these issues can be particularly challenging when comparing the performance of firms in different countries around the world.

One way to use a firm's accounting statements to measure its competitive advantage is through the use of accounting ratios. **Accounting ratios** are simply numbers taken from a firm's financial statements that are manipulated in ways that describe various aspects of a firm's performance. Some of the most common accounting ratios that can be used to characterize a firm's performance are presented in Table 1.4. These ratio measures of firm accounting performance can be grouped into four categories: (1) **profitability ratios**, or ratios with some measure of profit in the numerator and some measure of firm size or assets in the denominator; (2) **liquidity ratios**, or ratios that focus on the ability of a firm to meet its short-term financial obligations; (3) **leverage ratios**, or ratios that focus on the level of a firm's financial flexibility, including its ability to obtain more debt; and (4) **activity ratios**, or ratios that focus on the level of activity in a firm's business.

Of course, these ratios, by themselves, say very little about a firm. To tell us how a firm is performing, its accounting ratios must be compared with some standard. In general, that standard is the average of accounting ratios of other firms in the same industry. Using ratio analysis, a firm earns **above average accounting performance** when its performance is greater than the industry

tories tend to raise a firm's reported cost of goods sold and reduce its reported profits (and tax liability) compared to FIFO. U.S., Canadian, and Japanese firms can use either LIFO or FIFO methods of accounting for inventory. In the United Kingdom, Brazil, and New Zealand, both methods are legal, but most firms use FIFO; in Australia, LIFO is illegal.

Countries also vary in the extent to which they allow firms to operate multiple sets of books, one for financial reporting and one for tax reporting. For example, in the United States, most firms have two sets of books. The first presents the financial status of the firm to the financial community. The second reports the financial status of the firm to the government for tax purposes. Not surprisingly, it is usually the case that the performance of a firm as reported to the financial community is more positive than the performance of a firm as

reported to the government. After all, firms—just like most people—don't like to pay taxes. However, in Germany, firms are not allowed to keep two sets of books. The accounting numbers they report to the financial community are also used to establish their tax liability. In an effort to reduce this liability, it is not uncommon for German firms to engage in accounting practices that have the effect of reducing their reported performance. Thus, when comparing U.S. and German firms in the same industry, it is important to recognize that legal differences between these countries have the effect of biasing the reported performance of the German firms down, when compared to U.S. firms. This means, for example, that just because Daimler-Chrysler's reported accounting performance is, say, lower than Ford's in a given year, the difference between the actual performance of these firms may

not be as large as implied by a simple accounting ratio analysis.

All of this greatly complicates the application of accounting measures of competitive advantage for firms that are headquartered in different countries, especially when those countries have important differences in their accounting rules and regulations. However, over time, as markets have become more global, differences in accounting standards have tended to shrink. While we certainly are not in a world where the standard accounting practices of Japan are the same as the standard accounting practices in Germany, these differences have become smaller over time.

Sources: F. Choi (1997). *International accounting and finance handbook*, 2nd ed. New York: Wiley; F. Choi and R. Levich (1990). *The capital market effects of international accounting diversity*. Homewood, IL: Dow-Jones Irwin; R. Griffin and M. Pustay (1999). *International business*, 2nd ed. Reading, MA: Addison-Wesley.

average. Such firms typically have competitive advantages, sustained or otherwise. A firm earns **average accounting performance** when its performance is equal to the industry average. These firms generally enjoy only competitive parity. A firm earns **below average accounting performance** when its performance is less than the industry average. These firms generally experience competitive disadvantages.

Consider, for example, the performance of Apple Computer. Apple's financial statements for 2001 and 2002 are presented in Table 1.5. Losses in this table are presented in parentheses. Several ratio measures of accounting performance are calculated for Apple in these two years in Table 1.6.

Clearly, Apple's accounting performance improved from 2001 to 2002. After all, Apple lost money in 2001 and made a little bit of money in 2002. In fact, while Apple underperformed its industry in 2001, it performed roughly on par with its industry in 2002. The median ROA for firms in the computer and office equipment industry in 2001 and 2002 was zero percent. The median ROE for firms in this industry in 2001 and 2002 was three percent. Apple's current and quick ratio suggests that the firm, despite losing money in 2001, was not threatened with bankruptcy. Indeed, with only 35 percent of its total assets in debt, Apple actually has some debt capacity to grow future business opportunities.

Table 1.4   **Common Ratios to Measure a Firm's Accounting Performance**

Ratio	Calculation	Interpretation
Profitability Ratios		
1. Return on total assets (ROA)	$\dfrac{\text{profits after taxes}}{\text{total assets}}$	A measure of return on total investment in a firm. Larger is usually better.
2. Return on equity (ROE)	$\dfrac{\text{profits after taxes}}{\text{total stockholders' equity}}$	A measure of return on total equity investment in a firm. Larger is usually better.
3. Gross profit margin	$\dfrac{\text{sales} - \text{cost of goods sold}}{\text{sales}}$	A measure of sales available to cover operating expenses and still generate a profit. Larger is usually better.
4. Earnings per share (EPS)	$\dfrac{\text{profits (after taxes)}\ \text{prefered stock dividends}}{\text{number of shares of common stock outstanding}}$	A measure of profit available to owners of common stock. Larger is usually better.
5. Price earnings ratio (p/e)	$\dfrac{\text{current market price/share}}{\text{after-tax earnings/share}}$	A measure of anticipated firm performance—high p/e ratio tends to indicate that the stock market anticipates strong future performance. Larger is usually better.
6. Cash flow per share	$\dfrac{\text{after-tax profits} + \text{depreciation}}{\text{number of common shares outstanding}}$	A measure of funds available to fund activities above current level of costs. Larger is usually better.
Liquidity Ratios		
1. Current ratio	$\dfrac{\text{current assets}}{\text{current liabilities}}$	A measure of the ability of a firm to cover its current liabilities with assets that can be converted into cash in the short term. Recommended in the range of 2 to 3.
2. Quick ratio	$\dfrac{\text{current assets} - \text{inventory}}{\text{current liabilities}}$	A measure of the ability of a firm to meet its short-term obligations without selling off its current inventory. A ratio of 1 is thought to be acceptable in many industries.
Leverage Ratios		
1. Debt to assets	$\dfrac{\text{total debt}}{\text{total assets}}$	A measure of the extent to which debt has been used to finance a firm's business activities. The higher, the greater the risk of bankruptcy.
2. Debt to equity	$\dfrac{\text{total debt}}{\text{total equity}}$	A measure of the use of debt versus equity to finance a firm's business activities. Generally less than 1.
3. Times interest earned	$\dfrac{\text{profits before interest and taxes}}{\text{total interest charges}}$	A measure of how much a firm's profits can decline and still meet its interest obligations. Should be well above 1.
Activity Ratios		
1. Inventory turnover	$\dfrac{\text{sales}}{\text{inventory}}$	A measure of the speed with which a firm's inventory is turning over.
2. Accounts receivable turnover	$\dfrac{\text{annual credit sales}}{\text{accounts receivable}}$	A measure of the average time it takes a firm to collect on credit sales.
3. Average collection period	$\dfrac{\text{accounts receivable}}{\text{average daily sales}}$	A measure of the time it takes a firm to receive payment after a sale has been made.

Table 1.5   **Apple Computer's Financial Statements for 2001 and 2002 (numbers in millions)**

	2002	2001
Net sales	5,742	5,363
Cost of goods sold	4,139	4,128
Gross margin	1,603	1,235
Selling, general and administrative expenses	1,111	1,138
Other operating expenses	475	441
Total operating expenses	1,586	1,579
Operating income (loss)	17	(344)
Other income, net	70	292
Total income (loss), before tax	87	(52)
Provision for (benefit from) income taxes	22	(15)
Net income, after taxes	65	(37)
Inventories	45	11
Total current assets	5,388	5,143
Total assets	6,289	6,021
Total current liabilities	1,658	1,518
Total liabilities	2,203	2,101
Total shareholders' equity	4,095	3,920
Total assets	6,298	6,021

Economic Measures of Competitive Advantage

The great advantage of accounting measures of competitive advantage is that they are relatively easy to compute. All publicly traded firms have to make their accounting statements available to the public. Even privately owned firms will typically release some information about their accounting performance. Once you have access to these statements, it is quite easy to calculate various accounting ratios. Comparing these ratios to industry averages can tell you quite a bit about a firm's competitive position.

However, accounting measures of competitive advantage have at least one significant limitation. Earlier, economic profit was defined as the difference between the perceived benefit associated with purchasing a firm's products or services and the cost of producing and selling that product or service. There is one important component of cost that is typically not included in most accounting measures of competitive advantage: that is the cost of the capital a firm employs to produce and sell its products. The **cost of capital** is the rate of return that a firm promises to pay its suppliers of capital to induce them to invest in the firm. Once

Table 1.6   **Some Accounting Ratios for Apple Computer in 2001 and 2002**

	2002	2001
Return on Assets	0.13	(.006)
Return on Equity	.016	(.009)
Gross Profit Margin	.279	.231
Current Ratio	3.25	3.38
Quick Ratio	3.22	3.38
Debt to Assets	.350	.349
Debt to Equity	.538	.536

these investments are made, a firm can use this capital to produce and sell products and services. However, a firm must provide the promised return to its sources of capital if it expects to obtain more investment capital in the future. **Economic measures of competitive advantage** compare a firm's level of return to its cost of capital instead of to the average level of return in the industry.

Generally, there are two broad categories of sources of capital: **debt** (capital from banks and bondholders) and **equity** (capital from individuals and institutions that purchase a firm's stock). The **cost of debt** is equal to the interest that a firm must pay its debt holders (adjusted for taxes) in order to induce those debt holders to lend money to a firm. The **cost of equity** is equal to the rate of return a firm must promise its equity holders in order to induce these individuals and institutions to invest in a firm. A firm's **weighted average cost of capital** or **WACC** is simply the percentage of a firm's total capital that is debt times the cost of debt plus the percentage of a firm's total capital that is equity times the cost of equity. A simple approach to measuring a firm's WACC is described in the Strategy in Depth feature.

Conceptually, a firm's cost of capital is the level of performance a firm must attain if it is to satisfy the economic objectives of two of its critical stakeholders: debt holders and equity holders. A firm that earns above its cost of capital is likely to be able to attract additional capital, as debt holders and equity holders will scramble to make additional funds available for this firm. Such a firm is said to be earning **above normal economic performance** and will be able to use its access to cheap capital to help grow and expand its business. A firm that earns its cost of capital is said to have **normal economic performance**. This level of performance is said to be "normal" because this is the level of performance that most of a firm's equity and debt holders expect. Firms that have normal economic performance are able to gain access to the capital they need to survive, although they are not prospering. Growth opportunities may be somewhat limited for these firms. In general, firms with competitive parity usually have normal economic performance. A firm that earns less than its cost of capital is in the process of liquidating. Such **below normal economic performance** implies that a firm's debt and equity holders will be looking for alternative ways to invest their money, someplace where they can earn at least what they expect to earn, that is, normal economic performance. Unless a firm having below normal performance changes, its long-term viability will come into question. Obviously, firms that have a competitive disadvantage generally have below normal economic performance.

Measuring a firm's performance relative to its cost of capital has several advantages for strategic analysis. Foremost among these is the notion that a firm that earns at least its cost of capital is satisfying two of its most important stakeholders—debt holders and equity holders. Despite the advantages of comparing a firm's performance to its cost of capital, this approach has some important limitations as well.

For example, it can sometimes be difficult to calculate a firm's cost of capital. This is especially true if a firm is **privately held**—that is, has stock that is not traded on public stock markets, or is a division of a larger company. For example, it would be very difficult to calculate the cost of capital for many of the firms competing in the music download-for-a-fee business. Several of these firms are not publicly traded (e.g., Rhapsody). Some are divisions of publicly traded firms (e.g., iTunes Music Store is a division of Apple Computer). In these situations, it may be necessary to use accounting ratios to measure a firm's performance.

Strategy in Depth

A firm's weighted average cost of capital (WACC) can be an important benchmark against which to compare a firm's performance. However, calculating this number can sometimes be tricky. Fortunately, it is possible to obtain all the information needed to calculate a firm's WACC—at least for publicly traded firms—from information published in outlets such as Moody's, Standard and Poor's, Dun and Bradstreet, and Value Line. These publications are in every major business school library in the world, and are also online.

To calculate a firm's WACC, five pieces of information are required: (1) a firm's debt rating, (2) its marginal tax rate, (3) its Beta, (4) the risk-free and market rates of return in the years you are calculating a firm's WACC, and (5) information about a firm's capital structure.

Typically, a firm's debt rating will be presented in the form of a series of letters, for example, AA or BBB−. Think of these ratings as grades for a firm's riskiness: an "A" is less risky than an "AA" which is less risky than a "BBB+", and so forth. At any given point in time, there is a market-determined interest rate for a firm with a given debt rating. Suppose that the market-determined interest rate for a firm with a BBB debt rating was 7.5 percent. This is a firm's before-tax cost of debt. However, since, in the United States, interest payments are tax deductible, this before-tax cost of debt has to be adjusted for the tax savings a firm has from using debt. If a firm is reasonably large, then it will almost certainly have to pay the

Estimating a Firm's Weighted Average Cost of Capital

largest marginal tax rate, which in the United States has been 39 percent. So, the after-tax cost of debt in this example is (1 − .39) (7.5) or 4.58 percent.

A firm's Beta is a measure of how highly correlated the price of a firm's equity is to the overall stock market. Betas are published for most publicly traded firms. The risk-free rate of return is the rate the U.S. federal government has to pay on its long-term bonds to get investors to buy these bonds, and the market rate of return is the return investors would obtain if they purchased one share of each of the stocks traded on public exchanges. Historically, this risk-free rate of return has been low: around 3 percent. The market rate of return has averaged around 8.5 percent in the United States. Using these numbers, and

assuming that a firm's Beta is equal to 1.2, the cost of a firm's equity capital can be estimated using the Capital Asset Pricing Model, or CAPM, as follows:

Cost of Equity = Risk Free Rate of Return + (Market Rate of Return − Risk Free Rate of Return) Beta

For our example, this equation is:

$$9.6 = 3.0 + (8.5 - 3.0)1.2$$

Since firms obtain no tax advantages from using equity capital, the before- and after-tax cost of equity is the same.

To calculate a firm's WACC, simply multiple the percentage of a firm's total capital that is debt times the after-tax cost of debt and add it to the percentage of a firm's total capital that is equity times the cost of equity. If a firm has total assets of $5 million, and stockholders' equity of $4 million, then it must have debt with a market value of $1 million. The WACC for this hypothetical firm thus becomes:

WACC = (Stockholders' Equity/Total Assets) Cost of Equity + (Debt/Total Assets) After Tax Cost of Debt
= 4/5 (9.6) + 1/5 (4.58)
= 7.68 + .916
= 8.59

Obviously, firms can have a much more complicated capital structure than this hypothetical example. Moreover, the taxes a firm pays can be quite complicated to calculate. There are also some problems using the CAPM to calculate a firm's cost of equity. However, even with these caveats, this approach usually gives a reasonable approximation to a firm's weighted average cost of capital.

Moreover, some have suggested that while accounting measures of competitive advantage understate the importance of a firm's equity and debt holders in evaluating a firm's performance, economic measures of competitive advantage exaggerate the importance of these two particular stakeholders, often to the disadvantage of other stakeholders in a firm. These issues are discussed in more detail in the Ethics and Strategy feature.

The Relationship Between Economic and Accounting Performance Measures

The correlation between economic and accounting measures of competitive advantage is high. That is, firms that perform well using one of these measures usually perform well using the other. Conversely, firms that do poorly using one of these measures normally do poorly using the other. Thus, the relationships between competitive advantage, accounting performance, and economic performance depicted in Figure 1.5 generally hold.

However, it is possible for a firm to have above average accounting performance and simultaneously have below normal economic performance. This could happen, for example, when a firm is not earning its cost of capital but has above industry average accounting performance. Also, it is possible for a firm to have below average accounting performance and above normal economic performance. This could happen when a firm has a very low cost of capital and is earning at a rate in excess of this cost, but still below the industry average

Emergent Versus Intended Strategies

The simplest way of thinking about a firm's strategy is to assume that firms choose and implement their strategies exactly as described by the strategic management process in Figure 1.1. That is, they begin with a well-defined mission and objectives, they engage in external and internal analyses, they make their strategic choices, and then they implement their strategies. And there is no doubt that this describes the process for choosing and implementing a strategy in many firms.

For example, FedEx, the world leader in the overnight delivery business, entered this industry with a very well-developed theory about how to gain competitive advantages in this business. Indeed, Fred Smith, the founder of FedEx (originally known as Federal Express), first articulated this theory as a student in a term paper for an undergraduate business class at Yale University. Legend has it that he only received a "C" on the paper—but the company that was founded on the theory of competitive advantage in the overnight delivery business developed in that paper has done extremely well. Founded in 1971, FedEx had 2004 sales in excess of $24 billion, profits of $838 million, and employed almost 200,000 around the world.[9]

Figure 1.5   Competitive Advantage and Firm Performance

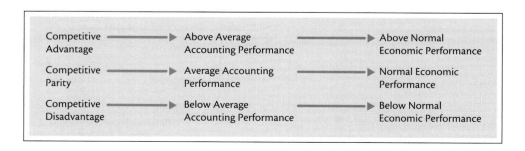

Ethics and Strategy

Considerable debate exists about the role of a firm's equity and debt holders versus its other stakeholders in defining and measuring a firm's performance. These other stakeholders include a firm's suppliers, its customers, its employees, and the communities within which it does business. Like equity and debt holders, these other stakeholders make investments in a firm. They too expect some compensation for making these investments.

On the one hand, some argue that if a firm maximizes the wealth of its equity holders, it will automatically satisfy all of its other stakeholders. This view of the firm depends on what is called the residual claimants view of equity holders. This view is that equity holders only receive payment on their investment in a firm after all the legitimate claims by a firm's other stakeholders are satisfied. Thus, a firm's equity holders, in this view, only receive payment on their investments in a firm after that firm's employees are compensated, after its suppliers are paid, after its customers are satisfied, and after it takes care of its obligations to the communities within which it does business. By maximizing returns to its equity holders, a firm is ensuring that its other stakeholders are fully compensated for investing in a firm.

On the other hand, some argue that the interests of equity holders and

Stockholders Versus Stakeholders

a firm's other stakeholders often collide, and that a firm that maximizes the wealth of its equity holders does not necessarily satisfy its other stakeholders. For example, where a firm's customers may want it to sell higher-quality products at lower prices, a firm's equity holders may want it to sell low-quality products at higher prices—this obviously would increase the amount of money left over to pay off a firm's equity holders. Also, where a firm's employees may want it to adopt policies that lead to steady performance over long periods of time—because this will lead to stable employment—a firm's equity holders may be

more interested in its maximizing its short-term profitability, even if this hurts employment stability. The interests of equity holders and the broader community may also clash, especially when it is very costly for a firm to engage in environment-friendly behavior that could reduce its short-term performance.

This debate manifests itself in a variety of ways. For example, many groups that oppose the globalization of the economy do so on the basis that firms make production, marketing, and other strategic choices in ways that maximize profits for equity holders, often to the detriment of a firm's other stakeholders. These people are concerned about the effects of globalization on employees, on the environment, and on the cultures in the developing economies where global firms sometimes locate their manufacturing and other operations. Managers in global firms respond by saying they have a responsibility to maximize the wealth of their equity holders. Given the passions that surround this debate, it is unlikely that these issues will be resolved soon.

Sources: T. Copeland, T. Koller, and J. Murrin (1995). *Valuation: Measuring and managing the value of companies*. New York Wiley; L. Donaldson (1990). "The ethereal hand: Organizational economics and management theory." *Academy of Review*, 15, pp. 369–381.

Other firms have also begun operations with a well-defined, well-formed strategy, but have found it necessary to modify this strategy so much once it is actually implemented in the marketplace that it bears little resemblance to the theory with which the firm started. **Emergent strategies** are theories of how to gain competitive advantage in an industry that emerge over time or that have been radically reshaped once they are initially implemented.[10] The relationship between a firm's intended and emergent strategies is depicted in Figure 1.6.

Figure 1.6 Mintzberg's Analysis of the Relationship Between Intended and Realized Strategies

Sources: Reprinted from "Strategy formation in an adhocracy," by H. Mintzberg and A. McHugh, published in *Administrative Science Quarterly*, 30, No. 2, June 1985, by permission of *Administrative Science Quarterly*. Copyright © 1985 by *Administrative Science Quarterly*.

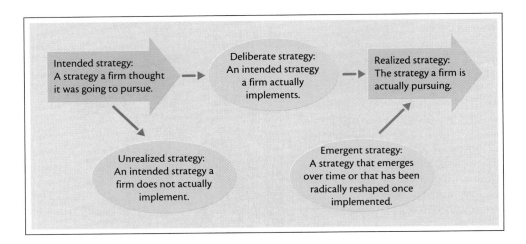

Several well-known firms have strategies that are at least partly emergent. For example, Johnson & Johnson was originally only a supplier of antiseptic gauze and medical plasters. It had no consumer business at all. Then, in response to complaints about irritation caused by some of its medical plasters, J&J began enclosing a small packet of talcum powder with each of the medical plasters it sold. Soon customers were asking to purchase the talcum powder by itself and the company introduced "Johnson's Toilet and Baby Powder." Later an employee invented a ready-to-use bandage for his wife. It seems she often cut herself while using knives in the kitchen. When J&J marketing managers learned of this invention, they decided to introduce it into the marketplace. J&J's Band-Aid products have since become the largest selling brand category at J&J. Overall, J&J's intended strategy was to compete in the medical products market, but its emergent consumer products strategies now generate over 40 percent of total corporate sales.

Another firm with what turns out to be an emergent strategy is the Marriott Corporation. Marriott was originally in the restaurant business. In the late 1930s, Marriott owned and operated eight restaurants. However, one of these restaurants was close to a Washington, D.C., airport. Managers at this restaurant noticed that airline passengers would come into the restaurant to purchase food to eat on their trip. J. Willard Marriott, the founder of the Marriott Corporation, noticed this trend and negotiated a deal with Eastern Airlines whereby Marriott's restaurant would deliver prepackaged lunches directly to Eastern's planes. This arrangement was later extended to include American Airlines. Over time, providing food service to airlines became a major business segment for Marriott. Although Marriott's initial intended strategy was to operate in the restaurant business, it became engaged in the emergent food service business at over 100 airports throughout the world.[11]

Some firms have almost entirely emergent strategies. PEZ Candy, Inc., for example, manufactures and sells small plastic candy dispensers with cartoon and movie character heads, along with candy refills. This privately held firm has made few efforts to speed its growth, yet demand for current and older PEZ products continues to grow. In the 1990s, PEZ doubled the size of its manufacturing operation to keep up with demand. Old PEZ dispensers have become something of a collector's item. Several national conferences on PEZ collecting have been held, and some particularly rare PEZ dispensers were once auctioned at Christie's. This demand has enabled PEZ to raise its prices without increases in advertising, sales personnel, and movie tie-ins so typical in the candy industry.[12]

Of course, one might argue that emergent strategies are only important when a firm fails to implement the strategic management process effectively. After all, if this process is implemented effectively, then would it ever be necessary to fundamentally alter the strategies that a firm has chosen?

In reality, it will often be the case that at the time a firm chooses its strategies, some of the information needed to complete the strategic management process may simply not be available. As suggested earlier, in this setting a firm simply has to make its "best bet" about how competition in an industry is likely to emerge. In such a situation, a firm's ability to change its strategies quickly to respond to emergent trends in an industry may be as important a source of competitive advantage as the ability to complete the strategic management process. For all these reasons, emergent strategies may be particularly important for entrepreneurial firms, as described in the Strategy in the Emerging Enterprise feature.

Why You Need to Know About Strategy

At first glance, it may not be obvious why students would need to know about strategy and the strategic management process. After all, the process of choosing and implementing a strategy is normally the responsibility of senior managers in a firm, and most students are unlikely to be senior managers in large corporations until many years after graduation. Why study strategy and the strategic management process now?

In fact, there are at least three very compelling reasons why it is important to study strategy and the strategic management process now. First, it can give you the tools you need to evaluate the strategies of firms that may employ you. We have already seen how a firm's strategy can have a huge impact on its competitive advantage. Your career opportunities in a firm are largely determined by that firm's competitive advantage. Thus, in choosing a place to begin or continue your career, understanding a firm's theory of how it is going to gain a competitive advantage can be essential in evaluating the career opportunities in a firm. Firms with strategies that are unlikely to be a source of competitive advantage will rarely provide the same career opportunities as firms with strategies that do generate such advantages. Being able to distinguish between these types of strategies can be very important in your career choices.

Second, once you are working for a firm, understanding that firm's strategies, and your role in implementing those strategies, can be very important for your personal success. It will often be the case that expectations of how you perform your function in a firm will change, depending on the strategies a firm is pursuing. For example, as we will see in Part Two of this book, the accounting function plays a very different role in a firm pursuing a cost leadership strategy versus a product differentiation strategy. Marketing and manufacturing also play very different roles in these two types of strategies. Your effectiveness in a firm can

Strategy in the Emerging Enterprise

Every entrepreneur—and would-be entrepreneur—is familiar with the drill: If you want to receive financial support for your idea, you need to write a business plan. Business plans are typically 25 to 30 pages long. Most begin with an Executive Summary; then move quickly to describing an entrepreneur's business idea, why customers will be interested in this idea, how much it will cost to realize this idea; and usually end with a series of charts that project a firm's cash flows over the next five years.

Of course, since these business ideas are often new and untried, no one—including the entrepreneur—really knows if customers will like this idea well enough to buy from this firm. No one really knows how much it will cost to build these products or produce these services—they've never been built or produced before. And certainly, no one really knows what a firm's cash flows will look like over the next five years or so. Indeed, it is not unusual for entrepreneurs to constantly revise their business plan to reflect new information they have obtained about their business idea and its viability. It is not even unusual for entrepreneurs to fundamentally revise their central business idea as they begin to pursue it in earnest.

The truth is, most decisions about whether or not to create an entrepreneur-

Emergent Strategies and Entrepreneurship

ial firm take place under conditions of high uncertainty and high unpredictability. In this setting, the ability to adjust on the fly, to be flexible, and to recast your business idea in ways that are more consistent with customer interests may be a central determinant of a firm's ultimate success. This, of course, suggests that emergent strategies are likely to be very important for entrepreneurial firms.

This view of entrepreneurship is different from the popular stereotype. In the popular view, entrepreneurs are assumed to be hit by a "blinding rush of

insight" about a previously unexploited market opportunity. In reality, entrepreneurs are more likely to experience a series of smaller insights about market opportunities. But typically, these periods of insight will be preceded by periods of disappointment, as an entrepreneur discovers that what he or she thought was a new and complete business model is, in fact, either not new or not complete or both. In the popular view, entrepreneurship is all about creativity, about being able to see opportunities others cannot see. In reality, entrepreneurship may be more about tenacity than creativity, as entrepreneurs build their firms step-by-step out of the uncertainty and unpredictability that plague their decision making. In the popular view, entrepreneurs can envision their success well before it occurs. In reality, while entrepreneurs may dream about financial and other forms of success, they usually do not know the exact path they will take, nor what success will actually look like, until after they have arrived.

Sources: S. Alvarez and J. Barney (2004). "Organizing rent generation and appropriation: Toward a theory of the entrepreneurial firm," *Journal of Business Venturing*, 19, pp. 621–636; W. Gartner (1988). "Who is the entrepreneur? is the wrong question." *American Journal of Small Business*, 12, pp. 11–32; S. Sarasvathy (2001). "Causation and effectuation: Toward a theoretical shift from economic inevitability to entrepreneurial contingency." *Academy of Management Review*, 26, pp. 243–264.

be reduced by doing accounting, marketing, and manufacturing as if your firm was pursuing a cost leadership strategy when it is actually pursuing a product differentiation strategy.

Finally, while it is true that strategic choices are generally limited to very experienced senior managers in large organizations, in smaller and entrepreneurial firms many employees end up being involved in the strategic management process. If you choose to work for one of these smaller or entrepreneurial firms—even if it is not right after graduation—you could very easily find yourself to be part of the strategic management team, implementing the strategic management process, and choosing which strategies this firm should implement. In this setting, a familiarity with the essential concepts that underlie the choice and implementation of a strategy may turn out to be very helpful.

The Strategic Management Process in an International Context

Thus far, the description of the strategic management process has ignored the fact that most firms make strategic choices within a global competitive context. Indeed, there are currently relatively few firms that do not have to consider some aspects of global competition when they make their strategic choices. How are these global considerations incorporated into the strategic management process?

There are two ways that this can happen. First, some have suggested that global strategies are a unique category of strategy, separate from the business and corporate strategies listed under the strategic choice section of the strategic management process in Figure 1.4. The logic behind this conclusion is straightforward: Conceiving of and implementing international strategies requires a set of skills that are qualitatively different from the skills required to conceive of and implement either business or corporate strategies. For example, those that pursue international opportunities for competitive advantage must know about legal systems in different countries; must understand differences in consumer tastes and culture; and must be able to operate simultaneously in different time zones, different languages, and different currencies—all while trying to identify and exploit opportunities for competitive advantage around the world.

A second perspective on international strategies acknowledges that these strategies do often place special demands on the managers and firms that pursue them, but that international strategies, in fact, are just one way—albeit a very important way—that firms can pursue their business or corporate strategies. That is, rather than being a separate type of strategy, this perspective suggests that international strategies may be a means by which a firm realizes competitive advantages from implementing its business or corporate strategies.

Take, for example, a cost leadership business strategy. As will be described in detail in Chapter 4, one very common feature of firms that pursue a low-cost strategy is low-cost manufacturing. Now, many low-cost firms develop their own low-cost manufacturing capability. However, more and more, firms are beginning to outsource their manufacturing to firms that have significant manufacturing cost advantages. In many cases, these firms are outsourcing to firms located in China, Malaysia, the Philippines, or other countries in Asia. In this setting, the decision to outsource manufacturing to an Asian company is driven by the desire to have the low-cost manufacturing needed to implement a cost leadership strategy. That is, the decision to "go international" is a means to an end—the implementation of a cost leadership strategy—rather than an end in and of itself.

A similar conclusion can be made about a firm's decision to begin selling in countries outside its home market. If a firm has decided it needs to diversify its operations—a classic corporate strategy that will be discussed in detail in Chapter 7—it may begin to sell into multiple geographic markets. If those geographic markets happen to span country borders, then this firm is pursuing an international strategy. However, as before, the decision to go international in this setting is a means to an end—diversifying a firm's operations—rather than an end in and of itself.

The perspective adopted in this book is that international strategies are typically used by firms to help them realize a particular business or corporate strategy. That said, it is also acknowledged that pursuing a particular business or corporate strategy through international means can create unique challenges, and opportunities, for firms. Thus, each chapter in this book will include a section that examines the challenges and opportunities associated with completing a particular stage of the strategic management process in an international context.

SUMMARY

A firm's strategy is its theory of how   to gain competitive advantages. These theories, like all theories, are   based on assumptions and hypotheses about how competition in an   industry is likely to evolve. When those assumptions and hypotheses are consistent with the actual evolution of competition in an industry, a firm's strategy is more likely to be able to generate a competitive advantage.

One way that a firm can choose its strategies is through the strategic management process. This process is a set of analyses and decisions that increase the likelihood that a firm will be able to choose a "good" strategy, that is, a strategy that will lead to a competitive advantage.

The strategic management process begins when a firm identifies its mission, or its long-term purpose. This mission is often written down in the form of a mission statement. Mission statements, by themselves, can have no impact on performance, can enhance a firm's performance, or can hurt a firm's performance. Objectives are measurable milestones firms use to evaluate whether or not they are accomplishing their mission. External and internal analyses are the processes through which a firm identifies its environmental threats and opportunities and organizational strengths and weaknesses. Armed with these analyses, it is possible for a firm to engage in strategic choice. Strategies can be classified into two categories: business-level strategies (including cost leadership and product differentiation) and corporate-level strategies (including vertical integration, strategic alliances, diversification, and mergers and acquisitions). Strategy implementation follows strategic choice and involves choosing organizational structures, management control policies, and compensation schemes that support a firm's strategies.

The ultimate objective of the strategic management process is the realization of competitive advantage. A firm has a competitive advantage if it is creating more economic value than its rivals. Economic value is defined as the difference between the perceived customer benefits from purchasing a product or service from a firm and the total economic cost of developing and selling that product or service. Competitive advantages can be temporary or sustained. Competitive parity exists when a firm creates the same economic value as its rivals. A competitive disadvantage exists when a firm creates less economic value than its rivals, and it can be either temporary or sustained.

There are two popular measures of a firm's competitive advantage: accounting performance and economic performance. Accounting performance measures competitive advantage using various ratios calculated with a firm's profit and loss and balance sheet statements. A firm's accounting performance is compared with the average level of accounting performance in a firm's industry. Economic performance compares a firm's level of return to its cost of capital. A firm's cost of capital is the rate of return it had to promise to pay to its debt and equity investors to induce them to invest in the firm.

While many firms use the strategic management process to choose and implement strategies, not all strategies are chosen this way. Some strategies emerge over time, as firms respond to unanticipated changes in the structure of competition in an industry.

There are at least three reasons why students need to understand strategy and the strategic management process. First, it can help in deciding where to work. Second, once you have a job, it can help you to be successful in that job. Finally, if you have a job in a small or entrepreneurial firm, you may become involved in strategy and the strategic management process from the very beginning.

While pursuing international opportunities for competitive advantage can create unique challenges and opportunities for firms, in this book such international strategies are analyzed as different ways that firms can realize the competitive advantages associated with the business and corporate strategies identified in the strategic management process. That said, the unique challenges and opportunities associated with using international operations to realize these business and corporate strategies will be examined in each chapter of the book.

CHALLENGE QUESTIONS

1. Some firms widely publicize their corporate mission statements by including them in annual reports, on company letterheads, and in corporate advertising. What, if anything, does this practice say about the ability of these mission statements to be sources of sustained competitive advantage for a firm? Why?

2. There is little empirical evidence that having a formal, written mission statement improves a firm's performance. Yet many firms spend a great deal of time and money developing mission statements. Why?

3. Is it possible to distinguish between an emergent strategy and an ad hoc rationalization of a firm's past decisions?

4. Both external and internal analyses are important in the strategic management process. Is the order in which these analyses are done important? If yes, which should come first—external analysis or internal analysis? If the order is not important, why not?

5. Will a firm that has a sustained competitive disadvantage necessarily go out of business? How about a firm with below average accounting performance over a long period of time? How about a firm with below normal economic performance over a long period of time?

6. Can more than one firm have a competitive advantage in an industry at the same time? Is it possible for a firm to simultaneously have a competitive advantage and a competitive disadvantage?

PROBLEM SET

1. Write objectives for each of the following mission statements.

(a) We will be a leader in pharmaceutical innovation.
(b) Customer satisfaction is our primary goal.
(c) We promise on-time delivery.
(d) Product quality is our first priority.

2. Rewrite each of the following objectives to make them more helpful in guiding a firm's strategic management process.

(a) We will introduce five new drugs.
(b) We will understand our customers' needs.
(c) Almost all of our products will be delivered on time.
(d) The number of defects in our products will fall.

3. Do firms with the following financial results have below normal, normal, or above normal economic performance?

(a) ROA = 14.3%, WACC = 12.8%
(b) ROA = 4.3%, WACC = 6.7%
(c) ROA = 6.5%, WACC = 9.2%
(d) ROA = 8.3%, WACC = 8.3%

4. Do these same firms have below average, average, or above average accounting performance?

(a) ROA = 14.3%, Industry Avg. ROA = 15.2%
(b) ROA = 4.3%, Industry Avg. ROA = 4.1%
(c) ROA = 6.5%, Industry Avg. ROA = 6.1%
(d) ROA = 8.3%, Industry Avg. ROA = 9.4%

5. Is it possible for a firm to simultaneously earn above normal economic returns and below average accounting returns? How about below normal economic returns and above average accounting returns? Why or why not? If this can occur, which measure of performance is more reliable: economic performance or accounting performance? Why?

6. Examine the following corporate Web sites and determine if the strategies pursued by these firms were emergent, deliberate, or both emergent and deliberate. Justify your answer with facts from these Web sites.

(a) www.walmart.com

(b) www.ibm.com

(c) www.homedepot.com

(d) www.cardinal.com

7. Using the information below, calculate this firm's ROA, ROE, Gross Profit Margin, and Quick Ratio. If this firm's WACC is 6.6 percent and the average firm in its industry has an ROA of 8 percent, is this firm earning above or below normal economic performance and above or below average accounting performance?

Net Sales	6,134	Operating Cash	3,226	Net Current Liabilities	1,549
Cost of Goods Sold	(4438)	Accounts Receivable	681	Long-Term Debt	300
Selling, General Admin. Expense	(996)	Inventories	20	Deferred Income Taxes	208
Other Expenses	(341)	Other Current Assets	0	Preferred Stock	0
Interest Income	72	Total Current Assets	3,927	Retained Earnings	0
Interest Expense	(47)	Gross Prop., Plant, Equip.	729	Common Stock	3,104
Provision for Taxes	(75)	Accumulated Depreciation	(411)	Other Liabilities	0
Other Income	245	Book Value of Fixed Assets	318	Total Liabilities and Equity	5,161
Net Income	554	Goodwill	0		
		Net Other Operating Assets	916		
		Total Assets	5,161		

END NOTES

1. This approach to defining strategy was first suggested in Drucker, P. (1994). "The theory of business." *Harvard Business Review*, 75, September/October, pp. 95–105.
2. Bart, C. K., and M. C. Baetz (1998). "The relationship between mission statements and firm performance: An exploratory study." *Journal of Management Studies*, 35(6), pp. 823–854.
3. See www.enron.com.
4. See Emshwiller, J., D. Solomon, and R. Smith (2004). "Lay is indicted for his role in Enron collapse." *Wall Street Journal*, July 8, pp. A1 + and Gilmartin, R. (2005). "The fought the law," *Business Week*, January 10, p. 82–83.
5. These performance results were presented originally in Collins, J. C., and J. I. Porras (1997). *Built to last: Successful habits of visionary companies*. New York: HarperCollins.
6. Quoted in Collins, J. C., and J. I. Porras (1997). *Built to last: successful habits of visionary companies*, New York: HarperCollins.
7. See Theroux, J., and J. Hurstak (1993). "Ben & Jerry's Homemade Ice Cream Inc.: Keeping the mission(s) alive." Harvard Business School, Case no. 9-392-025; and Applebaum, A. (2000). "Smartmoney.com: Unilever feels hungry, buys Ben & Jerry's." *Wall Street Journal*, April 13, pp. B1 +.

8. This definition of competitive advantage has a long history in the field of strategic management. For example, it is closely related to the definitions provided in Barney (1986, 1991) and Porter (1985). It is also consistent with the value-based approach described in Peteraf (2001), Brandenburger and Stuart (1999), and Besanko, Dranove, and Shanley (2000). For more discussion on this definition, see Peteraf and Barney (2004).
9. FedEx's history is described in Trimble, V. (1993). *Overnight success: Federal Express and Frederick Smith, its renegade creator*. New York: Crown.
10. Mintzberg, H. (1978). "Patterns in strategy formulation." *Management Science*, 24(9), pp. 934–948, and Mintzberg, H. (1985). "Of strategies, deliberate and emergent." *Strategic Management Journal*, 6(3), pp. 257–272. Mintzberg has been most influential in expanding the study of strategy to include emergent strategies.
11. The J&J and Marriott emergent strategy stories can be found in Collins, J. C., and J. I. Porras (1997). *Built to last: Successful habits of visionary companies*. New York: HarperCollins.
12. See McCarthy, M. J. (1993). "The PEZ fancy is hard to explain, let alone justify." *Wall Street Journal*, March 10, p. A1, for a discussion of PEZ's surprising emergent strategy.

2

Evaluating a Firm's External Environment

Can TiVo Change the Way You Watch TV?

You want to enter and compete in the consumer electronics industry? Are you out of your mind!? There are few industries as competitive as the worldwide consumer electronics industry. It is populated by huge companies—like Sony, and Mitsubishi, and Philips, and Panasonic, and Sharp, and it goes on and on—all of which have established global brand names and enormous research and development capabilities; they have the world's best and most efficient manufacturing facilities, and enormous marketing skills. Rivalry in the industry is rabid, with prices constantly dropping and profit margins constantly being squeezed. And yet, this is also an industry characterized by high levels of innovation. Virtually every day, some huge consumer electronics firm somewhere is announcing a radical new digital technology that will change the way we listen to music, watch TV, take pictures, communicate with others, and so forth.

And TiVo wants to enter this industry. Some may ask, what is TiVo? Founded in 1997, TiVo sells what might be described as a "super VCR." Essentially a box with a large hard drive in it, the TiVo system can be used to record TV shows digitally. Sounds simple enough, but it has some interesting applications—like the ability to "pause" a TV show in order to

1. Describe the dimensions of the general environment facing a firm and how this environment can affect a firm's opportunities and threats.

2. Describe how the structure-conduct-performance paradigm suggests that industry structure can influence a firm's competitive choices.

3. Describe the "five forces model of industry attractiveness" and indicators of when each of these forces will improve or reduce the attractiveness of an industry.

4. Describe the difference between rivals and substitutes.

5. Discuss the role of complements in analyzing competition within an industry.

6. Describe four generic industry structures and specific strategic opportunities in those industries.

7. Describe the impact of tariffs, quotas, and other nontariff barriers to entry on the cost of entry into new geographic markets.

8. Describe the differences between multinational, global, and transnational opportunities.

---

answer the door or the telephone; the ability to record more than one show simultaneously; and most ominously, the ability to enable viewers to skip commercials entirely. To skip commercials, all TiVo users have to do is start recording a show at its normal start time, but start watching the show a few minutes later. Then, when a commercial comes on the recorded show, just touch a button, and the TiVo system automatically skips the commercial. How about that—commercial-free television on commercial channels? The possibility that their expensive commercials are being skipped has forced some firms to rethink their advertising strategies.

The TiVo recorder sounds like a great product, but breaking into the consumer electronics industry is not easy—even if you have a "better mousetrap." Current consumer electronics firms have huge scale advantages in research and development, product differentiation, manufacturing, and distribution. Other firms are beginning to market products that function the same way as TiVo. Substitutes for some

of the TiVo's features—including the most widely distributed weekly magazine in the United States, *TV Guide*—are well-entrenched with consumers. And most problematic of all is the TV watcher—the quintessential "couch potato" with a remote in one hand and a beer in the other. Are consumers likely to change the way they watch TV?

So, TiVo faces some tough challenges. But, it is using some clever strategies to try to overcome these problems. For example, instead of just selling its own "box," TiVo is partnering with other large consumer electronics firms—including DirectTV and

Sony—to put TiVo technology in the products of these other firms. Also, to gain access to distribution, TiVo is partnering with firms like Best Buy to make its products more widely available.

By 2002, TiVo had a base of over 422,000 customers and was optimistic that it would have over a million customers in a few years. Most analysts agree that, at one million customers, TiVo will

become a viable consumer electronics firm.

Sources: D. Foust and B. Grow (2004). "Coke: Wooing the TiVo generation." *BusinessWeek*, March 1, 2004, pp. 77 +; S. Kirsner (2002). "Can TiVo go prime time?" *Fast Company*, August 2002, pp. 82 +; www.TiVo.com

T he strategic management process described in Chapter 1 suggested that one of the critical determinants of a firm's strategies is the threats and opportunities in its competitive environment. If a firm understands these threats and opportunities, it is one step closer to being able to choose and implement a "good strategy," that is, a strategy that leads to competitive advantage.

You can see how a knowledge of the threats and opportunities in the global consumer electronics industry helped TiVo choose its strategy—although, it is probably too early to tell if the strategy TiVo has chosen will be a source of competitive advantage. Because TiVo understands the high level of rivalry in this industry, it has partnered with some much larger firms, including Sony and DirecTV, to gain access to some of their competitive strengths. Because TiVo understands the high cost of entry into this market, it has partnered with some important electronics distributors, including Best Buy, to reduce those costs. All these actions have the effect of reducing the competitive threat these firms would have otherwise presented to TiVo as it tried to expand its business.

However, it is not enough to recognize that it is important to understand the threats and opportunities in a firm's competitive environment. What is also required is a set of tools that managers can apply to systematically complete this external analysis part of the strategic management process. Moreover, these tools must be rooted in a strong theoretical base, so that managers know they have not been developed in an arbitrary way. Fortunately, such tools exist and will be described in this chapter.

Understanding a Firm's General Environment

Any analysis of the threats and opportunities facing a firm must begin with an understanding of the general environment within which a firm operates. This **general environment** consists of broad trends in the context within which a firm operates that can have an impact on a firm's strategic choices. As depicted in Figure 2.1, the general environment consists of six interrelated elements: technological change, demographic trends, cultural trends, the economic climate, legal and political conditions, and specific international events. Each of these elements of the general environment is discussed below.

In 1899, Charles H. Duell, Commissioner of the United States patent office, said, "Everything that can be invented has been invented."[1] He was wrong. Technological changes over the last few years have had significant impacts on the ways firms do business and on the products and services they sell. These impacts have been most obvious for technologies that build on digital information—including computers, the Internet, wireless telephones, and so forth. Many of us

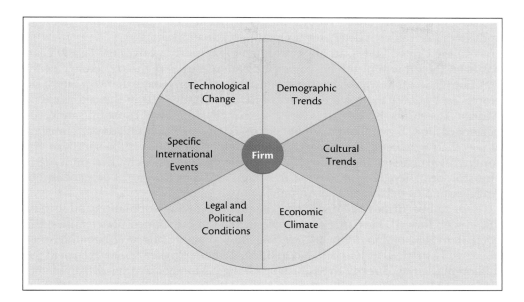

Figure 2.1 The General Environment Facing Firms

routinely use digital products or services that did not exist just five years ago—including TiVo. However, rapid technological innovation has not been restricted to digital technologies. Biotechnology has also made rapid progress over the last 10 years. New kinds of medicines are now being created. As important, biotechnology holds the promise of developing entirely new ways of both preventing and treating disease.[2]

Technological change creates both opportunity—as firms begin to explore how to use technology to create new products and services—and threats—as technological change forces firms to rethink their technological strategies. Indeed, in Chapter 1 we saw how one technological innovation—downloading digital music from the Internet—has created a threat to the profitability of record companies and an opportunity for firms like Apple's iTunes and Sony Connect to increase the sale of their portable digital listening devices.[3] This is almost always the case with technological change—it creates threats for some firms and opportunities for others.

A second element of the general environment facing firms is demographic trends. **Demographics** is the distribution of individuals in a society in terms of age, sex, marital status, income, ethnicity, and other personal attributes that may determine buying patterns. Understanding this basic information about a population can help a firm determine whether or not its products or services will appeal to customers and how many potential customers for these products or services it might have.

Some demographic trends are very well known. For example, everyone has heard of the "baby boomers"—adults who were born shortly after World War II. This large population has had an impact on the strategies of many firms, especially as they have grown older and have had more disposable income. However, other demographic groups have also had an impact on firm strategies. This is especially true in the automobile industry. For example, minivans were invented to meet the demands of "soccer moms"—women who live in the suburbs and have young children. The 3-series BMW seems to have been designed for "Yuppies"—the young, urban, and upwardly mobile adults of the 1970s and 1980s, while the Jeep Liberty and Nissan Exterra seem to have been designed for the so-called X-generation—young men and women currently in their twenties and either just out of college on anticipating graduation shortly.

In the United States, an important demographic trend over the last 20 years has been the growth of the Hispanic population. In 1990, the percentage of the U.S. population that was black was greater than the percentage that was Hispanic. However, by 2000, there were more people of Latin descent in the country than African Americans. By 2010, it is expected that Hispanics will constitute almost 15 percent of the U.S. population, while the percentage of blacks will remain constant at less than 8 percent. These trends are particularly notable in the southern and southwestern parts of the country. For example, 36 percent of children under 18 in Houston are Hispanic, 39 percent in Miami and San Diego, 53 percent in Los Angeles, and 61 percent in San Antonio.

Of course, firms have become aware of this growing population and its buying power. Indeed, Hispanic disposable income in the United States jumped 29 percent, to $652 billion, from 2001 to 2003. In response, firms have begun marketing directly to the U.S. Hispanic population. In 2003, Procter & Gamble spent $90 million marketing directly to Spanish-speaking customers. Procter & Gamble has also formed a 65-person bilingual team to manage the marketing of products to Hispanics. Indeed, Procter & Gamble expects that the Hispanic population will be the cornerstone of its sales growth in North America.[4]

Firms can try to exploit their understanding of a particular demographic segment of the population to create a competitive advantage—as is the case with Procter & Gamble and the U.S. Hispanic population—but focusing on too narrow a demographic segment can limit the demand for a firm's products. The WB, the alternative television network created by Time Warner in 1995, has faced this dilemma. Initially, the WB found success in producing shows for teens—classics like *Dawson's Creek* and *Buffy the Vampire Slayer*. However, in 2003, the WB saw an 11 percent drop in its viewership and a $25 million drop in its advertising revenues. While not leaving its traditional demographic behind, the WB is currently producing some programs that will appeal to older viewers. Whether or not older viewers will even consider watching a show on the WB is still not known. But, according to Garth Ancier, WB Chair, "To the degree that we have presented ourselves as just a teenage network, that's been a very large mistake on our part."[5]

A third element of a firm's general environment is cultural trends. **Culture** is the values, beliefs, and norms that guide behavior in a society. These values, beliefs, and norms define what is "right and wrong" in a society, what is acceptable and unacceptable, what is fashionable and what is unfashionable. Failure to understand changes in culture, or differences between cultures, can have a very large impact on the ability of a firm to gain a competitive advantage.

This becomes most obvious when firms operate in multiple countries simultaneously. Even seemingly small differences in culture can have an impact. For example, advertisements in the United States that end with a person putting their index finger and thumb together mean that a product is "okay"; in Brazil, the same symbol is vulgar and offensive. Ads in the United States that have a bride dressed in white may be very confusing to the Chinese, because in China white is the traditional color worn at funerals. In Germany, women typically purchase their own engagement rings while in the United States men purchase engagement rings for their fiancées. And what might be appropriate ways to treat women colleagues in Japan or France would land most men in U.S. firms in serious trouble. Understanding the cultural context

Global Perspectives

It may have begun with Pokémon, Hello Kitty, and Mighty Morphin Power Rangers, but Japanese style is rapidly becoming an important design feature in many products sold around the world and in the United States. While it is difficult to describe a single simple element of this Japanese style, much of the new Japanese look is derived from a particular form of Japanese cartoon animation called *anime*. Whether in films or in two-inch-thick comic books called *manga*, anime is characterized by highly stylized arts-based movements of characters with white, round, oversized eyes, dark black pupils, and a shock of unruly hair. Colors in anime are bold, the action furious. Characters clash in mythic adventures that pit good against evil in the science fiction of the future.

But this look—stylized, colorful, futuristic—has moved way beyond cartoons, comic books, and action figures. Elements of this Japanese look show up in many products sold around the world. These include the stylized action sequences in a movie like *The Last Samurai*; in

Pokémon Invades Louis Vuitton

cell phones built by Sony Ericsson that will soon be imported from Japan into the United States; in cars with futuristic designs like Nissan's full-size truck, the Titan; and even in Louis Vuitton's line of Murakami handbags—designed by Japanese artist Takashi Murakami—that now generates $300 million in sales worldwide.

Even cultural icons in the United States are being replaced by Japanese-influenced products. For example, in the 1980s and 1990s, street racers in the United States used to modify their American-made V8 Camaros and Firebirds to race on city streets. But, with the popularity of the movie *Fast and Furious*, American cars are being replaced, more and more often, with modified Japanese cars—Toyotas, Hondas, and Nissans replacing Camaro and Firebirds as the preferred hot rod of today's street racers. A similar transition from Harley-Davidson "Hogs" to Suzuki, Kawasaki, and Honda "pocket rockets" is taking place among those who race motorcycles.

And while it is a long way from Pokémon and Hello Kitty to Murakami handbags and Suzuki motorcycles racing down winding roads, all of these products are connected by a common Japanese look traceable to a uniquely Japanese art form, anime.

Sources: C. Palmeri and N. Byrnes (2004). "Is Japanese style taking over the world?" *BusinessWeek*, July 26, pp. 56 +; G. Parker (2004). "Students used to take Japanese for jobs; now it's for fun." *Wall Street Journal*, August 5, pp. A1 +; C. Matlack, R. Tiplady, D. Brady, R. Berner, and H. Tashiro (2004). "The Vuitton machine." *BusinessWeek*, March 22, pp. 98 +.

---

within which a firm operates is important in evaluating the ability of a firm to generate competitive advantages.[6]

However, cultural differences can also be a source of opportunity for firms. This is especially the case if a firm in one culture is able to identify and popularize elements taken from a different culture. As described in the Global Perspectives feature, this transfer of cultural elements is beginning to accelerate from the Japanese culture to the U.S. marketplace.

A fourth element of a firm's general environment is the current economic climate. The **economic climate** is the overall health of the economic systems within which a firm operates. The health of the economy varies over time in a distinct pattern: Periods of relative prosperity, when demand for goods and services is high and unemployment is low, are followed by periods of relatively low prosperity, when demand for goods and services is low and unemployment is high. When activity in an economy is relatively low, the economy is said to be in **recession**. A severe recession that lasts for several years is known as a **depression**. This alternating pattern of prosperity followed by recession, followed by prosperity, is called the **business cycle**.

Throughout the 1990s, the world, and especially the United States, enjoyed a period of sustained economic growth. Some observers even speculated that the government had become so skilled at managing demand in the economy through adjusting interest rates that a period of recession did not necessarily have to follow a period of sustained economic growth. Of course, the business cycle reared its ugly head again in 1999 with a sudden downturn in stock markets around the world, beginning with the technology sector in the United States and spreading to the entire world economy by 2000. Over a period of just a few months, much of the economic value that had been created through the 1990s disappeared. CEOs of Internet companies that had once been valued at billions of dollars now found themselves managing Web sites that were treated as virtually worthless in the market.

However, for every downturn in the economic climate, there is an upturn. For example, at one point in 1999, Amazon.com's stock was valued at $100 per share, for a market value of almost $50 billion. At $50 billion, Amazon's market value was greater than the market value of Ford and General Electric. By 2000, Amazon's stock had fallen to $6 per share; but just three years later, in 2003, Amazon's stock had rebounded to $50 per share and its market value to $21 billion. As important, in 2004 it was on track for annual sales of $7 billion and $400 million in earnings.[7] The ability to survive the technology bust of 1999 has positioned Amazon.com—along with other Internet firms including eBay, Google, and Yahoo!—to be a dominant player in the Internet for the foreseeable future.

A fifth element of a firm's general environment is legal and political conditions. The legal and political dimensions of an organization's general environment are the laws and the legal system's impact on business, together with the general nature of the relationship between government and business. These laws and the relationship between business and government can vary significantly around the world. For example, in Japan, business and the government are generally seen has having a consistently close and cooperative relationship. Indeed, some have observed that one of the reasons that the Japanese economy has been growing so slowly over the last decade is the reluctance of the government to impose economic restructuring that would hurt the performance of some Japanese firms—especially the largest Japanese banks. In the United States, on the other hand, the quality of the relationship between business and the government tends to vary over time. In some administrations, rigorous antitrust regulation and tough environmental standards—both seen as inconsistent with the interests of business—dominate. In other administrations, antitrust regulation is less rigorous and the imposition of environmental standards is delayed, suggesting a more "pro-business" perspective.

A final attribute of a firm's general environment is specific international events. These include events such as civil wars, political coups, terrorism, wars between countries, famines, and country or regional economic recessions. All of these specific events can have an enormous impact on the ability of a firm's strategies to generate competitive advantage.

Of course, one of the most important of these specific events to have occurred over the last several decades was the terrorist attacks on New York City and Washington, D.C., on September 11, 2001. Beyond the tragic loss of life, these attacks had important business implications as well. For example, most U.S. airlines have yet to fully recover from the drop in demand that followed 9/11. Insurance companies had to pay out billions of dollars in unanticipated claims as a result of the attacks. Defense contractors saw demand for their products soar as the United States and some of its allies began waging war in Afghanistan and then Iraq.

A firm's general environment defines the broad contextual background within which it operates. Understanding this general environment can help a firm identify some of the threats and opportunities it faces. However, it is usually the case that this general environment has an impact on a firm's threats and opportunities through its impact on a firm's more local environment. Thus, while analyzing a firm's general environment is an important step in any application of the strategic management process, this general analysis must be accompanied by an analysis of a firm's more local environment if the threats and opportunities facing a firm are to be fully understood. Specific tools for analyzing a firm's local environment, together with the theoretical perspectives from which these tools have been derived, are discussed below.

The Structure-Conduct-Performance Model of Firm Performance

In the 1930s, a group of economists began developing an approach for understanding the relationship between a firm's environment, its behavior, and performance. The original objective of this work was to describe conditions under which competition in an industry would *not* develop. Understanding when competition was not developing in an industry assisted government regulators in identifying industries where competition-enhancing regulations should be implemented.[8]

The theoretical framework that developed out of this effort became known as the **structure-conduct-performance model (S-C-P)** and is summarized in Figure 2.2. The term **structure** in this model refers to industry structure, measured by such factors as the number of competitors in an industry, the heterogeneity of products in an industry, the cost of entry and exit in an industry, and so forth. **Conduct** refers to the strategies that firms in an industry implement. **Performance** in the S–C–P model has two meanings: the performance of individual firms and

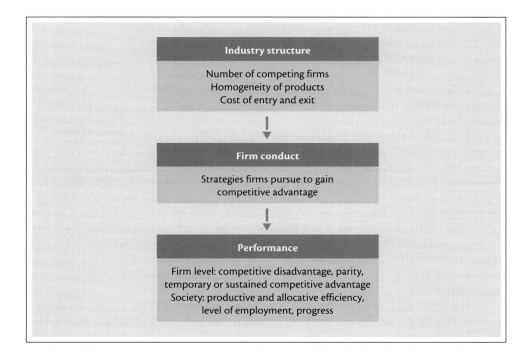

Figure 2.2   The Structure-Conduct-Performance Model

Ethics and Strategy

Is a Firm Gaining a Competitive Advantage Good for Society?

One of the basic tenets of economic theory is that society is better off when industries are very competitive. Industries are very competitive when there are large numbers of firms operating in an industry, when the products and services that these firms sell are similar to each other, and when it is not very costly for firms to enter into or exit these industries. Indeed, as is described in more detail in the Strategy in Depth feature, these industries are said to be perfectly competitive.

The reasons that society is better off when industries are perfectly competitive are well known. In such industries, firms must constantly strive to keep their costs low, their quality high, and, when appropriate, must constantly be innovating if they are to even survive. Low costs, high quality, and appropriate innovation are generally consistent with the interests of a firm's customers and thus consistent with the overall welfare of society.

Indeed, concern for **social welfare**, or the overall good of society, is the primary reason the S-C-P model was developed. This model was to be used to identify industries where perfect competition was not occurring, and thus where social welfare was not being maximized. With these industries identified, the government could

then engage in activities to increase the competitiveness of these industries, thereby increasing social welfare.

Strategic management scholars turned the S-C-P model upside down by using it to describe industries where firms could gain competitive advantages and attain above average performance. However, some have asked, if strategic management is all about creating and exploiting competitive imperfections in industries, is strategic management also all about reducing the overall good of society for advantages to be gained by a few firms? It is not surprising that individuals who are more interested in

improving society than improving the performance of a few firms question the moral legitimacy of the field of strategic management.

However, there is another view about strategic management and social welfare. The S-C-P model assumes that any competitive advantages a firm has in an industry must hurt society. The alternative view is that at least some of the competitive advantages may exist because that firm addresses customer needs more effectively than its competitors. From this perspective, competitive advantages are not bad for social welfare; they are actually good for social welfare.

Of course, both perspectives can be true. For example, a firm like Microsoft has engaged in activities that at least some courts have concluded are inconsistent with social welfare. On the other hand, Microsoft also sells applications software that is routinely ranked among the best in the industry, actions that are consistent with meeting customer needs in ways that maximize social welfare.

Sources: J. B. Barney (1986). "Types of competition and the theory of strategy." *Academy of Management Review*, 11, pp. 791–800; H. Demsetz (1973). "Industry structure, market rivalry, and public policy." *Journal of Law and Economics*, 16, pp. 1–9; M. Porter (1981). "The contribution of industrial organization to strategic management." *Academy of Management Review*, 6, pp. 609–620.

the performance of the economy as a whole. While both these definitions of performance in the S-C-P model are important, as is suggested in Chapter 1, the strategic management process is much more focused on the performance of individual firms than on the performance of the economy as a whole. That said, the relationship between these two types of performance can sometimes be complex, as described in the Ethics and Strategy feature.

The logic that links industry structure to conduct and performance is well known. Attributes of the industry structure within which a firm operates define the range of options and constraints facing a firm. In some industries, firms have very few options and face many constraints. In general, firms in these industries can gain only competitive parity. In this setting, industry structure completely determines both firm conduct and long-run firm performance.

However, in other, less competitive industries firms face fewer constraints and a greater range of conduct options. Some of these options may enable them to obtain competitive advantages. However, even when firms have more conduct options, industry structure still constrains the range of those options. Moreover, as will be shown in more detail later in this chapter, industry structure also has an impact on how long firms can expect to maintain their competitive advantages in the face of increased competition.

The Five Forces Model of Environmental Threats

As a theoretical framework, the S-C-P model has proven to be very useful in informing both research and government policy. However, in this form, this model can sometimes be awkward to use to identify threats in a firm's local environment. Fortunately, several scholars have developed models of environmental threats based on the S-C-P model that are highly applicable in identifying threats facing a particular firm. The most influential of these models was developed by Professor Michael Porter and is known as the "five forces framework."[9] The **five forces framework** identifies the five most common threats faced by firms in their local competitive environments and the conditions under which these threats are more or less likely to be present. The relationship between the S-C-P model and the five forces framework is discussed in the Strategy in Depth feature.

To a firm seeking competitive advantages, an **environmental threat** is any individual, group, or organization outside a firm that seeks to reduce the level of that firm's performance. Threats increase a firm's costs, decrease a firm's revenues, or in other ways reduce a firm's performance. In S-C-P terms, environmental threats are forces that tend to increase the competitiveness of an industry and force firm performance to competitive parity level. The five common environmental threats identified in the "five forces framework" are: (1) the threat of entry, (2) the threat of rivalry, (3) the threat of substitutes, (4) the threat of suppliers, and (5) the threat of buyers. The five forces framework is summarized in Figure 2.3.

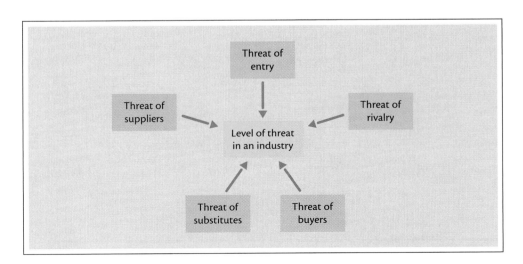

Figure 2.3 Five Forces Model of Environmental Threats

Source: M. E. Porter (1980). Adapted with the permission of The Free Press, a division of Simon & Schuster Adult Publishing Group.

Strategy in Depth

The relationship between the five forces framework and the S-C-P model turns on the relationship between the threats identified in this framework and the nature of competition in an industry. When all five threats are very high, competition in an industry begins to approach what economists call perfect competition. When all five threats are very low, competition in an industry begins to approach what economists call a monopoly. Between perfect competition on the one hand, and monopoly on the other, economists have identified two other types of competition in an industry—monopolistic competition and oligopoly—where the five threats identified in the framework are moderately high. These four types of competition, and the expected performance of firms in these different industries, are summarized in the table below.

Industries are **perfectly competitive** when there are large numbers of competing firms, products being sold are homogeneous with respect to cost and product attributes, and entry and exit are very low cost. Examples of such perfectly competitive industries include the spot market for crude oil.

The S-C-P Model and the Five Forces Framework

Firms in these industries can expect to earn only competitive parity.

In **monopolistically competitive industries**, there are large numbers of competing firms and low-cost entry into and exit from the industry. However, unlike the case of perfect competition, products in these industries are not homogeneous with respect to costs or product attributes. Examples of monopolistically competitive industries include

toothpaste, shampoo, golf balls, and automobiles. Firms in such industries can earn competitive advantages.

Oligopolies are characterized by a small number of competing firms, by homogeneous products, and by costly entry and exit. Examples of oligopolistic industries include the U.S. automobile and steel industries in the 1950s and the U.S. breakfast cereal market today. Currently, the top four producers of breakfast cereal account for about 90 percent of the breakfast cereal sold in the United States. Firms in such industries can earn competitive advantages.

Finally, **monopolistic industries** consist of only a single firm. Entry into this type of industry is very costly. There are few examples of purely monopolistic industries. Historically, for example, the U.S. Post Office had a monopoly on home mail delivery. However, this monopoly has been challenged in small-package delivery by FedEx, larger-package delivery by UPS, and in mail delivery by e-mail. Monopolists can generate competitive advantages—although they are sometimes managed very inefficiently.

Source: J. Barney (2002). *Gaining and sustaining competitive advantage*, 2nd ed. Upper Saddle River, NJ.

Types of Competition and Expected Firm Performance

Type of Competition	Attributes	Examples	Expected Firm Performance
Perfect competition	Large number of firms Homogeneous products Low-cost entry and exit	Stock market Crude oil	Competitive Parity
Monopolistic Competition	Large number of firms Heterogeneous products Low-cost entry and exit	Toothpaste Shampoo Golf balls Automobiles	Competitive Advantage
Oligopoly	Small number of firms Homogenous products Costly entry and exit	U.S. steel and and autos in the 1950s U.S. breakfast cereal	Competitive Advantage
Monopoly	One firm Costly entry	Home mail delivery	Competitive Advantage

The Threat of Entry

The first environmental threat identified in the five forces framework is the threat of new entry. **New entrants** are firms that have either recently begun operations in an industry or that threaten to begin operations in an industry soon. For Amazon.com, in the online book-ordering business, Barnes & Noble.com and Borders.com are new entrants. Amazon largely invented this way of selling books, and both Barnes & Noble and Borders recently entered this market, even though both these firms already operated in the traditional book sales industry. For ESPN in the television sports industry, both the Fox Sports Regional Network and the College Sports Television (CSTV) network are new entrants. The Fox Regional Sports Network consists of several regional sports channels that broadcast both national and regional sporting events, sports news shows, and sports entertainment shows—including *The Best Damn Sports Show, Period.* CSTV is a new (founded in spring of 2003) sports cable and satellite channel that specializes in college sports.

According to the S-C-P model, new entrants are motivated to enter into an industry by the superior profits that some incumbent firms in that industry may be earning. Firms seeking these high profits enter the industry, thereby increasing the level of industry competition and reducing the performance of incumbent firms. With the absence of any barriers, entry will continue as long as any firms in the industry are earning competitive advantages, and entry will cease when all incumbent firms are earning competitive parity.

The extent to which new entry acts as a threat to an incumbent firm's performance depends on the cost of entry. If the cost of entry into an industry is greater than the potential profits a new entrant could obtain by entering, then entry will not be forthcoming, and new entrants are not a threat to incumbent firms. But if the cost of entry is lower than the return from entry, entry will occur until the profits derived from entry are less than the costs of entry.

The threat of entry depends upon the cost of entry, and the cost of entry, in turn, depends upon the existence and "height" of barriers to entry. **Barriers to entry** are attributes of an industry's structure that increase the cost of entry. The greater the cost of entry, the greater the height of these barriers. With significant barriers to entry in place, potential entrants will not enter into an industry even though incumbent firms are earning competitive advantages.

Four important barriers to entry have been identified in the S-C-P and strategy literatures. These four barriers, listed in Table 2.1, are (1) economies of scale, (2) product differentiation, (3) cost advantages independent of scale, and (4) government regulation of entry.[10]

Economies of Scale as a Barrier to Entry

Economies of scale exist in an industry when a firm's costs fall as a function of that firm's volume of production. **Diseconomies of scale** exist when a firm's costs rise as a function of that firm's volume of production. The relationship between

Table 2.1 **Barriers to Entry into an Industry**

1. Economies of scale.
2. Product differentiation.
3. Cost advantages independent of scale.
4. Government regulation of entry.

Figure 2.4   Economies of Scale and the Cost of Production

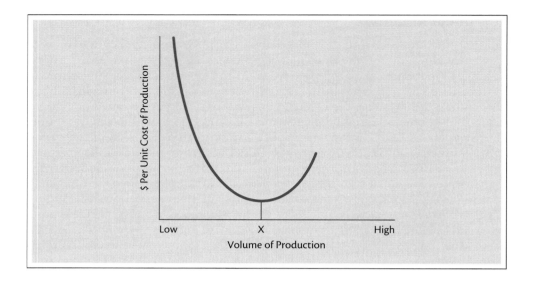

economies of scale, diseconomies of scale, and a firm's volume of production is summarized in Figure 2.4. As a firm's volume of production increases, its costs begin to fall. This is a manifestation of economies of scale. However, at some point, a firm's volume of production becomes too large and its costs begin to rise. This is a manifestation of diseconomies of scale. For economies of scale to act as a barrier to entry, the relationship between the volume of production and firm costs must have the shape of the line in Figure 2.4. This curve suggests that any deviation, positive or negative, from an optimal level of production (point X in Figure 2.4) will lead a firm to experience much higher costs of production.

To see how economies of scale can act as a barrier to entry, consider the following scenario. Imagine an industry with the following attributes. There are five incumbent firms (each firm has only one plant); the optimal level of production in each of these plants is 4,000 units (X = 4,000 units); total demand for the output of this industry is fixed at 22,000 units; the economies-of-scale curve is as depicted in Figure 2.4; and products in this industry are very homogeneous. Total demand in this industry (22,000 units) is greater than total supply (5 × 4,000 units = 20,000). Everyone knows that when demand is greater than supply, prices go up. This means that the five incumbent firms in this industry will have high levels of profit. The S–C–P model suggests that, absent barriers, these superior profits should motivate entry.

However, look at the entry decision from the point of view of potential entrants. Certainly, incumbent firms are earning superior profits, but potential entrants face an unsavory choice. On the one hand, new entrants could enter the industry with an optimally efficient plant and produce 4,000 units. However, this form of entry will lead industry supply to rise to 24,000 units (20,000 + 4,000). Suddenly, supply will be greater than demand (24,000 > 22,000), and all the firms in the industry, including the new entrant, will earn negative profits. On the other hand, the new entrant might enter the industry with a plant of smaller-than-optimal size (for example, 1,000 units). This kind of entry leaves total industry demand larger than industry supply (22,000 > 21,000). However, the new entrant faces a serious cost disadvantage in this case because it does not produce at the low-cost position on the economies-of-scale curve. Faced with these bleak alternatives, the potential entrant simply does not enter even though incumbent firms are earning positive profits.

Of course, there are other options for potential entrants, besides entering at the efficient scale and losing money or entering at an inefficient scale and losing money. For example, potential entrants can attempt to expand the total size of the market (that is, increase total demand from 22,000 to 24,000 units or more) and enter at the optimal size. Potential entrants can also attempt to develop new production technology, shift the economies-of-scale curve to the left (thereby reducing the optimal plant size), and enter. Or, potential entrants may try to make their products seem very special to their customers, enabling them to charge higher prices to offset higher production costs associated with a smaller-than-optimal plant.[11]

Any of these firm actions may enable entry into an industry. However, these actions are costly. If the cost of engaging in these "barrier-busting" activities is greater than the return from entry, entry will not occur, even if incumbent firms are earning positive profits.

Historically, economies of scale acted as a barrier to entry into the worldwide steel market. To fully exploit economies of scale, traditional steel plants had to be very large. If new entrants into the steel market had built these efficient and large steel-manufacturing plants, they would have had the effect of increasing the steel supply over the demand for steel, and the outcome would have been reduced profits for both new entrants and incumbent firms. This discouraged new entry. However, in the 1970s, the development of alternative mini-mill technology shifted the economies-of-scale curve to the left by making smaller plants very efficient in addressing some segments of the steel market. This shift had the effect of decreasing barriers to entry into the steel industry. Recent entrants, including Nucor Steel and Chaparral Steel, now have significant cost advantages over firms still using outdated, less efficient production technology.[12]

Product Differentiation as a Barrier to Entry

Product differentiation means that incumbent firms possess brand identification and customer loyalty that potential entrants do not possess. Brand identification and customer loyalty serve as entry barriers because new entrants not only have to absorb the standard costs associated with starting production in a new industry; they also have to absorb the costs associated with overcoming incumbent firms' differentiation advantages. If the cost of overcoming these advantages is greater than the potential return from entering an industry, entry will not occur, even if incumbent firms are earning positive profits.

There are numerous examples of industries where product differentiation tends to act as a barrier to entry. In the brewing industry, for example, substantial investments by Budweiser, Miller, and Coors (among other incumbent firms) in advertising (will we ever forget the Budweiser frogs?) and brand recognition have made large-scale entry into the U.S. brewing industry very costly.[13] E. & J. Gallo Winery, a U.S. winemaker, faces product differentiation barriers to entry in its efforts to sell Gallo wine in the French market. The market for wine in France is huge—the French consume 16.1 gallons of wine per person per year, for a total consumption of over 400 million cases of wine, while U.S. consumers drink only 1.8 gallons of wine per person per year, for a total consumption of less than 200 million cases. Despite this difference, intense loyalties to local French vineyards have made it very difficult for Gallo to break into this huge French market—a market where American wines are still given as "gag gifts" and only American theme restaurants carry U.S. wines on their menus. Gallo is attempting to overcome this product differentiation advantage of French wineries by emphasizing its California roots—roots that many French consider to be exotic—and downplaying the fact that it is a U.S. company, corporate origins that are less attractive to many French consumers.[14]

Table 2.2   **Sources of Cost Advantage, Independent of Scale, That Can Act as Barriers to Entry**

Proprietary Technology: When incumbent firms have secret or patented technology that reduces their costs below the costs of potential entrants, potential entrants must develop substitute technologies to compete. The cost of developing this technology can act as a barrier to entry.

Managerial Know-how: When incumbent firms have taken-for-granted knowledge, skills, and information that take years to develop, not possessed by potential entrants. The cost of developing this know-how can act as a barrier to entry.

Favorable Access to Raw Materials: When incumbent firms have low-cost access to critical raw materials not enjoyed by potential entrants. The cost of gaining similar access can act as a barrier to entry.

Learning-Curve Cost Advantages: When the cumulative volume of production of incumbent firms gives them cost advantages not enjoyed by potential entrants. These cost disadvantages of potential entrants can act as a barrier to entry.

Cost Advantages Independent of Scale as Barriers to Entry

In addition to the barriers previously cited, incumbent firms may have a whole range of cost advantages, independent of economies of scale, compared to new entrants. These cost advantages can act to deter entry, because new entrants will find themselves at a cost disadvantage vis-à-vis incumbent firms with these cost advantages. New entrants can engage in activities to overcome the cost advantages of incumbent firms, but as the cost of overcoming them increases, the economic profit potential from entry is reduced. In some settings, incumbent firms enjoying cost advantages, independent of scale, can earn superior profits and still not be threatened by new entry because the cost of overcoming those advantages can be prohibitive. Examples of these cost advantages, independent of scale, are presented in Table 2.2 and include: (1) proprietary technology, (2) managerial know-how, (3) favorable access to raw materials, and (4) learning-curve cost advantages.

Proprietary Technology. In some industries, **proprietary** (that is secret or patented) **technology** gives incumbent firms important cost advantages over potential entrants. To enter these industries, potential entrants must develop their own substitute technologies or run the risks of copying another firm's patented technologies. Both of these activities can be costly. Numerous firms in a wide variety of industries have discovered the sometimes substantial economic costs associated with violating another firm's patented proprietary technology. For example, in 1991, Eastman Kodak had to pay Polaroid $873 million for violating patents; in 1997, Intel had to pay Digital $700 million for violating patents; in 2002, Roche Holding had to pay Igen International $505 million for violating patents; and in 2002, Genentech had to pay City of Hope National Medical Center $500 million for violating patents.

Indeed, in the United States, at least 20 firms have had to pay some other firm over $100 million for violating this other firm's patents. And this does not include the numerous patent infringement suits that are settled out of court, suits that involve literally billions of dollars exchanging hands. Obviously, if an industry has several firms with proprietary technologies, these technologies can substantially increase the cost of entry into that industry.[15]

Managerial Know-How. Even more important than technology per se as a barrier to entry is the managerial know-how built up by incumbent firms over their history.[16] **Managerial know-how** is the often-taken-for-granted knowledge and information that are needed to compete in an industry on a day-to-day basis.[17] Know-how includes information about countless details (that has taken years, sometimes decades, to accumulate) in a firm that enables a firm to interact with customers and suppliers, to be innovative and creative, to manufacture quality products, and so forth. Typically, new entrants will not have access to this know-now and it will often be costly for them to build it quickly.

One industry where this kind of know-how is a very important barrier to entry is the pharmaceutical industry. Success in this industry depends critically on having high-quality research and development skills. The development of world-class research and development skills takes decades, as firms accumulate the knowledge, abilities, ideas—the know-how—needed to succeed. New entrants face enormous cost disadvantages for decades as they attempt to develop these abilities, and thus entry into the pharmaceutical industry has been quite limited.[18]

Favorable Access to Raw Materials. Incumbent firms may also have cost advantages, compared to new entrants, based on favorable access to raw materials. If, for example, there are only a few sources of high-quality iron ore in a specific geographic region, steel firms that have access to these sources may have a cost advantage over steel firms that must ship their ore in from distant sources.[19]

Learning-Curve Cost Advantages. It has been shown that in certain industries (such as airplane manufacturing), the cost of production falls with the cumulative volume of production. Over time, as incumbent firms gain experience in manufacturing, their costs fall below those of potential entrants. Potential entrants, in this context, must endure substantially higher costs while they gain experience, and thus they may not enter, despite possible superior profits being earned by incumbent firms. These learning-curve economies are discussed in more detail in Chapter 4.

Government Policy as a Barrier to Entry

Governments, for their own reasons, may decide to increase the cost of entry into an industry. This occurs most frequently when a firm operates as a government-regulated monopoly. In this setting, the government has concluded that it is in a better position to ensure that specific products or services are made available to the population at reasonable prices than competitive market forces. Industries such as electric power generation and elementary and secondary education have been (and to some extent, continue to be) protected from competitive entry by government restrictions on entry.

While the government has acted to restrict competitive entry in many industries in the past, the number of such industries and the level of this entry restriction have both fallen dramatically over the last several years. Indeed, in the United States, deregulation in the electric power generation industry has been occurring at a rapid pace. And while the bankruptcy of Enron may delay the relaxing of government-imposed barriers to entry into this industry, most observers agree that these restrictions will continue to be less important in the future. Entry is even occurring in the primary and secondary school industry with the creation of "charter schools"—often private schools that provide educational alternatives to public school systems.

The Threat of Rivalry

New entrants are an important threat to the ability of firms to maintain or improve their level of performance, but they are not the only threat in a firm's environment. A second environmental threat in the five forces framework is **rivalry**—the intensity of competition among a firm's direct competitors. Both Barnes & Noble .com and Borders.com have become rivals of Amazon.com. CBS, NBC, Fox, USA Networks, and TNN—to name a few—are all ESPN rivals.

Rivalry threatens firms by reducing their economic profits. High levels of rivalry are indicated by such actions as frequent price cutting by firms in an industry (for example, price discounts in the airline industry), frequent introduction of new products by firms in an industry (for example, continuous product introductions in consumer electronics), intense advertising campaigns (for example, Pepsi versus Coke advertising), and rapid competitive actions and reactions in an industry (competing airlines quickly matching the discounts of other airlines).

Some of the attributes of an industry that are likely to generate high levels of rivalry are listed in Table 2.3. First, rivalry tends to be high when there are numerous firms in an industry and these firms tend to be roughly the same size. Such is the case in the laptop personal computer industry. Worldwide, over 120 firms have entered the laptop computer market, and no one firm dominates in market share. Since the early 1990s, prices in the laptop market have been declining 25 to 30 percent a year. Profit margins for laptop personal computer firms that used to be in the 10 to 13 percent range have rapidly fallen to 3 and 4 percent.[20]

Second, rivalry tends to be high when industry growth is slow. When industry growth is slow, firms seeking to increase their sales must acquire market share from established competitors. This tends to increase rivalry. Intense price rivalry emerged in the U.S. fast-food industry—with 99-cent Whoppers at Burger King and "dollar menus" at Wendy's and McDonald's—when the growth in this industry declined.[21]

Third, rivalry tends to be high when firms are unable to differentiate their products in an industry. When product differentiation is not a viable strategic option, firms are often forced to compete only on the basis of price. Intense price competition is typical of high-rivalry industries. In the airline industry, for example, intense competition on longer routes—such as between Los Angeles and New York and Los Angeles and Chicago—has kept prices on these routes down. There are relatively few product differentiation options on these routes. However, by creating hub-and-spoke systems, certain airlines (American, United, Delta) have been able to develop regions of the United States where they are the dominant carrier. These hub-and-spoke systems enable airlines to partially differentiate their products geographically and thus reduce the level of rivalry in segments of this industry.[22]

Finally, rivalry tends to be high when production capacity is added in large increments. If, in order to obtain economies of scale, production capacity must be

Table 2.3   **Attributes of an Industry That Increase the Threat of Rivalry**

1. Large number of competing firms that are roughly the same size
2. Slow industry growth
3. Lack of product differentiation
4. Capacity added in large increments

added in large increments, an industry is likely to experience periods of oversupply after new capacity comes on line. This overcapacity often leads to price cutting. Much of the growing rivalry in the commercial jet industry between Boeing and AirBus can be traced to the large manufacturing capacity additions made by AirBus when it entered the industry.[23]

The Threat of Substitutes

A third environmental threat in the five forces framework is substitutes. The products or services provided by a firm's rivals meet approximately the same customer needs in the same ways as the products or services provided by the firm itself. **Substitutes** meet approximately the same customer needs but do so in different ways. Close substitutes for Amazon.com include Barnes & Noble, Borders, and Waldenbooks book stores. Television is a somewhat more distant substitute for Amazon, because the popularity of television comedies, dramas, and documentaries dampens demand for books. Substitutes for ESPN include sports magazines, sports pages in the newspapers, and actually attending sporting events.

Substitutes place a ceiling on the prices firms in an industry can charge and on the profits firms in an industry can earn. In the extreme, substitutes can ultimately replace an industry's products and services. This happens when a substitute is clearly superior to previous products. Examples include electronic calculators as substitutes for slide rules and mechanical calculators, electronic watch movements as substitutes for pin–lever mechanical watch movements, and compact discs as substitutes for long-playing (LP) records (although some audiophiles continue to argue for the sonic superiority of LPs). An open question remains about the extent to which online downloading of music is a substitute for compact discs.

Substitutes are playing an increasingly important role in reducing the profit potential in a wide variety of industries. For example, in the legal profession, private mediation and arbitration services are becoming viable substitutes for lawyers. Computerized texts are becoming viable substitutes for printed books in the publishing industry. Television news programs, especially services like CNN, are very threatening substitutes for weekly news magazines, including *Time* and *Newsweek*. In Europe, so–called superstores are threatening smaller food shops. Minor league baseball teams are partial substitutes for major league teams. Cable television is a substitute for broadcast television. Groups of "Big Box" retailers are substitutes for traditional shopping centers. Private mail delivery systems (like those in the Netherlands and Australia) are substitutes for government postal services. Home financial planning software is a partial substitute for professional financial planners.[24]

The Threat of Suppliers

A fourth environmental threat in the five forces framework is suppliers. **Suppliers** make a wide variety of raw materials, labor, and other critical assets available to firms. Suppliers can threaten the performance of firms in an industry by increasing the price of their supplies or by reducing the quality of those supplies. Any profits that were being earned in an industry can be transferred to suppliers in this way. For Amazon, book publishers and, more recently, book authors are critical suppliers, along with the employees that provide programming and logistics capabilities to Amazon. Critical suppliers for ESPN include

Table 2.4   **Indicators of the Threat of Suppliers in an Industry**

1. Suppliers' industry dominated by small number of firms.
2. Suppliers sell unique or highly differentiated products.
3. Suppliers are *not* threatened by substitutes.
4. Suppliers threaten forward vertical integration.
5. Firms are *not* important customers for suppliers.

sports leagues—such as the NFL and the NHL—as well as TV personalities that staff ESPN television shows.

Some supplier attributes that can lead to high levels of threat are listed in Table 2.4. First, a firm's suppliers are a greater threat if the *suppliers'* industry is dominated by a small number of firms. In this setting, a firm has little choice but to purchase supplies from these firms. These few firms thus have enormous flexibility to charge high prices, to reduce quality, or in other ways to squeeze the profits of the firms to which they sell. Much of Microsoft's power in the software industry reflects its dominance in the operating system market, where Windows remains the de facto standard for most personal computers. For now, at least, if a company wants to sell personal computers, it is going to need to interact with Microsoft. It will be interesting to see if Linux-based PCs become more powerful, thereby limiting some of Microsoft's power as a supplier.

Conversely, when a firm has the option of purchasing from a large number of suppliers, suppliers have less power to threaten a firm's profits. For example, as the number of lawyers in the United States has increased over the years (up 40 percent since 1981, currently close to one million), lawyers and law firms have been forced to begin competing for work. Some corporate clients have forced law firms to reduce their hourly fees and to handle repetitive simple legal tasks for low flat fees.[25]

Second, suppliers are a greater threat when what they supply is unique or highly differentiated. There was only one Michael Jordan, as a basketball player, as a spokesperson, and as a celebrity (but *not* as a baseball player). Jordan's unique status gave him enormous bargaining power as a supplier and enabled him to extract much of the economic profit that would otherwise have been earned by the Chicago Bulls and Nike. Currently, there is only one Le Bron James. In the same way, Intel's unique ability to develop, manufacture, and sell microprocessors gives it significant bargaining power as a supplier in the personal computer industry.

The uniqueness of suppliers can operate in almost any industry. For example, in the highly competitive world of television talk shows, some guests, as suppliers, can gain surprising fame for their unique characteristics. For example, one woman was a guest on eight talk shows. Her claim to fame: She was the tenth wife of a gay, con-man bigamist. Talk show hosts can also exercise significant power as suppliers. King World, the distributor of the *Oprah* talk show, has depended on *Oprah* for as much as 40 percent of its revenues. This, of course, has given the show's host, Oprah Winfrey, significant leverage in negotiating with King World.[26]

Third, suppliers are a greater threat to firms in an industry when suppliers are *not* threatened by substitutes. When there are no effective substitutes, suppliers can take advantage of their position to extract economic profits from firms they supply. Both Intel (in microprocessors) and Microsoft (in PC operating systems) have been accused of exploiting their unique product positions to extract profits from customers.

When there are substitutes for supplies, supplier power is checked. In the metal can industry, for example, steel cans are threatened by aluminum and plastic containers as substitutes. In order to continue to sell to can manufacturers, steel companies have had to keep their prices lower than what would otherwise have been the case. In this way, the potential power of the steel companies is checked by the existence of substitute products.[27]

Fourth, suppliers are a greater threat to firms when they can credibly threaten to enter into and begin competing in a firm's industry. This is called **forward vertical integration**, where suppliers cease to be suppliers alone and become suppliers *and* rivals. The threat of forward vertical integration is partially a function of barriers to entry into an industry. When an industry has high barriers to entry, suppliers face significant costs of forward vertical integration, and thus forward integration is not as serious a threat to the profits of incumbent firms (vertical integration is discussed in detail in Chapter 6).

Finally, suppliers are a threat to firms when firms are *not* an important part of suppliers' business. Steel companies, for example, are not too concerned with losing the business of a sculptor or of a small construction company. However, they are very concerned about losing the business of the major can manufacturers, major white-goods manufacturers (that is, manufacturers of refrigerators, washing machines, dryers, and so forth), and automobile companies. Steel companies, as suppliers, are likely to be very accommodating and willing to reduce prices and increase quality for can manufacturers, white-goods manufacturers, and auto companies. Smaller, "less important" customers, however, are likely to be subject to greater price increases, lower-quality service, and lower-quality products.

The Threat of Buyers

The final environmental threat in the five forces framework is buyers. **Buyers** purchase a firm's products or services. Where sellers act to increase a firm's costs, buyers act to decrease a firm's revenues. Amazon.com's buyers include all those who purchase books online as well as those who purchase advertising space on Amazon's Web site. ESPN's buyers include all those who watch sports on television as well as those who purchase advertising space on the network. Some of the important indicators of the threat of buyers are listed in Table 2.5.

First, if a firm has only one buyer, or a small number of buyers, these buyers can be very threatening. Firms that sell a significant amount of their output to the U.S. Department of Defense recognize the influence of this buyer on their operations. Reductions in defense spending have forced defense companies to try even harder to reduce costs and increase quality to satisfy government

Table 2.5   **Indicators of the Threat of Buyers in an Industry**

1. Number of buyers is small.
2. Products sold to buyers are undifferentiated and standard.
3. Products sold to buyers are a significant percentage of a buyer's final costs.
4. Buyers are *not* earning significant economic profits.
5. Buyers threaten backward vertical integration.

demands. All these actions reduce the economic profits of these defense-oriented companies.[28] Firms that sell to large retail chains have also found it difficult to maintain high levels of profitability. Powerful retail firms—like Wal-Mart and Home Depot—can make significant and complex logistical and other demands on their suppliers and, if suppliers fail to meet these demands, buyers can "fire" their suppliers. These demands can have the effect of reducing the profits of suppliers.

Second, if the products or services that are being sold to buyers are standard and not differentiated, then the threat of buyers can be greater. For example, farmers sell a very standard product. It is very difficult to differentiate products like wheat, corn, or tomatoes (although this can be done to some extent through the development of new strains of crops, the timing of harvests, no use of pesticides, and so forth). In general, wholesale grocers and food brokers can always find alternative suppliers of basic food products. These numerous alternative suppliers increase the threat of buyers and force farmers to keep their prices and profits low. If any one farmer attempts to raise prices, wholesale grocers and food brokers simply purchase their supplies from some other farmer.

Third, buyers are likely to be more of a threat when the supplies they purchase are a significant portion of the costs of their final products. In this context, buyers are likely to be very concerned about the costs of their supplies and constantly on the lookout for cheaper alternatives. For example, in the canned food industry, the cost of the can itself can constitute up to 40 percent of a product's final price. Not surprisingly, firms like Campbell Soup Company are very concerned about keeping the price of the cans they purchase as low as possible.[29]

Fourth, buyers are likely to be more of a threat when they are *not* earning significant economic profits. In these circumstances, buyers are likely to be very sensitive to costs and insist on the lowest possible cost and the highest possible quality from suppliers. This effect can be exacerbated when the profits suppliers earn are greater than the profits buyers earn. In this setting, a buyer would have a strong incentive to enter into its supplier's business to capture some of the economic profits being earned by the supplier. This strategy of **backward vertical integration** is discussed in more detail in Chapter 6.

Finally, buyers are more of a threat to firms in an industry when they have the ability to vertically integrate backward. In this case, buyers become both buyers and rivals and lock in a certain percentage of an industry's sales. The extent to which buyers represent a threat to vertically integrate, in turn, depends on the barriers to entry that are not in place in an industry. If there are significant barriers to entry, buyers may not be able to engage in backward vertical integration, and their threat to firms is reduced.

The Five Forces Model and Average Industry Performance

The five forces model has three important implications for managers seeking to choose and implement strategies. First, this model describes the most common sources of local environmental threat in industries. These are the threat of entry, the threat of rivalry, the threat of substitutes, the threat of suppliers, and the threat of buyers. Second, this model can be used to characterize the overall level of threat in an industry. Finally, since the overall level of threat in an industry is, according to S-C-P logic, related to the average level of performance of a firm in an industry, the five forces model can also be used to anticipate the average level of performance of firms in an industry.

Of course, it will rarely be the case that all five forces in an industry will be equally threatening at the same time. This can sometimes complicate the anticipation of the

Table 2.6   **Estimating the Level of Average Performance in an Industry**

	Industry I	**Industry II**	**Industry III**	**Industry IV**
Threat of Entry	High	Low	High	Low
Threat of Rivalry	High	Low	Low	High
Threat of Substitutes	High	Low	High	Low
Threat of Suppliers	High	Low	Low	High
Threat of Buyers	High	Low	High	Low
Expected Average Firm Performance	High	Low	?	?

average level of firm performance in an industry. Consider, for example, the four industries in Table 2.6. It is easy to anticipate the average level of performance of firms in the first two industries: In Industry I, this performance will be high; in Industry II, this performance will be low; however, in Industries III and IV it is somewhat more complicated. In these mixed situations, the real question to ask in anticipating the average performance of firms in an industry is: "Are one or more threats in this industry powerful enough to appropriate most of the profits that firms in this industry might generate?" If the answer to this question is yes, then the anticipated average level of performance will be low. If the answer is no, then this anticipated performance will be high.

Even more fundamentally, the five forces framework can be used only to anticipate the average level of firm performance in an industry. This is all right if a firm's industry is the primary determinant of its overall performance. However, as described in the Research Made Relevant feature, research suggests that the industry a firm operates in is far from the only determinant of its performance.

Another Environmental Force: Complementors

Recently, Professors Adam Brandenburger and Barry Nalebuff have suggested that another force needs to be added to Porter's five forces framework.[30] These authors distinguish between competitors and what they call a firm's complementors. If you were the CEO of a firm, this is how you could tell the difference between your competitors and your complementors. Another firm is a **competitor** if your customers value your product less when they have this other firm's product than when they have your product alone. Rivals, new entrants, and substitutes can all be seen as specific examples of competitors. On the other hand, another firm is a **complementor** if your customers value your product more when they have this other firm's product than when they have your product alone.

Consider, for example, the relationship between producers of television programming and cable television companies. The value of these firms' products partially depends on the existence of each other. Television producers need outlets for their programming. The growth in the number of channels on cable television provides more of these outlets and thus increases the value of these production firms. On the other hand, cable television companies can continue to add channels, but those channels need content. So, the value of cable television companies depends partly on the existence of television production firms. Since the value of television producing companies is greater when cable television firms exist, and since the value of cable television companies is greater when television producing companies exist, these types of firms are complements.

Brandenburger and Nalebuff go on to argue that an important difference between complementors and competitors is that a firm's complementors help

Research Made Relevant

For some time now, scholars have been interested in the relative impact of the attributes of the industry within which a firm operates and the attributes of a firm, itself, on its performance. The first work in this area was published by Richard Schmalansee. Using a single year's worth of data, Schmalansee estimated the variance in the performance of firms that was attributable to the industries within which firms operated versus other sources of performance variance. Schmalansee's conclusion was that approximately 20 percent of the variance in firm performance was explained by the industry within which a firm operated—a conclusion consistent with the S-C-P model and its emphasis on industry as a primary determinant of a firm's performance.

Richard Rumelt identified some weaknesses in Schmalansee's research. Most important of these was that Schmalansee had only one year's worth of data with which to examine the effects of industry and firm attributes on firm

The Impact of Industry and Firm Characteristics on Firm Performance

performance. Rumelt was able to use four year's worth of data, which allowed him to distinguish between stable and transient industry and firm effects on firm performance. Rumelt's results were consistent with Schmalansee's in one sense: Rumelt also found that about 16

percent of the variance in firm performance was due to industry effects versus Schmalansee's 20 percent. However, only about half of this industry effect was stable. The rest represented year-to-year fluctuations in the business conditions in an industry. This result is broadly inconsistent with the S-C-P model.

Rumelt also examined the impact of firm attributes on firm performance and found that over 80 percent of the variance in firm performance was due to these firm attributes, but that over half of this 80 percent (46.38%) was due to stable firm effects. The importance of stable firm differences in explaining differences in firm performance is also inconsistent with the S-C-P framework. These results are consistent with another model of firm performance called the Resource-Based View, which will be described in Chapter 3.

Sources: R. P. Rumelt (1991). "How much does industry matter?" *Strategic Management Journal,* 12, pp. 167–185; R. Schmalansee (1985). "Do markets differ much?" *American Economic Review,* 75, pp. 341–351.

increase the size of a firm's market, while a firm's competitors divide this market among a set of firms. Based on this logic, these authors suggest that while it is usually the case that a firm will want to discourage the entry of competitors into its market, it will usually want to encourage the entry of complementors. Returning to the television producers/cable television example, television producers will actually want cable television companies to grow and prosper and constantly add new channels, while cable television firms will want television show producers to grow and constantly create new and innovative programming. If the growth of either of these businesses slows, it hurts the growth of the other.

Of course, the same firm can be a complementor for one firm and a competitor for another. For example, the invention of satellite television and the popularization of DirecTV and the Dish Network represent a competitive challenge to cable television companies. That is, DirecTV and, say, Time Warner Cable, are competitors. However, DirecTV and television production companies are complementors to each other. In deciding whether or not to encourage the entry of new complementors, a firm has to weigh the extra value these new complementors will create against the competitive impact of this entry on a firm's current complementors.

It is also the case that a single firm can be both a competitor and a complementor to the same firm. This is very common in industries where it is important to create technological standards. Without standards about, for example, the size of a CD, how information on a CD will be stored, how this information will be read, and so forth, consumers will often be unwilling to purchase a CD player. With standards in place, however, sales of a particular technology can soar. To develop technology standards, firms must be willing to cooperate. This cooperation means that, with respect to the technology standard, these firms are complementors. And indeed, when these firms act as complementors, their actions have the effect of increasing the total size of the market. However, once these firms cooperate to establish standards, they begin to compete to try to obtain as much of the market they jointly created as possible. In this sense, these firms are also competitors.

Understanding when firms in an industry should behave as complementors and when they should behave as competitors is sometimes very difficult. It is even more difficult for a firm that has interacted with other firms in its industry as a competitor to change its organizational structure, formal and informal control systems, and compensation policy and start interacting with these firms as a complementor, at least for some purposes. Learning to manage what Brandenburger and Nalebuff call the "Jekyll and Hyde" dilemma associated with competitors and complementors can distinguish excellent from only average firms.

Industry Structure and Environmental Opportunities

Identifying environmental threats is only half the task in accomplishing an external analysis. Such an analysis must also identify opportunities. Fortunately, the same S-C-P logic that made it possible to develop tools for the analysis of environmental threats can also be used to develop tools for the analysis of environmental opportunities. However, instead of identifying the threats that are common in most industries, opportunity analysis begins by identifying several generic industry structures and then describing the strategic opportunities that are available in each of these different kinds of industries.[31]

Of course, there are many different generic industry structures. However, four are very common and will be the focus of opportunity analysis in this book. These four are: (1) fragmented industries, (2) emerging industries, (3) mature industries, and (4) declining industries. A fifth industry structure—international industries—will be discussed later in the chapter. The kinds of opportunities typically associated with these industry structures are presented in Table 2.7.

Table 2.7 **Industry Structure and Environmental Opportunities**

Industry structure	Opportunities
Fragmented industry	Consolidation
Emerging industry	First-mover advantages
Mature industry	Product refinement
	Investment in service quality
	Process innovation
Declining industry	Leadership
	Niche
	Harvest
	Divestment

Opportunities in Fragmented Industries: Consolidation

Fragmented industries are industries in which a large number of small or medium-sized firms operate and no small set of firms has dominant market share or creates dominant technologies. Most service industries, including retailing, fabrics, and commercial printing, to name just a few, are fragmented industries.

Industries can be fragmented for a wide variety of reasons. For example, there may be few barriers to entry into a fragmented industry, thereby encouraging numerous small firms to enter. There may be few, if any, economies of scale, and even some important diseconomies of scale, thus encouraging firms to remain small. Also, there may be a need for close local control over enterprises in an industry—for example, local movie houses and local restaurants, to ensure quality and to minimize losses from theft.

The major opportunity facing firms in fragmented industries is the implementation of strategies that begin to consolidate the industry into a smaller number of firms. Firms that are successful in implementing this **consolidation strategy** can become industry leaders and obtain benefits from this kind of effort, if they exist.

Consolidation can occur in several ways. For example, an incumbent firm may discover new economies of scale in an industry. In the highly fragmented funeral home industry, Service Corporation International (SCI) found that the development of a chain of funeral homes gave it advantages in acquiring key supplies (coffins) and in the allocation of scarce resources (morticians and hearses). By acquiring numerous previously independent funeral homes, SCI was able to substantially reduce its costs and gain higher levels of economic performance.[32]

Incumbent firms sometimes adopt new ownership structures to help consolidate an industry. Kampgrounds of America (KOA) uses franchise agreements with local operators to provide camping facilities to travelers in the fragmented private camping grounds industry. KOA provides local operators with professional training, technical skills, and access to brand name reputation. Local operators, in return, provide KOA with local managers who are intensely interested in the financial and operational success of their campgrounds. Similar franchise agreements have been instrumental in the consolidation of other fragmented industries, including fast foods (McDonald's), muffler repair (Midas), and motels (La Quinta, Holiday Inn, Howard Johnson's).[33]

The benefits of implementing a consolidation strategy in a fragmented industry turn on the advantages larger firms in such industries gain from their larger market share. As will be discussed in Chapter 4, firms with large market share can have important cost advantages. Large market share can also help a firm differentiate its products.

Opportunities in Emerging Industries: First-Mover Advantages

Emerging industries are newly created or newly re-created industries formed by technological innovations, changes in demand, the emergence of new customer needs, and so forth. Over the last 30 years, the world economy has been flooded by emerging industries, including the microprocessor industry, the personal computer industry, the medical imaging industry, and the biotechnology industry, to name a few. Firms in emerging industries face a unique set of opportunities, the exploitation of which can be a source of superior performance for some time for some firms.

The opportunities that face firms in emerging industries fall into the general category of first-mover advantages. **First-mover advantages** are advantages that come to firms that make important strategic and technological decisions early in the development of an industry. In emerging industries, many of the rules of the game and standard operating procedures for competing and succeeding have yet to be established. First-moving firms can sometimes help establish the rules of the game and create an industry's structure in ways that are uniquely beneficial to them. In general, first-mover advantages can arise from three primary sources: (1) technological leadership, (2) preemption of strategically valuable assets, and (3) the creation of customer-switching costs.[34]

First-Mover Advantages and Technological Leadership

Firms that make early investments in particular technologies in an industry are implementing a **technological leadership strategy**. Such strategies can generate two advantages in emerging industries. First, firms that have implemented these strategies may obtain a low-cost position based on their greater cumulative volume of production with a particular technology. These cost advantages have had important competitive implications in such diverse industries as the manufacture of titanium dioxide by DuPont and Procter & Gamble's competitive advantage in disposable diapers.[35]

Second, firms that make early investments in a technology may obtain patent protections that enhance their performance.[36] Xerox's patents on the xerography process and General Electric's patent on Edison's original light bulb design were important for these firms' success when these two industries were emerging.[37] However, although there are some exceptions (for example, the pharmaceutical industry and specialty chemicals), patents, per se, seem to provide relatively small profit opportunities for first-moving firms in most emerging industries. One group of researchers found that imitators can duplicate first movers' patent–based advantages for about 65 percent of the first mover's costs.[38] These researchers also found that 60 percent of all patents are imitated within four years of being granted—without legally violating patent rights obtained by first movers. As we will discuss in detail in Chapter 3, patents are rarely a source of sustained competitive advantage for firms, even in emerging industries.

First-Mover Advantages and Preemption of Strategically Valuable Assets

First movers that invest only in technology usually do not obtain sustained competitive advantages. However, first movers that move to tie up strategically valuable resources in an industry before their full value is widely understood can gain sustained competitive advantages. **Strategically valuable assets** are resources required to successfully compete in an industry. Firms that are able to acquire these resources have, in effect, erected formidable barriers to imitation in an industry. Some strategically valuable assets that can be acquired in this way include access to raw materials, particularly favorable geographic locations, and particularly valuable product market positions.

When an oil company like Royal Dutch Shell (because of its superior exploration skills) acquires leases with greater development potential than was expected by its competition, the company is gaining access to raw materials in a way that is likely to generate sustained competitive advantages. When Wal–Mart opens stores in medium-sized cities before the arrival of its competition, Wal-Mart is making it difficult for the competition to enter into this market. And when breakfast cereal companies expand their product lines to include all possible combinations of wheat, oats, bran, corn, and sugar, they are using a first-mover advantage to deter entry.[39]

First-Mover Advantages and Creating Customer-Switching Costs

Firms can also gain first-mover advantages in an emerging industry by creating customer-switching costs. **Customer-switching costs** exist when customers make investments in order to use a firm's particular products or services and when these investments are not useful in accomplishing this. These investments tie customers to a particular firm and make it more difficult for customers to begin purchasing from different firms.[40] Such switching costs are important factors in industries as diverse as applications software for personal computers, prescription pharmaceuticals, and groceries.[41]

In applications software for personal computers, users make very significant investments to learn how to use a particular software package. Once computer users have learned how to operate particular software, they are unlikely to switch to new software, even if that new software system is superior to what they currently use. Such a switch would require learning the new software and how it is similar to and different form the old software. For these reasons, some computer users will continue to use outdated software, even though new software performs much better.

Similar switching costs can exist in some segments of the prescription pharmaceutical industry. Once medical doctors become familiar with a particular drug, its applications, and side effects, they are sometimes reluctant to change to a new drug, even if that new drug promises to be more effective than the older, more familiar drug. Trying the new drug requires learning about its properties and side effects. Even if the new drug has received government approvals, its use requires doctors to be willing to "experiment" with the health of their patients. Given these issues, many physicians are unwilling to rapidly adopt new drug therapies. This is one reason that pharmaceutical firms spend so much time and money using their sales forces to educate their physician customers. This kind of education is necessary if a doctor is going to be willing to switch from an old drug to a new drug.

Customer-switching costs can even play a role in the grocery store industry. Each grocery store has a particular layout of products. Once customers learn where different products in a particular store are located, they are not likely to change stores, because in so doing they would have to relearn the location of products. Many customers want to avoid the time and frustration associated with wandering around a new store looking for some obscure product. Indeed, the cost of switching stores may be large enough to enable some grocery stores to charge higher prices than what would be the case without customer-switching costs.

First-Mover Disadvantages

Of course, the advantages of first moving in emerging industries must be balanced against the risks associated with exploiting this opportunity. Emerging industries are characterized by a great deal of uncertainty. When first-moving firms are making critical strategic decisions, it may not be at all clear what the right decisions are. In such highly uncertain settings, a reasonable strategic alternative to first moving may be retaining flexibility. Where first-moving firms attempt to resolve the uncertainty they face by making decisions early and then trying to influence the evolution of an emerging industry, they use flexibility to resolve this uncertainty by delaying decisions until the economically correct path is clear and then moving quickly to take advantage of that path.

Opportunities in Mature Industries: Product Refinement, Service, and Process Innovation

Emerging industries are often formed by the creation of new products or technologies that radically alter the rules of the game in an industry. However, over time, as these new ways of doing business become widely understood, as technologies diffuse through competitors, and as the rate of innovation in new products and technologies drops, an industry begins to enter the mature phase of its development. As described in the Strategy in the Emerging Enterprise feature, this change in the nature of a firm's industry can be difficult to recognize and can create both strategic and operational problems for a firm.

Common characteristics of **mature industries** include: (1) slowing growth in total industry demand, (2) the development of experienced repeat customers, (3) a slowdown in increases in production capacity, (4) a slowdown in the introduction of new products or services, (5) an increase in the amount of international competition, and (6) an overall reduction in the profitability of firms in the industry.[42]

The fast-food industry in the United States has become mature over the last 10 to 15 years. In the 1960s, there were only three large national fast-food chains in the United States: McDonald's, Burger King, and Dairy Queen. Through the 1980s, all three of these chains grew rapidly, although the rate of growth at McDonald's outstripped the growth rate of the other two firms. During this time period, however, other fast-food chains also entered the market. These included some national chains, such as Kentucky Fried Chicken, Wendy's, and Taco Bell, and some strong regional chains such as Jack in the Box and In and Out Burger. By the early 1990s, growth in this industry had slowed considerably. McDonald's announced that it was having difficulty finding locations for new McDonald's that did not impinge on the sales of already existing McDonald's. Except for non-U.S. operations, where competition in the fast-food industry is not as mature, the profitability of most U.S. fast-food companies did not grow as much in the 1990s as it did in the 1960s through the 1980s. Indeed, by 2002, all the major fast-food chains were either not making very much money, or like McDonald's, actually losing money.[43]

Opportunities for firms in mature industries typically shift from the development of new technologies and products in an emerging industry to a greater emphasis on refining a firm's current products, an emphasis on increasing the quality of service, and a focus on reducing manufacturing costs and increased quality through process innovations.

Refining Current Products

In mature industries such as home detergents, motor oil, and kitchen appliances, there are likely to be few, if any, major technological breakthroughs. However, this does not mean that there is not innovation in these industries. Innovation in these industries focuses on extending and improving current products and technologies. In home detergents, innovation recently has focused on changes in packaging and on selling more highly concentrated detergents. In motor oil, recent packaging changes (from fiber foil cans to plastic containers), additives that keep oil cleaner longer, and oil formulated to operate in four-cylinder engines are recent examples of this kind of innovation. In kitchen appliances, the availability of refrigerators with crushed ice and water through the door, commercial-grade stoves for home use, and dishwashers that automatically adjust the cleaning cycle depending on how dirty the dishes are, are recent improvements.[44]

Strategy in the Emerging Enterprise

*I*t began with a 5,000-word e-mail sent by Steve Balmer, CEO at Microsoft, to all 57,000 employees. Where previous e-mails from Microsoft founder Bill Gates—including one in 1995 calling on the firm to learn how to "ride the wave of the Internet"—inspired the firm to move on to conquer more technological challenges, Balmer's e-mail focused on Microsoft's current state and called on the firm to become more focused and efficient. Balmer also announced that Microsoft would cut its costs by $1 billion during the next fiscal year. One observer described it as the kind of e-mail you would expect to read at Procter & Gamble, not at Microsoft.

And then the other shoe dropped. In a surprise move, Balmer announced that Microsoft would distribute a large portion of its $56 billion cash reserve in the form of a special dividend to stockholders. In what is believed to be the largest such cash dispersion ever, Microsoft will distribute $32 billion to its stockholders, and use an additional $30 billion to buy back stock. Bill Gates, alone, will receive a $3.2 billion cash dividend. These changes would mean that Microsoft's capital structure would be more similar to, say, Procter & Gamble than to an entrepreneurial, high-flying software company.

What is happening at Microsoft? Is it the case that management at Microsoft has concluded that the PC software industry is no longer emerging, but has matured to the point that Microsoft will actually have to alter some of its traditional strategies? Most observers believe

Microsoft Grows Up

that Balmer's e-mail, and the decision to reduce its cash reserves, signal that, in fact, Microsoft has come to this conclusion. In fact, while most of Microsoft's core businesses—its Windows operating systems, its PC applications software, and its server software—are still growing at the rate of about $3 billion a year, if they were growing at historical rates, these businesses would be generating $7 billion in new revenues each year. Moreover, Microsoft's new businesses—video games, Internet services, business software, and software for phones and handheld computers—are adding less than $1 billion in new revenues each year. That is, growth in Microsoft's new businesses is not offsetting slower growth in its traditional businesses.

Other indicators of the growing maturity of the PC software industry, and Microsoft's strategic changes, also

exist. For example, during 2003 and 2004, Microsoft resolved most of the outstanding antitrust litigation it was facing, abandoned its employee stock option plan in favor of a stock-based compensation scheme popular with slower-growth firms, improved its systems for receiving and acting on feedback from customers, and improved the quality of its relationships with some of its major rivals, including Sun Microsystems, Inc. These are all the actions of a firm that recognizes that the rapid growth opportunities that existed in the software industry when Microsoft was a new company do not exist any more.

What Microsoft has to do now is to get its entire organization—all its employees, suppliers, and even its customers—used to the idea that high growth has been abandoned as a goal and replaced by maximizing returns for Microsoft's shareholders. Whether Microsoft will be able to retain all of its high-flying technical and managerial talent in this new world is yet to be seen. Microsoft may also have to get used to not being able to easily attract all the best technical and managerial talent it wants. But, if the PC software industry has really evolved from being an emerging to a mature industry, these are the kinds of strategic changes that a firm like Microsoft will have to make if it wants to retain its place in the industry.

Sources: J. Greene (2004). "Microsoft's midlife crisis." *BusinessWeek*, April 19, 2004, pp. 88 +; R. Guth and S. Thurm (2004). "Microsoft to dole out its cash hoard." *Wall Street Journal*, Wednesday, July 21, 2004, pp. A1 +, S. Hamm (2004). "Microsoft's worst enemy: Success." *BusinessWeek*, July 19, 2004, p. 33.

Emphasis on Service

When firms in an industry have only limited ability to invest in radical new technologies and products, efforts to differentiate products often turn toward the quality of customer service. A firm that is able to develop a reputation for high-quality customer service may be able to obtain superior performance even though the products it sells are not highly differentiated.

This emphasis on service has become very important in a wide variety of industries. For example, in the convenience food industry, one of the major reasons for slower growth in the fast-food segment has been a growth in the so-called "casual dining" segment. This segment includes restaurants such as Chili's and Applebee's. The food sold at fast-food restaurants and casual dining restaurants overlaps—they both sell burgers, soft drinks, salads, chicken, desserts, and so forth—although many consumers believe that the quality of food is superior in the casual dining restaurants. In an addition to any perceived differences in the food, however, the level of service in the two kinds of establishments varies significantly. At fast-food restaurants, food is handed to consumers on a tray; in casual dining restaurants, waiters and waitresses actually bring food to consumers on a plate. This level of service is one reason that casual dining is growing in popularity.[45]

Process Innovation

A firm's **processes** are the activities it engages in to design, produce, and sell its products or services. **Process innovation**, then, is a firms effort to refine and improve its current processes. Several authors have studied the relationship between process innovation, product innovation, and the maturity of an industry.[46] This work, summarized in Figure 2.5, suggests that in the early stages of industry development, product innovation is very important. However, over time, product innovation becomes less important, and process innovations designed to reduce manufacturing costs, increase product quality, and streamline management become more important. In mature industries, firms can often gain an advantage by manufacturing the same product as competitors, but at a lower cost. Alternatively, firms can manufacture a product that is perceived to be of higher quality and do so at a competitive cost. Process innovations facilitate both the reduction of costs and the increase in quality.

The role of process innovation in more mature industries is perhaps best exemplified by the improvement in quality in U.S. automobiles. In the 1980s, Japanese firms like Nissan, Toyota, and Honda sold cars that were of significantly higher quality than U.S. firms General Motors, Ford, and Chrysler. In the face of that competitive disadvantage, these U.S. firms engaged in numerous process reforms to improve the quality of their cars. In the 1980s, U.S. manufacturers were being cited for car body panels that did not fit well, bumpers that were hung crookedly on cars, and for putting the wrong engine in a car. Now, the differences

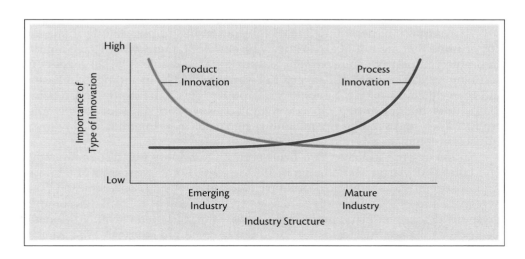

Figure 2.5 Process and Product Innovation and Industry Structure

Source: Taken from Hayes and Wheelwright, "The dynamics of process-product life cycles." *Harvard Business Review*, March-April, pp. 127–136.

in quality between newly manufactured U.S. and Japanese automobiles are very small. Indeed, one well-known judge of initial manufacturing quality—J. D. Powers—now focuses on items like the quality of a car's cup holders and the maximum distance at which a car's keyless entry system still works to establish quality rankings. The really significant quality issues of the 1980s are virtually gone. [47]

Opportunities in Declining Industries: Leadership, Niche, Harvest, and Divestment

A **declining industry** is an industry that has experienced an absolute decline in unit sales over a sustained period of time.[48] One of the most obvious examples of a declining industry is the U.S. defense business. During the Cold War, the U.S. defense industry constituted a significant portion of the country's Gross Domestic Product (GDP). Since the end of the Cold War in 1987, this industry has experienced a significant decline in sales. Between 1987 and 1995, total employment in the U.S. defense business dropped by 800,000, and this does not include 400,000 fewer people serving in the military. While the Gulf War and the Iraq War slowed this rate of decline for a time, the U.S. defense business continues to be a declining industry.

Obviously, firms in a declining industry face more threats than opportunities. Rivalry in a declining industry is likely to be very high, as is the threat of buyers, suppliers, and substitutes. However, even though threats are significant, there are opportunities that firms must recognize and, where appropriate, exploit. The major strategic options that firms in this kind of industry face are leadership, niche, harvest, and divestment.

Market Leadership

An industry in decline is often characterized by overcapacity in manufacturing, distribution, and so forth. Reduced demand often means that firms in this kind of industry will have to endure a significant shakeout period. A **shakeout period** exists when total supply in an industry is reduced by bankruptcies, acquisitions, and business closings. After a shakeout has occurred, a smaller number of lean and focused firms may enjoy a relatively benign environment with few threats and several opportunities. If a firm has decided to wait out the shakeout in hopes of better environmental conditions in the future, it should consider becoming a **market leader** in the pre–shakeout industry, most typically by becoming the firm with the largest market share in that industry.

The purpose of becoming a market leader in this setting is to facilitate the exit of firms that are not likely to survive a shakeout, thereby obtaining a more favorable competitive environment as quickly as possible. Market leaders in declining industries can facilitate exit in a variety of ways, including: purchasing and then de-emphasizing competitors' product lines, purchasing and retiring competitors' manufacturing capacity, manufacturing spare parts for competitors' product lines, and sending unambiguous signals of their intention to stay in an industry and remain a dominant firm.

In the defense industry, two firms seem to exemplify this leadership strategy: Loral and Martin Marietta. From 1987 to 1996, Loral spent over $1.8 billion buying several high-technology military electronics businesses, including Ford Aerospace and LTV's missile division. Clearly, management at Loral was committed to the defense industry. In the early 1990s, Martin Marietta acquired General Electric's aerospace businesses for $1 billion in preferred stock. In 1994, Martin

Marietta consolidated its position even more substantially with its $10 billion merger with Lockheed, and adopted a new name—Lockheed Martin. As is the case at Loral, top management at Lockheed Martin was convinced that the defense business would remain viable—after an industry shakeout—and wanted to be well positioned to exploit any possible opportunities there. Indeed, given the commitment of both Loral and Lockheed Martin to being market leaders in the declining defense industry, it was not too surprising when Lockheed Martin purchased most of Loral's assets for over $10 billion in 1996. This new firm had combined 2004 sales of over $32 billion.[49]

Market Niche

A firm following a leadership strategy in a declining industry attempts to facilitate exit by other firms, but a firm following a **niche strategy** in a declining industry reduces its scope of operations and focuses on narrow segments of the declining industry. If only a few firms choose this niche, then these firms may have a favorable competitive setting, even though the industry as a whole is facing shrinking demand.

In the defense industry, several smaller firms seem to be implementing niche strategies. Applied Signal Technology, a supplier of microwave and radio frequency components to Raytheon and Lockheed Martin, grew from $40 million in sales in 1990 to $117 million in 1997 by acquiring unwanted businesses and divisions from other firms. However, in most of these acquisitions, Applied Signal Technology remained focused on its relatively narrow market segment—microwave and radio frequency components. In 2003, Applied Signal Technology had sales of over $95 million and profits of $8.6 million. It seems likely that Applied Signal Technology will be a major player in this narrow segment of the defense industry.[50]

Harvest

Leadership and niche strategies, though differing along several dimensions, have one attribute in common: Firms that implement these strategies intend to remain in the industry despite its decline. Firms pursuing a **harvest** strategy in a declining industry do not expect to remain in the industry over the long term. Instead, they engage in a long, systematic, phased withdrawal, extracting as much value as possible during the withdrawal period. Firms can implement a harvest strategy by reducing the range of products they sell, reducing their distribution network, eliminating less profitable customers, reducing product quality, reducing service quality, deferring maintenance and equipment repair, and so forth. In the end, after a period of harvesting in a declining industry, firms can either sell their operations in an industry (to a market leader) or simply cease operations.

In the defense industry, GM's Hughes Electronics has been engaging in a harvest strategy. In the late 1990s, Hughes consolidated its four separate missile plants into a single facility. This consolidation enabled Hughes to reduce its R&D expenditures and manufacturing costs, although it also limited the range of missile products the company was manufacturing. GM completed the harvesting of Hughes' defense business by selling it to Raytheon Corporation for $9.5 billion in 1997.[51]

Divestment

The final opportunity facing firms in a declining industry is divestment. Like a harvest strategy, the objective of **divestment** is to extract a firm from a declining industry. However, unlike harvest, divestment occurs quickly, often soon after a pattern of decline is established. Firms without established competitive advantages may find divestment a superior option to harvest, because they have few competitive advantages they can exploit through harvesting.

In the defense business, divestment is the stated strategy of General Dynamics, at least in some of its business segments. General Dynamics' managers recognized early that the shrinking defense industry could not support all the incumbent firms. When General Dynamics concluded that it could not remain a leader in some of its businesses, it decided to divest those, to concentrate on a few remaining businesses. Since 1991, General Dynamics has sold businesses worth over $2.83 billion, including its missile systems business, its Cessna aircraft division, and its tactical aircraft division (maker of the very successful F–16 aircraft and partner in the development of the next generation of fighter aircraft, the F–22). These divestitures have left General Dynamics in just three businesses: armored tanks, nuclear submarines, and space launch vehicles. During this time, General Dynamics has returned almost $4.5 billion to its investors, has seen its stock go as high as $110 per share, and provided a total return to stockholders that at one time totaled 555 percent.[52]

Threat and Opportunity Analysis in an International Context

Obviously, the analysis of threats and opportunities in a firm's environment is not complete until the international dimensions of that environment are considered. Both threat analysis—using the five forces framework and the concept of complementors—and opportunity analysis—focusing on international opportunities—can be applied in this international context. Each of these international extensions will be considered in turn.

Analysis of Environmental Threats in an International Context

All of the threats identified in the five forces framework apply to the analysis of international competitive threats. It is certainly the case that a firm's rivals, new entrants, substitutes, suppliers, and buyers can all be international firms. Indeed, there is nothing in the five forces framework that cannot be applied in understanding international firms as a source of competitive threat.

However, of the five forces identified by Porter, it is usually the case that one of these—the threat of entry—is particularly salient in the analysis of international threats. This is because important barriers to entry still exist in international business. These barriers to entry typically fall into one of three categories: tariffs, quotas, or nontariff trade barriers.

Tariffs as a Barrier to Entry

Tariffs are taxes levied on goods or services imported into a country. Tariffs have the effect of increasing the price of an imported good or service, sometimes well above the price of the same good or service produced by a domestic firm. There are three types of tariffs: **ad valorem tariffs** (where the tariff is calculated as a percentage of the market value of an import, regardless of its weight or volume), **specific tariffs** (where the tariff is calculated as a percentage of the weight or volume of the goods being imported, regardless of its market value), and **compound tariffs** (where both the market value and the weight or volume are used in calculating a tariff).

Calculating the tariffs on specific imported items can be quite complex since different products can have different tariffs, and determining which product category a particular import falls into can be very ambiguous. For example, leather ski gloves imported into the United States are subject to a 5.5 percent ad valorem tariff. But if those ski gloves are designed for cross country skiing, they are subject to only a 3.5 percent ad valorem tariff. In one case, a firm was looking to import "Reindeer Caps" from China. These were hats to be worn primarily at Christmas parties, with fabric reindeer antlers that would play various Christmas carols and shout "Merry Christmas." For tariff purposes, were these caps toys, a hat, or a festive article? These three product categories actually carry different tariffs in the United States.[53]

Quotas as a Barrier to Entry

Quotas are a numerical limit on the number of particular items that are allowed to be imported into a country. Quotas have been used in many countries to protect politically powerful domestic industries, including textiles, automobiles, and agriculture. And while quotas do not raise the price of imported goods directly, they have the effect of reducing the supply of these goods in a particular country. This reduced supply, in turn, typically raises the price of those products or services that are sold within a country.

Nontariff Trade Barriers

Besides quotas, countries can use a variety of other nontariff mechanisms to increase the cost of entry into a geographic market. The other **nontariff trade barriers** include establishing product performance standards that cannot be met by imports, restricting access to domestic distribution channels, imposing local purchasing requirements for government purchases, and a variety of environmental and labor regulations that foreign firms must meet if they are to do business in a country. Often, domestic firms do not have to meet the same standards as firms looking to import into a country. When this is the case, these other nontariffs activities clearly act as a barrier to entry.

For example, entry into Japanese markets has historically been very difficult because of other nontariff trade barriers.[54] In the early 1990s, International Game Technology (IGT), a leading U.S. manufacturer of slot machines, sought entry into the large Japanese gambling market (Japan has over two-thirds of the world's slot machines, approximately 800,000 in total). IGT's entry was deterred, however, because its slot machines did not meet government slot machine standards. Unfortunately, knowledge about what these standards were was available only to members of the Japanese industry's trade association, and to become a member of this trade association, a firm needed to have been manufacturing slot machines in Japan for at least three years. It took several years for IGT to overcome this "Catch-22" barrier to entry.[55]

Similar barriers exist to entry into the Japanese beer industry. Four firms—Kirin, Asahi, Sapporo, and Suntory—dominate this industry with over 78 percent of the Japanese beer market. In order for foreign firms to begin producing beer in Japan, they must obtain a license from the ministry of finance (MOF). However, to obtain such a license, a firm must already be producing 2 million liters of beer in Japan. This barrier to entry has effectively limited non-Japanese beers to the expensive import market in Japan.[56]

Why Do Governments Impose Tariff and Nontariff Barriers to Entry?

Given that the effect of tariff and nontariff barriers to entry is almost always to raise the price of goods or services in a country, an important question becomes: Why would governments choose to erect such barriers? First, like any other tax, tariffs raise revenue for the government. Indeed, tariffs are often more politically palatable than other forms of taxation because they are hidden in the price of the goods or services a person buys. A tariff is not added to the base price of a product or service as is the case with a sales tax. Nor do tax payers receive a bill from the government every six months as is the case with property taxes. Indeed, consumers pay for this tax and they do not even have to file an income tax return to do so.

Second, tariff and nontariff barriers have the effect of strengthening demand for products and services produced by domestic firms. This can give domestic firms time to build their capabilities before engaging in full-fledged global competition. It can also secure higher levels of employment in an industry. Both tariff and nontariff barriers to entry can be politically very beneficial to a government.

Analysis of Opportunities in an International Context

Not only can threat analysis be extended to an international context, but opportunity analysis can as well. Indeed, it is an assumption of business in the twenty-first century that competitive opportunities are becoming more international in scope. Even industries that appear likely to be national or regional in focus (Broadway plays, for example, are by definition produced only in New York City) have, over the last several years, become more international in character (many major Broadway hits are transfers from the West End in London, and regional traveling companies exhibit these plays throughout the world). International competition has some very obvious effects on the level and kinds of opportunities in an industry.[57] Opportunities in international industries generally fall into three large categories: multinational opportunities, global opportunities, and transnational opportunities.

Multinational Opportunities

Firms pursuing **multinational opportunities** in international industries operate simultaneously in several national or regional markets, but these operations are independent of each other and are free to choose how to respond to the specific needs of each national or regional marketplace. Some well-known firms that have pursued multinational international opportunities include Nestlé and General Motors. Only a small percentage of Nestlé's products are sold throughout the entire world. Rather, managers within each country where Nestlé operates have the responsibility to discern local tastes, design products to be consistent with those tastes, and to market these specially designed products locally. In a similar way, GM encourages very little interaction between its U.S. and European operations. Cars designed for the European market and sold under GM's Opal brand name have infrequently been sold in the United States and relatively few Chevrolets and Oldsmobiles designed for the U.S. market are sold in Europe.

Pursuing multinational opportunities in international industries has at least two advantages. First, this strategy enables firms to respond rapidly to changing conditions in a country or region. If threats or opportunities appear in one part of the world but not in others, a multinational firm can quickly move to neutralize threats or exploit opportunities in those geographic regions where it is needed. For example, by operating at least partially as a multinational, McDonald's enables many of its European franchises to sell beer and wine alongside Big Macs and fries. Such sales do not represent an opportunity in McDonald's home market of the United States.

Second, although there are relatively few operational interactions between divisions and headquarters in a multinational company, impressive organizational resources can be quickly marshaled should they be required to exploit an opportunity or neutralize a threat in a particular country or region. McDonald's, for example, has been able to use all of its technological and management skills to open franchises in Moscow and other eastern European cities.[58]

Global Opportunities

Where firms pursuing multinational opportunities operate in countries or regions in an independent manner, those pursuing **global opportunities** seek to optimize production, distribution, and other business functions throughout the world in addressing all the markets in which they operate. If manufacturing costs are very low and quality is very high in plants located in Singapore, global organizations will locate manufacturing facilities there. If particular research and development skills and technology are widely available in Great Britain, global organizations will locate their R&D operations there. If capital is less costly in New York, global organizations will locate their financial functions there. In this manner, the cost and quality of each organizational function can be optimized. Examples of global organizations include IBM and Ford Motor Company. Global strategies have the obvious advantage of locating operations in geographic positions that reduce costs and maximize quality in all business functions.

However, global strategies also have some costs and risks associated with them. First, because the delivery of products or services in a global organization requires inputs from numerous operations all over the world, a global strategy puts a great deal of emphasis on coordination. Coordination can be difficult across divisions within a single country; it can be even more difficult across divisions in different countries or regions. Differences in language, culture, legal systems, and traditional business practices may complicate these coordination efforts.

Second, locating interdependent units in geographically disparate areas can create significant transportation costs. The very low cost of manufacturing automobile transmissions in Mexico may be effectively increased by the need to transport those transmissions to Japan to be installed in automobiles. This is less of a problem for a firm that ships products that are relatively light, small, and have very high profit margins.

Finally, exploiting global strategies may limit a firm's ability to respond to local needs, opportunities, and threats. Firms pursuing global opportunities in international industries are well designed to respond to global markets and less well designed to respond to a series of local markets. If the structure of the markets in which a firm operates does not significantly vary by country or region, a global approach may be a particularly attractive opportunity.

Transnational Opportunities

Recently, another opportunity has been described in international industries: to operate as a transnational firm. Some have argued that the traditional tradeoff between global integration and local responsiveness can be replaced by this transnational approach that exploits the advantages of both global integration and local responsiveness. Firms exploiting a **transnational opportunity** in an international industry treat their global operations as an integrated network of distributed and interdependent resources and capabilities.[59] In this context, a firm's operations in each country are not simply independent activities attempting to respond to local market needs; they are also repositories of ideas, technologies, and management approaches that the firm might be able to use and apply in its other global operations. Put differently, operations in different countries can be thought of as "experiments" in the creation of capabilities. Some of these experiments will work and generate important new capabilities for an entire firm; others will fail to have such benefits for a firm.

When an operation in a particular country develops a capability in manufacturing a particular product, providing a particular service, or engaging in a particular activity that can be used by other countries, the country operating with this capability can achieve global economies of scale by becoming the firm's primarily supplier of this product, service, or activity. In this way, local responsiveness is retained as country managers constantly search for new capabilities that enable them to maximize profits in their particular markets, and global integration and economies of scale are realized as country operations that have developed unique capabilities become suppliers for all other country operations. Firms that pursue transnational strategies include Hewlett-Packard and Honda.

SUMMARY

The strategic management process requires that a firm engage in an analysis of threats and opportunities in its competitive environment before a strategic choice can be made. This analysis begins with understanding the general environment within which a firm operates. This general environment has six components: technological change, demographic trends, cultural trends, economic climate, legal and political conditions, and specific international events. While some of these components of the general environment can affect a firm directly, more frequently they affect a firm through their impact on its local environment.

The theoretical framework that enables the analysis of a firm's local environment and links the structure of the industry within which a firm operates, its strategic alternatives, and firm performance is called the Structure-Conduct-Performance (or S-C-P) model. In this model, structure is defined as industry structure and includes those attributes of a firm's industry that constrain a firm's strategic alternatives and performance. Conduct in this model is defined as a firm's strategies. Performance in this model refers either to the performance of a firm in an industry, or the performance of the entire economy—although the former definition of performance is more important for most strategic management purposes.

The S-C-P model can be used to develop tools for analyzing threats in a firm's competitive environment. The most influential of these tools is called the "five forces framework." These five forces are: the threat of entry, the threat of rivalry, the threat of substitutes, the threat of suppliers, and the threat of buyers. The threat of entry depends on the existence and "height" of barriers to entry. Common barriers to entry include economies of scale, product differentiation, cost advantages independent of scale, and government regulation on entry. The threat of rivalry depends on the number and competitiveness of firms in an industry. The threat of rivalry is high in an industry when there are large numbers of competing firms, competing firms are roughly the same size and have the same influence, growth in an industry is slow, there is no product differentiation, and productive capacity is added in large increments. The threat of substitutes depends on how close substitute products and services are—in performance and cost—to products and services in an industry. Where rivals all meet the same customer needs in approximately the same way, substitutes meet the same customer needs, but do so in very different ways. The threat of suppliers in an industry depends on the number and distinctiveness of the products suppliers provide to an industry. The threat of suppliers increases when a supplier's industry is dominated by a few firms, when suppliers sell unique or highly differentiated products, when suppliers are not threatened by substitutes, when suppliers threaten forward vertical integration, and when firms are not important customers for suppliers. Finally, the threat of buyers depends on the number and size of an industry's customers. The threat of buyers is greater when the number of buyers is small, products sold to buyers are undifferentiated and standard, products sold to buyers are a significant percentage of a buyer's final costs, buyers are not earning significant profits, and when buyers threaten backward vertical integration. Taken together, the level of these threats in an industry can be used to determine the expected average performance of firms in an industry.

One force in a firm's environment not included within the five forces framework is complementors. Where competitors (including rivals, new entrants, and substitutes) compete with a firm to divide profits in a market, complementors increase the total size of the market. If you are a CEO of a firm, you know another firm is a complementor when the value of your products to your customers is higher in combination with this other firm's products than when customers use your products alone. Where firms have strong incentives to reduce the entry of competitors, they can sometimes have strong incentives to increase the entry of complementors.

The S-C-P model can also be used to develop tools for analyzing strategic opportunities in an industry. This is done by identifying generic industry structures and the strategic opportunities available in these different kinds of industries. Four common industry structures are: fragmented industries, emerging industries, mature industries, and declining industries. The primary opportunity in fragmented industries is consolidation. In emerging industries, the most important opportunity is first-mover advantages from technological leadership, preemption of strategically valuable assets, or creation of customer-switching costs. In mature industries, the primary opportunities are product refinement, service, and process innovation; and in declining industries, opportunities include market leadership, niche, harvest, and divestment.

Threat and opportunity analysis can be applied in an international context as well. In this context, all the five forces may be operating. However, barriers to entry are a particularly important consideration for firms contemplating international operations. In this context, barriers to entry can take one of three forms: tariffs, quotas, and other nontariff barriers. All these barriers typically have the effect of increasing the price of goods or services in a country. Finally, in international industries, opportunities include multinational, global, and transnational strategies.

CHALLENGE QUESTIONS

1. Your former college roommate calls you and asks to borrow $10,000 so that he can open a pizza restaurant in his hometown. In justifying this request, he argues that there must be significant demand for pizza and other fast food in his hometown because there are lots of such restaurants already there and three or four new ones are opening each month. He also argues that demand for convenience food will continue to increase and he points to the large number of firms that now sell frozen dinners in grocery stores. Will you lend him the money? Why or why not?

2. According to the five forces model, one potential threat in an industry is buyers. Yet unless buyers are satisfied, they are likely to look for satisfaction elsewhere. Can the fact that buyers can be threats be reconciled with the need to satisfy buyers?

3. Government policies can have a significant impact on the average profitability of firms in an industry. Government, however, is not included as a potential threat in the five forces model. Should the model be expanded to include government (to make a "six forces" model)? If yes, why? If no, why not?

4. How would you add complementors to the five forces model? In particular, if an industry has large numbers of complementors, does that make it a more attractive industry, a less attractive industry, or does it have no impact at all on the attractiveness of an industry? Justify your answer.

5. Opportunities analysis seems to suggest that there are strategic opportunities in almost any industry—even declining industries. If that is true, is it fair to say that there is really no such thing as an unattractive industry? If yes, what implications does this have for the five forces model? If no, describe an industry that has no opportunities.

6. Is the evolution of industry structure from an emerging industry to a mature industry to a declining industry inevitable? Why or why not?

PROBLEM SET

1. Perform a five forces analysis on the following two industries:

The Pharmaceutical Industry

The pharmaceutical industry consists of firms that develop, patent, and distribute drugs. Although there are not significant production economies in this industry, there are important economies in research and development. Product differentiation exists as well, because firms often sell branded products. Firms compete in research and development. However, once a product is developed and patented, competition is significantly reduced. Recently, the increased availability of generic, nonbranded drugs has threatened the profitability of some drug lines. Once an effective drug is developed, there are usually few, if any, alternatives to that drug. Drugs are manufactured from commodity chemicals usually available from numerous suppliers. Major customers include doctors and patients. Recently, increased costs have led the federal government and insurance companies to pressure drug companies to reduce their prices.

The Textile Industry

The textile industry consists of firms that manufacture and distribute fabrics for use in clothing, furniture, carpeting, and so forth. Several firms have invested heavily in sophisticated manufacturing technology, and many lower-cost firms located in Asia have begun fabric production. Textiles are not branded products. Recently, tariffs on some imported textiles have been implemented. There are numerous firms in this industry; the largest have less than 10 percent market share. Traditional fabric materials (such as cotton and wool) have recently been threatened by the development of alternative chemical-based materials (such as nylon and rayon), although many textile companies have begun manufacturing with these new materials as well. Most raw materials are widely available, although some synthetic products may be periodically in short supply. There are numerous textile customers, but textile costs are usually a large percentage of their final product's total costs. Many users shop around the world for the low prices on textiles.

2. Perform an opportunities analysis on the following industries:

Since the tragedies of 9/11, the U.S. airline industry has seen a consistent drop-off in sales. This has forced many U.S. airline companies to cut back their employment, and several—including USAir and United—have had to declare bankruptcy.

The U.S. beer industry is dominated by three companies: Anheuser-Busch, the Miller Brewing Company, and Adolf Coors. In addition, there are several regional brewers and a large number of very small micro-brewers that manufacture and sell beer in small quantities.

There are over 3,000 property and automobile insurance companies in the United States. The largest companies, including GEICO, Progressive, Allstate, and Safeco, control less than 20 percent of the property and automobile market.

Portable memory chips—sometimes worn around the neck like a necklace—may be an important substitute for floppy discs. These memory chips come in various sizes (from 64K to 256K) and range in price from $6 to $150. They plug into a computer's UBS port, self-load, and act like another hard drive in your computer.

In 2003, the German firm DHL acquired the U.S. firm Airborne Express, to become the third largest player in the small-package delivery business—behind UPS and FedEx. Shipments overseas continue to be a growing part of this industry.

3. For each of the following firms, identify at least two competitors (either rivals, new entrants, or substitutes) and two complementors.

(a) Yahoo!
(b) Microsoft
(c) Dell
(d) Boeing
(e) McDonald's

END NOTES

1. See (2003). *The big book of business quotations*. New York: Basic Books, p. 209.
2. See Weintraub, A. (2004). "Repairing the engines of life." *BusinessWeek*, May 24, 2004, pp. 99 + for a discussion of recent developments in biotechnology research and the business challenges they have created.
3. See the opening case in Chapter 1.
4. See Grow, B. (2004). "Hispanic nation." *BusinessWeek*, March 15, 2004, pp. 59 +.
5. Barnes, B. (2004). "The WB grows up." *Wall Street Journal*, July 19, 2004, pp. B1 +.
6. These and other cultural differences are described in Rugman, A., and R. Hodgetts (1995). *International business*. New York: McGraw-Hill. A discussion of the dimensions along which country cultures can vary is presented in a later chapter.
7. See Deutschman, A. (2004). "Inside the mind of Jeff Bezos." *Fast Company*, August 2004, pp. 53 +.
8. Early contributors to the structure-conduct-performance model include Mason, E. S. (1939). "Price and production policies of large scale enterprises." *American Economic Review*, 29, pp. 61—74; and Bain, J. S. (1956). *Barriers to new competition*. Cambridge, MA: Harvard University Press. The major developments in this framework are summarized in Bain, J. S. (1968). *Industrial organization*. New York: John Wiley & Sons, Inc.; and Scherer, F. M. (1980). *Industrial market structure and economic performance*. Boston: Houghton Mifflin. The links between this framework and work in strategic management are discussed by Porter, M. E. (1981a). "The contribution of industrial organization to strategic management." *Academy of Management Review*, 6, pp. 609–620; and Barney, J. B. (1986c). "Types of competition and the theory of strategy: Toward an integrative framework." *Academy of Management Review*, 1, pp. 791–800.
9. The five forces framework is described in detail in Porter, M. E. (1979). "How competitive forces shape strategy." *Harvard Business Review*, March/April, pp. 137–156; and Porter, M. E. (1980). *Competitive Strategy*. New York: Free Press.
10. These barriers were originally proposed by Bain, J. S. (1968). *Industrial organization*. New York: John Wiley & Sons, Inc.; and Porter, M. E. (1980). *Competitive strategy*. New York: Free Press.. It is actually possible to estimate the "height" of barriers to entry in an industry by comparing the cost of entry into an industry with barriers and the cost of entry into that industry if barriers did not

exist. The difference between these costs is the "height" of the barriers to entry.

11. Another alternative would be for a firm to own and operate more than one plant. If there are economies of scope in this industry, a firm might be able to enter and earn above normal profits. An economy of scope exists when the value of operating in two businesses simultaneously is greater than the value of operating in these two businesses separately. The concept of economy of scope is explored in more detail in Part Three of this book.

12. See Ghemawat, P., and H. J. Stander III (1992). "Nucor at a crossroads." Harvard Business School Case no. 9-793039.

13. See Montgomery, C. A., and B. Wernerfelt (1991). "Sources of superior performance: Market share versus industry effects in the U.S. brewing industry." Management Science, 37, pp. 954–959.

14. Stecklow, S. (1999). "Gallo woos French, but don't expect Bordeaux by the jug." Wall Street Journal, Friday, March 26, pp. A1 +.

15. See www.bustpatents.com/awards.html.

16. See Kogut, B., and U. Zander (1992). "Knowledge of the firm, combinative capabilities, and the replication of technology." Organization Science, 3, pp. 383–397; and Dierickx, I., and K. Cool (1989). "Asset stock accumulation and sustainability of competitive advantage." Management Science, 35, pp. 1504–1511. Both emphasize the importance of know-how as a barrier to entry into an industry. More generally, intangible resources are seen as particularly important sources of sustained competitive advantage. This will be discussed in more detail in Chapter 5.

17. See Polanyi, M. (1962). Personal knowledge: Towards a post critical philosophy. London: Routledge & Kegan Paul; and Itami, H. (1987). Mobilizing invisible assets. Cambridge, MA: Harvard University Press.

18. See Henderson, R., and I. Cockburn (1994). "Measuring competence: Exploring firm effects in pharmaceutical research." Strategic Management Journal, 15, pp. 361–374.

19. See Scherer, F. M. (1980). Industrial market structure and economic performance. Boston: Houghton Mifflin.

20. See Saporito, B. (1992). "Why the price wars never end." Fortune, March 23, pp. 68–78; and Allen, M., and M. Siconolfi (1993). "Dell Computer drops planned share offering." Wall Street Journal, February 25, p. A3.

21. Chartier, John (2002). "Burger battles." CNN/Money, http://money.cnn.com, December 11.

22. See Ghemawat, P., and A. McGahan (1995). "The U.S. airline industry in 1995." Harvard Business School Case No. 9-795-113.

23. Labich, K. (1992). "Airbus takes off." Fortune, June 1, pp. 102–108.

24. See Pollock, E. J. (1993). "Mediation firms alter the legal landscape." Wall Street Journal, March 22, p. B1; Cox, M. (1993). "Electronic campus: Technology threatens to shatter the world of college textbooks." Wall Street Journal, June 1, p. A1; Reilly, P. M. (1993). "At a crossroads: The instant-new age leaves Time magazine searching for a mission." Wall Street Journal, May 12, p. A1; Rohwedder, C. (1993). "Europe's smaller food shops face finis." Wall Street Journal, May 12, p. B1; Fatsis, S. (1995). "Major leagues keep minors at a distance." Wall Street Journal, November 8, pp. B1 +; Norton, E., and G. Stem (1995). "Steel and aluminum vie over every ounce in a car's construction." Wall Street Journal, May 9, pp. A1 + Paré, T. P. (1995). "Why the banks lined up against Gates.' Fortune, May 29, p. 18; "Hitting the mail on the head." The Economist, April 30, 1994, pp. 69–70; Pacelle, M. (1996). "'Big Boxes' by discounters are booming." Wall Street Journal, January 17, p. A2; and Pope, K., and L. Cauley (1998). "In Battle for TV ads, cable is now the enemy." Wall Street Journal, May 6, pp. B1 +.

25. Tully, S. (1992). "How to cut those #$%* legal costs." Fortune, September 21, pp. 119–124.

26. Jensen, E. (1993). "Tales are oft told as TV talk shows fill up airtime." Wall Street Journal, May 25, p. A1; (1995). Jensen, E. "King World ponders life without Oprah." Wall Street Journal, September 26, p. B1.

27. See DeWitt, W. (1997). "Crown Cork & Seal/Carnaud Metalbox." Harvard Business School Case No. 9-296-019.

28. Perry, N. J. (1993). "What's next for the defense industry." Fortune, February 22, pp. 94–100.

29. See "Crown Cork and Seal in 1989." Harvard Business School Case No. 5-395-224.

30. See Brandenburger, A., and B. Nalebuff (1996). Co-opetition. New York: Doubleday.

31. This approach to studying opportunities was also first suggested in Porter, M. E. (1980). Competitive strategy. New York: Free Press.

32. Jacob, R. (1992). "Service Corp. International: Acquisitions done the right way." Fortune, November 16, p. 96.

33. Porter, M. E. (1980). Competitive strategy. New York: Free Press.

34. For the definitive discussion of first-mover advantages, see Lieberman, M., and C. Montgomery (1988). "First-mover advantages." Strategic Management Journal, 9, pp. 41—58.

35. See Ghemewat, P. (1991). Commitment. New York: Free Press.

36. See Gilbert, R. J., and D. M. Newbery (1982). "Preemptive patenting and the persistence of monopoly." American Economic Review, 72(3), pp. 514–526.

37. See Bresnahan, T. F. (1985). "Post-entry competition in the plain paper copier market." American Economic Review, 85, pp. 15–19, for a discussion of Xerox's patents; and Bright, A. A. (1949). The electric lamp industry. New York: Macmillan, for a discussion of General Electric's patents.

38. See Mansfield, E., M. Schwartz, and S. Wagner (1981). "Imitation costs and patents: An empirical study." Economic Journal, 91, pp. 907–918.

39. See Main, O. W. (1955). The Canadian nickel industry. Toronto: University of Toronto Press, for a discussion of asset preemption in the oil and gas industry; Ghemawat, P. (1986). "Wal-Mart store's discount operations." Harvard Business School Case No. 9-387-018, for Wal-Mart's preemption strategy; Schmalensee, R. (1978). "Entry deterrence in the ready-to-eat breakfast cereal industry." Bell Journal of Economics, 9(2), pp. 305—327; and Robinson, W. T., and C. Fornell (1985). "Sources of market pioneer advantages in consumer goods industries." Journal of Marketing Research, 22(3), pp. 305–307, for a discussion of preemption in the breakfast cereal industry. In this latter case, the preempted valuable asset is shelf space in grocery stores.

40. Klemperer, P. (1986). "Markets with consumer switching costs." Doctoral thesis, Graduate School of Business, Stanford University; and Wernerfelt, B. (1986). "A special case of dynamic pricing policy." Management Science, 32, pp. 1562–1566.

41. See Gross, N. (1995). "The technology paradox." BusinessWeek, March 6, pp. 691–719; Bond, R. S., and D. F. Lean (1977). Sales, promotion, and product differentiation in two prescription drug markets. Washington, D. C.: U.S. Federal Trade Commission; Montgomery, D. B. (1975). "New product distribution: An analysis of supermarket buyer decision." Journal of Marketing Research, 12, pp. 255–264; Ries, A., and J. Trout (1986). Marketing warfare. New York: McGraw-Hill; and Davidson, J. H. (1976). "Why most new consumer brands fail." Harvard Business Review, 54, March/April, pp. 117–122, for a discussion of switching costs in these industries.

42. Porter, M. W. (1980). Competitive strategy. New York: Free Press.

43. Gibson, R. (1991). "McDonald's insiders increase their sales of company's stock." Wall Street Journal, June 14, p. A1; and Chartier, John (2002). "Burger Battles." CNN/Money, http://money.cnn.com, December 11.

44. Descriptions of these product refinements can be found in Demetrakakes, P. (1994). "Household-chemical makers concentrate on downsizing." Packaging, 39(1), p. 41; Reda, S. (1995). "Motor oil: Hands-on approach." Stores, 77(5), pp. 48–49; and Quinn, J. (1995). "KitchenAid." Incentive, 169(5), pp. 46–47.

45. Chartier, John (2002). "Burger Battles." CNN/Money, http://money.cnn.com, December 11.

46. See Hayes, R. H., and S. G. Wheelwright (1979). "The Dynamics of process-product life cycles." Harvard Business Review, March/April, p. 127.

47. See www.jdpowers.com.

48. See Porter, M. E. (1980). Competitive strategy. New York: Free Press; and Harrigan, K. R. (1980). Strategies for declining businesses. Lexington, MA: Lexington Books.

49. The strategies at Loral and Martin Marietta are described in Perry, N. J. (1993). "What's next for the defense industry." Fortune, February 22, pp. 94–100; Pare, T. P. (1994). "The new merger boom." Fortune, November 28, pp. 95–106; Brull, S. (1999). "A new

satellite system clambers onto the launchpad." *BusinessWeek*. September 6, p. 35; and Crock, S. (2000). "Can Lockheed Martin pull out of dry dock?" *BusinessWeek*, May 1, p. 148. Lockheed Martin is currently evaluating which of its defense businesses it might want to divest.

50. Perry, N. J. (1993). "What's next for the defense industry." *Fortune*, February 22, pp. 94–100; and *www.appsi.com*.

51. Perry, N. J. (1993). "What's next for the defense industry." *Fortune*, February 22, pp. 94–100; and *www.Raytheon.com*.

52. See Smith, L. (1993). "Can defense pain be turned to gain?" *Fortune*, February 8, pp. 84–96; Perry, N. J. (1993). "What's next for the defense industry." *Fortune*, February 22, pp. 94–100; and Dial, J., and K. J. Murphy (1995). "Incentive, downsizing, and value creation at General Dynamics." *Journal of Financial Economics*, 37, pp. 261–314.

53. U.S. customs decided that this item should be treated as a hat and charge a compound tariff of 37.7 cents per kilogram plus 13.4 percent of the market value of these items. See Griffin, R., and M. Pustay (1999). *International business*. Reading, MA: Addison-Wesley, pp. 215–216.

54. See Tuller, L. W. (1991). *Going global: New opportunities for growing companies to compete in world markets*. Homewood, IL: Irwin. Given Japan's recent economic troubles, some of these difficulties in entering the Japanese markets seem to be going away.

55. Schlesinger, J. M. (1993). "Tough gamble: A slot-machine maker trying to sell in Japan hits countless barriers." *Wall Street Journal*, May 11, p. A1.

56. (1994). "Only here for the Biru." *The Economist*, May 14, pp. 69–70.

57. See Bartlett, C. A., and S. Ghoshal (1989). *Managing across borders: The transnational solution*. Boston: Harvard Business School Press; and Bartlett, C., and S. Ghoshal (1993). "Beyond the M-form: Toward a managerial theory of the firm." *Strategic Management Journal*, 14, pp. 23–46

58. Blackman, A. (1990). "Moscow's Big Mac attack." *Time*, February 5, p. 51; and Bartlett, C. A., and S. Ghoshal (1989). *Managing across borders: The transnational solution*. Boston, MA: Harvard Business School Press.

59. Bartlett, C. A., and S. Ghoshal (1989). *Managing across borders: The transnational solution*. Boston, MA: Harvard Business School Press.

Evaluating a Firm's Internal Capabilities

Electronic Arts— They're in the Game

Video games are serious business, and no one treats them more seriously than Electronic Arts (EA). With 13 production studios around the world, EA is the largest and most successful video game firm in the world. With 27 titles selling more than one million units each, EA had sales of almost $3.0 billion and profits of $577 million in 2004. Some of the best known EA video games include *The Sims* and *Harry Potter* games (each with more than 10 million units sold) and the *FIFA Soccer, James Bond, Madden NFL Football,* and *Medal of Honor* games (each with more than five million units sold).

In 2002, domestic video game sales of $10 billion actually outstripped domestic box office receipts—video games are actually a larger industry than the movies! And video games aren't designed just for teenage boys anymore.

One-third of adults over the age of 18 play video games. Twenty-two percent of these people play five or more hours a week. And the development of games like *The Sims*—where players compete by building relationships rather than killing opponents—has helped increase the number of women and girls who play video games. Currently, about 46 percent of those who play video games are female. Moreover, with the introduction of games based on the *Harry Potter* novels, kids younger than 14 are now playing video games.

Learning Objectives

After reading this chapter, you should be able to:

1. Describe the critical assumptions of the resource-based view.

2. Describe four types of resources and capabilities.

3. Apply the VRIO framework to identify the competitive implications of a firm's resources and capabilities.

4. Apply value chain analysis to identify a firm's valuable resources and capabilities.

5. Describe the kinds of resources and capabilities that are likely to be costly to imitate.

6. Describe how a firm uses its structure, formal and informal control processes, and compensation policy to exploit its resources.

7. Discuss how the decision to imitate or not imitate a firm with a competitive advantage affects the competitive dynamics in an industry.

8. Discuss how firms can exploit their current resources or develop new resources through their international operations.

So, how does EA stay at the forefront of this intensely competitive and dynamic industry? Some observers suggest that EA is able to combine the creativity usually associated with Hollywood movies, the technological sophistication usually associated with Silicon Valley firms, and a business discipline usually associated with the best manufacturing firms in the world. Combining these three sometimes very different sets of skills sets EA apart from most of its competitors. Not only does EA routinely produce the most creative games; it is also among the most technically sophisticated, and most surprising of all, they are usually delivered on time and on budget.

The goal at EA is for each major product introduction to have at least one creative innovation (e.g., Snoop Dogg provided original background music for *NBA Live 2003*) and at least one technical innovation (e.g., a new "freestyle joystick" that increases the level of control in *NBA Live 2003*), and to do all of this while bringing a product out on time. After all, 80 percent of EA's revenues are generated during holiday sales. If an EA product misses this sales window, it will have to wait a full year for another opportunity.

The stakes for EA are huge. Each of its best-selling titles takes from 12 to 36 months to develop and costs from $5 to $10 million. But a successful title can generate hundreds of millions in sales. In fact, EA's *FIFA Soccer* has generated more than $1 billion in sales since it was first introduced in 1996. Its *Harry Potter*, *The Sims*, and *James Bond* titles—to name just a few—appear to be on track for this same level of success. But will EA be able to continue to develop its video game blockbusters?

Sources: "Computer games played by one in three adults." *Research Alert*, April 20, p. 10; "EA hits record financials." *Video Business*, May 12, p. 28; C. Salter (2002). "Playing to win." *Fast Company*, December pp. 80 +.

Most firms would like to have the kind of performance that Electronic Arts (EA) enjoys in the video game industry. Such sustained competitive advantages are the objective of the strategic management process described in Chapter 1. But, what is it about EA that enables this firm to gain and sustain its competitive advantage? What are its strengths, and how does it exploit them? What are its weaknesses and how does it avoid them? The purpose of this chapter is to describe a set of tools that can be used to answer these questions.

The Resource-Based View of the Firm

In Chapter 2, we saw that it was possible to take some theoretical models developed in economics—specifically the S-C-P model—and apply them to develop tools for analyzing a firm's external threats and opportunities. The same is true for analyzing a firm's internal strengths and weaknesses. However, where the tools described in Chapter 2 were based on the S-C-P model, the tools described in this chapter are based on the **Resource-Based View** of the Firm, or the **RBV**. The RBV is a model of firm performance that focuses on the resources and capabilities controlled by a firm as sources of competitive advantage.[1]

What Are Resources and Capabilities?

Resources in the RBV are defined as the tangible and intangible assets that a firm controls, which it can use to conceive of and implement its strategies. Examples of resources might include a firm's factories (a tangible asset), its products (a tangible asset), its reputation among customers (an intangible asset), and teamwork among its managers (an intangible asset). EA's tangible assets include its studios and its products. EA's intangible assets include the cooperation among its creative, technical, and business functions.

Capabilities are a subset of a firm's resources and are defined as tangible and intangible assets that enable a firm to take full advantage of other resources it controls. That is, capabilities alone do not enable a firm to conceive of and implement its strategies, but they enable a firm to use other resources to conceive of and implement such strategies. Examples of capabilities might include a firm's marketing skills and teamwork and cooperation among its managers. At EA, the cooperation among the creative, technical, and business functions is an example of a capability.

A firm's resources and capabilities can be classified into four broad categories: financial resources, physical resources, individual resources, and organizational resources. **Financial resources** include all the money, from whatever source, that firms use to conceive of and implement strategies. These financial resources include cash from entrepreneurs, from equity holders, from bondholders, and from banks. **Retained earnings**, or the profit that a firm made earlier in its history and invests in itself, are also an important type of financial resource.

Physical resources include all the physical technology used in a firm. This includes a firm's plant and equipment, its geographic location, and its access to raw materials. Specific examples of plant and equipment that are part of a firm's physical resources are a firm's computer hardware and software technology, robots used in manufacturing, and automated warehouses. Geographic location, as a type of physical resource, is important for firms as diverse as Wal-Mart (with its operations in rural markets generating, on average, higher returns than its operations in more competitive urban markets) and L. L. Bean (a catalogue retail firm that believes that its rural Maine location helps its employees identify with the outdoor lifestyle of many of its customers).[2]

Human resources include the training, experience, judgment, intelligence, relationships, and insight of *individual* managers and workers in a firm.[3] The importance of the human resources of well-known entrepreneurs such as Bill Gates (Microsoft) and Steve Jobs (currently at Apple) is broadly understood. However, valuable human resources are not limited to just entrepreneurs or senior managers. Each employee at a firm like Southwest Airlines is seen as essential for the overall success of the firm. Whether it is the willingness of the gate agent to joke with the harried traveler, or a baggage handler hustling to get a passenger's bag into a plane, or even a pilot's decision to fly in a way that saves fuel—all of these human resources are part of the resource base that has enabled Southwest to gain competitive advantages in the very competitive U.S. airline industry.[4]

Where human resources are an attribute of single individuals, **organizational resources** are an attribute of groups of individuals. Organizational resources include a firm's formal reporting structure; its formal and informal planning, controlling, and coordinating systems; its culture and reputation; as well as informal relations among groups within a firm and between a firm and those in its environment. At Southwest Airlines, relationships among individual resources are an important organizational resource. For example, it is not unusual to see the pilots at Southwest helping to load the bags on an airplane to ensure that the plane leaves on time. This kind of cooperation and dedication shows up in an intense loyalty between Southwest employees and the firm—a loyalty that manifests itself in low employee turnover and high employee productivity, even though over 80 percent of Southwest's employees are unionized.

Critical Assumptions of the Resource-Based View

The RBV rests on two fundamental assumptions about the resources and capabilities that firms may control. First, different firms may possess different bundles of resources and capabilities, even if they are competing in the same industry. This is the assumption of firm **resource heterogeneity**. Resource heterogeneity implies that for a given business activity, some firms may be more skilled in accomplishing this activity than other firms. In manufacturing, for example, Toyota continues to be more skilled than, say, General Motors. In product design, Apple continues to be more skilled than, say, IBM. In video games, EA continues to be more technically innovative and creative than most of its competitors.

Second, some of these resource and capability differences among firms may be long lasting. This is because it may be very costly for firms without certain resources and capabilities to develop or acquire them. This is the assumption of **resource immobility**. For example, Toyota has had its advantage in manufacturing for at least 30 years. Apple has had product design advantages over IBM since Apple was founded in the 1980s. And EA has had its skill advantages for at least 10 years. It is not that GM, IBM, and EA's competitors are unaware of their skill disadvantages. Indeed, some of these firms—notably GM and IBM—have made progress in addressing their disadvantages. However, despite these efforts, Toyota, Apple, and EA continue to enjoy skill advantages over their competition.

Taken together, these two assumptions make it possible to explain why some firms can outperform other firms, even if these firms are all competing in the same

Strategy in Depth

The theoretical roots of the Resource-based View can be traced to research done by David Ricardo in 1817. Interestingly enough, Ricardo was not even studying the profitability of firms way back then; he was interested in the economic consequences of owning more or less fertile farm land.

Unlike many other inputs into the production process, the total supply of land is relatively fixed and cannot be significantly increased in response to higher demand and prices. Such inputs are said to be **inelastic in supply**, because their quantity of supply is fixed and does not respond to price increases. In these settings, it is possible for those that own higher-quality inputs to gain competitive advantages.

Ricardo's argument concerning land as a productive input is summarized in Figure 3.1. Imagine that there are many parcels of land suitable for growing wheat. Also, suppose that the fertility of these different parcels varies from high fertility (low costs of production) to low fertility (high costs of production). It seems obvious that when the market price for wheat is low, it will only pay farmers with the most fertile land to grow wheat. Only these farmers will have costs low enough to make money when the market price for wheat is low. Also,

Ricardian Economics and the Resource-Based View

as the market price for wheat goes up, then farmers with progressively less fertile land will be able to use it to grow wheat. These observations lead to market supply curve in panel A of the figure: As prices (P) go up, supply (S) also goes up. At some point on this supply curve, supply will equal demand (D). This point determines the market price for wheat, given supply and demand. This price is called P^* in the figure.

Now consider the situation facing two different kinds of farmers. Ricardo assumed that both these farmers follow traditional economic logic by producing a quantity (q) such that their marginal cost (MC) equals their marginal revenue, that is, they produce enough wheat so that the cost of producing the last bushel of wheat equals the revenue they will get from selling that last bushel. However, this decision for the farm with less fertile land (in panel B of the figure) revenues that exactly equal the average total cost (ATC) of the only capital this farmer is assumed to employ cost of his land. On the other hand, the farmer with more fertile land (in panel C of the figure) has average total costs (ATC) less than the market-determined price and thus is able to earn an above-normal economic profit. This is because at the market determined price, P^*, $MC = ATC$ for the farmer with less fertile land, while $MC > ATC$ for the farmer with more fetile land.

In traditional economic analysis, the profit earned by the farmer with more fertile land should lead other farmers to enter into this market, to obtain some land and begin producing wheat. However, all the land that can be used to produce wheat in a way that generates at least a normal return given the market price P^* is already in production. In particular, there is no more very fertile land left, and fertile land (by

industry. If a firm possesses valuable resources and capabilities that few other firms possess, and if these other firms find it too costly to imitate these resources and capabilities, the firm that possesses these tangible and intangible assets can gain a sustained competitive advantage. The economic logic that underlies the Resource-Based View is described in more detail in the Strategy in Depth feature.

The VRIO Framework

Armed with the Resource-Based View, it is possible to develop a set of tools for analyzing all the different resources and capabilities a firm might possess and the potential of each of these to generate competitive advantages. In this way, it will

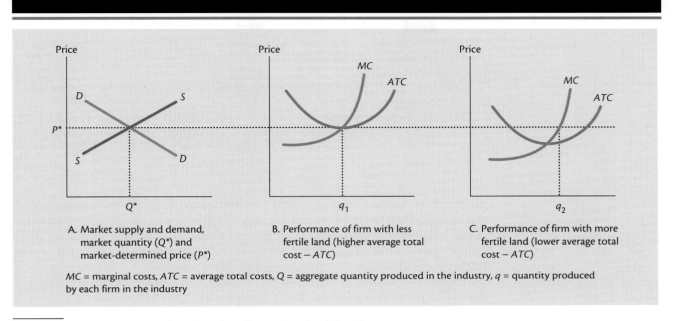

MC = marginal costs, ATC = average total costs, Q = aggregate quantity produced in the industry, q = quantity produced by each firm in the industry

Figure 3.1 The Economics of Land with Different Levels of Fertility

assumption) cannot be created. This is what is meant by land being inelastic in supply. Thus, the firm with more fertile land and lower production costs has a sustained competitive advantage over firms with less fertile land and higher production costs and is able to earn an above-normal economic profit.

Of course, at least two events can threaten this sustained competitive advantage. First, market demand may shift down and to the left. This would force farms with less fertile land to cease production and would also reduce the profit of the farms with more fertile land. If demand shifted far enough, this profit might disappear altogether.

Second, farms with less fertile land may discover low-cost ways of increasing their land's fertility, thereby reducing the competitive advantage of the farm with more fertile land. For example, farms with less fertile land may be able to use inexpensive fertilizers to increase their land's fertility. The existence of such low-cost fertilizers suggests that while

land may be in fixed supply, *fertility* may not be. If enough farms can increase the fertility of their land, then the profits originally earned by the farm with the more fertile land will disappear.

Of course, what the Resource-Based View does is recognize that land is not the only productive input that is inelastic in supply and that farmers are not the only firms that benefit from having such resources at their disposal.

Source: D. Ricardo (1817). *Principles of political economy and taxation.* London: J. Murray.

be possible to identify both a firm's internal strengths and its internal weaknesses. The primary tool for accomplishing this internal analysis is called the VRIO framework.[5] An acronym, the **VRIO framework** stands for four questions you must ask about a resource or capability to determine its competitive potential: the question of **V**alue, the question of **R**arity, the question of **I**mitability, and the question of **O**rganization. These four questions are summarized in Table 3.1.

The Question of Value

The **Question of Value** is: "Do resources and capabilities enable a firm to exploit an external opportunity or neutralize an external threat?" If a firm answers this

Table 3.1   **Questions Needed to Conduct a Resource-Based Analysis of a Firm's Internal Strengths and Weaknesses**

1. *The Question of Value:* Does a resource enable a firm to exploit an environmental opportunity and/or neutralize an environmental threat?
2. *The Question of Rarity:* Is a resource currently controlled by only a small number of competing firms?
3. *The Question of Imitability:* Do firms without a resource face a cost disadvantage in obtaining or developing it?
4. *The Question of Organization:* Are a firm's other policies and procedures organized to support the exploitation of its valuable, rare, and costly-to-imitate resources?

question "yes," then its resources and capabilities are valuable, and can be considered as firm *strengths*. If a firm answers this question "no," its resources and capabilities are *weaknesses*. There is nothing inherently valuable about a firm's resources and capabilities. Rather, they are only valuable to the extent that they enable a firm to enhance its competitive position. Sometimes, the same resources and capabilities can be strengths in one market and weaknesses in another. The Global Perspectives feature discusses this issue in more detail.

Valuable Resources and Firm Performance

Sometimes it is difficult to know for sure whether a firm's resources and capabilities really enable it to exploit its external opportunities or neutralize its external threats. Sometimes this requires detailed operational information that may not be readily available. Other times, the full impact of a firm's resources and capabilities on its external opportunities and threats may not be known for some time. Consider, for example, recent strategic decisions made by Yahoo! and described in the Strategy in the Emerging Enterprise feature on page 82.

One way to track the impact of a firm's resources and capabilities on its opportunities and threats is to examine the impact of using these resources and capabilities on a firm's revenues and costs. In general, firms that use their resources and capabilities to exploit opportunities or neutralize threats will see an increase in their net revenues, or a decrease in their net costs, or both, compared to the situation where they were not using these resources and capabilities to exploit opportunities or neutralize threats. That is, the value of these resources and capabilities will generally manifest itself in either higher revenues or lower costs or both, once a firm starts using them to exploit opportunities or neutralize threats.

Applying the Question of Value

The answer to the question of value, for many firms, has been "yes." That is, many firms have resources and capabilities that are used to exploit opportunities and neutralize threats, and the use of these resources and capabilities enables these firms to increase their net revenues or decrease their net costs. For example, Sony has a great deal of experience in designing, manufacturing, and selling miniaturized electronic technology. Sony has used these resources and capabilities to exploit opportunities, including video games, digital cameras,

Global Perspectives

Despite the best efforts of American college students, the consumption of beer in the United States is no longer growing. In an effort to expand their sales, both Anheuser-Busch and Miller Brewing are trying to enter the European market. Unfortunately, many Europeans don't like American beer. They consider it to be "watered-down" and "tasteless." None of this was helped when these two powerhouse U.S. firms first introduced their "light" beers to Europe. Unfortunately, "light beer" in Europe means "low alcohol content beer," and sales of Bud Light and Miller Light never met expectations. Indeed, Miller changed the name of its light beer in Europe to Miller Pilsner.

In an effort to grow their sales and overcome the perception that American beers are "lightweight," Anheuser-Busch and Miller are adopting very different strategies. Anheuser-Busch is actually playing up its American roots. It uses the same commercials in Europe as it does in the United States. The American eagle remains prominently displayed on the Budweiser can, and the Clydesdales still pull the old-fashioned beer wagon in some Budweiser ads. Anheuser-Busch is signing up European sports stars as spokespersons for Budweiser, and Bud just became the official beer of the 2006 Olympics in

Does It Pay to Be an American Beer in Europe?

Torino, Italy. Anheuser-Busch hopes that the European fascination with U.S. brands—including McDonald's Big Mac—will ultimately transfer to its products and will offset current tensions between the United States and Europe regarding the Iraq War. Currently only imported into Europe, Budweiser is priced as an expensive import beer and saw its market share in the United Kingdom—a critical beer-drinking market in Europe—go from 2.7 percent in 2000 to 2.9 percent in 2002.

Miller, on the other hand, downplays in American roots. Indeed, Miller

is trying to be seen as just another European beer company with an upscale product. For example, to serve the Russian market, Miller opened a Russian brewery just 84 miles from Moscow. Also, rather than using U.S.-based ads, Miller has developed a European ad campaign that markets its beer as part of a new, hipper lifestyle that is distinctly European, not made-over American. Miller's sales in Russia increased by 70 percent from 2002 to 2003 while the overall market for upscale beers in that country increased by only 30 percent. Miller is looking to repeat that success in other European countries.

So, is being an American beer a valuable resource or not? As suggested in the text, a resource is not inherently valuable or not valuable. It depends on the specific market demand for that resource. In the United States, being an American beer can be a valuable resource, but it may turn out to be less valuable in Europe.

Sources: J. Barney (2001). "Is the resource-based 'view' a useful perspective for strategic management research? Yes." *Academy of Management Review,* 26, pp. 41–56; D. Bilefsky and C. Lawton (2004). "In Europe, marketing beer as 'American' may not be a plus." *Wall Street Journal,* July 21, pp. B1 +.

computers and peripherals, handheld computers, home video and audio, portable audio, and car audio. 3M has used its resources and capabilities in substrates, coatings, and adhesives, along with an organizational culture that rewards risk-taking and creativity, to exploit opportunities in office products, including invisible tape and Post–it notes. Sony's and 3M's resources and capabilities—including their specific technological skills and their creative organizational cultures—made it possible for these firms to respond to, and even create, new opportunities.[6]

Strategy in the Emerging Enterprise

*E*ntrepreneurial firms, like all other firms, must be able to answer the Question of Value in the affirmative. This can sometimes be very problematic for entrepreneurial firms since the products or services they are providing to consumers may be entirely new. Anticipating whether or not a certain set of resources and capabilities is valuable when you are providing an entirely new product or service to the market can be very difficult. It is not unusual for entrepreneurial firms to adjust their strategies over time as they search for ways in which they can create value with the resources and capabilities they control.

Consider, for example, Yahoo! It began life as an Internet company that repackaged commodity information into formats that were easy for consumers to access. Combining both first-mover advantages and superior technology, Yahoo! became one of the most popular sites on the Web and serviced, over the years, more than 237 million customers. It seems likely that 237 million customers is a potentially valuable resource, and since its inception, Yahoo! has tried to find a way to make money by exploiting this resource.

Yahoo!'s first approach to exploiting this resource was to sell

Who Is Yahoo!?

advertising on its Web site. However, when the tech bubble burst in 1999–2000, it significantly reduced the demand for Web-based advertising, and Yahoo! had to explore alternative ways to use its customer-base resource to create value.

Its second approach was to charge its customers for using its services. Historically, Yahoo!'s services—including its e-mail system, its chat rooms, and its search engines—were free of charge to consumers. Beginning in 2001, Yahoo! began charging for these services. The theory was that if it

could generate $1,000 of revenue per customer a year, it could be a $237 billion company. Unfortunately, Yahoo!'s customers began using low-cost or free alternatives, and it was not able to generate sufficient revenue using its customer resource.

In 2003, Yahoo! decided to begin exploiting information it had about its customer base in a new way by selling its own services and the products and services of its partner firms to those customers. Or, as one observer put it, it became a "direct marketing and solicitation outfit, cold-calling families at dinner time, spamming their e-mail inboxes, and cluttering their mail with targeted appeals." The jury is still out on whether or not this strategy will allow Yahoo! to create value from its resources. On the one hand, it seems very likely that there are numerous firms that will be willing to pay Yahoo! for the information it controls about its 237 million customers. On the other hand, will those customers continue to return to Yahoo! when they know information about them is being sold to the highest bidder?

Sources: J. Ellis, H. Rubin, and K. Hammonds (2002). "FCMC." *Fast Company*, July, p. 113; B. Breen (2003). "She's helping Yahoo act normal." *Fast Company*, May, pp. 92 +; www.Yahoo.com.

Unfortunately, for other firms the answer to the question of value appears to be "no." Touted as a merger (AOL and Time Warner) to create a new kind of entertainment and media company, it is now widely recognized that Time Warner has been unable to marshall the resources necessary to create economic value. Time Warner wrote-off $90 billion in value in 2002; its stock price has been at record low levels, and there have been rumors that it will be broken up. Ironically, many of the segments of this diverse media conglomerate continue to create value. But the company as a whole has not realized the synergies that it was expected to generate when it was created. Put differently, these synergies—as resources and capabilities—are apparently not valuable.[7]

Using Value-Chain Analysis to Identify Potentially Valuable Resources and Capabilities

One way to identify potentially valuable resources and capabilities controlled by a firm is to study that firm's value chain. A firm's **value chain** is the set of business activities in which it engages to develop, produce, and market its products or services. Each step in a firm's value chain requires the application and integration of different resources and capabilities. Because different firms may make different choices about which value-chain activities they will engage in, they can end up developing different sets of resources and capabilities. This can be the case even if these firms are all operating in the same industry. These choices can have implications for the strategies a firm is pursuing, and, as is described in the Ethics and Strategy feature, they can also have implications for society more generally.

Consider, for example, the oil industry. Figure 3.2 provides a simplified list of all the business activities that must be completed if crude oil is to be turned into consumer products, like gasoline. These activities include exploring for crude oil, drilling for crude oil, pumping crude oil, shipping crude oil, buying crude oil, refining crude oil, selling refined products to distributors, shipping refined products, and selling refined products to final customers.

Different firms may make different choices about which of these stages in the oil industry they want to operate. Thus, these firms may have very different resources and capabilities. For example, exploring for crude oil is very expensive and requires substantial financial resources. It also requires access to land (a physical resource), the application of substantial scientific and technical knowledge (individual resources), and an organizational commitment to risk-taking and exploration (organizational resources). Firms that operate in this stage of the oil business are likely to have very different resources and capabilities than firms that, for example, sell refined oil products to final customers. To be successful in the retail stage of this industry, a firm needs retail outlets (such as stores and gas stations), which are costly to build and require both financial and physical resources. These outlets, in turn, need to be staffed by salespeople—individual resources— and marketing these products to customers through advertisements and other means can require a commitment to creativity—an organizational resource.

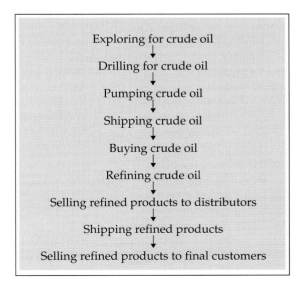

Figure 3.2 A Simplified Value Chain of Activities of Oil-Based Refined Products such as Gasoline and Motor Oil

Ethics and Strategy

Strategic management adopts the perspective of a firm's owners in discussing how to gain and sustain competitive advantages. Even when adopting a stakeholder perspective (see the Ethics and Strategy feature in Chapter 1), how a firm can improve its performance and increase the wealth of its owners still takes center stage.

However, an exclusive focus on the performance of a firm and the wealth of its owners can sometimes have broader effects—on society and on the environment—that are not fully recognized. Economists call these broader effects "externalities" because they are external to the core issue in economics and strategic management about how firms can maximize their performance. They are external to this issue because firms generally do not bear the full costs of the externalities their profit-maximizing behavior creates.

Externalities can take many forms. The most obvious of these has to do with pollution and the environment. If, for example, in the process of maximizing its performance, a firm engages in activities that pollute the environment, the impact of that pollution is an externality. Such pollution reduces our quality of life and hurts the environment, but the firm creating this pollution often does not bear the full costs of doing so.

Other externalities have to do with a firm's impact on the public's health. For example, when tobacco companies maximize their profits by selling tobacco to children, they are also creating a public health externality. Getting children hooked on tobacco early on might be good for the bottom line of a corporation, but it

Externalities and the Broader Consequences of Profit Maximization

increases the chances of these children developing lung cancer, emphysema, heart disease, and the other ailments associated with tobacco. Obviously, these individuals absorb most of the adverse consequences of these diseases, but society suffers as well from the high health care costs that are engendered.

Put differently, while adopting a simple profit-maximizing perspective in choosing and implementing strategies can have positive impacts for a firm, its owners, and its other stakeholders, it can also have negative consequences for society as a whole. Two broad solutions to this problem of externalities have been proposed. First, governments can take on the responsibility of directly monitoring and regulating the behavior of firms in areas where these kinds of externalities are likely to develop. Second, governments can use lawsuits and regulations to

ensure that firms directly bear more of the costs of any externalities their behavior might generate. Once these externalities are "internalized," it is then a matter of self-interest for firms not to engage in activities that generate negative externalities.

Consumers can sometimes also help internalize the externalities generated by a firm's behavior by adjusting their consumption patterns to buy products or services only from companies that do not generate negative externalities. Consumers can even be more proactive and let firms know which firm strategies are particularly troubling. For example, many consumers united to boycott firms with operations in South Africa when South Africa was still implementing a policy of apartheid. Ultimately, this pressure not only changed the strategies of many firms; it also helped change South Africa's domestic policies. More recently, consumer pressures on drug companies have forced these firms to make their AIDs drugs more accessible in less developed countries in Africa, and similar pressures have forced Nike to adjust the wages and working conditions of those individuals that manufacture Nike's shoes. To the extent that sufficient demand for "socially responsible firms" exists in the marketplace, it may make profit-maximizing sense for a firm to engage in socially responsible behavior by reducing the extent to which its actions generate negative externalities.

Sources: "AIDS in Africa." *British Medical Journal,* June 1, p. 456; J. S. Friedman (2003). "Paying for apartheid." *Nation,* June 6, pp. 7 +; L. Lee (2000). "Can Nike still do it?" *BusinessWeek,* February 21, pp. 121 +.

However, even firms that operate in the same set of value-chain activities in an industry may approach these activities very differently and therefore may develop very different resources and capabilities associated with these activities. For example, two firms may sell refined oil products to final customers. However, one of these firms may sell only through retail outlets it owns while the second may sell only through retail outlets it doesn't own. The first firm's financial and physical resources are likely to be very different from the second's, although these two firms may have similar individual and organizational resources.

Studying a firm's value chain forces us to think about firm resources and capabilities in a very disaggregated way. Although it is possible to characterize a firm's resources and capabilities more broadly, it is usually more helpful to think about how each of the activities a firm engages in affects its financial, physical, individual, and organizational resources. With this understanding, it is possible to begin to recognize potential sources of competitive advantage for a firm in a much more detailed way.

Because this type of analysis can be so helpful in identifying the financial, physical, individual, and organizational resources and capabilities controlled by a firm, several generic value chains for identifying them have been developed. The first, proposed by the management-consulting firm McKinsey and Company, is presented in Figure 3.3.[8] This relatively simple model suggests that the creation of value almost always involves six distinct activities: technology development, product design, manufacturing, marketing, distribution, and service. Firms can develop distinctive capabilities in any one or any combination of these activities.

Michael E. Porter has developed a second generic value chain.[9] This value chain, presented in Figure 3.4, divides value-creating activities into two large categories: primary activities and support activities. Primary activities include inbound logistics (purchasing, inventory, and so forth), production, outbound logistics (warehousing and distribution), sales and marketing, and service (dealer support and customer service). Support activities include infrastructure (planning, finance, information services, legal), technology development (research and development, product design), and human resource management and development. Primary activities are directly associated with the manufacture and distribution of a product. Support activities assist a firm in accomplishing its primary activities. As is the case with the McKinsey value chain, a firm can develop strengths or weaknesses in any one, or in any combination, of the activities listed in Porter's value chain. These activities, and how they are linked to one another, point to the kinds of resources and capabilities a firm is likely to have developed.

Figure 3.3   The Generic Value Chain Developed by McKinsey and Company

Technology development	Product design	Manufacturing	Marketing	Distribution	Service
Source	Function	Integration	Prices	Channels	Warranty Speed
Sophistication	Physical	Raw materials	Advertising/	Integration	Captive/independent
Patents	characteristics	Capacity	promotion	Inventory	Prices
Product/process	Aesthetics	Location	Sales force	Warehousing	
choices	Quality	Procurement	Package	Transport	
		Parts production	Brand		
		Assembly			

Figure 3.4   The Generic
Value Chain Developed by
Porter

Sources: Reprinted with
permission of The Free Press, a
division of Simon and Schuster
Adult Publishing Group, from
*Competitive Advantage: Creating and
Sustaining Superior Performance* by
Michael E. Porter. Copyright ©
1985 by The Free Press.

The Question of Rarity

Understanding the value of a firm's resources and capabilities is an important
first consideration in understanding a firm's internal strengths and weaknesses.
However, if a particular resource or capability is controlled by numerous competing firms, then that resource is unlikely to be a source of competitive advantage for any one of them. Instead, valuable but common (that is, not rare)
resources and capabilities are sources of competitive parity. Only when a
resource is not controlled by numerous other firms is it likely to be a source of
competitive advantage. These observations lead to the **Question of Rarity**:
"How many competing firms already possess particular valuable resources and
capabilities?"

Consider, for example, competition among television sports channels. All
the major networks broadcast sports. In addition, there are several sports-only
cable channels, including the best known all-sports channel, ESPN. Several years
ago, ESPN began televising what were then called alternative sports—
skateboarding, snowboarding, mountain bike riding, and so forth. The surprising
popularity of these programs led ESPN to package them into an annual competition called the "X-Games." "X" stands for extreme, and ESPN has definitely gone
to the extreme in including sports in the X-Games. The X-Games now include
sports such as sky-surfing, competitive high diving, competitive bungee cord
jumping, and so forth. ESPN broadcasts both a summer X-Games and a winter
X-Games. No other sports outlet has yet made such a commitment to so-called
extreme sports, and it has paid handsome dividends for ESPN—extreme sports
have very low cost broadcast rights and draw a fairly large audience. This commitment to extreme sports has been a source of at least a temporary competitive
advantage for ESPN.

Of course, not all of a firm's resources and capabilities have to be valuable
and rare. Indeed, most firms have a resource base that is composed primarily of
valuable but common resources and capabilities. These resources cannot be
sources of even temporary competitive advantage, but are essential if a firm is to
gain competitive parity. Under conditions of competitive parity, although no one
firm gains a competitive advantage, firms do increase their probability of survival.

Consider, for example, a telephone system as a resource or capability.
Because telephone systems are widely available and because virtually all organi-

zations have access to telephone systems, these systems are not rare and thus not a source of competitive advantage. However, firms that do not possess a telephone system are likely to give their competitors an important advantage and place themselves at a competitive disadvantage.

How rare a valuable firm resource or capability must be in order to have the potential for generating a competitive advantage varies from situation to situation. It is not difficult to see that if a firm's valuable resources and capabilities are absolutely unique among a set of current and potential competitors, they can generate a competitive advantage. However, it may be possible for a small number of firms in an industry to possess a particular valuable resource or capability and still obtain a competitive advantage. In general, as long as the number of firms that possess a particular valuable resource or capability is less than the number of firms needed to generate perfect competition dynamics in an industry, that resource or capability can be considered rare and a potential source of competitive advantage.

The Question of Imitability

V R I O

Firms with valuable and rare resources are often strategic innovators, for they are able to conceive of and engage in strategies that other firms cannot because these other firms lack the relevant resources and capabilities. These firms may gain the first-mover advantages discussed in Chapter 2.

Valuable and rare organizational resources, however, can be sources of sustained competitive advantage only if firms that do not possess them face a cost disadvantage in obtaining or developing them, compared to firms that already possess them. These kinds of resources are **imperfectly imitable**.[10] These observations lead to the **Question of Imitability**: "Do firms without a resource or capability face a cost disadvantage in obtaining or developing it compared to firms that already possess it?"

Imagine an industry with five essentially identical firms. Each of these firms manufactures the same products, uses the same raw materials, and sells the products to the same customers through the same distribution channels. It is not hard to see that firms in this kind of industry will have normal economic performance. Now, suppose that one of these firms, for whatever reason, discovers or develops a heretofore unrecognized valuable resource and uses that resource either to exploit an external opportunity or neutralize an external threat. Obviously, this one firm will gain a competitive advantage over the others.

This firm's competitors can respond to this competitive advantage in at least two ways. First, they can ignore the success of this one firm and continue as before. This action, of course, will put them at a competitive disadvantage. Second, these firms can attempt to understand why this one firm is able to be successful and then duplicate its resources to implement a similar strategy. If competitors have no cost disadvantages in acquiring or developing the needed resources, then this imitative approach will generate competitive parity in the industry.

Sometimes, however, for reasons that are discussed later, competing firms may face an important cost disadvantage in duplicating a successful firm's valuable resources. If this is the case, this one innovative firm may gain a **sustained competitive advantage**—an advantage that is not competed away through strategic imitation. Firms that possess and exploit costly-to-imitate, rare, and valuable resources in choosing and implementing their strategies may enjoy a period of sustained competitive advantage.[11]

For example, other sports networks have observed the success of ESPN's X-Games and are beginning to broadcast these competitions. NBC, for example, has developed its own version of the X-Games, called the "Gravity Games," and even the Olympics have included sports that were previously perceived as being "too extreme" for this mainline sports competition. Several Fox sports channels broadcast programs that feature extreme sports, and at least one new cable channel (Fuel) broadcasts only extreme sports. Whether these efforts will be able to attract the competitors that the X-Games attract, whether winners at these other competitions will gain as much status in their sports as do winners of the X-Games, and whether these other competitions and programs will gain the reputation among viewers enjoyed by ESPN will go a long way to determining whether ESPN's competitive advantage in extreme sports is temporary or sustained.[12]

Forms of Imitation: Direct Duplication and Substitution

In general, imitation occurs in one of two ways: **direct duplication** or **substitution**. Imitating firms can attempt to directly duplicate the resources possessed by the firm with a competitive advantage. Thus, NBC sponsoring an alternative extreme games competition can be thought of as an effort to directly duplicate the resources that enabled ESPN's X-Games to be successful. If the cost of this direct duplication is too high, then a firm with these resources and capabilities may obtain a sustained competitive advantage. If this cost is not too high, then any competitive advantages in this setting will only be temporary.

Imitating firms can also attempt to substitute other resources for a costly-to-imitate resource possessed by a firm with a competitive advantage. Extreme sports shows and an extreme sports cable channel are potential substitutes for ESPN's X-Game strategy. These shows appeal to much the same audience as the X-Games, but do not require the same resources as an X-Game strategy requires (e.g., because they are not competitions, they do not require the network to bring together a large number of athletes all at once). If substitute resources exist, and if imitating firms do not face a cost disadvantage in obtaining them, then the competitive advantage of other firms will only be temporary. However, if these resources have no substitutes, or if the cost of acquiring these substitutes is greater than the cost of obtaining the original resources, then competitive advantages can be sustained.

Why Might It Be Costly to Imitate Another Firm's Resources or Capabilities?

A variety of authors have studied the reasons why it might be costly for one firm to imitate the resources and capabilities of another firm. Four sources of costly imitation have been noted.[13] These are summarized in Table 3.2 and discussed below.

Unique Historical Conditions. It may be the case that a firm was able to acquire or develop its resources and capabilities in a low-cost manner because of its unique historical conditions. The ability of firms to acquire, develop, and use resources often depends upon their place in time and space. Once time and history pass, firms that do not have space-and-time–dependent resources face a significant cost disadvantage in obtaining and developing them, because doing so would require them to re-create history.[14]

ESPN's early commitment to extreme sports is an example of these unique historical conditions. The status and reputation of the X-Games was created because ESPN happened to be the first major sports outlet that took these compe-

Table 3.2   **Sources of Costly Imitation**

Unique Historical Conditions: When a firm gains low-cost access to resources because of its place in time and space, other firms may find these resources to be costly to imitate. Both first-mover advantages and path dependence can create unique historical conditions.

Causal Ambiguity: When competitors cannot tell, for sure, what enables a firm to gain an advantage, that advantage may be costly to imitate. Sources of causal ambiguity include when competitive advantages are based on "taken-for-granted" resources and capabilities, when multiple nontestable hypotheses exist about why a firm has a competitive advantage, and when a firm's advantages are based on complex sets of interrelated capabilities.

Social Complexity: When the resources and capabilities a firm uses to gain a competitive advantage involve interpersonal relationships, trust, culture, and other social resources that are costly to imitate in the short term.

Patents: Only a source of sustained competitive advantage in a few industries, including pharmaceuticals and specialty chemicals.

titions seriously. The X-Games apparently became the most important competition in many of these extreme sports. Indeed, for snow boarders, winning a gold medal in the X-Games is almost as important—if not more important—as winning a gold medal in the Winter Olympics. Other sports outlets that hope to be able to compete with the X-Games will have both the status of ESPN as "the worldwide leader in sports" and its historical advantage in extreme sports to overcome. Overcoming these advantages is likely to be very costly, making competitive threats from direct duplication, at least, less significant.

Of course, firms can also act to increase the costliness of imitating the resources and capabilities they control. ESPN is doing this by expanding its coverage of extreme sports, and by engaging in a "grassroots" marketing campaign that engages young, "extreme athletes" in local competitions. The purpose of these efforts is clear: to keep ESPN's status as the most important source of extreme sports competitions intact.[15]

There are at least two ways that unique historical circumstances can give a firm a sustained competitive advantage. First, it may be that a particular firm is the first in an industry to recognize and exploit an opportunity, and being first gives a firm one or more of the first-mover advantages discussed in Chapter 2. Thus, although in principle other firms in an industry could have exploited an opportunity, that only one firm did so makes it more costly for other firms to imitate this original firm.

A second way that history can have an impact on a firm builds on the concept of **path dependence**.[16] A process is said to be path dependent when events early in the evolution of a process have significant effects on subsequent events. In the evolution of competitive advantage, path dependence suggests that a firm may gain a competitive advantage in the current period based on the acquisition and development of resources in earlier periods. In these earlier periods, it is often not clear what the full future value of particular resources will be. Because of this uncertainty, firms are able to acquire or develop these resources for less than what will turn out to be their full value. However, once the full value of these resources is revealed, other firms seeking to acquire or develop these resources will need to pay their full known value, which (in general) will be greater than the costs incurred by the firm that acquired or developed these resources in some earlier period. The cost of acquiring both duplicate and substitute resources would rise once their full value became known.

Consider, for example, a firm that purchased land for ranching some time ago and discovered a rich supply of oil on this land in the current period. The difference between the value of this land as a supplier of oil (high) and the value of this land for ranching (low) is a source of competitive advantage for this firm. Moreover, other firms attempting to acquire this or adjacent land will now have to pay for the full value of the land in its use as a supply of oil (high) and thus will be at a cost disadvantage compared to the firm that acquired it some time ago for ranching.

Causal Ambiguity. A second reason why a firm's resources and capabilities may be costly to imitate is that imitating firms may not understand the relationship between the resources and capabilities controlled by a firm, and that firm's competitive advantage. In other words, the relationship between firm resources and capabilities and competitive advantage may be **causally ambiguous**.

At first, it seems unlikely that causal ambiguity about the sources of competitive advantage for a firm would ever exist. Managers in a firm seem likely to understand the sources of their own competitive advantage. If managers in one firm understand the relationship between resources and competitive advantage, then it seems likely that managers in other firms would also be able to discover these relationships and thus would have a clear understanding of which resources and capabilities they should duplicate or seek substitutes for. If there are no other sources of cost disadvantage for imitating firms, imitation should lead to competitive parity and normal economic performance.[17]

However, it is not always the case that managers in a particular firm will fully understand the relationship between the resources and capabilities they control and competitive advantage. This lack of understanding could occur for at least three reasons. First, it may be that the resources and capabilities that generate competitive advantage are so taken for granted, so much a part of the day-to-day experience of managers in a firm, that these managers are unaware of them.[18] Organizational resources and capabilities such as teamwork among top managers, organizational culture, relationships among other employees, and relationships with customers and suppliers may be almost "invisible" to managers in a firm.[19] If managers in firms that have such capabilities do not understand their relationship to competitive advantage, managers in other firms face significant challenges in understanding which resources they should imitate.

Second, managers may have multiple hypotheses about which resources and capabilities enable their firm to gain a competitive advantage, but they may be unable to evaluate which of these resources and capabilities, alone or in combination, actually create the competitive advantage. For example, if one asks successful entrepreneurs what enabled them to be successful, they are likely to reply with several hypotheses such as "hard work, willingness to take risks, and a high-quality top management team." However, if one asks what happened to unsuccessful entrepreneurs, they too are likely to suggest that their firms were characterized by "hard work, willingness to take risks, and a high-quality top management team." It may be the case that "hard work, willingness to take risks, and a high-quality top management team" are important resources and capabilities for entrepreneurial firm success, but other factors may also play a role. Without rigorous experiments, it is difficult to establish which of these resources have a causal relationship with competitive advantage and which do not.

Finally, it may be that not just a few resources and capabilities enable a firm to gain a competitive advantage but that literally thousands of these organizational attributes, bundled together, generate these advantages. When the resources and capabilities that generate competitive advantage are complex networks of relationships between individuals, groups, and technology, imitation can be costly.

Consider, again, Electronic Arts—the company with which this chapter began. The broad strategic goals that EA has for each of its major products—to have both creative and technological achievements—are easy to state. But it is the way that EA manages the creative and technological process that makes the achievement of these goals costly for others to imitate. For example, programmers are expected to share computer programs across products when they develop a new feature that might be relevant to other games. A couple of times each year, the senior management team at EA gathers to meet with a diverse group of artists to learn about the creative process. These managers talk about movement with interpretive dancers, they talk about creativity with performance artists, and they talk about structural design with sculptors. Recently, EA hired script writers from Hollywood who introduced a whole new approach to writing the stories associated with their computer games. No single one of these processes by itself would give EA its competitive advantage. But, in combination, these processes and many hundreds of others are very difficult to describe, let alone imitate.[20]

Whenever the sources of competitive advantage are widely diffused across people, locations, and processes in a firm, those sources will be costly to imitate. Perhaps the best example of such a resource is knowledge itself. To the extent that valuable knowledge about a firm's products, processes, customers, and so on, is widely diffused throughout an organization, competitors will have difficulty imitating that knowledge and it can be a source of sustained competitive advantage.[21]

Social Complexity. A third reason that a firm's resources and capabilities may be costly to imitate is that they may be socially complex phenomena, beyond the ability of firms to systematically manage and influence. When competitive advantages are based in such complex social phenomena, the ability of other firms to imitate these resources and capabilities, either through direct duplication or substitution, is significantly constrained. Efforts to influence these kinds of phenomena are likely to be much more costly than they would be if these phenomena developed in a natural way over time in a firm.[22]

A wide variety of firm resources and capabilities may be **socially complex**. Examples include the interpersonal relations among managers in a firm, a firm's culture, and a firm's reputation among suppliers and customers.[23] Notice that in most of these cases it is possible to specify how these socially complex resources add value to a firm. Thus, there is little or no causal ambiguity surrounding the link between these firm resources and capabilities and competitive advantage. However, understanding that an organizational culture with certain attributes or quality relations among managers can improve a firm's efficiency and effectiveness does not necessarily imply that firms lacking these attributes can engage in systematic effort to create them, or that low-cost substitutes for them exist. For the time being, such social engineering may be beyond the abilities of most firms. At the very least, such social engineering is likely to be much more costly than it would be if socially complex resources evolved naturally within a firm.[24]

It is interesting to note that firms seeking to imitate complex physical technology often do not face the cost disadvantages of imitating complex social phenomena. A great deal of physical technology (machine tools, robots, and so forth) can be purchased in supply markets. Even when a firm develops its own unique

Research Made Relevant

*M*ost empirical tests of the Resource-Based View have focused on the extent to which history, causal ambiguity, and social complexity have an impact on the ability of firms to gain and sustain competitive advantages. Among the most important of these tests has been research that examines the extent to which human resource practices that are likely to generate socially complex resources and capabilities are related to firm performance. This area of research is known as Strategic Human Resources Management.

The first of these tests was conducted as part of a larger study of efficient low cost manufacturing in the worldwide automobile industry. A group of researchers from the Massachusetts Institute of Technology developed rigorous measures of the cost and quality of over 70 manufacturing plants that assembled mid-size sedans around the world. They discovered that, at the time of their study, only six of these plants had simultaneously low costs and high-quality manufacturing—a position that obviously would give these plants a competitive advantage in their marketplace.

In trying to understand what distinguished these six plants from

Strategic Human Resource Management Research

the others in the sample, these researchers found that, not surprisingly, these six plants had the most modern and up-to-date manufacturing technology. However, so did many of the less effective plants. What distinguished these effective plants was not their manufacturing technology, per se, but their human resource (HR) practices. These six plants all implemented a bundle of such practices that included participative decision making, quality circles, and an emphasis on team production.

One of the results of these efforts—and another distinguishing feature of these six plants—was a high level of employee loyalty and commitment to a plant, together with a belief that plant managers would treat employees fairly. These socially complex resources and capabilities are just the types of resources that the RBV suggests should be sources of sustained competitive advantage.

Later work has followed up on this approach and has examined the impact of HR practices on firm performance outside the manufacturing arena. Using a variety of measures of firm performance and several different measures of HR practices, the results of this research continue to be very consistent with resource-based logic. That is, firms that are able to use HR practices to develop socially complex human and organizational resources are able to gain competitive advantages over firms that do not engage in these practices.

Sources: J. P. Womack, D. I. Jones, and D. Roos (1990). *The machine that changed the world.* New York: Rawson; M. Huselid (1995). "The impact of human resource management practices on turnover, productivity, and corporate financial performance." *Academy of Management Journal,* 38, pp. 635–672; J. B. Barney and P. Wright (1998). "On becoming a strategic partner." *Human Resource Management,* 37, pp. 31–46.

physical technology, reverse engineering tends to diffuse this technology among competing firms in a low-cost manner. Indeed, the costs of imitating a successful physical technology are often lower than the costs of developing a new technology.[25]

Although physical technology is usually not costly to imitate, the application of this technology in a firm is likely to call for a wide variety of socially complex organizational resources and capabilities. These organizational resources may be costly to imitate, and, if they are valuable and rare, the combination of physical and socially complex resources may be a source of sustained competitive advantage. The importance of socially complex resources and capabilities for firm performance has been studied in detail in the field of strategic human resource management, as described in the Research Made Relevant feature.

Patents. At first glance, it might appear that a firm's patents would make it very costly for competitors to imitate its products.[26] Patents do have this effect in some industries. For example, patents in the pharmaceutical and specialty chemical industry effectively foreclose other firms from marketing the same products until a firm's patents expire. As suggested in Chapter 2, patents can raise the cost of imitation in a variety of other industries as well.

However, from another point of view, a firm's patents may decrease, rather than increase, the costs of imitation. When a firm files for patent protection, it is forced to reveal a significant amount of information about its product. Governments require this information to ensure that the technology in question is patentable. By obtaining a patent, a firm may provide important information to competitors about how to imitate its technology.

Moreover, most technological developments in an industry are diffused throughout firms in that industry in a relatively brief period of time, even if the technology in question is patented, because patented technology is not immune from low-cost imitation. Patents may restrict direct duplication for a time, but they may actually increase the chances of substitution by functionally equivalent technologies.[27]

The Question of Organization

VRIO

A firm's potential for competitive advantage depends on the value, rarity, and imitability of its resources and capabilities. However, to fully realize this potential, a firm must be organized to exploit its resources and capabilities. These observations lead to the **Question of Organization**: "Is a firm organized to exploit the full competitive potential of its resources and capabilities?"

Numerous components of a firm's organization are relevant to the question of organization, including its formal reporting structure, its formal and informal management control systems, and its compensation policies. A firm's **formal reporting structure** is a description of who in the organization reports to whom; it is often embodied in a firm's **organizational chart**. **Management control systems** include a range of formal and informal mechanisms to ensure that managers are behaving in ways consistent with a firm's strategies. **Formal management controls** include a firm's budgeting and reporting activities that keep people higher up in a firm's organizational chart informed about the actions taken by people lower down in a firm's organizational chart. **Informal management controls** might include a firm's culture and the willingness of employees to monitor each others' behavior. **Compensation policies** are the ways that firms pay employees. Such policies create incentives for employees to behave in certain ways.

These components of a firm's organization are often called **complementary resources and capabilities** because they have limited ability to generate competitive advantage in isolation. However, in combination with other resources and capabilities, they can enable a firm to realize its full potential for competitive advantage.[28]

For example, it has already been suggested that ESPN may have a sustained competitive advantage in the extreme sports segment of the sports broadcasting industry. However, if ESPN's management had not taken advantage of its opportunities in extreme sports by expanding coverage, ensuring that the best competitors come to ESPN competitions, adding additional competitions, and changing up older competitions, then its potential for competitive advantage would not have been fully realized. Of course, the reason that ESPN has done all these things is because it has an appropriate organizational structure, management controls, and employee compensation policies. By themselves, these attributes of ESPN's organization could not be a source of competitive advantage; however, this organization was essential for ESPN to realize its full competitive advantage potential.

Having an appropriate organization in place has enabled ESPN to realize the full competitive advantage potential of its other resources and capabilities. Having an inappropriate organization in place prevented Xerox from taking full advantage of some of its most critical valuable, rare, and costly-to-imitate resources and capabilities.

Through the 1960s and early 1970s, Xerox invested in a series of very innovative technology development research efforts. It managed this research effort by creating a stand-alone research center in Palo Alto, California (Palo Alto Research Center—PARC), and by assembling a large group of highly creative and innovative scientists and engineers to work there. Left to their own devices, these scientists and engineers at Xerox PARC developed an amazing array of technological innovations: the personal computer, the "mouse," Windows-type software, the laser printer, the "paperless office," Ethernet, and so forth. In retrospect, it is clear that the market potential of these technologies was enormous. Moreover, because they were developed at Xerox PARC, they were rare. Xerox might have been able to gain some important first-mover advantages if the organization had been able to translate these technologies into products, thereby increasing the cost to other firms of imitating these technologies.

Xerox possessed the resources and capabilities but did not have an organization in place to take advantage of them. No structure existed whereby Xerox PARC innovations could become known to managers at Xerox. Indeed, most Xerox managers—even many senior managers—were unaware of these technological developments through the mid-1970s. Once they finally became aware of them, very few of the technologies survived Xerox's highly bureaucratic product development process, a process where product development projects were divided into hundreds of minute tasks and progress in each task was reviewed by dozens of large committees. Even innovations that survived the product development process were not exploited by Xerox managers, because management compensation at Xerox depended almost exclusively on maximizing current revenue. Short-term profitability was relatively less important in compensation calculations, and the development of markets for future sales and profitability was essentially irrelevant. Xerox's formal reporting structure, its explicit management control systems, and its compensation policies were all inconsistent with exploiting the valuable, rare, and costly-to-imitate resources it had developed. Not surprisingly, the company failed to exploit any of its potential sources of sustained competitive advantage.[29]

Applying the VRIO Framework

The questions of value, rarity, imitability, and organization can be brought together into a single framework to understand the return potential associated with exploiting any of a firm's resources or capabilities. This is done in Table 3.3. The relationship of the VRIO framework to strengths and weaknesses is presented in Table 3.4.

If a resource or capability controlled by a firm is not valuable, it will not enable a firm to choose or implement strategies that exploit environmental opportunities or neutralize environmental threats. Organizing to exploit this resource will increase a firm's costs or decrease its revenues. These types of resources are

Table 3.3 **The VRIO Framework**

Is a resource or capability:				
Valuable?	**Rare?**	**Costly to imitate?**	**Exploited by organization?**	**Competitive implications**
No	—	—	No	Competitive disadvantage
Yes	No	—	↑	Competitive parity
Yes	Yes	No	⇕	Temporary competitive advantage
Yes	Yes	Yes	Yes	Sustained competitive advantage

weaknesses. Firms will either have to fix these weaknesses or avoid using them when choosing and implementing strategies. If firms do exploit these kinds of resources and capabilities, they can expect to put themselves at a competitive disadvantage compared to firms that either do not possess these nonvaluable resources or do not use them in conceiving and implementing strategies.

If a resource or capability is valuable but not rare, exploitation of this resource in conceiving and implementing strategies will generate competitive parity. Exploiting these types of resources will generally not create competitive advantages, but failure to exploit them can put a firm at a competitive disadvantage. In this sense, valuable-but-not-rare resources can be thought of as organizational strengths.

If a resource or capability is valuable and rare but not costly to imitate, exploiting this resource will generate a temporary competitive advantage for a firm. A firm that exploits this kind of resource is, in an important sense, gaining a first-mover advantage, because it is the first firm that is able to exploit a particular resource. However, once competing firms observe this competitive advantage, they will be able to acquire or develop the resources needed to implement this strategy through direct duplication or substitution at no cost disadvantage compared to the first-moving firm. Over time, any competitive advantage that the first mover obtained would be competed away as other firms imitate the resources needed to compete. Consequently, this type of resource or capability can be thought of as an organizational strength and as a **distinctive competence**.

If a resource or capability is valuable, rare, and costly to imitate, exploiting it will generate a sustained competitive advantage. In this case, competing firms face a significant cost disadvantage in imitating a successful firm's resources and

Table 3.4 **The Relationship Between the VRIO Framework and Organizational Strengths and Weaknesses**

Is a resource or capability:				
Valuable?	**Rare?**	**Costly to imitate?**	**Exploited by organization?**	**Strength or weakness**
No	—	—	No	Weakness
Yes	No	—	↑	Strength
Yes	Yes	No	⇕	Strength and distinctive competence
Yes	Yes	Yes	Yes	Strength and sustainable distinctive competence

capabilities. As suggested earlier, this competitive advantage may reflect the unique history of the successful firm, causal ambiguity about which resources to imitate, the socially complex nature of these resources and capabilities, or any patent advantages a firm might posses. In any case, attempts to compete away the advantages of firms that exploit these resources will not generate competitive advantage or even competitive parity for imitating firms. Even if these firms are able to acquire or develop the resources or capabilities in question, the very high costs of doing so would put them at a competitive disadvantage. These kinds of resources and capabilities are organizational strengths and **sustainable distinctive competencies**.

The question of organization operates as an adjustment factor in the VRIO framework. For example, if a firm has a valuable, rare, and costly-to-imitate resource and capability but fails to organize itself to take full advantage of this resource, some of its potential competitive advantage could be lost (this is the Xerox example). Extremely poor organization, in this case, could actually lead a firm that has the potential for competitive advantage to gain only competitive parity or competitive disadvantages.

Applying the VRIO Framework to Dell Computer

To examine how the VRIO framework can be applied in analyzing real strategic situations, consider the competition position of Dell Computer. Most observers agree that Dell Computer has been able to gain a sustained competitive advantage in the very competitive personal computer industry. By applying the VRIO framework to Dell's value chain, it is possible to begin to identify the sources of that advantage. Figure 3.5 applies a version of the generic value chain developed by McKinsey and Company (see Figure 3.2) to Dell Computer.[30]

Notice that Dell is not engaged in very many stages of the value chain. Indeed, one of the critical aspects of Dell's ability to generate economic value is

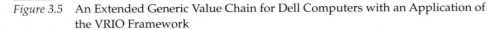

Figure 3.5   An Extended Generic Value Chain for Dell Computers with an Application of the VRIO Framework

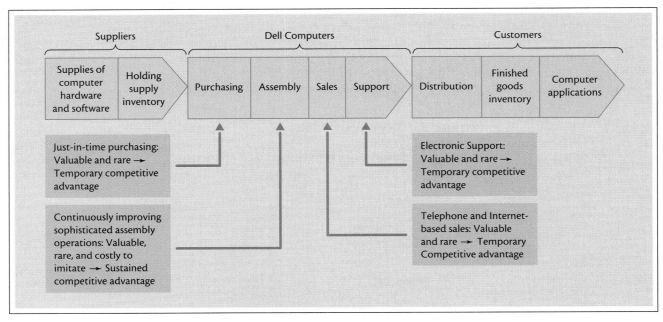

that it has adopted a strategy that enables it to focus only on those aspects of the value chain where it has either a temporary or sustained competitive advantage. This approach to deciding which stages of the value chain to enter into is discussed in more detail in Chapter 6.

Dell has at least a temporary competitive advantage in purchasing. This advantage stems from several factors, including Dell's volume of sales, which makes it an important customer to its suppliers. Dell can use its volume to obtain price reductions on many of the supplies it purchases. However, although its size is a valuable asset in this function, it is neither rare nor costly to imitate. After all, HP/Compaq and IBM both have large sales and thus enjoy similar volume advantages.

More important than Dell's size is the way that Dell manages its purchasing function. It purchases just the supplies it needs to complete production and expects its suppliers—both large and small—to make numerous deliveries to its production facilities, sometimes several times a day. In this way, Dell has been able to shift the costs of having an inventory of supplies from itself to its suppliers. This approach to purchasing is relatively unusual (that is, rare) in the personal computer industry. However, it is becoming the standard for efficient manufacturing in large numbers of industries, including the automobile industry. For this reason, although purchasing may be a source of temporary competitive advantage, it seems imitable and thus not likely to be a source of sustained competitive advantage.

Dell assembly operations, on the other hand, may be a source of sustained competitive advantage. Attention to detail, increased speed and efficiency, and high quality are all built into Dell assembly operations. This is true even though Dell assembles customized personal computers by offering numerous different option combinations, and often relies on outside companies to do its assembly.

For example, in building one type of computer, Dell engineers were able to reduce the number of times a computer had to be touched during the assembly process from 130 to 60. In another stage of the operation, Dell was able to modify the assembly process so that instead of requiring six screws to secure a subassembly, only a single screw was required—without the loss of quality. This attention to detail has led Dell to receive over 200 patents on assembly operations. And unlike product patents, patents on assembly operations are often costly to imitate because they are usually part of an integrated production system. Using language developed earlier in this chapter, Dell's advantage in assembly is based on numerous little decisions, decisions that are virtually invisible to competitors.

Moreover, Dell's relentless emphasis on process improvement is deeply ingrained in its socially complex culture. These attributes of the assembly process suggest that it is valuable, rare, and costly to imitate, and thus is likely to be a source of sustained competitive advantage for Dell.

Sales and support at Dell are managed through both telephone and Internet operations. Although Dell currently has a head start in these areas of its business, it is unlikely that other personal computer firms will ignore similar opportunities.[31] However, Dell currently does have a reputation for its e-commerce capabilities. This reputation among customers will probably mean that Dell will continue to enjoy these advantages beyond the time that competitors actually catch up to its sales and service strategy.

Dell does not engage in distribution, transportation, inventory holding, and computer applications stages of the value chain. Again, this enables it to concentrate on only those aspects of the value chain that are either a source of temporary or sustained competitive advantage. Given its strategy, it is not surprising that Dell's performance has been outstanding, even though it operates in a very competitive industry.

Imitation and Competitive Dynamics in an Industry

Suppose a firm in an industry has conducted an analysis of its resources and capabilities, concludes that it possesses some valuable, rare, and costly-to-imitate resources and capabilities, and uses these to choose a strategy that it implements with the appropriate organizational structure, formal and informal management controls, and compensation policies. The Resource-Based View suggests that this firm will gain a competitive advantage even if it is operating in what a five forces analysis (see Chapter 2) would suggest is a very unattractive industry. Examples of firms that have competitive advantages in unattractive industries include Southwest Airlines, Nucor Steel, Wal-Mart, and Dell Computers, to name a few.

Given that a particular firm in an industry has a competitive advantage, how should other firms respond? Decisions made by other firms given the strategic choices of a particular firm define the nature of the **competitive dynamics** that exist in an industry. In general, other firms in an industry can respond to the advantages of a competitor in one of three ways. First, they can choose to not respond at all. For example, when Airbus decided to build a super-jumbo airliner designed to dominate international travel for the next 30 years, Boeing did nothing. Second, they can choose to alter some of their business tactics. For example, when Southwest Airlines began operating out of Philadelphia's airport and charged very low airfares, US Airways—the airline that used to dominate the Philadelphia market—lowered its fares as well. Finally, they can choose to alter their strategy—their theory of how to gain competitive advantage (see Chapter 1). For example, when Dell's direct and Internet-based approach to selling personal computers became dominant, Gateway computers decided to abandon its retail stores in favor of a direct and Internet-based approach.[32] The choice of responses a firm makes determines the structure of the competitive dynamics in an industry.

Not Responding to Another Firm's Competitive Advantage

There are at least three reasons why a firm might not respond to another firm's competitive advantage. First, this firm might have its own competitive advantage. By responding to another firm's competitive advantage it might destroy, or at least compromise, its own sources of competitive advantage. For example, digital time keeping has made accurate watches available to most consumers at reasonable prices. Firms like Casio have a competitive advantage in this market because of their miniaturization and electronic capabilities. Indeed, Casio's market share and performance in the watch business continue to climb over the years. How should Rolex—a manufacturer of very expensive, nonelectronic watches—respond to Casio? Rolex's decision has been: Not at all. Rolex appeals to a very different market segment than Casio. Should Rolex change its strategies—even if it replaced its mechanical self-winding design with the technologically superior digital design—it could easily compromise its competitive advantage in its own niche market.[33] In general, when a firm already possesses its own sources of competitive advantage, it will not respond to different sources of competitive advantage controlled by another firm.

Second, a firm may not respond to another firm's competitive advantage because it does not have the resources and capabilities to do so. A firm with insufficient or inappropriate resources and capabilities—be they physical, financial, human, or organizational—will typically not be able to imitate a successful firm's resources either through direct duplication or substitution. This may very well be the case with USAir and Southwest Airlines. Southwest's managerial resources and capabilities may simply be beyond the ability of USAir to imitate. In this setting, USAir is likely to find itself at a sustained competitive disadvantage.[34]

Finally, a firm may not respond to the advantages of a competitor because it is trying to reduce the level of rivalry in an industry. Any actions a firm takes that have the effect of reducing the level of rivalry in an industry and that also do not require firms in an industry to directly communicate or negotiate with each other can be thought of as **tacit cooperation**. Explicit cooperation, where firms do directly communicate and negotiate with each other, is discussed in detail in Chapter 9's analysis of strategic alliances.

Reducing the level of rivalry in an industry can benefit all those firms operating in that industry. This decision can have the effect of reducing the quantity of goods and services provided in an industry to below the competitive level, actions which will have the effect of increasing the prices of these goods or services. When tacit cooperation has the effect of reducing supply and increasing prices, it is known as **tacit collusion**. Tacit collusion can be illegal in some settings. However, firms can also tacitly cooperate along other dimensions besides quantity and price. These actions can also benefit all the firms in an industry and are typically not illegal.[35]

For example, it may be that firms can tacitly agree not to invest in certain kinds of research and development. Some forms of R&D are very expensive, and while these investments might end up generating products or services that could benefit customers, firms might still prefer to avoid the expense and risk. Firms can also tacitly agree not to market their products in certain ways. For example, before regulations compelled them to do so, most tobacco companies had already decided not to put cigarette vending machines in locations usually frequented by children, even though these machines could have generated significant revenues. Also, firms can tacitly cooperate by agreeing not to engage in certain manufacturing practices, such as outsourcing to third world countries and engaging in environmentally unsound practices.

All of these actions can have the effect of reducing the level of rivalry in an industry. And reducing the level of rivalry can have the effect of increasing the average level of performance for a firm in an industry. However, tacit cooperative relationships among firms are sometimes difficult to maintain. Typically, in order for tacit cooperation to work, an industry must have the structural attributes described in Table 3.5. First, there must be relatively few firms in the industry. Informally communicating and coordinating strategies among a few firms is difficult enough; it is even more difficult when there are large numbers of firms in an industry. For this reason, tacit cooperation is a viable strategy only when an industry is an oligopoly (see Chapter 2).

Second, firms in this industry must be homogeneous with respect to the products they sell and their cost structure. Heterogeneous products makes it too

Table 3.5 **Attributes of Industry Structure That Facilitate the Development of Tacit Cooperation**

1. Small Number of Competing Firms
2. Homogeneous Products and Costs
3. Market Share Leader
4. High Barriers to Entry

easy for a firm to "cheat" on its tacitly cooperative agreements by modifying its products, and heterogeneous cost means that the optimal level of output for a particular firm may be very different than the level agreed to through tacit cooperation. In this setting, a firm might have a strong incentive to increase its output and upset cooperative agreements.

Third, there typically has to be a strong market share leader in an industry if firms in that industry are going to tacitly cooperate. This would be a relatively large firm that typically establishes an example of the kind of behavior that will be mutually beneficial in an industry, and other firms in the industry sometimes fall into line with this example. Indeed, it is often this market share leader that will choose not to respond to the competitive actions of another firm in the industry in order to maintain cooperative relations in that industry.

Finally, the maintenance of tacit cooperation in an industry almost always requires the existence of high barriers to entry. If tacit cooperation is successful, the average performance of firms in an industry will improve. However, this higher level of performance can induce other firms to enter into this industry (see Chapter 2). Such entry will increase the number of firms in an industry and make it very difficult to maintain tacitly cooperative relationships. Thus, it must be very costly for new firms to enter into an industry in order for those in that industry to maintain their tacit cooperation. The higher these costs, the higher the barriers to entry.

Changing Tactics in Response to Another Firm's Competitive Advantage

Tactics are the specific actions a firm takes to implement its strategies. Examples of tactics can include decisions firms make about various attributes of their products—including size, shape, color, and price—specific advertising approaches adopted by a firm, and specific sales and marketing efforts. Generally, firms change their tactics much more frequently than they change their strategies.[36]

When competing firms are pursuing approximately the same strategies, the competitive advantages that any one firm might enjoy at a given point in time are most likely due to the tactics that that firm is pursuing. In this setting, it is not unusual for competing firms to change their tactics by imitating the tactics of the firm with an advantage in order to reduce this advantage. While changing one's tactics in this manner will only generate competitive parity, that is usually better than the competitive disadvantage these firms were experiencing previously.

Several industries provide excellent examples of these kinds of tactical interactions. In consumer goods, for example, if one company's sales increase by adding a "lemon scent" to laundry detergent, then lemon scents start showing up in everyone's laundry detergent. When Coke brings out C2—a soft drink with half the sugar and half the carbs of regular Coke—can Pepsi's low sugar/low carb product be far behind? And when Delta Airlines cuts it airfares, can American and United be far behind? Not surprisingly, these kinds of tactical changes, because they initially may be valuable and rare, are seldom costly to imitate and thus are typically only sources of temporary competitive advantage.

Sometimes, rather than simply imitating the tactics of a firm with a competitive advantage, a firm at a disadvantage may "leap frog" its competitors by developing an entirely new set of tactics. Procter & Gamble engaged in this strategy when it introduced its laundry detergent, Tide, in a new, concentrated formula. This new Tide required new manufacturing and packaging equipment—the smaller box could not be filled in the current manufacturing lines in the industry—which meant that Tide's competitors had to take more time in imitating the concentrated laundry detergent tactic than other tactics pursued in this industry. But, nevertheless, in a few short weeks, other firms in this market were introducing their own versions of concentrated laundry detergent.

Indeed, some firms can become so skilled at innovating new products and other tactics that this innovative capability can be a source of sustained competitive advantage. Consider, for example, the performance of Sony. Most observers agree that Sony possesses some special management and coordination skills that enable it to conceive, design, and manufacture high-quality miniaturized consumer electronics. However, virtually every time Sony brings out a new miniaturized product, several of its competitors quickly duplicate that product through reverse engineering, thereby reducing Sony's technological advantage. In what way can Sony's socially complex miniaturization resources and capabilities be a source of sustained competitive advantage when most of Sony's products are quickly imitated through direct duplication?

After Sony introduces each new product, it experiences a rapid increase in profits attributable to the new product's unique features. This increase, however, leads other firms to reverse-engineer the Sony product and introduce their own version. Increased competition results in a reduction in the profits associated with a new product. Thus, at the level of individual products, Sony apparently enjoys only temporary competitive advantages. However, looking at the total returns earned by Sony across all of its new products over time makes clear the source of Sony's sustained competitive advantage: By exploiting its resources and capabilities in miniaturization, Sony is able to constantly introduce new and exciting personal electronics products. No one of these products generates a sustained competitive advantage. But over time, across several such product introductions, Sony's resource and capability advantages lead to sustained competitive advantages.[37]

Changing Strategies in Response to Another Firm's Competitive Advantage

Finally, firms sometimes respond to another firm's competitive advantage by changing their strategies. Obviously, this does not occur very often and it typically only occurs when another firm's strategies usurp a firm's competitive advantage. In this setting a firm will not be able to gain even competitive parity if it maintains its strategy, even if it implements that strategy very effectively.

Changes in consumer tastes, in population demographics, and in the laws that govern a business can all have the effect of rendering what once was a valuable strategy as valueless. However, nothing has this impact more frequently than changes in technology. For example, no matter how well-made a mechanical calculator, is it is simply inferior to an electronic calculator. No matter how efficient the telegraph was in its day, it is an inferior technology to the telephone. And no matter how quickly one's fingers can move the beads on an abacus, an electronic cash register is a better way of keeping track of sales and making change in a store.

When firms change their strategies, they must proceed through the entire strategic management process, as described in Chapter 1. However, these firms will often have difficulty abandoning their traditional strategies. For most firms, their strategy helps define what they do and who they are. Changing its strategy often requires a firm to change its identity and its purposes. These are difficult changes to make and many firms wait to change their strategy until absolutely forced to do so by disastrous financial results. By then these firms not only have to change their strategy—with all that implies—they have to do so in the face of significant financial pressures.

The ability of virtually all strategies to generate competitive advantages typically expires, sooner or later. In general, it is much better for a firm to change its strategy before that strategy is no longer viable. In this way, a firm can make a planned move to a new strategy that maintains whatever resources and capabilities it still possesses while it develops the new resources and capabilities it will need to compete in the future.

Implications of the Resource-Based View

The Resource-Based View and the VRIO framework can be applied to individual firms to understand whether or not these firms will gain competitive advantages, how sustainable these competitive advantages are likely to be, and what the sources of these competitive advantages are. In this way, the Resource-Based View and the VRIO framework can be understood as important complements to the threats and opportunities analyses described in Chapter 2.

However, beyond what these frameworks can say about the competitive performance of a particular firm, the Resource-Based View has some broader implications for managers seeking to gain competitive advantages. Some of these broader implications are listed in Table 3.6 and discussed below.

Where Does the Responsibility for Competitive Advantage in a Firm Reside?

First, the Resource-Based View suggests that competitive advantages can be found in several of the different resources and capabilities a firm controls. These resources and capabilities are not limited to those that are directly controlled by a

Table 3.6   **Broader Implications of the Resource-Based View**

1. The responsibility for competitive advantage in a firm:
   Competitive advantage is every employee's responsibility.
2. Competitive parity and competitive advantage:
   If all a firm does is what its competition does, it can gain only competitive parity. In gaining competitive advantage, it is better for a firm to exploit its own valuable, rare, and costly-to-imitate resources than to imitate the valuable and rare resources of a competitor.
3. Difficult to implement strategies:
   As long as the cost of strategy implementation is less than the value of strategy implementation, the relative cost of implementing a strategy is more important for competitive advantage than the absolute cost of implementing a strategy. Firms can systematically overestimate and underestimate their uniqueness.
4. Socially complex resources:
   Not only can employee empowerment, organizational culture, and teamwork be valuable; they can also be sources of sustained competitive advantage.
5. The role of the organization:
   Organization should support the use of valuable, rare, and costly-to-imitate resources. If conflicts between these attributes of a firm arise, change the organization.

firm's senior managers. Thus, the responsibility for creating, nurturing, and exploiting valuable, rare, and costly-to-imitate resources and capabilities for competitive advantage is not restricted to senior managers, but falls on every employee in a firm. To do this, employees should go beyond defining their jobs in functional terms and instead define their jobs in competitive and economic terms.

Consider a simple example. In a recent visit to a very successful automobile manufacturing plant, the plant manager was asked to describe his job responsibilities. He said, "My job is to manage this plant in order to help the firm make and sell the best cars in the world." In response to a similar question, the person in charge of the manufacturing line also said, "My job is to manage this manufacturing line in order to help the firm make and sell the best cars in the world." A janitor was also asked to describe his job responsibilities. Although he had not been present in the two earlier interviews, the janitor responded, "My job is to keep this facility clean in order to help the firm make and sell the best cars in the world."

Which of these three employees is most likely to be a source of sustained competitive advantage for this firm? Certainly, the plant manager and the manufacturing line manager *should* define their jobs in terms of helping the firm make and sell the best cars in the world. However, it is unlikely that their responses to this question would be any different than the responses of other senior managers at other manufacturing plants around the world. Put differently, while the definition of these two managers' jobs in terms of enabling the firm to make and sell the best cars in the world is valuable, it is unlikely to be rare and thus likely to be a source of competitive parity, not competitive advantage. On the other hand, a janitor that defines his or her job as helping the firm make and sell the best cars in the world instead of simply to clean the facility is, most would agree, quite unusual. Because it is rare, it might be a source of at least a temporary competitive advantage.[38]

Now the value created by one janitor defining his or her job in these competitive terms rather than functional terms is not huge, but suppose that all the employees in this plant defined their jobs in these terms. Suddenly, the value that might be created could be substantial. Moreover, the organizational culture and tradition in a firm that would lead employees to define their jobs in this way is likely to be costly for other firms to imitate. Thus, if this approach to defining job responsibilities is broadly diffused in a particular plant, it seems likely to be valuable, rare, and costly to imitate and thus a source of sustained competitive advantage, assuming the firm is organized to take advantage of this unusual resource.

In the end, it is clear that competitive advantage is too important to remain the sole property of senior management. To the extent that employees throughout an organization are empowered to develop and exploit valuable, rare, and costly-to-imitate resources and capabilities in the accomplishment of their job responsibilities, a firm may actually be able to gain sustained competitive advantages.

Competitive Parity and Competitive Advantage

Second, the Resource-Based View suggests that if all a firm does is create value in the same way as its competitors, the best performance it can ever expect to gain is competitive parity. To do better than competitive parity, firms must engage in valuable and rare activities. They must do things to create economic value that other firms have not even thought of, let alone implemented.

This is especially critical for firms that find themselves at a competitive disadvantage. Such a firm certainly should examine its more successful competition, understand what has made this competition so successful, and, where imitation is very low cost, should imitate the successful actions of its competitors. In this sense, benchmarking a firm's performance against the performance of its competitors can be extremely important.

However, if this is all that a firm does, it can only expect to gain competitive parity. Gaining competitive advantage depends on a firm discovering its own unique resources and capabilities and how they can be used in choosing and implementing strategies. For a firm seeking competitive advantage, it is better to be excellent in how it develops and exploits its own unique resources and capabilities than it is to be excellent in how it imitates the resources and capabilities of other firms.

This does not imply that firms must always be "first movers" to gain competitive advantages. Some firms develop valuable, rare, and costly-to-imitate resources and capabilities in being efficient second movers—that is, in rapidly imitating and improving on the product and technological innovations of other firms. Rather than suggesting that firms must always be first movers, the Resource-Based View suggests that, in order to gain competitive advantages, firms must implement strategies that rely on valuable, rare, and costly-to-imitate resources and capabilities, whatever those strategies or resources might be.

Difficult-to-Implement Strategies

Third, as firms contemplate different strategic options, they often ask how difficult and costly it will be to implement different strategies. As long as the cost of implementing a strategy is less than the value that a strategy creates, the Resource-Based View suggests that the critical question facing firms is not "Is a strategy easy to implement or not?" but rather, "Is this strategy easier for us to implement than it is for our competitors to implement?" Firms that already possess the valuable, rare, and costly-to-imitate resources needed to implement a strategy will, in general, find it easier (that is, less costly) to implement a strategy than firms that first have to develop the required resources and then implement the proposed strategy. For firms that already possess a resource, strategy implementation can be natural and swift.

In understanding the relative costs of implementing a strategy, firms can make two errors. First, they can overestimate the uniqueness of the resources they control. Although every firm's history is unique and no two management teams are exactly the same, this does not always mean that a firm's resources and capabilities will be rare. Firms with similar histories operating in similar industries will often develop similar capabilities. If a firm overestimates the rarity of its resources and capabilities, it can overestimate its ability to generate competitive advantages.

For example, when asked what their most critical sources of competitive advantage are, many firms will cite the quality of their top management team, the quality of their technology, and their commitment to excellence in all that they do. When pushed about their competitors, these same firms will admit that they too have high-quality top management teams, high-quality technology, and a commitment to excellence in all that they do. Although these three attributes can be sources of competitive parity, they cannot be sources of competitive advantage.

Second, firms can sometimes underestimate their uniqueness and thus underestimate the extent to which the strategies they pursue can be sources of sustained competitive advantage. When firms possess valuable, rare, and costly-to-imitate resources, strategy implementation can be relatively easy. In this context, it seems reasonable to expect that other firms will be able to quickly imitate this "easy-to-implement" strategy. Of course, this is not the case if these resources controlled by a firm are, in fact, rare and costly to imitate.

In general, firms must take great care not to overestimate or underestimate their uniqueness. An accurate assessment of the value, rarity, and imitability of a firm's resources is necessary to develop an accurate understanding of the relative costs of implementing a firm's strategies and thus the ability of those strategies to generate competitive advantages. Often, firms must employ outside assistance in helping them describe the rarity and imitability of their resources, even though managers in firms will generally be much more familiar with the resources controlled by a firm than outsiders. However, outsiders can provide a measure of objectivity in evaluating the uniqueness of a firm.

Socially Complex Resources

Over the last several decades much has been written about the importance of employee empowerment, organizational culture, and teamwork for firm performance. Most of this work suggests that firms that empower employees, that have an enabling culture, and that encourage teamwork will, on average, make better strategic choices and implement them more efficiently than firms without these organizational attributes. Using the language of the Resource-Based View, most of this work has suggested that employee empowerment, organizational culture, and teamwork, at least in some settings, are economically valuable.

Resource-based logic acknowledges the importance of the value of these organizational attributes. However, it also suggests that these socially complex resources and capabilities can be rare and costly to imitate—and it is these attributes that make it possible for socially complex resources and capabilities to be sources of sustained competitive advantage. Put differently, the Resource-Based View actually extends and broadens traditional analyses of the socially complex attributes of firms. Not only can these attributes be valuable, but they can also be rare and costly to imitate and thus sources of sustained competitive advantage.

The Role of Organization

Finally, resource-based logic suggests that an organization's structure, control systems, and compensation policies should support and enable a firm's efforts to fully exploit the valuable, rare, and costly-to-imitate resources and capabilities it controls. These attributes of organization, by themselves, are usually not sources of sustained competitive advantage.

These observations suggest that if there is a conflict between the resources a firm controls and that firm's organization, the organization should be changed. However, it is often the case that once a firm's structure, control systems, and compensation policies are put in place they remain, regardless of whether or not they are consistent with a firm's underlying resources and capabilities. In such settings, a firm will not be able to realize the full competitive potential of its underlying resource base. To the extent that a firm's resources and capabilities are continuously evolving, its organizational structure, control systems, and compensation policies must also evolve. For these attributes of organization to evolve, managers must be aware of their link with a firm's resources and capabilities and of organizational alternatives.

Internal Analysis in an International Context

The Resource-Based View and the VRIO framework can also be applied in the analysis of firm decisions to enter into international markets. This logic suggests two broad reasons why firms may begin operating in multiple businesses: (1) to take advantage of current resource and capability advantages in new geographic markets and (2) to develop new resource and capability advantages by beginning to operate in new geographic markets. Organizing to implement these international strategies is also important. However, since exploitation of international markets is almost always a specific example of a corporate diversification strategy, the discussion of how to organize such international ventures will be delayed until Chapter 8's analysis of implementing corporate diversification strategies.

Exploiting Current Resource Advantages in New Markets

Suppose a firm already has a sustained competitive advantage in its domestic market. One logical way for a firm with such an advantage to increase its growth and profitability is to exploit those same capabilities in new geographic markets by beginning international operations. However, that a firm's resources are valuable, rare, and costly to imitate in one country does not necessarily mean they will be in a different country.

Several firms have been successful in using their competitive advantage in one country to gain competitive advantages in another country. Coca-Cola, for example, has used its strong brand name—Coke—as a way of entering markets around the world. Currently, Coca-Cola actually sells more Coke products outside of the United States than it sells domestically. Sony used its technical and innovative capabilities, honed in its hypercompetitive home Japanese market, to become a dominant player in the U.S. consumer electronics market. And BMW used its engineering skills developed by building cars to run at 120 mph on the German autobahn to become an important part of the luxury sports sedan market in the United States. In all these cases, what were valuable, rare, and costly-to-imitate resources or capabilities in a firm's home market also turned out to be valuable, rare, and costly-to-imitate resources in nondomestic markets as well.

However, that a resource or capability is a source of sustained competitive advantage in one country does not guarantee that it will also be valuable, or valuable and rare, or valuable, rare, and costly to imitate in another country. For example, Disney has tried to leverage its brand name and its ability to create and manage theme parks internationally. Its theme park in Asia, Tokyo Disneyland, has been a significant financial success. However, the Disney Company has only a small financial stake in Tokyo Disneyland so this theme park's financial success has not benefited Disney that much. On the other hand, Disney's theme park in Europe, EuroDisney, just outside of Paris, France, has been a financial drag on the Disney Company. After several financial restructuring efforts, EuroDisney is finally beginning to have a positive impact on the financial position of Disney Company. But it has taken many years and many millions of dollars to get EuroDisney on a financially secure footing. Apparently, the "Disney experience" at EuroDisney is simply not as valuable as the "Disney experience" in Florida, California, or Tokyo.[39]

When contemplating the exploitation of a firm's valuable, rare, and costly-to-imitate resources and capabilities in a new geographic market, all four of the VRIO questions are important. Certainly, the value of a firm's resources in a new market may differ from the value of those same resources in its home market.

EuroDisney is an example of this problem. Also, if a firm is contemplating entry into a more competitive market than its home market, it is likely that what were rare and costly-to-imitate resources in the home market will be less rare and less costly to imitate in a new, more competitive, geographic market. As some authors have observed, firms looking to take advantage of their resources in new geographic markets are more likely to be successful if their home markets are highly competitive in the first place.[40] If a firm's valuable resources are a source of sustained competitive advantage in a highly competitive home market they are more likely to be sources of sustained competitive advantage in other, less competitive, geographic markets—assuming, of course, they are still valuable.

Developing New Resources and Capabilities in New Markets

One of the most compelling reasons for firms to begin operations outside their domestic markets is to develop new resources and capabilities. By beginning such operations, firms can gain a greater understanding of their strengths and weakness. By exposing these resources and capabilities to new competitive contexts, traditional resources can be modified and new resources can be developed.

Of course, for international operations to affect a firm's resources and capabilities, firms must learn from their experiences in nondomestic markets. Learning in this context is anything but automatic. Many firms that begin operations in a nondomestic market encounter challenges and difficulties and then immediately withdraw from their international efforts. Other firms continue to try to operate internationally but are unable to learn how to modify and change the core resources. One study identified three critical determinants of the ability of a firm to develop new resources and capabilities through its international operations: the intent to learn, the transparency of learning partners, and the receptivity to learning.[41]

A firm that has a strong intent to learn from its international operations is more likely to learn than a firm without this intent. Moreover, this intent must be communicated to all those who work in a firm's international activities. Compare, for example, a quote from a manager whose firm failed to learn from its international operations with a quote from a manager whose firm was able to learn from these operations.[42]

> Our engineers were just as good as [our partner's]. In fact, theirs were narrower technically, but they had a much better understanding of what the company was trying to accomplish. They knew they were there to learn, our people didn't.

> We wanted to make learning an automatic discipline. We asked the staff every day, "What did you learn from [our partner] today?" Learning was carefully monitored and recorded.

Obviously, the second firm was in a much better position than the first to learn from its international operations and to develop new resources and capabilities.

The transparency of learning partners is also an important determinant of the ability to develop new resources and capabilities from international operations. Some international business partners are more open and accessible than others. These differences can reflect different organizational philosophies, practices, and procedures, as well as differences in the culture of a firm's home country. For example, knowledge in Japanese and many other Asian cultures tends to be context-specific and deeply embedded in the broader social system. This makes it difficult for many Western managers to understand and appreciate the subtlety of

Japanese business practices and Japanese culture. This, in turn, limits the ability of Western managers to learn from their operations in the Japanese market or from their Japanese partners.[43]

In contrast, knowledge in most Western cultures tends to be less context-specific, less deeply embedded in the broader social system. Such knowledge can be written down, can be taught in classes, and can be transmitted, all at a relatively low cost. Japanese managers working in Western economies are more likely to be able to appreciate and understand Western business practices and thus more able to learn from their operations in the West and from their Western partners.

Finally, firms vary in their receptiveness to learning about new resources and capabilities. A firm's receptiveness to such learning is affected by its culture, its operation procedures, and its history. Research suggests that, before firms can learn from their international operations, they must be prepared to unlearn. Unlearning requires a firm to modify or abandon traditional ways of engaging in business. Unlearning can be difficult, especially if a firm has a long history of success using old patterns of behavior, and if those old patterns of behavior are reflected in its organizational structure, formal and informal management controls, and compensation policies.

SUMMARY

The Resource-Based View (RBV) is an economic theory that suggests that firm performance is a function of the types of resources and capabilities firms control. Resources are the tangible and intangible assets a firm uses to conceive of and implement its strategies. Capabilities are a subset of resources and enable a firm to take advantage of its other resources. Resources and capabilities can be categorized into financial, physical, human, and organizational resource categories.

The RBV makes two assumptions about resources and capabilities: the assumption of resource heterogeneity (that some resources and capabilities may be heterogeneously distributed across competing firms) and the assumption of resource immobility (that this heterogeneity may be long lasting). These two assumptions can be used to describe conditions under which firms will gain competitive advantages by exploiting their resources.

A tool for analyzing a firm's internal strengths and weaknesses can be derived from the RBV. Called the VRIO framework, this tool asks four questions about a firm's resources and capabilities in order to evaluate their competitive potential. These questions are: the Question of Value, the Question of Rarity, the Question of Imitability, and the Question of Organization.

A firm's resources and capabilities are valuable when they enable it to exploit external opportunities or neutralize external threats. Such valuable resources and capabilities are a firm's strengths. Resources and capabilities that are not valuable are a firm's weaknesses. Using valuable resources to exploit external opportunities or neutralize external threats will have the effect of increasing a firm's net revenues or decreasing its net costs.

One way to identify a firm's valuable resources and capabilities is by examining its value chain. A firm's value chain is the list of business activities it engages in to develop, produce, and sell its products or services. Different stages in this value chain require different resources and capabilities, and differences in value-chain choices across firms can lead to important differences among the resources and capabilities controlled by different companies. Two generic value chains have been developed, one by McKinsey and Company and the second by Michael Porter.

Valuable and common (that is, not rare) resources and capabilities can be a source of competitive parity. Failure to invest in such resources can create a competitive disadvantage for a firm. Valuable and rare resources can be a source of at least a temporary competitive advantage. There are fewer firms able to control such a resource and still exploit it as a source of at least temporary competitive advantage than there are firms that will generate perfect competition dynamics in an industry.

Valuable, rare, and costly-to-imitate resources and capabilities can be a source of sustained competitive advantage. Imitation can occur through direct duplication or through substitution. There are at least four reasons a firm's resources and capabilities may be costly to imitate: unique historical circumstances, causal ambiguity, socially complex resources and capabilities, and patents.

To take full advantage of the potential of its resources and capabilities, a firm must be appropriately organized. A firm's organization consists of its formal reporting structure, its formal and informal control processes, and its compensation policy. These are complementary resources in that they are rarely sources of competitive advantage on their own.

The VRIO framework can be used to identify the competitive implications of a firm's resources and capabilities—whether they are a source of competitive disadvantage, competitive parity, temporary competitive advantage, or sustained competitive advantage— and the extent to which these resources and capabilities are strengths or weaknesses.

When a firm faces a competitor that has a sustained competitive advantage, it can not respond, can change its tactics, or change its strategies. There are at least three reasons why a firm may choose not to respond in this setting. First, a response might weaken its own sources of sustained competitive advantage. Second, a firm may not have the resources required to respond. Third, a firm may be trying to create or maintain tacit cooperation within an industry.

The RBV has a series of broader managerial implications as well. For example, this logic suggests that competitive advantage is every employee's responsibility. It also suggests that if all a firm does is what its competition does, it can gain only competitive parity, and that in gaining competitive advantage it is better for a firm to exploit its own valuable, rare, and costly-to-imitate resources than to imitate the valuable and rare resources of a competitor. Also, resource-based logic implies that as long as the cost of strategy implementation is less than the value of strategy implementation, the relative cost of implementing a strategy is more important for competitive advantage than the absolute cost of implementing a strategy. It implies as well that firms can systematically overestimate and underestimate their uniqueness. With regard to a firm's resources and capabilities, resource-based logic suggests that not only can employee empowerment, organizational culture, and teamwork be valuable; they can also be sources of sustained competitive advantage. Also, if conflicts arise between a firm's valuable, rare, and costly-to-imitate resources and a firms organization, the organization should be changed.

Finally, resource-based theory and the VRIO framework can also be applied in an international context. In general, firms pursue international opportunities to either exploit their currently valuable, rare, and costly-to-imitate resources and capabilities in new markets or to develop new resources and capabilities. The ability to develop new resources and capabilities through international operations depends on a firm's intent to learn, the transparency of its international business partners, and its receptiveness to learning.

CHALLENGE QUESTIONS

1. Which approach to strategy formulation is more likely to generate economic profits: (a) evaluating external opportunities and threats and then developing resources and capabilities to exploit these opportunities and neutralize these threats or (b) evaluating internal resources and capabilities and then searching for industries where they can be exploited? Why?

2. Which firm will have a higher level of economic performance: (a) a firm with valuable, rare, and costly-to-imitate resources and capabilities operating in a very attractive industry or (b) a firm with valuable, rare, and costly-to-imitate resources and capabilities operating in a very unattractive industry? Assume both these firms are appropriately organized. Explain your answer.

3. Which is more critical to sustaining human life—water or diamonds? Why do firms that provide water to customers generally earn lower economic performance than firms that provide diamonds?

4. Will a firm currently experiencing competitive parity be able to gain sustained competitive advantages by studying another firm that is currently experiencing sustained competitive advantages? Why or why not?

5. Your former college roommate calls you and asks to borrow $10,000 so that he can open a pizza restaurant in his hometown. He acknowledges that there is a high degree of rivalry in this market, that the cost of entry is low, and that there are numerous substitutes for pizza, but he believes that his pizza restaurant will have some sustained competitive advantages. For example, he is going to have sawdust on his floor, a variety of imported beers, and a late-night delivery service. Will you lend him the money? Why or why not?

6. In the text, it is suggested that Boeing did not respond to Airbus's announcement of the development of a super-jumbo aircraft. Assuming this aircraft will give Airbus a competitive advantage in the segment of the air-

liner business that supplies airplanes for long international flights, why did Boeing not respond?

a. Does it have its own competitive advantage that it does not want to abandon?

b. Does it not have the resources and capabilities needed to respond?

c. Is it trying to reduce the level of rivalry in this industry?

7. Which firm is more likely to be successful in exploiting its sources of sustained competitive advantage in its home market in a highly competitive, nondomestic market: a firm from a less competitive home country or a firm from a more competitive home country? Why?

8. What are some indicators that a firm is engaging in an international strategy to develop new resources and capabilities?

PROBLEM SET

1. Apply the VRIO framework in the following settings. Will the actions described be a source of competitive disadvantage, parity, temporary advantage, or sustained competitive advantage, and why?

(a) Procter Gamble introduces new, smaller packaging for its laundry detergent Tide.

(b) American Airlines announces a 5 percent across-the-board reduction in airfares.

(c) The Korean automobile firm Hyundai announces a 10-year, 100,000 mile warranty on its cars.

(d) Microsoft makes it easier to transfer data and information from Microsoft Word to Microsoft Excel.

(e) Merck is able to coordinate the work of its chemists and biologists in the development of new drugs.

(f) Ford patents a new kind of brake pad for its cars.

(g) Ashland Chemical, a specialty chemical company, patents a new specialty chemical.

(h) The New York Yankees sign all-star pitcher Randy Johnson to a long-term contract.

(i) Michael Dell uses the money he has made from Dell Computers to purchase the Dallas Cowboys football team.

(j) Ted Turner uses the money he has made from his broadcasting empire to purchase the Atlanta Braves baseball team.

2. Identify three firms you might want to work for. Using the VRIO framework, evaluate the extent to which the resources and capabilities of these firms gives them the potential to realize competitive disadvantages, parity, temporary advantages, or sustained advantages. What implications, if any, does this analysis have for the company you might want to work for?

3. You have been assigned to estimate the present value of a potential construction project for your company. How would you use the VRIO framework to construct the cash flow analysis that is a part of any present-value calculation?

END NOTES

1. The term "the Resource-Based View" was coined by Wernerfelt, B. (1984). "A resource-based view of the firm." *Strategic Management Journal*, 5, pp. 171–180. Some important early contributors to this theory include Rumelt, R. P. (1984). "Toward a strategic theory of the firm." In R. Lamb (ed.), *Competitive strategic Management* (pp. 556–570). Upper Saddle River, NJ: Prentice Hall; and Barney, J. B. (1986). "Strategic factor markets: Expectations, luck and business strategy." *Management Science*, 32, pp. 1512–1514. A second wave of important early resource-based theoretical work includes Barney, J. B. (1991). "Firm resources and sustained competitive advantage." *Journal of Management*, 7, pp. 49–64; Dierickx, I., and K. Cool (1989). "Asset stock accumulation and sustainability of competitive advantage." *Management Science*, 35, pp. 1504–1511; Conner, K. R. (1991). "A historical comparison of resource-based theory and five schools of thought within industrial organization economics: Do we have a new theory of the firm?" *Journal of Management*, 17(1), pp. 121–154; and Peteraf, M. A. (1993). "The cornerstones of competitive advantage: A resource-based view." *Strategic Management Journal*, 14, pp. 179–191. A review of much of this early theoretical literature can be found in Mahoney, J. T., and J. R. Pandian (1992). "The resource-based view within the conversation of strategic management." *Strategic Management Journal*, 13, pp. 363–380. The theoretical perspective has also spawned a growing body of empirical work, including Brush, T. H., and K. W. Artz (1999). "Toward a contingent resource-based theory." *Strategic Management Journal*, 20, pp. 223–250; Marcus, A., and D. Geffen (1998). "The dialectics of competency acquisition." *Strategic Management Journal*, 19, pp. 1145–1168; Brush, T. H., P. Bromiley, and M. Hendrickx (1999). "The relative influence of industry and corporation on business segment performance." *Strategic Management Journal*, 20, pp. 519–547; Yeoh, P.-L., and K. Roth (1999). "An empirical analysis of sustained advantage in the U.S. pharmaceutical industry." *Strategic Management Journal*, 20, pp. 637–653; Roberts, P. (1999). "Product innovation, product-market competition and persistent profitability in the U.S. pharmaceutical industry." *Strategic Management Journal*, 20, pp. 655–670; Gulati, R. (1999). "Network location and learning." *Strategic Management Journal*, 20, pp. 397–420; Lorenzoni, G., and A. Lipparini (1999). "The leveraging of interfirm relationships as a distinctive organizational capability." *Strategic Management Journal*, 20, pp. 317–338; Majumdar, S. (1998). "On the utilization of resources." *Strategic Management Journal*, 19(9) pp. 809–831; Makadok, R. (1997). "Do inter-firm differences in capabilities affect strategic pricing dynamics?" *Academy of Management Proceedings '97*, pp. 30–34; Silverman, B. S., J. A. Nickerson, and J. Freeman (1997). "Profitability, transactional alignment, and organizational mortality in the U.S. trucking industry." *Strategic Management Journal*, 18 (Summer special issue), pp. 31–52; Powell, T. C., and A. Dent-Micallef (1997). "Information technology as competitive advantage." *Strategic Management Journal*, 18(5), pp. 375–405; Miller, D., and J. Shamsie (1996). "The Resource-Based View of the firm in two environments." *Academy of Management Journal*, 39(3), pp. 519–543; and Maijoor, S., and A. Van Witteloostuijn (1996). "An empirical test of the resource-based theory." *Strategic Management Journal*, 17, pp. 549–569; Barnett, W. P., H. R. Greve, and D. Y. Park (1994). "An evolutionary model of organizational performance." *Strategic Management Journal*, 15 (Winter special issue), pp. 11–28; Levinthal, D., and J. Myatt (1994). "Co-evolution of capabilities and industry: The evolution of mutual fund processing." *Strategic Management Journal*, 17, pp. 45–62; Henderson, R., and I. Cockburn (1994). "Measuring competence? Exploring firm effects in pharmaceutical research." *Strategic Management Journal*, 15, pp. 63–84; Pisano, G. P. (1994). "Knowledge, integration, and the locus of learning: An empirical analysis of process development." *Strategic Management Journal*, 15, pp. 85–100; and Zajac, E. J., and J. D. Westphal (1994). "The costs and benefits of managerial incentives and monitoring in large U.S. corporations: When is more not better?" *Strategic Management Journal*, 15, pp. 121–142.

2. Ghemawat, P. (1986). "Wal-Mart stores' discount operations." Harvard Business School Case No. 9-387-018, on Wal-Mart; Kupfer, A. (1991). "The champion of cheap clones." *Fortune*, September 23, pp. 115–120; and Holder, D. (1989). "L. L. Bean, Inc.—1974." Harvard Business School Case No. 9-676-014, on L. L. Bean. Some of Wal-Mart's more recent moves, especially its international acquisitions, are described in Laing, J. R. (1999). "Blimey! Wal-Mart." *Barron's*, 79, p. 14. L. L. Bean's lethargic performance in the 1990s, together with its turnaround plan, is described in Symonds, W. (1998). "Paddling harder at L.L. Bean." *BusinessWeek*, Dec. 7, p. 72.

3. For an early discussion of the importance of human capital in firms, see Becker, G. S. (1964). *Human capital*. New York: Columbia University Press.

4. Heskett, J. L., and R. H. Hallowell (1993). "Southwest Airlines: 1993 (A)." Harvard Business School Case No. 9-695-023.

5. See Jay Barney (1991). "Firm resources and sustained competitive advantage." *Journal of Management*, 17, pp. 99–120.

6. See Schlender, B. R. (1992). "How Sony keeps the magic going." *Fortune*, February 24, pp. 75–84; and (1999). "The weakling kicks back." *The Economist*, July 3, p. 46, for a discussion at Sony. See Krogh, L., J. Praeger, D. Sorenson, and J. Tomlinson (1988). "How 3M evaluates its R&D programs." *Research Technology Management*, 31, pp. 10–14.

7. George Anders (2002). "AOL's true believers." *Fast Company*, July pp. 96 +.

8. See Grant, R. M. (1991). *Contemporary strategy analysis*. Cambridge, MA: Basil Blackwell.

9. Porter, M. E. (1987). *Competitive advantage*. New York: Free Press.

10. Lipman, S., and R. Rumelt (1982). "Uncertain imitability: An analysis of interfirm differences in efficiency under competition." *Bell Journal of Economics*, 13, pp. 418–438; Barney, J. B. (1986). "Strategic factor markets: Expectations, luck and business strategy." *Management Science*, 32, pp. 1512–1514; and Barney, J. B. (1986). "Organizational culture: Can it be a source of sustained competitive advantage?" *Academy of Management Review*, 11, pp. 656–665.

11. Note that the definition of sustained competitive advantage presented here, though different, is consistent with the definition given in Chapter 1. In particular, a firm that enjoys a competitive advantage for a long period of time (the Chapter 1 definition) does not have its advantage competed away through imitation (the Chapter 3 definition).

12. See Breen, Bill (2003). "What's selling in America." *Fast Company*, January, pp. 80 +.

13. These explanations of costly imitation were first developed by Dierickx, I., and K. Cool (1989). "Asset stock accumulation and sustainability of competitive advantage." *Management Science*, 35, pp. 1504–1511; Barney, J. B. (1991). "Firm resources and sustained competitive advantage." *Journal of Management*, 7, pp. 49–64; Mahoney, J. T., and J. R. Pandian (1992). "The resource-based view within the conversation of strategic management." *Strategic Management Journal*, 13, pp. 363–380; and Peteraf, M. A. (1993). "The cornerstones of competitive advantage: A resource-based view." *Strategic Management Journal*, 14, pp. 179–191.

14. Dierickx, I., and K. Cool (1989). "Asset stock accumulation and sustainability of competitive advantage." *Management Science*, 35,

pp. 1504–1511. In economics, the role of history in determining competitive outcomes was first examined by Arthur, W. B. (1989). "Competing technologies, increasing returns, and lock-in by historical events." *Economic Journal*, 99, pp. 116–131.

15. See Breen, Bill (2003). "What's selling in America." *Fast Company*, January, pp. 80 +.

16. This term was first suggested by Arthur, W. B. (1989). "Competing technologies, increasing returns, and lock-in by historical events." *Economic Journal*, 99, pp. 116–131. A good example of path dependence is the development of Silicon Valley and the important role that Stanford University and a few early firms played in creating the network of organizations that has since become the center of much of the electronics business. See Alley, J. (1997). "The heart of Silicon Valley." *Fortune*, July 7, pp. 86 +.

17. Reed, R., and R. J. DeFillippi (1990). "Causal ambiguity, barriers to imitation, and sustainable competitive advantage." *Academy of Management Review*, 15(1), pp. 88–102, suggest that causal ambiguity about the sources of a firm's competitive advantage need only exist among a firm's competitors for it to be a source of sustained competitive advantage. Managers in a firm, they argue, may fully understand the sources of their advantage. However, in a world where employees freely and frequently move from firm to firm, such special insights into the sources of a firm's competitive advantage would not remain proprietary for very long. For this reason, for causal ambiguity to be a source of sustained competitive advantage, both the firm trying to gain such an advantage and those trying to imitate it must face similar levels of causal ambiguity. Indeed, Wal-Mart recently sued Amazon.com for trying to steal some of its secrets by hiring employees away from Wal-Mart. See Nelson, E. (1998). "Wal-Mart accuses Amazon.com of stealing its secrets in lawsuit." *Wall Street Journal*, October 19, p. B10. For a discussion of how difficult it is to maintain secrets, especially in a world of the World Wide Web, see Farnham, A. (1997). "How safe are your secrets?" *Fortune*, September 8, pp. 114 +. The international dimensions of the challenges associated with maintaining secrets are discussed in Robinson, E. (1998). "China spies target corporate America." *Fortune*, March 30, pp. 118 +.

18. Itami, H. (1987). *Mobilizing invisible assets*, Cambridge, MA: Harvard University Press.

19. See Barney, J. B., and B. Tyler (1990). "The attributes of top management teams and sustained competitive advantage." In M. Lawless and L. Gomez-Mejia (eds.), *Managing the High Technology Firm* (pp. 33–48). Greenwich, CT: JAI Press, on teamwork in top management teams; Barney, J. B. (1986). "Organizational culture: Can it be a source of sustained competitive advantage?" *Academy of Management Review*, 11, pp. 656–665, on organizational culture; Henderson, R. M., and I. Cockburn, (1994). "Measuring competence? Exploring firm effects in pharmaceutical research." *Strategic Management Journal*, 15, pp. 63–84, on relationships among employees; and Dyer, J. H., and H. Singh (1998). "The relational view: Cooperative strategy and sources of interorganizational competitive advantage." *Academy of Management Review*, 23(4), pp. 660–679, on relationships with suppliers and customers.

20. Management at Electronic Arts is described in Salter, Chuck (2002). "Playing to win." *Fast Company*, December, pp. 80 +.

21. For a discussion of knowledge as a source of competitive advantage in the popular business press, see Stewart, T. (1995). "Getting real about brain power." *Fortune*, November 27, pp. 201 +; Stewart, T. (1995). "Mapping corporate knowledge." *Fortune*, October 30, pp. 209 +. For the academic version of this same issue, see Simonin, B. L. (1999). "Ambiguity and the process of knowledge transfer in strategic alliances." *Strategic Management Journal*, 20(7), pp. 595–623; Spender, J. C. (1996). "Making knowledge the basis of a dynamic theory of the firm." *Strategic Management Journal*, 17 (Winter special issue), pp. 109–122; Hatfield, D. D., J. P. Liebeskind, and T. C. Opler (1996). "The effects of corporate restructuring on aggregate industry specialization." *Strategic Management Journal*, 17, pp. 55–72; and Grant, R. M. (1996). "Toward a knowledge-based theory of the firm." *Strategic Management Journal*, 17 (Winter special issue), pp. 109–122.

22. Porras, J., and P. O. Berg (1978). "The impact of organizational development." *Academy of Management Review*, 3, pp. 249–266, have done one of the few empirical studies on whether or not systematic efforts to change socially complex resources are effective. They found that such efforts are usually not effective. Although this study is getting older, it is unlikely that current change methods will be any more effective than the methods examined by these authors.

23. See Hambrick, D. (1987). "Top management teams: Key to strategic success." *California Management Review*, 30, pp. 88–108, on top management teams; Barney, J. B. (1986). "Organizational culture: Can it be a source of sustained competitive advantage?" *Academy of Management Review*, 11, pp. 656–665, on culture; Porter, M. E. (1980). *Competitive strategy*. New York: Free Press; and Klein, B., and K. Leffler (1981). "The role of market forces in assuring contractual performance." *Journal of Political Economy*, 89, pp. 615–641, on relations with customers.

24. See Harris, L. C., and E. Ogbonna (1999). "Developing a market oriented culture: A critical evaluation." *Journal of Management Studies*, 36(2), pp. 177–196.

25. Lieberman, M. B. (1987). "The learning curve, diffusion, and competitive strategy." *Strategic Management Journal*, 8, pp. 441–452, has a very good analysis of the cost of imitation in the chemical industry. See also Lieberman, M. B., and D. B. Montgomery (1988). "First-mover advantages." *Strategic Management Journal*, 9, pp. 41–58.

26. Rumelt, R. P. (1984). "Toward a strategic theory of the firm." In R. Lamb (ed.), *Competitive strategic management* (pp. 556–570). Upper Saddle River, NJ: Prentice Hall, among others, cites patents as a source of costly imitation.

27. There is currently significant debate about the patentability of different kinds of products. For example, while typefaces are not patentable (and cannot be copyrighted), the process for displaying typefaces may be. See Thurm, S. (1998). "Copy this typeface? Court ruling counsels caution." *Wall Street Journal*, July 15, pp. B1 +.

28. For an insightful discussion of these complementary resources, see Amit, R., and P.J.H. Schoemaker (1993). "Strategic assets and organizational rent." *Strategic Management Journal*, 14(1), pp. 33–45.

29. See Kearns, D. T., and D. A. Nadler (1992). *Prophets in the dark*. New York: HarperCollins; and Smith, D. K., and R. C. Alexander (1988). *Fumbling the future*. New York: William Morrow.

30. Information about Dell Computers was taken from Brown, E. (1999). "America's most admired companies." *Fortune*, March 1, pp. 68 +; Kirkpatrick, D. (1998). "The second coming at Apple." *Fortune*, November 9, pp. 96 +; and Hamel, G., and J. Sampler (1998). "The e-corporation." *Fortune*, December 7, pp. 80 +.

31. Indeed, many other firms, including Compaq and Hewlett-Packard, have begun using the net to sell their products. See McWilliams, G. (1998). "Mimicking Dell, Compaq to sell its PC directly." *Wall Street Journal*, November 11, pp. B1 +

32. (2004). "Gateway will close remaining retail stores." *Wall Street Journal*, April 2, p. B2; Michaels, D. (2004). "AA Airbus, picturing huge jet was easy; building it was hard." *Wall Street Journal*, May 27, pp. A1 +; Zeller, W., A. Michael, and L. Woellert (2004). "The airline debate over cheap seats." *Wall Street Journal*, May 24, pp. A1 +.

33. (2004). "Casio." *Marketing*, May 6, p. 95; Weisul, K. (2003). "When time is money—and art." *BusinessWeek*, July 21, p. 86.

34. That said, there have been some "cracks" in Southwest's capabilities armor lately. Its CEO suddenly resigned, and its level of profitability dropped precipitously in 2004. Whether these are indicators that Southwest's core strengths are being dissipated or there are short-term problems is not yet known. However, Southwest's stumbling would give USAir some hope. Trottman, M., S. McCartney, and J. Lublin (2004). "Southwest's CEO abruptly quits 'draining job'." *Wall Street Journal*, July 16, pp. A1 +.

35. One should consult a lawyer before one gets involved in these forms of tacit cooperation.

36. This aspect of the competitive dynamics in an industry is discussed in Smith, K. G., C. M. Grimm, and M. J. Gannon (1992). *Dynamics of competitive strategy*. Newberry Park, CA: Sage.

37. Schlender, B. R. (1992). "How Sony keeps the magic going." *Fortune*, February 24, pp. 75–84.

38. Personal communication.

39. Collis, D. (1988). "The Walt Disney Company (A): Corporate strategy." HBS Case No. 1-388-147; Rukstad, N. M., and D. Collis (2001). "The Walt Disney Company: The entertainment king." HBS Case No. 9-701-035.

40. Porter, M. E. (1990). *The competitive advantage of nations*. New York: Free Press.

41. See Hamel, G. (1991). "Competition for competence and inter-partner learning within international strategic alliances." *Strategic Management Journal*, 12, pp. 83–103.

42. Quoted in Hamel, G. (1991). "Competition for competence and inter-partner learning within international strategic alliances." *Strategic Management Journal*, 12, p. 86.

43. See, for example, Peterson, R. B., and J. Y. Shimada (1978). "Sources of management problems in Japanese-American joint ventures." *Academy of Management Review*, 3, pp. 796–804.

PART 1 CASES

Case 1–1: Roadway Express, Inc.*

As the summer of 1997 came to a close, a cloud hovered over the future of Roadway Express, Inc. Although Roadway had just come off a prosperous year in 1996 following two years of red ink, their contract with the Teamsters Union was set to expire on March 31, 1998. The Teamsters, which set wages and benefits for most of Roadway Express, Inc. workforce, had just completed what many considered a dramatic bargaining victory over United Parcel Service. Following a strike by the Teamsters which severely hampered UPS and slowed commerce in the U.S. economy as a whole, UPS made sweeping concessions to the union on wages, benefits, and rules governing the use of part-time and temporary workers. Many observers believed that the Teamsters would be emboldened to seek similar victories in upcoming bargaining. Roadway and other national less-than-truckload (LTL) trucking firms appeared to be the likely next target. Roadway faced the challenge of both continuing to respond to intense competition from nonunion carriers while being threatened with the increased costs that a new labor agreement was likely to bring. Could Roadway absorb the kind of increases in wages and benefits that UPS had conceded to and still be able to compete with nonunion carriers on freight rates? If not, what were their strategic alternatives?

History of Roadway Express, Inc.

Though Roadway Express, Inc. had existed as a corporate entity for only a short time, its history in LTL trucking was a long one. Roadway Express had been a subsidiary of

Roadway Services, Inc., but was spun off January 2, 1996. The former parent company, which was renamed Caliber System, Inc., focused more on regional and interregional freight transport using nonunion carriers. Though Roadway Express had existed as a stand-alone entity only since 1996, it had been active in LTL trucking since the former parent company was founded in 1930. For decades Roadway Express had been among the six largest providers of LTL transportation. In 1996 Roadway was considered one of the "Big Four" national LTL carriers along with Yellow Freight, ABF Freight Systems, and Consolidated Freightways. Roadway also offered service to and from another 62 countries worldwide. The carrier shipped general commodity freight in the United States and within Canada and Mexico through its subsidiaries. General commodity freight included apparel, appliances, automotive parts, chemicals, food, furniture, glass, machinery, metal and metal products, nonbulk petroleum products, rubber, textiles, wood, and miscellaneous manufactured products. Roadway's primary focus was on freight services involving city-to-city routes that required two days or longer in transit.

U.S. Trucking Industry

Analysts generally divided the U.S. trucking industry into two categories: less-than-truckload (LTL) carriage and truckload (TL) carriage. LTL service involved the transit of loads of less than 10,000 pounds. For a national LTL firm, this service typically involved a hub-and-spoke network of terminals and consolidation centers to efficiently transport freight. Freight was collected from shippers, and then taken to terminals. Terminals were large warehouses with many large loading ramps and garage doors to facilitate rapid unloading, sorting, and reloading of freight. At the terminals, freight was unloaded, resorted, and then reloaded on to trucks. Freight on these reloaded trucks was then routed to regional consolidation centers where

*This case was prepared by William Hesterly for the purposes of class discussion. The section on regulation in the trucking industry borrows heavily from Bryan S. Silverman, Jack A. Nickerson, and John Freeman, "Profitability, Transactional Alignment, and Organizational Mortality in the U.S. Trucking Industry," *Strategic Management Journal*, 1997, 18, 31–52.

it was again unloaded, resorted, and reloaded on to other trucks bound either for final destinations are other terminals. The handling and rerouting involved in LTL shipments necessitated sophisticated logistics systems, so that carriers could track any item shipped. TL carriage, on the other hand, involved shipments of freight greater than 10,000 pounds. These shipments generally went directly to the destination without the unloading, sorting, and reloading typical of LTL shipments. With TL carriage, trucks picked up a full truckload of goods from the sender and then transported them directly to the receiver of the shipment with no handling of the goods in between. Because TL shipments required no intermediate handling, TL carriers did not need the advanced tracking and logistics systems characteristic of the LTL market.

The U.S. trucking industry had been heavily regulated through much of its history, but had been largely deregulated in 1980. The Interstate Commerce Commission (ICC) had regulated competition in trucking beginning in 1935. Regulation was a response to intense lobbying from railroads who were threatened by the growth of the trucking industry. The ICC restricted the entry of new firms and the growth of existing firms. Prospective entrants into a market were required to obtain certification before they were able to operate. When a prospective entrant applied for certification to operate on a particular route, carriers who already served the market where the entrant intended to operate were given the opportunity to protest the need for a new entrant. Existing carriers generally did make such protests. The result of this process was that the ICC usually offered a certificate to a new carrier only after existing carriers were given the chance to offer the services proposed by entrants. The net effect of this regulation was that for many years the number of trucking firms remained almost constant. In 1960, there were 16,276 ICC regulated carriers compared to 16,005 in 1975. Prices were also tightly regulated. Price floors were established by regional pricing bureaus. These price floors essentially precluded any price competition between carriers.

The Motor Carrier Act of 1980 deregulated both entry and price. The Act greatly eased the restrictions on new carriers and gave carriers pricing freedom. By the end of 1991 there were 47,890 ICC certified carriers in operation. This figure did not include another 100,000 or more individual owner-operators who served as independent contractors for trucking firms. Another significant presence in the industry were private trucking fleets that served the in-house needs of large firms such as grocery or discount chains. Many of the ICC certified carriers were owner-operators or small, nonunion firms that focused on specific city-to-city routes. Pricing freedom resulted in sharply reduced rates in many cases. A sharp increase in the number of carriers ceasing operations or filing for bankruptcies also followed the 1980 Act.

LTL Market

The LTL market included two segments, long-haul and regional. National LTLs used a network of costly hubs (consolidation centers) and spokes (terminals) to distribute freight. Analysts had estimated that 400 terminals and 13–15 hubs would be adequate to offer national service. Many of the regional carriers, in contrast, were able to service their geographic areas with much less investment in network infrastructure. Major LTL carriers had reduced their consolidation centers and terminals by 25 percent between 1992 and 1996. This reduction had cut costs and shortened transit times where goods had been handled less. The number of times goods were handled directly affected shipping costs. Large LTLs handled freight an average of 1.9 times per shipment in the early 1990s.[1] Industry analysts estimated that a national LTL could save $750,000 for every .1 reduction in the number of times a shipment was handled.

Competition for freight was based primarily on price and service. The most important component of service was transit time. The hub and spoke system made competing on transit time more difficult. Carriers could reduce transit time through more direct routes as opposed to routing shipments through hubs. This avoided much of the time needed in handling and sorting goods. Some carriers had also adopted "sleeper" teams of drivers to reduce transit times. A sleeper team involved the use of two drivers and allowed a truck to operate for a greater proportion of time since regulations limited the number of hours an operator could drive in a day. Service on timing of deliveries had improved significantly and had reached the point where some carriers were offering two- and three-day guaranteed delivery schedules for the first time in national LTL shipments. Regional shipments typically involved less handling of freight.

Labor

The largest component of costs for LTL carriers was labor. National LTL firms were covered under a uniform bargaining agreement with the International Brotherhood of Teamsters which industry participants termed "the contract." The contract stipulated wages, benefits, and various rules regarding aspects such as what a union member could or could not do in a job, the use of nonunion labor by carriers, and the use of temporary and part-time workers. Many of the regional carriers were nonunion and thus enjoyed lower labor costs and freedom from inflexible union rules. For example, the agreement with the Teamsters banned union drivers from loading or unloading within 75 miles of a terminal. This lack of flexibility meant that if no dock workers were available, then cargo sat idle.

Equipment and Fuel

Aside from labor, equipment and fuel were the other major costs for LTLs. Several major tractor manufacturers supplied trucks to the industry. The most commonly used size trucks could be purchased for little more than $100,000. Little savings could be gained by purchasing in volume. Fuel constituted a major cost for trucking firms. Firms used swaps, options, and long-term contracts to hedge against fluctuating fuel costs. For example, approximately 20 percent of Yellow Corp. anticipated fuel costs for 1997 were covered under various types of agreements. Changes in fuel costs typically exerted a short-term impact on profitability. If fuel prices rose dramatically, carriers were often not successful in fully passing the increased costs on to customers. Thus, profits dropped. On the other hand, when fuel prices fell significantly, carriers sometimes experienced a short-term profit windfall.

Customers

Millions of customers purchased freight services. No single customer accounted for a large percentage of the industry's revenue. Competition for freight was based primarily on price and service. Customers tended to be price sensitive. In many cases, they would switch from one carrier to another for a small price savings, even as small as less than one percent. The most important element of service was transit time. While customers valued reliability and on-time delivery, these service elements were often taken for granted and were not criteria by which carriers could differentiate themselves. Some customers were coming to rely on LTLs for more than just the physical transport of goods. These customers (package recipients) wanted carriers to be able to locate shipments on demand and verify that senders were shipping the required goods. In effect, they sought to outsource much of the shipping and receiving function to LTLs. Such demands required LTLs to make additional technology investments and develop additional logistical capabilities.

Non-LTL Freight Services

Customers had alternatives to LTL in shipping goods. TL carriers were viable for large shipments. Premium freight such as Federal Express and UPS was suitable for smaller, time-sensitive shipments. And, intermodal (or multimodal) which involved the use of both trucks and rail to ship goods was being used increasingly.

Truckload Freight. Since TL shipping required no intermediate handling of freight, its cost structure was much different than LTL. TL carriers did not require investments in terminals, consolidation centers, or in logistics and tracking systems. Most TL carriers were nonunion and were able to pay drivers

less than union wages. To become a TL carrier required little more than to purchase or lease a truck and a chauffeur's license. Many small firms competed in the TL segment. Revenues from TL freight had risen to $98.8 billion in 1995 from $71.1 billion in 1991 (see Exhibit 1). This compared to $58.1 billion in 1995 and $46.6 billion for LTL. LTL tonnage rose 3 percent in 1996 while truckload tonnage dropped 2.8 percent.

Intermodal transport involved combining multiple means of transportation such as rail, trucking, or ocean shipping to transport goods. Most often, intermodal involved combining a rail segment with truck transport to deliver goods. Trailers that could be either pulled by trucks or carried on railway flatcars made intermodal feasible. Since railroads had costs as much as 10–15 percent below that of trucks for long haul transport, and trucks could provide the convenience of door-to-door pick-up and delivery, intermodal was seen as a way to achieve greater efficiency without sacrificing service. Roadway was a leader in using intermodal. It found significant savings by using rail for over 23 percent of its total line-haul miles. Yellow and CFMF also used intermodal for over 20 percent of their miles. ABF, with less than 10 percent of its miles in intermodal, used intermodal less than the rest of the big four LTL carriers. The LTL industry had also increased its use of intermodal, going from 11.1 percent of vehicle miles in 1994 to 21 percent in 1997. There were drawbacks in using intermodal, however. Intermodal typically took longer to ship goods than did trucks because of the use of rail. Thus, some observers believed that intermodal involved a tradeoff in service to customers who were sensitive to the time required to deliver freight. Another obstacle in the use of intermodal was that the 1994 agreement with the Teamsters limited intermodal use to no more than 28 percent of vehicle miles.

Premium Freight providers such as Federal Express and UPS were the likely choice for shippers who had small packages to send or who needed next-day delivery. The premium providers both restricted and to a large extent standardized the size of packages they processed. This allowed them to achieve a high degree of automation and efficiency in their operations. Like the LTL firms, premium freight carriers possessed national networks of terminals and the ability to pick up and deliver packages. UPS, with its fleet of trucks and network infrastructure, possessed many of the same assets and capabilities as LTL carriers. UPS did some LTL shipping and clearly possessed the capacity to enter more heavily into the LTL segment if it chose to do so.

Competitors

Roadway's three major national competitors were Yellow Freight System, CF MotorFreight, and ABF Freight Systems. Like Roadway, each had experienced a decline in

Exhibit 1   Trucking and Courier Services (SIC 421)—Estimated Motor Carrier Revenue, by Size of Shipments Commodities Handled, and Origin and Destination of Shipments: 1991 Through 1995.

	Millions of Dollars					% Change				% Total Motor Carrier Revenue				
	1995	1994	1993	1992	1991	1995	1994	1993	1992	1995	1994	1993	1992	1991
Total Motor Carrier Revenue	155,971	149,160	135,383	127,049	117,732	4.6	10.2	6.6	7.9	100.0	100.0	100.0	100.0	100.0
Size of Shipments														
Less-than-truckload	58,147	55,445	52,075	49,119	46,626	4.9	6.5	6.0	5.3	37.3	37.2	38.5	38.7	39.6
Truckload	97,824	93,715	83,308	77,930	71,106	4.4	12.5	6.9	9.6	62.7	62.8	61.5	61.3	60.4
Commodities Handled														
Agricultural and food products	23,156	21,795	19,941	19,390	17,850	6.20	9.30	2.80	8.60	14.80	14.60	14.70	15.30	15.20
Mining products, unrefined	3,125	2,631	2,259	1,890	1,748	18.80	16.50	19.50	8.10	2.00	18	1.70	1.50	1.50
Building materials	8,502	8,904	8,477	7,247	5,966	-4.5	5.00	17.00	21.50	5.50	6.00	6.30	5.70	5.10
Forestry, wood, and paper products	11,613	10,959	9,304	8,441	7,559	6.00	17.80	10.20	11.70	7.40	7.30	69	66	6.40
Chemicals and allied products	7,431	7,049	6,607	6,350	6,071	5.40	6.70	4.00	4.60	4.80	47	49	50	5.20
Petroleum and petroleum products	3,888	4,044	3,746	3,734	3,954	-3.9	8.00	0.30	-5.6	2.50	2.70	2.80	2.90	3.40
Metals and metal products	14,085	13,193	12,018	11,038	10,697	6.80	9.80	89	3.20	9.00	88	89	97	91
Household goods	10,886	9,772	8,647	8,144	7,416	11.40	13.00	6.20	9.80	70	66	64	64	6.30
Other manufactured products	21,818	21,842	18,696	17,109	15,733	-0.1	16.80	9.30	8.70	14.00	14.60	13.80	13.50	134
Other goods	51,467	48,971	45,688	43,706	40,738	5.10	7.20	4.50	7.30	33.00	32.80	33.70	34.40	34.60

operating margins in the decade preceding 1997. In 1987, each had enjoyed operating margins in the four to five percent range. Those margins had declined to less than three percent for all four by 1996 (see Exhibit 4).

Roadway's largest competitor with 1996 revenues of over $2 billion was **Yellow Freight System, Inc.** Yellow Freight was the largest division of The Yellow Corporation accounting for 77 percent of its revenues. Yellow Corporation also operated three regional LTL carriers: Preston Trucking Company, Saia Motor Freight, and WestEx. Another subsidiary, Yellow Technology Services provided logistical solutions to customers. Yellow Freight expanded internationally in the 1990s. Expansion into Asia in 1996 followed a move into Europe four years earlier. International expansion was a top priority for the firm in 1997.

Yellow Freight had implemented a vigorous cost reduction program. Cost savings from improvements in pickup and delivery and reduced general and administrative expenses had been achieved. The carrier reduced terminals from 449 in 1995 to 334 in 1996. This reduction along with a write-off of computer software resulted in a $46.1 million special charge. Yellow Freight also sought to improve its operations in other ways. Organization restructuring into five geographic business units was implemented by Yellow Freight to give front line employees more authority to respond quickly to customer requests.

Yellow Corporation did not report financial results for Yellow Freight, but the corporation as a whole had lost money in 1996, 1995, and 1994. Yellow Freight instituted a general rate increase of 5.8 percent in January 1996, which applied to customers without long-term contracts. Tonnage declined by 2.8 percent while revenue per ton increased by 2.4 percent. Operating expenses for Yellow Freight were up just 0.6 percent in 1996 despite higher fuel costs and the 3.8 percent increase in union wages and benefits imposed on all the national LTLs.

CF MotorFreight (CFMF) was spun off from Consolidated Freightways, which subsequently changed its name to CNF. CFMF had been the poorest performer of the national LTLs despite extensive cost reduction efforts. CFMF had reduced the number of its terminals from 650 in 1992 to 380 in 1995. Routes had also been restructured to reduce freight handling and increase the amount of city-to-city shipments. Despite these efforts CFMF had not been able to achieve profitability. With CNF's other subsidiaries all occupying leadership positions in their niches, some analysts believed the spin off was part of an effort to emphasize CNF's other businesses.

ABF Freight Systems had become a national LTL carrier after deregulation by pursuing a strategy of aggressive acquisi-

tions. Historically, ABF had fewer terminals and consolidation centers than the other of the "big four," but still operated more than 300 terminals. ABF also enjoyed the highest operating margins of any of the "big four" and the highest growth rate.

In addition to the "big four" several interregional carriers and many regional firms competed for LTL business. These firms tended to be nonunion and enjoy cost advantages because of their lower labor costs, lower investment in infrastructure, and more direct routing which reduced handling. As a result, the regional and interregional LTLs enjoyed higher operating margins than the "big four" (see Exhibit 2). Despite the numerous competitors, though, capacity in the industry had declined in the mid 1990s. Some regional carriers, such as Viking Freight, had attempted to forge virtual national carriers out of networks of regional truckers, but none had succeeded.

Roadway's Strategy

Marketing

Roadway's marketing strategy centered around developing stable, long-term relationships with customers. Yet, Roadway served over 500,000 customers in 1996. No customer accounted for more than 2 percent of total revenues in 1996 and the ten largest customers accounted for less than 10 percent of revenues that year. Nevertheless, Roadway worked with individual customers to identify possible efficiencies in serving a specific account where both the customer and

Exhibit 2   Commercial Freight Distribution—1996

	Bil. $	% of Total
Trucking		
Private, interstate	110	24.4
Private, local	90	60
National TL	60	13.3
Local TL, for-hire	40	8.9
LTL, national	9	2.0
LTL, regional	9	2.0
Package/express (ground)	24	5.3
Total trucking	342	75.8
Railroad	36	8.0
Pipeline (oil & gas)	26	5.8
Air freight, domestic	25	5.5
Air freight, international	15	3.3
Water (Great Lakes/rivers)	7	1.6
TOTAL	451	100.0

Source: Standard and Poor's *Industry Survey:* "Transportation: Commercial," January 22, 1998.

Exhibit 3   Trucking Industry Operating Statistics

CARRIER	REVENUES (MIL$)		OPERATING INCOME (MIL$)		LTLREVENUES (MIL. $)		TLREVENUES (MIL $)		LTLTONNAGE (TONS)		TLTONNAGE (MIL. TONS)		MILES (MILLIONS)		INTERMODAL MILES (MILLIONS)	
	1995	1996	1995	1996	1995	1996	1995	1996	1995	1996	1995	1996	1995	1996	1995	1996
1. Roadway Express	2,255	2,339	(21.2)	36.7	2,038	2,128	217.2	211.3	6.0	6.2	1.4	1.4	500.7	487.2	147.8	168.0
2. Yellow Corp.	2,339	2,324	(6.4)	30.1	2,116	2,109	221.6	213.4	6.9	6.7	1.6	1.5	614.5	582.4	124.1	128.8
3. Consolidated Frways	2,015	2,052	(51.6)	(79.3)	1,834	1,868	178.7	183.3	5.6	5.7	1.2	1.2	476.8	448.3	133.8	120.3
4. Conway Western	1,049	1,171	95.4	101.3	978	1,094	71.1	77.2	4.5	4.7	0.8	0.8	271.5	295.6	2.1	1.7
5. ABF Freight	1,006	1,103	(6.4)	(8.4)	895	983	110.5	113.7	2.9	3.0	0.8	0.8	296.5	285.0	19.2	31.0
6. Overnite Trans.	976	961	(29.7)	(48.0)	872	896	103.8	65.4	4.0	4.2	1.5	1.2	306.1	275.5	47.4	45.8
7. American Freightways	572	729	30.8	27.1	528	680	44.9	48.8	2.9	3.6	0.5	0.6	182.2	237.3	0.0	0.0
8. USF Holland Mtr. Ex.	527	595	43.7	51.4	478	542	49.7	53.6	2.9	3.3	0.6	0.7	139.0	155.3	0.0	0.0
9. Watkins Motor Lines	475	535	24.2	28.1	421	479	50.1	52.2	1.2	1.3	0.3	0.3	182.1	198.7	0.0	5.1
10. Southeastern Freight Lines	264	304	20.5	17.2	237	277	26.1	27.7	1.6	1.8	0.6	0.6	63.4	82.6	1.8	2.8
Total	11,478	12,114	99.3	156.2	10,397	11,061	1,074.7	1,046.6	38.4	40.6	9.4	•9.0	3,032.8	3,047.9	476.2	503.5

Source: American Trucking Associations.

Exhibit 4   Comparison of LTLs on Key Measures

Company	Revenues[1] ($mil)	Operating margin[2]	5-year growth rate[3]	5-year return on capital[4]
Unionized national LTLs				
ABF Freight System	$1,105	2.8%	7.1%	8.7%
Consolidated Freightways	2,238	0.9	0.0	−10.0
Roadway Express	2,523	2.2	2.8	16.6
Yellow Freight System	2,408	2.5	0.3	7.7
Nonunion regional LTLs				
AAA Cooper Transportation	316	10.3	12.1	40.0
Estes Express Lines	356	13.2	23.4	29.1
USF Bestway	121	11.9	6.1	25.8
Nonunion interregional LTLs				
American Freightways	794	4.7	29.8	12.9
Con-Way Transportation	1,374	8.7	15.1	41.0
Old Dominion Freight Line	308	5.6	13.4	17.3

[1] For the 12 months ended June 30.   [2] Excludes special charges.   [3] For period ended Dec. 31, 1996.
[4] Operating income over shareholders' equity plus long-term debt.

Sources: Forbes. Company reports; Transportation Technical Services' Blue Book of Trucking Companies; Alex. Brown & Sons.

Roadway could benefit. Despite this emphasis, Roadway had not been immune from aggressive price competition. Profit margins suffered during 1995 as the firm lost $12.7 million during a year of intense discounting. Freight rates rose 5.7 percent in 1996 and Roadway adopted a less lenient discount policy. Rates had remained stable in 1996 and early 1997. Roadway attributed the increased stability in rates to a reduction in industry capacity. Roadway offered or negotiated discounts with many customers. These discounts were negotiated on an account-by-account basis.

Technology and Operations

Roadway operated 30 major consolidation/distribution centers and 424 terminal facilities in 1996. The 30 centers were located in strategic locations throughout the United States Of the 424 terminal facilities, Roadway owned 285 and leased the other 139. These leases were generally for terms of three years or less. The company owned 9,665 tractors and 30,082 trailers. For tractors and trailers used for intercity transport, the average age was 7.6 and 9.0 years respectively. Freight handling capacity was typically measured by the number of loading spaces. Roadway owned 11,861 spaces and leased another 1,905. Consolidation centers accounted for 5,340 of these loading spaces.

Cost reductions were attributed to several improvements. Increased use of rail lines to transport freight in linehaul

operations was a major element in cost reduction. Roadway also had achieved a leaner network infrastructure. Roadway's 424 terminals was down from 585 at the beginning of 1995. The company planned to reduce its network by another 30 terminals in 1997. Roadway executives anticipated that the elimination of these terminals would reduce fixed costs and increase network utilization. Claims on freight shipped declined by 11.2 percent in 1996, which indicated improved freight handling. Roadway attributed this improvement to network refinements which reduced the number of times freight was handled in unloading, sorting, and reloading. Improved freight handling techniques were also cited as a reason for the decline in claims. A decline in depreciation expenses was another reason cited for the reduction in costs. The decline resulted from fewer terminals, a greater proportion of fully depreciated equipment, and limited capital expenditures in prior years.

Human Resources

Approximately 75 percent of Roadway's 25,500 employees were represented by unions. Most were represented by the International Brotherhood of Teamsters. Wages and benefits were governed by the Master Freight Agreement ("The Contract"). Under the contract, union labor wages and benefits increased 3.8 percent in 1996 and another 3.8 percent on April 1, 1997. LTL drivers received, on average, wages of $18 to $19 an hour and pensions of $2,500 a month. On average,

Exhibit 5   Statements Of Consolidated Income, Roadway Express, Inc. and Subsidiaries

	1996	1995	1994
	(dollars in thousands, except per share data)		
Revenue	2,372,718	2,288,844	2,171,117
Operating expenses:			
Salaries, wages and benefits	1,544,926	1,545,000	1,512,235
Operating supplies and expenses	409,900	395,170	388,268
Purchased transportation	193,640	158,494	105,486
Operating taxes and licenses	75,041	74,720	74,031
Insurance and claims	50,856	54,826	46,913
Provision for depreciation	62,681	71,669	75,750
Net gain on sale of carrier operating property	(8,256)	(267)	(2,628)
Total operating expenses	2,328,788	2,299,612	2,200,055
Operating income (loss)	43,930	10,768	28,938
Other (expense) income:			
Interest expense	(1,764)	(3,098)	(3,218)
Other, net	304	(9)	1,443
	(1,460)	(3,107)	(1,775)
Income (loss) before income taxes	42,470	(13,875)	(30,713)
Provision (benefit) for income taxes	20,582	(1,206)	(9,268)
Net income (loss)	21,888	(12,669)	(21,445)
Net income (loss) per share	1.07	(0.62)	(1.04)
Average number of common shares outstanding	20,533,219	20,556,714	20,556,714

Roadway's union workers were paid more than 20 percent more than their counterparts in nonunion LTLs. In their 1997 agreement with UPS, the Teamsters had negotiated a 15.5 percent wage increase in wages to an average of $23.05 an hour. The agreement also included a 50 percent increase in pensions to $3,000 a month for drivers with 30 years of service. UPS had contended that the strike was premeditated and intended to prop up the Teamsters' image and political clout in the months leading up to the union's presidential election. One effect of the UPS strike was that it led shipping customers to place greater importance on using multiple transportation providers, so that subsequent strikes would have less impact on their businesses. Roadway experienced a 24-day strike by the Teamsters in April of 1994 following the expiration of the previous Master Freight Agreement. The Master Freight Agreement was scheduled to expire on March 31, 1998. Many observers expected the Teamsters to push for major concessions from the national LTL carriers on wages and benefits. Historically, the Teamsters had not given ground on wage rates and benefits even though their membership had significantly declined.

While many industry observers had noted the high cost and relative lack of flexibility of Teamsters' labor, Roadway's company documents argued that the Teamsters' provided advantages for the carrier. Among the advantages noted were a stable workforce, a very low turnover rate of under 3 percent, and experienced employees who understood the LTL business and thus made fewer mistakes and were more efficient. Another advantage of Teamster labor cited by Roadway was an outstanding safety record, which led to greater reliability and less freight damage and claims for shippers.

Notes

[1]   Cavanaugh, Sheila C., "CF MotorFreight in 1992." *Harvard Business School Press*, 1993.

Case 1–2: Michelin and the Global Tire Industry in 1999*

On September 8, 1999, Michelin, the world's leading maker of automotive tires, unveiled excellent first-half results: net profits had risen by 20 percent to FF2.1 billion. In the same breath, the company announced 7,500 job cuts across Europe, equivalent to 10 percent of its European workforce, in order to increase productivity by 20 percent over the next three years. "In this period of world-wide consolidation, it is imperative that we reinforce our leadership and our efficiency," it declared.

The announcement set off a storm of protest. "I do not believe that this decision is a given irreversible," commented the Socialist Prime Minister, Lionel Jospin. "We must all mobilise when this kind of decision is considered." Although Jospin acknowledged that the days when the State had to authorise redundancies were over, his remarks raised fears of a government-backed strike. Michelin shares rose by 12.6 percent but only a few days later, a court ordered Michelin to suspend a layoff procedure at one of its 24 plants in France.

While the announced cutbacks seemed inexplicable to many, the company's new head, Edouard Michelin, knew that the good half-year results were due to exceptional buoyancy in the car and truck markets and to sharp falls in raw material costs. He also knew that such favourable conditions might not last.

Edouard Michelin, aged 36 and the fourth generation Michelin to head the group, had succeeded his father François only three months earlier. The new plan was his first major strategic decision. In February 1999, archrival Goodyear had unveiled an alliance with Japanese tire maker Sumitomo Rubber that would relegate Michelin to second place worldwide. Tie-ups were being hatched across the industry and a new period of restructuring was looming. As the 20th century drew to an end, the tire industry looked set for another mega-battle. Wrote an industry expert: "If an entrepreneur developed a business plan which promised the returns that the tire industry has actually been making over the last decade, no venture capitalist would agree to finance it."[1] The scion of the House of Michelin faced a significant challenge.

The Tire Industry: A History

While the concept of air-filled tires dates from 1846, the tire industry was born at the end of the 19th century when several firms started manufacturing bicycle tires in both Europe and the United States. The most innovative companies would later become industry leaders: Britain's Dunlop invented the original rubber tire, with a carcass made of fabric layers. In the United States Goodyear patented the first tubeless pneumatic tire in 1903. France's Michelin developed the removable tire and Germany's Continental was the first to develop tread patterns in 1904.

Quality improved dramatically during the first half of the 20th century. In the 1920s, carbon black was introduced. A tire's average lifespan under normal conditions increased from nine months in 1910 to three years by 1937. The development of synthetic rubber (butadiene) in the 1930s and 1940s further improved the quality of raw materials while reducing their cost.

Michelin's Radial Innovation

Most innovations in tires had been incremental rather than revolutionary but there was one major exception: the radial tire launched by Michelin in 1946. The radial had two to three times the lifespan of a traditional "bias" (or "crossply') design and it reduced fuel consumption dramatically. It was also safer than the bias tire which was prone to blowouts. However, production required massive investment in new facilities and rivals, especially United States giants Goodyear and Firestone, which had made huge investments to produce bias tires, did all they could to delay

*This case was written by Karel Cool, the BP Chaired Professor of European Competitiveness, and Francesca Gee, Research Associate, both at INSEAD. It is intended to be used as a basis for class discussion rather than to illustrate either effective or ineffective handling of an administrative situation. Copyright © 2002 INSEAD-CEDEP, Fontainebleau, France.

acceptance. In 1966, Armstrong Rubber Company launched a higher quality bias tire that incorporated a belt between the plies and the tread, and other United States manufacturers rallied around this bias belted tire. Despite its obvious inferiority to the radial, the bias belted tire achieved rapid acceptance in the United States, equipping 82 percent of new cars by 1972.

The radial did eventually succeed. Initially, demand built up as Americans became familiar with radials mounted on imported cars. Prices also fell as Michelin gained production experience. In the early 1970s, the French company built two dedicated plants (in Canada in 1971 and in the United States in 1975) to make radials. The 1973 oil shock made the radial's fuel savings even more attractive. Eventually, United States manufacturers were forced to develop their own radials and invest massively in new plants. Goodyear for instance devoted an estimated US$2 billion to convert to radial production in the early 1970s. It was now a race for survival, and major tire makers rushed to bring their own radials to market. The results in terms of product quality were often disastrous: abnormally high rates of tread reparations and blowouts forced Firestone to recall its first radial line, the 500 series, in 1978 at a cost of US$147 million. In Europe, both Kléber (France) and Metzeler (Austria) had to recall their products.

A Painful Round of Consolidation

Firestone's difficulties hurt its share price, attracting interest from "corporate raiders". In 1981, the Tisch brothers accumulated a large holding of Firestone shares, prompting the company to buy back its stock. The following year, Firestone suffered a new round of "greenmail" from raider Carl Icahn and had to buy back yet more stock to remain independent. Icahn repeated his raiding strategy in 1983 on Goodrich which also defended itself by buying back its stock and by splitting its tire and chemical businesses. In 1985 Icahn continued, this time targeting Uniroyal, which subsequently went private in a leveraged buy-out.

The most spectacular shareholder action was against Goodyear in 1986 by British businessman Sir James Goldsmith. After three years of high earnings, Goodyear had gone on a spending spree, acquiring various oil and aerospace businesses. Goldsmith's line of attack was that Goodyear should re-focus on tire making. Goodyear fought back but eventually adopted the very course of action proposed by Goldsmith. The company sold its new businesses but had to spend US$2.6 billion to buy back the shares accumulated by Goldsmith and friends. Goodyear's debt spiralled from US$1.1 billion at the end of 1985 to US$3.6 billion two years later.

The tire industry entered a painful round of consolidation as competitors fought over acquisitions. 1986 saw a merger between Goodrich and Uniroyal. While Uniroyal was strong in original equipment (OE) and the supply of private-label tires, Goodrich had a strong aftermarket brand, especially in high-performance tires. The two had few manufacturing synergies, however, leaving little scope for rationalisation. After the merger, earnings continued to disappoint.

In Europe, Dunlop was left bankrupt after a failed merger with Pirelli and had to find a new partner. In 1984, it sold its European and North American interests to Sumitomo Rubber for US$240 million. In 1987, as the US dollar continued its plunge against other currencies, Continental purchased General Tire of the United States and announced a strategic partnership with two Japanese manufacturers, Yokohama and Toyo, to develop truck tire plants in the United States. Pirelli bid US$1.8 billion for Firestone but Bridgestone, which in 1983 had bought a Firestone plant in Tennessee, entered a counter-bid and won the day, forking out a hefty US$2.6 billion. Pirelli consoled itself with the acquisition of the much smaller Armstrong tire.

By 1989, while a price war fed by overcapacity was raging, Michelin, then the world number two, overcame its long-standing reluctance to make acquisitions and purchased Uniroyal-Goodrich for US$1.5 billion, thus becoming the world's largest tire maker. By then, Uniroyal-Goodrich had already sold its European operations and licensed the Uniroyal brand in Europe to Continental. Lastly, in 1991, Continental rebuffed a bid by Pirelli.

The restructuring of the industry then came to a halt. Goodyear, burdened by heavy debt, was the only major player who had not been able to afford a significant acquisition. Exhibit 1 shows changes in the industry's structure over the last 20 years.

Exhibit 1   The Changing Structure of the World Tire Industry, 1978 and 1998

Rank	1978	1998
1	Goodyear (US)	Bridgestone (Japan)
2	Michelin (France)	Michelin (France)
3	Firestone (US)[a]	Goodyear (US)
4	Bridgestone (Japan)	Continental (Germany)
5	Dunlop (UK)[b]	Sumitomo (Japan)[c]
6	Uniroyal (US)[d]	Pirelli (Italy)
7	Uniroyal (US)[e]	Yokohama (Japan)
8	Pirelli (Italy)	Cooper (US)
9	General Tire (US)[e]	Toyo (Japan)
10	Yokohama (Japan)	Kumho (South Korea)

[a] Acquired by Bridgestone.
[b] Acquired by Sumitomo.
[c] In the process of forming a series of joint ventures with Goodyear.
[d] Acquired by Michelin.
[e] Acquired by Michelin.
[e] Acquired by Continental.

The Tire Industry in the 1990s

The price war had left the industry reeling and a painful period of restructuring and cost cutting followed. Overall industry productivity increased through changes such as the introduction of continuous shift working. By 1993, Michelin, Bridgestone and Goodyear together had 52 percent of the global market. The top ten firms had about 80 percent of world production. This would not change significantly until 1999 (See Exhibits 2 and 3).

Exhibit 2   Global Tire Company Rankings (in millions of dollars, translated at average annual currency exchange rates)

No	Co./Headquarters	1998 Tire Sales	1998 % of total corp. sales	1997 Tire Sales	1997 % of total corp. sales	1996 Tire Sales	1996 % of total corp. sales
1	Michelin et Cie Clermont-Ferrand, France	$*12,916.3	*93%	$*12,718	*94%	$*13,100	94%
2	Bridgestone Corp. # Tokyo	*12,634	*74%	*12,920	*72%	*12,900	72%
3	Goodyear Tire & Rubber Co. # 1,2 Akron, Ohio	11,311.0	85%	*11,850	*85%	*11,705	*84%
4	Continental A.G. # Hanover, Germany	*4,334.0	*58%	*4,355	*68%	*4,866	*70%
5	Sumitomo Rubber Industries Ltd # 2 Kobe, Japan	*3,750.0	*75%	*3,800	*75%	*4,000	*75%
6	Pirelli S.p.A. # Milan, Italy	3,005.8	49%	*3,020	*46%	*3,000	*45%
7	Yokohama Rubber Co. Ltd. † Tokyo, Japan	2,193.5	70%	*2,343	*70%	*2,600	*70%
8	Cooper Tire & Rubber Co. Findlay, Ohio	1,447.4	77%	*1,449	80%	*1,372	*85%
9	Toyo Tire & Rubber Co. Ltd. † Osaka, Japan	1,120.2	60%	1,283	59%	1,378	57%
10	Kumho & Co. Seoul, South Korea	965.5	*91%	1,241	89%	1,355	89%
11	Hankook Tire Manufacturing Co. Ltd. Seoul, South Korea	*905.0	*94%	*1,095	*94%	1,135	93%
12	Ohtsu Tire & Rubber Co. Ltd. Osaka, Japan	616.1	83%	668	84%	897	95%
13	MRF Ltd. † Chennai, India	537.7	98%	534	92%	551	96%
14	Cheng Shin Rubber Co. Yuanlin, Taiwan	497.5	100%	410	100%	375	99%
15	Shanghai Tire & Rubber Co. Ltd. Shanghai, China	461.7	99%	518	99%	423	90%
16	J.K. Industries Ltd. † New Delhi, India	357.7	91%	409	92%	255	83%
17	Apollo Tires Ltd. † Kerala, India	*346.3	100%	375	100%	353	100%
18	Shandong Triangle Group Co. Ltd. Shandong, China	330.9	100%	255	100%	214	N.A.
19	Co. Industria de Llantes (Euzkadi) 3 Mexico City, Mexico	328.0	100%	312	95%	286	95%
20	Shandong Chengshan Rubber Co. Ltd. Chengshan, China	326.2	N.A.	236	97%	227	N.A.

* = Estimated
\# = Non-tire portion of company-owned retail activities factored out
† = fiscal year ends other than Dec. 31
N.A. = not available; N.R. = not ranked

Source: http://www.tirebusiness.com/subscriber/global99.phtml.

Exhibit 3   The World's Leading Tire Manufacturers, 1998

		Country	Total sales (US$ m)	Tire Sales (US$ m)	% of sales	Market share (%)
1	Bridgestone	Japan	17,944	12,920	72	18.6
2	Michelin	France	13,675	12,718	93	18.3
3	Goodyear	US	13,941	11,850	85	17.1
4	Continental	Germany	6,404	4,355	68	6.3
5	Sumitomo	Japan	5,067	3,800	75	5.5
6	Pirelli	Italy	6,565	3,020	46	4.4
7	Yokohama	Japan	3,347	2,343	70	3.4
8	Cooper	US	1,811	1,449	80	2.1
9	Toyo	Japan	2,175	1,283	59	1.8
10	Kumho	South Korea	1,394	1,241	89	1.8
11	Hankook	South Korea	1,165	1,095	94	1.6
12	Ohtsu	Japan	795	668	84	1.0
13	MRF	India	580	534	92	0.8
14	Shanghai	China	523	518	99	0.7
15	Chen Shin	Taiwan	410	410	100	0.6

Source: Crain Communications.

After experiencing a lean period from 1990 to 1993, the tire industry returned to profitability in 1994 as the market tightened (cuts in global capacity had produced a shortage) and natural rubber prices surged, enabling manufacturers to impose higher prices. Between 1994 and 1998 retail prices for tires rose every year. Goodyear led the way in North America with 3–5 percent increases in November 1994, quickly followed by Michelin (3 percent). By 1998, retail prices had increased by an aggregate 13.6 percent in Europe and 21.5 percent in North America. The big change however was in the original equipment market where the indexing of prices resulted in upward corrections of 20 percent or more. This enabled leaders Goodyear and Michelin not only to make up for the surge in raw material prices but also to improve margins.

At the same time, several tire makers formed alliances and joint ventures. In Europe, they started moving into the former Communist states to create a low-cost manufacturing base and establish themselves in growth markets. Sumitomo and Continental were the first to make acquisitions, followed by Goodyear and Michelin.

In 1997, a severe crisis hit most of Asia and other emerging markets around the world. Desperate for foreign currencies, tire makers in those countries reacted by increasing their exports, flooding developed countries with cheap tires. By 1999, Asia was well on its way to recovery. Meanwhile, major developed markets were enjoying strong growth: in North America, truck sales had grown by 9.3 percent in the first half of the year, while passenger car sales increased by 6 percent; in Europe, the increases were 2.4 percent and 3.7 percent respectively. (Exhibit 4 gives sales growth data.) The tire industry had a turnover of US$70 billion.

The Global Market for Tires

Market Segments: Passenger Car Tires and Truck Tires

Of the nearly one billion tires made in 1998, 700 million were for passenger cars and 250 million for trucks; the balance being made up of agricultural or other technical tires. Exhibit 5 gives tire production by type; Exhibit 6 shows market size in Asia, Europe and North America. Car owners, particularly in Europe, were increasingly demanding high performance tires, designed to provide more "grip." They were more expensive, produced higher margins, and tended to wear down faster.

Truck tires were a specific segment. Because they made up as much as 5 percent of the total costs of running a

Exhibit 4   World Growth Rates for Passenger CarTires and Truck Tires Sales, 1992–1998 (Average annual % growth)

	Passenger car tires	Truck tires
Western Europe	1.8	2.9
Eastern Europe	6.1	−0.9
North America	2.3	3.4
South America	3.7	2.3
Asia	3.5	5.6
Other	3.0	6.4
World	**2.6**	**3.8**

Source: EIU.

Exhibit 5   World Tire Production by Type, 1998

Production	m units
Passenger tires	700
Truck tires	249
Agricultural tires	16
Total	**965**

Source: EIU World Tire Industry 1998.

commercial vehicle fleet, large truck fleets often bought tires in bulk from manufacturers. Differences in performance, such as durability and fuel economy, could prove critical. Retreading could considerably increase the lifespan of a truck tire, which could be driven up to 600,000 miles (970,000 km).

Demand for truck tires was driven by underlying economic conditions, much more so than demand for passenger car tires. In a recession, trucks drove fewer miles, reducing tire wear (especially since fleets used to swap tires when trucks lay idle). Demand picked up very quickly at the end of a downturn.

Although the truck tire segment differed significantly from the much larger passenger car tire segment, there were some major synergies: technological improvements on large tires were often used for smaller tires. Large

retailers also preferred to buy from manufacturers that provided full lines of both passenger car and truck tires.

Market Segments: Original Equipment and Replacement

Another dimension of market segmentation was between tires sold to original equipment (OE) manufacturers, to be fitted onto new vehicles, and those sold in the replacement market. About 30 percent of passenger car tires and 20 percent of truck tires were sold in the OE market (See Exhibit 7).

The OE market was smaller and far less profitable. Margins were low as a result of carmakers" buying power and because tire makers believed car owners would replace their tires with the brand originally fitted on their car.[2] (In the truck segment, virtually all fleets replaced worn-out tires with the original brand.) Most major tire manufacturers started making losses on OE sales during the price war of the late 1980s. Even after price rises in 1994 through 1998, OE sales remained a low-margin business. Costly research and development work was mostly carried out for OE manufacturers that had a strong influence on product design. OE sales were also highly cyclical since they were linked to sales of new vehicles.

The replacement market was both bigger and more profitable. In the early 1980s, a tire sold as a replacement

Exhibit 6   The Market for Tires in Asia, Europe, and North America, 1992–1998

(m units)	1992	1993	1994	1995	1996	1997	1998
Asia							
Car tires	101.2	106.5	111.2	118.6	125.2	131.3	123.4
% change	*–*	*5.2*	*4.4*	*6.7*	*5.6*	*4.9*	*–6.0*
Truck tires	73.6	77.2	79.9	84.7	95.1	103.4	101.5
% change	*–*	*4.9*	*3.5*	*6.0*	*12.3*	*8.7*	*–1.8*
Total	**174.8**	**183.7**	**191.1**	**203.3**	**220.3**	**234.7**	**224.9**
Europe							
Car tires	213.1	210.8	219.0	232.1	236.6	241.9	246.1
% change	*–*	*–1.1*	*3.9*	*6.0*	*1.9*	*2.2*	*1.7*
Truck tires	46.8	45.3	45.0	46.6	48.3	50.2	50.0
% change	*–*	*–3.2*	*–0.7*	*3.6*	*3.6*	*3.9*	*–0.4*
Total	**259.9**	**256.1**	**264.0**	**278.7**	**284.9**	**291.1**	**296.1**
North America							
Car tires	233.4	241.8	249.6	254.9	255.0	260.2	267.7
% change	*–*	*3.6*	*3.2*	*2.1*	*0.0*	*2.0*	*2.9*
Truck tires	47.8	48.6	50.0	53.4	54.4	57.3	58.4
% change	*–*	*1.7*	*2.9*	*6.8*	*1.9*	*5.3*	*1.9*
Total	**281.2**	**290.4**	**299.6**	**308.3**	**309.4**	**317.5**	**326.1**

Exhibit 7   World Tire Sales by Market, 1998

(m units)	Passenger car	% of total	Truck	% of total
OE	217.7	31	50.6	20
Replacement	482.4	69	198.2	80
Total	700.1	100	248.8	100

Source: EIU.

cost about 35 percent more than in the OE market and the gap widened to nearly 100 percent during the price war. For truck tires, the price differential was about 50 percent. As the battle for market share raged in the late 1980s, retail sales margins fell too. Replacement sales were also more stable. Customer needs were more varied: motorists, for instance, were demanding new products such as high-performance tires and winter tires; safety was increasingly a concern.

Regional Differences

Geographically, the market was concentrated in North America, Western Europe, and Japan that accounted for over three-quarters of passenger car tire sales and half of all truck tires sales. North America and Europe dominated the passenger car market, while Asia dominated the market for light and standard truck tires. There were other differences between regions. Japanese tire makers were relatively more dependent on their domestic auto industry, hence on OE sales, while in North America, OE accounted for only 12 percent of total sales. (The United States had a larger replacement market because vehicles there drove longer distances and tire quality was generally poorer.) The United States also had a more fragmented replacement market, with budget private brands and associate brands accounting for half of total sales. (See Exhibits 8 and 9 for a breakdown of car and truck tire sales in the OE and RE segments per region in 1998 as well as an estimate for 2005).

Making Tires

Raw Materials

A tire was made up of about 100 components. Natural and synthetic rubbers accounted for about 50 percent of raw materials costs although the proportion of natural was falling steadily (to about 47 percent of total rubber weight). More synthetic rubber was used for passenger car tires and more natural rubber was used for utility tires. Carbon black, which gave the tire its rigidity, made up about one

Exhibit 8   Tire Sales in 1998 (m Units)

	Car tires		Truck tires	
	OE	RE	OE	RE
W. Europe	69.6	131.9	7.6	22.2
E. Europe and Russia	11.3	33.3	5.1	15.1
N. America	66.1	201.6	9.3	49.1
S. America	8.0	29.0	2.5	18.1
Asia	58.9	64.5	21.8	79.7
Others	3.8	22.1	4.3	14.0
Total	217.7	482.4	50.6	198.2

Source: World Tire Industry, EIU, 1999.

quarter of purchases. All in all, petroleum derivatives made up about 60 percent of purchases. Michelin had developed with Rhône-Poulenc a silica compound that replaced carbon black in low rolling resistance ("green") tires. Steel cord, used to make radial belts and the carcass of larger tires, was also a major component. Many tire manufacturers had a degree of vertical integration, owning hevea plantations and synthetic rubber production plants, but none was entirely self-sufficient.

Since 1979, natural rubber prices had been propped up by the INRO cartel, whose members were both producer countries and consumers. This had encouraged overproduction and the perpetuation of nearly half-a-million small, inefficient rubber plantations. Prices soared in 1994 and 1995 as world demand surged. After mid-1998, they fell precipitously, spurred by the collapse of INRO in 1999.

Over three-quarters of the world output of synthetic rubber was absorbed by the tire industry. The price of the main ingredients, styrene and butadiene (both petroleum derivatives), soared in 1994 and 1995 due to saturated capacity in the chemicals industry. Afterwards it fell steadily in line with oil prices.

Exhibit 9   Tire Sales Forecast for 2005 (m Units)

	Car tires		Truck tires	
	OE	RE	OE	RE
W. Europe	67.2	140.8	8.0	24.8
E. Europe and Russia	14.6	40.2	5.9	17.9
N. America	69.4	211.9	9.2	52.0
S. America	9.0	40.0	2.8	24.4
Asia	67.8	81.2	24.6	89.4
Others	14.2	23.6	4.8	17.6
Total	242.2	537.6	55.3	226.1

Source: World Tire Industry, EIU, 1999.

In the first half of 1999 alone, raw materials costs, which represented roughly 20 percent of sales, dropped by 7 percent, reflecting a 13 percent fall in natural rubber prices and lower crude oil prices. (This amounted to a 1.5 percent fall in total production costs.) About two thirds of purchases were either dollar-denominated or directly affected by dollar fluctuations.

Research and Development

To be a full line tire provider required continued investment in Research and Development (R&D) to meet the demands of OE manufacturers in an increasingly segmented end-market. The major players spent on average 2.8 percent of sales on R&D. (Exhibit 10)

Tire design was a compromise between various properties, with each market segment preferring a different set of characteristics. The main qualities sought were good tread wear, low rolling resistance, and superior traction. Improving any of these usually meant compromising other qualities. For instance, it was not possible to reduce rolling resistance too much without affecting braking performance.

Major changes were in the making: carmakers were planning to start outsourcing tire-wheel assembly that would itself become part of a larger suspension system including brakes, springs, and shock absorbers.[3] Computers played a growing role in simulating vehicle dynamics; they were used to optimise the strength, durability and vehicle dynamics behaviour of new systems before actual prototypes were built.

The most dramatic recent innovation was the run-flat tire. While it seemed the perfect answer to carmakers' desire to eliminate the cumbersome spare tire, it had a major drawback: few motorists were actually able to detect when a tire lost pressure. This meant that run-flats would have to be fitted with pressure monitoring systems. Goodyear had been the first in this new segment with the EMT, priced about 20 percent more than a radial tire. Since then, Michelin had introduced the more sophisticated PAX system, which could run longer while offering better fuel economy. Bridgestone's offering was the Firehawk SH30.

Another major area of development was the intelligent tire where a chip in the tire read out and kept records of exact tire pressures and temperatures. This promised to be particularly useful for truck fleets as it would obviate the need for manual inspections that were time-consuming and far less reliable.

Manufacturing

Tire plants were very labour-intensive and only became profitable when running at very high capacity utilisation levels. In 1999, industry-wide overcapacity was estimated at nearly 30 percent. See Exhibit 11 for plant locations of the major players. Major manufacturers all developed their own machinery. Continuous work with three shifts, seven days a week was a major change introduced in the 1990s. The industry as a whole had probably doubled productivity since 1994, having already doubled it in the five previous years, and further gains were expected.

As carmakers increasingly moved towards global construction, they expected tire suppliers to produce for them locally, albeit to high international quality standards. In order to differentiate their models, many OEMs now requested tires to be designed specifically for a particular model, sometimes in a particular market. This forced tire manufacturers to produce smaller runs.

In 1999, the five biggest tire makers were developing new manufacturing processes that would, they hoped, dramatically reduce capital and labour costs. These processes were closely guarded secrets. Michelin had led the way with its C3M process. Goodyear's Impact process and Bridgestone's Tochigi—the latter believed to be completely automated—also claimed huge savings. "A paradigm shift is taking place," wrote industry expert Neil Mullineux,[4] adding that the new processes would further widen the gap between the three leaders and the followers. However, implementation had not taken place quickly.

Marketing

Customers for replacement car tires were commonly divided into three groups. While price was an important variable, only 20–25 percent of buyers sought the lowest prices, regardless of brand or retail outlet. Most fell into either the "brand conscious" or "store reliant" categories.

	Sales	R&D	% of
Exhibit 10	**R&D Expenditure in the Tire Industry, 1998**		
Company	Sales (US$m)	R&D expenditure	% of sales
Michelin	13,645.9	680.0[1]	5.0
Goodyear	13,155.2	384.1	2.9
Bridgestone	17,940.5	317.5	1.8
Continental	6,447.2	260.0	4.0
Pirelli	6,611.7	208.4	3.2
Sumitomo	5,071.1	150.0	3.0
Yokohama	3,422.1	114.0	3.3
Toyo	2,159.0	50.0	2.3
Cooper	1,813.0	21.7	1.2
Kumho	1,314.7	40.0	3.0
Hankook	1,218.1	37.8	3.1
Others	13,326.0	133.0	1.0
Total	**86,125.0**	**2,397.0**	**2.8**

[1] Estimated.

Exhibit 11   The Market Leaders' Plants in Europe, North America, and Asia

Includes plants making tires for passenger cars, light trucks, trucks and buses, agricultural, motorcycles, earthmovers, industrial, aircraft, and racing. Joint ventures are not included in the total; they are mentioned in footnotes.

Europe

	1990 Plants	1990 Employees	1993 Plants	1996 Plants	1996 Employees	1998 Plants	1998 Employees
Michelin	31	70,813	30	32	50,057	31	62,980[1]
Bridgestone/Firestone	6	7,160	5	5	6,715	6	5,930
Goodyear	6	8,975	7	7	15,300	6	12,357
Continental	9	8,803	12	12	18,000	10[2]	11,941
Sumitomo/Dunlop	6	70	65	8	6,665	8	6,401
Pirelli	10	11,700	9	8	7,215	8	7,210
Yokohama	0	0	0	0	0	0	0
Toyo	0	0	0	0	0	0	0
Cooper	0	0	0	0	0	1	750
Kumho	0	0	0	0	0	0	0

[1] N/A for Aranda del Duero and Valladolid plants.   [2] Also has a joint venture in Bulgaria with Barum, employing 3,700.

North America*

	1990 Plants	1990 Employees	1993 Plants	1996 Plants	1996 Employees	1998 Plants	1998 Employees
Michelin	15	21,382	13	13	17,450	15	17,400
Bridgestone/Firestone	7	10,855	7	9	11,355	10	12,777[1]
Goodyear	13	19,908	13	12	20,680	12	20,680
Continental	5	6,335	4	4[2]	5,609	4[3]	4,509
Sumitomo/Dunlop	3	3,103	NA	2	2,700	2	2,640
Pirelli	3	2,450	3	2	1,255	1	630
Yokohama	1	500	1	1[4]	831	1[5]	831
Toyo	0	0	0	0[6]	0	0[7]	0
Cooper	3	3,150	4	4	4,200	4	4,250
Kumho	0	0	0	0	0	0	0

*North America includes Canada and the United States.   [1] The number of employees for the Aiken, South Carolina, plant is not available.   [2] Continental also has a joint venture with Yokohama and Toyo, employing 431.   [3] Id.   [4] Yokohama also has a joint venture with Continental and Toyo, employing 431.   [5] Id.   [6] Toyo has a joint venture with Continental and Yokohama, employing 431.   [7] Id.

Asia

	1990 Plants	1990 Employees	1993 Plants	1996 Plants	1996 Employees	1998 Plants	1998 Employees
Michelin	3	NA	3	2[1]	450[2]	2[3]	1,300
Bridgestone	12	12,719	13	13	12,455	15	12,674
Goodyear	5	3,885	6[4]	9	4,273[5]	8[6]	4,973
Continental	1	1,000	1	1	1,000	0	0
Sumitomo[7]	3	3,250	NA	4	2,430	5	4,330
Yokohama	6	5,676	6	7	6,758	6[8]	6,130
Toyo	2	1,900	3.5	3	2,170	2	1,750
Cooper	0	0	0	0	0	0	0
Kumho	1	1,300	2	2[9]	2,860	2	2,860
Hankook			3	3	4,590[10]	3	4,310

[1] Michelin also has two joint ventures in Thailand with Siam Tire, employing a total of 1,755.   [2] The number of employees for Michelin's Shen Yang joint venture is not available.   [3] Michelin also has three joint ventures in Thailand with Siam Tire, employing a total of 2,601.   [4] Goodyear also has a joint venture with Toyo in Japan.   [5] Goodyear also has a joint venture with CEAT in India, for which the number of employees is not available, and a joint venture with Toyo in Japan employing 260.   [6] Goodyear also has several joint ventures: with CEAT in India (number of employees not available), with Dalian Rubber in China (300 employees), and with Toyo in Japan (255 employees).   [7] Includes Ohtsu.   [8] Yokohama also has a joint venture in Vietnam with Mitsubishi and Southern Rubber (number of employees not available).   [9] Kumho also has two joint ventures in China (number of employees not available).   [10] The total does not include employees in the Kumsan plant, whose number is not available.

Source: European Rubber Journal.
The main countries included under Asia are China, India, Indonesia, Japan, Malaysia, Nepal, Pakistan, Philippines, South Korea, Sri Lanka, Taiwan, Thailand, and Vietnam. Michelin is present in Japan, Thailand; Goodyear in India, Indonesia, Malaysia, Philippines, Taiwan, Thailand; Bridgestone in Japan, Indonesia, Taiwan, Thailand; Continental in Pakistan (until 1996); Sumitomo and Toyo in Japan; Yokohama in Japan (and in South Korea through a joint venture); Kumho in South Korea.

In the truck tire market, technical criteria mattered more than brand image. Truck fleets were getting bigger. In the United States, the trucking industry was increasingly concentrated, with 3 percent of fleets operating 50 percent of the vehicles on the road. This was leading to greater standardisation of tire fitments. In Europe concentration was less advanced, although in the United Kingdom, 1 percent of fleets already operated 40 percent of trucks.[5]

The Big Three's goal was to cover all segments, with different brands, so dealers could offer a full range. This strategy, also known as "good, better, best," had been implemented in the United States by both Michelin (with the Michelin-BF Goodrich-Uniroyal brand trio) and Bridgestone, whose brand was complemented by Dayton and Firestone. Goodyear had lacked a middle-market brand, but would soon have Sumitomo's widely known Dunlop brand.

Globally, each of the Big Three had some problems. Bridgestone, whose reputation in its home market was excellent, suffered from low recognition in Europe and North America, where Firestone was better known. Michelin was highly reputed worldwide, but its subsidiary brands were not: Goodrich was little known outside the United States, Kléber was only strong in France, and Michelin had relinquished its mid-market Uniroyal brand in Europe to Continental. Goodyear was well positioned as a premium brand, but Kelly was not well known outside North America.

Private brand tires had captured a significant market share but were no longer seen as the major threat. They had grown vigorously in the 1970s and 1980s, especially in the United States, but in the 1990s the majors fought back more aggressively with their own associate brands. In the United States, private brands accounted for about 30 percent of the market; associate brands for 20 percent.

Distribution

In distribution too, the major trend was consolidation, both at the wholesale and retail levels. Replacement tires had traditionally been sold through wholesalers or distributors, whose market share was steadily declining. As independent retailers consolidated, they increasingly purchased tires directly from the manufacturer. As a result, large US distributors were consolidating, and some were acquiring retail chains in order to protect their market share.

Distribution to end-consumers was dominated by independent dealers in all three major markets, as it had been since the early days. In fact, the share of independent dealers, large and small, had grown significantly in the 1980s, mainly at the expense of service stations. In the 1990s in North America, the 30 largest retail chains had about half of the market.[6] Smaller dealers rushed to join groups that provided volume buying and joint services such as advertising and training.[7] (Exhibit 12 shows retail market shares.)

Exhibit 12   US Replacement Passenger Tire Sales by Outlet, 1972, 1986 and 1998 (% share)

	1972	1986	1998
Small independents	31.6	44.8	31.2
Large regional independents	2.5	10.3	23.4
Mass merchandisers	25.4	16.7	16.9
Manufacturer outlets	11.4	11.5	9.1
Warehouse clubs	0.0	2.6	6.5
Service stations	22.8	7.7	9.0
Other[1]	6.3	6.4	9.0
Total	**100.0**	**100.0**	**100.0**

[1]Other comprises car dealers, auto parts stores, and garages.

In Europe, the top 25 independent dealers accounted for 25–30 percent of sales, and concentration was due to increase as British, German and other retail chains expanded beyond their home market. They often formed buying groups, pooling their buying and marketing functions to negotiate better terms. Kwik-Fit, a subsidiary of Ford Motor Company, was Europe's largest independent retailer with more than 1,600 shops under several brands: the flagship Kwik-Fit (in the United Kingdom, Ireland, Belgium, and Holland), Speedy (in France, Belgium, and Spain), Pitstop (in Germany), and a group of small chains that kept their local identities.[8] Multinational marketing cooperatives were also growing with networks such as Point S, Tecar, and Vulcopneu attracting growing numbers of dealers in France, Germany, Italy, and Spain with advantageous purchasing conditions and the prospect of regional marketing clout. They were a growing force behind the growth of private brands and leading outlets for cheaper tire imports, especially from Asia.[9]

In Japan, distribution was consolidating as the share of mass merchandisers such as Autobacs and Yellow Hat increased. (Exhibit 13 shows details.) There too, the growth of chains that negotiated large discounts or bulk orders threatened to erode the pricing power of manufacturers.

The tire makers needed the feedback provided by retail activities, and the marketing muscle afforded by a retail chain. They did not, however, aim at increasing their chains of company-owned outlets; franchising was seen as a better route as owned stores were usually loss making or turning only a tiny profit. The situation was different in the truck segment where closer control was sought in order to better serve truck fleets, especially through services such as retreading.

Pricing

In the OE market, prices were set through an auction process. Carmakers asked tire manufacturers to submit bids for a

Exhibit 13	Tire Distribution Outlets in Japan, 1988 and 1998 (%)	
	1988	**1998**
Car dealers	30	27
Auto speciality stores	22	30
Service stations	16	18
Tire shops		
Company	6	6
independent	7	8
Discount/DIY	7	9
Other	12	3
Total	**100**	**100**

Source: EIU.

certain price and quantity. They then asked all bidders to match the lowest price. Supply contracts were typically for three years, with prices renegotiated every year. In replacement tires, the Big Three set prices in their domestic market.

Retail prices had fallen significantly. According to an industry expert, "tire prices. . . are below what they were five and 10 years ago. And the consumer is getting an unbelievably high quality, highly technical product for a very, very low price. However, when the consolidation moves (among dealers) are completed a higher price structure will result."[10]

Michelin's Competitors

Goodyear Tire and Rubber

Goodyear's origins dated back to 1898, when Frank and Charles Seiberling founded a tire and rubber company in Akron, Ohio, and named it after Charles Goodyear who had invented the vulcanisation process in 1839.[11] By 1916, when the pneumatic truck tire was introduced, Goodyear was the world's largest tire maker. In 1935 it acquired tire maker Kelly-Springfield, and two years later it began making tires from synthetic rubber. After World War II, Goodyear was a leader in new technologies such as polyester tire cord (1962).

It came under attack when Michelin's radial tires started making inroads in North America, and was forced to invest over US$3 billion to develop its own radials in the late 1970s. Later, the company invested in oil and aerospace. After Goldsmith's 1986 hostile bid, the company was burdened by debt from buying back a large proportion of its shares and suffered greatly from the 1980's recession, overcapacity, and price-cutting.

Goodyear returned to profitability in 1991 after starting to supply private brands to Wal-Mart, Kmart and Sears and implementing drastic cost cutting through layoffs and plant closures. In 1996, chairman Samir Gibara had

announced that its goal was to become the low-cost producer among the majors, partly by building plants or acquiring companies in low-cost countries, but also by keeping US costs under tight control.

In 1999 Goodyear was poised to win back the global leadership position that it had held for much of its history, after unveiling in February a cleverly negotiated alliance with Sumitomo. Goodyear would receive Sumitomo's Dunlop brand in North America and Europe and a 10 percent stake in Sumitomo in exchange for its own operations in Japan, a 1.4 percent capital stake and US$936 million in cash. The deal would enable Goodyear to rationalise the companies' production facilities, especially in Europe where it would become a strong number two. About one-quarter of Goodyear's sales came from other rubber industrial and consumer products (belts, hoses, tank tracks) and from a wide range of synthetic rubber, resins, and organic chemicals. It owned more than 900 retail tire outlets in the United States.

Bridgestone/Firestone

Formed in 1931 by Shojiro Ishibashi (Ishibashi means "stone bridge" in Japanese), Bridgestone began making bicycles tires in 1946 and signed a technical assistance pact with Goodyear five years later. It experienced fast growth in the 1970s thanks to the expansion of the Japanese automotive industry.

The 1988 acquisition of Firestone was initially disastrous (General Motors immediately dropped Firestone as a supplier). Bridgestone only moved to cut production costs drastically in 1991. It imposed continuous shift working, alienating the United Rubber Workers (URW). For years, its US operations were plagued with labour disputes. However, continuous shifts did become the norm throughout the industry and in 1996 Bridgestone reached an agreement with the URW. (GM too returned, naming Bridgestone/Firestone 1995 Supplier of the Year.)

To improve its distribution, Bridgestone renamed in 1992 its 1,550 North American MasterCare auto service centres "Tire Zone at Firestone" and took the then unheard-of step of selling rival Michelin tires. Bridgestone's retail channels also included large US retailers such as Sears and Montgomery Ward and its own outlets in Japan.

Its new process technology, Tochigi, was believed to be revolutionary: a 5,060 sq. meter–plant, opened at a cost of US$22 million, could produce 2,500 passenger tires per day with only 18 people. Batch sizes could be as small as 30, and changes in size or type of model took only 30 seconds. It had 40 tire plants worldwide, and was boosting operations in emerging markets such as China, India, and Russia. Aside from tires for heavy equipment (off-road mining vehicles) and aircraft, it made a variety of products: automotive belts and hoses, building materials, golf and tennis balls. Prior to the Goodyear-Sumitomo deal, its stated goal had been to win 20 percent of the world market by 2000 by becoming the clear number two in both Europe and the United States.

Continental Gummi

Well behind Michelin, Continental was the number two in Europe, its largest market by far. This position was now being challenged by the Goodyear-Sumitomo alliance. In 1998 Continental had taken the bold step of acquiring ITT's brake and chassis systems activities and was turning itself into a systems supplier with strong innovation capabilities. The synergies between tires and brake systems could give it a significant cost advantage in the growing area of vehicle control systems and in run-flat tires.

Sumitomo Rubber Industries

Part of Sumitomo Group, one of the largest *keiretsu* in Japan, Sumitomo had gained a measure of internationalisation and widened its business portfolio thanks to its acquisition of Dunlop. More than half its sales were made in Japan; 24 percent came from nontire businesses (sporting equipment and industrial components). Sumitomo had gone through a difficult patch in 1994 and 1995, with a long strike in the United States and the earthquake in Kobe where its head office, main research centre and one plant were located. As a result it was highly indebted.

Pirelli

Pirelli had recently been relaunched with two core businesses (tires and cables), and was pursuing a growth strategy in both. In tires, where it was a replacement market specialist, its global market share was weak, except in high-performance tires. Like Continental, its strategy was to develop technologically advanced tires, capable of commanding higher prices, while meeting demand for cheaper products from plants in Eastern Europe and other low-cost countries. Pirelli had a high market share in Latin America.

In cables, Pirelli had a much stronger position and was at the top of many high-tech fields. However synergies between the two businesses were few and the tire division had been seen as a possible acquisition target. Yet the company seemed determined to stick with tires for the time being, after announcing in February 1999 an agreement with Cooper that covered distribution, purchasing and marketing in North and Latin America.

The "Small Six"

Several other players had a substantial tire production capacity, including three Japanese and two South Korean companies. Cooper Tire and Rubber had by far the best efficiency and profitability of all the major tire makers[12] despite its fast growth (50 percent in four years). A low-cost producer, it targeted budget replacement tires and private label production. Its strategy was to manufacture low-technology tires that required low investment and R&D spending. Its 1997 acquisition of UK company Avon, said to offer "enormous cost reductions and product enhancement opportunities," and the alliance with Pirelli reflected Cooper's desire to expand in Europe.

Hankook and Kumho, two South Korean companies that had grown together with their country's automotive industry, were low cost producers that could potentially threaten the majors. Their technology and products were catching up fast and they had significant market share in Europe (25 percent of the UK replacement market[13]). However, this dramatic rise, fuelled by years of heavy investment, had plunged them deeply into the red. They had been battered by the plunge of the Korean won in 1997 (they paid for purchases in dollars). Both remained strongly dependent on their home market which accounted for about 50 percent of sales. Kumho, the more diversified of the two, had such high gearing that it only survived with help from South Korea's banks.

Among Japanese players, Yokohama had less than 4 percent of the world market. Only 72 percent of total sales came from tires. Toyo, also highly diversified, had a noticeable presence in bus and heavy truck tires, and made three-quarters of its sales in Japan. A market follower, it struggled to improve its dismal financial performance. Ohtsu was 41

Exhibit 14   Profitability (Return on Sales, Return on Assets) of the Tire Industry

| | 1994 | | 1995 | | 1996 | | 1997 | |
	ROS	ROA	ROS	ROA	ROS	ROA	ROS	ROA
Industry	6.7	6.9	7.0	7.4	7.8	8.4	7.9	8.7
Big three	8.2	8.5	8.5	9.1	9.3	10.3	9.3	10.6
Next three	3.7	3.8	4.7	5.1	5.2	5.4	5.8	5.7
Small six	5.5	5.1	5.2	4.8	6.1	5.6	5.4	5.1

Source: World Tire Industry, EIU, 1999.

Exhibit 15a	Tire Manufacturers Market Share in Europe, 1993 and 1998	
	1993	**1998**
Michelin	31.9	27.5
Continental	13.9	18.8
Goodyear	13.1	13.7
Pirelli	9.2	9.5
Bridgestone	9.3	9.2
Sumitomo	9.3	8.1
Others	13.3	13.2
Total	100	100

Source: World Tire Industry, EIU, 1999.

Exhibit 15b	Tire Manufacturers Market Share in North America, 1996 and 1998	
	1996	**1998**
Goodyear	36.4	36.1
Michelin	21.7	21.6
Bridgestone/Firestone	16.2	18.6
Continental General	7.1	6.4
Cooper	6.1	6.3
Dunlop	4.1	3.8
Yokohama	2.3	1.8
Pirelli	1.8	1.6
Toyo	1.3	1.0
Total	100	100

Source: World Tire Industry, EIU, 1999.

percent-controlled by Sumitomo Rubber, whose R&D department and sales and marketing staff it shared. It sold 75 percent of its output in Japan. Exhibit 14 gives an overview of the profitability of the tire industry as a whole and the different groups of tire makers in specific. Exhibits 15a and 15b show the market shares of the major competitors in Europe and North America. Exhibit 16 shows financial data on Goodyear, Bridgestone, Continental and Cooper.

Michelin et Cie: Company History

Michelin, still controlled by the founding family, had revolutionised tire design with the invention of the radial tire and still enjoyed a formidable technical reputation. It was the least diversified of the Big Three, with 93 percent of its revenues from tires, but had a small (and profitable) sideline in maps and travel guides. Both the guides and the Michelin Man, Bibendum, had given it worldwide recognition.

The company began as an agricultural machinery business in Clermont-Ferrand in the Auvergne region of central France. In 1863, it started using rubber to make joints and seals. The Michelin brothers (André, 1853–1931, a successful businessman, and Edouard, 1854–1940, a Parisian artist) took over the company and in 1889 renamed it Compagnie Générale des Etablissements Michelin. That year a British cyclist touring the Auvergne punctured his Dunlop pneumatic tire and sought help from the brothers. After analysing the tire, Edouard found that filling them with air would make cycling more comfortable. Pneumatic tires were initially glued to the rims and required hours to change. In 1891, Edouard made a removable bicycle tire that could be changed in only 15 minutes.

The Michelins promoted their tires by persuading cyclists to use them in long-distance races. They made their first car tires for the 1895 Paris-Bordeaux-Paris motor race.

In 1898 André realised that a stack of tires with arms resembled a man, and designed the now-famous Bibendum.[14] The Michelin Guide was launched in 1900 as a marketing tool; it was initially offered free of charge to motorists.

The company started its international expansion in 1905, when it opened an office in London, and soon built factories in Turin (1906) and New Jersey (1908). More plants were opened in the 1920s and 1930s in Germany, Argentina, Spain, Czechoslovakia, and Belgium. Michelin's technological innovations included detachable rims and spare tires (1906), tubeless tires (1930), treads (1934), and modern low-profile tires (1937). During the 1930s Depression, Michelin accepted a majority stake in Citroën, later converted into a minority interest in Peugeot, in lieu of payment for tires.

Research conducted during World War II by Michelin produced substitutes for natural rubber and new tire designs. The radial, launched in 1946 as the X tire, was fitted on Citroëns in 1951. A second generation of radials (X-AS) was introduced in 1965, shortly before the patent on the X tire was due to expire. (The company believed that even without patent protection, its manufacturing know-how provided considerable competitive advantage.)

Once the radial had taken hold, it turned Michelin into a world leader. Although the company's expansion was largely confined to Europe in the 1950s, in the 1960s it grew worldwide. (Sears started selling Michelin radials in 1966.) Michelin was the world's 10th largest tire supplier in 1960, progressing to 6th by 1970 and 3rd in 1974. In 1978 it overtook Firestone to move into second place with 17 percent of the world market.

In 1971, Michelin exported over 40 percent of the output of its French plants; more than 75 percent of total sales were made outside France. The resulting transportation costs ate up most of its premium price margin. (Around that time,

Exhibit 16   Financial Data on Michelin's Major Competitors

	Goodyear		Continental		Cooper		Bridgestone	
	31-Dec-98	31-Dec-97	31-Dec-98	31-Dec-97	31-Dec-98	31-Dec-97	31-Dec-98	31-Dec-97
	Mil USD	Mil USD	Mil DEM	Mil DEM	Mil USD	Mil USD	Mil JPY	Mil JPY
Assets								
Cash & S.T. Investments	239	259	731	889	42	53	63,805	52,337
Receivables (Net)	1,771	1,734	1,736	1,171	320	292	410,826	428,870
Total Inventories	2,165	1,835	1,936	1,420	186	192	305,444	318,685
Current Assets–Total	4,529	4,164	5,028	4,015	569	555	861,252	891,290
Long Term Receivables	174	190	2	1	n.a.	n.a.	23,861	15,119
Invest. in Uncons. Subsidiaries	111	125	116	100	n.a.	n.a.	18,335	15,390
Property Plant & Equip–Net	4,359	4,150	4,522	2,966	885	860	764,445	713,486
Property Plant & Equip–Gross	9,753	9,234	11,907	9,001	1,509	1,399	1,800,398	1,700,368
Other Assets	1,417	1,289	3,115	526	87	81	46,445	51,091
Total Assets	10,589	9,917	12,829	7,649	1,541	1,496	1,755,302	1,727,094
Liabilities & Shareholders' Equity								
Accounts Payable	1,132	1,178	1,270	769	95	100	169,428	183,437
ST Debt & Curr Portion LT Debt	789	507	583	401	8	11	222,184	254,260
Other Current Liabilities	352	422	562	387	54	42	308,118	330,795
Current Liabilities–Total	3,277	3,251	2,431	1,671	193	200	699,730	768,492
Long Term Debt	1,187	845	3,805	1,038	205	206	161,363	119,934
Provs For Risks & Charges	1,946	1,946	3,560	2,184	152	145	168,382	169,117
Other Liabilities	176	225	28	40	49	38	38,463	39,999
Total Liabilities	6,585	6,266	9,855	4,946	673	662	1,003,421	1,033,635
Minority Interest	259	256	341	292	0	0	54,456	52,077
Common Equity	3,746	3,396	2,632	2,410	868	834	697,424	641,382
Total Liab & Shareholders' Equity	10,589	9,917	12,829	7,649	1,541	1,496	1,755,302	1,727,094
Number of Employees	96,950	95,472	62,357	44,797	10,766	10,456	97,767	96,204
Income Statement								
Net Sales or Revenues	12,626	13,155	13,189	11,186	1,876	1,813	2,236,698	2,170,802
Cost of Goods Sold (Excl Dep)	9,185	9,577	8,988	7,439	1,444	1,404	1,301,920	1,182,477
Depreciation, Depletion & Amort	488	469	711	602	102	94	107,473	200,830
Gross Income	2,953	3,109	3,489	3,146	331	315	827,305	787,495
Selling, Gen & Adm Expenses	1,881	1,890	2,517	2,383	121	106	594,194	580,037
Other Operating Expenses	0	0	373	278	0	0	0	0
Operating Expenses–Total	11,554	11,935	12,588	10,701	1,666	1,604	2,003,587	1,963,344
Operating Income	1,072	1,220	600	485	210	209	233,111	207,457
Extraordinary Credit–Pretax	30	0	0	0	0	0	0	0
Extraordinary Charge–Pretax	16	265	0	0	0	0	4,624	112,787
Non-Operating Interest Income	13	23	44	36	0	0	4,633	4,555
Other Income/Expense Net	83	−13	190	128	4	1	−30,903	−11,889
Earnings Bef Int & Taxes (EBIT)	1,182	964	839	661	213	210	202,217	87,336
Interest Expense on Debt	154	126	228	202	15	17	18,416	19,779
Pretax Income	1,034	845	611	459	198	195	183,801	67,557
Income Taxes	286	241	198	137	71	72	77,888	24,263
Net Income Before Pref Div	682	559	376	277	127	122	104,626	39,158

Source: Worldscope Disclosure Database, March 2000.

sales were growing by about 16 percent p.a. on an average operating margin of 13 percent.) The company decided to manufacture in North America and opened in 1971 a cluster of three radial plants (each plant was due to specialise in a specific stage of production) in Canada. This was followed by a similar cluster in South Carolina (1975). In both cases Michelin chose greenfield sites to avoid unionisation.

In 1975 Michelin introduced its third-generation radial, the TRX.[15] With performance levels far outrunning its rivals, it once more set world standards for engineering. But the TRX had a drawback: it was designed for smaller wheels and would only succeed if carmakers agreed to change wheel size. Michelin offered to share product specifications with other tire makers and to supply OEMs at a discount. The response was less than enthusiastic.

By the late 1970s, despite its investment in new radial plants, Michelin lagged in productivity as US rivals built increasingly efficient factories. Competitors could now claim that they made better tires. Pirelli's P6 and P7 ranges, which could be fitted on standard wheels, rivalled the TRX in looks and performance and the All Season tire developed by Goodyear was cutting into Michelin's US market share. The second oil crisis in 1980 plunged the company into the red. Between 1981 and 1984, Michelin lost nearly FF9 billion and in 1985 was forced to seek a FF4 billion distress credit; this was arranged at favourable interest rates – probably with help from the French government.

In 1983 Michelin embarked on the first of a long series of cost-cutting plans. This paternalistic employer was finding itself forced to cut capacity and reduce headcount. In 1985 favourable market conditions returned the company to profit (but only by FF1 billion). It finally dropped the TRX and replaced it with a new generation, the MX high performance tire. Profits hit a peak of FF2.6 billion in 1988. The cash flow helped reduce debt levels and interest charges (which fell from 8.2 percent of revenues in 1984 to 4.5 percent in 1986).

Michelin was late in developing a strategy for Asia. In 1986 it set up a joint venture in South Korea with Woo-Pong that eventually failed. In 1987 the company built a plant in Thailand. Joint ventures in Japan (with Okamoto) and Malaysia followed in 1988 and 1989.

Uniroyal-Goodrich and Later Acquisitions

By 1988, Michelin was not producing enough tires in North America and exports from France posed insoluble logistical problems, not to mention high costs. Its premium ranges had won market share in both OE and replacement in the United States, but it lacked access to independent retail outlets. Meanwhile Uniroyal-Goodrich, which had an excellent distribution network, was looking for a buyer. In 1989, Michelin acquired the company for US$1.52 billion (including US$810 million in assumed debt). The acquisition turned Michelin into the world's largest tire manufacturer and the chief tire supplier to GM, whose needs it covered by more than 50 percent.

The acquisition was far from an unmitigated success. "Economies of scale really do matter in the tire business," wrote *The Economist*, "but Michelin seemed so obsessed with Uniroyal-Goodrich's market share in America that it paid far too high a price for a technologically backward company loaded with debt."[16] Uniroyal-Goodrich's entire production tool had to be restructured, at a cost of US$4 billion. Michelin eventually decided to close down all of Uniroyal-Goodrich's bias tire plants— half the company's factories in the United States. On top of the US$4 billion capital investment, Michelin had to amortise US$360 million in goodwill over 20 years. In one year, its debt doubled to FF44.7 billion. Michelin, which posted a FF5.2 billion loss for 1990, launched a drastic rationalisation program in the United States, closing down aged plants, reducing the workforce and negotiating a new contract with the United Rubber Workers.

In 1991 and 1992, Michelin implemented a new FF3 billion cost-cutting program, laying off 16,000 employees (including 4,900 in France) and putting an annual cap of FF3 billion on new investment. Another FF3.5 billion cost-reduction plan was unveiled in 1993, with 10,000 more staff laid off in Europe and North America (8 percent of the total workforce); European plants were also specialised and the Michelin and Uniroyal-Goodrich sales operations in North America merged. In 1995, Uniroyal-Goodrich was in working order at last.

Also in 1995, the company turned its efforts to a wide-ranging reorganisation effort under the aegis of young Edouard Michelin. Managers were asked to carry out cross-departmental audits over a six-month period. In February 1996, Edouard was ready to present the new organisation. The company's highly centralised regional structure was replaced with nine so-called "tactical operational units" (TOUs), each covering a major product line. As profit centres, TOUs were accountable for their results. Each had its own product development, marketing, manufacturing, and sales departments. International coordination was ensured by four regional executives, and 12 "group services" provided support to the TOUs. Only one area remained under central control: research and development. (The new structure is shown in Exhibit 17.) The company commented at the time: "The internationalisation of the car and tire markets calls for a consistent approach on all continents, while remaining close to the needs of each individual market." Even more surprising to outsiders, for the first time Michelin unveiled an organisation chart in which key positions were filled by young executives.

Exhibit 17   Michelin Organization

Michelin's nine product lines

- Passenger Car & Light Truck Tires
- Truck Tires
- Earthmover Tires
- Agricultural Tires
- Aircraft Tires
- Two-wheel Tires
- Components (rubber and elastomers, reinforcement materials, etc.)
- Suspension Systems (wheels, anti-vibration equipment, assemblages)
- Tourism Services

12 Group Services provide support to the different divisions:

- Purchasing
- Audit
- Communication
- Finance
- Information Services
- Legal
- Logistics
- Personnel
- Plans and Results
- Quality, General Organization, Information Systems
- Security
- Public Relations

After expanding in North America, Michelin turned to central Europe and to its perennial weak point, Asia. In 1995, it bought a majority interest in Polish tire manufacturer Stomil and the next year acquired 90 percent of Taurus, which made most of Hungary's rubber. In 1996, it joined forces with Continental to make private-label tires for independent distributors and in 1997, it acquired 51 percent of German wheel maker Mannesmann Kronprinz. Total sales increased by 8 percent in 1996 and 12 percent in 1997. In China, where Michelin had opened a commercial office in Beijing in 1989, it created a joint venture in Shen Yang that made radials for the Chinese market. But it still lacked a presence in the large Indian market.

Later acquisitions included Colombian tire maker Icollantas, with factories in Bogota and Cali, in 1998. In 1999, the purchase of Tire Centers Inc, a distributor and retreader of truck tires, underlined Michelin's determination to become a major player in US retreading.[17]

Michelin in 1999

By 1999, Michelin had 82 manufacturing plants in 19 countries. It was unique among the Big Three in making nearly 90 percent of sales outside its home market (about 49 percent in Europe and 34 percent in North America). Michelin marketed a range of 28,000 products, with tires ranging from less than 200 grams to over five tons for all types of vehicles, "from bicycles to the space shuttle." Every day it made more than 830,000 tires as well as over 76,000 inner tubes, 4 million kilometres of wires, 88,000 wheels, and 70,000 tourist maps and guides. Passenger car tires were estimated to account for 47 percent of total sales, and truck tires for 37 percent. Replacement tires represented 70 percent of total tire sales.

A major recent innovation was the Energy[18] "green" tire, which reduced rolling resistance by 35 percent[19] and fuel consumption by 5 percent by adding silica to the rubber mix. (Rival offerings claimed no more than 3 percent fuel savings.) Michelin also had a highly successful 80,000-mile tire, the XH4 Long Life, for the US replacement market. The Classic range was aimed at the budget European market and Michelin had a new high performance range, the Pilot.

In 1997, the company had introduced its PAX run-flat that could travel 200 km after a puncture. While the PAX out-performed competing products, owing to carmakers' distaste for single sourcing, Michelin had to license the technology to its rivals to gain widespread acceptance. In February 1999, it concluded a deal with Pirelli. By then the PAX was available on a few models, such as the Renault Twingo and the Cherokee Jeep.[20]

Production

Michelin had by far the largest workforce in the industry. It employed over 127,000 in 1998, compared with 96,000 for both Goodyear and Bridgestone. It had built eight small plants to implement the C3M process.[21] C3M was believed to require about half of the capital costs of an equivalent conventional plant and only one-tenth of the labour. Manufacturing was radically different: a flow-line process made components in their final form (all rubber parts were built directly onto the drum), eliminating the conventional batch production of sub-components.

Michelin grew 25,000 hectares of rubber in Nigeria and Brazil to experiment with ways to improve quality and boost production. Company policy was "to maintain its independence in the technological and procurement aspects". There was one area where it tried to keep everything in-house: it designed and manufactured most of its tire-making machinery.

Retailing

Like other tire makers, Michelin relied on independent retailers for most of its sales, but in the 1980s it had started increasing its ownership of retail outlets. European retailing operations had been consolidated under the Euromaster brand with about 1,300 outlets in nine countries (including 550 in the UK and 300 in France). The outlets also sold tires from other manufacturers, and offered a variety of services: exhaust, shock absorbers, batteries, brakes. In the United States, Michelin used a multitude of distribution channels, including thousands of independent dealers and mass merchandiser points of sale (such as Sears, Wal-Mart, Western Auto Group), as well as major membership clubs. Michelin also serviced over 50,000 US truck fleets, including UPS.

Research and Development

Michelin spent 5 percent of sales on R&D, far more than any of its rivals. The company strongly believed that its success was due to its commitment to R&D and innovation. Investment in process technology, which Michelin saw as its strength, remained a priority; it had spent several decades developing C3M and unveiled it in 1992. New tire concepts were developed at company Technology Centres in Europe, the United States and Japan that were equipped with large-scale computing facilities to carry out sophisticated simulations. Prototypes were checked out at four testing sites (in France, Spain, the United States, and Japan) recreating the various conditions in which tires were used.

Despite its leadership, Michelin had sometimes been slow to implement its own innovations. Improvements in radial design had remained under test in Clermont-Ferrand while rivals introduced better products in the late 1970s and 1980s. More recently, competitors had been able to catch up in process technology as Michelin delayed the introduction of C3M. Michelin had sometimes snubbed competitors' innovations. For instance, it had lost market share for ignoring Goodyear's all season tire, explaining that the radial had always been "all season." In 1999, Michelin had been caught unprepared by a sudden surge in demand for high performance tires.[22]

Ownership and Legal Structure

Even after Michelin had become a global manufacturer, the family had remained strongly in control. More than 500 Michelin family members[23] owned a substantial but undisclosed share—variously estimated at 10–40 percent—of the holding company, Compagnie Générale des Etablissements Michelin. Control was exerted through an unusual legal status of "Société en commandite par actions," retained by Michelin since it was first founded. Patents and other intellectual property were held by the holding company, which received royalties from the operating company.

The group was headed by three managing partners ("gérants") who enjoyed extensive powers in exchange for unlimited liability for the company's losses. They received no salary, but were paid a substantial share of the profits. It was almost impossible for nonfamily shareholders to dismiss a gérant. A nine-member executive committee had been created recently to assist and advise the gérants.

The commandite, a legal form dating back to the 18th century (when seafaring captains used it to raise finance for voyages of bounty), was ferociously criticised by outside investors. Other French companies (most family-owned businesses) had long since adopted the limited liability (société anonyme) structure. The benefits of the commandite were thus described by François Michelin, in 1992: "It allows us to move much faster, to be protected from outside pressure when taking decisions. . . . Do you know that Japan is nothing more than a huge commandite, through its banking system? It lets us take a long term view." Seven years later, his son Edouard was equally adamant: "I don't feel ashamed of being a commandite. I am convinced there is an innovative and modern way to be a commandite."[24]

The Michelin Dynasty

Ever since its founding in 1898, Michelin had been run by a family member. The only exception had been the 15 sombre years following the death in 1940 of founder Edouard Michelin, whose two sons had been killed in a car crash. The elder Edouard had then asked his son-in-law to act as caretaker until the orphaned François (young Edouard's father) was able to take over. François's reign lasted nearly 45 years.

Secret, enigmatic, and unpredictable, François Michelin was a boss unlike any other. A fellow industrialist described him as "a disconcerting yet engaging man, who provokes admiration and fear."[25] A devout Roman Catholic, dedicated to his family, in times of trouble he was as likely to seek help from God as from his managers, and religion tainted the sense of fairness with which he ran his business.

Ignoring charges of parochialism, "Monsieur François" preferred to stay in the Auvergne, away from power-broking in Paris, and his top managers had to live there too. The local people (Auvergnats) were known for their conservative, sober, thrifty—some said stingy—habits, which François Michelin readily adopted. He dressed modestly, and for years drove a small Citroën 2CV.

Corporate Culture and Management

Because of the family ownership structure, Michelin had long been extremely centralised and secretive. "The smallest leak would be suicide," said François Michelin. Until the 1990s there was no formal organisational chart, and the company did not use formal titles (except for the financial director and plant managers). Managers simply introduced themselves as Mr. So-and-so from Michelin. (Insiders could guess someone's role from his place in the internal directory.) Departments were known by a one- or two-letter code: SG for Accounting, K for legal, and F for Research. Top management, the "gérance," was known as Service S. François Michelin, who liked to quote the Chinese saying: "You are a prisoner of your next word," shunned the media and public pronouncements. Speeches were factual, reflecting the company's belief in hard facts.

Instead of graduates from the "grandes écoles" and MBAs, Michelin recruiters preferred to hire local young engineers who would develop with the company, which offered them a lifelong career.[26] François Michelin himself spent nearly five years learning basic manufacturing and sales skills before taking on the company's leadership. His credo, often preached to his workforce, went as follows: "All those who work for Michelin have a common goal: to make the best possible product for the customer."[27]

As a family-dominated company Michelin had always been able to take a long term view and used this to full effect with its strategic planning. It also felt a particular responsibility for the welfare of employees, even though it had started laying off staff in the 1980s. (In Clermont-Ferrand itself, the workforce had fallen to 15,000 from 30,000.) In its early years the company had invested in housing, schools, hospitals, nurseries, and shops, creating a veritable "Michelinville" that it only gradually sold or handed over to local authorities. François Michelin had taken a dim view of trade unions, which he tolerated only as a necessary evil.

While operations reflected his own thriftiness, with modestly equipped premises and ceaseless efforts to save on "unnecessary" expenses, there was one area where nothing seemed too expensive: research and development, often described as "the boss's mistress." François Michelin valued engineering excellence above all else—certainly marketing or finance. Inventories were allowed to swell far beyond expected orders in order to accommodate powerful plant managers (75 stock days in June 1999, against the industry average of 54). The company's best marketing tool, François Michelin believed, were its products.

"Young Edouard"

In April, 1999, Michelin shareholders received a letter from the company: "Your managing partners feel that Mr Edouard Michelin, who has been playing a major role in the group's strategy and operational management, should henceforward officially speak for your company. . ." At the shareholders' meeting in June, Edouard was named head of the group, although his father would remain a "gérant" for a further three years.

Little was known about Edouard, who cultivated the discretion becoming to a Michelin. Born in 1963, François's youngest son had been carefully groomed for leadership. His upbringing in Clermont-Ferrand had been provincial and deeply religious. (Two of his five siblings had taken holy orders.) During the holidays, he sometimes worked in a Michelin workshop or as a company messenger. He graduated in engineering from one of France's prestigious "grandes écoles," the Ecole Centrale and served as a submarine officer for two years. Bright, but quiet and unprepossessing, with a penchant for humour, he was married with five children and particularly enjoyed mountain hiking, theology, and Gregorian plainchant.

Edouard had joined Michelin in 1989, spending three months in training with other cadres taken on that year, followed by four months as a worker at two company plants. He moved up to supervisor, and then became production manager at the Puy-en-Velay plant making giant earthmover tires. In 1991, he was made a "gérant" and posted to the US. Working with Carlos Ghosn, the Brazilian executive later known as "le Cost Cutter" at Renault and Nissan, Edouard earned his spurs as president and chief operating officer for Michelin North America. He ran the group's eight North American production plants, Michelin's most modern. He later described the experience as seminal: "The North American market is hyper competitive. All the tire makers are there, as well as all the OE manufacturers. And distribution plays a huge role: half the market is dominated by private distributor brands."[28] He also said: "In North America we are a younger organisation, our teams are smaller and more reactive to the market."[29]

In 1993 "young Edouard", as he was known, returned to Clermont-Ferrand and took on greater responsibilities, soon sharing decision-making with his father. A convert to methods such as removing managers to empower employees, he started overruling the old guard and urging new ideas. Asked about his role, he once described it as "speeding up project management and innovation. . . fine-tuning rather than revolutionising."[30] Before the major reorganisation in 1996, he was credited with engineering a FF3.5 billion cost cutting effort launched in April 1993, as well as the 1994 decision to hike OE prices, although he was characteristically modest about his own contribution to the latter: "Let's say that my father paved the way through two years of consistent efforts, and that I acted as a catalyst in a decision that was vital for our House." In 1995 Edouard, described by his father as an "iconoclast" ("I took it as an invitation to be myself"), broke with tradition by putting 4,000 managers through training sessions that stressed the importance of marketing, service, and profitability. He also set up an incentive pay scheme linked to corporate and personal performance for managers.

The Challenge for Bibendum

In recent years, especially since the acquisition of Uniroyal-Goodrich, Michelin had become more responsive to the outside world, for instance allowing journalists to visit some of its factories, "once almost as tough to enter as the no man's land between the two Koreas."[31] Yet the continued secretiveness and family control, not to mention the commandite structure, still infuriated investors and analysts. The company's share price had not always performed well, as shown in Exhibit 18. Exhibit 19 gives Michelin financial data.

While the announced layoffs were welcomed by the financial markets, they enraged the company's larger constituency, from workers and trade unions all the way up to the French government, and Michelin had to scale down its job-reduction plan within days. Analysts meanwhile were blaming the slow roll-out of the C3M technology on a desire to avoid labour unrest and a political backlash. Michelin's slow progress in Asia was another weakness.

In his first speech as head of the group, to the June 1999 shareholders meeting, Edouard Michelin said he intended to focus on five key areas: product performance, globalisation, productivity gains, management efficiency, and lastly, "reliable, reactive control of the group so as to increase its robustness." In a later interview, he emphasised delegation, empowerment, and accountability so as to make time for more important activities: new countries and strategic opportunities, and promised to focus more on customer demand. For instance, customers would soon be able to order tires via the Internet and, in some cases, plan their own tire designs from a range of primary colours. About his father he said: "I think in terms of vision of the industry . . . we are very close. In terms of method, we are very different. That's normal: I represent a new generation."[32]

The task facing Edouard Michelin was huge: he had to usher into the 21st century a firm that came, from many points of view, straight out of the 19th. "His heritage is a vast empire, powerful yet archaic, domineering yet indebted, an embattled world leader. . .", a French journalist wrote.[33] For the first time in 40 years, a new man was at the controls. Would he be enough of an iconoclast to ensure Michelin's continued preeminence?

Exhibit 18   Share Price

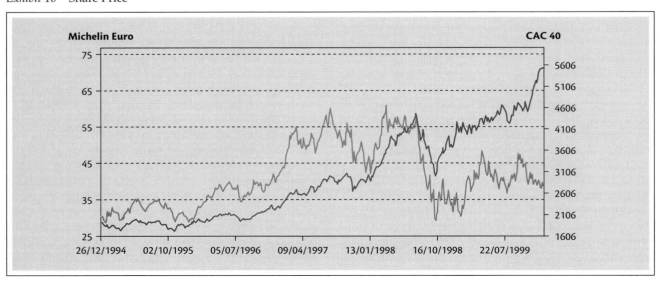

Exhibit 19   Financial Data on Compagnie Générale des Etablissements Michelin

	12/31/1998 Mil FRF	12/31/1997 Mil FRF	12/31/1996 Mil FRF	12/31/1995 Mil FRF	12/31/1994 Mil FRF	12/31/1993 Mil FRF
Assets						
Cash & S.T. Investments	7,368	7,407	6,909	5,239	3,817	2,212
Receivables (Net)	15,738	15,653	15,271	14,837	15,290	15,945
Total Inventories	17,845	16,177	15,981	14,577	13,655	15,541
Current Assets–Total	40,951	39,236	38,162	34,653	32,761	33,698
Long Term Receivables	110	117	106	129	142	206
Invest. in Uncons. Subsidiaries	89	253	211	317	324	322
Other Investments	2,485	2,363	1,919	1,910	2,697	2,772
Property Plant & Equip–Net	32,392	30,889	28,061	26,000	26,890	29,582
Property Plant & Equip–Gross	80,411	78,315	72,157	66,576	66,449	67,436
Other Assets	8,167	8,860	7,743	7,419	7,424	8,108
Total Assets	84,193	81,718	76,202	70,429	70,238	74,689
Liabilities & Shareholders' Equity						
Accounts Payable	8,612	6,976	5,693	6,071	5,316	4,970
ST Debt & Curr Portion LT Debt	11,654	8,973	13,112	8,043	7,969	10,474
Other Current Liabilities	9,028	9,448	9,116	9,481	9,540	9,298
Current Liabilities–Total	29,294	25,397	27,921	23,596	22,825	24,742
Long Term Debt	13,601	15,105	16,502	22,676	23,928	26,754
Provs For Risks & Charges	12,067	13,635	12,778	10,119	12,598	14,020
Deferred Income	n.a.	n.a.	n.a.	n.a.	n.a.	n.a.
Deferred Taxes	358	346	416	318	349	363
Other Liabilities	1,273	1,294	1,165	770	1,099	838
Total Liabilities	56,593	55,776	58,782	57,478	60,800	66,718
Minority Interest	2,003	1,902	1,399	1,126	734	695
Common Equity	25,597	24,040	16,021	11,825	8,704	7,275
Total Liab & Shareholders' Equity	84,193	81,718	76,202	70,429	70,238	74,689
Number of Employees	127,241	123,254	119,780	114,397	117,776	124,575
Income Statement						
Net Sales or Revenues	81,900	79,692	71,246	66,110	67,221	63,298
Cost of Goods Sold (Excl Dep)	55,441	55,274	50,068	46,773	48,752	47,585
Depreciation, Depletion & Amort	4,911	4,608	5,654	5,449	5,818	6,277
Gross Income	21,548	19,810	15,523	13,888	12,651	9,436
Selling, Gen & Adm Expenses	n.a.	n.a.	n.a.	n.a.	n.a.	n.a.
Other Operating Expenses	17,528	15,181	10,961	9,809	9,412	9,139
Operating Expenses–Total	77,880	75,063	66,684	62,031	63,982	63,001
Operating Income	4,021	4,629	4,562	4,080	3,239	297
Extraordinary Credit–Pretax	2,093	1,842	1,375	3,483	2,679	2,295
Extraordinary Charge–Pretax	2,102	1,945	3,184	3,831	3,418	5,199
Non-Operating Interest Income	1,269	1,303	1,233	1,291	1,664	1,446
Other Income/Expense Net	3,220	2,636	3,295	1,743	1,580	1,576
Earnings Bef Int & Taxes (EBIT)	8,500	8,466	7,281	6,765	5,745	416
Interest Expense on Debt	2,732	2,788	2,723	2,819	3,443	4,113
Pretax Income	5,768	5,677	4,559	3,946	2,302	–3,697
Income Taxes	2,018	1,570	1,355	984	940	280
Net Income Before Pref Div	3,513	3,883	2,891	2,796	1,291	–3,670

Source: Worldscope Disclosure Database, March 2000.

Notes

1 Neil Mullineux, *World Tire industry*, EIU, 1999.

2 *Tires: Wearing thin*, Dresdner Kleinwort Benson Securities, 20 July 1999. This was truer in Europe than in the US, where drivers easily changed brands.

3 "Computer skills needed in tires," *European Rubber Journal*, Global Tire Report, 1998.

4 Neil Mullineux, o.c., 1999.

5 *Global Tire Report*, 1997–98.

6 *Global Tire Report*, 1998–99, p. 21.

7 *Modern Tire Dealer*, January 1997.

8 Hoovers' Web site.

9 *Global Tire Report*, 1996–97.

10 Saul Ludwig, in *Modern Tire Dealer*, January 1997.

11 The heat treatment that binds the tire's many ingredients into a resilient structure and gives it its final size, shape and tread pattern.

12 Cooper's net profit margin had slowed down slightly in 1998, but at 6.8 percent it was still well above the industry average. Goodyear's net profit margin was 5.4 percent and Michelin's 4.4 percent.

13 *EIU.*

14 It was shown holding a glass full of nails, with the Latin caption: "Nunc est bibendum" (Let's drink now), to underline the greater resistance to punctures of Michelin Tires.

15 TR stands for "tension répartie", referring to the tire's evenly distributed stress design.

16 June 30, 1990.

17 *Modern Tire Dealer*, January 1998.

18 XFE—Xtra Fuel Economy—in the United States.

19 The original X radial reduced rolling resistance over bias designs by 34%. Between its launch—1947—and 1990, manufacturers had managed to reduce rolling resistance only by a further 10%.

20 Reuter's, March 9, 1999.

21 *Les Echos*, June 1999.

22 See *Tire Business*, October 25, 1999.

23 *Financial Times*, December 20, 1999.

24 "Edouard Michelin: The new head of Michelin," *The Financial Times*, December 20, 1999.

25 *L'Usine nouvelle*, September 21, 1989.

26 In 1999, they had started to recruit MBA's at INSEAD, however.

27 Freydet and Pingaud, *Les patrons face à la gauche*, 1982, Paris: Ramsay.

28 "Les héritiers: Edouard Michelin," by Pascal Galinier, *Le Nouvel Economiste*, July 13, 1995.

29 *Le Nouvel Economiste*, July 13, 1995.

30 *Le Nouvel Economiste*, July 13, 1995.

31 *Financial Times*, December 20, 1999.

32 *Financial Times*, December 20, 1999.

33 *Le Nouvel Economiste*, July 13, 1995.

Case 1–3: Apple's iTunes

Changing the Face of Online Music Retailing*

"The iTunes Music Store is changing the way people buy music."[1]

—**Steve Jobs, Apple's CEO, in June 2003.**

"The iTunes Music Store has defined what it means for people to have music instantly–and legally–at their fingertips."[2]

—**Doug Morris, CEO, Universal Music Group, June 24, 2003.**

Apple Spells Success With iTunes

In June 2003, Apple Computer Inc (Apple)[3] announced that its Internet-based music selling initiative, the iTunes Music Store (iTunes), had sold more than three million songs in the first month of its launch. This figure, far beyond even the company's expectations, took the music retailing industry by surprise. All those who had predicted doom for iTunes at the time of its launch, watched in disbelief as Apple reported total sales of five million songs by the end of the second month. The music store was reportedly attracting a growing audience day by day owing to its simplicity and ease of use (Refer to Exhibit 1 for a look at the iTunes Web page).

iTunes was now being labeled by industry analysts as a revolutionary concept that was all set to change the way music was traded—offline as well as online. Commenting on this, Doug Morris, CEO, Universal Music Group, said, "iTunes is pushing us into the future of how music is produced and consumed."[4] Using iTunes, songs could be downloaded at a nominal charge for each song, and copied to or played on portable music players such as Apple's iPod. Apart from being simple to use, iTunes reportedly offered good quality music downloads as compared to the other music download services available on the Internet.

More significantly, iTunes had emerged as a legal alternative to downloading music using file swapping services like KaZaA, Morpheus, and the erstwhile Napster.

Corporate players were happy that there seemed to be hope for legal, paid music downloading services. Industry observers as well as companies in the music and Internet businesses were liberal in praising iTunes, calling it one of the best things to have happened to the ailing music industry (Refer to Exhibit 2 for information about the major players in the industry).

Commenting on how iTunes had shown that selling music over the Internet was viable and safe, David Goldberg, General Manager for Music, Yahoo, said, "Apple's service shows there is consumer demand, and it shows they have built a great product."[5] Roger Ames, Chairman and CEO of Warner Music Group, said, "Everyone in our industry is looking for a solution, and Apple is leading the way with the iTunes Music Store."[6]

Background Note—Emergence of Online Music Distribution

The music industry across the globe can broadly be divided into three segments: creation, marketing, and distribution. Music artists create music, which is marketed and distributed by a network of record labels, distributors, retailers, broadcasters and DJs/clubs. Labels (record companies) play an important role in all three stages by providing capital and the marketing know-how to create, promote, and distribute music. Music marketing takes place through branding, community building, and information dissemination. Music is sold in "containers" like compact discs (CDs) and audio cassettes[7] through distribution channels. Another form of music distribution is conducting public and private music shows.

The business of music involves many intermediaries between artists (creators) and customers (end users). Each

*This case was written by **V. Sarvani,** under the direction of **A. Mukund,** ICFAI Center for Management Research (ICMR). It is intended to be used as a basis for class discussion rather than to illustrate either effective or ineffective handling of a management situation. The case was compiled from published sources. ©2003, ICFAI Center for Management Research (ICMR), Hyderabad, India. Used with permission.

Free 30-second, full-quality previews of any song

Download music

Exclusive artists and tracks

Scroll through the latest releases and staff favorites

Browse entire store library by genre, artist, and album

Search for any artist, song, or album plus power search

Top song downloads

Top album downloads

Exhibit 1   The iTunes Music Store Web page

Source: www.apple.com.

intermediary adds to the final cost of the product. Therefore, some record companies like Bertelsmann combine the roles of multiple intermediaries to reduce overall costs by selling music directly to their club members at low prices. Another way to reduce the cost of promotion and distribution was to sell music in the form of albums containing many solos.[8] Companies such as EMI, Warner, and BMG have been doing this for a long time.

Record companies have always been a dominating force in this industry since they control major marketing and distribution channels. They exert their might by binding individual artists to long-term contracts. Most of the artists bound themselves to record companies lured by the latter's financial muscle, experience, and marketing prowess—all of which were necessary to succeed in the business, and none of which the artists had. This also meant that emerging artists could not compete on their own as they did not have access to big companies. Therefore, they either had to be "lucky or resourceful enough" for a record

company to spot and sign them, or they had to be content with operating in niche markets. Due to the clout labels wielded on the industry, they reportedly took away a huge share (around 80 to 90 percent) of profits.

The practice of selling music in the album format forced music artists to compose several solos in order to make the end product commercially viable. Under pressure from their labels, the trend of artists composing just three or four good songs emerged. These songs were then packaged along with fillers (songs that seemed to be there just to fill out the CD) and marketed by the record companies. Typically, customers had to pay $15 to $20 per CD for an album. However, music lovers recognized the trickery behind this strategy. They argued that it was not justifiable that an individual should buy an entire album to listen to just one or two songs he or she liked. This had been a sore point with music customers all over the world, considering the fact that the cost of manufacturing a CD or audio cassette was less than a dollar.

Exhibit 2   A Note on the Major Players in the Music Industry

In 2002, the global recording music market was estimated to be worth $32 billion. The market was mainly dominated by five major recording labels, Universal Music Group, Sony Music, Warner Music, EMI Music, and BMG Music, in the given order. Apart from them, many thousands of small record companies and individual players existed in the market. Most of these smaller players operated on a regional basis, with a few local record companies ruling the roost in most countries of the world.

The Universal Music Group was the world's number one music company; it was formed in 1998 as a result of the merger between Polygram (Europe) and the US-based MCA/Universal Group. Before being acquired by Vivendi Universal in 2000, it was the flagship brand of Seagram, a Canadian beverages company. In 2001, Universal posted revenues of $6.2 billion.

Sony Music Entertainment was the US-based music subsidiary of Japan's Sony Corporation. The number two player in the industry, Sony comprised a huge portfolio of artists and record labels including Columbia Records, Epic Records, Legacy Recording, Sony Classic, Sony Nashville, and Sony Wonder. The company's revenues in 2001 stood at $4.6 billion.

Warner Music group, the worlds number three music company, comprised some of the world's leading record companies like Electra Entertainment Group, the Atlantic Group, Rhino Entertainment, Word Entertainment, and Warner Bros. Records Inc. The company operated in more than 70 countries. In 2001, Warner Music posted revenues of $3.9 billion.

EMI Music was the UK's leading record company. With a presence in over 30 countries, the company included record labels like Virgin Records, EMI Music Publishing, EMI Records, Capitol Records, and Angel Records. In 2001, EMI's revenues amounted to $3.8 billion.

BMG Music was the third largest music distributor and the leading distributor of singles in the US. The company operated in ten countries around the world. BMG earned revenues of Ä2.7 billion in 2002, 44.1 percent from North America, 8.8 percent from Germany, 28.1 percent from Europe (excluding Germany), and the remaining from other countries.

After the emergence of online music distribution, many Internet companies established online music stores in association with the recording labels. Some of the well-known stores were MP3.com, MusicMatch.com, Pressplay (from Sony), and LaunchCast (from Yahoo).

Source: Compiled from various sources.

Music enthusiasts found an answer to their problems in the Internet. As the use of the Internet spread phenomenally in the 1990s, the music retailing landscape changed. Companies like Amazon.com and CDNow began selling CDs and audio cassettes over the Internet. This model was better than the existing set up in many ways. Companies did not have to invest heavily in maintaining a physical store and inventory, and customers could search from a large database of artists which was much more convenient than traveling to physical retail stores to buy CDs.

Although selling music on the Internet removed certain logistics costs from the business, the issue of customers being charged excessively for CDs or audio cassettes remained unanswered. This led to the emergence of digital distribution of music, that is, downloading of music in digital format from the Internet to the personal computers of users. Using Internet audio technologies like MP3, Real Audio, and Microsoft's Windows Media Player, music could be converted into software (digital files) and compressed[9] and transferred over the net.

Due to the ease of transferring music in the above manner, and the fact that MP3 technology was a freeware (not the property of any company), music lovers took to online transferring in a major way. By the late 1990s, the industry even saw the emergence of portable digital music players from companies such as Creative Labs and Samsung that played MP3 songs.

The Debate on Online Music Distribution

By 2000, two kinds of services took shape in the field of online music distribution: free to share and subscription based. Free to share services such as Napster ran on peer-to-peer (P2P) technology wherein, using file-sharing networks, it became possible to swap music files from one system to another. Such services became extremely popular because of the ease of use and the availability of a wide selection of songs. But above all, their popularity was due to the fact that they were entirely free. Napster, launched in mid-1999,

Exhibit 3   A Note on Music Piracy

The International Federation of Phonographic Industry (IFPI), an organization that represented 1,500 record companies in 70 countries around the world, estimated the value of the global music piracy market at $4.6 billion in 2002, an increase of 7 percent over 2001. This excluded the estimated losses due to distribution of unauthorized files over the Internet and private copying by individuals. The global music piracy market was reportedly bigger than any individual national music market except the United States and Japan.

Music piracy included disc piracy (pressed disks and CD-R) and audio cassette piracy. Disc piracy was estimated to be around 1.1 billion units in 2002, an increase of 14 percent over 2001, and more than double the units sold in 1999 (510 million units). According to IFPI findings, every one in three disks, and two in five audio cassettes, were pirated. However, the threat to the industry from the Internet, that is, digital music piracy, had emerged as the biggest menace by the 21st century. According to a research study conducted by RIAA in early 2002, 50 percent of music buyers who downloaded music from the Internet made illegal copies of it in 2001, as against 13 percent in 2000.

The pressed disks (mass produced in factories by using a mould or press of a single master disk), dominated the piracy market in Asia (especially in China and Indonesia) and Russia. According to IFPI reports, more than three-fourths of the world's pressed disks were sold in these regions. CD-R piracy, wherein copies are created by burning CDs, was prevalent in Latin America and Southern Europe. Reportedly, CD-R piracy was considered to be a major threat because of the ease of mass pirate production with the help of legally available low-cost and high-speed CD burners. Due to the widespread music piracy, global recording music sales fell by 7 percent in value and 8 percent in units in 2002.

The music piracy menace prompted major players in the industry to take various combative measures. They campaigned to the effect that piracy was unethical and some of the record labels even released CDs that incorporated piracy protection technology. However, these measures were not considered to be foolproof. The companies also backed legal digital music download services, which failed due to complexity in usage.

IFPI even organized a "Digital Download Day" in Europe in January 2003. On this day, the music industry, including the major labels as well as the small and individual labels, offered consumers in France, Germany, Spain, Italy, and the United Kingdom free downloadable songs at their Web sites. This move was aimed at making users aware of the evils of music piracy and to educate them on where and how to download quality legal digital music. Despite all the above measures and the emergence of easy to use, affordable and legal digital music download services, the menace of music piracy was expected to continue plaguing the industry.

Source: Compiled from various sources.

---

became extremely popular with 1.6 million people using its services during the height of its popularity in early 2000.

However, these P2P services gave rise to music piracy since they violated music copyrights and intellectual property rights of music companies. By making available songs that were the "property" of record companies at no cost, the business of these companies was under threat (Refer to Exhibit 3 for a note on music piracy).

The Recording Industry Association of America (RIAA)[10] strongly condemned the use of P2P technology stating that it was illegal. This was because the technology allowed users to copy and download music without payment and without the express permission of the rights' owners. The most popular of such services, Napster, became the first target of RIAA's ire when the latter filed a copyright infringement suit against it. In mid-2001, Napster was shut down after the courts ruled in favor of RIAA.

This development did not deter P2P technology service providers and its users from floating similar services like KaZaA, BearShare, Grokster, and Morpheus. After the closure of Napster, P2P technology became even more popular. According to a market survey conducted by RIAA, an estimated 2.6 billion copyrighted files were traded over P2P networks every month. This seemed to be true considering that KaZaA attracted 100 million users in July 2002.

Reportedly, the P2P Web sites were responsible for sales in the music industry declining alarmingly. Some companies even tried adopting new technologies that made it impossible for customers to copy songs sold in the CD format. In fact, an album released by Sony Music in early 2002 (featuring popular singer Celine Dion) could not be played on computers. If customers tried to do so, their computers crashed due to the technology used. However, this move evoked strong protests from many customers. Other music companies too tried out similar tactics—but to no avail. As piracy continued eating into the industry's fortunes, many debt-ridden media conglomerates even began considering selling their music businesses.

The other mode of online music distribution, subscription-based services, levied a subscription fee on registered users as well as a charge for each song downloaded. These services entered into revenue-sharing agreements with record companies to provide users with a wide selection of songs. Reportedly, RIAA member companies had agreed to make their songs available on the subscription-based Web sites, since this seemed to be a better alternative to file-swapping services.

In mid-2003, some popular subscription-based services included America Online's MusicNet, Full Audio's MusicNow, RealOne's Rhapsody, Music Match's MX, EMusic, and Pressplay. The subscription fee varied according to the services offered. Pressplay charged a monthly fee of $9.95 for providing unlimited streaming and downloading of songs. These songs could not be burned (copied) onto a CD. However, by paying a higher monthly fee of $17.95, users could burn 10 songs per month. An additional $1 was charged for each extra song burned.

Similarly, Rhapsody charged a monthly fee of $9.95 and an additional 75 cents per song to burn a CD. MusicNow charged $9.95 per month and an additional 99 cents per song to burn a CD. MX charged a monthly fee starting from $4.95 for unlimited streaming, but did not allow burning to CD. Another service, EMusic, offered unlimited streaming and burning for a monthly fee of $9.95. However, the selection did not include big label artists but songs and music from independent artists (Refer to Exhibit 4 for a comparison of online music services on various parameters).

While record companies claimed that subscription-based services were the answer to the menace of P2P networks, music buyers had a different story to tell. They argued that buying a music album was easier than keeping track of the pricing options from such services. Due to pressure from record labels, all the subscription-based services offered music with many restrictions on how and where it could be used. For instance, most fee-based services had made burning CDs either too costly and complicated, or impossible altogether.

Due to the above reasons, the subscription model never really became popular with music lovers. Meanwhile, the record companies attempted to provide "pay per song" services as well, although at prices as high as $3.99 per song. This move was a miserable failure. The music industry's woes worsened when a federal court judge, in April 2003, ruled that file swapping services like Streamcast (parent of Morpheus) and Grokster were legal technological tools similar to video cassette recorders and copy machines. The ruling stated that the Web sites were not liable for its users who engage in copyrights infringements as these technologies had other valuable uses also.

Although the ruling was a setback to RIAA, the fact that the law had recognized that individual users were accountable for illegally using P2P networks, came as a boon. In early 2003, reportedly, RIAA was planning to take action against individuals engaging in music piracy. Some industry observers felt that this development would deter many music file swappers and they would start using paid services.

However, P2P services continued to flourish. Reportedly, the number of people using KaZaA (offering around 719,280,000 MP3 files) was 230 million by May 2003. A survey conducted by Ipsos Insight, a US-based market research firm, in June 2003, revealed that in the United States alone, there were more than 21 million people using P2P services every month. These figures were further substantiated by Big Champagne (an online media research firm), which reported that in 2002–2003 around 3.4 million MP3 files were being traded every month through KaZaA and Grokster.

Contrary to what RIAA believed, many analysts said that the reason users did not turn to legal music download services was not that they did not want to pay, but because these services did not offer wide selections and the ability to copy music files to computer hard drives, CDs, and portable players. Supporting the above stand, Josh Bernoff (Bernoff) of Forrester Research, said, "The reason people use free services is because they did not find what they were looking for—not that they did not want to pay."[11]

That music listeners liked to download music from the Internet was an established fact. However, when the subscription model seemed to be failing, the industry was at a loss to find a solution to the problem of illegal swapping of music files.

iTunes Provides a Solution

Aware of the shortcomings of the existing models of online music retailing, Apple's CEO Steve Jobs, reportedly, said that though free services offered a vast selection of songs for unlimited downloads, their quality was poor and performance unreliable. Also, subscription-based services were not popular due to the limitations they imposed on downloading songs—many even suspended access to songs when the subscriptions expired.

Jobs believed that the problem of music piracy was a behavioral one and technological solutions could not tackle it. He felt that users resorted to piracy because they were not offered any viable alternative for buying music at a reasonable price. Peter Lowe (Lowe), Director, Marketing Consumer Application, Apple, said, "In future the real

Exhibit 4   Online Music Services*

	Name	Tracks	Charges	Features
P2P services				
1	KaZaA	719,280,000 MP3 files	Free	Unlimited downloads, can be copied to any number of CDs and computer hard disks.
2	Grokster	Unlimited	Free	Unlimited downloads, can be copied to any number of CDs and computer hard disks.
3	Morpheus	Unlimited	Free	Unlimited downloads, can be copied to any number of CDs and computer hard disks.
Subscription based services				
1	MusicNet	300,000	$4 (monthly fee) $9 (monthly fee) $18 (monthly fee)	Download and stream 20 songs. Restricted user rights for different songs. Download and stream unlimited tracks. Restricted user rights for different songs. Download and stream unlimited number of tracks; allows to burn 10 tracks.
2	Music Now	Limited	$9.95 (monthly fee)	One time download only. Different licensing terms for different songs. Compatible only with Windows Media Player. Additional cost of 99 cents per song to burn a CD.
3	Rhapsody	Limited	$9.95 (monthly fee)	For downloading songs only and an additional cost of 75 cents/song to burn a CD.
4	Pressplay	Limited Limited	$9.95 (monthly fee) $17.95 (monthly fee)	Unlimited streaming and downloading of songs to a computer hard disk. Cannot copy songs to a CD. Burn 10 songs per month and an additional 1$ per extra song.
5	MX	Limited	$4.95 (monthly fee)	Unlimited streaming but no downloading. Cannot burn CDs.
6	EMusic	Limited	$9.95 (monthly fee)	Unlimited streaming. Cannot burn CDs.
Pay Per Song Services				
1	iTunes	200,000	99 cents/song. $10 for certain albums.	Uniform rights for all songs, no restriction on copying songs to any number of CDs and Macintoshes. Songs can be transferred to any number of portable digital players. Compatible only with Macintoshes.
2	BuyMusic	300,000	79 cents–$1.29 per song. Individual albums between $7.95 and $12.	Restrictions on CD burning. Varying rights for different songs. Not compatible with all portable digital players.

Source: Compiled from various sources.   *The list is not exhaustive.

sea-changes in our industry will be driven by things that truly empower users, rather than tech-fads."[12]

Commenting on the belief that Apple could offer a solution to change this behavioral pattern, Lowe said, "We fundamentally believe that most people are honest. The illegal file-sharing services have prospered because there have been no elegant legal alternatives. We think if you give people great value, a really good selection of music, and fast, good-quality downloads, they will use the service in preference to the illegal ones."[13] Analysts summed up Apple's stand as "an approach that makes buying music online easier rather than trying to make pirating it harder."

Apple's decision to launch iTunes thus seemed to offer a solution to some of the difficulties faced by the music buyers as well as the music industry. iTunes offered several improvements to the services offered by P2P and subscription-based services. Launched on April 28, 2003, iTunes was not a subscription-based service—it charged 99 cents for every song downloaded, had a library of 200,000 music tracks, did not enforce any restrictions on use of the songs, and provided the option of burning CDs—all packaged in an easy to use, no frills Web site. Apple seemed to have devised a business model that combined both the advantages of subscription-based services (legality) and free services (easy to use and low or zero costs).

For obtaining the music tracks, the company entered into a revenue sharing agreement with five of the big music labels in the country: BMG, EMI, Sony, Universal, and Warner. Analysts expressed surprise over the ready support Apple got from the big labels. While some perceived this move as an indication that the music industry was ready to shift from the traditional business model to the cost-effective online model, others believed that it was an experimental venture.

By agreeing to tie-up with Apple, the industry had given a clear signal that it was willing to try out new business models rather than allow illegal services to continue. Commenting on this, a music label executive said, "Until Apple, it was not cool to buy digital music. This was about getting to that pivotal group of people—the people who buy the cool sneakers and wear the right clothes—and showing them that legally downloading music could be cooler than stealing it."[14]

However, some reports stated that Apple's (particularly Jobs') popularity among elite influencers in the music industry (and Hollywood), helped the company get the required licenses to create a viable service. A digital music analyst at the US-based research firm, Raymond James & Associates, stated that even if iTunes' market was limited [iTunes was compatible only with Macintoshes[15] (Mac) that comprised only 3 percent of desktops globally], the segment was big enough for record labels to test a new business model for online music retailing.

Interestingly, apart from the deal from record labels, iTunes also featured songs from 80 to 100 independent artists. Some of the songs at the store were accompanied by their respective videos also. The store also had exclusive songs from 20 popular artists, including Bob Dylan and U2. Although the music store had a limited collection of songs, the database was expected to be enhanced depending upon the response received from users.

iTunes gave users 30 seconds to listen to songs before deciding to buy. This was a unique feature that was not available at other online services. Even at physical record stores, users were allowed to listen to songs only from those CDs which the music companies were promoting at

that point of time. Analysts considered this feature of iTunes as a sensible move since it allowed users to be sure about their purchase decisions.

Another innovative feature was that users were allowed to compile their own albums from the existing library of songs. This addressed the decades old problem of music lovers having to buy a complete album, when they liked only a couple of songs on it. Not only did this eliminate the need to pay a high price for CDs, the fee of 99 cents per song was affordable for a majority of online music buyers. An analyst based in New York commented, "Under a dollar is a fair price. A whole CD from a retail store costs at least 15 bucks."[16] This feature was expected to have another advantage—if fillers did not sell, record labels could decide not to force artists to produce them. This would, in turn, lead to an overall improvement in the quality of the albums.

The licensing terms of iTunes did not put any restrictions on the users as it allowed them to save songs on their hard disk, burn them onto a CD, or transfer them onto digital music players. Apple offered a broad set of rights across all its music, which was considered a commendable achievement. The only major restriction Apple imposed was not allowing the copying of more than 10 songs per CD of an individual artist. This was done in order to prevent users from burning such a "collection" on a large number of CDs and making money out of it.

Thus, iTunes was the first paid service that gave all the rights to the users, in sharp contrast to other music stores that offered complicated, different rights for different sets of music (certain songs could not be copied onto a CD or transferred to other computers or portable music players). Analysts observed that by removing the complexities in the licensing terms that confused users, iTunes had made it easy to purchase music online.

The service was launched only for Mac users. To use the service, Mac users had to download the iTunes software, which was available free at Apple's Web sites. As users began burning songs as many times as they wanted on a CD, and transferred the songs to a number of iPods (a portable music player offered by Apple), they began appreciating iTunes more.

The response to iTunes vindicated the move by Jobs, Lowe, and Apple—one millions songs were sold within the first week of launch, setting a new record for online music sales (downloads). Company reports revealed that more than 46 percent of songs were purchased as albums and around 80 percent of available songs at the store were purchased at least once. According to Jobs, the best part about the whole business was, "It is not stealing, which is good karma."[17] As mentioned earlier, sales increased to over five million songs by the end of eight weeks. Jobs said, "Selling five million songs in the first eight weeks has far surpassed our expectations, and clearly illustrates that many customers are hungry for a legal way to acquire their music online."[18]

Looking at the financial performance of iTunes, since revenues were shared between Apple, record labels, and artists, the company would earn relatively less (estimated $2 million) in the first quarter of the services' launch. However, Apple did not have to spend on the infrastructure of iTunes as the software already existed in Macs.[19] Their only expenditure was on building the Web site. Therefore, the incremental cost was much less than that spent by other online music stores, who had to build everything from scratch. Company watchers believed that Apple stood to gain a lot from iTunes in the long run.

iTunes—Facing Competition

Although iTunes was considered a remarkable improvement over the previous services available in the market, it did have some drawbacks. First, critics argued that the collection of songs at the store was limited (200,000), and did not give much choice to the users. Second, songs downloaded from iTunes could be played only in Macs since the software was not compatible with Windows-based PCs.

The biggest problem, however, was the emergence of similar services that had been inspired by the growing popularity of iTunes. All these new services were working on a Windows version to tap the 97 percent of the global PC market that iTunes could not reach out to. Commenting on this, Bernoff, said, "The race has been on since iTunes was launched to produce a similar service for the Windows market."[20]

One such service was BuyMusic.com (BuyMusic), launched by Buy.com, an online retailer, on July 22, 2003. BuyMusic offered 300,000 tracks from five of the major record labels and also from hundreds of independent artists. BuyMusic also operated on a pay per download basis and charged between 79 cents and $1.29 per track. Individual albums were sold at prices ranging from $7.95 to $12. Songs downloaded from this site were in the Windows Media Audio (WMA) format and could be listened to using Windows Media Player (Version 9). Since WMA files could not be transferred over P2P file sharing services, BuyMusic scored over iTunes (which offered MP3 files) in terms of piracy prevention.[21]

The first Windows-based service similar to iTunes, BuyMusic, was expected to take the market by storm. However, this did not happen due to a host of reasons. While BuyMusic marketed itself as a store that sold songs starting from 79 cents, the Web site reportedly had only one song for that price, the prices for the rest of the songs ranged between 99 cents and $1.29. Also, it limited the number of times a song could be burned on CDs (ranging from one to 10 for different songs). It also limited the number of computers and portable MP3 players users could transfer the songs to. Moreover, the songs which were in the WMA format, were reportedly not compatible with many portable digital music players including popular ones like iPod. BuyMusic, reportedly, had many technical glitches as well, such as its search engine not returning results for search queries.

There were other Web sites like Full Audio's MusicNow (improved version) and AOL's MusicNet. Tracks at MusicNow were priced at $1 each, in addition to a monthly subscription of $10. The songs were compatible with Windows, could be burned on a CD and transferred to those portable players which could read WMA files. The Web site also offered good quality radio streaming. However, the collection available was, reportedly, not considered good as it comprised songs mostly from jam bands (those who compose songs by fusion of various music genres—these bands were not as popular as mainstream commercial bands and the quality of their songs was believed to be not very good).

AOL's MusicNet had a library of over 300,000 songs that were offered on a monthly subscription basis. The Web site offered three subscription options: $4 to download and stream 20 songs, $9 to download and stream any number of tracks, and $18 to burn 10 tracks and to download and stream an unlimited number of tracks. However, to access these services, users had to be AOL subscribers. Also, songs from MusicNet could not be transferred to any portable player.

A legal version of the defunct Napster was also expected to be launched by the end of 2003. Reportedly, the new version would feature 500,000 tracks from five of the major record labels and a number of independent artists. Napster planned to offer various options to users, like pay per download, monthly subscription, Internet radio streaming or combinations of these. Napster's comeback was expected to give tough competition to iTunes in 2004. Companies like Microsoft, AOL and Yahoo were also expected to launch similar services by the end of 2003.

Market observers pointed out that though competition seemed to be intensifying for iTunes, until now none of the new services matched it on the user friendliness front. Moreover, the limitations faced by iTunes were considered far less than those experienced by other services. Also, in the short-term, the success of iTunes was believed to be more "symbolic" than in terms of financial viability. A source at Warner Brothers said that Apple's business model had "A real business potential for selling downloads."[22]

Though the market scenario in 2003 seemed bright, analysts at Jupiter Research stated that, despite the hype generated by iTunes, online music sales for 2003 would not generate more than $80 million. Analysts expected the market to grow to $3.8 billion in 2008, as compared to an earlier estimate of $5.1 billion by 2007. However, most industry observers were optimistic and believed that the results shown by iTunes could be the beginning of a revolution long-delayed—a financially viable, legal online music distribution system.

The Future of iTunes—Not Sweet Music All Along

The going seemed to be smooth for iTunes in mid-2003, with the music industry as well as customers apparently happy with the service. Thus, the opposition to iTunes from popular music bands such as Red Hot Chilli Peppers and Metallica, was totally unexpected. These artists argued that they would lose creative control of their albums if companies like Apple were allowed to sell songs individually. In a statement made to Reuters, Mark Reiter of Q Prime Management Company, which managed Red Hot Chili Peppers, Metallica, and many other artists, said, "Our artists would rather not contribute to the demise of the album format."[23]

Analysts refuted this argument saying that if music artists refused to sell individual songs through legal Web sites like iTunes, the consequences would only be adverse. This was because music lovers would inevitably find and download songs through the innumerable file sharing services available on the Internet. Industry observers said that cooperating with legal Web sites was a practical and sensible way of combating piracy.

Supporting this argument was a statement from a Metallica fan, Marc McCoy, who bought two songs of Metallica's latest music album, St. Anger, instead of buying the whole album. Referring to the PC version of Windows, he said, "When iTunes for Windows rears its head, we will see who is in control."[24] Analysts argued that instead of

opposing pay per download Web sites, artists should be able to use this technology for their benefit.

In July 2003, Apple announced that it was preparing to release the Windows version of the iTunes software to address what had been termed as the service's biggest weakness. Analysts observed that with this, Apple's online music business could grow seven-fold Charles Wolf, an analyst at Needham & Co, estimated that through iTunes (with Windows and Mac versions), Apple could capture 20 percent of the pay per download music market. This would translate into $600 million in annual revenues and about $50 million to $60 million in operating income.

Considering the fact that this amount was almost equal to Apple's total profits in 2002 ($65 million), the potential for iTunes seemed immense. Commenting on the above, Wolf said, "Apple is abandoning its strategy of confining its software to the Mac platform. This overdue move will enable it to target its digital entertainment products and services at the entire market, not just the 5 percent Apple currently addresses."[25]

The most positive outcome of the iTunes story, however, would perhaps be that the stranglehold of record companies on the music business would loosen, and the industry would become more artist and customer friendly. Commenting on how iTunes had played a pioneering role in this, one of the world's most successful and popular music stars, Michael Jackson, said, "We should look to new technologies, like Apple's new music store, for solutions. It is the fans that drive the success of the music business; I wish this would not be forgotten."[26]

Questions for Discussion

1. Examine the structure and functioning of the music industry and comment on how technological advancements over the years have impacted its functioning.

2. What were the reasons that led to the emergence of digital music distribution? What steps did the music industry take to address the issue of music piracy in the wake of the growing popularity of P2P services?

3. Examine the advantages and disadvantages of subscription-based services as compared to P2P networks. What were the reasons that contributed to the popularity of P2P services and the failure of subscription-based services?

4. Would you agree that music piracy is more of a behavioral issue on the part of customers than a technological one? Is iTunes the solution to the industry's problems? What were the reasons for the rapid acceptance of iTunes by customers?

5. Given the level of competition in the business of digital distribution of music, which direction is the iTunes Music Store headed in? If you were sitting at the Apple headquarters, what strategy framework would you design to ensure that iTunes sustains the growth momentum it picked up in mid-2003?

Notes

1   "Apple touts iTunes success," www.pcworld.com, June 24, 2003.
2   "Apple touts iTunes success," www.pcworld.com, June 24, 2003.
3   The US-based Apple manufactures and sells personal computers and other personal computing solutions (hardware and software). It owns a network of retail stores

where it sells Apple offerings and third-party products. For the nine-month period ended June 28, 2003, Apple posted $4.49 billion in revenues and a net profit of $25 million. The company, renowned for its innovative products, was ranked ninth among global PC manufacturers and had a 2.1 percent market share in the first quarter of 2003 (2.9 percent in the US).

4   "The Chilli Peppers' sour grapes over iTunes," *BusinessWeek*, July 16, 2003.

5   "Big names ready to rival Apple," www.pcworld.com, June 10, 2003.

6   "Apple touts iTunes success," www.pcworld.com, June 24, 2003.

7   The music industry evolved through adapting itself to many technological innovations over the past century. Media technologies evolved from vinyl to audio cassettes to CDs and mini discs. Technological advances in playback devices helped in this growth through gramophones and large stereo systems to portable digital audio devices.

8   Individual songs are referred to as solos—a collection of such songs forms an "album."

9   Typically, a three-minute song after digital conversion occupied 30 megabytes of computer memory space. By using technologies such as MP3, the 30 MB song file could be compressed into a 3 MB file. This made it easier for Internet browsers to transfer the file in a short span of time.

10   RIAA was a trade group which represented the biggest music record labels like Universal Music, Warner Music, Sony Music, Bertelsmann AG, and the EMI Group.

11   "Music downloads: Is it time to pay?" www.pcworld.com, June 5, 2003.

12   "iTunes for Windows: Coming soon?" www.pcworld.com, June 16, 2003.

13   "iTunes for Windows Coming soon," www.pcworld.com, June 16, 2003.

14   "Where 'think different' is taking Apple," *BusinessWeek*, August 5, 2003.

15   Launched in the early 1980s, the Mac was considered to be a significant technological advancement over the existing computers in the industry as it could provide several functions other than calculation. Although Macs were superior technologically to Windows-based PCs offered by Microsoft, they were not widely used by people due to their high price. Comparatively, Windows-based PCs were cheaper and affordable by most people. Due to its mass appeal, Windows PCs were more popular than Macs. Over the decades, Macs evolved into a niche product, catering to a small segment of loyal customers.

16   "Music downloads: Is it time to pay," www.pcworld.com, June 5, 2003.

17   "Apple unveils online music service," www.pcworld.com, April 28, 2003.

18   "Apple touts iTunes success," www.pcworld.com, June 24, 2003.

19   Launched in January 2001, the iTunes software was used for managing digital audio files for Macs.

20   "BuyMusic.com offers tunes for Windows," www.pcworld.com, July 22, 2003.

21   WMA incorporates an anti-piracy technology called Digital Rights Management (DRM) which prevents users from making copies of music files.

22   "iTunes Music Store 'best news' music industry has had," http://maccentral.mcworld.com, July 21, 2003.

23   "The Chilli Peppers sour grapes over iTunes," *BusinessWeek*, July 16, 2003.

24   "Why iTunes has bands on run," *BusinessWeek*, July 30, 2003.

25   "iTunes store puts company at the forefront of the digital media market," www.sunspot.net, July 24, 2003.

26   "Pop Star Michael Jackson lauds Apple's iTunes," http://maccentral.macworld.com, July 22, 2003.

Additional Readings & References

1.   Gross D Robin, "**Right here right now: The new music industry,**" www.ibslaw.com, 1998,

2.   Prof Parikh, Mihir, **The Music Industry in the Digital World: Waves of Change**, www.ite.poly.edu, June 16, 1999.

3.   Haddad Charles, **Apple's iTunes: Best of Show**, *BusinessWeek*, January 24, 2001.

4.   Mariano Gwendolin, Borland John, **Looking for the Next Napster**, http://news.com.com, July 05, 2001.

5. Pastore Michael, **Online Music Sales Grow: Labels Prepare for Digital Downloads**, http://cyberatlas.internet.com, July 24, 2001.
6. Wilcox Joe, **Apple to Unveil Digital Music Device**, http://news.com.com, October 17, 2001.
7. **Dion's CDs Can Crash PCs**, http://news.bbc.co.uk, April 05, 2002.
8. Leyden John, **Marker Pens, Sticky Tape Crack Music CD Protection**, www.theregister.co.uk, May 05, 2002.
9. **Music Piracy Rises Worldwide**, http://news.bbc.co.uk, June 11, 2002.
10. Borland John, Fried Ian, **Apple Preparing Digital Music Service**, http://news.com.com, March 04, 2003.
11. Salkever Alex, **Apple's Chance to Get Online Music Right**, BusinessWeek, March 12, 2003.
12. Fried Ian, **Apple Tunes Up for Music Pitch**, http://news.com.com, April 21, 2003.
13. Borland John, **Judge: File-Swapping Tools are Legal**, http://zdnet.com.com, April 25, 2003.
14. Borland John, **Apple Unveils Music Store**, http://zdnet.com.com, April 28, 2003.
15. **Apple Launches Online Music Service With Support from Major Record Companies**, www.foxnews.com, April 28, 2003.
16. **Apple Unveils Online Music Service**, www.pcworld.com, April 28, 2003.
17. Hansen Evan, Wilcox Joe, **Apple's Tunes Could Threaten Microsoft**, http://zdnet.com.com, April 30, 2003.
18. Salkever Alex, **Steve Jobs Pied Piper of Online Music**, BusinessWeek, April 30, 2003.
19. Hinson Byron, **iTunes for Windows—Will it Take Off**, www.activewin.com, May 01, 2003.
20. Salkever Alex, **A Talk With iTunes' Conductor**, BusinessWeek, May 07, 2003.
21. **Apple's Continued iTunes Music Store Success Means Staying Ahead of Piracy**, www.macdailynews.com, June 04, 2003.
22. McLaughlin Laurianne, **Music Downloads: Is It Time to Pay**, www.pcworld.com, June 05, 2003.
23. **Big Names Ready to Rival Apple**, www.pcworld.com, June 10, 2003.
24. **iTunes for Windows Coming Soon**, www.pcworld.com, June 16, 2003.
25. **Apple Touts iTunes Success**, www.pcworld.com, June 24, 2003.
26. **New Offensive Against Swappers**, www.arabtimesonline.com, June 28, 2003.
27. DeLong Ve James, **Musical Scares**, www.techcentralstation.com, July 01, 2003.
28. Colliano Del Jerry, **Metallica Disses Apple iTunes**, www.audiorevolution.com, July 09, 2003.
29. Teather David, **Music Industry Hails Drop in Piracy**, www.guardian.co.uk, July 15, 2003.
30. Haddad Charles, **The Chili Peppers' Sour Grapes Over iTunes**, BusinessWeek, July 16, 2003.
31. Gowan Michael, **Apple's iTunes Music Store is a Winner**, www.pcworld.com, July 2003.
32. Cohen Peter, **iTunes Music Store "Best News" Music Industry Has Had**, http://maccentral.macworld.com, July 21, 2003.
33. Cohen Peter, **Pop star Michael Jackson lauds iTunes Music Store**, http://maccentral.macworld.com, July 22, 2003.
34. **BuyMusic.com offers Tunes for Windows**, www.pcworld.com, July 22, 2003.
35. Zeiler David, **Apple's Music Lessons**, www.sunspot.net, July 24, 2003.
36. Levitus Bob, **BuyMusic Isn't Comparable to Mac's iTunes**, www.chron.com, July 25, 2003.
37. Harwood Susie, **Napster 2.0 to Launch for Christmas**, www.netimperative.com, July 29, 2003.
38. Haddad Charles, **Why iTunes has Bands on the Run**, BusinessWeek, July 30, 2003.
39. Gibson Owen, **Legal Downloads Won't Make Up for Drop in CD Sales, Record Labels Told**, www.guardian.co.uk, July 30, 2003.
40. www.ifpi.org

Case 1–4: Wal-Mart Stores Inc.*

As recently as 1979, Wal-Mart had been a regional retailer little known outside the South with only 229 discount stores compared to the industry leader Kmart's 1,891 stores. In less than 25 years, Wal-Mart had risen to become the largest U.S. corporation in sales. With over $258 billion (see Exhibits 1 and 2) in revenues Wal-Mart had far eclipsed Kmart, whose sales had fallen to a fraction of Wal-Mart's. Yet another measure of Wal-Mart's dominance was that it accounted for approximately 17 percent of general merchandise, apparel, and furniture sales in the United States by 1996[1] and as much as 30 percent of goods such as hair products and disposable diapers. *Forbes* put Wal-Mart's success into perspective:

> With 3,550 stores in the U.S. and 1,000 Supercenters to be added in the next five years, all that's left for Wal-Mart is mop-up. It already sells more toys than Toys "R" Us, more clothes than the Gap and Limited combined and more food than Kroger. If it were its own economy, Wal-Mart Stores would rank 30th in the world, right behind Saudi Arabia. Growing at 11 percent a year, Wal-Mart would hit half a trillion dollars in sales by early in the next decade.[2]

The central question facing Wal-Mart, however, was how to continue its remarkable growth (see Exhibit 3). Many observers believed that Wal-Mart was facing a maturing market and would no longer see the growth rates it had enjoyed previously. Domestic growth opportunities in its core business, discount retail centers, were largely limited to the Northeast and West Coast—areas that were notorious for their high costs and mobilization of neighborhood opposition to new Wal-Marts. Supercenters had provided significant growth for Wal-Mart, but it was not clear how long they could deliver the company's customary growth rates. Wal-Mart faced problems in other business areas as well. The Wal-Mart-owned Sam's Club warehouse stores had not measured up to Costco, its leading competitor. International operations were another challenge for Wal-Mart. Faced with slowing growth domestically, it had tried to capitalize on international opportunities. These international efforts, however, had met with only mixed success at best.

Wal-Mart was also a target for critics who attacked its record on social issues.[3] Wal-Mart had been blamed for pushing production from the United States to low-wage overseas producers. Some claimed that Wal-Mart had almost single-handedly depressed wage growth in the U.S. economy. Democratic presidential candidates John Kerry and Howard Dean had both singled out Wal-Mart for criticism in the 2004 U.S. presidential campaign. For many, Wal-Mart had become a symbol of capitalism that had run out of control. Indeed, *Time* magazine asked, "Will Wal-Mart Steal Christmas?"[4] Much of the criticism directed at Wal-Mart did not go beyond angry rhetoric. In many cases, however, Wal-Mart had faced stiff community opposition to building new stores.

With such challenges, some investment analysts questioned whether it was even possible for a company like Wal-Mart, with over $250 billion in sales, to sustain its accustomed high growth rates. To do so, Wal-Mart would have to address a number of challenges such as maturing markets, competition in discount retailing from both traditional competitors and specialty retailers, aggressive efforts by competitors to imitate Wal-Mart's products and processes, and international expansion. Indeed, some believed that Wal-Mart would need to find new businesses if it were to continue its historic success.

The Discount Retail Industry

General retailing in the United States evolved dramatically during the twentieth century. Before 1950, general retailing most often took the form of Main Street department stores. These stores typically sold a wide variety of general merchandise. Department stores were also different from other retailers in that they emphasized service and credit. Before World War II, few stores allowed customers to take goods directly from shelves. Instead, sales clerks served customers at store counters. Not until the 1950s did self-help department stores begin to spread. Discount retail stores also began to emerge in the late 1950s. Discount retailers emphasized low prices and generally offered less service, credit, and return privileges. Their growth was spawned by the repeal of fair trade laws in many states. Many states had passed such laws during the Depression to protect local grocers from chains such as the Atlantic & Pacific Company. The laws fixed prices so that local merchants could not be undercut on price. The repeal of these laws freed discounters to offer prices below the manufacturer's suggested retail price.

*This case was prepared by William Hesterly for the purpose of classroom discussion.

Exhibit 1   Wal-Mart Stores, Inc., Earnings Statement, 1999–2004

Year Ended	1/31/04	1/31/03	1/31/02	1/31/01	1/31/00
Net Sales	256,329	229,616	204,011	191,329	165,013
Other Income	2,352	1,961	1,812	1,787	1,796
Rental Income	—	—	—	—	—
Total Revenue	**258,681**	**231,577**	**205,823**	**193,116**	**166,809**
Cost of Sales	198,747	178,299	159,097	150,255	129,664
General & Admin.	44,909	39,983	35,147	31,550	27,040
Debt Interest	729	799	1,080	1,104	756
Capital Lease Exp.	267	260	274	279	266
Interest Income	(164)	(132)	(171)	(188)	—
Total Operating Expense	**244,488**	**219,209**	**195,427**	**183,000**	**157,726**
Operating Income	**14,193**	**12,368**	**10,396**	**10,116**	**9,083**
Net Income Before Taxes	**14,193**	**12,368**	**10,396**	**10,116**	**9,083**
Provision for Income Taxes	5,118	4,357	3,765	3,692	3,338
Net Income After Taxes	**9,075**	**8,011**	**6,631**	**6,424**	**5,745**
Minority Interest	(214)	(193)	(183)	(129)	(170)
Net Income Before Extra. Items	8,861	7,818	6,448	6,295	5,575
Income from Discont.	193	137	144	—	—
Accounting Change	—	0.00	0.00	0.00	(198)
Net Income	**9,054**	**7,955**	**6,592**	**6,295**	**5,377**
Income Available to Com Excl ExtraOrd	**8,861**	**7,818**	**6,448**	**6,295**	**5,575**
Income Available to Com Incl ExtraOrd	**9,054**	**7,955**	**6,592**	**6,295**	**5,377**
Basic Weighted Average Shares	4,363	4,430	4,465	4,465	4,451
Basic EPS Excluding ExtraOrdinary Items	**2.03**	**1.76**	**1.44**	**1.41**	**1.25**
Basic EPS Including ExtraOrdinary Items	**2.08**	**1.80**	**1.48**	**1.41**	**1.21**
Dilution Adjustment	0.00	0.00	0.00	0.00	0.00
Diluted Net Income	9,054	7,955	6,592	6,295	5,377
Diluted Weighted Average Shares	4,373	4,446	4,481	4,484	4,474
Diluted EPS Excluding ExtraOrd. Items	**2.03**	**1.76**	**1.44**	**1.40**	**1.25**
Diluted EPS Including ExtraOrd. Items	**2.07**	**1.79**	**1.47**	**1.40**	**1.20**
DPS-Common Stock	0.36	0.30	0.28	0.24	0.20
Gross Dividends-Common Stock	1,569	1,328	1,249	1,070	890

Exhibit 2   Wal-Mart Stores, Inc., Balance Sheet, 1999–2004

Year Ended	1/31/04	1/31/03	1/31/02	1/31/01	1/31/00
Cash/Equivalents	5,199	2,736	2,161	2,054	1,856
Receivables	1,254	1,569	2,000	1,768	1,341
Inv.-Replac.Cost	—	—	22,749	21,644	20,171
LIFO Reserve	—	—	(135)	(202)	(378)
Prepaid Expenses	1,356	837	1,103	1,291	1,366
Recoverable Cost	—	—	—	—	—
Inventories	26,612	24,401	—	—	—
Assets Discont.	0.00	1,179	—	—	—
Total Current Assets	34,421	30,722	27,878	26,555	24,356
Land	12,699	11,202	10,241	9,433	8,785
Building	38,966	33,345	28,527	24,537	21,169
Fixtures	17,861	15,640	14,135	12,964	10,362
Trans. Equipment	1,269	1,099	1,089	879	747
Depreciation	(15,594)	(13,116)	(11,436)	(10,196)	(8,224)
Net Leases	—	—	—	—	—
Capital Leases	5,092	4,814	4,626	4,620	4,285
Amortization	(1,763)	(1,610)	(1,432)	(1,303)	(1,155)
Goodwill/Intang.	9,882	9,389	8,566	9,059	9,392
Other	2,079	2,594	1,333	1,582	632
Assets Discont.	0.00	729	—	—	—
Total Assets	104,912	94,808	83,527	78,130	70,349
Commercial Paper	3,267	1,079	743	2,286	3,323
Accounts Payable	19,332	16,829	15,617	15,092	13,105
Accrued Liabs.	10,342	8,857	7,174	6,355	6,161
Accrued Taxes	1,377	748	1,343	841	1,129
Cur.Port.LT Debt	2,904	4,536	2,257	4,234	1,964
Cur.Port.Cap.Lse.	196	176	148	141	121
Short Term Debt	—	—	—	—	—
Liabs. Discont.	0.00	294	—	—	—
Total Current Liabilities	37,418	32,519	27,282	28,949	25,803
Long Term Debt	17,102	16,597	15,687	12,501	13,672
Capital Leases	2,997	3,000	3,045	3,154	3,002
Total Long Term Debt	20,099	19,597	18,732	15,655	16,674
Liabs. Discont.	0.00	10	—	—	—
Deferred Taxes	2,288	1,859	1,204	1,043	759
Minority Inter.	1,484	1,362	1,207	1,140	1,279
Total Liabilities	61,289	55,347	48,425	46,787	44,515
Common Stock	431	440	445	447	446
Paid In Capital	2,135	1,954	1,484	1,411	714
Retained Erngs.	40,206	37,576	34,441	30,169	25,129
Other Comprehen.	851	(509)	(1,268)	—	—
Trans. Adjust.	—	—	—	(684)	(455)
Total Equity	43,623	39,461	35,102	31,343	25,834
Total Liabilities & Shareholders' Equity	104,912	94,808	83,527	78,130	70,349
S/O-Common Stock	4,311	4,395	4,453	4,470	4,457
Total Common Shares Outstanding	4,311	4,395	4,453	4,470	4,457
T/S-Common Stock	—	—	—	—	—
Total Preferred Shares Outstanding	—	—	—	—	—
Employees	1,500,000	1,400,000	1,383,000	1,244,000	1,140,000
Number of Common Shareholders	333,604	330,000	324,000	317,000	307,000

Among discount retailers, there were both general and specialty chains. General chains carried a wide assortment of hard and soft goods. Specialty retailers, on the other hand, focused on a fairly narrow range of goods such as office products or sporting goods. Specialty discount retailers such as Office Depot, Home Depot, Staples, and Circuit City began to enjoy widespread success in the 1980s. One result of the emergence of both general and specialty discount retailers was the decline of some of the best known traditional retailers. Moderate-priced retailers such

Exhibit 3   Wal-Mart Stores, Inc., Performance by Segment

Wal-Mart Stores Segment

Fiscal Year	Segment Net Sales Increase from Prior Fiscal Year	Segment Operating Income (in Billions)	Segment Operating Income Increase from Prior Year	Operating Income as a Percentage of Segment Sales
2003	**12.9%**	**$ 11.9**	**16.2%**	**7.6%**
2002	14.1%	$ 10.2	6.3%	7.3%
2001	12.1%	$ 9.6	10.5%	7.9%

SAM'S CLUB Segment

Fiscal Year	Segment Net Sales Increase from Prior Fiscal Year	Segment Operating Income (in Billions)	Segment Operating Income Increase from Prior Year	Operating Income as a Percentage of Segment Sales
2003	**7.8%**	**$ 1.028**	**0.0%**	**3.2%**
2002	9.7%	$ 1.028	9.1%	3.5%
2001	8.1%	$ 0.942	10.8%	3.5%

Net Sales

The Company and each of its operating segments had net sales (in millions) for the three fiscal years ended January 31, 2003 as follows:

Fiscal Year	Wal-Mart Stores	SAM'S CLUB	International	Other	Total Company	Total Company Increase from Prior Fiscal Year
2003	**$ 157,121**	**$ 31,702**	**$ 40,794**	**$ 14,907**	**$ 244,524**	**12%**
2002	139,131	29,395	35,485	13,788	217,799	14%
2001	121,889	26,798	32,100	10,542	191,329	16%

as Sears and JCPenney had seen their market share decline in response to the rise of discount stores.

A number of factors explained why discount retailers had enjoyed such success at the expense of general old-line retailers. Consumers' greater concern for value, broadly defined, was perhaps most central. Value in the industry was not precisely defined, but involved price, service, quality, and convenience. One example of this value orientation was in apparel. Consumers who once shunned the private label clothing lines found in discount stores as a source of stigma were increasingly buying labels such as Wal-Mart's Kathie Lee line. According to one estimate, discount stores were enjoying double-digit growth in apparel while clothing sales in department stores had decreased by 3 percent since 1991.[5]

Another aspect of consumers' concern for value involved price. Retail consumers had shown a greater sensitivity to price than in the pre-1990s period. They were less reliant on established brand names in a wide variety of goods and showed a greater willingness to purchase the private label brands of firms such as JCPenney, Sears, Kmart, and Wal-Mart. Convenience had also taken on greater importance for customers. As demographics shifted to include more working mothers and longer workweeks, many American workers placed a greater emphasis on fast, efficient shopping trips. More consumers desired "one-stop shopping" where a

broad range of goods were available in one store, to minimize the time they spent shopping. This trend accelerated in the 1990s with the spread of supercenters. Supercenters, which combined traditional discount retail stores with supermarkets under one roof, grew to more than $100 billion in sales by 2001 and blurred some of the traditional lines in retailing.

Larger firms had an advantage in discount retailing. The number of multistore chains had risen dramatically. Also, the number of retail business failures had risen markedly in the mid-1990s. Most of these failures were individual stores and small chains, but some discount chains such as Venture, Bradlee, and Caldor had filed for bankruptcy. Large size enabled firms to spread their overhead costs over more stores. Larger firms were also able to distribute their advertising costs over a broader base. Perhaps the greatest advantage of size, however, was in relationships with suppliers. Increased size led to savings in negotiating price reductions but it also helped in other important ways. Suppliers were more likely to engage in arrangements with large store chains such as cooperative advertising and electronic data interchange links.

The Internet posed a greater threat to discount retailers as more people became comfortable with shopping online. By 2004, the number of Internet users had increased dramatically over the nearly 37 million users just eight years earlier. Internet shopping was appealing because of the convenience and selection available, but perhaps the most attractive aspect was the competitive pricing. Some Internet retailers were able to offer steep discounts because of lower overhead costs. Additionally, customers were able to quickly compare prices between different Internet retailers. Despite the great promise of Internet retailing, however, only a few specialty retailers had been profitable. Many traditional retailers had either initiated their own Web sites or had plans to do so.

Large discount retailers such as Wal-Mart derived considerable purchasing clout with suppliers because of their immense size. Even many of the company's largest suppliers gained a high proportion of their sales from Wal-Mart (see Exhibit 4). Suppliers with over $1 billion in sales such as Newell, Fruit of the Loom, Rubbermaid, Sunbeam, and Fieldcrest Cannon received over 15 percent of their sales from Wal-Mart. Many of these large manufacturers also sold a substantial proportion of their output to Kmart, Target, and other discount retailers. Frequently, smaller manufacturers were even more reliant on the large discount retailers such as Wal-Mart. For example, Wal-Mart accounted for as much as 50 percent of revenues for many smaller suppliers.

Private label goods offered by discount stores had become much more important in the 1990s and presented new challenges in supplier relationships. Managing private labels required a high level of coordination between designers and manufacturers (who were often foreign). Investment in systems that could track production and inventory were also necessary.

Technology investments in sophisticated inventory management systems, state-of-the-art distribution centers, and other aspects of logistics were seen as critically important for all discount retailers. Discount retailers were spending large sums on computer and telecommunications technology in order to lower their costs in these areas. The widespread use of Universal Product Codes (UPC) allowed

Exhibit 4   Proportion of Sales that Suppliers Receive from Wal-Mart

Revenues	Total 1995	from Wal-Mart	Operating Margin	12-month price change
Newell/housewares, home furnishings	$2,498	15%	20.7%	17%
Fruit of the Loom/apparel	2,478	16%	17.0	300%
Rubbermaid/plastic and rubber products	2,329	15	20.7	−10
Springs Industries/finished fabrics, home furnishings	2,233	12	10.9	10
Westpoint Stevens/linens, home furnishings	1,651	10	1.3	43
Sunbeam/household appliances	1,202	17	10.7	−33
Fieldcrest Cannon/linens, home furnishings	1,095	18	9.4	−13
First Brands/household products	1,053	12	15	38
Coleman/recreational gear	902	10+	14.7	12
Huffy/recreational gear	685	10+	4.6	−31
Roadmaster Industries/recreational gear	675	28	8	−37
Paragon Trade Brands/diapers	519	15	12.7	90
Playtex Products/personal care products	471	15	28.8	10
Ekco Group/housewares	270	10+	17.8	−2
Royal Appliance Manufacturing/vacuum cleaners	270	23	7	−19
Crown Crafts/textiles, home furnishings	214	16	12.3	−39
Armor All Products/auto polishes, protectants	204	20	20.5	−23
Toastmaster/home appliances	187	30	7.3	−38
Windmere/personal care products	185	18	10.6	−4
National Presto Industries/home appliances	123	35	19.8	3
Empire of Carolina/toys	119	17	5.6	−11
General Housewares/household products	117	13	10.6	−32
Safety lst/child safety products	70	18	16.9	−50
National Picture & Frame/frames, mirrors	61	36	14.2	−3
Ohio Art/toys	43	20	5.9	48

Dollar amounts are in millions.

Source: Forbes, March 11, 1996.

retailers to more accurately track inventories for shop-keeping units (SKUs) and better match inventory to demand. Discount retailers also used electronic data interchange (EDI) to shorten the distribution cycle. EDI involved the electronic transmission of sales and inventory data from the registers and computers of discounters directly to suppliers' computers. Often replenishment of inventories was triggered without human intervention. Thus, EDI removed the need for several intermediate steps in procurement such as data entry by the discounter, ordering by purchasers, data entry by the supplier, and even some production scheduling by supplier managers. Wal-Mart was also pushing the adoption of radio frequency identification (RFID), a new technology for tracking and identifying products. RFID promised to eliminate the need for employees to scan UPC codes and would also dramatically reduce shrinkage, another term for shoplifting and employee pilferage. In November of 2003, Wal-Mart announced that large suppliers would have until January 2005 to implement RFID while smaller suppliers would have until January 2006. Suppliers anticipated that RFID would be costly to implement, but the benefits for Wal-Mart were estimated to be as high as $8 billion in labor savings and $2 billion in reducing shrinkage.

Another important aspect of managing inventory was accurate forecasting. Having the right quantity of products in the correct stores was essential to success. Stories of retailers having an abundance of snow sleds in Florida stores while stores in other areas with heavy snowfall had none were common examples of the challenges in managing inventory. Discounters used variables such as past store sales, the presence of competition, variation in seasonal demand, and year-to-year calendar changes to arrive at their forecasts.

Point-of-sale (POS) scanning enabled retailers to gain information for any purchase on the dollar amount of the purchase, category of merchandise, color, vendor, and SKU number. POS scanning, while valuable in managing inventory, was also seen as a potentially significant marketing tool. Databases of such information offered retailers the potential to "micromarket" to their customers. Upscale department stores had used the POS database marketing more extensively than discounters. Wal-Mart, however, had used such information. For example, POS data showed that customers who purchased children's videos typically bought more than one. Based on this finding, Wal-Mart emphasized placing other children's videos near displays of hot-selling videos.

Competitors

Competition in discount retailing came from both general and specialty discount stores. Among the general discount retailers, Wal-Mart was the largest, followed by Target and Kmart. Kmart had nearly 10 times more sales than the next-largest retailers Dollar General and ShopKo (see Exhibit 5). The most formidable specialty discount retailers included office supply chains such as Office Depot with over $12 billion in sales and Staples with approximately $13 billion, Toys "R" Us with over $11 billion, Circuit City in electronics with nearly $10 billion, and Payless Shoesource with almost $3 billion. In warehouse clubs, Costco and Sam's Club dominated. Costco was the leader with over $42 billion in sales, followed by Sam's Warehouse Club. No other warehouse club chains had sales of even one-sixth of Sam's Club. Wal-Mart was the leader in supercenter chains with more than double the sales of the number-two firm in the category, Grand Rapids, Michigan–based Meijer. Meijer was followed by Fred Meyer, the pioneer in the supercenter format, and by Super Kmart Centers.

Once Wal-Mart's largest competitor, Kmart had experienced a long slide in performance. Kmart operated approximately 1,500 stores at the beginning of 2004 and had sales of $23 billion in 2003, down from $36 billion just four years earlier. Traditionally, Kmart's discount philosophy had differed from Wal-Mart's. Kmart discount centers sought to price close to, but not necessarily lower than, Wal-Mart's everyday low prices. More emphasis was placed on sale items at Kmart. Pricing strategy revolved around several key items that were advertised in Kmart's 73 million advertising circulars distributed in newspapers each Sunday. These items were priced sharply lower than competitors' prices. The effective implementation of this

Exhibit 5   Discount Department Store Industry Comparisons

	Kmart	Wal-Mart	Target	JCPenney	Sears	Discount Store Average
Sales per Sq. Ft.	$ 201	$ 334	$ 225	$ 174	$ 375	$ 253
Comp. Sales Growth	2.50%	4.90%	6.00%	3.40%	5.80%	3.50%
Total Selling Sq. Ft.(millions)	156	252	79	135	83	NA
Total Stores	2,261	2,558	735	4,084	3,372	NA

Source: Kmart annual report and Wal-Mart 10K.

strategy had been impeded by Kmart's difficulty in keeping shelves stocked with sale items and by Wal-Mart's willingness to match Kmart's sale prices. An attempt to imitate Wal-Mart's everyday low pricing strategy failed to deliver sales growth at the same time it squeezed margins, so Kmart returned to its traditional pricing strategy in 2003.

Performance at Kmart had suffered dramatically in the 1990s. It experienced losses of over $300 million from 1993 to 1995 and by 1995 had seen its debt rating fall below investment grade. Various attempts to revitalize the company had fallen short of restoring profitability. A restructuring that closed over 200 stores in the mid-1990s and shuttered another 600 stores in 2002-2003 did not result in profitability in any year from 2001 to 2004. Sales per square foot dropped to $212 in 2002, which was down from $236 a year earlier. By 2004, there was some indication that all the restructuring might have eventually paid off as Kmart reported profitability in the first three quarters of the year. It was still plagued, however, by declining same-store sales. Some suggested that Kmart's primary goal was to serve as a cash cow for ESL Investments, Inc., and its founder Eddie Lampert. Assisted by $3.8 billion in accumulated tax credits, Kmart had generated over $2 billion in positive cash flow in the first three quarters of 2004. The presumption was cash would be used to fund other investments by ESL.[6]

Kmart sought to follow Wal-Mart's pattern in many of its activities. The company expressed a commitment to building a strong culture that emphasized performance, teamwork, and respect for individuals who, borrowing from Wal-Mart, were referred to as associates. Establishing such a culture was particularly challenging in the midst of workforce reductions that had taken Kmart from 373,000 employees in 1990 to 307,000 at the end of 1995, and then an even more precipitous drop to 158,000 in 2004. Kmart had also adopted Wal-Mart departmental structure within stores. Another area in which Kmart emulated Wal-Mart was in offering larger income potential to store managers. Each store manager's bonus was linked to an index of customer satisfaction. Kmart had also sought to close the gap between it and Wal-Mart in technology and distribution. The company made large information technology investments in the mid-1990s.

Although it had been criticized for several years for being slow to adapt, Kmart had shown a new aggressiveness in exploring new store concepts beginning in the mid-1990s. Developing new formats was the company's highest strategic priority. Like Wal-Mart, Kmart had begun to emphasize supercenters (combination supermarkets and discount centers). The first Super Kmart Center was opened in 1992. Kmart had also experimented with another store format in 1995 and subsequently converted a majority of its stores to this format. Dubbed the Big Kmart or high-frequency format, it involved converting traditional stores to a new format which changed the appearance, layout, and product mix of stores. The Big Kmart format emphasized frequently purchased products such as paper goods, dry groceries, soaps, and other consumable items. In both the supercenters and the Big Kmart format, Kmart's goal was to price high-frequency items 1 to 3 percent below leading competitors.

Kmart's strategy in 2004 focused on three major initiatives. First, it defined itself as "the store of the neighborhood." Ethnic groups such as Asians and African Americans were a particular focus of Kmart's neighborhood strategy. Individual store managers were given greater autonomy to customize their merchandise assortments to suit local community needs. A second emphasis in Kmart's strategy was on exclusive branded products. Its most prominent brands included Martha Stewart in home products, Jaclyn Smith and Kathy Ireland in women's apparel, and Route 66 in men's and women's apparel. The "top sellers" program also focused on improving sales and in-stock positions for each of the store's top 300 selling items. Additionally, with further testing of the "store of the future" prototype, significant improvements in the customer shopping experience were expected. The third prong in Kmart's strategy was to further rationalize its operations. Kmart intended to focus more on higher-performing products and to continue to eliminate underperforming stock-keeping units (SKUs) and reallocate shelf space to more profitable items. The company claimed that it had significantly improved the inventory management practices around forecasting and replenishment that had plagued it so often in the past. These practices were particularly critical to a focus on highly advertised products.

Target, Wal-Mart's other large national competitor, was owned by Target Corporation, formerly Dayton Hudson Corporation, based in Minneapolis, Minnesota. Along with Target, the corporation owned Mervyn's, a middle-market promotional department store. It also owned other upscale department stores including Marshall Fields, which operated in several midwestern states. In 2003, Target's 1,225 stores accounted for $41.3 billion of Target Corporation's $48.2 billion in sales and $3.5 billion of its $3.7 billion in profits. Target operated stores in 47 states including 119 SuperTarget stores in 19 states. Target was considered an "upscale discounter." The median income of Target shoppers was $57,000 and more than 75 percent had attended or completed college.[7] Target attracted a more affluent clientele through a more trendy and upscale product mix and through a store ambience that differed from most discounters in aspects such as wider aisles and brighter lighting. Target had also introduced a proprietary credit card, the Target Guest Card, to differentiate it from other discounters. Pricing at Target was generally not as low as Wal-Mart but was lower than middle-market department stores such as JCPenney and Mervyn's. As with Wal-Mart and Kmart, supercenters were also high on Target's list of strategic priorities. The supercenters, named SuperTargets, had opened in many cities and the company planned to aggressively grow in this area. Promotions were an important part of Target's marketing approach. Each week over 100 million Target advertising circulars were distributed in Sunday newspapers. Holiday promotions were also emphasized at Target. Like Kmart, Target had traditionally focused much of its effort on metropolitan areas. In the late 1990s, over half of its stores were in 30 metropolitan markets. Target's philanthropic activities gave it greater visibility. Each year, the company gave 5 percent of its pretax earnings to nonprofit organizations. St. Jude Children's Research Hospital and local schools were perhaps Targest's highest philanthropic priorities.

Wal-Mart's History

Wal-Mart was started in 1962 by Sam Walton. The discount retail industry was then in its infancy. A couple of regional firms had experimented with discount retailing, but that year three major retail firms joined Wal-Mart in entering the discount industry. Kresge Corporation started Kmart, Dayton Hudson began Target, and the venerable F.W. Woolworth initiated Woolco. Sam Walton had been the most successful franchisee in the Ben Franklin variety store chain, but discount stores threatened the success of his 18 stores. Walton was convinced that discount retailing would have a bright future even though most in the industry were highly skeptical of the concept. Indeed, Walton was quickly rebuffed in his efforts to convince Ben Franklin and others to provide financial backing for his proposed venture into discounting. With no major chains willing to back him, Walton risked his home and all his property to secure financing for the first Wal-Mart in Rogers, Arkansas.

Of the four new ventures in discount retailing started that year, Wal-Mart seemed the least likely to succeed. Most Wal-Mart stores were in northwestern Arkansas and adjacent areas of Oklahoma, Missouri, and Kansas. Walton had started his retailing career with Ben Franklin in small towns because his wife Helen did not want to live in any city with a population of over 10,000 people. He had chosen northwestern Arkansas as a base because it allowed him to take advantage of the quail-hunting season in four states. Wal-Mart was, in Sam Walton's words, "underfinanced and undercapitalized"[8] in the beginning. Nevertheless, Walton sought to grow Wal-Mart as fast as he could because he feared new competitors would preempt growth opportunities if Wal-Mart did not open stores in new towns. After five years, Wal-Mart had 19 stores and sales of $9 million. In contrast, Kmart had 250 stores and $800 million in sales.

Walton retained many of the practices regarding customer service and satisfaction that he had learned in the variety stores business. The central focus of Wal-Mart, however, was on price. Walton sought to make Wal-Mart the low-priced provider of any product it sold. As Walton said,

What we were obsessed with was keeping our prices below everybody else's. Our dedication to that idea was total. Everybody worked like crazy to keep the expenses down. We didn't have systems. We didn't have ordering programs. We didn't have a basic merchandise assortment. We certainly didn't have any sort of computers. In fact, when I look at it today, I realize that so much of what we did in the beginning was really poorly done. But we managed to sell our merchandise as low as we possibly could and that kept us right-side up for the first ten years. . . . The idea was simple: when customers thought of Wal-Mart, they should think of low prices and satisfaction guaranteed. They could be pretty sure they wouldn't find it any cheaper anywhere else, and if they didn't like it, they could bring it back.[9]

By 1970, Wal-Mart had expanded to 30 stores in the small towns of Arkansas, Missouri, and Oklahoma. Sam Walton, however, was personally several million dollars in debt. For Wal-Mart to expand beyond its small region required an infusion of capital beyond what the Walton family could provide. Walton thus decided to offer Wal-Mart stock publicly. The initial public offering yielded nearly $5 million in capital. By the early 1990s, 100 shares of that initial stock offering would increase in value from $1,650 to over $3,000,000.

The other problem that plagued Wal-Mart in its early years was finding a way to keep its costs down. Large vendors were reluctant to call on Wal-Mart and, when they did do business with the company, they would dictate the price and quantity of what they sold. Walton described the situation as , "I don't mind saying that we were the victims of a good bit of arrogance from a lot of vendors in those days. They didn't need us, and they acted that way."[10] Another problem that contributed to high costs was distribution. Distributors did not service Wal-Mart with the same care that they did its larger competitors. Walton saw that "the only alternative was to build our own warehouse so we could buy in volume at attractive prices and store the merchandise."[11]

Wal-Mart increased from 32 stores in 1970 to 859 stores 15 years later. For much of that time Wal-Mart retained its small-town focus. Over half its stores were in towns with populations of under 25,000. Because of its small-town operations, Wal-Mart was not highly visible to many others in the retail industry. By 1985, though, that had changed. *Forbes* named Sam Walton the richest man in America. Furthermore, Wal-Mart had begun to expand from its small town base in the South and had established a strong presence in several large cities. By the 1990s, it had spread throughout the United States in both large cities and small towns.

Wal-Mart in 2004

By the beginning of 2004, Wal-Mart's activities had spread beyond its historical roots in domestic discount centers (see Exhibits 6–8). The number of domestic discount centers had declined to 1,568 from a high 1,995 in 1996. Many discount centers had been converted to supercenters, which had almost tripled in the previous five years to 1,251 stores. Wal-Mart Supercenters combined full-line supermarkets and discount centers into one store. Wal-Mart also operated 525 Sam's Clubs, which were warehouse membership clubs. In 1999, Wal-Mart opened its first Neighborhood Markets, which were supermarkets, and it had 49 in operation by 2004.

Operations

From its beginning, Wal-Mart had focused on everyday low prices (EDLP). EDLP saved on advertising costs and on labor costs since employees did not have to rearrange stock before and after sales. The company changed its traditional slogan, "Always the Lowest Price," in the 1990s to "Always Low Prices. Always." Despite the change in slogan, however, Wal-Mart continued to price goods lower than its competitors. When faced with a decline in profits in the late 1990s, Wal-Mart considered raising margins.[12] Instead of pricing 7 to 8 percent below competitors, some managers believed that pricing only about 6 percent below would raise gross margins without jeopardizing sales. Some investment analysts believed that raising prices would not only boost Wal-Mart's profits but Kmart's also. Other managers and board members, however, were skeptical that price hikes would work at Wal-Mart. They reasoned that Wal-Mart's culture and identity were so closely attached to low prices that broad price increases would clash with the company's bedrock beliefs. It would be difficult to convince managers and associates who had prided themselves on Wal-Mart's low-price philosophy that higher prices were needed. Another concern was that competitors might seize any opportunity to narrow the gap with Wal-Mart.

Wal-Mart had pioneered the use of technology in retail operations for many years and still possessed significant advantages over its competitors. It was the leader in forging EDI links with suppliers. Its Retail Link technology gave over 3,200 vendors POS data and authorization to replace inventory for approximately 2,000 stores.[13] The fine-tuning of its Retail Link system allowed Wal-Mart to reduce inventory by 25 percent of SKUs while still increasing sales in the mid-1990s. Competitors traditionally faced high costs in developing a proprietary EDI system to rival Wal-Mart's. Connecting seamlessly with a large number of suppliers was a daunting task given the complexity and cost of dealing with a large variety of computer and information systems. A recent trend, however, was emergence of intermediaries who provided EDI links between purchasers and suppliers. With the inter-

mediaries, retailers could simply send all their EDI data to one source and various manufacturers could also reduce their difficulties in connecting with a large number of buyers by using one intermediary for transactions with many customers. Such intermediaries also made EDI a more feasible alternative for smaller retailers, who lacked the scale necessary to implement their own EDI systems. In August 2002, Wal-Mart informed suppliers that they would be required to do EDI exchanges over the Internet using AS2, a software package from Isoft Corp. The software package cost as little at $300 for suppliers to connect only with Wal-Mart, though a typical installation could cost much more. Some suppliers were given as little as six weeks to be fully operable on AS2. The transition to Internet-based EDI was nearly complete by November 2003 with 98 percent of Wal-Mart's EDI exchanges taking place over the Internet.[14] Competitors had responded to Wal-Mart's advantage in logistics and EDI by forming cooperative exchanges, but, despite their efforts, a large gap remained between Wal-Mart and its competitors.[15] As a result, Wal-Mart possessed a substantial advantage in information about supply and demand, which reduced both the number of items that were either overstocked or out of stock.

November 2003 was also notable for another Wal-Mart technological initiative. It announced plans to implement radio frequency identification (RFID) to all products by January 2005. Smaller suppliers were given an extra year to comply with this demand. RFID, as its name implies, involves the use of tags that transmitt radio signals. It had the potential to track inventory more precisely than traditional methods and to eventually reduce much of the labor involved in activities such as manually scanning bar codes for incoming goods. Some analysts estimated that Wal-Mart's cost savings from RFID could run as high $8 billion.[16]

Technology was only one area where Wal-Mart exploited advantages through its relationships with suppliers. Wal-Mart's clout was clearly evident in the payment terms it had with its suppliers. Suppliers frequently offered 2 percent discounts to customers who paid their bills within 15 days. Wal-Mart typically paid its bills at close to 30 days from the time of purchase but still usually received a 2 percent discount on the gross amount of an invoice rather than the net amount.[17] Several suppliers had attributed performance problems to Wal-Mart's actions. Rubbermaid, for example, had enjoyed rapid growth in revenue and profits before 1995. In 1995, however, it experienced higher raw materials costs. Wal-Mart and other large discount retailers, however, did not allow Rubbermaid to pass its higher costs along in the form of higher prices. At the same time, Wal-Mart gave more shelf space to Rubbermaid's lower-cost competitors. As a result, Rubbermaid's profits dropped by 30 percent and it was forced to cut its workforce by over 1,000 employees.[18] Besides pushing for low prices, the large discounters also required

Exhibit 6   Wal-Mart's Store Count in the United States, end of year, 1996

State	Wal-Mart Stores	Supercenters	Sam's Clubs
Alabama	65	11	8
Alaska	3		3
Arizona	31		6
Arkansas	58	19	4
California	88		26
Colorado	34	2	9
Connecticut	6		3
Delaware	2		1
Florida	116	16	34
Georgia	79	6	15
Hawaii	4		1
Idaho	7		1
Illinois	101	3	24
Indiana	66	6	14
Iowa	45		6
Kansas	43	3	5
Kentucky	60	8	5
Louisiana	62	13	9
Maine	19		3
Maryland	19		10
Massachusetts	23		5
Michigan	39		21
Minnesota	33		9
Mississippi	47	10	4
Missouri	81	27	11
Montana	6		1
Nebraska	13	4	3
Nevada	9		2
New Hampshire	15		4
New Jersey	14		6
New Mexico	19		3
New York	46	4	17
North Carolina	82	1	13
North Dakota	8		2
Ohio	70		22
Oklahoma	61	17	6
Oregon	17		
Pennsylvania	47	5	14
Rhode Island	4		1
South Carolina	49	3	8
South Dakota	8		1
Tennessee	69	19	9
Texas	185	56	51
Utah	13		5
Vermont	1		
Virginia	43	4	10
Washington	13		2
West Virginia	12	2	3
Wisconsin	51		11
Wyoming	9		2
U.S. Totals:	**1,995**	**239**	**433**

Exhibit 6 (continued)   Wal-Mart Store Count in the United States, End of Year, 2003

Fiscal 2003 End-of-Year Store Count

State	Discount Stores	Supercenters	Sam's Clubs	Neighborhd Markets
Alabama	34	49	9	2
Alaska	6	0	3	0
Arizona	24	17	10	0
Arkansas	35	43	4	6
California	133	0	30	0
Colorado	17	29	14	0
Connecticut	27	2	3	0
Delaware	3	3	1	0
Florida	66	87	37	1
Georgia	42	61	20	0
Hawaii	6	0	1	0
Idaho	5	11	1	0
Illinois	81	33	27	0
Indiana	42	42	14	0
Iowa	27	24	7	0
Kansas	29	23	6	0
Kentucky	34	41	5	0
Louisiana	35	47	12	0
Maine	12	9	3	0
Maryland	32	5	13	0
Massachusetts	41	1	3	0
Michigan	48	14	22	0
Minnesota	34	9	12	0
Mississippi	21	41	5	1
Missouri	56	58	14	0
Montana	5	6	1	0
Nebraska	10	11	3	0
Nevada	11	7	5	0
New Hampshire	19	6	4	0
New Jersey	30	0	8	0
New Mexico	6	18	5	0
New York	52	22	18	0
North Carolina	47	52	17	0
North Dakota	8	0	2	0
Ohio	70	28	26	0
Oklahoma	41	40	7	12
Oregon	24	3	0	0
Pennsylvania	50	43	20	0
Rhode Island	8	0	1	0
South Carolina	22	37	9	0
South Dakota	6	4	2	0
Tennessee	33	57	15	2
Texas	117	155	68	24
Utah	6	15	7	1
Vermont	4	0	0	0
Virginia	21	52	13	0
Washington	29	6	2	0
West Virginia	8	20	3	0
Wisconsin	49	20	11	0
Wyoming	2	7	2	0
U.S. Totals:	**1,568**	**1,258**	**525**	**49**

Exhibit 7   International Wal-Mart Stores in 1996

Country	Wal-Mart Stores	Supercenters	Sam's Clubs	Neighborhd Markets
Argentina	0	1	2	0
Brazil	0	2	3	0
Canada	131	0	0	0
Mexico*	85	1328	0	0
Puerto Rico	7	0	4	0

*Mexico includes 3 Superamas, 25 Bodegas, 4 Aurreras, 48 Vips, and 5 Suburbias

suppliers to pick up an increasing amount of inventory and merchandising costs. Wal-Mart, for example, required large suppliers such as Procter & Gamble to place large contingents of employees at its Bentonville, Arkansas, headquarters in order to service its account. A *Fast Company* article on Wal-Mart interviewed several former suppliers of the company and concluded that "To a person, all those interviewed credit Wal-Mart with a fundamental integrity in its dealings that's unusual in the world of consumer goods, retailing, and groceries. Wal-Mart does not cheat its suppliers, it keeps its word, it pays its bills briskly. 'They are tough people but very honest; they treat you honestly,' says Peter Campanella, a former Corning manager."[19]

Although several companies such as Rubbermaid and the pickle vendor Vlasic had experienced dramatic downfalls largely through being squeezed by Wal-Mart, other companies suggested that their relationship with Wal-Mart had made them much more efficient.[20] Some critics suggested, however, that these extreme efficiency pressures had driven many suppliers to move production from the United States to nations such as China that had much lower wages. Wal-Mart set standards for all of its suppliers in areas such as child labor and safety. A 2001 audit, however, revealed that as many as one-third of Wal-Mart's international suppliers were in "serious violation" of the standards.[21] Wal-Mart pursued steps to help suppliers address the violations, but it was unclear how successful these efforts were.

At the heart of Wal-Mart's success was its distribution system. To a large extent it had been born out of the necessity of servicing so many stores in small towns while trying to maintain low prices. Wal-Mart used distribution centers to achieve efficiencies in logistics. Initially, distribution centers were large facilities—the first were 72,000 square feet—that served 80 to 100 Wal-Mart stores within a 250-mile radius. Newer distribution centers were considerably larger than the early ones and in some cases served a wider geographical radius. In the early 1990s, over 85 percent of Wal-Mart's products were distributed through distribution centers, in contrast to only 50 percent for Kmart. As a result, Wal-Mart had far more distribution centers than any of its competitors. Cross-docking was a particularly important practice of these centers.[22] In cross-docking, goods were delivered to distribution centers and often simply loaded from one dock to another or even from one truck to another without ever sitting in inventory. Cross-docking reduced Wal-Mart's cost of sales by 2 to 3 percent compared to competitors. Cross-docking was receiving a great deal of attention among retailers with most attempting to implement it for a greater proportion of goods. It was extremely difficult to manage, however, because of the close coordination and timing required between the store,

Exhibit 8   International Wal-Mart Stores in 2004

Country	Wal-Mart Stores	Supercenters	Sam's Clubs	Neighborhd Markets
Argentina	0	11	0	0
Brazil	0	13	10	2
Canada	231	0	4	0
China	0	28	4	2
Germany	0	92	0	0
Mexico*	487	83	53	0
Puerto Rico*	9	3	9	32
United Kingdom*	255	12	0	0

*Mexico includes 44 Superamas, 140 Bodegas, 4 Aurreras, 251 Vips, and 52 Suburbias   *Puerto Rico includes 32 Amigos
*U.K. includes 253 ASDA Stores and 2 George Stores

manufacturer, and warehouse. As one supplier noted, "Everyone from the forklift driver on up to me, the CEO, knew we had to deliver on time. Not 10 minutes late. And not 45 minutes early, either. . . . The message came through clearly: You have this 30-second delivery window. Either you're there or you're out."[23] Because of the close coordination needed, cross-docking required an information system which effectively linked stores, warehouses, and manufacturers. Most major retailers were finding it difficult to duplicate Wal-Mart's success at cross-docking.

Wal-Mart's logistics system also included a fleet of over 2,000 company-owned trucks. It was able to routinely ship goods from distribution centers to stores within 48 hours of receiving an order. Store shelves were replenished twice a week on average in contrast to the industry average of once every two weeks.[24]

Wal-Mart stores typically included many departments in areas such as soft goods/domestics, hard goods, stationery and candy, pharmaceuticals, records and electronics, sporting goods, toys, shoes, and jewelry. The selection of products varied from one region to another. Department managers and in some cases associates (or employees) had the authority to change prices in response to competitors. This was in stark contrast to the traditional practice of many chains where prices were centrally set at a company's headquarters. Wal-Mart's use of technology was particularly useful in determining the mix of goods in each store. The company used historical selling data and complex models that included many variables such as local demographics to decide what items should be placed in each store.

Unlike many of its competitors, Wal-Mart had no regional offices. Instead, regional vice presidents maintained their offices at company headquarters in Bentonville, Arkansas. The absence of regional offices was estimated to save Wal-Mart as much as 1 percent of sales. Regional managers visited stores from Monday to Thursday of each week. Each Saturday at 7:30 A.M., regional vice presidents and a few hundred other managers and employees met with the firm's top managers to discuss the previous week's results and discuss different directions for the next week. Regional managers then conveyed information from the meeting to managers in the field via the videoconferencing links that were present in each store.

Sam's Club

A notable exception to Wal-Mart's dominance in discount retailing was in the warehouse club segment. Despite significant efforts by Wal-Mart's Sam's Club, Costco was the established leader. Sam's Club had far more stores than Costco—532 to 312—yet, Costco still reported 5 percent more sales. Costco stores averaged almost twice the revenue per store as Sam's with $112 million versus $63 million per store for Sam's Club (see Exhibit 9).

To the casual observer, Costco and Sam's Clubs appeared to be very similar. Both charged small membership fees—$45 at Costco and $30 at Sam's—and both were "warehouse" stores that sold goods from pallets. The goods were often packaged or bundled into larger quantities than typical retailers offered. Beneath these similarities, however, were important differences. Costco focused on more upscale small business owners and consumers while Sam's, following Wal-Mart's pattern, had positioned itself more to the mass middle market. Relative to Costco, Sam's was also concentrated more in smaller cities.

Exhibit 9   Costco Versus Sam's Club*

	Costco	Sam's Club
Year founded	1983	1983
U.S. revenues (year ended Aug. 31, 2003)	$34.4 billion	$32.9 billion (est.)
Presidents (or equivalents, since founding)	one	seven
Membership cardholders	42 million	46 million
Members' average salary	$95,333	N.A.
Annual membership fees	$45	$30–35
U.S. warehouses worldwide)	312 (423 worldwide)	532 (604
Average annual sales (per U.S. location)	$112 million	$63 million
Average transaction	$94	$78
Average sales per square foot	$797	$497
Starting hourly wage	$10	N.A.
Employee turnover per year	23%	45% (WalMart)
Private label (as % of sales)	15%	10%

Source: Heylar, John "The only company Wal-Mart fears" Fortune, November 24, 2003.

Consistent with its more upscale strategy, Costco stocked more luxury and premium branded items than Sam's Club had traditionally done. This changed somewhat when Sam's began to stock more high-end merchandise after the 1990s, but some questioned whether or not its typical customers demanded such items. A Costco executive pointed to the differences between Costco and Sam's customers by describing a scene where a Sam's customer responded to a $39 price on a Ralph Lauren Polo shirt by saying, "Can you imagine? Who in their right mind would buy a T-shirt for $39?" Despite the focus on pricier goods, Costco still focused intensely on managing costs and keeping prices down. Costco set a goal of 10 percent margins and capped markups at 14 percent (compared to the usual 40 percent markup by department stores). Managers were discouraged from exceeding the margin goals.

Some analysts claimed that Sam's Club's lackluster performance was a result of a copycat strategy. Costco was the first of the two competitors to sell fresh meat and produce, gasoline, and introduce a premium private label for many goods. In each case, Sam's followed suit two to four years later.

> "By looking at what Costco did and trying to emulate it, Sam's didn't carve out its own unique strategy," says Michael Clayman, editor of the trade newsletter Warehouse Club Focus. And at least one of the "me too" moves made things worse. Soon after Costco and Price Club merged in 1993, Sam's bulked up by purchasing Pace warehouse clubs from Kmart. Many of the 91 stores were marginal operations in marginal locations. Analysts say that Sam's Club management became distracted as it tried to integrate the Pace stores into its system.[25]

To close the gap against Costco, Wal-Mart started in 2003 to integrate the activities of Sam's Club and Wal-Mart more. Buyers for the two coordinated their efforts to get better prices from suppliers. Like Wal-Mart, Sam's was also promoting the use of RFID to lower costs.

Culture

Perhaps the most distinctive aspect of Wal-Mart was its culture. To a large extent, Wal-Mart's culture was an extension of Sam Walton's philosophy and was rooted in the early experiences and practices of Wal-Mart. The Wal-Mart culture emphasized values such as thriftiness, hard work, innovation, and continuous improvement. As Sam Walton wrote,

> Because wherever we've been, we've always tried to instill in our folks the idea that we at Wal-Mart have our own way of doing things. It may be different and it may take some folks a while to adjust to it at first. But it's straight and honest and basically pretty simple to figure it out if you want to. And whether or not other folks want to accommodate us, we pretty much stick to what we believe in because it's proven to be very, very successful.[26]

Wal-Mart's thriftiness was consistent with its obsession with controlling costs. One observer joked that "The Wal-Mart folks stay at Mo 3, where they don't even leave the light on for you."[27] This was not, however, far from the truth. Sam Walton told of early buying trips to New York where several Wal-Mart managers shared the same hotel room and walked everywhere they went rather than use taxis. One of the early managers described how these early trips taught managers to work hard and keep costs low:

> From the very beginning, Sam was always trying to instill in us that you just didn't go to New York and roll with the flow. We always walked everywhere. We never took cabs. And Sam had an equation for the trips: expenses should never exceed 1 percent of our purchases, so we would all crowd in these little hotel rooms somewhere down around Madison Square Garden. . . . We never finished up until about twelve-thirty at night, and we'd all go out for a beer except Mr. Walton. He'd say, "I'll meet you at breakfast at six o'clock." And we'd say, "Mr. Walton, there's no reason to meet that early. We can't even get into the buildings that early." And he'd just say, "We'll find something to do."[28]

The roots of Wal-Mart's emphasis on innovation and continuous improvement can also be seen in Sam Walton's example. Walton's drive for achievement was evident early in life. He achieved the rank of Eagle Scout earlier than anyone previously had in the state of Missouri. Later, in high school, he quarterbacked the undefeated state champion football team and played guard on the undefeated state champion basketball team while serving as student body president. This same drive was evident in Walton's early retailing efforts. He studied other retailers by spending time in their stores, asking endless questions, and taking notes about various store practices. Walton was quick to borrow a new idea if he thought it would increase sales and profits. When, in his early days at Ben Franklin, Walton read about two variety stores in Minnesota that were using self-service, he immediately took an all-night bus ride to visit the stores. Upon his return from Minnesota, he converted one of his stores to self-service, which, at the time, was only the third variety store in the United States to do so. Later, he was one of the first to see the potential of discount retailing.

Walton also emphasized always looking for ways to improve. Wal-Mart managers were encouraged to critique their own operations. Managers met regularly to discuss their store operations. Lessons learned in one store were quickly spread to other stores. Wal-Mart managers also carefully analyzed the activities of their competitors and tried to borrow practices that worked well. Sam Walton stressed the importance of observing what other firms did well rather than what they did wrong. Another way in which Wal-Mart had focused on improvement from its earliest days was in information and measurement. Long before Wal-Mart had any computers, Sam Walton would personally enter measures on several variables for each store into a ledger he carried with him. Information technology enabled Wal-Mart to extend this emphasis on information and measurement.

International Operations

Wal-Mart's entry into the international retail arena had been somewhat recent. As late as 1992, Wal-Mart's entire international operations consisted of only 162,535 square feet of retail space in Mexico. By 1996, however, Wal-Mart operated 276 stores outside of the United States. The company's largest international presence was in Canada and Mexico. Following a 1994 acquisition of Woolco's Canadian stores, Wal-Mart operated 131 discount centers in Canada in 1996. With its Mexican partner Cifra, Wal-Mart had opened 85 discount centers, 13 supercenters, and 28 Sam's Clubs in Mexico. Wal-Mart expanded its international expansion into South America in 1996 by opening three stores in Argentina and five in Brazil. Expansion plans called for more stores in Mexico and South America as well as entry into the Asian market with stores in China, Indonesia, and additional stores in Hong Kong where it had two Sam's Clubs. Wal-Mart had continued its international expansion by entering Europe via major acquisitions in Germany and the United Kingdom.

Although it was the company's fastest-growing division, Wal-Mart's performance in international markets had been mixed or as *Forbes* put it, "Overseas, Wal-Mart has won some—and lost a lot."[29] Over 80 percent of Wal-Mart's international revenue came from only three countries: Canada, Mexico, and the United Kingdom (see Exhibit 10).

Wal-Mart had tried a variety of approaches and faced a diverse set of challenges in the different countries they entered. Entry into international markets had ranged from greenfield development to franchising, joint ventures, and acquisitions. Each country that Wal-Mart had entered had presented new and unique challenges. In China, Wal-Mart had to deal with a backward supply chain. It had to negotiate a Japanese environment that was hostile to large chains and protective of its small retailers. Strong foreign competitors were the problem in Brazil and Argentina. Labor unions had plagued Wal-Mart's entry into Germany along with unforeseen difficulties in integrating acquistions. Mistakes in choosing store locations had hampered the company in South Korea and Hong Kong.

Wal-Mart approached it international operations with much the same philosophy they had used in the United States "We're still very young at this, we're still learning,"[30] stated John Menzer, chief executive of Wal-Mart International. Menzer's approach was to have country presidents make decisions. His thinking was that it would facilitate the faster implementation of decisions. Each country president made decisions regarding his own sourcing, merchandising, and real estate. Menzer concluded, "Over time all you really have is speed. I think that's our most important asset."[31]

In most countries, entrenched competitors responded vigorously to Wal-Mart's entry. For example, Tesco, the United Kingdom's biggest grocer, responded by opening supercenters. In China, Lianhua and Huilan, the two largest retailers, merged in 2003 into one state-owned entity named the Bailan Group. Wal-Mart was also not alone among major international retailers in seeking new growth in South America and Asia. One international competitor, the French retailer Carrefour, was already the leading retailer in Brazil and Argentina. Carrefour expanded into China in the late 1990s with a hypermarket in Shanghai. In Asia, Makro, a Dutch wholesale club retailer, was the regional leader. Both of the European firms were viewed as able, experienced competitors. The Japanese retailer, Yaohan, moved its headquarters from Tokyo to Hong Kong with the aim of becoming the world's largest retailer. Helped by the close relationship between chairman Kazuo Wada and Deng Xiaoping, Yaohan was the first foreign retail firm to receive a license to operate in China and planned to open over a

---

Exhibit 10   Sales Growth by Region

Country	Sales 2003 ($mil)	Annualized growth 2001–2003
Argentina	$122	2%
Brazil	388	13
Canada	7,165	15
China	673	30
Germany	2,743	-7
Mexico	10,659	17
Puerto Rico	2,413	30
South Korea	836	30
United Kingdom	21,740	14
USA	209,509	11

1,000 stores there. Like Wal-Mart, these international firms were motivated to expand internationally by slowing growth in their own domestic markets. Some analysts feared that the pace of expansion by these major retailers was faster than the rate of growth in the market and could result in a price war. Like Wal-Mart, these competitors had also found difficulty in moving into international markets and adapting to local differences. Both Carrefour and Makro had experienced visible failures in their international efforts. Folkert Schukken, chairman of Makro, noted this challenge: "We have trouble selling the same toilet paper in Belgium and Holland." The chairman of Carrefour, Daniel Bernard, agreed, "If people think that going international is a solution to their problems at home, they will learn by spilling their blood. Global retailing demands a huge investment and gives no guarantee of a return."[32]

It was not known what Wal-Mart's next international moves would be. The *Wall Street Journal* reported that the French hypermarket firm Carrefour might be an acquisition target. There were also rumors that Wal-Mart might acquire the Esselunga chain of Italy or the Daiei or Aeon chains in Japan.

Notes

[1]   Standard and Poor's Industry Surveys. *Retailing: General*, February 5, 1998.
[2]   Upbin, Bruce. "Wall-to-wall Wal-Mart." *Forbes*, April 12, 2004.
[3]   Nordlinger, Jay. "The new colossous: Wal-Mart is America's store, and the world's and its enemies are sadly behind." *National Review*, April 19, 2004.
[4]   Nordlinger, Jay. "The new colossous: Wal-Mart is America's store, and the world's and its enemies are sadly behind." *National Review*, April 19, 2004.
[5]   Standard and Poor's Industry Surveys. *Retailing: General*, February 5, 1998.
[6]   Berner, Robert. "The next Warren Buffett?" *BusinessWeek*, November 22, 2004.
[7]   Standard and Poor's Industry Surveys. *Retailing: General*, February 5, 1998.
[8]   Walton, Sam (with John Huey). *Sam Walton: Made in America*. New York: Doubleday, p. 63.
[9]   Walton, Sam (with John Huey). *Sam Walton: Made in America*. New York: Doubleday, pp. 64–65.
[10] Walton, Sam (with John Huey). *Sam Walton: Made in America*. New York: Doubleday, p. 66.
[11] *Forbes*, August 16, 1982, p. 43
[12] Pulliam, Susan. "Wal-Mart considers raising prices, drawing praise from analysts, but concern from board." *Wall Street Journal*, March 8, 1996, p. C2.
[13] Standard and Poor's Industry Surveys. *Retailing: General*, February 5, 1998.
[14] Zimmerman, Ann. "B-2-B—Internet 2.0: To sell goods to Wal-Mart, get on the Net." *Wall Street Journal*, November 21, 2003, p. B1
[15] Useem, Jerry. "America's most admired companies." *Fortune*, February 18, 2003.
[16] Boyle, Matthew. *Fortune*, November 10, 2003, p. 46.
[17] Schifrin, Matthew. "The big squeeze." *Forbes*, March 11, 1996.
[18] Schifrin, Matthew. "The big squeeze." *Forbes*, March 11, 1996.
[19] Fishman, Charles. "The Wal-Mart you don't know." *Fast Company*, December 2003, p. 73.
[20] Fishman, Charles. "The Wal-Mart you don't know." *Fast Company*, December 2003.
[21] Wal-Mart Web site.
[22] Stalk, George, Philip Evans, and Lawrence E. Schulman. "Competing on capabilities: The new rules of corporate strategy." *Harvard Business Review*, March/April 1992, pp. 57–68.
[23] Fishman, Charles. "The Wal-Mart you don't know." *Fast Company*, December 2003, p. 73.
[24] Stalk, George, Philip Evans, and Lawrence E. Schulman. "Competing on capabilities: The new rules of corporate strategy." *Harvard Business Review*, March/April 1992, pp. 57–68.
[25] Helyar, John. "The only company Wal-Mart fears." *Fortune*, November 24, 2003, p. 158.
[26] Walton, Sam (with John Huey). *Sam Walton: Made in America*. New York: Doubleday, p. 85.
[27] Loeb, Marshall. "Editor's desk: The secret of two successes." *Fortune*, May 2, 1994.
[28] Walton, Sam (with John Huey). *Sam Walton: Made in America*. New York: Doubleday, p. 84.
[29] Upbin, Bruce. "Wall-to-wall Wal-Mart." *Forbes*, April 12, 2004.
[30] Upbin, Bruce. "Wall-to-wall Wal-Mart." *Forbes*, April 12, 2004.
[31] Upbin, Bruce. "Wall-to-wall Wal-Mart." *Forbes*, April 12, 2004.
[32] *Fortune*, "Retailers go global" February 20, 1995.

Case 1–5: Harlequin Enterprises: The Mira Decision[1]

During June 1993, Harlequin management was deciding whether or not to launch MIRA, a new line of single-title women's fiction novels. With the increased popularity of single-title women's fiction, Harlequin's leading position as the world's largest romance publisher was being threatened. While Harlequin was the dominant and very profitable producer of *series* romance novels, research indicated that many customers were reading as many *single-title* romance and women's fiction books as series romances. Facing a steady loss of share in a growing total women's fiction market, Harlequin convened a task force in December 1992 to study the possibility of relaunching a single-title women's fiction program. Donna Hayes, vice-president of direct marketing, stated:

> Industry trends reveal that demand for single-title women's fiction continues to grow while demand for series romance remains stable. Our strengths lie in series romance . . . by any account, launching MIRA (single-title) will still be a challenge for us. How do we successfully launch a single-title women's fiction program?

Tentatively named "MIRA," Harlequin's proposed single-title program would focus exclusively on women's fiction. Management hoped MIRA's launch would provide the opportunity to continue Harlequin's history of strong revenue growth. Hayes, leader of the MIRA team, knew this was a significant decision for Harlequin. Several years earlier an attempt at single-title publishing—Worldwide Library—had failed. Before going to her executive group for approval, Hayes thought about the decisions the company faced if it wished to enter single-title women's fiction publishing: What were the growth and profitability implications if Harlequin broadened its scope from series romance to single-title women's fiction? What fundamental changes would have to be made to Harlequin's current business model? Did the company have the necessary resources and capabilities to succeed in this new arena? If the company proceeds, how should it go about launching MIRA?

The Publishing Industry[2]

Apart from educational material, traditional single-title book publishing was typically a high-risk venture. Each book was a new product with all the risks attendant on any new product introduction. The risks varied with the author's reputation, the subject matter and thus the predictability of the market's response. Among the numerous decisions facing the publisher were selecting manuscripts out of the thousands submitted each year, deciding how many copies to print and deciding how to promote the book.

Insiders judged one key to success in publishing was the creative genius needed to identify good young authors among the hundreds of would-be writers, and then publish and develop them through their careers. Years ago, Sol Stein of Stein and Day Publishers had commented; "Most successful publishers are creative editors at heart and contribute more than risk capital and marketing expertise to the books they publish. If a publisher does not add value to what he publishes, he's a printer, not a publisher."

Traditional single-title publishers allowed distributors 50 percent margins (from which the retailer's margin would come).[3] Some other typical costs included royalty payments of more than 12 percent, warehouse and handling costs of four percent, and selling expenses at 5.5 percent. Advertising generally required six percent and printing costs[4] required another 12 percent. The remainder was earnings before indirect overhead. Typically, indirect overhead accounted for two percent of the retail price of a book. Because of author

Ken Mark prepared this case under the supervision of Professors Rod White and Mary Crossan solely to provide material for class discussion. The authors do not intend to illustrate either effective or ineffective handling of a managerial situation. The authors may have disguised certain names and other identifying information to protect confidentiality.

advances, pre-publication promotion and fixed costs of printing break-even volumes were significant. And if the publisher failed to sell enough books, the losses could be substantial. Harlequin's core business, series romance fiction was significantly different from traditional single-title publishing.

Harlequin Enterprises Limited

The word romance and the name Harlequin had become synonymous over the last half-century. Founded in 1949, Harlequin began applying its revolutionary approach to publishing—a packaged, consumer-goods strategy—in 1968 shortly after acquiring the publishing business of U.K.-based Mills & Boon. Each book was part of an identifiable product line; consistently delivering the expected benefit to the consumer. With a growth rate of 25 percent per year during the 1970s, Harlequin became the world's largest publisher of women's series romance fiction. It was during this time that Torstar, a newspaper publisher, acquired all of Harlequin Enterprises Ltd.

Over the years, many book publishers had attempted to enter Harlequin's segment of the industry. All had eventually withdrawn. Only once had Harlequin's dominance in series romance fiction been seriously challenged. The "romance wars" began in 1980 when Harlequin took over U.S. distribution of its series products from Simon & Schuster (S&S), a large U.S.-based single-title publisher with established paperback distribution. Subsequently, S&S began publishing series romance fiction under the Silhouette imprint. After several years, a truce was negotiated between Harlequin and S&S. Harlequin acquired Silhouette, S&S's series romance business, and S&S got a 20-year deal as Harlequin's sole U.S. distributor for series fiction.

During the late 1980s and early 1990s, growth in the series market slowed. Harlequin was able to maintain revenues by publishing longer and more expensive series products and generally raising prices. However, as shown in Table 1, global unit volume was no longer growing.

Harlequin's Target Market and Products

Harlequin books were sold in more than 100 international markets in more than 23 languages around the world. Along with romance fiction, Harlequin participated in the series mystery and male action-adventure markets under its Worldwide Library and Gold Eagle imprints. Harlequin had an estimated 20 million readers in North America and 50 million readers around the world.

With a median age of 41, the Harlequin's romance series reader was likely to be married, well educated, and working outside the home. More than half of Harlequin readers spent at least three hours reading per week. Harlequin series readers were brand loyal; a survey indicated four out of five readers would continue to buy Harlequin books in the next year. Larry Heisey, Harlequin's former chief executive officer and chairman, expanded on the value of Harlequin's products: "I think our books are so popular because they provide relaxation and escape. . . . We get many letters from people who tell us how much these books mean to them."

While Harlequin had advertised its series product on television, current marketing efforts centred on print media. Harlequin advertised in leading women's magazines such as *Cosmopolitan, Glamour, Redbook, Good Housekeeping,* and general interest magazines such as *People.* The print advertisement usually featured one of Harlequin's series products and also promoted the company's brands.

Romance Series Product: Well Defined and Consistent

Under the Harlequin and Silhouette brands, Harlequin published 13 different series with 64 titles each month. Each series was distinctly positioned, featuring a particular genre (e.g., historical romances) or level of explicitness. Isabel Swift, editorial director of Silhouette, described the different types of series books published by Harlequin:

> Our different lines deliver different promises to our readers. For example, Harlequin Temptation's tagline is sassy, sexy and seductive, *promising that each story will deliver a sexy, fun, contemporary romance between one man and one woman. Whereas the Silhouette Romance title, in comparison, is a tender read within a framework of more traditional values.*

Overall, the product portfolio offered a wide variety of stories to capture readers' interests. For the positioning of Harlequin's series, see Exhibit 1. Sold in more than a

Table 1   **Total Unit Sales (in $000s)**

Year	1988	1989	1990	1991	1992	1993
Operating Revenue	344,574	326,539	348,358	357,013	417,884	443,825
Operating Profit	48,142	56,217	57,769	52,385	61,842	62,589
Total Unit Sales	202	191	196	193	205	199

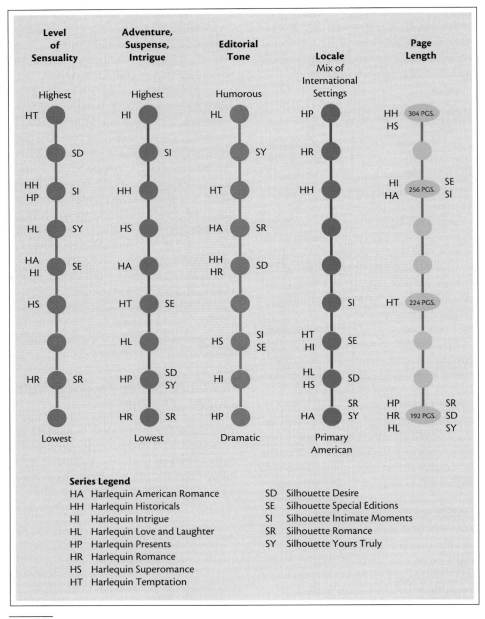

Exhibit 1 Harlequin/Silhouette Series Positioning Scales

Source: Company files.

dozen countries, Harlequin had the ability to publish series books worldwide. The average retail price of a Harlequin series novel was $4.40,[5] significantly less than the $7 retail price for the typical single-title paperback novel, and much less than the $15 to $25 for longer, hardcover titles by best-selling authors.

Harlequin's series romance product was fundamentally different from that of traditional single-title publish-ers: content, length, artwork size, basic formats, and print were all well defined to ensure a consistent product. Each book was not a new product, but rather an addition to a clearly defined product line. Unlike single-title books, Harlequin's series products had a common format. They measured 105 millimetres by 168 millimetres and fit neatly into specially designed racks located primarily in super-markets and drugstores. Most product lines were 192 to

Exhibit 2   Typical Harlequin Series Romance Products

Source: Company files.

256 pages in length; some were up to 304 pages in length. Cover designs differed slightly by product line and country, but the look and feel was similar (see Exhibit 2).

Harlequin provided prospective series romance authors with plot, style, and book length guidelines. However, crafting the stories still demanded skill and work. As David Galloway, chief executive officer of Torstar, Harlequin's parent company, and the former head of Harlequin observed:

> The books are quite simply good stories. If they weren't, we wouldn't be getting the repeat purchases we do. A lot of writers think they can dash off a Harlequin, but they can't. We've had submissions from PhD's in English who can certainly write but they can't tell a story.

To ensure a consistent product emerged, Harlequin's editors assessed many elements including plot, story line, main character(s), setting, percentage of romance in the plot, level of realism, level of fantasy, sensuality, social and/or individual problems, happy ending, and reading impact. Even though many different authors contributed to series romance, Harlequin's editors ensured a consistent finished product, satisfying the needs of their loyal series romance readers. The consequences of this uniformity were significant. The reader was buying a Harlequin novel, and advertising promoted the Harlequin brands rather than a particular book or author.

Bookstores were not the primary channel for series romance novels. Most retail purchases were made at supermarkets or drugstores and increasingly mass merchandisers like Wal-Mart. But many avid Harlequin readers got the product delivered to their home every month through Harlequin's direct mail service. The standardized size and format made warehousing and distribution more efficient. In addition, the product's consistency enabled standing

Exhibit 3   Comparing Harlequin's Series Business Model and a Traditional Publisher's

	Harlequin Series	Single-title Publisher
Editorial	Emphasizes consistency within established guidelines	Requires separate judgment on potential consumer demand for each manuscript
Rights	Uses standardized contract	Can be a complex process, involving subrights, hard/soft deals, advances, and tying up authors for future books
Author Management	Less dependent on specific authors	Vulnerable to key authors changing publisher
Production	Uses consistent format with focus on efficiency	Emphasizes package, size, and format—cost control secondary
Marketing	Builds the imprint/series	Builds each title/author
Distribution	Supermarkets, drugstores, mass merchandisers, big-box bookstores. Large direct mail	Bookstores (all types) Book clubs and mass merchandisers
Selling	Emphasizes servicing, rack placement, and order regulation	Cover, in-store placement, critical reviews, special promotional tactics (e.g., author signings)
Order Regltn/Information Systems	Utilizes very sophisticated shipping and returns handling procedures	Historically has not received much attention, and hence, is not as sophisticated

order distribution to retail. As Pam Laycock, director of new product development, explained:

> A major contributor to our success as a series publisher is our standing order distribution. Each series is distributed to a retail location in a predetermined configuration—for example in a series where we publish four titles per month, a retailer may take six copies per title and this level of distribution is generally agreed upon and maintained for the entire year. This approach enables us to more accurately predict monthly print quantities and achieve significant print cost effectiveness.

Orders (and sales) for conventional single-title books were not as predictable. Another significant difference was that series romance books were part of Harlequin's standing order distribution plan. And more like magazines, they were displayed on retail shelves for four weeks. Harlequin's distributors then removed and returned any unsold books, and replaced them with the next month's offerings. By comparison, single-title books were typically displayed at retail from six to 12 months or more.

Harlequin's series romance business did not generate or even encourage best-sellers. "Best-sellers (in series romance) would ruin our system," a Harlequin insider stated. "Our objective is consistency in volume. We have no winners and no losers." Unsold books could be returned to the publisher for credit. A consequence of Harlequin's even and predictable

sales was that order regulation and returns could be more easily optimized to maximize the contribution to profits.

A comparison of Harlequin's series business model and the operations of traditional "one-off" publishers is presented in Exhibit 3.

With a consistent quality product, standing orders, predictable retail traffic patterns and the ability to produce and deliver books at low costs, Harlequin had achieved great success. Harlequin's series romance business had consistently earned a return on sales of 15 percent. As shown in Exhibit 4, this figure compared favorably with larger traditional publishers.

Loriana Sacilotto, director of retail marketing, explained why Harlequin out-performed other traditional single-title publishers:

> There are a variety of reasons why other publishers do not achieve the same margins we enjoy. The main reason is that they are broad in their publishing focus whereas we focus on women's fiction. They don't have the same reader recognition, trust and relationships. We invest in it.

Harlequin Business System

The Global Author–Editor Team. Harlequin had established a strong level of reader trust and brand equity by consistently delivering quality content. Editors in three acquisi-

Exhibit 4   Comparison of Harlequin's Performance With Traditional Publisher—1993 (in millions of dollars)

	Harlequin[a]	Simon & Schuster[b]	Harper/Avon[c]
Sales Revenue	417.8	1,929.0	1,210.4
Operating Profit	61.8	218.4	160.8
Identifiable Assets	319.2	2,875.8	2,528.0
R.O.S	14.8%	11.3%	13.2%
R.O.I.A.	19.4%	7.6%	6.4%

[a] Canadian dollars   [b] U.S. dollars (Cdn$1.20 = US$1)   [c] Australian dollars (Cdn$0.80 = AUD$1)

tion centres in Toronto, New York, and London were responsible for working closely with 1,300-plus authors to develop and publish more than 1,000 new titles annually. In addition to the work of its regular writers, Harlequin received approximately 30,000 unsolicited manuscripts per year. Typically, about 100 of these were accepted in any given year.

Series authors received royalties of 13 percent of retail book price. Harlequin's typical series authors had more than 100,000 of each of their books distributed worldwide.

Harlequin's series romance product focused solely on *front-list* sales. In the publishing world, front-list sales referred to the first print runs of a book supporting its initial market launch. *Back-list* referred to books reprinted and reissued years after the book's initial run (often to support an author's subsequent books). Harlequin's series romance novels—unlike a traditional publisher's single-title books—were not available on back-list. However, Harlequin retained these rights.

Printing was a highly competitive business and Harlequin subcontracted its requirements. Costs per series book were typically $0.44 per book compared to the competitors' average costs of $0.88 per single-title soft cover book.

Distribution, Selling and Promotion. With its standing orders, Harlequin's distribution costs per book were $0.18, with selling expenses at an average of $0.09 per book. Because it was the dominant player in series romance, Harlequin had relatively low advertising and promotion costs—about $0.22 per book.

In Canada, Harlequin had its own distribution. Elsewhere in the world, independent distributors were employed. In the United States, Pocketbooks, the sales division of Simon & Schuster, a large traditional publisher, handled Harlequin's series romance books. Supermarkets, drugstores, discount department stores, and mass merchandisers accounted for 70 percent of North American retail sales. Specialty big-box bookstores like Barnes and Noble and other chains and independent bookstores accounted for the remainder of retail sales. Globally Harlequin's prod-

ucts were in over 250,000 retail outlets. Eighty thousand of these outlets were in North America; almost 50,000 of these were supermarkets and drugstores. Harlequin's series products were in 70 percent of supermarkets but only 55 percent of bookstores. In Europe, kiosks and tobacconists accounted for the largest proportion of retail outlets.

The direct channel handled direct-to-reader book sales. Harlequin's "Reader Service" book club was an important source of sales and profits. Investing in advertising to acquire readers, this direct mail operation offered frequent Harlequin readers the possibility of purchasing every book the company published, delivered right to their doorstep. In the United States, six books were sold through the book club for every 10 sold at retail. Furthermore, a book sold through the book club yielded Harlequin the full cover price, whereas a book sold at retail netted the company approximately half the retail price, and required advertising, distribution costs, and the acceptance of returns from retailers.

Rise of Single-title Romance

The proliferation of titles and authors during the "Romance Wars" had resulted in the emergence of single-titles as a significant factor in the women's romance fiction market. Exhibit 5 provides the sales breakdown for romance novels.

Exhibit 5   Romance Novel Sales in North America (millions of units)

	1985	1986	1987	1988	1989	1990
Harlequin series romance	77	79	80	82	83	85
Other romance series publishers	12	12	13	13	14	14
Single-title romance books by other publishers	72	79	86	94	102	112
Total romance books	161	170	179	189	199	211

Exhibit 6 Range of Worldwide Titles (1987)

Book Title	Type/Genre	Unit Sales Data	Harlequin Series Author?
Longest Pleasure	Romance	304,000	Yes
Quarantine	Horror	62,000	No
Eve of Regression	Psychological Thriller	55,000	No
War Moon	Suspense	72,000	No
Illusion	Psychological Suspense	35,000	No
Dream Escape	Romance	297,000	Yes
Alien Planet	Science Fiction	71,000	No

In an attempt to capitalize on reader's growing appetite for single-titles, Harlequin launched Worldwide Library in 1986, its first single-title publishing program. This move also gave Harlequin's more accomplished series authors another outlet. Laycock commented:

Several authors who began their writing careers with Harlequin writing series romance wanted broader opportunities—opportunities that they saw in the single-title women's fiction publishing arena. Prior to the launch of Worldwide Library, Harlequin didn't have publishing opportunities to meet the desires of these authors. As a result, authors would seek out competitive publishers to support their single-title works.

By 1988, Worldwide was shut down as a result of several problems. "Worldwide could never decide if it was a romance program, a women's fiction program or a general fiction program," a Harlequin insider commented. Exhibit 6 illustrates a list of typical titles published at Worldwide.

With the shutdown of Worldwide Library, popular authors moved to other publishers. As shown in Exhibit 7, other publishers continued to exploit the popularity of single-title romance novels.

Eager to find ways to grow its publishing business, Harlequin's management reexamined the publishing market. A broader analysis revealed that although Harlequin's series romance had captured well over 80 percent of the North American series romance market by 1990, Harlequin's estimated share of the North American *women's fiction* market was only about five percent. Table 2 provides a breakdown of the women's fiction market. There was substantial overlap in the readership of series romance fiction and other fiction. Mark Mailman, vice-president of market research and analysis added:

One compelling reason to get into single-title publishing is that when we look at our research on customers, they're reading 20 Harlequin books and 20 single-title books from other publishers. We have an opportunity to take a greater share of that market.

Harlequin's Single-Title Task Force

Faced with slow or no growth in series romance, a Harlequin task force convened in 1992 to study the feasibility of launching a new women's fiction single-title program. To begin, they examined why Worldwide had failed and concluded that overall lack of success was attributable to: editorial parameters that were too broad; less than optimal North American retail distribution; very few Worldwide titles distributed through the direct-to-reader channel; global support for the program was not timely and universal; the selection of authors and titles was unsuccessful. The task force report stated:

In the past few years, sell-through efficiencies in the supermarket channels are not as great as the sell-through efficiencies in both mass merchandisers and bookstores. The more efficient retailer knew that the

Exhibit 7 Monthly Single Title Romance Output Analysis North America Market

Single Title Romance by Category	1985	1989	1991
Contemporary	2	6	12
Historical	22	37	43
Regency	6	8	17
Total	**30**	**51**	**72**

By Publisher			
Zebra (Kensington Publishing)	5	15	21
Bantam/Dell	2	2	8
Diamond	0	0	4
Harper Paperbacks	0	0	3
Avon	4	5	6
Jove	2	2	4
Leisure Books	3	3	5
NAL/Signet	6	7	8
Pocket Books (Simon & Schuster)	1	6	3
Ballantine/Fawcett, Onyx, SMP	4	7	7
Warner Books/Popular Library	3	4	3
Total	**30**	**51**	**72**

Source: Company files.

Table 2 **North American Women's Fiction Market Size Estimate, 1993**
(As a percentage of overall segment sizes in US$ millions)

	General Fiction	Romance	Mystery	Sci-Fi	Total Fiction
Total Segment Size	**2,222**	**1,220**	**353**	**476**	**4,271**
Estimated Women's Fiction Share of Segment	60%	100%	60%	38%	69%

consumer was spending her discretionary reading dollar to buy a diversity of romantic reads, including those that had previously been thought of as mainstream.

Since a single-title strategy requires a single-title solicitation from the sales force and more expensive single-title packaging, two of Harlequin's strategic lynchpins of our earlier decades have to be rethought (for single-title): standing order program and same format production. However, Harlequin can still capitalize on its global base and its ability to distribute widely to points of purchase that women visit on a regular basis.

MIRA Launch Decision

The task force was preparing its recommendation for MIRA, Harlequin's proposed women's fiction single-title program. The addition of single titles would make a welcome contribution to overhead costs. Currently, indirect overhead costs per series novel were $0.09 per book. Because infrastructure was already in place, it was estimated that MIRA novels would not incur additional indirect overhead costs. Printing costs for single-titles were expected to be $0.71 per book (350 pages on average). Estimated advertising and promotional costs for new single-titles were six percent of (the higher) retail price.

Author Management

In the single-title market, authors were categorized into three groups, based on their sales potential: brand new, mid-list, and best-seller (see Exhibit 8). Depending on the author group royalties, sales and promotional support varied. Best-selling authors were expected to sell more than a million books. Publishers were known to sign established authors for up to a five-book contract with large multimillion dollar advances. It had not been determined whether MIRA should follow suit. In addition to author advances, typical royalties per MIRA-type book were estimated to be 13 percent of the $6.75 retail price.

A Different Format

Women's fiction books were expected to have many differences from well-defined series romance books. Unlike series romance, topics would cover a broader range of seg-

ments including general fiction, science fiction, and mystery. Women's fiction books would be longer in length: 100,000 to 400,000 words compared with a series romance book length of 75,000 words. Naturally, book sizes would be bigger in terms of page length: from 250 to 400 pages versus a norm of 192 to 304 pages for series romance.

Distribution

Harlequin had a strong distribution network for its series romances through supermarkets, drugstores, and discount department stores. Single-title women's fiction novels required more mainstream distribution focusing on retail bookstores. In addition, standing order distribution, a hallmark of Harlequin's series romance business model, would have to be abandoned in favor of relying on orders generated by the distributor's sales force for single-titles.

Success in the United States would be key for MIRA, and in this market, Harlequin relied upon Simon and Schuster's sales force. Since S&S was a major single-title publisher, Harlequin did not know how much support MIRA would be afforded. Harlequin was considering offering better margins to the distributors than those it offered for series romance distribution. Expenses for single-title distribution were expected to be $0.27 per book.

MIRA books would rely more heavily upon distribution through bookstores when distributed through the same channels as the series product. Retailers would be encouraged to shelve MIRA books separately from the series offering. The more intensive selling effort for single titles would require four percent of the single title retail price. The new single-title program planned to offer $3.38 in margin to the distribution channel for single-title books (50 percent of the typical retail price of $6.75) versus $2.42 for series books (45 percent of the $4.40 suggested retail price).

Acquiring Single-title Rights

Harlequin subsidiaries in some countries were already buying rights to publish single-titles. By launching MIRA Harlequin could negotiate better global-author deals. The task force report added: "By acquiring mainstream titles through a central acquiring office, the collective clout of Harlequin could

Exhibit 8   General Industry Contract Terms For Fiction Category By Author Group

	Brand New Author	Mid-List Author	Best-Selling Author
Advance	$10,000 to $30,000	$80,000 to $200,000	$1 million to $5 million
Royalties	5% to 13%	8% to 15%	10% to 17%
Overseas Publishing Schedule	Within 18 months	Within 12 months	Simultaneous
Overseas Publishing Markets	Major markets	All markets	All markets
Minimum Distribution	30,000 to 80,000	100,000 to 400,000	>1 million
Promotional Support per	Possibly some support (up to $50,000)	Support ($100,000)	Very strong support book (more than $300,000)

Sources: Industry sources and casewriter estimates.

create the likelihood of better-selling mainstream titles marketed by all countries in the global enterprise."

Harlequin's author and editor relationships remained strong, so much so that many series authors were enthusiastic about maintaining a long-term relationship with a trusted editor as they pursued their break-out mainstream book. With MIRA, these authors could remain loyal to Harlequin.

How Best to Proceed

There were many issues to be resolved prior to any launch of MIRA. Most pressing was the question of whether Harlequin had the resources and capabilities to succeed in its new women's fiction segment. Certainly there were elements of its series business model that could be transferred to the broader women's fiction market. But what were the gaps? What else did Harlequin need?

Hayes had a several options if MIRA was launched. Several established best-selling authors had begun their writing careers with Harlequin and had moved on to writing single-title books. These authors had established reputations. Harlequin could approach one or more of these authors to sign with MIRA/Harlequin. Such an

arrangement would involve a multi-book contract and substantial advances. While risky, this approach would ensure that MIRA's launch attracted attention.

A different, seemingly less risky alternative was to tap into Harlequin's extensive back-list collection and reissue a selection of novels by current best-selling authors currently signed with rival single-title publishers. The physical size of the book and page length could be extended to 250 pages from 192 by adjusting format. In addition, a new, MIRA-branded cover could be produced to repackage the books. Coincident with the launch of this back-list, Harlequin's editors would cultivate and develop existing series authors, encouraging them to write single-title books for MIRA.

Returning to the strategic dilemma that Harlequin faced, Swift commented on the challenge of successfully launching MIRA:

Our biggest challenge is the requirement to publish on a title-by-title basis. Every new book will have to stand on its own, with its own cover, a new marketing plan and possibly even an author tour. Can we as a company develop the flexibility to remain nimble? How patient should we be in waiting for success? Given Worldwide's poor results, how should we approach this challenge?

Notes

[1] To protect confidentiality, all financial information within this case study has been disguised.

[2] This section is adapted from the Richard Ivey School of Business #9A87M002 Harlequin Enterprises Limited—1979, Peter Killing.

[3] All amounts are a percentage of the suggested retail price.

[4] Numbers are for the typical paperback. Hardcover books cost more to produce, but as a percentage of its higher retail price, printing costs were roughly the same proportion.

[5] All amounts in Cdn$ unless otherwise specified.

2
BUSINESS LEVEL STRATEGIES

4

Cost Leadership

It is already the largest firm in the United States, with 2002 revenues of almost $250 billion, profits of over $8 billion, and almost 1.5 million employees. Not bad for a company that began with a single store in 1945, had only 38 stores in 1970, and now has over 4,000 stores!

So, how has Wal-Mart done it, and can it keep it going? At Wal-Mart's current growth rate of 16 percent per year it will be the first company with over $1 trillion in sales within 10 years. At that

Can Wal-Mart Keep It Going?

size, Wal-Mart would have more than 5 million employees—about half the size of the U.S. military during World War II and more people than are employed by the U.S. government. Wal-Mart's sales would approximately equal the Gross Domestic Product (GDP) of the United Kingdom and be sub-

stantially larger than the GDP of Australia, Canada, and Spain; and nearly 10 percent of the GDP of the United States.

The strategy behind this growth is remarkably simple. Wal-Mart exploits its enormous size to get the best prices possible from its suppliers and then passes most of these savings on to customers. This enables people of modest means to purchase items that historically have only been available to wealthier consumers. Only firms with Wal-Mart's huge purchasing power can implement this

Learning Objectives

After reading this chapter, you should be able to:

1. Define cost leadership.

2. Identify six reasons firms can differ in their costs.

3. Identify four reasons economies of scale can exist and four reasons diseconomies of scale can exist.

4. Explain the relationship between cost advantages due to learning curve economies and a firm's market share, as well as the limitations of this logic.

5. Identify how cost leadership helps neutralize each of the major threats in an industry.

6. Identify the bases of cost leadership that are more likely to be rare and costly to imitate.

7. Explain how firms use a functional organizational structure to implement business-level strategies like cost leadership.

8. Describe the formal and informal management controls and compensation policies firms use to implement cost leadership strategies.

9. Explain how international operations can affect a firm's cost position.

---

strategy—and there are no other retail firms with Wal-Mart's purchasing power.

Of course, the path to endless growth at Wal-Mart is far from certain. The firm faces both external and internal challenges. Externally, several cities around the United States have successfully fought off Wal-Mart's attempt to build new stores in their communities. These cities argue that Wal-Marts tend to destroy traditional downtown shopping areas, part of a small town lifestyle that citizens in these cities don't want to lose. Also, Wal-Mart has yet to prove that it can export its strategy around the world. While its operations in the United Kingdom are profitable, it has taken years for its operations in Mexico to begin to turn a profit, and there is some uncertainty about Wal-Mart's long term success in Germany.

Internally, Wal-Mart faces the difficult challenge of expanding its size without losing the unique organizational culture that has helped it get to its current level of success. Indeed, many observers have been surprised that Wal-Mart has been able to retain the enthusiastic, down home, "rah-rah" culture originally created by Sam Walton, the founder of Wal-Mart. This culture, which helps create a sense of loyalty between Wal-Mart and its employees, requires continuous investment to remain healthy and vital. And the question remains: "Is it really possible to have a culture that unites 5 million employees?"

Sources: J. Collins (2003). "Bigger, better, faster." *Fast Company*, June, pp. 74 +; B. Breen (2003). "What's selling in America?" *Fast Company*, January, pp. 80 +; P. Ghemewat (1993). "Wal-Mart discount store operations." Harvard Business School Case No. 9-387-018.

Wal-Mart's success has, to this point in time, been almost unimaginable. It is especially striking since one of its major competitors—Kmart—was going through bankruptcy at the same time that Wal-Mart was becoming the largest firm in the United States. And Wal-Mart and Kmart sell just about the same products. Why is it that two firms operating in the same industry, selling the same products to the same customers, can have such different levels of performance? Well, as we have seen, Wal-Mart has been able to use its volume of sales to extract low prices from its suppliers, which it then passes on to customers in the form of lower prices. This is a classic cost leadership strategy, the business strategy that is the topic of this chapter. Kmart has been unable to implement a similar strategy and thus has not enjoyed the same success.

What Is Business-Level Strategy?

Part One of this book introduced you to the basic tools required to conduct a strategic analysis: tools for analyzing external threats and opportunities (in Chapter 2) and tools for analyzing internal strengths and weaknesses (in Chapter 3). Once you have completed these two analyses, it is possible to begin making strategic choices. As was explained in Chapter 1, strategic choices fall into two large categories: business strategies and corporate strategies. **Business-level strategies** are actions firms take to gain competitive advantages in a single market or industry. **Corporate-level strategies** are actions firms take to gain competitive advantages by operating in multiple markets or industries simultaneously.

The two business-level strategies discussed in this book are cost leadership (this chapter) and product differentiation (Chapter 5). The importance of these two business-level strategies is so widely recognized that they are often called **generic business strategies**.

What Is Cost Leadership?

A firm that chooses a **cost leadership business strategy** focuses on gaining advantages by reducing its costs to below those of all its competitors. This does not mean that this firm abandons other business or corporate strategies. Indeed, a single-minded focus on *just* reducing costs can lead a firm to make low-cost products that no one wants to buy. However, a firm pursuing a cost leadership strategy focuses much of its effort on keeping its costs low.

Numerous firms have pursued cost leadership strategies. Wal-Mart clearly follows this strategy, as does Timex and Casio in the watch industry and BIC in the disposable pen and razor market. All these firms advertise their products. However, these advertisements tend to emphasize reliability and low prices—the kinds of product attributes that are usually emphasized by firms pursuing cost leadership strategies.

In automobiles, Hyundai has implemented a cost leadership strategy with its emphasis on low-priced cars for basic transportation. Like Timex, Casio, and BIC, Hyundai spends a significant amount of money advertising its products, but its advertisements tend to emphasize its sporty styling and high gas mileage. Hyundai is positioned as a fun and inexpensive car, not a high-performance sports car or a luxurious status symbol. Hyundai's ability to sell these fun and inexpensive automobiles depends on its design choices (keep it simple) and its low manufacturing costs.[1]

Table 4.1   **Important Sources of Cost Advantages for Firms**

1. Size differences and economies of scale
2. Size differences and diseconomies of scale
3. Experience differences and learning-curve economies
4. Differential low-cost access to productive inputs
5. Technological advantages independent of scale
6. Policy choices

Sources of Cost Advantages

There are many reasons why an individual firm may have a cost advantage over its competitors. Cost advantages are possible even when competing firms produce similar products. Some of the most important of these sources of cost advantage are listed in Table 4.1, and discussed in this section.

Size Differences and Economies of Scale

One of the most widely cited sources of cost advantages for a firm is its size. When there are significant economies of scale in manufacturing, marketing, distribution, service, or other functions of a business, larger firms (up to some point) have a cost advantage over smaller firms. The concept of economies of scale was first defined in Chapter 2. **Economies of scale** are said to exist when the increase in firm size (measured in terms of volume of production) is associated with lower costs (measured in terms of average costs per unit of production), as depicted in Figure 4.1. As the volume of production in a firm increases, the average cost per unit decreases until some optimal volume of production (point X) is reached, after which the average costs per unit of production begin to rise because of **diseconomies of scale** (a concept discussed in more detail later in this chapter).

If the relationship between volume of production and average costs per unit of production depicted in Figure 4.1 holds, and if a firm in an industry has the largest volume of production (but not greater than the optimal level, X), then that firm will have a cost advantage in that industry. There are several reasons why increasing the volume of production in a firm can reduce a firm's costs.

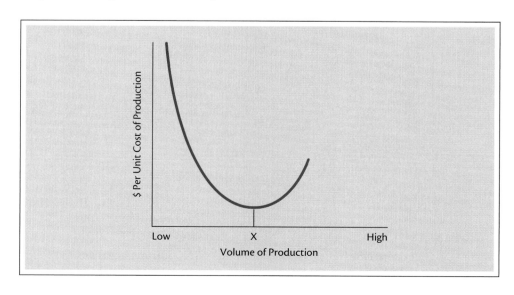

Figure 4.1   Economies of Scale

Table 4.2   **Why Higher Volumes of Production in a Firm Can Lead to Lower Costs**

> With higher production volume . . .
> 1. firms can use specialized machines . . .
> 2. firms can build larger plants . . .
> 3. firms can increase employee specialization . . .
> 4. firms can spread overhead costs across more units produced . . .
>   . . . which can lower per unit production costs.

Some of the most important of these reasons are summarized in Table 4.2 and discussed below.

Volume of Production and Specialized Machines. When a firm has high levels of production, it is often able to purchase and use specialized manufacturing tools that cannot be kept in operation in small firms. Manufacturing managers at BIC Corporation, for example, have emphasized this important advantage of high volumes of production. A former director of manufacturing at BIC once observed:

> *We are in the automation business. Because of our large volume, one tenth of 1 cent in savings turns out to be enormous. . . . One advantage of the high–volume business is that you can get the best equipment and amortize it entirely over a short period of time (4 to 5 months). I'm always looking for new equipment. If I see a cost–savings machine, I can buy it. I'm not constrained by money.*[2]

Only firms with BIC's level of production in the pen industry have the ability to reduce their costs in this manner.

Volume of Production and the Cost of Plant and Equipment. High volumes of production may also allow a firm to build larger manufacturing operations. In some industries, the cost of building these manufacturing operations per unit of production is lower than the cost of building smaller manufacturing operations per unit of production. Thus large-volume firms, other factors being equal, will be able to build lower per unit cost manufacturing operations and will have lower average costs of production.

The link between volume of production and the cost of building manufacturing operations is particularly important in industries characterized by **process manufacturing**—chemical, oil refining, paper and pulp manufacturing, and so forth. Because of the physical geometry of process manufacturing facilities, the costs of constructing a processing plant with increased capacity can be expected to rise as the two–thirds power of a plant's capacity. This is because the area of the surface of some three-dimensional containers (such as spheres and cylinders) increases at a slower rate than the volume of these containers. Thus, larger containers hold greater volumes and require less material per unit volume for the outside skins of these containers. Up to some point, increases in capacity come at a less-than-proportionate rise in the cost of building this capacity.[3]

For example, it might cost a firm $100 to build a plant with a capacity of 1,000 units, for a per-unit average cost of $.01. But, assuming the "two-thirds rule" applies, it might cost a firm $465 to build a plant with a capacity of 10,000 units ($465 = 10,000^{2/3}$), for a per unit average cost of $.0046. The difference between $.01 per unit and $.0046 per unit represents a cost advantage for a large firm.

Volume of Production and Employee Specialization. High volumes of production are also associated with high levels of employee specialization. As workers specialize in accomplishing a narrow task, they can become more and more efficient at this task, thereby reducing their firm's costs. This reasoning applies both in specialized manufacturing tasks (such as the highly specialized manufacturing functions in an assembly line) and in specialized management functions (such as the highly specialized managerial functions of accounting, finance, and sales).

Smaller firms often do not possess the volume of production needed to justify this level of employee specialization. With smaller volumes of production, highly specialized employees may not have enough work to keep them busy an entire workday. This low volume of production is one reason why smaller firms often have employees that perform multiple business functions and often use outside contract employees and part-time workers to accomplish highly specialized functions like accounting, taxes, and human resource management.

Volume of Production and Overhead Costs. A firm with high volumes of production has the luxury of spreading its overhead costs over more units and thereby reducing the overhead costs per unit. Suppose, in a particular industry, that the operation of a variety of accounting, control, and research and development functions, regardless of a firm's size, is $100,000. Clearly, a firm that manufactures 1,000 units is imposing a cost of $100 per unit to cover overhead expenses. However, a firm that manufactures 10,000 units is imposing a cost of $10 per unit to cover overhead. Again, the larger-volume firm's average per unit costs are lower than the small-volume firm's average per unit cost.

Size Differences and Diseconomies of Scale

Just as economies of scale can generate cost advantages for larger firms, important diseconomies of scale can actually increase costs if firms grow too large. As Figure 4.1 shows, if the volume of production rises beyond some optimal point (point X in the figure), this can actually lead to an increase in per-unit costs. If other firms in an industry have grown beyond the optimal firm size, a smaller firm (with a level of production closer to the optimal) may obtain a cost advantage even when all firms in the industry are producing very similar products. Some important sources of diseconomies of scale for a firm are listed in Table 4.3 and discussed in this section.

Physical Limits to Efficient Size. Applying the two–thirds rule to the construction of manufacturing facilities seems to imply, for some industries at least, that larger is always better. However, there are some important physical limitations to the size of some manufacturing processes. Engineers have found, for example, that cement kilns develop unstable internal aerodynamics above 7 million barrels per year capacity. Others have suggested that scaling up nuclear reactors from small installations to huge facilities generates forces and physical processes that, though nondetectable in smaller facilities, can become significant in larger operations. These physical limitations on manufacturing processes reflect the underlying physics and engineering in a manufacturing process and suggest when the cost curve in Figure 4.1 will begin to rise.[4]

Table 4.3   **Major Sources of Diseconomies of Scale**

When the volume of production gets too large . . .
1. physical limits to efficient size . . .
2. managerial diseconomies . . .
3. worker de-motivation. . . .
4. distance to markets and suppliers . . .
   . . . can increase per-unit costs.

Managerial Diseconomies. Although the underlying physics and engineering in a manufacturing process have an important impact on a firm's costs, managerial diseconomies are perhaps an even more important cause of these cost increases. As a firm increases in size, it often increases in complexity, and the ability of managers to control and operate it efficiently becomes limited.

One well-known example of a manufacturing plant that grew too large and thus became inefficient is Crown, Cork and Seal's can-manufacturing plant in Philadelphia. Through the early part of this century, this Philadelphia facility handled as many as 75 different can-manufacturing lines. The most efficient plants in the industry, however, were running from 10 to 15 lines simultaneously. The huge Philadelphia facility was simply too large to operate efficiently and was characterized by large numbers of breakdowns, a high percentage of idle lines, and poor-quality products.[5]

Worker De-Motivation. A third source of diseconomies of scale depends on the relationship between firm size, employee specialization, and employee motivation. It has already been suggested that one of the advantages of increased volumes of production is that it allows workers to specialize in smaller and more narrowly defined production tasks. With specialization, workers become more and more efficient at the particular task facing them.

However, a significant stream of research suggests that these types of very specialized jobs can be unmotivating for employees. Based on motivational theories taken from social psychology, this work suggests that as workers are removed further from the complete product that is the end result of a manufacturing process, the role that a worker's job plays in the overall manufacturing process becomes more and more obscure. As workers become mere "cogs in a manufacturing machine," worker motivation wanes, and productivity and quality can both suffer.[6]

Distance to Markets and Suppliers. A final source of diseconomies of scale can be the distance between a large manufacturing facility and the place where the goods in question are to be sold, or the places where essential raw materials are purchased. Any reductions in cost attributable to the exploitation of economies of scale in manufacturing may be more than offset by large transportation costs associated with moving supplies and products to and from the manufacturing facility. Firms that build highly efficient plants without recognizing these significant transportation costs may put themselves at a competitive disadvantage compared to firms with slightly less efficient plants but plants that are located nearer suppliers and key markets.

Experience Differences and Learning-Curve Economies

A third possible source of cost advantages for firms in a particular business depends on their different cumulative levels of production. In some circumstances, firms with the greatest experience in manufacturing a product or service will have the lowest costs in an industry and thus will have a cost-based advantage. The link between cumulative volumes of production and cost has been formalized in the concept of the **learning curve**. The relationship between cumulative volumes of production and per unit costs is graphically represented in Figure 4.2.

The Learning Curve and Economies of Scale. As depicted in Figure 4.2, the learning curve is very similar to the concept of economies of scale. However, there are two important differences. First, where economies of scale focuses on the relationship between the volume of production at a given point in time and average unit costs, the learning curve focuses on the relationship between the *cumulative* volume of production—that is, how much a firm has produced over time—and average unit costs. Second, where diseconomies of scale are presumed to exist if a firm gets too

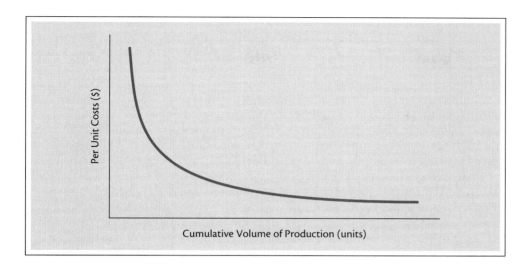

Figure 4.2 The Learning Curve and the Cost of Production

large, there is no corresponding increase in costs in the learning-curve model as the cumulative volume of production grows. Rather, costs continue to fall until they approach the lowest technologically possible cost.

The Learning Curve and Cost Advantages. The learning-curve model is based on the empirical observation that the costs of producing a unit of output fall as the cumulative volume of output increases. This relationship was first observed in the construction of aircraft before World War II. Research then showed that the labor costs per aircraft fell by 20 percent each time the cumulative volume of production doubled.[7] A similar pattern has been observed in numerous industries, although the rate of cost reduction may vary. Some of these industries include the manufacture of ships, computers, spacecraft, and semiconductors. In all these cases, increases in cumulative production have been associated with the improvement of work methods, a fine-tuning of the production operation, and detailed learning about how to make production as efficient as possible.

However, learning-curve cost advantages are not restricted to manufacturing. Learning can be associated with any business function, from purchasing raw materials to distribution and service. Also, there can be important learning effects in service industries as well. The learning curve applies whenever the cost of accomplishing a business activity falls as a function of the cumulative number of times a firm has engaged in that activity.[8]

The Learning Curve and Competitive Advantage. The learning-curve model summarized in Figure 4.2 has been used to develop a model of cost-based competitive advantage that links learning with market share and average production costs. The major proponent of the application of this learning-curve logic to create competitive advantage has been the Boston Consulting Group.[9]

The logic behind this application of the learning-curve model is straightforward: The first firm that successfully moves down the learning curve will obtain a cost advantage over rivals. To move a production process down the learning curve, a firm needs to have higher levels of cumulative volume of production. Of course, firms that are successful at producing high volumes of output need to sell that output to customers. In selling this output, firms are, in effect, increasing their market share. Thus, to drive down the learning-curve and obtain a cost advantage, firms must aggressively acquire market share.

This application of learning-curve logic has been criticized by a wide variety of authors.[10] Two criticisms are particularly salient. First, although the acquisition of market share is likely to allow a firm to reduce its production costs, the acquisition of share itself is expensive. To acquire share, firms must often increase advertising and other marketing expenditures and reduce prices. Indeed, research suggests that the costs that firms will need to absorb in order to acquire market share will often equal the value of that market share in lowering a firm's production costs. Thus, efforts to move down the learning-curve quickly, by acquiring market share, are likely to generate only normal economic performance. This may have occurred in the consolidation of the U. S. beer industry, as described in the Research Made Relevant feature.

The second major criticism of this application of the learning-curve model is that there is, in this logic, no room for any other business or corporate strategies. In other words, this application of the learning-curve implicitly assumes that firms can compete only on the basis of their low costs and that any other strategies are not possible. Most industries, however, are characterized by opportunities for at least some of these other strategies, and thus this strict application of the learning-curve model can be misleading.[11]

These criticisms aside, it is still the case that in many industries, firms with larger cumulative levels of production, other things being equal, will have lower average production costs. Thus, experience in all the facets of production can be a source of cost advantage even if the single–minded pursuit of market share to obtain these cost reductions may not give a firm above-normal economic returns.

Differential Low-Cost Access to Productive Inputs

Besides economies of scale, diseconomies of scale, and learning-curve cost advantages, differential low-cost access to productive inputs may create cost differences among firms producing similar products in an industry. **Productive inputs** are any supplies used by a firm in conducting its business activities; they include, among other things, labor, capital, land, and raw materials. A firm that has differential low-cost access to one or more of these factors is likely to have lower economic costs compared to rivals.

Consider, for example, an oil company with fields in Saudi Arabia compared to an oil company with fields in the North Sea. The cost of obtaining crude oil for the first firm is considerably less than the cost of obtaining crude oil for the second. North Sea drilling involves the construction of giant offshore drilling platforms, housing workers on floating cities, and transporting oil across an often-stormy sea. Drilling in Saudi Arabia requires only the simplest drilling technologies because the oil is found relatively close to the surface.

Of course, in order to create a cost advantage, the cost of acquiring low-cost productive inputs must be less than the cost savings generated by these factors. For example, even though it may be much less costly to drill for oil in Saudi Arabia than in the North Sea, if it is very expensive to purchase the rights to drill in Saudi Arabia compared to the costs of the rights to drill in the North Sea, the potential cost advantages of drilling in Saudi Arabia can be lost. As with all sources of cost advantages, firms must be careful to weigh the cost of acquiring that advantage against the value of that advantage for the firm.

Differential access to raw materials like oil, coal, and copper ore can be important determinants of a cost advantage. However, differential access to other productive inputs can be just as important. For example, it may be easier (that is, less costly) to recruit highly trained electronics engineers for firms located near where these engineers receive their schooling than for firms located some distance

Research Made Relevant

*I*n the 1960s and early 1970s, the U.S. beer market was highly fragmented—with numerous small, regional brewers dominating their local markets. Today, three brewers—Anheuser-Busch, Miller Brewing Company and Coors Brewing Company—dominate the industry, with well over 85 percent of the U.S. beer market. So, how did this industry consolidation occur, and did today's big beer companies create economic value by increasing their market share? This is the subject of an article by Cynthia Montgomery and Birger Wernerfelt.

These authors begin by observing that we know that market share can create value for a firm—among other things, it can reduce costs if learning-curve economies are operating. However, since market share can create value, wouldn't it often be the case that a competitive market for market share might develop? That is, if several firms in an industry were all trying to acquire market share—by increasing their advertising, reducing their prices, and so forth—wouldn't the "price" of acquiring that share go up, to the point perhaps, that the price of acquiring additional share might actually be greater than the value of that share? If this happened, then firms that are successful in acquiring share might actually destroy some of their economic value.

Well, this is exactly what happened in the U.S. beer industry. All but one of the top six brewers in the United States saw at least some increases in their market share—Anheuser-Busch's share increased 10.8 percent and Miller's share increased

The Consolidation of the U.S. Beer Market—Did Bud Pay Too Much?

16.3 percent. Only Schlitz saw a reduction in share, of 2.1 percent. However, using a market-based measure of performance similar to those described in Chapter 1, Montgomery and Wernerfelt showed that increases in market share actually destroyed economic value for firms in the U.S. beer industry. Moreover, the more share a firm acquired, the greater the negative impact on a firm's value: Miller and Anheuser-Busch destroyed more value than Schlitz, a firm that lost 2.1 percentage points in share but saw its economic value actually increase!

None of these results is inconsistent with the notion that high market share can, among other things, reduce a firm's costs. However, these results do suggest that if several equally skilled and resourced firms are all attempting to acquire market share, the price of doing so can sometimes rise to be equal

to, or perhaps even greater than, the value that share would create for a firm.

Of course, the performance measure that was used in this research was relatively short term in orientation. It may be the case that Anheuser-Busch and Miller have been able to create value with their market share in ways that could not have been anticipated when they first acquired this share. This suggests that while acquiring market share in a competitive situation may not generate short- to medium-term profits, it may be profitable in the long run—if a firm with large market share is able to leverage that resource in creative ways that were not anticipated when it originally acquired its share advantage.

This research has become very important recently as another wave of consolidations seems to be occurring in the beer industry. Interbrew SA, a European brewer, recently merged with the leading brewer in South America. Anheuser-Busch recently purchased Harbin Brewery Group, Ltd., a regional brewer in China. And Coors and Molson are investigating a possible merger. Whether this current round of consolidations will see firms overpaying for market share, as was the case in the last round of consolidations, is still an open question.

Source: R. Frank, D. Berman, and E. Cherney (2004). "Molson family fight threatens merger with Coors." *Wall Street Journal*, Friday, July 23, pp. A1 +; C. Lawton (2004). "Coors investors may not want to mix drinks." *Wall Street Journal*, Tuesday, July 20, pp. C1 +; C. Montgomery and B. Wernerfelt (1991). "Sources of superior performance: Market share versus industry effects in the U.S. Brewing industry." *Management Science*, 37, pp. 954–959.

away. This lower cost of recruiting is a partial explanation of the development of geographic technology centers like Silicon Valley in California, Route 128 in Massachusetts, and the Research Triangle in North Carolina. In all three cases, firms are located physically close to several universities that train the engineers that are the lifeblood of high-technology companies. The search for low-cost labor can create ethical dilemmas, as described in the Ethics and Strategy feature.

Technological Advantages Independent of Scale

Another possible source of cost advantage in an industry may be the different technologies that firms employ to manage their business. It has already been suggested that larger firms may have technology–based cost advantages reflecting their ability to exploit economies of scale (for example, the two-thirds rule). Here, technology–based cost advantages that do not depend upon economies of scale are discussed.

Traditionally, discussion of technology–based cost advantages has focused on the machines, computers, and other physical tools that firms use to manage their business. Clearly, in some industries, these physical technology differences between firms can create important cost differences—even when the firms in question are approximately the same size in terms of volume of production. In the steel industry, for example, technological advances can substantially reduce the cost of producing steel. Firms with the latest steel-manufacturing technology will typically enjoy some cost advantage compared to similar-sized firms without the latest technology. The same applies in the manufacturing of semiconductors, automobiles, consumer electronics, and a wide variety of other products.[12]

These physical technology cost advantages apply in service firms as well as in manufacturing firms. For example, early in its history, Charles Schwab, a leading discount brokerage, purchased a computer system that enabled Schwab to complete customer transactions more rapidly and at a lower cost than rivals.[13] Kaiser-Permanente, the largest HMO in the United States, has invested in information technology that doctors can use to avoid incorrect diagnoses and procedures that can adversely affect a patient's health. By avoiding these medical mistakes, Kaiser-Permanente can substantially reduce its costs of providing medical service.[14]

However, the concept of technology can be easily broadened to include not just the physical tools that firms use to manage their business, but any processes within a firm used in this way. This concept of firm technology includes not only the **technological hardware** of companies—the machines and robots—but also the **technological software** of firms—things like the quality of relations between labor and management, an organization's culture, and the quality of managerial controls. All these characteristics of a firm can have an impact on a firm's economic costs.[15]

Again, Wal-Mart is an example of a firm that understands the importance of technological software to realize a cost leadership strategy. Wal-Mart's culture of enthusiasm and commitment—complete with Saturday morning employee meetings where the Wal-Mart cheer is shouted and the Wal-Mart song is played—is central to involving all of Wal-Mart's employees in reducing its costs, allowing Wal-Mart to charge lower prices.

Policy Choices

Thus far this discussion has focused on reasons why a firm can gain a cost advantage despite producing products that are similar to competing firms' products. When firms produce essentially the same outputs, differences in economies of scale, learning-curve advantages, differential access to productive inputs, and differences in technology can all create cost advantages (and disadvantages) for

Ethics and Strategy

*O*ne of the most important productive inputs in almost all companies is labor. Getting differential low-cost access to labor can give a firm a cost advantage.

This search for low labor costs has led some firms to engage in an international "Race to the Bottom." It is well known that the wage rates of most U.S. and Western European workers are much higher than the wage rates of workers in other, less developed parts of the world. While a firm might have to pay its employees $20 per hour (in wages and benefits) to make sneakers and basketball shoes in the United States, that same firm may only have to pay an employee in the Philippines, or Malaysia, or China $1.00 per day to make the same sneakers and basketball shoes—shoes the firm might be able to sell for $150 a pair in the United States and Europe. Thus, many firms look to overseas manufacturing as a way to keep their labor cost low.

But this search for low labor cost has some important unintended consequences. First, the location of the lowest cost labor rates in the world changes over time. It used to be that Mexico had the lowest labor rates, then Korea and the Philippines, then Malaysia, then China. As the infrastructures of each of these countries evolve to the point that they can support worldwide manufacturing, firms abandon their relation-

The Race to the Bottom

ships with firms in prior countries in search of still lower costs in new countries. The only way former "low-cost centers" can compete is to drive their costs even lower.

This sometimes leads to a second unintended consequence of the "race to the bottom": horrendous working conditions and low wages in these low-cost manufacturing settings. Employees earning $1 for working a 10-hour day, six days a week may look good on the corporate bottom line, but many observers are deeply concerned about the moral and ethical issues associated with this strategy. Indeed, several companies—including Nike and Kmart—have been forced to increase the wages

and improve the working conditions of many of their overseas employees.

An even more horrific result of this "race to the bottom" has been the reemergence of what amounts to slavery in some Western European countries and some parts of the United States. In search of the promise of a better life, illegal immigrants are sometimes brought to Western European countries or the United States and forced to work in illegal, underground factories. These illegal immigrants are sometimes forced to work as many as 20 hours a day, for little or no pay—supposedly to "pay off" the price of bringing them out of their less developed countries. And because of their illegal status and language barriers, they often do not feel empowered to go to the local authorities.

Of course, the people who create and manage these facilities are criminals and deserve contempt. But, what about the companies that purchase the services of these illegal and immoral manufacturing operations? Aren't they also culpable, both legally and morally?

Sources: R. DeGeorge (2000). "Ethics in international business—A contradiction in terms?" *Business Credit*, 102, pp. 50 +; G. Edmondson, K. Carlisle, I. Resch, K. Nickel Anhalt, and H. Dawley (2000). "Workers in bondage." *BusinessWeek*, November 27, pp. 146 +; D. Winter (2000). "Facing globalization." *Ward's Auto World*, 36, pp. 7 +.

them. However, firms can also make choices about the kinds of products and services they will sell—choices that have an impact on their relative cost position. These choices are called **policy choices**.

In general, firms that are attempting to implement a cost leadership strategy will choose to produce relatively simple standardized products that sell for relatively low prices compared to the products and prices firms pursuing other business or corporate strategies choose. These kinds of products often tend to have high volumes of sales, which (if significant economies of scale exist) tend to reduce costs even further.

These kinds of choices in product and pricing tend to have a very broad impact on a cost leader's operations. In these firms, the task of reducing costs is not delegated to a single function or a special task force within the firm but is the responsibility of every manager and employee. Cost reduction sometimes becomes the central objective of the firm. Indeed, in this setting, management must be constantly alert to cost-cutting efforts that reduce the ability of the firm to meet customers' needs. This kind of cost-cutting culture is central to Wal-Mart's ability to implement its cost leadership strategy.

 ## The Value of Cost Leadership

There is little doubt that cost differences can exist among firms, even when those firms are selling very similar products. Policy choices about the kinds of products firms in an industry choose to produce can also create important cost differences. But, under what conditions will these kinds of cost advantages actually create value for a firm?

It was suggested in Chapter 3 that one way to tell if a resource or capability—like the ability of a firm to have a cost advantage—actually creates value for a firm is by whether or not that resource or capability enables a firm to neutralize its external threats or exploit its external opportunities. The ability of a cost leadership position to neutralize external threats will be examined here. The ability of such a position to enable a firm to exploit opportunities will be left as an exercise. The specific economic consequences of cost leadership are discussed in the Strategy in Depth feature.

Cost Leadership and the Threat of Entry

A cost leadership competitive strategy helps reduce the threat of new entrants by creating cost–based barriers to entry. Recall that many of the barriers to entry cited in Chapter 2, including economies of scale and cost advantages independent of scale, assume that incumbent firms have lower costs than potential entrants. If an incumbent firm is a cost leader, for any of the reasons just listed, then new entrants may have to invest heavily to reduce their costs prior to entry. Often, new entrants will enter using another business strategy (for example, product differentiation) rather than attempting to compete on costs.

Cost Leadership and the Threat of Rivalry

Firms with a low-cost position also reduce the threat of rivalry. The threat of rivalry is reduced through pricing strategies that low-cost firms can engage in and through their relative impact on the performance of a low-cost firm and its higher-cost rivals.

Cost leader firms have two choices in pricing their products or services. First, these firms can set their prices equal to the prices of higher-cost competitors. Assuming that there are few opportunities for other firms to implement product differentiation strategies, customers will be indifferent about purchasing goods or services from the low-cost firm or from its high-cost rivals. However, at these competitive prices, high-cost firms are likely to earn normal economic performance, while the cost leader firm is earning above-normal performance.

Second, low-cost firms can price their goods or services slightly below the prices of their high-cost rivals. Again, assuming little product differentiation, customers will no longer be indifferent about which firm they prefer to buy from. Obviously, the lower prices of the low-cost firm will attract numerous customers, rapidly increasing the market share of the low-cost firm.

Strategy in Depth

*A*nother way to demonstrate that cost leadership can be a source of economic value is to directly examine the economic profits generated by a firm with a cost advantage operating in an otherwise very competitive industry. This is done in Figure 4.3.

The firms depicted in this figure are **price takers**—that is, the price of the products or services they sell is determined by market conditions and not by individual decisions of firms. This implies that there is effectively no product differentiation in this market and that no one firm's sales constitute a large percentage of this market.

The price of goods or services in this type of market (P^*) is determined by aggregate industry supply and demand. This industry price determines the demand facing an individual firm in this market. Because these firms are price takers, the demand facing an individual firm is horizontal—that is, firm decisions about levels of output have a negligible impact on overall industry supply and thus a negligible impact on the market-determined price. As is well known, a firm in this setting maximizes its economic performance by producing a quantity of output (Q) so that marginal revenue equals marginal cost (MC). The ability of firms to earn economic profits in this setting depends upon the relationship between the market-determined price (P^*) and the average total

The Economics
of Cost Leadership

cost (ATC) of a firm at the quantity it chooses to produce.

Firms in the market depicted in Figure 4.3 fall into two categories. All but one firm have the average-total-cost curve ATC_2 and marginal-cost curve

MC_2. However, one firm in this industry has the average-total-cost curve ATC_1 and marginal-cost curve MC_1. Notice that ATC_1 is less than ATC_2 at the performance-maximizing quantities produced by these two kinds of firms (Q_1 and Q_2, respectively). In this particular example, firms with common average-total-cost curves are earning zero economic profits, while the low-cost firm is earning an economic profit (equal to the shaded area in the figure). A variety of other examples could also be constructed: The cost leader firm could be earning zero economic profits while other firms in the market are incurring economic losses; the cost leader firm could be earning substantial economic profits while other firms are earning smaller economic profits; the cost leader firm could be incurring small economic losses while the other firms are incurring substantial economic losses; and so forth. However, in all these examples, the cost leader's economic performance is greater than the economic performance of other firms in the industry. Thus, cost leadership can have an important impact on a firm's economic performance.

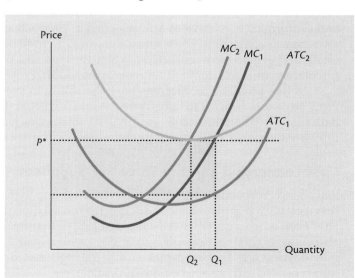

Figure 4.3 Cost Leadership and Economic Performance

Each of these alternatives has strengths and weaknesses. Keeping prices equal to the competition's prices enables a low-cost firm to earn large margins on its sales. As important, this pricing approach at least partially conceals the fact that the low-cost firm has a cost advantage. Concealing this information reduces the chances that competitors will imitate the low-cost firm, thereby reducing its cost advantage. However, keeping prices equal to a competitor's prices does sacrifice market share and sales volume.

Setting the low-cost firm's prices below the prices of competing firms has the opposite effects. Such a pricing strategy can significantly increase a firm's market share and total volume of sales, but at the cost of some of the profit margin of the low-cost firm. Also, setting prices to this lower level sends a signal to competitors that lower costs are possible. Such a signal may motivate competitors to try to reduce their costs, either through implementing their own cost leadership competitive strategies or through implementing strategies that reduce costs.

In the end, the choice between these two pricing strategies depends upon the ability of competing firms to respond to the cost advantages of cost leaders. If the potential responses of competing firms are likely to be very detrimental to the cost leader, then this firm should set its prices equal to competitors' prices, sacrificing some market share for increased profit margins and the release of less information. However, if competitive reactions are not likely to threaten the cost leader, then dropping prices below competitors' prices should increase overall economic performance through increased volumes of profitable sales.

More generally, these strategic pricing options, and the potential above-normal economic performance they hold, are available only to cost leaders. These strategies enable a low-cost firm to earn above-normal economic returns even if the industry within which this firm operates is characterized by intense rivalry.

Cost Leadership and the Threat of Substitutes

As suggested in Chapter 2, substitutes become a threat to a firm when their cost and performance, relative to a firm's current products or services, become more attractive to customers. Thus, when the price of crude oil goes up, substitutes for crude oil become more attractive. When the cost and performance of electronic calculators improve, demand for mechanical adding machines disappears.

In this situation, cost leaders have the ability to keep their products and services attractive relative to substitutes. While high-cost firms may have to charge high prices to cover their costs, thus making substitutes more attractive, cost leaders can keep their prices low and still earn normal or above-normal economic profits.

Cost Leadership and the Threat of Suppliers

Suppliers can become a threat to a firm by charging higher prices for the goods or services they supply or by reducing the quality of those goods or services. However, when a supplier sells to a cost leader, that firm has greater flexibility in absorbing higher-cost supplies than does a high-cost firm. Higher supply costs may destroy any above-normal profits for high-cost firms but still allow a cost leader firm to earn an above-normal profit.

Cost leadership based on large volumes of production and economies of scale can also reduce the threat of suppliers. Large volumes of production imply large purchases of raw materials and other supplies. Suppliers are not likely to jeopardize these sales by threatening their customers. Indeed, as was suggested earlier, buyers are often able to use their purchasing volume to extract volume discounts from suppliers.

Cost Leadership and the Threat of Buyers

Cost leadership can also reduce the threat of buyers. Powerful buyers are a threat to firms when they insist on low prices or higher quality and service from their suppliers. Lower prices threaten firm revenues; higher quality can increase a firm's costs. Cost leaders can have their revenues reduced by buyer threats and still have normal or above-normal performance. These firms can also absorb the greater costs of increased quality or service and may still have a cost advantage over their competition.

Buyers can also be a threat through backward vertical integration. Being a cost leader deters buyer backward vertical integration, because a buyer that vertically integrates backward will often not have costs as low as an incumbent cost leader. Rather than vertically integrating backwards and increasing its cost of supplies, powerful buyers usually prefer to continue purchasing from their low-cost suppliers.

Finally, if cost leadership is based on large volumes of production, then the threat of buyers may be reduced, because buyers may depend on just a few firms for the goods or services they purchase. This dependence reduces the willingness of buyers to threaten a selling firm.

Cost Leadership and Sustained Competitive Advantage   V R I O

Given that cost leadership can be valuable, an important question becomes, "Under what conditions will firms implementing this business strategy be able to maintain that leadership to obtain a sustained competitive advantage?" If cost leadership strategies can be implemented by numerous firms in an industry, or if no firms face a cost disadvantage in imitating a cost leadership strategy, then being a cost leader will not generate a sustained competitive advantage for a firm. As was suggested in Chapter 3, the ability of a valuable cost leadership competitive strategy to generate a sustained competitive advantage depends on that strategy being rare and costly to imitate, either through direct duplication or substitution. As suggested in Tables 4.4 and 4.5, the rarity and imitability of a cost leadership strategy depend, at least in part, on the sources of that cost advantage.

The Rarity of Sources of Cost Advantage

Some of the sources of cost advantage listed in Table 4.4 are likely to be rare among a set of competing firms; others are less likely to be rare. Sources of cost advantage that are likely to be rare include learning-curve economies (at least in emerging industries), differential low-cost access to productive inputs, and technological "software." The remaining sources of cost advantage are less likely to be rare.

Table 4.4   **The Rarity of Sources of Cost Advantage**

Likely-to-be-rare sources of cost advantage	Less-likely-to-be-rare sources of cost advantage
Leaving-curve economies of scale (especially in emerging businesses)	Economies of scale (except when efficient plant size approximately equals total industry demand)
Differential low-cost access to productive inputs	Diseconomies of scale
Technological "software"	Technological hardware (unless a firm has proprietary hardware development skills)
	Policy choices

Table 4.5   **Direct Duplication of Cost Leadership**

	Source of cost advantage	Basis for costly duplication		
		History	Uncertainty	Social complexity
Low-cost duplication possible	1. Economies of scale	—	—	—
	2. Diseconomies of scale	—	—	—
May be costly to duplicate	3. Learning-curve economies	*	—	—
	4. Technological "hardware"	—	*	*
	5. Policy choices	*	—	—
Usually costly to duplicate	6. Differential low-cost access to productive inputs	***	—	**
	7. Technological "software"	***	**	***

— = not a source of costly imitation   * = somewhat likely to be a source of costly imitation   ** = likely to be a source of costly imitation
*** = very likely to be a source of costly imitation

Rare Sources of Cost Advantage

Early in the evolution of an industry, substantial differences in the cumulative volume of production of different firms are not unusual. Indeed, this was one of the major benefits associated with first-mover advantages, discussed in Chapter 2. These differences in cumulative volume of production, in combination with substantial learning-curve economies, suggest that in some settings, learning-curve advantages may be rare and thus a source of at least temporary competitive advantage.

The definition of differential access to productive inputs implies that this access is often rare. Certainly, if large numbers of competing firms have this same access, then it cannot be a source of competitive advantage.

Technological software is also likely to be rare among a set of competing firms. These software attributes represent each firm's path through history. If these histories are unique, then the technological software they create may also be rare. Of course, if several competing firms experience similar paths through history, the technological software in these firms is less likely to be rare.

Less Rare Sources of Cost Advantage

When the efficient size of a firm or plant is significantly smaller than the total size of an industry, there will usually be numerous efficient firms or plants in that industry, and a cost leadership strategy based on economies of scale will not be rare. For example, if the efficient firm or plant size in an industry is 500 units, and the total size of the industry (measured in units produced) is 500,000 units, then there are likely to be numerous efficient firms or plants in this industry, and economies of scale are not likely to give any one firm a cost–based competitive advantage.

Cost advantages based on diseconomies of scale are also not likely to be rare. It is unusual for numerous firms to adopt levels of production in excess of optimal levels. If only a few firms are too large in this sense, then several competing firms in an industry that are *not* too large will have cost advantages over the firms that are too large. However, because several firms will enjoy these cost advantages, they are not rare.

One important exception to this generalization may be when changes in technology significantly reduce the most efficient scale of an operation. Given such changes in technology, several firms may be inefficiently large. If a small number of firms happen to be sized appropriately, then the cost advantages these firms obtain in this way may be rare. Such changes in technology have made large integrated steel producers "too big" relative to smaller mini-mills. Thus, mini-mills have a cost advantage over larger integrated steel firms.

Technological hardware is also not likely to be rare, especially if it is developed by suppliers and sold on the open market. However, if a firm has proprietary technology development skills, it may possess rare technological hardware that creates cost advantages.

Finally, policy choices by themselves are not likely to be a rare source of cost advantage, particularly if the product or service attributes in question are easy to observe and describe.

The Imitability of Sources of Cost Advantage

Even when a particular source of cost advantage is rare, it must be costly to imitate in order to be a source of sustained competitive advantage. Both direct duplication and substitution, as forms of imitation, are important. Again, the imitability of a cost advantage depends, at least in part, on the source of that advantage.

Easy-to-Duplicate Sources of Cost Advantage

In general, economies of scale and diseconomies of scale are relatively easy-to-duplicate bases of cost leadership. As can be seen in Table 4.5, these sources of cost advantage do not build on history, uncertainty, or socially complex resources and capabilities and thus are not protected from duplication for these reasons.

For example, if a small number of firms does obtain a cost advantage based on economies of scale, and if the relationship between production scale and costs is widely understood among competing firms, then firms at a cost disadvantage will rapidly adjust their production to exploit these economies of scale. This can be done by either growing a firm's current operations to the point that the firm exploits economies or by combining previously separate operations to obtain these economies. Both actions enable a firm at a cost disadvantage to begin using specialized machines, reduce the cost of plant and equipment, increase employee specialization, and spread overhead costs more effectively.

Indeed, perhaps the only time economies of scale are not subject to low-cost duplication is when the efficient size of operations is a significant percentage of total demand in an industry. Of course, this is the situation described in Chapter 2's discussion of economies of scale as a barrier to entry. For example, as suggested earlier, BIC Corporation, with its dominant market share in the disposable pen market, has apparently been able to gain and retain an important cost advantage in that market based on economies of scale. BIC's ability to retain this advantage reflects the fact that the optimal plant size in the disposable pen market is a significant percentage of the pen market, and thus economies of scale act as a barrier to entry in that market.

Like economies of scale, in many settings diseconomies of scale will not be a source of sustained competitive advantage for firms that have *not* grown too large. In the short run, firms experiencing significant diseconomies can shrink the size of their operations to become more efficient. In the long run, firms that fail to adjust their size will earn below-normal economic performance and cease operations.

Although in many ways reducing the size of operations to improve efficiency seems like a simple problem for managers in firms or plants, in practice it is often a difficult change to implement. Because of uncertainty, managers in a firm or plant that is too large may not understand that diseconomies of scale have increased their costs. Sometimes, managers conclude that the problem is that employees are not working hard enough, that problems in production can be

Strategy in the Emerging Enterprise

Baseball in the United States has a problem. Most observers agree that it is better for fans if there is competitive balance in the league—that is, if, at the beginning of the year, the fans of several teams believe that their team has a chance to go to the World Series and win it all. However, the economic reality of competition in baseball is that only a small number of financially successful teams in large cities—the New York Yankees, the Los Angeles Dodgers—have the resources necessary to compete for a spot in the World Series year after year. So called "small market teams," like the Pittsburgh Pirates or the Milwaukee Brewers—may be able to compete every once in a while, but these exceptions prove the general rule—teams from large markets usually win the World Series.

And then there is Oakland and the Oakland A's. Oakland (with a population of just over 400,000) is the smallest—and least glamorous—of the three cities

The Oakland A's: Inventing a New Way to Play Competitive Baseball

in the San Francisco Bay Area, the other two being San Francisco and San Jose. The A's play in an outdated stadium—Network Associates Coliseum—to an average crowd of 26,787 fans—ranking

eighteenth among the 30 major league baseball teams in the United States. In 2003, the A's player payroll was $49 million, about one-third of the Yankees' player payroll.

Despite these liabilities, from 1998 to 2000, the A's compiled a win–loss record of 456 wins and 353 losses—second in the American league behind the Yankees. And, the team made money!

What is the "secret" to the A's success? Their general manager, William Lamar Beane, says that it has to do with three factors: how players are evaluated, making sure that every personnel decision in the organization is consistent with this approach to evaluation, and ensuring that all personnel decisions are thought of as business decisions.

The criteria used by the A's to evaluate players are easy enough to state. For batters, the A's focus on on-base percentage (i.e., how often a batter reaches base) and total bases (a measure of the ability

fixed, and so forth. These firms or plants may continue their inefficient operations for some time, despite costs that are higher than the industry average.[16]

Other psychological processes can also delay the abandonment of operations that are too large. One of these phenomena is known as **escalation of commitment**: Sometimes, managers committed to an incorrect (cost-increasing or revenue-reducing) course of action *increase* their commitment to this action as its limitations become manifest. For example, a manager who believes that the optimal firm size in an industry is larger than the actual optimal size may remain committed to large operations despite costs that are higher than the industry average.[17]

For all these reasons, firms suffering from diseconomies of scale must often turn to outside managers to assist in reducing costs. Outsiders bring a fresh view to the organization's problems and are not committed to the practices that generated the problems in the first place.[18]

Bases of Cost Leadership That May Be Costly to Duplicate

Although cost advantages based on learning-curve economies are rare (especially in emerging industries), they are usually not costly to duplicate. As suggested in Chapter 2, for learning-curve cost advantages to be a source of sustained competitive advantage, the learning obtained by a firm must be proprietary. Most recent empirical work suggests that in most industries learning is not proprietary and

of a batter to hit for power)—that is, they focus on the ability of players to get on base and score. For pitchers, the A's focus on the percentage of first pitches that are strikes and the quality of a pitcher's fast ball. First-pitch strikes and throwing a good fast ball are correlated with keeping runners off base. Thus, not surprisingly, the A's criteria for evaluating pitchers are the reverse of their criteria for evaluating hitters.

While these evaluation criteria are easy to state, getting the entire organization to apply them consistently in scouting, choosing, developing, and managing players is much more difficult. Almost every baseball player and fan has his or her own favorite way to evaluate players. However, if you want to work in the A's organization, you must be willing to let go of your personal favorite and evaluate players the A's way. The result is that players that come through the A's farm system—the minor leagues where younger players are developed until they

are ready to play in the major leagues—learn a single way of playing baseball instead of learning a new approach to the game every time they change managers or coaches. One of the implications of this consistency has been that the A's farm system has been among the most productive in baseball.

This consistent farm system enables the A's to treat personnel decisions—including decisions about whether or not they should re-sign a star player or let him go to another team—as business decisions. The A's simply do not have the resources necessary to play the personnel game the same way as the Los Angeles Dodgers or the New York Yankees. When these teams need a particular kind of player, they go and sign one. Oakland has to rely more on its farm system. But because its farm system performs so well, the A's can let so-called "superstars" go to other teams, knowing that they are likely to have a younger—and cheaper—player in the minor

leagues, just waiting for the chance to play in "the show"—the players' nickname for the major leagues. This allows the A's to keep their payroll costs down and remain profitable, despite relatively small crowds, while still fielding a team that competes virtually every year for the right to play in the World Series.

Of course, an important question becomes: How sustainable is the A's competitive advantage? The evaluation criteria, themselves, are not a source of sustained competitive advantage. However, the socially complex nature of how these criteria are consistently applied throughout the A's organization may be a source of sustained competitive advantage in enabling the A's to gain the differential access to low-cost productive inputs—in this case, baseball players.

Sources: K. Hammonds (2003). "How to play Beane ball." *Fast Company*, May, pp. 84 +; M. Lewis (2003). *Moneyball*. New York; Norton; A. McGahan, J. F. McGuire, and J. Kou (1997). "The baseball strike." Harvard Business Review Case No. 9-796-059.

thus can be rapidly duplicated as competing firms move down the learning-curve by increasing their cumulative volume of production.[19]

However, the fact that learning is not costly to duplicate in *most* industries does not mean it is never costly to duplicate. In some industries the ability of firms to learn from their production experience may vary significantly. For example, some firms treat production errors as failures and systematically punish employees who make those errors. These firms effectively reduce risk-taking among their production employees and thus reduce the chances of learning how to improve their production process. Alternatively, other firms treat production errors as opportunities to learn how to improve their production process. These firms are likely to move rapidly down the learning-curve and retain cost advantages, despite the cumulative volume of production of competing firms. These different responses to production errors reflect the organizational cultures of these different firms. Because organizational cultures are socially complex, they can be very costly to duplicate.[20]

Because technological hardware can usually be purchased across supply markets, it is also not likely to be difficult to duplicate. Sometimes, however, technological hardware can be proprietary, or closely bundled with other unique, costly-to-duplicate resources controlled by a firm. In this case, technological hardware *can* be costly to duplicate.

It is unusual, but not impossible, for policy choices, per se, to be a source of sustained competitive cost advantages for a firm. As suggested earlier, if the policies in question focus on easy-to-observe and easy-to-describe product characteristics, then duplication is likely, and cost advantages based on policy choices will be temporary. However, if policy choices reflect complex decision processes within a firm, teamwork among different parts of the design and manufacturing process, or any of the software commitments discussed previously, then policy choices can be a source of sustained competitive advantage, as long as only a few firms have the ability to make these choices.

Indeed, most of the successful firms that operate in unattractive industries make policy choices that are costly to imitate because they reflect historical, causally ambiguous, and socially complex firm processes. Thus, for example, Dell's low product inventory strategy—a policy with clear low-cost implications—actually reflects the complex linkage between various parts of the value-chain within Dell, an unwavering commitment to manufacturing flexibility and efficiency, and an organizational culture that focuses on Web-based sales. Wal-Mart's supply chain management strategy—again, a policy with clear low-cost implications—actually reflects Wal-Mart's unique history, its socially complex relations with suppliers, and its unique organizational culture. And Southwest Airlines' low-price pricing strategy— a strategy that reflects Southwest's low-cost position—is possible because of the kind of airplane fleet Southwest has built over time, the commitment of its employees to Southwest's success, a charismatic founder (Herb Kelleher), and its unique organizational culture. Because these policies reflect costly-to-imitate attributes of these firms, they can be sources of sustained competitive advantage.

However, for these and other firms, it is not these policy choices, per se, that create sustainable cost leadership advantages. Rather, it is how these policies flow out of the historical, causally ambiguous, and socially complex processes within a firm that makes them costly to duplicate. This has been the case for the Oakland A's baseball team, as described in the Strategy in the Emerging Enterprise Feature.

Costly-to-Duplicate Sources of Cost Advantage

Differential access to low-cost productive inputs and technological software is usually a costly-to-duplicate basis of cost leadership. This is because these inputs often build on historical, uncertain, and socially complex resouces and capabilities. As suggested earlier, differential access to productive inputs often depends on the location of a firm. Moreover, to be a source of economic profits, this valuable location must be obtained before its full value is widely understood. Both these attributes of differential access to productive inputs suggest that if, in fact, it is rare, it will often be costly to duplicate. First, some locations are unique and cannot be duplicated. For example, most private golf clubs would like to own courses with the spectacular beauty of Pebble Beach in Monterey, California, but there is only one Pebble Beach—a course that runs parallel to some of the most beautiful oceanfront scenery in the world. Although "scenery" is an important factor of production in running and managing a golf course, the re-creation of Pebble Beach's scenery at some other location is simply beyond our technology.

Second, even if a location is not unique, once its value is revealed, acquisition of that location is not likely to generate economic profits. Thus, for example, although being located in Silicon Valley provides access to some important low-cost productive inputs for electronics firms, firms that moved to this location after its value was revealed have substantially higher costs than firms that moved there before its full value was revealed. These higher costs effectively reduce the economic profit that otherwise could have been generated. Referring to the discussion in Chapter 3, these arguments suggest that gaining differential access to productive inputs in a way that generates economic profits may reflect a firm's unique path through history.

Technological software is also likely to be difficult to duplicate and often can be a source of sustained competitive advantage. As suggested in Chapter 3, the values, beliefs, culture, and teamwork that constitute this software are socially complex and may be immune from competitive duplication. Firms with cost advantages rooted in these socially complex resources incorporate cost savings in every aspect of their organization; they constantly focus on improving the quality and cost of their operations, and they have employees who are firmly committed to, and understand, what it takes to be a cost leader. Other firms may talk about low costs; these firms live cost leadership. Dell, Wal-Mart, and Southwest are all examples of such firms. If there are few firms in an industry with these kinds of beliefs and commitments, then they can gain a sustained competitive advantage from their cost advantage.

Substitutes for Sources of Cost Advantage

In an important sense, all of the sources of cost advantage listed in this chapter are at least partial substitutes for each other. Thus, for example, one firm may reduce its cost through exploiting economies of scale in large-scale production, and a competing firm may reduce its costs through exploiting learning-curve economies and large cumulative volume of production. If these different activities have similar effects on a firm's cost position, and if they are equally costly to implement, then they are strategic substitutes for each other.

Because of the substitute effects of different sources of cost advantage, it is not unusual for firms pursuing cost leadership to simultaneously pursue *all* the cost-reduction activities discussed in this chapter. Implemention of this *bundle* of cost-reducing activities may have few substitutes. If duplicating this bundle of activities is also rare and difficult, then a firm may be able to gain a sustained competitive advantage from doing so.

Several of the other strategies discussed in later chapters can also have the effect of reducing a firm's costs and thus may be substitutes for the sources of cost reduction discussed in this chapter. For example, one common motivation for firms implementing strategic alliance strategies is to exploit economies of scale in combination with other firms. Thus, a strategic alliance that reduces a firm's costs may be a substitute for a firm exploiting economies of scale on its own to reduce its costs. As is discussed in more detail in Chapter 8, many of the strategic alliances among aluminum mining and smelting companies are motivated by realizing economies of scale and cost reduction. Also, corporate diversification strategies often enable firms to exploit economies of scale across different businesses within which they operate. In this setting, each of these businesses—treated separately—may have scale disadvantages; but collectively, their scale creates the same low-cost position as that of an individual firm that fully exploits economies of scale to reduce costs in a single business (see Chapter 9).

Organizing to Implement Cost Leadership

VRIO

As is the case with all strategies, firms seeking to implement cost leadership strategies must adopt an organizational structure, management controls, and compensation policies that reinforce this strategy. Some key issues associated with using these organizing tools to implement cost leadership are summarized in Table 4.6.

Organizational Structure in Implementing Cost Leadership

As suggested in Table 4.6, firms implementing cost leadership strategies will generally adopt what is known as a **functional organizational structure**.[21] An example of a functional organization structure is presented in Figure 4.4. Indeed, this

Table 4.6   **Organizing to Realize the Full Potential of Cost Leadership Strategies**

Organization structure: Functional structure with
1. Few layers in the reporting structure
2. Simple reporting relationships
3. Small corporate staff
4. Focus on narrow range of business functions

Management control systems
1. Tight cost control systems
2. Quantitative cost goals
3. Close supervision of labor, raw material, inventory, and other costs
4. A cost leadership philosophy

Compensation policies
1. Reward for cost reduction
2. Incentives for all employees to be involved in cost reduction

functional organizational structure is the structure used to implement all business-level strategies a firm might pursue, although this structure is modified when used to implement these different strategies.

In a functional structure, each of the major business functions is managed by a **functional manager**. For example, if manufacturing, marketing, finance, accounting, and sales are all included within a functional organization, then a manufacturing manager leads that function, a marketing manager leads that function, a finance manager leads that function, and so forth. In a functional organizational structure, all these functional managers report to one person. This person has many different titles—including President, CEO, Chair, or Founder. However, for purposes of this discussion, this person will be called the **chief executive officer (CEO)**.

The CEO in a functional organization has a unique status. Everyone else in this company is a functional specialist. The manufacturing people manufacture, the marketing people market, the finance people finance, and so forth. Indeed, there is only one person in the functional organization that has to have a multifunctional perspective—the CEO. This role is so important that sometimes the functional organization is called a **U-form structure**, where the "U" stands for "unitary"—because there is only one person in this organization that has a broad, multifunctional corporate perspective.

When used to implement a cost leadership strategy, this U-form structure is kept as simple as possible. As suggested in Table 4.6, firms implementing cost leadership strategies will have relatively few layers in their reporting structure. Complicated reporting structures, including **matrix structures** where one employee reports to two or more people, are usually avoided.[22] Corporate staff in

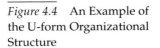

Figure 4.4   An Example of the U-form Organizational Structure

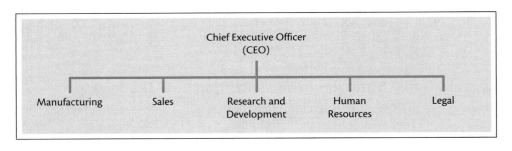

these organizations is kept small. Such firms do not operate in a wide range of business functions, but instead operate only in those few business functions where they have valuable, rare, and costly-to-imitate resources and capabilities.

One excellent example of a firm pursuing a cost leadership strategy is Nucor Steel. A leader in the mini–mill industry, Nucor has only 5 layers in its reporting structure, compared to 12 to 15 in its major higher-cost competitors. Most operating decisions at Nucor are delegated to plant managers, who have full profit-and-loss responsibility for their operations. Corporate staff at Nucor is small and focuses its efforts on accounting for revenues and costs and on exploring new manufacturing processes to further reduce Nucor's operating expenses and expand its business opportunities. Nucor's former president, Ken Iverson, believed that Nucor does only two things well: build plants efficiently and run them effectively. Thus Nucor focuses its efforts in these areas and subcontracts many of its other business functions, including the purchase of its raw materials, to outside vendors.[23]

Responsibilities of the CEO in a Functional Organization

The CEO in a U-form organization has two basic responsibilities: (1) to formulate the strategy of the firm and (2) to coordinate the activities of the functional specialists in the firm to facilitate the implementation of this strategy. In the special case of a cost leadership strategy, the CEO must decide on which bases such a strategy should be founded—including any of those listed in Table 4.1—and then must coordinate functions within a firm to make sure that the economic potential of this strategy is fully realized.

Strategy Formulation. The CEO in a U-form organization engages in strategy formulation by applying the strategic management process described in Chapter 1. A CEO establishes the firm's mission and associated objectives. He or she evaluates environmental threats and opportunities, understands the firm's strengths and weaknesses, and then chooses one or more of the business and corporate strategies discussed in this book. In the case of a cost leadership strategy, the application of the strategic management process must lead a CEO to conclude that the best chance for achieving a firm's mission is for that firm to adopt a cost leadership business-level strategy.

Although the responsibility for strategy formulation in a U-form organization ultimately rests with the CEO, this individual needs to draw on the insights, analysis, and involvement of functional managers throughout the firm. CEOs who fail to involve functional managers in strategy formulation run several risks. First, strategic choices made in isolation from functional managers may be made without complete information. Second, limiting the involvement of functional managers in strategy formulation can limit their understanding of, and commitment to, the chosen strategy. This can severely limit their ability, and willingness, to implement any strategy—including cost leadership—that is chosen.[24]

Coordinating Functions for Strategy Implementation. Even the best formulated strategy is competitively irrelevant if it is not implemented. And the only way that strategies can be effectively implemented is if all the functions within a firm are aligned in a way consistent with this strategy.

For example, compare two firms pursuing a cost leadership strategy. All but one of the first firm's functions—marketing—are aligned with this cost leadership strategy. All of the second firm's functions—including marketing— are aligned with this cost leadership strategy. Because marketing is not aligned with the first firm's cost leadership strategy, this firm is likely to advertise products that it does not sell. That is, this firm might advertise its products on the basis of their style and performance, but sell products that are reliable (but

Table 4.7   **Common Misalignments Between Business Functions and a Cost Leadership Strategy**

	When Function is *Aligned* with Cost Leadership Strategies	When Function is *Misaligned* with Cost Leadership Strategies
Manufacturing	Lean, low cost, good quality	Inefficient, high cost, poor quality
Marketing	Emphasize value, reliability, and price	Emphasize style and performance
R&D	Focus on product extensions and process improvements	Focus on radical new technologies and products
Finance	Focus on low cost and stable financial structure	Focus on non-traditional financial instruments
Accounting	Collect cost data and adopt conservative accounting principles	Collect no-cost data and adopt very aggressive accounting principles
Sales	Focus on value, reliability, and low price	Focus on style and performance and high price

not stylish) and inexpensive (but not high performers). A firm that markets products it does not actually sell is likely to disappoint its customers. On the other hand, the second firm that has all of its functions—including marketing—aligned with its chosen strategy is more likely to advertise products it actually sells and thus is less likely to disappoint its customers. In the long run, it seems reasonable to expect this second firm to outperform the first firm, at least with respect to implementing a cost leadership strategy.

Of course, alignment is required of all of a firm's functional areas, not just marketing. Also, misalignment can emerge in any of a firm's functional areas. Some common misalignments between a firm's cost leadership strategy and its functional activities are listed in Table 4.7.

Management Controls in Implementing Cost Leadership

As suggested in Table 4.6, cost leadership firms are typically characterized by very tight cost-control systems; frequent and detailed cost-control reports; an emphasis on quantitative cost goals and targets; and close supervision of labor, raw materials, inventory, and other costs. Again, Nucor is an example of a cost leadership firm that has implemented these kinds of control systems. At Nucor, groups of employees are given weekly cost and productivity improvement goals. Groups that meet or exceed these goals receive extra compensation. Plant managers are held responsible for cost and profit performance. A plant manager who does not meet corporate performance expectations cannot expect a long career at Nucor. Similar group-oriented cost-reduction systems are in place at some of Nucor's major competitors, including Chaparral Steel.[25]

Less formal management control systems also drive a cost-reduction philosophy at cost leadership firms. For example, although Wal-Mart is one of the most successful retail operations in the world, its Arkansas headquarters is plain and simple. Indeed, some have suggested that Wal-Mart's headquarters looks like a warehouse. Its style of interior decoration was once described as "early bus station." Regional vice presidents at Wal-Mart travel every week, from Monday to Thursday, meet all day Friday, attend a company–wide meeting on Saturday morning, and then have late Saturday and Sunday off, just in time to start traveling again on Monday. This schedule enables Wal-Mart to reduce its costs by 2 percent of sales by *not* opening independent regional offices. Wal-Mart even involves its customers in reducing costs by asking them to "help keep your costs low" by returning shopping carts to the designated areas in Wal-Mart's parking lots.[26]

Compensation Policies and Implementing Cost Leadership Strategies

As suggested in Table 4.6, compensation in cost leadership firms is usually tied directly to cost-reducing efforts. Such firms often provide incentives for employees to work together to reduce costs and increase or maintain quality, and they expect *every* employee to take responsibility for both costs and quality. For example, an important expense for retail stores like Wal-Mart is "shrinkage"—a nice way of saying people steal stuff. About half the shrinkage in most stores comes from employees stealing their own companies' products.

Wal-Mart used to have a serious problem with shrinkage. Among other solutions (including hiring "greeters" whose real job is to discourage shoplifters), Wal-Mart developed a compensation scheme that took half the cost savings created by reduced shrinkage and shared it with employees in the form of a bonus. With this incentive in place, Wal-Mart's shrinkage problems dropped significantly.

Even apparently small cost savings can be important for firms implementing a cost leadership strategy. Ford Motor used compensation policies to help discover cost reductions in manufacturing the Ford Taurus. Cost reductions included redesigning door hinge pins (to save $2 per car), the use of splash shields under wheel wells made out of recycled plastic (to save 45 cents per car), and the use of a part from the Lincoln Continental to reinforce sheet metal under seats (to save $1.50 per car). Collectively, these small improvements have trimmed $180 from the cost of producing each Taurus. This could lead to additional profits of almost $73 million for the Taurus line of products.[27]

Cost Leadership in an International Context

As has already been suggested in this chapter, one of the most common reasons that a firm begins international operations is to reduce its cost position. International operations can reduce a firm's costs in at least three ways: (1) by increasing sales to realize economies of scale, (2) by gaining access to low-cost labor, and (3) by gaining access to low-cost raw materials.

Gaining access to new customers for a firm's current products or services can increase a firm's volume of sales. If a firm's production process is sensitive to economies of scale, this increased volume of sales can reduce its costs and enable it to gain cost advantages in both its domestic and nondomestic operations. Many scholars, over many years, have pointed out the potential of international operations to generate economies of scale.[28] Most recognize that the realization of economies of scale from international operations requires a high degree of integration across firm borders. Integration must focus on those aspects of a firm's operations where economies of scale can be realized. For example, McDonald's attempts to generate training-based economies of scale through the operation of a single management training center for all of its international operations. Firms in the float glass, color television, and chemical industries have all attempted to exploit manufacturing economies of scale through their international operations.[29]

Many firms in the worldwide automobile industry have attempted to realize manufacturing economies of scale through their international operations. According to one estimate, the minimum efficient scale of a single compact-car manufacturing plant is 400,000 units per year.[30] Such a plant would produce approximately 20 percent of all the automobiles sold in Britain, Italy, or France. Obviously, to exploit this 400,000-cars-per-year manufacturing efficiency, European automobile firms have had to sell cars in more than just a single-country market. Thus, the implementation of an international strategy has been essential if these firms were to recognize manufacturing economies of scale.

Global Perspectives

The Rise of the Maquiladora

One interesting example of firms gaining access to low labor costs through their international strategies is maquiladoras. Maquiladoras are manufacturing plants owned by non-Mexican companies operated in Mexico near the U.S. border. The primary driver behind maquiladora investment is lower labor costs than similar plants located in the United States. In addition, firms exporting from maquiladoras to the United States have to pay duties only on the value added that was created in Mexico; maquiladoras do not have to pay Mexican taxes on the goods processed in Mexico. Also, the cost of the land on which plants are built in Mexico is substantially lower than the cost would be in the United States. However, despite these other advantages, a study by the Banco de Mexico suggests that without the 20 percent cost-of-labor advantage, most maquiladoras would not be profitable.

Given the cost advantages in operating maquiladoras, it is not surprising that investment in this particular international strategy has increased substantially over time. In 1965, there were only 12 maquiladora plants. By 1990, approximately 1,700 were in operation. By 1999, over 3,100 maquiladoras, employing over 1 million people, were in operation. Most of these were U.S. firms operating plants in Mexico. Currently, only oil generates more foreign currency for Mexico than maquiladoras.

Sources: A. DePalma (1994). "Trade pact is spurring Mexican deals in the U.S." *New York Times*, March 17, pp. C1, 3; M. Celestino (1999). "Manufacturing in Mexico." *World Trade*, 12, July, pp. 36–42.

Similar economies of scale through international operations can be found through research and development and marketing.

It has already been suggested that firms can engage in international operations to gain access to low-cost labor. As the lowest cost labor in the world shifted from Japan (right after World War II) to South Korea, then to Taiwan, Singapore, and Malaysia, and still later to China, Mexico, and Vietnam, some firms have changed their manufacturing operations accordingly. For example, Mineba, a Japanese ball bearing company, began manufacturing in Japan, shifted its operations to Singapore in the 1970s, and has been operating in Thailand since the 1980s. Hewlett-Packard operates manufacturing and assembly operations in Malaysia and Mexico, Mitsubishi Motors recently opened a manufacturing operation in Vietnam, General Motors operates assembly plants in Mexico, and Motorola has operations in China. All these investments were motivated, at least partly, by the availability of low-cost labor in these countries.[31] One interesting approach to gaining access to the low-cost labor market while still remaining close to the boundaries of the United States is described in the Global Perspectives feature.

Finally, firms can engage in international operations to gain access to low-cost raw materials. Indeed, historically, this was the most traditional reason that firms began international operations. For example, in 1600, the British East India Company was formed with an initial investment of 70,000 £ to manage trade between England and the Far East, including India. In 1601, the third British East India Company fleet sailed for the Indies to buy cloves, pepper, silk, coffee, saltpeter, and other products. This fleet generated a return on investment of 234 percent. These profits led to the formation of the Dutch East India Company in 1602 and the French East India Company in 1664. Similar firms were organized to manage trade in the New World. The Hudson Bay Company was chartered in 1670 to manage the fur trade, and the rival North West Company was organized in 1784 for the same purpose. All these organizations were created to gain access to low-cost raw materials and products that were available only in nondomestic markets.[32]

Gaining access to low-cost raw materials is still an important reason why some firms engage in international enterprise. In some industries, including the oil and gas industry, virtually the only reason why firms have begun international operations is to gain access to low-cost raw materials.

SUMMARY

There are several reasons that firms producing essentially the same products can have different costs. Some of the most important of these are: (1) size differences and economies of scale, (2) size differences and diseconomies of scale, (3) experience differences and learning-curve economies, (4) differential access to productive inputs, and (5) technological advantages independent of scale. In addition, firms competing in the same industry can make policy choices about the kinds of products and services to sell that can have an important impact on their relative cost position. Cost leadership in an industry can be valuable by assisting a firm in reducing the threat of each of the five forces in an industry outlined in Chapter 2.

Each of the sources of cost advantage discussed in this chapter can be a source of sustained competitive advantage if it is rare and costly to imitate. Overall, leaning-curve economies, differential access to productive inputs, and technological "software" are more likely to be rare than other sources of cost advantage. Differential access to productive inputs and technological "software" is more likely to be costly to imitate—either through direct duplication or through substitution—than the other sources of cost advantage. Thus, differential access to productive inputs and technological "software" will often be more likely to be a source of sustained competitive advantage than cost advantages based on other sources.

Of course, to realize the full potential of these competitive advantages, a firm must be organized appropriately. Organizing to implement a strategy always involves a firm's organizational structure, its management control systems, and its compensation policies. The organizational structure used to implement cost leadership—and other business strategies—is called a functional or U-form structure. The CEO is the only person in this structure who has a corporate perspective. The CEO has two responsibilities: to formulate a firm's strategy and to implement it by coordinating functions within a firm. Ensuring that a firm's functions are aligned with its strategy is essential to successful strategy implementation.

When used to implement a cost leadership strategy, the U-form structure generally has few layers, simple reporting relationships, a small corporate staff; and it focuses on a narrow range of business functions. The management control systems used to implement these strategies generally include tight cost controls; quantitative cost goals; close supervision of labor, raw materials, inventory and other costs; and a cost leadership culture and mentality. Finally, compensation policies in these firms typically reward cost reduction and provide incentives for everyone in the organization to be part of the cost-reduction effort.

Firms often pursue a cost leadership strategy by engaging in international operations, and such operations can affect their cost structure in at least three ways: (1) firms can use international sales to exploit economies of scale, (2) firms can operate facilities around the world to gain access to low-cost labor, and (3) firms can operate internationally to gain access to low-cost raw materials.

CHALLENGE QUESTIONS

1. Wal-Mart, Timex, Casio, and Hyundai are all cited as examples of firms pursuing cost leadership strategies, but these firms make substantial investments in advertising, which seems more likely to be associated with a product differentiation strategy. Are these firms really pursuing a cost leadership strategy or are they pursuing a product differentiation strategy by emphasizing their lower costs?

2. When economies of scale exist, firms with large volumes of production will have lower costs than firms with smaller volumes of production. The realization of these economies of scale, however, is far from automatic. What actions can firms take to ensure that they realize whatever economies of sale are created by their volume of production?

3. Firms engage in an activity called "forward pricing" when they estab-lish, during the early stages of the learning-curve, a price for their products that is lower than their actual costs, in anticipation of lower costs later on, after significant learning has occurred. Under what conditions, if any, does forward pricing make sense? What risks, if any, do firms engaging in forward pricing face?

4. One way of thinking about organizing to implement cost leadership strategies is that firms that pursue this strategy should be highly centralized, have high levels of direct supervision, and keep employee wages to an absolute minimum. Another approach is to decentralize decision-making authority—to ensure that individuals who know the most about reducing costs make decisions about how to reduce costs. This, in turn, would imply less direct supervision and somewhat higher levels of employee wages (why?). Which of these two approaches seems more reasonable? Under what conditions would these different approaches make more or less sense?

5. International operations can reduce a firm's costs by generating economies of scale that it would not otherwise enjoy or by giving a firm access to low-cost labor and/or raw materials. The first of these strategies involves mostly exporting products made in a firm's home country to a nondomestic market while the second involves mostly importing products made outside a firm's home market to its home market. Describe the differences between these two strategies in terms of the types of investments that firms following these two strategies must make in their non-domestic markets and the different management control problems these firms are likely to face.

PROBLEM SET

1. The economies of scale curve in Figure 4.1 can be represented algebraically in the following equation:

$$\text{Average costs} = a + bQ + cQ^2$$

where Q is the quantity produced by a firm.; and a, b, and c are coefficients that are estimated from industry data. For example, it has been shown that that economies of scale curve for savings and loan companies in the U.S. is:

$$\text{Average costs} = 2.38 - .615A + .54A^2$$

where A is a savings and loan's total assets. Using this equation, what is the optimal size of a savings and loan? (Hint: Plug in different values of A and calculate Average costs. The lowest possible Average costs is the optimal size for a savings and loan.)

2. The learning-curve depicted in Figure 4.2 can be represented algebraically in the following equation:

$$\text{Average time to produce x units} = ax^{-\beta}$$

where x is the total number of units produced by a firm in its history, a is the amount of time it took a firm to produce its first unit, and β is a coefficient that describes the rate of learning in a firm.

Suppose it takes a team of workers 45 hours to assemble their first product (a = 45) and 40.5 hours to assemble their second product. When a firm doubles its production (in this case, from one to two units) and cuts its production time (in this case, from 45 hours to 40.5

hours), learning is said to have occurred (in this case a 40.5/45 or 90% learning-curve). The β for a 90% learning-curve is .3219. Thus, this firm's learning-curve is:

$$\text{Average time to produce x units} = 45x^{-.3219}$$

What is the average amount of time it will take this firm to produce 6 products? (Hint: Simply plug "6" in for "X" in the equation and solve.) What is the total time it took this firm to produce these 6 products? (Hint: Simply multiply the number of units produced "6" by the average time it will take to produce these 6 products.) What is the average time it will take this firm to produce 5 products? What is the total time it will take this firm to produce 5 products? So, what is the total time it will take this firm to produce its sixth product? (Hint: Subtract the total time needed to produce five products from the total time needed to produce six products.)

Suppose a new firm is going to start producing these same products. Assuming this new firm doesn't learn anything from established firms, what will its cost disadvantage be when it assembles its first product? (Hint: Compare the costs of the experienced firm's sixth product with the cost of the new firm's first product.)

END NOTES

1. Weiner, S. (1987). "The road most traveled." *Forbes*, October 19, pp. 60–64.
2. Christensen, C. R., N. A. Berg, and M. S. Salter (1980). *Policy formulation and administration: A casebook of senior management problems in business*, 8th ed. Homewood, IL: Irwin, p. 163.
3. Scherer, F. M. (1980). *Industrial market structure and economic Performance.* Boston: Houghton Mifflin; Moore, F. T. (1959). "Economies of scale: Some statistical evidence." *Quarterly Journal of Economics*, 73, pp. 232–245; and Lau, L. J., and S. Tamura (1972). "Economies of scale, technical progress, and the nonhomothetic leontief production function." *Journal of Political Economy*, 80, pp. 1167–87.
4. Scherer, F. M. (1980). *Industrial market structure and economic performance.* Boston: Houghton Mifflin; and Perrow, C. (1984). *Normal accidents: Living with high-risk technologies.* New York: Basic Books.
5. Hamermesh, R. G., and R. S. Rosenbloom (1989). "Crown Cork and Seal Co., Inc." Harvard Business School Case No. 9-388-096.
6. See Hackman, J. R., and G. R. Oldham (1980). *Work redesign.* Reading, MA: Addison-Wesley.
7. This relationship was first noticed in 1925 by the commander of Wright-Patterson Air Force Base in Dayton, Ohio.
8. Learning-curves have been estimated for numerous industries. Boston Consulting Group (1970). "Perspectives on experience." Boston: BCG, presents learning curves for over 20 industries while Lieberman, M. (1984). "The learning curve and pricing in the chemical processing industries". *Rand Journal of Economics*, 15, pp. 213–228, estimates learning curves for 37 chemical products.
9. Henderson, B. (1974). *The experience curve reviewed III—How does it work?* Boston: Boston Consulting Group; and Boston Consulting Group (1970). "Perspectives on experience". Boston: BCG.
10. Hall, G., and S. Howell (1985). "The experience curve from the economist's perspective." *Strategic Management Journal*, 6, pp. 197–212.
11. Hill, C. W. L. (1988). "Differentiation versus low-cost or differentiation and low-cost: A contingency framework". *Academy of Management Review*, 13(3), pp. 401–412.
12. See Ghemawat, P., and H. J. Stander III (1992). "Nucor at a cross-roads." Harvard Business School Case No. 9-793-039 on technology in steel manufacturing and cost advantages; Shaffer, R. A. (1995). "Intel as conquistador." *Forbes*, February 27, p. 130 on technology in semi-conductor manufacturing and cost advantages; Monteverde, K., and D. Teece (1982). "Supplier switching costs and vertical integration in the automobile industry." *Rand Journal of Economics*, 13(1), pp. 206–213; and McCormick, J., and N. Stone (1990). "From national champion to global competitor: An interview with Thomson's Alain Gomez." *Harvard Business Review*, May/June, pp. 126–135 on technology in consumer electronic manufacturing and cost advantages.
13. Schultz, E. (1989). "Climbing high with discount brokers." *Fortune*, Fall (special issue), pp. 219–223.
14. Schonfeld, Erick (1998). "Can computers cure health care?" *Fortune*, March 30, pp. 111 +.
15. Ibid.
16. See Meyer, M. W., and L. B. Zucker (1989). *Permanently failing organizations.* Newbury Park, CA: Sage.
17. Staw, B. M. (1981). "The escalation of commitment to a course of action." *Academy of Management Review*, 6, pp. 577–587.
18. Hesterly, W. S. (1989). *Top management succession as a determinant of firm performance and de-escalation: An agency problem,* Unpublished doctoral dissertation, University of California, Los Angeles.
19. Barney, J. B. (1986). "Organizational culture: Can it be a source of sustained competitive advantage?" *Academy of Management Review*, 11, pp. 656–665.
20. See Spence, A. M. (1981). "The learning-curve and competition." *Bell Journal of Economics*, 12, pp. 49–70, on why learning needs to be proprietary; Mansfield, E. (1985). "How rapidly does new industrial technology leak out?" *Journal of Industrial Economics*, 34(2), pp. 217–223; Lieberman, M. B. (1982). *The learning-curve, pricing and market structure in the chemical processing industries.* Unpublished doctoral dissertation, Harvard University; Lieberman, M. B. (1987). "The learning curve, diffusion, and competitive strategy." *Strategic Management Journal*, 8, pp. 441–452 on why it usually is not proprietary.
21. Williamson, O. (1975). *Markets and hierarchies.* New York: Free Press.
22. Davis, S. M., and P. R. Lawrence (1977). *Matrix.* Reading, MA: Addison-Wesley.
23. See Ghemawat, P., and H. J. Stander III (1992). "Nucor at a cross-roads." Harvard Business School Case No. 9-793-039.
24. See Floyd, S. W. and B. Woldridge (1992). "Middle management involvement in strategy and its association with strategic type: A research note." *Strategic Management Journal*, 13, pp. 153–167.
25. Ibid.
26. Walton, S. (1992). *Sam Walton, made in America: My story.* New York: Doubleday.
27. See Suris, O. (1996). "How Ford cut costs on its 1997 Taurus, little by little." *Wall Street Journal*, July 18, pp. B1 +.
28. See Fayerweather, J. (1969). *International business management.* New York: McGraw-Hill, and Porter, M. E. (1982). "How global companies win out." *Harvard Business Review*, September/October, pp. 98–108.
29. See Serwer, A. (1994). "McDonald's conquers the world." *Fortune*, October 17, pp. 103–116; Prahalad, C. K., and Y. Doz (1987). *The multinational mission.* New York: Free Press; and Bartlett, C. A., and S. Shoshal (1989). *Managing across borders: The transnational solution.* Boston: Harvard Business Press.
30. See Porter, M. E. (1986). "Competition in international industries: A conceptual framework." In M. E. Porter (ed.), *Competition in international industries.* Boston: Harvard Business School Press.
31. See Collis, D. J. (1991). "A resource-based analysis of international competition: The case of the bearing industry." *Strategic Management Journal*, 12 (Summer Special Issue), pp. 49–68; and Engardio, P. (1993). "Motorola in China: A great leap forward." *BusinessWeek*, May 17, pp. 58–59.
32. See Trager, J. (1992). *The people's chronology.* New York: Henry Holt.

5

Product Differentiation

Sexy. Glamorous. Mysterious. Victoria's Secret is the world's leading specialty retailer of lingerie and beauty products. With 2002 sales of almost $3.6 billion, and operating profits of $614 million, Victoria's Secret sells its mix of sexy lingerie, prestige fragrances, and fashion-inspired collections through over 1,000 retail stores and through the almost 400 million catalogues it distributes each year.

But all this glamour and success leaves the two central questions about this firm unanswered: "Who is Victoria?" and "What is her secret?"

Who Is Victoria, and What Is Her Secret?

It turns out that Victoria is a retired fashion model who lives in an up-and-coming fashionable district in London. She has a committed relationship and is thinking about starting a family. However, these maternal instincts are balanced by Victoria's adventurous and sexy side. She loves good food, classical music, and great wine. She travels frequently and is as much at home in New York, Paris, and Los Angeles as she is in London. Her fashion tastes are edgy enough to never be boring, but practical enough to never be extreme. Her lingerie is an essential part of her wardrobe. Sexy and alluring while never cheap, trashy, or vulgar, Victoria's lingerie is the perfect complement to her overall lifestyle. Most importantly, while Victoria knows she is beautiful and sexy, she also knows that it is

144

Learning Objectives

After reading this chapter, you should be able to:

1. Define product differentiation.

2. Describe eleven bases of product differentiation and how they can be grouped into three categories.

3. Describe how product differentiation is ultimately limited only by managerial creativity.

4. Describe how product differentiation can be used to neutralize environmental threats and exploit environmental opportunities.

5. Describe those bases of product differentiation that are not likely to be costly to duplicate, those that may be costly to duplicate, and those that will often be costly to duplicate.

6. Describe the main substitutes for product differentiation strategies.

7. Describe how organizational structure, control processes, and compensation policies can be used to implement product differentiation strategies.

8. Discuss whether or not it is possible for a firm to implement cost leadership and product differentiation strategies simultaneously, and why or why not.

9. Discuss the trade-off between local responsiveness and international integration as firms pursue product differentiation strategies around the world.

her brains, not her looks, that have enabled her to succeed in life.

This is who Victoria is. This is the woman that Victoria's Secret's designers design for, the woman Victoria's Secret's marketers create advertising for, and the woman to whom all Victoria's Secret's sales associates are trained to sell.

And this is her secret— Victoria doesn't really exist. Or, more precisely, the number of real women in the entire world who are like Victoria is very small—no more than a handful. So why would a company like Victoria's Secret organize all of its design, marketing, and sales efforts

around meeting the lingerie needs of a woman who, for all practical purposes, doesn't really exist?

Victoria's Secret knows how few of its actual customers are like Victoria. However, it is convinced that many of its customers would like to be treated as if they were Victoria, if only for a few hours, when they come into a Victoria's Secret store. Victoria's Secret is not just selling lingerie; it is selling an opportunity, almost a fantasy, to be like Victoria—to live in an exciting and sexy city, to travel the world, to

have refined yet edgy tastes. To buy and wear Victoria's Secret lingerie is—if only for a moment or two— an opportunity to experience life as Victoria experiences life.

Practically speaking, building an entire company around meeting the needs of a customer who does not actually exist creates some interesting problems. You can't just call Victoria on the phone and ask her about trends in her lifestyle; you can't form a focus group of people like Victoria and ask them to evaluate new lines of lingerie. In a sense, not only has Victoria's Secret invented Victoria; it also had to invent Victoria's lifestyle—and the lingerie, fragrances, and accessories that go along with that lifestyle. And as long as the lifestyle that the Company invents for Victoria is desirable to, but just beyond the reach of, its actual customers, Victoria's Secret will continue to be able to sell a romantic fantasy—along with its bras and panties.

Source: www.limitedbrands.com; www.victoriassecret.com.

Victoria's Secret uses the fictional character "Victoria" to help implement its product differentiation strategy.

What Is Product Differentiation?

Where Wal-Mart exemplifies a firm pursuing a cost leadership strategy, Victoria's Secret exemplifies a firm pursuing a product differentiation strategy. **Product differentiation** is a business strategy whereby firms attempt to gain a competitive advantage by increasing the perceived value of their products or services relative to the perceived value of other firms' products or services. These other firms can be either that firm's rivals or firms that provide substitute products or services. By increasing the perceived value of its products or services, a firm will be able to charge a higher price than it would otherwise. This higher price can increase a firm's revenues and can generate competitive advantages.

A firm's attempts to create differences in the relative perceived value of its products or services often are made by altering the objective properties of those products or services. Rolex attempts to differentiate its watches from Timex and Casio watches by manufacturing them with solid gold cases. Mercedes attempts to differentiate its cars from Hyundai's cars through sophisticated engineering and high performance. Victoria's Secret attempts to differentiate its shopping experience from Wal-Mart, and other retailers, through the merchandise it sells and the way it sells it.

While firms often alter the objective properties of their products or services in order to implement a product differentiation strategy, the existence of product differentiation, in the end, is *always* a matter of customer perception. Products sold by two different firms may be very similar, but if customers believe the first is more valuable than the second, then the first product has a differentiation advantage.

In the world of "craft" or "microbrewery" beers for example, image among consumers about where a beer is brewed may be very different from how a beer for example is actually brewed. Boston Beer Company, for example, sells Samuel Adams Beer. Customers can tour the Boston Beer Company, where they will see a small row of fermenting tanks and two 10-barrel kettles being tended by a brewmaster wearing rubber boots. However, Samuel Adams Beer is not actually brewed in this small factory. Instead, it is brewed—in 200-barrel steel tanks—in Cincinnati, Ohio, by the Hudepohl-Schoenling Brewing Company, a contract brewing firm that also manufactures Hudy Bold Beer and Little Kings Cream Ale. Maui Beer Company's Aloha Lager brand is brewed in Portland, Oregon, and Pete's Wicked Ale (a craft beer that claims it is brewed "one batch at a time. Carefully.") is brewed in batches of 400 barrels each by Stroh Brewery Company, makers of Old Milwaukee Beer. However, the more consumers believe there are important differences between these "craft" beers and more traditional brews—despite many of their common manufacturing methods—the more willing they will be to pay more for a craft beer. This willingness to pay more suggests that an important "perceptual" basis of product differentiation exists for these craft beers.[1] If products or services are *perceived* as being different in a way that is valued by consumers, then product differentiation exits.

Just as perceptions can create product differentiation between products that are essentially identical, the lack of perceived differences between products with very different characteristics can prevent product differentiation. For example, consumers with an untrained palate may not be able to distinguish between two different wines, even though expert wine tasters would be very much aware of their differences. Those who are not aware of these differences, even if they exist, will not be willing to pay more for one wine over the other. In this sense, for these consumers at least, these two wines, though different, are not differentiated.

Product differentiation is always a matter of customer perceptions, but firms can take a variety of actions to influence these perceptions. These actions can be thought of as different bases of product differentiation.

Bases of Product Differentiation

A wide variety of authors, drawing on both theory and empirical research, have developed lists of ways firms can differentiate their products or services.[2] Some of these are listed in Table 5.1. While the purpose of all these bases of product differentiation is to create the perception that a firm's products or services are unusually valuable, different bases of product differentiation attempt to accomplish this objective in different ways. For example, the first four bases of product differentiation listed in Table 5.1 attempt to create this perception by focusing directly on the attributes of the products or services a firm sells. The second three attempt to create this perception by developing a relationship between a firm and its customers. The last five attempt to create this perception through linkages within and between firms. Of course, these bases of product differentiation are not mutually exclusive. Indeed, firms will often attempt to differentiate their products or services along multiple dimensions simultaneously. An empirical method for identifying ways that firms have differentiated their products is discussed in the Research Made Relevant feature.

Table 5.1   **Ways Firms Can Differentiate Their Products**

To differentiate their products, firms can focus directly
on the attributes of it products or services, or

1. Product features
2. Product complexity
3. Timing of product introduction
4. Location

on relationships between itself and its customers, or

5. Product customization
6. Consumer marketing
7. Product reputation

on linkages within or between firms

8. Linkages among functions within a firm
9. Linkages with other firms
10. Product mix
11. Distribution channels
12. Service and support

Source: M.C. Porter, (1980). *Competitive Strategy*-New York: Free Press. And R.E. Caves, and P. Williamson (1985). "What is product differentiation, really?" *Journal of Industrial Economics*, 34, pp. 113–132.

Research Made Relevant

Of all the possible bases of product differentiation that might exist in a particular market, how does one pinpoint those bases of product differentiation that have actually been used to differentiate products in that market? Research in strategic management and marketing has shown that the bases of product differentiation can be identified using multiple regression analysis to estimate what are called **hedonic prices**. A hedonic price is that part of the price of a product or service that is attributable to a particular characteristic of that product or service.

The logic behind hedonic prices is straightforward. If customers are willing to spend more for a product with a particular attribute than they are willing to spend for that same product without that attribute, then that attribute differentiates the first product from the second. That is, this attribute is a basis of product differentiation in this market.

Consider, for example, the price of used cars. The market price of a used car can be determined through the use of a variety of used car buying guides. These guides typically establish the base price of a used car. This base price typically includes product features that are common to almost all cars—a radio, a standard engine, a

Discovering the Bases of Product Differentiation

heater/defroster. Because these product attributes are common to virtually all cars, they are not a basis for product differentiation.

However, in addition to these common features, the base price of an automobile is adjusted depending on some less common features—a high-end stereo system, a larger engine, air conditioning. How much the base price of the car is adjusted when these features are added—$300 for a high-end stereo, $500 for a larger engine, $200 for air conditioning—are the hedonic prices of these product attributes. These product attributes differen-

tiate well-equipped cars from less-well-equipped cars and, since consumers are willing to pay more for well-equipped cars, can be thought of as bases of product differentiation in this market.

Multiple regression techniques are used to estimate these hedonic prices in the following way. For the simple car example above, the following regression equation is estimated:

$$Price = a_1 + b_1(Stereo) + b_2(Engine) + b_3(AC)$$

where Price is the retail price of cars, Stereo is a variable describing whether or not a car has a high-end stereo, Engine is a variable describing whether or not a car has a large engine, and AC is a variable describing whether or not a car has air conditioning. If the hedonic prices for these features are those suggested earlier, the results of running this regression analysis would be:

$$Price = \$7,800 + \$300(Stereo) + \$500(Engine) + \$200(AC)$$

where $7,800 is the base price of this type of used car.

Source: D. Hay and D. Morris (1979). *Industrial economics: Theory and evidence.* Oxford: Oxford University Press; K. Cowling and J. Cubbin (1971). "Price, quality, and advertising competition." *Economica*, 38, pp. 378–394.

Focusing on the Attributes of a Firm's Products or Services

Product Features. The most obvious way that firms can try to differentiate their products is by altering the features of the products they sell. One industry where firms are constantly modifying product features to attempt to differentiate their products is the automobile industry. Chrysler, for example, introduced the "cab forward" design to try to give its cars a distinctive look, while Audi went with a more radical flowing and curved design to differentiate its cars. For emergency situations, General Motors introduced the "On Star" system which instantly connects drivers to GM operators 24 hours a day, while Mercedes-Benz continued to develop its "crumple zone" system to ensure passenger safety in a crash. In body construction, General Motors continues to develop its "uni-body" construction system, where different parts of a car are welded to each other rather than built on a single frame, while Jaguar introduced a 100 percent aluminum body to help differentiate its top-of-the-line model from other luxury cars. Mazda continues to tinker with the motor and suspension of its sporty Miata, while Nissan introduced the 350 Z—a continuation of the famous 240 Z line—and Porsche changed from air-cooled to water-cooled engines in its 911 series of sports cars. All these—and many more—changes in the attributes of automobiles are examples of firms trying to differentiate their products by altering product features.

Product Complexity. Product complexity can be thought of as a special case of altering a product's features to create product differentiation. In a given industry, products can vary significantly in their complexity. The BIC "crystal pen" for example, has only a handful of parts, while a Cross pen or a Mount Blanc pen has many more parts. To the extent that these differences in product complexity convince consumers that the products of some firms are more valuable than the products of other firms, product complexity can be a basis of product differentiation.

Timing of Product Introduction. Introducing a product at the right time can also help create product differentiation. As suggested in Chapter 2, in some industry settings (that is, in emerging industries) *the* critical issue is to be a first mover—to introduce a new product before all other firms. Being first in emerging industries can enable a firm to set important technological standards, preempt strategically valuable assets, and develop customer-switching costs. These first-mover advantages can create a perception among customers that the products or services of the first-moving firm are somehow more valuable than the products or services of other firms.[3]

First moving has been an important determinant of perceived differences in the quality of education at universities in the United States and worldwide. In the United States, the first few universities founded (for example, Harvard and Yale) are seen as more prestigious than more recently founded state schools. In the United Kingdom, the oldest universities (including Oxford and Cambridge) are also widely perceived to be superior to more recently founded universities. Regardless of whether the date of founding of a university has an impact on the quality of education one receives, if there is a *perceived* link between founding date and quality, founding date acts as a timing-based source of product differentiation.[4]

Timing-based product differentiation, however, does not depend only on being a first mover. Sometimes, a firm can be a later mover in an industry but introduce products or services at just the right time and thereby gain a competitive advantage. This can happen when the ultimate success of a product or service depends on the availability of complementary products or technologies. For example, the domination of Microsoft's MS-DOS operating system, and thus ultimately, the domination of Windows, was only possible because IBM introduced its version of the personal computer. Without the IBM PC, it would have been difficult for any operating system—including MS-DOS—to have such a large market presence.[5]

Location. The physical location of a firm can also be a source of product differentiation.[6] Consider, for example, Disney's operations in Orlando, Florida. Beginning with The Magic Kingdom and Epcot Center, Disney built a world-class destination resort in Orlando. Over the years, Disney has added numerous attractions to its core entertainment activities, including MGM Studios, over 11,000 Disney-owned hotel rooms, a $100 million sports center, an automobile racing track, an after-hours entertainment district, and most recently, a $1 billion theme park called "The Animal Kingdom"—all in and around Orlando. Now, families can travel from around the world to Orlando, knowing that in a single location they can enjoy a full range of Disney adventures.[7]

Focusing on the Relationship Between a Firm and Its Customers

Product Customization. Products can also be differentiated by the extent to which they are customized for particular customer applications. Product customization is an important basis for product differentiation in a wide variety of industries, from enterprise software to bicycles.

Enterprise software is software that is designed to support all of a firm's critical business functions, including human resources, payroll, customer service, sales, quality control, and so forth. Major competitors in this industry include PeopleSoft and Oracle. However, although these firms sell basic software packages, most firms find it necessary to customize these basic packages to meet their specific business needs. The ability to build complex software packages that can also be customized to meet the specific needs of a particular customer is an important basis of product differentiation in this marketplace.

In the bicycle industry, consumers can spend as little as $50 on a bicycle, and as much as—well, almost as much as you want on a bicycle, easily in excess of $10,000. High-end bicycles use, of course, the very best components—like brakes and gears. But what really distinguishes these bicycles is their customized fit. Firms that sell these customized bicycles build a strong and lightweight frame that is custom fit to you and to your individual riding style. Much of the competition in this high end of the industry focuses on different ways of customizing this fit and different space-age materials that can be used to build the frames. Once a serious rider becomes accustomed to a particular customization approach, it is very difficult for that rider to switch to suppliers that might have an alternative approach to customization.

Consumer Marketing. Differential emphasis on consumer marketing has been a basis for product differentiation in a wide variety of industries. Through advertising and other consumer marketing efforts, firms attempt to alter the perceptions of current and potential customers, whether or not specific attributes of a firm's products or services are altered.

For example, in the soft drink industry, Mountain Dew—a product of PepsiCo—was originally marketed as a fruity, lightly carbonated drink, that tasted as light as a "morning dew in the mountains." However, beginning in the late 1990s, Mountain Dew's marketing efforts changed dramatically. "As light as a morning dew in the mountains" became "Do the Dew," and Mountain Dew focused its marketing efforts on young, mostly male, extreme sports-oriented consumers. Young men riding snowboards, roller blades, mountain bikes, and skateboards—mostly upside down—became central to most Mountain Dew commercials. Mountain Dew became a sponsor of a wide variety of extreme sports contests and an important sponsor of the X-games on ESPN. And will we ever forget the confrontation between the young Dew enthusiast and a mountain ram over a can of Mountain Dew in a meadow? Note that this radical repositioning of Mountain Dew depended entirely on changes in consumer marketing. The features of the underlying product were not changed at all.

Reputation. Perhaps the most important relationship between a firm and its customers depends on a firm's reputation in its marketplace. Indeed, a firm's **reputation** is really no more than a socially complex relationship between a firm and its customers. Once developed, a firm's reputation can last a long time, even if the basis for that reputation no longer exists.[8]

A firm that has tried to exploit its reputation for cutting-edge entertainment is MTV, a division of Viacom, Inc. While several well-known video artists—including Madonna—have had their videos banned from MTV, it has still been able to develop a reputation for risk-taking on television. MTV believes that its viewers have come to expect the unexpected in MTV programming. One of the first efforts to exploit, and reinforce, this reputation for risk-taking was *Beavis and Butthead*, an animated series on MTV starring two teenage boys with serious social and emotional development problems. More recently, MTV exploited its reputation by inventing an entirely new genre of television—"reality TV"—through its *Real World* and *House Rules* programs. Not only are these shows cheap to produce, they build on the reputation that MTV has for providing entertainment that is a little risky, a little sexy, and a little controversial. Indeed, MTV has been so successful in providing this kind of entertainment that it had to form an entirely new cable station—MTV 2—to actually show music videos.[9]

Focusing on Links Within and Between Firms

Linkages Between Functions. A less obvious but still important way in which a firm can attempt to differentiate its products is through linking different functions within the firm. For example, research in the pharmaceutical industry suggests that firms vary in the extent to which they are able to integrate different scientific specialties—such as genetics, biology, chemistry, and pharmacology—to develop new drugs. Firms that are able to form effective multidisciplinary teams to explore new drug categories have what some have called an **architectural competence**, that is, the ability to use organizational structure to facilitate coordination among scientific disciplines to conduct research. Firms that have this competence are able to more effectively pursue product differentiation strategies—by introducing new and powerful drugs—compared to firms that do not have this competence. And in the pharmaceutical industry, where firms that introduce such drugs can experience very large positive returns, the ability to coordinate across functions is an important source of competitive advantage.[10]

Links with Other Firms. Another basis of product differentiation is linkages with other firms. Here, instead of differentiating products or services on the basis of linkages between functions within a single firm or linkages between different products, differentiation is based on explicit linkages between one firm's products and the products or services of other firms.

This form of product differentiation has increased in popularity over the last several years. For example, with the growth in popularity of stock car racing in the United States, more and more corporations are looking to link their products or services with famous names and cars in NASCAR. Firms such as Kodak, Circuit City, Gatorade, McDonald's, Home Depot, The Cartoon Network, True Value, and Pfizer (manufacturers of Viagra) have all been major sponsors of NASCAR teams. In one year, the Coca-Cola Corporation filled orders for over 200,000 NASCAR-themed vending machines. Visa struggled to keep up with demand for its NASCAR affinity cards, and over 1 million NASCAR Barbies were once sold by Mattel—generating revenues of about $50 million. Notice that none of these firms sells products for automobiles. Rather, these firms seek to associate themselves with NASCAR because of the popularity of this sport.[11]

Another product with which firms often seek to link their own products and services is movies, especially summer "blockbuster" movies. This can be done in at least two ways. First, firms may **co-brand** their product with a movie.[12] That is, they may tie the brand of their product to the brand of another firm's product. For example, McDonald's often uses characters from movies as toys in its Happy Meals. This first occurred in 1979, when a McDonald's Happy Meal featured action figures from *Star Trek: The Motion Picture*. Second, firms can attempt to place their products in a movie. Such product placements can be as simple as having an actor drink from a can of Coca-Cola after defeating the bad guys or as complicated as introducing a new product to the market by having an actor use this product in a movie. Both BMW and Aston-Martin used this kind of product placement in James Bond movies to introduce new cars to the automobile market—although the cars that were actually sold did not include machine guns and rockets.

In general, linkages between firms that differentiate their products are examples of cooperative strategic alliance strategies. The conditions under which cooperative strategic alliances create value and are sources of sustained competitive advantage are discussed in detail in Chapter 9.

Product Mix. One of the outcomes of links among functions within a firm and links between firms can be changes in the mix of products a firm brings to the market. This mix of products or services can be a source of product differentiation, especially when (1) those products or services are technologically linked or (2) when a single set of customers purchases several of a firm's products or services.

For example, technological interconnectivity is an extremely important selling point in the information technology business and thus an important basis of potential product differentiation. However, seamless interconnectivity—where Company A's computers talk to Company B's computers across Company C's data line merging a database created by Company D's software with a database created by Company E's software to be used in a calling center that operates with Company F's technology—has been extremely difficult to realize. For this reason, some information technology firms try to realize the goal of interconnectivity by adjusting their product mix, that is, by selling a bundle of products whose interconnectivity they can control and guarantee to customers. This goal of selling a bundle of interconnected technologies can influence a firm's research and development, strategic alliance, and merger and acquisition strategies, since all these activities can influence the set of products a firm brings to market.

Shopping malls are an example of the second kind of linkage among a mix of products—where products have a common set of customers. Many customers prefer to go to one location, to shop at several stores at once, rather than travel to a series of locations to shop. This one-stop shopping reduces travel time and helps turn shopping into a social experience. Mall development companies have recognized that the value of several stores brought together in a particular location is greater than the value of those stores if they were isolated, and they have invested to help create this mix of retail shopping opportunities.[13]

Distribution Channels. Linkages within and between firms can also have an impact on how a firm chooses to distribute its products, and distribution channels can be a basis of product differentiation. For example, in the soft drink industry, Coca-Cola, PepsiCo, and Seven-Up all distribute their drinks through a network of independent and company-owned bottlers. These firms manufacture key ingredients for their soft drinks and ship these ingredients to local bottlers, who add carbonated water, package the drinks in bottles or cans, and distribute the final product to soft drink outlets in a given geographic area. Each local bottler has exclusive rights to distribute a particular brand in a geographic location.

Canada Dry has adopted a completely different distribution network. Instead of relying on local bottlers, Canada Dry packages its final product in several locations and then ships its soft drinks directly to wholesale grocers, who distribute them to local grocery stores, convenience stores, and other retail outlets.

One of the consequences of these alternative distribution strategies is that Canada Dry has a relatively strong presence in grocery stores but a relatively small presence in soft drink vending machines. The vending machine market is dominated by Coca-Cola and PepsiCo. These two firms have local distributors that maintain and stock vending machines. Canada Dry has no local distributors and is able to get its products into vending machines only when they are purchased by local Coca-Cola or Pepsi distributors. These local distributors are likely to purchase and stock Canada Dry products such as Canada Dry ginger ale, but they are contractually prohibited from purchasing Canada Dry's various cola products.[14]

Service and Support. Finally, products have been differentiated by the level of service and support associated with them. Some firms in the home appliance market, including General Electric, have not developed their own service and support network and instead rely on a network of independent service and support operations throughout the United States. Other firms in the same industry, including Sears, have developed their own service and support network.[15]

Differences in service and support have recently become a major point of differentiation in the automobile industry. Such firms as Lexus (a division of Toyota) and Saturn (a division of General Motors) compete not only on the basis of product quality but also on the basis of the level of service and support they provide. To emphasize its willingness to provide service and support, Saturn once advertised that one of its customers needed to replace a defective seat in a Saturn car. The customer lived in the Alaskan wilderness, and Saturn sent a customer service representative there for just a single day to replace the defective seat.

Product Differentiation and Creativity

The bases of product differentiation listed earlier in Table 5.1 indicate a broad range of ways in which firms can differentiate their products and services. In the end, however, any effort to list all possible ways to differentiate products and services is doomed to failure. Product differentiation is ultimately an expression of the creativity of individuals and groups within firms. It is limited only by the opportunities that exist, or that can be created, in a particular industry and by the willingness and ability of firms to creatively explore ways to take advantage of those opportunities. It is not unreasonable to expect that the day some academic researcher claims to have developed the definitive list of bases of product differentiation, some creative engineer, marketing specialist, or manager will think of yet another way to differentiate his or her product.

The Value of Product Differentiation

VRIO

In order to have the potential for generating competitive advantages, the bases of product differentiation upon which a firm competes must be valuable. The market conditions under which product differentiation can be valuable are discussed in the Strategy in Depth feature. More generally, in order to be valuable, bases of product differentiation must enable a firm to neutralize its threats and/or exploit its opportunities.

Product Differentiation and Environmental Threats

Successful product differentiation helps a firm respond to each of the environmental threats identified in the five forces framework. For example, product differentiation helps reduce the threat of new entry by forcing potential entrants to an industry to absorb not only the standard costs of beginning business but also

Strategy in Depth

The two classic treatments of the relationship between product differentiation and firm value, developed independently and published at approximately the same time, are by Edward Chamberlin and Joan Robinson.[16]

Both Chamberlin and Robinson examine product differentiation and firm performance relative to perfect competition. As explained in Chapter 2, under perfect competition, there are assumed to be numerous firms in an industry, each controlling a small proportion of the market, and the products or services sold by these firms are assumed to be identical. Under these conditions, firms face a horizontal demand curve (because they have no control over the price of the products they sell), and they maximize their economic performance by producing and selling output such that marginal revenue equals marginal costs. The maximum economic performance a firm in a perfectly competitive market can obtain, assuming no cost differences across firms, is normal economic performance.

When firms sell differentiated products, they gain some ability to adjust their prices. A firm can sell its output at very high prices and produce relatively smaller amounts of output, or it can sell its output at very low prices and produce relatively greater amounts of output. These trade-offs

The Economics
of Product Differentiation

between price and quantity produced suggest that firms selling differentiated products face a downward-sloping demand curve, rather than the horizontal demand curve for firms in a perfectly competitive market. Firms selling differentiated products and facing a downward-sloping demand curve are in an industry structure described by Chamberlin as **monopolistic competition**. It is as if, within the market niche defined by a firm's differentiated product, a firm possesses a monopoly.

Firms in monopolistically competitive markets still maximize their economic profit by producing and selling a quantity of products such that

marginal revenue equals marginal cost. The price that firms can charge at this optimal point depends on the demand they face for their differentiated product. If demand is large, then the price that can be charged is greater; if demand is low, then the price that can be charged is lower. However, if a firm's average total cost is below the price it can charge (that is, if average total cost is less than the demand-determined price), then a firm selling a differentiated product can earn an above-normal economic profit.

Consider the example presented in Figure 5.1. Several curves are relevant in this figure. First, notice that the demand (D) facing a firm in this industry is downward sloping. This means that the industry is not perfectly competitive and that a firm has some control over the prices it will charge for its products. Also, the marginal-revenue curve (MR) is downward sloping and everywhere lower than the demand curve. Marginal revenue is downward sloping because in order to sell additional levels of output of a single product, a firm must be willing to lower its price. The marginal-revenue curve is lower than the demand curve because this lower price applies to all the products sold by a firm, not just to any additional products the firm sells. The marginal-cost curve (MC) is upward sloping, indicating that in order to produce

the additional costs associated with overcoming incumbent firms' product differentiation advantages. The relationship between product differentiation and new entry has already been discussed in Chapter 2.

Product differentiation reduces the threat of rivalry, because each firm in an industry attempts to carve out its own unique product niche. Rivalry is not reduced to zero, for these products still compete with one another for a common set of customers, but it is somewhat attenuated because the customers each firm seeks are different. For example, both a Rolls Royce and a Hyundai satisfy the same basic

additional outputs, a firm must accept additional costs. The average-total-cost curve (*ATC*) can have a variety of shapes, depending on the economies of scale, the cost of productive inputs, and other cost phenomena described in Chapter 4.

These four curves (demand, marginal revenue, marginal cost, and average total cost) can be used to determine the level of economic profit for a firm under monopolistic competition. In order to maximize profit, the firm produces an amount (Q_e) such that marginal costs equal marginal revenues. To determine the price of a firm's output at this level of production, a vertical line is drawn from the point where marginal costs equal marginal revenues. This line will intersect with the demand curve. Where this vertical line intersects demand, a horizontal line is drawn to the vertical (price) axis to determine the price a firm can charge. In the figure, this price is P_e. At the point P_e, average total cost is less than the price. The total revenue obtained by the firm in this situation (price x quantity) is indicated by

the shaded area in the figure. The economic profit portion of this total revenue is indicated by the cross-hatched section of the shaded portion of the figure. Because this cross-hatched section is above average total costs in the figure, it represents a competitive advantage. If this section was below average total costs, it would represent a competitive disadvantage.

Chamberlin and Robinson go on to discuss the impact of entry into the market niche defined by a firm's differentiated product. As discussed in Chapter 2, a basic assumption of S-C-P models is that the existence of above-normal economic performance motivates entry into an industry or into a market niche within an industry. In monopolistically competitive industries, such entry means that the demand curve facing incumbent firms shifts downward and to the left. This implies that an incumbent firm's customers will buy less of its output if it maintains its prices or (equivalently) that a firm will have to lower its prices to maintain its current volume of sales. In the long run, entry into this market niche can lead to a situation where the price of goods or services sold when a firm produces output such that marginal cost equals marginal revenue is exactly equal to that firm's average total cost. At this point, a firm earns zero economic profits even if it still sells a differentiated product.

Sources: E. H. Chamberlin (1933). *The economics of monopolistic competition.* Cambridge, MA: MIT Press; J. Robinson (1934). "What is perfect competition?" *Quarterly Journal of Economics,* 49, pp. 104–120.

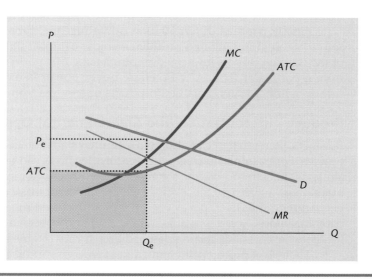

Figure 5.1   Product Differentiation and Firm Performance: The Analysis of Monopolistic Competition

consumer need—transportation—but it is unlikely that potential customers of Rolls Royce will also be interested in purchasing a Hyundai or vice versa.

Product differentiation also helps firms reduce the threat of substitutes by making a firm's current products appear more attractive than substitute products. For example, fresh food can be thought of as a substitute for frozen processed foods. In order to make its frozen processed foods more attractive than fresh foods, products like Stouffer's and Swanson are marketed heavily through television advertisements, newspaper ads, point-of-purchase displays, and coupons.

Product differentiation can also reduce the threat of suppliers. Powerful suppliers can raise the prices of the products or services they provide. Often, these increased supply costs must be passed on to a firm's customers in the form of higher prices if a firm's profit margin is not to deteriorate. A firm without a highly differentiated product may find it difficult to pass its increased costs on to customers, because these customers will have numerous other ways to purchase similar products or services from a firm's competitors. However, a firm with a highly differentiated product may have loyal customers or customers who are unable to purchase similar products or services from other firms. These types of customers are more likely to accept increased prices. Thus, a powerful supplier may be able to raise its prices, but, up to some point, these increases will not reduce the profitability of a firm selling a highly differentiated product.

The relationship between sugar suppliers and soft drink manufacturers over the last 30 years has had many of these characteristics. In the 1970s, sugar was a major ingredient in soft drinks. However, in the early 1980s, sugar prices rose suddenly. At first, soft drink companies were able to pass these increased costs on to customers in the form of increased prices. Customer loyalty to soft drink brands, and dislike for soft drink substitutes, kept customers purchasing soft drinks despite increased prices. However, as sugar prices continued to rise, several alternatives to sugar were developed. First, expensive sugar from sugar cane was supplemented by less expensive high-fructose corn syrup. Second, aspartame, a low-calorie sugar substitute (marketed under the brand name NutraSweet) was developed. Thus, although soft drink firms could raise their prices in response to increased sugar costs, at some point these higher prices led to the development of sugar substitutes that reduced the power of sugar suppliers over the soft drink industry.[17]

Finally, product differentiation can reduce the threat of buyers. When a firm sells a highly differentiated product, it enjoys a "quasi-monopoly" in that segment of the market. Buyers interested in purchasing this particular product must buy it from a particular firm. Any potential buyer power is reduced by the ability of a firm to withhold highly valued products or services from a buyer.

Product Differentiation and Environmental Opportunities

Product differentiation can also help a firm take advantage of environmental opportunities. For example, in fragmented industries firms can use product differentiation strategies to help consolidate a market. In the office-paper industry, Xerox has used its brand name to become the leading seller of paper for office copy machines and printers. Arguing that its paper is specially manufactured to avoid jamming in its own copy machines, Xerox was able to brand what had been a commodity product and facilitate the consolidation of what had been a very fragmented industry.[18]

The role of product differentiation in emerging industries has been discussed in Chapter 2. By being a first mover in these industries, firms can gain product differentiation advantages based on perceived technological leadership, preemption of strategically valuable assets, and buyer loyalty due to high switching costs.

In mature industries, product differentiation efforts often switch from attempts to introduce radically new technologies to product refinement as a basis of product differentiation. For example, in the mature retail gasoline market, firms attempt to differentiate their products by selling slightly modified gasoline (cleaner-burning gasoline, gasoline that cleans fuel injectors, and so forth) and by altering the product mix (linking gasoline sales with convenience stores). In mature markets, it is sometimes difficult to find ways to actually refine a product or service. In such settings, firms can sometimes be tempted to exaggerate the extent to which they have

Ethics and Strategy

One of the most common ways to try to differentiate a product is to make claims about that product's performance. In general, high-performance products command a price premium over low-performance products. However, the potential price advantages enjoyed by high-performance products can sometimes lead firms to make claims about their products that, at the least, strain credibility, and at the most, simply lie about what their products can do.

Some of these claims are easily dismissed as harmless exaggerations. Few people actually believe that using a particular type of whitening toothpaste is going to make your in-laws like you, or that not wearing a particular type of deodorant is going cause patrons in a bar to collapse when you lift your arms in victory after a foosball game. These exaggerations are harmless and present few ethical challenges.

However, in the field of health care, exaggerated product performance claims can have serious consequences. This can happen when a patient takes a medication with exaggerated performance claims in lieu of a medication with more modest, although accurate, performance claims. A history of false medical performance claims in the United States led to the formation of the Federal Drug Administration (FDA), a federal regulatory agency charged with evaluating the efficacy of drugs before they are marketed. Historically, the FDA has adopted the "gold standard" of drug approval—not only must a drug demon-

Product Claims and the Ethical Dilemmas in Health Care

strate that it does what it claims, it must also demonstrate that it does not do any significant harm to the patient. Patients can be confident that drugs that pass the FDA approval process meet the highest standards in the world.

However, this "gold standard" of approval creates important ethical dilemmas—mostly stemming from the time it takes a drug to pass FDA inspections. This process can take between five and seven years. During FDA trials, patients that might otherwise benefit from a drug are not allowed to use it because it hasn't yet received FDA approval. Thus, while the FDA approval process may work very well for people who may need a drug sometime in the future, it works less well for those who need a drug right now.

A growing suspicion among some consumers that the FDA process may prevent effective drugs from being marketed has helped feed the growth of alternative treatments—usually based on some herbal or more natural formula. Such treatments are careful to note that their claims—everything from re-growing hair to losing weight to enhancing athletic performance to quitting smoking—have not been tested by the FDA. And yet, these claims are still made.

Some of these performance claims seem at least reasonable. For example, it is now widely accepted that ephedra does behave as an amphetamine, and thus is likely to enhance strength and athletic performance. Others—including those that claim that a mixture of herbs can actually increase the size of male genitals—seem far-fetched, at best. Indeed, a recent analysis of herbal treatments making this claim found no ingredients that could have this effect, and found an unacceptably high concentration of bacteria from animal feces that can cause serious stomach disorders. Firms that sell products on the basis of exaggerated and unsubstantiated claims face their own ethical dilemmas. And without the FDA to ensure product safety and efficacy, the adage "caveat emptor"—or, let the buyer beware— seems like good advice.

Sources: J. Angwin (2003). "Some 'enlargement pills' pack impurities." *Wall Street Journal*, April 8, p. B1; G. Pisano (1991). "Nucleon, Inc." Harvard Business School Case No. 9-692-041.

refined and improved their products or services. The implications of these exaggerations are discussed in the Ethics and Strategy feature.

Product differentiation can also be an important strategic option in a declining industry. Product-differentiating firms may be able to become leaders in this kind of industry (based on their reputation, on unique product attributes, or on some other product differentiation basis). Alternatively, highly differentiated firms may be able to discover a viable market niche that will enable them to survive despite the overall decline in the market.

Finally, the decision to implement a product differentiation strategy can have a significant impact on how a firm acts in a global industry. For example, several firms in the retail clothing industry with important product differentiation advantages in their home markets are beginning to enter into the U.S. retail clothing market. These firms include Sweden's H & M Hennes & Mauritz AB with its emphasis on "cheap chic," the Dutch firm Mexx (a division of Liz Claiborne), the Spanish company Zara (a division of Inditex SA), and the French sportswear company Lacoste (a division of Devanlay SA).[19]

Product Differentiation and Sustained Competitive Advantage

Product differentiation strategies add value by enabling firms to charge for their products or services prices that are greater than its average total cost. Firms that implement this strategy successfully can reduce a variety of environmental threats and exploit a variety of environmental opportunities. However, as discussed in Chapter 3, the ability of a strategy to add value to a firm must be linked with rare and costly-to-imitate organizational strengths in order to generate a sustained competitive advantage. Each of the bases of product differentiation listed earlier in this chapter varies with respect to how likely it is to be rare and costly to imitate.

Rare Bases for Product Differentiation

The concept of product differentiation generally assumes that the number of firms that have been able to differentiate their products in a particular way is, at some point in time, smaller than the number of firms needed to generate perfect competition dynamics. Indeed, the reason that highly differentiated firms can charge a price for their product that is greater than average total cost is because these firms are using a basis for product differentiation that few competing firms are also using.

Ultimately, the rarity of a product differentiation strategy depends on the ability of individual firms to be creative in finding new ways to differentiate their products. As suggested earlier, highly creative firms will be able to discover or create new ways to do this. These kinds of firms will always be one step ahead of the competition, for rival firms will often be trying to imitate these firms' last product differentiation move while creative firms are working on their next one.

The Imitability of Product Differentiation

Valuable and rare bases of product differentiation must be costly to imitate if they are to be sources of sustained competitive advantage. Both direct duplication and substitution, as approaches to imitation, are important in understanding the ability of product differentiation to generate competitive advantages.

Direct Duplication of Product Differentiation

As discussed in Chapter 4, firms that successfully implement a cost leadership strategy can choose whether or not they want to reveal this strategic choice to their competition by adjusting their prices. If they keep their prices high—despite their cost advantages—the existence of those cost advantages may not be revealed to competitors. Of course, other firms—like Wal-Mart—who are confident that their cost advantages cannot be duplicated at low cost are willing to reveal their cost advantage through charging lower prices for their products or services.

Firms pursuing product differentiation strategies usually do not have this option. More often than not, the act of selling a highly differentiated product or service reveals the basis upon which a firm is trying to differentiate its products. In fact, most firms go to great lengths to let their customers know how they are differentiating their products; and in the process of informing potential customers they also inform their competitors. Indeed, if competitors are not sure how a firm is differentiating its product, all they need to do is purchase that product themselves. Their own experience with the product—its features and other attributes—will tell them all they need to know about this firm's product differentiation strategy.

Knowing how a firm is differentiating its products, however, does not necessarily mean that competitors will be able to duplicate the strategy at low cost. The ability to duplicate a valuable and rare product differentiation strategy depends on the basis upon which a firm is differentiating its products. As suggested in Table 5.2, some bases of product differentiation—including the use of product features—are almost always easy to duplicate. Others—including product mix, links with other firms, product customization, product complexity, and consumer marketing—can sometimes be costly to duplicate. Finally, still other bases of product differentiation—including links between functions, timing, location, reputation, distribution channels, and service and support—are usually costly to duplicate.

How costly it is to duplicate a particular basis of product differentiation depends on the kinds of resources and capabilities that basis uses. When those resources and capabilities are acquired in unique historical settings, when there is some uncertainty about how to build these resources and capabilities, or when these resources and capabilities are socially complex in nature, then product differentiation strategies that exploit these kinds of resources and capabilities will be costly to imitate. These strategies can be a source of sustained competitive advantage for a firm. However, when a product differentiation strategy exploits resources and capabilities that do not possess these attributes, then those strategies are likely to be less costly to duplicate, and even if they are valuable and rare, will only be sources of temporary competitive advantage.

Bases of Product Differentiation That Are Easy to Duplicate. The one basis of product differentiation in Table 5.2 that is identified as almost always being easy to duplicate is product features. This is ironic since product features are by far the most popular way for firms to try to differentiate their products. Rarely do product features, by themselves, enable a firm to gain sustained competitive advantages from a product differentiation strategy.

For example, virtually every one of the product features used in the automobile industry to differentiate the products of different automobile companies has been duplicated. Chrysler's "cab forward" design has been incorporated in the design of many manufacturers. The curved, sporty styling of the Audi has surfaced in cars manufactured by Lexus and General Motors. GM's "On Star" system has been duplicated by Mercedes. Mercedes' crumple zone technology has become the industry standard as has GM's uni-body construction method. Indeed, only the Mazda Miata, Nissan 350 Z, and the Porsche 911 have remained unduplicated—and this has little to do with the product features of these cars and much more to do with their reputation.

The only time product features, per se, can be a source of sustained competitive advantage for a firm is when those features are protected by patents. However, as was discussed in Chapters 2 and 3, even patents provide only limited protection from direct duplication, except in very unusual settings.

Table 5.2   **Bases of Product Differentiation and the Cost of Duplication**

	History	Uncertainty	Social complexity
Low-cost duplication usually possible			
1. Product features	—	—	—
May be costly to duplicate			
2. Product mix	*	*	*
3. Links with other firms	*	—	**
4. Product customization	*	—	**
5. Product complexity	*	—	*
6. Consumer marketing	—	**	—
Usually costly to duplicate			
7. Links between functions	*	*	**
8. Timing	***	*	—
9. Location	***	—	—
10. Reputation	***	**	***
11. Distribution channels	**	*	**
12. Service and support	*	*	**

— = Not likely to be a source of costly duplication   * = Somewhat likely to be a source of costly duplication
** = Likely to be a source of costly duplication   *** = Very likely to be a source of costly duplication

While product features, by themselves, are usually not a source of sustained competitive advantage, they can be a source of a temporary competitive advantage. During the period of time when a firm has a temporary competitive advantage from implementing a product differentiation strategy based on product features, it may be able to attract new customers. Once these customers try this product, they may discover other features of a firm's products that make them attractive. If these other features are costly to duplicate, then they can be a source of sustained competitive advantage, even though the features that originally attracted a customer to a firm's products will often be rapidly duplicated by competitors.

Bases of Product Differentiation That May Be Costly to Duplicate. On the other hand, some bases of product differentiation may sometimes be costly to duplicate, at least in some circumstances. The first of these, listed in Table 5.2, is product mix.

Duplicating the features of another firm's products is usually not difficult. However, if that firm brings a series of products to market, if each of these products has unique features, and most importantly, if the products are highly integrated with each other, then this mix of products may be costly to duplicate. Certainly, the technological integration of the mix of information technology products sold by IBM and other firms has been relatively difficult to duplicate for firms that do not manufacture all these products themselves.

On the other hand, when this basis of a product mix advantage is a common customer, then duplication is often less difficult. Thus, while having a mall that brings several stores together in a single place is a source of competitive advantage over stand-alone stores, it is not a competitive advantage over other malls that provide the same service. Since there continue to be opportunities to build such malls, the fact that malls make it easier for a common set of customers to shop does not give any one mall a sustained competitive advantage.

Links with other firms may also be costly to duplicate, especially when those links depend on socially complex relationships. Setting up a racing team to compete in NASCAR requires a great deal of time and effort. However, most of the skills needed to set up a team are widely available and thus not likely to be a source of competitive advantage for any one firm. The same is probably true for fast-food companies—like McDonald's marketing its Happy Meals using characters from a single summer movie. However, to develop a marketing relationship between a firm and a movie studio such that a firm can plan its marketing efforts years in advance requires a great deal of coordination and cooperation. Thus, to the extent that McDonald's has that kind of relationship with a movie studio, or to the extent that BMW and Aston Martin coordinate their product development cycle with the release of a particular movie, these links with other firms may be costly to duplicate and a source of sustained competitive advantage.

The extent to which interfirm links can provide sources of sustained competitive advantage is discussed in more detail in Chapter 9.

In the same way, product customization and product complexity are often easy-to-duplicate bases of product differentiation. However, sometimes the ability of a firm to customize its products for one of its customers depends on the close relationships it has developed with those customers. Product customization of this sort depends on the willingness of a firm to share often-proprietary details about its operations, products, research and development, or other characteristics with a supplying firm. Willingness to share this kind of information, in turn, depends on the ability of each firm to trust and rely on the other. The firm opening its operations to a supplier must trust that that supplier will not make this information broadly available to competing firms. The firm supplying customized products must trust that its customer will not take unfair advantage of it. If two firms have developed these kinds of socially complex relationships, and few other firms have them, then links with other firms will be costly to duplicate and a source of sustained competitive advantage.

The product customization seen in both enterprise software and in high-end customized bicycles has these socially complex features. In a real sense, when these products are purchased, a relationship with a supplier is being established— a relationship that is likely to last a long period of time. Once this relationship is established, partners are likely to be unwilling to abandon it, unless, of course, a party to the exchange tries to take unfair advantage of another party to that exchange. This possibility is discussed in detail in Chapter 9.

Finally, consumer marketing, though a very common form of product differentiation, is often easy to duplicate. Thus, while Mountain Dew has established itself as the "Extreme Games" drink, other drinks, including Gatorade, have also begun to tap into this market segment. Of course, every once in a while an advertising campaign or slogan, a point-of-purchase display, or some other attribute of a consumer marketing campaign will unexpectedly catch on and create greater-than-expected product awareness. In beer, marketing campaigns such as "Tastes great, less filling," "Why ask why," the "Budweiser Frogs," and "What's Up?" have had these unusual effects. If a firm, in relation with its various consumer marketing agencies, is systematically able to develop these superior consumer marketing campaigns, then it may be able to obtain a sustained competitive advantage. However, if such campaigns are unpredictable and largely a matter of a firm's good luck, they cannot be expected to be a source of sustained competitive advantage.

Bases of Product Differentiation That Are Usually Costly to Duplicate. The remaining bases of product differentiation listed in Table 5.2 are usually costly to duplicate. Firms that differentiate their products on these bases may be able to obtain sustained competitive advantages.

Linkages across functions within a single firm are usually a costly-to-duplicate basis of product differentiation. Where linkages with other firms can be either easy or costly to duplicate, depending on the nature of the relationship that exists between firms, linkages across functions within a single firm usually require socially complex, trusting relations. There are numerous built-in conflicts between functions and divisions within a single firm. Organizations that have a history and culture that support cooperative relations among conflicting divisions may be able to set aside functional and divisional conflicts to cooperate in delivering a differentiated product to the market. However, firms with a history of conflict across functional and divisional boundaries face a significant, and costly, challenge in altering these socially complex, historical patterns.

Indeed, the research on architectural competence in pharmaceutical firms suggests that not only do some firms possess this competence, but that other firms do not. Moreover, despite the significant advantages that accrue to firms with this competence, firms without this competence have, on average, been unable to develop it. All this suggests that such a competence, if it is also rare, is likely to be costly to duplicate and thus a source of sustained competitive advantage.

Timing is also a difficult-to-duplicate basis of product differentiation. As suggested in Chapter 3, it is difficult (if not impossible) to recreate a firm's unique history. If that history endows a firm with special resources and capabilities it can use to differentiate its products, this product differentiation strategy can be a source of sustained competitive advantage. Rivals of a firm with such a timing-based product differentiation advantage may need to seek alternative ways to differentiate their products. Thus, it is not surprising that universities that compete with the oldest universities in the country find alternative ways to differentiate themselves—through their size, the quality of the extramural sports, through their diversity—rather than relying on their age.

Location is often a difficult-to-duplicate basis of product differentiation. This is especially the case when a firm's location is unique. For example, research on the hotel preferences of business travelers suggests that location is a major determinant of the decision to stay in a hotel. Hotels that are convenient to both major transportation and commercial centers in a city are preferred, other things being equal, to hotels in other types of locations. Indeed, location has been shown to be a more important decision criterion for business travelers than price. If only a few hotels in a city have these prime locations, and if no further hotel development is possible, then hotels with these locations can gain sustained competitive advantages.

Of all the bases of product differentiation listed in this chapter, perhaps none is more difficult to duplicate than a firm's reputation. As suggested earlier, a firm's reputation is actually a socially complex relationship between a firm and its customers, based on years of experience, commitment, and trust. Reputations are not built quickly, nor can they be bought and sold. Rather, they can only be developed over time by consistent investment in the relationship between a firm and its customers. A firm with a positive reputation can enjoy a significant competitive advantage, whereas a firm with a negative reputation, or no reputation, may have to invest significant amounts over long periods of time to match the differentiated firm.

Distribution channels can also be a costly-to-duplicate basis of product differentiation, for at least two reasons. First, relations between a firm and its distribution channels are often socially complex and thus costly to duplicate. Second, the supply of distribution channels may be limited. Firms that already have access to these channels may be able to use them, but firms that do not have such access may be forced to create their own or develop new channels. Creating new channels, or developing entirely new means of distribution, can be difficult and costly undertakings.[20] These costs are one of the primary motivations underlying many international joint ventures (see Chapter 9).

Finally, level of service and support can be a costly-to-duplicate basis of product differentiation. In most industries, it is usually not too costly to provide a minimum level of service and support. In home electronics, this minimum level of service can be provided by a network of independent electronic repair shops. In automobiles, this level of service can be provided by service facilities associated with dealerships. In fast foods, this level of service can be provided by a minimum level of employee training.

However, moving beyond this minimum level of service and support can be difficult for at least two reasons. First, increasing the quality of service and support may involve substantial amounts of costly training. McDonald's has created a sophisticated training facility (Hamburger University) to maintain its unusually high level of service in fast foods. General Electric has invested heavily in training for service and support over the last several years. Many Japanese automakers spent millions on training employees to help support auto dealerships, before they opened U.S. manufacturing facilities.[21]

More important than the direct costs of the training needed to provide high-quality service and support, these bases of product differentiation often reflect the attitude of a firm and its employees toward customers. In many firms throughout the world, the customer has become "the bad guy." This is, in many ways, understandable. Employees tend to interact with their customers less frequently than they interact with other employees. When they do interact with customers, they are often the recipients of complaints directed at the firm. In these settings, hostility toward the customer can develop. Such hostility is, of course, inconsistent with a product differentiation strategy based on customer service and support.

In the end, high levels of customer service and support are based on socially complex relations between firms and customers. Firms that have conflicts with their customers may face some difficulty duplicating the high levels of service and support provided by competing firms.

Substitutes for Product Differentiation

The bases of product differentiation outlined in this chapter vary in how rare they are likely to be and in how difficult they are to duplicate. However, the ability of the bases of product differentiation to generate a sustained competitive advantage also depends on whether low-cost substitutes exist.

Substitutes for bases of product differentiation can take two forms. First, many of the bases of product differentiation listed in Table 5.1 can be partial substitutes for each other. For example, product features, product customization, and product complexity are all very similar bases of product differentiation and thus can act as substitutes for each other. A particular firm may try to develop a competitive advantage by differentiating its products on the basis of product customization only to find that its customization advantages are reduced as another firm alters the features of its products. In a similar way, linkages between functions, linkages between firms, and product mix, as bases of product differentiation, can also be substitutes for each other. IBM links its sales, service, and consulting functions to differentiate itself in the computer market. Other computer firms, however, may develop close relationships with computer service companies and consulting firms to close this product differentiation advantage. Given that different bases of product differentiation are often partial substitutes for each other, it is not surprising that firms pursue these multiple bases of product differentiation simultaneously.

Second, other of the strategies discussed throughout this book can be substitutes for many of the bases of product differentiation listed in Table 5.1. One firm may try to gain a competitive advantage through adjusting its product mix, and another firm may substitute strategic alliances to create the same type of product differentiation. For example, Southwest Airline's continued emphasis on friendly, on-time, low cost service and United Airlines' emphasis on its links to Lufthansa and other worldwide airlines through the Star Alliance can both be seen as product differentiation efforts that are at least partial substitutes.[22]

In contrast, some of the other bases of product differentiation discussed in this chapter have few obvious close substitutes. These include timing, location, distribution channels, and service and support. To the extent that these bases of product differentiation are also valuable, rare, and difficult to duplicate, they may be sources of sustained competitive advantage.

VRIO

Organizing to Implement Product Differentiation

As was suggested in Chapter 3, the ability to implement a strategy depends on the adjustment of a firm's structure, its management controls, and its compensation policies to be consistent with that strategy. Where strategy implementation for firms adopting a cost leadership strategy focuses on reducing a firm's costs and increasing its efficiency, strategy implementation for a firm adopting a product differentiation strategy must focus on innovation, creativity, and product performance. Where cost-leading firms are all about customer value, product-differentiating firms are all about style. How the need for style is reflected in a firm's structure, controls, and compensation policies is summarized in Table 5.3.

Organizational Structure and Implementing Product Differentiation

Both cost leadership and product differentiation strategies are implemented through the use of a functional or U-form organizational structure. However, where the U-form structure used to implement a cost leadership strategy has few layers, simple reporting relationships, a small corporate staff, and focuses on only a few business functions, the U-form structure for a firm implementing a product differentiation strategy can be somewhat more complex. For example, these firms often use temporary cross-divisional *and* cross-functional teams to manage the development and implementation of new, innovative, and highly differentiated products. These teams bring individuals from different businesses and different functional areas together to cooperate on a particular new product or service.

One firm that has used these cross-divisional and cross-functional teams effectively is the British advertising agency WPP. WPP owns several very large advertising agencies, several public relations firms, several marketing research companies, and so forth. Each of these businesses operates relatively independently in most areas. However, the corporation has identified a few markets where cross-divisional and cross-functional collaboration is important. One of these is the health care market. To

Table 5.3   **Organizing to Implement Product Differentiation Strategies**

Organizational Structure:
1. Cross-divisional/cross-functional product development teams
2. Complex matrix structures
3. Isolated pockets of intense creative efforts: Skunk works

Management Control Systems:
1. Broad decision-making guidelines
2. Managerial freedom within guidelines
3. A policy of experimentation

Compensation Policies:
1. Rewards for risk-taking, not punishment for failures
2. Rewards for creative flair
3. Multidimensional performance measurement

exploit opportunities in this health care market, WPP, the corporation, forms teams of advertising specialists, market research specialists, public relations specialists, and so on, drawn from each of the businesses it owns. The resulting cross-divisional teams are given the responsibility of developing new and highly differentiated approaches to developing marketing strategies for their clients in the health care industry.[23]

The creation of cross-divisional, or cross-functional teams often implies that a firm has implemented some form of matrix structure. As suggested in Chapter 4, a **matrix structure** exists when individuals in a firm have two or more "bosses" simultaneously. Thus, for example, if a person from one of WPP's advertising agencies is assigned temporarily to a or cross-divisional team, that person has two bosses: the head of the temporary team he/she has been assigned to and his/her boss back in the advertising agency. Managing two bosses simultaneously can be very challenging, especially when they have conflicting interests, and, as we will see in Chapter 8, the interests of these multiple bosses *will* often conflict.

A particularly important form of the cross-divisional or cross-functional team exists when this team is relieved of all other responsibilities in the firm and focuses all its attention on developing a new innovative product or service. The best known example of this approach to developing a differentiated product occurred at the Lockheed Corporation during the 1950s and 1960s when small groups of engineers were put on very focused teams to develop sophisticated and top secret military aircraft. These teams would have a section of the Lockheed facility dedicated to their efforts and designated as off-limits to almost all other employees. The joke was that these intensive creative efforts were so engaging that members of these teams actually would forget to shower—hence their name "**Skunk Works**." Such skunk works have been used by numerous firms to focus the creative energy required to develop and introduce highly differentiated products.[24]

Management Controls and Implementing Product Differentiation

The first two management controls helpful for implementing product differentiation listed in Table 5.3—broad decision-making guidelines and managerial freedom within those guidelines—often go together, even though they sound somewhat contradictory. These potential contradictions are discussed in the Strategy in the Emerging Enterprise feature. Managing these contradictions is one of the central challenges of firms looking to implement product differentiation strategies.

Broad decision-making guidelines help bring order to what otherwise might be a chaotic decision-making process. When managers have no constraints in their decision making, they can make decisions that are disconnected from each other and inconsistent with a firm's overall mission and objectives. This results in decisions that are either not implemented or not implemented well.

On the other hand, if these decision-making guidelines become too narrow, they can stifle creativity within a firm. As was suggested earlier, a firm's ability to differentiate its products is limited only by its creativity. Thus, decision guidelines must be narrow enough to ensure that the decisions made are consistent with a firm's mission and objectives. However, these guidelines must be broad enough so that managerial creativity is not destroyed. In well-managed firms implementing product differentiation strategies, as long as managerial decisions fall within the broad decision-making guidelines in a firm, managers have the right—in fact, are expected—to make creative decisions.

A firm that has worked hard to reach this balance between chaos and control is 3M. In an effort to provide guiding principles that define the range of acceptable decisions at 3M, its senior managers have developed a set of innovating principles. These are presented in Table 5.4 and define the boundaries of innovative chaos at

Strategy in the Emerging Enterprise

*I*n the 1950s, a well-known economist named Joseph Schumpeter suggested that only very large and profitable companies have the resources necessary to invest in creating new and highly innovative products and services. His conclusion suggested that the social evils caused by economic power being concentrated in the hands of a relatively few large and powerful organizations was simply the price society had to pay for innovations that could benefit consumers.

The economic history of the last 30 years or so suggests that one of Schumpeter's key assumptions—that only large firms can afford to be innovative—is wrong. Indeed, over this time period, it is clear that a great deal of innovation has occurred through the creation of entrepreneurial firms. Firms such as Dell, Microsoft, Intel, Apple, Home Depot, Cisco, Gateway, Sun, Office Depot, Nike, Oracle, PeopleSoft, Foot Locker, Amazon.com, and Starbucks have all been sources of major innovations in their industries, and all were begun as entrepreneurial ventures in the last 30 years. Indeed, given the impact of these and other entrepreneurial ventures on the worldwide economy during this time period, it is possible to call the last 30 years the "era of the entrepreneur."

What is it about entrepreneurial firms that enables them to develop innovations that sometimes come to dominate a market? Some scholars have sug-

Can Only Small Firms Be Innovative?

gested that the small size and lack of resources that characterize entrepreneurial start-ups, far from limiting their innovativeness, actually facilitate innovation.

For example, entrepreneurial firms have relatively little to lose when engaging in innovation. If the market accepts their innovation, great; if it doesn't, move on to the next innovation. Established firms, on the other hand, may have a significant stake in an older technology, an older distribution system, or an older type of customer. Established firms may be unwilling to cannibalize the sales of their current products for new and innovative products.

Moreover, small entrepreneurial firms have relatively few bureaucratic controls. Information and ideas flow freely in these organizations. Such information flow tends to facilitate innovation. Larger firms, on the other hand, have usually installed numerous bureaucratic controls that impede cross-functional communication, and thus slow innovation.

Indeed, some have even argued that the types of people that are attracted to small entrepreneurial firms tend to be more innovative than people that are attracted to larger, more stable companies. People who are comfortable with risk-seeking and creativity may be attracted to an entrepreneurial firm, while people who are less comfortable with risk-seeking and creativity may be attracted to larger, more stable firms.

Whatever the reasons, many large firms have come to realize that they cannot afford to be "out-innovated" and "out-maneuvered" by entrepreneurial start-ups. In response, larger firms have begun to adopt policies and procedures that try to create the kind of innovativeness and creativity one often sees in entrepreneurial firms. Some firms—like 3M (see Table 5.4)—have been quite successful in this effort. Others have been less successful.

Sources: C. Christensen (1997). *The innovator's dilemma*. Boston: Harvard Business School Press; J. Schumpeter (1942). *Capitalism, socialism and democracy*. New York: Harper and Rowe; T. Zenger and E. Rasmusen (1990). "Diseconomies of scale in employment contracts." *Journal of Law, Economics, and Organization*, 6, pp. 65–98.

3M. Within these boundaries, managers and engineers are expected to be creative and innovative in developing highly differentiated products and services.[25]

Another firm that has managed this tension well is British Airways (BA). BA has extensive training programs to teach its flight attendants how to provide world-class service, especially for its business-class customers. This training constitutes standard operating procedures that give purpose and structure to BA's efforts to provide a differentiated service in the highly competitive airline industry. Interestingly, however, BA also trains its flight attendants in when to violate these standard policies and procedures. By recognizing that no set of management controls can ever anticipate all the special situations that can occur when provid-

Table 5.4   **Guiding Innovative Principles at 3M***

1. **Vision.** Declare the importance of innovation; make it part of the company's self-image. "Our efforts to encourage and support innovation are proof that we really do intend to achieve our vision of ourselves . . . that we intend to become what we want to be . . . as a business and as creative individuals."

2. **Foresight.** Find out where technologies and markets are going. Identify articulated and unarticulated needs of customers. "If you are working on a next-generation medical imaging device, you'll probably talk to radiologists, but you might also sit down with people who enhance images from interplanetary space probes."

3. **Stretch goals.** Set goals that will make you and the organization stretch to make quantum improvements. Although many projects are pursued, place your biggest bets on those that change the basis of competition and redefine the industry. "We have a number of stretch goals at 3M. The first states that we will drive 30 percent of all sales from products introduced in the past 4 years. . . . To establish a sense of urgency, we've recently added another goal, which is that we want 10 percent of our sales to come from products that have been in the market for just 1 year . . . Innovation is time sensitive . . . you need to move quickly."

4. **Empowerment.** Hire good people and trust them, delegate responsibilities, provide slack resources, and get out of the way. Be tolerant of initiative and the mistakes that occur because of that initiative. "William McKnight [a former chairman of 3M] came up with one way to institutionalize a tolerance of individual effort. He said that all technical employees could devote 15 percent of their time to a project of their own invention. In other words, they could manage themselves for 15 percent of the time. . . . The number is not so important as the message, which is this: The system has some slack in it. If you have a good idea, and the commitment to squirrel away time to work on it and the raw nerve to skirt your lab manager's expressed desires, then go for it.

   Put another way, we want to institutionalize a bit of rebellion in our labs. We can't have all our people off totally on their own . . . we do believe in

   discipline . . . but at the same time 3M management encourages a healthy disrespect for 3M management. This is not the sort of thing we publicize in our annual report, but the stories we tell—with relish—are frequently about 3Mers who have circumvented their supervisors and succeeded.

   We also recognize that when you let people follow their own lead . . . everyone doesn't wind up at the same place. You can't ask people to have unique visions and march in lockstep. Some people are very precise, detail-oriented people . . . and others are fuzzy thinkers and visionaries . . . and this is exactly what we want."

5. **Communications.** Open, extensive exchanges according to ground rules in forums that are present for sharing ideas and where networking is each individual's responsibility. Multiple methods for sharing information are necessary. "When innovators communicate with each other, you can leverage their discoveries. This is critically important because it allows companies to get the maximum return on their substantial investments in new technologies. It also acts as a stimulus to further innovation. Indeed, we believe that the ability to combine and transfer technologies is as important as the original discovery of a technology."

6. **Rewards and recognition.** Emphasize individual recognition more than monetary rewards through peer recognition and by choice of managerial or technical promotion routes. "Innovation is an intensely human activity." "I've laid out six elements of 3M's corporate culture that contribute to a tradition of innovation: vision, foresight, stretch goals, empowerment, communication, and recognition. . . . The list is . . . too orderly. Innovation at 3M is anything but orderly. It is sensible, in that our efforts are directed at reaching our goals, but the organization . . . and the process . . . and sometimes the people can be chaotic. We are managing in chaos, and this is the right way to manage if you want innovation. It's been said that the competition never knows what we are going to come up with next. The fact is, neither do we."

*As expressed by W. Coyne (1996) *Building a tradition of innovation.* The Fifth U.K. Innovation Lecture, Department of Trade and Industry, London. Cited in Van de Ven et al. (1999), pp. 198–200.

ing service to customers, BA empowers its employees to meet specific customer needs. This enables BA to have both a clearly defined product differentiation strategy and the flexibility to adjust this strategy as the situation dictates.[26]

Firms can also facilitate the implementation of a product differentiation strategy by adopting a **policy of experimentation**. Such a policy exists when firms are committed to engage in several related product differentiation efforts simultaneously. That these product differentiation efforts are related suggests that a firm has some vision about how a particular market is likely to unfold over time. However, that there are several of these product differentiation efforts occurring simultaneously suggests that a firm is not overly committed to a particular narrow vision about how a market is going to evolve. Rather, several different experiments facilitate the exploration of different futures in a marketplace. Indeed, successful experiments can actually help define the future evolution of a marketplace.

Consider, for example, Charles Schwab, the innovative discount broker. In the face of increased competition from full-service and Internet-based brokerage firms, Schwab engaged in a series of experiments to discover the next generation of products it could offer to its customers and the different ways it could differentiate those products. Schwab investigated a software for simplifying online mutual fund selection, online futures trading, and online company research. It also formed an exploratory alliance with Goldman Sachs to evaluate the possibility of enabling Schwab customers to trade in initial public offerings. Not all of Schwab's experiments led to the introduction of highly differentiated products. For example, based on some experimental investments, Schwab decided not to get into the credit card market. However, by experimenting with a range of possible product differentiation moves, it was able to develop a range of new products for the fast-changing financial services industry.[27]

Compensation Policies and Implementing Product Differentiation Strategies

The compensation policies used to implement product differentiation listed in Table 5.3 very much complement the organizational structure and managerial controls listed in that table. For example, a policy of experimentation has little impact on the ability of a firm to implement product differentiation strategies if every time an innovative experiment fails, individuals are punished for taking risks. Thus, compensation policies that reward risk-taking and celebrate a creative flair help to enable a firm to implement its product differentiation strategy.

Consider, for example, Nordstrom's. Nordstrom's is a department store that celebrates the risk-taking and creative flair of its associates as they try to satisfy their customers' needs. The story is often told of a Nordstrom's sales associate who allowed a customer to return a set of tires to the store because she wasn't satisfied with them. What makes this story interesting—whether or not it is true—is that Nordstrom's doesn't sell tires. But this sales associate felt empowered to make what is obviously a risky decision, and this decision is celebrated within Nordstrom's as an example of the kind of service that Nordstrom's customers should expect.

The last compensation policy listed in Table 5.4 is multidimensional performance measurement. In implementing a cost leadership strategy, compensation should focus on providing appropriate incentives for managers and employees to reduce costs. Various forms of cash payments, stock, and stock options can all be tied to the attainment of specific cost goals and thus can be used to create incentives for realizing cost advantages. Similar techniques can be used to create incentives for helping a firm implement its product differentiation advantage. However, since the implementation of a product differentiation strategy generally involves the integration of multiple business functions, often through the use of product development teams, compensation schemes designed to help implement this strategy must generally recognize its multifunctional character.

Thus, rather than focusing only on a single dimension of performance, these firms often examine employee performance along multiple dimensions simultaneously. Examples of such dimensions include not only a product's sales and profitability, but customer satisfaction, an employee's willingness to cooperate with other businesses and functions within a firm, an employee's ability to effectively facilitate cross-divisional and cross-functional teams, and an employee's ability to engage in creative decision making.

Can Firms Implement Product Differentiation and Cost Leadership Simultaneously?

The arguments developed in Chapter 4 and in this chapter suggest that cost leadership and product differentiation business strategies, under certain conditions, can both create sustained competitive advantages. Given the beneficial impact of both strategies on a firm's competitive position, an important question becomes: "Can a single firm simultaneously implement both strategies?" After all, if each separately can improve a firm's performance, wouldn't it be better for a firm to implement both?

No: These Strategies Cannot Be Implemented Simultaneously

A quick comparison of the organizational requirements for the successful implementation of cost leadership strategies and product differentiation strategies presented in Table 5.5 summarizes one perspective on the question of whether or not these strategies can be implemented simultaneously. In this view the organizational requirements of these strategies are essentially contradictory. Cost leadership requires simple reporting relationships, but product differentiation requires cross-divisional/cross-functional linkages. Cost leadership requires intense labor supervision, but product differentiation requires less intense supervision of creative employees. Cost leadership requires rewards for cost reduction, but product

Table 5.5 **The Organizational Requirements for Implementing Cost Leadership and Product Differentiation Strategies**

Cost leadership	*Product differentiation*
Organizational structure	**Organizational structure**
1. Few layers in the reporting structure	1. Cross-divisional/cross-functional product development teams
2. Simple reporting relationships	2. Willingness to explore new structures to exploit new opportunities
3. Small corporate staff	3. Isolated pockets of intense creative efforts
4. Focus on narrow range of business functions	
Management control systems	**Management control systems**
1. Tight cost-control systems	1. Broad decision-making guidelines
2. Quantitative cost goals	2. Managerial freedom within guidelines
3. Close supervision of labor, raw material, inventory, and other costs	3. Policy of experimentation
4. A cost leadership philosophy	
Compensation policies	**Compensation policies**
1. Reward for cost reduction	1. Rewards for risk-taking, not punishment for failures
2. Incentives for all employees to be involved in cost reduction	2. Rewards for creative flair
	3. Multidimensional performance measurement

Figure 5.2 Simultaneous Implementation of Cost Leadership and Product Differentiation Competitive Strategies: Being "Stuck in the Middle"

Source: M. E. Porter (1980). *Competitive strategy: techniques for analyzing industries and competitors.* New York: Free Press, a Division of Simon & Schuster Adult Publishing Group.

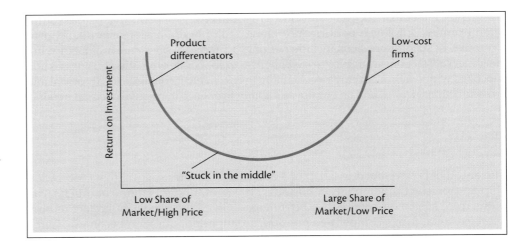

differentiation requires rewards for creative flair. It is reasonable to ask, "Can a single firm combine these multiple contradictory skills and abilities?"

Some have argued that firms that attempt to implement both strategies will end up doing neither well. This logic leads to the curve pictured in Figure 5.2. This figure suggests that there are often only two ways to earn superior economic performance within a single industry: (1) by selling high-priced products and gaining small market share (product differentiation) or (2) by selling low-priced products and gaining large market share (cost leadership). Firms that do not make this choice of strategies (medium price, medium market share) or that attempt to implement both strategies will fail. These firms are said to be "stuck in the middle."[28]

Yes: These Strategies Can Be Implemented Simultaneously

More recent work contradicts assertions about being "stuck in the middle." This work suggests that firms that are successful in both cost leadership and product differentiation can often expect to gain a sustained competitive advantage. This advantage reflects at least two processes.

Differentiation, Market Share, and Low-Cost Leadership

First, firms that are able to successfully differentiate their products and services are likely to see an increase in their volume of sales. This is especially the case if the basis of product differentiation is attractive to a large number of potential customers. Thus, product differentiation can lead to increased volumes of sales. It has already been established (in Chapter 4) that an increased volume of sales can lead to economies of scale, learning, and other forms of cost reduction. So, successful product differentiation can, in turn, lead to cost reductions and a cost leadership position.[29]

This is the situation that best describes McDonald's. McDonald's has traditionally followed a product differentiation strategy, emphasizing cleanliness, consistency, and fun in its fast-food outlets. Over time, McDonald's has used its differentiated product to become the market share leader in the fast-food industry. This market position has enabled it to reduce its costs, so that it is now the cost leader in fast foods as well. Thus, McDonald's level of profitability depends both on its product differentiation strategy and its low-cost strategy. Either one of these two strategies by itself would be difficult to overcome; together they give McDonald's a very costly-to-imitate competitive advantage.[30]

Managing Organizational Contractions

Product differentiation can lead to high market share and low costs. It may also be the case that some firms develop special skills in managing the contradictions that are part of simultaneously implementing low-cost and product differentiation strategies. Some recent research on automobile manufacturing helps describe these special skills.[31] Traditional thinking in automotive manufacturing was that plants could either reduce manufacturing costs by speeding up the assembly line or increase the quality of the cars they made by slowing the line, emphasizing team-based production, and so forth. In general, it was thought that plants could not simultaneously build low-cost/high-quality (that is low cost *and* highly differentiated) automobiles.

Several researchers at the Massachusetts Institute of Technology examined this traditional wisdom. They began by developing rigorous measures of the cost and quality performance of automobile plants and then applied these measures to over 70 auto plants throughout the world that assembled mid-size sedans. What they discovered was six plants in the entire world that had, at the time this research was done, very low costs *and* very high quality.[32]

In examining what made these six plants different from other auto plants, the researchers focused on a broad range of manufacturing policies, management practices, and cultural variables. Three important findings emerged. First, these six plants had the best manufacturing technology hardware available—robots, laser-guided paint machines, and so forth. However, since many of the plants in the study had these same technologies, manufacturing technology by itself was not enough to make these six plants special. In addition, policies and procedures at these plants implemented a range of highly participative, group-oriented management techniques, including participative management, team production, and total quality management. As important, employees in these plants had a sense of loyalty and commitment toward the plant they worked for—a belief that they would be treated fairly by their plant managers.

What this research shows is that firms *can* simultaneously implement cost leadership and product differentiation strategies if they learn how to manage the contradictions inherent in these two strategies. The management of these contradictions, in turn, depends on socially complex relations among employees, between employees and the technology they use, and between employees and the firm for which they work. These relations are not only valuable (because they enable a firm to implement cost leadership and differentiation strategies) but also socially complex and thus likely to be costly to imitate and a source of sustained competitive advantage.

Recently, many scholars have backed away from the original "stuck in the middle" arguments and now suggest that low-cost firms must have competitive levels of product differentiation to survive, and that product differentiation firms must have competitive levels of cost to survive.[33] So, for example, a firm like the fashion design company Versace—the ultimate product differentiating firm—has recently had to hire a new CEO and controller to help control its costs.[34]

Product Differentiation in an International Context

The tension that sometimes exists between cost leadership and product differentiation strategies domestically can also exist internationally. Here, this tension is manifest by the need for firms to simultaneously be responsive to local market needs while still integrating operations across multiple countries. On the one hand, local responsiveness enables a firm to implement a product differentiation strategy internationally, and failure to do so can lead to marketing blunders, some of which are described in the Global Perspectives feature. On the other hand, global integration can enable a firm to gain the cost advantages associated with international operations, as described in Chapter 4.

Global Perspectives

Lack of local responsiveness has led to some well-known—and sometimes quite funny—international product differentiation blunders. For example, General Motors once introduced the Chevrolet Nova to South America, even though "No va" in Spanish means "it won't go." When Coca-Cola was first introduced in China, it was translated into Ke-kou-ke-la, which turns out to mean either "bite the wax tadpole" or "female horse stuffed with wax," depending on which dialect was being spoken. Coca-Cola reintroduced its product with the name Ke-kou-ko-le, which roughly translates into "happiness in the mouth."

Coca-Cola is not the only beverage firm to run into problems internationally. Pepsi's slogan "Come alive with the Pepsi generation" was translated into "Pepsi will bring your ancestors back from the dead" in Taiwan. In Italy, a marketing campaign for Schweppes tonic water was translated into Schweppes toilet water—not a terribly appealing drink. Bicardi developed a fruity drink called "Pavian." Unfortunately, "Pavian" means baboon in German. Coors used its "Turn it loose" slogan when selling beer in Spain and Latin America.

International Marketing Blunders

Unfortunately, "Turn it loose" was translated into "Suffer from diarrhea."

Food companies have had similar problems. Kentucky Fried Chicken's slogan "Finger-lickin' good" translates into "eat your fingers off" in Chinese. In Arabic, the "Jolly Green Giant" translates into "Intimidating Green Ogre." Frank Perdue's famous catch phrase—"It takes a tough man to make a tender chicken"—takes on a slightly different meaning when translated into Spanish—

"It takes a sexually stimulated man to make a chicken affectionate." And Gerber found that it was unable to sell its baby food—with pictures of cute babies on the jar—in Africa because the tradition in Africa is to put pictures of what is inside the jar on the label. Think about it.

Other product differentiation blunders include Colgate's decision to introduce Cue toothpaste in France, even though Cue is the name of a French pornographic magazine; an American T-shirt manufacturer who wanted to print up T-shirts in Spanish that said "I saw the Pope" (el Papa) but instead printed up T-shirts that said "I saw the potato" (la papa); and Salem cigarettes, whose slogan "Salem—feeling free" translated into Japanese as "When smoking Salem, you feel so refreshed that your mind seems to be free and empty." What were they smoking?

However, of all these marketing blunders, perhaps none tops Electrolux—a Scandinavian vacuum cleaner manufacturer. While its marketing slogan for the U.S. market does rhyme—"Nothing sucks like an Electrolux"—it doesn't really communicate what the firm had in mind.

Source: www.relojournal.com.

Traditionally, it has been thought that firms had to choose between local responsiveness and international integration. For example, firms like CIBA-Geigy (a Swiss chemical company), Nestlé (a Swiss food company), and Philips (a Dutch consumer electronics firm) have chosen to emphasize local responsiveness. Nestlé, for example, owns nearly 8,000 brand names worldwide. However, of those 8,000 brands, only 750 are registered in more than 1 country, and only 80 are registered in more than 10 countries. Nestlé adjusts its product attributes to the needs of local consumers, adopts brand names that resonate with those consumers, and builds its brands for long-run profitability by country. For example, in the United States, Nestlé's condensed milk carries the brand name "Carnation" (obtained through the acquisition of the Carnation Company); in Asia, this same product carries the brand name "Bear Brand." Nestlé delegates brand management authority to country managers, who can (and do) adjust traditional marketing and manufacturing strategies in accordance with local tastes and preferences. For example, Nestlé's Thailand management group dropped traditional coffee-marketing efforts that focused on taste, aroma, and stimulation and instead began selling coffee as a drink that promotes relaxation and romance. This marketing strategy resonated with Thais experiencing urban stress, and it prompted Nestlé coffee sales in Thailand to jump dramatically.[35]

Of course, all this local responsiveness comes at a cost. Firms that emphasize local responsiveness are often unable to realize the full economic value possible by integrating their operations across country borders. Numerous firms have focused on appropriating this economic value and have pursued a more integrated international strategy. Examples of such firms include IBM, General Electric, Toyota Motor Corporation, and most major pharmaceutical firms, to name just a few.

Internationally integrated firms locate business functions and activities in countries that have a comparative advantage in these functions or activities. For example, the production of components for most consumer electronics is research intensive, capital intensive, and subject to significant economies of scale. To manage component manufacturing successfully, most internationally integrated consumer electronics firms have located their component operations in technologically advanced countries like the United States and Japan. However, because the assembly of these components into consumer products is labor intensive, most internationally integrated consumer electronics firms have located their assembly operations in countries with relatively low labor costs, including Mexico and China.

Of course, one of the costs of locating different business functions and activities in different geographic locations is that these different functions and activities must be coordinated and integrated. Operations in one country might very efficiently manufacture certain components. However, if the wrong components are shipped to the assembly location, or if the right components are shipped at the wrong time, any advantages that could have been obtained from exploiting the comparative advantages of different countries can be lost. Shipping costs can also reduce the returns on international integration.

To ensure that different operations in internationally integrated firms are appropriately coordinated, these firms typically manufacture more standardized products, using more standardized components, than do locally responsive firms. Standardization enables these firms to realize substantial economies of scale and other advantages, but it can limit their ability to respond to the specific needs of individual markets. When international product standards exist, as in the personal computer industry and the semiconductor chip industry, such standardization is not problematic. Also, when local responsiveness requires only a few modifications of a standardized product (for example, changing the shape of the electric plug or changing the color of a product), international integration can be very effective. However, when local responsiveness requires a great deal of local knowledge and product modifications, international integration can create problems for a firm pursuing an international product differentiation strategy.

Recently, it has been suggested that the traditional trade-off between international integration and local responsiveness can be replaced by a **transnational strategy** that exploits all the advantages of both international integration and local responsiveness.[36] Firms implementing a transnational strategy treat their international operations as an integrated network of distributed and interdependent resources and capabilities. In this context, a firm's operations in each country are not simply independent activities attempting to respond to local market needs; they are also repositories of ideas, technologies, and management approaches that the firm might be able to use and apply in its other international operations. Put differently, operations in different countries can be thought of as "experiments" in the creation of new resources and capabilities. Some of these experiments will work and generate important new resources and capabilities; others will fail to have such benefits for a firm.

When a particular country operation develops a competence in manufacturing a particular product, providing a particular service, or engaging in a particular activity that can be used by other country operations, the country operation with this competence can achieve international economies of scale by becoming the firm's primary supplier of this product, service, or activity. In this way, local responsiveness is retained as country managers constantly search for new competencies that enable them to maximize profits in their particular markets, and international integration and economies are realized as country operations that have developed unique competencies become suppliers for all other country operations.

SUMMARY

Product differentiation exists when customers perceive a particular firm's products to be more valuable than other firms' products. Although differentiation can have several bases, it is, in the end, always a matter of customer perception. Bases of product differentiation include: (1) attributes of the products or services a firm sells (including product features, product complexity, the timing of product introduction, and location); (2) relations between a firm and its customers (including product customization, consumer marketing, and reputation); and (3) links within and between firms (including links between functions, links with other firms, a firm's product mix, its distribution system, and its level of service and support). However, in the end, product differentiation is limited only by the creativity of a firm's managers.

Product differentiation is valuable to the extent that it enables a firm to set its prices higher than what it would otherwise be able to. Each of the bases of product differentiation identified can be used to neutralize environmental threats and exploit environmental opportunities. The rarity and imitability of bases of product differentiation vary. Highly imitable bases of product differentiation include product features. Somewhat imitable bases include product mix, links with other firms, product customization, and consumer marketing. Costly-to-imitate bases of product differentiation include linking business functions, timing, location, reputation, and service and support.

The implementation of a product differentiation strategy involves management of organizational structure, management controls, and compensation policies. Structurally, it is not unusual for firms implementing product differentiation strategies to use cross-divisional and cross-functional teams, together with teams that are focused exclusively on a particular product differentiation effort, so-called "skunk works." Managerial controls that provide free managerial decision-making within broad decision-making guidelines can be helpful in implementing product differentiation strategies, as is a policy of experimentation. Finally, compensation policies that tolerate risk-taking and a creative flair and that measure employee performance along multiple dimensions simultaneously can also be helpful in implementing product differentiation strategies.

A variety of organizational attributes is required to successfully implement a product differentiation strategy. Some have argued that contradictions between these organizational characteristics and those required to implement a cost leadership strategy mean that firms that attempt to do both will perform poorly. More recent research notes the relationship between product differentiation, market share, and low costs and observes that some firms have learned to manage the contradictions between cost leadership and product differentiation.

These same tensions can manifest themselves for firms pursuing international strategies. Product differentiation, internationally, requires responsiveness to local markets; cost leadership, internationally, requires a firm to integrate its global operations. Some authors have suggested that a transnational strategy can enable a firm to be both locally responsive and globally integrated.

CHALLENGE QUESTIONS

1. Although cost leadership is, perhaps, less relevant for firms pursuing product differentiation, costs are not totally irrelevant. What advice about costs would you give a firm pursuing a product differentiation strategy?

2. Product features are often the focus of product differentiation efforts. Yet product features are among the easiest-to-imitate bases of product differentiation and thus among the least likely bases of product differentiation to be a source of sustained competitive advantage. Does this seem paradoxical to you? If no, why not? If yes, how can you resolve this paradox?

3. What are the strengths and weaknesses of using regression analysis and hedonic prices to describe the bases of product differentiation?

4. "Monopolistic competition" is the term that Chamberlin developed to describe firms pursuing a product differentiation strategy in a competitive industry. However, it is usually the case that firms that operate in monopolies are less efficient and less competitive than firms that operate in more competitive settings (see Chapter 3). Does this same problem exist for firms operating in a "monopolistic competition" context? Why or why not?

5. Implementing a product differentiation strategy seems to require just the right mix of control and creativity. How do you know if a firm has the right mix? Is it possible to evaluate this mix before problems associated with being out of balance manifest themselves? If yes, how? If no, why not?

6. A firm with a highly differentiated product can increase the volume of its sales. Increased sales volumes can enable a firm to reduce its costs. High volumes with low costs can lead a firm to have very high profits, some of which the firm can use to invest in further differentiating its products. What advice would you give a firm whose competition is enjoying this product differentiation and cost leadership advantage?

7. What kinds of organizational and management problems is a firm trying to implement a transnational strategy (as a way to resolve conflicts between product differentiation and cost leadership strategies internationally) likely to face? (Hint: See Table 5.5.)

8. Is a firm implementing a transnational strategy just "stuck in the middle" internationally? If yes, why? If no, why not?

PROBLEM SET

1. For each of the listed products, describe at least two ways they are differentiated.

(a) Ben & Jerry's ice cream
(b) The Hummer H2
(c) The X-Games
(d) The Back Street Boys
(e) The movies *Animal House* and *Caddyshack*
(f) Fredrick's of Hollywood
(g) Taco Bell

2. Which, if any of these bases of product differentiation (in question #1) are likely to be sources of sustained competitive advantage, and why?

3. Suppose you obtained the following regression results, where the starred (*) coefficients are statistically significant. What could you say about the bases of product differentiation in this market? (Hint: A regression coefficient is statistically significant when it is so large that its effect is very unlikely to have emerged by chance.)

$$\text{House Price} = \$125{,}000^* + \$15{,}000^*(\text{More than 3 bedrooms})$$
$$+ \$18{,}000^*(\text{More than 3,500 square feet})$$
$$+ \$150(\text{Has plumbing}) + \$180(\text{Has lawn})$$
$$+ \$17{,}000^*(\text{Lot larger than 1/2 acre})$$

How much would you expect to pay for a 4-bedroom, 3,800-square-foot house on a one-acre lot? How much for a 4-bedroom, 2,700-square-foot house on a 1/4-acre lot? Do these results say anything about the sustainability of competitive advantages in this market?

4. Which of the following management controls and compensation policies is consistent with implementing cost leadership? With product differentiation? With both cost leadership and product differentiation? With neither cost leadership nor product differentiation?

(a) Firm-wide stock options

(b) Compensation that rewards each function separately for meeting its own objectives

(c) A detailed financial budget plan

(d) A document that describes, in detail, how the innovation process will unfold in a firm

(e) A policy that reduces the compensation of a manager who introduces a product that fails in the market

(f) A policy that reduces the compensation of a manager who introduces several products that fail in the market

(g) The creation of a purchasing council to discuss how different business units can reduce their costs

5. Identify three industries or markets that have the volume–profit relationship described in Figure 5.2. Which firms in this industry are implementing cost leadership strategies? Which are implementing product differentiation strategies? Are there any firms "stuck in the middle?" If yes, who are they? If no, why not? Are there any firms implementing both cost leadership and product differentiation strategies? If yes, who? If no, why not?

END NOTES

1. See Ono, Y. (1996). "Who really makes that cute little beer? You'd be surprised." *Wall Street Journal*, April 15, pp. A1 +. Since this 1996 article, some of these craft beer companies have changed the way they manufacture the beers to be more consistent with the image they are trying to project.
2. See Porter, M. E. (1980). *Competitive strategy*. New York: Free Press, and Caves R. E., and P. Williamson (1985). "What is product differentiation, really?" *Journal of Industrial Organization Economics*, 34, pp. 113–132.
3. Lieberman, M. B., and D. B. Montgomery (1988). "First-mover advantages." *Strategic Management Journal*, 9, pp. 41–58.
4. London, H. (1995). "Bait and switch in academe." *Forbes*, May 22, p. 120.
5. Carroll, P. (1993). *Big blues: The unmaking of IBM*. New York: Crown Publishers.
6. These ideas were first developed in Hotelling, H. (1929). "Stability in competition." *Economic Journal*, 39, pp. 41–57; Ricardo, D. (1817). *Principles of political economy and taxation*. London: J. Murray.
7. See Gunther, M. (1998). "Disney's Call of the Wild." *Fortune*, April 13, pp. 120–124.
8. The idea of reputation is explained in Klein, B., and K. Leffler (1981). "The role of market forces in assuring contractual performance." *Journal of Political Economy*, 89, pp. 615–641.
9. See Robichaux M., (1995). "It's a book! A T-shirt! A toy! No, just MTV trying to be Disney." *Wall Street Journal*, February 8, pp. A1 +.
10. See Henderson, R., and I. Cockburn (1994). "Measuring competence? Exploring firm effects in pharmaceutical research." *Strategic Management Journal*, 15, pp. 63–84.
11. See Johnson, R. (1999). "Speed sells." *Fortune*, April 12, pp. 56–70. In fact, NASCAR fans either love or hate Jeff Gordon.
12. See Carvell, T. (1998). "How Sony created a monster." *Fortune*, June 8, pp. 162 +; and Gibson, R. (1999). "Star Wars' tie-in is more a menace than a hit at Tricon." *Wall Street Journal*, July 21, p. A5.
13. Kotler, P. (1986). *Principles of marketing*. Upper Saddle River, NJ: Prentice Hall.
14. Porter, M. E., and R. Wayland (1991). "Coca-Cola vs. Pepsi-Cola and the soft drink industry." Harvard Business School Case No. 9-391-179.
15. Ghemawat, P. (1993). "Sears, Roebuck and Company: The merchandise group." Harvard Business School Case No. 9-794-039.
16. Chamberlin, E. H. (1933). *The theory of monopolistic competition*. Cambridge, MA: Harvard University Press; Robinson, J. (1934). "What is perfect competition?" *Quarterly Journal of Economics*, 49, pp. 104–120.
17. Casey, J. (1976). "High fructose corn syrup." *Research Management*, 19, pp. 27–32.
18. Welsh, J. (1998). "Office-paper firms pursue elusive goal: Brand loyalty." *Wall Street Journal*, September 21, p. B6.
19. See White, E., and K. Palmer (2003). "U.S. retailing 101." *Wall Street Journal*, August 12, pp. B1 +.
20. See Hennart, J. F. (1988). "A transaction cost theory of equity joint ventures." *Strategic Management Journal*, 9, pp. 361–374.
21. Deutsch, C. H. (1991). "How is it done? For a small fee…." *New York Times*, October 27, p. 25; Armstrong, L. (1991). "Services: The customer as 'Honored Guest'." *BusinessWeek*, October 25, p. 104.
22. See Rankin, A. (1998). "Dave Mathews band succeeds by marching to its own drummer." *Columbus Dispatch*, August 2, pp. F1 +; and Yoffie, D. (1994). "Swissair's alliances (A)." Harvard Business School Case No. 9-794-152.
23. "WPP—Integrating icons." Harvard Business School Case No. 9-396-249.
24. Orosz, J. J. (2002). "Big funds need a 'Skunk Works' to stir ideas." *Chronicle of Philanthropy*, June 27, p. 47.
25. Van de Ven, A., D. Polley, R. Garud, and S. Venkatraman (1999). *The innovation journey*. New York: Oxford, pp. 198-200.
26. Prokesch, S. (1995). "Competing on customer service: An interview with British Airways' Sir Colin Marshall." *Harvard Business Review*, November/December, p. 101.
27. Position, L. L. (1999). "David S. Pottruck." *BusinessWeek*, September 27, EB 51.
28. Porter, M. E. (1980). *Competitive strategy*. New York: Free Press.
29. Hill, C. W. L. (1988). "Differentiation versus low cost or differentiation and low cost: A contingency framework." *Academy of Management Review*, 13(3), pp. 401–412.
30. Gibson, R. (1995). "Food: At McDonald's, new recipes for buns, eggs." *Wall Street Journal*, June 13, p. B1.
31. Originally discussed in the Strategy in Depth feature in Chapter 3.
32. Womack, J. P., D. I. Jones, and D. Roos (1990). *The machine that changed the world*. New York: Rawson.
33. Porter, M. E. (1985). *Competitive advantage*. New York: Free Press.
34. Agins, Teri, and Alessandra Galloni (2003). "Facing a squeeze, Versace struggles to trim the fat." *Wall Street Journal*, September 30, pp. A1 +.
35. Rapoport, C. (1994). "Nestlé's brand building machine." *Fortune*, September 19, pp. 147–156.
36. See Bartlett, C. A., and S. Ghoshal (1989). *Managing across borders: The transnational solution*. Boston: Harvard Business School Press.

Case 2–1: The British Motorcycle Industry at a Crossroads*

By 1975, the collapse of the British motorcycle makers was nearly complete. In the face of competition from Honda and other Japanese rivals, British production had fallen from 130,000 bikes in 1960 to 20,000 in 1974 and seemed unlikely to recover in 1975.[1] A single British company, Norton Villiers Triumph (NVT), remained in operation. The company, a recent combination of often-reorganized Norton Villiers and failing BSA/Triumph, lost £5.1 million in 1974 on sales of roughly £16 million.[2] In March, 1975, Britain's Secretary of State for Industry asked consultants from the Boston Consulting Group (BCG) to identify and evaluate strategic alternatives for the last British motorcycle producer and its suppliers. This case summarizes what the consultants discovered as they sized up the global motorcycle industry and Britain's position in it.

Markets and Products

British motorcycles were sold mostly in North America and Europe. In total, consumers bought more than 1.4 million motorcycles in those regions in 1974.[3] Buyers in these areas used motorcycles mostly for recreation, not for basic transportation, and with the introduction of new recreational products such as off-road bikes and so-called superbikes,

unit sales had risen nearly 16% per year since 1968. Demand appeared to be reaching saturation, however, and the BCG consultants forecast a 4–5% annual growth rate for the coming years.[4]

Nine out of ten motorcycle buyers in the U.S., the world's largest motorcycle market, were men, and more than half were younger than 25. The typical buyer shopped for eight weeks before purchasing and gathered information from many sources, including other motorcycle owners (consulted by 85% of buyers), dealers (82%), cycling magazines (69%), manufacturers' literature (52%), competition results (39%), and test drives (38%).[5] Exhibit 1 shows the product attributes that buyers considered most important.

Exhibit 1 Factors Influencing U.S. Motorcycle Buyers

Product Attribute	Percent of Buyers Rating Attribute Important or Very Important
Quality of workmanship	94.6
Availability of parts	91.6
Handling/performance	88.9
Power/acceleration	85.9
Styling/appearance	84.6
Recommendation of owners/friends	81.3
Dealer's reputation	80.4
Dealer's service	76.9
Resale value	74.8
Warranty coverage	72.1
Economy of operation	63.9
Test drive	56.3
Owned same make before	34.3

Source: AHF Marketing Research, Inc., "The Market for New Motorcycles," 1973, reported in D. Purkayastha and R.D. Buzzell, "Note on the Motorcycle Industry – 1975," HBS case 578–210, p. 4.

*Professor Jan W. Rivkin prepared this case from published sources, especially the report "Strategy Alternatives for the British Motorcycle Industry" by the Boston Consulting Group Limited, published in 1975 by Her Majesty's Stationery Office. The case is designed to be taught with the earlier cases "Honda (A)" (384–049) and "Honda (B)" (384–050). HBS cases are developed solely as the basis for class discussion. Cases are not intended to serve as endorsements, sources of primary data, or illustrations of effective or ineffective or ineffective management. Reprinted by permission of Harvard Business School Press. ©2003 President and Fellows of Harvard College.

Exhibit 2   Size and Growth of U.S. Motorcycle Market, by Displacement Class

Class	Units sold in 1974 (000s)	Retail value in 1974 ($ mm)	Average retail price in 1974 ($)	Unit CAGR, 1968–74 (%)
<125 cc	276	81	293	2.2
125–349 cc	382	339	887	12.8
350–449 cc	200	230	1,150	25.8
450–749 cc	173	186	1,076	16.7
750 cc and above	128	288	2,253	46.7
Total	1,159	1,124	970	15.2

Source: Motorcycle Industry Council, reported in BCG, "Strategy Alternatives for the British Motorcycle Industry," Appendix pp. 7–8, 18–20.

Products ranged from small bikes designed for economical commuting to luxurious superbikes equipped for cross-country cruising to rugged off-road cycles with studded tires. Bikes were often classified by engine displacement, which corresponded roughly to size and engine power. Common categories included learner's bikes (<125 cc displacement), intermediate bikes (125–349 cc), medium bikes (350–449 cc), big bikes (450–749 cc), and superbikes (≥750 cc).[6] Exhibit 2 breaks down the U.S. market by displacement class and shows the recent growth rate in each class. First-time buyers typically started with a small-displacement motorcycle, then traded up over time, usually within a year. When trading up, roughly a third of buyers stayed with the same brand.[7]

Prices typically rose in line with displacement, as shown in Exhibit 3 for 1969 and 1975. Within a displacement class, however, competitors did set different prices from one another. BCG's consultants felt that demand for a particular model would neither rise nor fall much as long as the model's price was within 10% of the typical price for its displacement class. Premiums greater than 10% would cut demand for the model significantly, and premiums above 40% would wipe out essentially all demand.[8]

Competitors

The dominant dynamic in the global motorcycle industry during the 1960s and early 1970s was the rise of Japanese competitors, led by Honda. The story of Honda's overseas expansion is laid out in related case studies.[9] Honda's Japanese rivals – Yamaha, Kawasaki, and Suzuki – differed from Honda in several ways, but for simplicity in this case,

we will take Honda as representative of the Japanese competitors. Exhibit 4 shows the shifts in sales and market share in the United States between 1968 and 1974. Exhibit 5 shows the number of models offered by each competitor in 1968 and 1974, by displacement class. In its globalization efforts, Honda had succeeded first in the market for small motorcycles, but then expanded into larger displacement classes.

In the United States, Honda and the other Japanese rivals faced Harley-Davidson, BMW, and NVT. Harley-Davidson maintained a loyal following in the U.S., both because it was the last U.S.-made option for patriotic customers and because its big, tough bikes closely matched a big, tough set of leather-clad customers. Observers noted that Harley was among the few brand names that customers commonly tattooed on their bodies. In 1975, Harley was petitioning the U.S. International Trade Commission to raise tariffs on motorcycles in order to protect U.S. employment. BMW produced motorcycles only in the 600–900 cc range and made 25,000 machines per year worldwide. Expansion plans called for an output of 45,000 machines per year by 1980. All BMW models were variants of a single engine and frame design, a design which led *Motorcycle Magazine* to name the BMW 750 the best superbike in the world in 1973.[10] With a reputation for very high quality, BMW charged a premium of 30–40% over rival bikes of equal displacement.

In the past, NVT and its predecessors had produced a full range of motorcycles. Individual models had been withdrawn, however, as each became unprofitable. Since the early 1960s, lack of model profitability had prompted the British to exit the 175, 250, 350, 500, and 650 cc classes.[11] In 1975, all of NVT's remaining models had displacements of 740 cc or greater. British makers had introduced no gen-

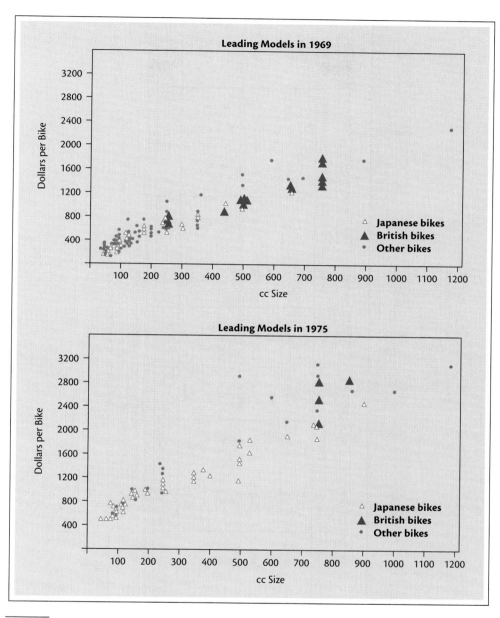

Exhibit 3   Price/Displacement Relationship

Source: NADA Motorcycle Appraisal Guide, reported in BCG, "Strategy Alternatives for the British Motorcycle Industry," Appendix pp. 51, 53.

uinely new models since Triumph's Trident in 1968 though many models had been "uprated" to higher displacements. Exhibit 6 shows British output over time.

British motorcycles had been popular around the world at least since Marlon Brando rode astride a Triumph in the 1954 motorcycle-gang film *The Wild One* (a film whose violent themes caused it to be banned in Britain for more than a decade). Triumphs continued to make regular appearances in Hollywood films in the 1970s. British bikes had a traditional reputation for premium quality finish,

Exhibit 4 Sales and Market Shares in the United States

Competitor	Units sold (000s)		Retail value ($ mm)		Unit share (%)		Average price ($)		Number of models		Units per model (000s)	
	1968	1974	1968	1974	1968	1974	1968	1974	1968	1975	1968	1974/75
Honda	161.1	433.8	98.4	477.7	37.5	37.4	611	1,101	21	26	7.7	16.7
Yamaha	58.2	205.1	31.2	215.4	13.5	17.7	536	1,050	22	29	2.6	7.1
Kawasaki	19.9	129.6	8.9	147.0	4.6	11.2	446	1,134	15	23	1.3	5.6
Suzuki	23.0	108.5	8.7	98.1	5.3	9.4	379	904	4	24	5.7	4.5
Harley-Davidson	26.3	57.9	27.8	111.8	6.1	5.0	1,056	1,930	6	15	4.4	3.9
BMW	2.4	9.0	3.1	25.8	0.6	0.8	1,305	2,854	3	4	0.8	2.3
NVT	27.8	13.9	34.5	26.3	6.5	1.2	1,242	1,893	20	17	1.4	0.8
Others	111.3	201.1		21.9	25.9	17.4		109				
Total	430.0	1,159.0		1,124.0				970				

Note: Differences in average prices across competitors reflect differences in displacement-class mixes, not just discounts given or premiums commanded within a displacement class. The average price shown here for NVT differs from the price shown in Exhibit 7 primarily because of price adjustments and inflation between 1974 and 1975.

Source: R.L. Polk and BCG estimates, reported in BCG, "Strategy Alternatives for the British Motorcycle Industry," Appendix p. 23. NADA Motorcycle Appraisal Guide, reported in D. Purkayastha and R.D. Buzzell, "Note on the Motorcycle Industry – 1975," HBS case 578–210, p. 21. Casewriter calculations.

Exhibit 5   Models Offered in Each Displacement Class

Competitor	Under 125 cc 1968	Under 125 cc 1975	125–349 cc 1968	125–349 cc 1975	350–449 cc 1968	350–449 cc 1975	450–749 cc 1968	450–749 cc 1975	750 cc and above 1968	750 cc and above 1975
Honda	10	14	9	6	2	3	0	3	0	0
Yamaha	11	12	11	11	0	4	0	2	0	0
Kawasaki	3	10	9	6	0	4	3	2	0	1
Suzuki	1	10	2	7	0	3	1	4	0	0
Harley-Davidson	3	3	2	2	0	0	1	4	0	6
BMW	0	0	0	0	0	0	3	2	0	2
NVT	0	0	3	0	2	0	15	7	0	10

Note: "New" NVT models in 1975 with displacements 750 cc and above are actually models that had displacements of 450-749 cc in 1968 and were modified slightly to have larger displacements.

Source: NADA Motorcycle Appraisal Guide, reported in D. Purkayastha and R.D. Buzzell, "Note on the Motorcycle Industry – 1975," HBS case 578–210, p. 21.

elegant styling, superior handling, and high performance (e.g., quick acceleration and high top speeds). By 1975, however, new Japanese machines such as the Kawasaki Z-1 easily topped the British bikes in performance tests, and technological changes had improved their handling characteristics. New Japanese models incorporated features such as electric starters, disc brakes, and five-speed transmissions, features which British makers struggled to add to existing models. British motorcycles were also known for their mechanical failures, particularly oil leaks. Warranty claims were resisted by dealers, and spare parts were hard to come by.[12] Observers joked that British bikes were particularly popular among riders who enjoyed fixing their own machines.

British models tended to be priced at or slightly above the prices of Japanese models with comparable displacements, but pricing patterns varied widely over time. In 1973, for instance, Triumph's Bonneville 750 model was priced 12% below the Honda 750 in the U.S.; indeed, 1973 was the only year since 1968 that Triumph had not lost market share in the U.S. In 1975, in an effort to regain profitability, NVT priced its models nearly $400 above comparable Japanese models.[13] A typical NVT bike had a retail price of $2,495 while a comparable Honda 750 was priced at $2,112.

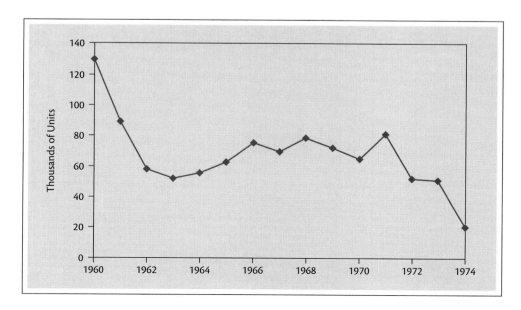

Exhibit 6   U.K. Production of Motorcycles

Source: Motorcycle and Cycle Trader, reported in BCG, "Strategy Alternatives for the British Motorcycle Industry," pp. 7–8, 18–20.

Exhibit 7   Costs Incurred to Bring a British Motorcycle to Market in the United States, 1975

Item	Dollars
Retail price	2,495
Dealer markup	648
Wholesale price	1,847
Production costs:	
Engine and frame parts	484
Assembly	121
Raw materials and components	606
Subtotal	1,211
Research and development	116
Selling and distribution costs:	
Ocean freight	60
Packing	40
Duty	75
Advertising and promotions	58
Other selling and distribution	267
Subtotal	500
Total costs	1,827
Profit contribution	20

Source: Casewriter calculations and estimates based on BCG, "Strategy Alternatives for the British Motorcycle Industry."

Design and Production

Exhibit 7 lays out the costs incurred to bring a typical British motorcycle to market in the United States. More than two-thirds of the manufacturer's costs were incurred before the machine left the factory. Design of a motorcycle preceded production, which involved the procurement of raw materials and components, the production of engine parts, the production of frame parts, and assembly. Honda and NVT took very different approaches to each of these steps.

Design. At Honda, marketing personnel performed a commercial evaluation of any new product or feature and production engineers assessed its costs before design of the product or feature began. Design followed a precise program, with regular checkpoints and reassessments and with special attention to a design's implications for unit costs. Honda's subsidiary, the Honda R&D Company, employed 1,300 people, or 0.75 people per $1 million of corporate motorcycle sales. Each Honda R&D employee, it was estimated, earned $17,000 per year in 1975, and personnel accounted for roughly half of total R&D expenses.

Honda claimed that its design personnel could take an idea from conception to production in 18 months.[14]

NVT's engineering staff numbered roughly 100, or 2.7 people per $1 million of corporate sales. The staff tended to focus on "pure" design considerations and would use nonstandard parts and unusual fittings if necessary to improve performance, handling, or styling. The joints between crankcase parts and cylinder block, for instance, met in a "T" shape, consistent with classic British styling but nearly impossible to seal tightly. Projects were controlled informally, with virtually no paperwork. The engineering staff estimated that a minimum of 18 months was required to move an idea from conception to a complete set of drawings and 18 more months were needed to tool up for production.[15]

Production of engine and frame parts. Honda carried out its global production of nearly 2 million bikes per year in four very modern plants in Japan. Plants were specialized: one plant, for instance, made only engines. In the formation and machining of engine and frame parts, Honda made extensive use of relatively automated die-casting techniques and machine tools. BCG's consultants estimated that a company unfamiliar with automated technology, such as NVT, might have to invest $48 million in plant and equipment with a 10-year depreciable life in order to adopt the technology. The technology would reduce the total cost per unit of such a company—fixed costs per unit plus variable costs per unit—once its production of similar components exceeded 50,000 unit per year. (Below this volume, older manual technology would lead to a lower total cost per unit than the automated systems.) Because Honda grouped its many models into families that used similar components, it was not unusual for Honda to require 100,000 units of a particular component each year, worldwide. Beyond the cost savings attained by employing automated equipment at large scale, Honda enjoyed the benefits of extensive production experience. BCG estimated that accumulated experience might have reduced Honda's unit costs of engine and frame part production by 20% or even more.[16]

Honda's machine tools were highly specialized, and many were custom-made by its 1,400-person Honda Engineering subsidiary. Honda Engineering delivered machine tools less than six months after an order was placed. Delivery times of 18 months were common on the open market.[17]

NVT produced its motorcycles in three factories in Wolverhampton, Small Heath, and Meriden, all in the Midlands section of England. Factory buildings dated from the First World War period. Small Heath was multistory, and Wolverhampton, with many separate buildings, was described by BCG consultants as "rather confused."[18]

Within the buildings, general purpose, labor intensive machines were used to manufacture engine and frame parts. At Wolverhampton, it was estimated that 80 percent of machine tools were more than 15 years old. It was not unusual for parts for a single motorcycle to come from machine tools of quite different vintages and tolerances. The costs associated with parts production were essentially all variable, since the fixed costs associated with plant and equipment were nearly completely depreciated. Though BCG consultants detected a strong, downward sloping experience curve for Japanese manufacturers, they found no association between unit costs and accumulated production experience for NVT.[19]

Assembly. Assembly of finished product was the least automated and most labor-intensive stage of Honda's production process. Most of the 16,400 employees at Honda's four factories were involved in assembly. (The average factory laborer at Honda earned $8,500 in 1975.) Powered conveyors and sophisticated factory control techniques allowed Honda to keep assembly cycle times down to a bare minimum.

In NVT's factories, most of the 2,950 employees manned the machine tools that produced engine and frame parts, but a significant minority were involved in assembly. (The average factory laborer at NVT earned $5,800 in 1975.) It was estimated that the average Honda assembler could put together 2.3 motorcycles in the time it took the average NVT assembler to make one. The difference arose in part because Honda made many simple, small-displacement motorcycles with few parts. For bikes of equal displacement, the ratio was perhaps 1.5 to 1.[20]

A series of layoffs, mergers, and reorganizations had left labor relations strained and worker morale low at NVT's three factories. Morale was somewhat better at Meriden than elsewhere. When Norton Villiers and BSA/Triumph merged in 1973, management tried to close Meriden, but workers occupied the factory in protest. The sit-in led to the establishment of the Meriden Workers' Cooperative which, with an infusion of cash from the British government, purchased most of the assets at Meriden. Thus Meriden was formally owned by the workers, though in practice it operated as part of NVT.[21]

Procurement of raw materials and components. Honda worked closely with its suppliers to reduce working capital and to co-locate production, in some cases even allowing suppliers to set up within Honda plants. Honda also suggested new production methods and technologies to suppliers and worked with them to integrate R&D plans. Suppliers tended to invest in automated production techniques, and they appeared to enjoy benefits of automation, scale, and experience similar in proportion to those enjoyed by Honda itself in its production of engine and frame parts. The typical Honda supplier earned a return on assets in the 6–10% range.[22]

NVT suppliers tended to use production techniques comparable to those of NVT itself, not the latest, high-volume production techniques. Exceptions arose when NVT procured parts from large auto industry suppliers such as Dunlop. Such suppliers considered NVT a very small customer.[23]

Selling and Distribution

The distribution subsidiaries of Honda, NVT, and other competitors sold motorcycles to independent dealerships, which in turn sold the machines to riders. The subsidiaries handled physical distribution, deployed advertising and promotions to pull consumers into dealerships, and gave dealers incentives and support to push bikes through the channel.

Physical distribution was straightforward. The companies bought freight services and packing materials in competitive markets on equal terms. When shipping abroad, they also paid duties. In the United States, duties on a motorcycle totaled about 3% of the cycle's retail price.

Advertising and promotion expenditures focused on television spots and on ads in consumer and trade magazines. In the United States in 1975, Honda and NVT had consumer advertising and promotion budgets of $10 million and $800,000, respectively.

Dealer relations included the most complicated aspects of the selling and distribution task. In the United States, most dealerships were small businesses with annual sales of less than $200,000 and single-digit net margins. The number of American dealers had swelled from roughly 3,000 in 1960 to 10,000 in 1974.[24] The distribution subsidiary of each motorcycle maker fielded a sales force that reached out to the numerous dealers and, in many cases, convinced dealers to offer its brand of bike exclusively. On an on-going basis, the motorcycle makers supported dealers by distributing spare parts, paying for service that was performed under warranty, helping with product display and market planning, training sales staff, and providing financial assistance if needed.

In 1975, Honda sold its motorcycles in the United States through 1,974 dealers, 84% of which sold Honda bikes exclusively. Honda was known among dealers for extensive sales support, for generous financial assistance that could be used to modernize showrooms, and for a computerized system that made 14,000 spare parts for its diverse product line readily available. In its early days in the U.S., Honda had also offered dealers an unusually fat markup between the wholesale price and the suggested retail price. By 1975, however, because of the rapid turnover of Honda-branded inventory, dealers were willing to accept a dollar markup on each Honda bike that was as much as $120 lower than the markup on each British cycle.[25]

NVT's U.S. distribution network was in flux in 1975. Prior to the merger, in 1972, BSA/Triumph had 850 dealers in the U.S. and Norton had 750. By 1975, Triumph was down to 408 dealers, 7% of which sold Triumph machines exclusively; the number of Norton dealers was not reported by the BCG consultants. NVT hoped to whittle the total number of U.S. dealers down to 400 eventually. NVT offered considerably less support to its dealers than did Honda or other Japanese competitors.[26]

The BCG consultants argued that unit costs associated with selling and distribution should fall as a company's overall sales volume in a market, its volume per model, and its volume per dealer rose, and unit costs should rise as a company offered its dealers more extensive support. Exhibit 8 gives data on a number of these factors. The consultants also noted a strong pattern across companies: for virtually all companies, including Honda and NVT, total selling and distribution costs were 20% of overall retail sales.[27]

Overall Performance. NVT's 1974 loss of £5.1 million, or $12.1 million, on sales of £16 million, or $37 million, overstated the company's desperation slightly. The loss included a substantial charge associated with the merger of Norton Villiers and BSA/Triumph. Even excluding the charge, however, NVT lost money in 1974. The company felt that because of price increases it had made between 1974 and 1975, bikes sold in the U.S. during 1975 would make a small but positive contribution to covering the company's modest overhead expenses. This positive contribution is reflected in Exhibit 7.

Worldwide, Honda had motorcycle revenue of $1.7 billion in 1974. Honda's profit margins were difficult to determine precisely because the company participated in other businesses, especially the auto market, where it was in the midst of an expensive effort to expand around the world. Observers speculated that return on sales in the motorcycle business was in the single digits, with substantially higher margins possible for large-displacement bikes.

Strategic Alternatives

Having analyzed the motorcycle industry and Britain's place in it, the BCG consultants began to formulate strategic alternatives for NVT. They first laid out some broad objectives. They then identified a set of options that might meet the objectives. All but three options seemed highly unlikely to work. For each of those three, the BCG team made a detailed projection of volumes, prices, costs, and required investments. From each projection came a forecast of operating results, financial returns, employment levels, and the industry's contribution to the U.K. balance of payments. The team also examined the sensitivity of each forecast to competitive price cuts and to errors in the volume projection, and it assessed the implementation risks associated with each option. The consultants stopped short of a final recommendation, however. The choice among the viable options, the consultants noted, was likely to involve "non-commercial considerations outside the scope of the study."[28]

Exhibit 8   Dealer Networks in the United States, 1974/75

Competitor	Units sold (000s)	Retail value ($ mm)	Number of dealers	Percent exclusive dealers	Units per model (000s)	Retail volume per dealer ($000)
Honda	433.8	477.7	1,974	84	16.7	242
Yamaha	205.1	215.4	1,515	71	7.1	142
Kawasaki	129.6	147.0	1,018	61	5.6	144
Suzuki	108.5	98.1	1,103	84	4.5	89
Harley-Davidson	57.9	111.8	390	79	3.9	287
BMW	9.0	25.8	NA	NA	2.3	NA
NVT	13.9	26.3	408*	7	0.8	64*

*Number of Triumph dealers only. Retail volume per dealer figure assumes that all NVT volume goes through the 408 Triumph dealers.

Source: Exhibit above. *Motorcycle Dealer News* Survey, R.L. Polk, and BCG estimates, reported in BCG, "Strategy Alternatives for the British Motorcycle Industry," Appendix p. 25.

Notes

1   Boston Consulting Group, "Strategy Alternatives for the British Motorcycle Industry," London: Her Majesty's Stationery Office, 1975 (hereafter referred to as "SABMI"), p. 6.

2   "SABMI," p. 36 and Appendix pp. 204–206.

3   "SABMI," p. 5.

4   "SABMI," pp. 10–13.

5   D. Purkayastha and R.D. Buzzell, "Note on the Motorcycle Industry – 1975," HBS case 578–210, p. 4.

6   "SABMI," Appendix p. 9.

7   D. Purkayastha and R.D. Buzzell, "Note on the Motorcycle Industry – 1975," HBS case 578–210, p. 4.

8   "SABMI," pp. 70–73.

9   R.T. Pascale and E.T. Christiansen, "Honda (A)," HBS case 384–049 and "Honda (B)," HBS case 384–050.

10 "SABMI," p. 26.

11 "SABMI," p. 28.

12 "SABMI," p. 27.

13 "SABMI," pp. 28–29.

14 "SABMI," p. 62. The casewriter estimated the annual salary of each R&D employee by taking the monthly salary of a factory laborer given on p. 54 of "SABMI" and assuming that each R&D employee earned a salary twice that of a factory laborer.

15 "SABMI," p. 58.

16 "SABMI," pp. 59–61. The $48 million figure comes from the discussion of strategic alternatives, "SABMI," Exhibit 28, assuming an exchange rate of 0.42 £/$. The ten-year depreciable life is an estimate provided by the casewriter. The 20% cost reduction associated with experience is derived from "SABMI," Exhibit 13.

17 "SABMI," p. 61.

18 "SABMI," p. 57.

19 "SABMI," pp. 46, 56–57.

20 "SABMI," pp. 54, 56, 60, 62 and casewriter estimates.

21 "SABMI," Appendix p. 204.

22 "SABMI," pp. 63–64.

23 "SABMI," pp. 58–59.

24 D. Purkayastha and R.D. Buzzell, "Note on the Motorcycle Industry – 1975," HBS case 578–210, pp. 5–6.

25 "SABMI," p. 30, Appendix pp. 25–29, and casewriter estimates.

26 "SABMI," p. 30, Appendix pp. 25–29.

27 "SABMI," p. 40.

28 "SABMI," p. ix.

Case 2–2: JetBlue Airways

Neeleman's Future Bet[*]

The goal was to create an airline that had not only the lowest cost on a seat/mile basis but also had the best product. If you have a business and you can give the best value to people and produce the lowest cost, you will survive.

–David Neeleman, Founder and CEO. JetBlue Airways[1]

Introduction

JetBlue Airways (JetBlue) had started operations in February 2000, as a low-fare, low-cost, high frills, point-to-point domestic airline, flying between New York City and Ft. Lauderdale, Florida. By 2004, its fleet size had increased to 57 Airbus A320s and served about 22 cities in 11 US including Puerto Rico. JetBlue flew both short and long haul flights[2] and carried approximately nine million passengers in 2003 (one million in 2000) through its 246 daily flights. While the US airline industry had collectively lost $5.3 billion in 2003, JetBlue reported net income of $103 million.[3] Even though the US airline industry had not fully recovered from the aftermath of the terrorist attacks in 2001, founder and CEO David Neeleman (Neeleman) had charted out an aggressive growth plan for his company. By 2010, he expected to increase the fleet size to 290[4] aircraft and employ about 25,000 people (In 2003, employee strength was about 6,000). In addition to offering flights between major cities, Neeleman had also planned to serve the smaller regional cities and to that effect, he had ordered 100 Embraer 190 aircraft (100 seats). Neeleman's broad plan was to add one aircraft every three weeks in 2004 and about one in every ten days the following year.

While founding JetBlue, Neeleman's aim was "to bring humanity back to air travel and make flying more enjoyable." To differentiate the start-up, he acquired a fleet of brand new Airbus A320s equipped with leather seats and provided 24 channels of Live Satellite TV at every seat for free. Instead of providing meals, the airline served "all you can eat" gourmet snacks like blue terra chips and muffins. JetBlue offered advance purchase fares that were 30%–40% lower and walk up fares that were 60%–70% lower than those of the major carriers. It became the first carrier to introduce the concept of a "paperless cockpit" and made flight booking 100% ticketless. Along with the low fares and emphasis on technology, JetBlue was known to offer friendly customer service and had one of the lowest customer complaint rates in the industry. With a combination of low fares and friendly service, JetBlue had won the prestigious Conde Nast Travelers Award for the best domestic airlines consecutively in 2002 and 2003.

While Neeleman was confident of his growth plan, many predicted that the competitive scenario would intensify in the years to come. In addition to competing with the major carriers such as American, United, Delta, Continental, Northwest, US Airways, Southwest, etc., JetBlue now faced a new breed of low-cost carriers such as AirTran, Song (promoted by Delta), Ted (a unit of United), etc., and also the likely threat from Virgin Group's foray into domestic airline in future.[5] As a result of increased competition and price-cutting by major players, JetBlue's operating margins had declined to 12.5% in the first quarter of 2004, from about 15.9% a quarter ago.[6] Also, for the first time in its operating history, in December 2003, JetBlue was forced out of a city (Atlanta) because of the increased competition from Delta and AirTran. The two airlines, with primary hub operations in Atlanta, had successfully offered cheaper flights than JetBlue over a period of time and many airlines were eyeing to repeat a similar feat to protect their major markets. Not only that, players such as Delta were being counter offensive by increasing their presence in JetBlue's east coast base, JFK International Airport in New York City.

Many industry experts predicted that JetBlue's aggressive growth plans might not be sustainable over long periods of time and compared its business model to that of People Express Airlines that had gone bankrupt during the mid-1980s. A magazine article stated:[7]

[*]This case was written by **Shahida Kathawala**, under the direction of **Senthil Ganesan**, ICFAI Business School Case Development Centre. It is intended to be used as the basis for class discussion rather than to illustrate either effective or ineffective handling of a management situation. The case was compiled from published sources. ©ICFAI University Press and ICFAI Business School Case Development Centre, 2004. Reprinted with permission. www.icfaipress.org/www.icfaipress.org/books.

"If there's one airline that serves as a cautionary tale for JetBlue, it's People Express Airlines. Back in the early 1980s, it revolutionized air travel, offering dirt-cheap fares, preaching customer focus, and priding itself on an energetic staff. Its charismatic and boyish fortysomething founder, Donald Burr, was featured on magazine covers and on TV. The airline reached a billion dollars in annual sales in less than five years. Sound familiar? Then, at approximately the same point JetBlue finds itself today—on the verge of becoming big—People Express stretched too far. Its systems couldn't handle rapidly increasing volume, and it also choked on an acquisition. People Express wound up with a one-way ticket to oblivion just a year later."

The US Airline Industry

The passenger airlines industry in the US was fragmented into three classes: the traditional carriers, the regional carriers and the low-cost carriers (LCC). While the traditional segment was dominated by the six network carriers, American Airlines, United Airlines, Delta Airlines, US Airways, Continental, and Northwest Airlines, the regional segment comprised of players such as Comair, American Eagle, Atlantic South East, SkyWest, and Mesa. The major players in the LCC segment were Southwest, AirTran and JetBlue.

The segmentation was done on the basis of how the carriers transported the passengers. While the network carriers relied on a hub and spoke arrangement through which they gathered passengers at the collection points (hubs) and from there, dispersed them to their destination cities, the LCC used the point-to-point model by providing connections only between origination and destination cities. The regional carriers operated as feeder airlines for the majors by funneling traffic from the less traveled cities (spokes) to the hubs of the major carriers.

As the majors used the hub and spoke arrangement, it led to increased investment and expenses as flights had to converge at the hubs simultaneously so that travelers could be sorted out and dispersed to catch the connecting flight. This also required increased number of ground crew to handle the traffic, unload and reload baggage resulting in under utilization of the aircraft as they had to be stationed on the ground for a longer time to collect the travelers coming on different flights. Due to these additional expenses, the majors incurred 40% higher expenditure than the LCC.

In contrast, by flying point to point, the LCC were able to reduce their operating costs by increasing flight frequency, utilizing their aircrafts better and employing lesser number of people per flight. To profitably sustain point to point flying, LCC only targeted cities with a minimum of a million potential annual airline passengers (an analysis of the US domestic market suggested that point to point traffic was 1.6 to 2 times more profitable than the connecting traffic), Among the three segments, the LCC were considered the fastest growing with a rapidly growing market share (Exhibit 1). The low-cost model in the US was pioneered by Southwest when it began operations in 1971. With the deregulation of the industry in 1978, many new low-cost airlines entered the market. However, the majors succeeded in putting most of them out of business by way of predatory pricing and intense government lobbying.[8] The start-ups also made the mistake of launching with insufficient capital, choosing wrong routes to operate on, and having less than satisfactory operational efficiency.

Although the majors were able to wipe out the new carriers, their operating costs increased substantially during the 1980s. This was due to employing multi-aircraft fleet, the development of hub and spoke system which increased labor costs and the maintenance of the expensive frequent flier programs. In the early 1990s, due to the US economic downslide, traffic declined and as a result, the majors faced huge financial losses. To tide over the period, the majors consolidated their hubs and decreased their capacity. This downturn in the airline industry resulted in launching of new LCC such as National and ValuJet that took advantage of unused capacity at the airports and the availability of surplus aircraft. But, by the mid-1990s, the economy improved substantially thus leading to increased travel demands. The majors capitalized on this trend and recovered their high costs by increasing the air fares especially for their business travelers.[9]

The majors again came under severe pressure in 2000 due to a number of factors. First, the technology bubble burst dragging the economy down with it and second, the increased use of Internet made airfares transparent. As a result, business travelers switched either to the LCC or the economy class of the majors. The combined effect of the slowing economy and the tragic events of September 2001 led to substantial decrease in the air traffic with enplanements declining from 48 million to 31 million and capacity declining from 79 million available seat miles (ASM) in September 2000 to 65 million ASM in September 2001. This resulted in heavy losses for the airline industry and pushed United and US Airways into bankruptcy.[10] Despite a government bailout worth $15 billion, the industry collectively lost around $21 billion between 2001 and 2003. The only profitable carriers during this entire period were Southwest and JetBlue (Exhibit 2).

Due to their better economic health, the LCC took advantage of the woes of the major airlines post 2001 and increased their services to markets left vacant by them. JetBlue, for example, added new flights to Las Vegas, Denver and Salt Lake City. It also increased its capacity by

Exhibit 1   Growth in the Market Share of LCC, 1990–2002

Table 1: Market Share of Domestic Origin & Destination Passengers, 1990–2002

	1990	1991	1992	1993	1994	1995	1996	1997	1998	1999	2000	2001	2002
AirTran[†]				0.0	0.6	1.4	1.0	0.9	1.2	1.3	1.5	1.6	1.9
ATA	0.1	0.1	0.1	0.4	0.7	1.0	0.9	0.8	1.1	1.2	1.3	1.6	1.9
Frontiar				0.0	0.2	0.3	0.3	0.3	0.5	0.6	0.6	0.8
JetBlue											0.3	0.8	1.3
Southwest	7.0	8.2	9.6	11.3	12.7	13.6	14.1	13.8	13.8	14.3	14.9	16.2	15.8
Other LCCs			0.2	1.9	2.4	2.3	2.8	2.4	2.2	2.2	2.0	2.1	2.0
Total LCCs	7.0	8.3	10.0	13.7	16.3	18.4	19.0	18.2	18.5	19.4	20.6	22.9	23.7
Alaska	1.8	1.9	1.9	2.0	2.6	2.9	3.1	3.0	3.1	3.0	2.9	3.0	3.2
America West	3.8	4.3	3.6	3.4	3.3	3.4	3.3	3.3	3.2	3.2	3.4	3.6	3.8
American	14.8	15.3	16.2	14.7	12.7	11.5	11.0	10.7	10.8	10.4	10.9	10.8	14.1
Continental	6.8	7.4	7.4	7.3	8.3	7.2	6.5	6.6	7.0	6.9	6.7	6.9	6.8
Delta	12.6	15.0	15.5	15.0	14.8	13.4	14.8	15.7	16.2	15.9	16.1	15.2	16.0
Northwest	7.1	7.3	7.5	7.3	7.1	7.4	7.5	7.6	7.0	7.6	7.6	7.6	7.6
TWA*	3.9	3.8	4.1	3.6	3.6	3.6	3.5	3.6	3.9	3.8	3.8	3.2	
United	11.5	12.8	12.7	11.8	11.2	11.9	11.9	12.1	13.2	12.7	11.7	11.0	10.2
US Airways	14.0	13.1	12.4	11.8	12.3	10.7	10.1	10.7	10.7	10.2	10.4	10.3	9.6
Other Carriers	16.6	10.8	8.8	9.5	7.7	9.7	9.2	8.7	6.6	6.9	5.9	5.6	5.1
Total	100.0	100.0	100.0	100.0	100.0	100.0	100.0	100.0	100.0	100.0	100.0	100.0	100.0

*Acquired by A.M.R. Corporation in 2001. [†]Data for AirTran and ValuJet combined.

Source: U.S. DOT DE1A Database, 1990–2002. Data for 2002 is from the first and second quaters.

44% on the lucrative New York-Florida routes by adding seven new flights as Delta, American, and United had cut back their services on these routes. In all, the majors reduced their seating capacity by 15% in three years since 2001 and collectively laid off 100,000 workers. In their efforts to cut costs further, the majors started moving in the direction of becoming 100% ticketless by selling it over the net. Continental, for example, had laid off a large number

Exhibit 2   Comparison of the Net Income of the Network Carriers and the LCC, 2001–2003 (All figures in millions of dollars)

Airline	2001	2002	2003
American Airlines	(1762)	(3511)	(1228)
United	(2145)	(3212)	(2808)
Delta	(1216)	(1272)	(773)
Continental	(95)	(441)	38
Northwest	(423)	(798)	236
AirTran	(2)	11	100
Southwest	**511**	**241**	**442**
JetBlue	**38**	**55**	**104**

Source: Compiled from - (a) www.finance.yahoo.com, (b) www.hoovers.com

of its reservation agents and was planning to lay off 500 more by the end of 2004. Some airlines like American altered their flight schedules to "de-peak" the hubs, i.e., it implemented rolling waves of connecting flights instead of holding planes on the ground in anticipation of any particular connection. This initiative helped it to reduce its fleet by five planes and use fewer gates. In addition, American also simplified its fleet from 12 aircraft types to only 5, thus helping it to reduce costs on maintenance and engineering. On the other hand, to compete against the LCC, majors such as Delta and United launched their own low fare airlines; Song and Ted respectively.

Analysts estimated that by the summer of 2004, traffic would return to the September 2000 level and with the improving economy, the majors would become profitable in 2004. But due to the crisis in Middle East and the increased fuel costs, the majors continued to reel under the impact of high costs and ended the first quarter of 2004 in losses. Fuel costs had touched a high of $35 a barrel in the first quarter of 2004 as against an average of $31 a barrel in 2003 and unlike the LCC, some of the majors were unable to hedge fuel due to high debts and ongoing bankruptcy proceedings.[11] The combined losses for American Airlines, United Airlines, Delta, Northwest, Continental, and US Airways for the first quarter of 2004 ending March 31st were $1.54 billion. On the other hand, Southwest, AirTran, and JetBlue ended the quarter with combined profits of $45.3 million.

In a forecast by the FAA (Federal Aviation Administration) of the US, it was estimated that by 2015, the LCC would account for 50% of all domestic passengers flown, the number of which was expected to increase to a billion over the forecast period. The FAA also estimated that the LCC would grow at a rate of 6.4% annually as compared to 3.4% growth rate for the network carriers. Also, analysts were of the opinion that the major growth would come from increase in point to point traffic in the mid-sized cities. As such, it was estimated that the aircraft fleet would include more of the 80–100 and 100–125 seat regional crafts. It was predicted that the former segment would grow to 6% from 2% over the period 2003 to 2012 while the latter segment would grow from 11% to 16% over the same period.

JetBlue: Genesis and Growth

Even after a large number of LCC had failed, Neeleman felt the need for a low-cost airline in the US market. Neeleman was an aviation industry veteran who had co-founded Morris Air in the early 1980s along with June Morris, Morris Air was a low-cost carrier and was based on the Southwest model. As Neeleman himself acknowledged:[12]

> "He (Herb Kelleher) was my idol. I studied what Kelleher was doing and tried to do it a bit better."

Neeleman not only replicated Southwest's strategy of keeping costs low by turning around planes quickly but also introduced other innovative cost-cutting concepts. He came up with electronic ticketing and encouraged travel agents to take reservation calls at home. By 1992, Morris Air had grown to a fleet of 21 Boeing 737s and was all set for an IPO when Southwest acquired it for $130 million. Following this, Neeleman joined Southwest as the Senior Vice President but was fired within the first year and was made to sign a non-compete agreement for five years.

Eventually, Neeleman started working as a consultant for the Canadian low-fare start up, WestJet Airlines. In the mid 1990s, he improvised on the online reservation system he had developed at Morris Air, named it as Open Skies,[13] and sold it to Hewlett Packard in 1999. Even before the non-compete agreement with Southwest was to expire, Neeleman along with his lawyer and JetBlue's eventual Vice President, Tom Kelly (Kelly) raised $130 million from investors such as George Soros, Chase Manhattan Bank, etc. for his start up. Neeleman himself invested $4 million.

To begin operations, Neeleman recruited various industry veterans such as Dave Barger (Dave), who had spent 10 years running Continental's Newark hub, for the position of Chief Operating Officer (COO). Neeleman also brought in two top executives from Southwest. John Owens, who had been the treasurer at Southwest for 14 years, joined JetBlue as the Chief Financial Officer (CFO) and Ann Rhoades (Rhoades), who was the head of human resources at Southwest, joined JetBlue as its HR head. For the marketing department, Neeleman hired Amy Curtis McIntyre (Curtis), who had previously worked as a marketing executive at Virgin Atlantic.

The airline, now christened JetBlue Airways, placed an order worth $4 billion with Airbus for 75 A320s. JetBlue launched operations with its inaugural flight in February 2000 between John F Kennedy Airport (JFK, New York) and Fort Lauderdale, Florida. This long haul flight proved to be a major revenue generator and by the end of its first year, JetBlue expanded to 5 cities in Florida and operated 9 daily flights. In August 2001, JetBlue started operations from Long Beach, California, its second focus city after New York and in 2002, came out with its initial public offering (IPO). The company raised $158.4 million dollars by offering 14% of the shares (5.87 million shares). JetBlue also launched its True Blue Flight gratitude (customer loyalty) program the same year. JetBlue continued on its growth strategy in 2003 and placed an order for 100 Embraer 190 aircrafts to serve mid-sized cities. The airline planned to start its operations with the Embraer in mid-2005.

The JetBlue Experience

> "Our mission is to stimulate traffic, have the lowest fares, the lowest cost, and the best product."
>
> David Neeleman[14]

Operations

Going against conventional wisdom, Neeleman chose JFK airport as the airline's base. Most of the majors avoided JFK for domestic services as it was an international airport and that New Yorkers would avoid it for domestic travel as it was farther from Manhattan than either LaGuardia or Newark airports.[15] Neeleman, on the other hand, figured that since JFK was an international airport and was crowded from only 3pm-9pm with flights, he could use the remaining non-peak hours for spacing about 80% of his flights. Also Neeleman saw a huge untapped market in New York because in spite of being the largest travel market in the US, the city lacked a LCC presence.

But to fly from JFK during the peak hours, it was necessary to get slot exemptions.[16] Normally, if an airline wanted these slots, it either had to purchase them from an existing air carrier or from the Department of Transportation (DOT). But, Neeleman with the backing of a strong Washington lobby and the promise of serving upstate New York cities

(Buffalo, Syracuse, and Rochester) was able to get exemption for 75 slots at JFK. By basing his operations there, Neeleman was able to avoid the hubs of the majors and at the same time, target the nineteen million New Yorkers who lived within a sixty mile radius of the city. JetBlue thus became the "local hometown airline for New York." JFK also had distinct advantages over both Newark and LaGuardia airports in terms of infrastructure. JFK occupied over four times the space as LaGuardia and twice the space as Newark. Also, JFK had four runways as compared to two intersecting ones at LaGuardia and three at Newark.

In the same way, when Neeleman had to choose an operations base on the West Coast, instead of opting for the crowded Los Angeles Airport (LAX)[17], he targeted the Long Beach airport (LGB, California), about 25 miles from LAX. But, LGB was environmentally protected and as such only 41 flights were allowed landing and take-off rights. Out of the 41 slots, American Airlines and America West were using 14 slots and Neeleman got the remaining 27 slots for use till 2003.[18] By basing operations at LGB, JetBlue was able to target the six million people living within 20 miles of LGB and 16 million people living in Los Angeles Metropolitan Area. By basing operations in the underserved airports, Neeleman was not only able to avoid the hubs of the majors but was also able to lower the airport and gate rent.

For the fleet, Neeleman chose the Airbus A320s over Boeing B737s. Not only were the A320s technologically more advanced but were also more fuel efficient and had a wider body than the B737s. Also, as a single aircraft type was used expenses on inventory and spare parts stock were reduced. Moreover, the airline spent less on training of the pilots (with a multi-aircraft fleet, an additional eight weeks of training was required for moving a pilot from one category of plane to the next) and maintenance crew who became experts in dealing with the A320s over time. In addition, JetBlue became the first start up to begin with a brand new fleet of A320s. As the new planes required less maintenance, they were grounded for fewer hours and could be flown for longer durations and over longer distances. As such, the average stage length[19] for JetBlue planes was 1272 miles against the domestic industry average of 900 miles. To further increase utilization of its aircraft, JetBlue flew red eye flights (flights starting late night and reaching the destination early morning). Also, small innovations like using leather seats instead of cloth seats helped in faster cleaning and turnaround for the aircraft. Additionally, along with the crew members, even the pilots helped in cleaning the aircrafts and carrying the luggage. As a result, JetBlue was able to turn-around its flight within 30 minutes which was as fast as Southwest. As a result, JetBlue's planes flew 13 hours a day against 9

for United, US Airways, and American and 11 for Southwest.

To keep labor costs low, the company had a pay package through which it gave the employees a percentage of their gross salary in profit sharing (that amounted to $31 million in 2003). Employees were also encouraged to take up stock options by setting aside 10% of their wages. As a result, the company was able to make low cash payments. Also, as JetBlue was a young start up, it could afford to negotiate low pay packages for its pilots due to their limited seniority. For the traditional carriers, benefits like medical coverage and pension plans accounted for 47% of the salary of an employee. However, as JetBlue was not unionized, it offered 401 (k) plans to its employee but refrained from providing costly pension plans. Therefore, against the airline industry average where labor costs accounted for 40% of the revenues; at JetBlue, this figure was pegged at 25%.

In 2001, JetBlue started a fuel hedging program so that fluctuating fuel prices would not impact the airline adversely. The company thus saved $1.2 million in 2002 and $3.6 million in 2003. JetBlue was also hedged at mid $20s for 40% of its total fuel requirement[20] in 2004 when most of the majors were shelling out close to $35 per barrel. Moreover, since its planes were new; they burnt less fuel per mile unlike the older industry fleet. Another cost-saving measure taken by Neeleman was the non-meal policy of the airline. JetBlue provided snacks rather than full meals on its flight. JetBlue thus saved an average of $15 million annually.

JetBlue also made efficient use of technology to reduce costs. From the start, it focused its efforts on online ticket reservations and was the first airline to be 100% ticketless (ticket confirmations were received online or by fax). By the end of 2003, 75% of its sales were through its own Web site. Selling tickets this way cost the company only 1% of the ticket price. This was much below the 7–9% costs that were incurred by selling through traditional means such as travel agents. Also, JetBlue saved on expenses by not having any downtown reservation offices like the major airlines had. Rather, Neeleman had come up with the innovative concept of home-based reservation agents. These agents numbered around 700 and were based in Salt Lake City, Utah. To make the concept work, JetBlue provided these agents with computers and two phone lines to handle calls. By using home-based agents, JetBlue saved 20% on transaction costs on every flight that was booked. These members were paid around $8.25 per hour against the industry average of $12. Yet another manner in which technology was efficiently utilized was the introduction of "paperless cockpits." For this, JetBlue equipped each of its pilots and technicians with laptops so that they had ready access to the updated flight manuals and could rapidly adjust to any changing conditions. This helped reduce flight times.

For 2003, JetBlue's operating costs per seat mile were 6.08 cents compared to 6.51 cents at Southwest and an average of 10–11 cents for the major carriers.

Building the Brand

"Our new business comes to us from word-of-mouth. When we first built this airline, we wanted to build a company with a great brand. We knew that it wasn't an ad agency that could build our brand. They can bring them (customers) to us, but we're going to bring them back. They'll come back because they really like the experience."

–David Neeleman[21]

"You start by getting the product right, getting your attitude right, getting everyone internally understanding the mission. Then you move to telling the story through PR. You build the advertising last, and that way you can live on realistic budgets."

–Amy Curtis McIntyre, VP-Marketing[22]

The first challenge the marketing team of the company faced was to select a name for the airline. The name that Neeleman had initially filed with the DOT was "New Air" but the marketing team was not convinced by it. The marketing team was very clear that they did not want either geographic descriptions like Southwest and Northwest or made up words like Hiway Air. Everyone from friends, family, and neighbors chipped in with ideas and 200 names were suggested in total varying from Idlewild Transportation (after the original name for JFK) to Imagine Air, Liberty Air, Yes!, The Competition, Home, The High Road, Civilization, Fresh Air, New York Air, Gotham, Taxi, The Big Apple, Blue, It, Egg and many more. Curtis wanted Neeleman to choose "Taxi" because it was a New York airline and she felt Taxi would lend it a New York feel. But, Taxi was ultimately dropped as it was found in focus groups that although 50% of the respondents associated the word Taxi with Checker Cabs of New York in the forties, the other half linked it to an unsafe ride in an unclean cab by a person who had an unclear grasp over English. Neeleman liked "Blue" but the entire team agreed that it would not be possible to trademark just the word "Blue."

Ultimately, the management turned to Landor Associates, a division of Young & Rubicam ad agency for a name for the airline. Landor came up with "True Blue." Curtis liked "Blue" as it conveyed skies, friendship, and loyalty. But even "True Blue" had to be dropped as the team

learned that it was already owned by Thrifty Rent-A-Car for its internal customer service initiative. Finally a week and a half before the launch, while Neeleman and Curtis were discussing the name over the phone, she came up with the name "JetBlue" that Neeleman instantly liked. He reasoned:[23]

"Jet made it sound real, like it wasn't a puddle jumper, and the blue had that association with the wild blue yonder."

Once the airline was christened, it took to the skies from JFK. For its first flight, its one way fares ranged from $79–$159. The advance purchase fares of the airlines were 30–40% lower and walk up fares were 60–70% lower than those of the major airlines. Initially, the advertisements emphasized the low fares and targeted the 8 million bargain hungry New Yorkers who lived in a five mile radius around JFK. These low fares were the first reason why the young college students and the elderly people tried JetBlue.

JetBlue was also effectively able to stimulate traffic by converting drivers into fliers on short haul routes. For example, before JetBlue launched its services to Burlington (Vermont) from JFK, the average fare for the route was $375. But, JetBlue pegged its fares from $49–$105 and people who had to drive for six hours previously now flew to their destination in 55 minutes. The increase in traffic due to low fares was described by the industry as the "JetBlue Effect."

JetBlue was able to fill 73% of its seats in the first year of its operations by emphasizing the low fares. However, the marketing team felt that JetBlue should highlight the various product innovations along with its superior customer service and target the nineteen million Manhattanites living in a sixty mile radius around New York. As Gareth Edmondson Jones, the airlines spokesperson, put it:[24]

"We want that "aspirational" audience. We see our customers as the same ones who can afford more but shop at Target because their stuff is hip but inexpensive."

To differentiate JetBlue on dimensions other than price, the management gave the airline a distinctive appeal through various innovations. For example, the color blue was prominently used to differentiate the brand. From having blue ticket counters to blue color on its tailfins, JetBlue also served blue potato chips on its flight. Even the designer-created uniforms of the flight crew were dark blue in color and so were the pilots' shirts. For the same reason, Neeleman decided to use leather seats instead of the standard cloth seats in his new aircrafts. The leather seats cost twice as much as cloth but they also lasted twice as long. Also, all its seats were equipped with Live Satellite TV which provided 24 channels to choose from. This service was offered free to the customers. Additionally, all the aircrafts were fitted with 156 seats[25] as opposed to the maximum 180 seat capacity of the A320 so that 34 inches of leg space could be provided to the passengers as against the industry standard of 31 inches. Thus, JetBlue had billboard ads which promised Free Live TV with every ticket purchase to spots that emphasized the low fares along with its brand new fleet of aircrafts, leather seats, more legroom, and e-tickets. JetBlue, through its distinctive style, wanted its customers to recall a time when flying was a more sophisticated and a less common venture.

Even after the events of September 11, 2001, when the rest of the industry was urging the Americans to shake off their fear of flying, the marketing department at JetBlue decided against such a campaign as it didn't feel right for New Yorkers. Instead, they ran an ad saying:[26]

"We know you need time to heal. JetBlue will be here when you're ready to fly again."

To instill a sense of security following the attacks, Neeleman installed bulletproof Kevlar doors and titanium bolts in the entire fleet.

In addition to providing low fares and high frills, JetBlue's management understood the importance of good customer service. As Neeleman put it:[27]

"Our low fares will get you to fly us, and our great service will get you to come back."

A survey conducted by JetBlue's own marketing department showed that the number one reason people recommended the airlines to their friends was its service. The airlines estimated that 74% of its first-time passengers chose the airline because of good word of mouth. Even the advertising emphasized its friendly customer service. For example, one of the spots known as "Subway" depicted what a subway car might be like if it were a JetBlue flight. Crew members danced through the car, inserted pillows under passengers' heads, placed blankets over sleeping bodies, poured coffee in the cup that a beggar was using to collect change and so on.

JetBlue took various steps to avoid any inconvenience to its customers. For example, flights at JetBlue were never overbooked. Also, unlike at Southwest, seats on JetBlue were pre-assigned and it charged only $25 for flight change unlike the other airlines that charged $125. To make check-in quick and easy for the passengers, JetBlue had a number of roaming ticket agents with portable equipments who would check-in the passengers, print boarding passes and check luggage. Not only that, JetBlue in collaboration with IBM rolled out 150 self service kiosks at various airports. These kiosks allowed customers to check in, selector change their assigned seat, and obtain a boarding pass. JetBlue also provided free Internet access in its terminal and was considering providing Wi-Fi[28] too. These initiatives made the airline very popular with the business travelers though JetBlue had never targeted this segment. Another reason business people preferred JetBlue was that unlike other LCC that flew only short haul, JetBlue flew transcontinental.[29]

The management and the staff at JetBlue converted every contact with the customers into a branding experience. For example, in one instance, a flight to Rochester, NY was 20 minutes late. Neeleman himself apologized to the passengers and helped the crew clean up the aircraft. In another instance, one of JetBlue's planes skidded off the icy runaway after landing at JFK. The shaken passengers were served breakfast, issued free round-trip tickets and provided with a cell phone. This resulted in 160 people telling the media that the experience was not that bad. In the same manner, to make its customers feel relaxed and stress free while flying after 9/11 attacks, JetBlue introduced "Airplane Yoga," instructional cards on how to perform simple Yoga movements.

On popular customer demand, JetBlue introduced a TrueBlue Frequent Flier Program for its frequent fliers. The TrueBlue program was totally online without any statements, mailings, partners or the ability to earn 'rewards' any other way but by obtaining free tickets for flying in markets served by the airline. Through this program, members earned points instead of miles which were to be used within a year's time. Two points were earned for a short flight, four for a medium flight and six for a long flight. Along with it, members who booked through the company's Web site, earned double points. On earning 100 points, the members became eligible for a free round trip. By 2003, JetBlue had a total of 1.3 million TrueBlue members.

For its special emphasis on customer service, JetBlue was voted the best airline in terms of overall quality and customer service in a survey conducted by University of Nebraska and Wichita State University. For 2003, JetBlue was named the second best domestic airline for its customer service by the *Travel & Leisure* World's Best Service Readers' Poll Awards. For its hip and humorous advertising, JetBlue was awarded Marketer of the Year Award by Advertising Age in 2002 and Marketing Award by Airline Business in 2003.

Through a combination of award winning customer service and advertising, JetBlue was able to stimulate demand in the markets it entered and the airline had one of the highest load factors in the industry with an average of 82% of its seats filled in the years 2001–2003.[30]

Company Culture and HR Practices

"Our crew members are the product; they are the airline."

–David Neeleman[31]

Neeleman had hired Rhoades as the Vice President of HR. Before the first plane flew, she decided to develop the core values at JetBlue. Instead of having a mission statement, the airlines operated by the five core values of safety,

---

Exhibit 3   JetBlue Airways: Core Values

Safety: We commit to "Safety First"; Comply with all Regulatory Agencies; Set and Maintain Consistently High Standards; Ensure the Security of Crewmembers and Customers; Never Compromise Safety.

Caring: Maintain Respectful Relationships with Crewmembers and Customers; Strive to be a Role Model at Work and in the Community; Embrace a Healthy Balance between Work and Family; Take Responsibility for Personal and Company Growth.

Integrity: Demonstrate Honesty, Trust and Mutual Respect; Give the JetBlue Values a "Heartbeat"; Never Compromise the Values for Short-Term Results; Possess and Demonstrate Broad Business Knowledge; Commit to Self Improvement.

Fun: Exhibit a Sense of Humor and the Ability to Laugh at Self; Add Personality to the Customer Experience; Demonstrate and Create Enthusiasm for the Job; Seek to Convert a Negative Situation into a Positive Customer Experience; Create a Friendly Environment Where Taking Risks is Okay.

Passion: Strive to Meet the Diverse Needs of Crewmembers and Customers; Champion Tean Spirif; Crave and Deliver Superior Performance; Enjoy Overcoming Barriers to Good Service; Look for Innovative Solutions to Business Issues.

Source: www.jetblue.com

---

caring, fun, integrity and passion. These five core values defined the culture at JetBlue and influenced all the decisions taken by the company (Exhibit 3).

JetBlue employed a total of 6,000+ "crew members" (as employees at JetBlue were addressed) by 2003 and this number was likely to increase to 25,000 by 2010. The screening process at JetBlue was totally paperless as all applicants submitted their resumes online. Since the computers handled the screening, the process was faster and required less manpower. Also, through the online process the airline was successfully able to discourage applicants who lacked computer skills for working at a technology intensive airline.

JetBlue hired people who were team players and risk takers. In every interview, the applicants were confronted with a battery of questions asking them to describe situations where they had broken any rule for a coworker. Only those people were hired who had the ability to break rules and make decisions. Through this policy, the company's goal was to develop a "disciplined culture of excellence" so that members could make quick decisions at the front line without waiting for the managers. For a group like pilots who needed to be tech savvy, although computer skills were not tested physically, they were confronted with a battery of questions related to IT skills during their screening process. Each new hire was then provided with a laptop and was given ample time and training to learn the systems documentation. Also at JetBlue, the first group of pilots hired the subsequent groups and so did the mechanists which increased the chances of right fit and helped in maintaining the esprit de corps among the crew members.

Every person who was hired at JetBlue met the CEO, the heads of operations and human resources on the first day of their jobs. Neeleman made finding the right employees such a priority that in a given year, 130,000 applicants were screened for 2,300 jobs.

To maintain the feel of a small organization and a strong company culture, the management felt the need of customer service training along with the operational training for all the groups of employees including the pilots and the mechanics. As Mike Barger (Barger), the director of training at JetBlue, put it:[32]

"I've always believed that a good percentage of training is cultural—the energy, the transfer of the facilitator's passion to the students. In a service industry like ours, the energy is as important as the technical skill."

Barger had devoted his initial years imparting training to each discipline separately but in due course of time, felt that the system was somewhat fragmented and led to operational inefficiencies. He envisioned training at JetBlue as a centralized and cohesive function. Also, he had discovered that the JetBlue trainers were great operational doers but not great educators. Barger's desire to convert doers into educators led him to Doug Lynch, the assistant dean of the school of continuing and professional studies at New York University (NYU). With his collaboration, Barger set up a centralized training department called JetBlue University (JBU). Through this, Barger wanted to instill the importance of corporate culture and customer service in JetBlue's faculty. According to Barger, airline customers expected that maintenance people knew how to fix planes and pilots knew how to fly planes. But what created the customer delight and the niche in the market were the service aspects—like experiencing the reservation personnel and the customer service crew checking in passengers for the flight or the flight attendants taking care of the passengers on board.

JBU and NYU developed a three phase program, known as Principles of Leadership (POL) for the 150 faculty members it planned to have by the end of 2004. Through POL 101, they were trained in providing traditional classroom teaching; POL 201 covered the practical aspects of training and third phase of the program was meant to deal with specialized training. Most of JetBlue's faculty was selected from operations as they had the right mix of operational excellence and cultural fit.

By the end of 2003, 700 of JetBlue's leaders including captains had been educated through POL 101 and POL 201, which was made mandatory training for all the leaders in 2004. One of the major reasons for the development of the POL program was the need to preserve the culture of JetBlue. As the number of people increased, the management found that the culture of JetBlue had started to strain. In a staff survey conducted in 2002, Neeleman discovered that one-third of the employees were unhappy with the management style of their superiors. The chief reason was that the employees were being promoted too fast without the commensurate training required for their jobs.

JBU was to be based in Orlando, Florida and the construction work had begun in early 2004. The campus was to house College of Flight In-flight and Operations. Through such initiatives, JetBlue wanted to instill leadership with emphasis on five basic principles:

- Treat your People Right
- Communicate with Your Team
- Inspire Greatness in Others
- Encourage Initiative and Innovation; and
- Do the Right Thing

At JetBlue, employee satisfaction was at the core of high employee productivity and the HR department would go to great lengths to ensure that the crew members were happy and content. For example, the payroll department came to work on a Saturday (which is an off day) to hand produce 300 checks that were miscalculated due to a programming error so that the employees would not face any inconvenience the next week. Also, different policies were developed for different groups of "crew members" as it was believed that employees should be treated fairly and not equally as people were not equal. As Rhoades, Executive VP-HR, put it:[33]

> "We look at each work group and address what they want to have happen, not what the company thinks should happen. Our style is accommodation."

For example, three different work schedules were developed for the flight attendants depending on the hours they wanted to work. There was a traditional flight attendant schedule, a college-student program and a JetBlue Friends Crew program. The traditional schedule was aimed at people who wanted to work more hours than the industry norms whereas the college-student program was designed for young people who wanted to have fun and travel for a year before moving on to the next stage. Through the JetBlue Friends Crew Program, two people were hired to share a schedule. The friends were interviewed together and if they were hired, the airline gave them the schedule and left it to them to decide on the shifts. This program gave the flexibility to the airline to hire great people who could not normally work as flight attendants.

For its 700 reservationists, instead of placing them in cubicles to answer calls all day, JetBlue provided them with a PC, two telephone lines, a pager and gave them the flexibility to work from home. The reservationists were so content that the turnover rate was less than 1% and there were 2,500 people in line for the job.

At JetBlue, hierarchy was downplayed by eliminating titles. Every airport employee from supervisor onwards was addressed as a crew member and was considered an equal partner in the airlines' success. Also, every JetBlue officer owned a "JetBlue city." This required the officer to visit the city four times a year for one full day to apprise the members on how the company was doing and "to reach out" to the airport authorities like tower staff, crash/fire rescue team and so on. The company also had monthly open house meetings at its JFK base and on-the-road sessions for its staff to express their views and share their opinions.

Furthermore, to involve the crew members in the running of the airlines and to provide them with a sense of ownership, JetBlue came up with some innovative ideas. For example, crew members were involved in the "No Plain Jane Plain Name Contest" for naming the JetBlue aircrafts with the word blue in it. They came up with names like Bada Bing Bada Blue, Born to be Blue, Ol' Blue Eyes, Cool Blue and Estrella Azul (Blue Star). The winners along with a guest of their choice were awarded trips to Toulouse, France (final assembly plant of Airbus Industrie) to take part in the delivery of aircraft. Even when the decision had to be taken about the flight crews' uniforms, a lot of research was done to find out the right color and style. As Curtis put it:[34]

> "They are our ambassadors; the uniform has to say the right thing."

Even while deciding on the color of the aircraft, input was taken from the mechanics as to which paint looked good and at the same time, was easy for them to clean and maintain.

The airline also made novel use of technology inhouse. For example, monthly e-mails were sent to every JetBlue employee on the company's progress, its financial results and the competitors' standing. In addition, staff stories about teamwork and motivation were shared via the intranet and online sessions were held for executives to discuss hot topics within the company.

Neeleman himself played a big part in shaping the corporate culture. He flew on at least one flight every month, worked with the crew serving snacks, picking up trash, cleaning the plane after it landed, and throwing bags at the ramp. This gave the crew members a sense of pride and increased their loyalty towards the airlines.

Another instance that increased the crew members' loyalty towards JetBlue was Neeleman's decision against laying off any employees in the aftermath of September 11, 2001 when the airline industry was laying off thousands of workers. One case in point was the treatment of the employees hired in early September to begin operations at the Washington Dulles Airport. Though the service was postponed and began only in November, none of the new hires were laid off. Instead, they were provided with computers and phone lines to support the reservations staff.

Since JetBlue's crewmembers were highly motivated and satisfied, it was the only airline that was not unionized in the domestic airline industry.

The Challenges Ahead

Although JetBlue was one of the profitable airlines in the US, analysts were worried about its ability to maintain its low costs and maintain its growth. Though at 6.09 cents it had the lowest operating costs per seat mile in the industry, expenses were bound to rise as insurance costs, fuel costs and maintenance charges increased as it added new planes.

Exhibit 4	Comparison of the RASM* and CASM* of JetBlue Airways and the Major Airlines for 2003 (All data in cents)	
Airlines	**RASM**	**CASM**
JetBlue Airways	**6.85**	**6.08**
American Airlines	8.53	9.49
United	9.40	10.5
Delta	8.88	10.71
Continental	8.55	9.76
Northwest	8.99	10.23
US Airways	10.62	11.68
Southwest	8.07	7.82
AirTran	8.34	8.26

*Revenue per available seat mile
*Cost per available seat mile

Source: Annual reports of the various airlines

Also, JetBlue had low labor costs as it provided stock option to its 6,000+ workforce. However, with declining stock price (from around $45 in late 2003 to about $27 in June 2004), many felt that the stock options would no longer be an ideal compensation and that employees might be tempted to get unionized.

Analysts were also worried about the aggressive growth strategy of the airline. Within 3 years of its operations, its fleet size had increased to 57 A320s and it was adding one new aircraft every three weeks. In contrast, Southwest in 30 years of its operations had increased its fleet to only 393 B737s. Further, JetBlue was planning to add 16 new A320s in 2004, increasing its overall capacity by 35–37% over 2003. The increase in capacity was expected to lower the revenue available per seat mile which at 6.85 cents for 2003 was lower than that of Southwest at 8.07 cents (Exhibit 4). The company thus forecasted its operating margin in the range of 13–15% on a fuel neutral basis which was much lower than the 17% operating margins for 2003 which included fuel costs. Also, over 3 years of its operations from 2000–2002, JetBlue added services to 19 cities but in 2003, it added only one new city, San Diego to its list. Instead of blanketing the country too rapidly, Neeleman started "connecting the dots" by adding flights between existing cities as it was the most cost-effective method to add capacity.

Along with rising expenses, competition was likely to heat up once the majors improved their financials by curtailing costs and streamlining operations. The majors were targeting JetBlue by not only increasing operations from their existing bases but by also introducing low cost subsidiary. For example, Delta had plans of increasing domestic operations from JFK and would invest $300 million to upgrade its facilities at JFK and add new destinations like Denver and San Diego and increase frequencies to Los Angeles, San Francisco, etc. Delta had already introduced Song, its low cost subsidiary, to take on JetBlue in the leisure markets of Florida. Song provided services from all the three major New York airports giving it an advantage over JetBlue. (Like JetBlue, it had leather seats and offered Live satellite TV at every seat. It also provided in-seat Internet access, 80 pay-per-view films, multichannel MP3 audio and an a la carte menu priced from $2–$8). In the same manner, when JetBlue expanded into Boston, it came into direct competition with American Airlines on the routes from Boston to Orlando and Fort Lauderdale (Florida). American responded by slashing fares to JetBlue's levels. The predatory pricing by the majors had a negative impact on JetBlue's operating margins for the first quarter which fell to a low of 12.5% from a high of 15.9% a quarter ago.

Annexure I   JetBlue Airways: Income Statement 2001–2003
(Amounts in thousands of U.S. dollars except share prices)

Income Statement	Dec 03	Dec 02	Dec 01
Operating Revenues			
Passenger	965,091	615,171	310,498
Other	310,498	20,020	9,916
Total Revenues	998,351	635,191	320,414
Operating Expenses			
Salaries, wages, and benefits	267,334	162,191	84,762
Aircraft Fuel	147,316	76,271	41,666
Landing Fees and Other Rents	68,691	43,881	27,342
Aircraft Rent	59,963	40,845	32,927
Sales and Marketing	53,587	44,345	28,305
Depreciation and Amortization	50,397	26,922	10,417
Maintenance Material and Repairs	23,114	8,926	4,705
Others	159,116	126,823	63,483
Total Operating Expenses	829,518	530,204	293,607
Operating Income	168,833	104,987	26,807
Other Income (Expense)			
Interest Expense	(28,897)	(21,009)	(14,132)
Capitalized Interest	5,203	5,325	8,043
Interest Income and Other	7,539	5,314	2,491
Government Compensation	22,761	407	18,706
Total Other Income (Expense)	6,606	(9,963)	15,108
Income Before Income Taxes	175,439	95,024	41,915
Income Tax Expense	71,541	40,116	3,378
Net Income	103,898	54,908	38,537
Preferred Stock Dividends	–	(5,955)	(16,970)
Net Income Applicable to Common Stockholders	103,898	48,953	21,567
Earnings Per Common Share:			
Basic	1.07	0.73	4.39
Diluted	0.97	0.56	0.51

Source: www.jetblue.com

Annexure II   JetBlue Airways: Balance Sheet 2001–2003
(Amounts in thousands of U.S. dollars)

Balance Sheet	Dec 03	Dec 02	Dec 01
Assets			
Current Assets			
Cash and Cash Equivalents	570,695	246,752	117,522
Short Term Investments	36,610	11,101	–
Net Receivables	16,723	14,777	20,791
Inventory	8,295	4,840	2,210
Other Current Assets	13,417	5,589	3,742
Total Current Assets	645,740	283,059	144,265
Long-Term Investments	–	–	–
Property Plant and Equipment	1,420,691	997,161	504,878
Goodwill	–	–	–
Intangible Assets	62,256	68,278	–
Accumulated Amortization	–	–	–
Other Assets	57,070	30,425	24,630
Total Assets	2,185,757	1,378,923	673,773

Annexure II   JetBlue Airways: Balance Sheet 2001–2003 (Amounts in thousands of U.S. dollars) *(continued)*

Balance Sheet	Dec 03	Dec 02	Dec 01
Liabilities			
Current Liabilities			
Accounts Payable	137,915	197,231	58,794
Short/Current Long-Term Debt	96,985	72,433	83,766
Other Current Liabilities	134,719	–	51,566
Total Current Liabilities	369,619	269,664	194,126
Long-Term Debt	1,011,610	639,498	290,665
Other Liabilities	34,362	16,543	7,335
Deferred Long-Term Liability Charges	99,030	38,545	3,373
Minority Interest	–	–	–
Negative Goodwill	–	–	
Total Liabilities	1,514,621	964,250	495,499
Stockholders' Equity			
Miscellaneous Stocks Options Warrants	–	–	–
Redeemable Preferred Stock	–	–	210,441
Preferred Stock	–	–	–
Common Stock	1,021	638	44
Retained Earnings	119,689	15,791	(33,117)
Treasury Stock	–	–	–
Capital Surplus	552,375	407,471	3,889
Other Stockholder Equity	(1,949)	(9,227)	(2,983)
Total Stockholder Equity	671,136	414,673	(32,167)
Net Tangible Assets	$608,880	$346,395	($32,167)

Source: www.finance.yahoo.com

Annexure III   JetBlue Airways: Flight Schedule

Origin	Destination	Daily Round-trip Flights Scheduled as of 3/15/04	Service Commenced	Daily Round-trip Flights at Start of Service
New York, NY	Fort Lauderdale, FL	16	February 2000	2
	Buffalo, NY	5	February 2000	3
	Tampa, FL	6	March 2000	3
	Orlando, FL	9	June 2000	2
	Oakland, CA	6	July 2000	1
	Ontario, CA	1	August 2000	1
	Rochester, NY	4	August 2000	2
	Burlington, VT	3	September 2000	2
	West Palm Beach, FL	8	October 2000	1
	Fort Myers, FL	6	November 2000	1
	Salt Lake City, UT	1	November 2000	1
	Seattle, Washington	1	May 2001	1
	Syracuse, NY	3	May 2001	3
	Denver, CO	1	May 2001	1
	New Orleans, LA	1	July 2001	2
	Long Beach, CA	6	August 2001	2
	San Juan, PR	4	May 2002	2
	Las Vegas, NV	5	November 2002	1
	San Diego, CA	3	June 2003	1
	Sacramento, CA	1	March 2004	1

Annexure III   JetBlue Airways: Flight Schedule *(continued)*

Origin	Destination	Daily Round-trip Flights Scheduled as of 3/15/04	Service Commenced	Daily Round-trip Flights at Start of Service
Long Beach, CA	Washington D.C.	3	May 2002	2
	Oakland, CA	6	September 2002	9
	Las Vegas, NV	2	October 2002	3
	Salt Lake City, UT	1	October 2002	1
	Fort Lauderdale, FL	1	May 2003	1
Washington D.C.	Fort Lauderdale, FL	3	November 2001	2
	Oakland, CA	2	May 2002	2
Boston, MA	Orlando, FL	4	January 2004	2
	Fort Lauderdale, FL	2	January 2004	1
	Tampa, FL	2	January 2004	2
	Denver, CO	1	January 2004	1
	Long Beach, CA	2	January 2004	2

Source: www.jetblue.com

While JetBlue was able to fill 79.9% of its seats (on capacity increase of 44.6%) year on year, its revenue per mile decreased 7.9% to 6.85 cents over the previous year.

Competition was also bound to increase from LCC like Southwest and AirTran as both were moving into JetBlue's territory. While Southwest was changing its business model for the first time in 30 years and entering principal airports like Philadelphia and Pittsburgh and started flying long haul, AirTran was revamping its fleet with new Boeing 737s, flying transcontinental (between Atlanta, its hub and Los Angeles, Las Vegas, and Denver) instead of its traditional north south routes and providing perks like increased leg room and leather seats. In addition, JetBlue was likely to face new competition from Virgin Group, which had plans to introduce domestic airline service.

In spite of these impending challenges, JetBlue continued on its growth strategy and planned to consolidate opera-

Annexure IV   JetBlue Airways: Route Map

Source: www.jetblue.com

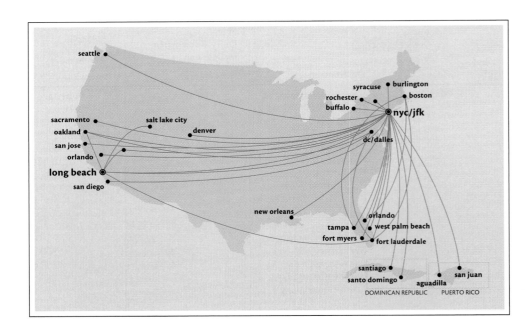

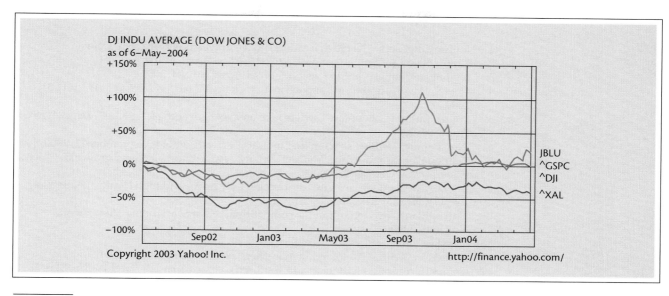

DJ INDU AVERAGE (DOW JONES & CO)
as of 6–May–2004

Copyright 2003 Yahoo! Inc.   http://finance.yahoo.com/

Annexure V   JetBlue's Stock Performance Compared with S&P, Dow Jones and the AMEX Airline Index (2002–2004)

Source: www.finance.yahoo.com

tions at JFK by increasing the number of its flights by 35% for 2004 summer months. Neeleman also had plans of starting operations from La Guardia, NY in the summer. Analysts believed that instead of cannibalizing demand at JFK, Neeleman would introduce services to new cities like Dallas, Houston, and Chicago. JetBlue was also waiting for federal approval for flying internationally to the Dominican Republic and had plans to fly to Mexico and Caribbean in the future. Due to the complexities involved in international flying, analysts were, however, worried that JetBlue might lose its cost advantage due to lower utilization of its planes, increased crew requirement and the need for interlining with various domestic players in the international markets it entered.

Moreover, Neeleman had also placed orders for 100 new Embraer 190 jet aircraft worth $3 billion.[35] Through this deal, Neeleman wanted to target the mid-sized cities in the US which the regional carriers were serving through the smaller 50 and 70 seat jets. In comparison with these smaller jets, the Embraer 190 were more fuel efficient, had 40% lower operating costs and were more comfortable. Also, Neeleman planned to utilize these jets at the rate of 11 hrs per day as against 8 hrs per day for the current regional jets. Through the Embraer, which had a range of 2000 nautical miles, JetBlue could fly from additional 900 cities with a minimum of 200–500 passengers each way (JetBlue had

traditionally targeted cities which had a minimum of 600 passengers each way. That gave the airlines 300 potential cities to choose from). In addition, through these jets JetBlue could increase frequencies between New York and upstate cities like Syracuse and Rochester which it was already servicing with the A320s. These jets could also be used alternately with the A320s in seasonal markets. But, analysts were concerned that the smaller jet strategy of JetBlue could backfire as adding a new plane to the fleet could increase the maintenance costs and the training costs of the pilots. In addition, it could complicate labor relations as pilots operating the smaller planes were paid less than their counterparts operating the bigger ones.

With JetBlue's high growth business model and the increased competitive pressures in the market, S&P analysts estimated that JetBlue would have revenue growth of 40% for 2004 and that earnings at 35% for the next five years. But, JP Morgan analysts had differing views as they estimated a double digit growth in the overall industry capacity to negatively impact JetBlue's growth prospects. As one analyst put it:[36]

> "The industry is unsheathing its own capacity dagger . . . and I expect a pronounced negative impact on JetBlue both this year and next. The industry is gunning for JetBlue."

References

1. Johnson, Rebecca, "Name that airline," www.travelandleisure.com, October 1999.
2. Grant, Elaine X, "Southwest with a twist," *Travel Agent*, March 61, 2000.
3. Shillinglaw, James, "JetBlue vision," *Travel Agent*, July 24, 2000.
4. Goetzl, David, "JetBlue asks sponsors to pick up TV tab," *Advertising Age*, July 31, 2000.
5. Young, Susan J., "Low-fare carriers take on majors over the long haul," *Travel Agent*, August 7, 2000.
6. Tsui, Bonnie, "JetBlue soars in first months," *Advertising Age*, September 11, 2000.
7. Zellner, Wendy and Arndt, Michael, "Many new airlines will never grow old," *BusinessWeek*, October 23, 2000.
8. Goetzl, David, "JetBlue's growth strategy: Low prices and high loyalty," *Advertising Age*, October 23, 2000.
9. Harris, Elana, "Undercutting the competition," *Sales & Marketing Management*, November 2000.
10. "Upstart with a difference," *Time*, January 22, 2001.
11. Naughton, Keith, "Try lounging in leather," *Newsweek*, March 23, 2001.
12. Compart, Andrew, "JetBlue to add southern California base," *Travel Weekly*, May 28, 2001.
13. Browner, Eryn, "Smokeless Herb," www.fortune.com, May 28, 2001.
14. Feldman, Joan M, "JetBlue loves New York," *Air Transport World*, June 2001.
15. "In new cockpits paper's passe," *Aviation Week and Space Technology*, July 16, 2001.
16. Shannon, Darren, "Three of a kind," *Travel Agent*, July 23, 2001.
17. Donnelly, Sally B., "Blue skies," *Time*, July 30, 2001.
18. Rottier, Amy, "The skies are JetBlue," *Workforce*, September 2001.
19. Feldman, Joan M., "Connecting the dots," *Air Transport World*, October 2001.
20. Zellner, Wendy, "The little birds grow stronger," *BusinessWeek*, November 5, 2001.
21. DiMassimo, Mark, "Sky high," *Adweek* Western Edition, November 26, 2001.
22. Judge, Paul C., "How will your company adapt," *Fast Company*, December 2001.
23. Newman, Michael, "Onward & upward," *Gallup Management Journal*, December 15, 2001.
24. Tsao, Amy, "Thinking of taking off with JetBlue," *BusinessWeek Online*, April 5, 2002
25. Begun, Bret, "Moving into the future," *Newsweek*, April 29, 2002.
26. Baker, Robert, "Is JetBlue flying too high," *BusinessWeek*, April 29, 2002.
27. Shifrin, Carol, "Born to be Blue," *Airline Business*, June 2002.
28. Scelfo, Julie, "Remain seated," *Newsweek*, June 3, 2002.
29. Arndt, Michael and Zellner, Wendy, "American draws a bead on JetBlue," *BusinessWeek*, June 24, 2002.
30. Landis, David, "What price airlines," *Kiplinger's Personal Finance*, August 2002.
31. Labetti, Kristi Sue, "Motivating a blue streak," *Potentials*, September 2002.
32. Wells, Melanie, "Lord of the skies," www.fortune.com, October 2002.
33. Cogswell, David, "JetBlue provides Vermont with boost in airlift," *Travel Weekly*, December 16, 2002.
34. Compart, Andrew, "JetBlue posed to take Delta in its home town," *Travel Weekly*, February 24, 2003.
35. Marcial, Gene G., "At JetBlue the sky's the limit," *BusinessWeek*, March 24, 2003.
36. Pachetti Nick and Neeleman, David, "JetBlue skies," *Money*, April 2003.
37. Pilling, Mark, "Price promise," *Airline Business*, April 2003.
38. Amdt Michael and Zellner, Wendy, "Can anything fix the airlines," *BusinessWeek*, April 7, 2003.
39. "JetBlue aims to be the best," *Business Travel World*, May 2003.
40. Gajilan, Ailyn Tobias, "The amazing JetBlue," www.fortune.com, May 17, 2003.
41. Kaufman, David, "Song's lure," *Kiplinger's Personal Finance*, June 2003.
42. Zellner, Wendy, "JetBlue strafes the big boys again," www.businessweekonline.com, June 13, 2003.
43. "JetBlue remains bullish on Embraer 190 contract despite share price setback," *Flight Daily News*, June 15, 2003.

44. Fiorino, Frances, "The $3-billion 'Effect'," *Aviation Week and Space Technology*, June 16, 2003.
45. Field, David, "JetBlue refocuses with regional jet buy," *Airline Business*, July 2003.
46. Jonas, David, "Delta broadens discounts," *Business Travel News*, July 7, 2003.
47. Bond, David, "JetBlue rolls on," *Aviation Week and Space Technology*, July 28, 2003.
48. Corridore, Jim, "Open skies for JetBlue," *BusinessWeek Online*, July 29, 2003.
49. Field, David, "Low-fare carriers sustain growth plan," *Airline Business*, August 2003.
50. Compart, Andrew, "Delta teaches JetBlue a lesson in Atlanta," *Travel Weekly*, November 3, 2003.
51. Jonas, David, "Buyers: JetBlue wins big in the smaller carrier sector," *Business Travel News*, November 10, 2003.
52. Piazza, Johanna, "JetBlue's planned expansion into Boston should help Logan," *The Bond Buyer*, November 14, 2003.
53. Bartlett, Michael, "A management message right out of the (Jet) Blue," *The Credit Union Journal*, December 8, 2003.
54. Comiteau, Jennifer, "Neeleman on the spot," *Adweek*, December 22–29, 2003.
55. Zellner, Wendy, "Folks are finally packing their bags," *BusinessWeek*, January 12, 2004.
56. Donnelly, Sally B., "Friendlier skies," *Time*, January 26, 2004.
57. Jonas, David, "Delta, JetBlue NY duel spells lower fares, more flights," *Business Travel News*, February 9, 2004.
58. Bond, David, "Slugging it out," *Aviation Week and Space Technology*, February 9, 2004.
59. Zellner, Wendy, "Is JetBlue's flight plan flawed?" www.businessweek.com, February 16, 2004.
60. Flottau, Jens, "On a roll," *Aviation Week and Space Technology*, February 16, 2004.
61. Alexander, Keith L., "The math flies," www.washingtonpost.com, February 29, 2004.
62. "How JetBlue partnered with NYU to develop its training department," www.ioma.com, March 2004.
63. Brodsky, Norm, "Learning from JetBlue," *Inc.*, March 2004.
64. Capell, Kerry and Zellner, Wendy, "Richard Branson's next big adventure," *BusinessWeek*, March 8, 2004.
65. Arndt, Michael, "Flying budget but in style," *BusinessWeek*, March 15, 2004.
66. Haji, Salim, "Low-cost carriers flying high," www.fool.com, March 18, 2004.
67. Watts, William L and Cole, August, "JetBlue tops airline quality study," www.CBSMarketWatch.com, April 5, 2004.

Notes

1. *Business Travel World*, May 2003.
2. 93% of JetBlue's business consisted of long haul flights.
3. Till 2003, JetBlue has reported twelve consecutive profitable quarters.
4. In contrast, it had taken Southwest 30 years to grow to a fleet of 393 B737s.
5. Virgin USA is expected to begin operations in 2005 either from Boston's Logan International Airport, Washington Dulles International, or San Francisco International Airport.
6. In spite of decline in its operating margins, JetBlue had the highest margins among all the US carriers.
7. Salter, Chuck, "And Now the Hard Part," *Fast Company*, May 2004.
8. Out of the fifty carriers that were launched in the decade after the deregulation, only one, America West, was able to survive but even it faced repeated bankruptcy.
9. The business fliers were charged a premium of 30% over the economy class.
10. United Airlines came out of bankruptcy in March 2003 with a concession of $1.24 billion from the federal government.
11. Every $1 per barrel rise in fuel price resulted in cost increase of $500 million for the airline industry. Southwest was hedged at $24, JetBlue at $27.63, Delta, at $26.10, AirTran at $31.80 and Continental at $32 for 2004. The cost per barrel had increased to $40 by June 2004.

12 "The Amazing JetBlue," *Fortune Small Business*, www.fortune.com, May 17, 2003.

13 An online ticketing system.

14 Zellner, Wendy "JetBlue Strafes the Big Boys Again," www.businessweekonline.com, June 13th 2003.

15 From Wall Street in downtown New York City, JFK was 19 miles away, compared to Newark (13 miles) and LaGuardia (12 miles).

16 Take off and landing rights granted at peak hours to the airlines by Department of Transportation.

17 LAX was the third largest airport in the US based on 2002 passenger traffic and served three-fourths of the domestic arrivals to California.

18 JetBlue had to renegade three slots to American and two slots to Alaska Airlines as American threatened to sue it otherwise. American's contention was that as JetBlue was not using all the slots immediately, the slots should be assigned to it rather than be used gradually by JetBlue to increase flights over the course of three years from 2001–2003.

19 Represents average number of miles flown per flight.

20 JetBlue's fuel consumption had increased from 105,515 thousand gallons in 2002 to 173,157 thousand gallons in 2003.

21 Comiteau, Jennifer, "Neeleman on the Spot," *Adweek*, 22-29, December 2003.

22 Bloom, Jonah, "Upstart JetBlue Marketer of the Year," *Advertising Age*. December 9, 2002.

23 Johnson, Rebecca, "Name that Airline," www.travelandleisure.com, October 1999.

24 Donnelly, Sally B., "Blue Skies," *Time*, July 30, 2001.

25 Initially the number of seats was 162 but JetBlue decreased it to 156 to provide increased leg room.

26 Judge, Paul C, "How will your Company Adapt," *Fast Company*, December 2001.

27 Grant, Elaine X, "Southwest with a twist," *Travel Agent*, March 6th 2000.

28 Wi-Fi is short for Wireless Fidelity. Wi-Fi permits a person with wireless enabled computer to connect to the Internet by moving within 15 meters or an access point called hotspot.

29 By 2001, business travelers accounted for 50% of profits per flight.

30 The average load factor for the industry was in the low 70s.

31 Shifrin, Carol, "Born to be Blue," *Airline Business*, June 2002.

32 "How JetBlue Partnered with NYU to Develop its Training Program," www.ioma.com, March 2004.

33 Rottier, Ann, "The Skies are JetBlue," *Workforce*, September 2001.

34 Op.cit, "Upstart JetBlue Marketer of the Year."

35 The first seven crafts were to be delivered in the year 2005 and the remaining at the rate of 18 per year by 2011. JetBlue also had an option for 100 additional Embraer jets after 2011.

36 Velocci, Anthony L, "Market Focus," *Aviation Week and Space Technology*, January 12, 2004.

Case 2–3: The Levi's Personal Pair Proposal[1]

"I'll have my recommendation to you by the end of the week." Heidi Green hung up the phone and surveyed her calendar for appointments that could be pushed into the next week. It was a rainy afternoon in December of 1994 and she had yet to recover from the pre-holiday rush to get product out to retailers.

She had three days to prepare a presentation for the Executive Committee on a new concept called Personal Pair. Custom Clothing Technology Corporation (CCTC) had approached Levi Strauss with the joint venture proposal that would marry Levi's core products with the emerging technologies of mass customization. Jeans could be customized in style and fit to meet each customer's unique needs and taste. If CCTC was correct, this would reach the higher end of the jeans market, yielding stronger profit margins due to both the price premium and the streamlined production process involved.

On the other hand, the technology was new to Levi Strauss and the idea could turn out to be an expensive and time-consuming proposal that would come back later to haunt her, since she would have to manage the venture. The initial market studies seemed supportive, but there was no way to know how customers would respond to the program since there was nothing quite like it out there. She also was unsure whether the program would work as smoothly in practice as the plan suggested.

Company Background and History

Levi Strauss and Co. is a privately held company owned by the family of its founder, Levi Strauss. The Bavarian immigrant was the creator of durable work pants from cloth used for ships' sails, which were reinforced with his patented rivets. The now-famous "waist-overalls," were originally created over 130 years ago for use by California gold rush workers. These were later seen as utilitarian farm- or factory-wear. By the 1950s, Levi's jeans had acquired a Hollywood cachet, as the likes of Marilyn Monroe, James Dean, Marlon Brando, Elvis, and Bob Dylan proudly wore them, giving off an air of rebellious hipness. The jeans would become a political state-

ment and an American icon, as all jeans soon became known generically as "Levi's." The baby boomer generation next adopted the jeans as a fashion statement, and from 1964–1975, the company's annual sales grew tenfold, from $100 million to $1 billion.[2] By the late 1970s, Levi's had become synonymous with the terms, "authentic," "genuine," "original," and "real," and wearing them allowed the wearer to make a statement. According to some who recognize the brand's recognition even over that of Coke, Marlboro, Nike, or Microsoft, "Levi Strauss has been, and remains, both the largest brand-apparel company in the world and the number one purveyor of blue jeans in the world."

While blue jeans remain the company's mainstay, the San Francisco–based company also sells pants made of corduroy, twill and various other fabrics, as well as shorts, skirts, jackets, and outerwear. The company, with its highly recognizable brand name, holds a top position in many of its markets, and is sold in more than 80 countries. More than half of the company's revenue was from its U.S. sales; nevertheless, Europe and Asia are highly profitable markets. Latin America and Canada are secondary markets, with smaller contributions to overall profits. As the graphic (right) shows, apparel imports were increasing faster than exports during this period.

The company's non-denim brand, Dockers, was introduced in 1986, and is sold in the U.S., Canada, Mexico, and Europe. While it is composed of both women's and

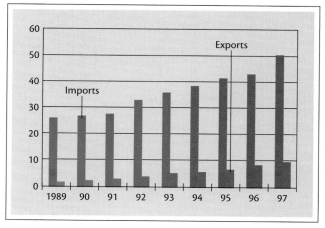

Import and Exports of Apparel (In billions of dollars)

Source: U.S. Department of Commerce.

The Levi's Personal Pair Proposal. Used with permission of Professor Russell Coff and the Goizueta Business School.

men's clothing, the men's line of khaki pants occupies the leading position in U.S. sales of khaki trousers and sells well with baby boomers. Sales of Dockers have steadily increased with the rise in casual workplaces, and this line of non-denim products has helped in allowing Levi's to be less reliant on the denim industry.

Competition and the Denim Industry

Denim is "one of the fastest-growing apparel fabrics," and sales have been increasing approximately 10% per year. According to some surveys, an average American consumer owns 17 denim items, which includes 6–7 pairs of jeans.[3] Levi Strauss and Company held the largest market share in 1990, at 31%, followed by VF Corporation's Lee and Wrangler (17.9%), designer labels (6%), The Gap (3%), and department store private labels (3.2%). By 1995, women's jeans had grown to a $2 billion market, of which Levi's held first place.

However, at the same time, many jeans producers were starting to move production to low-cost overseas facilities, which allowed for cost (especially labor) advantages. As the graph (below) shows, this trend was represented throughout the apparel industry and is clearly visible in employment statistics. Indeed, JCPenney, one of Levi's long-time partners, had become a competitor by introducing a cheaper alternative, the Arizona label. They and other rivals had realized that by sourcing all production in cheap overseas facilities they could enter the business with a cost advantage over Levi Strauss.

Levi's as a private company, which viewed itself as having a strong "social conscience," wanted to avoid being seen as exploiting disadvantaged workers. Accordingly,

they preferred to have their jeans "U.S.-made," and Levi Strauss was a leader in providing generous salary and benefits packages to its employees.

Accordingly, it did not relish the notion of entering into price-based competition with rivals committed to overseas production. Their delayed response led to some significant incursions by rivals into Levi's core product arenas.

Levi's also wanted to avoid price-based competition because they had a history of brand recognition and brand loyalty. They were accustomed to the Levi's brand carrying enough clout to justify a reasonable price premium. However, over the years, the brand name carried less cachet, and as hundreds of competitors with similar products dotted the landscape, it became necessary to create valued features that would help to differentiate the product in the eyes of consumers.

Levi Strauss' financial performance is summarized in Exhibit 1 for the period from 1990–1994. While the company was profitable throughout the period, revenue growth had clearly slowed and income growth was quite uneven. This is especially apparent for 1994, the current year, where net income dropped by 35% due to fierce competition for market share and narrowing margins.

Cost Structure

Exhibit 2 provides an estimate of the cost and margins on an average pair of jeans sold through Levi's two outlets. Much of their product is sold through wholesale channels, to be distributed by competing retailers. However, Levi's maintains a chain of Original Levi's Stores (OLS) primarily to help keep them closer to the customer. The profit per pair of jeans is about 30% lower in the wholesale channel ($2 as opposed to $3). This is driven by the 30% margin that accrues to the channel, and which is somewhat balanced by the higher costs of operating the OLS outlets (especially the additional SG&A costs for operating the stores).

Exhibit 2 also indicates the ongoing investment per pair of jeans. Once this is considered, the wholesale outlets are nearly twice as profitable—the pre-tax return on invested capital is 15%, as opposed to 8%. Here, the OLS outlets require additional investment in inventory ($8/pair), which is normally borne by the retailer, and the capital tied up in the retail stores ($20/pair).

Mass Customization

Mass customization uses emerging communication and computer technologies to bypass the limitations of traditional mass production methods. From a strategic standpoint, the concept is based on the idea that "the ultimate niche is a market of one."[4] Previously, it was thought that highly-customized products were necessarily expensive to produce;

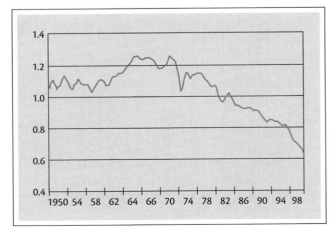

U.S. Apparel Industry Employment (Production workers, in millions)

Source: Bureau of Labor Statistics.

Exhibit 1   Levi Strauss Financial Performance

	1994	1993	1992	1991	1990
Income Statement					
Net sales	$6,074,321	$5,892,479	$5,570,290	$4,902,882	$4,247,150
Cost of goods	$3,632,406	$3,638,152	$3,431,469	$3,024,330	$2,651,338
Gross Profit	$2,441,915	$2,254,327	$2,138,821	$1,878,552	$1,595,812
Selling G&A Exp	$1,472,786	$1,394,170	$1,309,352	$1,147,465	$922,785
Non Operating Income	−$18,410	$8,300	−$142,045	$31,650	−$36,403
Interest Exp	$19,824	$37,144	$53,303	$71,384	$82,956
Income Before Taxes	$930,895	$831,313	$634,121	$691,353	$553,668
Taxes	$373,402	$338,902	$271,673	$324,812	$288,753
Net Inc Before Ext Items	$557,493	$492,411	$362,448	$366,541	$264,915
Ext Items	−$236,517	$0	−$1,611	−$9,875	−$13,746
Net Income	$320,976	$492,411	$360,837	$356,666	$251,169
Growth					
Sales Growth	3.1%	5.8%	13.6%	15.4%	
Net Income Growth	−34.8%	36.5%	1.2%	42.0%	
Key Financial Ratios					
Quick ratio	1.57	1.03	0.76	0.87	0.73
SG&A/Sales	24.25	23.66	23.51	23.4	21.73
Receivables Turnover	6.68	6.87	7.67	7.31	6.88
Inventories Turnover	7.76	7.44	7.64	7.5	7.29
Total Debt/Equity	2.57	10.57	34.39	71.82	22.21
Net inc/Sales	5.28	8.36	6.48	7.27	5.91
Net inc/Total assets	8.18	15.84	12.53	13.54	10.51

however, with the advent of various information technologies, meeting the customer's needs for flexibility and greater choice in the marketplace is becoming more and more economical.

> "A silent revolution is stirring in the way things are made and services are delivered. Companies with millions of customers are starting to build products designed just for you. You can, of course, buy a Dell computer assembled to your exact specifications. . . . But you can also buy pills with the exact blend of vitamins, minerals, and herbs that you like, glasses molded to fit your face precisely, CD's with music tracks that you choose, cosmetics mixed to match your skin tone, textbooks whose chapters are picked out by your professor, a loan structured to meet your financial profile, or a night at a hotel where everyone knows your favorite wine. And if your child does not like any of Mattel's 125 different Barbie dolls, she will soon be able to design her own."[5]

There is, of course, a delicate balance between providing consumers enough flexibility to meet their needs without so much that the decision-making process becomes perplexing and the company's costs spiral out of control trying to meet the customers' phantom needs.

In the early 90s, Levi Strauss found itself facing a dual set of competitors. There were the low-cost, high-volume producers with a distinct advantage over Levi's, and there were also the higher-cost producers of jeans that targeted the affluent end of the denim-buying public. As a high-volume producer with a cost disadvantage, Levi's increasingly found itself at a disadvantage in both the upper and lower ends of the apparel market.

Personal Pair Proposal

Proponents of the Personal Pair project envisioned a niche that would allow Levi's to avoid competing against the low-cost high-volume producers. Market research revealed that only a quarter of women were truly happy with the fit of their jeans, and the company hoped to attract higher-income customers who would be willing to pay a little extra for a perfect fit.

In addition, a mass customization model could lower costs as well as provide the differentiation advantage since the re-engineered process is often more efficient once new technologies are applied. For example, the mass customization model, which operates on the "pull-driven" approach of

Exhibit 2 Profitability Analysis of Women's Jeans

	Wholesale Channel	Original Levi's Store Channel	Personal Pair?	Notes
Operations, per pair				
Gross Revenue	$35	$50		$50 retail price with a 30% channel margin.
Less	(3)	(5)		Avg. channel markdowns of $5; 60% born by mfg.
markdowns				
Net Revenue	32	45		
Costs				
Cotton	5	5		
Mfg.	7	7		High labor content since all jeans hand-sewn.
conversion				Wholly-owned distribution network for OLS
Distribution	9	11		channel. Add $2 for warehouse to store.
Total	21	23		
COGS				
Gross Margin	11	22		
SG&A	9[1]	19[2]		
Profit Before	$2	$3		
Tax				
Investment, per pair				
Inventory	$4	$12		77 days for Levi's wholesale channel & 240 days for OLS stores to include retail inventory.
Less A/P	(1)	(1)		Reflects 27 days of Accounts Payable.
Accounts	4	0		51-day collection period for wholesale. Retail customers pay immediately.
Receivable				
Net working				
capital	7	11		
Factory PP&E	5	5		Reflects a sales to fixed asset turnover of 5.33.
Distribution				
PP&E	1	2		Doubled for OLS channel due to additional retail distribution investment (estimate).
Retail Store	0	20		$2.4M/OLS store for 120,000 pairs sold/yr (est.).
Total Investment	$13	$38		
Pre-tax return on invested capital	15%	8%		

[1] At $9, a little higher than Levi's overall 25% SG&A due to supply chain problems with women's jeans.
[2] The additional $10 reflects an average 22% store expense for retail clothiers (Compact Disclosure database).

Source: Adapted from Carr, 1998.

having the customer drive the production process, would lower distribution costs and inventories of unsold products.

Personal Pair was a jeans customization program made possible through a joint venture with Custom Clothing Technology Corporation (CCTC), in Newton, Massachusetts. CCTC approached Levi Strauss, described the potential of its technology and suggested that, together, the two companies could enter the mass customization arena.

The Personal Pair proposal reflected a form of collaborative customization. This approach helps customers who find the array of choices in the marketplace overwhelming, to narrow down their specific needs. The company enters into a dialogue with customers to help them understand what they need, and is then able to provide specialized products that meet that specific need. Collaborative customizers are able to keep inventories of finished products at a minimum, which brings new products to market faster. That is, they manufacture products in a "just-in-time" fashion to respond to specific customer requests.

How it would work. Original Levi's Stores (OLS) would be equipped with networked PC's and Personal Pair kiosks. Trained sales clerks would measure customers' waist, hips, rise, and inseam, resulting in one of 4,224 possible size combinations—a dramatic increase over the 40 combinations normally available to customers. The computer would then generate a code number that corresponded to one of 400 prototype pairs of jeans kept in the kiosk. Within three tries, more measurements would be taken and a perfect fit would be obtained; the customer would then pay for the jeans and opt for Federal Express delivery ($5 extra) or store pickup, with a full money-back guarantee on every pair.

The order was then sent to CCTC in Boston via a Lotus Notes computer program. This program would "translate" the order and match it with a pre-existing pattern at the Tennessee manufacturing facility. The correct pattern would be pulled, "read," and transferred to the cut station, where each pair was cut individually. A sewing line composed of eight flexible team members would process the order, it would be sent to be laundered, and would be inspected and packed for shipping. A bar code would be sewn into each pair to simplify reordering details, and the customer would have a custom-fit pair within three weeks.

Once the program was underway, the proposal suggested that about half of the orders would be from existing customers. Reordering would be simplified and encouraged by the bar code sewn into each pair. In addition, reorders could be handled through a web-based interface.

Pricing. There was some question about how much of a price premium the new product would command. The proposal called for a $15 premium (over the standard $50/pair off the rack) and focus groups suggested that women, in particular, would consider this a fair price to pay for superior fit. However, other's argued that this price point was a bit optimistic, suggesting that $5 or $10 might be more realistic given the lower-priced alternatives.

Planned scope. The initial proposal was to equip four Original Levi's Stores (OLS) with Personal Pair kiosks and specialized PC's. Once the systems were worked out, this would be expanded to more than 60 kiosks across the U.S. and Canada. In addition, they envisioned opening kiosks in London where they estimated that the product would command a premium of £19 over the original £46 price for standard jeans. The jeans would still be produced in Tennessee and shipped via Federal Express.

Cost impact. Although the new process would require some investments in technology and process changes, many other costs were projected to drop. These are illustrated by the complex supply chain for the OLS channel (Exhibit 3) and the relatively simple supply chain for the proposed Personal Pair program (Exhibit 4).

- The most obvious ongoing cost savings would be in distribution. Here, the order is transmitted electronically and the final product is shipped directly to the customer at his/her expense. These costs would be nearly eliminated in the proposed program.
- Manufacturing and raw materials would not change much since all jeans are hand sewn and would use the same materials for the traditional and mass-customized processes.
- The portion of SG&A expenses attributable to retail operations would be reduced if 50% of the sales are reorders that do not incur incremental costs in the retail stores ($5/pair savings). However, CCTC would incur its own SG&A costs that would have to be considered (about $3/pair).
- Finally, no price adjustments would be needed in such a tight channel since there would be no inventory of finished product. In the retail channel, about one third of jeans are sold at a discount to clear out aging stock (the discounts average 30%).[6]

Investment impact. While the factory PP&E was not projected to change much (they would continue to use the same facilities), a number of other factors would impact the invested capital tied up in a pair of jeans (both positively and negatively) under the proposed program:
Increases in invested capital:

- First, there would be an initial $3 million required to integrate the systems of CCTC with Levi's existing systems. This was relatively small since it was a matter of integrating existing systems in the two companies.
- CCTC would also require additional IT investments estimated at $10/pair to maintain the system and upgrade it regularly as scale requirements increased.
- In addition, the kiosks would take up about one third of the space in the OLS retail stores (about $7/pair for retail space).

Decreases in invested capital:

- The required inventory was significantly lower under the proposed program. Recent estimates calculated Levi's average inventory at about 8 months.[7] In contrast, the Personal Pair program called for no inventory of finished product and only a small inventory of raw materials (about $1/pair).
- Finally, the proposal suggested that accounts receivable would lead to a net gain of about $2/pair since customers would have paid about 3 weeks prior to receiving the product (similar to the Amazon.com model).

Cost-efficient Mass Customization. In order for a company to transform an existing product into one that is cost-efficient to mass produce, certain product modifications must be made. The Personal Pair proposal incorporated several of

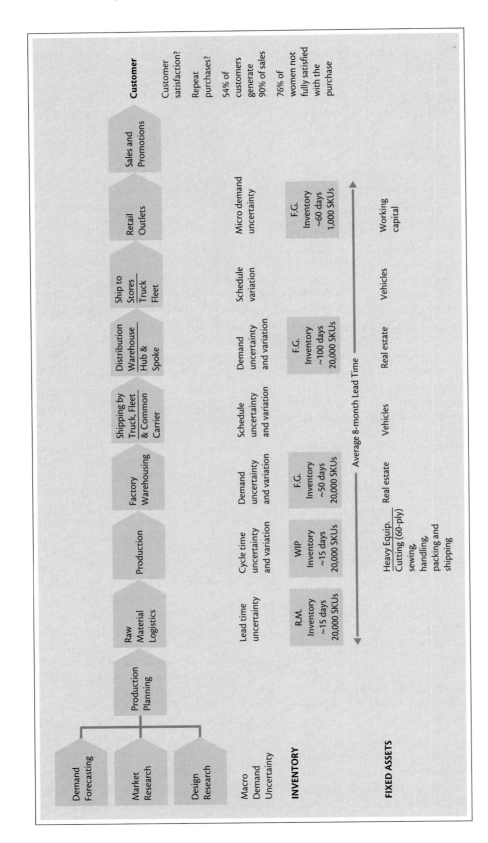

Exhibit 3 Traditional Original Levi's Store Supply Chain

Source: Adapted from Carr, 1998.

| Personal Pair kiosk in retail store | EDI link to manufacturing via CCTC | Raw material logistics | Manufacturing the one pair of jeans* | Pack pair for daily pickup at factory by FedEx | FedEx directly to customer |

Exhibit 4   Personal Pair Value Chain

*Although this approach changes cutting from 60-ply to one, it does not otherwise change manufacturing since jeans were, and are, sewn one pair at a time.

the key elements suggested as helpful for implementing successful mass-customization programs.[8]

First, it is important to introduce the differentiating component of the product (that which must be customized) as late in the production process as possible. For example, paint is not mixed by the manufacturer, but at the point of sale, after being demanded by individual customers. Unfortunately, the making of personalized jeans would not lend itself to a differentiating component late in the production process. Therefore, in this case, the customizing would have to take place at the beginning of the process.

Then, it is helpful if either the product or the process of manufacturing can be easily separated into production modules. Steps in the process can then be reassembled in a different order. For example, a sweater manufacturer might wait until the last possible moment to dye its products in different colors for each season, instead of dying the wool first and knitting the sweaters. This allows for much more flexibility and helps the manufacturer to keep up with fast moving fashion trends. The Personal Pair proposal suggested that the manufacturing process would be modified to allow for better flow—specifically teams would be used to allow for more flexibility and handling of custom products. Unfortunately, since elements in the jean manufacturing process do not always come together in the same way, it would be important that employees accumulate a large range of skills to accommodate idiosyncratic problems that cannot be anticipated.

Finally, it is helpful if either the products or the sub-processes in the manufacturing chain are standardized. This allows for more efficient production and inventory management, whether it be for different types of domestic uses or different markets (for example, international as well as domestic markets were served by a printer manufacturer that allowed all its printers to be adjusted for both 110/220-volt usage). Here, the Personal Pair proposal called for a complex computer program with computerized patterns that were then beamed directly to the cutting floor. This would help them to integrate some technology-enhanced sub-processes with existing standard labor-intensive manufacturing methods.

It also goes without saying that all the parts of the new mass customization process need to come together in an "instantaneous, costless, seamless and frictionless manner."[9]

The Decision. As Heidi leaned back and gazed outside at the rain-soaked plaza, she considered the pros and cons to the proposal. The proposal carried several risks that she could not fully quantify. First, there was the ability of Levi Strauss to implement new technologies. Second, the cost savings in the proposal were based on CCTC's estimates in their proposal for the program. Would the program still be successful if the costs turned out to be very different? Third, market research indicated that women were not satisfied about fit. How much would they be willing to pay for a better fit?

On another level, she wondered about the competition. If the program were successful, would their low-cost rivals dive into this market as well? Did Levi's have any advantage here? What if they did not move forward with the proposal? Would one of their rivals partner with CCTC?

Bibliography

1   Aron, Laurie Joan. "From push to pull: The supply chain management shifts." *Apparel Industry Magazine*, June 1998, Volume 59, Issue 6, pp. 58–59.

2   *Apparel Industry Magazine*. "Jeanswear gets squeezed: Plants close at Levi's." VF, March 1999, Volume 60, Issue 3, p. 10.

3   Billington, Jim. "How to Customize for the Real World" *Harvard Management Update*, Reprint #U9704A, 1997.

4   Bounds, Wendy. "Inside Levi's race to restore a tarnished brand." *Wall Street Journal*, August 4, 1998, p. B1.

5   Carr, Lawrence, William Lawler, and John Shank. "Levi's Personal Pair cases A, B, and Teaching Note." F.W. Olin Graduate School of Business, Babson College, December 1998, #BAB020, BAB021, and BAB520.

6   Chaplin, Heather. "The Truth Hurts." *American Demographics*, April 1999, Volume 21, Issue 4, pp. 68–69.

7   Charlet, Jean-Claude, and Erik Brynjolfsson. "BroadVision." *Stanford University Graduate School of Business Case* #OIT-21, March 1998.

8   Church, Elizabeth. "Personal Pair didn't fit into Levi Strauss's plans." *The Globe and Mail*, May 27, 1999, p. B13.

9   Collett, Stacy. "Levi shuts plants, misses trends." *Computerworld*, March 1, 1999, p. 16.

10   *Economist, The*. "Keeping the customer satisfied." July 14, 2001, pp. 9–10.
     Economist, The. Special Report. "Mass customization: A long march." July 14, 2001, pp. 63–65.

11   Ellison, Sarah. "Levi's is ironing some wrinkles out of its sales." *Wall Street Journal*, February 12, 2001, p. B9.

12   Espen, Hal. "Levi's Blues." *New York Times Magazine*, March 21, 1999, p. 6.

13   Esquivel, Josephine R., and Huong Chu Belpedio. Textile and Apparel Suppliers Industry Overview, Morgan Stanley Dean Witter, March 14, 2001, pp. 1–72.

14   Feitzinger, Edward, and Hau L. Lee. "Mass customization at Hewlett-Packard: The power of postponement." *Harvard Business Review*, January-February 1997, Reprint #97101, pp. 116–121.

15   FITCH Company Reports, Levi Strauss and Co., February 15, 2001, www.fitchratings.com.

16   FITCH Company Reports, Levi Strauss and Co., October 31, 2000, www.fitchratings.com.

17   FITCH Company Reports, Levi Strauss and Co., March 18, 1999, www.fitchratings.com.

18   Gilbert, Charles. "Did modules fail Levi's or did Levi's fail modules?" *Apparel Industry Magazine*, September 1998, Volume 59, Issue 9, pp. 88–92.

19   Gilmore, James H. "The four faces of mass customization." *Harvard Business Review*, January-February 1997, Reprint #97103, pp. 91–101.

20   Ginsberg, Steve. "Ripped Levi's: Blunders, bad luck take toll." *San Francisco Business Times*, December 11–17, 1998, Vol. 13, Issue 18.

21   Hill, Suzette. "Levi Strauss and Co.: Icon in revolution." *Apparel Industry Magazine*, January 1999, Volume 60, Issue 1, pp. 66–69.

22   Hill, Suzette. "Levi Strauss puts a new spin on brand management." *Apparel Industry Magazine*, November 1998, pp. 46–47.

23   Hofman, Mike. "Searching for the mountain of youth." *Inc.*, December 1999, Volume 21, Issue 18, pp. 33–36.

24   Homer, Eric. "Levi's zips up first ever private deal." *Private Placement Letter*, July 23, 2001.

25   Hunt, Bryan C., and Mark O. Doehla. Denim Industry, *FirstUnion Industry Report*, February 23, 1999.

26   Jastrow, David. "Saying no to Web sales." *Computer Reseller News*, November 29, 1999, Issue 871, p. 73.

27   Johnson, Greg. "Jeans war: Survival of the fittest." *Los Angeles Times*, December 3, 1998, p. C1.

28   King, Ralph T., Jr. "Jeans therapy: Levi's factory workers are assigned to teams, and morale takes a hit." *Wall Street Journal*, May 20, 1998, p. A1.

29   Laberis, Bill. "Levi's shows it may not be driver it pretends to be." *Computerworld*, April 12, 1999, Vol. 33, Issue 15, p. 36.

30   Lee, Julian. "Can Levi's ever be cool again?" *Marketing*, April 15, 1999, pp. 28–29.

31   Lee, Louise. "Can Levi's be cool again?" *BusinessWeek*, March 13, 2000, pp. 144–148.

32   Levi Strauss and Company Promotional Materials.

33   Levine, Bettijane. "Fashion fallout from the Levi Strauss layoffs." *Los Angeles Times*, March 1, 1999, p. 1.

34   Magretta, Joan. "The power of virtual integration: An interview with Dell Computer's Michael Dell." *Harvard Business Review*, March-April 1998, Reprint #98208, pp. 73–84.

35   Meadows, Shawn. "Levi shifts on-line strategy." *Bobbin*, January 2000, Vol. 41, Issue 5, p. 8.

36   Merrill Lynch Company Report, Levi Strauss and Co., Global Securities Research and Economics Group, March 23, 2001.

37   Merrill Lynch Company Report, Levi Strauss and Co., Global Securities Research and Economics Group, January 11, 2001.

38   Merrill Lynch Company Report, Levi Strauss and Co., Global Securities Research and Economics Group, September 20, 2000.

39   Munk, Nina. "How Levi's trashed a great American brand." *Fortune*, April 12, 1999, Vol. 139, Issue 7, pp. 82–90.

40   *New York Times*. "The view from outside: Levi's needs more than a patch." February 28, 1999, p. 4.

41   Pine, B. Joseph II. "Serve each customer efficiently and uniquely." *Network Transformation*, BCR, January 1996, pp. 2–5.

42   Pine, B. Joseph II, Bart Victor, and Andrew C. Boynton. "Making mass customization work." *Harvard Business Review*, September-October 1993, Reprint #93509, pp. 108–116.

43   Pressler, Margaret Webb. "Mending time at Levi's: Jeans maker struggles to recapture youth market, reshape its culture." *Washington Post*, April 12, 1998, p. HO1.

44   Reidy, Chris. In marketplace, they're no longer such a great fit." *Boston Globe*, February 23, 1999, p. A1.

45   Reda, Susan. "Internet Channel Conflicts." *Stores*, December 1999, Vol. 81, Issue 12, pp. 24–28.

46   Robson, Douglas. "Levi showing new signs of fraying in San Francisco." *San Francisco Business Times*, October 15, 1999, Volume 14, Issue 10, p. 1.

47   Rosenbush, Steve. "Personalizing service on Web." *USAToday*, November 16, 1998, p. 15E.

48   Schoenberger, Karl. "Tough jeans, a soft heart and frayed earnings." *New York Times*, June 25, 2000, p. 3.

49   Schonfeld, Erick. "The customized, digitized, have-it-your-way economy. "*Fortune*, September 28, 1998.

50   Stoughton, Stephanie. "Jeans market now a tight fit for Levi's; Denim leader missed marketing opportunities, failed to spot trends." *Washington Post*, February 23, 1999, p. E1.

51   Trebay, Guy. "What's stonewashed, ripped, mended and $2,222?" *New York Times*, April 17, 2001, p. 10, col. 1.

52   Voight, Joan. "Red, white, and blue: An American icon fades away." *Adweek*, April 26, 1999, Vol. 40, Issue 17, pp. 28–35.

53   Watson, Richard T., Sigmund Akselsen, and Leyland F. Pitt. "Attractors: Building mountains in the flat landscape of the World Wide Web." *California Management Review*, Volume 40, Number 2, Winter 1998, pp. 36–54.

54   Zito, Kelly. "Levi reveals rare look at inner secrets." *San Francisco Chronicle*, May 6, 2000, p. B1.

Notes

1   This case was prepared by Farah Mihoubi under the supervision of Associate Professor Russell Coff of the Goizueta Business School, as the basis for class discussion, rather than to illustrate either effective or ineffective management. Information assembled from published sources and interviews with company sources. Copyright 2001, by the Goizueta Business School, Case and Video Series, Atlanta, Georgia, 30322, U.S.A. All rights reserved.

2   Espen, 1999.

3   Levine, 1999.

4   Schonfeld, 1998.

5   Schonfeld, 1998.

6   Carr, 1998.

7   Carr, 1998.

8   Billington, 1997.

9   Pine, Victor, and Boynton, 1993, p. 112.

Case 2–4: Kodak

Betting on Digital Imaging*

We have a goal of becoming a $20 billion company by 2010, reflecting a healthy mix of businesses that are commercial and consumer, traditional and digital, new and established—and all of them taking advantage of the opportunities available in the $385 billion infoimaging market.

Daniel Carp, Chairman and CEO, Eastman Kodak[1]

Introduction

In September 2003, Daniel Carp (Carp), Chairman and CEO of Kodak, unveiled a strategic plan to invest $3 billion in the company's consumer, health and commercial digital businesses. This plan seemed essential as many industry experts had predicted an annual drop of 10–12% in Kodak's traditional film sales over the next three years.[2] Carp's plan was to cut dividend by 72% from $1.80 (in 2002) to $0.50 a share and invest the $3 billion thus saved into digital businesses. He predicted that the plan would increase the company's revenues from $13 billion in 2003 to about $16 billion in 2006.

To implement his plan, Carp, along with Antonio Perez,[3] realigned Kodak's divisions into five business groups. All the consumer businesses were put under the newly formed "Digital & Film Imaging Systems" (D&FIS) group. The new group consisted of seven strategic product and service groups (SPGs):

- The Home Printing group that was responsible for the development of home printing products;
- Consumer Output group that handled retail services, camera phone printing, wholesale printing, the Picture Center Online services and Picture Maker kiosks;
- Professional Output division responsible for the Pro Studio solutions, Pro Lab solutions, the paper and chemical product platform, Event Imaging Solutions, professional digital cameras, etc;
- The Film Capture group that handled professional and consumer films, single-use cameras and film cameras;
- The Digital Capture group that was responsible for consumer digital still cameras, memory and all digital camera accessories;
- Entertainment Imaging group responsible for the motion picture film and digital services for the entertainment industry; and
- The Digital Imaging group that focused on online, mobile imaging and software services.

The other business groups were Commercial Printing, Health, Commercial Imaging, and Display (Exhibit 1).

Many viewed Carp's plan with skepticism as the company had undergone repeated restructurings since the 1980s, and yet sales had been on a decline from $19 billion in 1991 to $13 billion in 2003 (Annexure I and Annexure II). Carp's announcement prompted a 14% drop in the company's stock price[4] (Annexure III) signaling growing investor doubt about the prospects of the company. Industry analysts too echoed the market sentiments. According to Harbir Singh, a professor of management at the Wharton School of the University of Pennsylvania:

"Kodak must shift from the chemicals industry that has been its mainstay for 123 years into consumer electronics, where profit margins are thinner and competitors such as Hewlett–Packard are entrenched."[5]

One former HP executive commented:

"They know more about the science of imaging, photographs and what people want to do with them than any company in the world. They have great technical capabilities, but they've lacked focus and application."[6]

Background Note

Eastman Kodak Company (Kodak) was founded in 1880 by George Eastman when he invented and patented a dry-plate formula[7] and a machine for preparing large number of plates. In 1888, the company introduced its first snapshot camera with the slogan "You press the button, we do the rest." And, in

*This case was written by **Shahida K** and **Senthil Ganesan**, under the direction of **Gopal Saxena**, ICFAI Business School Case Development Centre. It is intended to be used as the basis for class discussion rather than to illustrate either effective or ineffective handling of a management situation. The case was compiled from published sources. ©ICFAI University Press and ICFAI Business School Case Development Centre, 2004. Reprinted with permission. www.icfaipress.org/www.icfaipress.org/books.

Exhibit 1   Kodak Business Segments

Segment	Business
Digital and Film Imaging Systems Group	Consumer Film products Print Film Professional Film products Traditional and inkjet photo paper Chemicals Traditional and digital cameras Photo processing equipment and services Digitization services including online services
Health Imaging Group	Traditional analog products Medical Films Chemicals Processing equipment Digital medical imaging products Digital print films Laser imagers Computed and digital radiography systems Picture archiving and communications system Radiology Information systems
Commercial Imaging Group	Document scanners Micrographics Microfilm Optics and optical systems
Commercial Printing Group	Wide format inkjet printers Graphic arts material Digital production presses Digital production printing systems
Display	Organic light emitting diode (OLED) Displays, imaging sensor solutions

Source: www.kodak.com.

1900, The Brownie camera was introduced at a price of $1. In the decades to follow, Kodak continued introducing new products and, by 1962, had reached sales of $1 billion. By the mid-1970s, Kodak controlled 90% of the film market and 85% of the camera sales in the US, and by the early 1980s had sales of $10 billion and income of $923 million. Soon thereafter, growth began to decelerate due to increased competition from Fuji Photo Film Company (Japan) and the advent of new filmless camera technology. In 1981, Sony Corporation introduced Mavica, a filmless camera that recorded images on a computer chip. The Mavica was not initially successful but slowly increased the presence of filmless technologies.

To counter the new competition, Kodak, in 1982, introduced a disk-film camera, a miniaturized camera that used electronics to make operations automatic. However, the camera was unsuccessful as the prints were grainy and Kodak eventually stopped production in 1988. During the same period, the company, under Chairman and CEO Colby Chandler (Chandler) and President Kay Whitmore (Whitmore, Chairman and CEO from 1990 to 1993), made

several non-core acquisitions like Atex (a supplier of word-processing systems to newspaper publishers), Sterling Drug (1988) etc. Not only were these businesses unprofitable over time, but also increased the debt levels of the company (After the Sterling acquisition, the long term debt level of Kodak stood at $7 billion).

While Kodak focused away from its core business, rival Fuji Film made inroads into the US market and quickly gained a 12% market share. In 1987, Fuji introduced the first disposable camera, thereby making its presence stronger in the market. Competition also intensified from rivals like Sony, Nikon, Canon, etc. that introduced digital cameras. Another challenge Kodak faced was the growing demand for inexpensive store brands. By 1992, store brands accounted for 15% of the US market, reducing Kodak's share to about 70%. Kodak's revenues now stood at $20 billion and income at about $994 million.

To improve its financial situation, Kodak laid off thousands of workers. This plan, however, did little to cut costs as many workers were given generous severance

Annexure I   Eastman Kodak: Income Statement 2001–2003
(Amounts in millions of U.S. dollars)

Income Statement	Dec 03	Dec 02	Dec 01
Revenue	13,317.0	12,835.0	13,234.0
Cost of Goods Sold	8,203.0	7,407.0	7,905.0
Gross Profit	5,114.0	5,428.0	5,329.0
Gross Profit Margin	38.4%	42.3%	40.3%
SG&A Expense	3,429.0	3,292.0	3,406.0
Depreciation & Amortization	830.0	818.0	919.0
Operating Income	855.0	1,318.0	1,004.0
Operating Margin	6.4%	10.3%	7.6%
Nonoperating Income	(51.0)	(84.0)	(18.0)
Nonoperating Expenses	148.0	173.0	219.0
Income Before Taxes	172.0	963.0	108.0
Income Taxes	(66.0)	153.0	32.0
Net Income After Taxes	238.0	810.0	76.0
Continuing Operations	238.0	793.0	76.0
Discontinued Operations	27.0	(23.0)	0.0
Total Operations	265.0	770.0	76.0
Total Net Income	265.0	770.0	76.0
Net Profit Margin	2.0%	6.0%	0.6%
Diluted EPS from Continuing Operations ($)	0.83	2.72	0.26
Diluted EPS from Discontinued Operations ($)	0.09	(0.08)	0.00
Diluted EPS from Total Operations ($)	0.92	2.64	0.26
Diluted EPS from Total Net Income ($)	0.92	2.64	0.26
Dividends per Share	1.15	1.80	2.21

Source: www.hoovers.com.

packages. Many senior and experienced workers opted for these buyouts, thus leaving the company with relatively inexperienced personnel. Thus, waste levels, inefficiencies and customer complaints increased dramatically. Kodak initiated another round of restructuring in 1993; this time it reduced its management levels from seven to five, eliminated 2,000 jobs in administration and R&D and trimmed its $1.6 billion R&D budget by $100 million. Kodak's debt had by now increased to $9.5 billion against shareholder's equity of $4.5 billion. Dissatisfied with Whitmore's performance, the board fired him in 1993 and appointed George Fisher (Fisher) as the Chairman and CEO.

Fisher's strategy was simple: to sell both film and digital imaging products. He stressed the need for focusing on five links of the imaging chain: image capture, processing, storage, output and delivery of images on a worldwide basis. He also sold off all unrelated businesses acquired under Chandler and Whitmore, thereby reducing the company's long-term debt from $7.8 billion to $1.6 billion.

Fisher increased focus on digital products and soon formed the Digital and Applied Imaging division to synergize all the scattered digital imaging projects of the company. He also announced alliances with IBM, Microsoft, Sprint, Kinko and Hewlett Packard (HP)[8] to further develop the digital imaging portfolio. Fisher reasoned:

"There are many dimensions to imaging—capturing, processing, manipulation, output and communications. In all aspects of these, Kodak has some capability. But consumers want all of them. So we more or less filled in the blanks with these deals, because we didn't have time to do it on our own."[9]

For the traditional film business, Kodak introduced its Funtime film thus entering the low-end film market after years of internal debate. To expand the market of disposable cameras, the fastest growing part of the film business, the company introduced telephoto, panoramic, portrait, and underwater versions. Fisher also targeted emerging markets like India and China to increase revenues in the film business and signed a partnership deal with a distributor in China (China, then, was a Fuji stronghold). By the end of 1994, about 45% of Kodak's revenue and 75% of profit came from film business. The digital business accounted for about $500 million in revenues and no profits.

Continuing with its digital strategy, Kodak, in 1995, introduced its first consumer digital camera (DC-40), priced at $1,000. In 1996, Kodak introduced its Advantix camera that was based on "advanced photo system,"[10] developed in partnership with Fuji, Minolta, Nikon, and Canon. With $500 million invested in the product by 1997, Kodak did not make enough cameras to supply dealers and had intro-

| **Annexure II** | **Eastman Kodak: Balance Sheet 2001–2003 (Amounts in millions of U.S. dollars except per share amount)** | | |

Balance Sheet	Dec 03	Dec 02	Dec 01
Assets			
Current Assets			
Cash	1,250.0	569.0	448.0
Net Receivables	2,389.0	2,234.0	2,337.0
Inventories	1,075.0	1,062.0	1,137.0
Other Current Assets	741.0	669.0	761.0
Total Current Assets	5,455.0	4,534.0	4,683.0
Net Fixed Assets	5,094.0	5,420.0	5,659.0
Other Noncurrent Assets	4,269.0	3,415.0	3,020.0
Total Assets	14,818.0	13,369.0	13,362.0
Liabilities and Shareholders' Equity			
Current Liabilities			
Accounts Payable	3,707.0	3,351.0	3,276.0
Short-Term Debt	946.0	1,442.0	1,534.0
Other Current Liabilities	654.0	584.0	544.0
Total Current Liabilities	5,307.0	5,377.0	5,354.0
Long-Term Debt	2,302.0	1,164.0	1,666.0
Other Noncurrent Liabilities	3,945.0	4,051.0	3,448.0
Total Liabilities	11,554.0	10,592.0	10,468.0
Shareholders' Equity			
Preferred Stock Equity	0.0	0.0	0.0
Common Stock Equity	3,264.0	2,777.0	2,894.0
Total Equity	3,264.0	2,777.0	2,894.0
Shares Outstanding (mil.)	286.6	285.9	290.9

Source: www.hoovers.com.

| **Exhibit 2** | **Kodak: Segment Wise Revenue Split-Up (in $ Million)*** | | |

Segment	2003	2002	2001
Photography			
Inside the US	$3,812	$4,034	$4,482
Outside the US	5,420	4,968	4,921
Total Photography	**9,232**	**9,002**	**9,403**
Health Imaging			
Inside the US	1,061	1,088	1,089
Outside the US	1,370	1,186	1,173
Total Health Imaging	**2,431**	**2,274**	**2,262**
Commercial Imaging			
Inside the US	912	818	820
Outside the US	647	638	634
Total Commercial Imaging	**1,559**	**1,456**	**1,454**
All Other			
Inside the US	44	53	68
Outside the US	51	50	24
Total All Other	**95**	**103**	**110**
Total Net Sales	13,317	12,835	13,229

*Kodak would report revenues based on the new structure from 2004 onwards. *Source:* Kodak 2003 10K Report.

duced the line before there were enough processors to develop the pictures. Also, with the large number of digital cameras available in the market, most of the early adopters turned to the digital cameras instead. Kodak's next digital camera, the DC-25, also failed to make an impact. So, after investing millions of dollars on digital imaging, Kodak kept losing money. To make matters worse, Kodak faced increased pressure from Fuji Film that resorted to aggressive price cutting (with film prices about 25% less than that of Kodak). As a result, in 1997, Kodak generated earnings of $5 million on revenue $14.7 billion. Immediately, Fisher announced elimination of 20,000 jobs, including 200 executives, in order to cut $1 billion in costs by 1999.

Till 1997, Fisher had concentrated on two markets for digital photo processing – the home digital darkroom[11] and the kiosk-based digital imaging[12]—but now he decided to concentrate only on the kiosks. Kodak had already installed 13,000 kiosks by then and the initiative was to install more while its competitors chose the other alternative.

To focus Kodak on digital product development efforts, Carp (the then President of the company) formed a new operating team in 1998 to study problems in the capture, storage, and application of digital images. To focus the company's efforts on "digitization,"[13] Kodak also acquired a 51% share

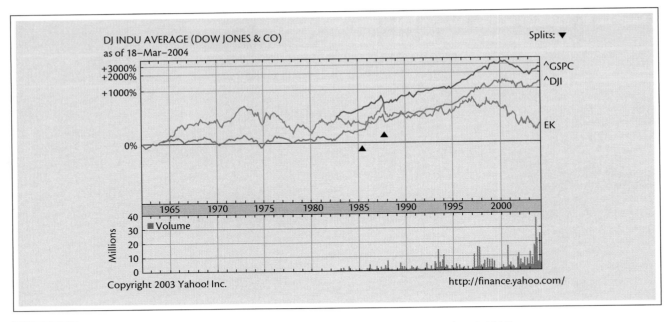

Annexure III   Eastman Kodak's Performance Compared with S&P and Dow Jones (1965–2004)

Source: http://finance.yahoo.com.

in PictureVision (an online photofinishing firm) and integrated PictureVision's PhotoNet Internet-based imaging service with the products and services of the Kodak Picture Network (KPN).[14] Kodak's efforts paid off and by 1998, Kodak's share of the digital camera market stood at 20% with product prices ranging from below $1,000 to $15,000. Kodak ended 1998 with earnings of $1.4 billion on sales of $13 billion, but with the digital business still making losses.

The year 1999 was a turning point for the digital imaging industry as for the first time the 2 megapixel cameras were introduced.[15] Two million digital cameras were sold in 1999 and industry groups estimated that film would grow by only 1% till 2003 and thereafter decline. Kodak, on the other hand forecasted that film would grow by 5% annually and a major part of its revenue would come from it. Kodak ended 1999 with earnings of $1.4 billion on sales of $14 billion.

In January 2000, more than a year before his contract was to expire, Fisher stepped down and was replaced by Carp. Carp began focusing Kodak on the digital trinity of image capture, services, and image output.

Kodak Under Daniel Carp

When Carp took over, the company was under a lot of pressure to improve its digital product portfolio. Having invested more than $5 billion in digital businesses over the past ten years, Kodak had earned only $20 million on it in 1999. On the other hand, traditional film business still produced 80% of the revenue but grew at only 2% a year.[16] So, Carp wanted Kodak to focus on image capture (cameras), services (online photo manipulation) and image output (digital kiosks, inkjet printers, paper, and inks). He was optimistic about the future and commented:

"We happen to be in a business that is going to explode, digital means more picture-taking, whether they are health pictures, professional pictures or consumer pictures. And with that comes more and more output."[17]

Carp continued investing in digital cameras even though they were losing $75 million on $400 million of sales annually.[18] Kodak, in 2001, introduced its "EasyShare" digital cameras in the US. The EasyShare cameras came with a docking station that recharged the camera and docked to the PC, transferring photos to the computer at the click of a button. Kodak counted on more consumers taking print-outs and thus driving sales of its photofinishing paper, with the simplification of the uploading process. The cameras were a big hit with the customers but they accounted for only $500 million[19] of Kodak's $13 billion 2001 sales. While digital camera sales increased to 9 million units in 2001, prices of digital cameras fell from an average of $460 in 2000 to $300 in 2002.[20] Kodak also expanded its product portfolio by introducing digital offerings for the professional and entertainment imaging industry.

To capture a significant share of the online photofinishing business, Carp continued to invest in PhotoNet, building a massive repository of images online for customers and retailers. Carp also launched Kodak's own website, Print@Kodak, selling its services to old-line retailers and websites like Ememories, PhotoPoint, MyFamily.com and Snapfish. Buying prints off the web was already a $425 million business, with Kodak holding a 15% share of the market.[21] Kodak already led in photo-quality paper for inkjets, with a 40% share.[22] In 2001, Kodak acquired Ofoto Inc. that offered processing of digital media and traditional film, providing private online image storage, sharing and editing of images. Kodak also increased the number of its kiosks to 24,000 in the US and 35,000 worldwide.[23]

The company ended 2001 with net earnings of $75 million dollars on sales of $13 billion as the world economy became sluggish and the traditional film business in the US declined by 5%. The company announced 7,500 job cuts and reorganized its business around strategic product groups. These groups were

- The Photography group, which included consumer imaging, digital & applied imaging, photography portion of Kodak professional and the entertainment-imaging unit;
- The Health-imaging group;
- The Commercial imaging group, including document imaging, graphics and commercial printing; and
- The Component group that included the flat-panel display technology used in devices like cell phones.

The regrouping was done to make the groups more autonomous and accountable for their performance.

With the economic growth continuing to be sluggish in 2002 also, Carp continued to invest in the emerging markets with Kodak achieving increase of 25% in China, 20% in Russia and 8% in India.[24] Kodak also offered its premium products like Max HQ or the Max Versatility film to increase revenues from high-end film sales. To increase demand and revenues from print outs and its photofinishing services, Kodak introduced Perfect Touch Processing service that scanned film negatives and applied special software to provide richer color, more detail and fewer dark shadows in the picture. The new technology increased photofinishing volumes by more than 20%.[25]

Kodak ended 2003 with revenues of $13 billion with a $4 billion digital portfolio. Kodak's digital camera sales grew by 100% in 2003 and the product turned profitable in the second quarter of the year. The EasyShare cameras and the media (printing paper) generated $75 million in sales in 2003. For the first time in 2003, digital camera sales surpassed film sales in the US. It was forecast that worldwide 53 million digital camera units would be sold in 2004 (Exhibits 3 and 4) with digital cameras completely replacing reloadable film cameras (excluding one-time use cameras) by 2008 (Annexure IV). Digital camera sales were expected to increase at a CAGR of 15%.[26] However, film sales were expected to decline 10–12% annually from 2004–2006 (Exhibit 5). Kodak, thus, unveiled its new digital strategy in September 2003 to move away from traditional businesses and towards the digital by investing $3 billion in consumer, commercial and health imaging businesses. Kodak also announced more lay-offs, reducing the number of its employees from 70,000 in 2002 to 62,000 at the end of 2003.

Kodak's New Initiative

To reach the targeted revenue of $16 billion by 2006, Carp focused on the high growth areas and planned to reinvest the earning from the traditional business in the digital business.

Exhibit 3   Worldwide Still Camera Sales (in millions of units)

Millions of units	1999	2000	2001	2002	2003*
Digital-still cameras					
Worldwide	**5.5**	**11.0**	**18.5**	**30.5**	**50.0**
The Americas	2.0	4.3	6.5	11.5	17.0
Europe	1.1	2.3	4.6	9.0	18.0
Japan	1.8	3.6	5.9	6.7	9.0
Rest of the World	0.6	0.8	1.5	3.3	6.0
Analog-still cameras					
Worldwide	**67.0**	**71.0**	**66.0**	**63.0**	**57.0**
The Americas	16.8	20.6	19.0	19.0	16.0
Europe	20.1	20.6	20.0	19.0	17.0
Japan	6.0	5.7	4.0	3.5	2.0
Rest of the World	24.1	24.1	23.0	21.5	22.0

Notes: *Projections made in November 2003.   *Source:* PMA Research.

Exhibit 4   Shipments of Imaging Devices Worldwide

Source: www.gaiatec.com.

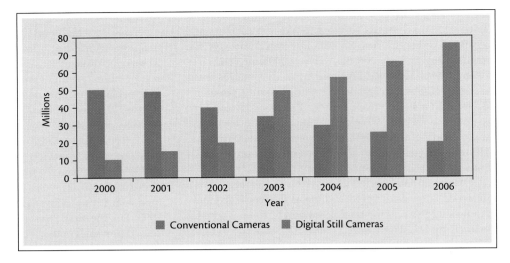

He also intended to develop a new low cost, more efficient business model for the traditional photography business. Working on this strategy, Carp in early 2004 announced reduction of total manufacturing square footage by one-third and of the work force by another 15,000 to 20,000 or 20% over the next three years. These measures were taken to generate savings of $800 million to $1 billion by 2007.

Traditional Film Business

In its core photography business, Kodak increased its efforts in the markets of India, China, Russia, and Eastern Europa.[27] While it discontinued reloadable 35mm cameras in the US, Canada and Western Europe and the Advanced Photo System worlwide, it continued to make high performance 35mm and APS film worldwide. In China, Kodak's strategy was to focus more on the interests of first-time photography users. As a result, Kodak signed a 20-year agreement with Lucky Film Corp., the largest color film manufacturer of China, to acquire 20% of the company. Kodak paid $100 million for the deal and provided Lucky with technical assistance, equipment upgrades and training over time. Kodak also promised to respect the three principles of cooperation, allowing Lucky to maintain its brand, majority ownership and management control in the joint venture. According to Carp, in the long term, Kodak

> *". . . would rather consumers who come in at the low end have a good experience with photography. Eventually, we'll graduate them to Kodak product. If they come in, and their first experience is not a good one, they'll spend their money on something else."* [28]

In return, Lucky was to pay Kodak for the use of selected technology and give dividends on the share owned by Kodak. Through this deal, Kodak was able to stall Fuji in the Chinese market where it was the second largest player after Kodak. Also, for the high-end film market, Kodak introduced KODAK PLUS Digital Film, the KODAK High Definition One-Time-Use Camera and KODAK MAX Versatility Film, all of which offered increased image clarity, versatility and easy conversion to digital formats.

Annexure IV   US One-Time-Use Camera Sales (1987–2004)

Source: www.pmai.org.

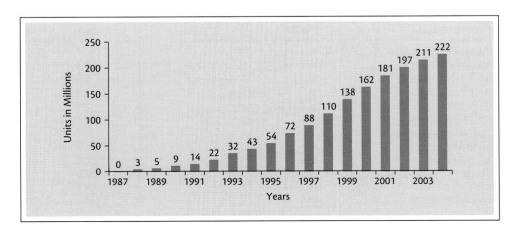

Digital Business
Image Capture

Growing its digital camera portfolio, Kodak also extended its line of EasyShare cameras by introducing six new models. These cameras were not only compact in size, but they also delivered good picture quality. In addition, they were compatible with the Kodak EasyShare printer dock. Through this feature, the digital camera could be directly connected to the printer and photos could be easily printed at home, with or without the computer. Prices of digital cameras ranged from $99.95 to $499.95.

Digital Service and Image Output

To enable customers to click and process pictures anytime and anywhere, Kodak introduced the kmobile service in partnership with Cingular Wireless, Nokia, and AT&T Wireless. Kodak's initiative was based on the increasing use of mobile phones for imaging and the forecast by market research firms that more than 97 million camera-enabled mobile phones would be in use by 2004. Through this service, the subscribers could sign up at www.kmobile.com to store, organize, share, and view their digital pictures and phone-captured video for a fee of $2.99 per month. According to Bernard Masson, president (D&FIS) and senior vice president, Kodak,

"As an example of Kodak's aggressive pursuit of the digital imaging market, these new services and agreements place Kodak at the forefront of the mobile imaging industry, with products and services that help people take, view, print and share pictures wherever they are, whenever they want. Whether online or through kiosks at retail locations, Kodak's mobile imaging services now give consumers places to print all their mobile images."[29]

Kodak, in partnerhip with Microsoft, introduced the television-friendly version of Ofoto to work, with Windows Media Center Edition 2004 PCs. This service enabled Ofoto members to view and share their online photos anytime on the TV set.

Further consolidating its market share in photofinishing paper, Kodak introduced KODAK Ultima Picture Paper with COLORLAST considered to be the world's longest lasting inkjet photo paper. Targeting the minilab (these were $100,000 photo processing machines that were placed behind store counters and could process 2,000 photos an hour) market,[30] Kodak in collaboration with Noritsu, maker of photofinishing equipments, introduced the QSS 3200 digital minilab portfolio. These minilabs were equally productive whether the input was from traditional film or digital media. The number of digital minilabs worldwide was estimated to increase from 61,900 in 2003 to 88,500 in 2004.[31] Kodak also introduced the KODAK Picture Maker G3 Film

Annexure V   The Various Camera Models Offered by the Top Seven Companies

Name	Type	Megapixels*	Price
Sony CyberShot DSC-F717	Advanced	5.02	$629.95
Sony CyberShot DSC-V1	Advanced	5	$444.00
Sony CyberShot DSC-T1	Ultra Compact	5	$547.98
Kodak EasyShare DX4530	Point and Shoot	5	$249.99
Kodak Easyshare CX6300	Point and Shoot	3.1	$157.99
Kodak EasyShare DX6400	Point and Shoot	4	$235.00
Canon EOS 10D	SLR	6.3	$1499.95
Canon Powershot A80	Advanced	4	$330.00
Canon Powershot A60	Point and Shoot	2	$159.94
Olympus C-5000 Zoom	Advanced	5	$269.99
Olympus C-750 Ultra Zoom	Extended Zoom	4	$437.99
Olympus E-1	SLR	5.5	$1799.00
Nikon D2H	SLR	4.1	$3199.95
Nikon D100	SLR	6.1	$1499.95
Nikon Coolpix 4300	Advanced	4	$339.95
Fuji FinePix S7000	Advanced	6.3	$550.00
Fuji FinePix S5000	Extended Zoom	3.1	$329.95
Fuji FinePix F410	Ultra Compact	3.1	$439.94
HP Photosmart 945	Extended Zoom	5.1	$449.00
HP Photosmart 735	Point and Shoot	3.2	$189.94
HP Photosmart 435	Point and Shoot	3.1	$121.72

*The picture quality or the resolution of a digital picture is measured in pixels. The higher the pixels the better is the print quality of the photos.
Source: www.digitalcamera-hq.com.

Exhibit 5 US Amateur
Film Sales, 1990–2004
(in millions of units)

Note: Includes one-time-use
camers.
Source: www.pmai.org.

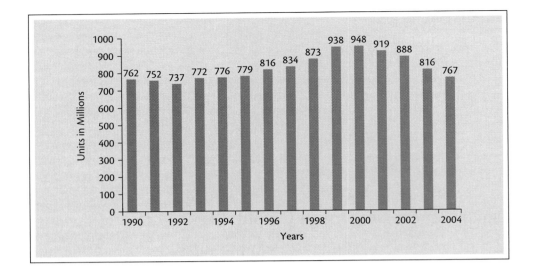

Processing Station, expanding its kiosk family to enable digitization of photos from a 35mm film roll (Exhibit 6).

Through all these innovations, Kodak tried to strengthen its position in the highly competitive digital product market and ward off competition not only from traditional competitors like Fuji, but also from the new world competitors like Sony, Hewlett Packard, and others (Exhibit 7, 8 and Annexure IV).

Competitive Scenario

Digital camera sales reached 50 million units worldwide in 2003 and it was forecasted that the sales would increase over the next four years at a CAGR of 15%. Europe was leading North America and Japan in this transition from film to digital. Worldwide, Sony had the largest share of the camera market with 18%, followed by Canon at 16%, Olympus at 13%, and Kodak at 12%.

On the other hand, to position itself in the photofinishing market, Kodak acquired the online photofinishing site, Ofoto, and developed Print@Kodak through which digital camera users could upload, store, and order print-outs of their pictures online. It was estimated that a total of 31 billion print-outs would be taken by 2006. However, Kodak faced stiff competition from online sites like clubphoto, Imagestation, shutterfly, and others.

Sony Corporation

Sony, headquartered in Tokyo, had sales of $22 billion for the third quarter ended December 31st 2003, up 0.7% from the previous quarter. The electronics segment that sold digital cameras and CCDs (charge coupled devices) recorded sales of $14

Exhibit 6   The Picture Maker Kiosk Family of Kodak

Picture Maker G3 Order Station LS: Allowed consumers to preview and select their film or digital images and print them to the retailer's on-site digital lab system by connecting directly to a digital minilab. One of Kodak's thermal printers could also be added to produce prints in seconds.

Picture Maker G3 Digital Station LS: Provided consumers with a quick and easy way to make prints from any digital camera card. This stand-alone kiosk allowed consumers to preview and select the pictures they wanted and enhance, edit and print images in minutes or write to a KODAK Picture CD. A smaller, 17-inch cabinet offered a more compact option for retailers.

Picture Maker G3 Print Station: Served as the full-service member of the Picture Maker family bringing all of the functionality of the Order and Digital Stations to the original Picture Maker. This kiosk was available in a 24-inch or 36-inch screen model, accepted original prints, compact disk, floppy and digital media and offered popular editing-enhancement features. The Picture Maker offered print sizes ranging from ID size to 8 x 10 and could easily print or write images to a KODAK Picture CD.

Picture Maker G3 Film Processing Station: Offered the first self-service kiosk system that connected to a KODAK Picture Maker G3 station to enable consumers to quickly print photo quality Kodak pictures in minutes from their 35mm film cameras. The Film Processing Station let consumers preview and select the pictures they wanted, zoom & crop, eliminate red-eye, adjust colors, and print the quantities and size of the pictures they wanted. Consumers received high quality prints and a KODAK Picture CD with an index print of each roll.

Source: www.kodak.com.

Exhibit 7 US Digital Camera Market, Q3 2003

	Shipments '000	Market Share, %	Growth from Q3 2002, %
Sony	800	22.4	11.1
Kodak	625	17.5	66.7
Canon	550	15.4	83.3
Olympus	414	11.6	13.8
Nikon	340	9.5	58.1
FujiFilm	270	7.5	−3.6
HP	245	6.8	113.0
Other	334	9.3	−85.6
Total	3578	100	39.2

Source: "Has Kodak missed the moment," *The Economist*, December 30, 2003.

billion, up 0.4% over the previous year, but its operating income dropped 39.7% to $493 million over the same period. The decline was due to restructuring expenses, a reduction in digital camera prices, and strengthening of the Yen against the US dollar. Sony had started a restructuring plan in 1999 to transform the company to have a highly profitable cost structure with an operating income margin of 10% by the year 2007.

Sony had a focused strategy to pursue growth in its Audio and Video category (a part of the electronics segment that manufactured imaging products like digital cameras and components like CCDs). The company strategically chose to create a more attractive product line up in high growth markets like digital cameras, Liquid Crystal Display and Plasma Display Panel.

In the US market, Sony's digital cameras included the Mavica and Cyber-shot brands with prices ranging from $200–$1,000, targeting both the amateur and the professional photographers. To make printing easy for the camera users, Sony along with Canon, Fuji, HP, Olympus, and Seiko Epson had developed the PictBridge which enabled a digital camera to directly connect to a printer through a USB port. Sony also introduced the Digital Photo Printer with built-in photo editing for easy photo printing without a PC.

Canon Inc.

Headquartered in Tokyo, Canon ended 2003 with sales of $29 billion, an increase of 8.8% over the previous year and earnings of $2.5 billion, an increase of 44%. Canon had a worldwide market share of 17% in digital cameras and it leveraged its expertise in optical and image processing activities to continually introduce new digital cameras. Canon introduced six new digital models in 2003–2004. Camera segment as a whole (digital still cameras, camcorders,

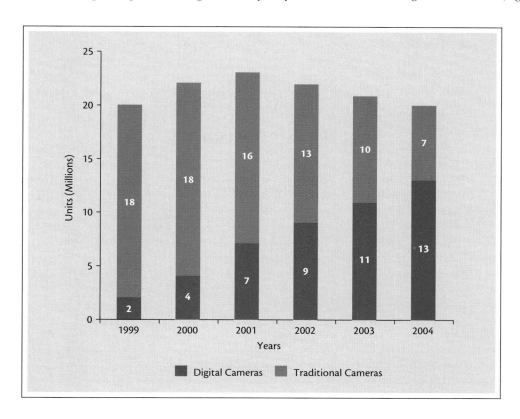

Exhibit 8 Camera Sales in the US

Source: http://gaiatec.com.

and film cameras) had sales growth of 34.5% totaling $6 billion. Operating profit from the segment reached $1 billion, an increase of 79.7%. All the digital cameras manufactured by Canon were compatible with the PictBridge standard. Canon was targeting the home printing market capitalizing on its strong position in both inkjet printer (worldwide share of 25%) and digital cameras.

Olympus

Headquartered in Tokyo, Olympus Optical Co. Ltd. had four major business groups—the imaging systems group which included the digital cameras, film cameras, recorders and magneto-optical disk drives, the medical systems group, the industrial systems group and the life sciences group which was formed in 2003. Olympus ended 2003 with operating income of $520 million on sales of $4.7 billion, an increase of 6.8% and 47.4% year-on year respectively.

Sales of its imaging group increased to $2 billion with an operating income of $152 million. Growth in the digital camera market was the main reason behind the company's strong performance with sales of digital cameras increasing 26.8% to $1.4 billion. The company's digital cameras faced losses till 2002 but by shifting manufacturing facilities from Japan to China, the company capitalized on lower manufacturing costs in China. Olympus' digital camera sales increased to 4.4 million units worldwide in 2003. To make sharing, editing, and printing of photos easier for the camera users, Olympus introduced the digital photo services by Ofoto (wholly owned Kodak subsidiary). Olympus also offered various printers for the camera users to print their digital images at home along with its Pictorico Paper. All its digital cameras had the PicBridge standard to make prints directly from the camera.

Nikon

Nikon Corporation's business was aligned by three business companies: the Imaging Company (digital cameras and digital imaging equipment business), Precision Equipment Company (IC steppers and LCD steppers), Instruments Company (microscopes, measuring equipment and inspection instrument) and others. Nikon's business strategy for the imaging company was centered on three areas:

- expand dominance in the digital SLR (Single Lens Reflex)[32] market;
- boost market share in the medium and popular-class consumer digital cameras; and
- cut costs by expanding overseas manufacturing (China) and promoting in-house production. Nikon had an 11% share of the 24.55 million shipment units of digital camera (sold in the Japanese market and exported by the Japanese manufacturers).

Fuji Film

Fuji Film ended 2003 with an operating income of $1.3 billion (a decrease of 5% over 2002) on sales of $20 billion (an increase of 4.4% over 2002) due to strong sales of digital cameras, digital minilabs, and other digital related products. To compete in the changing environment, Fuji Film adopted a "Hybrid Imaging" business strategy that integrated the latest electronics technologies with their traditional imaging expertise.

Fuji Film's business was divided into three segments: the Imaging Solutions segment that included film, film cameras, digital cameras, lab equipment, color paper, chemicals and services for photofinishing; the Information Solutions segment that included graphic arts systems products, medical imaging products, LCD materials and recording media; and the Document Solutions segment (which operated as a consolidated subsidiary of Fuji and Xerox, Fuji Xerox Co. Ltd) that comprised of copying machines, printers, fax machines, and consumables for document service applications in offices. The above three segments contributed 28.9%, 33.2% and 37.9% respectively to the total revenue.

Fuji introduced new digital camera models that incorporated the PictBridge standard for easy home printing. To complete its home printing portfolio, Fuji also marketed the Premium Plus Inkjet Photo Printer. Through Fuji's Web site, the camera users were also given an option to upload and store their pictures online.

On the photofinishing side, Fuji was the market leader in the digital minilab segment with its Digital Minilab Frontier series. FujiFilm was also making inroads in the kiosk market (Kodak had the largest market share), as retailers who purchased its Frontier minilabs were also buying its Aladdin and PrintPix kiosks.

Hewlett Packard

The company's products and services were categorized into the following major categories: the imaging and printing group which included the printer hardware, all-in-ones, digital cameras and scanners and associated supplies and accessories; the enterprise systems group which provided the key technology components of the IT infrastructure: the personal systems group that included desktop PCs, notebooks, workstations, smart handheld and personal devices, and the services.

The contribution of the printing and imaging group to the total revenue for 2003 was $21.2 billion. The corporate strategy of HP was to provide high tech products at low costs by leveraging its size and large product portfolio to provide the best experience to the customer. HP unplike Kodak, placed bets on the home digital darkroom and introduced products in every category to enable camera users to print pictures at

Exhibit 9   Leading Online Photofinishing Services

Name	Web site	Storage/Sharing	Cost/print-out (4 by 6) and CD
Ofoto	www.ofoto.com	Free	29 cents for digital print, $4 for film roll*
Club Photo	www.clubphoto.com	Free for 90 days. Thereafter charges $24.95 year	25 cents for digital print, $1 for a film roll. Album CD cost $7.95
Imagestation	www.imagestation.com	Free	24 cents for digital rent
MSN Photos	photos.msn.com	$10/month for non-subscribers	49 cents for digital print. Uses Print@FujiColor for its photofinishing services
Shutterfly	www.shutterfty.com	Free	25 cents to 39 cents for digital print, $3.99 for a film roll. Uses Fuji Paper
Snapfish	www.snapfish.com	Free	19 cents for digital print, $2.99 for a film roll. Uses Kodak paper

*Film roll photos were digitized and loaded to these Web sites. Both of Kodak's Web sites had Picture Perfect Picture Processing incorporated.

Source: www.forbes.com and respective web sites.

home. The Photosmart line of HP digital cameras featured printers with memory card slots and printer docks that allowed cameras to connect directly to the printer. In addition, HP was the market leader in inkjet printers, laser printers cartridges and printing paper, with margins of 65% on inkjet paper and ink and roughly 30% on laser printing supplies.[33]

The Online Photofinishing Sites

Online photofinishing sites were the online counterparts of the brick and mortar retailers, providing another link for consumers to take print-outs of their digital or film photos from the comfort of their home. In addition, these sites also provided free sharing and storage of photos online. They only charged for the prints customers wanted.

Kodak provided this service through Ofoto and the Kodak Picture Center. Kodak also had collaboration with sites like Snapfish to provide prints on its photo paper. Other online photofinishing sites included Sony's Imagestation, Club Photo, MSN Photos, all providing free uploading, sharing and editing of pictures and charging a fee for the printing and storage (Exhibit 9, 10, and 11).

Camera Phones

Another threat facing the entire digital still camera industry came from the introduction of new and trendy mobile camera phones. The sales of camera enabled phones had increased to 81 million units worldwide by the end of 2003, with half the global market for camera phones in Japan. However, the

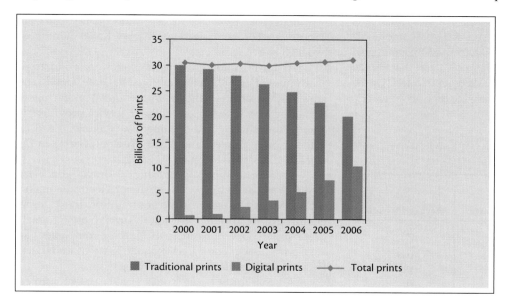

Exhibit 10   Print Volumes in Billions (Traditional vs. Digital Prints)

Source: www.pmai.org.

Exhibit 11 Volume of Digital Prints Made by Various Methods

Source: www.pmai.org.

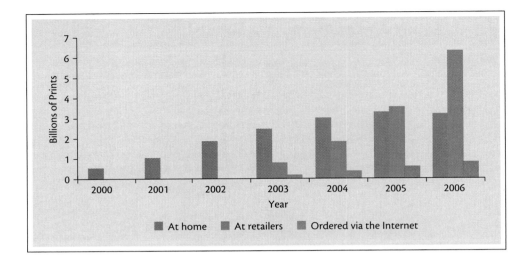

balance was expected to shift towards China from 2004. The global handset shipments for 2004 were estimated to be in the range of 580–585 million units, whereas the total camera phone shipments were expected to increase to 97 million units over the same period. It was expected that as the memory, battery life, and picture resolution of the mobile camera phones became better, these high-end phones could be in direct competition with the digital camera vendors like Kodak and Sony. Nokia had already introduced camera phones with 1 megapixel picture resolution in the market. The major players in 2003 in the camera phone market were NEC of Japan, Nokia, Samsung, Panasonic, and Sony Ericsson. (Exhibit 12)

Future Outlook

The photography industry worldwide had witnessed key changes in 2003. It was during this year that for the first time sales of digital cameras outnumbered that of the traditional ones in the US. It was estimated that about 53 million digital cameras would be sold worldwide in 2004 and that annual growth rate for the coming years would be around 15%. On the other hand, the film sales were expected to drop about 10–12%

Exhibit 12	Worldwide Camera Phone Market Share	
	Shipments (in millions of units)	**Market Share%**
NEC	13.1	26
Nokia	11	21.5
Samsung	10	19.6
Panasonic	9.2	18
Sony Ericsson	8.2	16

Source: www.msnbc.msn.com.

for 2003–2006. This situation posed great challenges for Kodak as it still relied on film products for about 60% of revenues.

Carp's restructuring plan in September 2003 aimed at diverting resources towards the digital businesses, and he hoped that the company's revenue would, as a result, increase to $16 billion by 2006. As of 2003, Kodak's sales from digital cameras were $75 million, with volumes increasing by 100%. In the US Kodak with an 18% market share, was behind Sony which had a share of 22%. However, worldwide, Kodak had a share of 12% in digital cameras as compared to Sony's 18%, Canon's 16% and Olympus 13%.

Carp employed various initiatives to build the digital business. He increased Kodak's stake in Chinon Industries (Japan) from 59% to 89% to speed up development of digital cameras and improve manufacturing margins. Kodak expanded its line of "EasyShare" cameras by introducing six new models that combined higher picture quality with compact design. For the professional market, Kodak introduced two high-end SLR cameras.

As for the photofinishing market, Kodak addressed all avenues of growth. It had invested in Ofoto, kiosks, and minilabs. To address the mobile camera phone users, Kodak tied up with various cellular service providers to offer picture sharing and printing. For example, it tied up with Cingular Wireless and AT&T Wireless offering in US, with NTT DoCoMo in Japan.

In spite of these opportunities, threats did exist. Kodak was competing with consumer electronic majors such as Sony, HP, etc. which were traditionally strong in manufacturing and had learned to survive on extremely slim margins. Operating margins for these companies varied from 5–10% as compared to about 30% that Kodak had got used to in its film business over the years.

Another threat facing Kodak was the patent infringement suit filed by Sony, alleging that Kodak had infringed on ten of its patents that covered basic technologies related to CCDs. Kodak had earlier filed a suit that Sony had infringed on 10 of its patents that covered various aspects of capturing, storing and displaying digital images. While the outcome of the lawsuit was uncertain, Kodak stood to gain if it won the battle. Winning the case would help Kodak charge licensing fees from Sony for every unit of camera sold. Kodak already had licensing agreement with about 10 digital camera makers, which included Olympus, Sanyo, etc.

Yet another problem facing Kodak was the increase in demand for mobile camera phones. The sales of camera phones had increased to 57 million units worldwide by the end of 2003 and were expected to reach to 97 million units by 2004. It was estimated that over the period of 2003–2006, camera phones would reduce sales of digital cameras by 7.7% and result in the decrease of the shipment value of more than $2.7 billion.

In the traditional film segment, Kodak focused on high value films such as the KODAK PLUS Digital Film and the KODAK MAX Versatility film and pinned its hopes on emerging markets such as India, Russia and China to drive film revenue growth. In China, Kodak had a 20% stake in Lucky Film, the largest film manufacturer in the country. However, Kodak faced a setback when Lucky reported a 36% decline in its profits ($9.67 million) for the year 2003 over the previous year due to a combination of factors like decline in tourism (because of the SARS scare), competition from contraband brands and increasing use of digital cameras.

In addition to these initiatives, Carp also announced further cost cutting measures. He planned to reduce total manufacturing square footage by one-third and of the work force by another 15,000 to 20,000 over the next three years. These measures were expected to generate savings of $800 million to $1 billion by 2007.

Even with these strategies in place, there were mixed responses from industry experts. One expert commented:

". . . . . . I'm surprised that they are acting as quickly as they have. If they can get this cash cow film to generate enough profits to sustain the growth that they want to have on the digital side that may work." [34]

While another said:

"I think the long-term trend, that these guys are on the wrong side of the fence, continues, they have legacy issues that a lot of their competitors don't have." [35]

Additional Readings & References

1. Eisenstodt, Gale and Feldman Amy, "Sharply focused," www.forbes.com, December 24, 1990.
2. Alex Taylor III, "Higher rewards in lowered goals," www.fortune.com, March 8, 1993.
3. Loomis J. Carol, "Managing the battle to shape up Kodak," www.fortune.com, May 31, 1993.
4. Chakravarty, N. Subrata and Feldman, Amy, "The road not taken," www.forbes.com, September 30, 1993.
5. Nulty, Peter, "Kodak grabs for growth again," www.fortune.com, May 16, 1994.
6. Nulty, Peter, "Digital Imaging had better boom before Kodak film busts," www.fortune.com, May 1, 1995.
7. Koprowski, Gene, "George Fisher," www.forbes.com, June 5, 1995.
8. Rotenier, Nancy, "Back in focus," www.forbes.com, January 1, 1996.
9. Grant, Linda, "The Bears back off Kodak," www.fortune.com, June 24, 1996.
10. Chakravarty, N. Subrata, "How an outsider's vision saved Kodak," www.forbes.com, January 13, 1997.
11. Grant, Linda, "Can Fischer Focus Kodak?" www.fortune.com, January 13, 1997.
12. Smith, Geoffrey, Wolverton, Brad and Palmer, Ann Therese, "A Dark Kodak moment," www.businessweek.com, August 4, 1997.
13. Smith, Geoffrey and Symonds, William, "Can George Fischer fix Kodak," www.businessweek.com, October 20, 1997.
14. Grant, Linda, "What's ailing Kodak? Fuji," www.fortune.com, October 27, 1997.
15. Smith, Geoffrey, "Kodak's focus may be too narrow," www.businessweek.com, November 24, 1997.
16. Grant, Linda, "Why Kodak still isn't fixed," www.fortune.com, May 11, 1998.
17. Chakravarty, N. Subrata and Gordon, Joanne, "Vindication," www.forbes.com, September 7, 1998.
18. Himowitz J. Michael, "Kodak's cool digital pix site," www.fortune.com, September 28, 1998.
19. Symonds, William and Smith, Geoffrey, "Fischer's photo finish," www.businessweek.com, June 21, 1999.
20. Webb, Chanoine, "The picture just keeps getting darker at Kodak," www.fortune.com, June 21, 1999.
21. Smith, Geoffrey, "Film vs Digital: Can Kodak build a bridge?" www.businessweek.com, September 2, 1999.

22. Bruce, Upbin, "Kodak's digital moment," www.forbes.com, August 21, 2000.
23. Tsao, Amy, "Kodak: Not enough positive development," www.businessweek.com, November 26, 2001.
24. Smith, Geoffrey, and Faith, Keenan, "Kodak is the picture of digital success," www.businessweek.com, January 4, 2002.
25. Serwer, Andy, "Kodak in the noose," www.fortune.com, February 4, 2002.
26. Tsao, Amy, "Kodak's place in the big picture," www.businessweek.com, January 8, 2003.
27. Keenan, Faith and Schottenstein, Cathy, "Big yellow's digital dilemma," www.businessweek.com, March 24, 2003.
28. Robinson, Peter, "Kodak like IBM and Polaroid before it, faces battle to adapt," www.detnews.com, September 29, 2003.
29. "Kodak's profit down 63 percent," The Associated Press, October 28, 2003.
30. Ferrari, Alicia, "The Push for more digital photo prints," www.forbes.com, October 30, 2003.
31. Patsuris, Penelope, "The fight ahead for Fuji," www.forbes.com, October 31, 2003.
32. Symonds, C. William, "The Kodak revolt is short sighted," www.businessweek.com, November 3, 2003.
33. Patsuris, Penelope, "Kodak polishes its (Mobile) Image," www.forbes.com, November 12, 2003.
34. "Has Kodak missed the moment," The Economist, December 30, 2003.
35. Rand, Ben, "Kodak's carp: No time to be timid," www.democratandchronicle.com, January 23, 2004.
36. Dobbin, Ben, "Kodak focus on digital", www.twincities.com, January 23, 2004.
37. "Kodak sues Sony oper patents," New York Times News Service, March 11, 2004.
38. "Camera phones intensity competition in Asian mobile market," www.channelnewsasia.com, March 14, 2004.
39. "Lucky Film net profit down 36%," Asia intelligence wire, March 29, 2004.
40. Wakabayashi, Daisuke and Layne, Nathan, "Sony sues Kodak over digital camera patents," www.finance.yahoo.com, April 1, 2004.
41. "Sony still in top on digital camera market," www.finance.yahoo.com, April 2, 2004.
42. Cary, Peter, Hedges J. Stephen, Hawkins, Dana and Headden, Susan, "Loser layoffs," www.bus.colorado.edu.
43. Wenhao, Zhang, "Is Kodak playing Santa Claus," www.caijing.com.

Web sites

1 www.dpreview.com
2 www.pmai.org
3 www.photomarketing.com
4 www.gaiatec.com
5 www.digitalcamera-hq.com
6 www.photo-news.com
7 www.ce.org
8 www.photoreporter.com
9 www.infotrends-rgi.com
10 www.kellogg.nwu.edu
11 www.seyboldreport.com
12 www.idc.com

Notes

1 www.kodak.com.
2 Kodak controlled two-thirds of the film market in the US. Worldwide Kodak's share of the film market was 40%.
3 Antonio Perez, the President and COO of Kodak, served as President and CEO of HP's inkjet imaging business. During the five years in which Perez led the business, the installed base of inkjet printers grew from 17 million to 100 million worldwide.
4 Kodak's share price had dwindled from a high of $94 in early 1997 to $27 on the eve of this announcement, As of April 2003, Kodak with a market cap of $7 billion has been delisted from the DJIA.
5 Robinson, Peter, "Kodak like IBM and Polaroid before it, faces battle to adapt," www.detnews.com, September 29, 2003.
6 Symonds, William C, "The Kodak revolt is short sighted," www.businessweek.com, November 3, 2003.

7   Before this invention, the wet plates were used in photography. These had to be coated with chemicals, exposed at once and developed while still wet. Dry plates, on the other hand, could be exposed and developed at the photographer's convenience.

8   With Microsoft, Kodak developed software that would help computer users to touch up, crop, and otherwise manipulate photos—a digital darkroom. Except for the one with Microsoft, all other alliances fell apart.

9   Koprowski, Gene, "George Fisher," www.forbes.com, June 5, 1995.

10 The camera stored pictures on conventional film rather than compact disks and allowed picture takers to switch between three different size photographs on the same roll, it also imprinted digital information about the kind of shot, lighting conditions and the date onto the film, so that photo-finishing machines could process the film correctly.

11 Home digital darkrooms enabled the consumer to make prints from digital photos at home. This was made possible by uploading digital photos to the PC, manipulating them with software and printing them through an inkjet printer on a photo paper.

12 With kiosk-based digital imaging, customers could take their digital media, memory stick or card and insert it in the kiosk, manipulate the required photos and take a print-out through the installed printers.

13 Pictures could be taken by digital cameras—or by standard cameras on traditional film and then scanned into computers or onto CDs—for manipulating, storage, retrieval, and printing.

14 Through this service, customers, for an extra five or six dollars, could have their photos digitized and scanned from a negative to be posted at www.kodak.photonet.com— PhotoNet's Web site. These images could then be downloaded on the PC, sent to others for viewing via e-mail or used to make electronic greeting cards.

15 The picture quality or the resolution of a digital camera is measured in pixels. The higher the pixels, the better is the print quality of the photos.

16 Bruce, Upbin, "Kodak's digital moment," www.forbes.com, August 21, 2000.

17 op. cit, "Kodak's digital moment."

18 op. cit, "Kodak's digital moment."

19 Geoffrey, Smith and Faith, Keenan, "Kodak is the picture of digital success," www.businessweek.com, January 4, 2002.

20 ibid.

21 ibid. By 2001 only 15 to 20% of the digital photos were being printed.

22 ibid.

23 Kiosks were paced at $15,000 a piece and generated $200 million in sales by 1999.

24 51% of Kodak's revenue came from outside the US.

25 www.kodak.com.

26 www.dpreview.com.

27 Kodak's worldwide market share for film sales was 40% compared to Fuji's 35%.

28 www.Photomarketing.com.

29 www.kodak.com.

30 Fuji was the market leader in this segment with 5,000 labs in place which was equivalent to 60% of the US market in 2003.

31 The total number of minilabs operating worldwide was forecasted to increase from 298,800 to 355,700.

32 SLR cameras are advanced cameras that provide various options to the photographer for precisely controlling the focus and composition of a picture, selecting and changing lenses, choosing film exposures from a selection of automatic and semi-automatic light metering modes and manually adjusting the shutter and lens openings to shut. These cameras are used by most professional photographers, camera hobbyists, and photography students. Another type of cameras are the point and shoot cameras. These are compact in size, affordable and easy to use as most of the functions are automated.

33 Alica, Ferrari, "The Push for more digital photo prints," www.forbes.com, October 30, 2003.

34 Rand, Ben, "Kodak's Carp: No time to be timid,"; www.democratandchronicle.com, January 23, 2004.

35 ibid.

Case 2–5: Nike, Inc. in 1998*

In the late 1990s, Nike, Inc., was considered by many to be the most powerful and influential force in sports. So popular was its Air Jordan brand, for example, that the company refrained from introducing new products on school days in an effort to combat truancy. One journalist concluded that it was "difficult to locate a three-year-old—or, for that matter, a Trobriand Islander or an Inuit hunter—who can't tell you that Jordan is a Nike man."[1]

As 1998 drew to a close, however, the company's vulnerability was exposed. Nike's stock had fallen 20 percent in the previous year (see Exhibit 1). Phil Knight, the firm's founder and largest shareholder, had experienced an estimated decline in value of $700 million of his Nike stock. Nike faced multiple challenges in 1998. The Asian economic collapse had led to plummeting sales growth in a region Nike had counted on for high growth. Changes in fashion also threatened the firm's core athletic footwear business as many so-called Generation X consumers were choosing "brown shoes" such as hiking boots over sports shoes. Public relations had also become a problem for Nike as its image had been attacked on several fronts. In some circles Nike had become, in Knight's words, the "great satan [of American Capitalism] . . . synonymous with slave wages, forced overtime and arbitrary abuse."[2] Garry Troudeau had used his Doonesbury cartoon column to criticize Nike for its overseas labor practices.

Faced with these challenges, Nike's managers confronted important decisions about how to turn the company's performance around. Did Nike need to reinvent itself again as it had in the 1980s? Clearly, one of Knight's favorite mottos, "There is no finish line," was applicable to Nike's circumstances in 1998.

Nike's History

The Nike story began when Phil Knight and Bill Bowerman met at the University of Oregon in 1957. Knight was a member of the Oregon track team which Bowerman coached. Both Knight and Bowerman shared a dissatisfaction with the mostly German running shoes that were available at the time. After leaving Oregon, Knight went on to receive an MBA at Stanford. While at Stanford, Knight developed, for a class assignment, a business plan for how low-priced, well-merchandised shoes from Japan could end German domination of running shoes in the United States. After receiving his MBA, Knight traveled to Japan to explore the possibility of importing running shoes. Onitsuka Tiger, a Japanese manufacturer of athletic shoes, agreed to supply Knight. When asked by Tiger what firm he represented, Knight quickly made up a name, Blue Ribbon Sports, thus giving a name to his new venture.

Blue Ribbon Sports enjoyed modest success in its early years. Knight started Blue Ribbon Sports by importing his first shoes—200 pairs—from Onitsuka Tiger in late 1962. In 1964, Knight and Bowerman both contributed $500 and continued importing shoes from Tiger. In the early days of Blue Ribbon Sports, Knight maintained a job as a Price Waterhouse accountant. On the side, he sold track shoes out of the trunk of his Plymouth Valiant at local track meets. Blue Ribbon Sports sold 1,300 pairs of shoes in 1964 for $8,000 in revenue. In 1968, one of Bowerman's early designs, the Cortez, became one of Tiger's top-selling models. By 1969, with sales nearing $300,000, Knight was able to quit his job and focus his efforts full-time on his fledgling shoe company.

Tiger and Nike split in a dispute over distribution rights in 1972. Having lost their Japanese supplier, Knight and Bowerman decided to design and distribute their own line of shoes. Blue Ribbon Sports launched the Nike brand at the 1972 Olympic trials. The name Nike was taken from the Greek goddess of victory while the swoosh emblem was designed by a student for $35. Knight and Bowerman persuaded some runners in the 1972 Olympic trials to wear their shoes. A major breakthrough occurred the next year when the legendary distance runner, Steve Prefontaine, became the first major track star to wear Nike shoes. Nike also achieved its first major technical innovation in the early 1970s. Bowerman designed the waffle sole when he used his waffle iron to mold a piece of rubber for a sole. The shoe offered greater traction and cushioning than other shoes. The introduction of the waffle trainer coincided with a jogging boom in the United States. By 1974, the waffle-soled shoes became the top-selling training shoe in the United States. Nike gained nearly 50 percent of the rapidly growing U.S. market for running shoes by the time of its first public stock offering in December 1980.

In the early 1980s, Nike lost its number-one position in the U.S. athletic shoe market. Reebok capitalized on the boom in aerobics with its aerobic shoe lines, to overtake Nike. Nike responded with a reemphasis on technical innovation, and by moving beyond running shoes to other sports shoes. Nike introduced what was probably the most successful athletic shoe in history—the Air Jordan—in 1985. Another highly successful move beyond running shoes was the first cross-trainer shoes in 1987. That year, Nike also introduced

*This case was written by William Hesterly for the purpose of classroom discussion.

Exhibit 1   Nike Financial Summary

FINANCIAL HISTORY

(in millions, except per shared data and financial ratios)

	98	97	96	95	94	93	92	91	90	89
YEAR ENDED MAY 31										
Revenues	$9,553.1	$9,186.5	$6,470.6	$4,760.8	$3,789.7	$3,931.0	$3,405.2	$3,003.6	$2,235.2	$1,710.8
Gross margin	3,487.6	3,683.5	2,563.9	1,895.6	1,488.2	1,544.0	1,316.1	1,153.1	851.1	636.0
Gross margin %	36.5%	40.1%	39.6%	39.8%	39.3%	39.3%	38.7%	38.4%	38.1%	37.2%
Restructuring charge	129.9	–	–	–	–	–	–	–	–	–
Net income	399.6	795.8	553.2	399.7	298.8	365	329.2	287.0	243.0	167.0
Basic earnings per common share	1.38	2.76	1.93	1.38	1.00	1.20	1.09	0.96	0.81	0.56
Diluted earnings per common share	1.35	2.68	1.88	1.36	0.99	1.18	1.07	0.94	0.80	0.56
Average common shares outstanding	288.7	288.4	286.6	289.6	298.6	302.9	301.7	300.4	299.1	297.7
Diluted average common shares outstanding	295	297	293.6	294	301.8	308.3	306.4	304.3	302.7	300.6
Cash dividends declared per common share	0.46	0.38	0.29	0.24	0.20	0.19	0.15	0.13	0.10	0.07
Cash flow from operations	517.5	323.1	339.7	254.9	576.5	265.3	435.8	11.1	127.1	169.4
Price range of common stock										
High	64.125	76.375	52.063	20.156	18.688	22.563	19.344	13.625	10.375	4.969
Low	37.750	47.875	19.531	14.063	10.781	13.750	8.781	6.500	4.750	2.891
AT MAY 31										
Cash and equivalents	$108.6	$445.4	$262.1	$216.1	$518.8	$291.3	$260.1	$119.8	$90.4	$85.7
Inventories	1,396.6	1,338.6	931.2	629.7	470.0	593	471.2	586.6	309.5	222.9
Working capital	1,828.8	1964.0	1,259.9	938.4	1,208.4	1,165.2	964.3	662.6	561.6	419.6
Total assets	5,397.4	5361.2	3,951.6	3,142.7	2,373.8	2,186.3	1,871.7	1,707.2	1,093.4	824.2
Long-term debt	379.4	296.0	9.6	10.6	12.4	15	69.5	30	25.9	34.1
Redeemable Preferred Stock	0.3	0.3	0.3	0.3	0.3	0.3	0.3	0.3	0.3	0.3
Common shareholders' equity	3261.6	3155.9	2,431.4	1,964.7	1,740.9	1,642.8	1,328.5	1,029.6	781.0	558.6
Year-end stock price	46.000	57.500	50.188	19.719	14.750	18.125	14.500	9.938	9.813	4.750
Market capitalization	13,201.1	16,633.0	14,416.8	5,635.2	4,318.8	5,499.3	4,379.6	2,993.0	2,942.7	1,417.4
FINANCIAL RATIOS										
Return on equity	12.5%	28.5%	25.2%	21.6%	17.7%	24.5%	27.9%	31.7%	36.3%	34.5%
Return on assets	7.4%	17.1%	15.6%	14.5%	13.1%	18.0%	18.4%	20.5%	25.3%	21.8%
Inventory turns	4.4	4.8	5	5.2	4.3	4.5	3.9	4.1	5.2	5.1
Current ratio at May 31	2.1	2.1	1.9	1.8	3.2	3.6	3.3	2.1	3.1	2.9
Current ratio at May 31 (diluted)	34.1	21.5	16.6	14.5	14.9	15.3	13.5	10.5	12.2	8.6
GEOGRAPHIC REVENUES										
United States	$5,452.5	$5,529.1	$3,964.7	$2,997.9	$2,432.7	$2,528.8	$2,270.9	$2,141.5	$1,755.5	$1,362.2
Europe	2,143.7	1,833.7	1,334.3	980.4	927.3	1085.7	919.8	664.7	334.3	241.4
Asia/Pacific	1,255.7	1,245.2	735.1	515.6	283.4	178.2	75.7	56.2	29.3	32
Canada, Latin America, and other	701.2	578.5	436.5	266.9	146.3	138.3	138.8	141.2	116.1	75.2
Total Revenues	$9,553.1	$9,186.5	$6,470.6	$4,760.8	$3,789.7	$3,931.0	$3,405.2	$3,003.6	$2,235.2	$1,710.8

what was perhaps its most important technical innovation— the air sole. Air soles, invented by former NASA engineer Frank Rudy, placed pressurized gas into urethane bags. When placed in a shoe's sole these bags compressed on impact to absorb shock, then quickly rebounded to their original shape in time for the next impact. Air soles could be configured for different sports and athletes' needs by modifying the placement, amount of pressure, and shape of the gas-filled bags. The air sole reestablished Nike as the technological leader in athletic footwear. The company also placed an unprecedented focus on advertising. Nike's "Just Do It" ad campaign debuted in 1988. The combined effect of the technical innovation, new advertising emphasis, and the broadened product line was a surge in sales as revenues almost doubled within two years.

After 1990, Nike's success continued as it gained momentum in international markets (see Exhibits 2 and 3) at the same time it expanded into sports equipment and increased its penetration in sports apparel (see Exhibit 4). In 1991, Nike reported that international sales had increased 80 percent to $860 million and a year later passed the $1 billion mark in international revenue. In 1992, Nike also opened its first NIKETOWN. NIKETOWNs were upscale retail stores in major cities. While some retailers feared that NIKETOWNs would have an adverse impact on sales, Nike managers contended that NIKETOWN was intended to promote its brand name more than to directly sell products. One journalist

Exhibit 2   Nike Footwear and Apparel Revenues by Geographic Region (in millions)

	1995	1996	1997	1998
Europe	$969	$1,293	$1,789	$2,063
Asia-Pacific	518	731	1,242	1,244
Americas	230	311	447	589
U.S.A.	2,278	3,604	5,160	5,055

reported that, within a few weeks of opening, the Chicago NIKETOWN had usurped the Lincoln Park Zoo and the Shedd Aquarium as the most popular tourist attraction in Chicago.[3] The year 1992 also marked another potentially important strategic move for the comapany: It moved into sports equipment with its acquisition of hockey equipment manufacturer Bauer. The Bauer acquisition was Nike's first move into sports equipment.

The Market for Sports Footwear and Apparel in 1998

Athletic footwear was considered a mature industry in 1998. Wholesale sales were greater than $9 billion in 1995. Overall industry growth had been a moderate 6 percent to 9 percent for most of the 1990s. Some of the largest firms in the industry,

Exhibit 3   Total Revenue, Operating Income, and Assets by Geographic Region

Revenues			
United States	$5,452.5	$5,529.1	$3,964.7
Europe	2,143.7	1,833.7	1,334.3
Asia/Pacific	1,255.7	1,245.2	535.1
Americas	701.2	578.5	436.5
Total Revenues	$9,553.1	$9,186.5	$6,470.6
Operating Income			
United States	598.3	969.0	697.1
Europe	185.6	170.6	145.7
Asia/Pacific	(34.6)	175.0	123.6
Americas	140.5	71.3	55.9
Less corporate interest and other income (expense) and other eliminations	(236.8)	(90.7)	(123.2)
Total Operating Income	$653.0	$1,295.2	$899.1
Assets			
United States	$3,115.2	$2,994.0	$2,372.0
Europe	1,409.4	1,272.9	941.5
Asia/Pacific	480.7	665.8	386.5
Americas	372.7	328.7	188.8
Total identifiable assets	5,378.0	5,261.4	3,888.8
Corporate cash and eliminations	19.4	99.8	62.8
Total Assets	$5,397.4	$5,361.2	$3,951.6

Exhibit 4   Nike Sales by Broad Product Areas, 1996–1998 (in thousands)

	1998	1997	1996
United States footwear	$3,498.7	$3,753.5	$2,772.5
United States apparel	1,556.3	1,406.6	831.3
Total United States	5,055.0	5,160.1	3,603.8
Non-U.S. footwear	2,460.3	2,391.0	1,682.3
Non-U.S. apparel	1,435.5	1,086.9	651.4
Total Non-U.S.	3,895.8	3,477.9	2,333.7
Other and other brands	602.3	548.5	533.1
Total Nike	$9,553.1	$9,186.5	$6,470.6

Source: Annual Report.

such as Nike, Reebok, and Adidas, had experienced much faster growth, as had some small-niche producers.

A number of designers planned to introduce new lines of athletic footwear in 1997 and 1998. Tommy Hilfiger, Ralph Lauren, Calvin Klein, Donna Karan, and Nautica all were expected to introduce shoes aimed at fashion-conscious leisure shoe wearers.[4]

Nike and other major athletic shoemakers saw shoe sales suffer in 1998 at the same time that smaller competitors flourished. Reebok was expected to post a 47 percent decline in earnings while other established companies such as Converse and Fila anticipated losses. Smaller competitors such as Candie's and Global Sports expected gains of 83 percent and 67 percent, respectively. Analysts pointed to a possible shift in consumer tastes as one reason for the lackluster performance of the established firms compared to smaller competitors in the industry. Brian Eisenbarth, an analyst for Collins, Inc., said, "There appears to be a rebellion going on among teens and preteens against the big traditional franchises of the industry, along with their high prices. Generally any shoe priced over $80 is having a hard time leaving the store."[5]

The increasing popularity of "brown" shoes was another blow to athletic shoemakers (see Exhibit 5). Brown footwear included shoes such as Hush Puppies, Timberland, and work or hiking boots. One estimate suggested that the shift to brown shoes had cut 20 percent out of athletic shoe sales.[6] The threat of brown shoes to athletic footwear was heightened because a high percentage (one industry rule of thumb was 80 percent)[7] of athletic shoes were not bought for any athletic purpose.

Another trend observed by industry analysts was a shift away from basketball shoes. Firms such as Converse and Fila, which had narrower product lines and were thus more dependent on basketball shoes, were more adversely affected than firms with more diverse product lines such as Nike and Reebok. One exception to the downward trend in basketball shoe sales was Nike's new Brand Jordan. The Brand Jordan shoes had enjoyed a successful brand launch.

In contrast to larger shoe companies, smaller-niche competitors such as Vans, Airwalk, Etnies, and DC had revenue increases ranging from 20 percent to 50 percent. Candie's was another firm experiencing an upsurge in sales. With an emphasis on women ages 19 to 30 and shoes that sold for an average of $35 a pair, Candie's sales had increased 39 percent over 1997. Global Sports was another competitor that had experienced high growth. Its growth was attributed to its success in women's shoes and Yukon, a lower-priced line of outdoor footwear.

Perhaps the biggest beneficiary of the shift in consumer tastes was Vans Inc. Sales for Vans were up 21 percent in late 1998. The main appeal of Vans' shoes was to "the anti-establishment crowd looking for something other than traditional sneakers."[8] Its shoes were particularly popular with stunt bikers and boarders. Boarders participated in various sports based on boards: skateboards, snowboards, wakeboards, and allterrrain boards. In 1998, it

Exhibit 5   Men's and Women's Shoe Sales by Type

Type	Million Pairs		Million $	
	1991	1995	1991	1995
Dress	234.1	180.1	$8,142	$6,396
Casual	178.2	167.6	5,065	5,149
Sandals	63.9	96.4	1,375	1,923
Athletic/Tennis	367.7	350.8	11,702	11,408
Work/Duty	35.9	45.6	1,799	2,400
Western/casual boot	12.4	15.1	921	955
Sport/hiking boot	6.1	35.1	320	1,444
Other	73.8	79.7	2,688	2,833
Total	972.1	970.4	$32,012	$32,510

Source: Standard & Poor's Industry Survey, "Apparel and Footwear," August 21, 1997.

was estimated that there were 6.5 million skateboarders, 4.5 million snowboarders, 1.5 million stunt bikers, 2 million wakeboarders, and 1 million allterrain boarders. These figures were expected to expand anywhere from double to six times in the three years following 1998.[9] Boarding was characterized by a strong anti-establishment culture. And, for many boarders, Nike represented the establishment. Some boarders wore buttons with the slogan "Don't Do It" in a clear contradiction of Nike's famous slogan.[10] Another sign of the anti-establishment ethos of the board sports participants was that many top snowboarders skipped the 1998 Olympics in Nagano, Japan.

Vans shoes were not only more appealing to the boarding set for cultural reasons; they were also cheaper. Vans shoes averaged $45 to $50 in price compared to $70 to $75 for Nike. Vans also did not have to participate in large endorsements. One of its top athletes, street luger Lee Dancie, was paid only $100,000 a year to wear Vans. Many Vans endorsers reported that they had refused offers from larger companies.[11] Vans sponsored alternative sporting events in snowboarding, skateboarding, and stunt bike exhibitions.

Another area affected by changes in consumer tastes was the sale of tennis shoes. Fewer people were playing tennis than in earlier decades. The U.S. tennis association estimated that there were 34 million tennis players over the age of 12 in 1974 but only 19.5 million in 1996.[12] Nike's global sales of tennis shoes grew 11.5 percent in 1998 to 15 million pairs. In 1998, Nike began an ad campaign aimed at attracting tennis players back to the game. The television ads sought to remind viewers in an offbeat way about what they liked about tennis.

The largest competitors in athletic footwear were Nike, Reebok, Adidas, and Fila. They were joined by a number of other firms such as Converse, New Balance, and others (see Exhibit 6). For the most part, these second-tier firms had narrower product lines than the top four. For example, Converse focused more on basketball shoes while ASICS tended to specialize in running shoes. There were also a number of smaller-niche firms in athletic footwear in 1998. For example, Vans, Etnies, and DC focused on the market for skateboarders and other "boarders."

Reebok was Nike's largest U.S. competitor with over $3.6 billion in sales in 1997. Like Nike, Reebok was experiencing a significant downturn in results. Earnings were down 49 percent for the first quarter of 1998 and both prices and orders had declined, suggesting a dark outline for the next year. Reebok sold shoes under the Reebok brand name as well as under the Rockport, Greg Norman, and Ralph Lauren Footwear brands. Rumors floated in the 1998 that Reebok was a likely acquisition target for another consumer products company.[13]

Next to Reebok, Nike's largest competitors were the European companies Adidas-Salomon AG and Fila Holding S.P.A. The German-based Adidas had once dominated much of the athletic footwear market in Europe and North America. Following the 1972 Olympics, however, Adidas had lost its leading position in North America to Nike and Reebok. In 1997, Adidas had apparel and footwear sales of over $3.7 billion. Adidas-Salomon was formed out of Adidas' $1.4 billion purchase of Salomon, the French maker of skis and other sporting goods including Taylor Made golf clubs. Adidas-Salomon had set a goal to become the world's second-largest sports company after Nike. The merger with Salomon had not gone as smoothly as hoped, but analysts believed that, except for Taylor Made, the company was positioned well for 1998. The Italian firm Fila was the fourth-largest athletic footwear maker behind Nike, Reebok, and Adidas with 1996 sales of $1.2 billion. Sales had flattened for Fila in 1997 and 1998 after a

Exhibit 6   Branded U.S. Athletic Footwear Market (in millions of dollars)

Brand	Sales			Market Share (%)		
	1994	**1995**	**1996**	**1994**	**1995**	**1996**
1. Nike	2,017	2,529	3,261	30.8	37.4	43.4
2. Reebok	1,410	1,405	1,210	21.5	20.8	16.1
3. Fila	291	380	575	4.4	5.6	7.7
4. Adidas	331	355	390	5.1	5.2	5.2
5. Keds	305	245	200	4.7	3.6	2.7
6. New Balance	130	151	200	2.0	2.2	2.7
7. Converse	298	208	190	4.6	3.1	2.5
8. Airwalk	102	126	158	1.6	1.9	2.1
9. L.A. Gear	296	193	140	4.5	2.9	1.9
10. ASICS	187	122	131	2.9	1.8	1.7

Source: Standard & Poor's Industry Survey, "Apparel and Footwear," August 21, 1997; Sporting Goods Intelligence.

period of rapid growth. Fila was attempting to shed its fashion reputation in favor of one rooted more in performance. Baketball and tennis shoes were the products for which Fila was best known. As a result, the company had been severely affected by the downturn in basketball shoes.

Nike in 1998

Although Nike had traditionally been identified as a shoe company, the firm had consistently extended its scope over its history. When growth had slowed during 1993–1994, Nike made a greater commitment to product areas beyond shoes. Phil Knight maintained, "We decided we're a sports company, not just a shoe company."[14] Design, development, and worldwide marketing of high-quality footwear, apparel, equipment, and accessory products were Nike's principal business activities. Its internal emphasis was on design, development, and marketing rather than manufacturing. Nike did virtually no manufacturing. Instead, essentially all of its products were manufactured by independent contractors. Most footwear products were produced outside the United States, while apparel products were produced both in the United States and abroad.

Products

Nike athletic footwear products were designed primarily for specific athletic use, although a large percentage of the products were worn for casual or leisure purposes. The company placed considerable emphasis on high-quality construction and innovative design. Running, basketball, children's, cross-training, and women's shoes were the top-selling products in 1998 and were expected to continue to lead in sales for the foreseeable future. Training, running, basketball, kids', and Brand Jordan were the largest product categories for Nike, accounting for 80 percent of sales in fiscal 1998. Overall, U.S. footwear had decreased by 7 percent in revenue in 1998 and 3 percent in pairs sold. Nike had enjoyed considerable success in establishing its shoes in other sports beyond running and basketball. Shoes designed for outdoor activities, tennis, golf, soccer, baseball, football, bicycling, volleyball, wrestling, cheerleading, aquatic activities, and other athletic and recreational uses contributed substantially to Nike's sales. Golf and soccer, particularly, were bright spots, with sales increases in 1998 of 71 percent and 74 percent, but outdoor and tennis sales had dropped by 7 percent and 14 percent, respectively.

Apparel. Although Nike had established itself by selling shoes, active sports apparel as well as athletic bags and accessory items were increasingly important to its sales. Apparel and accessories were designed to complement Nike's athletic footwear products; they featured the same trademarks and were sold through the same marketing and distribution channels. In some instances, Nike sought to bundle apparel and footwear into collections. For example, the Air Jordan model of basketball shoes would be coupled with apparel. Apparel sales had increased for nearly all categories in 1998. Training apparel was up 10 percent, accessories 6 percent, kids' 41 percent, T-shirts 5 percent, and golf 57 percent, all enjoying increases. Team sports apparel, with an 8 percent drop, was the only apparel area to show a significant decrease. Broken down by region, U.S. apparel had increased by 11 percent while European apparel was up 35 percent.

Nike owned a handful of wholly owned subsidiaries that marketed products in different markets. It sold a line of dress and casual footwear and accessories for men, women, and children under the brand name Cole Haan through its wholly owned subsidiary, Cole Haan Holdings Incorporated. Another wholly owned subsidiary, Sports Specialties Corporation, sold a line of headwear with licensed team logos under the brand name "Sports Specialties." Bauer Inc., headquartered in Montreal, manufactured and distributed ice skates, skate blades, in-line roller skates, protective gear, hockey sticks, and hockey jerseys and accessories under the Bauer® brand name. Bauer also offered products for street, roller, and field hockey. Finally, Nike sold small amounts of various plastic products to other manufacturers through NIKE IHM, Inc. (formerly Tetra Plastics, Inc.).

Sports Equipment. Sports equipment was an area of growing importance to Nike. It had moved into sports equipment during the 1990s, and several items were sold under the Nike brand name, including sport balls, timepieces, eyewear, skates, and bats for softball and baseball. Some of the most visible product introductions had not performed well. Hockey sticks and basketballs, for example, had experienced disappointing sales.[15] Industry observers rumored that Nike would expand into other areas of equipment such as golf. Andrew Mooney, who headed Nike's sports equipment division, summarized the company's ambition in sports equipment, "Within a few years, the equipment division will be Nike's fastest growing division."[16]

Jordan Brand. Nike launched its JORDAN brand in October 1997. JORDAN extended Nike's relationship with Michael Jordan, who had endorsed Nike since the early 1980s. Some credited the introduction of the Air Jordan shoe in 1984 with catapulting Nike from close head-to-head competition with Reebok to clear dominance in the industry. Nike promoted JORDAN as "a pure, authentic basketball brand of premium, high-performance basketball footwear and apparel inspired by the performance, vision and direct involvement of Michael Jordan."[17] While growth was flat across the industry for basketball footwear, the JORDAN brand shoes were seen as a clear success. Nike believed the brand would show similar market strength into the next century.

Women's Products. Another area of promising growth for Nike was in products targeted to women. Women's participation in sports had increased by 30 percent in the decade preceding 1998 while participation in team and individual sports combined had increased by 26 percent. The growth in women's participation appeared to be accelerating.[18] Nike planned new lines of shoes for fall 1998, which contained a new footbed designed specifically for women. It also had initiated women's concept shops with retail partners such as Dick's and The Finish Line.

Marketing

Nike's marketing efforts centered around the relentless promotion of its brand name. The company sought to promote the Nike brand image as representing technical superiority, performance, and "the free-flowing spirit of the athlete."[19] An ongoing concern for Nike was that its performance image would be diluted. Knight worried (in 1994) that "We've moved away from our heritage and more toward fashion."[20] Managers at Nike were keenly conscious that brand leadership was difficult to sustain in footwear and apparel over long periods of time. According to Knight:

> The brand cycles in this industry last only around seven years. You've got to reawaken the customer every season, yet there are these larger cycles. First, Converse had its day, then Adidas, then Nike. The cycle took us from zero to a billion dollars in a short time, and suddenly Reebok had its years in the sun. Then Nike was reinvented during the late '80s, and now we're back on top. . . . If we're a giant, then we're a pretty fragile giant. Every six months is like a new life. We can't take our eye off the ball, because if we lose it, we'll have a bitch of a time getting it back.[21]

Advertising. Nike placed great importance on advertising and promoting its brand name. Its $900 million global "demand creation" budget was divided into $500 million for sports marketing and $400 million for communication.[22] The communications budget's main component was advertising while athlete and team endorsements constituted the lion's share of sports marketing.

Nike was one of the most recognized brands in the world and its swoosh was one of the best known product symbols. Knight sought to extend the Nike brand name further:

> These products and the way we present them to the world is our greatest asset, our brand name. Not a brand name equivalent yet to Coca-Cola or even Gillette but we're not "too far" behind. That's one of our big goals as a company—to reach that next level.[23]

Nike's advertising was distinctive. Many of its ads neither promoted a specific product nor even mentioned the firm's name. Instead, as one *Fortune* article stated, "they come across as demonstrations of a passion for sport, as spoken by athletes like Michael Jordan."[24] Advertising slogans such as "Bo Knows" and "Just Do It" had gained almost universal recognition and association with the Nike brand name.

So ubiquitous were Nike's symbol and slogan "Just Do It" that overexposure was a concern. In 1998, Nike replaced its "Just Do It" ads with others featuring the slogan "I Can." This led some in the media to conclude that Nike had retired the "Just Do It" slogan. In a press release, the company flatly stated that conclusion was wrong.[25] The use of the swoosh symbol was also modified somewhat in 1998. Nike began to use its wordmark "nike" instead of the swoosh to sign off its advertising and on its letterhead and business cards. A Nike press release answered speculation by the *New York Post* with a press release that "emphatically" denied the retiring of the swoosh. Gordon Thompson, Nike's vice president of design, emphasized that "It is the Swoosh that has brought us to prominence, and it isn't going away. The Swoosh will still be used in its most powerful form—on product."[26]

Endorsements. Nike aggressively sought endorsements from top athletes and teams in several sports. Regardless of the sport, the company sought to have the best athletes in those sports wear its shoes, because it believed that if the best athletes in a sport wore its shoes then serious athletes would also choose Nike as would, eventually, more casual participants. One example was a model of tennis shoes that went from sales of 10,000 pairs one year in the 1980s to 1.5 million the next, after the world's best known player, John McEnroe, started wearing them.

The most visible endorsers of Nike were Michael Jordan, Tiger Woods, and Ronaldo, the world's top-ranked athletes in basketball, golf, and soccer, respectively. Jordan was nearing the end of his basketball career, which led some to question whether shoes bearing his name would continue to attract consumers in the same numbers. Woods and Ronaldo were both in their early twenties in 1998. Like Jordan, both were viewed as uniquely gifted athletes with a flair for the spectacular, and both were predicted to dominate their sports as Jordan had done in basketball. Nike had also aggressively obtained endorsements from top women athletes such as track star Marion Jones and soccer player Mia Hamm. It had also sponsored the U.S. Olympic women's teams in soccer, softball, and volleyball. These endorsements were viewed as one reason that Nike's sales to women and girls had grown to about 25 percent of sales in 1998 from less than 15 percent in 1993.[27]

Endorsement expenses were up 47 percent in 1998. This increase was largely attributed to the cost of new contracts in soccer. In October 1998, Nike announced a decision to cut its budget of sports star endorsements by $100 million. The company planned to shift the amount cut from endorsements to spending on advertising. The reduction in endorsement spending followed an industry trend. Reebok had dropped 700 athletes from its endorsement list, including basketball player Shaquille O'Neal. Other companies had also reduced the amounts paid to athletes for endorsements while some, such as New Balance, shunned athlete endorsements altogether.[28] Despite the reduction, Nike emphasized that it was "totally committed to sports marketing athletes' and teams' endorsements as a fundamental pillar of success for this business and this industry."[29] Company managers believed that renewal costs would be lower on expired contracts and that with less competition for star athletes it would have a greater advantage in obtaining desired endorsements.

Distribution. Nike was the largest seller of athletic footwear and athletic apparel in the world. Its products were sold to approximately 19,700 retail accounts in the United States and through a mix of independent distributors, licensees, and subsidiaries in approximately 110 countries around the world.

During fiscal 1998, the United States accounted for approximately 57 percent of total revenues for Nike. Its products were sold through a broad array of retail outlets, including department stores; footwear stores; sporting goods stores; skating, tennis, and golf shops; and other specialty retail stores. Although Nike sold to approximately 19,500 retail accounts, its largest customer, Foot Locker, accounted for 11 percent of its global sales. Retailers generally conceded that they had benefited from Nike's dramatic growth. Many retailers, however, resented the company's policies on pricing, which limited their flexibility, and what they considered the miserly way in which Nike distributed some products. Another concern of many retailers was that their success had become too entwined with Nike's and that they would thus suffer from a downturn in Nike's performance.[30]

Nike had pioneered its "Futures' ordering program, which became a model for other consumer products manufacturers. The futures program required retailers to order five to six months in advance of delivery. Many retailers complained that "Futures" shifted the risk of excess inventory from Nike to them. Nike guaranteed that 90 percent of retailers' orders would be delivered within a set time period at a fixed price. Approximately 85 percent of Nike's domestic footwear was shipped under the futures program in fiscal year 1998. This compared to 93 percent of shipments in 1997 and 88 percent in 1996 that were made through the futures program, which was also used for apparel shipments. Nike made 84 percent of its domestic apparel shipments under the futures program in 1998. As of May 31, 1998, its worldwide futures orders for athletic footwear and apparel equaled $4.2 billion, compared to $4.9 billion as of May 31, 1997. Futures orders in May were scheduled for delivery from June through November of 1998. Nike expected, based on past experience, that approximately 95 percent of these orders would be filled in that time period, although orders might be cancelable.

Sales for footwear and apparel in the United States were solicited primarily through 21 Nike sales offices; the company used 10 independent sales representatives for specialty products such as golf, cycling, water sports, and outdoor wear.

Nike retailed directly to consumers in some instances; its most visible retail operations were its 12 NIKETOWN stores. Nike also owned and operated 111 other stores. Approximately 60 of these were factory outlet stores that sold mostly B-grade and close-out merchandise; 35 were Cole Haan stores and 10 were employee-only stores.

Manufacturing

Almost all of Nike's products were manufactured by a number of independent contractors in different countries. For footwear, 37 percent were manufactured in the People's Republic of China, Indonesia accounted for 34 percent, Vietnam 11 percent, Thailand 10 percent, the Philippines 4 percent, South Korea 2 percent, and Taiwan 2 percent. Nike also had has manufacturing agreements with independent factories in Argentina, Brazil, Italy, and Mexico. The largest supplier of Nike footwear accounted for only about 8 percent of production. The manufacturing of apparel was distributed differently than footwear. Approximately 53 percent of Nike's apparel sold in the United States was also produced domestically. The apparel produced in the United States was done so by independent contract manufacturers, most of which were located in the southern states. The apparel sold in international markets was manufactured outside the United States and was manufactured by independent contractors located in 30 countries, primarily in Bangladesh, Hong Kong, Indonesia, Malaysia, Mexico, the Philippines, Singapore, Sri Lanka, Taiwan, and Thailand.

Because of the large proportion of Nike's products manufactured overseas, import duties were a concern. Trade relations with China were a source of almost annual contention in the U.S. Congress each year. Nevertheless, "normal trade relations" (formerly "most favored nation") trading status had been granted to China each year since 1980. Revocation of normal trade relations status, however, would substantially raise tariffs on goods imported from China. Some European countries limited through import quotas the number of shoes manufactured in China, Indonesia, and Thailand that could be sold in a given year.

Nike had received widespread criticism for treatment of workers producing its products in Vietnam, Indonesia, and other Asian countries. The heated rhetoric against Nike was evident in one estimate which suggested that the $20 million paid to Michael Jordan to endorse Nike products was equal to the pay of 350,000 third world workers.[31] An Ernst & Young report on the labor conditions at subcontractor plants was leaked to the press, although it had been prepared for internal use. The report found a number of unhealthy conditions, including high levels of carcinogens.[32]

In response to these criticisms, Nike announced several initiatives in May 1998 that were designed to address the conditions of those producing Nike goods. These were summarized in its 1998 annual report (see Exhibit 8). Included in the recommendations were actions such as expanding independent monitoring; raising minimum age requirements for workers; and strengthening environmental, health, and safety standards.

Research and Development

Nike believed that its research and development efforts were a key factor in its success. During fiscal 1998, the company spent approximately $106.7 million on product research, development, and evaluation, compared to $73.2 million in 1997, and $46.8 million in 1996. Great importance was placed on technical innovations that reduced or eliminated injury, aided athletic performance, and maximized comfort. Nike employed specialists in the areas of biomechanics, exercise physiology, engineering, industrial design, and related fields. It also used people outside the company in its research efforts. Research committees and advisory boards made up of athletes, coaches, trainers, equipment managers, orthopedists, podiatrists, and other experts reviewed designs, materials, and concepts for product improvement. Testing also received considerable emphasis at Nike. Employee athletes wear-tested and evaluated products during the design and development process.

One of Nike's most important technical innovations involved its patented air technology. Air technology involved using pressurized gas encapsulated in polyurethane for cushioning. Nike had an exclusive, worldwide license to make and sell footwear using patented "air" technology, but some of the early Nike Air patents expired in 1997. The expiration raised the possibility that competitors might employ certain types of air technology. Later Nike Air patents were not due to expire for several years; the company sought patent rights for any inventions it viewed as valuable. Nike managers believed, however, that the firm's patent position was less important than skills in design, research and development, and marketing.

While Nike managers believed that their research and development was the most advanced in the industry, concern grew in the 1980s that their technical proficiency was not leading to the development of new products as quickly as needed. Knight was particularly chagrined at Reebok's comparative success in aerobic shoes, a market that Nike had almost entirely missed at one point. In response, Nike

instituted (in 1987) a more market-based organization toward product development. The footwear division was divided into smaller units that specialized in individual sports. Cross-functional teams were formed between production, sales, and advertising with the intent of developing a more unified approach to product development.

International

International Markets. With an aging U.S. population (see Exhibit 7), international markets were seen as an important source of growth, Nike marketed its products in approximately 110 countries outside of the United States in 1998. Non-U.S. sales accounted for 43 percent of total revenues in fiscal 1998, compared to 38 percent in 1997 and 36 percent in 1996. The largest international operations for Nike in 1998 were Japan, the United Kingdom, Canada, France, Italy, and Spain. Japan's sales were up 4 percent in 1998, the United Kingdom 11 percent, Canada 32 percent, France 15 percent, Italy 35 percent, and Spain 40 percent. Nike's sales had declined in Korea (29%) and Germany (6%). Overall, European sales increased 6 percent in footwear and 35 percent for apparel, while Asian apparel increased by 34 percent, but Asian footwear was down 8 percent.

Independent distributors, licensees, subsidiaries, and branch offices were all used to market and distribute products outside the United States Nike operated 25 distribution centers in Europe, Asia, Canada, Latin America, and Australia, and also distributed through independent distributors and licensees. Nike estimated that its products were sold through approximately 31,000 retail accounts outside the United States. The futures program was also an important part of operations outside the United States Nike sold through its futures program in Japan, Canada, and in many other countries in Asia, South America, and Europe. Efforts were also being made to develop the futures program in several countries where the program had not been offered.

Nike had moved aggressively to gain a larger share of the soccer market. Its managers believed that soccer was important to the future of the company. Because jerseys, which were controlled by teams and national soccer federations, were the most important advertising vehicles for the sport, Nike had formed lucrative endorsement agreements with a number of national teams. Brazil's national team agreed to endorse Nike products for $200 million over ten years while the United States and Italy settled for $120 million over eight years and $25 million for five years, respectively. One estimate placed Nike's long-term commitments to soccer teams and players at $680 million at the same time that soccer products contributed only 2 percent of the company's sales.[33]

The anti-establishment, confrontational style of doing business that characterized Nike did not always work well in

Exhibit 7	U.S. Population Projections						

	1997		2005		2015	
Age Group	Number Thousands		Number Thousands		Number Thousands	
Under 5 yrs.	19,229	7.2	19,127	6.7	21,174	6.8
5 to 14 yrs.	39,059	14.6	40,147	14.0	40,795	13.2
15 to 19 yrs.	19,013	7.1	20,997	7.3	21,194	6.8
20 to 24 yrs.	17,287	6.5	19,960	7.0	21,876	7.1
25 to 29 yrs.	18,848	7.0	18,057	6.3	20,836	6.7
30 to 34 yrs.	20,775	7.8	18,249	6.4	20,248	6.5
35 to 39 yrs.	22,607	8.4	19,802	6.9	18,872	6.1
40 to 44 yrs.	21,323	8.0	22,363	7.8	18,726	6.0
45 to 49 yrs.	18,442	6.9	21,988	7.7	19,594	6.3
50 to 54 yrs.	15,149	5.7	19,518	6.8	21,602	7.0
55 to 64 yrs.	21,816	8.2	29,606	10.4	39,650	12.8
65 yrs. & over	34,518	12.9	36,970	12.9	45,832	14.8
All ages	267,645	100.0	285,981	100.0	310,134	100.0

Source: U.S. Department of Commerce.

the soccer market. Gaining endorsements from teams and national federations was a particularly political process. Nike's approach to advertising and promotion in soccer grew less confrontational with some success. "For a long time, they were just the brash Americans throwing money at soccer. But as you watch the World Cup now, you're very conscious of the swoosh," according to John Boulter, former head of sports marketing at Reebok.[34] Adidas was the world leader in the soccer market and had traditionally enjoyed close ties to the governing bodies of soccer. Much of Nike's progress in soccer had come at Adidas' expense. For example, in the 1994 World Cup in the United States, Adidas sponsored 10 teams and Nike none. In the 1998 World Cup in France, however, both companies sponsored six teams. Adidas responded by spending an additional $25 million to have its name appear on stadium billboards. Overall, Adidas spent $100 million on the World Cup compared to $40 million for Nike.

In September 1998, orders in the Asia-Pacific region were down 56 percent and 24 percent in the Americas.[35]

Asian Turmoil. After a period of rapid growth, Nike's sales in Asia flattened in 1998. Asia-Pacific sales grew by approximately 41 percent and 69 percent in 1996 and 1997 but less than 1 percent in 1998. Much of the drop-off in the growth of Asian sales was attributed to the economic turmoil many Asian economies experienced in 1998. Futures orders in the region were up 55 percent as fiscal 1998 began. Management had expected Asian revenues to almost double in 1998.[36] One analyst suggested that Nike had "grossly miscalculated how strong demand would be overseas" and ended up "stuck with up to a year's worth of inventory in Japan and elsewhere in

Asia."[37] Knight acknowledged that the company had not been able to adjust production quickly enough for the changes in the Asian market. Excess inventory was a more severe problem in Asia where Nike had no outlets for leftover shoes except in the United States, where factory outlet stores and other discount retailers helped sell close-out models. In his letter to shareholders, Knight indicated that "To come back does not mean Asia has to be booming again, but it does mean we need to see the bottom of the slide, so that retailers are again confident enough to order several months in advance. Asia is a big part of this company's heritage and it remains a big part of its future."

Another reason offered for Nike's troubles in Asia went beyond economic cycles. Some analysts predicted that the shift to brown shoes in the United States would send a fashion signal to the rest of the world and begin a downward spiral for athletic footwear.[38]

Management

From its early years, Nike had an expressed preference for talent over industry experience in choosing managers. Its managerial ranks included lawyers, architects, teachers, editors, and accountants who switched professions in joining Nike. Many former pro and college athletes worked for the firm.

Management depth was a great concern for Phil Knight in 1998. At various points in its history, Nike had lost waves of managers who had become wealthy through stock options and then left the company either for retirement or other challenges. When Nike's stock hit dramatic highs in 1997 and early 1998, the company had experienced a significant exodus of managers. In his annual letter to

Exhibit 8   Excerpts from Nike's 1998 Annual Report on Improving Worker Conditions

Expanding Independent Monitoring: Working with NGO (nongovernment organization) participation, Nike will initially focus on Vietnam, Indonesia, and China. The ultimate goal is to establish a global system of independent certification of the company's labor practices, much the same way financial information in this annual report is certified.

Raising Minimum Age Requirements: Nike has increased the minimum age of footwear factory workers to 18 and the minimum age for all other light manufacturing workers (apparel, accessories, equipment) to 16. There is no tolerance for exception.

Strengthening Environmental, Health, and Safety Standards: Nike launched the Environmental, Health, and Safety Management System (EHSMS) in June of 1998. The program, developed with two consultant groups (The Gauntlett Group and Environmental Resources Management), will provide every factory where Nike footwear is made the tools and training to effectively manage and ensure continuous improvement throughout their environmental, health, and safety programs. The program helps each factory develop a fully functioning EHSMS by June 2001.

Key Environmental, Health, and Safety Initiatives: (a) Indoor air testing of all footwear factories, and the monitoring of any necessary corrective measures to bring air quality to OSHA levels. (b) Accelerated replacement of petroleum-based, organic solvents with safer water-based compounds. In an average month, nine of ten Nike shoes are made with water-based adhesives, with parallel substitutions underway for primers, degreasers, and cleaners used in traditional footwear production.

Expanded Worker Education: The Jobs + Education program offers footwear factory workers educational opportunities, such as middle school and high school equivalency courses. The classes will be free and scheduled during nonwork hours. Factory participation is voluntary, but by 2002 Nike will order only from footwear factories that offer some form of after-hours education.

Increasing Support of the Micro-enterprise Loan Program: The Jobs + Micro-enterprise Program will provide loans to women to create small businesses. Building on a successful program already responsible for 1,000 loans in Vietnam, Nike will expand the program to reach an equal number of families in Indonesia, Thailand, and Pakistan.

Building Understanding: Through the Rising Tides program, Nike is providing research grants and logistical support to universities and colleges to expand the academic body of knowledge on corporate responsibility, contract manufacturing, and development issues involving Nike and other companies. Nike will also convene a series of open forums to foster dialogue with factory workers and partners, academics, NGOs, and others interested in these issues.

We are serious about these initiatives. We recognize that there is no finish line. Our goal is continuous improvement. Based on our new initiatives, we have amended and are enforcing the Nike Code of Conduct that directs our factory partners accordingly. Nike will sever its business relationship with any manufacturer refusing to meet these standards or exhibiting a pattern of violations. In the last year, Nike has terminated business with eight factories in four countries for not meeting our Code of Conduct requirements.

---

shareholders, Knight summarized the challenges of maintaining an effective management team:

> *The first question you should ask is: What are we doing to upgrade management? First, for those who are used to TV sitcom problems being solved in 30 minutes, I have bad news. It's going to take some time. Our approach is a simple one: We bring in talented newcomers, push a very good bench along a little faster than planned, and weave it all into a strong culture. This will actually change our culture—a little bit, not a lotta bit—recognizing our greater size and more sizable challenges.[39]*
>
> *We have lost experienced people for whom the stock option program has created lifetime financial security. Add that to the incredible competitive nature of our industry and you're going to see key contributors leave for other challenges.[40]*

Other managers had departed Nike over the years for positions at other shoe companies. For example, in the early

1990s, Tom Carmody had taken a high-level position with Reebock and one of Nike's top marketers, Rob Strasser, left the company to become the head of Adidas U.S.A.

Culture

Nike's culture was well known in the sports industry for emphasizing a distinctive set of values. The Nike culture was credited with helping the company maintain a competitive focus unmatched in the industry. According to one Reebok executive, "They [Nike] have tremendous focus and consistency. That discipline is very important."[41] A *Business Week* article concluded that "The relentless spotlight on sports and performance results in the design of shoes athletes really wear."[42] "We knew instinctively what was a Nike thing to do and what wasn't a Nike thing to do," according Tom Carmody, a former Nike executive speaking of the early days. So strong was the identification with Nike's culture that managers who left for competitors reported being shunned by their former co-workers at Nike. Nike approached its rivalry with Reebok with particular zeal. Reebok's Paul Fireman noted, "At the end of a contest, I'd shake hands and walk away. I think [Knight] would throw a shovel of dirt on the grave."[43]

The company's values were viewed by Nike employees as contributing to the goal of "enhancing people's lives through sports and fitness." Executives stressed Nike's commitment to "keeping the magic of sports alive." Knight was quoted as saying that sport "is the culture of the United States" and that it would, in time, define the culture of the entire world.[44] Nike values focused on sports and performance. Employees viewed Nike as "'an athlete's company,' an organization run for and by athletes."[45] So strong was the emphasis on sports that one managerial candidate with both Ph.D. and law degree credentials was dismissed from consideration when he could not answer the question, "Who is Deion Sanders?"[46] The emphasis on performance was evident in the company's attitude toward fashion. The word "fashion" was not used at Nike except occasionally by Knight. Instead, "design" was the preferred term in the company. "We work hard to convey that performance, not image, is everything," asserted Knight.[47] Over time, however, Nike had grudgingly come to a recognition that style and appearance were important in its products.

A *Wall Street Journal* article suggested that Knight had "suffused his company with the idea of the intense, inwardly focused competitor. Heroes and hero worship abound at his Nike home office in Oregon, where every building seems to be named for a sports star."[48] Nike's values were embodied in sports heroes. Buildings were named after such famous sports figures as marathoner Joan Benoit Samuelson, baseball pitcher Nolan Ryan, and football coach Joe Paterno. No sports figure was more central to Nike's culture than Steve Prefontaine, the U.S. distance runner who had died in a 1975 car accident. Knight offered this view of Prefontaine's impact on Nike:

> To many he was the greatest U.S. middle-distance runner ever, but to me he was more than that. Pre was a rebel from a working class background, a guy full of cockiness and pride and guts. Pre's spirit is the cornerstone of this company's soul.[49]

Nike was seen as an iconoclastic, anti-establishment company, an image the company cultivated by its association with controversial athletes such as Prefontaine, John McEnroe, Ilie Nastase, Deion Sanders, and Charles Barkley. In its early years, Nike focused its competitive culture and anti-establishment zeal on overtaking Adidas as the number-one athletic shoe company. Adidas was viewed within Nike as an elitist company that capitalized on its close ties with international sports authorities. People at Nike viewed themselves, of whom many were former competitive runners, as having "authenticity." As Katz noted, "The word is repeated like a mantra in Beaverton. Authentic shoes for authentic athletes."[50]

Knight's role in preserving and articulating Nike's values was central. He was quick to respond to instances that he thought challenged the company's values. For example, when one of Nike's athletes, tennis player Andre Agassi, appeared in a Canon camera commerical with the slogan, "Image is Everything," Knight quickly reminded Nike employees that image was not a core Nike value. A 1994 *BusinessWeek* article described Knight as "An enigmatic, private man . . . [who] has been known to retreat from Nike's day-to-day activities for months at a stretch, only to reappear when the company is drifting. That being the case today, 'Knight is reengaging' says Chris Van Dyke, head of Nike's Outdoor Div."[51]

Nike was particularly concerned about inculcating its culture abroad. An example of this concern was evident in *BusinessWeek*'s account of Yukihiro Akimoto, who was chosen to head Nike's Japanese operations after building Kentucky Fried Chicken's Japanese business.

> A smoker whose idea of recreation was such mild recreation as golf, Akimoto was brought to Beaverton for a four-month immersion class in Nike culture and operations. He threw away his cigarettes and started running. When he returned to Tokyo in December, he banned smoking at Nike Japan Corp.—a big deal in the heavy-puffing country—and pushed Nike's Japanese employees to train for this year's Hawaii marathon. Nike's improved communication with the affiliate paid some early dividends: It led to the creation of a special lightweight running shoe designed specifically for Asian feet.[52]

Notes

1   Katz, Donald. "Triumph of the swoosh." *Sports Illustrated*, August 16, 1993, pp. 54–73.
2   Jenkins, Holman W. "Business world: The rise and stumble of Nike." *Wall Street Journal*, June 3, 1998, p. A19.
3   Katz, Donald. "Triumph of the swoosh." *Sports Illustrated*, August 16, 1993, pp. 54–73.
4   Standard & Poor's, "Apparel and footwear industry survey," August 21, 1997.
5   Dow Jones Newswires. "Smaller sneaker makers walk all over big ones in 3Q," October 8, 1998.
6   Jenkins, Holman W. "Business world: The rise and stumble of Nike." *Wall Street Journal*, June 3, 1998, p. A19.
7   Ibid.

8   Dow Jones Newswires. "Smaller sneaker makers walk all over big ones in 3Q," October 8, 1998.

9   Pereira, Joseph. "Going to extremes: Board-riding youths take sneaker maker on a fast ride uphill—For Generation Y, rebellion and Vans shoes are cool; Nike and baseball aren't—'Elvises' go to 'Cube Farms.'" *Wall Street Journal*, April 16, 1998, p. A1.

10   Ibid.

11   Ibid.

12   Beatty, Sally. "Nike serves up tennis-gear ad that plays sudden death game." *Wall Street Journal*, August 26, 1998, p. B2.

13   *BusinessWeek*, "A buyer may be on Reebok's heels." June 15, 1998, p. 114.

14   Lieber, Ronald B. "Just redo it." *Fortune*, June 23, 1997, p. 72.

15   O'Harrow, Robert, Jr. "Nike's downward swoosh; Changing tastes, Asia crisis halt athletic shoe giant's winning streak." *Washington Post*, January 18, 1998, p. H2.

16   Eubanks, Steve. "Where does Nike fit into this picture?" *Golf World*, January 30, 1998, p. 58.

17   Nike Annual Report, 1998.

18   Standard & Poor's, "Apparel and Footwear Industry Survey," August 21, 1997.

19   *BusinessWeek*. "Can Nike just do it? "April 18, 1994, pp. 86–90. Yang, Dori Jones and Michael Oneal

20   Ibid.

21   Katz, Donald. "Triumph of the swoosh." *Sports Illustrated*, August 16, 1993, pp. 54–73.

22   Nike Press Release. "Nike: No fundamental change in sports marketing strategy." October. 1, 1998.

23   Nike Annual Report, 1998.

24   Lieber, Ronald B. "Just redo it." *Fortune*, June 23, 1997, p. 72.

25   Nike Press Release, "Instant Replay: Nike & the Swoosh," September 15, 1998.

26   Ibid.

27   Munk, Nina. "Girl power." *Fortune*, December. 8, 1997, pp. 132–140.

28   Richards, Bill. "Nike says it plans to cut $100 million on spending for star endorsements." *Wall Street Journal*, October. 2, 1998.

29   Nike VP Andy Mooney quoted in Nike Press Release, "Nike: No fundamental change in sports marketing strategy." October. 1, 1998.

30   Steinhauer, Jennifer. "With no big rival, it calls the shots in athletic shoes." *New York Times*, June 7, 1997.

31   Jenkins, Holman W. "Business world: The rise and stumble of Nike." *Wall Street Journal*, June 3, 1998, p. A19.

32   O'Harrow, Robert, Jr. "Nike's downward swoosh; changing tastes, Asia crisis halt athletic shoe giant's winning streak." *Washington Post*, January. 18, 1998, p. H2.

33   Fatsis, Stefan. "World Cup 1998: Into the quarterfinals—Nike tackles soccer, nicely." *Wall Street Journal*, July 2, 1998, p. A12

34   Ibid.

35   Dow Jones Newswires. "Nike up 10.6% as company makes progress on turnaround." September 18, 1998.

36   Sellers, Patricia. "Four reasons Nike's not cool." *Fortune*, March 30, 1998, p. 26.

37   O'Harrow, Robert, Jr. "Nike's downward swoosh; changing tastes, Asia crisis halt athletic shoe giant's winning streak." *Washington Post*, January. 18, 1998, p. H2.

38   Ibid.

39   Nike Annual Report, 1998.

40   Nike Annual Report, 1998.

41   *BusinessWeek*. "Can Nike just do it?" April 18, 1994, pp. 86–90.

42   Ibid.

43   Katz, Donald. "Triumph of the swoosh." *Sports Illustrated*, August 16, 1993, pp. 54–73.

44   Ibid.

45   Ibid.

46   Ibid.

47   Ibid.

48   Jenkins, Holman W. "Business world: The rise and stumble of Nike." *Wall Street Journal*, June 3, 1998, p. A19.

49   Katz, Donald. "Triumph of the swoosh." *Sports Illustrated*, August 16, 1993, pp. 54–73.

50   Ibid.

51   *BusinessWeek*. "Can Nike just do it?" April 18, 1994, pp. 86–90.

52   Ibid.

3

CORPORATE STRATEGIES

6

Vertical Integration

The box promised that it would be easy to install. It promised that your new software would be "plug-and-play compatible" with your system. But, here you are; three hours into installation and all you get is helpful error messages like "System Error No. 1257-3"—whatever that means. So, you decide to call the help line. But who are you calling?

The package from your tax service arrived on time. All it requires is your signature, and you can safely file your taxes. And then—the tax refund. Those tickets to Cancun are

Who Am I Calling?

just dying to be purchased. However, as you look over your return, you are not sure about how a certain deduction is calculated. A mistake on your tax return can be very costly, so you decide to call the help line. But who are you calling?

Last month was a great month—concerts, new music, new clothes, a road trip. But it was very

expensive—maybe too expensive. The day of reckoning— when the credit card bill comes in the mail—finally arrives. $1,600! How can the bill be that much? You quickly look over the list of charges and see that you were double billed for that great hotel in Florida. Well, this will be easy to fix—just call the customer service line. But who are you calling?

Until recently, it was easy to know who you were calling to receive these kinds of services. If, for example, your software was an IBM product and you called the

178

Learning Objectives

After reading this chapter, you should be able to:

1. Define vertical integration, forward vertical integration, and backward vertical integration.

2. Discuss how vertical integration can create value by reducing the threat of opportunism.

3. Discuss how vertical integration can create value by enabling a firm to exploit its valuable, rare, and costly-to-imitate resources and capabilities.

4. Discuss how vertical integration can create value by enabling a firm to retain its flexibility.

5. Describe conditions under which vertical integration may be rare and costly to imitate.

6. Describe how the functional organization structure, management controls, and compensation policies are used to implement vertical integration.

7. Describe different degrees of vertical integration in an international context.

IBM help line, you would talk to an IBM employee located somewhere in the United States. If you had a problem with you tax return, you would call your tax preparer—a firm like H&R Block—and talk to an employee located somewhere in the United States. And if you had a problem with your credit card bill, you would call the credit card company and talk to one of its employees in the United States.

But in the last ten years, all of this has changed. First, large corporations started to hire smaller companies to staff and manage their call centers. Firms like Convergys locate call centers near universities and colleges and hire engineering and computer science students to answer questions about software; they hire accounting students to answer questions about tax returns and other students to answer questions about credit card bills. All this is cheaper than these large corporations hiring full-time employees to answer these questions—and the quality of these services can be very good.

However, the search for high-quality, low-cost services has led some corporations to look beyond the borders of the United States for companies to manage their call centers and help lines. Many of these services are now provided by companies operating out of India. That's right—you may call the same 800 help line number you always have, but the person you get on the other end may actually live in India.

Research shows that shifting operations to firms in India can reduce a corporation's costs by 40 to 60 percent. And with India's schools turning out

260,000 well-trained engineers each year, the quality of the service you receive on the other end of the line that connects you to a call center in India may be just as good as the service you received in the past.

And it isn't just call centers that are moving to India. Some of the Web sites you visit, the electronics you use, the financial analyses you read—even your credit worthiness—are designed, written, and evaluated by firms in India. One study estimates that by 2008, the information technology and back-office work done in India will employ over 4 million people, be worth over $57 billion, and account for 7 percent of India's Gross Domestic Product (GDP). Currently, GE Capital employs 16,000 people in India to help manage paper work; GE's John Welch Technology Center employs 1,800 people in India to develop and design new products; IBM employs 10,000 people in India to provide information technology services and software; Oracle employs 6,000 people in India to develop new software and provide software services; and Intel employs 1,700 people in India to help design chips and software. These trends are likely to continue for some time.

So, the next time you call a help line to install your software, update your tax return, or check your credit card bill, ask the people on the other end of the line who they are and where they live. More and more, they are not likely to be employees of the firm you thought you were calling. And more and more, they don't even live in the United States.

Sources: M. Kripalani and P. Engardio (2003). "The rise of India." *BusinessWeek*, December 8, pp. 66 +; C. Hawn (2004). "The global razor's edge." *Fast Times*, February, pp. 27 +; K. J. Delaney (2003). "Outsourcing jobs—and workers—to India." *Wall Street Journal*, October 13, pp. B1 +.

The decision to hire another company to provide services for a firm's customers is an example of a decision that determines the level of a firm's vertical integration. This is the case, whether the company that is hired to perform these services is located in the United States or India.

What Is Corporate Strategy?

Vertical integration is the first corporate strategy examined in detail in this book. As suggested in Chapter 1, **business strategy** is a firm's theory of how to gain competitive advantage in a single business or industry. The two business strategies discussed in this book are cost leadership and product differentiation. **Corporate strategy** is a firm's theory of how to gain competitive advantage by operating in several businesses simultaneously. Decisions about whether or not to vertically integrate often determine whether or not a firm is operating in a single business or industry or multiple businesses or industries. Other corporate strategies discussed in this book include strategic alliances, diversification, and mergers and acquisitions.

What Is Vertical Integration?

The concept of a firm's value chain was first introduced in Chapter 3. As a reminder, a **value chain** is that set of activities that must be accomplished to bring a product or service from raw materials to the point that it can be sold to a final customer. A simplified value chain of the oil and gas industry, originally presented in Figure 3.1, is reproduced in Figure 6.1.

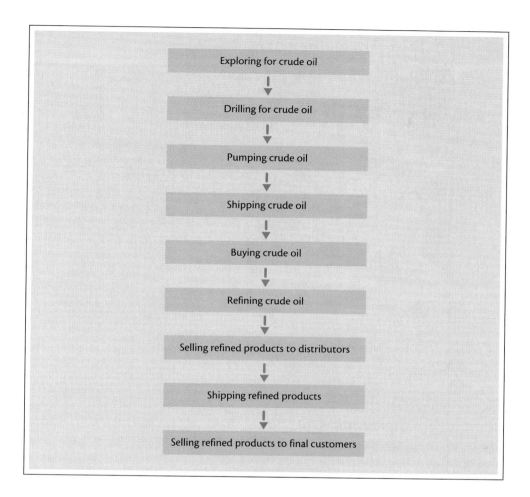

A firm's level of **vertical integration** is simply the number of steps in this value chain that a firm accomplishes within its boundaries. More vertically integrated firms accomplish more stages of the value chain within their boundaries than less vertically integrated firms. A more sophisticated approach to measuring the degree of a firm's vertical integration is presented in the Strategy in Depth feature.

A firm engages in **backward vertical integration** when it incorporates more stages of the value chain within its boundaries and those stages bring it closer to the beginning of the value chain, that is, closer to gaining access to raw materials. When computer companies developed all their own software, they were engaging in backward vertical integration, because these actions are close to the beginning of the value chain. When they began using independent companies operating in India to develop this software, they were less vertically integrated backward.

A firm engages in **forward vertical integration** when it incorporates more stages of the value chain within its boundaries and those stages bring it closer to the end of the value chain, that is, closer to interacting directly with final customers. When companies staffed and operated their own call centers in the United States, they were engaging in forward vertical integration, because these activities brought them closer to the ultimate customer. When they started using independent companies in India to staff and operate these centers, they were less vertically integrated forward.

Strategy in Depth

It is sometimes possible to directly observe which stages of the value chain a firm is engaging in and thus the level of that firm's vertical integration. Sometimes, however, it is more difficult to directly observe a firm's level of vertical integration. This is especially the case when a firm believes that its level of vertical integration is a potential source of competitive advantage and thus is not likely to reveal this information freely to competitors.

In this situation, it is possible to get a sense of the degree of a firm's vertical integration—though not a complete list of the steps in the value chain integrated by the firm—from a close examination of the firm's **value added as a percentage of sales**. Valued added as a percentage of sales measures that percentage of a firm's sales that is generated by activities done within the boundaries of a firm. A firm with a high ratio between value added and sales has brought many of the value-creating activities associated with its business inside its boundaries, consistent with a high level of vertical integration. A firm with a low ratio between value added and sales does not have, on average, as high a level of vertical integration.

Value added as a percentage of sales is computed using the following equation in Exhibit 1.

The sum of net income and income taxes is subtracted in both the

Measuring Vertical Integration

numerator and the denominator in this equation to control for inflation and changes in the tax code over time. Net income, income taxes, and sales can all be taken directly from a firm's profit-and-loss statement. Value added can be calculated using the equation in Exhibit 2.

Again, most of the numbers needed to calculate value added can be found either in a firm's profit-and-loss statement or in its balance sheet.

Sources: A. Laffer (1969). "Vertical integration by corporations: 1929–1965." *Review of Economics and Statistics*, 51, pp. 91– 93; I. Tucker and R. P. Wilder (1977). "Trends in vertical integration in the U.S. manufacturing sector." *Journal of Industrial Economics*, 26, pp. 81–94; K. Harrigan (1986). "Matching vertical integration strategies to competitive conditions." *Strategic Management Journal*, 7, pp. 535–555.

Exhibit 1

$$\text{vertical integration}_i = \frac{\text{value added}_i - \left(\text{net income}_i + \text{income taxes}_i\right)}{\text{sales}_i - \left(\text{net income}_i + \text{income taxes}_i\right)}$$

where,

$\text{vertical integration}_i$ = the level of vertical integration for firm$_i$

value added_i = the level of value added for firm$_i$

net income_i = the level of net income for firm$_i$

income taxes_i = firm$_i$'s income taxes

sales_i = firm$_i$'s sales

Exhibit 2

value added = depreciation + amortization + fixed charges + interest expense + labor and related expenses + pension and retirement expenses + income taxes + net income (after taxes) + rental expense

Of course, in choosing how to organize its value chain, a firm has more choices than just to vertically integrate or not vertically integrate. Indeed, between these two extremes, a wide range of somewhat vertically integrated options exist. These alternatives include various types of strategic alliances and joint ventures, the primary topic of Chapter 9.

The Value of Vertical Integration

The question of vertical integration—which stages of the value chain should be included within a firm's boundaries and why—has been studied by many scholars for almost 100 years. The reason this question has been of such interest was first articulated by Nobel Prize–winning economist Ronal Coase. In a famous article originally published in 1937, Coase asked a simple question: Given how efficiently markets can be used to organize economic exchanges among thousands, even hundreds of thousands, of separate individuals, why would markets, as a method for managing economic exchanges, ever be replaced by firms? In markets, almost as if by magic, Adam Smith's "invisible hand" coordinates the quantity and quality of goods and services produced with the quantity and quality of goods and services demanded through the adjustment of prices—all without a centralized controlling authority. In firms, on the other hand, centralized bureaucrats monitor and control subordinates who, in turn battle each other for "turf" and control of inefficient internal "fiefdoms." Why would the "beauty" of the invisible hand ever be replaced by the clumsy "visible hand" of the modern corporation?[1]

Coase began to answer his own question when he observed that sometimes the cost of using a market to manage an economic exchange must be higher than the cost of using vertical integration and bringing an exchange within the boundary of a firm. Over the years, efforts have focused on identifying the conditions under which this would be the case. The resulting work has described several different situations where vertical integration can either increase a firm's revenues or decrease its costs compared to not vertically integrating, that is, several situations where vertical integration can be valuable. Three of the most influential of these explanations of when vertical integration can create value for a firm are discussed here.

Vertical Integration and the Threat of Opportunism

One of the best known explanations of when vertical integration can be valuable focuses on using vertical integration to reduce the threat of opportunism.[2] **Opportunism** exists when a firm is unfairly exploited in an exchange. Examples of opportunism include when a party to an exchange expects a high level of quality in a product it is purchasing, only to discover it has received a lower level of quality than it expected; when a party to an exchange expects to receive a service by a particular point in time and that service is delivered late (or early); and when a party to an exchange expects to pay a price to complete this exchange and its exchange partner demands a higher price than what was previously agreed to.

Obviously, when one of its exchange partners behaves opportunistically, this reduces the economic value of a firm. One way to reduce the threat of opportunism is to bring an exchange within the boundary of a firm, that is, to vertically integrate into this exchange. This way, managers in a firm can directly monitor and control this exchange instead of relying on the market to manage it. If the exchange that is brought within the boundary of a firm brings a firm closer to its ultimate suppliers, it is an example of backward vertical integration. If the exchange that is brought within the boundary of a firm brings a firm closer to its ultimate customer, it is an example of forward vertical integration.

Of course, firms should only bring market exchanges within their boundaries when the cost of vertical integration is less than the cost of opportunism. If the cost of vertical integration is greater than the cost of opportunism, then firms should not vertically integrate into an exchange. This is the case for both backward and forward vertical integration decisions.

So, when will the threat of opportunism be large enough to warrant vertical integration? Research has shown that the threat of opportunism is greatest when a party to an exchange has made what are called transaction-specific investments. A **transaction-specific investment** is any investment in an exchange that has significantly more value in the current exchange than it does in alternative exchanges. Perhaps the easiest way to understand the concept of a transaction-specific investment is through an example.

Consider the economic exchange between an oil refining company and an oil pipeline building company, depicted in Figure 6.2. As can be seen in the figure, this oil refinery is built on the edge of a deep-water bay. Because of this, the refinery has been receiving supplies of crude oil from large tanker ships. However, an oil field exists several miles distant from the refinery, but the only way to transport crude oil from the oil field to the refinery is with trucks—a very expensive way to move crude oil, especially compared to large tankers. But, if the oil refining company could find a way to get crude oil from this field cheaply, it would probably make this refinery even more valuable.

Enter the pipeline company. Suppose this pipeline company approaches the refinery and offers to build a pipeline from the oil field to the refinery. In return, all the pipeline company expects is for the refinery to promise to buy a certain number of barrels of crude at an agreed-to price for some period of time, say, five years, through the pipeline. If reasonable prices can be negotiated, the oil refinery is likely to find this offer attractive, for the cost of crude oil carried by the pipeline is likely to be lower than the cost of crude oil delivered by ship or by truck. Based on this analysis, so far, the refinery and the oil pipeline company are likely to cooperate and the pipeline is likely to be built.

Now, five years go by, and it's time to renegotiate the contract. Which of these two firms has made the largest transaction-specific investments? Remember

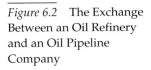

Figure 6.2 The Exchange Between an Oil Refinery and an Oil Pipeline Company

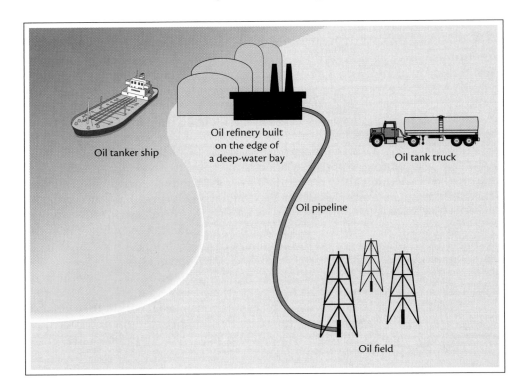

that a transaction-specific investment is any investment in an exchange that is more valuable in that particular exchange than in alternative exchanges.

What specific investments has the refinery made? Well, how much is this refinery worth if this exchange with the pipeline company is not renewed? Its value would probably drop some—remember that oil through the pipeline is probably cheaper than oil through ships or trucks. So, if the refiner doesn't use the pipeline any longer, it will have to use these alternative supplies. This will reduce its value some—say from $1 million to $900,000. This $100,000 difference is the size of the transaction-specific investment made by the refining company.

However, the transaction-specific investment made by the pipeline firm is probably much larger. Suppose the pipeline is worth $750,000 as long as it is pumping oil to the refinery. But if it is not pumping oil, how much is it worth? Not very much. An oil pipeline that is not pumping oil has limited alternative uses. It has value either as scrap or (perhaps) as the world's largest enclosed water slide. If the value of the pipeline is only $10,000 if it is not pumping oil to the refinery, then the level of transaction specific investment made by the pipeline firm is substantially larger than that made by the firm that owns the refinery: $750,000 – $10,000, or $740,000 for the pipeline company versus $100,000 for the refining company.

So who is at greater risk of opportunism when the contract between the refinery and the pipeline company is renegotiated—the refinery or the pipeline company? Obviously, the pipeline company has more to lose. If it cannot come to an agreement with the oil refining company, it will lose $740,000. If the refinery cannot come to an agreement with the pipeline company, it will lose $100,000. Knowing this, the refining company can squeeze the pipeline company during the renegotiation by insisting on lower prices or more timely deliveries of higher-quality crude oil, and the pipeline company really can't do much about it.

Of course, managers in the pipeline firm are not stupid. They know that after the first five years of their exchange with the refining company they will be in a very difficult bargaining position. So, in anticipation, they will insist on much higher prices for building the oil pipeline in the first place than would otherwise be the case. This will drive up the cost of building the pipeline, perhaps to the point that it is no longer cheaper than getting crude oil from ships. If this is the case, then the pipeline will not be built, even though if it could be built and the threat of opportunism eliminated, both the refining company and the pipeline company would be better off.

One way to solve this problem is for the oil refining company to buy the oil pipeline company—that is, for the oil refinery to backward vertically integrate.[3] When this happens, the incentive for the oil refinery to exploit the vulnerability of the pipeline company will be reduced. After all, if the refinery business tries to rip-off the pipeline business, it only hurts itself, since it owns the pipeline business.

This, then, is the essence of opportunism-based explanations of when vertical integration creates value: Transaction-specific investments make parties to an exchange vulnerable to opportunism and vertical integration solves this vulnerability problem. Using language developed in Chapter 3, this approach suggests that vertical integration is valuable when it reduces threats from a firm's suppliers or buyers due to any transaction-specific investments a firm has made.

Vertical Integration and Firm Capabilities

A second approach to vertical integration decisions focuses on a firm's capabilities and its ability to generate sustained competitive advantages.[4] This approach has two broad implications. First, it suggests that firms should vertically integrate into those business activities where they possess valuable, rare, and costly-to-imitate resources and capabilities. This way, firms can appropriate at least some of the profits that using these capabilities to exploit environmental opportunities will create. Second, this approach also suggests that firms should not vertically integrate into business activities where they do not possess the resources necessary to gain competitive advantages. Such vertical integration decisions would not be a source of profits to a firm, since they do not possess any of the valuable, rare, or costly-to-imitate resources needed to gain competitive advantages in these business activities. Indeed, to the extent that some other firms have competitive advantages in these business activities, vertically integrating into them could put a firm at a competitive disadvantage.

This, then, is the essence of the capabilities approach to vertical integration: If a firm possesses valuable, rare, and costly-to-imitate resources in a business activity, it should vertically integrate into that activity; otherwise, no vertical integration. This perspective can sometimes lead to vertical integration decisions that conflict with decisions derived from opportunism-based explanations of vertical integration.

Consider, for example, firms acting as suppliers to Wal-Mart. As described in Chapter 4, Wal-Mart has a huge competitive advantage in the discount retail industry. In principle, firms that sell to Wal-Mart could vertically integrate forward into the discount retail market to sell their own products. That is, these firms could begin to compete against Wal-Mart. However, such efforts are not likely to be a source of competitive advantage for these firms. Wal-Mart's resources and capabilities are just too extensive and costly to imitate for most of these suppliers. So, instead of forward vertical integration, most of these firms sell their products through Wal-Mart.

Of course, the problem is that by relying so much on Wal-Mart, these firms are making significant transaction-specific investments. If they stop selling to Wal-Mart, they may go out of business. However, this decision will have a limited impact on Wal-Mart. Wal-Mart can go to any number of suppliers around the world who are willing to replace this failed firm. So, Wal-Mart's suppliers are at risk of opportunism in this exchange, and indeed, it is well known that Wal-Mart can squeeze its suppliers, in terms of the quality of the products it purchases, the price at which it purchases them, and the way in which these products are delivered.

So the tension between these two approaches to vertical integration becomes clear. Concerns about opportunism suggest that Wal-Mart's suppliers should vertically integrate forward. Concerns about having a competitive disadvantage if they do vertically integrate forward suggest that Wal-Mart's suppliers should not vertically integrate. So, should they or shouldn't they vertically integrate?

Not many of Wal-Mart's suppliers have been able to resolve this difficult problem. Most do not vertically integrate into the discount retail industry. However, they try to reduce the level of transaction-specific investment they make with Wal-Mart by supplying other discount retailers, both in the United States and abroad. They also try to use their special capabilities to differentiate their products so much that Wal-Mart's customers insist on Wal-Mart selling these products. And these firms constantly search for cheaper ways to make and distribute higher-quality products.

Vertical Integration and Flexibility

A third perspective on vertical integration focuses on the impact of this decision on a firm's flexibility. **Flexibility** refers to how costly it is for a firm to alter its strategic and organizational decisions. Flexibility is high when the cost of changing strategic choices is low; flexibility is low when the cost of changing strategic choices is high.

So, which is less flexible: vertical integration or no vertical integration? Research suggests that, in general, vertically integrating is less flexible than not vertically integrating.[5] This is because once a firm has vertically integrated, it has committed its organizational structure, its management controls, and its compensation policies to a particular vertically integrated way of doing business. Undoing this decision often means changing these aspects of an organization.

Suppose, for example, that a vertically integrated firm decides to get out of a particular business. To do this, this firm will have to sell or close its factories, (actions that can adversely affect both the employees it has to lay off and those that remain), alter its supply relationships, hurt customers that have come to rely on this firm as a partner, and change the internal reporting structure of the firm. On the other hand, if a non–vertically integrated firm decides to get out of a business, it simply stops. It cancels whatever contracts it might have had in place and ceases operations in that business. The cost of exiting a non–vertically integrated business is generally much lower than the cost of exiting a vertically integrated business.

Of course, flexibility is not always valuable. In fact, flexibility is only valuable when the decision-making setting a firm is facing is uncertain. A decision-making setting is **uncertain** when the future value of an exchange cannot be known when investments in that exchange are being made. In such settings, less vertical integration is better than more vertical integration. This is because vertically integrating into an exchange is less flexible than not vertically integrating into an exchange. If an exchange turns out not to be valuable, it is usually more costly for firms that have vertically integrated into an exchange to exit that exchange compared to firms that have not vertically integrated.

Consider, for example, a pharmaceutical firm making investments in biotechnology. The outcome of biotechnology research is very uncertain. If a pharmaceutical company vertically integrates into a particular type of biotechnology research by hiring particular types of scientists, building an expensive laboratory, and developing the other skills necessary to do this particular type of biotechnology research, it has made a very large investment. Now suppose that this research turns out not to be profitable. This firm has made huge investments that now have little value. As important, it has failed to make investments in other areas of biotechnology that could turn out to be valuable.

A flexibility-based approach to vertical integration suggests that, rather than vertically integrating into a business activity whose value is highly uncertain, firms should not vertically integrate and, instead, form a strategic alliance to manage this exchange. A strategic alliance is more flexible than vertical integration but still gives a firm enough information about an exchange to estimate its value over time.

An alliance has a second advantage in this setting. The downside risks associated with investing in a strategic alliance are known and fixed. They equal the cost of creating and maintaining the alliance. If an uncertain investment turns out not to be valuable, parties to this alliance know the maximum amount they can lose—an amount equal to the cost of creating and maintaining the alliance. On the other hand, if this exchange turns out to be very valuable, then maintaining an alliance can give a firm access to this huge upside potential. These aspects of strategic alliances will be discussed in more detail in Chapter 9.

Each of these explanations of vertical integration has received significant empirical attention in the academic literature. Some of these studies are described in the Research Made Relevant feature.

Research Made Relevant

Of the three explanations of verti-cal integration discussed here, opportunism-based explanations are the oldest, and thus have received the greatest empirical support. One review of this empirical work, by Professor Joe Mahoney of the University of Illinois, observes that the core asser-tion of this approach—that high levels of transaction-specific investment lead to higher levels of vertical integra-tion—receives consistent empirical support.

More recent work has begun to examine the trade-offs among these three explanations of vertical integra-tion by examining their effects on verti-cal integration simultaneously. For example, Professor Tim Folta of Purdue University examined the opportunism and flexibility approaches to vertical integration simultaneously. His results show that the basic assertion of the opportunism approach still holds. However, when he adds uncertainty to his empirical analysis, he finds that firms engage in less vertical integra-

Empirical Tests of Theories
of Vertical Integration

tion than those in which they would otherwise engage. In other words, firms apparently worry not only about transaction-specific investments when they make vertical integration choices; they also worry about how costly it is to reverse those investments in the face of high uncertainty.

An even more recent study by Michael Leiblein of The Ohio State University and Doug Miller of Tulane University, examines all three of these explanations of vertical integration simultaneously. These authors study vertical integration decisions in the semiconductor manufacturing indus-try and find that all three explanations hold. That is, firms in this industry worry about transaction-specific investment, the capabilities they pos-sess, the capabilities they would like to possess, and the uncertainty of the markets within which they operate when they make vertical integration choices.

Sources: J. Mahoney (1992). "The choice of orga-nizational form: Vertical financial ownership versus other methods of vertical integration." *Strategic Management Journal*, 13, pp. 559–584; T. Folta (1998). "Governance and uncertainty: The trade-off between administrative control and commitment." *Strategic Management Journal*, 19, pp. 1007–1028; M. Leiblein and D. Miller (2003). "An empirical examination of transaction- and firm-level influences on the vertical boundaries of the firm." *Strategic Management Journal*, 24(9), pp. 839–859.

Applying the Theories to the Management of Call Centers

So, what do these three theories say about how call centers should be managed? Each of these theories will be discussed in turn.

Transaction-Specific Investments and Managing Call Centers

When applying opportunism-based explanations of vertical integration, start by looking for actual or potential transaction-specific investments that would need to be made in order to complete an exchange. High levels of such investments sug-gest the need for vertical integration; low levels of such investments suggest that vertically integrating this exchange is not necessary.

In the context of call centers, when this approach to providing customer ser-vice was first developed in the 1980s, it required substantial levels of transaction-specific investment. First, a great deal of special purpose equipment had to be pur-chased. And while this equipment could be used for any call center, it had little value except within a call center. Thus, this equipment was an example of a some-what specific investment.

More importantly, in order to provide service in call centers, call center employees would have to be fully aware of all the problems that are likely to emerge with the use of a firm's products. This requires a firm to study its products very closely and then to train call center employees to be able to respond to any problems customers might have. This training was sometimes very complex and very time-consuming and represented substantial transaction-specific investments on the part of call center employees. Only employees that worked full-time for a large corporation—where job security was usually high for productive workers—would be willing to make these kinds of specific investments. Thus, vertical integration into call center management made a great deal of sense.

However, as information technology improved, firms found it was possible to train call center employees much faster. Now, all call center employees had to do was follow scripts that were pre-written and pre-loaded on their computers. By asking a few pre-scripted questions, call center employees could diagnose most problems. And solutions to those problems were also included on an employee's computer. Only really unusual problems could not be handled by employees working off these computer scripts. Because the level of specific investment required to use these scripts was much lower, employees were willing to work for companies without the job security usually associated with large firms. Indeed, call centers became good part-time and temporary employment opportunities. Since the level of specific investment required to work in these call centers was much lower, not vertically integrating into call center management made a great deal of sense.

Capabilities and Managing Call Centers

In opportunism-based explanations of vertical integration, you start by looking for transaction-specific investments and then make vertical integration decisions based on these investments. In capability-based approaches, you start by looking for valuable, rare, and costly-to-imitate resources and capabilities, and then make vertical integration decisions appropriately.

In the early days of call center management, how well a firm operated its call centers could actually be a source of competitive advantage. During this time period, the technology was new, and the training required to answer a customer's questions was extensive. Firms that developed special capabilities in managing these processes could gain competitive advantages and thus would vertically integrate into call center management.

However, over time, as more and more call center management suppliers were created, and as the technology and training required to staff a call center became more widely available, the ability of a call center to be a source of competitive advantage for a firm dropped. That is, the ability to manage a call center was still valuable, but it was no longer rare or costly to imitate. In this setting, it is not surprising to see firms getting out of the call center management business, outsourcing this business to low-cost specialist firms, and focusing on those business functions where they might be able to gain a sustained competitive advantage.

Flexibility and Managing Call Centers

Opportunism logic suggests starting with a search for transaction-specific investments; capabilities logic suggests starting with a search for valuable, rare, and costly-to-imitate resources and capabilities. Flexibility logic suggests starting by looking for sources of uncertainty in an exchange.

One of the biggest uncertainties in providing customer service through call centers is the question: Can the people staffing the phones actually help a firm's customers? This is a particularly troubling concern for firms that are selling complex products that can have numerous different kinds of problems. A variety of technological solutions have been developed to try to address this uncertainty. But, if a firm vertically integrates into the call center management business, it is committing to a particular technological solution. This solution may not work, or may not work as well as some other solutions.

In the face of this uncertainty, maintaining relationships with several different call center management companies—each of whom have adopted different technological solutions to the problem of how to use call center employees to assist customers who are using very complex products—gives a firm technological flexibility that it would not otherwise have. Once a superior solution is identified, then a firm no longer needs this flexibility and may choose to vertically integrate into call center management or not—depending on opportunism and capabilities considerations.

Integrating Different Theories of Vertical Integration

At first glance, having three different explanations about how vertical integration can create value seems troubling. After all, won't these explanations sometimes contradict each other?

The answer to this question is: Yes. We have already seen such a contradiction in the case of opportunism and capabilities explanations of whether or not Wal-Mart suppliers should forward vertically integrate into the discount retail industry.

However, more often than not, these three explanations are complementary in nature. That is, applying these three approaches generally leads to the same conclusions about how a firm should vertically integrate, not different conclusions. Moreover, sometimes it is simply easier to apply one of these approaches to evaluate a firm's vertical integration choices than the other two. Having a "tool kit" that includes three explanations of vertical integration enables the analyst to choose the approach that is most likely to be a source of insight in a particular situation.

Even when these explanations make contradictory assertions about vertical integration, having multiple approaches can be helpful. In this context, having multiple explanations can highlight the trade-offs that a firm is making when choosing its vertical integration strategy. Thus, for example, if opportunism-based explanations suggest that vertical integration is necessary because of high transaction-specific investments, capabilities-based explanations caution about the cost of developing the resources and capabilities necessary to vertically integrate and flexibility concerns caution about the risks that committing to vertical integration imply, and the costs and benefits of whatever vertical integration decision is ultimately made can be understood very clearly.

Overall, having three explanations of vertical integration has several advantages for those looking to analyze the vertical integration choices of real firms. Of course, applying these explanations can create important ethical dilemmas for a firm, especially when it becomes clear that a firm needs to become less vertically integrated than it has historically been. Some of these dilemmas are discussed in the Ethics and Strategy feature.

Vertical Integration and Sustained Competitive Advantage

Of course, in order for vertical integration to be a source of sustained competitive advantage, not only must it be valuable (because it responds to threats of opportunism; enables a firm to exploit its own or other firms' valuable, rare,

Ethics and Strategy

*I*magine a firm that has successfully operated in a vertically integrated manner for decades. Employees come to work, they know their jobs, they know how to work together effectively, they know where to park. The job is not just the economic center of their lives; it has become the social center as well. Most of their friends work in the same company, in the same function, as they do. The future appears to be much as the past—stable employment and effective work, all aiming toward a comfortable and well-planned retirement. And then the firm adopts a new outsourcing strategy. It changes its vertical integration strategy by becoming less vertically integrated and purchasing services from outside suppliers that it used to obtain internally.

The economics of outsourcing can be compelling. Outsourcing can help firms reduce costs and focus their efforts on those business functions that are central to their competitive advantage. When done well, outsourcing creates value—value that firms can share with their owners, their stockholders.

Indeed, outsourcing is becoming a trend in business. In 2000, companies that specialize in providing outsourced services had worldwide sales of over $1

The Ethics of Outsourcing

trillion. As important, the size of this outsourced services market doubled from 1997 to 2000. By 2015, some observers predict that an additional 3.3 million jobs in the United States will be outsourced, many to operations overseas.

But what of the employees whose jobs are taken away? What of their lifetime of commitment, their steady and reliable work? What of their stable and secure retirement? Outsourcing often devastates lives, even as it creates economic value. Of course, some firms go out of their way to soften the impact of

outsourcing on their employees. Those that are near retirement age are often given an opportunity to retire early. Others receive severance payments in recognition of their years of service. Other firms hire "out placement" companies—firms that specialize in placing suddenly unemployed people in new jobs and new careers.

But all these efforts to soften the blow do not make the blow go away. Many employees assume that they have an implicit contract with the firms they work for. That contract is: "As long as I do my job well, I will have a job." That contract is being replaced with: "As long as a firm wants to employ me, I will have a job." In this world, it is not surprising that many employees now look first to maintain their employability in their current job—by receiving additional training and experiences that might be valuable at numerous other employers—and are concerned less with what they can do to improve the performance of the firm they work for.

Sources: S. Steele-Carlin (2003). "Outsourcing poised for growth in 2002." *FreelanceJobs News*.com, October 20; (2003). "Who wins in off shoring?" *McKinseyQuarterly*.com, October 20.

and costly-to-imitate resources; or because it gives a firm flexibility); it must also be rare and costly to imitate, and a firm must be organized to implement it correctly.

The Rarity of Vertical Integration

A firm's vertical integration strategy is rare when few competing firms are able to create value by vertically integrating in the same way. A firm's vertical integration strategy can be rare because it is one of a small number of competing firms that are able to vertically integrate efficiently or because it is one of a small number of firms that are able to adopt a non–vertically integrated approach to managing an exchange.

Rare Vertical Integration

A firm may be able to create value through vertical integration, when most of its competitors are not able to create value through vertical integration, for at least three reasons. Not surprisingly, these reasons parallel the three explanations of vertical integration presented in this chapter.

Rare Transaction-Specific Investment and Vertical Integration. First, a firm may have developed a new technology, or a new approach to doing business, that requires its business partners to make substantial transaction-specific investments. Firms that engage in these activities will find it in their self-interest to vertically integrate, while firms that have not engaged in these activities will not find it in their self-interest to vertically integrate. If these activities are rare and costly to imitate, they can be a source of competitive advantage for a vertically integrating firm.

For example, the opening case in this chapter suggests that many firms in the computer industry are outsourcing their call centers to India. However, one firm—Dell Computers—recently brought one of its call centers back from India and re–vertically integrated into this business. The call center Dell brought back within its boundaries provides technical support to its corporate customers.[6] The problems faced by corporate customers are typically much more complicated than the problems faced by individual consumers. Thus, it is much more difficult to provide call center employees the training they need to address corporate problems. Moreover, because corporate technologies change more rapidly than many consumer technologies, keeping call center employees up-to-date on how to service corporate customers is also more complicated than having call center employees provide services to its noncorporate customers. Because Dell needs the people staffing its corporate call centers to make substantial specific investments in its technology and in understanding its customers, it has found it necessary to bring these individuals within the boundaries of the firm and to re–vertically integrate the operation of this particular type of service center.

If Dell, through this vertical integration decision, is able to satisfy its customers more effectively than its competitors, and if the cost of managing this call center is not too high, then this vertical integration decision is both valuable and rare and thus a source of at least a temporary competitive advantage for Dell.

Rare Capabilities and Vertical Integration. A firm like Dell might also conclude that it has unusual skills, either in operating a call center, or in providing the training that is needed to staff certain kinds of call centers. If those capabilities are valuable and rare, then vertically integrating into businesses that exploit these capabilities can enable a firm to gain at least a temporary competitive advantage. Indeed, the belief that a firm possesses valuable and rare capabilities is often a justification for rare vertical integration decisions in an industry. Consider, for example, MTV's decision to enter the Indian market, described in the Global Perspectives feature.

Rare Uncertainty and Vertical Integration. Finally, a firm may be able to gain an advantage from vertically integrating when it resolves some uncertainty it faces sooner than its competition. Suppose, for example, that several firms in an industry all begin investing in a very uncertain technology. Flexibility logic suggests that, to the extent possible, these firms will prefer to not vertically integrate into the manufacturing of this technology until its designs and features stabilize and market demand for this technology is well established.

However, imagine that one of these firms is able to resolve these uncertainties before any other firm. This firm no longer needs to retain the flexibility that is so valuable under conditions of uncertainty. Instead, this firm might be able to,

Global Perspectives

MTV has a dominant brand in music television in the United States and much of western Europe. Given that this brand is valuable, rare, and costly to imitate in these markets, it is not surprising that MTV has decided to continue its international expansion by moving into Malaysia, Japan, India, and other countries in Asia. However, Viacom—MTV's corporate parent—is finding it necessary to modify much of its content as it tries to introduce MTV in these Asian markets.

For example, when MTV first entered India in 1991, it presented content originally produced for its U.S. station and for the rest of Asia. This included rock-and-roll videos, rap videos, and English-speaking vee-jays. Later, it presented reruns of *The Osbournes*. The only problem with this strategy was that Indian teenagers don't like rock-and-roll videos, rap videos, and English-speaking vee-jays, and were totally mystified by *The Osbournes*. Another successful U.S. MTV product—*MTV Grind*—about spring break, was too risqué for an Indian audience and was cancelled soon after it was first shown.

To respond to this local market, MTV has had to develop more locally oriented fare, including *Roadies*, a show based loosely on MTV's popular *Road*

Producing a Hindi Version of *The Osbournes*

Rules program. However, unlike *Road Rules*—where contestants ride across America in a comfortable RV—in *Roadies*, four young men and three young women ride across India on two-wheeled motor scooters. Moreover, all of MTV India's vee-jays now speak Hinglish—a combination of Hindi and English—and present popular Indian music videos.

An even more radical departure for MTV India is its new youth-oriented soap opera *Kitna Mast Hai Zindagi*, which means *It's a Beautiful Life*. What is most unusual about this

production is that, unlike most of the other programming on MTV India, this show is not produced by MTV itself. In an effort to gain a true "Indian" feel to this new soap, MTV India actually outsourced its production to an Indian production company. This company, Balaji Telefilms, already produces a successful prime time soap opera on another Indian cable channel.

These efforts are beginning to pay some dividends in the Indian market. In 2003, MTV India had revenues of about $25 million and generated "several million" in profits—a very small amont of money for $27 billion Viacom, but a respectful level of performance in a difficult market. However, MTV India has many challenges left if it is to reach a size and profitability level that will make it an important business for Viacom. For example, currently MTV India is broadcast in Hinglish and reaches the Hindi-speaking population. However, large regions of India speak Tamil, Telegu, and Punjabi, not Hindi. What if someone who speaks Telegu says, "I want my MTV"? How will MTV India respond?

Sources: M. Gunther (2004). "MTV's passage to India." *Fortune*, August 9, pp. 117 +. © 2004 Time Inc. All rights reserved.

---

say, design special purpose machines that can very efficiently manufacture this technology. Such machines are not flexible, but they can be very efficient.

Of course, for outside vendors to use these new machines, they would have to make substantial transaction-specific investments. Outside vendors may be reluctant to make these investments. In this setting, this firm may find it necessary to vertically integrate to be able to use its machines to produce this technology. Thus, this firm, by resolving uncertainty faster than its competitors, is able to gain some of the advantages of vertical integration sooner than its competitors. While the competition is still focusing on flexibility in the face of uncertainty, this firm gets to focus on production efficiency in meeting customers' product demands. This can obviously be a source of competitive advantage.

Rare Vertical Dis-Integration

Each of the examples of vertical integration and competitive advantage described so far focus on a firm's ability to vertically integrate to create competitive advantage. However, firms can also gain competitive advantages through their decisions to vertically dis-integrate, that is, through the decision to outsource an activity that used to be within the boundaries of the firm. Whenever a firm is among the first in its industry to conclude that the level of specific investment required to manage an economic exchange is no longer high, or that a particular exchange is no longer rare or costly to imitate, or that the level of uncertainty about the value of an exchange has increased, it may be among the first in its industry to vertically dis-integrate this exchange. Such activities, to the extent they are valuable, will be rare, and thus a source of at least a temporary competitive advantage.

The Imitability of Vertical Integration

The extent to which these rare vertical integration decisions can be sources of sustained competitive advantage depends, as always, on the imitability of the rare resources that gives a firm at least a temporary competitive advantage. Both direct duplication and substitution can be used to imitate another firm's valuable and rare vertical integration choices.

Direct Duplication of Vertical Integration

Direct duplication occurs when competitors develop or obtain the resources and capabilities that enable another firm to implement a valuable and rare vertical integration strategy. To the extent that these resources and capabilities are path dependent, socially complex, or causally ambiguous, they may be immune from direct duplication and thus can be a source of sustained competitive advantage.

With respect to outsourcing call centers to India, it seems that the very popularity of this strategy suggests that it is highly imitable. Indeed, this strategy is becoming so common that firms that move in the other direction by vertically integrating a call center and managing it in the United States (like Dell) make news.

But the fact that many firms are outsourcing their call centers to India does not mean that they are all equally successful in doing so. These differences in performance may reflect some subtle and complex capabilities that some of these outsourcing firms possess that others do not. These are the kinds of resources and capabilities that may be sources of sustained competitive advantage.

Some of the resources that might enable a firm to implement a valuable and rare vertical integration strategy may not be susceptible to direct duplication. These might include a firm's ability to analyze the attributes of its economic exchanges and its ability to conceive of and implement vertical integration strategies. Both of these capabilities may be socially complex and path dependent—built up over years of experience.

Substitutes for Vertical Integration

The major substitute for vertical integration—strategic alliances—is the major topic of Chapter 9. So an analysis of how strategic alliances can substitute for vertical integration will be delayed until then.

Organizing to Implement Vertical Integration

V R I O

Organizing to implement vertical integration involves the same organizing tools as implementing any business or corporate strategy: organizational structure, management controls, and compensation policies.

Organizational Structure and Implementing Vertical Integration

The organizational structure that is used to implement a cost leadership and product differentiation strategy—the functional or U-form structure—is also used to implement a vertical integration strategy. Indeed, each of the exchanges included within the boundaries of a firm as a result of vertical integration decisions are incorporated into one of the functions in a functional organizational structure. Decisions about which manufacturing activities to vertically integrate into determine the range and responsibilities of the manufacturing function within a functionally organized firm; decisions about which marketing activities to vertically integrate into determine the range and responsibilities of the marketing function within a functionally organized firm; and so forth. Thus, in an important sense, vertical integration decisions made by a firm determine the structure of a functionally organized firm.

The CEO in this vertically integrated, functionally organized firm has the same two responsibilities that were first identified in Chapter 4: strategy formulation and strategy implementation. However, these two responsibilities take on added dimensions when implementing vertical integration decisions. In particular, while the CEO must take the lead in making decisions about whether or not each individual function should be vertically integrated into a firm, this person must also work to resolve conflicts that naturally arise between vertically integrated functions. The approach of one reluctant CEO to this management challenge is described in the Strategy in the Emerging Enterprise feature.

Resolving Functional Conflicts in a Vertically Integrated Firm

From a CEO's perspective, coordinating functional specialists to implement a vertical integration strategy almost always involves conflict resolution. Conflicts among functional managers in a U-form organization are both expected and normal. Indeed, if there is no conflict among certain functional managers in a U-form organization, then some of these managers probably are not doing their jobs. The task facing the CEO is not to pretend this conflict does not exist, or to ignore it, but to manage it in a way that facilitates strategy implementation.

Consider, for example, the relationship between manufacturing and sales managers. Typically, manufacturing managers prefer to manufacture a single product with long production runs. Sales managers, however, generally prefer to sell numerous customized products. Manufacturing managers generally do not like large inventories of finished products; sales managers generally prefer large inventories of finished products that facilitate rapid deliveries to customers. If these various interests of manufacturing and sales managers do not, at least sometimes, come into conflict in a vertically integrated U-form organization, then the manufacturing manager is not focusing enough on cost reduction and quality improvement in manufacturing or the sales manager is not focusing enough on meeting customer needs in a timely way, or both.

Strategy in the Emerging Enterprise

With revenues close to $1 billion a year, this woman heads one of the most successful multimedia companies in the United States. One of the businesses she owns—Harpo, Inc.—produces one of the most successful daytime television shows ever (with revenues of over $300 million a year); a magazine with the most successful launch ever and currently 2.5 million paid subscribers (more than *Vogue* and *Fortune*); and a movie production unit. One investment banker estimates that if Harpo, Inc. was a publicly traded firm, it would be valued at $575 million. Other properties she owns—including investments, real estate, a stake in the cable television channel Oxygen, and stock options in Viacom—generate another $468 million in revenues per year.

And Oprah Winfrey does not consider herself to be a CEO.

Certainly, her decision-making style is not typical of most CEOs. She has been quoted as describing her business decision-making as "leaps of faith" and "If I called a strategic planning meeting, there would be dead silence, and then people would fall out of their chairs laughing."

Oprah, Inc.

One the other hand, she has made other decisions that put her firmly in control of her empire. For example, in 1987, she hired a tough Chicago entertainment attorney— Jeff Jacobs—as president of Harpo, Inc. Where Oprah's business decisions are made from her gut and from her heart, Jacobs makes sure that the numbers add up to more revenues and profits for Harpo. She has also been unwilling to license her name to other firms, unlike Martha Stewart who licensed her name to Kmart. Oprah has made strategic alliances with King World (to distribute her TV show), with ABC (to broadcast her movies), with Hearst (to distribute her magazine), and with Oxygen (to distribute some other television programs). But she has never given up control of her business. And she has not taken her firm public. She was once quoted as saying "If I lost control of my business, I'd lose myself—or at least the ability to be myself."

To help control this growing business, Oprah and Jacobs hired a chief operating officer (COO), Tim Bennett, who then created several functional departments, including accounting, legal, and human resources, to help manage the firm. With 221 employees, an office, and a real organization, Harpo is a real company, and Oprah is a real CEO—albeit a CEO with a slightly different approach to making business decisions.

Sources: P. Sellers (2002). "The Business of being Oprah." *Fortune*, April 1, pp. 50 +; Oprah.com; Hoovers.com, "Harpo Inc.," October 20, 2003.

Numerous other conflicts arise among functional managers in a vertically integrated U-form organization. Accountants often focus on maximizing managerial accountability and close analysis of costs; R&D managers may fear that such accounting practices will interfere with innovation and creativity. Finance managers often focus on the relationship between a firm and its external capital markets; human resource managers are more concerned with the relationship between a firm and external labor markets.

In this context, the CEO's job is to help resolve conflicts in ways that facilitate the implementation of the firm's strategy. Functional managers do not have to "like" each other. However, if a firm's vertical integration strategy is correct, the reason that a function has been included within the boundaries of a firm is that this decision creates value for the firm. Allowing functional conflicts to get in the way of taking advantage of each of the functions within a firm's boundaries can destroy this potential value.

Management Controls and Implementing Vertical Integration

While having the correct organizational structure is important for firms implementing their vertical integration strategies, that structure must be supported by a variety of management control processes. Among the most important of these processes are the budgeting process and the management committee oversight process, which can also help CEOs resolve the functional conflicts that are common within vertically integrated firms.

The Budgeting Process

Budgeting is one of the most important control mechanisms available to CEOs in vertically integrated U-form organizations. Indeed, in most U-form companies, enormous management effort goes into the creation of budgets and the evaluation of performance relative to budgets. Budgets are developed for costs, revenues, and a variety of other activities performed by a firm's functional managers. Often, managerial compensation and promotion opportunities depend on the ability of a manager to meet budget expectations.

Although budgets are an important control tool, they can also have unintended negative consequences. For example, the use of budgets can lead functional managers to overemphasize short-term behavior that is easy to measure and underemphasize longer-term behavior that is more difficult to measure. Thus, for example, the strategically correct thing for a functional manager to do might be to increase expenditures for maintenance and management training, thereby ensuring that the function will have both the technology and the skilled people needed to do the job in the future. An overemphasis on meeting current budget requirements, however, might lead this manager to delay maintenance and training expenditures. By meeting short-term budgetary demands, this manager may be sacrificing the long-term viability of this function and thereby compromising the long-term viability of the firm.

CEOs can do a variety of things to counter the "short-termism" effects of the budgeting process. For example, research suggests that evaluating a functional manager's performance relative to budgets can be an effective control device when (1) the process used in developing budgets is open and participative, (2) the process reflects the economic reality facing functional managers and the firm, and (3) quantitative evaluations of a functional manger's performance are augmented by qualitative evaluations of that performance. Adopting an open and participative process for setting budgets helps ensure that budget targets are realistic and that functional managers understand and accept them. Including qualitative criteria for evaluation reduces the chances that functional managers will engage in behaviors that are very harmful in the long run but enable them to make budget in the short run.[7]

The Management Committee Oversight Process

In addition to budgets, vertically integrated U-form organizations can use various internal management committees as management control devices. Two particularly common internal management committees are the **executive committee** and the **operations committee** (although these committees have many different names in different organizations).

The executive committee in a U-form organization typically consists of the CEO and two or three key functional senior managers. It normally meets weekly and reviews the performance of the firm on a short-term basis. Functions represented on this committee generally include accounting, legal, and other functions (such as manufacturing or sales) that are most central to the firm's short-term business success. The fundamental purpose of the executive committee is to track the short-term performance of the firm, to note and correct any budget variances for functional managers, and to respond to any crises that might emerge. Obviously, the executive committee can help avoid many functional conflicts in a vertically integrated firm before they arise.

In addition to the executive committee, another group of managers meets regularly to help control the operations of the firm. Often called the operations committee, this committee typically meets monthly and usually consists of the CEO and each of the heads of the functional areas included in the firm. The executive committee is a subset of the operations committee.

The primary objective of the operations committee is to track firm performance over time intervals slightly longer than the weekly interval of primary interest to the executive committee and to monitor longer-term strategic investments and activities. Such investments might include plant expansions, the introduction of new products, and the implementation of cost-reduction or quality improvement programs. The operations committee provides a forum in which senior functional managers can come together to share concerns and opportunities and to coordinate efforts to implement strategies. Obviously, the operations committee can help resolve functional conflicts in a vertically integrated firm after they arise.

In addition to these two standing committees, various other committees and task forces can be organized within the U-form organization to manage specific projects and tasks. These additional groups are typically chaired by a member of the executive or operations committee and report to one or both of these standing committees as warranted.

Compensation in Implementing Vertical Integration Strategies

Organizational structure and management control systems can have an important impact on the ability of a firm to implement its vertical integration strategy. However, a firm's compensation policies can be important as well.

We have already seen how compensation can play a role in implementing cost leadership and product differentiation, and how compensation can be tied to budgets to help implement vertical integration. However, the three explanations of vertical integration presented in this chapter have important compensation implications as well. We will first discuss the compensation challenges these three explanations suggest and then discuss ways these challenges can be addressed.

Compensation Challenges

Opportunism-based Vertical Integration and Compensation Policy. For example, when opportunism-based approaches to vertical integration are applied to the exchange between a firm and its employees, this suggests that employees who make firm-specific investments in their jobs will often be able to create more value for a firm than employees who do not make firm-specific investments. Firm-specific investments are a type of transaction-specific investment. Where transaction-specific investments are investments that have more value in a particular exchange than in alternative exchanges, **firm-specific investments** are investments made by employees that have more value in a particular firm than in alternative firms.[8]

Examples of firm-specific investments include an employee's understanding of a particular firm's culture, his/her personal relationships with others in the firm, and an employee's knowledge about a firm's unique business processes. All this knowledge can be used by an employee to create a great deal of value in a firm. However, this knowledge has almost no value in other firms. The effort to create this knowledge is thus a firm-specific investment.

Despite the value that an employee's firm-specific investments can create, opportunism-based explanations of vertical integration suggest that employees will often be reluctant to make these investments because, once they do, they become vulnerable in their exchange with this firm. For example, an employee who has made very significant firm-specific investments may not be able to quit and go to work for another company, even if her or she is passed over for promotion, does not receive a raise, or is even actively discriminated against. This is because by quitting this firm, this employee loses all the investment he or she made in this particular firm. Since this employee has few employment options other than his or her current firm, this firm can treat this employee badly and the employee can do little about it. This is why employees are often reluctant to make firm-specific investments.

But the firm needs its employees to make such investments if it is to realize its full economic potential. Thus, one of the tasks of compensation policy is to create incentives for employees whose firm-specific investments could create great value to actually make those investments.

Capabilities and Compensation. Capability explanations of vertical integration also acknowledge the importance of firm-specific investments in creating value for a firm. Indeed, many of the valuable, rare, and costly-to-imitate resources and capabilities that can exist in a firm are a manifestation of firm-specific investments made by a firm's employees. However, where opportunism explanations of vertical integration tend to focus on firm-specific investments made by individual employees, capabilities explanations tend to focus on firm-specific investments made by groups of employees.[9]

In Chapter 3, it was suggested that one of the reasons that a firm's valuable and rare resources may be costly to imitate is that these resources are socially complex in nature. Socially complex resources reflect the teamwork, cooperation, and culture that have evolved within a firm—capabilities that can increase the value of a firm significantly, but capabilities that other firms will often find costly to imitate, at least in the short to medium term. Moreover, these are capabilities that exist because several employees—not just a single employee—have made specific investments in a firm.

From the point of view of designing a compensation policy, capabilities analysis suggests that not only should a firm's compensation policy encourage employees whose firm-specific investments could create value to actually make those investments; this theory also recognizes that these investments will often be collective in nature—that, for example, until all the members of a critical management team make firm-specific commitments to that team, that team's ability to create and sustain competitive advantages will be significantly limited.

Flexibility and Compensation. Flexibility explanations of vertical integration also have some important implications for compensation. In particular, since the creation of flexibility in a firm depends on employees being willing to engage in activities that have fixed and known downside risks and significant upside potential, it follows that compensation that has fixed and known downside risks and significant upside potential would encourage employees to choose and implement flexible vertical integration strategies.

Table 6.1   **Types of Compensation and Approaches to Making Vertical Integration Decisions**

Opportunism Explanations	Salary Cash Bonuses for individual performance Stock Grants for individual performance
Capabilities Explanations	Cash Bonuses for corporate or group performance Stock Grants for corporate or group performance
Flexibility Explanations	Stock Options for individual, corporate, or group performance

Compensation Alternatives

Table 6.1 lists several compensation alternatives and how they are related to each of the three explanations of vertical integration discussed in this chapter. Not surprisingly, opportunism-based explanations suggest that compensation that focuses on individual employees and how they can make firm-specific investments will be important for firms implementing their vertical integration strategies. Such individual compensation includes an employee's salary, cash bonuses based on individual performance, and **stock grants**—or payments to employees in a firm's stock—based on individual performance.

Capabilities explanations of vertical integration suggest that compensation that focuses on groups of employees making firm-specific investments in valuable, rare, and costly-to-imitate resources and capabilities will be particularly important for firms implementing their vertical integration strategies. Such collective compensation includes cash bonuses based on a firm's overall performance and stock grants based on a firm's overall performance.

Finally, flexibility logic suggests that compensation that has fixed and known downside risk and significant upside potential is important for firms implementing their vertical integration strategies. **Stock options**, where employees are given the right but not the obligation to purchase stock at predetermined prices, are a form of compensation that has these characteristics. Stock options can be granted based on an individual employee's performance or the performance of the firm as a whole.

The task facing CEOs looking to implement a vertical integration strategy through compensation policy is to determine what kinds of employee behavior they need to have for this strategy to create sustained competitive advantages and then to use the appropriate compensation policy. Not surprisingly, most CEOs find that all three explanations of vertical integration are important in their decision making and thus, not surprisingly, many firms adopt compensation policies that feature a mix of the compensation policies listed in Table 6.1. Thus, most firms use both individual and corporate-wide compensation schemes along with salaries, cash bonuses, stock grants, and stock options for employees who have the greatest impact on a firm's overall performance.

Vertical Integration in an International Context

Examples of vertical integration strategies that lead firms to begin operations beyond their home country borders—in particular, outsourcing to India—have already been featured in this chapter. Currently, the trend in vertical integration decisions in an international context seems to be for firms to reduce their level of

Table 6.2   **Vertical Integration Options When Pursuing International Market Opportunities**

Not Vertically Integrated	*Somewhat Vertically Integrated*	*Vertically Integrated*
Importing/Exporting	Licensing Strategic Alliances Joint Ventures	Foreign Direct Investment

vertical integration by outsourcing functions that used to be within their boundaries to independent foreign operations. However, in some settings, firms exploit international market opportunities not by outsourcing to independent foreign firms, but by entering those international markets in a vertically integrated way.

The vertical integration options available to firms pursuing an international strategy are listed in Table 6.2. These options range from non–vertically integrated (exporting/importing), to somewhat vertically integrated (licensing, strategic alliances, joint ventures), to fully vertically integrated (foreign direct investment). Each of these options is discussed briefly below.

Firms can maintain traditional arm's-length market relationships between themselves and their nondomestic customers and still implement international strategies. They do this by simply importing supplies from nondomestic sources or by exporting their products or services to nondomestic markets. In this way, firms limit any foreign direct investment into nondomestic markets. Of course, firms that adopt this non-vertically integrated approach generally have to work with some partner or partners to receive, market, and distribute their products in a nondomestic market. However, it is possible for exporting firms to use relatively simple contracts to manage their relationships with these foreign partners and thereby maintain arm's-length relationships with them.

The advantages of adopting a non–vertically integrated approach in engaging in an international strategy includes its relatively low cost and the limited risk exposure that firms that pursue international opportunities in this manner face. Firms that are just beginning to consider international strategies can use non–vertically integrated approaches to test international waters—to find out if there is demand for their current products or services, to develop some experience operating in nondomestic markets, or to begin to develop relationships that could be valuable in subsequent international strategy efforts. If firms discover that there is not much demand for their products or services in a nondomestic market, or if they discover that they do not have the resources and capabilities to effectively compete in those markets, they can simply cease their international operations. The direct cost of ceasing these operations can be quite low, especially if a firm's volume of international activity is small and the firm has not invested in plant and equipment internationally. Certainly, if a firm has limited its foreign direct investment, it does not risk losing this investment if it ceases international operations.

If a firm decides to move beyond non–vertically integrated approaches in pursuing international strategies, a wide range of somewhat vertically integrated approaches is available. These approaches range from simple **licensing arrangements**, where a domestic firm grants a firm in a nondomestic market the right to use its products and brand names to sell products in that nondomestic market; to full-blown joint ventures, where a domestic firm and a nondomestic firm create an independent organizational entity to manage international efforts. Again these options will be discussed in depth in Chapter 9.

Finally, firms may decide to integrate in their international operations by acquiring a firm in a nondomestic market or by forming a new wholly owned subsidiary to manage their operations in a nondomestic market. Obviously, both of these international investments involve substantial direct foreign investment by a firm over long periods of time. These investments are subject to both political and economic risks and should be undertaken only if the value they create is significant.

Although vertical integration in international operations can be expensive and risky, it can have some important advantages for internationalizing firms. First, this approach to internationalization can enable a firm to realize any sources of value that might exist in an international opportunity. Moreover, integration enables managers to use a wider range of organizational controls to limit the threats from any transaction-specific investments that have been made. Finally, unlike strategic alliances, where any profits from international operations must be shared with international partners, integrating into international operations enables firms to capture all the economic profits from their international operations.

SUMMARY

Vertical integration is defined as the number of stages in an industry's value chain that a firm has brought within its boundaries. Forward vertical integration is vertical integration that brings a firm closer to its ultimate customer; backward vertical integration is vertical integration that brings a firm closer to the sources of its raw materials. In making their vertical integration decisions for a particular business activity, firms can choose to be not vertically integrated, somewhat vertically integrated, or vertically integrated.

Vertical integration can create value in three different ways: First, by reducing opportunistic threats from a firm's buyers and suppliers due to any transaction-specific investments it may have made. A transaction-specific investment is an investment that has more value in a particular exchange than in any alternative exchanges. Second, vertical integration can create value by enabling a firm to exploit its valuable, rare, and costly-to-imitate resources and capabilities. Firms should vertically integrate into activities where they enjoy such advantages and should not vertically integrate into other activities. Third, vertical integration typically only creates value under conditions of low uncertainty. Under high uncertainty, vertical integration can commit a firm to a costly-to-reverse course of action and the flexibility of a non–vertically integrated approach may be preferred.

Often, these three different approaches to vertical integration will generate similar conclusions. However, even when they suggest different vertical integration strategies, they can still be helpful to management.

The ability of valuable vertical integration strategies to generate a sustained competitive advantage depends on how rare and costly to imitate these strategies are. Vertical integration strategies can be rare in two ways: (1) when a firm is vertically integrated while most competing firms are not vertically integrated and (2) when a firm is not vertically integrated while most competing firms are. These rare vertical integration strategies are possible when firms vary in the extent to which the strategies they pursue require transaction-specific investments; firms vary in the resources and capabilities they control; or firms vary in the level of uncertainty they face.

The ability to directly duplicate a firm's vertical integration strategies depends on how costly it is to directly duplicate the resources and capabilities that enable a firm to pursue these strategies. The closest substitute for vertical integration—strategic alliances—is discussed in more detail in Chapter 9.

Organizing to implement vertical integration depends on a firm's organizational structure, its management controls, and its compensation policies. The organizational structure most commonly used to implement vertical integration is the functional or U-form organization which involves cost leadership and product differentiation strategies. In a vertically integrated U-form organization, the CEO has to focus not only on deciding which functions to vertically integrate into, but also how to resolve conflicts that inevitably arise in a functionally organized vertically integrated firm. Two management controls that can be used to help implement vertical integration strategies and resolve these functional conflicts are the budgeting process and management oversight committees.

Each of the three explanations of vertical integration suggests different kinds of compensation policies that a firm looking to implement vertical integration should pursue. Opportunism-based explanations suggest individual-based compensation—including salaries and cash bonus and stock grants based on individual performance—while capabilities explanations suggests group-based compensation—including cash bonuses and stock grants based on corporate or group performance—and flexibility explanations suggest flexible compensation—including stock options based on individual, group, or corporate performance. Because all three approaches to vertical integration are often operating in a firm, it is not surprising that many firms employ all these devices in compensating employees whose actions are likely to have a significant impact on firm performance.

Firms in an international context also can choose to not be vertically integrated, somewhat vertically integrated, or vertically integrated. Firms choose to be not vertically integrated when they engage in arm's-length importing or exporting. They choose to be somewhat vertically integrated when they engage in licensing, strategic alliances, or joint ventures; and they choose vertical integration when they engage in foreign direct investment.

CHALLENGE QUESTIONS

1. Some firms have engaged in backward vertical integration strategies in order to appropriate the economic profits that would have been earned by suppliers selling to them. How is this motivation for backward vertical integration related to the opportunism logic for vertical integration described in this chapter? (*Hint*: Compare the competitive conditions under which firms may earn economic profits to the competitive conditions under which firms will be motivated to avoid opportunism through vertical integration.)

2. You are about to purchase a used car. What kinds of threats do you face in this purchase? What can you do to protect yourself from these threats? How is buying a car like and unlike vertical integration decisions?

3. What are the competitive implications for firms if they assume that all potential exchange partners cannot be trusted?

4. Common conflicts between sales and manufacturing are mentioned in the text. What conflicts might exist between R&D and manufacturing? Between finance and manufacturing? Between marketing and sales? Between accounting and everyone else? What could a CEO do to help resolve these conflicts?

5. Under what conditions would you accept a lower-paying job instead of a higher-paying job? What implications does your answer have for your potential employer's compensation policy?

6. According to opportunism-based explanations of vertical integration, when should a firm pursue foreign direct investment? According to capabilities-based explanations, when should it pursue these investments? According to flexibility explanations, when should it pursue these investments?

PROBLEM SET

1. Which of the following two firms is more vertically integrated? How can you tell?

(a) Firm A has included manufacturing, sales, finance, and human resources within its boundaries and has outsourced legal and customer service.

(b) Firm B has included manufacturing, sales, legal, and customer service within its boundaries and has outsourced finance and human resources.

2. What is the level of transaction-specific investment for each firm in the following transactions? Who in these transactions is at greater risk of being taken unfair advantage of?

(a) Firm I has built a plant right next door to Firm II. Firm I's plant is worth $5 million if it supplies Firm II. It is worth $200,000 if it does not supply Firm II. Firm II has three alternative suppliers. If it receives supplies from Firm I, it is worth $10 million. If it does not receive supplies from Firm I, it is worth $9.8 million.

(b) Firm A has just purchased a new computer system that is only available from Firm B. Firm A has redesigned its entire production process around this new computer system. The old production process is worth $1 million, the new process is worth $12 million. Firm B has several hundred customers for its new computer system.

(c) Firm Alpha, a fast-food restaurant company, has a contract with Firm Beta, a movie studio. After negotiating with several other potential partners, Firm Alpha agreed to a contract that requires Firm Alpha to pay Firm Beta $5 million per year for the right to use characters from Firm Beta's movies in its packaged meals for children. Demand for children's movies has recently dropped.

(d) Firm I owns and runs a printing press. Firm J uses the services of a printing press. Historically, Firm I has sold its services to many customers. However, it was recently approached by Firm J to become its exclusive supplier of printing press services. Currently, Firm I is worth $1 million. If it became the sole supplier to Firm J, it would be worth $8 million. To complete this deal, Firm I would have to stop supplying its current customers and modify its machines to meet Firm J's needs. No other firm needs the same services as Firm J. Firm J contacted several other suppliers who said they would be willing to become a sole supplier for Firm J before deciding to propose this arrangement with Firm I.

3. What recommendation would you make in each of these situations, vertical integration or non–vertical integration, and why?

(a) Firm A needs a new and unique technology for its product line. There are no substitute technologies. Should Firm A make this technology or buy it?

(b) Firm I has been selling its products through a distributor for some time. It has become the market share leader. Unfortunately, this distributor has not been able to keep up with the evolving technology and customers are complaining. There are no alternative distributors available. Should Firm I keep its current distributor or should it begin distribution on its own?

(c) Firm Alpha has manufactured its own products for years. Recently, however, one of these products has become more and more like a commodity. Several firms are now able to manufacture this product at the same price and quality as Firm Alpha. However, they do not have Firm Alpha's brand name in the marketplace. Should Firm Alpha continue to manufacture this product or should it outsource it to one of these other firms?

(d) Firm I is convinced that a certain class of technologies holds real economic potential. However, it does not know, for sure, which particular version of this technology is going to dominate the market. There are eight competing versions of this technology currently, but ultimately, only one will dominate the market. Should Firm I invest in all eight of these technologies itself? Should it invest in just one of these technologies? Should it partner with other firms that are investing in these different technologies?

END NOTES

1. Coase, R. (1937). "The nature of the firm." *Economica*, 4, pp. 386–405.
2. This explanation of vertical integration is known as transactions cost economics in the academic literature. See Williamson, O. (1975). *Markets and hierarchies: Analysis and antitrust implications*. New York: Free Press; Williamson, O. (1985). *The economic institutions of capitalism*. New York: Free Press; and Klein, B., R. Crawford, and A. Alchian (1978). "Vertical integration, appropriable rents, and the competitive contracting process." *Journal of Law and Economics*, 21, pp. 297–326.
3. Another option—forming an alliance between these two firms—is discussed in more detail in Chapter 9.
4. This explanation of vertical integration is known as the capabilities-based theory of the firm in the academic literature. It draws heavily from the resource-based view described in Chapter 3. See Barney, J. B. (1991). "Firm resources and sustained competitive advantage." *Journal of Management*, 17, pp. 99–120; Barney, J. B. (1999). "How a firm's capabilities affect boundary decisions." *Sloan Management Review*, 40(3);

Conner, K. R., and C. K. Prahalad (1996). "A resource-based theory of the firm: Knowledge versus opportunism." *Organization Science*, 7, pp. 477–501.
5. This explanation of vertical integration is known as real-options theory in the academic literature. See Kogut, B. (1991). "Joint ventures and the option to expand and acquire." *Management Science*, 37, pp. 19–33.
6. Kripalani, M., and P. Engardio (2003). "The rise of India." *BusinessWeek*, December 8, pp. 66 +.
7. See Gupta, A. K. (1987). "SBU strategies, corporate-SBU relations and SBU effectiveness in strategy implementation." *Academy of Management Journal*, 30(3), pp. 477–500.
8. Becker, G. S. (1993). *Human capital: A theoretical and empirical analysis, with special reference to education*. Chicago: University of Chicago Press.
9. Barney, J. B. (1991). "Firm resources and sustained competitive advantage." *Journal of Management*, 17, pp. 99–120.

7

Corporate Diversification

Even its logo is foreboding: Two slashes of green, crossing, on a black background, as if an alien is trying to push through the sides of a box that has held it prisoner, revealing a terrifying world within. Microsoft's initial entry into the competitive world of video game consoles, X-Box was designed to thrill gamers and terrify competitors. It also represented a significant diversification move on the part of Microsoft.

Until X-Box, Microsoft was a software company. Its first prod-

X-Box Is Coming

ucts were applications software for Apple II computers. It then acquired the rights to a PC operating system called QDOS (for "Quick and Dirty Operating System"), renamed it MSDOS (for "Microsoft Disc Operating System"), and MSDOS became the standard of PC operating systems in the industry. MSDOS was later

replaced by Windows, an operating system that emulated much of the user interface pioneered by Apple. However, because of the domination of MSDOS, Windows became the de facto standard operating system in PCs—and still is, despite the recent growth of an open-source operating system called Linux.

Microsoft followed up its PC operating system by diversifying into application software designed to operate effectively with Windows. Virtually every application

Learning Objectives

After reading this chapter, you should be able to:

1. Define corporate diversification and describe five types of corporate diversification.

2. Specify the two conditions that a corporate diversification strategy must meet in order to create economic value.

3. Define the concept of "economies of scope" and identify eight potential economies of scope a diversified firm might try to exploit.

4. Identify which of these economies of scope a firm's outside equity investors are able to realize on their own at low cost.

5. Specify the circumstances under which a firm's diversification strategy will be rare.

6. Indicate which of the economies of scope identified in this chapter are more likely to be subject to low-cost imitation and which are less likely to be subject to low-cost imitation.

7. Identify two potential substitutes for corporate diversification.

8. Identify economies of scope that can be realized through international operations.

developed by Microsoft—from Word, to Excel, to Power Point—has become the de facto standard application in the industry. More recently, Microsoft has diversified its software even more by developing both operating systems and applications for servers (larger computers used to connect multiple users most frequently purchased by companies), a variety of Internet applications (e.g., MSN), enterprise software for small and medium-sized firms (i.e., software that lets these firms do their bookkeeping efficiently), and Windows-type software for phones and PDAs (personal digital assistants or handheld computers).

In the process of developing this diversified portfolio of software, Microsoft has become a huge success. Its sales grew an average of 36 percent a year through the 1990s. Its current market value is $279 billion, and it generates $1 billion a month in profits. Given its success in developing and selling software, an obvious question becomes: Why did this software company decide to bring out hardware—the X-Box console—to compete in the video game market?

At least three reasons for this have been suggested. First, by the time Microsoft decided to enter the video game market, there were already several well-established video game development companies—not the least of which was Entertainment Arts (see Chapter 3). These firms had already demonstrated the ability to develop popular games. Given that Microsoft did not have these game development skills, it concluded that it could outsource game development to firms that did, and focus instead on the console.

Second, the video game software market, while it is software, is very different from any of the other software markets in which Microsoft operates. Microsoft's markets focus on using computers to accomplish very utilitarian tasks. Also, once users learn a Microsoft product, it is very unlikely that they will change. Video game software is more of a "hit" market—where firms have to introduce new games, these new games have to break new technical and playing ground, and old titles are constantly being replaced by new or updated titles. While computer operators might use the same copy of Windows or Word for several years and then update these copies when new versions come out, video game players are looking for new titles and new versions every year or more frequently.

The console market, on the other hand, is more like Microsoft's traditional software

market. There has historically been a five-year product life cycle in consoles—once a console is developed, it remains largely unchanged for five years. This enables game developers to discover and then fully exploit the technical capabilities of a console in their games. Only after these technical capabilities are fully exploited do console manufacturers consider bringing out new ones.

Finally, Microsoft has been very interested in linking its current software products with the Internet. In a famous e-mail to Microsoft employees, founder Bill Gates argued that unless Microsoft learned how to integrate its software with the Internet it would struggle in the long run. X-Box is one area where this linkage is very natural. In fact, X-Box has become a leader in Internet-based video

gaming through its "X-Box Live" option. As a further entree into the Internet, X-Box is of strategic importance at Microsoft.

So far, the X-Box has not had a huge impact on Microsoft's performance. Current revenues for the games and home entertainment divisions at Microsoft hovers around $3.5 billion. However, these activities are yet to generate significant profits. Despite this lackluster performance, Microsoft remains committed to X-Box. Indeed, it currently has plans to introduce a new X-Box model after only four years, shortening by one year the traditional product life cycle in the video game console industry.

Sources: J. Greene (2004). "Microsoft's midlife crisis." *BusinessWeek*, April 19; R. Guth and S. Thurm (2004). "Microsoft to dole out its cash horde." *Wall Street Journal*, July 21, pp. A1 +; B. R. Schendler (1995). "What Bill Gates really wants." *Fortune*, January 16, pp. 34–63.

Microsoft is like most large firms in the United States and the world: It has diversified operations. Indeed, virtually all of the 500 largest firms in the United States and the 500 largest firms in the world are diversified, either by product or geographically. Large single-business firms are very unusual. However, like most of these large diversified firms, Microsoft has diversified along some dimensions, but not along others.

What Is Corporate Diversification?

A firm implements a **corporate diversification strategy** when it operates in multiple industries or markets simultaneously. When a firm operates in multiple industries simultaneously, it is said to be implementing a **product diversification strategy**. When a firm operates in multiple geographic markets simultaneously, it is said to be implementing a **geographic market diversification**

strategy. When a firm implements both of these types of diversification simultaneously, it is said to be implementing a **product-market diversification strategy**. Just how geographically diversified firms really are is examined in the Global Perspectives feature.

We have already seen glimpses of these diversification strategies in the discussion of vertical integration strategies in Chapter 6. Sometimes, when a firm vertically integrates backward or forward, it begins operations in a new product or geographic market. This happened to computer software firms when they began manning their own call centers. These firms moved from the "computer software development" business to the "call center management" business when they vertically integrated forward. In this sense, when firms vertically integrate, they may also be implementing a diversification strategy. However, the critical difference between the diversification strategies studied here and vertical integration (discussed in Chapter 6) is that in this chapter, product market diversification is the primary objective of these strategies, whereas in Chapter 6, such diversification was often a secondary consequence of pursuing a vertical integration strategy.

Types of Corporate Diversification

Firms vary in the extent to which they have diversified the mix of businesses they pursue. Perhaps the simplest way of characterizing differences in the level of corporate diversification focuses on the relatedness of the businesses pursued by a firm. As shown in Figure 7.1, firms can pursue a strategy of **limited corporate diversification**, of **related corporate diversification**, or of **unrelated corporate diversification**.

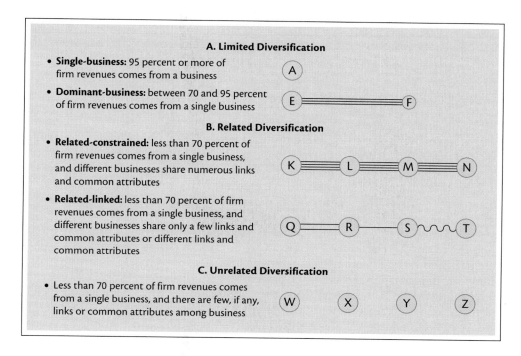

A. Limited Diversification

- **Single-business:** 95 percent or more of firm revenues comes from a business
- **Dominant-business:** between 70 and 95 percent of firm revenues comes from a single business

B. Related Diversification

- **Related-constrained:** less than 70 percent of firm revenues comes from a single business, and different businesses share numerous links and common attributes
- **Related-linked:** less than 70 percent of firm revenues comes from a single business, and different businesses share only a few links and common attributes or different links and common attributes

C. Unrelated Diversification

- Less than 70 percent of firm revenues comes from a single business, and there are few, if any, links or common attributes among business

Figure 7.1   Levels and Types of Diversification

Global Perspectives

The same headline seems to appear in every newspaper, in every business book, and in every business class: Business is Becoming More Global. The implication is clear: Firms ignore the global nature of their business at their own peril.

In one sense, it is clear that business is becoming more and more global. Large firms, whether headquartered in the United States or abroad, are seeing an ever-larger percentage of their revenues coming from nondomestic sources. Indeed, some firms—like McDonald's and Coca-Cola—are seen not just as global firms, but as exporters of U.S. culture around the world. On the other hand, a careful analysis of where large diversified firms actually sell their products and services tells a somewhat different story. One recent study found that "global diversification" is not really that "global."

In particular, these authors divided the world's economy into three

How Global Are Globally Diversified Firms?

great markets: North America, Europe, and Asia. They then examined the number of firms that have significant sales in just one of these three geographic markets, in two of these markets, and in all three of these markets. The "globalization of business" hypoth-

esis suggests that large numbers of firms will have significant operations in all three of these markets. This is not the case.

Based on a list of 365 of the largest corporations in the world, this study found that only 9 (2.4 percent) had 20 percent or more of their sales in all three of these global regions, only 25 (5.0 percent) had 20 percent or more of their sales in two of these global regions, while 320 (84.2 percent) had 20 percent or more of their sales in just one of these global regions. This suggests that while it may not be uncommon for firms to sell outside their home country to neighboring countries, it is somewhat more uncommon for firms to have significant sales outside their geographic region.

The list of truly global firms, that is, firms that had significant sales in all three regional economies, includes many of the usual suspects, such as IBM, Sony, Philips Electronics, Nokia, Intel, Canon, and Coca-Cola. However,

Limited Corporate Diversification

A firm has implemented a strategy of **limited corporate diversification** when all or most of its business activities fall within a single industry and geographic market (see Panel A of Figure 7.1). Two kinds of firms are included in this corporate diversification category: **single-business firms** (firms with greater than 95 percent of their total sales in a single product market) and **dominant-business firms** (firms with between 70 percent and 95 percent of their total sales in a single product market).

Differences between single-business and dominant-business firms are represented in Panel A of Figure 7.1. The firm pursing a single-business corporate diversification strategy engages in only one business, Business A. An example of a single-business firm is the WD-40 Company of San Diego, California. This company manufactures and distributes only one product—the spray cleanser and lubricant WD-40. The dominant-business firm pursues two businesses, Business E and a smaller Business F that is tightly linked to Business E. An example of a dominant business firm is Donato's Pizza. Donato's Pizza does the vast majority of its business in a single product—pizza—in a single market—the United States.

several supposedly "global" firms did not show up on this list. For example, Toyota, Unilever, Motorola, Sun Microsystems, 3M, McDonald's, Michelin, and Kodak all have significant sales in two regions of the world, but not all three. For example, only 7.7 percent of Toyota's total sales comes from Europe; only 14 percent of Motorola's total sales comes from Europe; only 14.8 percent of McDonald's total sales comes from Asia; and only 17.2 percent of Kodak's sales comes from Asia.

The list of large firms that have significant sales in only one geographic region is also interesting. This list includes Wal-Mart (94.1 percent of sales in North America), General Motors (81.1 percent in North America), General Electric (59.1 percent in North America), Mitsubishi (86.8 percent in Asia), Volkswagen (68.2 percent in Europe), Ford (66.7 percent in North America) and Phillip Morris (57.9 percent in North America). Some of these firms—

including GM and GE—are thought of as truly international giants. But what this research shows is that even these giant international firms are still tied to their historical geographic homes.

These findings have significant implications for the management of international firms. First, they suggest that the products and services of most international firms are not equally accessible across the globe. This is true despite efforts by multinational firms to modify their products to be responsive to local demand. Second, these results suggest that many sources of competitive advantages for firms are valuable only within specific geographic regions and not broadly around the globe. Finally, because firms may have very different market positions in different geographic regions of the world, it may be necessary for these firms to adopt very different strategies in these regions. For exam-

ple, Toyota—a firm that has significant sales in Asia and North America—may be able to leverage its reputation for quality by introducing a new brand of luxury automobile—the Lexus. However, because Toyota has such a small market presence in Europe, it has less of a reputation for quality to build on in Europe and thus has been unable to successfully launch the Lexis brand there. Toyota may have to adopt a different approach to the European luxury market or wait to enter that market until its sales in Europe increase dramatically.

Sources: A. Rugman and A. Verbeke (2004). "A perspective on regional and global strategies of multinational enterprises." *Journal of International Business Studies*, 35, pp. 3–18; A. Rugman and A. Verbeke (2002). "A note on the transnational solution and the transaction cost theory of multinational strategic management." *Journal of International Business Studies*, 23, pp. 761–771.

However, Donato's also owns a subsidiary that makes a machine that automatically slices and puts pepperoni on pizzas. Not only does Donato's use this machine in its own pizzerias, it also sells this machine to food manufacturers that make frozen pepperoni pizza.

In an important sense, firms pursuing a strategy of limited corporate diversification are not leveraging their resources and capabilities beyond a single product or market. Thus, the analysis of limited corporate diversification is logically equivalent to the analysis of business-level strategies (discussed in Part 2 of this book). Because these kinds of strategies have already been discussed, the remainder of this chapter focuses on corporate strategies that involve higher levels of diversification.

Related Corporate Diversification

As a firm begins to engage in businesses in more than one product or market, it moves away from being a single-business or dominant-business firm and begins to adopt higher levels of corporate diversification. When less than 70 percent of a firm's revenue comes from a single product market and these multiple lines of business are linked, the firm has implemented a strategy of **related corporate diversification**.

The multiple businesses that a diversified firm pursues can be related in two ways (see Panel B in Figure 7.1). If all the businesses in which a firm operates share a significant number of inputs, production technologies, distribution channels, similar customers, and so forth, this corporate diversification strategy is called **related-constrained**. This strategy is termed "constrained" because corporate managers pursue business opportunities in new markets or industries only if those markets or industries share numerous resource and capability requirements with the businesses the firm is currently pursuing. Commonalities across businesses in a strategy of related-constrained diversification are represented by the linkages among Businesses K, L, M, and N in the related-constrained section of Figure 7.1.

PepsiCo is an example of a related-constrained diversified firm. While PepsiCo is operating in multiple businesses around the world, all of its businesses focus on providing snack-type products, either food or beverages. PepsiCo is not in the business of making or selling more traditional types of food—like pasta, or cheese, or breakfast cereal. Moreover, PepsiCo attempts to use a single, firm-wide capability to gain competitive advantages in each of its businesses—its ability to develop and exploit well-known brand names. Whether it's Pepsi, or Doritos, or Mountain Dew, or Big Red, PepsiCo is all about building brand names. In fact, PepsiCo has 16 brands that generate $1 billion or more in revenues each year. That is more so-called "power brands" than Nestlé, Procter & Gamble, or Coca-Cola![1]

If the different businesses that a single firm pursues are linked on only a couple of dimensions, or if different sets of businesses are linked along very different dimensions, that corporate diversification strategy is called **related-linked**. For example, Business Q and Business R may share similar production technology, Business R and Business S may share similar customers, Business S and Business T may share similar suppliers, and Business Q and Business T may have no common attributes. This strategy is represented in the related-linked section of Figure 7.1 by businesses with relatively few links between them and with different kinds of links between them (i.e., straight lines and curved lines).

An example of a related-linked diversified firm is Disney. Disney has evolved from a single-business firm (when it did nothing but produce animated motion pictures), to a dominant business firm (when it produced family-oriented motion pictures and operated a theme park), to a related-constrained diversified firm (when it produced family-oriented motion pictures, operated multiple theme parks, and sold products through its Disney Stores). Recently, it has become so diversified that it has taken on the attributes of related-linked diversification. While much of the Disney empire still builds on characters developed in its animated motion pictures, it also owns and operates businesses—including a movie studio that produces movies more appropriate for mature audiences, several hotels and resorts that have little or nothing to do with Disney characters, and a television network (ABC) that broadcasts non-Disney-produced content—that are less directly linked to these characters. This is not to suggest that Disney is pursuing an unrelated diversification strategy. After all, most of its businesses are in the entertainment industry, broadly defined. Rather, this is only to suggest that it is no longer possible to find a single thread—like a Mickey Mouse or a Lion King—that connects all of Disney's business enterprises. In this sense, Disney has become a related-linked diversified firm.[2]

Unrelated Corporate Diversification

Firms that pursue a strategy of related corporate diversification have some type of linkages among most, if not all, the different businesses they pursue. However, it is possible for firms to pursue numerous different businesses and for there to be *no* linkages among them (see Panel C of Figure 7.1). When less than 70 percent of a firm's revenues is generated in a single product market, and when a firm's businesses share few, if any, common attributes, then that firm is pursuing a strategy of **unrelated corporate diversification**.

General Electric is an example of a firm pursuing an unrelated diversification strategy. GE's mix of businesses includes commercial finance and leasing (revenues of $23 billion), insurance (revenues of $22.6 billion), turbines and other technologies to generate electricity (revenues of $18 billion), commercial finance including a large credit card business (revenues of $15 billion), jet engines (revenues of $15 billion), consumer and industrial products including light bulbs (revenues of $13 billion), medical imaging devices (revenues of $11.5 billion), entertainment businesses including NBC (revenues of $8.3 billion), advanced materials including artificial diamonds (revenues of $7.8 billion), equipment services including the leasing and management of railroad boxcars (revenues of $4.4 billion), and water treatment and security services (revenues of $3.5 billion). It is difficult to see how any of these businesses are closely related to each other. Indeed, GE tends to manage each of its businesses as if they were stand-alone entities—a management approach consistent with a firm implementing an unrelated diversified corporate strategy.[3]

The Value of Corporate Diversification

V R I O

In order for corporate diversification to be economically valuable, two conditions must hold. First, there must be some valuable economy of scope among the multiple businesses in which a firm is operating. Second, it must be less costly for managers in a firm to realize these economies of scope than for outside equity holders on their own. If outside investors could realize the value of a particular economy of scope on their own, and at low cost, then they would have few incentives to "hire" managers to realize this economy of scope for them. Each of these requirements for corporate diversification to add value for a firm will be considered below.

What Are Valuable Economies of Scope?

Economies of scope exist in a firm when the value of the products or services it sells increases as a function of the number of businesses that firm operates in. The term "scope" in this definition refers to the range of businesses in which a diversified firm operates. For this reason, only diversified firms can, by definition, exploit economies of scope. Economies of scope are valuable to the extent that they increase a firm's revenues or decrease its costs, compared to what would be the case if these economies of scope were not exploited.

A wide variety of potentially valuable sources of economies of scope have been identified in the literature. Some of the most important of these are listed in Table 7.1 and discussed below. How valuable economies of scope actually are, on average, has been the subject of a great deal of research summarized in the Research Made Relevant feature.

Research Made Relevant

*I*n 1994, Lang and Stulz published a sensational article that suggested that, on average, when a firm began implementing a corporate diversification strategy, it destroyed about 25 percent of its market value. Lang and Stulz came to this conclusion by comparing the market performance of firms pursuing a corporate diversification strategy with portfolios of firms pursuing a limited diversification strategy. Taken together, the market performance of a portfolio of firms that were pursuing a limited diversification strategy was about 25 percent higher than the market performance of a single diversified firm operating in all of the businesses included in this portfolio. These results suggested that not only were economies of scope not valuable, but, on average, efforts to realize these economies actually destroyed economic value. Similar results were published by Comment and Jarrell using different measures of firm performance.

Not surprisingly, these results generated quite a stir. If Lang and Stulz were correct, then diversified firms—no matter what kind of diversification strategy they engaged in—destroyed an enormous amount of economic value. This could lead to a fundamental restructuring of the U.S. economy.

However, more recent research has significantly tempered Lang and Stulz's conclusions. Two new findings suggest that, even if there is a 25 percent discount, diversification can still add value. First, Villalonga and others found that firms pursuing diversification

How Valuable Are Economies of Scope, on Average?

strategies were generally performing more poorly before they began diversifying than firms that never pursued diversification strategies. Thus, while it might appear that diversification leads to a significant loss of economic value, in reality that loss of value occurred before these firms began implementing a diversification strategy. Indeed, some more recent research suggests that these relatively poor-performing firms may actually increase their market value over what would have been the case if they did not diversify.

Second, Miller found that firms that find it in their self-interest to diversify do so in a very predictable pattern. These firms tend to diversify into the most profitable new business first, the second most profitable business second, and so forth. Not surprisingly, the fiftieth

diversification move made by these firms might not generate huge additional profits. However, these profits—it turns out—are still, on average, positive. Since multiple rounds of diversification increase profits at a decreasing rate, the overall average profitability of diversified firms will generally be less than the overall average profitability of firms that do not pursue a diversification strategy—thus, a substantial difference between the market value of nondiversified and diversified firms might exist. However, this discount, per se, does not mean that the diversified firm is destroying economic value. Rather, it may mean only that a diversifying firm is creating value in smaller increments as it continues to diversify.

Currently, most scholars believe that exploiting economies of scope through corporate diversification, on average, increases a firm's market value. This does not mean, of course, that all diversification strategies will create economic value. Managers must carefully plan which economies of scope they will realize through their diversification moves and how to efficiently realize those economies through their organization.

Sources: H. P. Lang and R. Stulz (1994). "Tobin's *q*, corporate diversification, and firm performance." *Journal of Political Economy*, 102, pp. 1248–1280; R. Comment and G. Jarrell (1995). "Corporate focus and stock returns." *Journal of Financial Economics*, 37, pp. 67–87; D. Miller (2004). "Firms' technological resources and the performance effects of diversification: A longitudinal study." Forthcoming, *Strategic Management Journal*; B. Villalonga (2004). "Does diversification cause the 'diversification discount'?" *Financial Management*, 33(2), pp. 5–28.

Diversification to Exploit Operational Economies of Scope

Sometimes, economies of scope may reflect operational links among the businesses a firm engages in. **Operational economies of scope** typically take one of two forms: shared activities and shared core competencies.

Table 7.1   **Different Types of Economies of Scope**

1. Operational economies of scope
   - Shared activities
   - Core competencies

2. Financial economies of scope
   - Internal capital allocation
   - Risk reduction
   - Tax advantages

3. Anticompetitive economies of scope
   - Multipoint competition
   - Exploiting market power

4. Employee and stakeholder incentives for diversification
   - Maximizing management compensation

Shared Activities. In Chapter 3, it was suggested that value-chain analysis can be used to describe the specific business activities of a firm. This same value-chain analysis can also be used to describe the business activities that may be shared across several different businesses within a diversified firm. These **shared activities** are potential sources of operational economies of scope for diversified firms.

Consider, for example, the hypothetical firm presented in Figure 7.2. This diversified firm engages in three businesses: A, B, and C. However, these three

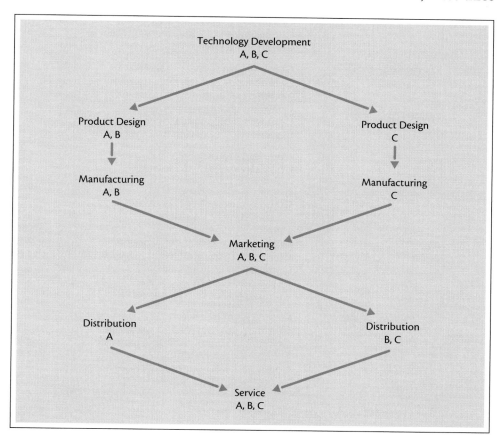

Figure 7.2   A Hypothetical Firm Sharing Activities Among Three Businesses

businesses share a variety of activities throughout their value chains. For example, all three draw on the same technology development operation. Product design and manufacturing are shared in businesses A and B and separate for business C. All three businesses share a common marketing and service operation. Business A has its own distribution system.

These kinds of shared activities are quite common among both related-constrained and related-linked diversified firms. At Texas Instruments, for example, a variety of electronics businesses share some research and development activities and often share common manufacturing locations. Procter & Gamble's numerous different consumer products businesses often share common manufacturing locations and rely on a common distribution network (through retail grocery stores).[4] Some of the most common shared activities in diversified firms, and their location in the value chain, are summarized in Table 7.2.

Many of the shared activities listed in Table 7.2 can have the effect of reducing a diversified firm's costs. For example, if a diversified firm has a purchasing function that is common to several of its different businesses it can often obtain volume discounts on its purchases that would otherwise not be possible. Also, by

Table 7.2   **Possible Shared Activities and Their Place in the Value Chain**

Value chain activity	Shared activities
Input activities	Common purchasing
	Common inventory control system
	Common warehousing facilities
	Common inventory delivery system
	Common quality assurance
	Common input requirements system
	Common suppliers
Production activities	Common product components
	Common product components manufacturing
	Common assembly facilities
	Common quality control system
	Common maintenance operation
	Common inventory control system
Warehousing and distribution	Common product delivery system
	Common warehouse facilities
Sales and marketing	Common advertising efforts
	Common promotional activities
	Cross-selling of products
	Common pricing systems
	Common marketing departments
	Common distribution channels
	Common sales forces
	Common sales offices
	Common order processing services
Dealer support and service	Common service network
	Common guarantees and warranties
	Common accounts receivable management systems
	Common dealer training
	Common dealer support services

Sources: Porter, M. E. (1985). *Competitive advantage.* New York: Free Press, Rumelt, R. P. (1974). *Strategy, structure, and economic performance.* Cambridge, MA: Harvard University Press, Ansoff, H. I. (1965). *Corporate strategy.* New York: McGraw-Hill.

manufacturing products that are used as inputs into several of a diversified firm's businesses, the total costs of producing these products in a firm can be reduced. A single sales force representing the products or services of several different businesses within a diversified firm can reduce the cost of selling these products or services. Firms such as IBM, Hewlett-Packard, and General Motors have all used shared activities to reduce their costs in these ways.

Failure to exploit shared activities across businesses can lead to out-of-control costs. For example, Kentucky Fried Chicken, when it was a division of PepsiCo, encouraged each of its regional business operations in North America to develop their own quality improvement plans. The result was enormous redundancy and at least three conflicting quality efforts—all leading to higher-than-necessary costs. In a similar way, Levi Strauss's unwillingness to centralize and coordinate order processing led to a situation where six separate order-processing computer systems operated simultaneously. This costly redundancy was ultimately replaced by a single, integrated ordering system shared across the entire corporation.[5]

Shared activities can also increase the revenues in diversified firms' businesses. This can happen in at least two ways. First, it may be that shared product development and sales activities may enable two or more businesses in a diversified firm to offer a bundled set of products to customers. Sometimes, the value of these "product bundles" is greater than the value of each product separately. This additional customer value can generate revenues greater than what would have been the case if the businesses were not together and sharing activities in a diversified firm.

In the telecommunications industry, for example, separate firms sell telephones, access to telephone lines, equipment to route calls in an office, mobile telephones, and paging services. A customer that requires all these services could contact five different companies. Each of these five different firms would likely possess its own unique technological standards and software, making the development of an integrated telecommunications system for the customer difficult at best. Alternatively, a single diversified firm sharing sales activities across these businesses could significantly reduce the search costs of potential customers. This one-stop shopping is likely to be valuable to customers, who might be willing to pay a slightly higher price for this convenience than they would pay if they purchased these services from five separate firms. Moreover, if this diversified firm also shares some technology development activities across its businesses, it might be able to offer an integrated telecommunications network to potential customers. The extra value of this integrated network for customers is very likely to be reflected in prices that are higher than would have been possible if each of these businesses were independent or if activities among these businesses were not shared. Most of the regional telephone operating companies in the United States—including Bell South and Southwestern Bell—are attempting to gain these economies of scope.[6]

Such product bundles are important in other firms as well. Many grocery stores now sell prepared foods alongside traditional grocery products in the belief that busy customers want access to all kinds of food products—in the same location.[7]

Second, shared activities can enhance business revenues by exploiting the strong, positive reputations of some of a firm's businesses in other of its businesses. For example, if one business has a strong positive reputation for high-quality manufacturing, other businesses sharing this manufacturing activity will gain some of the advantages of this reputation. And, if one business has a strong positive reputation for selling high-performance products, other businesses sharing sales and marketing activities with this business will gain some of the advantages of this reputation. In both cases, businesses that draw on the strong reputation of another business through shared activities with that business will have larger revenues than they would were they operating on their own.

The Limits of Activity Sharing. Despite the potential of activity sharing to be the basis of a valuable corporate diversification strategy, this approach has three important limits.[8] First, substantial organizational issues are often associated with a diversified firm's learning how to manage cross-business relationships. Managing these relationships effectively can be very difficult, and failure can lead to excess bureaucracy, inefficiency, and organizational gridlock. These issues are discussed in detail in Chapter 8.

Second, sharing activities may limit the ability of a particular business to meet its specific customers' needs. For example, if two businesses share manufacturing activities, they may reduce their manufacturing costs. However, to gain these cost advantages, these businesses may need to build products using somewhat standardized components that do not fully meet their individual customers' needs. Businesses that share distribution activities may have lower overall distribution costs but be unable to distribute their products to all their customers. Businesses that share sales activities may have lower overall sales costs but be unable to provide the specialized selling required in each business.

One diversified firm that has struggled with the ability to meet the specialized needs of customers in its different divisions is General Motors. To exploit economies of scope in the design of new automobiles, GM shared the design process across its several automobile divisions. The result, through much of the 1990s, was "cookie-cutter"–looking cars—the traditional distinctiveness of several GM divisions, including Oldsmobile and Cadillac, was all but lost.[9]

Third, if one business in a diversified firm has a poor reputation, sharing activities with that business can reduce the quality of the reputation of other businesses in the firm.

Taken together, these limits on activity sharing can more than offset any possible gains. Indeed, over the last decade, more and more diversified firms have been abandoning efforts at activity sharing in favor of managing each business's activities independently. For example, ABB, Inc. (a Swiss engineering firm) and CIBA-Geigy (a Swiss chemicals firm) have adopted explicit corporate policies that restrict almost all activity sharing across businesses.[10] Other diversified firms, including Nestlé and General Electric, restrict activity sharing to just one or two activities (such as research and development or management training). However, to the extent that a diversified firm can exploit shared activities while avoiding these problems, shared activities can add value to a firm.

Core Competencies. Recently, a second operational linkage among the businesses of a diversified firm has been described. Unlike shared activities, this linkage is based on different businesses in a diversified firm sharing less tangible resources such as managerial and technical know-how, experience, and wisdom. This source of operational economy of scope has been called a firm's core competence.[11] **Core competence** has been defined by Prahalad and Hamel as "the collective learning in the organization, especially how to coordinate diverse production skills and integrate multiple streams of technologies." Core competencies are complex sets of resources and capabilities that link different businesses in a diversified firm through managerial and technical know-how, experience, and wisdom.[12]

Two firms that have well-developed core competencies are 3M and Johnson & Johnson. 3M has a core competence in substrates, adhesives, and coatings.

Collectively, employees at 3M know more about developing and applying adhesives and coatings on different kinds of substrates than do employees in any other organization. Over the years, 3M has applied these resources and capabilities in a wide variety of products, including Post-it notes, magnetic tape, photographic film, pressure-sensitive tape, and coated abrasives. At first glance, these widely diversified products seem to have little or nothing in common. Yet they all draw on a single core set of resources and capabilities in substrates, adhesives, and coatings.

Johnson & Johnson has a core competence in developing or acquiring pharmaceutical and medical products and then marketing them to the public. Many of Johnson & Johnson's products are dominant in their market segments—Johnson & Johnson's in baby powder, Ethicon in surgical sutures, and Tylenol in pain relievers. And while these products range broadly from those sold directly to consumers (e.g., the BandAid brand of adhesive bandages) to highly sophisticated medical technologies sold only to doctors and hospitals (e.g., Ethicon sutures), all of Johnson & Johnson's products build on the same ability to identify, develop, acquire, and market products in the pharmaceutical and medical products industry.

To understand how core competencies can reduce a firm's costs or increase its revenues, consider how these core competencies emerge over time. Most firms begin operations in a single business. Imagine that a firm has carefully evaluated all of its current business opportunities and has fully funded all of those with a positive net present value. Any of the above-normal returns that this firm has left over after fully funding all its current positive net present value opportunities can be thought of as **free cash flow**.[13] Firms can spend this free cash in a variety of ways: They can spend it on benefits for managers; they can give it to shareholders through dividends or by buying back a firm's stock; they can use it to invest in new businesses.

Suppose a firm chooses to use this cash to invest in a new business. In other words, suppose this firm chooses to implement a diversification strategy. If this firm is seeking to maximize the return from implementing this diversification strategy, which of all the possible businesses that it could invest in should it invest in? Obviously, a profit-maximizing firm will choose to begin operations in a business where it has a competitive advantage. What kind of business is likely to generate this competitive advantage for this firm? The obvious answer is a business where the same underlying resources and capabilities that gave this firm an advantage in its original business are still valuable, rare, and costly to imitate. Consequently, this first diversification move sees the firm investing in a business that is closely related to its original business, in that both businesses draw on a common set of underlying resources and capabilities where the firm already has a competitive advantage.

Put another way, a firm that diversifies by exploiting its resource and capability advantages in its original business will have lower costs than firms that begin a new business without these resource and capability advantages, or higher revenues than firms lacking these advantages, or both. As long as this firm organizes itself to take advantage of these resource and capability advantages in its new business, it should earn high profits in its new business, along with the profits it will still be earning in its original business.[14] This can be true for even relatively small firms, as described in the Strategy in the Emerging Enterprise feature.

Of course, over time this diversified firm is likely to develop new resources and capabilities through its operations in the new business. These new resources and capabilities enhance the entire set of skills that a firm might be able to bring to still another business. Using the profits it has obtained in its previous businesses, this

Strategy in the Emerging Enterprise

W. L. Gore & Associates is best known for manufacturing a water- and wind-proof but breathable fabric that is used to insulate winter coats, hiking boots, and a myriad of other outdoor apparel products. This fabric—known as Gore-Tex—has a brand name in its market niche every bit as strong as any of the brand names controlled by PepsiCo. or Procter & Gamble. The "Gore-Tex" label attached to any outdoor garment promises waterproof comfort in even the harshest conditions.

But W. L. Gore & Associates did not start out in the outdoor fabric business. Indeed, for the first 10 years of its existence, W. L. Gore sold insulation for wires and similar industrial products using a molecular technology originally developed by DuPont—a technology most of us know as Teflon. Only 10 years after its initial founding did the founder's son, Bob Gore, discover that it was possible to stretch the Teflon molecule to form a strong and porous material that is chemically inert, has a low friction coefficient, functions within a wide temperature range, does not age, and is extremely strong. This is the material called Gore-Tex.

Gore-Tex and Guitar Strings

By extending its basic technology, W. L. Gore and Associates has been able to diversify well beyond its original wire insulation business. With 2003 sales of $1.35 billion, the company currently has operations in medical products (including synthetic blood vessels and patches for soft tissue regeneration), electronics products (including wiring board materials and computer chip components), industrial products (including filter bags for environmental protection and sealants for chemical manufacturing), and fabrics (including Gore-Tex fabric, Wind-Stopper fabric, and CleanStream filters).

And Gore continues to discover new ways to exploit its competence in the Teflon molecule. In 1997, a team of Gore engineers developed a cable made out of the Teflon molecule for use to control puppets at Disney's theme parks. Unfortunately, these cables did not perform up to expectations and were not sold to Disney. However, some guitar players discovered these cables and began using them as strings for their guitars. They found out that these "Gore-Tex" strings sounded great and lasted five times as long as alternative guitar strings. So Gore entered yet another market—the $100 million fretted-stringed-instrument business—with its Elixir brand of guitar strings. Currently, W. L. Gore is the second-largest manufacturer in this market.

The flexibility of the Teflon molecule—and W. L. Gore's ability to explore and exploit that flexibility—has created a diversified company whose original objective was simply to sell insulation for wires.

Sources: www.gore.com; D. Sacks (2003). "The Gore-Tex of guitar strings." *Fast Times,* December, p. 46.

firm is likely to enter another new business. Again, choosing from among all the new businesses it could enter, it is likely to begin operations in a business where it can exploit its now-expanded resource and capability advantages to obtain a competitive advantage, and so forth.

After a firm has engaged in this diversification strategy several times, the resources and capabilities that enable it to operate successfully in several businesses are its core competencies. A firm develops these core competencies by transferring the technical and management knowledge, experience, and wisdom it developed in earlier businesses to its new businesses. A firm that has just begun this diversification process has implemented a dominant-business strategy. If all of a firm's businesses share the same core competencies, then that firm has implemented a strategy of related-constrained diversification. If different businesses exploit different sets of resources and capabilities, that firm has implemented a strategy of related-linked diversification. In any case, these core competencies enable firms to have lower costs or higher revenues as they include more businesses in their diversified portfolio, compared to firms without these competencies.

Of course, not all firms develop core competencies in this logical and rational manner. That is, sometimes a firm's core competencies are examples of the emergent strategies described in Chapter 1. Indeed, as described in Chapter 1, Johnson & Johnson is an example of a firm that has a core competence that emerged over time. However, no matter how a firm develops core competencies, to the extent that they enable a diversified firm to have lower costs or larger revenues in its business operations, these competencies can be thought of as sources of economies of scope.

Some diversified firms realize the value of these kinds of core competencies through shared activities. For example, as suggested earlier, 3M has a core competence in substrates, adhesives, and coatings. To exploit this, 3M has adopted a multitiered product innovation process. In addition to product innovations within each business unit separately, 3M also supports a corporate research and development lab that seeks to exploit and expand its core competence in substrates, adhesives, and coatings. Since the corporate R&D laboratory is shared by all of 3M's different businesses, it can be thought of as a shared activity.

However, other firms realize the value of their core competencies without shared activities. While Johnson & Johnson has a core competence in developing, acquiring, and marketing pharmaceutical and medical products, it does not realize this core competence through shared activities. Indeed, each of J&J's businesses is run very independently. For example, while one of its most successful products is Tylenol, the fact that the company that manufactures and distributes Tylenol—McNeil—is actually a division of Johnson & Johnson is not printed on any Tylenol packaging. If you did not know that Tylenol was a J&J product, you could not tell from the bottles of Tylenol you buy.

While J&J does not use shared activities to realize the value of its core competencies, it does engage in other activities to realize this value. For example, it is not uncommon for members of the senior management team of each of the businesses in J&J's portfolio to have obtained managerial experience in some other J&J business. That is, J&J identifies high-potential managers in one of its businesses and uses this knowledge by giving these managers additional responsibilities in another J&J business. This ability to leverage its management talent across multiple businesses is an example of a firm's core competence, although the realization of the value of that competence does not depend on the existence of a shared activity.

Sometimes, because a firm's core competence is not reflected in specific shared activities, it is easy to conclude that it is not exploiting any economies of scope in its diversification strategy. Diversified firms that are exploiting core competencies as an economy of scope, but are not doing so with any shared activities, are sometimes called **seemingly unrelated diversified firms**. They may appear to be unrelated diversified firms, but are, in fact, related diversified firms without any shared activities.

One example of a seemingly unrelated diversified firm is the British company Virgin Group. Operating in a wide variety of businesses—everything from record producing, music retailing, air and rail travel, soft drinks, spirits, mobile phones, cosmetics, retail bridal shops, financial services, and providing gas and electricity, to hot air ballooning—the Virgin Group is clearly diversified. There are also few, if any, shared activities in this firm. However, there are at least two core competencies that cut across all the business activities in the group—the brand name "Virgin" and the eccentric marketing and management approach of Virgin's founder, Richard Branson. Branson is the CEO who walked down a "catwalk" in a wedding gown to help publicize the opening of Virgin Brides—the Virgin Group's line of retail bridal shops. Branson is also the CEO who had all of Virgin Air's airplanes repainted with the British "Union Jack" and the slogan "Britain's Real Airline" when British Airways eliminated the British Flag from its airplanes. Whether or not these two core competencies create sufficient value to justify the Virgin Group's continued existence, and whether or not they will continue beyond Branson's affiliation with the group, are still open questions.

Limits of Core Competencies. Just as there are limits to the value of shared activities as sources of economies of scope, so there are limits to core competencies as sources of these economies. The first of these limitations stems from important organizational issues to be discussed in Chapter 8. The way that a diversified firm is organized can either facilitate the exploitation of core competencies or prevent this exploitation from occurring.

A second limitation of core competencies is a result of the intangible nature of these economies of scope. Whereas shared activities are reflected in tangible operations in a diversified firm, core competencies may be reflected only in shared knowledge, experience, and wisdom across businesses. The intangible character of these relationships is emphasized when they are described as a **dominant logic** in a firm, or a common way of thinking about strategy across different businesses.[15]

The intangibility of core competencies can lead diversified firms to make two kinds of errors in managing relatedness. First, intangible core competencies can be illusory inventions by creative managers who link even the most completely unrelated businesses and thereby justify their diversification strategy. A firm that manufactures airplanes and running shoes can rationalize this diversification by claiming to have a core competence in managing transportation businesses. A firm operating in the professional football business and the movie business can rationalize this diversification by claiming to have a core competence in managing entertainment businesses. Such **invented competencies** are not real sources of economies of scope.

Second, a diversified firm's businesses may be linked by a core competence, but this competence may affect these businesses' costs or revenues in a trivial way. Thus, for example, all of a firm's businesses may be affected by government actions, but the impact of these actions on costs and revenues in different businesses may be quite small. A firm may have a core competence in managing relationships with the government, but this core competence will not reduce costs or enhance revenues for these particular businesses very much. Also, each of a diversified firm's businesses may use some advertising. However, if advertising does not have a major impact on revenues for these businesses, core competencies in advertising are not likely to significantly reduce a firm's costs or increase its revenues. In this case, a core competence may be a source of economies of scope, but the value of those economies may be very small.

Diversification to Exploit Financial Economies of Scope

A second class of motivations for diversification shifts attention away from operational linkages among a firm's businesses and toward financial advantages associated with diversification. Three financial implications of diversification have been studied: diversification and capital allocation, diversification and risk reduction, and tax advantages of diversification.

Diversification and Capital Allocation. Capital can be allocated to businesses in one of two ways. First, businesses operating as independent entities can compete for capital in the external capital market. They do this by providing a sufficiently high return to induce investors to purchase shares of their equity, by having a sufficiently high cash flow to repay principal and interest on debt, and in other ways. Alternatively, a business can be part of a diversified firm. That diversified firm competes in the external capital market and allocates capital among its various businesses. In a sense, diversification creates an **internal capital market** in which businesses in a diversified firm compete for corporate capital.[16]

For an internal capital market to create value for a diversified firm, it must offer some efficiency advantages over an external capital market. It has been suggested that a potential efficiency gain from internal capital markets depends on the greater amount and quality of information that a diversified firm possesses about the businesses it owns, compared with the information that external suppliers of capital possess. Owning a business gives a diversified firm access to detailed and accurate information about the actual performance of the business, its true future prospects, and thus the actual amount and cost of the capital that should be allocated to it. External sources of capital, in contrast, have relatively limited access to information and thus have a limited ability to judge the actual performance and future prospects of a business.

Some have questioned whether a diversified firm, as a source of capital, actually has more and better information about a business it owns, compared to external sources of capital. After all, independent businesses seeking capital have a strong incentive to provide sufficient information to external suppliers of capital to obtain required funds. However, a firm that owns a business may have at least two informational advantages over external sources of capital.

First, although an independent business has an incentive to provide information to external sources of capital, it also has an incentive to downplay or even not report any negative information about its performance and prospects. Such negative information would raise an independent firm's cost of capital. External sources of capital have limited ability to force a business to reveal all information about its performance and prospects and thus may provide capital at a lower cost than they would if they had full information. Ownership gives a firm the right to compel more complete disclosure, although even here full disclosure is not guaranteed. With this more complete information, a diversified firm can allocate just the right amount of capital, at the appropriate cost, to each business.

Second, an independent business may have an incentive not to reveal all the positive information about its performance and prospects. In Chapter 3, the ability of a firm to earn economic profits was shown to depend on the imitability of a firm's resources and capabilities. An independent business that informs external sources of capital about all of its sources of competitive advantage is also informing its potential competitors about these sources of advantage. This information sharing increases the probability that these sources of advantage will be imitated. Because of the competitive implications of sharing this information, firms may choose not to share it, and external sources of capital may underestimate the true performance and prospects of a business.

A diversified firm, however, may gain access to this additional information about its businesses without revealing it to potential competitors. This information enables the diversified firm to make more informed decisions about how much capital to allocate to a business and about the cost of that capital, compared to the external capital market.[17]

Over time, there should be fewer errors in funding businesses through internal capital markets, compared to funding businesses through external capital markets. Fewer funding errors, over time, suggest a slight capital allocation advantage for a diversified firm, compared to an external capital market. This advantage should be reflected in somewhat higher rates of return on invested capital for the diversified firm, compared to the rates of return on invested capital for external sources of capital.

However, the businesses within a diversified firm do not always gain cost-of-capital advantages by being part of a diversified firm's portfolio. Several authors have argued that because a diversified firm has lower overall risk (see the following discussion), it will have a lower cost of capital, which it can pass along to the businesses within its portfolio. Although the lower risks associated with a diversified firm may lower the firm's cost of capital, the appropriate cost of capital to businesses within the firm depends on the performance and prospects of each of those businesses. The firm's advantages in evaluating its businesses' performances and prospects result in more appropriate capital allocation, not just in lower cost of capital for those businesses. Indeed, a business's cost of capital may be lower than what it could have obtained in the external capital market (because the firm is able to more fully evaluate the positive aspects of that business), or it may be higher than what it could have obtained in the external capital market (because the firm is able to more fully evaluate the negative aspects of that business).

Of course, if these businesses also have lower cost or higher revenue expectations because they are part of a diversified firm, then those cost/revenue advantages will be reflected in the appropriate cost of capital for these businesses. In this sense, any operational economies of scope for businesses in a diversified firm may be recognized by a diversified firm exploiting financial economies of scope.

Limits on Internal Capital Markets. Although internal capital allocation has several potential advantages for a diversified firm, several limits of this process also exist. First, the level and type of diversification that a firm pursues can affect the efficiency of this allocation process. A firm that implements a strategy of unrelated diversification, where managers have to evaluate the performance and prospects of numerous very different businesses, puts a greater strain on the capital allocation skills of its managers than does a firm that implements related diversification. Indeed, in the extreme, the capital allocation efficiency of a firm pursuing broad-based unrelated diversification will probably not be superior to the capital allocation efficiency of the external capital market.

Second, the increased efficiency of internal capital allocation depends on managers in a diversified firm having better information for capital allocation than the information available to external sources. However, this higher-quality information is not guaranteed. The incentives that can lead managers to exaggerate their performance and prospects to external capital sources can also lead to this behavior within a diversified firm. Indeed, several examples of business managers falsifying performance records to gain access to more internal capital have been reported.[18] Research suggests that capital allocation requests by managers are routinely discounted in diversified firms in order to correct for these managers' inflated estimates of the performance and prospects of their businesses.[19]

Finally, not only do business managers have an incentive to inflate the performance and prospects of their business in a diversified firm, but managers in charge of capital allocation in these firms may have an incentive to continue investing in a business despite its poor performance and prospects. The reputation and status of these managers often depend on the success of these business investments, because often they initially approved them. These managers often continue throwing good money at these businesses in hope that they will someday improve, thereby justifying their original decision. Organizational psychologists call this process **escalation of commitment** and have presented numerous examples of managers' becoming irrationally committed to a particular investment.[20]

Indeed, research on the value of internal capital markets in diversified firms suggests that, on average, the limitations of these markets often outweigh their advantages. For example, even controlling for firm size, excessive investment in poorly performing businesses in a diversified firm reduces the market value of the average diversified firm.[21] However, the fact that many firms do not gain the advantages associated with internal capital markets does not necessarily imply that no firms gain these advantages. If only a few firms are able to obtain the advantages of internal capital markets while successfully avoiding their limitations, this financial economy of scope may be a source of at least a temporary competitive advantage.

Diversification and Risk Reduction. Another possible financial economy of scope for a diversified firm has already been briefly mentioned—that is, the riskiness of the cash flows of diversified firms is lower than the riskiness of the cash flows of undiversified firms. Consider, for example, the riskiness of two businesses operating separately, compared to the risk of a diversified firm operating in those same two businesses simultaneously. If both these businesses are very risky on their own, and the cash flows from these businesses are not highly correlated over time, then combining these two businesses into a single firm will generate a lower level of overall risk for the diversified firm than for each of these businesses on their own.

This lower level of risk is due to the low correlation between the cash flows associated with these two businesses. If Business I is having a bad year, Business II might be having a good year, and a firm that operates in both of these businesses simultaneously can have moderate levels of performance. In another year, Business II might be off while Business I is having a good year. Again, the firm operating in both these businesses can have moderate levels of performance. Firms that diversify to reduce risk will have relatively stable returns over time, especially as they diversify into many different businesses with cash flows that are not highly correlated over time.

Tax Advantages of Diversification. Another financial economy of scope from diversification stems from possible tax advantages of this corporate strategy. These possible tax advantages reflect one or a combination of two effects. First, a diversified firm can use losses in some of its businesses to offset profits in others, thereby reducing its overall tax liability. Of course, substantial losses in some of its businesses may overwhelm profits in other businesses, forcing businesses that would have remained solvent if they were independent to cease operation. However, as long as business losses are not too large, a diversified firm's tax liability can be reduced. Empirical research suggests that diversified firms do, sometimes, offset profits in some businesses with losses in others, although the tax savings of these activities are usually small.[22]

Second, because diversification can reduce the riskiness of a firm's cash flows, it can also reduce the probability that a firm will declare bankruptcy. This can increase a firm's debt capacity. This effect on debt capacity is greatest when the cash flows of a diversified firm's businesses are perfectly and negatively correlated. However, even when these cash flows are perfectly and positively correlated, there can still be a (modest) increase in debt capacity.

Debt capacity is particularly important in tax environments where interest payments on debt are tax deductible. In this context, diversified firms can increase their leverage up to their debt capacity and reduce their tax liability accordingly. Of course, if interest payments are not tax deductible, or if the marginal corporate tax rate is relatively small, then the tax advantages of diversification can be quite small. Recent empirical work suggests that diversified firms do have greater debt capacity than undiversified firms. However, low marginal corporate tax rates, at least in the United States, make the accompanying tax savings on average relatively small.[23]

Diversification to Exploit Anticompetitive Economies of Scope

A third group of motivations for diversification is based on the relationship between diversification strategies and various anticompetitive activities by firms. Two specific examples of these activities are (1) multipoint competition to facilitate mutual forbearance and tacit collusion and (2) exploiting market power.

Multipoint Competition. Multipoint competition exists when two or more diversified firms simultaneously compete in multiple markets. For example, Hewlett-Packard and IBM compete in both the personal computer market and the market for computer printers. Michelin and Goodyear compete in both the U.S. automobile tire market and the European automobile tire market. Disney and AOL/Time Warner compete in both the movie production and book publishing businesses.

Multipoint competition can serve to facilitate a particular type of tacit collusion called **mutual forbearance**. Firms engage in **tacit collusion** when they cooperate to reduce rivalry below the level expected under perfect competition. Consider the situation facing two diversified firms, A and B. These two firms operate in the same businesses, I, II, III, and IV (see Figure 7.3). In this context, any decisions that Firm A might make to compete aggressively in Businesses I and III must take into account the possibility that Firm B will respond by com-

Figure 7.3 Multipoint Competition Between Hypothetical Firms A and B

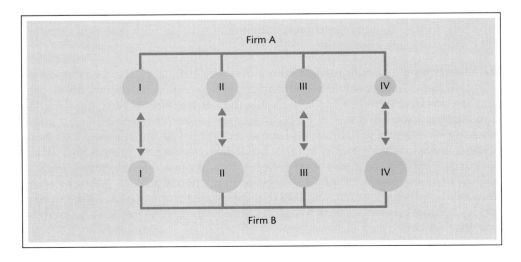

peting aggressively in Businesses II and IV and vice versa. The potential loss that each of these firms may experience in some of its businesses must be compared to the potential gain that each might obtain if it exploits competitive advantages in other of its businesses. If the present value of gains does not outweigh the present value of losses from retaliation, then both firms will avoid competitive activity. Refraining from competition is mutual forbearance.[24]

Mutual forbearance as a result of multipoint competition has occurred in several industries. For example, this form of tacit collusion has been described as existing between Michelin and Goodyear, Maxwell House and Folger's, Caterpillar and John Deere, and BIC and Gillette.[25] Another clear example of such cooperation can be found in the airline industry. For example, America West began service into the Houston Intercontinental Airport with very low introductory fares. Continental Airlines, the dominant firm at Houston Intercontinental, rapidly responded to America West's low Houston fares by reducing the price of its flights from Phoenix, Arizona, to several cities in the United States. Phoenix is the home airport of America West. Within just a few weeks, America West withdrew its low introductory fares in the Houston market, and Continental withdrew its reduced prices in the Phoenix market. The threat of retaliation across markets apparently led America West and Continental to tacitly collude on prices.[26]

However, sometimes multipoint competition does not lead to mutual forbearance. Consider, for example, the conflict between The Walt Disney Company and Time Warner in the early 1990s. As mentioned earlier, Disney operates in the theme park, movie and television production, and television broadcasting industries. Time Warner operates in the theme park and movie and television production industries and also operates a very large magazine business (*Time, People, Sports Illustrated*, and so forth). From 1988 through 1993, Disney spent over $40 million in advertising its theme parks in Time Warner magazines. Despite this substantial revenue, Time Warner began an aggressive advertising campaign aimed at wooing customers away from Disney theme parks to its own. Disney retaliated by canceling all of its advertising in Time Warner magazines. Time Warner responded to Disney's actions by canceling a corporate meeting to be held in Florida at Disney World. Disney responded to Time Warner's meeting cancellation by refusing to broadcast Time Warner theme park advertisements on its Los Angeles television station.[27]

Some recent research investigates the conditions under which mutual forbearance strategies are pursued, as well as conditions under which multipoint competition does not lead to mutual forbearance.[28] In general, the value of the threat of retaliation must be substantial for multipoint competition to lead to mutual forbearance. However, not only must the payoffs to mutual forbearance be substantial, but the firms pursuing this strategy must have strong strategic linkages among their diversified businesses. This suggests that firms pursuing mutual forbearance strategies based on multipoint competition are usually pursuing a form of related diversification.

Diversification and Market Power. Internal allocations of capital among a diversified firm's businesses may enable it to exploit in some of its businesses the market power advantages it enjoys in other of its businesses. For example, suppose that a firm is earning monopoly profits in a particular business. This firm can use some of these monopoly profits to subsidize the operations of another of its businesses. This cross-subsidization can take several forms, including **predatory pricing**— that is, setting prices so that they are less than the subsidized business's costs. The effect of this cross-subsidy may be to drive competitors out of the subsidized business and then to obtain monopoly profits in that subsidized business. In a sense, diversification enables a firm to apply its monopoly power in several different businesses. Economists call this a **deep pockets model** of diversification.[29]

Diversified firms with operations in regulated monopolies have been criticized for this kind of cross-subsidization. For example, most of the regional telephone companies in the United States are engaging in diversification strategies. The consent decree that forced the breakup of AT&T expressly forbade cross-subsidies between these regional companies' telephone monopolies and other business activities, under the assumption that such subsidies would give these firms an unfair competitive advantage in their diversified business activities.[30]

Although these market power economies of scope, in principle, may exist, relatively little empirical work documents their existence. Indeed, research on regulated utilities diversifying into nonregulated businesses in the 1980s suggests not that these firms use monopoly profits in their regulated businesses to unfairly subsidize nonregulated businesses, but that the poor management skills developed in the regulated businesses tend to make diversification less profitable rather than more profitable.[31] Nevertheless, the potential that large diversified large firms have to exercise market power and to behave in socially irresponsible ways has led some observers to call for actions to curtail both the economic and political power of these firms. These issues are discussed in the Ethics and Strategy feature.

Firm Size and Employee Incentives to Diversify

Employees may have incentives to diversify that are independent of any benefits from other sources of economies of scope. This is especially the case for employees in senior management positions and employees with long tenure in a particular firm. These employee incentives reflect the interest of employees to diversify because of the relationship between firm size and management compensation.

Research over the years demonstrates conclusively that the primary determinant of the compensation of top managers in a firm is not the economic performance of the firm but the size of the firm, usually measured in sales.[32] Thus, managers seeking to maximize their income should attempt to grow their firm. One of the easiest ways to grow a firm is through diversification, especially unrelated diversification through mergers and acquisitions. By making large acquisitions, a diversified firm can grow substantially in a short period of time, leading senior managers to earn higher incomes. All of this is independent of any economic profit that diversification may or may not generate. Senior managers need only worry about economic profit if the level of that profit is so low that unfriendly takeovers are a threat or so low that the board of directors may be forced to replace management.

Recently, the traditional relationship between firm size and management compensation has begun to break down. More and more, the compensation of senior managers is being tied to economic performance of firms. In particular, the use of stock and other forms of deferred compensation makes it in management's best interest to be concerned with a firm's economic performance. These changes in compensation do not necessarily imply that firms will abandon all forms of diversification. They do suggest that firms will abandon those forms of diversification that do not generate real economies of scope.

Can Equity Holders Realize These Economies of Scope on Their Own?

Earlier in this chapter, it was suggested that for a firm's diversification strategies to create value, two conditions must hold. First, these strategies must exploit valuable

Ethics and Strategy

*I*n 1999, a loose coalition of union members, environmentalists, youth, indigenous peoples, human rights activists, and small farmers took to the streets of Seattle, Washington, to protest a meeting of the World Trade Organization (WTO) and to fight against the growing global power of corporations. Government officials and corporate officers alike were confused by these protests. After all, hadn't world trade increased 11.5 times from 1950 to 1995 ($0.4 trillion to $5 trillion in constant 1997 dollars), and hadn't the total economic output of the entire world gone from $6.4 trillion in 1950 to $35.5 trillion in 1995 (again, in constant 1997 dollars)? Why protest a global economic system—a system that was enhancing the level of free trade and facilitating global economic efficiency—that was so clearly improving the economic well-being of the world's population?

The protestors' message to government and big business was that these aggregate growth numbers masked more truth than they told. Yes, there has been economic growth. But that growth has benefited only a small percentage of the world's population. Most of the population still struggles to survive. The combined net worth of 358 U.S. billionaires in the early 1990s ($760 billion) was equal to the combined net worth of the 2.5 billion poorest people on the earth! Eighty-three percent of the world's total income goes to the richest fifth of the population while the poorest fifth of the world's population receives only 1.4 percent of the world's total income. Currently, 45 to 70 million people worldwide have

Globalization and the Threat of the Multinational Firm

had to leave their home countries to find work in foreign lands and approximately 1.2 billion people around the world live on less than $1 a day. Even in relatively affluent societies like the United States, people are finding it increasingly difficult to meet their financial obligations. Falling real wages, economic insecurity, and corporate downsizing have led many people to work longer hours or hold two or three jobs. While the number of billionaires in the world continues to grow, the number of people facing mind-numbing and strength-robbing poverty grows even faster.

The causes of this apparent contradiction—global economic growth linked with growing global economic decay—are numerous and complex. However, one explanation focuses on the growing economic power of the diversified multi-national corporation. The size of these institutions can be immense—many international

diversified firms are larger than the entire economies of many nations. And these huge institutions, with a single-minded focus on maximizing their performance, can make profit-making decisions that adversely affect their suppliers, their customers, their employees, and the environment, all with relative impunity. Armed with the unspoken mantra that "Greed is Good," these corporations can justify almost any action, as long as it increases the wealth of its shareholders.

Of course, even if one accepts this hypothesis—and it is far from being universally accepted—solutions to the growing power of internationally diversified firms are not obvious. The problem is that one way that firms become large and powerful is by being able to meet customer demands effectively. Thus, firm size, per se, is not necessarily an indication that a firm is behaving in ways inconsistent with the public good. Government efforts to restrict the size of firms simply because they are large could easily have the effect of making citizens worse off. On the other hand, once firms are large and powerful, they may very well be tempted to exercise that power in ways that benefit themselves at great cost to society.

Whatever the causes and solutions to these problems, the protests in Seattle in 1999 have at least one clear message—global growth for growth's sake is no longer universally accepted as the correct objective of international economic policy.

Sources: D. C. Korten (2001). *When corporations rule the world*, 2nd ed. Bloomfield, CT: Kumarian Press; H. Demsetz (1973). "Industry structure, market rivalry, and public policy." *Journal of Law and Economics*, 16, pp. 1–9.

Table 7.3   **The Competitive Implications of Different Economies of Scope**

Type of Economy of Scope	Are They Valuable?	Can They be Realized by Equity Holders on Their Own?	Positive Returns to Equity Holders?
1. *Operational economies of scope*			
Shared activities	Possible	No	Possible
Core competencies	Possible	No	Possible
2. *Financial economies of scope*			
Internal capital allocation	Possible	No	Possible
Risk reduction	Possible	Yes	No
Tax advantages	Possible—small	No	Possible—small
3. *Anticompetitive economies of scope*			
Multipoint competition	Possible	No	Possible
Exploiting market power	Possible	No	Possible
4. *Employee incentives for diversification*			
Maximizing management compensation	No	No	No

economies of scope. Potentially valuable economies of scope were presented in Table 7.1 and discussed in the previous section. Second, it must be less costly for managers in a firm to realize these economies of scope than for outside equity holders on their own. If outside equity holders could realize a particular economy of scope on their own, without a firm's managers, at low cost, why would they want to hire managers to do this for them by investing in a firm and providing capital to managers to exploit an economy of scope?

Table 7.3 summarizes the discussion on the potential value of the different economies of scope listed in Table 7.1. It also suggests which of these economies of scope will be difficult for outside equity investors to exploit on their own and thus which bases of diversification are most likely to create positive returns for a firm's equity holders.

Most of the economies of scope listed in Table 7.3 cannot be realized by equity holders on their own. This is because most of them require activities that equity holders cannot engage in or information that equity holders do not possess. For example, shared activities, core competencies, multipoint competition, and exploiting market power all require the detailed coordination of business activities across multiple businesses in a firm. While equity holders may own a portfolio of equities, they are not in a position to coordinate business activities across this portfolio. In a similar way, internal capital allocation requires information about a business's prospects that is simply not available to a firm's outside equity holders.

Indeed, the only two economies of scope listed in Table 7.3 that do not have the potential for generating positive returns for a firm's equity holders are diversification in order to maximize the size of a firm—since firm size, per se, is not valuable—and diversification to reduce risk—since equity holders can do this on their own at very low cost by simply investing in a diversified portfolio of stocks. Indeed, while risk reduction is often a published rationale for many diversification moves, this rationale, by itself, is not directly consistent with the interests of a firm's equity holders. However, some scholars have suggested that this strategy may directly benefit other of a firm's stakeholders and thus indirectly benefit its equity holders. This possibility is discussed in detail in the Strategy in Depth feature.

Overall, this analysis of possible bases of diversification suggests that related diversification is more likely to be consistent with the interests of a firm's equity holders than unrelated diversification. This is because the one economy of scope listed in Table 7.3 that is the easiest for outside equity holders to duplicate—risk reduction—is the only economy of scope that an unrelated diversified firm can try to realize. All the other economies of scope listed in Table 7.3 require coordination and information sharing across businesses in a diversified firm that are very difficult to realize in unrelated diversified firms. Indeed, the preponderance of empirical research suggests that related diversified firms outperform unrelated diversified firms.[33]

Corporate Diversification and Sustained Competitive Advantage

V R I O

Table 7.3 describes those economies of scope that are likely to create real economic value for diversifying firms. It also suggests that related diversification can be valuable while unrelated diversification is usually not valuable. However, as we have seen with all the other strategies discussed in this book, the fact that a strategy is valuable does not necessarily imply that it will be a source of sustained competitive advantage. In order for diversification to be a source of sustained competitive advantage, it must be not only valuable but also rare and costly to imitate, and a firm must be organized to implement this strategy. The rarity and imitability of diversification are discussed in this section; organizational questions are deferred until the next.

The Rarity of Diversification

At first glance, it seems clear that diversification per se is usually not a rare firm strategy. Most large firms have adopted some form of diversification, if only the limited diversification of a dominant-business firm. Even many small and medium-sized firms have adopted different levels of diversification strategy.

However, the rarity of diversification depends not on diversification per se but on how rare the particular economies of scope associated with that diversification are. If only a few competing firms have exploited a particular economy of scope, that economy of scope can be rare. If numerous firms have done so, it will be common and not a source of competitive advantage.

The Imitability of Diversification

Both forms of imitation—direct duplication and substitution—are relevant in evaluating the ability of diversification strategies to generate sustained competitive advantages even if the economies of scope that they create are rare.

Direct Duplication of Diversification

The extent to which a valuable and rare corporate diversification strategy is immune from direct duplication depends on how costly it is for competing firms to realize this same economy of scope. As suggested in Table 7.4, some economies of scope are, in general, more costly to duplicate than others.

Strategy in Depth

Risk-Reducing Diversification and a Firm's Other Stakeholders

*A*lthough diversifying in order to reduce risk generally does not directly benefit outside equity investors in a firm, it can *indirectly* benefit outside equity investors through its impact on the willingness of other stakeholders in a firm to make firm-specific investments. A firm's **stakeholders** include all those groups and individuals who have an interest in how a firm performs. In this sense, a firm's equity investors are one of a firm's stakeholders. Other firm stakeholders include employees, suppliers, and customers.

Firm stakeholders make **firm-specific investments** when the value of the investments they make in a particular firm is much greater than the value of those same investments would be in other firms. Consider, for example, a firm's employees. An employee with a long tenure in a particular firm has generally made substantial **firm-specific human capital investments**. These investments include understanding a particular firm's culture, policies, and procedures; knowing the "right" people to contact to complete a task; and so forth. Such investments have significant value in the firm where they are made. Indeed, such firm-specific knowledge is generally necessary if an employee is to be able to help a firm conceive and implement valuable strategies.

However, the specific investments that an employee makes in a particular firm have almost no value in other firms. If a firm were to cease operations, employees would instantly lose almost all the value of any of the firm-specific investments they had made in that firm.

Suppliers and customers can also make these firm-specific investments. Suppliers make these investments when they customize their products or services to the specific requirements of a particular customer. They also make firm-specific investments when they forgo opportunities to sell to other firms in order to sell to a particular firm. Customers make firm-specific investments when they customize their operations to fully utilize the products or services of a particular firm. Also, by developing close relationships with a particular firm, customers may forgo the opportunity to develop relationships with other firms. These too are firm-specific investments made by customers. If a firm were to cease operations, suppliers and customers would instantly lose almost the entire value of the specific investments they have made in this firm.

Although the firm-specific investments made by employees, suppliers, and customers are risky—in the sense that almost their entire value is lost if the firm in which they are made ceases operations—they are extremely important if a firm is going to be able to generate economic profits. As was suggested in Chapter 3, valuable, rare, and costly-to-imitate resources and capabilities are more likely to be a source of sustained competitive advantage than resources and capabilities without these attributes. Firm-specific investments are more likely to have these attributes than non-firm-specific investments. Non-firm-specific investments are investments that can generate value in numerous different firms.

Thus, valuable, rare, and costly-to-imitate firm-specific investments

Table 7.4 Costly Duplication of Economies of Scope

Less costly-to-duplicate economies of scope	Costly-to-duplicate economies of scope
Shared activities	Core competencies
Risk reduction	Internal capital allocation
Tax advantages	Multipoint competition
Employee compensation	Exploiting market power

made by a firm's employees, suppliers, and customers can be the source of economic profits. And because a firm's outside equity holders are residual claimants on the cash flows generated by a firm, these economic profits benefit equity holders. Thus, a firm's outside equity holders generally will want a firm's employees, suppliers, and customers to make specific investments in a firm because those investments are likely to be sources of economic wealth for outside equity holders.

However, given the riskiness of firm-specific investments, employees, suppliers, and customers will generally only be willing to make these investments if some of the riskiness associated with making them can be reduced. Outside equity holders have little difficulty managing the risks associated with investing in a particular firm, because they can always create a portfolio of stocks that fully diversifies this risk at very low cost. This is why diversification that reduces the riskiness of a firm's cash flows does not generally directly benefit a firm's outside equity holders. However, a firm's employees, suppliers, and customers usually do not have these low-cost diversification opportunities. Employees, for example, are rarely able to make firm-specific human capital investments in a large enough number of different firms to

fully diversify the risks associated with making them. And although suppliers and customers can diversify their firm-specific investments to a greater degree than employees—through selling to multiple customers and through buying from multiple suppliers—the cost of this diversification for suppliers and customers is usually greater than the costs that are born by outside equity holders in diversifying their risk.

Because it is often very costly for a firm's employees, suppliers, and customers to diversify the risks associated with making firm-specific investments on their own, these stakeholders will often prefer that a firm's managers help manage this risk for them. Managers in a firm can do this by diversifying the portfolio of businesses in which a firm operates. If a firm is unwilling to diversify its portfolio of businesses, then that firm's employees, suppliers, and customers will generally be unwilling to make specific investments in that firm. Moreover, because these firm-specific investments can generate economic profits, and because economic profits can directly benefit a firm's outside equity holders, equity holders have an indirect incentive to encourage a firm to pursue a diversification strategy, even though that strategy does not directly benefit them.

Put differently, a firm's diversification strategy can be thought of as compensation for the firm-specific investments that a firm's employees, suppliers, and customers make in a firm. Outside equity holders have an incentive to encourage this compensation in return for access to some of the economic profits that these firm-specific investments can generate. In general, the greater the impact of the firm-specific investment made by a firm's employees, suppliers, and customers on the ability of a firm to generate economic profits, the more likely that pursuing a corporate diversification strategy is indirectly consistent with the interests of a firm's outside equity holders. In addition, the more limited the ability of a firm's employees, suppliers, and customers to diversify the risks associated with making firm-specific investments at low cost, the more that corporate diversification is consistent with the interests of outside equity investors.

Sources: J. B. Barney (1991). "Firm resources and sustained competitive advantage." *Journal of Management,* 17, pp. 99–120; R. M. Stulz (1996). "Rethinking risk management." *Journal of Applied Corporate Finance,* Fall, pp. 8–24; K. Miller (1998). "Economic exposure and integrated risk management." *Strategic Management Journal,* 33, pp. 756–779; R. Amit and B. Wernerfelt (1990). "Why do firms reduce business risk?" *Academy of Management Journal,* 33. pp. 520–533.

Shared activities, risk reduction, tax advantages, and employee compensation as bases for corporate diversification are usually relatively easy to duplicate. Because shared activities are based on tangible assets that a firm exploits across multiple businesses, such as common R&D labs, common sales forces, and common manufacturing, they are usually relatively easy to duplicate. The only duplication issues for shared activities concern developing the cooperative cross-business relationships that often facilitate the use of shared activities—issues discussed in the next chapter. Moreover, because risk reduction, tax advantages, and employee compensation motives for diversifying can be accomplished through both related and unrelated diversification, these motives for diversifying tend to be relatively easy to duplicate.

On the other hand, other economies of scope are much more difficult to duplicate. These difficult-to-duplicate economies of scope include core competencies, internal capital allocation efficiencies, multipoint competition, and exploitation of market power. Because core competencies are more intangible, their direct duplication is often challenging. The realization of capital allocation economies of scope requires very substantial information-processing capabilities. These capabilities are often very difficult to develop. Multipoint competition requires very close coordination between the different businesses in which a firm operates. This kind of coordination is socially complex and thus may often be immune from direct duplication. Finally, exploitation of market power may be costly to duplicate because it requires that a firm must possess significant market power in one of its lines of business. A firm that does not have this market power advantage would have to obtain it. The cost of doing so, in most situations, would be prohibitive.

Substitutes for Diversification

Two obvious substitutes for diversification exist. First, instead of obtaining cost or revenue advantages from exploiting economies of scope *across* businesses in a diversified firm, a firm may decide to simply grow and develop each of its businesses separately. In this sense, a firm that successfully implements a cost leadership strategy or a product differentiation strategy in a single business can obtain the same cost or revenue advantages it could have obtained by exploiting economies of scope, but without having to develop cross-business relations. Growing independent businesses within a diversified firm can be a substitute for exploiting economies of scope in a diversification strategy.

One firm that has chosen this strategy is Nestlé. Nestlé exploits few, if any, economies of scope among its different businesses. Rather, it has focused its efforts on growing each of its international operations to the point that they obtain cost or revenue advantages that could have otherwise been obtained in some form of related diversification. Thus, for example, Nestlé's operation in the United States is sufficiently large to exploit economies of scale in production, sales, and marketing, without reliance on economies of scope between U.S. operations and operations in other countries.[34]

A second substitute for exploiting economies of scope in diversification can be found in strategic alliances. By using a strategic alliance, firms may be able to gain the economies of scope they could have obtained if they had carefully exploited economies of scope across businesses they own. Thus, for example, instead of a firm exploiting research and development economies of scope between two businesses it owns, it could form a strategic alliance with a different firm and form a joint research and development lab. Instead of a firm exploiting sales economies of scope by linking its businesses through a common sales force, it might develop a sales agreement with another firm and obtain cost or revenue advantages in this way.

Corporate Diversification in an International Context

Each of the ways that a strategy of corporate diversification can add value, as summarized in Table 7.1, can also be an explanation of why firms pursuing an international strategy can also create value. This is because a firm pursuing an international strategy is pursuing, at least, a strategy of geographic diversification and perhaps a strategy of product-market diversification. In this sense, an international strategy can be thought of as a special case of a corporate diversification strategy. Indeed, some of the economies of scope listed in Table 7.1 are likely to be more valuable in an international context than in a domestic-only context. One of these economies of scope is described in the Global Perspectives feature.

However, pursuing international diversification opportunities can create unique challenges for a firm. Two of these challenges have to do with unique financial risks and the political risks associated with pursuing an international diversification strategy.

Financial Risks and International Diversification

As firms begin to pursue international strategies, they may expose themselves to financial risks that are less obvious within a single domestic market. In particular, currency fluctuations can significantly affect the value of a firm's international investments. Such fluctuations can turn what had been a losing investment into a profitable investment (this is the good news). They can also turn what had been a profitable investment into a losing investment (this is the bad news). In addition to currency fluctuations, different rates of inflation across countries can require very different managerial approaches, business strategies, and accounting practices. Certainly, when a firm first begins international operations, these financial risks can seem daunting.

Fortunately, it is now possible for firms to hedge many of these risks, through the use of a variety of financial instruments and strategies. The development of money markets, together with growing experience in operating in high-inflation economies, has substantially reduced the threat of these financial risks for firms pursuing international strategies. Of course, the benefits of these financial tools and experience in high-inflation environments do not accrue to firms automatically. Firms seeking to implement international strategies must develop the resources and capabilities they will need to manage these financial risks. Moreover, these hedging strategies can do nothing to reduce the business risks that firms assume when they enter into nondomestic markets. For example, it may be that consumers in a nondomestic market simply do not want to purchase a firm's products or services, in which case this economy of scope cannot be realized. Moreover, these financial strategies cannot manage political risks that can exist for firms pursuing an international strategy.

Political Risks and International Diversification

The political environment is an important consideration in all strategic decisions. Changes in the political rules of the game can have the effect of increasing some environmental threats, reducing others, and thereby changing the value of a firm's resources and capabilities. However, the political environment can be even more problematic as firms pursue international strategies.

Types of Political Risks

Politics can affect the value of a firm's international strategies at the macro and micro levels. At the macro level, broad changes in the political situation in a country can change the value of an investment. For example, after the Second World War, nationalist governments came to power in many countries in the Middle East. These governments expropriated, for little or no compensation, many of the

Global Perspectives

For firms not pursuing an international strategy, diversification can help reduce taxes because of its impact on a firm's debt capacity. The logic that links diversification, debt capacity, and taxes has already been discussed in this chapter: Because diversified firms generally have a low probability of bankruptcy, banks and other sources of debt are more willing to lend to these firms than they would otherwise; since interest payments on debt are tax deductible, a more highly leveraged firm, other factors being equal, will have lower taxes than a less leveraged firm. Thus, corporate diversification can affect a firm's tax liability. However, empirical work on the effect of diversification on tax liability suggests that, on average, this effect is not very large.

However, tax savings can be much more important for firms operating in an international context. Such firms can reduce their tax liability by using internal transfer prices to shift firm profits from high-tax locations to low-tax locations and can locate their operations in what are known as "tax havens."

As will be described in Chapter 8 in detail, a **transfer price** is the price that one part of a diversified firm charges another part of the firm for products or services. These transfer prices can have a substantial impact on the reported profits of a particular unit within a diversified firm. This impact of transfer pricing on a unit's reported profits is what creates the tax-reduction

Using International Strategies to Avoid Taxes

opportunity in an international setting. Suppose one of these units (for example, the unit selling a product or service) is in a high-tax country, while the second unit (for example, the unit buying a product or service) is in a low-tax country. By setting the transfer price in this example very high, the corporation is essentially transferring profits that would otherwise be attributed to the first unit to the second unit. It is also shifting those profits from a high-tax country to a low-tax country, thereby reducing its tax liability.

Of course, national tax authorities (like the IRS) do not approve of such actions and try to prevent firms from using internal transfer prices to avoid paying taxes. They do this by making sure that a firm's internal transfer prices are reasonable and justifiable. However, as we will see in Chapter 8, it is very difficult to calculate the "optimal transfer price" in most settings. Only when it is apparent that the sole purpose of setting a transfer price was to avoid taxes can firms be prevented from engaging in this strategy.

A second way that firms can use their international operations to avoid taxes is by establishing operations in what is known as a **tax haven**. A tax haven is a country that charges little or no corporate tax. In this tax avoidance strategy, a firm uses transfer prices, licensing fees, dividends, and other activities to book revenues and profits generated in high-tax countries to the operations in the tax haven. Countries that have emerged as tax havens over the last decade or so include Bermuda, the Cayman Islands, Granada, the Netherland Antilles, Liechtenstein, and Luxembourg. Currently, there are more foreign-owned firms registered in the Cayman Islands than there are people who live in the Cayman Islands. Banks on the Caymans have attracted over $300 billion in deposits from foreign investors, or roughly $9.4 million for each person who lives on the Caymans. Obviously, these tax havens are attracting a large number of firms and private investors.

Sources: "Cleaning up by cleaning up." *Euromoney*, April, pp. 73–77; H. French (1991). "Offshore banking gets new scrutiny with BCCI scandal." *New York Times*, September 29, p. 7.

assets of oil and gas companies located in their countries. Expropriation of foreign company assets also occurred when the Shah of Iran was overthrown, when a communist government was elected in Chile, and when new governments came to power in Angola, Ethiopia, Peru, and Zambia.[35]

Government upheaval and the attendant risks to international firms are facts of life in some countries. Consider, for example, oil-rich Nigeria. Since its independence in 1960, Nigeria has experienced several successful coups d'état, one civil war, two civil governments, and six military regimes.[36] The prudent course of action for firms engaging in business activities in Nigeria is to expect the current government to change and to plan accordingly.

Of course, government changes are not always bad for international firms. The fall of the Soviet Union and the introduction of capitalism into eastern Europe have created enormous opportunities for firms pursuing international strategies. For example, Volkswagen has invested $6 billion in a Czech automobile firm; Opel (General Motors' European division) has invested $680 million in a car-manufacturing facility in the former East Germany; and General Electric has invested $150 million in a light-bulb manufacturing operation in Hungary since the fall of the Soviet Union.[37]

At the micro level, politics in a country can affect the fortunes of particular firms in particular industries. For example, the success of Japanese automobile companies in the U.S. market has subjected these firms to a variety of political challenges, including local-content legislation and voluntary import quotas. These political risks exist even though there have been no major macro changes in the political system in the United States.[38]

Quantifying Political Risks

Political scientists have attempted to quantify the political risk that firms seeking to implement international strategies are likely to face in different countries. Although different studies vary in detail, the country attributes listed in Table 7.5 summarize most of the important determinants of political risk for firms pursuing international strategies.[39] Firms can apply the criteria listed in the table by evaluating the political and economic conditions in a country and by adding up the scores associated with these conditions. The most recent rankings of the political risks associated with conducting business in different countries are interesting. Not surprisingly, countries in western Europe and North America are the least risky. The least risky country within which to do business in the entire world is Luxembourg, followed by Switzerland, Norway, Denmark, the United States, and Sweden. On the other hand, countries currently experiencing civil unrest and revolution are among the most risky. The most risky country in the world, overall, is North Korea. Other very risky countries include Afghanistan, Iraq, Cuba, the Marshall Islands, and Zaire. Countries in Asia range from very low risk (Singapore and Japan, numbers 17 and 18 overall) to very high risk (North Korea). Countries in Africa and South America, on the other hand, tend to be relatively risky.

Managing Political Risk

Unlike financial risks, there are relatively few tools for managing the political risks associated with pursuing an international strategy. Obviously, one option would be to pursue international opportunities only in countries where political risk is very small. However, it is often the case that significant business opportunities exist in politically risky countries precisely because they are politically risky. Alternatively, firms can limit their investment in politically risky environments. However, these limited investments may not enable a firm to take full advantage of whatever economies of scope might exist by engaging in business in that country.

One approach to managing political risk is to see each of the determinants of political risk as negotiation points as a firm enters into a new country market. In many circumstances, those in a nondomestic market have just as much interest in a firm doing business in a new market as does the firm contemplating entry. International firms can sometimes use this bargaining power to negotiate

Table 7.5   **Quantifying Political Risks from International Operations**

	Low	High
The political economic environment		
1. Stability of the political system	3	14
2. Imminent internal conflicts	0	14
3. External threats to stability	0	12
4. Degree of control of the economic system	5	9
5. Reliability of country as a trade partner	4	12
6. Constitutional guarantees	2	12
7. Effectiveness of public administration	3	12
8. Labor relations and social peace	3	15
Domestic economic conditions		
1. Size of the population	4	8
2. Per capita income	2	10
3. Economic growth over the last 5 years	2	7
4. Potential growth over the next 3 years	3	10
5. Inflation over the last 2 years	2	10
6. Availability of domestic capital markets to outsiders	3	7
7. Availability of high-quality local labor force	2	8
8. Possibility of employing foreign nationals	2	8
9. Availability of energy resources	2	14
10. Environmental pollution legal requirements	4	8
11. Transportation and communication infrastructure	2	14
External economic relations		
1. Import restrictions	2	10
2. Export restrictions	2	10
3. Restrictions on foreign investments	3	9
4. Freedom to set up or engage in partnerships	3	9
5. Legal protection for brands and products	3	9
6. Restrictions on monetary transfers	2	8
7. Revaluation of currency in the last 5 years	2	7
8. Balance-of-payments situation	2	9
9. Drain on hard currency through energy imports	3	14
10. Financial standing	3	8
11. Restrictions of the exchange of local and foreign currencies	2	8

Source: Adapted from E. Dichtl and H. G Koeglmayr (1986). "Country Risk Ratings." *Management Review*, 26(4), pp. 2–10. Reprinted with permission.

entry conditions that reduce, or even neutralize, some of the sources of political risk in a country. Of course, no matter how skilled a firm is in negotiating these entry conditions, a change of government or changes in laws can quickly nullify any agreements.

A final approach to managing political risk is to turn the threat into an opportunity. One firm that has been successful in this way is Schlumberger, an international oil services company. Schlumberger has headquarters in New

York, Paris, and the Caribbean; it is a truly international company. Schlumberger management has adopted a policy of strict neutrality in interactions with governments in the developing world. Because of this policy, the company has been able to avoid political entanglements and continues to do business where many firms find the political risks too great. Put differently, Schlumberger has developed valuable, rare, and costly-to-imitate resources and capabilities in managing political risks and is using these resources to generate high levels of economic performance.[40]

SUMMARY

Firms implement corporate diver- sification strategies that range from limited diversification (single- business, dominant-business) to related diversification (related- constrained, related-linked) to unrelated diversification. In order to be valuable, corporate diversification strategies must reduce costs or increase revenues by exploiting economies of scope that outside equity holders cannot realize on their own at low cost.

Several motivations for implementing diversification strategies exist, including exploiting operational economies of scope (shared activities, core competencies), exploiting financial economies of scope (internal capital allocation, risk reduction, obtaining tax advantages), exploiting anticompetitive economies of scope (multipoint competition, market power advantages), and employee incentives to diversify (maximizing management compensation). All of these reasons for diversifying, except diversifying to maximize management compensation, have the potential for creating economic value for a firm. Moreover, a firm's outside equity holders will find it costly to realize all of these bases for diversification, except risk reduction. Thus, neither diversifying to maximize management compensation nor diversifying to reduce risk is directly consistent with the wealth maximizing interests of a firm's equity holders. This analysis also suggests that, on average, related diversified firms will outperform unrelated diversified firms.

The ability of a diversification strategy to create sustained competitive advantages depends not only on the value of that strategy but also on its rarity and imitability. The rarity of a diversification strategy depends on the number of competing firms that are exploiting the same economies of scope through diversification. Imitation can occur either through direct duplication or through substitutes. Costly-to-duplicate economies of scope include core competencies, internal capital allocation, multipoint competition, and exploitation of market power. Other economies of scope are usually less costly to duplicate. Important substitutes for diversification are when relevant economies are obtained through the independent actions of businesses within a firm and when relevant economies are obtained through strategic alliances.

Firms that pursue international business opportunities are implementing a geographic diversification strategy and may be implementing a product-market diversification strategy. All the economies of scope that can exist for firms pursuing a diversification strategy within a country can also exist for firms pursuing a diversification strategy internationally. However, two unique challenges are associated with international diversification: financial risks and political risks.

This discussion set aside important organizational issues in implementing diversification strategies. These issues are examined in detail in the next chapter.

CHALLENGE QUESTIONS

1. One simple way to think about relatedness is to look at the products or services a firm manufactures. The more similar these products or services are, the more related is the firm's diversification strategy. However, will firms that exploit core competencies in their diversification strategies always produce products or services that are similar to each other? Why or why not?

2. A firm implementing a diversification strategy has just acquired what it claims is a strategically related target firm but announces that it is not going to change this recently acquired firm in any way. Will this type of diversifying acquisition enable the firm to realize any valuable economies of scope that could not be duplicated by outside investors on their own? Why or why not?

3. One of the reasons why internal capital markets may be more efficient

than external capital markets is that firms may not want to reveal full information about their sources of competitive advantage to external capital markets, in order to reduce the threat of competitive imitation. This suggests that external capital markets may systematically undervalue firms with competitive advantages that are subject to imitation. Do you agree with this analysis? If yes, how could you trade on this information in your own investment activities? If no, why not?

4. A particular firm is owned by members of a single family. Most of the wealth of this family is derived from the operations of this firm, and the family does not want to "go public" with the firm by selling its equity position to outside investors. Will this firm pursue a highly related diversification

strategy or a somewhat less related diversification strategy? Why?

5. Under what conditions will a related diversification strategy not be a source of competitive advantage for a firm?

6. Suppose a firm has invested heavily in an oil-rich country with an unstable government. If this government was to fall, this firm is likely to lose its investment in this country, and the price of crude oil is likely to go up substantially. Also, suppose this firm has purchased equity positions in a large number of other oil firms that do not have investments in this particular country. In what ways can these equity investments be thought of as a hedge against a firm losing its investment in the unstable country? What, if anything, does your analysis say about the ability of firms to manage political risks indirectly?

PROBLEM SET

1. Visit the corporate Web sites for the following firms. How would you characterize the corporate strategies of these companies? Are they following a strategy of limited diversification, related diversification, or unrelated diversification?

(a) ExxonMobil
(b) Google
(c) General Motors
(d) Jet Blue
(e) Citigroup
(f) Entertainment Arts
(g) IBM
(h) Dell
(i) Berkshire Hathaway

2. Consider the following list of strategies. In your view, which of these strategies are examples of potential economies of scope underlying a corporate diversification strategy?

For those strategies that are an economy of scope, which economy of scope are they? For those strategies that are not an economy of scope, why aren't they?

(a) The Coca-Cola Corporation replaces its old diet cola drink (Tab) with a new diet cola drink called Diet Coke.

(b) Apple Computer introduces an I-Pod MP3 player with a larger memory.

(c) PepsiCo distributes Lay's Potato Chips to the same stores where it sells Pepsi.

(d) Kmart extends is licensing arrangement with Martha Stewart for four years.

(e) Wal-Mart uses the same distribution system to supply its Wal-Mart stores, its Wal-Mart SuperCenters (Wal-Mart stores with grocery stores in them), and its Sam's Clubs.

(f) Head Ski Company introduces a line of tennis rackets.

(g) General Electric borrows money from BankAmerica at 3 percent interest and then makes capital available to its jet engine subsidiary at 8 percent interest.

(h) McDonald's acquires Boston Market and Chipotle (two restaurants where many customers sit in the restaurant to eat their meals).

(i) A venture capital firm invests in a firm in the biotechnology industry and a firm in the entertainment industry.

(j) Another venture capital firm invests in two firms in the biotechnology industry.

3. Consider the following facts. The standard deviation of the cash flows associated with Business I is .8. The larger this standard deviation, the riskier a business's future cash flows are likely to be. The standard deviation of the cash flows associated with Business II is 1.3. That is, Business II is riskier than Business I. Finally, the correlation between the cash flows of these two businesses over time is −.8. This means that when Business I is up, Business II tends to be down, and vice versa. Suppose one firm owns both of these businesses.

(a) Assuming that Business I constitutes 40 percent of this firm's revenues and Business II constitutes 60 percent of its revenues, calculate the riskiness of this firm's total revenues using the following equation:

$$sd_{I,II} = \sqrt{w^2 sd_I^2 + (1-w)^2 sd_{II}^2 + 2w(1+w)\left(r_{I,II} sd_I sd_{II}\right)}$$

Where $w = .40$; $sd_I = .8$, $sd_{II} = 1.3$, and $r_{I,II} = -.8$.

(b) Given this result, does it make sense for this firm to own both Business I and Business II? Why or why not?

END NOTES

1. See Sellers, Patricia (2004). "The brand king's challenge." *Fortune*, April 5, pp. 192 +.
2. The Walt Disney Company (A). Harvard Business School Case No. 1-388-147.
3. Useem, Jerry (2004). "Another boss, another revolution." *Fortune*, April 5, pp. 112 +.
4. See Burrows, P. (1995). "Now, TI means 'taking initiative'." *BusinessWeek*, May 15, pp. 120–121; and Rogers, A. (1992). "It's the execution that counts." *Fortune*, November 30, pp. 80–83; Wallas, J., and J. Erickson (1993). *Hard drive: Bill Gates and the making of the Microsoft empire*. New York: Harper Business; and Porter, M. E. (1981). "Disposable diaper industry in 1974." Harvard Business School Case No. 9-380-175. Whether or not Microsoft continues to share activities across operating systems and applications software was one of the key issues at stake in the Microsoft antitrust suit. A more general discussion of the value of shared activities can be found in St. John, C. H., and J. S. Harrison (1999). "Manufacturing-based relatedness, synergy, and coordination." *Strategic Management Journal*, 20, pp. 129–145.
5. See Fuchsberg, G. (1992). "Decentralized management can have its drawbacks." *Wall Street Journal*, December 9, p. B1.
6. See Crockett, R. (2000). "A Baby Bell's growth formula." *BusinessWeek*, March 6, pp. 50–52; and Crockett, R. (1999). "The last monopolist." *BusinessWeek*, April 12, p. 76.
7. de Lisser, E. (1993). "Catering to cooking-phobic customers, supermarkets stress carryout. " *Wall Street Journal*, April 5, p. B1.

8. See, for example, Davis, P., R. Robinson, J. Pearce, and S. Park (1992). "Business unit relatedness and performance: A look at the pulp and paper industry." *Strategic Management Journal*, 13, pp. 349–361.

9. Loomis, C. J. (1993). "Dinosaurs?" *Fortune*, May 3, pp. 36–42.

10. Rapoport , C. (1992). "A tough Swede invades the U.S." *Fortune*, June 29, pp. 776–779.

11. Prahalad, C. K., and G. Hamel (1990). "The core competence of the organization." *Harvard Business Review*, 90, p. 82.

12. See also Grant, R. M. (1988). "On 'dominant logic' relatedness and the link between diversity and performance." *Strategic Management Journal*, 9, pp. 639–642; Chatterjee, S., and B. Wernerfelt (1991). "The link between resources and type at diversification: Theory and evidence." *Strategic Management Journal*, 12, pp. 33–48; Markides, C., and P. J. Williamson (1994). "Related diversification, core competencies, and corporate performance." *Strategic Management Journal*, 15, pp. 149–165; Montgomery, C. A., and B. Wernerfelt (1991). "Sources of superior performance: Market share versus industry effects in the U.S. brewing industry." *Management Science*, 37, pp. 954–959; Liedtka, J. M. (1996). "Collaborating across lines of business for competitive advantage." *Academy of Management Executive*, 10(2), pp. 20–37; and Farjoun, M. (1998). "The independent and joint effects of the skill and physical bases of relatedness in diversification." *Strategic Management Journal*, 19, pp. 611–630.

13. Jensen, M. C. (1986). "Agency costs of free cash flow, corporate finance, and takeovers." *American Economic Review*, 76, pp. 323–329.

14. See Nayyar, P. (1990). "Information asymmetries: A source of competitive advantage for diversified service firms." *Strategic Management Journal*, 11, pp. 513–519; and Robins, J., and M. Wiersema (1995). "A resource-based approach to the multibusiness firm: Empirical analysis of portfolio interrelationships and corporate financial performance." *Strategic Management Journal*, 16, pp. 277–299, for a discussion of the evolution of core competencies.

15. Prahalad, C. K., and R. A. Bettis (1986). "The dominant logic: A new linkage between diversity and performance." *Strategic Management Journal*, 7(6), pp. 485–501.

16. See Williamson, O. E. (1975). *Markets and hierarchies: Analysis and antitrust implications.* New York: Free Press.

17. See Liebeskind, J. P. (1996). "Knowledge, strategy, and the theory of the firm." *Strategic Management Journal*, 17 (Winter Special Edition), pp. 93–107.

18. Perry, L. T., and J. B. Barney (1981). "Performance lies are hazardous to organizational health." *Organizational Dynamics*, 9(3), pp. 68–80.

19. Bethel, J. E. (1990). *The capital allocation process and managerial mobility: A theoretical and empirical investigation.* Unpublished doctoral dissertation, University of California at Los Angles.

20. Staw, B. M. (1981). "The escalation of commitment to a course of action." *Academy of Management Review*, 6, pp. 577–587.

21. See Comment, R., and G. Jarrell (1995). "Corporate focus and stock returns." *Journal of Financial Economics*, 37, pp. 67–87; Berger, P. G., and E. Otek (1995). "Diversification's effect on firm value." *Journal of Financial Economics*, 37, pp. 39–65; Maksimovic, V., and G. Phillips (1999). "Do conglomerate firms allocate resources inefficiently?" Working paper, University of Maryland; Matsusaka, J. G., and V. Nanda (1998). Internal capital markets and corporate refocusing." Working paper, University of Southern California; Palia, D. (1998). "Division-level overinvestment and agency conflicts in diversified firms." Working paper, Columbia University; Rajan, R., H. Servaes, and L. Zingales (1997). "The cost of diversity: The diversification discount and inefficient investment." Working paper, University of Chicago; Scharfstein, D. S. (1997). "The dark side of internal capital markets II: Evidence from diversified conglomerates." NBER [National Bureau of Economic Research]. Working paper; Shin, H. H., and R. M. Stulz (1998). "Are internal capital markets efficient?" *The Quarterly Journal of Economics*, May, pp. 551–552. But Houston and James (1998) show that internal capital markets can create competitive advantages for firms: Houston, J., and C. James (1998). "Some evidence that banks use internal capital markets to lower capital costs." *Journal of Applied Corporate Finance*, 11(2), pp. 70–78.

22. Scott, J. H. (1977). "On the theory of conglomerate mergers." *Journal of Finance*, 32, pp. 1235–1250.

23. See Brennan, M. (1979). "The pricing of contingent claims in discrete time models." *Journal of Finance*, 34, pp. 53–68; Cox, J., S. Ross, and M.

Rubinstein (1979). "Option pricing: A simplified approach." *Journal of Financial Economics*, 7, pp. 229–263; and Stapleton, R. C. (1982). "Mergers, debt capacity, and the valuation of corporate loans." In M. Keenan and L. J. White (eds.), *Mergers and acquisitions.* Lexington, MA: D. C. Heath, Chapter 2; and Galai, D., and R. W. Masulis (1976). "The option pricing model and the risk factor of stock." *Journal of Financial Economics*, 3, pp. 53–82.

24. See Karnani, A., and B. Wernerfelt (1985). "Multiple point competition." *Strategic Management Journal*, 6, pp. 87–96; Bernheim, R. D., and M. D. Whinston (1990). "Multimarket contact and collusive behavior." *Rand Journal of Economics*, 12, pp. 605–617; Tirole, J. (1988). *The theory of industrial organization.* Cambridge, MA: MIT Press; Gimeno, J., and C. Y. Woo (1999). "Multimarket contact, economies of scope, and firm performance." *Academy of Management Journal*, 43(3), pp. 239–259; Korn, H. J., and J. A. C. Baum (1999). "Chance, imitative, and strategic antecedents to multimarket contact." *Academy of Management Journal*, 42(2), pp. 171–193; Baum, J. A. C., and H. J. Korn (1999). "Dynamics of dyadic competitive interaction." *Strategic Management Journal*, 20, pp. 251–278; Gimeno, J. (1999). "Reciprocal threats in multimarket rivalry: Staking our 'spheres of influence' in the U.S. airline industry." *Strategic Management Journal*, 20, pp. 101–128; Gimeno, J., and C. Y. Woo (1996). "Hypercompetition in a multimarket environment: The role of strategic similarity and multimarket contact in competitive de-escalation." *Organization Science*, 7(3), pp. 322–341; Ma, H. (1998). "Mutual forbearance in international business." *Journal of International Management*, 4(2), pp. 129–147; McGrath, R. G., and M.-J. Chen (1998). "Multimarket maneuvering in uncertain spheres of influence: Resource diversion strategies." *Academy of Management Review*, 23(4), pp. 724–740; Chen, M.-J. (1996). "Competitor analysis and interfirm rivalry: Toward a theoretical integration." *Academy of Management Review*, 21(1), pp. 100–134; Chen, M.-J., and K. Stucker (1997). "Multinational management and multimarket rivalry: Toward a theoretical development of global competition." *Academy of Management Proceedings 1997*, pp. 2–6; and Young, G., K. G. Smith, and C. M. Grimm (1997). "Multimarket contact, resource heterogeneity, and rivalrous firm behavior." *Academy of Management Proceedings 1997*, pp. 55–59. This idea was originally proposed by Edwards, C. D. (1955). "Conglomerate bigness as a source of power." In *Business concentration and price policy.* NBER Conference Report. Princeton, NJ: Princeton University Press.

25. See Karnani, A., and B. Wernerfelt (1985). "Multiple point competition." *Strategic Management Journal*, 6, pp. 87–96.

26. This is documented by Gimeno, J. (1994). "Multipoint competition, market rivalry and firm performance: A test of the mutual forbearance hypothesis in the United States airline industry, 1984–1988." Unpublished doctoral dissertation, Purdue University.

27. See Landro, L., P. M. Reilly, and R. Turner (1993). "Cartoon clash: Disney relationship with Time Warner is a strained one." *Wall Street Journal*, April 14, p. A1; and Reilly, P. M., and R. Turner (1993). "Disney pulls ads in tiff with *Time.*" *Wall Street Journal*, April 2, p. B1. The growth and consolidation of the entertainment industry since the early 1990s has made Disney and Time Warner (especially after its merger with AOL) large entertainment conglomerates. It will be interesting to see if these two larger firms will be able to find ways to tacitly collude or will continue the competition begun in the early 1990s.

28. The best work in this area has been done by Gimeno, J. (1994). "Multipoint competition, market rivalry and firm performance: A test of the mutual forbearance hypothesis in the United States airline industry, 1984–1988." Unpublished doctoral dissertation, Purdue University. See also Smith, F., and R. Wilson (1995). "The predictive validity of the Karnani and Wernerfelt model of multipoint competition." *Strategic Management Journal*, 16, pp. 143–160.

29. See Tirole, J. (1988). *The theory of industrial organization.* Cambridge, MA: MIT Press.

30. Carnevale, M. L. (1993). "Ring in the new: Telephone service seems on the brink of huge innovations." *Wall Street Journal*, February. 10, p. A1.

31. See Russo, M. V. (1992). "Power plays: Regulation, diversification, and backward integration in the electric utility industry." *Strategic Management Journal*, 13, pp. 13–27. Recent work by Jandik and Makhija indicates that when a regulated utility diversifies out of a

regulated industry, it often earns a more positive return than when an unregulated firm does this [Jandik, T., and A. K. Makhija (1999). "An Empirical Examination of the Atypical Diversification Practices of Electric Utilities: Internal Capital Markets and Regulation." Fisher College of Business, Ohio State University, working paper (September).] This work shows that regulators have the effect of making a regulated firm's internal capital market more efficient. Differences between Russo's (1992) findings and Jandik and Makhija's (1999) findings may have to do with when this work was done. Russo's (1992) research may have focused on a time period before regulatory agencies had learned how to improve a firm's internal capital market. However, even though Jandik and Makhija (1999) report positive returns from regulated firms diversifying, these positive returns do not reflect the market power advantages of these firms.

32. Finkelstein, S., and D. C. Hambrick (1989). "Chief executive compensation: A study of the intersection of markets and political processes." *Strategic Management Journal*, 10, pp. 121–134.

33. See William, J., B. L. Paez, and L. Sanders (1988). "Conglomerates revisited." *Strategic Management Journal*, 9, pp. 403–414; Geringer, J. M., S. Tallman, and D. M. Olsen (2000). "Product and international diversification among Japanese multinational firms." *Strategic Management Journal*, 21, pp. 51–80; Nail, L. A., W. L. Megginson, and C. Maquieira (1998). "How stock-swap mergers affect shareholder (and bondholder) wealth: More evidence of the value of corporate 'focus'." *Journal of Applied Corporate Finance*, 11(2), pp. 95–106; G. R. Carroll; L. S. Bigelow; M.-D. L. Seidel; L. B. Tsai (1966)." "The fates of *De Novo* and *De Alio* producers in the American automobile industry 1885—1981." *Strategic Management Journal*, 17 (Special

Summer Issue), pp. 117–138; Nguyen, T. H., A. Seror, and T. M. Devinney (1990). "Diversification strategy and performance in Canadian manufacturing firms." *Strategic Management Journal*, 11, pp. 411–418; and Amit, R., and J. Livnat (1988). "Diversification strategies, business cycles and economic performance." *Strategic Management Journal*, 9, pp. 99–110, for a discussion of corporate diversification in the economy over time.

34. The Nestlé story is summarized in Templeman, J. (1993). "Nestlé: A giant in a hurry." *BusinessWeek*, March 22, pp. 50–54.

35. See Rugman, A., and R. Hodgetts (1995). *Business: A strategic management approach*. New York: McGraw-Hill.

36. Glynn, M. A. (1993). "Strategic planning in Nigeria versus U.S.: A case of anticipating the (next) coup." *Academy of Management Executive* 7(3), pp. 82–83.

37. See Roth, T. (1990). "Bid size showed VW's eagerness to buy Skoda." *Wall Street Journal*, December 11, p. A15; and Tully, S. (1990). "GE in Hungary: Let there be light." *Fortune*, October 22, pp. 137–142.

38. See Ring, P. S., S. A. Lenway, and M. Govekar (1990). "Management of the political imperative in international business." *Strategic Management Journal*, 11, pp. 141–151.

39. Dichtl, E., and H. G. Koeglmayr (1986). "Country risk ratings." *Management Review*, 26(4), pp. 2–10; O'Leary, M. (2002) "Analysts take an optimistic view." *Euromoney*, September, pp. 208–216; Hoti, S. (2004). "Snapshot images of country risk ratings: An international comparison." Unpublished, Department of Economics, University of Western Australia.

40. See Auletta, K. (1983). "A certain poetry—Parts I and II." *The New Yorker*, June 6, pp. 46–109; June 13, pp. 50–91.

8

Organizing to Implement Corporate Diversification

During 2002 and 2003, it seemed like you couldn't open the newspaper without reading about yet another example of corporate corruption. The list of former senior managers recently convicted, currently on trial, or awaiting trial is depressingly long: Samuel D. Walsa (ImClone Systems, Inc.); Frank Quattrone (an investment banker at Credit Suisse First Boston); Dennis Kozlowski and Mark H. Swartz (Tyco International); Bernard J. Ebbers and Scott D. Sullivan

Corporate Crooks

(WorldCom, Inc.); Richard Scrushy (HealthSouth Corp.); Andrew Fastow and David W. Delainey (Enron); and Martha Stewart (Martha Stewart Living Inc.). And this corruption isn't limited to just the United States Calisto Tanzi, founder and former CEO of the Italian dairy and food products firm Parmalat, has

been jailed, along with his son and several members of Parmalat's top management team, for corruption and accounting fraud.

What is wrong? Is the current generation of senior managers simply less honest or less ethical than previous generations? Or has the level of dishonesty remained the same, but the effectiveness of government enforcement improved? And why did it take so many years for the transgressions of Enron and WorldCom and other firms to be revealed?

Learning Objectives

After reading this chapter, you should be able to:

1. Describe the multidivisional, or M-form, structure and how it is used to implement a corporate diversification strategy.

2. Describe the roles of the board of directors, institutional investors, the senior executive, corporate staff, division general managers, and shared activity managers in making the M-form structure work.

3. Describe how three management control processes—measuring divisional performance, allocating corporate capital, and transferring intermediate products—are used to help implement a corporate diversification strategy.

4. Describe the role of management compensation in helping to implement a corporate diversification strategy.

Where were the checks and balances supposedly built into the capitalist system? Where were the boards of directors, the banks, institutional investors, external auditors, the press?

One explanation of the current level of business corruption begins by observing that the economic climate of the 1990s led to growth expectations that were greater than what could be sustained by the underlying business models of many large firms. Faced with the choice between dampening those expectations (and having the price of their firm's stock drop significantly) or

"cooking the books" to keep the price up, many managers took the latter course. This was a particularly tempting option since many of these managers owned a great deal of their company's stock. As these first efforts at "earnings management" were augmented by even more creative forms of accounting, companies and managers created an accounting "house of cards" so fragile that even the smallest of events could send it tumbling down.

And then it came crashing down, and the list of managerial felons grew ever longer.

Obviously, the components of corporate governance that were supposed to rein in these kinds of abuses—the boards of directors, banks, institutional investors, external auditors, the press— failed too many times, and new legislation that strengthened the control of corporations was passed, at least in the United States.

But this episode in the history of the corporation strikes another cautionary note. Despite the lengthy list of corporate misdeeds uncovered during the first years of the twenty-first century, the vast majority of corporations in the United States and around the world followed the rules, did not engage in unethical practices, and continued to manage their businesses in fiscally sound ways. Put differently, our recent experiences remind us both of the importance of diligence in monitoring the business practices of large firms and of the fact that most of that monitoring effort reveals remarkably few unethical practices.

Sources: "On Trial." *BusinessWeek*, January 12, 2004, pp. 80–81; Alessandra Galloni, David Reilly, and Carrick Mollenkamp (2004). "Italy's Parmalat probe looks to Bank of America in London." *Wall Street Journal*, March 8, p. B6; Gail Edmondson, David Fairlamb, and Nanete Byrnes (2004). "The milk just keeps on spilling." *BusinessWeek*, January 26, pp. 54 +.

Τhis chapter is about how the large diversified firm—the kind of firm at the center of so much of the business corruption recently reported in the popular press—is managed and governed efficiently. The chapter explains how many of the checks and balances described in the opening case act to assure that the corporation is managed in a way that is consistent with the interests of its owners—equity holders—as well as the interests of its other stakeholders. The three components of organizing to implement any strategy, first identified in Chapter 3—organizational structure, management controls, and compensation policy—are also important in implementing corporate diversification strategies.

Organizational Structure and Implementing Corporate Diversification

The most common organizational structure for implementing a corporate diversification strategy is the **M-form**, or **multidivisional**, structure. A typical M-form structure, as it would appear in a firm's annual report, is presented in Figure 8.1.

Figure 8.1   An Example of M-Form Organizational Structure as Depicted in a Firm's Annual Report

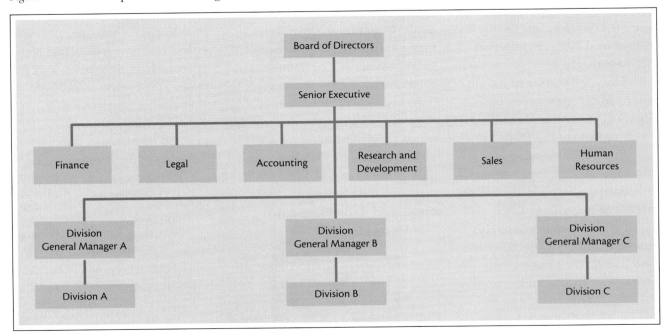

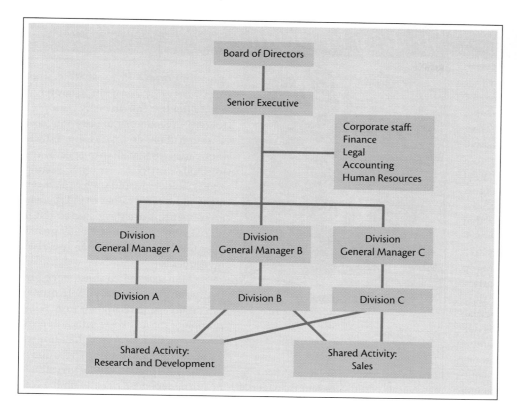

Figure 8.2 An M-Form Structure Redrawn to Emphasize Roles and Responsibilities

This same structure is redrawn in Figure 8.2 to emphasize the roles and responsibilities of each of the major components of the M-form organization.[1]

In the multidivisional structure, each business that the firm engages in is managed through a division. Different firms have different names for these **divisions**—strategic business units (SBUs), business groups, companies. Whatever their names, the divisions in an M-form organization are true **profit-and-loss centers**: Profits and losses are calculated at the level of the division in these firms.

Different firms use different criteria for defining the boundaries of profit-and-loss centers. For example, General Electric defines its divisions in terms of the types of products each one manufactures and sells (for example, consumer electronics, nuclear, medical imaging, and so forth). Nestlé defines its divisions with reference to the geographic scope of each of its businesses (North America, South America, and so forth). General Motors defines its divisions in terms of the brand names of its products (Cadillac, Chevrolet, Saturn, and so forth). However they are defined, divisions in an M-form organization should be large enough to represent identifiable business entities but small enough so that each one can be managed effectively by a division general manager. Indeed, each division in an M-form organization typically adopts a U-form structure (see the discussion of the U-form structure in Chapters 4, 5, and 6), and the division general manager takes on the role of a U-form senior executive for his or her division.

The M-form structure is designed to create checks and balances for managers that increase the probability that a diversified firm will be managed in ways consistent with the interests of its equity holders. The roles of each of the major elements of the M-form structure in accomplishing this objective are summarized in Table 8.1 and discussed below. Some of the conflicts of interest that might emerge between a firm's equity holders and its managers are described in the Strategy in Depth feature.

Strategy in Depth

*I*n Chapter 7, it was suggested that sometimes it is in the best interest of equity holders to delegate to managers the day-to-day management of their equity investments in a firm. This will be the case when equity investors cannot realize a valuable economy of scope on their own while managers *can* realize that economy of scope.

Several authors suggest that whenever one party to an exchange delegates decision-making authority to a second party, an **agency relationship** has been created between these parties. The party delegating this decision-making authority is called the **principal**; the party to whom this authority is delegated is called the **agent**. In the context of corporate diversification, an agency relationship exists between a firm's outside equity holders (as principals) and its managers (as agents) to the extent that equity holders delegate the day-to-day management of their investment to those managers.

The agency relationship between equity holders and managers can be very effective as long as managers make investment decisions that are consistent with equity holders' interests. Thus, if equity holders are interested in maximizing the rate of return on their investment in a firm and if managers make their investment decisions with this objective in mind, then equity holders will have few concerns about delegating the day-to-day management of their investments to managers. Unfortunately, in numerous situations the interests of a firm's outside equity holders and its managers do not coincide. When parties in an agency relationship differ in their decision-making objectives, **agency problems** arise. Two common agency problems

Agency Conflicts Between Managers and Equity Holders

have been identified: investment in managerial perquisites and managerial risk aversion.

Managers can decide to take some of a firm's capital and invest it in **managerial perquisites** that do not add economic value to the firm but do directly benefit those managers. Examples of such investments include lavish offices, fleets of corporate jets, and corporate vacation homes. Dennis Kozlowski, former CEO of Tyco International, is accused of "stealing" $600 million in these kinds of managerial perquisites from his firm. The list of goods and services that Kozlowski lavished on himself and those close to him is truly astounding—a multimillion-dollar birthday party for his wife, a $6,000 wastebasket, a $15,000 umbrella stand, a $144,000 loan to a board member, toga-clad waiters at an event, and so on.

As outrageous as some of these managerial perquisites can be, the second source of agency problems—managerial risk aversion—is probably

more important in most diversified firms. As discussed in Chapter 7, equity holders can diversify their portfolio of investments at very low cost. Through their diversification efforts, they can eliminate all firm-specific risk in their portfolios. In this setting, equity holders would prefer managers make more risky rather than less risky investments, since the expected return on risky investments is usually greater than the expected return on less risky investments.

Managers, in contrast, have limited ability to diversify their human capital investments in their firm. Some portion of these investments is specific to a particular firm and has limited value in alternative uses. The value of a manager's human capital investment in a firm depends critically on the continued existence of the firm. Thus managers are *not* indifferent to the riskiness of investment opportunities in a firm. Very risky investments may jeopardize a firm's survival and thus eliminate the value of a manager's human capital investments. These incentives can lead managers to be more risk averse in their decision making than equity holders would like them to be.

One of the purposes of the M-form structure, and indeed of all aspects of organizing to implement corporate diversification, is to reduce these agency problems.

Sources: M. C. Jensen and W. H. Meckling (1976). "Theory of the firm: Managerial behavior, agency costs, and ownership structure." *Journal of Financial Economics*. 3, pp. 305–360; J. Useem (2003). "The biggest show." *Fortune*, December 8, pp157+; R. Lambert (1986). "Executive effort and selection of risky projects." *Rand Journal of Economics*, 13(2), pp. 369–378.

Table 8.1   **The Roles and Responsibilities of Major Components of the M-Form Structure**

Component	Activity
Board of directors	Monitor decision-making in a firm to ensure that it is consistent with the interests of outside equity holders
Institutional investors	Monitor decision-making to ensure that it is consistent with the interests of major institutional equity investors
Senior executives	Formulate corporate strategies consistent with equity holders' interests and assure strategy implementation

Strategy formulation:

- Decide the businesses in which the firm will operate
- Decide how the firm should compete in those businesses
- Specify the economies of scope around which the diversified firm will operate

Strategy implementation:

- Encourage cooperation across divisions to exploit economies of scope
- Evaluate performance of divisions
- Allocate capital across divisions

| Corporate staff | Provides information to the senior executive about internal and external environments for strategy formulation and implementation |
| Division general managers | Formulate divisional strategies consistent with corporate strategies and assure strategy implementation |

Strategy formulation:

- Decide how the division will compete in its business, given the corporate strategy

Strategy implementation:

- Coordinate the decisions and actions of functional managers reporting to the division general manager to implement divisional strategy
- Compete for corporate capital allocations
- Cooperate with other divisions to exploit corporate economies of scope

| Shared activity managers | Support the operations of multiple divisions |

The Board of Directors

One of the major components of an M-form organization is a firm's **board of directors**. In principle, all of a firm's senior managers report to the board. The board's primary responsibility is to monitor decision making in the firm, to ensure that it is consistent with the interests of outside equity holders.

Research Made Relevant

There has been a great deal of research on when boards of directors are more or less effective in ensuring that firms are managed in ways consistent with the interests of equity holders. Three issues have received particular attention: The roles of insiders (i.e., managers) and outsiders on the board; whether or not the board chair and the senior executive should be the same or different people; and whether the board should be active or passive.

With respect to insiders and outsiders on the board, in one way this seems like a simple problem. Because the primary role of the board of directors is to monitor managerial decisions to ensure that they are consistent with the interests of equity holders, it follows that the board should consist primarily of outsiders because they face no conflict of interest in evaluating managerial performance. Obviously, managers, as inside members of the board, face significant conflicts of interest in evaluating their own performance.

Research on outsider members of boards of directors tends to support this point of view. Outside directors, as compared to insiders, tend to focus more on monitoring a firm's economic

**The Effectiveness
of Boards of Directors**

performance than on other measures of firm performance. Obviously, a firm's economic performance is most relevant to its equity investors. Outside board members are also more likely than inside members to dismiss CEOs following poor performance. Also, outside board members have a stronger incentive than inside members to maintain their reputations as effective monitors. This incentive by itself can lead to more effective monitoring by outside board

members. Moreover, the monitoring effectiveness of outside board members seems to be enhanced when they personally own a substantial amount of a firm's equity.

However, the fact that outside members face fewer conflicts of interest in evaluating managerial performance compared to management insiders on the board does not mean that there is no appropriate role for inside board members. Managers bring something to the board that cannot be easily duplicated by outsiders—detailed information about the decision-making activities inside the firm. This is precisely the information that outsiders need to effectively monitor the activities of a firm, and it is information available to them only if they work closely with insiders (managers). One way to gain access to this information is to include managers as members of the board of directors. Thus, while most work suggests that a board of directors should be composed primarily of outsiders, there is an important role for insiders/managers to play as members of a firm's board.

There is currently some debate about whether the roles of board chair and CEO should be combined or sepa-

A board of directors typically consists of 10 to 15 individuals drawn from a firm's top management group and from individuals outside the firm. A firm's **senior executive** (often identified by the title president or chief executive officer or CEO), its chief financial officer (CFO), and a few other senior managers are usually on the board—although managers on the board are typically outnumbered by outsiders. The firm's senior executive is often but not always the **chairman of the board** (a term used here to denote both female and male senior executives). The task of managerial board members—including the board chair—is to provide other board members information and insights about critical decisions being made in the firm and the effect those decisions are likely to have on a firm's equity holders. The task of outsiders on the board is to evaluate the past, current, and future performance of the firm, and of its senior managers, to ensure that the actions taken in the firm are consistent with equity holders' interests.[2]

rated and, if separated, what kinds of people should occupy these positions. Some have argued that the roles of CEO and chairman of the board should definitely be separated and that the role of the chairman should be filled by an outside (nonmanagerial) member of the board of directors. These arguments are based on the assumption that only an outside member of the board can ensure the independent monitoring of managerial decision making. Others have argued that effective monitoring often requires more information than what would be available to outsiders and thus that the roles of board chair and CEO should be combined and filled by a firm's senior manager.

Empirical research on this question suggests that whether these roles of CEO and chairman should be combined or not depends on the complexity of the information analysis and monitoring task facing the CEO and chairman. Brian Boyd has found that combining the roles of CEO and chairman is positively correlated with firm performance when firms operate in slow-growth and simple competitive environments—environments that do not overtax the cognitive capability of a single individual. This finding suggests that combining these roles does not necessarily increase conflicts between a firm and its equity holders. This research also found that separating the roles of CEO and board chair is positively correlated with firm performance when firms operate in high-growth and very complex environments. In such environments, a single individual cannot fulfill all the responsibilities of both CEO and chairman and thus the two roles need to be held by separate individuals.

Finally, with respect to active versus passive boards, historically the boards of major firms have been relatively passive and would take dramatic action, such as firing the senior executive, only if a firm's performance was significantly below expectations for long periods of time. However, more recently, boards have become more active proponents of equity holders' interests. This recent surge in board activity reflects a new economic reality: If a board does not become more active in monitoring firm performance, then other monitoring mechanisms will. Consequently, the board of directors has become progressively more influential in representing the interests of a firm's equity holders.

However, board activity can go too far. To the extent that the board begins to operate a business on a day-to-day basis, it goes beyond its capabilities. Boards rarely have sufficient detailed information to manage a firm directly. When it is necessary to change a firm's senior executive, boards will usually not take on the responsibilities of that executive, but rather will rapidly identify a single individual—either an insider or outsider—to take over this position.

Sources: E. Zajac and J. Westphal (1994). "The costs and benefits of managerial incentives and monitoring in large U.S. corporations: When is more not better?" *Strategic Management Journal,* 15, pp. 121–142; P. Rechner and D. Dalton (1991). "CEO duality and organizational performance: A longitudinal analysis." *Strategic Management Journal,* 12, pp. 155–160; S. Finkelstein and R. D'Aveni (1994). "CEO duality as a double-edged sword: How boards of directors balance entrenchment avoidance and unity of command." *Academy of Management Journal,* 37, pp. 1079–1108; B. K. Boyd (1995). "CEO duality and firm performance: A contingency model." *Strategic Management Journal,* 16, pp. 301–312; F. Kesner and R. B. Johnson (1990). "An investigation of the relationship between board composition and stockholder suits." *Strategic Management Journal,* 11, pp. 327–336.

Boards of directors are typically organized into several subcommittees. An **audit committee** is responsible for ensuring the accuracy of accounting and financial statements. A **finance committee** maintains the relationship between the firm and external capital markets. A **nominating committee** nominates new board members. A **personnel and compensation committee** evaluates and compensates the performance of a firm's senior executive and other senior managers. Often, membership on these standing committees is reserved for external board members. Other standing committees reflect specific issues for a particular firm and are typically open to external and internal board members.[3]

Over the years, a great deal of research has been conducted about the effectiveness of boards of directors in ensuring that a firm's managers make decisions in ways consistent with the interests of its equity holders. Some of this work is summarized in the Research Made Relevant feature.

Global Perspectives

The Family Firm in the United States and the World

How common is it for large diversified firms around the world to be owned or dominated by single families? Most people are surprised to find out just how common family-dominated firms are in the United States. Indeed, one-third of the firms in the Standard & Poor's 500 have their founding families still involved in day-to-day management. Such firms include Marriott, Walgreens, Wrigley, Alberto-Culver, Campbell Soup, Dell Computer, and Wal-Mart.

However, as important as these family-dominated firms are in the U.S. economy, they are not the dominant force that such firms are in many countries around the world. In fact, one recent study found that they can be a very important force in the economy of many countries. For example, in New Zealand, 9 of the 20 largest firms in the economy are family dominated; in Argentina, 13 of the 20 largest firms in the economy are family dominated; in Mexico, all 20 of the 20 largest firms in the economy are

family dominated. By comparison, only 4 of the 20 largest firms in the United States are family dominated, and only 1 of the 20 largest firms in the United Kingdom is family dominated.

These results suggest that the model of corporate governance that is

normally taught in the United States—with large numbers of shareholders owning stock in professionally managed firms—is actually the exception around the world. In many countries—including Argentina, Belgium, Canada, Denmark, Greece, Hong Kong, Israel, Mexico, New Zealand, Portugal, Singapore, South Korea, Sweden, and Switzerland—over one-third of the 20 largest firms are dominated by family owners.

Family ownership of large diversified corporations has advantages and disadvantages. On the positive side, many of the agency problems (see the Strategy in Depth feature) that exist in professionally managed firms are less important in family-dominated firms. After all, managers in family-dominated firms are not "playing" with other people's money, they are "playing" with their own family's money. Family-dominated firms can also make strategic decisions faster than large bureaucratic firms, they tend to create a sense of loyalty among

Institutional Owners

Historically, the typical large diversified firm has had its equity owned in small blocks by millions of individual investors. The exception to this general rule was family-owned or -dominated firms, a phenomenon that is discussed in more detail in the Global Perspectives feature. When a firm's ownership is spread among millions of small investors, it is difficult for any one of these investors to have a large enough ownership position to influence management decisions directly. The only course of action open to such investors if they disagree with management decisions is to sell their stock.

However, the growth of institutional owners has changed the ownership structure of many large diversified firms over the last several years. **Institutional owners** are usually pension funds, mutual funds, insurance companies, or other groups of individual investors that have joined together to manage their investments. In 1970, institutions owned 32 percent of the equity traded in the United States. By 1990, institutions owned 48 percent of this equity. In 2002, they owned 62 percent of the equity traded in the United States.[4]

their employees, and they tend to invest for long-term growth rather than being forced to respond to short-term fluctuations in the stock market. Indeed, in the United States over the last 10 years, family-dominated firms have outperformed non-family-dominated firms—in terms of income growth—21 percent to 11.5 percent.

On the other hand, family-dominated firms have some significant limitations as well. First, since senior leadership positions in these firms, and especially those outside the United States, tend to be reserved for family members, such firms often do not have access to the broader professional management skills available to non-family-dominated firms. Also, since family interests tend to weigh heavily in strategic decision making in these firms, outside investors will often be reluctant to invest in such firms. This suggests that family-dominated firms may often face important capital constraints. Finally, because much

of a particular family's wealth tends to be tied up in the family firm, it is difficult for family members to purchase equities and other investments to diversify their personal investment portfolios. Thus, in order to obtain the benefits of portfolio diversification for their family owners, family-dominated firms often engage in a strategy of unrelated diversification. As was suggested in Chapter 7, this is a very expensive way for a firm's owners to diversify their risk.

Overall, while family-dominated businesses can have advantages and disadvantages, research indicates that the predominance of family-dominated businesses in a country's economy is negatively correlated with the overall level of growth in that economy. Countries whose economies are dominated by family-owned businesses tend to grow less quickly than countries whose economies are not dominated by family-owned businesses. This negative correlation probably reflects the

primary reason that family firms are still important in many economies around the world. When individuals in a country are not confident that the legal and political system will protect their personal property rights, they develop alternative ways to protect those rights. Large and powerful family firms are another way of protecting personal property rights. This suggests that the sanctity of personal property rights in a country explains both the level of economic growth in that country and the extent to which family firms dominate a country's economy.

Sources: R. Morck and B. Yeung (2004). "Family control and the rent-seeking society." *Entrepreneurship: Theory and Practice,* Summer, pp. 391–409; R. LaPorta, F. Lopez-de-Salinas, A. Shleifer, and R. Vishny (1999). "Corporate ownership around the world." *Journal of Finance,* 54, pp. 471–520; J. Weber, L. Lavelle, T. Lowry, W. Zellner, and A. Barrett (2003). "Family, Inc." *BusinessWeek,* November 10, pp. 100 +.

Institutional investors can use their investment clout to insist that a firm's management behaves in ways consistent with the interests of equity holders. Observers who assume that institutional investors are interested more in maximizing the short-term value of their portfolios than in the long-term performance of firms in those portfolios fear that such power will force firms to make only short-term investments. Recent research in the United States and Japan, however, suggests that institutional investors are not unduly myopic. Rather, as suggested earlier, these investors use approximately the same logic equity investors use when evaluating the performance of a firm. For example, one group of researchers examined the impact of institutional ownership on research and development investments in R&D–intensive industries. R&D investments tend to be longer term in orientation. If institutional investors are myopic, they should influence firms to invest in relatively less R&D, in favor of investments that generate shorter-term profits. This research showed that high levels of institutional ownership did not adversely affect the level of R&D in a firm. These findings are consistent with the notion that institutional investors are not inappropriately concerned with the short term in their monitoring activities.[5]

More generally, other researchers have shown that high levels of institutional ownership leads firms to sell strategically unrelated businesses. This effect of institutional investors is enhanced if, in addition, outside directors on a firm's board have substantial equity investments in the firm. Given the discussion of the value of unrelated diversification in Chapter 7, it seems clear that these divestment actions are typically consistent with maximizing the present value of a firm.[6]

The Senior Executive

As suggested in Table 8.1, the senior executive (the president or CEO) in an M-form organization has two responsibilities: strategy formulation and strategy implementation. Strategy formulation entails deciding which set of businesses a diversified firm will operate in and strategy implementation focuses on encouraging behavior in a firm that is consistent with this strategy. Each of these responsibilities of the senior executive are discussed in turn.

Strategy Formulation

At the broadest level, deciding which businesses a diversified firm should operate in is equivalent to discovering and developing valuable economies of scope among a firm's current and potential businesses. If these economies of scope are also rare and costly to imitate, they can be a source of sustained competitive advantage for a diversified firm.

The senior executive is uniquely positioned to discover, develop, and nurture valuable economies of scope in a diversified firm. Every other manager in this kind of firm either has a divisional point of view (for example, division general managers and shared activity managers) or is a functional specialist (for example, corporate staff and functional managers within divisions). Only the senior executive has a truly corporate perspective. However, the senior executive in an M-form organization should involve numerous other divisional and functional managers in strategy formulation to ensure complete and accurate information as input to the process and a broad understanding of and commitment to that strategy once it has been formulated.

Strategy Implementation

As is the case for senior executives in a U-form structure, strategy implementation in an M-form almost always involves resolving conflicts among groups of managers. However, instead of simply resolving conflicts between functional managers (as is the case in a U-form), senior executives in M-form organizations must resolve conflicts within and between each of the major managerial components of the M-form structure: corporate staff, division general managers, and shared activity managers. Various corporate staff managers may disagree about the economic relevance of their staff functions, corporate staff may come into conflict with division general managers over various corporate programs and activities, division general managers may disagree with how capital is allocated across divisions, division general managers may come into conflict with shared activity managers about how shared activities should be managed, shared activity managers may disagree with corporate staff about their mutual roles and responsibilities, and so forth.

Obviously, the numerous and often conflicting relationships among groups of managers in an M-form organization can place significant strategy implementation burdens on the senior executive.[7] While resolving these numerous conflicts, however, the senior executive needs to keep in mind the reasons why the firm began pursuing a diversification strategy in the first place: to exploit real economies of scope that outside investors cannot realize on their own. Any strategy implementation decisions that jeopardize the realization of these real economies of scope are inconsistent with the underlying strategic objectives of a diversified firm. These issues are analyzed in detail later in this chapter, in the discussion of management control systems in the M-form organization.

The Office of the President: Chairman, CEO, and COO

It is often the case that the roles and responsibilities of the senior executive in an M-form organization are greater than what can be reasonably managed by a single individual. This is especially likely if a firm is broadly diversified across numerous complex products and markets. In this situation, it is not uncommon for the tasks of the senior executive to be divided among two or three people: the **chairman of the board**, the **chief executive officer**, and the **chief operating officer (COO)**. The primary responsibilities of each of these roles in an M-form organization are listed in Table 8.2. Together, these roles are known as the **office of the president**. In general, as the tasks facing the office of the president become more demanding and complex, the more likely it is that the roles and responsibilities of this office will be divided among two or three people.

Corporate Staff

The primary responsibility of **corporate staff** is to provide information about the firm's external and internal environments to the firm's senior executive. This information is vital for both the strategy formulation and the strategy implementation responsibilities of the senior executive. Corporate staff functions that provide information about a firm's external environment include finance, investor relations, legal affairs, regulatory affairs, and corporate advertising. Corporate staff functions that provide information about a firm's internal environment include accounting and corporate human resources. These corporate staff functions report directly to a firm's senior executive and are a conduit of information to that executive.

Corporate and Divisional Staff

Many organizations re-create some corporate staff functions within each division of the organization. This is particularly true for internally oriented corporate staff functions such as accounting and human resources. At the division level, divisional staff managers usually have a direct, "solid-line" reporting relationship to their respective corporate staff functional managers and a less formal, "dotted-line" reporting relationship to their division general manager. The reporting relationship between the divisional staff manager and the corporate staff manager is the link that enables the corporate staff manager to collect the information that the senior executive requires for strategy formulation and implementation. The senior executive can also use this corporate staff–division staff relationship to communicate corporate policies and procedures to the divisions, although these policies can also be communicated directly by the senior executive to division general managers.

Table 8.2   **Responsibilities of Three Different Roles in the Office of the President**

Chairman of the board	Supervision of the board of directors in its monitoring role
Chief executive officer	Strategy formulation
Chief operating officer	Strategy implementation

Although divisional staff managers usually have a less formal relationship with their division general managers, in practice division general managers can have an important influence on the activities of divisional staff. After all, divisional staff managers may formally report to corporate staff managers, but they spend most of their time interacting with their division general managers and with the other functional managers who report to their division general managers. These divided loyalties can sometimes affect the timelines and accuracy of the information transmitted from divisional staff managers to corporate staff managers and thus affect the timeliness and accuracy of the information the senior executive uses for strategy formulation and implementation.

Nowhere are these divided loyalties potentially more problematic than in accounting staff functions. Obviously, it is vitally important for the senior executive in an M-form organization to receive timely and accurate information about divisional performance. If the timeliness and accuracy of that information are inappropriately affected by division general managers, the effectiveness of senior management can be adversely affected. Moreover, in some situations, division general managers can have very strong incentives to affect the timeliness and accuracy of divisional performance information, especially if a division general manager's compensation depends on this information or if the capital allocated to a division depends on this information.

Efficient monitoring by the senior executive requires that corporate staff, and especially the accounting corporate staff function, remain organizationally independent of division general managers—thus the importance of the solid-line relationship between divisional staff managers and corporate staff managers. Nevertheless, the ability of corporate staff to obtain accurate performance information from divisions also depends on close cooperative working relationships between corporate staff, divisional staff, and division general managers—thus the importance of the dotted-line relationship between divisional staff managers and division general managers. How one maintains the balance between, on the one hand, the distance and objectivity needed to evaluate a division's performance and, on the other hand, the cooperation and teamwork needed to gain access to the information required to evaluate a division's performance distinguishes excellent from mediocre corporate staff managers.

Overinvolvement in Managing Division Operations

Over and above the failure to maintain a balance between objectivity and cooperation in evaluating divisional performance, the one sure way that corporate staff can fail in a multidivisional firm is to become too involved in the day-to-day operations of divisions. In an M-form structure, the management of such day-to-day operations is delegated to division general managers and to functional managers who report to division general managers. Corporate staff managers collect and transmit information; they do not manage divisional operations.

One way to ensure that corporate staff does not become too involved in managing the day-to-day operations of divisions is to keep corporate staff small. This is certainly true for some of the best-managed diversified firms in the world. For example, just 1.5 percent of Johnson & Johnson's 82,700 employees work at the firm's headquarters, and only some of those individuals are members of the corporate staff. Hanson Industries has in its U.S. headquarters 120 people who help manage a diversified firm with $8 billion in revenues. Clayton, Dubilier, and Rice, a management buyout firm, has only 11 headquarters staff members overseeing eight businesses with collective sales of over $6 billion.[8]

Division General Manager

Division general managers in an M-form organization have primary responsibility for managing a firm's businesses from day to day. Division general managers have full profit-and-loss responsibility and typically have multiple functional managers reporting to them. As general managers, they have both strategy formulation and strategy implementation responsibilities. On the strategy formulation side, division general managers choose strategies for their divisions, within the broader strategic context established by the senior executive of the firm. Many of the analytical tools described in Parts 1 and 2 of this book can be used by division general managers to make these strategy formulation decisions.

The strategy implementation responsibilities of division general managers in an M-form organization parallel the strategy implementation responsibilities of senior executives in U-form organizations. In particular, division general managers must be able to coordinate the activities of often-conflicting functional managers in order to implement a division's strategies.

In addition to their responsibilities as a U-form senior executive, division general managers in an M-form organization have two additional responsibilities: to compete for corporate capital and to cooperate with other divisions to exploit corporate economies of scope. Division general managers compete for corporate capital by promising high rates of return on capital invested by the corporation in their business. In most firms, divisions that have demonstrated the ability to generate high rates of return on earlier capital investments gain access to more capital or to lower-cost capital, compared to divisions that have not demonstrated a history of such performance.

Division general managers cooperate to exploit economies of scope by working with shared activity managers, corporate staff managers, and the senior executive in the firm to isolate, understand, and use the economies of scope around which the diversified firm was originally organized. Division general managers can even become involved in discovering new economies of scope that were not anticipated when the firm's diversification strategy was originally implemented but nevertheless may be both valuable and costly for outside investors to create on their own.

Of course, a careful reader will recognize a fundamental conflict between the last two responsibilities of division general managers in an M-form organization. These managers are required to compete for corporate capital and to cooperate to exploit economies of scope at the same time. Competition is important, because it leads division general managers to focus on generating high levels of economic performance from their divisions. If each division is generating high levels of economic performance, then the diversified firm as a whole is likely to do well also. However, cooperation is important to exploit economies of scope that are the economic justification for implementing a diversification strategy in the first place. If divisions do not cooperate in exploiting these economies, there are few, if any, justifications for implementing a corporate diversification strategy, and the diversified firm should be split into multiple independent entities. The need to simultaneously compete and cooperate puts significant managerial burdens on division general managers. It is likely that this ability is both rare and costly to imitate across most diversified firms.[9]

Shared Activity Managers

One of the potential economies of scope identified in Chapter 7 was shared activities. Divisions in an M-form organization exploit this economy of scope when one or more of the stages in their value chains are managed in common. Typical examples of activities shared across two or more divisions in a multidivisional firm include common sales forces, common distribution systems, common manufacturing facilities, and common research and development efforts (also see Table 7.2). The primary responsibility of the individuals who manage shared activities is to support the operations of the divisions that share the activity.

The way in which M-form structure is often depicted in company annual reports (as in Figure 8.1) tends to obscure the operational role of shared activities. In this version of the M-form organizational chart, no distinction is made between corporate staff functions and shared activity functions. Moreover, it appears that managers of shared activities report directly to a firm's senior executive, just like corporate staff. These ambiguities are resolved by redrawing the M-form organizational chart to emphasize the roles and responsibilities of different units within the M-form (as in Figure 8.2). In this more accurate representation of how an M-form actually functions, corporate staff groups are separated from shared activity managers, and each is shown reporting to its primary internal "customer." That "internal customer" is the senior executive for corporate staff groups and two or more division general managers for shared activity managers.

Shared Activities as Cost Centers

Shared activities are often managed as cost centers in an M-form structure. That is, rather than having profit-and-loss responsibility, **cost centers** are assigned a budget and manage their operations to that budget. When this is the case, shared activity managers do not attempt to create profits when they provide services to the divisions they support. Rather, these services are priced to internal customers in such a way that the shared activity just covers its cost of operating.

Because cost center shared activities do not have to generate profits from their operations, the cost of the services they provide to divisions can be less than the cost of similar services provided either by a division itself or by outside suppliers. If a shared activity is managed as a cost center, and the cost of services from this shared activity is *greater than* the cost of similar services provided by alternative sources, then either this shared activity is not being well managed, or it was not a real economy of scope in the first place. However, when the cost of services from a shared activity is *less than* the cost of comparable services provided by a division itself or by an outside supplier, then division general managers have a strong incentive to use the services of shared activities, thereby exploiting an economy of scope that may have been one of the original reasons why a firm implemented a corporate diversification strategy.

Shared Activities as Profit Centers

Some diversified firms are beginning to manage shared activities as profit centers, rather than as cost centers. Moreover, rather than requiring divisions to use the services of shared activities, divisions retain the right to purchase services from internal shared activities or from outside suppliers or to provide services for themselves. In this setting, managers of shared activities are required to compete for their internal customers on the basis of the price and quality of the services they provide.[10]

One firm that has taken this profit center approach to managing shared activities is ABB, Inc., a Swiss engineering firm. ABB eliminated almost all its corporate staff and reorganized its remaining staff functions into shared activities. Shared activities in ABB compete to provide services to ABB divisions. Not only do some traditional shared activities—such as research and development and sales—compete for internal customers, but many traditional corporate staff functions—such as human resources, marketing, and finance—do as well. ABB's approach to managing shared activities has resulted in a relatively small corporate staff and in increasingly specialized and customized shared activities.[11]

Of course, the greatest risk associated with treating shared activities as profit centers and letting them compete for divisional customers is that divisions may choose to obtain no services or support from shared activities. Although this course of action may be in the self-interest of each division, it may not be in the best interest of the corporation as a whole if, in fact, shared activities are an important economy of scope around which the diversified firm is organized.

In the end, whether a shared activity is managed as a cost center or as a profit center, the task facing the managers of shared activities is the same: to provide such highly customized and high-quality services to divisional customers at a reasonable cost that those internal customers will not want to seek alternative suppliers outside the firm or provide those services themselves. In an M-form organization, the best way to ensure that shared activity economies of scope are realized is for shared activity managers to satisfy their internal customers.

Management Controls and Implementing Corporate Diversification

The M-form structure presented in Figures 8.2 and 8.3 is complex and multifaceted. However, no organizational structure by itself is able to fully implement a corporate diversification strategy. The M-form structure must be supplemented with a variety of management controls. Three of the most important management controls in an M-form structure—systems for evaluating divisional performance, for allocating capital across divisions, and for transferring intermediate products between divisions—are discussed in this section.[12]

Evaluating Divisional Performance

Because divisions in an M-form structure are profit-and-loss centers, evaluating divisional performance should, in principle, be straightforward: Divisions that are very profitable should be evaluated more positively than divisions that are less profitable. In practice, this seemingly simple task is surprisingly complex. Two problems typically arise: (1) How should division profitability be measured? and (2) How should economy-of-scope linkages between divisions be factored into divisional performance measures?

Measuring Divisional Performance

Accounting Measures of Divisional Performance. Both accounting and economic measures of performance can be used in measuring the performance of divisions within a diversified firm. Common accounting measures of divisional performance include the return on the assets controlled by a division, the return on a division's sales, and a division's sales growth. These accounting measures of divisional performance are then compared with some standard to see if a division's performance exceeds or falls short of that standard. Diversified firms use three different standards of comparison when evaluating the performance of a division: (1) a hurdle rate that is common across all the different business units in a firm, (2) a division's budgeted level of performance (which may vary by division), and (3) the average level of profitability of firms in a division's industry.

Each of these standards of comparison has its strengths and weaknesses. For example, if a corporation has a single hurdle rate of profitability that all divisions must meet or exceed, there is little ambiguity about the performance objectives of divisions. On the other hand, such a single standard ignores important differences in performance that might exist across divisions.

Comparing a division's actual performance to its budgeted performance allows the performance expectations of different divisions to vary, but the budgeting process is time-consuming and fraught with political intrigue. One study showed that corporate managers routinely discount the sales projections and capital requests of division managers on the assumption that division managers are trying to "game" the budgeting system.[13] Moreover, division budgets are usually based on a single set of assumptions about how the economy is going to evolve, how competition in a division's industry is going to evolve, and what actions that division is going to take in its industry. When these assumptions no longer hold, budgets are redone—a costly and time-consuming process that has little to do with generating value in a firm.

Finally, while comparing a division's performance with the average level of profitability of firms in a division's industry also allows performance expectations to vary across divisions within a diversified firm, this approach lets other firms determine what is and is not excellent performance for a division within a diversified firm. This approach can also be manipulated: By choosing just the "right" firms with which to compare a division's performance, almost any division can be made to look like it's performing better than its industry average.[14]

No matter what standard of comparison is used to evaluate a division's accounting performance, most accounting measures of divisional performance have a common limitation. All these measures have a short-term bias. This short-term bias reflects the fact that all these measures treat investments in resources and capabilities that have the potential for generating value in the long run as costs during a particular year. In order to reduce costs in a given year, division managers may sometimes forgo investing in these resources and capabilities, even if they could be a source of sustained competitive advantage for a division in the long run.

Economic Measures of Divisional Performance. Given the limitations of accounting measures of divisional performance, several firms have begun adopting economic methods of evaluating this performance. Economic methods build on accounting methods, but adjust those methods to incorporate short-term investments that may generate long-term benefits. Economic methods also compare a division's performance with a firm's cost of capital (see Chapter 1). This avoids some of the gaming that can characterize the use of other standards of comparison in applying accounting measures of divisional performance.

Perhaps the most popular of these economically oriented measures of division performance is known as **economic value added** or **EVA**.[15] EVA is calculated by subtracting the cost of capital employed in a division from that division's earnings in the following manner:

$$EVA = \text{adjusted accounting earnings}$$
$$- (\text{weighted average cost of capital} \times \text{total capital employed by a division})$$

Several of the terms in the EVA formula require some discussion. For example, the calculation of economic value added begins with a division's "adjusted" accounting earnings. These are a division's traditional accounting earnings, adjusted so that they approximate what would be a division's economic earnings. Several adjustments to a division's accounting statements have been described in the literature. For example, traditional accounting practices require R&D spending to be deducted each year from a division's earnings. This can lead division general managers to underinvest in longer-term R&D efforts. In the EVA measure of divisional performance, R&D spending is added back into a division's performance, and R&D is then treated as an asset and depreciated over some period of time.

One consulting firm (Stern Stewart) that specializes in implementing EVA-based divisional evaluation systems in multidivisional firms makes up to 40 "adjustments" to a division's standard accounting earnings so that they more closely approximate economic earnings. Many of these adjustments are proprietary to this consulting firm. However, the most important adjustments—like how R&D should be treated—are broadly known.

The terms in parentheses in the EVA equation reflect the cost of investing in a division. Rather than using some alternative standard of comparison, EVA applies financial theory and multiplies the amount of money invested in a division by a firm's weighted average cost of capital. A firm's weighted average cost of capital is the amount of money a firm could earn if it invested in any of its other divisions. In this sense, a firm's weighted average cost of capital can be thought of as the opportunity cost of investing in a particular division, as opposed to investing in any other division in the firm.

By adjusting a division's earnings, and accounting for the cost of investing in a division, economic value added is a much more accurate estimate of a division's economic performance than are traditional accounting measures of performance. The number of diversified firms evaluating their divisions with EVA-based measures of divisional performance is impressive and growing. These firms include AT&T, Coca-Cola, Quaker Oats, CSX, Briggs and Stratton, and Allied Signal. At Allied Signal, divisions that do not earn their cost of capital are awarded the infamous "leaky bucket" award. If this performance is not improved, division general managers are replaced. The use of EVA has been touted as the key to creating economic wealth in a diversified corporation. Even the U.S. Postal Service is exploring the application of EVA to its operations.[16]

Economies of Scope and the Ambiguity of Divisional Performance

Whether a firm uses accounting measures to evaluate the performance of a division or uses economic measures of performance like EVA, divisional performance in a well-managed diversified firm can never be evaluated unambiguously. Consider a simple example.

Suppose that in a particular multidivisional firm there are only two divisions (Division A and Division B) and one shared activity (research and development). Also, suppose that the two divisions are managed as profit-and-loss centers and that the R&D shared activity is managed as a cost center. To support this R&D effort, each division pays $10 million per year and has been doing so for 10 years. Finally, suppose that after 10 years of effort (and investment) the R&D group develops a valuable new technology that perfectly addresses Division A's business needs.

Obviously, no matter how divisional performance is measured, it is likely to be the case that Division A's performance will rise relative to Division B's performance. In this situation, what percentage of Division A's improved performance should be allocated to Division A, what percentage should be allocated to the R&D group, and what percentage should be allocated to Division B?

The managers in each part of this diversified firm can make compelling arguments in their favor. Division general manager A can reasonably argue that without Division A's efforts to exploit the new technology, the full value of the technology would never have been realized. The R&D manager can reasonably argue that without the R&D effort, there would not have been a technology to exploit in the first place. Finally, division general manager B can reasonably argue that without the dedicated long-term investment of Division B in R&D, there would have been no new technology and no performance increase for Division A.

That all three of these arguments can be made suggests that, to the extent that a firm exploits real economies of scope in implementing a diversification strategy, it will not be possible to unambiguously evaluate the performance of individual divisions in that firm. The fact that there are economies of scope in a diversified firm means that all of the businesses a firm operates in are more valuable bundled together than they would be if kept separate from one another. Efforts to evaluate the performance of these businesses as if they were separate from one another are futile.

One solution to this problem is to force businesses in a diversified firm to operate independently of each other. If each business operates independently, then it will be possible to unambiguously evaluate its performance. Of course, to the extent that this independence is enforced, the diversified firm is unlikely to be able to realize the very economies of scope that were the justification for the diversification strategy in the first place.

Divisional performance ambiguity is bad enough when shared activities are the primary economy of scope that a diversified firm is trying to exploit. This ambiguity increases dramatically when the economy of scope is based on intangible core competencies. In this situation, it is shared learning and experience that justify a firm's diversification efforts. The intangible nature of these economies of scope multiplies the difficulty of the divisional evaluation task.

Even firms that apply rigorous EVA measures of divisional performance are unable to fully resolve these performance ambiguity difficulties. For example, the Coca-Cola division of the Coca-Cola Company has made enormous investments in the Coke brand name over the years, and the Diet Coke division has exploited some of that brand name capital in its own marketing efforts. Of course, it is not clear that all of Diet Coke's success can be attributed to the Coke brand name. After all, Diet Coke has developed its own creative advertising, has developed its own loyal group of customers, and so forth. How much of Diet Coke's success—as measured through that division's economic value added—should be allocated to the Coke brand name (an investment made long before Diet Coke was even conceived), and how much should be allocated to the Diet Coke division's efforts? EVA measures of divisional performance do not resolve ambiguities created when economies of scope exist across divisions.[17]

In the end, the quantitative evaluation of divisional performance—with either accounting or economic measures—must be supplemented by the experience and judgment of senior executives in a diversified firm. Only by evaluating a division's performance numbers in the context of a broader, more subjective evaluation of the division's performance can a true picture of divisional performance be developed.

Allocating Corporate Capital

Another potentially valuable economy of scope outlined in Chapter 7 (besides shared activities and core competencies) is internal capital allocation. In that discussion, it was suggested that for internal capital allocation to be a justification for diversification, the information made available to senior executives allocating capital in a diversified firm must be superior, in both amount and quality, to the information available to external sources of capital in the external capital market. Both the quality and the quantity of the information available in an internal capital market depend on the organization of the diversified firm.

One of the primary limitations of internal capital markets is that division general managers have a strong incentive to overstate their division's prospects and understate its problems, in order to gain access to more capital at lower costs.

Having an independent corporate accounting function in a diversified firm can help address this problem. However, given the ambiguities inherent in evaluating divisional performance in a well-managed diversified firm, independent corporate accountants do not resolve all these informational problems.

In the face of these challenges, some firms use a process called **zero-based budgeting** to help allocate capital. In zero-based budgeting, corporate executives create a list of all capital allocation requests from divisions in a firm, rank them from "most important" to "least important," and then fund all the projects a firm can afford, given the amount of capital it has available. In principle, with zero-based budgeting, no project will receive funding for the future simply because it received funding in the past. Rather, each project has to stand on its own merits each year by being included among the important projects the firm can afford to fund.

While zero-based budgeting has some attractive features, it has some important limitations as well. For example, evaluating and ranking all projects in a diversified firm from "most important" to "least important" is a very difficult task. It requires corporate executives to have a very complete understanding of the strategic role of each of the projects being proposed by a division, as well as an understanding of how these projects will affect the short-term performance of divisions.

In the end, no matter what process firms use to allocate capital, allocating capital inside a firm in a way that is more efficient than what could be done by external capital markets requires the use of information that is not available to those external markets. Typically, that information will be intangible, tacit, and complex. Corporate managers looking to realize this economy of scope must find a way to use this kind of information effectively.[18] The difficulty of managing this process effectively may be one of the reasons why internal capital allocation often fails to qualify as a valuable economy of scope in diversified firms.[19]

Transferring Intermediate Products

The existence of economies of scope across multiple divisions in a diversified firm often means that products or services produced in one division are used as inputs for products or services produced by a second division. Such products or services are called **intermediate products or services**. Intermediate products or services can be transferred between any of the units in an M-form organization. This transfer is, perhaps, most important and problematic when it occurs between profit center divisions.

The transfer of intermediate products or services among divisions is usually managed through a **transfer-pricing system**: One division "sells" its product or service to a second division for a transfer price. Unlike a market price, which is typically determined by market forces of supply and demand, transfer prices are set by a firm's corporate management to accomplish corporate objectives.

Setting Optimal Transfer Prices

From an economic point of view, the rule for establishing the optimal transfer price in a diversified firm is quite simple: The transfer price should be the value of the opportunities forgone when one division's product or service is transferred to another division. Consider the following example. Division A's marginal cost of production is $5 per unit, but Division A can sell all of its output to outside customers for $6 per unit. If Division A can sell all of its output to outside customers for $6 per unit, the value of the opportunity forgone of transferring a unit of production from Division A to Division B is $6—the amount of money that Division A forgoes by transferring its production to Division B instead of selling it to the market.

However, if Division A is selling all the units it can to external customers for $6 per unit but still has some excess manufacturing capacity, the value of the opportunity forgone in transferring the product from Division A to Division B is only $5 per unit—Division A's marginal cost of production. Because the external market cannot absorb any more of Division A's product at $6 per unit, the value of the opportunity forgone when Division A transfers units of production to Division B is not $6 per unit (Division A can't get that price) but only $5 per unit.[20]

When transfer prices are set equal to opportunity costs, selling divisions will produce output up to the point that the marginal cost of the last unit produced equals the transfer price. Moreover, buying divisions will buy units from other divisions in the firm as long as the net revenues from doing so just cover the transfer price. These transfer prices will lead profit-maximizing divisions to optimize the diversified firm's profits.

Difficulties in Setting Optimal Transfer Prices

Setting transfer prices equal to opportunity costs sounds simple enough, but it is very difficult to do in real diversified firms. Establishing optimal transfer prices requires information about the value of the opportunities forgone by the "selling" division. This, in turn, requires information about this division's marginal costs, its manufacturing capacity, external demand for its products, and so forth. Much of this information is difficult to obtain. Moreover, it is rarely stable. As market conditions change, demand for a division's products can change, marginal costs can change, and the value of opportunities forgone can change. Also, to the extent that a selling division customizes the products or services it transfers to other divisions in a diversified firm, the value of the opportunities forgone by this selling division become even more difficult to calculate.

Even if this information could be obtained and updated rapidly, division general managers in selling divisions have strong incentives to manipulate the information in ways that increase the perceived value of the opportunities forgone by their division. These division general managers can thus increase the transfer price for the products or services they sell to internal customers and thereby appropriate for their division profits that should have been allocated to buying divisions.

Setting Transfer Prices in Practice

Because it is rarely possible for firms to establish an optimal transfer-pricing scheme, most diversified firms must adopt some form of transfer pricing that attempts to approximate optimal prices. Several of these transfer-pricing schemes are described in Table 8.3. However, no matter what particular schemes a firm uses, the transfer prices it generates will, at times, create inefficiencies and conflicts in a diversified firm. Some of these inefficiencies and conflicts are described in Table 8.4.[21]

The inefficiencies and conflicts created by transfer-pricing schemes that only approximate optimal transfer prices mean that few diversified firms are ever fully satisfied with how they set transfer prices. Indeed, one study found that as the level of resource sharing in a diversified firm increases (thereby increasing the importance of transfer-pricing mechanisms), the level of job satisfaction for division general managers decreases.[22]

It is not unusual for a diversified firm to change its transfer-pricing mechanisms every few years in an attempt to find the "right" transfer-pricing mechanism. Economic theory tells us what the "right" transfer-pricing mechanism is: Transfer prices should equal opportunity cost. However, this "correct" transfer-price mechanism cannot be implemented in most firms. Firms that continually change their transfer-pricing mechanisms generally find that all

Table 8.3 **Alternative Transfer Pricing Schemes**

Exchange autonomy	■ Buying and selling division general managers are free to negotiate transfer price without corporate involvement. ■ Transfer price is set equal to the selling division's price to external customers.
Mandated full cost	■ Transfer price is set equal to the selling division's actual cost of production. ■ Transfer price is set equal to the selling division's standard cost (that is, the cost of production if the selling division were operating at maximum efficiency).
Mandated market based	■ Transfer price is set equal to the market price in the selling division's market.
Dual pricing	■ Transfer price for the buying division is set equal to the selling division's actual or standard costs. ■ Transfer price for the selling division is set equal to the price to external customers or to the market price in the selling division's market.

Source: R. Eccles (1985). *The transfer pricing problem: A theory for practice.* Lexington, MA: Lexington Books. Used with permission of Rowman and Littlefield Publishing Group.

these systems have some weaknesses. In choosing which system to use, a firm should be less concerned about finding the right transfer-pricing mechanism and more concerned about choosing a transfer-pricing policy that creates the fewest management problems—or at least the kinds of problems that the firm can manage effectively. Indeed, some scholars have suggested that the search for optimal transfer pricing should be abandoned in favor of treating transfer pricing as a conflict resolution process. Viewed in this way, transfer pricing highlights differences between divisions and thus makes it possible to begin to resolve those differences in a mutually beneficial way.[23]

Table 8.4 **Weaknesses of Alternative Transfer-Pricing Schemes**

1. Buying and selling divisions negotiate transfer price.
   - ■ What about the negotiating and haggling costs?
   - ■ The corporation risks not exploiting economies of scope if the right transfer price cannot be negotiated.

2. Transfer price is set equal to the selling division's price to external customers.
   - ■ Which customers? Different selling division customers may get different prices.
   - ■ Shouldn't the volume created by the buying division for a selling division be reflected in a lower transfer price?
   - ■ The selling division doesn't have marketing expenses when selling to another division. Shouldn't that be reflected in a lower transfer price?

3. Transfer price is set equal to the selling division's actual costs.
   - ■ What are those actual costs, and who gets to determine them?
   - ■ *All* the selling division's costs, or only the costs relevant to the products being purchased by the buying division?

4. Transfer price is set equal to the selling division's standard costs.
   - ■ Standard costs are the costs the selling division would incur if it were running at maximum efficiency. This hypothetical capacity subsidizes the buying division.

5. Transfer price is set equal to the market price.
   - ■ If the product in question is highly differentiated, there is no simple "market price."
   - ■ Shouldn't the volume created by the buying division for a selling division be reflected in a lower transfer price?
   - ■ The selling division doesn't have marketing expenses when selling to a buying division. Shouldn't that be reflected in a lower transfer price?

6. Transfer price is set equal to actual costs for the selling division and to market price for the buying division.
   - ■ This combination of schemes simply combines other problems of setting transfer prices.

Overall, the three management control processes described here—measuring divisional performance, allocating corporate capital, and transferring intermediate products—suggest that the implementation of a corporate diversification requires a great deal of management skill and experience. They also suggest that sometimes diversified firms may find themselves operating businesses that no longer fit with the firm's overall corporate strategy. What happens when a division no longer fits with a firm's corporate strategy is described in the Strategy in the Emerging Enterprise feature.

Compensation Policies and Implementing Corporate Diversification

A firm's compensation policies constitute a final set of tools for implementing corporation diversification. Traditionally, the compensation of corporate managers in a diversified firm has been only loosely connected to the firm's economic performance. One important study examined the relationship between executive compensation and firm performance and found that differences in CEO cash compensation (salary plus cash bonus) are not very responsive to differences in firm performance.[24] In particular, this study showed that a CEO of a firm whose equity holders lost, collectively, $400 million in a year earned average cash compensation worth $800,000, while a CEO of a firm whose equity holders gained, collectively, $400 million in a year earned average cash compensation worth $1,040,000. Thus, an $800 million difference in the performance of a firm only had, on average, a $204,000 impact on the size of a CEO's salary and cash bonus. Put differently, for every million dollars of improved firm performance, CEOs, on average, get paid an additional $255. After taxes, increasing a firm's performance by a million dollars is roughly equal in value to a good dinner at a nice restaurant.

However, this same study was able to show that if a substantial percentage of a CEO's compensation came in the form of stock and stock options in the firm, changes in compensation would be closely linked with changes in the firm performance. In particular, the $800 million difference in firm performance just described would be associated with a $1.2 million difference in the value of CEO compensation, if CEO compensation included stock and stock options in addition to cash compensation. In this setting, an additional million dollars of firm performance increases a CEO's salary by $667.

These and similar findings reported elsewhere have led more and more diversified firms to include stock and stock options as part of the compensation package for the CEO. As important, many firms now extend this noncash compensation to other senior managers in a diversified firm, including division general managers. For example, the top 1,300 managers at General Dynamics receive stock and stock options as part of their compensation package. Moreover, the cash bonuses of these managers also depend on General Dynamics' stock market performance. At Johnson & Johnson, all division general managers receive a five-component compensation package. The level of only one of those components, salary, does not vary with the economic profitability of the business over which a division general manager presides. The level of the other four components—a cash bonus, stock grants, stock options, and a deferred income package—varies with the economic performance of a particular division. Moreover, the value of some of these variable components of compensation also depends on Johnson & Johnson's long-term economic performance.[25]

To the extent that compensation in diversified firms gives managers incentives to make decisions consistent with stockholders' interests, they can be an important part of the process of implementing corporate diversification. However, the sheer size of the compensation paid to some CEOs raises ethical issues for some. These ethical issues are discussed in the Ethics and Strategy feature on page 269.

Strategy in the Emerging Enterprise

A **corporate spin-off** exists when a large, typically diversified firm divests itself of a business in which it has historically been operating and the divested business operates as an independent entity. Thus, corporate spin-offs are different from asset divestitures, where a firm sells some of its assets, including perhaps a particular business, to another firm. Spin-offs are a way that new firms can enter into the economy.

Spin-offs can occur in numerous ways. For example, a business might be sold to its managers and employees who then manage and work in this independently operating firm. Alternatively, a business unit within a diversified firm may be sold to the public through an **initial public offering**, or **IPO**. Sometimes, the corporation spinning a business unit off will retain some ownership stake in the spin-off; other times, this corporation will sever all financial links with the spun-off firm.

In general, there are three broad reasons why large diversified firms might spin off businesses they own. First, the efficient management of these businesses may require very specific skills that are not available in a diversified firm. For example, suppose a diversified manufacturing firm finds itself operating in an R&D-intensive industry. The management skills required to manage manufacturing efficiently can be very different from the management skills required to manage R&D. If a diversified firm's skills do not match the skills required in a particular business, that business might be spun off.

Second, anticipated economies of scope between a business and the rest of a diversified firm may turn out to not be valuable. For example, PepsiCo acquired Kentucky Fried Chicken, Pizza Hut, and

Transforming Big Business into Entrepreneurship

Taco Bell, anticipating important marketing synergies between these fast-food restaurants and PepsiCo's soft drink business. Despite numerous efforts to realize these synergies, they were not forthcoming. Indeed, several of these fast-food restaurants began losing market share because they were forced to sell Pepsi rather than Coca-Cola products. After a few years, PepsiCo spun off its restaurants into a separate business.

Finally, it may be necessary to spin a business off in order to fund other of a firm's businesses. Large diversified firms may face capital constraints due to, among other things, their high level of debt. In this setting, firms may need to spin off a business in order to raise capital to invest in other parts of the firm. Moreover, spinning off a part of the business that is particularly costly in terms of the capital it consumes may not only be a source of funds for other parts of this firm's business; it can also reduce the demand for that capital within a firm.

Research in corporate finance suggests that corporations are most likely to spin off businesses that are unrelated to a firm's corporate diversification strategy; those that are poorly performing compared to other businesses a firm operates in; and relatively small businesses. Also, the amount of merger and acquisition activity in a particular industry will determine which businesses are spun off. The greater the level of this activity in an industry, the more likely that a business owned by a corporation in such an industry will be spun off. This is because the level of merger and acquisition activity in an industry is an indicator of the number of people and firms that might be interested in purchasing a spun-off business. On the other hand, when there is not much merger and acquisition activity in an industry, businesses in that industry are less likely to be spun off, even if they are unrelated to a firm's corporate diversification strategy, are poorly performing, or small. In such settings, large firms are not likely to obtain the full value associated with spinning off a business and thus are reluctant to do so.

Whatever the conditions that lead a large diversified firm to spin off one of its businesses, this process is important for creating new firms in the economy.

Sources: F. Schlingemann, R. Stulz, and R. Walkling (2002). "Divestitures and the liquidity of the market for corporate assets." *Journal of Financial Economics*, 64, pp. 117–144; G. Hite, J. Owens, and R. Rogers (1987). "The market for inter-firm asset sales: Partial sell-offs and total liquidations." *Journal of Financial Economics*, 18, pp. 229–252; P. Berger and E. Ofek (1999). "Causes and consequences of corporate focusing programs." *Review of Financial Studies*, 12, pp. 311–345.

Organizing to Implement Corporate Diversification in an International Context

Since international strategies are really just a special case of corporate diversification strategies, it follows that many of the issues firms face in implementing corporate diversification strategies would also exist for firms implementing international strategies. It also follows that many of the organizational tools used to implement corporate diversification strategies can be used to implement international strategies.

Despite these similarities, there are some differences between how corporate diversification within a country and corporate diversification across multiple countries is implemented. Differences in organizational structure, management controls, and compensation policies will all be briefly discussed.

Firms pursuing an international strategy have four basic organizational structural alternatives, listed in Table 8.5 and discussed later. Although each of these structures has some special features, they are all special cases of the M-form structure.

Some firms organize their international operations as a **decentralized federation**. In this organizational structure, each country in which a firm operates is organized as a full profit-and-loss division headed by a division general manager who is typically the president of the company in that particular country. In a decentralized federation, there are very few shared activities or other economies of scope among different divisions or country companies; corporate headquarters plays a limited strategic role. Corporate staff functions are generally limited to the collection of accounting and other performance information from divisions or country companies and to reporting this aggregate information to appropriate government officials and to financial markets. Most employees within the divisions or country companies in a decentralized federation may not even be aware that they are part of a larger, internationally diversified firm. Both strategic and operational decision making are delegated to division general managers or country company presidents in a decentralized federation organizational structure. There are relatively few examples of pure decentralized federations in today's world economy, but firms like Nestlé, CIBA-Geigy, and Electrolux have many of the attributes of this type of structure.

A second structural option for international firms is the **coordinated federation**. In a coordinated federation, each country operation is organized as a full profit-and-loss center, and division general managers can be presidents of country companies. However, unlike the case in a decentralized federation, strategic and operational decisions are not fully delegated to division general managers. Operational decisions are delegated to division general managers or country presidents, but broader strategic decisions are made at corporate headquarters.

Table 8.5 **Structural Options for Firms Pursuing International Strategies**

Decentralized federation	Strategic and operational decisions are delegated to divisions or country companies.
Coordinated federation	Operational decisions are delegated to divisions or country companies; strategic decisions are retained at corporate headquarters.
Centralized hub	Strategic and operational decisions are retained at corporate headquarters.
Transnational structure	Strategic and operational decisions are delegated to those operational entities that maximize responsiveness to local conditions and international integration.

Sources: C. A. Bartlett, and S. Ghoshal (1989). *Managing across borders: The transnational solution.* Boston: Harvard Business School Press.

Ethics and Strategy

Steve Jobs, CEO of Apple Computer, was hailed as a modern-day hero when he refused to accept any salary upon returning, in 1997, to the firm he founded. At the time, Apple was going through some rough times. People were being laid off, investments in new technologies curtailed. And Steve Jobs, being sensitive to the economic condition of the firm—and being already independently wealthy—decided to take the radical step of receiving no salary.

However, six years later, in 2003, Steve Jobs—although he still received no regular salary—received $74.8 million in total compensation. Assuming that Mr. Jobs worked 50 hours a week and took two weeks' vacation, this means that he earned just under $30,000 an hour in 2003. Even if this total is considered as compensation for his six years of service at Apple, Steve Jobs still earned—based on his 2003 compensation—the equivalent of $5,000 per hour since he returned to Apple in 1997.

But Jobs did not receive the highest hourly pay of a CEO in 2003. He was only number two. Number one was Reuben Mark, CEO of Colgate-Palmolive. Again, assuming he worked 50 hours a week for 50 weeks, Mr. Mark earned $56,440 per hour. Of this income, $5.1 million came in the form of salary and bonus and $136 million came in the form of long-term compensation—stock, stock options, and so forth.

Of course, what is remarkable about the hourly incomes of Steve Jobs and Reuben Mark is that they are not all that remarkable. The CEO of United

When Is Enough Too Much?

Technologies earned $28,200 per hour, the CEO of Cendant earned $21,700 per hour, the CEO of Citigroup earned $21,640 per hour, and so forth. Indeed, the average hourly wage of the top 20 highest paid CEOs in the United States in 2003 was $18,619. To put that in a different context, the median family income in the United States in 2002 was $42,409. This means that the average top paid CEO in the United States in 2003 needed to work just over two hours and fifteen minutes to earn as much as the median family in the United States.

These levels of compensation would seem more reasonable if they were closely tied to the performance of a firm. Of course, some are. For example, during his time as CEO of Colgate-Palmolive, Mr. Mark helped increase this firm's stock price by 286 percent, compared to the 114 percent gain of the

Standard & Poor's 500 Stock Index over the same time period. But the overall correlation between CEO compensation and firm performance is not very high. For example, Margaret Whitman (CEO of eBay) was paid "only" $3.4 million even though shareholders of eBay earned a 292 percent return in 2003, while Larry Elison (CEO of Oracle) was paid $746.7 million even though shareholders of Oracle lost 54 percent of the value of their investment in the firm. Warren Buffett (CEO of Berkshire Hathaway) was paid only $1 million while his investors received a 19 percent return on their investment; Jozef Straus (CEO of JDS Uniphase) was paid $151.9 million while his investors received a negative 91 percent return on their investment.

Apologists for these high levels of CEO compensation suggest that they simply reflect the result of market forces in the labor market for CEOs. An alternative explanation is that high CEO compensation, especially when it is unrelated to a firm's performance, may reflect more of a CEO's power and influence over his/her board of directors than any competitive market process. If the latter explanation is true, such levels of CEO compensation may not be consistent with the interests of a firm's equity holders.

Moreover, all of this begs the simple moral question: Is anyone really worth $56,000 an hour?

Sources: L. Lavelle (2004). "Executive pay." *BusinessWeek,* April 19, pp. 106 +; S. Finkelstein and D. C. Hambrick (1996). "Chief executive compensation: A study of the intersection of markets and political processes." *Strategic Management Journal,* 10, pp. 121–134.

Moreover, coordinated federations attempt to exploit various shared activities and other economies of scope among their divisions or country companies. It is not uncommon for coordinated federations to have corporately sponsored central research and development laboratories, corporately sponsored manufacturing and technology development initiatives, and corporately sponsored management training and development operations. There are numerous examples of coordinated federations in today's world economy, including General Electric, General Motors, IBM, and Coca-Cola.

A third structural option for international firms is the **centralized hub**. In centralized hubs, operations in different companies may be organized into profit-and-loss centers, and division general managers may be country company presidents. However, most of the strategic and operational decision making in these firms takes place at the corporate center. The role of divisions or country companies in centralized hubs is simply to implement the strategies, tactics, and policies that have been chosen at headquarters. Of course, divisions or country companies are also a source of information for headquarters staff when these decisions are being made. However, in centralized hubs, strategic and operational decision rights are retained at the corporate center. Many Japanese and Korean firms are managed as centralized hubs, including Toyota, Mitsubishi, and NEC (in Japan) and Goldstar, Daewoo, and Hyundai (in Korea).

A fourth structural option for international firms is the **transnational structure**. This structure is most appropriate for implementing the transnational strategy described in previous chapters. In many ways, the transnational structure is similar to the coordinated federation. In both, strategic decision-making responsibility is largely retained at the corporate center, and operational decision making is largely delegated to division general managers or country presidents. However, important differences also exist.

In a coordinated federation structure, shared activities and other cross-divisional or cross-country economies of scope are managed by the corporate center. Thus, for many of these firms, if research and development is seen as a potentially valuable economy of scope, a central research and development laboratory is created and managed by the corporate center. In the transnational structure, these centers of corporate economies of scope may be managed by the corporate center. However, they are more likely to be managed by specific divisions or country companies within the corporation. Thus, for example, if one division or country company develops valuable, rare, and costly-to-imitate research and development capabilities in its ongoing business activities in a particular country, that division or country company could become the center of research and development activity for the entire corporation. If one division or country company develops valuable, rare, and costly-to-imitate manufacturing technology development skills in its ongoing business activities in a particular country, that division or country company could become the center for manufacturing technology development for the entire corporation.

The role of corporate headquarters in a transnational structure is to constantly scan business operations across different countries for resources and capabilities that might be a source of competitive advantage for other divisions or country companies in the firm. Once these special skills are located, corporate staff must then determine the best way to exploit these economies of scope—whether they should be developed within a single division or country company (to gain economies of scale) and then transferred to other divisions or country companies, or developed through an alliance between two or more divisions or country companies (to gain economies of scale) and then transferred to other divisions or country companies, or redeveloped for the entire firm at corporate headquarters. These options are not available to decentralized federations (which always allow individual divisions or country companies to develop their own competencies), coordinated federations, or centralized hubs (which always develop corporate-wide economies of scope at the corporate level). Firms that have been successful in adopting this transnational structure include Ford (Ford Europe has become a leader for automobile design in all of the Ford Motor Company) and Ericson (Ericson's Australian subsidiary developed this Swedish company's first electronic telecommunication switch, and corporate headquarters was able to help transfer this technology to other Ericson subsidiaries).

It should be clear that the choice among these four approaches to managing international strategies depends on the trade-offs that firms are willing to make between local responsiveness and international integration (see Figure 8.3). Firms that seek to maximize their local responsiveness will tend to choose a decentralized federation structure. Firms that seek to maximize international integration in their operations will typically opt for centralized hub structures. Firms that seek to balance the need for local responsiveness and international integration will typically choose centralized federations. Firms that attempt to optimize both local responsiveness and international integration will choose a transnational organizational structure.

Of course, none of the organizational structures described in Table 8.5 can stand alone without the support of a variety of management control systems and management compensation policies. All the management control processes discussed previously, including evaluating the performance of divisions, allocating capital, and managing the exchange of intermediate products among divisions, are also important for firms organizing to implement an international strategy. Moreover, the same management compensation challenges and opportunities discussed previously apply in the organization of international strategies as well.

However, as is often the case when organizing processes originally developed to manage diversification within a domestic market are extended to the management of international diversification, many of the management challenges highlighted earlier in this chapter are exacerbated in an international context. This puts an even greater burden on senior managers in an internationally diversified firm to choose control systems and compensation policies that create incentives for division general managers or country presidents to appropriately cooperate to realize the economies of scope that originally motivated the implementation of an international strategy.

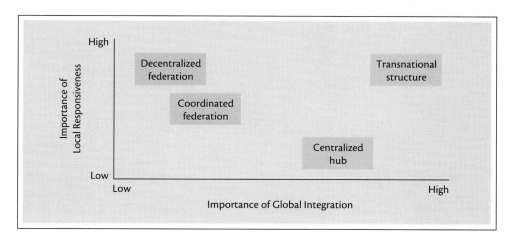

Figure 8.3 Local Responsiveness, International Integration, and Organizational Structure

Sources: From R. Grant (1991). *Contemporary strategy analysis.* Cambridge, MA: Basil Blackwell. Reprinted with permission.

SUMMARY

To be valuable, diversification strategies must exploit valuable economies of scope that cannot be duplicated by outside investors at low cost. However, to realize the value of these economies of scope, firms must organize themselves appropriately. A firm's organizational structure, its management control processes, and its compensation policies are all relevant in implementing a corporate diversification strategy.

The best organizational structure for implementing a diversification leveraging strategy is the multidivisional, or M-form, structure. The M-form structure has several critical components including the board of directors, institutional investors, the senior executive, corporate staff, division general managers, and shared activity managers.

This organizational structure is supported by a variety of management control processes. Three critical management control processes for firms implementing diversification strategies are (1) evaluating the performance of divisions, (2) allocating capital across divisions, and (3) transferring intermediate products between divisions. The existence of economies of scope in firms implementing corporate diversification strategies significantly complicates the management of these processes.

Finally, a firm's compensation policies are also important for firms implementing a diversification strategy. Historically, management compensation has been only loosely connected to a firm's economic performance, but the last few years have seen the increased popularity of using stock and stock options to help compensate managers. Such compensation schemes help reduce conflicts between managers and outside investors, but the absolute level of CEO compensation is still very high, at least in the United States.

These same implementation issues exist for firms looking to diversify their operations internationally. In this international context, firms can choose between a decentralized federation, a coordinated federation, a centralized hub, and a transnational organizational structure. The effectiveness of these different approaches depends on the relative importance of local responsiveness and global integration.

CHALLENGE QUESTIONS

1. Agency theory has been criticized for assuming that managers, left on their own, will behave in ways that reduce the wealth of outside equity holders when, in fact, most managers are highly responsible stewards of the assets they control. This alternative view of managers has been called *stewardship theory*. Do you agree with this criticism of agency theory? Why or why not?

2. Suppose that the concept of the stewardship theory is correct and that most managers, most of the time, behave responsibly and make decisions that maximize the present value of the assets they control. What implications, if any, would this supposition have on organizing to implement diversification strategies?

3. The M-form structure enables firms to pursue complex corporate diversification strategies by delegating different management responsibilities to different individuals and groups within a firm. Will there come a time when a firm becomes too large and too complex to be managed even through an M-form structure? In other words, is there a natural limit to the efficient size of a diversified firm?

4. Most observers agree that centrally planned economies fail because it is impossible for bureaucrats in large government hierarchies to coordinate different sectors of an economy as efficiently as market mechanisms do. Many diversified firms, however, are as large as some economies and use private sector hierarchies to coordinate diverse business activities in a firm. Are these large, private sector hierarchies somehow different from the government hierarchies of

centrally planned economies? If yes, in what way? If no, why do these large, private sector hierarchies continue to exist?

5. Suppose that the optimal transfer price between one business and all other business activities in a firm is the market price. What does this condition say about whether this firm should own this business?

6. Suppose a firm pursuing an international diversification strategy requires neither local responsiveness nor global integration to realize valuable economies of scope that cannot be duplicated by outside equity holders at low cost. What type of organizational structure should this firm pursue?

PROBLEM SET

1. Which elements of the M-form structure (the board of directors, the office of the CEO, corporate staff, division general managers, shared activity managers) should be involved in the following business activities? If more than one of these groups should be involved, indicate their relative level of involvement (e.g., 20 percent office of the CEO, 10 percent shared activity manager, 70 percent division general manager). Justify your answers.

(a) Determining the compensation of the CEO.

(b) Determining the compensation of the Corporate Vice President of Human Resources.

(c) Determining the compensation of a Vice President of Human Resources in a particular business division.

(d) Deciding to sell a business division.

(e) Deciding to buy a relatively small firm whose activities are closely related to the activities of one of the firm's current divisions.

(f) Deciding to buy a larger firm that is not closely related to the activities of any of a firm's current divisions.

(g) Evaluating the performance of the Vice President of Sales, a manager whose sales staff sells the products of three divisions in the firm.

(h) Evaluating the performance of the Vice President of Sales, a manager whose sales staff sells the products of only one division in the firm.

(i) How much money to invest in a corporate R&D function.

(j) How much money to invest in an R&D function that supports the operations of two divisions within the firm.

(k) Whether or not to fire an R&D scientist.

(l) Whether or not to fire the Vice President of Accounting in a particular division.

(m) Whether or not to fire the corporation's Vice President of Accounting.

(n) The decision to take a firm public by selling stock in the firm to the general public for the first time.

2. Consider the following facts. Division A in a firm has generated $847,000 of profits on $24 million worth of sales, using $32 million worth of dedicated assets. The cost of capital for this firm is 9 percent, and the firm has invested $7.3 million in this division.

(a) Calculate the ROS and ROA of Division A. If the hurdle rate for ROS and ROA in this firm are, respectively, .06 and .04, has this division performed well?

(b) Calculate the EVA of Division A (assuming that the reported profits have already been adjusted). Based on this EVA has this division performed well?

(c) Suppose you were CEO of this firm, how would you choose between ROS/ROA and EVA for evaluating this division?

3. Suppose that Division A sells an intermediate product to Division B. Choose one of the ways of determining transfer prices described in this chapter (not setting transfer prices equal to the selling firm's opportunity costs) and show how Division Manager A can use this mechanism to justify a higher transfer price, while Division Manager B can use this mechanism to justify a lower transfer price. Repeat this exercise with another approach to setting transfer prices described in the chapter.

END NOTES

1. The structure and function of the multidimensional firm was first described by Chandler, A. (1962). *Strategy and structure: Chapters in the history of the industrial enterprise.* Cambridge, MA: MIT Press; The economic logic underlying the multidimensional firm was first described by Williamson, O. E. (1975). *Markets and hierarchies: Analysis and antitrust implications.* New York: Free Press; Empirical examinations of the impact of the M-form or firm performance include Armour, H. O., and D. J. Teece (1980). "Vertical integration and technological innovation." *Review of Economics and Statistics*, 60, pp. 470–474; There continues to be some debate about the efficiency of the M-form structure. See Freeland, R. F. (1966). "The myth of the M-form? Governance, consent, and organizational change." *American Journal of Sociology*, 102(2), pp. 483–626; and Shanley, M. (1996). "Straw men and M-form myths: Comment on Freeland." *American Journal of Sociology*, 102(2), pp. 527–536.

2. See Finkelstein, S., and R. D'Aveni (1994). "CEO duality as a double-edged sword: How boards of directors balance entrenchment avoidance and unity of command." *Academy of Management Journal*, 37, pp. 1079–1108.

3. Kesner, I. F. (1988). "Director's characteristics and committee membership: An investigation of type, occupation, tenure and gender." *Academy of Management Journal*, 31, pp. 66–84; Zahra, S. A., and J. A. Pearce II (1989). "Boards of directors and corporate financial performance: A review and integrative model." *Journal of Management*, 15, pp. 291–334.

4. *Investor Relations Business* (2000). "Reversal of fortune: Institutional ownership is declining," May 1, pp. 8–9; Federal Reserve Board (2004). "Flow of funds report."

5. See Hansen, G. S., and C. W. L. Hill (1991). "Are institutional investors myopic? A time-series study of four technology-driven industries." *Strategic Management Journal*, 12, pp. 1–16.

6. See Bergh, D. (1995). "Size and relatedness of units sold: An agency theory and resource-based perspective." *Strategic Management Journal*, 16, pp. 221–239; and Bethel, J., and J. Liebeskind (1993). "The effects of ownership structure on corporate restructuring." *Strategic Management Journal*, 14, pp. 15–31.

7. Burdens that are well described by Westley, F., and H. Mintzberg (1989). "Visionary leadership and strategic management." *Strategic Management Journal*, 10, pp. 17–32.

8. See Dumaine, B. (1992). "Is big still good?" *Fortune*, April 20, pp. 50–60.

9. See Golden, B. (1992). "SBU strategy and performance: The moderating effects of the corporate–SBU relationship." *Strategic Management Journal*, 13, pp. 145–158; Berger, P., and E. Otek (1995). "Diversification effect on firm value." *Journal of Financial Economics*, 37, pp. 36–65; Lang, H. P., and R. Stulz (1994). "Tobin's q, corporate diversification, and firm performance." *Journal of Political Economy*, 102, pp. 1248–1280; Rumelt, R. (1991). "How much does industry matter?" *Strategic Management Journal*, 12, pp. 167–185.

10. See Halal, W. (1994). "From hierarchy to enterprise: Internal markets are the new foundation of management." *The Academy of Management Executive*, 8(4), pp. 69–83.

11. Bartlett, C., and S. Ghoshal (1993). "Beyond the M-form: Toward a managerial theory of the firm." *Strategic Management Journal*, 14, pp. 23–46.

12. See Simons, R. (1994). "How new top managers use control systems as levers of strategic renewal." *Strategic Management Journal*, 15, pp. 169–189.

13. Bethel, J. E. (1990). "The capital allocation process and managerial mobility: A theoretical and empirical investigation." Unpublished doctoral dissertation, UCLA.

14. Some of these are described in Duffy, M. (1989). "ZBB, MBO, PPB, and their effectiveness within the planning/marketing process." *Strategic Management Journal*, 12, pp. 155–160.

15. See Stern, J., B. Stewart, and D. Chew (1995). "The EVA financial management system." *Journal of Applied Corporate Finance*, 8, pp. 32–46; and Tully, S. (1993). "The real key to creating wealth." *Fortune*, September 20, pp. 38–50.

16. Applications of EVA are described in Tully, S. (1993). "The real key to creating wealth." *Fortune*, September 20, pp. 38–50; Tully, S. (1995). "So, Mr. Bossidy, we know you can cut. Now show us how to grow." *Fortune*, August 21, pp. 70–80; Tully, S. (1995). "Can EVA deliver profits to the post office?" *Fortune*, July 10, p. 22.

17. A special issue of the *Journal of Applied Corporate Finance* in 1994 addressed many of these issues.

18. See Priem, R. (1990). "Top management team group factors, consensus, and firm performance." *Strategic Management Journal*, 11, pp. 469–478; and Wooldridge, B., and S. Floyd (1990). "The strategy process, middle management involvement, and organizational performance." *Strategic Management Journal*, 11, pp. 231–241.

19. A point made by Westley, F. (1900). "Middle managers and strategy: Microdynamics of inclusion." *Strategic Management Journal*, 11, pp. 337–351; Lamont, O. (1997). "Cash flow and investment: Evidence from internal capital markets." *The Journal of Finance*. 52(1), pp. 83–109; Shin, H. H., and R. M. Stulz (1998). "Are internal capital markets efficient?" *Quarterly Journal of Economics*, May,

pp. 531–552; and Stein, J. C. (1997). "Internal capital markets and the competition for corporate resources." *The Journal of Finance*, 52(1), pp. 111–133.

20. See Brickley, J., C. Smith, and J. Zimmerman (1996). *Organizational architecture and managerial economics approach*. Homewood, IL: Irwin; and Eccles, R. (1985). *The transfer pricing problem: A theory for practice*. Lexington, MA: Lexington Books.

21. See Cyert, R., and J. G. March (1963). *A behavioral theory of the firm*. Upper Saddle River, NJ: Prentice Hall; Swieringa, R. J., and J. H. Waterhouse (1982). "Organizational views of transfer pricing." *Accounting, Organizations & Society*, 7(2), pp. 149–165; and Eccles, R. (1985). *The transfer pricing problem: A theory for practice*. Lexington, MA: Lexington Books.

22. Gupta, A. K., and V. Govindarajan (1986). "Resource sharing among SBUs: Strategic antecedents and administrative implications." *Academy of Management Journal*, 29, pp. 695–714.

23. A point made by Swieringa, R. J., and J. H. Waterhouse (1982). "Organizational views of transfer pricing." *Accounting, Organizations and Society*, 7(2), pp. 149–165.

24. Jensen, M. C., and K. J. Murphy (1990). "Performance pay and top management incentives." *Journal of Political Economy*, 98, pp. 225–264.

25. See Dial, J., and K. J. Murphy (1995). "Incentive, downsizing, and value creation at General Dynamics." *Journal of Financial Economics*, 37, pp. 261–314, on General Dynamics' compensation scheme, and Aguilar, F. J., and A. Bhambri (1983). "Johnson & Johnson (A)." Harvard Business School Case No. 384-053, on Johnson & Johnson's compensation scheme.

9

Strategic Alliances

Original Programming at HBO

Sex and the City, The Sopranos, and *Band of Brothers*—all these programs have at least three things in common. First, they have all been among the most critically acclaimed programs on television. *Sex and the City* routinely earned the Emmy for Best Comedy Series, *The Sopranos* was nominated for the Best Dramatic Series Emmy every year it was on television, and *Band of Brothers*—a ten-part mini-series that documents the history of the 101st Airborne during World War II—won numerous Emmys the year it was broadcast. Second, they have been among the most-watched shows on cable television. Indeed, in its fourth year, *The Sopranos* became the most-watched series ever on premium cable television and led HBO to its highest ratings ever. Finally, all three of these shows were co-produced by HBO—a division of AOL Time Warner—through HBO's Original Programming Division.

This has not always been the case. Originally, HBO presented only material produced by others—in particular, movies. Indeed, for many years, competition between HBO and other premium cable channels focused exclusively on which of these channels would gain the broadcast rights to which movies. The resulting competition

Learning Objectives

After reading this chapter, you should be able to:

1. Define a strategic alliance and give three specific examples of strategic alliances.

2. Describe nine different ways that alliances can create value for firms and how these nine sources of value can be grouped into three large categories.

3. Describe how adverse selection, moral hazard, and hold-up can threaten the ability of alliances to generate value.

4. Describe the conditions under which a strategic alliance can be rare and costly to directly duplicate.

5. Describe the conditions under which "going it alone" and acquisitions are not likely to be substitutes for alliances.

6. Describe how contracts, equity investments, firm reputations, joint ventures, and trust can all reduce the threat of cheating in strategic alliances.

7. Describe the role of strategic alliances in an international context.

led to substantial increases in rights fees—the fee a cable channel pays a movie's producers for the right to broadcast that movie. This competition hurt the profitability of many premium cable channels, including HBO.

However, beginning in the mid-1990s, HBO began producing, or co-producing, its own programming. This began slowly, with a few low-budget movies and sports programs (e.g., *NFL This Week* and various boxing matches). However, by the late 1990s, original programming had become an important part of HBO's weekly schedule. Most of this original programming was produced through partnerships between HBO Original Productions and independent production companies, including Steven Spielberg's production company Dreamworks and Tom Hanks's production company Playtone. And in the summer of 2003, HBO announced that it would enter into similar partnerships to begin producing movies for theatrical release.

The entry of HBO into partnerships to produce original programming has increased its prof-

itability. It has also shifted the basis of competition in the premium cable market from "Who can broadcast the biggest movies?"—a competition that was making movie producers wealthy but reducing the profits of premium cable channel companies—to "Who can develop the most cutting-edge, provocative, and popular entertainment on television?"

This shift in strategy at HBO has also had an impact on the content of broadcast network shows. ABC, NBC, CBS, Fox, and the WB have all had to increase the quality and "cutting-edge" feel of their series and other programs if these programs are to attract viewers away from the shows broadcast on HBO. Shows like *Frasier*, *Will and Grace*, *NYPD Blue*, *Law and Order*, *The West Wing*, *24*, and *Boomtown* have all incorporated comedic and dramatic elements first pioneered on television in shows co-produced by HBO.

While HBO is now committed to using partnerships to co-produce much of its entertainment programming, other premium channels have not yet made such a commitment. For example, Cinemax (a division of HBO), Starz (a 12-channel premium service), and the Sundance Channel all have very little self-produced content. Indeed, the only other premium cable channels that are following HBO's lead are Showtime—the second-largest premium cable channel—and the Independent Film Channel—which has begun investing in the production of independent films for theatrical release.

Sources: www.AOLTW.com; www.HBO.com.

HBO's decision to begin producing its own shows is an example of a backward vertical integration decision—the kind of decision discussed in Chapter 6. However, rather than fully incorporating the production process within its boundaries, HBO uses partnerships with independent producers to create virtually all of its original content. These partnerships are an example of strategic alliances.

The use of strategic alliances to manage economic exchanges has grown substantially over the last several years. In the early 1990s, strategic alliances were relatively uncommon, except in a few industries—including the entertainment industry. However, by the late 1990s, they had become much more common in a wide variety of industries. High-technology firms like IBM and Cisco were creating alliances with hundreds of partners. Over 450 alliances between large pharmaceutical firms and biotechnology firms were created in 1997 and 1998 alone. Even firms in more traditional industries—including firms in the U.S. automobile industry—began using alliances to manage their international expansion. Currently, alliances account for over 35 percent of the revenue of the largest 1,000 firms in the United States.[1]

What Is a Strategic Alliance?

A **strategic alliance** exists whenever two or more independent organizations cooperate in the development, manufacture, or sale of products or services. As shown in Figure 9.1, strategic alliances can be grouped into three broad categories: nonequity alliances, equity alliances, and joint ventures.

In a **nonequity alliance**, cooperating firms agree to work together to develop, manufacture, or sell products or services, but they do not take equity positions in each other or form an independent organizational unit to manage their cooperative efforts. Rather, these cooperative relations are managed through the use of various forms of contracts. **Licensing agreements** (where one firm allows others to use its brand name to sell products), **supply agreements** (where one firm agrees to supply others), and **distribution agreements** (where one firm agrees to distribute the products of others) are examples of nonequity strategic alliances. Most of the alliances between HBO and independent producers take the form of nonequity supply agreements.

In an **equity alliance**, cooperating firms supplement contracts with equity holdings in alliance partners. For example, when General Motors began importing small cars manufactured by Isuzu, not only did these partners have supply con-

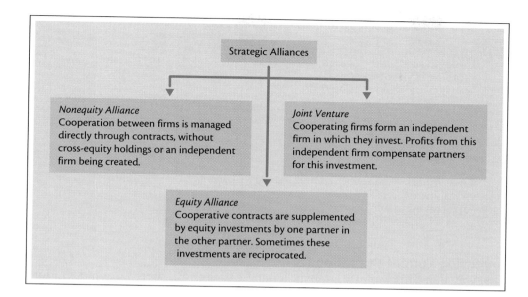

Figure 9.1 Types of Strategic Alliances

tracts in place, but GM purchased 34.2 percent of Isuzu's stock. Ford had a similar relationship with Mazda, and DaimlerChrysler had a similar relationship with Mitsubishi.[2] Equity alliances are also very common in the biotechnology industry. Large pharmaceutical firms like Pfizer and Merck own equity positions in several start-up biotechnology companies.

In a **joint venture**, cooperating firms create a legally independent firm in which they invest and from which they share any profits that are created. Some of these joint ventures can be very large. For example, Dow and Corning's joint venture Dow-Corning is a *Fortune* 500 company on its own. SBC and BellSouth are co-owners of the joint venture Cingular, one of the largest wireless phone companies in the United States—especially after its recent acquisition of AT&T Wireless Service. And CFM—a joint venture between General Electric and SNECMA (a French Aerospace firm)—is one of the world's leading manufacturers of jet engines for commercial aircraft. If you have ever flown on a Boeing 737, then you have placed your life in the hands of this joint venture because it manufactures the engines for virtually all of these aircraft.

How Do Strategic Alliances Create Value?

Like all the strategies discussed in this book, strategic alliances create value by exploiting opportunities and neutralizing threats facing a firm. Some of the most important opportunities that can be exploited by strategic alliances are listed in Table 9.1. Threats to strategic alliances are discussed later in this chapter.

Strategic Alliance Opportunties

Opportunities associated with strategic alliances fall into three large categories. First, these alliances can be used by a firm to improve the performance of their current operations. Second, alliances can be used to create a competitive environment favorable to superior firm performance. Finally, they can be used to facilitate a firm's entry into or exit from new markets or industries.

Table 9.1   **Ways Strategic Alliances Can Create Economic Value**

Helping firms improve the performance of their current operations
1. Exploiting economies of scale
2. Learning from competitors
3. Managing risk and sharing costs

Creating a competitive environment favorable to superior performance
4. Facilitating the development of technology standards
5. Facilitating tacit collusion

Facilitating entry and exit
6. Low-cost entry into new industries and new industry segments
7. Low-cost exit from industries and industry segments
8. Managing uncertainty
9. Low-cost entry into new markets

Improving Current Operations

One way that firms can use strategic alliances to improve their current operations is to use alliances to realize economies of scale. The concept of economies of scale was first introduced in Chapter 2. **Economies of scale** exist when the per unit cost of production falls as the volume of production increases. Thus, for example, while the per unit cost of producing one Bic pen would be very high, the per unit costs of producing 50 million Bic pens can be very low.

To realize economies of scale, firms have to have a large volume of production, or at least a volume of production large enough so that the cost advantages associated with scale can be realized. Sometimes—as was described in Chapters 2 and 4—a firm can realize these economies of scale by itself; other times, it can't. When a firm cannot realize the cost savings from economies of scale all by itself, it may join in a strategic alliance with other firms. Jointly, these firms may have sufficient volume to be able to gain the cost advantages of economies of scale.

But, why wouldn't a firm be able to realize these economies all by itself? There are several reasons why a firm may have to turn to alliance partners to help realize economies of scale. For example, if the volume of production required to realize these economies is very large, a single firm might have to dominate an entire industry in order to obtain these advantages. It is often very difficult for a single firm to obtain such a dominant position in an industry. And even if it does so, it may be subject to anti-monopoly regulation by the government. Also, while a particular part or technology may be very important to several firms, no one of these firms may generate sufficient demand for this part or technology to realize economies of scale in its development and production. In this setting as well, independent firms may join together to form an alliance to realize economies of scale in the development and production of the part or technology.

Firms can also use alliances to improve their current operations by learning from their competitors. As suggested in Chapter 3, different firms in an industry may have different resources and capabilities. These resources can give some firms competitive advantages over others. Firms that are at a competitive disadvantage may want to form alliances with the firms that have an advantage in order to learn about their resources and capabilities.

General Motors formed this kind of alliance with Toyota. In the early 1990s, GM and Toyota jointly invested in a previously closed General Motors plant in Fremont, California. This joint venture—called NUMI—was to build compact cars to be distributed through GM's distribution network. But why did GM decide to build these cars in an alliance with Toyota? Obviously, it could have built them in any of its own plants. However, GM was very interested in learning about how Toyota was able to manufacture high-quality small cars at a profit. Indeed, in the NUMI plant, Toyota agreed to take total responsibility for the manufacturing process, using former General Motors employees to install and operate the "lean manufacturing" system that had enabled Toyota to become the quality leader in the small-car segment of the automobile industry. However, Toyota also agreed to let GM managers work in the plant and directly observe how Toyota managed this production process. Since its inception, GM has rotated thousands of its managers from other GM plants through the NUMI plant so that they can be exposed to Toyota's lean manufacturing methods.

It's clear why GM would want this alliance with Toyota. But, why would Toyota want this alliance with GM? Certainly, Toyota was not looking to learn about lean manufacturing, per se. However, since Toyota was contemplating entering the United States by building its own manufacturing facilities, it did need to learn how to implement lean manufacturing in the United States with U.S. employees. Thus, Toyota also had something to learn from this alliance.

When both parties to an alliance are seeking to learn something from that alliance, an interesting dynamic called a "learning race" can evolve. This dynamic is described in more detail in the Strategy in Depth feature.

Finally, firms can use alliances to improve their current operations through sharing costs and risks. Indeed, most of HBO's alliances with independent producers are created to share costs and risks. Producing new television shows can be costly. Development and production costs can run into the hundreds of millions of dollars, especially for long and complicated mini-series like HBO's *Band of Brothers*. And, despite audience testing and careful market analyses, the production of these new shows is also very risky. Even bankable stars like Dustin Hoffman and Warren Beatty—remember *Ishtar*?—and Ben Affleck and Jennifer Lopez—remember *Gigli*?—cannot guarantee success.

In this context, it is not surprising that HBO decides to not "go it alone" in its production efforts. If HBO was to be the sole producer of its original programming, not only would it have to absorb all the production costs, but it would also bear all the risk if a production turned out not to be successful. Of course, by getting other firms involved in its production efforts, HBO also has to share whatever profits a particular production generates. Apparently, HBO has concluded that sharing this upside potential is more than compensated for by sharing the costs and risks of these productions.

Creating a Favorable Competitive Environment

Firms can also use strategic alliances to create a competitive environment that is more conducive to superior performance. This can be done in at least two ways. First, firms can use alliances to help set technology standards in an industry. With these standards in place, technology-based products can be developed and consumers can be confident that the products they buy will be useful for some time to come.

Such technologic standards are particularly important in what are called **network industries**. Such industries are characterized by **increasing returns to scale**. Consider, for example, fax machines. How valuable is one fax machine, all by itself? Obviously, not very valuable. Two fax machines that can talk to each other are a little more valuable, three that can talk to each other are still more valuable, and so forth. The value of each individual fax machine depends on the total number of fax machines that can talk to each other that are in operation. This is

Strategy in Depth

A **learning race** exists in a strategic alliance when both parties to that alliance seek to learn from each other, but when the rate at which these two firms learn varies. In this setting, the first firm to learn what it wants to learn from an alliance has the option to begin to underinvest in, and perhaps even withdraw from, an alliance. In this way, the firm that learns the fastest is able to prevent the slow-learning firm from learning all it wanted from an alliance. If, outside of this alliance, these firms are competitors, winning a learning race can create a sustained competitive advantage for the fast-learning firm over the slow-learning firm.

There are a variety of reasons why firms in an alliance may vary in the rate they learn from each other. First, they may be looking to learn different things, and some things are easier to learn than others. For example,

Winning Learning Races

in the GM–Toyota example, GM wanted to learn about how to use "lean manufacturing" to build high-quality small cars profitably. Toyota wanted to learn how to apply the "lean manufacturing" skills it already pos-

sessed in the United States. Which of these is easier to learn—about "lean manufacturing" or about how to apply "lean manufacturing" in the United States?

An argument can be made that GM's learning task was much more complicated than Toyota's. At the very least, in order for GM to apply knowledge about "lean manufacturing" gleaned from Toyota, it would have to transfer that knowledge to several of its currently operating plants. Using this knowledge would require these plants to change their current operations—a difficult and time-consuming process. Toyota, on the other hand, only had to transfer its knowledge of how to operate a "lean manufacturing" operation in the United States to its other U.S. plants—plants that at the time this alliance was first created had yet to be built. Because GM's learning task was

---

what is meant by increasing returns to scale—the value (or returns) on each product increases as the number of these products (or scale) increases.

Now, if there are 100 million fax machines in operation, but none of these machines can talk to each other, none of these machines has any value whatsoever—except as a large paper weight. For their full value to be realized, they must be able to talk to each other. And to talk to each other, they must all adopt the same—or at least compatible—communication standards. This is why setting technology standards is so important in network industries.

There are two ways that these standards can be set. First, different firms can introduce different standards, and consumers can decide which they prefer. This is how the standard for home videotapes was set. Sony sold one type of videotape machine—the Betamax—and Matsushita sold a second type of videotape machine—VHS. These two technologies were incompatible. Some consumers preferred Beta and purchased Sony's technology. Others preferred VHS and bought Matsushita's technology. However, since Matsushita licensed its VHS technology to numerous other firms, while Sony refused to do so, more and more consumers started buying VHS machines, until VHS became the de facto standard. This was the case even though most observers agreed that Beta was superior to VHS on several dimensions.

Of course, the biggest problem with letting customers and competition set technology standards is that customers may end up purchasing technologies that

more complicated than Toyota's, it is very likely that Toyota's rate of learning was greater than GM's.

Second, firms may differ in terms of their ability to learn. This ability has been called a firm's **absorptive capacity**. Firms with high levels of absorptive capacity will learn at higher rates than firms with low levels of absorptive capacity, even if these two firms are trying to learn exactly the same things in an alliance. Absorptive capacity has been shown to be an important organizational capability in a wide variety of settings.

Third, firms can engage in activities to try to slow the rate of learning of their alliance partners. For example, while firms might make their technology available to an alliance partner—thereby fulfilling the alliance agreement—they may not provide all the know-how necessary to exploit this technology. This can slow a partner's learning. Also, a firm might withhold critical employees from an alliance, thereby slowing the learning of an alliance partner. All these actions, to the extent that they slow the rate of a partner's learning without also slowing the rate at which the firm engaging in these activities learns, can help this firm win a learning race.

While learning race dynamics have been described in a wide variety of settings, they are particularly common in relations between entrepreneurial and large firms. In these alliances, entrepreneurial firms are often looking to learn about all the managerial functions required to bring a product to market, including manufacturing, sales, distribution, and so forth. This is a difficult learning task. Large firms in these alliances, on the other hand, often are only looking to learn about the entrepreneurial firm's technology. This is a less difficult learning task. Because the learning task facing entrepreneurial firms is more challenging than that facing their large-firm partners, larger firms in these alliances typically win the learning race. Once these large firms learn what they want from their alliance partners, they often underinvest or even withdraw from these alliances. This is why, in one study, almost 80 percent of the managers in entrepreneurial firms felt unfairly exploited by their large-firm alliance partners.

Sources: S. A. Alvarez and J. B. Barney (2001). "How entrepreneurial firms can benefit from alliances with large partners." *Academy of Management Executive*, 15, pp. 139–148; G. Hamel (1991). "Competition for competence and inter-partner learning within international alliances." *Strategic Management Journal*, 12, pp. 83–103; W. Cohen and D. Levinthal (1990). "Absorptive capacity: A new perspective on learning and innovation." *Administrative Science Quarterly*, 35, pp. 128–152.

are incompatible with the standard that is ultimately set in the industry. What about all those consumers who purchased Beta products? For this reason, customers may be unwilling to invest in a new technology until the standards of that technology are established.

This is where strategic alliances come in. Sometimes, firms form strategic alliances, the sole purpose of which is to evaluate and then choose a technology standard in an industry. With such a standard in place, technologies can be turned into products that customers are likely to be more willing to purchase, since they know that they will compatible with industry standards for at least some period of time. Thus, in this setting—network industries with increasing returns to scale where standards are important—strategic alliances can be used to create a more favorable competitive environment.

Such alliances have been important in setting standards in a wide variety of industries, including the mobile telephone industry. The history of standard-setting in this industry, and how it has affected competition in the mobile phone industry around the world, is described in the Global Perspectives feature.

Another incentive for cooperating in strategic alliances is that such activities may facilitate the development of tacit collusion. As explained in Chapter 3, **collusion** exists when two or more firms in an industry coordinate their strategic choices to reduce competition in an industry. This reduction in competition usually

Global Perspectives

The mobile telephone industry is a classic example of a network industry—that is, an industry with increasing returns to scale where standards are important. The more people that own mobile phones that can talk to each other, the more valuable those mobile phones are. Because of the role that standards play in realizing these increasing returns to scale, standard-setting has been an important determinant of competition in the mobile phone industry around the world.

However, this standard-setting process has been anything but smooth; nor has there been agreement around the world about what the technological standard in the industry should be. While alliances can facilitate the creation of standards, sometimes sets of competing alliances can make it more difficult, not less difficult, to create a standard for an entire industry. This has been the case in the worldwide mobile telecommunications industry.

The first round of technical standards in mobile telephones was developed in the early 1980s. In the United States, the federal government adopted Ameritech's AMPS standard and required all mobile phone operators to use this analogue system. In Europe, two analogue standards emerged: NMT-450, developed by an alliance between Ericsson and Nokia, dominant in the Scandinavian countries and much of continental Europe; and TACS, developed by an alliance between Vodaphone and Cellnet for operations in the United Kingdom and Italy. Many

Can You Hear Me Now?

mobile phones operating in the United Kingdom still use the TACS standard. And in Japan, two additional analogue standards were created—NTT, created by Nippon Telephone and Telegraph, and JTACS, created in by an alliance that involved Toyota Motor Corporation. None of these standards were compatible with each other. A person with a phone that operated on, say, the NMT-450 standard could not talk to a person with a phone operating on, say, the AMPS standard.

The emergence of digital technology in the late 1980s led to a new round of standard-setting. In the United States, several potential standards were allowed to compete. The two dominant competing digital standards in the United States were known as TDMA and CDMA. In Europe, an alliance among all the major mobile phone companies, with government support, devel-

oped a single pan-European standard known as GSM—Global System for Mobile Communication. In Japan, two competing digital standards emerged: PDC, supported by an alliance that included Nissan Motors, and PHS, a system that relies on a dense network of antennas each with a very restricted range to provide mobile telephone services. Countries around the world have generally adopted one or more of these standard technologies. As was the case with analog standards, none of these digital standards are compatible.

This cacophony of standards has led to a search for a third-generation standard that would be applicable around the world. This standard—known as 3G—would have to be backward compatible (i.e., previous standards would have to be able to operate in conjunction with the new standard) and facilitate the full range of digital communications technology around the world. Two standards are currently competing for the right to become the worldwide 3G standard: UMTS, a standard supported by an alliance of European and Japanese mobile telecommunications companies, and CDMA-2000, a standard supported by most American mobile telecommunications companies. How this standards competition will unfold is still not entirely known.

Sources: www.cellular-news.com/history_of_tele-coms/; C. Arnst, S. Jackson, and M. Shari (1995). "The last frontier: Telecommunications in developing countries." *BusinessWeek*, September 18, pp. 98 +; T. Rapport (1996). *Wireless communications: principles and practices.* Upper Saddle River, NJ: Prentice Hall.

makes it easier for colluding firms to earn high levels of performance. A common example of collusion is when firms cooperate to reduce the quantity of products being produced in an industry in order to drive prices for these products up. **Explicit collusion** exists when firms directly communicate with each other to coordinate their levels of production, their prices, and so forth. Explicit collusion is illegal in most countries.

Since managers that engage in explicit collusion can end up in jail, most collusion that exists in the economy must be tacit in character. **Tacit collusion** exists when firms coordinate their production and pricing decisions, not by directly communicating with each other, but by exchanging signals with other firms about their intent to cooperate. Examples of such signals might include public announcements about price increases, public announcements about reductions in a firm's productive output, public announcements about decisions not to pursue a new technology, and so forth.

Sometimes, signals of intent to collude are very ambiguous. For example, when firms in an industry do not reduce their prices in response to a decrease in demand, they may be sending a signal that they want to collude, or they may be attempting to exploit their product differentiation to maintain high margins. When firms do not reduce their prices in response to reduced supply costs, they may be sending a signal that they want to collude, or they may be individually maximizing their economic performance. In both these cases, a firm's intent to collude or not, as implied by its activities, is ambiguous at best.

In this context, strategic alliances can facilitate tacit collusion. Separate firms, even if they are in the same industry, can form strategic alliances. Although communication between these firms cannot legally include sharing information about prices and costs for products or services that are produced outside the alliance, such interaction does help create the social setting within which tacit collusion may develop.[3] As suggested in the Research Made Relevant feature, most early research on strategic alliances focused on their implications for tacit collusion. More recently, research suggests that alliances do not usually facilitate tacit collusion, although this is still a possibility.

Facilitating Entry and Exit

A final way that strategic alliances can be used to create value is by facilitating either a firm's entry into a new market or industry or its exit from a market or industry. Strategic alliances are particularly valuable in this context when the value of market entry or exit is uncertain. Entry into an industry can require skills, abilities, and products that a potential entrant does not possess. Strategic alliances can help a firm enter a new industry by avoiding the high costs of creating these skills, abilities, and products.

For example, recently DuPont wanted to enter into the electronics industry. However, building the skills and abilities needed to develop competitive products in this industry can be very difficult and costly. Rather than absorb these costs, DuPont developed a strategic alliance (DuPont/Philips Optical) with an established electronics firm, Philips, to distribute some of Philips's products in the United States. In this way DuPont was able to enter into a new industry (electronics) without having to absorb all the costs of creating electronics resources and abilities from the ground up.

Of course, for this joint venture to succeed, Philips must have had an incentive to cooperate with DuPont. Where DuPont was looking to reduce its cost of

Research Made Relevant

Several authors have concluded that joint ventures, as a form of alliance, do increase the probability of tacit collusion in an industry. As reviewed in books by Scherer and Barney, one study found that joint ventures created two industrial groups, besides U.S. Steel, in the U.S. iron and steel industry in the early 1900s. In this sense, joint ventures in the steel industry were a substitute for U.S. Steel's vertical integration and had the effect of creating an oligopoly in what (without joint ventures) would have been a more competitive market. Other studies found that over 50 percent of joint venture parents belong to the same industry. After examining 885 joint venture bids for oil and gas leases, yet another study found only 16 instances where joint venture partners competed with one another on another tract in the same sale. These results suggest that joint ventures might encourage subsequent tacit collusion among firms in the same industry.

In a particularly influential study, Pfeffer and Nowak found that joint ventures were most likely in industries of moderate concentration. These authors argued that in highly concentrated industries—where there

Do Strategic Alliances Facilitate Tacit Collusion?

were only a small number of competing firms—joint ventures were not necessary to create conditions conducive to collusion. In highly fragmented industries, the high levels of industry concentration conducive to tacit collusion could not be created by joint ventures. Only when joint venture activity could effectively create concentrated industries—that is, only when industries were moderately concentrated—were joint ventures likely.

Scherer and Barney also review more recent work that disputes these findings. Joint ventures between firms in the same industry may be valuable for a variety of reasons that have little or nothing to do with collusion. Moreover, by using a lower level of aggregation, several authors have disputed the finding that joint ventures are most likely in moderately concentrated industries. The original study defined industries using very broad industry categories—"the electronics industry," "the automobile industry," and so forth. By defining industries less broadly—"consumer electronics" and "automobile part manufacturers"—subsequent work found that 73 percent of the joint ventures had parent firms coming from different industries. Although joint ventures between firms in the same industry (defined at this lower level of aggregation) may have collusive implications, subsequent work has shown that these kinds of joint ventures are relatively rare.

Sources: F. M. Scherer (1980). *Industrial market structure and economic performance.* Boston: Houghton Mifflin; J. B. Barney (2002). *Gaining and sustaining competitive advantage,* 2nd ed. Upper Saddle River, NJ: Prentice Hall; J. Pfeffer and P. Nowak (1976). "Patterns of joint venture activity: Implications for anti-trust research." *Antitrust Bulletin,* 21, pp. 315–339.

entry into a new industry, Philips was looking to reduce its cost of continued entry into a new market: the United States. Philips used its alliance with DuPont to sell in the United States the compact discs it already was selling in Europe.[4] The role of alliances in facilitating entry into new geographic markets will be discussed in more detail later in this chapter.

Alliances to facilitate entry into new industries can be valuable even when the skills needed in these industries are not as complex and difficult to learn as skills in the electronics industry. For example, rather than develop their own frozen novelty foods, Welch Foods, Inc., and Leaf, Inc. (maker of Heath candy bars), asked Eskimo Pie to formulate products for this industry. Eskimo Pie developed Welch's frozen grape juice bar and the Heath toffee ice cream bar. These firms then split the profits derived from these products.[5] As long as the cost of using an alliance to enter a new industry is less than the cost of learning new skills and capabilities, an alliance can be a valuable strategic opportunity.

Some firms use strategic alliances as a mechanism to withdraw from industries or industry segments in a low-cost way. Firms are motivated to withdraw from an industry or industry segment when their level of performance in that business is less than what was expected and when there are few prospects of its improving. Often, when a firm desires to exit an industry or industry segment, it will need to dispose of the assets it has developed to compete in that industry or industry segment. These assets often include tangible resources and capabilities such as factories, distribution centers, and product technologies, and intangible resources and capabilities such as brand name, relationships with suppliers and customers, a loyal and committed workforce, and so forth.

Firms will often have difficulty in obtaining the full economic value of these tangible and intangible assets as they exit an industry or industry segment. This reflects an important information asymmetry that exists between the firms that currently own these assets and firms that may want to purchase these assets. By forming an alliance with a firm that may want to purchase its assets, a firm is giving its partner an opportunity to directly observe how valuable those assets are. If those assets are actually valuable, then this "sneak preview" can lead the assets to be more appropriately priced and thereby facilitate the exit of the firm that is looking to sell its assets. These issues will be discussed in more detail in Chapter 10's discussion of mergers and acquisitions.

One firm that has used strategic alliances to facilitate its exit from an industry or industry segment is Corning. In the late 1980s, Corning entered into the medical diagnostics industry. After several years, however, Corning concluded that its resources and capabilities could be more productively used in other businesses. For this reason, it began to extract itself from the medical diagnostics business. However, to make sure it received the full value of the assets it had created in the medical diagnostics business, upon exiting, it formed a strategic alliance with the Swiss specialty chemical company Ciba-Geigy. Ciba-Geigy paid $75 million to purchase half of Corning's medical diagnostics business. A couple of years later, Corning finished exiting from the medical diagnostics business by selling its remaining assets in this industry to Ciba-Geigy. However, where Ciba-Geigy had paid $75 million for the first half of Corning's assets, it paid $150 million for the second half. Corning's alliance with Ciba-Geigy had made it possible for Ciba-Geigy to fully value Corning's medical diagnostics capabilities. Any information asymmetry that might have existed was reduced, and Corning was able to get more of the full value of its assets upon exiting this industry.[6]

Finally, firms may use strategic alliances to manage **uncertainty**. Under conditions of high uncertainty, firms may not be able to tell, at a particular point in time, which of several different strategies they should pursue. Firms in this setting have an incentive to retain the flexibility to move quickly into a particular market or industry once the full value of that strategy is revealed. In this sense, strategic alliances enable a firm to maintain a point of entry into a market or industry, without incurring the costs associated with full-scale entry.

Based on this logic, strategic alliances have been analyzed as **real options**.[7] In this sense, a joint venture is an option that a firm buys, under conditions of uncertainty, to retain the ability to move quickly into a market or industry if valuable opportunities present themselves. One way in which firms can move quickly into a market is simply to buy out their partner(s) in the joint venture. Moreover, by investing in a joint venture, a firm may gain access to the information it needs to evaluate full-scale entry into a market. In this approach to analyzing strategic alliances, firms that invest in alliances as options will acquire their alliance partners only after the market signals an unexpected increase in value of the venture—that is, only after uncertainty is reduced and the true, positive value of entering into a market is known. Empirical findings are consistent with these expectations.[8]

Given these observations, it is not surprising to see firms in new and uncertain environments develop numerous strategic alliances. This is one of the reasons that strategic alliances are so common in the biotechnology industry. While there is relatively little uncertainty that at least some drugs created through biotechnology will ultimately prove to be very valuable, which specific drugs will turn out to be the most valuable is very uncertain. Rather than investing in a small number of biotechnology drugs on their own, pharmaceutical companies have invested in numerous strategic alliances with small biotechnology firms. Each of these smaller firms represents a particular "bet" about the value of biotechnology in a particular class of drugs. If one of these "bets" turns out to be valuable, then the large pharmaceutical firm that has invested in that firm has the right, but not the obligation, to purchase the rest of this company. In this sense, from the point of view of the pharmaceutical firms, alliances between large pharmaceutical firms and small biotechnology firms can be thought of as real options.

Alliance Threats: Incentives to Cheat on Strategic Alliances

Just as there are incentives to cooperate in strategic alliances, there are also incentives to cheat on these cooperative agreements. Indeed, research shows that as many as one-third of all strategic alliances do not meet the expectations of at least one alliance partner.[9] While some of these alliance "failures" may be due to firms forming alliances that do not have the potential for creating value, some are also due to parties to an alliance cheating—that is, not cooperating in a way that maximizes the value of the alliance. Cheating can occur in at least the three different ways presented in Table 9.2: adverse selection, moral hazard, and holdup.[10]

Adverse Selection

Potential cooperative partners can misrepresent the skills, abilities, and other resources that they will bring to an alliance. This form of cheating, called **adverse selection**, exists when an alliance partner promises to bring to an alliance certain resources that it either does not control or cannot acquire. For example, a local firm engages in adverse selection when it promises to make available to alliance

Table 9.2 **Ways to Cheat in Strategic Alliances**

- *Adverse selection*: Potential partners misrepresent the value of the skills and abilities they bring to the alliance.
- *Moral hazard*: Partners provide to the alliance skills and abilities of lower quality than they promised.
- *Holdup*: Partners exploit the transaction-specific investments made by others in the alliance.

partners a local distribution network that does not currently exist. Firms that engage in adverse selection are not competent alliance partners.

Adverse selection in a strategic alliance is likely only when it is difficult or costly to observe the resources or capabilities that a partner brings to an alliance. If potential partners can easily see that a firm is misrepresenting the resources and capabilities it possesses, they will not create a strategic alliance with that firm. Armed with such understanding, they will seek a different alliance partner, develop the needed skills and resources internally, or perhaps forgo this particular business opportunity.

However, evaluating the veracity of the claims of potential alliance partners is often not easy. The ability to evaluate these claims depends on information that a firm may not possess. To fully evaluate claims about a potential partner's political contacts, for example, a firm needs its own political contacts; to fully evaluate claims about potential partners' market knowledge, a firm needs significant market knowledge. A firm that can completely, and at low cost, evaluate the resources and capabilities of potential alliance partners probably does not really need these partners in a strategic alliance. The fact that a firm is seeking an alliance partner is in some sense an indication that the firm has limited abilities to evaluate potential partners.

In general, the less tangible the resources and capabilities that are to be brought to a strategic alliance, the more costly it will be to estimate their value before an alliance is created, and the more likely it is that adverse selection will occur. Firms considering alliances with partners that bring intangible resources such as "knowledge of local conditions" or "contacts with key political figures" will need to guard against this form of cheating.

Moral Hazard

Partners in an alliance may possess high-quality resources and capabilities of significant value in an alliance but fail to make those resources and capabilities available to alliance partners. This form of cheating is called **moral hazard**. For example, a partner in an engineering strategic alliance may agree to send only its most talented and best trained engineers to work in the alliance but then actually send less talented, poorly trained engineers. These less qualified engineers may not be able to contribute substantially to making the alliance successful, but they may be able to learn a great deal from the highly qualified engineers provided by other alliance partners. In this way, the less qualified engineers effectively transfer wealth from other alliance partners to their own firm.[11]

Often both parties in a failed alliance accuse each other of moral hazard. This was the case in the recently abandoned alliance between Disney and Pixar, described in the Strategy in the Emerging Enterprise feature.

The existence of moral hazard in a strategic alliance does not necessarily mean that any of the parties to that alliance are malicious or dishonest. Rather, what often happens is that market conditions change after an alliance is formed, requiring one or more partners to an alliance to change their strategies.

For example, in the early days of the personal computer industry, Compaq Computer Corporation relied on a network of independent distributors to sell its computers. However, as competition in the personal computer industry increased, Internet, mail order, and so-called computer superstores became much more valuable distribution networks, and alliances between Compaq and its traditional distributors became strained. Over time, Compaq's traditional distributors were

Strategy in the Emerging Enterprise

In 1994, Pixar was a struggling start-up company in northern California that was trying to compete in an industry that really didn't yet exist—the computer graphics animated motion picture industry. Headed by the former founder of Apple Computer, Steven Jobs, Pixar was desperately looking for a partner that could help finance and distribute its new brand of animated movies. Who better, Pixar thought, than the world's leader in animated feature length films—Disney? And thus, a strategic alliance between Pixar and Disney was formed.

In the alliance, Disney agreed to help finance and distribute Pixar's films. In return, they would share in any profits these films generated. Also, Disney would retain the right to produce any sequels to Pixar's films—after first offering Pixar the right to make these sequels. This agreement gave Disney a great deal of control of any characters that Pixar created in movies distributed through Pixar's alliance with Disney. Of course, at the time the alliance was originally formed, there were no such characters. Indeed, Pixar had yet to produce any movies. So, because Pixar was a weak alliance partner, Disney was able to gain control of any characters Pixar developed in the future. Disney, after all, had the track record of success.

A funny thing happened over the next ten years. Pixar produced blockbuster animated features like *Toy Story* ($362 million in revenues in 1995); *A Bug's Life* ($363 million in revenues in 1998); *Toy Story 2* ($485 million in revenues in 1999); *Monsters, Inc.* ($524 million in revenues in 2001); and *Finding Nemo*

**Disney and Pixar Have
a Falling Out**

($844 million in revenues in 2003). During this same time period, Disney's traditional animated fare performed much more poorly—*Treasure Planet* generated only $112 million in revenues in 2002, *The Emperor's New Groove* only $169 million in revenues in 2000, and *Brother Bear* only $126 million in revenues in 2003. Disney's "big hit" during this time period was *Lilo & Stitch*, with 2002 revenues of $269 million—smaller than any of the movies produced by Pixar.

Oops! The firm with the "proven track record" of producing hit animated features—Disney—stumbled badly, and the upstart company with no track record—Pixar—had all the success. Since Disney did not have many of its own characters upon which to base sequels, it began to eye Pixar's characters. And Disney's approach to making sequels made Pixar's man-

agers blanche—poor production values, poorly developed story lines, limited distribution, lower-quality talent. Do you remember seeing the "direct to video hit," *The Lion King: Another Viewpoint*?

Fast forward to 2004. It's time to renew this alliance. But now Pixar has the upper hand, because it has the track record. Disney comes knocking and asks Pixar to redo the alliance. What does Pixar say, "Okay, but . . . we want control of our characters, we want Disney to act just as a distributor"—in other words, "We want Disney out of our business!" Disney balks at these demands, and Pixar—well, Pixar just cancelled the alliance.

But Disney is not done. It still controls the rights to characters created by Pixar while the old alliance with Disney was in place. So, in 2004, Disney announced that it would be producing *Toy Story 3* without Pixar's involvement. Whether this new production will be up to the standards established by Pixar, or be more similar to Disney's track record from 2000 on is yet to be seen. But for now, Disney seems to need Pixar more than Pixar needs Disney.

One final irony in this alliance. Some observers have suggested that Disney's inability to maintain its alliance with Pixar was one of the reasons that Comcast was able to launch an unfriendly takeover bid for Disney in February of 2004.

Sources: S. Levy and D. Jefferson (2004). "Hey Mickey, buzz off!" *BusinessWeek*, February 9, pp. 4; T. Lowry et al. (2004). "Megamedia mergers: How dangerous?" *BusinessWeek*, February 23, pp. 34 +.

unable to obtain all the inventory they wanted in a timely manner. Indeed, to satisfy the needs of large accounts, some traditional distributors actually purchased Compaq computers from local computer superstores and then shipped them to their customers. Compaq's shift from independent dealers to alternative distributors looked like moral hazard—at least from the point of view of the independent dealers. However, from Compaq's perspective, this change simply reflected economic realities in the personal computer industry.[12]

Holdup

Even if alliance partners don't engage in either adverse selection or moral hazard, another form of cheating may evolve. Once a strategic alliance has been created, partner firms may make investments that have value only in the context of that alliance and in no other economic exchanges. These are the transaction-specific investments mentioned in Chapter 6. For example, managers from one alliance partner may have to develop close, trusting relationships with managers from other alliance partners. These close relationships are very valuable in the context of the alliance but have limited economic value in other economic exchanges. Also, one partner may have to customize its manufacturing equipment, distribution network, and key organizational policies to cooperate with other partners. These modifications have significant value in the context of the alliance but do not help the firm, and may even hurt it, in economic exchanges outside the alliance. As was the case in Chapter 6, whenever an investment's value in its first-best use (in this case, within the alliance) is much greater than its value in its second-best use (in this case, outside the alliance), that investment is said to be **transaction specific**.[13]

When one firm makes more transaction-specific investments in a strategic alliance than partner firms make, that firm may be subject to the form of cheating called **holdup**. Holdup occurs when a firm that has not made significant transaction-specific investments demands returns from an alliance that are higher than what the partners agreed to when they created the alliance.

For example, suppose two alliance partners agree to a fifty–fifty split of the costs and profits associated with an alliance. To make the alliance work, Firm A has to customize its production process. Firm B, however, does not have to modify itself to cooperate with Firm A. The value to Firm A of this customized production process, if it is used in the strategic alliance, is $5,000. However, outside the alliance, this customized process is only worth $200 (as scrap).

Obviously, Firm A has made a transaction-specific investment in this alliance and Firm B has not. Consequently, Firm A may be subject to holdup by Firm B. In particular, Firm B may threaten to leave the alliance unless Firm A agrees to give Firm B part of the $5,000 value that Firm A obtains by using the modified production process in the alliance. Rather than lose all the value that could be generated by its investment, Firm A may be willing to give up some of its $5,000 to avoid gaining only $200. Indeed, if Firm B extracts up to the value of Firm A's production process in its next-best use (here, only $200), Firm A will still be better off continuing in this relationship rather than dissolving it. Thus, even though Firm A and Firm B agree on a fifty–fifty split from this strategic alliance, the agreement may be modified if one party to the alliance makes significant transaction-specific investments. Research on international joint ventures suggests that the existence of transaction-specific investments in these relationships often leads to holdup problems.[14]

Although holdup is a form of cheating in strategic alliances, the threat of holdup can also be a motivation for creating an alliance. Bauxite-smelting companies often join in joint ventures with mining companies in order to exploit economies of scale in mining. However, these firms have another option: They could choose to operate large and efficient mines by themselves and then sell the excess bauxite (over and above their needs for their own smelters) on the open market. Unfortunately, bauxite is not a homogeneous commodity. Moreover, different kinds of bauxite require different smelting technologies. In order for one firm to sell its excess bauxite on the market, other smelting firms would have to make enormous investments, the sole purpose of which would be to refine that particular firm's bauxite. These investments would be transaction specific and subject these other smelters to holdup problems.

In this context, a strategic alliance can be thought of as a way of reducing the threat of holdup by creating an explicit management framework for resolving holdup problems. In other words, although holdup problems might still exist in these strategic alliances, the alliance framework may still be a better way in which to manage these problems than attempting to manage them in arm's-length market relationships. Some of the ethical dimensions of adverse selection, moral hazard, and holdup are discussed in the Ethics and Strategy feature.

 ## Strategic Alliances and Sustained Competitive Advantage

The ability of strategic alliances to be sources of sustained competitive advantage, like all the other strategies discussed in this book, to be sources of sustained competitive advantage can be analyzed by using the VRIO framework developed in Chapter 3. An alliance is economically valuable when it exploits any of the opportunities listed in Table 9.1 but avoids the threats in Table 9.2. In addition, for a strategic alliance to be a source of sustained competitive advantage, it must be rare and costly to imitate.

The Rarity of Strategic Alliances

The rarity of strategic alliances does not only depend on the number of competing firms that have already implemented an alliance. It also depends on whether or not the benefits that firms obtain from their alliances are common across firms competing in an industry.

Consider, for example, the automobile industry in the United States. Over the last several years, strategic alliances have become very common in this industry, especially with Japanese auto firms. GM developed an alliance with Toyota that has already been described; Ford developed an alliance with Mazda before it purchased this Japanese firm outright; and DaimlerChrysler developed an alliance with Mitsubishi. Given the frequency with which alliances have developed in this industry, it is tempting to conclude that strategic alliances are rare and thus not a source of competitive advantage.

Closer examination, however, suggests that these alliances may have been created for different reasons. For example, until recently, GM and Toyota have cooperated only in building a single line of cars, the Chevrolet Nova. GM has been less interested in learning design skills from Toyota and has been more interested in learning about manufacturing high-quality small cars profitably. Ford and Mazda,

Ethics and Strategy

So, firms in strategic alliances can cheat on their alliance partners by engaging in adverse selection, moral hazard, or holdup. These three activities all have at least one thing in common—they all involve one alliance partner lying to another. And these lies can often pay off big, in the form of the lying firm appropriating more than its "fair share" of the value created in an alliance. Are alliances one place in the economy where the adage "cheaters never prosper" does not hold?

There is little doubt that, in the short run, firms that cheat on their alliance partners can gain some advantages. But research suggests that cheating does not pay in the long run, because firms that cheat on their alliance partners will find it difficult to form alliances with new partners and thus have many valuable exchange opportunities foreclosed to them.

One study that examined the long-term return to "cheaters" in strategic alliances examined alliances using a simple game called the "Prisoner's Dilemma." In a "Prisoner's Dilemma" game, firms have two options: to continue cooperating in a strategic alliance, or to "cheat" on that alliance through adverse selection, moral hazard, or

When It Comes to Alliances, Do "Cheaters Never Prosper?"

holdup. The payoffs to firms in this game depend on the decisions made by both firms. As shown in Table 9.3, if both firms decide to cooperate, they each get a good size payoff from the alliance ($3,000 in Table 9.3); if they both decide to cheat on the alliance, they each get a very small payoff ($1,000 in Table 9.3); and if one decides to cheat while the other decides to cooperate, then the cheating firm gets a very big payoff ($5,000 in Table 9.3) while the cooperating firm gets a very small payoff ($0 in Table 9.3).

If Firms One and Two in this game are going to engage in only one strategic alliance, then they have a very strong incentive to "cheat." The worst that could happen if they cheat is that they earn a $1,000 payoff; but there is a possibility of a $5,000 payoff. However, research has shown that if a firm is contemplating engaging in multiple strategic alliances over time, then the optimal strategy is to cooperate in all its alliances. This is true even if all these alliances are not with the same partner firm.

The specific "winning" strategy in repeated "Prisoner Dilemma" games is called a "tit-for-tat" strategy. "Tit-for-tat" means that Firm One will cooperate in an alliance as long as Firm Two cooperates. However, as soon as Firm Two cheats on an alliance, Firm One cheats as well. "Tit-for-tat" works well in this setting because adopting a cooperative posture in an alliance ensures that, most of the time, the alliance will generate a high payoff (of $3,000 in Table 9.3). However, by immediately responding to cheaters by cheating, the firm implementing a "tit-for-tat" strategy also minimizes the times when it will earn the lowest payoff in the table ($0). So, "tit-for-tat" maximizes the upside potential of an alliance while minimizing its downside.

All this analysis suggests that while cheating on an alliance can give a firm competitive advantages in the short to medium term; in the long run, "cheaters never prosper."

Sources: R. M. Axelrod (1984). *The evolution of cooperation.* New York: Basic Books; D. Ernst and J. Bleek (1993). *Collaborating to compete.* New York: Wiley.

Table 9.3   **Returns from Cooperating and Cheating in a "Prisoner's Dilemma"**

Firm One		Strategic Alliance	
		Cooperates	Cheats
	Cooperates	I: $3,000 II: $3,000	I: $5,000 II: $0
Firm Two			
	Cheats	I: $0 II: $5,000	I: $1,000 II: $1,000

in contrast, have worked closely together in designing new cars and have joint manufacturing operations. Indeed, Ford and Mazda have worked so closely together that Ford finally purchased Mazda. Mitsubishi has acted primarily as a supplier to DaimlerChrysler, and (until recently) there has been relatively little joint development or manufacturing. Thus, although all three U.S. firms have strategic alliances, the alliances serve different purposes and therefore each may be rare.[15]

One of the reasons why the benefits that accrue from a particular strategic alliance may be rare is that relatively few firms may have the complementary resources and abilities needed to form an alliance. This is particularly likely when an alliance is formed to enter into a new market and especially a new foreign market. In many less developed economies, only one local firm or very few local firms may exist with the local knowledge, contacts, and distribution network needed to facilitate entry into that market. Moreover, sometimes the government acts to limit the number of these local firms. Although several firms may seek entry into this market, only a very small number will be able to form a strategic alliance with the local entity and therefore the benefits that accrue to the allied firms will likely be rare.

The Imitability of Strategic Alliances

As discussed in Chapter 3, the resources and capabilities that enable firms to conceive and implement valuable strategies may be imitated in two ways: direct duplication and substitution. Both duplication and substitution are important considerations in analyzing the imitability of strategic alliances.

Direct Duplication of Strategic Alliances

Recent research suggests that successful strategic alliances are often based on socially complex relations among alliance partners.[16] In this sense, successful strategic alliances often go well beyond simple legal contracts and are characterized by socially complex phenomena such as a trusting relationship between alliance partners, friendship, and even (perhaps) a willingness to suspend narrow self-interest for the longer-term good of the relationship.

Some research has shown that the development of trusting relationships between alliance partners is both difficult and essential to the success of strategic alliances. In one study, the most common reason that alliances fail to meet the expectations of partner firms was the partners' inability to trust one another. Interpersonal communication, tolerance for cultural differences, patience, and willingness to sacrifice short-term profits for longer-term success were all important determinants of the level of trust among alliance partners.[17]

Of course, not all firms in an industry are likely to have the organizational and relationship-building skills required for successful alliance building. If these skills and abilities are rare among a set of competing firms and costly to develop, then firms that are able to exploit these abilities by creating alliances may gain competitive advantages. Examples of firms that have developed these specialized skills include Corning and Cisco, firms with several hundred strategic alliances each.[18]

Substitutes for Strategic Alliances

Even if the purpose and objectives of a strategic alliance are valuable and rare, and even if the relationships on which an alliance is created are socially complex and costly to imitate, that alliance will still not generate a sustained competitive advantage if low-cost substitutes are available. At least two possible substitutes for strategic alliances exist: "going it alone" and acquisitions.[19]

"Going It Alone". Firms "go it alone" when they attempt to develop all the resources and capabilities they need to exploit market opportunities and neutralize market threats by themselves. Sometimes "going it alone" can create the same—or even more—value than using alliances to exploit opportunities and neutralize threats. In these settings, "going it alone" is a substitute for a strategic alliance. However, in other settings, using an alliance can create substantially more value than "going it alone." In these settings, "going it alone" is not a substitute for a strategic alliance.

So, when will firms prefer an alliance over "going it alone?" Not surprisingly, the three explanations of vertical integration, discussed in Chapter 6, are relevant here as well. These three explanations focused on the threat of opportunism, the impact of firm resources and capabilities, and the role of uncertainty. If you need to review these three explanations, they are described in detail in Chapter 6. They are relevant here because "going it alone"—as a potential substitute for a strategic alliance—is an example of vertical integration. The implications of these three explanations for when strategic alliances will be preferred over "going it alone" are summarized in Table 9.4. If any of the conditions listed in Table 9.4 exist, then "going it alone" will not be a substitute for strategic alliances.

Recall from Chapter 6 that opportunism-based explanations of vertical integration suggest that firms will want to vertically integrate an economic exchange when they have made high levels of transaction specific investment in that exchange. That is, using language developed in this chapter, firms will want to vertically integrate an economic exchange when using an alliance to manage that exchange could subject them to holdup. Extending this logic to strategic alliances suggests that strategic alliances will be preferred over "going it alone" and other alternatives when the level of transaction-specific investment required to complete an exchange is moderate. If the level of this specific investment is low, then market forms of exchange will be preferred; if the level of this specific investment is high, then "going it alone" in a vertically integrated way will be preferred; if the level of this specific investment is moderate, then some sort of strategic alliance will be preferred. Thus, when the level of specific exchange in a transaction is moderate, then "going it alone" is not a substitute for a strategic alliance.

Capabilities explanations suggest that an alliance will be preferred over "going it alone" when an exchange partner possesses valuable, rare, and costly-to-imitate resources and capabilities. A firm without these capabilities may find them to be too costly to develop on their own. If a firm must have access to capabilities it cannot develop on its own, it must use an alliance to gain access to those capabilities. In this setting, "going it alone" is not a substitute for a strategic alliance.[20]

Finally, it has already been suggested that, under conditions of high uncertainty, firms may be unwilling to commit to a particular course of action by engaging

Table 9.4 **When Alliances Will Be Preferred Over "Going It Alone"**

Alliances will be preferred over "going it alone" when:

1. The level of transaction-specific investment required to complete an exchange is moderate.
2. An exchange partner possesses valuable, rare, and costly-to-imitate resources and capabilities.
3. There is great uncertainty about the future value of an exchange.

in an exchange within a firm. In such settings, firms may choose the strategic flexibility associated with alliances. As suggested earlier in this chapter, alliances can be thought of as real options that give a firm the right, but not the obligation, to invest further in an exchange—perhaps by bringing it within the boundaries of a firm—if that exchange turns out to be valuable sometime in the future. Thus, under conditions of high uncertainty, "going it alone" is not a substitute for strategic alliances.

Acquisitions. The acquisition of other firms can also be a substitute for alliances. In this case, rather than developing a strategic alliance or attempting to develop and exploit the relevant resources by "going it alone," a firm seeking to exploit the opportunities listed in Table 9.1 may simply acquire another firm that already possesses the relevant resources and capabilities. However, such acquisitions have four characteristics that often limit the extent to which they can act as substitutes for strategic alliances. These are summarized in Table 9.5.[21]

First, there may be legal constraints on acquisitions. These are especially likely if firms are seeking advantages by combining with other firms in their own industry. Thus, for example, using acquisitions as a substitute for strategic alliances in the aluminum industry would lead to a very concentrated industry and subject some of these firms to serious antitrust liabilities. These firms have acquisitions foreclosed to them and must look elsewhere to gain advantages from cooperating with their competition.

Second, as has already been suggested, strategic alliances enable a firm to retain its flexibility either to enter or not to enter into a new business. Acquisitions limit that flexibility, because they represent a strong commitment to engage in a certain business activity. Consequently, under conditions of high uncertainty, firms may choose strategic alliances over acquisitions as a way to exploit opportunities while maintaining the flexibility that alliances create.

Third, firms may choose strategic alliances over acquisitions because of the unwanted organizational baggage that often comes with an acquisition. Sometimes, the value created by combining firms depends on combining particular functions, divisions, or other assets in the firms. A strategic alliance can focus on exploiting the value of combining just those parts of firms that create the most value. Acquisitions, in contrast, generally include the entire organization, both the parts of a firm where value is likely to be created and parts of a firm where value is not likely to be created.

From the point of view of the acquiring firm, parts of a firm that do not create value are essentially unwanted baggage. These parts of the firm may be sold off subsequent to an acquisition. However, this sell-off may be costly and time-consuming. If enough baggage exists, firms may determine that an acquisition is not a viable option, even though important economic value could be created between a firm and a potential acquisition target. To gain this value, an alternative approach—a strategic alliance—may be preferred. These issues will be explored in more detail in Chapter 10.

Table 9.5   **Reasons Why Strategic Alliances May Be More Attractive than Acquisitions to Realize Exchange Opportunities**

Alliances will be preferred to acquisitions when:

1. There are legal constraints on acquisitions.
2. Acquisitions limit a firm's flexibility under conditions of high uncertainty.
3. There is substantial unwanted organizational "baggage" in an acquired firm.
4. The value of a firm's resources and capabilities depends on its independence.

Finally, sometimes a firm's resources and capabilities are valuable because that firm is independent. In this setting, the act of acquiring a firm can actually reduce the value of a firm. When this is the case, any value between two firms is best realized through an alliance, not an acquisition. For example, the international growth of numerous marketing-oriented companies in the 1980s led to strong pressures for advertising agencies to develop global marketing capabilities. During the 1990s, many domestic-only advertising firms acquired nondomestic agencies to form a few large international advertising agencies. However, one firm that was reluctant to be acquired in order to be part of an international advertising network was the French advertising company Publicis. Over and above the personal interests of its owners to retain control of the company, Publicis wanted to remain an independent French agency in order to retain its stable of French and French-speaking clients— including Renault and Nestlé. These firms had indicated that they preferred working with a French advertising agency and that they would look for alternative suppliers if Publicis were acquired by a foreign firm. Because much of the value that Publicis created in a potential acquisition depended on obtaining access to its stable of clients, the act of acquiring Publicis would have had the effect of destroying the very thing that made the acquisition attractive. For this reason, rather than allowing itself to be acquired by foreign advertising agencies, Publicis developed a complex equity strategic alliance and joint venture with a U.S. advertising firm, Foote, Coyne, and Belding. Although, ultimately, this alliance was not successful in providing an international network for either of these two partner firms, an acquisition of Publicis by Foote, Coyne, and Belding would almost certainly have destroyed some of the economic value that Publicis enjoyed as a stand-alone company.

Organizing to Implement Strategic Alliances

V R I O

One of the most important determinants of the success of strategic alliances is their organization. The primary purpose of organizing a strategic alliance is to enable partners in the alliance to gain all the benefits associated with cooperation while minimizing the probability that cooperating firms will cheat on their cooperative agreements. The organizing skills required in managing alliances are, in many ways, unique. It often takes some time for firms to learn these skills and thus to realize the full potential of their alliances. This is why some firms are able to gain competitive advantages from managing alliances more effectively than their competitors. Indeed, sometimes firms may have to choose alternatives to alliances—including "going it alone" and acquisitions—even when those alternatives are not preferred simply because they do not have the skills required to organize and manage alliances.

A variety of tools and mechanisms can be used to help realize the value and minimize the threat of cheating in alliances. These include: contracts, equity investments, firm reputations, joint ventures, and trust.

Explicit Contracts and Legal Sanctions

One way to avoid cheating in strategic alliances is for parties to an alliance to anticipate the ways in which cheating may occur (including adverse selection, moral hazard, and holdup) and to write explicit contracts that define legal liability if cheating does occur. Writing these contracts, together with the close monitoring of contractual compliance and the threat of legal sanctions, can reduce the probability of cheating. Earlier in this chapter, such strategic alliances were called non-equity alliances.

However, contracts sometimes fail to anticipate all forms of cheating that might occur in a relationship—and firms may cheat on cooperative agreements in subtle ways that are difficult to evaluate in terms of contractual requirements. Thus, for example, a contract may require parties in a strategic alliance to make available to the alliance certain proprietary technologies or processes. However, it may be very difficult to communicate the subtleties of these technologies or processes to alliance partners. Does this failure in communication represent a clear violation of contractual requirements, or does it represent a good-faith effort by alliance partners? Moreover, how can one partner tell whether it is obtaining all the necessary information about a technology or process when it is unaware of all the information that exists in another firm? Hence, although contracts are an important component of most strategic alliances, they do not resolve all the problems associated with cheating.

Although most contracts associated with strategic alliances are highly customized, these different contracts do have some common features. These common features are described in detail in Table 9.6. In general, firms contemplating a strategic alliance that will be at least partially governed by a contract will have to include clauses that address the issues presented in Table 9.6.

Table 9.6   **Common Clauses in Contracts Used to Govern Strategic Alliances**

Establishment Issues

Shareholdings
If an equity alliance or joint venture is to be formed, what percentage of equity is to be purchased by each firm involved in the alliance.

Voting rights
The number of votes assigned to each partner in an alliance. May or may not be equal to shareholding percentages.

Dividend percentage
How the profits from an alliance will be allocated among cooperating firms. May or may not be equal to shareholding percentages.

Minority protection
Description of the kinds of decisions that can be vetoed by firms with a minority interest in an alliance.

Board of directors
Initial board of directors, plus mechanisms for dismissing and appointing board members.

Articles of association
Procedures for passing resolutions, share issuance, share disposal, etc.

Place of incorporation
If a joint venture, geographic location of incorporation.

Advisors
Lawyers, accountants, and other consultants to the alliance.

Identification of parties
Legal entities directly involved in an alliance.

Operating Issues

Performance clauses

Duties and obligations of alliance partners, including warranties and minimum performance levels expected.

Noncompete clauses

Partners are restricted from entering the primary business of the alliance.

Nonsolicitation clauses

Partners are restricted from recruiting employees from each other.

Confidentiality clauses

Proprietary information from partners or from the alliance cannot be shared outside the alliance.

Licensing intellectual property rights

Who owns the intellectual property created by an alliance and how this property is licensed to other firms.

Liability

Liability of the alliance and liability of cooperating partners.

Changes to the contract

Process by which the contract can be amended.

Dispute resolution

Process by which disputes among partners will be resolved.

Termination Issues

Preemption rights

If one partner wishes to sell its shares, it must first offer them to the other partner.

Variations on preemption rights

Partners are forbidden to ever discuss the sale of their shares to an outsider without first informing their partner of their intention to do so.

Call options

When one partner can force the other partner to sell its shares to it. Includes discussion on how these shares will be valued and the circumstances under which a call option can be exercised.

Put options

A partner has the right to force another partner to buy its alliance shares.

Drag-along rights

One partner can arrange a sale to an outside firm and force the other partner to sell shares as well.

Tag-along rights

A partner can prevent the sale of the second partner's shares to an outside firm unless that outside firm also buys the first partner's shares.

Initial public offering (IPO)

Circumstances under which an IPO will be pursued.

Termination

Conditions under which contract can be terminated and consequences of termination for partners.

Sources: Adapted from E. Campbell and J. Reuer (2000). "Note on the legal negotiation of strategic alliance agreements." Unpublished working paper, Fontainbleau, France: INSEAD.

Equity Investments

The effectiveness of contracts can be enhanced by having partners in an alliance make equity investments in each other. When Firm A buys a substantial equity position in its alliance partner, Firm B, the market value of Firm A now depends, to some extent, on the economic performance of that partner. The incentive of Firm A to cheat Firm B falls, for to do so would be to reduce the economic performance of Firm B and thus the value of Firm A's investment in its partner. These kinds of strategic alliances are called equity alliances.

Many firms use cross-equity investments to help manage their strategic alliances. These arrangements are particularly common in Japan, where a firm's largest equity holders often include several of its key suppliers, including its main banks. These equity investments, because they reduce the threat of cheating in alliances with suppliers, can reduce these firms' supply costs. In turn, not only do firms have equity positions in their suppliers, but suppliers often have substantial equity positions in the firms to which they sell.[22]

Firm Reputations

A third constraint on incentives to cheat in strategic alliances exists in the effect that a reputation for cheating has on a firm's future opportunities. Although it is often difficult to anticipate all the different ways in which an alliance partner may cheat, it is often easier to describe after the fact how an alliance partner has cheated. Information about an alliance partner that has cheated is likely to become widely known. A firm with a reputation as a cheater is not likely to be able to develop strategic alliances with other partners in the future, despite any special resources or capabilities that it might be able to bring to an alliance. In this way, cheating in a current alliance may foreclose opportunities for developing other valuable alliances. For this reason, firms may decide not to cheat in their current alliances.[23]

There is substantial evidence that the effect of reputation on future business opportunities is important. Firms go to great lengths to make sure that they do not develop this negative reputation. Nevertheless, this reputational control of cheating in strategic alliances does have several limitations.[24]

First, subtle cheating in a strategic alliance may not become public, and if it does become public, the responsibility for the failure of the strategic alliance may be very ambiguous. In one equity joint venture attempting to perfect the design of a new turbine for power generation, financial troubles made one partner considerably more anxious than the other partner to complete product development. The financially healthy and thus patient partner believed that if the alliance required an additional infusion of capital, the financially troubled partner would have to abandon the alliance and would have to sell its part of the alliance at a relatively low price. The patient partner thus encouraged alliance engineers to work slowly and carefully in the guise of developing the technology to reach its full potential. The financially troubled and thus impatient partner encouraged alliance engineers to work quickly, perhaps sacrificing some quality to develop the technology sooner. Eventually, the impatient partner ran out of money, sold its share of the alliance to the patient partner at a reduced price and accused the patient partner of not acting in good faith to facilitate the rapid development of the new technology. The patient partner accused the other firm of pushing the technology too quickly, thereby sacrificing quality and, perhaps, worker safety. In some sense, both firms were cheating on their agreement to develop the new technology cooperatively. However, this cheating was subtle and difficult to spot and had relatively little impact on the reputation of either firm or on the ability of either firm to establish alliances in the future. It is likely that most observers would simply conclude that the patient partner obtained a windfall because of the impatient partner's bad luck.[25]

Second, although one partner to an alliance may be unambiguously cheating on the relationship, one or both of the firms may not be sufficiently connected into a network with other firms to make this information public. When information about cheating remains private, public reputations are not tarnished and future opportunities are not forgone. This is especially likely to happen if one or both alliance partners operate in less developed economies where information about partner behavior may not be rapidly diffused to other firms or to other countries.

Finally, the effect of a tarnished reputation, as long as cheating in an alliance is unambiguous and publicly known, may foreclose future opportunities for a firm, but it does little to address the current losses experienced by the firm that was cheated. Moreover, any of the forms of cheating discussed earlier—adverse selection, moral hazard, or holdup—can result in substantial losses for a firm currently in an alliance. Indeed, the wealth created by cheating in a current alliance may be large enough to make a firm willing to forgo future alliances. In this case, a tarnished reputation may be of minor consequence to a cheating firm.[26]

Joint Ventures

A fourth way to reduce the threat of cheating is for partners in a strategic alliance to invest in a joint venture. Creating a separate legal entity, in which alliance partners invest and from whose profits they earn returns on their investments, reduces some of the risks of cheating in strategic alliances. When a joint venture is created, the ability of partners to earn returns on their investments depends on the economic success of the joint venture. Partners in joint ventures have limited interests in behaving in ways that hurt the performance of the joint venture, because such behaviors end up hurting themselves. Moreover, unlike reputational consequences of cheating, cheating in a joint venture does not just foreclose future alliance opportunities; it can hurt the cheating firm in the current period as well.

Given the advantages of joint ventures in controlling cheating, it is not surprising that when the probability of cheating in a cooperative relationship is greatest, a joint venture is usually the preferred form of cooperation. There are some clear economies of scale in bauxite mining, for example. However, transaction-specific investments would lead to significant holdup problems in selling excess bauxite in the open market, and legal constraints prevent the acquisition of other smelter companies to create an intraorganizational demand for excess bauxite. Holdup problems would continue to exist in any mining strategic alliances that might be created. Nonequity alliances, equity alliances, and reputational effects are not likely to restrain cheating in this situation, because the returns on holdup, once transaction-specific investments are in place, can be very large. Thus, most of the strategic alliances created to mine bauxite take the form of joint ventures. Only this form of strategic alliance is likely to create incentives strong enough to significantly reduce the probability of cheating.[27]

Despite these strengths, joint ventures are not able to costlessly reduce all cheating in an alliance. Sometimes the value of cheating in a joint venture is sufficiently large that a firm cheats even though doing so hurts the joint venture and forecloses future opportunities. For example, through a joint venture, a particular firm may gain access to a technology that would be valuable if used in another of its lines of business. This firm may be tempted to transfer this technology to this other line of business even if it has agreed not to do so and even if doing so would limit the performance of its joint venture. Because the profits earned in this other line of business may have a greater value than the returns that could have been earned in the joint venture and the returns that could have been earned in the future with other strategic alliances, cheating may occur in a joint venture.

Trust

It is sometimes the case that alliance partners rely only on legalistic and narrowly economic approaches to manage their alliance. However, recent work seems to suggest that although successful alliance partners do not ignore legal and economic disincentives to cheating, they strongly support these narrower linkages with a rich set of interpersonal relations and trust. Trust, in combination with contracts, can help reduce the threat of cheating. More important, trust may enable partners to explore exchange opportunities that they could not explore if only legal and economic organizing mechanisms were in place.[28]

At first glance, this argument may seem far-fetched. However, some research offers support for this approach to managing strategic alliances, suggesting that successful alliance partners typically do not specify all the terms and conditions in their relationship in a legal contract and do not specify all possible forms of cheating and their consequences. Moreover, when joint ventures are formed, partners do not always insist on simple fifty–fifty splits of equity ownership and profit sharing. Rather, successful alliances involve trust, a willingness to be flexible, a willingness to learn, and a willingness to let the alliance develop in ways that the partners could not have anticipated.[29]

Commitment, coordination, and trust are all important determinants of alliance success. Put another way, a strategic alliance is a relationship that evolves over time. Allowing the lawyers and economists to too-rigorously define, a priori, the boundaries of that relationship may limit it and stunt its development.[30]

This "trust" approach also has implications for the extent to which strategic alliances may be sources of sustained competitive advantage for firms. The ability to move into strategic alliances in this trusting way may be very valuable over the long run. There is strong reason to believe that this ability is not uniformly distributed across all firms that might have an interest in forming strategic alliances and that this ability may be history-dependent and socially complex and thus costly to imitate. Firms with these skills may be able to gain sustained competitive advantages from their alliance relationships. The observation that just a few firms, including Corning and Cisco, are well known for their strategic alliance successes is consistent with the observation that these alliance management skills may be valuable, rare, and costly to imitate.

Strategic Alliances in an International Context

As suggested in Table 9.1, strategic alliances are especially important for firms looking to enter into new foreign markets. In this context, one partner typically brings products or services (as resources) to the alliance, and the other partner brings local knowledge, local distribution networks, and local political influence (as resources) to the relationship. The development of local distribution networks can be a costly and difficult process. Such actions generally require a great deal of knowledge about local conditions. Local alliance partners may already possess this knowledge. They may even already have a local distribution network in place. By cooperating with local partners, firms can substantially reduce the cost of entry into these markets.

Of course, some governments require new entrants to have local alliance partners. Governments see such relationships not only as a way to facilitate entry of foreign firms into their market place, but also as a way that domestic firms can learn from foreign firms. This has been the case with General Electric's entry into the Chinese electricity production market. The Chinese government has required GE, if it wants to sell its generators in China, to form joint ventures with local Chinese companies. This has enabled GE to sell over $900 million worth of generators in the Chinese market.

However, recently, China began to require GE to provide its Chinese joint venture partners information about its generator technology and information about how to manufacture that technology. GE has spent over $500 million developing its new line of generators and obviously does not want to share this knowledge with firms that might some day become its competitors. But the Chinese government is now saying: "If you want to sell in China, you need to share your technology." Several other firms, besides GE, have had to share technology with their Chinese alliance partners to continue doing business in China as well, including Motorola, Microsoft, Seimens, and Nokia.[31] These actions by the Chinese government have the effect of increasing the cost of entry into the Chinese market.

All the potential threats that exist in alliances—from adverse selection to moral hazard, from holdup to learning races—can exist in an international context. Indeed, while it is often the case that there will be important information asymmetries between firms in an alliance, these asymmetries are likely to be much greater when alliance partners come from different countries, operate in different cultures, and speak different languages.

Ironically, it is precisely these kinds of threats that often motivate firms to engage in alliances in exploiting international opportunities. These same kinds of threats exist if a firm vertically integrates into its international operations—either on its own or by acquiring another firm. However, once a firm has vertically integrated, it can be relatively costly for it to extract itself from this investment if it turns out that it has been unfairly taken advantage of in deciding to begin operations in a country. On the other hand, it is much less costly for a firm to withdraw from an international alliance. For these reasons, it is not unusual to observe firms, as they begin to explore international opportunities, to do so first by engaging in market-based forms of exchange (through simple importing or exporting), followed by nonequity alliances (including licensing agreements). Only after a firm has developed trust and confidence in its international partners will it be willing to engage in equity alliances and, perhaps, joint ventures. In the end, if it makes economic sense to do so, a firm may even decide to vertically integrate into its international operations. However, this is often the last step in exploiting international opportunities, not the first step.

Thus, while all the threats associated with alliances exist in an international context, so do all the tools that can be used to reduce these threats. Over time, firms can even develop very strong and trusting relationships with their international alliance partners—relationships that create all the economic value of vertical integration but do so at much lower cost.

SUMMARY

Strategic alliances exist whenever two or more organizations cooperate in the development, manufacture, or sale of products or services. Strategic alliances can be grouped into three large categories: nonequity alliances, equity alliances, and joint ventures.

There are three broad reasons why firms join in strategic alliances: to improve the performance of their current operations, to improve the competitive environment within which they are operating, and to facilitate entry or exit into markets and industries. Just as there are incentives to cooperate in strategic alliances, there are also incentives to cheat. Cheating generally takes one or a combination of three forms: adverse selection, moral hazard, or holdup.

Strategic alliances can be a source of sustained competitive advantage. The rarity of alliances depends not only on the number of competing firms that have developed an alliance but also on the benefits that firms gain through their alliances.

Imitation through direct duplication of an alliance may be costly because of the socially complex relations that underlie an alliance. However, imitation through substitution is more likely. Two substitutes for alliances may be "going it alone," where firms develop and exploit the relevant sets of resources and capabilities on their own, and acquisitions. Opportunism, capabilities, and uncertainty all have an impact on when "going it alone" will and will not be a substitute for a strategic alliance. Acquisitions may be a substitute for strategic alliances when there are no legal constraints in acquisitions, strategic flexibility is not an important consideration, when the acquired firm has relatively little unwanted "organizational baggage," and when the value of a firm's resources and capabilities does not depend on its remaining independent. However, when these conditions do not exist, acquisitions are not a substitute for alliances.

The key issue facing firms in organizing their alliances is to facilitate cooperation while avoiding the threat of cheating. Contracts, equity investments, firm reputations, joint ventures, and trust can all reduce the threat of cheating in different contexts. These tools can also be used to reduce the threats to alliances in an international context.

CHALLENGE QUESTIONS

1. One reason why firms might want to pursue a strategic alliance strategy is to exploit economies of scale. Exploiting economies of scale should reduce a firm's costs. Does this mean that a firm pursuing an alliance strategy to exploit economies of scale is actually pursuing a cost leadership strategy? Why or why not?

2. Consider the joint venture between General Motors and Toyota. GM has been interested in learning how to profitably manufacture high-quality small cars from its alliance with Toyota. Toyota has been interested in gaining access to GM's U.S. distribution network and in reducing the political liability associated with local content laws.

Which of these firms do you think is more likely to accomplish its objectives, and why? What implications, if any, does your answer have for a possible "learning race" in this alliance?

3. Some have argued that strategic alliances are one way in which firms can help facilitate the development of a tacit collusion strategy. In your view, what are the critical differences between tacit collusion strategies and strategic alliance strategies? How can one tell whether two firms are engaging in an alliance to facilitate collusion or are engaging in an alliance for other purposes?

4. Some have argued that alliances can be used to help firms evaluate the economic potential of entering into a new

industry or market. Under what conditions will a firm seeking to evaluate these opportunities need to invest in an alliance to accomplish this evaluation? Why couldn't such a firm simply hire some smart managers, consultants, and industry experts to evaluate the economic potential of entering into a new industry? What, if anything, about an alliance makes this a better way to evaluate entry opportunities than alternatives?

5. If adverse selection, moral hazard, and holdup are such significant problems for firms pursuing alliance strategies, why do firms even bother with alliances? Why don't they instead adopt a "go it alone" strategy to replace strategic alliances?

PROBLEM SET

1. Which of the following firms faces the greater threat of "cheating" in the alliances described, and why?

(a) Firm I and Firm II form a strategic alliance. As part of the alliance, Firm I agrees to build a new plant right next to Firm II's primary facility. In return, Firm II promises to buy most of the output of this new plant. Who is at risk, Firm I or Firm II?

(b) Firm A and Firm B form a strategic alliance. As part of the alliance, Firm A promises to begin selling products it already sells around the world in the home country of Firm B. In return, Firm B promises to provide Firm A with crucial contacts in its home country's government. These contacts are essential if Firm A is going to be able to sell in Firm B's home country. Who is at risk, Firm A or Firm B?

(c) Firm 1 and Firm 2 form a strategic alliance. As part of the alliance, Firm 1 promises to provide Firm 2 access to some new and untested technology that Firm 2 will use in its products. In return, Firm 2 will share some of the profits from its sales with Firm 1. Who is at risk, Firm 1 or Firm 2?

2. For each of the strategic alliances described in the above question, what actions could be taken to reduce the likelihood that partner firms will "cheat" in these alliances?

3. Examine the Web sites of the following strategic alliances and determine which of the sources of value presented in Table 9.1 are present:

(a) Dow-Corning (an alliance between Dow Chemical and Corning)
(b) CFM (an alliance between General Electric and SNECMA)
(c) Cingular (an alliance between SBC and BellSouth)
(d) NCAA (an alliance among colleges and universities in the United States)
(e) Visa (an alliance among banks in the United States)
(f) The alliance among United, Delta, Singapore Airlines, AeroMexico, Alitalia, and Korean Air.

END NOTES

1. See J. L. Badaracco and N. Hasagava (1988). "General Motors' Asian alliances." Harvard Business School, Case no. 9-388-094; D. Ernst and J. Bleeke (1993). *Collaborating to compete: Using strategic alliances and acquisitions in the global marketplace.* New York: Wiley; L. Doz & G. Hamel (1998). *Alliance advantage: The art of creating value through partnering*, Boston: Harvard Business School Press, xiii; R. D. Ireland, M. A. Hitt, & D. Vaidyanath (2202). Alliance management as a source of competitive advantage, *Journal of Management*, 28: 413–446; J. G. Coombs & D. J. Ketchen, 1999, Exploring interfirm cooperation and performance: Toward a reconciliation of predictions from the resource-based view and organizational economics, *Strategic Management Journal*, 20: 867–888.

2. Badaracco, J. L., and N. Hasegawa (1988). "General Motors' Asian alliances." Harvard Business School Case No. 9-388-094.

3. See Burgers, W. P., C. W. L. Hill, and W. C. Kim (1993). "A theory of global strategic alliances: The case of the global auto industry." *Strategic Management Journal*, 14, pp. 419–432.

4. See Freeman, A., and R. Hudson (1980). "Dupont and Philips plan joint venture to make, market laser disc products." *Wall Street Journal*, December 22, p. 10.

5. Teitelbaum, R. S. (1992). "Eskimo pie." *Fortune*, June 15, p. 123.

6. Nanda, A., and C. A. Bartlett (1990). "Corning Incorporated: A network of alliances." Harvard Business School Case No. 9-391-102.

7. See Knight, F. H. (1965). *Risk, uncertainty, and profit*. New York: John Wiley & Sons, Inc., on uncertainty; Kogut, B. (1991). "Joint ventures and the option to expand and acquire." *Management Science*, 37, pp. 19–33; Burgers, W. P., C. W. L. Hill, and W. C. Kim (1993). "A theory of global strategic alliances: The case of the global auto industry." *Strategic Management Journal*, 14, pp. 419–432; Noldeke, G., and K. M. Schmidt (1998). "Sequential investments and options to own." *Rand Journal of Economics*, 29(4), pp. 633–653; and Folta, T. B. (1998). "Governance and uncertainty: The tradeoff between administrative control and commitment." *Strategic Management Journal*, 19, pp. 1007–1028.

8. See Kogut, B. (1991). "Joint ventures and the option to expand and acquire. " *Management Science*, 37, pp. 19–33; and Balakrishnan, S., and M. Koza (1993). "Information asymmetry, adverse selection and joint-ventures." *Journal of Economic Behavior & Organization*, 20, pp. 99–117.

9. See, for example, Ernst, D., and J. Bleeke (1993). *Collaborating to compete: Using strategic alliances and acquisition in the global marketplace.* New York: John Wiley & Sons, Inc.

10. These terms are defined in Barney, J. B., and W. G. Ouchi (1986). *Organizational economics.* San Francisco: Jossey-Bass; and Holmstrom, B. (1979). "Moral hazard and observability." *Bell Journal of Economics*, 10(1), pp. 74–91. Problems of cheating in economic exchanges, in general, and in alliances in particular, are discussed by Gulati, R., and H. Singh (1998). "The architecture of cooperation: Managing coordination costs and appropriation concerns in strategic alliances." *Administrative Science Quarterly*, 43, pp. 781–814; Williamson, O. E. (1991). "Comparative economic organization: The analysis of discrete structural alternatives." *Administrative Science Quarterly*, 36, pp. 269–296; Osborn, R. N., and C. C. Baughn (1990). "Forms of interorganizational governance for multinational alliances." *Academy of Management Journal*, 33(3), pp. 503–519; Hagedorn, J., and R. Narula (1996). "Choosing organizational modes of strategic technology partnering: International and sectoral differences." *Journal of International Business Studies*, second quarter, pp. 265–284; Hagedorn, J. (1996). "Trends and patterns in strategic technology partnering since the early seventies." *Review of Industrial Organization*, 11, pp. 601–616; Kent, D. H. (1991). "Joint ventures vs. non-joint ventures: An empirical investigation." *Strategic Management Journal*, 12, pp. 387–393; and Shane, S. A. (1998). "Making new franchise systems work." *Strategic Management Journal*, 19, pp. 697–707.

11. Such alliance difficulties are described in Ouchi, W. G. (1984). *The M-form society: How American teamwork can capture the competitive edge.* Reading, MA: Addison-Wesley; and Bresser, R. K. (1988). "Cooperative strategy." *Strategic Management Journal*, 9, pp. 475–492.

12. Pope, K. (1993). "Dealers accuse Compaq of jilting them." *Wall Street Journal*, February 26, pp. 8, B1 +.

13. Williamson, O. E. (1975). *Markets and hierarchies: Analysis and antitrust implications.* New York: Free Press; Klein, B., R. Crawford, and A. Alchian (1978). "Vertical integration, appropriable rents, and the competitive contracting process." *Journal of Law and Economics*, 21, pp. 297–326.

14. See, for example, Yan, A., and B. Gray (1994). "Bargaining power, management control, and performance in United States-China joint ventures: A comparative case study." *Academy of Management Journal*, 37, pp. 1478–1517.

15. See Badaracco, J. L., and N. Hasegawa (1988). "General Motors' Asian alliances." Harvard Business School Case No. 9-388-094, on GM and Toyota; Patterson, G. A. (1991). "Mazda hopes to crack Japan's top tier." *Wall Street Journal*, September 20, pp. B1 +; and Williams, M., and M. Kanabayashi (1993). "Mazda and Ford drop proposal to build cars together in Europe." *Wall Street Journal*, March 4, p. A14, on Ford and Mazda; and Ennis, P. (1991). "Mitsubishi group wary of deeper ties to Chrysler." *Tokyo Business Today*, 59, July, p. 10, on DaimlerChrysler and Mitsubishi.

16. See, for example, Ernst, D., and J. Bleeke (1993). *Collaborating to compete: Using strategic alliances and acquisition in the global marketplace.* New York: John Wiley & Sons, Inc.; and Barney, J. B., and M. H. Hansen (1994). "Trustworthiness as a source of competitive advantage." *Strategic Management Journal*, 15, winter (special issue), pp. 175–190.

17. Ernst, D., and J. Bleeke (1993). *Collaborating to compete: Using strategic alliances and acquisition in the global marketplace.* New York: John Wiley & Sons, Inc.

18. Bartlett, C., and S. Ghoshal (1993). "Beyond the M-form: Toward a managerial theory of the firm." *Strategic Management Journal*, 14, pp. 23–46.

19. See Nagarajan, A., and W. Mitchell (1998). "Evolutionary diffusion: Internal and external methods used to acquire encompassing, complementary, and incremental technological changes in the lithotripsy industry." *Strategic Management Journal*, 19, pp. 1063–1077; Hagedoorn, J., and B. Sadowski (1999). "The transition from strategic technology alliances to mergers and acquisitions: An exploratory study." *Journal of Management Studies*, 36(1), pp. 87–107; and Newburry, W., and Y. Zeira (1997). "Generic differences between equity international joint ventures (EIJVs), international acquisitions (IAs) and International Greenfield investments (IGIs): Implications for parent companies." *Journal of World Business*, 32(2), pp. 87–102, on alliance substitutes.

20. Barney, J. B. (1999). "How a firm's capabilities affect boundary decisions." *Sloan Management Review*, 40(3), pp. 137–145.

21. See Hennart, J. F. (1988). "A transaction cost theory of equity joint ventures." *Strategic Management Journal*, 9, pp. 361–374; Kogut, B. (1988). "Joint ventures: Theoretical and empirical perspectives." *Strategic Management Journal*, 9, pp. 319–332; and Barney, J. B. (1999). "How a firm's capabilities affect boundary decisions." *Sloan Management Review*, 40(3), pp. 137–145, for a discussion of these limitations.

22. See Ouchi, W. G. (1984). *The M-form society: How American teamwork can capture the competitive edge.* Reading, MA: Addison-Wesley; and Barney, J. B. (1990). "Profit sharing bonuses and the cost of debt: Business finance and compensation policy in Japanese electronics firms." *Asia Pacific Journal of Management*, 7, pp. 49–64.

23. This is an argument developed by Barney, J. B., and M. H. Hansen (1994). "Trustworthiness as a source of competitive advantage." *Strategic Management Journal*, 15, winter (special issue), pp. 175–190; Weigelt, K., and C. Camerer (1988). "Reputation and corporate strategy: A review of recent theory and applications." *Strategic Management Journal*, 9, pp. 443–454; and Granovetter, M. (1985). "Economic action and social structure: The problem of embeddedness." *American Journal of Sociology*, 3, pp. 481–510.

24. See, for example, Eichenseher, J., and D. Shields (1985). "Reputation and corporate strategy: A review of recent theory and applications." *Strategic Management Journal*, 9, pp. 443–454; Beatty, R., and R. Ritter (1986). "Investment banking, reputation, and the underpricing of initial public offerings." *Journal of Financial Economics*, 15, pp. 213–232; Kalleberg, A. L., and T. Reve (1992). "Contracts and commitment: Economic and Sociological Perspectives on Employment Relations." *Human Relations*, 45(9), pp. 1103–1132; Larson, A. (1992). "Network dyads in entrepreneurial settings: A study of the governance of exchange relationships." *Administrative Science Quarterly*, March, pp. 76–104; Stuart, T. E., H. Hoang, and R. C. Hybels (1999).

"Interorganizational endorsements and the performance of entrepreneurial ventures." *Administrative Science Quarterly*, 44, pp. 315–349; Stuart, T. E. (1998). "Network positions and propensities to collaborate: An investigation of strategic alliance formation in a high-technology industry." *Administrative Science Quarterly*, 43(3), pp. 668–698; and Gulati, R. (1998). "Alliances and networks." *Strategic Management Journal*, 19, pp. 293–317.

25. Personal communication, April 8, 1986.

26. This same theoretic approach to firm reputation is discussed in Tirole, J. (1988). *The theory of industrial organization*. Cambridge, MA: MIT Press.

27. Scherer, F. M. (1980). *Industrial Market structure and economic performance*. Boston: Houghton Mifflin.

28. See again, Ernst, D., and J. Bleeke (1993). *Collaborating to compete: Using strategic alliances and acquisition in the global marketplace*. New York: John Wiley & Sons, Inc.; and Barney, J. B., and M. H. Hansen (1994). "Trustworthiness as a source of competitive advantage." *Strategic Management Journal*, 15, winter (special issue), pp. 175–190. In fact, there is a great deal of literature on the role of trust in strategic alliances. Some of the most interesting of this work can be found in Holm, D. B., K. Eriksson, and J. Johanson (1999). "Creating value through mutual commitment to business network relationships." *Strategic Management Journal*, 20, pp. 467–486; Lorenzoni, G., and A. Lipparini (1999). "The leveraging of interfirm relationships as a distinctive organizational capability: A longitudinal study." *Strategic Management Journal*, 20(4), pp. 317–338; Blois, K. J. (1999). "Trust in business to business relationships: An evaluation of its status." *Journal of Management Studies*, 36(2), pp. 197–215; Chiles, T. H., and J. F. McMackin (1996). "Integrating variable risk preferences, trust, and transaction cost economics." *Academy of Management Review*, 21(1), pp. 73–99; Larzelere, R. E., and T. L. Huston (1980). "The dyadic trust scale: Toward understanding interpersonal trust in close relationships." *Journal of Marriage and the Family*, August, pp. 595–604; Butler, J. K., Jr. (1983). "Reciprocity of trust between professionals and their secretaries." *Psychological Reports*, 53, pp. 411–416; Zaheer, A., and N. Venkatraman (1995). "Relational governance as an interorganizational strategy: An empirical test of the role of trust in economic exchange." *Strategic Management Journal*, 16, pp. 373–392; Butler, J. K., Jr., and R. S. Cantrell (1984). "A behavioral decision theory approach to modeling dyadic trust in superiors and subordinates." *Psychological Reports*, 55, pp. 19–28; Carney, M. (1998). "The competitiveness of networked production: The role of trust and asset specificity." *Journal of Management Studies*, 35(4), pp. 457–479.

29. Ernst, D., and J. Bleeke (1993). *Collaborating to compete: Using strategic alliances and acquisition in the global marketplace*. New York: John Wiley & Sons, Inc.

30. See Mohr, J., and R. Spekman (1994). "Characteristics of partnership success: Partnership attributes, communication behavior, and conflict resolution techniques." *Strategic Management Journal*, 15, pp. 135–152; and Zaheer, A., and N. Venkatraman (1995). "Relational governance as an interorganizational strategy: An empirical test of the role of trust in economic exchange." *Strategic Management Journal*, 16, pp. 373–392.

31. Kranhold, Kathryn (2004). "China's price for market entry: Give us your technology, too." *Wall Street Journal*, February 26, pp. A1 +.

10

Mergers and Acquisitions

It's as baffling as any mystery novel. One acquisition works while an apparently very similar acquisition does not work. How can this be?

Here are the facts: Two struggling Japanese automakers—Mitsubishi and Nissan—were acquired. DaimlerChrysler, a German and American company, acquired 37 percent of Mitsubishi's stock (a controlling interest) for $2.4 billion in 2001; Renault, a French company, acquired 38 percent of Nissan for $6 billion in 1998.

Before they were acquired, both Mitsubishi and Nissan had significant difficulties. Mitsubishi

The Case of the Twin Mergers

had a staggering debt load; it had few products under development, and miniscule sales in the most important car market in the world—the United States. Mitsubishi is, however, a member of one of the oldest and most powerful *keiretsu* in Japan. Its close links with other Japanese firms

suggested that Mitsubishi would probably have access to the low-cost capital it needed to invest in its turnaround.

If anything, Nissan was in worse shape. Indeed, $19 billion in debt, a faded brand name, and no products under development led DaimlerChrysler to turn its back on a potential acquisition of Nissan in favor of acquiring Mitsubishi. Renault was the only suitor left.

Learning Objectives

After reading this chapter, you should be able to:

1. Describe different types of mergers and acquisitions.

2. Estimate the return to the stockholders of bidding and target firms when there is no strategic relatedness between firms.

3. Describe different sources of relatedness between bidding and target firms.

4. Estimate the return to stockholders of bidding and target firms when there is strategic relatedness between firms.

5. Describe five reasons why bidding firms might still engage in acquisitions, even if on average they do not create value for a bidding firm's stockholders.

6. Describe three ways that bidding firms might be able to generate high returns for their equity holders through implementing mergers or acquisitions.

7. Describe the major challenges that firms integrating acquisitions are likely to face.

8. Discuss unique challenges to merger and acquisition strategies in an international context.

As soon as these acquisitions were complete, DaimlerChrysler reorganized and restructured Mitsubishi while Renault reorganized and restructured Nissan. By 2003, DaimlerChrysler had cut Mitsubishi's supplier costs by 15 percent, cut the workforce by 16 percent, doubled research and development spending compared to 2000, and hired several new world-class designers. Moreover, the Chrysler division of DaimlerChrysler had begun cooperating with Mitsubishi to develop new platforms for small and medium-sized cars. Soon, automobile platforms developed with Mitsubishi would be the basis for new models of the Dodge Neon, the Dodge Stratus, the Chrysler Sebring, a new Jeep SUV, and a new Chrysler PT Cruiser. Together, these cars represented about 20 percent of Chrysler's annual sales. At the end of this restructuring, Mitsubishi seemed poised to join with DaimlerChrysler to create a worldwide power in the automobile industry.

Over this same time period, Renault made its own changes in

Nissan. It closed five Nissan plants, reduced Nissan's workforce by 23,000, and began manufacturing more models in Nissan's efficient U.S. factories. These changes and investments led Nissan to lose $6.2 billion in 2000. Moreover, unlike Mitsubishi, Nissan was part of a relatively weak *keiretsu* in Japan. This meant that Nissan had to rely much more on Renault, and on its own capabilities, for the capital it needed to invest to become a world-class auto manufacturer. While a Renault–Nissan combination was not likely to be able to wield the worldwide clout of

DaimlerChrysler and Mitsubishi, it nevertheless appeared that Nissan was poised to restore some of the luster it had lost over the previous decade.

Jump to 2004. Nissan reported record profits. Its product line-up included such well-received models as the new Nissan 350Z sports car and the full-size Titan pickup. Nissan's market share in the U.S. market continued to improve, and it enjoyed some of the highest profit margins on its products in the industry. Mitsubishi, on the other hand, reported a $660 million loss. Its sales in the United States fell 26 percent and it had only 1.5 percent of the U.S. car market. Executives at DaimlerChrysler were beginning to despair. One Daimler executive was quoted as saying: "It's an absolute disaster. We can't sell it. It's worth nothing!" DaimlerChrysler almost seemed ready to write off its $2.4 billion investment in Mitsubishi, while Renault's investment in Nissan was beginning to show real dividends.

Why the difference between these two acquisitions? Some observers argued that DaimlerChrysler's efforts to restructure Mitsubishi never went far enough. Some actions not taken by Mitsubishi that might have helped turn things around included closing one plant in Japan, one plant in Australia, phasing out money-losing models in Japan, and shifting production to low-cost factories in China. However, while these actions might have improved Mitsubishi's financial position, other observers suggest a more subtle difference between the acquisition of Mitsubishi and the acquisition of Nissan.

Because Nissan was a member of a weak *keiretsu*, senior managers at Nissan knew that if they did not successfully turn this company around, it would go out of business. Literally, the entire livelihood for these Nissan managers was at risk, dependent on reawakening this once very successful company. On the other hand, since Mitsubishi was part of a much stronger *keiretsu*, its survival as an organization was never really in jeopardy. Historically, members of the Mitsubishi *keiretsu* have provided each other the cash and other resources they need to survive in even the most difficult times. Because their survival was never at risk, some senior managers at Mitsubishi were able to resist the cultural changes that are always part of a corporate restructuring. Despite the efforts of senior managers brought to Mitsubishi by DaimlerChrysler, these pockets of cultural resistance remained. Most observers agree that until Mitsubishi transforms its culture— a culture that is so reluctant to share bad news with senior managers that information about quality defects that should have led to product recalls was squelched for over 10 years—it will not be as successful an acquisition as Nissan.

Sources : G. Edmundson (2004). "Japan: A tale of two mergers." *BusinessWeek*, May 10, p. 42; D. Welch and G. Edmundson (2004). "A shaky automotive *menage a trois.*" *BusinessWeek*, May 10, pp. 40–41.

Mergers and acquisitions are one very common way that a firm can accomplish its vertical integration and diversification objectives. This can be seen in the opening case. Both DaimlerChrysler and Renault were looking to diversify their operations internationally to give themselves a more global reach than they traditionally had. DaimlerChrysler's acquisition of Mitsubishi and Renault's acquisition of Nissan accomplished this objective quite well. In addition, the Chrysler division of DaimlerChrysler was looking to outsource some aspects of the car development process—including the design of new automotive platforms. It needed a partner to work with and the recently acquired Mitsubishi became that partner. So, this acquisition also helped a division of DaimlerChrysler to accomplish its vertical integration objectives.

However, the story of the acquisitions of Mitsubishi and Nissan is a cautionary tale as well. While a firm may be able to accomplish its vertical integration and diversification objectives through mergers or acquisitions, it is sometimes difficult to generate real economic profit from doing so. Indeed, one of the strongest empirical findings in the fields of strategic management and finance is that, on average, the equity holders of target firms in mergers and acquisitions make money while the equity holders of bidding firms in these same mergers and acquisitions usually only "break even."

What Are Mergers and Acquisitions?

The terms "mergers" and "acquisitions" are often used interchangeably, even though they are not synonyms. A firm engages in an **acquisition** when it purchases a second firm. The form of this purchase can vary. For example, an acquiring firm can use cash it has generated from its ongoing businesses to purchase a target firm; it can go into debt to purchase a target firm; it can use its own equity to purchase a target firm; or it can use a mix of these mechanisms to purchase a target firm. Also, an acquiring firm can purchase all of a target firm's assets, it can purchase a majority of those assets (greater than 51 percent), or it can purchase a **controlling share** of those assets (i.e., enough assets so that the acquiring firm is able to make all the management and strategic decisions in the target firm).

Acquisitions also vary on several other dimensions. For example, **friendly acquisitions** occur when the management of the target firm wants the firm to be acquired. **Unfriendly acquisitions** occur when the management of the target firm does not want the firm to be acquired. Some unfriendly acquisitions are also known as **hostile takeovers**. Some acquisitions are accomplished through direct negotiations between an acquiring firm's managers and the managers of a target firm. This is especially common when a target firm is **privately held** (i.e., when it has not sold shares on the public stock market) or **closely held** (i.e., when it has not sold very many shares on the public stock market). Other acquisitions are accomplished by the acquiring firm publicly announcing that it is willing to purchase the outstanding shares of a potential target for a particular price. This price is normally greater than the current market price of the target firm's shares. The difference between the current market price of a target firm's shares and the price a potential acquirer offers to pay for those shares is known as an **acquisition premium**. This approach to purchasing a firm is called a **tender offer**. Tender offers can be made either with or without the support of the management of the target firm. Obviously, tender offers with the support of the target firm's management are typically friendly in character; those made without the support of the target firm's management are typically unfriendly.

It is usually the case that larger firms—in terms of sales or assets—acquire smaller firms. This was the case both for DaimlerChrysler's acquisition of Mitsubishi and Renault's acquisition of Nissan. On the other hand, when the assets of two similar-sized firms are combined, this transaction is called a **merger**. Mergers can be accomplished in many of the same ways as acquisitions, that is, using cash or stock to purchase a percentage of another firm's assets. Typically, however, mergers will not be unfriendly. In a merger, one firm purchases some percentage of a second firm's assets while the second firm simultaneously purchases some percentage of the first firm's assets. For example, DaimlerChrysler—the firm that purchased Mitsubishi (in the opening case)—was created as a merger between Daimler-Benz (the maker of Mercedes-Benz) and Chrysler. Daimler-Benz invested some of its capital in Chrysler, and Chrysler invested some of its capital in Daimler-Benz.

While mergers typically begin as a transaction between equals, that is, between firms of equal size and profitability, they often evolve after a merger such that one firm is more dominant in the management of the merged firm than the other. For example, most observers believe that Daimler (the German part of DaimlerChrysler) has become more dominant in the management of the combined firm than Chrysler (the American part). Indeed, while Daimler management may be willing to "write off" their interests in Mitsubishi as a bad investment, Chrysler management is very reluctant to do so, since they have worked with Mitsubishi to help develop platforms for many of Chrysler's best-selling cars. How long a Daimler-dominated DaimlerChrysler will put up with a "bad" investment that only helps the Chrysler part of the firm is an open question.[1] Put differently, while mergers usually start out as something different from acquisitions, they usually end up looking more like acquisitions than mergers.

V R I O   The Value of Mergers and Acquisitions

That merger and acquisition strategies are an important strategic option open to firms pursuing diversification and vertical integration strategies can hardly be disputed. The number of firms that have used merger and acquisition strategies to become diversified over the last few years is staggering. Worldwide, the total value of announced merger and acquisition activities was over $1.5 trillion in 2000, 2001, and 2002. And while the total level of these activities moderated somewhat in 2003, mergers and acquisitions have certainly not disappeared. For example, in 2003, over 200 publicly traded firms in the United States engaged in merger and acquisition activities. These firms ranged in size from Cardinal Health and Johnson & Johnson—two of the largest health care firms in the world—to Inflazyme Pharmaceuticals—a relatively small biotechnology start-up that acquired Glycodesign, Inc. Nor were these acquisitions limited to just a few industries. At least 26 occurred in health-related industries, 43 in the financial services industries, 20 in the mining and raw materials extraction industries, and 28 in high-technology industries.

The list of firms that engaged in mergers and acquisitions in 2003 was long and varied. For example, on October 29, 2003, Applied Micro Circuits purchased JNI Corporation for $7.00 cash per share, in a deal valued at $209.2 million. JNI made enterprise storage connectivity products that Applied Micro Circuits used in its products. On October 28, 2003, palmOne Inc. (maker of the famous Palm Pilot lines of PDAs) purchased Handspring, Inc. (maker of another PDA brand, Treo). On March 26, 2003, K2 (the ski and in-line skate manufacturer) extended its operations into the sporting goods industry by purchasing Rawlings Sporting Goods (manufacturer of, among other things, most of the baseball gloves used in major league baseball). Each Rawlings shareholder received 1.08 shares of K2 stock. On September 3, 2003, Univision Communications (the leading broadcaster of Spanish-language programming on television) purchased Hispanic Broadcasting Corporation (a firm that owns over 40 Spanish-language radio stations). On September 26, 2003, Linamar Corp. (a firm that sells machined parts to the worldwide automobile industry) purchased Mclaren Performance Technologies (the firm that was originally created to develop and build race engines for Mclaren Formula One race cars) for $.8875 per share. And on March 3, 2003, Penn National Gaming (an owner and operator of riverboat casinos and other gambling venues) expanded its geographic reach by acquiring Hollywood Casinos for $12.75 a share.

That mergers and acquisitions are common is clear. What is less clear is that they actually generate value for firms implementing these strategies. Two cases will be examined here: mergers and acquisitions between strategically unrelated firms and mergers and acquisitions between strategically related firms.

Mergers and Acquisitions: The Unrelated Case

Imagine the following scenario: One firm (the target) is the object of an acquisition effort, and 10 firms (the bidders) are interested in making this acquisition. Suppose the **current market value** of the target firm is $10,000—that is, the price of each of this firm's shares times the number of shares outstanding equals $10,000. Also, suppose the current market value of each of the bidding firms is $15,000.[2] Finally, suppose there is no strategic relatedness between these bidding firms and the target. This means that the value of any one of these bidding firms when combined with the target firm exactly equals the sum of the value of these firms as separate entities. In this example, since the current market value of the target is $10,000, and the current market value of the bidding firms is $15,000, the value of this target when combined with any of these bidders would be $25,000 ($10,000 + $15,000). Given this information, at what price will this target be acquired, and what are the economic performance implications for bidding and target firms at this price?

In this, and all acquisition situations, bidding firms will be willing to pay a price for a target up to the value that the target firm adds to the bidder once it is acquired. This price is simply the difference between the value of the two firms combined (in this case $25,000) and the value of the bidding firm by itself (in this case $15,000). Notice that this price does not depend on the value of the target firm acting as an independent business but, rather, depends on the value that the target firm creates when it is combined with the bidding firm. Any price for a target less than this value (i.e., less than $10,000) will be a source of economic profit for a bidding firm; any price equal to this value (i.e., equal to $10,000) will be a source of zero economic profits; and any price greater than this value (i.e., greater than $10,000) will be a source of economic losses for the bidding firm that acquires the target.

It is not hard to see that the price of this acquisition will quickly rise to $10,000 and that at this price the bidding firm that acquires the target will earn zero economic profits. The price of this acquisition will quickly rise to $10,000 because any bid less than $10,000 will generate economic profits for a successful bidder. These potential profits, in turn, will generate entry into the bidding war for a target. Because entry into the acquisition contest is very likely, the price of the acquisition will quickly rise to its value, and economic profits will not be created.

Moreover, at this $10,000 price, the target firm's equity holders will also gain zero economic profits. Indeed, for them, all that has occurred is that the market value of the target firm has been capitalized in the form of a cash payment from the bidder to the target. The target was worth $10,000, and that is exactly what these equity holders will receive.

Mergers and Acquisitions: The Related Case

The conclusion that the acquisition of strategically unrelated targets will generate only zero economic profits for both the bidding and the target firms is not surprising. It is very consistent with the discussion of the economic consequences of unrelated diversification in Chapter 7. There it was argued that there is no economic justification for a corporate diversification strategy that does not build on some type of economy of scope across the businesses within which a firm operates, and thus that unrelated diversification is not an economically viable corporate strategy. So, if there is any hope that mergers and acquisitions will be a source of superior performance for bidding firms, it must be because of some sort of strategic relatedness or economy of scope between bidding and target firms.

Types of Strategic Relatedness

Of course, bidding and target firms can be strategically related in a wide variety of ways. Three particularly important lists of these potential linkages are discussed here.[3]

The FTC Categories. Because mergers and acquisitions can have the effect of increasing (or decreasing) the level of concentration in an industry, the Federal Trade Commission (FTC) is charged with the responsibility of evaluating the competitive implications of proposed mergers or acquisitions. In principle, the FTC will disallow any acquisition involving firms with headquarters in the United States that could have the potential for generating monopoly (or oligopoly) profits in an industry. To help in this regulatory effort, the FTC has developed a typology of mergers and acquisitions (see Table 10.1). Each category in this typology can be thought of as a different way in which a bidding firm and a target firm can be related in a merger or acquisition.

According to the FTC, a firm engages in a **vertical merger** when it vertically integrates, either forward or backward, through its acquisition efforts. Vertical mergers could include a firm purchasing critical suppliers of raw materials (backward vertical integration) or acquiring customers and distribution networks (forward vertical integration). Applied Micro Circuits' acquisition of JDI is an example of a backward vertical integration. Disney's acquisition of Capital Cities/ABC can be understood as an attempt by Disney to forward vertically integrate into the entertainment distribution industry, while its acquisition of ESPN can be seen as backward vertical integration into the entertainment production business.[4]

A firm engages in a **horizontal merger** when it acquires a former competitor; palmOne's acquisition of Handspring is an example of a horizontal merger.

Table 10.1   **FTC Categories of Mergers and Acquisitions**

■ Vertical merger	A firm acquires former suppliers or customers.
■ Horizontal merger	A firm acquires a former competitor.
■ Product extension merger	A firm gains access to complementary products through an acquisition.
■ Market extension merger	A firm gains access to complementary markets through an acquisition.
■ Conglomerate merger	There is no strategic relatedness between a bidding and a target firm.

Obviously, the FTC is particularly concerned with the competitive implications of horizontal mergers because these strategies can have the most direct and obvious anticompetitive implications in an industry. For example, the FTC raised antitrust concerns in the proposed merger between Oracle and PeopleSoft, because these firms, collectively, dominated the enterprise software market. Similar concerns were raised in the proposed merger between British Petroleum and Arco and the proposed merger between Mobil and Exxon.

The third type of merger identified by the FTC is a **product extension merger**. In a product extension merger, firms acquire complementary products through their merger and acquisition activities. Examples include K2's acquisition of Rawlings Sporting Goods, Univision's acquisition of Hispanic Broadcasting, and Linamar's acquisition of Mclaren Performance Technology.

The fourth type of merger identified by the FTC is a **market extension merger**. Here, the primary objective is to gain access to new geographic markets. Examples include Penn National Gaming's acquisition of Hollywood Casinos.

The final type of merger or acquisition identified by the FTC is a **conglomerate merger**. For the FTC, conglomerate mergers are a residual category. If there are no vertical, horizontal, product extension, or market extension links between firms, the FTC defines the merger or acquisition activity between firms as a conglomerate merger. Given our earlier conclusion that mergers or acquisitions between strategically *unrelated* firms will not generate economic profits for either bidders or targets, it should not be surprising that there are currently relatively few examples of conglomerate mergers or acquisitions; however, at various times in history, they have been relatively common. In the 1960s, for example, many acquisitions took the form of conglomerate mergers. Research has shown that the fraction of single-business firms in the *Fortune* 500 dropped from 22.8 percent in 1959 to 14.8 percent in 1969, while the fraction of firms in the *Fortune* 500 pursuing unrelated diversification strategies rose from 7.3 percent to 18.7 percent during the same time period. These findings are consistent with an increase in the number of conglomerate mergers and acquisitions during the 1960s.[5]

Despite the popularity of conglomerate mergers in the 1960s, many mergers or acquisitions among strategically unrelated firms are divested shortly after they are completed. One study estimated that over one-third of the conglomerate mergers of the 1960s were divested by the early 1980s. Another study showed that over 50 percent of these acquisitions were subsequently divested. These results are all consistent with our earlier conclusion that mergers or acquisitions involving strategically unrelated firms are not a source of economic profits.[6]

Other Types of Strategic Relatedness. Although the FTC categories of mergers and acquisitions provide some information about possible motives underlying these corporate strategies, they do not capture the full complexity of the links that might exist between bidding and target firms. Several authors have attempted to develop more complete lists of possible sources of relatedness between bidding and target firms. One of these lists, developed by Professor Michael Lubatkin, is summarized in Table 10.2. This list includes **technical economies** (in marketing, production, and similar forms of relatedness), **pecuniary economies** (market power), and **diversification economies** (in portfolio management and risk reduction) as possible bases of strategic relatedness between bidding and target firms.

A second important list of possible sources of strategic relatedness between bidding and target firms was developed by Michael Jensen and Richard Ruback after a comprehensive review of empirical research on the economic returns to mergers and acquisitions. This list is summarized in Table 10.3 and includes the following factors as

Table 10.2 **Lubatkin's List of Potential Sources of Strategic Relatedness Between Bidding and Target Firms**

Technical economies	Scale economies that occur when the physical processes inside a firm are altered so that the same amounts of input produce a higher quantity of outputs. Sources of technical economies include marketing, production, experience, scheduling, banking, and compensation.
Pecuniary economies	Economies achieved by the ability of firms to dictate prices by exerting market power.
Diversification economies	Economies achieved by improving a firm's performance relative to its risk attributes or lowering its risk attributes relative to its performance. Sources of diversification economies include portfolio management and risk reduction.

Sources: M. Lubatkin (1983). "Mergers and the performance of the acquiring firm." *Academy of Management Review*, 8, pp. 218–225. © 1983 by Academy of Management. Reproduced with permission.

possible sources of economic gains in mergers and acquisitions: potential reductions in production or distribution costs (from economies of scale, vertical integration, reduction in agency costs, and so forth); the realization of financial opportunities (such as gaining access to underutilized tax shields, avoiding bankruptcy costs); the creation of market power; and the ability to eliminate inefficient management in the target firm.

To be economically valuable, links between bidding and target firms must meet the same criteria as diversification strategies (see Chapter 7). First, these links must build on real economies of scope between bidding and target firms. These economies of scope can reflect either cost savings or revenue enhancements that are created by combining firms. Second, not only must this economy of scope exist but it must be less costly for the merged firm to realize than for outside equity holders to realize on their own. As is the case with corporate diversification strategies, by investing in a diversified portfolio of stocks, outside equity investors can gain many

Table 10.3 **Jensen and Ruback's List of Reasons Why Bidding Firms Might Want to Engage in Merger and Acquisition Strategies**

To reduce production or distribution costs:
1. Through economies of scale.
2. Through vertical integration.
3. Through the adoption of more efficient production or organizational technology.
4. Through the increased utilization of the bidder's management team.
5. Through a reduction of agency costs by bringing organization-specific assets under common ownership.

Financial motivations:
1. To gain access to underutilized tax shields.
2. To avoid bankruptcy costs.
3. To increase leverage opportunities.
4. To gain other tax advantages.

To gain market power in product markets.

To eliminate inefficient target management.

Sources: M. C. Jensen and R. S. Ruback (1983). "The market for corporate control: The scientific evidence." *Journal of Financial Economics*, 11, pp. 5–50. Vol. II. © 1983.

of the economies associated with a merger or acquisition on their own. Moreover, investors can realize some of these economies of scope at almost zero cost. In this situation, it makes little sense for investors to "hire" managers in firms to realize these economies of scope for them through a merger or acquisition. Rather, firms should pursue merger and acquisition strategies only to obtain valuable economies of scope that outside investors find too costly to create on their own.

Economic Profits in Related Acquisitions

If bidding and target firms are strategically related, then the economic value of these two firms combined is greater than their economic value as separate entities. To see how this changes returns to merger and acquisition strategies, consider the following scenario: As before, there is one target firm and ten bidding firms. The market value of the target firm as a stand-alone entity is $10,000, and the market value of the bidding firms as stand-alone entities is $15,000. However, unlike the earlier scenario in this chapter, the bidding and target firms are strategically related. Any of the types of relatedness identified in Tables 10.1, 10.2, or 10.3 could be the source of these economies of scope. They imply that when any of the bidding firms and the target are combined, the market value of this combined entity will be $32,000—note that $32,000 is greater than the sum of $15,000 and $10,000. At what price will this target firm be acquired, and what are the economic profit implications for bidding and target firms at this price?

As before, bidding firms will be willing to pay a price for a target up to the value that a target firm adds once it is acquired. Thus, the maximum price bidding firms are willing to pay is still the difference between the value of the combined entity (here, $32,000) and the value of a bidding firm on its own (here, $15,000), or $17,000.

As was the case for the strategically unrelated acquisition, it is not hard to see that the price for actually acquiring the target firm in this scenario will rapidly rise to $17,000, because any bid less than $17,000 has the potential for generating profits for a bidding firm. Suppose that one bidding firm offers $13,000 for the target. For this $13,000, the bidding firm gains access to a target that will generate $17,000 of value once it is acquired. Thus, to this bidding firm, the target is worth $17,000, and a bid of $13,000 will generate $4,000 economic profit. Of course, these potential profits will motivate entry into the competitive bidding process. Entry will continue until the price of this target equals $17,000. Any price greater than $17,000 would mean that a bidding firm is actually losing money on its acquisition.[7]

At this $17,000 price, the successful bidding firm earns zero economic profits. After all, this firm has acquired an asset that will generate $17,000 of value and has paid $17,000 to do so. However, the owners of the target firm will earn an economic profit worth $7,000. As a stand-alone firm, the target is worth $10,000; when combined with a bidding firm, it is worth $17,000. The difference between the value of the target as a stand-alone entity and its value in combination with a bidding firm is the value of the economic profit that can be appropriated by the owners of the target firm.

Thus, the existence of strategic relatedness between bidding and target firms is not a sufficient condition for the equity holders of bidding firms to earn economic profits from their acquisition strategies. If the economic potential of acquiring a particular target firm is widely known and if several potential bidding firms can all obtain this value by acquiring a target, the equity holders of bidding firms will, at best, earn only zero economic profits from implementing an acquisition strategy. In this setting, a "strategically related" merger or acquisition will create economic value, but this value will be distributed in the form of economic profits to the equity holders of acquired target firms.

Since so much of the value created in a merger or acquisition is appropriated by the stockholders of the target firm, it is not surprising that many small and entrepreneurial firms look to be acquired as one way to compensate their owners for taking the risks associated with founding these firms. This phenomenon is discussed in more detail in the Strategy in the Emerging Enterprise feature.

Strategy in the Emerging Enterprise

*I*magine you are an entrepreneur. You have mortgaged your home, taken out loans, run up your credit cards, and put all you own on the line in order to help grow a small company. And finally, after years of effort, things start going well. Your product or service starts to sell, customers start to appreciate your unique value proposition, and you actually begin to pay yourself a reasonable salary. What do you do next to help grow your company?

Some entrepreneurs in this situation decide that maintaining their control of the firm is very important. These entrepreneurs may compensate certain critical employees with equity in the firm, but typically limit the number of outsiders who make equity investments in their firm. To grow these closely held firms, these entrepreneurs must rely on capital generated from their ongoing operations (called **retained earnings**) and debt capital provided by banks, customers, and suppliers. Entrepreneurs who decide to maintain control of their companies are compensated for taking the risks associated with starting a firm through the salary they pay themselves.

Other entrepreneurs get more outside equity investors involved in providing the capital a firm needs to grow. These outside investors might include wealthy individuals—called **business angels**—looking to invest in entrepreneurial ventures or **venture capital firms**. Venture capital firms typically raise money from numerous smaller investors which they then

Cashing Out

invest in a portfolio of entrepreneurial firms. Over time, many of these firms decide to "go public" by engaging in what is called an **initial public offering**, or **IPO**. In an IPO, a firm, typically working with an investment banker, sells its equity to the public at large. Entrepreneurs who decide to sell equity in their firm are compensated for taking the risks associated with starting a firm through the sale of their equity on the public markets through an IPO. An entrepreneur who receives compensation for risk-taking in this manner is said to be **cashing out**.

Finally, still other entrepreneurs may decide to not use an IPO to cash out, but rather to have their firm acquired by another, typically larger, firm. In this scenario, entrepreneurs are compensated by the acquiring firm for

taking the risks associated with starting a firm. Indeed, because the demand for IPOs has been volatile since the technology bubble burst of 2000, more and more smaller and entrepreneurial firms are looking to be acquired as a way for their founders to cash out. Moreover, since the stockholders of target firms typically appropriate a large percentage of the total value created by an acquisition, and since the founders of these entrepreneurial firms are also often large stockholders, being acquired is often a source of great wealth for an entrepreneurial firm's founders.

The choice between keeping a firm private, going public, or being acquired is a difficult and multidimensional one. Issues including the personal preferences of a firm's founders, demand for IPOs, how much capital a firm will need in order to continue to grow its business, and what other resources—besides capital—it will need to create additional value all play a role. In general, firms that do not need a great deal of money or other resources to grow will choose to remain private. Those that need only money to grow will choose IPOs, while those that need managerial or technical resources controlled by another firm to grow will typically be acquired. Of course, all this changes if entrepreneurs decide to maintain control of their firms because they want to.

Sources: R. Hennessey (2004). "Underwriters cut prices on IPOs as market softens." *Wall Street Journal*, May 27, p. C4; F. Vogelstein (2003). "Can Google grow up?" *Fortune*, December 8, pp. 102 +.

What Does Research Say About Returns to Mergers and Acqusitions?

The empirical implications of this discussion of returns to bidding and target firms in strategically related and strategically unrelated mergers and acquisitions have been examined in a variety of academic literatures. One study reviewed over 40 empirical merger and acquisition studies in the finance literature. This study concluded that acquisitions, on average, increased the market value of target firms by about 25 percent and left the market value of bidding firms unchanged. The authors of this report concluded that "corporate takeovers generate positive gains, ... target firm equity holders benefit, and ... bidding firm equity holders do not lose."[8] The way these studies evaluate the return to acquisition strategies is discussed in the Strategy in Depth feature.

Strategy researchers have also attempted to examine in more detail the sources of value creation in mergers and acquisitions and the question of whether these sources of value creation affect whether bidders or targets appropriate this value. For example, two well-known studies examined the impact of the type and degree of strategic relatedness (defined using the FTC typology summarized in Table 10.1) between bidding and target firms on the economic consequences of mergers and acquisitions.[9] These studies found that the more strategically related bidding and target firms are, the more economic value mergers and acquisitions create. However, like the finance studies, this work found that this economic value was appropriated by the owners of the target firm, regardless of the type or degree of relatedness between bidding and target firms. Bidding firms—even when they attempt to acquire strategically related targets—earn, on average, zero economic profits from their merger and acquisition strategies.

Why Are There So Many Mergers and Acquisitions?

Given the overwhelming empirical evidence that most of the economic value created in mergers and acquisitions is appropriated by the owners of the target firm most of the time, an important question becomes: " Why do managers of bidding firms continue to engage in merger and acquisition strategies?" Some possible explanations are summarized in Table 10.4 and discussed in this section.

To Ensure Survival
Even if mergers and acquisitions, on average, generate only zero economic profits for bidding firms, it may be necessary for bidding firms to engage in these activities to ensure their survival. In particular, if all of a bidding firm's competitors have been able to improve their efficiency and effectiveness

Table 10.4 **Possible Motivations to Engage in Mergers and Acquisitions Even Though They Usually Do Not Generate Profits for Bidding Firms**

1. To ensure survival
2. Free cash flow
3. Agency problems
4. Managerial hubris
5. The potential for above-normal profits

Strategy in Depth

By far, the most popular way to evaluate the performance effects of acquisitions for bidding firms is called **event study analysis**. Rooted in the field of financial economics, event study analysis compares the actual performance of a stock after an acquisition has been announced to the expected performance of that stock, if no acquisition had been announced. Any performance greater (or less) than what was expected in a short period of time around when an acquisition is announced is attributed to that acquisition. This **cumulative abnormal return** or **CAR** can be positive or negative, depending on whether the stock in question performs better or worse than what was expected without an acquisition.

The CAR created by an acquisition is calculated in several stages. First, the expected performance of a stock, without an acquisition, is estimated with the following regression equation:

$$E(R_{j,t}) = a_j + b_j R_{m,t} + e_{j,t}$$

Where $E(R_{j,t})$ is the expected return of stock j during time t, a_j is a constant (approximately equal to the rate of return on risk-free equities), b_j is an empirical estimate of the financial parameter β (equal to the covariance between the returns of a particular firm's stock and the average return of all stocks in the market, over time), $R_{m,t}$ is the actual average rate of return of all stocks in the market over time, and $e_{j,t}$ is an error term. The form of this equation is derived from the capital asset pricing model in finance. In this model, $E(R_{j,t})$ is simply the expected performance of a stock, given

Evaluating the Performance Effects of Acquisitions

the historical relationship between that stock and the overall performance of the stock market.

To calculate the unexpected performance of a stock, this expected level of performance is simply subtracted from the actual level of performance for a stock. This is done in the following equation:

$$XR_{j,t} = R_{j,t} - (a_j + b_j R_{m,t})$$

where $R_{j,t}$ is the actual performance of stock j during time t, and $XR_{j,t}$ is the unexpected performance of stock j during time t.

In calculating the CAR for a particular acquisition, it is necessary to sum the unexpected returns ($XR_{j,t}$) for a stock across the t periods when the stock market is responding to news about this acquisition. Most analyses of acquisitions examine the market's reaction one day before an acquisition is formally announced to three days after it is announced. The sum of these

unexpected returns over this time period is the CAR attributable to this acquisition.

This methodology has been applied to literally thousands of acquisition episodes. For example, when Manulife Financial purchased John Hancock Financial, Manulife's CAR was −10%, while John Hancock's CAR was +6%. When Anthem acquired Wellpoint, Anthem's CAR was −10% and Wellpoint's was +7%. When Bank of America acquired FleetBoston Financial, Bank of America's CAR was −9% and FleetBoston's was +24%. And when UnitedHealth acquired Mid Atlantic Medical, UnitedHealth's CAR was −4% and Mid Atlantic Medical's was +11%.

While the event study method has been used widely, it does have some important limitations. First, it is based entirely on the capital asset pricing model and there is some reason to believe that this model is not a particularly good predictor of a firm's expected stock price. Second, it assumes that a firm's equity holders can anticipate all the benefits associated with making an acquisition at the time that acquisition is made. Some scholars have argued that value creation continues long after an acquisition is announced as parties in this exchange discover value-creating opportunities that could not have been anticipated.

Sources: A. Arikan (2004). "Long-term returns to acquisitions: The case of purchasing tangible and intangible assets." Unpublished, Fisher College of Business, Ohio State University; S. J. Brown and J. B. Warner (1985). "Using daily stock returns: The case of event studies." *Journal of Financial Economics,* 14, pp. 3–31; D. Henry, M. Der Hovanseian, and D. Foust (2003). "M&A deals: Show me." *BusinessWeek,* November 10, pp. 38 +.

through a particular type of acquisition, then failing to make such an acquisition may put a firm at a competitive disadvantage. Here, the purpose of a merger or acquisition is not to gain competitive advantages but rather to gain competitive parity.

Many recent mergers among banks in the United States seem to have competitive parity and normal economic profits as an objective. Most bank managers recognize that changing bank regulations, increased competition from nonbanking financial institutions, and soft demand are likely to lead to a consolidation of the U.S. banking industry. To survive in this consolidated industry, many U.S. banks will have to merge. As the number of banks engaging in mergers and acquisitions goes up, the ability to earn superior profits from those strategies goes down. These lower returns from acquisitions have already reduced the economic value of some of the most aggressive acquiring banks. Despite these lower returns, acquisitions are likely to continue for the foreseeable future, as banks seek survival opportunities in a consolidated industry.[10]

Free Cash Flow

Another reason why firms may continue to invest in merger and acquisition strategies is that these strategies, on average, can be expected to generate at least competitive parity for bidding firms. This zero economic profit may be a more attractive investment for some firms than alternative strategic investments. This is particularly the case for firms that generate free cash flow.[11]

Free cash flow is simply the amount of cash a firm has to invest after all positive net present-value investments in its ongoing businesses have been funded. Free cash flow is created when a firm's ongoing business operations are very profitable but offer few opportunities for additional investment. One firm that seems to have generated a great deal of free cash flow over the last several years is Philip Morris. Philip Morris's retail tobacco operations are extremely profitable. However, regulatory constraints, health concerns, and slowing growth in demand limit investment opportunities in the tobacco industry. Thus, the amount of cash generated by Philip Morris's ongoing tobacco business has probably been larger than the sum of its positive net present-value investments in that business. This difference is free cash flow for Philip Morris.[12]

A firm that generates a great deal of free cash flow must decide what to do with this money. One obvious alternative would be to give it to stockholders in the form of dividends or stock buybacks. However, in some situations (for example, when stockholders face high marginal tax rates), stockholders may prefer a firm to retain this cash flow and invest it for them. When this is the case, how should a firm invest its free cash flow?

Because (by definition) no positive net present-value investment opportunities in a firm's ongoing business operations are available, firms have only two investment options: to invest their free cash flow in strategies that generated competitive parity or in strategies that generate competitive disadvantages. In this context, merger and acquisition strategies are a viable option, for bidding firms, on average, can expect to generate at least competitive parity. Put differently, while mergers and acquisitions may not be a source of superior profits, there are worse things you could do with your free cash flow.

Agency Problems

Another reason why firms might continue to engage in mergers and acquisitions, despite earning only competitive parity from doing so, is that mergers and acquisitions benefit managers directly, independent of any value they may or may not create for a bidding firm's stockholders. As suggested in Chapter 8, these conflicts of interest are a manifestation of agency problems between a firm's managers and its stockholders.

Merger and acquisition strategies can benefit managers—even if they do not directly benefit a bidding firm's equity holders—in at least two ways. First, managers can use mergers and acquisitions to help diversify their human capital investments in their firm. As discussed in Chapter 7, managers have difficulty diversifying their firm-specific human capital investments when a firm operates in a narrow range of businesses. By acquiring firms with cash flows that are not perfectly correlated with the cash flows of a firm's current businesses, managers can reduce the probability of bankruptcy for their firm and thus partially diversify their human capital investments in their firm.

Second, managers can use mergers and acquisitions to quickly increase firm size, measured in either sales or assets. If management compensation is closely linked to firm size, managers who increase firm size are able to increase their compensation. Of all the ways to increase the size of a firm quickly, growth through mergers and acquisitions is perhaps the easiest. Even if there are no economies of scope between a bidding and a target firm, an acquisition ensures that the bidding firm will grow by the size of the target (measured in either sales or assets). If there are economies of scope between a bidding and a target firm, the size of the bidding firm can grow at an even faster rate, as can the value of management's compensation, even though, on average, acquisitions do not generate wealth for the owners of the bidding firm.

Managerial Hubris

Another reason why managers may choose to continue to invest in mergers and acquisitions, despite the fact that, on average, they gain no profits from doing so, is the existence of what has been called **managerial hubris**.[13] This is the unrealistic belief held by managers in bidding firms that they can manage the assets of a target firm more efficiently than the target firm's current management. This notion can lead bidding firms to engage in acquisition strategies even though there may not be positive economic profits from doing so.

The existence of managerial hubris suggests that the economic value of bidding firms will fall once they announce a merger or acquisition strategy. Although managers in bidding firms might truly believe that they can manage a target firm's assets more efficiently than the target firm's managers, investors in the capital markets are much less likely to be caught up in this hubris. In this context, a commitment to a merger or acquisition strategy is a strong signal that a bidding firm's management has deluded itself about its abilities to manage a target firm's assets. Such delusions will certainly adversely affect the economic value of the bidding firm.

Of course, empirical work on mergers and acquisitions discussed earlier in this chapter has concluded that although bidding firms do not obtain profits from their merger and acquisition strategies, they also do not, on average, reduce their economic value from implementing these strategies. This is inconsistent with the "hubris hypothesis." However, the fact that, on average, bidding firms do not lose economic value does not mean that *some* bidding firms do not lose economic value. Thus, although it is unlikely that all merger and acquisition strategies are motivated by managerial hubris, it is likely that at least some of them are.[14]

The Potential for Economic Profits

A final reason why managers might continue to pursue merger and acquisition strategies is the potential that these strategies offer for generating profits for at least some bidding firms. The empirical research on returns to bidding firms in mergers and acquisitions is very strong. On average, bidding firms do not gain profits from their merger and acquisition strategies. However, the fact that bidding firms, *on average*, do not earn profits on these strategies does not mean that *all* bidding firms will *always* fail to earn profits. In some situations bidding firms may be able to gain competitive advantages from merger and acquisition activities. These situations are discussed in the following section.

Mergers and Acquisitions and Sustained Competitive Advantage

VRIO

We have already seen that the economies of scope that motivate mergers and acquisitions between strategically related bidding and target firms can be valuable. However, the ability of these economies to generate profits and competitive advantages for bidding firms depends not only on their economic value but also on the competitiveness of the market for corporate control through which these valuable economies are realized. The **market for corporate control** is the market that is created when multiple firms actively seek to acquire one or several firms. Only when the market for corporate control is imperfectly competitive might it be possible for bidding firms to earn profits from implementing a merger or acquisition strategy. To see how the competitiveness of the market for corporate control can affect returns to merger and acquisition strategies, we will consider three scenarios involving bidding and target firms and examine their implications for the managers of these firms.[15]

Valuable, Rare, and Private Economies of Scope

An imperfectly competitive market for corporate control can exist when a target is worth more to one bidder than it is to any other bidders and when no other firms—including bidders and targets—are aware of this additional value. In this setting, the price of a target will rise to reflect public expectations about the value of the target. Once the target is acquired, however, the performance of the special bidder that acquires the target will be greater than generally expected, and this level of performance will generate profits for the equity holders of the bidding firm.

Consider a simple case. Suppose the market value of bidder Firm A combined with target firms is $12,000, whereas the market value of all other bidders combined with targets is $10,000. No other firms (bidders or targets) are aware of Firm A's unique relationship with these targets, but they are aware of the value of all other bidders combined with targets (that is, $10,000). Suppose also that the market value of all bidding firms, as stand-alone entities, is $7,000. In this setting, Firm A will be willing to pay up to $5,000 to acquire a target ($12,000 − $7,000), and all other bidders will only be willing to pay up to $3,000 to acquire a target ($10,000 − $7,000).

Because publicly available information suggests that acquiring a target is worth $3,000 more than the target's stand-alone price, the price of targets will rapidly rise to this level, ensuring that if bidding firms, apart from Firm A, acquire a target, they will obtain no profits. If there is only one target in this market for corporate control, then Firm A will be able to bid slightly more than $3,000 (perhaps $3,001) for this target. No other firms will bid higher than Firm A because, from their point of view, the acquisition is simply not worth more than $3,000. At this $3,001 price, Firm A will earn a profit of $1,999—Firm A had to spend only $3,001 for a firm that brings $5,000 in value above its stand-alone market price. Alternatively, if there are multiple targets, then several bidding firms, including Firm A, will pay $3,000 for their targets. At this price, these bidding firms will all earn zero economic profits, except for Firm A, which will earn an economic profit equal to $2,000. That is, only Firm A will gain a competitive advantage from acquiring a target in this market.

In order for Firm A to obtain this profit, the value of Firm A's economy of scope with target firms must be greater than the value of any other bidding firms with that target. This special value will generally reflect unusual resources and capabilities possessed by Firm A—resources and capabilities that are more valuable in combination with target firms than are the resources and capabilities that other bidding firms possess. Put differently, to be a source of economic profits and competitive advantage, Firm A's link with targets must be based on firm resources and capabilities that are rare among those firms competing in this market for corporate control.

However, not only does Firm A have to possess valuable and rare links with bidding firms to gain economic profits and competitive advantages from its acquisition strategies, but information about these special economies of scope must not be known by other firms. If other bidding firms know about the additional value associated with acquiring a target, they are likely to try to duplicate this value for themselves. Typically, they would accomplish this by imitating the type of relatedness that exists between Firm A and its targets, by developing the resources and capabilities that enabled Firm A to have its valuable economies of scope with targets. Once other bidders developed the resources and capabilities necessary to obtain this more valuable economy of scope, they would be able to enter into bidding, thereby increasing the likelihood that the equity holders of successful bidding firms would earn no economic profits.

Target firms must also be unaware of Firm A's special resources and capabilities if Firm A is to obtain competitive advantages from an acquisition. If target firms were aware of this extra value available to Firm A, along with the sources of this value, they could inform other bidding firms. These bidding firms could then adjust their bids to reflect this higher value, and competitive bidding would reduce profits to bidders. Target firms are likely to inform bidding firms in this way because increasing the number of bidders with more valuable economies of scope increases the likelihood that target firms will extract all the economic value created in a merger or acquisition.[16]

Valuable, Rare, and Costly-to-Imitate Economies of Scope

The existence of firms that have valuable, rare, and private economies of scope with targets is not the only way that the market for corporate control can be imperfectly competitive. If other bidders cannot imitate one bidder's valuable and rare economies with targets, then competition in this market for corporate control will be imperfect, and the equity holders of this special bidding firm will earn economic profits. In this case, the existence of valuable and rare economies does not need to be private, because other bidding firms cannot imitate these economies, and therefore bids that substantially reduce the profits for the equity holders of the special bidding firm are not forthcoming.

Typically, bidding firms will be unable to imitate one bidder's valuable and rare economies of scope with targets when the strategic relatedness between the special bidder and the targets stems from some rare and costly-to-imitate resources or capabilities controlled by the special bidding firm. Any of the costly-to-imitate resources and capabilities discussed in Chapter 3 could create costly-to-imitate economies of scope between a firm and a target. If, in addition, these economies are valuable and rare, they can be a source of profits to the equity holders of the special bidding firm. This can happen even if all firms in this market for corporate control are aware of the more valuable economies of scope available to this firm and its sources. Although information about this special economy of scope is publicly available, equity holders of special bidding firms will earn a profit when acquisition occurs. The equity holders of target firms will not obtain all of this profit, because competitive bidding dynamics cannot unfold when the sources of a more valuable economy of scope are costly to imitate.

Of course, it may be possible for a valuable, rare, and costly-to-imitate economy of scope between a bidding and a target firm to also be private. Indeed, it is often the case that those attributes of a firm that are costly to imitate are also difficult to describe and thus can be held as proprietary information. In that case, the analysis of profits associated with valuable, rare, and private economies of scope presented earlier applies.

Unexpected Valuable Economies of Scope Between Bidding and Target Firms

Thus far, this discussion has adopted, for convenience, the strong assumption that the present value of the strategic relatedness between bidders and targets is known with certainty by individual bidders. This is, in principle, possible but certainly not likely. Most modern acquisitions and mergers are massively complex, involving numerous unknown and complicated relationships between firms. In these settings, unexpected events after an acquisition has been completed may make an acquisition or merger more valuable than bidders and targets anticipated it would be. The price that bidding firms will pay to acquire a target will equal the expected value of the target only when the target is combined with the bidder. The difference between the unexpected value of an acquisition actually obtained by a bidder and the price the bidder paid for the acquisition is a profit for the equity holders of the bidding firm.

Of course, by definition, bidding firms cannot expect to obtain unexpected value from an acquisition. Unexpected value, in this context, is a surprise, a manifestation of a bidding firm's good luck, not its skill in acquiring targets. For example, when the British advertising firm WPP acquired J. Walter Thompson for $550 million, it discovered some property owned by J. Walter Thomson in Tokyo. No one knew of this property when the firm was acquired. It turned out to be worth over $100 million after taxes, a financial windfall that helped offset the high cost of this acquisition. When asked, Martin Sorrel, president of WPP and the architect of this acquisition, admitted that this $100 million windfall was simply good luck.[17]

Implications for Bidding Firm Managers

The existence of valuable, rare, and private economies of scope between bidding and target firms, and of valuable, rare, and costly-to-imitate economies of scope between bidding and target firms suggests that although, on average, most bidding firms do not generate competitive advantages from their acquisition strategies, in some special circumstances it may be possible for them to do so. Thus, the task facing managers in firms contemplating merger and acquisition strategies is to choose strategies that have the greatest likelihood of being able to generate profits for their equity holders. Several important managerial prescriptions can be derived from this discussion. These "rules" for bidding firm managers are summarized in Table 10.5.

Search for Rare Economies of Scope

One of the main reasons why bidding firms do not obtain competitive advantages from acquiring strategically related target firms is that several other bidding firms value the target firm in the same way. When multiple bidders all value a target in the same way, competitive bidding is likely. Competitive bidding, in turn, drives out the potential for superior performance. To avoid this problem, bidding firms should seek to acquire targets with which they enjoy valuable and rare linkages.

Operationally, the search for rare economies of scope suggests that managers in bidding firms need to consider not only the value of a target firm when combined with their own company, but also the value of a target firm when combined with other potential bidders. This is important because it is the difference between the value of a particular bidding firm's relationship with a target and the value of other bidding firms' relationships with that target that defines the size of the potential economic profits from an acquisition.

In practice, the search for valuable and rare economies of scope is likely to become a search for valuable and rare resources already controlled by a firm that are synergistically related to a target. For example, if a bidding firm has a unique reputation in its product market, and if the target firm's products could benefit by association with that reputation, then the target firm may be more valuable to this particular bidder than to other bidders (firms that do not possess this special reputation). Also, if a particular bidder possesses the largest market share in its industry, the best distribution system, or restricted access to certain key raw materials, and if the target firm would benefit from being associated with these valuable and rare resources, then the acquisition of this target may be a source of economic profits.

The search for valuable and rare economies of scope as a basis of mergers and acquisitions tends to rule out certain interfirm linkages as sources of economic profits. For example, most acquisitions can lead to a reduction in overhead costs, because much of the corporate overhead associated with the target firm can be eliminated subsequent to acquisition. However, the ability to eliminate these overhead costs is not unique to any one bidder, and thus the value created by these reduced costs will usually be captured by the equity holders of the target firm.

Table 10.5   **Rules for Bidding Firm Managers**

1. Search for valuable and rare economies of scope.
2. Keep information away from other bidders.
3. Keep information away from targets.
4. Avoid winning bidding wars.
5. Close the deal quickly.
6. Operate in "thinly traded" acquisition markets.

Keep Information Away from Other Bidders

One of the keys to earning superior performance in an acquisition strategy is to avoid multiple bidders for a single target. One way to accomplish this is to keep information about the bidding process, and about the sources of economies of scope between a bidder and target that underlie this bidding process, as private as possible. In order for other firms to become involved in bidding for a target, they must be aware of the value of the economies of scope between themselves and that target. If only one bidding firm knows this information, and if this bidding firm can close the deal before the full value of the target is known, then it may gain a competitive advantage from completing this acquisition.

Of course, in many circumstances, keeping all this information private is difficult. Often, it is illegal. For example, when seeking to acquire a publicly traded firm, potential bidders must meet disclosure requirements that effectively reduce the amount of private information a bidder can retain. In these circumstances, unless a bidding firm has some valuable, rare, and costly-to-imitate economy of scope with a target firm, the possibility of economic profits coming from an acquisition is very low. It is not surprising that the research conducted on mergers and acquisitions of firms traded on public stock exchanges governed by the U.S. Securities and Exchange Commission (SEC) disclosure rules suggests that, most of the time, bidding firms do not earn economic profits from implementing their acquisition strategies.

However, not all potential targets are publicly traded. Privately held firms may be acquired in an information environment that can create opportunities for above-normal performance for bidding firms. Moreover, even when acquiring a publicly traded firm, a bidder does not have to release all the information it has about the potential value of that target in combination with itself. Indeed, if some of this value reflects a bidding firm's taken-for-granted "invisible" assets, it may not be possible to communicate this information. In this case, as well, there may be opportunities for competitive advantages for bidding firms.

Keep Information Away from Targets

Not only should bidding firms keep information about the value of their economy of scope with a target away from other bidders; they should also keep this information away from target firms. Suppose that the value of a target firm to a bidding firm is $8,000 but the bidding firm, in an attempt to earn economic profits, has bid only $5,000 for the target. If the target knows that it is actually worth $8,000, it is very likely to hold out for a higher bid. In fact, the target may contact other potential bidding firms and tell them of the opportunity created by the $5,000 bid. As the number of bidders goes up, the possibility of superior economic performance for bidders goes down. Therefore, to keep the possibility of these profits alive, bidding firms must not fully reveal the value of their economies of scope with a target firm. Again, in some circumstances, it is very difficult, or even illegal, to attempt to limit the flow of information to target firms. In these settings, superior economic performance for bidding firms is very unlikely.

Limiting the amount of information that flows to the target firm may have some other consequences as well. For example, it has been shown that a complete sharing of information, insights, and perspectives before an acquisition is completed increases the probability that economies of scope will actually be realized once it is completed.[18] By limiting the flow of information between itself and a target, a bidding firm may actually be increasing the cost of integrating the target into its ongoing business, thereby jeopardizing at least some of the superior economic performance that limiting information flow is designed to create. Bidding firms will need to carefully balance the economic benefits of limiting the information they share with the target firm against the costs that limiting information flow may create.

Avoid Winning Bidding Wars

It should be reasonably clear that if a number of firms bid for the same target, the probability that the firm that successfully acquires the target will gain competitive advantages is very low. Indeed, to ensure that competitive bidding occurs, target firms can actively encourage other bidding firms to enter into the bidding process. The implications of these arguments are clear: Bidding firms should generally avoid winning a bidding war. To "win" a bidding war, a bidding firm will often have to pay a price at least equal to the full value of the target. Many times, given the emotions of an intense bidding contest, the winning bid may actually be larger than the true value of the target. Completing this type of acquisition will certainly reduce the economic performance of the bidding firm.

The only time it might make sense to "win" a bidding war is when the winning firm possesses a rare and private or a rare and costly-to-imitate economy of scope with a target that is more valuable than the strategic relatedness that exists between any other bidders and that target. In this setting, the winning firm may be able to earn a profit if it is able to fully realize the value of its relationship with the target.

Close the Deal Quickly

Another rule of thumb for obtaining superior performance from implementing merger and acquisition strategies is to close the deal quickly. All the economic processes that make it difficult for bidding firms to earn economic profits from acquiring a strategically related target take time to unfold. It takes time for other bidders to become aware of the economic value associated with acquiring a target; it takes time for the target to recruit other bidders; information leakage becomes more of a problem over time; and so forth. A bidding firm that begins and ends the bidding process quickly may forestall some of these processes and thereby retain some superior performance for itself.

The admonition to close the deal quickly should not be taken to mean that bidding firms need to make their acquisition decisions quickly. Indeed, the search for valuable and rare economies of scope should be undertaken with great care. There should be little rush in isolating and evaluating acquisition candidates. However, once a target firm has been located and valued, bidding firms have a strong incentive to reduce the period of time between the first bid and the completion of the deal. The longer this period of negotiation the less likely it is that the bidding firm will earn economic profits from the acquisition.

Complete Acquisitions in "Thinly Traded" Markets

Finally, an acquisition strategy can be a source of economic profits to bidding firms if these firms implement this corporate strategy in what could be described as "thinly traded markets." In general, a **thinly traded market** is a market where there are only a small number of buyers and sellers, where information about opportunities in this market is not widely known, and where interests besides purely maximizing the value of a firm can be important. In the context of mergers and acquisitions, thinly traded markets are markets where only a few (often only one) firms are implementing acquisition strategies. These unique firms may be the only firms that understand the full value of the acquisition opportunities in this market. Even target firm managers may not fully understand the value of the economic opportunities in these markets, and if they do, they may have other interests besides maximizing the value of their firm if it becomes the object of a takeover.

In general, thinly traded merger and acquisition markets are highly fragmented. Competition in these markets occurs at the local level, as one local small firm competes with other local small firms for a common group of geographically defined customers. Most of these small firms are privately held. Many are sole proprietorships. Examples of these thinly traded markets have included, at various points in history, the printing industry, the fast-food industry, the used car industry, the dry cleaning industry, and the barber shop/hair salon industry.

As was suggested in Chapter 2, the major opportunity in all highly fragmented industries is consolidation. In the context of mergers and acquisitions, consolidation can occur by one firm (or a small number of firms) buying numerous independent firms to realize economies of scope in these industries. Often, these economies of scope reflect economies of scale in these industries—economies of scale that were not realized in a highly fragmented setting. As long as the number of firms implementing this consolidation strategy is small, then the market for corporate control in these markets will probably be less than perfectly competitive and opportunities for profits from implementing an acquisition strategy may be possible.

More generally, if a merger or acquisition contest is played out through full-page ads in the *Wall Street Journal*, the ability of bidding firms to gain competitive advantages from their acquisitions is limited. Such highly public acquisitions are likely to lead to very competitive markets for corporate control. Competitive markets for corporate control, in turn, assure that the equity holders of the target firm will appropriate any value that could be created by an acquisition. However, if these contests occur in obscure, out-of-the-way industries, it is more likely that bidding firms will be able to earn profits from their acquisitions.

Service Corporation International: An Example

Empirical research on mergers and acquisitions suggests that it is not easy for bidding firms to earn economic profits from these strategies. However, it may be possible for some bidding firms, some of the time, to do so. One firm that has been successful in gaining competitive advantages from its merger and acquisition strategies is Service Corporation International (SCI). SCI is in the funeral home and cemetery business. It grew from a collection of five funeral homes in 1967 to being the largest owner of cemeteries and funeral homes in the United States today. It has done this through an aggressive and what was until recently a highly profitable acquisitions program in this historically fragmented industry.

The valuable and rare economy of scope that SCI brought to the funeral home industry is the application of traditional business practices in a highly fragmented and not often professionally managed industry. SCI-owned funeral homes operate with gross margins approaching 30 percent, nearly three times the gross margins of independently owned funeral homes. Among other things, higher margins reflected savings from centralized purchasing services, centralized embalming and professional services, and the sharing of underutilized resources (including hearses) among funeral homes within geographic regions. SCI's scale advantages made a particular funeral home more valuable to SCI than to one of SCI's smaller competitors, and more valuable than if a particular funeral home was left as a stand-alone business.

Moreover, the funeral homes that SCI targeted for acquisition were, typically, family owned and lacked heirs to continue the business. Many of the owner or operators of these funeral homes were not fully aware of the value of their operations to SCI (they are morticians more than business managers), nor were they just interested in maximizing the sale price of their funeral homes. Rather, they were often looking to maintain continuity of service in a community, secure employment for

Global Perspectives

*I*n the late 1980s, managers at Ford Motor Company faced a problem. While Ford had been able to get its quality on par with the best manufacturers—through its "Quality Is Job One" program—worldwide competition in small and medium-sized cars had reduced the profit margin on Ford's small-car lines to almost nothing. The only cars that continued to deliver high profit margins to Ford were its luxury cars—the Lincoln and related cars. Unfortunately, Lincoln was an aging brand. It was being rapidly displaced in the highly profitable luxury car market by Mercedes-Benz and BMW—German automobiles that had more traction among younger car buyers than Lincoln. Moreover, Nissan (through its Infiniti division), Honda (through its Acura division), and Toyota (through its Lexus division) were beginning to invest in the luxury car market.

At the same time, managers at Jaguar also faced a problem. They were about to go out of business. Despite having a well-known brand and beautifully designed cars, Jaguar's quality problems had just about driven this firm out of business; its poor quality was legendary. The joke was that you had to buy two

Ford's Acquisition
of Jaguar

brand-new Jaguars—one to drive and one for parts. To give its customers some sense of security, Jaguar introduced a free towing service for new-car buyers. The service would tow your broken-down Jaguar to a Jaguar dealer free. The usage rate of this free towing service among Jaguar owners was 118 percent—essentially every Jaguar owner had to have his or her new car towed in for repairs and some more than once. In the J. D. Power ratings of initial quality, Jaguar

in the early 1990s was ranked ahead of only one other firm—Yugo. Yugo manufactured very low-quality, cheap cars for sale in Europe and import into the United States. Unfortunately, while Jaguar was manufacturing very low-quality cars for sale around the world, they were not cheap! What a deal—a luxury car price with Yugo quality!

The match between Ford and Jaguar seemed perfect. Ford needed a new luxury brand to compete with Mercedes, BMW, Lexus, and so forth; Jaguar had such a brand. Jaguar desperately needed to learn how to manufacture quality automobiles; Ford now knew how to do that. Assuming Ford could use its manufacturing skills with Jaguar without destroying the value of Jaguar's brand name, it seemed likely that a Ford acquisition of Jaguar would create real economic value.

But who would appropriate that value—Ford's stockholders or Jaguar's stockholders? To answer this question, it is necessary to understand if any other firms would profit from acquiring Jaguar in about the same way as Ford. What about General Motors? GM faced the same profit squeeze in small cars as Ford. It also had its own

their loyal employees, and ensure a comfortable (if not lavish) retirement for themselves. Being acquired by SCI was likely to be the only alternative to closing the funeral home once an owner or operator retired. Extracting less than the full value of the home when selling to SCI often seemed preferable to other alternatives.

Because SCI's acquisition of funeral homes exploited real and valuable economies of scope, this strategy had the potential for generating superior economic performance. Because SCI was, for many years, the only firm implementing this strategy in the funeral home industry, because the funeral homes that SCI acquired were generally not publicly traded, and because the owner or operators of these funeral homes often had interests besides simply maximizing the price of their operation when they sold it, it seems likely that SCI's acquisition strategy generated superior economic performance for many years. However, in the last several years, information about SCI's acquisition strategy has become widely

aging luxury line of cars—the Cadillac. And GM had also recently begun improving its manufacturing quality dramatically. Would GM be interested in purchasing Jaguar?

It turns out that while GM never made a formal offer for Jaguar, it did hold discussions about a possible acquisition. The bid that Ford made to take over Jaguar had to anticipate the possibility that GM was also interested. Initially, Ford paid $2.5 billion for Jaguar; since the acquisition, Ford has invested another $3.5 billion. Together, the almost $6 billion invested in Jaguar is almost $2.5 billion more than Jaguar's market price when it was a stand-alone company. This means that in order for this acquisition to pay off for Ford's stockholders, Ford must create more than $2.5 billion of extra value from its acquisition of Jaguar.

What has Ford done with Jaguar? First, and foremost, it helped Jaguar improve its quality problems. Indeed, Jaguar went from having the second-worst initial quality of any car manufacturer ranked by J. D. Powers in 1992 to having the best initial quality in 1999. Since 1999, Jaguar's rankings have dropped some, but it is still among the world's elite in initial qual-

ity rankings. However, it is reasonable to expect that much of the value created through this quality effort was anticipated in the price for Jaguar. That is, the value created here is part of the $2.5 billion premium paid for Jaguar. For it to be a source of profits for Ford's stockholders, Ford must create value in excess of this $2.5 billion.

Ford also helped Jaguar develop new models, including the mid-size "S-Type" and the smaller "X-Type" Jaguars. While these vehicles have dramatically increased Jaguar's volume of production, some observers worry that these automobile lines blur the distinction between the Ford and Jaguar brands. This is especially a problem for the "X-Type" or "baby Jag"—a car that looks disturbingly like a Hyundai Sonata. While it seems reasonable to assume that the premium paid for Jaguar anticipated Ford's ability to help Jaguar introduce some new models, the specific details of these models and their ultimate success would have been difficult to anticipate at the time Jaguar was acquired. If these models turn out to be successful, they may be a source of superior profits for Ford's shareholders.

More recently, Ford has used additional acquisitions to round out its

line of luxury cars—including its recent acquisition of Volvo and Range Rover. Ford is currently experimenting with the creation of single dealerships that sell Jaguars, Volvos, and Range Rovers. In this way, Ford's customers can gain access to a full line of luxury cars in a single location. It is also likely that these additional acquisitions were not anticipated at the time Ford acquired Jaguar. If this "one-stop-shop" approach to luxury car shopping ends up creating value, this value is also likely to be a source of superior performance to Ford's shareholders.

Of course, all this discussion begs a more fundamental question: Did Ford have to acquire Jaguar to obtain all the value described here? Couldn't Ford have created its own new luxury brand, the same way that Nissan, Honda, and Toyota did? And, which would have been cheaper—Ford paying a $2.5 billion premium for Jaguar or developing its own new luxury brand?

Sources: T. Luehrman (1991). "Jaguar plc, 1989." Harvard Business School Case No. 9-291-034; J. D. Powers (1999). "Jaguar is top make in initial quality." *Special Power Report*; J. Flint (2004). "Tarnished jewels." www.forbes.com, 01/27/04; D. Kiley (2001). "$29,950 soon can buy you a 'baby Jag." *USA Today*, February 14, p. 1.

known. This has led other funeral homes to begin bidding to acquire formerly independent funeral homes. Moreover, independent funeral home owners have become more aware of their full value to SCI. Although SCI's economy of scope with independent funeral homes is still valuable, it is no longer rare and thus no longer a source of economic profits to SCI. Put differently, the imperfectly competitive market for corporate control that SCI was able to exploit for almost 10 years has become more perfectly competitive. Future acquisitions by SCI are not likely to be a source of sustained competitive advantage and economic profit. For these reasons, SCI is currently reevaluating its corporate strategy, attempting to discover a new way that it might be able to generate superior profits.[19]

This same form of analysis can be applied to virtually any merger and acquisition strategy. Consider, for example, the acquisition discussed in the Global Perspectives feature.

Implications for Target Firm Managers

Although bidding firm managers can do several things to attempt to maximize the probability of earning economic profits from their merger and acquisition strategies, target firm managers can attempt to counter these efforts, to ensure that the owners of target firms appropriate whatever value is created by a merger or acquisition. These "rules" for target firm managers are summarized in Table 10.6

Seek Information from Bidders

One way a bidder can attempt to obtain superior performance from implementing an acquisition strategy is to keep information about the source and value of the strategic relatedness that exists between the bidder and target private. If that relationship is actually worth $12,000 but targets believe it is only worth $8,000, then a target might be willing to settle for a bid of $8,000 and thereby forgo the extra $4,000 it could have extracted from the bidder. Once the target knows that its true value to the bidder is $12,000, it is in a much better position to obtain this full value when the acquisition is completed. Therefore, not only should a bidding firm inform itself about the value of a target, target firms must inform themselves about their value to potential bidders. In this way, they can help obtain the full value of their assets.

Invite Other Bidders to Join the Bidding Competition

Once a target firm is fully aware of the nature and value of the economies of scope that exist between it and current bidding firms, it can exploit this information by seeking other firms that may have the same relationship with it and then informing these firms of a potential acquisition opportunity. By inviting other firms into the bidding process, the target firm increases the competitiveness of the market for corporate control, thereby increasing the probability that the value created by an acquisition will be fully captured by the target firm.

Delay But Do Not Stop the Acquisition

As suggested earlier, bidding firms have a strong incentive to expedite the acquisition process, to prevent other bidders from becoming involved in an acquisition. Of course, the target firm wants other bidding firms to enter the process. To increase the probability of receiving more than one bid, target firms have a strong incentive to delay an acquisition.

The objective, however, should be to delay an acquisition to create a more competitive market for corporate control, not to stop an acquisition. If a valuable economy of scope exists between a bidding and a target firm, the merger of these two firms will create economic value. If the market for corporate control within which this merger occurs is competitive, then the equity holders of the target firm will appropriate the full value of this economy of scope. Preventing an acquisition in this setting can be very costly to the equity holders of the target firm.

Table 10.6 **Rules for Target Firm Managers**

1. Seek information from bidders.
2. Invite other bidders to join the bidding competition.
3. Delay but do not stop the acquisition.

Target firm managers can engage in a wide variety of activities to delay the completion of an acquisition. Some common responses of target firm management to takeover efforts, along with their economic implications for the equity holders of target firms, are discussed in the Research Made Relevant feature.

Research Made Relevant

Managers in potential target firms can respond to takeover attempts in a variety of ways. As suggested in Table 10.7, some of these responses increase the wealth of target firm shareholders, some have no impact on target firm shareholders, and others decrease the wealth of target firm shareholders.

Management responses that have the effect of reducing the value of target firms include greenmail, standstill agreements, and "poison pills." Each of these is an anti-takeover action target firm managers can take that reduces the wealth of target firm equity holders. **Greenmail** is a maneuver in which a target firm's management purchases any of the target firm's stock owned by a bidder and does so for a price that is greater than the current market value of that stock. Greenmail effectively ends a bidding

The Wealth Effects of Management Responses to Takeover Attempts

firm's effort to acquire a particular target and does so in a way that can greatly reduce the wealth of a target firm's equity holders. Not only do these equity holders not appropriate any economic value that could have been created if an acquisition had been completed, but they have to bear the cost of the premium price that management pays to buy its stock back from the bidding firm.

Not surprisingly, target firms that resort to greenmail substantially reduce the economic wealth of their equity holders. One study found that the value of target firms that pay greenmail drops, on average, 1.76 percent. Another study reported a 2.85 percent drop in the value of such firms. These reductions in value are greater if greenmail leads to the cancellation of a takeover effort. Indeed, this second study found that such episodes led to a 5.50 percent reduction in the value of target firms. These reductions in value as a response to greenmail activities stand in marked contrast to the generally positive market response to efforts by a firm to repurchase its own shares in nongreenmail situations.

Standstill agreements are often negotiated in conjunction with greenmail. A standstill agreement is a contract between a target and a bidding firm wherein the bidding firm agrees not to attempt to take over the target for some period of time. When a target firm negotiates a standstill agreement, it prevents the current acquisition effort from being completed, and it reduces the number of bidders that might become involved in future acquisition efforts. Thus, the equity holders of this target firm forgo

Table 10.7   **The Wealth Effects of Target Firm Management Responses to Acquisition Efforts**

1. Responses that reduce the wealth of target firm equity holders:
   - Greenmail
   - Standstill agreements
   - Poison pills

2. Responses that do not affect the wealth of target firm equity holders:
   - Shark repellents
   - Pac Man defense
   - Crown jewel sale
   - Law suits

3. Responses that increase the wealth of target firm equity holders:
   - Search for white knights
   - Creation of bidding auctions
   - Golden parachutes

(continued)

any value that could have been created if the current acquisition had occurred, and they also lose some of the value that they could have appropriated in future acquisition episodes by the target's inviting multiple bidders into a market for corporate control.

Standstill agreements, either alone or in conjunction with greenmail, reduce the economic value of a target firm. One study found that standstill agreements that were unaccompanied by stock repurchase agreements reduced the value of a target firm by 4.05 percent. Such agreements, in combination with stock repurchases, reduced the value of a target firm by 4.52 percent.

So-called **poison pills** include any of a variety of actions that target firm managers can take to make the acquisition of the target prohibitively expensive. In one common poison-pill maneuver, a target firm issues rights to its current stockholders indicating that if the firm is acquired in an unfriendly takeover, it will distribute a special cash dividend to stockholders. This cash dividend effectively increases the cost of acquiring the target and can discourage otherwise interested bidding firms from attempting to acquire this target. Another poison-pill tactic substitutes the distribution of additional shares of a target firm's stock, at very low prices, for the special cash dividend. Issuing this low-price stock to current stockholders effectively undermines the value of a bidding firm's equity investment in a target and thus increases the cost of the acquisition. Other poison pills involve granting current stockholders other rights—rights that effectively increase the cost of an unfriendly takeover.

Although poison pills are creative devices that target firms can use to prevent an acquisition, they generally have not been very effective. If a bidding firm and a target firm are strategically related, the value that can be created in an acquisition can be substantial, and most of this value will be appropriated by the stockholders of the target firm. Thus, target firm stockholders have a strong incentive to see that the target firm is acquired, and they are amenable to direct offers made by a bidding firm to them as individual investors; these are called **tender offers**. However, to the extent that poison pills actually do prevent mergers and acquisitions, they are usually bad for the equity holders of target firms.

Target firm management can also engage in a wide variety of actions that have little or no impact on the wealth of a target firm's equity holders. One class of these responses is known as shark repellents. **Shark repellents** include a variety of relatively minor corporate governance changes that, in principle, are supposed to make it somewhat more difficult to acquire a target firm. Common examples of shark repellents include **supermajority voting rules** (which specify that more than 50 percent of the target firm's board of directors must approve a takeover) and state incorporation laws (in some states, incorporation laws make it difficult to acquire a firm incorporated in that state). However, if the value created by an acquisition is sufficiently large, these shark repellents will neither slow an acquisition attempt significantly nor prevent it from being completed.

Another response that does not affect the wealth of target firm equity

holders is known as the **Pac Man defense**. Targets using this tactic fend off an acquisition by taking over the firm or firms bidding for them. Just as in the old video game, the hunted becomes the hunter; the target turns the tables on current and potential bidders. It should not be too surprising that the Pac Man defense does not, on average, either hurt or help the stockholders of target firms. In this defense, targets become bidders, and we know from empirical literature that, on average, bidding firms earn only zero economic profits from their acquisition efforts. Thus, one would expect that, on average, the Pac Man defense would generate only zero economic profits for the stockholders of target firms implementing it.

Another ineffective and inconsequential response is called a **crown jewel sale**. The idea behind a crown jewel sale is that, sometimes, a bidding firm is interested in just a few of the businesses currently being operated by the target firm. These businesses are the target firm's "crown jewels." To prevent an acquisition, the target firm can sell off these crown jewels, either directly to the bidding firm or by setting up a separate company to own and operate these businesses. In this way, the bidding firm is likely to be less interested in acquiring the target.

A final, relatively ineffective defense that most target firm managers pursue is filing lawsuits against bidding firms. Indeed, at least in the United States, the filing of a lawsuit has been almost automatic as soon as an acquisition effort is announced. These suits, however, usually do not delay or stop an acquisition or merger.

Finally, as suggested in Table 10.7, some of the actions that the management of target firms can take to delay (but not stop) an acquisition actually benefit target firm equity holders. The first of these is the search for a **white knight**—another bidding firm that agrees to acquire a particular target in the place of the original bidding firm. Target firm management may prefer to be acquired by some bidding firms more than by others. For example, it may be that some bidding firms possess much more valuable economies of scope with a target firm than other bidding firms. It may also be that some bidding firms will take a longer-term view in managing a target firm's assets than other bidding firms. In both cases, target firm managers are likely to prefer some bidding firms over others.

Whatever motivation a target firm's management has, inviting a white knight to bid on a target firm has the effect of increasing by at least one the number of firms bidding for a target. If there is currently only one bidder, inviting a white knight into the bidding competition doubles the number of firms actually bidding for a target. As the number of bidders increases, the competitiveness of the market for corporate control and the likelihood that the equity holders of the target firm will appropriate all the value created by an acquisition also increase. On average, the entrance of a white knight into a competitive bidding contest for a target firm increases the wealth of target firm equity holders by 17 percent.

If adding one firm into the competitive bidding process increases the wealth of target firm equity holders

some, then adding more firms to the process is likely to increase this wealth even more. Target firms can accomplish this outcome by creating an **auction** among bidding firms. On average, the creation of an auction among multiple bidders increases the wealth of target firm equity holders by 20 percent.

A third action that the managers of a target firm can take to increase the wealth of their equity holders from an acquisition effort is the institution of **golden parachutes**. A golden parachute is a compensation arrangement between a firm and its senior management team that promises these individuals a substantial cash payment if their firm is acquired and they lose their jobs in the process. These cash payments can appear to be very large but are actually quite small in comparison to the total value that can be created if a merger or acquisition is completed. In this sense, golden parachutes are a small price to pay to give a potential target firm's top managers incentives not to stand in the way of completing a takeover of their firm. Put differently, golden parachutes reduce agency problems for the equity holders of a potential target firm by aligning the interests of top managers with the interests of that firm's stockholders. On average, when a firm announces golden parachute compensation packages for its top management team, the value of this potential target firm's equity increases by 7 percent.

Overall, there is substantial evidence that delaying an acquisition long enough to ensure that a competitive market for corporate control

emerges can significantly benefit the equity holders of target firms. One study found that when target firms did not delay the completion of an acquisition, their equity holders experienced, on average, a 36 percent increase in the value of their stock once the acquisition was complete. If, on the other hand, target firms *did* delay the completion of the acquisition, this average increase in value jumped to 65 percent.

Of course, target firm managers can delay too long. Delaying too long can create opportunity costs for their firm's equity holders, for these individuals do not actually realize the gain from an acquisition until it is completed. Also, long delays can jeopardize the completion of an acquisition, in which case the equity holders of the target firm do not realize any gains from the acquisition.

Sources: R. Walkling and M. Long (1984). "Agency theory, managerial welfare, and takeover bid resistance." *Rand Journal of Economics*, 15(1), pp. 54–68; R. D. Kosnik (1987). "Greenmail: A study of board performance in corporate governance." *Administrative Science Quarterly*, 32, pp. 163–185; J. Walsh (1989). "Doing a deal: Merger and acquisition negotiations and their impact upon target company top management turnover." *Strategic Management Journal*, 10, pp. 307–322; L. Y. Dann and H. DeAngelo (1983). Standstill agreements, privately negotiated stock repurchases, and the market for corporate control." *Journal of Financial Economics*, 11, pp. 275–300; M. Bradey and L. Wakeman (1983). "The wealth effects of targeted share repurchases." *Journal of Financial Economics*, 11, pp. 301–328; H. Singh and F. Haricento (1989). "Top management tenure, corporate ownership and the magnitude of golden parachutes." *Strategic Management Journal*, 10, pp. 143–156; T. A. Turk (1987). "The determinants of management responses to interfirm tender offers and their effect on shareholder wealth." Unpublished doctoral dissertation, Graduate School of Management, University of California at Irvine.

| VRIO | Organizing to Implement a Merger or Acquisition |

To realize the full value of any strategic relatedness that exists between a bidding and a target firm, the merged organizations must be appropriately organized. The realization of each of the types of strategic relatedness discussed earlier in this chapter requires at least some coordination and integration between the bidding and target firms after an acquisition has occurred. For example, to realize economies of scale from an acquisition, bidding and target firms must coordinate in the combined firm the functions that are sensitive to economies of scale. To realize the value of any technology that a bidding firm acquires from a target firm, the combined firm must use this technology in developing, manufacturing, or selling its products. To exploit underutilized leverage capacity in the target firm, the balance sheets of the bidding and target firms must be merged, and the resulting firm must then seek additional debt funding. To realize the opportunity of replacing the target firm's inefficient management with more efficient management from the bidding firm, these management changes must actually take place.

Post-acquisition coordination and integration is essential if bidding and target firms are to realize the full potential of the strategic relatedness that drove the acquisition in the first place. If a bidding firm decides not to coordinate or integrate any of its business activities with the activities of a target firm, then why was this target firm acquired? Just as corporate diversification requires the active management of linkages among different parts of a firm, mergers and acquisitions (as one way in which corporate diversification strategies can be created) require the active management of linkages between a bidding and a target firm.

Given that most merger and acquisition strategies are used to create corporate diversification strategies, the organizational approaches previously described for implementing diversification are relevant for implementing merger and acquisition strategies as well. Thus, mergers and acquisitions designed to create diversification strategies should be managed through the M-form structure. The management control systems and compensation policies associated with implementing diversification strategies should also be applied in organizing to implement merger and acquisition strategies. On the other hand, mergers and acquisitions designed to create vertical integration strategies should be managed through the U-form structure, with management controls and compensation policies consistent with this strategy.

Although, in general, organizing to implement merger and acquisition strategies can be seen as a special case of organizing to implement corporate diversification strategies or vertical integration strategies, implementing merger and acquisition strategies can create special problems. Most of these problems reflect the fact that operational, functional, strategic, and cultural differences between bidding and target firms involved in a merger or acquisition are likely to be much greater than these same differences between the different parts of a diversified or vertically integrated business that was not created through acquisition. The reason for this difference is that the firms involved in a merger or acquisition have had a separate existence, separate histories, separate management philosophies, and separate strategies.

Differences between bidding and target firms can manifest themselves in a wide variety of ways. For example, they may own and operate different computer systems, different telephone systems, and other conflicting technologies. These firms might have very different human resource policies and practices. One firm might have a very generous retirement and health care program; the other, a less generous program. One firm's compensation system might focus on high salaries; the other firm's compensation system might focus on large cash bonuses and stock options. Also, these firms might have very different relationships with customers. At one firm, customers might be thought of as business partners; in another, the relationship with customers might be more arm's-length in character. Integrating bidding and target firms may require the resolution of numerous differences.

Perhaps the most significant challenge in integrating bidding and target firms has to do with cultural differences.[20] In Chapter 3, it was suggested that it can often be difficult to change a firm's organizational culture. The fact that a firm has been acquired does not mean that the culture in that firm will rapidly change to become more like the culture of the bidding firm; cultural conflicts can last for very long periods of time. Indeed, the difference between the relative success of Renault's acquisition of Nissan and DaimlerChrysler's acquisition of Mitsubishi—discussed in the opening case of this chapter—has largely been attributed to the inability of Mitsubishi to modify its traditional management culture.

Cultural differences were apparently an important part of the post-merger integration challenges in the merger between Bank One and First Chicago Bank. Bank One had many operations and offices in small and medium-sized cities in the Midwest. First Chicago, on the other hand, was a more urban bank. Different kinds of employees may have been attracted to these different firms, leading to significant cultural clashes as these two firms sought to rationalize their combined operations.[21] Most reports suggest that First Chicago employees have come to dominate this "merger." Whether similar challenges will arise between the recently merged Bank One and J. P. Morgan is yet to seen.

Operational, functional, strategic, and cultural differences between bidding and target firms can all be compounded by the merger and acquisition process—especially if that process was unfriendly. Unfriendly takeovers can generate, in target firm management, anger and animosity toward the management of the bidding firm. Research has shown that top management turnover is much higher in firms that have been taken over compared to firms not subject to takeovers, reflecting one approach to resolving these management conflicts.[22]

The difficulties often associated with organizing to implement a merger and acquisition strategy can be thought of as an additional cost of the acquisition process. Bidding firms, in addition to estimating the value of the strategic relatedness between themselves and a target firm, also need to estimate the cost of organizing to implement an acquisition. The value that a target firm brings to a bidding firm through an acquisition should be discounted by the cost of organizing to implement this strategy. In some circumstances, it may be the case that the cost of organizing to realize the value of strategic relatedness between a bidding firm and a target may be greater than the value of that strategic relatedness, in which case the acquisition should not occur. For this reason, many observers argue that potential economies of scope between bidding and target firms are often not fully realized. For example, despite the numerous multimedia mergers in the 1990s (Time Warner, Turner Broadcasting, and AOL; The Walt Disney Company, Capital Cities/ABC, and ESPN; GE and NBC; Westinghouse and CBS), only Viacom and News Corporation seem to have been able to realize any important economies of scope.[23]

Although organizing to implement mergers and acquisitions can be a source of significant cost, it can also be a source of value and opportunity. Some scholars have suggested that value creation can continue to occur in a merger or acquisition long after the formal acquisition is complete.[24] As bidding and target firms continue to coordinate and integrate their operations, unanticipated opportunities for value creation can be discovered. These sources of value could not have been anticipated at the time a firm was originally acquired (and thus are, at least partially, a manifestation of a bidding firm's good luck), but bidding firms can influence the probability of discovering these unanticipated sources of value by learning to cooperate effectively with target firms while organizing to implement a merger or acquisition strategy.

Mergers and Acquisitions in an International Context

All the issues associated with mergers and acquisitions described thus far also apply to those that occur in an international setting. For example, firms exploring international merger and acquisition opportunities will need to follow the guidelines in Table 10.5 if they hope to gain competitive advantages from these strategies, while international targets need to follow the guidelines in Table 10.6 if they are to extract as much of the value created by an acquisition as possible. However, there is one aspect of international mergers and acquisitions that requires additional discussion: Challenges created for post-merger integration caused by cultural differences between countries.

We have already seen that post-merger integration usually involves resolving conflicts between the cultures of merged or acquired firms. However, when these organizational cultures reflect deep-seated country cultures, post-merger integration can be even more difficult. Thus, the integration of merged firms in an international context is often confounded by the need to discover how different country cultures can work together.

The most influential study of cultures around the world, by Geert Hofstede, suggests that cultures can be described as varying along the five dimensions presented in Figure 10.1.[25] Differences along each of these dimensions create potential challenges when integrating acquisitions conducted across country and cultural borders. These differences are rarely easy to resolve.

For example, a firm that operates in an individualistic culture may have a compensation scheme that celebrates individual achievement. If this firm acquires a company that operates in a collectivist culture, imposing an individualistic compensation policy can lead to misunderstanding and disagreement. Senior managers in a firm that operates in a culture that respects power may assume that their orders to employees in a firm that operates in a culture that only tolerates power will be carried out, while these employees will not do anything until they hear the boss's justification of those orders. A firm used to innovation and risk-seeking may be very frustrated if it acquires a company that operates in a culture that avoids uncertainty rather than celebrates it. Employees that work in a firm that operates in a culture that values material possessions and hard work to obtain those possessions may be shocked to see employees in an acquired firm that operates in a culture that values the quality of life over material possessions go home at 5:00 P.M.—even if the work for the day is not done. Finally, employees that work in a firm that operates in a culture that values looking to the future may find it very difficult to work with employees in a firm that operates in a culture that values looking to the past.

Of course, acquiring firms can engage in specific activities to modify some aspects of the culture of the firms they acquire. However, to the extent that the

Figure 10.1   Dimensions of Culture and Their Implications for Integration in International Acquisitions

Individualism ← **Social Orientation** → Collectivism
Individual interests   *Relative importance of individual*   *Group interests*
dominate   *and group interests*   *dominate*

Examples of Cultural Clashes in Post-Merger Integration:

Individualistic firm has individually oriented compensation policies while the collectivist firm has group-based compensation policies; individualistic firm has employees that make quick decisions on their own while the collectivist firm has employees who consult with others before making decisions.

Power Respect ← **Power Orientation** → Power Tolerance
Authority determined by a   *Basis on which power and*   *Authority determined by*
person's position in a firm   *authority are granted to others*   *its perceived correctness*

Examples of Cultural Clashes in Post-Merger Integration:

Employees in power respect firm do what they are told while employees in power tolerance firm wait to hear justifications before they do what they are told; employees in power respect firm are deferential to senior managers while employees in power tolerance firms may or may not be deferential depending on how effective senior managers have been in the past.

Uncertainty Acceptance ← **Uncertainty Orientation** → Uncertainty Avoidance
Change and new opportunities   *Emotional response to*   *Change and new opportunities*
valued   *change and new opportunities*   *not valued*

Examples of Cultural Clashes in Post-Merger Integration:

Employees in uncertainty acceptance firms are encouraged to think "outside the box" while employees in uncertainty avoidance firms are encouraged to reinforce the boundaries of the "box"; employees in uncertainty acceptance firms understand that failure sometimes accompanies risk-taking while employees in the uncertainty avoidance firm punish risk-takers for being foolish.

Aggressive Goal Behavior ← **Goal Orientation** → Passive Goal Behavior
Value material possessions   *Source of motivation to*   *Value quality of life and welfare*
    accomplish goals   *of others*

Examples of Cultural Clashes in Post-Merger Integration:

Employees in aggressive goal behavior firms willing to work long hours to accomplish objectives while employees in passive goal behavior firms will leave when work begins to interfere with the quality of life; employees in aggressive goal behavior firms look for tangible results from their work while employees in passive goal behavior firms are more interested in how others in a firm are faring.

Long-Term Outlook ← **Time Orientation** → Short-Term Outlook
Value patience, determination,   *Short- or long-term outlook*   *Tend to focus on the present or*
and hard work   *the past*

Examples of Cultural Clashes in Post-Merger Integration:

Employees in long-term outlook firms have long-term goals and objectives while employees in short-term outlook firms tend to be satisfied with the status quo; employees in long term outlook firms focus on the benefits of hard work while employees in short-term outlook firms focus on the benefits of traditional ways of doing things.

Source: G. Hofstede, 1980. *Culture's consequences: International differences in work-related values.*

organizational cultures of these acquired firms reflect differences in national cultures, there are few things that can be done to modify them. In such settings, acquiring firms must look to sources of value creation in an acquisition that do not depend on the integration of the organizational cultures of the bidding and target firms.

SUMMARY

Firms can use mergers and acquisition and vertical integration between strategically unrelated firms sitions to create corporate diversification strategies. Mergers or acquisitions can be expected to generate only competitive parity for both bidders and targets. Thus, firms contemplating merger and acquisition strategies must search for strategically related targets.

Several sources of strategic relatedness have been discussed in literature. On average, the acquisition of strategically related targets does create economic value, but most of that value is captured by the equity holders of target firms. The equity holders of bidding firms generally gain competitive parity even when bidding firms acquire strategically related targets. Empirical research on mergers and acquisitions is consistent with these expectations. On average, acquisitions do create value, but that value is captured by target firms, and acquisitions do not hurt bidding firms.

Given that most mergers and acquisitions generate only zero economic profits for bidding firms, an important question becomes: " Why are there so many mergers and acquisitions?" Explanations include (1) the desire to ensure firm survival, (2) the existence of free cash flow, (3) agency problems between bidding firm managers and equity holders, (4) managerial hubris, and (5) the possibility that some bidding firms might earn economic profits from implementing merger and acquisition strategies.

To gain competitive advantages and economic profits from mergers or acquisitions, these strategies must be either valuable, rare, and private or valuable, rare, and costly to imitate. In addition, a bidding firm may exploit unanticipated sources of strategic relatedness with a target. These unanticipated sources of relatedness can also be a source of economic profits for a bidding firm. These observations have several implications for the managers of bidding and target firms.

Organizing to implement a merger or acquisition strategy can be seen as a special case of organizing to implement a corporate diversification or vertical integration strategy. However, historical differences between bidding and target firms may make the integration of different parts of a firm created through acquisitions more difficult than if a firm is not created through acquisitions. Cultural differences between bidding and target firms are particularly problematic. Bidding firms need to estimate the cost of organizing to implement a merger or acquisition strategy and discount the value of a target by that cost. However, organizing to implement a merger or acquisition can also be a way that bidding and target firms can discover unanticipated economies of scope.

Post-merger integration challenges are likely to be particularly important for mergers and acquisitions in an international context. Important differences between the country cultures of different firms can raise the cost of post-merger integration. In these settings, it may be necessary for acquiring firms to find economies of scope to exploit that do not require the integration of cultures.

CHALLENGE QUESTIONS

1. Consider the following scenario: A firm acquires a strategically related target after successfully fending off four other bidding firms. Under what conditions, if any, can the firm that acquired this target expect to earn an economic profit from doing so?

2. Consider this scenario: A firm acquires a strategically related target; there were no other bidding firms. Is this acquisition situation necessarily different from the situation described in question 1? Under what conditions, if any, can the firm that acquired this target expect to earn an economic profit from doing so?

3. Some researchers have argued that the existence of free cash flow can lead managers in a firm to make inappro-priate acquisition decisions. To avoid these problems, these authors have argued that firms should increase their debt-to-equity ratio and "soak up" free cash flow through interest and princi-pal payments. Is free cash flow a sig-nificant problem for many firms? What are the strengths and weaknesses of increased leverage as a response to free cash flow problems in a firm?

4. The hubris hypothesis suggests that managers continue to engage in acquisitions, even though on average they do not generate economic prof-its, because of the unrealistic belief on the part of these managers that they can manage a target firm's assets more efficiently than that firm's cur-rent management. This type of sys-tematic nonrationality usually does not last too long in competitive mar-ket conditions: Firms led by man-agers with these unrealistic beliefs change, are acquired, or go bankrupt in the long run. Are there any attrib-utes of the market for corporate con-trol that suggest that managerial hubris could exist in this market, despite its performance-reducing implications for bidding firms? If yes, what are these attributes? If no, can the hubris hypothesis be a legitimate explanation for continuing acquisi-tion activity?

5. It has been shown that so-called poison pills rarely prevent a takeover from occurring. In fact, sometimes when a firm announces that it is insti-tuting a poison pill, its stock price goes up. Why could that happen?

PROBLEM SET

1. For each of the following scenarios, estimate how much value an acquisition will cre-ate, how much of that value will be appropriated by each of the bidding firms, and how much of that value will be appropriated by each of the target firms. In each of these scenar-ios, assume that firms do not face significant capital constraints.

(a) A bidding firm, A, is worth $27,000 as a stand-alone entity. A target firm, B, is worth $12,000 as a stand-alone entity, but $18,000 if it is acquired and integrated with Firm A. Several other firms are interested in acquiring Firm B, and Firm B is also worth $18,000 if it is acquired by these other firms. If A acquired B, would this acquisition create value? If yes, how much? How much of this value would the equity holders of A receive? How much would the equity holders of B receive?

(b) The same scenario as in a, except that the value of B, if it is acquired by the other firms interested in it, is only $12,000.

(c) The same scenario as in a, except that the value of B, if it is acquired by the other firms interested in it, is $16,000.

(d) The same scenario as in b, except that Firm B contacts several other firms and explains to them how they can create the same value with Firm B that Firm A does.

(e) The same scenario as in b, except that Firm B sues Firm A. After suing Firm A, Firm B installs a "supermajority" rule in how its board of directors operates. After putting this new rule in place, Firm B offers to buy back any stock purchased by Firm A for 20 per-cent above the current market price.

END NOTES

1. See Welch, David, and Gail Edmondson (2004). "A Shaky automotive *Menage à Trois*." *BusinessWeek*, May 10, pp. 40–41.

2. Here, and throughout this chapter, it is assumed that capital markets are semi-strong efficient, that is, all publicly available information about the value of a firm's assets is reflected in the market price of those assets. One implication of semi-strong efficiency is that firms will be able to gain access to the capital they need to pursue any strategy that generates positive present value. See Fama, E. F. (1970). "Efficient capital markets: A review of theory and empirical work." *Journal of Finance*, 25, pp. 383–417.

3. See Trautwein, I. (1990). "Merger motives and merger prescriptions." *Strategic Management Journal*, 11, pp. 283–295; and Walter, G., and J. B. Barney (1990). "Management objectives in mergers and acquisition." *Strategic Management Journal*, 11, pp. 79–86. The three lists of potential links between bidding and target firms were developed by the Federal Trade Commission; Lubatkin, M. (1983). "Mergers and the performance of the acquiring firm." *Academy of Management Review*, 8, pp. 218–225; and Jensen, M. C., and R. S. Ruback (1983). "The market for corporate control: The scientific evidence." *Journal of Financial Economics*, 11, pp. 5–50.

4. See Huey, J. (1995). "Eisner explains everything." *Fortune*, April 17, pp. 44–68; and Lefton, T. (1996). "Fitting ABC and ESPN into Disney: Hands in glove." *Brandweek*, 37(18), April 29, pp. 30–40.

5. See Rumelt, R. (1974). *Strategy, structure, and economic performance.* Cambridge, MA: Harvard University Press.

6. The first study was by Ravenscraft, D. J., and F. M. Scherer (1987). *Mergers, sell-offs, and economic efficiency.* Washington, DC: Brookings Institution. The second study was by Porter, M. E. (1987). "From competitive advantage to corporate strategy." *Harvard Business Review*, 3, pp. 43–59.

7. This is because, if the combined firm is worth $32,000, the bidder firm is worth $15,000 on its own. If a bidder pays, say, $20,000 for this target, it will be paying $20,000 for a firm that can only add $17,000 in value. So, a $20,000 bid would lead to a $3,000 economic loss.

8. This is Jensen, M. C., and R. S. Ruback (1983). "The market for corporate control: The scientific evidence." *Journal of Financial Economics*, 11, pp. 5–50.

9. See Lubatkin, M. (1987). "Merger strategies and stockholder value." *Strategic Management Journal*, 8, pp. 39–53; and Singh, H., and C. A. Montgomery (1987). "Corporate acquisition strategies and economic performance." *Strategic Management Journal*, 8, pp. 377–386.

10. See Grant, L. (1995). "Here comes Hugh." *Fortune*, August 21, pp. 43–52; Serwer, A. E. (1995). "Why bank mergers are good for your savings account." *Fortune*, October 2, p. 32; and Deogun, N. (2000). "Europe catches merger fever as global volume sets record." *Wall Street Journal*, January 3, p. R8.

11. The concept of free cash flow has been emphasized in Jensen, M. C. (1986). "Agency costs of free cash flow, corporate finance, and takeovers." *American Economic Review*, 76, pp. 323–329; and Jensen, M. (1988). "Takeovers: Their causes and consequences." *Journal of Economic Perspectives*, 2, pp. 21–48.

12. See Miles, R. H., and K. S. Cameron (1982). *Coffin nails and corporate strategies.* Upper Saddle River, NJ: Prentice Hall.

13. Roll, R. (1986). "The hubris hypothesis of corporate takeovers." *Journal of Business*, 59, pp. 205–216.

14. See Dodd, P. (1980). "Merger proposals, managerial discretion and stockholder wealth." *Journal of Financial Economics*, 8, pp. 105–138; Eger, C. E. (1983). "An empirical test of the redistribution effect in pure exchange mergers." *Journal of Financial and Quantitative Analysis*, 18, pp. 547–572; Firth, M. (1980). "Takeovers, shareholder returns, and the theory of the firm." *Quarterly Journal of Economics*, 94, pp. 235–260; Varaiya, N. (1985). "A test of Roll's hubris hypothesis of corporate takeovers." Working paper, Southern Methodist University, School of Business; Ruback, R. S., and W. H. Mikkelson (1984). "Corporate investments in common stock." Working paper, Massachusetts Institute of Technology, Sloan School of Business; Ruback, R. S. (1982). "The Conoco takeover and stockholder returns." *Sloan Management Review*, 14, pp. 13–33.

15. This section of the chapter draws on Barney, J. B. (1988). "Returns to bidding firms in mergers and acquisitions: Reconsidering the relatedness hypothesis." *Strategic Management Journal*, 9, pp. 71–78.

16. See Turk, T. A. (1987). "The determinants of management responses to interfirm tender offers and their effect on shareholder wealth." Unpublished doctoral dissertation, Graduate School of Management, University of California at Irvine. In fact, this is an example of an anti-takeover action that can increase the value of a target firm. These anti-takeover actions are discussed later in this chapter.

17. See Bower, J. (1996). "WPP-integrating icons." Harvard Business School Case No. 9-396-249.

18. See Jemison, D. B., and S. B. Sitkin (1986). "Corporate acquisitions: A process perspective." *Academy of Management Review*, 11, pp. 145–163.

19. Blackwell, R. D. (1998). "Service Corporation International." Presented to The Cullman Symposium, October, Columbus, OH.

20. Cartwright, S., and C. Cooper (1993). "The role of culture compatibility in successful organizational marriage." *The Academy of Management Executive*, 7(2), pp. 57–70; Chatterjee, S., M. Lubatkin, D. Schweiger, and Y. Weber (1992). "Cultural differences and shareholder value in related mergers: Linking equity and human capital." *Strategic Management Journal*, 13, pp. 319–334.

21. See Deogun, N. (2000). "Europe catches merger fever as global volume sets record." *Wall Street Journal*, January 3, p. R8.

22. See Walsh, J., and J. Ellwood (1991). "Mergers, acquisitions, and the pruning of managerial deadwood." *Strategic Management Journal*, 12, pp. 201–217; and Walsh, J. (1988). "Top management turnover following mergers and acquisitions." *Strategic Management Journal*, 9, pp. 173–183.

23. Landro, L. (1995). "Giants talk synergy but few make it work." *Wall Street Journal*, September 25, pp. B1 +.

24. See Haspeslagh, P., and D. Jemison (1991). *Managing acquisitions: Creating value through corporate renewal.* New York: Free Press.

25. See Hofstede, G. (1980). *Culture's consequences: International differences in work-related values.* Beverly Hills, CA: Sage Publications.

Case 3–1: e B a y

To Drop-Off or Not?*

"That's a source that didn't even exist 10 years ago. Four hundred thousand people make some money trading on eBay."

—Vice President Dick Cheney, on why official unemployment rates may be understated, September 9, 2004.

Meg Whitman spun her desk chair around to face her office window. As another busy week came to a close, the CEO of eBay gathered her thoughts as she surveyed the company's San Jose, California, campus. Watching the sun dip below the horizon, Whitman thought of the success that eBay had experienced under her leadership. However, she was concerned that a relatively small percentage of registered users were classified as active users—users who bought an item, listed an item, or bid on an item. This suggested that some people wishing to use the site balked and abandoned the system for some reason. The emergence of online auction drop-off stores was a new development poised to reverse this trend. Whitman wondered how best to position eBay to capitalize on this new industry.

Online Auction Industry

Since before the time of Socrates, Plato, and Alexander the Great, auctions have existed as a way of creating a market between buyers and sellers. Some of the earliest recorded auctions took place in ancient Babylon, where single women were auctioned to available men for marriage. The Romans advanced the concept of the auction to include agricultural products and goods produced by artisans. The rules that govern modern auctions come to us from Great Britain. With the founding of auction houses like Sotheby's and Christie's, rules such as "the winning bid is the highest bid," and "goods are sold as is" were formalized.[1]

One of the most attractive aspects of an auction is that buyers and sellers are matched and create a market where the price received for an item is the highest price that an individual buyer is willing to pay. Sellers typically allow buyers to inspect items available for sale. The logistics required to get groups of buyers and sellers together can limit the number of individuals that participate in an auction. Additionally, some items may not hold enough broad-based appeal to ever make a traditional auction attractive. Indeed, how many people can you pull together in Rhinelander, Wisconsin, to bid on a Star Wars R2-D2 action figure?

eBay History

With the rapid integration of the Internet into everyday life, this logistical limitation vanished. Suddenly, an inexpensive, relatively easy way of connecting large numbers of buyers with large numbers of sellers existed. This was the vision behind eBay when Pierre Omidyar and Jeff Skoll started the company in September 1995 as Auction Web.[2] Within a few weeks, high traffic forced Omidyar to move the site to a business account and begin charging users a listing fee for their auctions and commissions on sales. The site was renamed "eBay." eBay's founders sought to create a community of individuals who came together to communicate and trade obscure items (e.g., Pez dispensers).[3] This community gradually developed its own sense of values, which governed transactions between members of eBay. Exhibit 1 lists the values that guide eBay community members.

The founding belief that eBay was a "community" meant that community members, along with eBay management, were responsible for developing the enterprise. Member feedback was a huge driver behind changes.

*This case was written by Ida Abdalkhani, Austin Anderson, Neil Bansal, Ryan Furmick, Bob Hamzik, Avinash Wadhwa, and Esteban Zamora, November 16, 2004. Written under the direction of Professor Jay Barney.

Exhibit 2

Category	Q103 Global GMS
eBay Motors	$8.7B
Computers	$2.6B
Consumer Electronics	$2.5B
Books/Movies/Music	$2.4B
Clothing and Accessories	$2.2B
Sports	$2.0B
Collectibles	$1.6B
Home & Garden	$1.6B
Toys	$1.5B
Jewelry & Gemstones	$1.3B
Cameras & Photo	$1.2B
Business & Industrial	$1.1B

Source: Company reports. Note: Figures are annualized.

Omidyar was overwhelmed by e-mails asking him whether particular sellers were trustworthy. He responded by creating a voluntary, participant-driven reputation mechanism that allows community members to describe exceptional and forgettable service experiences. Buyers and sellers could leave one line of text feedback for each other about each transaction and a +1, −1, or 0 score. This mechanism helped foster a robust online community, where users discussed common interests on message boards and in chat rooms related to the auction categories. The simple one-line feedback mechanism developed over a period of time into an elaborate feedback forum, largely because a good reputation within the eBay community had become a precious resource. In addition to the feedback forum, eBay put in place the SafeHarbor™ program, which provides guidelines for trading, provides information to resolve user disputes, and responds to reports of misuse of the eBay service. eBay's trust and safety initiatives, including user identity verification, insurance, integrated escrow, authentication, and other proactive antifraud efforts, are key elements of its effort to make eBay a safe place to trade.

Developing the infrastructure to support buyers and sellers was one key component of eBay's strategy. Attracting buyers and sellers to the site was another component. However, to market the company, eBay initially spent nothing on advertising, allowing word of mouth from users to generate new traffic. eBay did cross-promote and partner with other online and offline auctioneers, Web portals, search engines, and new sites.[4] It became the exclusive consumer-to-consumer (C2C) auction site for AOL's Web sites and online service in September 1998.

The growth of the company created a gap in management capabilities and the service levels demanded by customers. Shortly before taking the company public, Omidyar brought Meg Whitman aboard to succeed him as CEO. At that time, community members were largely selling and buying collectibles and antiques. Whitman brought with her a Harvard Business School pedigree, marketing experience at Procter & Gamble and PepsiCo, and consulting experience at Bain & Co. She began to fill senior management positions with other former consultants. The ex-consultants' focus on gathering data and measuring performance meant that eBay's managers could better decide on which projects to spend money. Whitman began to segment eBay's product offerings into categories, such as collectibles, jewelry or apparel, each with its own category manager.[5] Exhibit 2 lists the product categories and the sales per category.

eBay's Performance Since Going Public

Seven months after Whitman's arrival, the firm went public. eBay's IPO in September 1998 was a frenzied event. The offer price of $18 quickly rose above $54 in early trading. The stock closed at $47.37 at the end of first-day trading.[6] Exhibit 3 provides a graphical view of eBay's share price since September 1998, and a comparison with the S&P 500 over a similar period. eBay's revenue performance has also been impressive. Table 1 shows the company's net revenues on a quarterly basis since 2002.

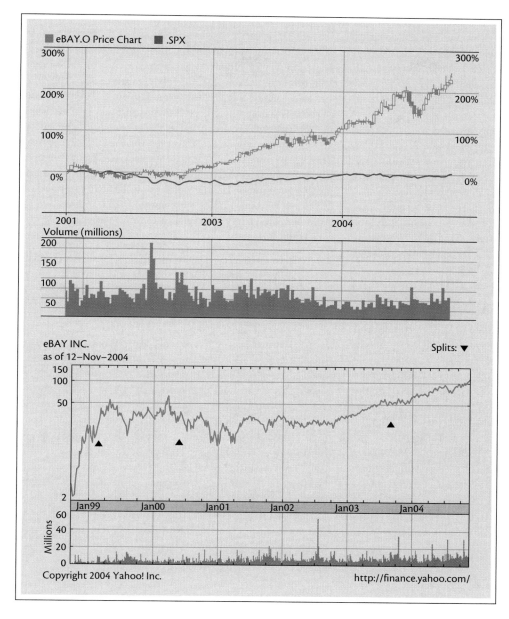

Exhibit 3   eBay Stock Price Performance

Triangles indicate a 3:1 stock split in March 1999, a 2:1 split in May 2000 and a 2:1 split in August 2003.

Table 1   **($ in thousands)**

	1Q02	**2Q02**	**3Q02**	**4Q02***	**1Q03**	**2Q03**
Net Revenues	$245,106	$266,287	$288,779	$413,928	$476,492	$509,269
Change versus prior quarter	12%	9%	8%	43%	15%	7%

	3Q03	**4Q03**	**1Q04**	**2Q04**	**3Q04**
Net Revenues	$530,942	$648,393	$756,239	$773,412	$805,876
Change versus prior quarter	4%	22%	17%	2%	4%

*Includes revenue from PayPal acquisition completed in October 2002.

A large portion of eBay's pre-2000 revenue came from collectibles. As eBay grew, it opened other product categories and specialty sites (e.g., motor vehicles). By 2004, its product categories spanned over 16,000 types of goods in 28 international markets. Both expansions involved partnerships and acquisitions of specialized and local auction Web sites.

To address the growing concerns of eBay users over payment speed and security, the company acquired PayPal in July 2002. PayPal is an online payment system that solves the problems associated with traditional payment methods such as money orders or personal checks. PayPal users fund their PayPal accounts using bank accounts or credit cards. When a customer pays for goods and services using PayPal's payment system, funds are transferred from his/her account to the PayPal seller's account. The PayPal seller can then withdraw these funds via bank account, debit card, or check. Alternatively, these funds can be used to make other PayPal purchases. Exhibit 4 depicts the PayPal payment process.[7]

By mid-2004, eBay reported 114 million registered users on eBay, reflecting a six-year CAGR of 126 percent. This figure includes all users who have an eBay log-in ID and password. Of these registered users, 41 million were active users—users who bid, bought, or listed over the preceding 12 months.[8] Exhibit 5 shows the growth in active users in the United States and Internationally. Analysts estimated that these users would list 1.389 billion items in fiscal 2004, and 1.807 billion in 2005.[9] eBay's growth explosion has made enforcing sanctions for site violations (e.g., fraud) more difficult. The growth of the company has also been marked by Web site attacks and outages. Disgruntled sellers in the eBay community recently filed a lawsuit for eBay's failure to remedy faulty billing.[10]

Online Auction Drop-Off

The online auction drop-off selling refers to the selling of items online for other people. There are a number of ways that this can be done, but the most common is for the seller or consignee to collect items for sale from the client or consignor. The consignee then handles the whole listing and selling process, and then pays the proceeds of the sale to the client, less an agreed-upon fee for the seller's services. If the item does not sell, it is either returned to the client or donated to charity. One great advantage of online auction drop-off selling is that the seller does not have to buy items up front—there is no risk of losing money on items that do not sell. Alternative approaches to online auction drop-off selling include:

- Offering it as a free service for friends, family, or charities
- Leaving the item with the owner and providing a listing service only
- Operating a retail store or "drop-off" location where customers leave items at the store

Exhibit 6 is a graphical depiction of the selling process completed by online auction drop-off stores. The emergence of retail brick-and-mortar storefronts to do eBay selling for customers has been a recent trend. Numerous auction drop-off stores have sprouted up all over the nation and the world. The industry is extremely fragmented, with several smaller players that compete with a number of major players. Some of the major competitors in this arena include AuctionDrop (www.auctiondrop.com), QuikDrop (www.quikdrop.com), and Trading Circuit (www.tradingcircuit.com).

Each of the players has adopted a unique business format to compete in this industry. Franchising, partnerships, retail implanting, and opening a central warehouse

Exhibit 4   PayPal Payment Process

Source: Company reports and JPMorgan.

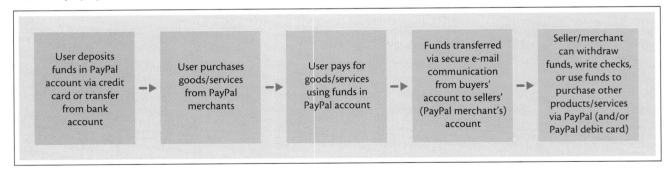

| User deposits funds in PayPal account via credit card or transfer from bank account | → | User purchases goods/services from PayPal merchants | → | User pays for goods/services using funds in PayPal account | → | Funds transferred via secure e-mail communication from buyers' account to sellers' (PayPal merchant's) account | → | Seller/merchant can withdraw funds, write checks, or use funds to purchase other products/services via PayPal (and/or PayPal debit card) |

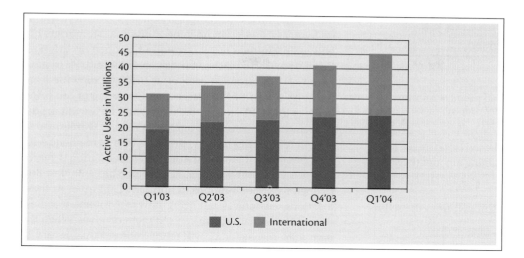

Exhibit 5   eBay Active User Growth

Source: Company reports and JPMorgan estmates.

with satellite stores are some major business formats deployed. Examples of fee structures that some drop-off store utilizes are outlined in Exhibit 7. The industry has two different types fee packages: basic and premium. The major difference between these two packages is that the premium package allows the seller to set a minimum opening bid price and/or reserve price (i.e., a minimum price that the seller is willing to accept) for the auction. This ensures that a drop-off store will not sell an item for less than the customer wishes to sell it for. Setting a reserve price and minimum starting price, however, decreases the probability that the item will sell. Because of this, eBay drop-off stores require a prepayment for the premium package.

Many predict that the online auction drop-off industry will become a big market. The majority of these consignment stores utilize eBay as their auction host of choice. There are only a select few that provide Yahoo! Auctions as a choice to customers. An executive from one of the many sprouting brick-and-mortar retail stores offering eBay selling services said that eBay itself is upping its estimate of the industry size for the drop-off services. Where once the firm estimated the potential revenue at $5 to $10 billion, it now deems it more likely to grow to $20 to $25 billion, according to AuctionDrop CEO Randy Adams.[11]

Online auction drop-off stores are expanding the eBay market. The drop-off store model has the full support of eBay, which it believes will open up business from potential sellers currently unwilling or unable to sell online themselves. eBay CEO Meg Whitman said recently: "We're excited about this. Clearly they are getting an incremental customer that would never have come to eBay on their own."[12]

Exhibit 6   Graphical Depiction of Auction Drop-off Selling Process

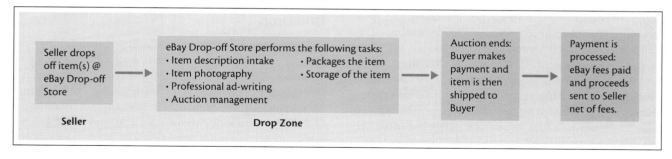

Exhibit 7   Online Auction Drop-Off Fee Structure Comparison

Name	Fee Structure
AuctionDrop	Basic Service–No prepayPremium Service–$19.99 prepay Minimum: $19.99 38% of the first $200 30% of the next $300 ($200.01–$500) 20% of the remaining amount (over $500) Special quotes for items estimated to sell at more than $5,000. The fees are calculated from the selling price: 38% of the first $200
QuikDrop	30% of the next $300 20% of the remaining (over $500) A $20.00 fee will be charged for items with a reserve price, Buy it Now, and/or high minimum bid.
Trading Circuit	Our commission is 35% of the first $500 of the item's final selling price and 25% of the remaining amount over $500. Note that there may also be other expenses associated with selling your item, including eBay charges.
DropSmart	30% of the first $500 20% of the remaining balance (over $500) $10 minimum commission Rates are applied on a per item basis. DropSmart incurs all listing fees.

Source: www.auctiondrop.com, www.quikdrop.com, www.tradingcircuit.com, www.dropsmart.com.

Players in the Online Auction Drop-Off Industry

AuctionDrop

Founded in December 2002 by Bill Rollinson and Andy Jeffrey, AuctionDrop received $3.2 million in venture capital funding from Mobius Venture Capital & Draper Associates. It opened its first location in California in March of 2003. Its goal was to have 100 stores in 10 major areas by 2005; however, it stumbled onto a new approach to the drop-off store market as it conducted its business. It now runs a model which includes a central warehouse where the entire selling process is completed, and individual storefronts with mini-warehouses for temporary storage. AuctionDrop is no longer planning on opening individual storefronts but will maintain the ones it currently has open on the West Coast. It has also reached an agreement with UPS to have "drop-off" locations at each of its 3,400 nationwide locations. As a result of this agreement, customers can bring items to any UPS store in the nation and UPS will take the item and send it to AuctionDrop's central warehouse to complete the eBay selling process. This agreement with UPS has helped AuctionDrop develop a national reach. Recently, AuctionDrop formed a partnership with Best Buy to open five pilot locations in northern California. At these locations, customers can bring unwanted items into Best Buy so that AuctionDrop can sell them on eBay. When the item sells, the customer will receive a Best Buy gift card in the amount of the item sold less any commissions to AuctionDrop.

AuctionDrop has averaged approximately 500 auctions per week since June of 2004 (see Exhibit 8). Despite having numerous drop-off locations, every store operates using a single eBay ID. This is because one central warehouse is controlling the entire listing and selling process. One advantage to having a central warehouse in control of the selling process is the ability to administer quality control and maintain a high feedback rating. AuctionDrop also averages a 90 percent sell-through rate,[13] compared to a much lower industry average. (See Exhibit 9.) A sell-through rate is a statistic that measures the success of auctions that are listed. Basically, a 90 percent sell-through rate signifies that 9 out of 10 auctions that AuctionDrop lists successfully result in sales. How do drop-off stores achieve much higher sell-through rates? AuctionDrop only accepts items for sale that meet certain criteria it has set. It uses databases such as Andale (www.andale.com) to access historical information on what sells, the amount it sells for, and the success rate for each sale. It also requires that an item have a perceived value of at least $75 in order to accept it for sale, recognizing that accepting any item lower than this value will not cover the costs or provide the required return.

QuikDrop

Another major player in the online auction drop-off industry, QuikDrop runs an individual storefront approach with each store operating as a franchise. Each individual store has its own eBay ID, since stores operate independently of each other. The cost of opening a QuikDrop varies depending on size and location. An applicant needs a minimum of $35,000 to open an average

QuikDrop store. Larger stores in higher-priced locations could require a minimum of $55,000. These figures include a franchise fee of $15,000 and the QuikFlow software license fee of $1,995. QuikFlow is proprietary software developed to connect each franchise to the QuikDrop network and completely automate administrative operations such as point-of-sale transactions, managing and billing bidder accounts, and paying customers for their items. In a few simple steps, a franchisee can sign up new customers and pre-set the billing parameters. QuikDrop also charges an ongoing monthly royalty fee of $1,800. The term of its franchise agreement is 15 years and is renewable for $2,500.[14] QuikDrop has averaged 1,200 auctions per week across all of its stores nationwide since June of 2004 (refer to Exhibit 8), and has diversified its business by utilizing its individual storefronts to do more than just sell items on eBay.

QuikDrop currently has 18 storefront locations and plans to open more in the next year. To open up franchise locations, QuikDrop needs to receive authorization from the territories in which it wishes to operate. Franchise contracts are currently in place to open over 500 stores in the United States and 100 stores internationally. QuikDrop currently has authorization to do business in the following regions: California, Texas, Alabama, Virginia, South Carolina, Florida, Pennsylvania, Nevada, New York, Kentucky, Illinois, Ohio, New Jersey, North Carolina, Indiana, Georgia, Oregon, Arizona, Ontario Canada, and Australia.

Trading Circuit

An eBay drop-off store that was started by Circuit City Trading Circuit utilizes existing excess capacity within Circuit City stores and is classified as a "retail implant." Trading Circuit started off with eight pilot locations in Georgia and Pennsylvania. Each Trading Circuit operates under different eBay user IDs. During this trial period, Trading Circuit averaged 438 auctions per week, which equated to approximately 55 auctions per storefront (refer to Exhibit 8). Trading Circuit initiated a referral program in which they offer $5 for every item brought in by the referred person.

In September of 2004, Trading Circuit shut down four of its eight pilot stores. Circuit City spokesperson Steve Mullen said Trading Circuit is a test business. It got "somewhat uneven results," he reported, and decided to close the four Atlanta centers to control costs and focus efforts on the Pittsburgh centers. "We are learning lots of lessons," Mullen said.[15] Trading Circuit currently operates six stores in Pennsylvania, Virginia,

and most recently in Oklahoma. Circuit City plans on rolling out Trading Circuit in all of its retail stores throughout the United States and Canada, depending on the success of these pilot locations.

Why Would People Choose Online Consignment?

There are several steps that are needed to sell on eBay, or any other auction site, for that matter. For many sellers the process seems easy because they enjoy doing it, but even for professionals who sell many items daily, the process can be very time-consuming.

An hour or more to sell an item may seem unrealistically long, but consider every part of the selling process step-by-step. Table 2 demonstrates the tasks required to sell an item using an online auction site. A seller could spend 5 to 30 minutes on each task:

It is likely that most households could easily find 10 or more items that are no longer of any use to them, and could raise upwards of several hundred dollars if they were to sell these items on eBay. However, many people are either too busy, do not enjoy working on computers, are not computer savvy, or simply cannot be bothered to sell their own property—these are the potential customers for online auction drop-off stores. Other common clients are businesses with slow-moving stock, particularly those with limited space to display their stock, such as car and antique dealers. Additional customers may also include businesses that have upgraded equipment among other things and wish to sell excess items on eBay but do not have the time or manpower to complete such an intense process.

Table 2

Researching prices
Taking photographs
Cropping, resizing, and editing photographs
Writing descriptions
Listing the item
Answering questions
Corresponding with the buyer
Paying in checks
Monitoring your bank account for checks to clear
Packing the item
Shipping the item
Updating spreadsheets or accounting software

Exhibit 8   Weekly Auction Counts, 2004

Name	eBay Auction ID	23-Jul	2-Jul	9-Jul	16-Jul	23-Jul	30-Jul	6-Aug
AuctionDrop	auctiondrop	532	489	359	421	475	584	719
Trading Circuit	Robinson (Pitt)	NA	NA	NA	NA	NA	NA	NA
Trading Circuit	Ross Park (Pitt)	NA	NA	NA	NA	NA	NA	NA
Trading Circuit	Wilkins (Pitt)	NA	NA	NA	NA	NA	NA	NA
Trading Circuit	Century (West Mifflin)	NA	NA	NA	NA	NA	NA	NA
Trading Circuit	Ardmore, OK	NA	NA	NA	NA	NA	NA	NA
Trading Circuit	Richmond, Virginia	NA	NA	NA	NA	NA	NA	NA
Trading Circuit Circuit City (reduced to 6 locations)	tradingcircuit1020, trading_circuit_730, trading_circuit_768, trading_circuit_770, trading_circuit_772, trading_circuit_773, trading_circuit_809, trading_circuit_781, trading_circuit_584, trading_circuit_111, quikdropvavir quikdroplv	52	291	613	539	482	470	396
QuikDrop	quikdropcaps1 quikdroptxdfw quikdropcasd	845	551	487	714	792	978	1308
NuMarkets	numarkets	1147	1302	2331	1446	1489	1629	2028
iSold it	isoldit isoldit_tx100	554	492	487	625	607	450	612
e-Powersellers	e-powersellers e-powersellers-cal	2552	2657	3245	2689	2657	2683	2770
AuctionASAP	auctionasap snappyauctions2	7	1	9	10	11	13	1
Snappy Auctions	snappyauctions snappyauctions4	206	173	157	154	120	172	128
AuctionBin	auctionbin	101	112	86	50	64	79	99
AuctionValet	myauctionvalet	61	65	105	78	97	95	86
ExpressDrop	expressdropchicago	114	147	86	114	106	130	155
eLOT	elotonline	194	192	187	199	213	183	167
AuctionWagon	auctionwagon	151	86	116	193	178	207	190
Cash it in	cashitinnow	110	79	87	91	83	75	93
NY Oasis	online_auction_service	539	867	1144	911	721	713	842
Auction it Easy	auctioniteasy	60	166	93	131	61	122	117
DropPro/Sell2All	droppro edropshop	2	0	1	0	0	0	0
DropSmart	dropsmart	147	142	141	171	144	135	134
ez Auction Stop	ezauctionstop	38	61	58	54	80	61	58
EZBayer	ezbayertx	91	105	85	150	100	110	99
AuctionHARBOR	auctionharbort1	159	170	99	99	114	61	92
Ways Center	wayscenter	202	183	171	220	232	212	215
1stopAuctions	1stopauctions	62	58	77	35	65	66	47
DigaDeal	digadealny	0	30	73	50	51	30	56
Auction-Fest	siempre26	14	29	5	28	4	12	16
AuctionFarm	palleyd	250	180	359	369	488	274	226
Auction Shoppe	auctionshoppe	31	28	33	50	36	50	72
AuctionGenie	yourauctiongenie	NA	NA	NA	NA	NA	5	6
United Auction Brokers	uabcorporate	NA	NA	NA	NA	NA	15	0
FastEZAuctions	fastezauction_san_diego	NA	NA	NA	NA	NA	NA	53
Auction Pointe	auction-pointe	61	61	21	119	20	0	NA
Drop n' Sell	dropnsell01	52	12	1	0	0	0	0

Source: eBay Historical Auction Data

13-Aug	20-Aug	27-Aug	13-Sep	22-Sep	22-Oct	29-Oct	Average Auctions Per week	Average Auctions Per Year
530	339	397	352	403	406	447	496	25812
NA	NA	NA	NA	NA	114	107	111	5746
NA	NA	NA	NA	NA	112	105	109	5642
NA	NA	NA	NA	NA	76	135	106	5486
NA	NA	NA	NA	NA	127	152	140	7254
NA	NA	NA	NA	NA	0	122	61	3172
NA	NA	NA	NA	NA	67	56	62	3198
501	491	313	529	579	496	677	495	25716
1381	1565	1416	1327	1453	NA	1645	1205	62669
2201	2330	2026	1711	2991	NA	1033	1972	102544
734	756	970	1061	1034	NA	NA	699	36322
2542	1001	1099	1223	1327	NA	NA	2204	114595
5	2	20	21	8	NA	NA	9	468
138	128	113	161	151	NA	NA	150	7804
125	77	150	59	84	NA	NA	91	4706
99	117	101	76	91	NA	NA	89	4641
122	102	126	100	135	NA	NA	120	6227
113	202	117	192	133	NA	NA	174	9065
104	99	143	59	98	NA	NA	135	7037
46	42	54	54	49	NA	NA	72	3740
609	854	731	847	277	NA	NA	755	39238
161	117	145	152	142	NA	NA	122	6357
11	16	19	8	14	NA	NA	6	308
41	22	29	52	65	NA	NA	102	5300
49	73	64	59	89	NA	NA	62	3224
77	123	134	143	110	NA	NA	111	5750
142	98	109	110	82	NA	NA	111	5785
242	188	180	160	200	NA	NA	200	10422
45	71	31	38	35	NA	NA	53	2730
43	65	49	60	82	NA	NA	49	2552
9	24	1	17	7	NA	NA	14	719
173	280	290	184	257	NA	NA	278	14430
57	61	53	74	85	NA	NA	53	2730
4	3	4	0	10	NA	NA	3	139
0	2	2	9	12	NA	NA	3	173
29	4	11	0	0	NA	NA	8	420
NA	NA	NA	NA	NA	NA	na	35	1833
1	NA	NA	NA	NA	NA	NA	8	429

Exhibit 9

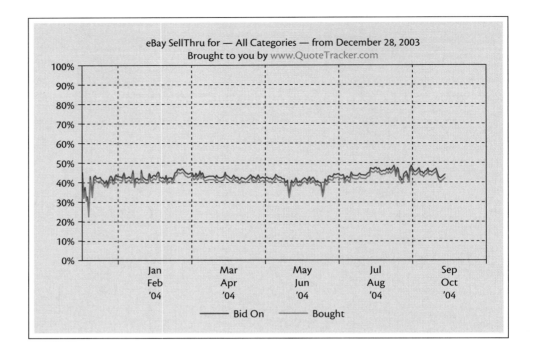

eBay SellThru for — All Categories — from December 28, 2003
Brought to you by www.QuoteTracker.com

——— Bid On   ——— Bought

An additional reason why customers would utilize the services of online auction drop-off stores is that these stores generally have experienced sellers who know the ins and outs of how to get maximum dollar for an auction. This involves anything from putting in key words in the subject line to attract bidders to taking professional photographs to ensure that bidders know what they are getting. Higher bids also result from a high feedback rating generally associated with the online auction drop-off stores. As these stores claim to get higher values for goods they sell compared to an average online seller, the commission charged to a customer is somewhat offset by the higher sale price.

Competitors

Yahoo!

Founded in 1994 by two Stanford Ph.D. candidates, David Filo and Jerry Yang, Yahoo! was one of the largest Web portals by the time it entered online auctions in September 1998. Headquartered in Summyvale, California, Yahoo! has operations in North America, Europe, Asia, Latin America, and Australia. The company's number one operating philosophy is to provide the best Internet experience for its users. To this end, Yahoo! provides services across four major segments: Search & Marketplace, Information & Content, Communications & Consumer Services, and Affiliate Services. Yahoo! Auctions and many of the company's revenue generating activities fall under the area of Search & Marketplace.

Going into 2003, the company had a positive outlook on long-term growth and revenue-generation. According to Susan Decker, Chief Financial Officer of Yahoo!, the company had a clear plan:

As we move into 2003, we continue to focus on maximizing long-term free cash flow per share. . . . Our long-term financial strategy of attracting significantly more revenue from our growing user base without commensurately increasing our expense appears to be gaining traction. In 2003, we expect strong growth in revenue, profitability and free cash flow, even as we continue to invest in areas that we expect will drive long-term growth.[16]

The company's broad offerings have enabled it to grow its user base greatly over the past year. Yahoo! has 263 Million unique users worldwide, up 23 percent from 2002. Approximately 50 percent of the users are classified as active registered users (log in once per month or more), up 30 percent from 2002.[17]

The company has also demonstrated phenomenal revenue growth of 71 percent over 2002. In 2003, revenues were at $1.6 billion, up from $953 million the previous year. Revenue is generated from three primary activities: marketing services, fees, and listings. Gross profits also increased to $1.3 billion, up from $790 million in 2002 and Net Income showed strong growth at $238 million, up from $43 million the previous year. Much of the total revenue increase is attributed to a growth in paying users and thus, fee revenues. Fees increased over 2002 due to a rise in the number of paying users. In 2003, Yahoo! had 4.9 million paying users, up from 2.2 million in 2002; a 123 percent increase. However, average revenue per user declined to $5 per month, down from $7 per month in 2002. This decline is attributed to user growth in the lower-priced offerings. Exhibit 10 shows the growth of 43 percent in fee revenues.

Paying users are currently "the fastest growing subset of users on the Yahoo! network."[18]

The current fee structure of Yahoo! Auctions generates revenues via both a list and final selling fee; buyers do not pay any fees. The listing fee starts at $0.05 and goes up to $0.75 (for items $50 and up). A final selling fee is also charged if the item sells and ranges from 2 percent for small-value items ($25 and less) to a graduated scale of 0.5 percent (for items with a closing price over $1,000).[19] Exhibit 11 provides further details on Yahoo! Auction's fee structure.

However, Yahoo! Auctions is still not a substantial player in the overall online auction market. The majority of online auction dollars go through eBay (64 percent). A dis-

Exhibit 10   Revenue Sources for eBay, Yahoo!, and Overstock.com

eBay Inc.   ($ in millions)

	2002	2003	2004E	2005E
Gross Merchandise Sales	$14,868.0	$23,779.0	$34,154.0	$46,162.0
% change Y-o-Y		60%	44%	35%
Payment Revenue	$159.8	$429.5	$647.2	$776.7
eBay Online Revenue	$949.2	$1,682.8	$2,479.3	$3,481.7
Total Transactions	$1,109.0	$2,112.2	$3,126.5	$4,258.4
3rd Party Advertising Revenue	$61.0	$47.1	$69.4	$80.0
End-to-end Services	$22.2	$5.7	–	–
Total Online Revenue	$1,192.3	$2,165.1	$3,195.9	$4,338.4
% change Y-o-Y		81.6%	47.6%	35.7%

Source: eBay Annual Reports; JP Morgan North America Equity Research, 07-Jun-2004.

Yahoo! Revenue-Mix   ($ in thousands)

	2002	2003	Yr-over-Yr Growth ($)	Yr-over-Yr Growth (%)
Marketing Srvs	$651,568	$1,199,733	$548,165	84%
Fees	$207,941	$298,192	$90,251	43%
Listings	$93,558	$127,172	$33,614	36%
Total Revenues	$953,067	$1,625,097	$672,030	71%

Source: Yahoo! Annual Report 2003.

Overstock Financials   ($ in thousands)

	2002	2003	Yr-over-Yr Growth ($)	Yr-over-Yr Growth (%)
Revenues (Sales)	$91,800	$238,900	$147,100	160%
Net Income (Loss)	($4,600)	($11,900)	($7300)	(158%)

Source: http://premium.hoovers.com.proxy.lib.ohio-state.edu/subscribe/co/fin/factsheet.xhtml?ID=105874.

tant second is uBid.com (14.7 percent). Yahoo! Auctions, Amazon auctions, and Egghead.com accounted for the rest of the top five online auction players, at less than 4 percent each. eBay also had the highest satisfaction and conversion rates among users.[20]

Overstock.com

Overstock.com's central organizing principle is to offer an online retail environment to provide consumers the opportunity to purchase brand-name merchandise at a discount. The merchandise itself is obtained from manufacturers holding excess production stock, or stock that is dated or even of the wrong color. In essence, the company functions primarily as a liquidator for manufacturers, distributors, importers, retailers, and catalog companies, selling their excess inventory.[21]

Overstock.com has its origins in Discounts Direct, a firm formed in 1997. In 1999, Overstock.com entered the e-commerce sphere. Company president and CEO Dr. Patrick Byrne, 42, earned his Ph.D. in Philosophy from Stanford, and is the son of former GEICO Insurance CEO, Jack Byrne, and a friend of Warren Buffett.[22] The company went public in 2002, and Byrne holds 40 percent of the shares. The company has a current market capitalization of $1.1 billion.

Overstock.com has been described as a "Persian bazaar," selling anything from books and music CDs, to electronics, jewelry and even luxury cruises. While it was originally conceived to sell this broad assortment of merchandise to retail customers in their homes, the company now also sells in small blocks to small business retailers through a sister site, www.overstockb2b.com. Additionally, the company often serves as a "fulfillment partner" for other merchants, selling their merchandise—which Overstock.com never actually owns or handles—via the Overstock.com Web site.

A relatively new player in the world of online commerce, Overstock.com has grown dramatically. Sales in 2000 were $25.5 million and had grown to $91.8 million in 2002, and to $238.9 million by 2003. But, as with many nascent Internet commerce companies, the net income picture is far less rosy: Annual net income in 2000 was a negative $21.3 million. This figure improved to negative $4.6 million by 2002, and was a negative $11.9 million in 2003.[23] Byrne has been successful in growing the business and making it competitive, and in September of 2004 attempted to translate that success beyond the world of simply selling excess merchandise, to compete in the online auction market. Under the name "Ocean," Overstock.com offers an auction venue similar to that of eBay.

Exhibit 11	Fee Structures of Main Online Auction Players: eBay, Yahoo! Auctions, Overstock.com Auctions

eBay

Charges two fee types: Graduated listing fee & final selling price percentage

Final value fee is only charged if item sells:

Closing Price	Final Value Fee
$0–$25	5.25% of the closing price
$25–$1,000	5.25% of the first $25 ($1.31) plus 2.75% of the remaining closing price
$1,000 and up	5.25% of the first $25 ($1.31) plus 2.75% of the first $25–$1,000 ($26.81) plus 1.5% of the remaining closing price

Yahoo! Auctions

Charges two fee types: Graduated listing fee & final selling price percentage

Starting Price or Reserve Price	Listing Fee
$0.01–$9.99	$0.05
$10.00–$24.99	$0.15
$25.00–$49.99	$0.35
$50.00 and up	$0.75

Final value fee is only charged if item sells:

Closing Price	Final Value Fee
$0–$25	2% of the closing price
$25–$1,000	2% of the first $25 ($0.50) plus 1% of the remaining closing price
$1,000 and up	2% of the first $25 ($0.50) plus 1% of the first $25–$1,000 ($9.75) plus 0.5% of the remaining closing price

Overstock.com Auctions

Charges two fee types: Graduated listing fees & final selling percentage

Starting Price or Reserve Price	Listing Fee
$0.01–$0.99	$0.20
$1.00–$9.99	$0.23
$10.00–$24.99	$0.40
$25.00–$49.99	$0.79
$50.00–$199.99	$1.58
$200.00–$499.99	$2.38
$500.00 and up	$3.17

Final value fee is only charged if item sells:

Closing Price	Final Value Fee
$0–$25	3.25% of closing price
$25–$1,000	2.00% of closing price
$1,000 and up	1.00% of closing price

Sources: http://pages.ebay.com/help/sell/fees.html; http://help.yahoo.com/help/auctions/afee/afee-06.html; http://auctionbytes.com/cab/pages/sitepricing.

Overstock.com will attempt to compete against eBay on price, charging 30 percent less to list items on its auction site, and it charges graduated insertion fees for placing an item on its site for auction (refer to Exhibit 11). For example, a $50 item would have an insertion fee of $1.58, and a $250 item, $2.38. Overstock.com also realizes revenue when an item is sold, charging a graduated percentage of the sale price. Items selling for less than $1,000 produce a 2 percent fee; items closing at more than $1,000 generate 1 percent for Overstock.com.[24]

Overstock is hoping to use its customer base from its fixed-price business to drive its success in the auction market. It is unclear what proportion of current customers will actually utilize the service, however. Early figures show growth in the number of products listed, from 400 in September, to over 17,700 in October.

Byrne is convinced that there is a place for Overstock.com Auctions:

> First there was "e-Bay" and now there is "o-cean"— the internal code name for Overstock.com Auctions. I think this will work for three reasons: 1) certain dynamics within eBay's marketplace are causing eBay's Powersellers to itch for an alternative; 2) our auction tab scratches that itch; and 3) the social networking imbedded within our auction tab may turn out to be powerful.[25]

Byrne's optimism must be tempered by the fact that successful online retailing and auctioning is somewhat like that of the brick-and-mortar variety in that it depends on the customer "seeing" the product. In the online world this is measured by number of unique visits to a Web site, among other metrics. Overstock.com has witnessed dramatic increases in sales through its retail business, and hopes this will continue in its auction site. But to offer some perspective on the level of success in being "seen" by customers, one can look at industry peers and their success in being "seen." In August 2004, eBay had 15.4 million visitors weekly to its site, Yahoo! had 2.9 million, and Overstock.com had 1.6 million.[26] (See Exhibit 12.)

Exhibit 12   Overview of Web Presence

Unique Web site Visitors (millions/week)

eBay	15.47
Yahoo Shopping	2.92
Overstock.com	1.62

Gender Differential (% Female)

eBay	48.7
Yahoo Shopping	53.2
Overstock.com	56.5

Source: http://www.internetretailer.com/dailynews.asp?id=12602.

It's clear that Overstock.com and its burgeoning auction site have a long hill to climb. The recent auction of the historic 700th home run ball of San Francisco Giants' left-fielder Barry Bonds for $804,000 is precisely the sort of high profile event the company needs to help draw the attention of potential users and to successfully launch its auction site.[27]

Conclusion

As the sun set on San Jose, Meg Whitman felt uncertain about how to best pursue the opportunities that online auction drop-off stores presented. It was clear to her that this industry presented unforeseen opportunities and their future impact on the online auction industry could be substantial. These stores could definitely help eBay grow the number of sellers and make the site more accessible to the general population or they could simply be just another fad that would eventually dissipate. As the final glimmers of sunlight beamed through her office window, she sat back and pondered the possible options.

Notes

1   Cassady, Ralph, *Auctions and auctioneering*. Berkeley: Univeristy of California Press, 1967. URL: http://www.agorics.com/Library/Auctions/auction9.html.
2   Bjornsson, Magus, "eBay: A concise analysis." 16-Mar-2001; URL: http://www.cs.brandeis.edu/~magnus.
3   Business Week Online, "Q&A with eBay's Pierre Omidyar." 3-Dec-2001; URL: http://www.businessweek.com/magazine/content/01_49/b3760605.htm.
4   "Z Auction and eBay announce strategic alliance." eBay Press Release, 10-Feb-1998.
5   Lashinsky, Adam, Fortune Magazine, "Meg and the machine." August 11, 2003.
6   Sullivan, Jennifer, Wired Magazine, "Investory frenzy over eBay IPO." 24-Sept-1998; URL: http://www.wired.com/news/print/0,1294,15212,00.html
7   Gaither, Chris, "eBay to acquire PayPal for $1.513 stock deal, unites online auction giant, net payment service." *The Boston Globe*, 9-Jul-2002.
8   eBay Inc. 2Q 2004 Financial Results, Press Release, July 21, 2004; URL: http://investor.ebay.com/news/Q204/EBAY072104-139863.pdf.
9   eBay presentation at 2004 Pacific Crest Technology Forum, 10-Aug-2004.
10 Matt Hines, "eBay sellers file billing suit." CNET News.com, 07-Jul-2004.
11 Marketing Vox News, "eBay drop-off stores optimistic." News Archives, 03-Feb-2004 http://www.marketingvox.com/archives/2004/02/03/ebay_dropoff_stores_optimistic/
12 The Retail Bulletin, "eBay drop-off stores herald $10bn sales boost." 21-Jul 2004; URL: http://www.theretailbulletin.com/index.php?page=5&cat=news&id=4403&size=up&PHPSESSID=9797d0bd1ab6b9d477e1f0ded843a79d.
13 Anne B. McDonald from the Sep-2004 issue of PC World Magazine, "Auction stores do ebay selling for you." URL: http://www.pcworld.com/news/article/0,aid,117090,pg,1,00.asp.
14 AuctionBytes.com, "Circuit City closes four ebay drop-off centers." URL: http://www.auctionbytes.com/cab/abn/y04/m10/i04/s02.
15 Ibid.
16 Matthew Clark, ENN electricnews.net, "Yahoo raises the bar for 2003." 16-Jan-2003; URL: http://www.enn.ie/news.html?code=8894192.
17 Yahoo! 2003 Annual Report, page #4, Terry S. Semel's letter to shareholders.
18 Ibid.
19 URL: http://help.yahoo.com/help/auctions/afee/afee-06.html.
20 Nielsen Net Ratings: Auction sites ever more popular." July 2, 2001; URL: http://www.nua.ie/surveys/index.cgi?f=VS&art_id=905356927&rel=true.
21 Company Profile, Overstock.com; URL: http://www.shareholder.com/overstock/history.cfm?page=do.
22 James K. Glassman, Tech Central Station, "Profit-from-doom Overstock boss prophesizes e-tailing's quick demise." URL: http://www.techcentralstation.com/011501L.html.
23 From Company's 10Q and 10K filings.
24 Ibid.
25 From the company's October 21, 2004, SEC Form 8-K.
26 Internet retailer, 06-Aug-2004; URL: http://www.internetretailer.com/dailynews.asp?id=12602.
27 Morningstar.com News, 27-Oct-2004, "Overstock.com auction closes for Barry Bonds' historic 700th home run ball." URL: http://news.morningstar.com/news/PR/M10/D27/1098907868159.html.

Case 3–2: Nucleon, Inc.*

Robert Moore, a recent graduate of a top-ranked M.B.A. program, now realized what it was like to be on the other side of a case study. It was December 1990 and Nucleon, the young biotechnology start-up at which he had recently become project manager, faced critical manufacturing choices. Moore and Jeff Hurst, the firm's CEO, had met to discuss the situation, and within the next few weeks, Hurst needed to present the company's manufacturing strategy to the board of directors. In the meantime, he asked Moore to evaluate in detail Nucleon's options and give his own recommendation.

Nucleon's first potential product, "cell regulating protein-1" (CRP-1), had been undergoing extensive experimentation and analysis in the company's R&D laboratories for several years. The next major hurdle was human clinical trials, which also typically took place over several years. However, before Nucleon could launch clinical trials, it had to decide how and where CRP-1 would be manufactured. To ensure participants' safety, the U.S. Food and Drug Administration (FDA) imposed strict guidelines; products being tested in humans had to be made in facilities certified for "clinical grade" production.[1]

Since CRP-1 was the company's first product to go into the clinic, Nucleon had no manufacturing facilities which met FDA requirements. It was faced with three options for supplying CRP-1 to the clinic: The first was to build a new 5000 square-foot pilot plant with enough capacity to supply all the CRP-1 needed for Phases I and II of clinical trials. The second option was to contract clinical manufacturing to an outside firm. And a third option was to license the manufacturing to another biotechnology company or to a pharmaceutical firm. Under this third option, the licensee would be responsible for all manufacturing, clinical development, and eventual marketing of CRP-1.

Definite risks and rewards were attached to each option, and Moore knew that the one ultimately chosen by Hurst would have long-term consequences for Nucleon's survival in the intensively competitive and high-stakes drug industry.

Background

Nucleon was founded in 1985 by Dr. Alan Ball, an internationally respected researcher at the Children's Hospital and an Associate Professor of Clinical Medicine at the Greaves Medical Center, to develop pharmaceutical products based on a class of proteins known as cell regulating factors. From 1985 to 1988, Dr. Ball and a small group of scientists who joined Nucleon researched ways of producing CRP-1 outside the human body. Although CRP-1 was a naturally occurring protein contained in human blood plasma, the amount that could be extracted was far too small to be of any commercial use.

Scientists first isolated a small amount of naturally occurring CRP-1 and determined the gene that instructed human cells how to produce CRP-1. The gene was then cloned. While this laboratory process for producing CRP-1 was still very small scale, it generated enough material to send to academic collaborators who were exploring the potential therapeutic uses of CRP-1. Although an actual product was still several years and millions of dollars away, early research indicated that CRP-1 had potential as a treatment for burns and kidney failure.

*Professor Gary Pisano wrote this case as the basis for class discussion rather than to illustrate either effective or ineffective handling of an administrative situation.

Data and names have been altered for purposes of confidentiality.

Reprinted by permission of Harvard School Press from Nucleon, Inc. by Professor Gary Pisano. Copyright © 1991 by the President and Fellows of Harvard College. To order copies or request permission to reproduce materials, call 1-800-545-7685, write Harvard Business School Publishing, Boston, MA 02163, or go to http://www.hbsp.harvard.edu. No part of this publication may be reproduced, stored in a retrieval system, used in a spreadsheet, or transmitted in any form or by any means—electronic, mechanical photocopying, recording, or otherwise—without the permission of Harvard Business School.

Strategy and Competition

Nucleon was one of over 200 firms founded since the mid-1970s to develop pharmaceutical technologies based on recent advances in molecular biology and immunology. This new field of R&D, commonly called "biotechnology," also attracted the attention of established companies. By 1989, most of the world's largest pharmaceutical enterprises, like Eli Lilly, Merck, and Hoffman LaRoche, had extensive in-house biotechnology R&D programs as well as collaborative ties with many of the new entrants.

Competition was intense. Scientists at both start-up and established companies were racing to be the first to clone certain genes and establish proprietary positions for their firms in emerging areas like cell regulating factors. Establishing a strong patent position was particularly important for small companies like Nucleon. Moore explained: "Given the enormous costs of developing and commercializing a new drug, potential investors want to see a strong proprietary position before they commit serious capital. Just one strong patent on the right molecule can ensure survival for years by allowing you to attract capital."

Biotechnology patent law, however, was as new and uncertain as the technology itself. Indeed, the legality of patenting a genetically engineered microorganism was only established in 1980 by a landmark United States Supreme Court decision, and the ensuing decade saw many legal battles over the scope and efficacy of specific patents. In some cases, two or more companies had claims on different proprietary elements of the same molecule. For example, one company might claim ownership of the molecule itself while another of the genetic sequence used to synthesize the molecule. Further, it was extremely difficult to patent the process technology used to obtain a biologically important molecule, even though the starting material and the resulting molecule were considered original enough to be patented. Given the lack of precedent, it was always difficult to predict how the courts would rule in any given situation.

Moreover, the United States Patent Office might take several years to process an application. And while few companies could afford to wait until a patent was granted before continuing development, there were big risks in going ahead with development before the granting of a patent. A company could spend tens of millions of dollars in clinical trials and manufacturing facilities yet wind up not having a proprietary position if the patent office denied the application. Even if patents were granted, it was always possible for a competitor to challenge them in court. While Nucleon believed it had a strong patent position on the CRP-1 molecule, its rights to other necessary proprietary components (such as the genetic sequence) were less certain.

Nucleon management believed that several factors were critical to the company's survival. As Hurst commented:

Given how small we are, it's absolutely essential that we pick the right projects. We can't hedge our bets with a big portfolio of projects, like the big pharmaceutical companies can. We've got to pick winners the first time.

Gordon Banks, Nucleon's vice president of R&D, and one of the leading scientists in the field of cell regulating factors added:

That's why it's so important for us to be at the leading edge of scientific research. This means not only attracting the best in-house scientists, but also maintaining close contact with universities. If someone at a university clones the genes for a new cell regulating factor, we want to know about it.

Nucleon management believed that it had found an attractive niche: relatively few firms were working on cell regulating proteins. Banks believed that the company's distinctive technical capability lay in its ability to identify potentially therapeutic cell regulating factors. Although Nucleon was a leader in cell regulating factors, the company was not free from competition. Other companies were developing drugs using somewhat similar technology. Also, many companies were using alternative technologies to develop drugs for some of the same diseases for which cell regulating factors were being developed. As Hurst commented, "We're a leader, but we're not alone. It's important for us to get our products into the clinic before others do."

Biotechnology firms were using different strategies for developing and commercializing their technologies. Virtually all the biotechnology companies started, like Nucleon, as specialized R&D laboratories. Over time, some vertically integrated into production, and a few of the oldest companies, like Genentech, were even vertically integrating into marketing. Nucleon was presently contemplating its manufacturing strategy. Its marketing strategy, however, was clear. Nucleon management believed that the company could not afford to market its products on its own. Instead, it planned to link up with established pharmaceutical companies, with strong distribution capabilities, to market its products. Hurst, who once worked in marketing for a large pharmaceutical company, noted:

Companies like Merck have hundreds of salespeople. They can reach every doctor's office in the country within one week. It would be crazy for a company like us to go up against them in marketing. Besides, our products are likely to be targeted at a variety of therapeutic markets. We would need a few hundred salespeople to market all these products directly. We're much better off linking up with the best company in each therapeutic market.

By December 1990, the privately held company had grown to 22 employees, 18 of whom were engaged in R&D; of these about one-third had PhDs from scientific disciplines such as biochemistry, molecular biology, protein chemistry, and immunology. Most of the R&D staff had been recruited from leading university research laboratories and were strongly attracted to cutting-edge, product-oriented research. Nucleon's size and entrepreneurial spirit created an academic atmosphere in R&D and tight links to the academic/scientific community.

Since its founding, Nucleon had raised approximately $6 million in venture capital and received research grants from the U.S. Department of Agriculture totaling $600,000.

Drug Development: From Research to Market

Establishing the safety and efficacy of products like CRP-1 that were based upon novel genetic engineering technology was enormously complex, time-consuming, and expensive. Nucleon's drug development process, divided into several distinct phases, is discussed below.

Research

Before launching a research project to develop a new drug, Nucleon management considered several factors in evaluating a project's profit potential. First, there had to be a chance of achieving a dominant proprietary position. Second, the market had to be large enough to justify the R&D investment. Finally, Nucleon wanted to develop drugs where no alternative treatments were available. During the research phase, Nucleon's scientists sought to identify and purify from human plasma minute quantities of cell regulating proteins that might have therapeutic value. Some critical information to pursue this research was obtained by perusing scientific literature or by consulting with leading academic researchers. Much necessary information, however, was still undiscovered and came only from in-house research and experimentation, which seldom moved in a straight-forward, logical manner but from one obstacle to the next. This could entail abandoning one strategy and starting over again.

Cloning and Purification

Products like CRP-1 and others that Nucleon intended to develop were fundamentally different from most drugs developed by pharmaceutical companies, which traditionally were synthetic chemicals. Chemical synthesis was effective for relatively small and simple molecules, but proteins like CRP-1 were simply too big and complex to be synthesized that way and instead were produced by genetic engineering.

Through genetic engineering, the scientist created a microscopic protein factory. The gene for the protein was identified, isolated, and cloned, then inserted into different strains of the bacterium *E. coli*. In theory, the genetically engineered bacteria could then produce the protein in a test tube or shake flask. However, since genetic engineering was still a relatively new scientific discipline, it was not always easy to either identify the relevant genes or to get "host" (genetically altered) bacteria to produce a specific protein. In practice, it was usually necessary to try different types of host cells to find one or more capable of producing the protein in quantities that could be scaled-up to an economically feasible process.

Only a few milligrams of protein could be produced from genetically engineered cells grown in shake flasks. Thus, an extensive amount of work then had to go into developing the processes for making each of these proteins in large quantity.

Pre-Clinical Research

Before a pharmaceutical was tested in humans it underwent pre-clinical evaluation, consisting of experiments in animals to evaluate its efficacy. Over six to eight months, increasing doses were administered to animals with and without the simulated disease. Another six months might be needed to evaluate the data.

By this point, the company might have spent $6 to $10 million in R&D and preparation of regulatory documents. Only after completing all the requisite animal tests, and having a suitable production process, could the company file for permission with the FDA to commence clinical trials in humans. Though Nucleon had not begun human clinical trials, management expected to file an application with the FDA to begin human trials for CRP-1 as a burn wound treatment in 1992. The company was also doing research to determine if CRP-1 might have other therapeutic applications. There was some preliminary data suggesting that it might treat kidney failure. Moore estimated that about another two years and $3 million of work were needed before the kidney failure application could be tested in the clinic.

Human Clinical Trials

Most governments required every new pharmaceutical product to undergo extensive clinical testing before it could be marketed widely, and the FDA regulations were considered the most stringent in the world. To meet them, any new drug, or any approved drug being modified for a different therapeutic application, had to undergo three phases of clinical trials.

Phase I trials assessed basic safety. During these trials, the drug was administered to a small group of healthy volunteers and any adverse reactions (such as fevers, dizziness, or nausea) were noted.[2] This phase usually required between 6 and 12 months. As long as there were no serious side effects, the product moved to Phase II trials where it was administered to a small group of patients having the disease the drug was presumed to treat. The patients were monitored to determine whether their condition improved as a result of the drug and whether they suffered any adverse side effects. It was during Phase II trials that appropriate dosages were determined. This phase typically required between one to two years to complete. If Phase II trials succeeded, the product then moved to Phase III trials.

Phase III trials assessed the product's efficacy with a relatively large sample of patients on a statistically rigorous basis. Typically, these trials involved multiple hospitals and could require from two to five years to complete. Because of the large number of patients, doctors, and hospitals involved, this stage was by far the most expensive. The costs of manufacturing the drug, administering it to patients, monitoring results, analyzing data, and preparing the requisite regulatory paperwork could run between $30–$100 million. It was imperative for regulatory reasons to manufacture the product with the same process that would be used when the product was marketed commercially. Any change in manufacturing would mean repeating human clinical trials to prove that the deviation did not alter the product's safety and efficacy. This also added significantly to the costs of running Phase III clinical trials.

The CRP-1 Project: Current Applications

Since Nucleon's founding, its main development project had been CRP-1 and most of the company's R&D resources had been focused on the CRP-1 projects. While CRP-1's commercialization was still a few years away, Nucleon's scientists and investors were optimistic about its potential. Exhibit 1 depicts the expected time to FDA approval. Initial research focused on developing two major therapeutic applications—one for topical treatment of burn wounds, the other for acute kidney failure. Both the burn wound and kidney failure markets were estimated to be similar in size. Furthermore, in 1988, the company had also begun investigating two new cell regulating factors, still in the

Exhibit 1	Approximate Time Frame for CRP-1 Project
April 1992	Begin Phase I Clinical Trials
December 1992	Begin Phase II Clinical Trials
December 1993	End Phase II Clinical Trials
June 1994	Begin Phase III Clinical Trials
December 1996	Complete Phase III Clinical Trials; File data with FDA
January 1998	Expected FDA approval and commencement of sales

early stages of research. Dr. Banks estimated that these could be ready for clinical trials in about four years if the company spent $10 million on each one.

One of the most critical activities currently taking place on the CRP-1 project was the development of a larger scale production process, with sufficient capacity to meet all clinical trial requirements. Every step of the process had to be carefully documented and validated to ensure that it could produce identical product from batch to batch.

Process Development and Manufacturing

CRP-1 production would require four basic process steps: 1) fermentation, 2) purification, 3) formulation, 4) filling and packaging (see Exhibit 2).

Fermentation Fermentation initially focused on growing the genetically engineered *E. coli* in small laboratory flasks; the process was then scaled up to successively larger vessels. Unfortunately, the process used to grow cells in a 1-liter glass bottle might not work when attempted in a 10-liter glass chamber or a 100-liter stainless steel tank (also known as a fermentor or bioreactor), given differences in heat exchange, tank aeration, and fermentor geometry. The kinds of nutrients cells were fed, bioreactor temperature, acidity level, oxygen flow rate into the bioreactor, and dozens of other process parameters, were all determined during fermentation process development.

While crude fermentation processes existed for over 6000 years, fermentation using genetically engineered cells dated to the early 1980s. Many biotechnology firms encountered major difficulties when trying to run pilot and commercial scale fermentation processes for the first time, as Dr. Ann Dawson, Nucleon's director of process science, explained:

There are so many unknowns and so many things which can go wrong. If a virus gets into your bioreactor, you could be shut down for weeks. Incredibly tight process control is an absolute must, and even then, you may still run into troubles.

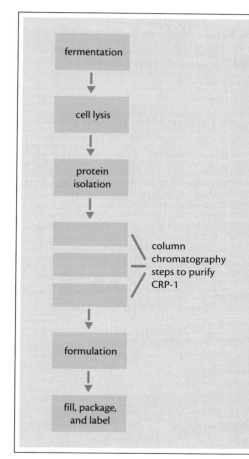

Fermentation: A process in which organisms such as bacteria or yeast are suspended in a nutrient growth medium, consisting of sugars, salts, and amino acids (protein building blocks), at an appropriate temperature and aeration level (oxygen and other gases) in order to promote these organisms' growth and metabolism. The desired products of the organisms' metabolism may be the whole organism itself, metabolic products, modified compounds, or in this case proteins.

Cell Lysis: In cases where the protein of interest is not excreted by the cell into the surrounding medium but remains inside, the cell needs to be broken open to obtain the protein. This process is know as cell lysis. Lysis can be done mechanically or chemically.

Isolation and Purification: After cells are lysed, the protein of interest must be isolated and purified from among all of the other contents of the cell. Initially, methods such as centrifugation (using centrifugal force to separate heavy and light debris) and chemical precipitation can be used to concentrate the mixture.

After a series of initial separation steps have been performed, finer, more precise separation techniques can be employed to isolate the protein of interest from other similar protein molecules. For example, chromatography isolated substances based upon their ability to separate between a liquid and a solid.

Formulation: In drug formulation, the protein of interest is put into an appropriate medium for administration as a therapeutic drug. The protein may by dissolved in purified water or another pure solvent such as ethanol for injection. In some cases, a protein must be formulated to be applied in a topical form such as a cream or put in an aerosol suspension. The challenge is to ensure the drug's safety and efficacy.

Filling: The therapeutic is then placed in an appropriate container under sterile conditions and is packaged and labeled.

Exhibit 2   Process Flow for CRP-11[1]

[1]Diagram does not include holding points where work-in-process is stored between operations. The diagram also does not include quality control steps which are conducted after every operation.

For regulatory reasons, it was absolutely critical to run the process exactly as specified. Such strict adherence to process specifications was necessary because even minor process deviations could impact product quality. In addition, the efficiency of the process could be severely affected by changes in any one of the key process parameters.

Because such production methods were new, process development required a great deal of trial-and-error and close collaboration between research scientists and process development scientists early on in the project. Research scientists had to design a process that worked in a test tube as well as on a larger scale, and process development scientists had to be aware of and understand the details of the product and its host cell. Some genetically-engineered cell lines, for example, were extremely difficult to grow large-scale. Dr. Dawson noted:

Ideally, we want the research scientists to work with only those cell lines which we know can be scaled-up. While I think they agree with this in principle, they really don't want to be constrained, particularly if they're having trouble getting expression with one of our "preferred" cell lines.

While much progress had been made over the past decade, many people considered biotechnology production processes very much an art. It was not unheard of for a process to work well in one facility but fail completely when transferred to another. One Nucleon researcher who had experience with such transfers explained:

You would be surprised at all the little things that could be done differently from one organization to another. Most of these things are so minor you would not even think of writing them down. But they make the difference between a successful and unsuccessful process.

Currently, Nucleon had scaled up the process for making CRP-1 to 10 liters, enough to supply material for its own biochemical studies, academic collaborators, and potential joint venture partners who wanted to evaluate the product. Early phase clinical trials were likely to require a 100-liter process, and commercial production a much larger scale process.

As complex as it was, bacterial fermentation was considered one of the more efficient ways of producing proteins like CRP-1. In some cases, product characteristics could be enhanced if a mammalian cell (e.g., from a mouse or human) rather than a bacterial cell was used as a host. Mammalian cell processes, while desirable from the product side, were much more complex than bacterial processes, not well understood, and much more expensive to maintain. Mammalian cells had to be fed more expensive nutrients, and they grew much more slowly than bacterial cells. They required different bioreactors, and even stricter adherence to original process specifications than bacterial cells. Dr. Dawson explained, "With bacterial cells, a one degree Centigrade temperature change can slow the growth rate and increase your costs, whereas mammalian cells might just die altogether."

Although most biotechnology companies had some experience with bacterial cell processes, many fewer had mammalian cell capabilities. Fortunately, CRP-1 could be produced using bacterial cells. The company's R&D lab, however, was already working on second generation CRP-1 molecules produced in mammalian cells. And biotechnology companies overall were unsure whether existing process development technology would be viable in the future to produce biological products.[3]

Purification. After fermentation, the cells would be broken apart and the CRP-1 protein separated from all other proteins and cell debris contained in the fermentation tank. A series of fractionation and centrifugation steps would isolate the cell protein from carbohydrates, fatty acids, and DNA. The CRP-1 containing protein mixture would then be purified in three additional steps using a filtration procedure known as column chromatography. Like fermentation, the purification process specified during process development had to be strictly followed during manufacturing. After purification, the material would be subjected to extensive quality testing to ensure that the product met the FDA's extremely high purity standards.

Formulation. Purification processes yielded nearly pure quantities of the protein of interest, for example CRP-1. At this stage, the product was made into the intended dosage form (e.g., oral, topical, injectable), and subjected to extensive quality testing. For burn treatment, CRP-1 would be formulated into a topical dosage form.

Filling and Packaging. During the final step, bulk quantities of the formulated product were put into tubes, bottles, or other vessels required for administration to patients. The sealed vessels were then inserted into packages, which were also sealed.

The Financial Environment

A critical issue affecting Nucleon was capital availability. The situation had changed dramatically since the late 1970s and early 1980s when investors lined up to provide capital to brand new biotechnology companies. By the mid- to late-1980s, private and public equity markets grew tighter, and venture capitalists, who expected investment returns of 30%, became more selective. The state of the public equity markets in 1990 made "going public" virtually impossible for a company like Nucleon; furthermore, potential corporate partners, who had been disappointed by previous biotechnology relationships, were unwilling to fund early stage projects. As Hurst described it:

> In the early 1980s, a company like ours could have gotten corporate funding with just our idea. By the mid-1980s, we probably would have needed to have started some lab work and have had some preliminary experimental data. Now, it's hard to get a large pharmaceutical company to talk to you unless you've got some solid Phase I and Phase II clinical results and can demonstrate that you've got a stable manufacturing process. And even then, they'll cut some pretty tough terms with you. When it comes to raising capital today, it's a buyers' market.

Nucleon was just about to receive another $6.0 million infusion from its venture capitalist. This funding, combined with existing cash on-hand, revenues, interest, and grants, would give Nucleon about $6.5 million. Furthermore, if CRP-1 showed promise in pre-clinical trials, Hurst felt that Nucleon could raise enough money to pursue Phase I and II clinical trials. Some analysts were predicting that by 1991 or 1992, Wall Street would once again find biotechnology stocks attractive and there would be opportunities for smaller companies to raise money by selling stock to the public. Others thought the capital situation would stay tight for at least several more years. The possibility that a long awaited "shake-out" was about to hit the biotechnology industry was making many investors cautious. One promising sign was that large corporations again seemed willing to fund some selected projects at very early stages of research. As Moore noted, "Today, some brand new start-ups in new fields, like antisense, are cutting some deals on projects which are still years away from the clinic."

Manufacturing Options for Phase I and Phase II CRP-1 Development

Nucleon management contemplated three options to produce clinical grade CRP-1: 1) build a new pilot facility, 2) contract CRP-1 production to a third-party, or 3) license manufacturing and marketing rights to another biotechnology company or pharmaceutical firm in exchange for up front cash payments and royalties on future product sales. Each option is described below.

The New Pilot Plant

Nucleon commissioned an engineering consulting firm to study the physical requirements and costs of a new pilot plant (Exhibit 3). The proposed 5000 square-foot plant would be fully equipped with all the state-of-the-art processing equipment and environmental controls necessary to meet clinical production standards. Planned capacity would meet Nucleon's requirements for Phase I and Phase II clinical trials. The pilot facility, however, could not be used to produce CRP-1 for Phase III trials, because it would not meet FDA manufacturing standards for those trials. It was beyond Nucleon's financial capability to build such a plant at this time.

The main advantage in building a pilot plant, as Moore saw it, was that it would enable the firm to develop the nucleus of a future larger-scale, in-house manufacturing capability. Because most of Nucleon's employees were PhD scientists engaged in R&D, it currently lacked supervisors and technicians who could carry out the maintenance, procurement, quality assurance, technical support, logistics, and other functions to operate even a small manufacturing plant. Recruiting people with the appropriate skills and getting the manufacturing organization to work effectively would take time. Supplying clinical trials would allow manufacturing time to accumulate experience dealing with many complicated technical and regulatory issues. Moore noted:

If Nucleon waits until Phase III trials to bring manufacturing in-house, we might find ourselves with a "green" manufacturing organization just when the stakes are highest. By starting now, we'll have the basic manufacturing skills in-house and ready to go when we are really going to need them. The second big advantage of the pilot facility is that it would keep control over process and quality procedures firmly in Nucleon's hands.

Dawson added, "Scaling up will be much easier if we have our own pilot plant to experiment in."

Of course, building a pilot plant was risky. Moore knew that despite its promise in laboratory experiments, it was uncertain at this point how well CRP-1 would work when tested in humans. Indeed, if the history of the pharmaceutical industry was any guide, most drugs that entered clinical trials never reached the market. This high risk of failure was offset somewhat by the fact that CRP-1 had several potential therapeutic applications. If clinical trials for burn wounds were not promising, it might be used in other applications. Nevertheless, Nucleon management had to consider the possibility of the pilot plant being idled if CRP-1 performed poorly in the clinic. Other products under development were still years away from requiring pilot manufacturing capabilities.

Another major risk involved process uncertainty. The pilot plant would be designed to produce products using bacterial fermentation; but the company was already in the early stages of developing a version in mammalian cells, which would require vastly different process development capabilities.

Some board members believed that Nucleon should focus all of its financial, managerial, and technical resources on R&D. Manufacturing, they felt, would only distract the company from its main mission of exploiting its unique scientific capabilities in the discovery of cell regulating proteins. According to Hurst:

Exhibit 3   **Time and Cost to Obtain Phase II Data for CRP-1 (Burn Treatment) Using a New Pilot Facility for Clinical-grade Production of CRP-1. Midrange estimate. ($000)**

Pilot Facility	1991	1992	1993	Total Thru 12/93
Construction and Equipment Costs	3,100	0	0	3,100
Variable Production Expenses and Overhead	0	800	1,204	2,004
Pre-Clinical Development	250	0	0	250
Clinical Trials (Phase I/II)	0	1,040	1,000	2,040
Total	3,350	1,840	2,204	7,394

Our venture capitalists are asking us where we, as a company, add the most value. As a small research-intensive company, we can be the "fastest guns on the block" when it comes to drug discovery. But that means funneling our limited resources into R&D. Some of our investors are concerned that we could get bogged down in manufacturing. On the other hand, it's getting to the point where anyone can clone a gene. I keep wondering whether we can still differentiate ourselves on R&D alone.

Contract Manufacturing

Contracting manufacturing was a second option for Phase I and Phase II CRP-1 development. The biggest advantage of this option was that it required no major capital investments on Nucleon's part. If CRP-1 failed, the contract could be easily terminated. Aside from relatively small termination penalties, the company would have little else at risk. Another advantage was that companies supplying contract manufacturing services had facilities and personnel in place.

Contract production was not inexpensive (see Exhibit 4). There were very few U.S. companies capable and willing to contract manufacture pharmaceuticals from bacteria. Nucleon management was meeting with several potential contractors. These included other biotechnology companies who had excess capacity. In recent years, many biotechnology companies had built GMP plants in anticipation of future products. When product approvals were delayed or even rejected by the FDA, these companies found themselves with tremendous excess manufacturing capacity. Because of mounting financial pressures, some of these companies were providing contract manufacturing services. Some industry experts believed that excess manufacturing capacity would continue to accumulate during the next few years.

One of contract manufacturing's biggest risks was confidential information disclosure. It was virtually impossible for any contractor to provide reliable time and cost estimates without knowing many proprietary product details. Moreover, the complexity of the products and processes

made estimates of time and cost painstaking; reaching an agreement could take many months. Even after a contract was signed, technology transfer and scale-up might take another nine months. Moore noted, "It will take about as much time to negotiate an agreement and transfer and validate the process as it will for us to build a pilot plant."

Although production contracts were negotiated typically for fixed quantities (e.g., 100 g of CRP-1 over 10 months), in contract negotiations, a balance needed to be struck. On one hand, it was risky to commit to large quantities of material—which might not be required if product specifications changed or the product was pulled from the clinic. On the other hand, short-term contracts usually involved a higher price to offset fixed costs of scale-up and batch set-ups.

Under either the pilot plant or the contract manufacturing option, Nucleon would retain ownership of the product rights at least until the commencement of Phase III clinical trials. At that point, the company would enter into licensing and marketing with a large corporate partner. The options for Phase III trials and beyond are discussed later.

Licensing the Product to Another Company

Rather than waiting until Phase III trials to enter a licensing deal, Nucleon could license the product immediately in exchange for fixed payments and future royalties. Under this option, the licensed partner, not Nucleon, would make all the requisite expenditures in clinical development, clinical manufacturing, regulatory filings, and commercial manufacturing and marketing. The partner would have the right to market CRP-1 to treat burn wounds. Nucleon would retain the right to develop CRP-1 for other therapeutic applications. Nucleon also would receive an upfront, fixed licensing fee and reimbursement for any additional development work it performed on the project. If and when CRP-1 was commercialized, Nucleon would receive royalties as a percentage of sales.

This licensing option had the chief benefit of generating cash immediately; it also spared Nucleon from making

---

Exhibit 4   Time and Cost to Obtain Phase II Clinical Trial Data for CRP-1 (Burn Treatment) Using Contract Production for Clinical-grade CRP-1

	1991	1992	1993	Total Thru 12/93
Contract Production and Related Expense	0	955	1,550	2,505
Pre-Clinical Development	250	0	0	250
Clinical Trials (Phase I/II)	0	1,040	1,000	2,040
Total	250	1,995	2,550	4,795

large capital investments in clinical development and manufacturing, and allowed the company to concentrate all of its financial and human resources on R&D. Of course, if the product turned out to be successful, Nucleon would receive far lower revenues than if it had made all of these investments itself. Some Nucleon employees viewed this option as "mortgaging away" the company's future.

Whether this option would mortgage the company's future depended upon the exact terms of the agreement that Nucleon could negotiate. While it was virtually impossible to know for sure what kind of deal could be struck, Nucleon management had conducted preliminary discussions with several firms. From these and consultations with the company's venture capitalists, Moore determined that Nucleon could expect to reach an agreement with the following terms:

Upon signing the contract Nucleon would get a $3 million payment. After the FDA approved CRP-1 for burn wounds, Nucleon would receive annual royalty payments from the partner equivalent to 5% of gross sales (see Exhibit 5).

Manufacturing Options for Phase III and Commercialization

One of the chief advantages of either in-house pilot manufacturing or contract manufacturing over immediate licensing was that it gave Nucleon more options if the project survived Phase I and Phase II trials. As noted earlier, under these two options, Nucleon intended to line up with a partner who would be responsible for conducting Phase III trials, handling regulatory filings and marketing the product. However, under such an arrangement, Nucleon could either retain commercial manufacturing responsibilities or license these to the partner. Each of these approaches are discussed below.

Vertically Integrate into Commercial Manufacturing

Before Phase III trials began, Nucleon could invest in a full-scale commercial manufacturing facility which met the FDA guidelines for Good Manufacturing Practice (see Exhibit 6). The FDA required that Phase III trials be supplied largely by the plant which would be used to supply the commercial market. Thus it would be necessary to commence construction in mid-1993 so that the plant could be fully validated and operational by the scheduled commencement of Phase III trials.

Moore estimated that the costs of such a facility would be about $20 million, and another $1 million in development resources would be required to perform

Exhibit 5   Estimated Gross Sales of CRP-1 (As Topical Burn Wound Treatment)

Year	Sales ($thousands)
1998	53,700
1999	99,500
2000	125,000
2001	130,000
2002	150,000

*After the year 2000, sales of CRP-1 as a burn wound treatment were expected to grow at approximately 5% per year, assuming no introduction of a substitute product.

scale-up. He and Nucleon's financial advisors believed that once the project cleared Phase II trials, it would have little difficulty raising the needed funds to build the plant. The company would also have to hire at least 20 people to handle such functions as procurement, quality control, maintenance, technical support, and logistics.[4]

It was difficult to know exactly what terms could be reached. If Nucleon built a commercial plant, it would be the sole supplier of CRP-1 to its marketing partner. Judging by what other firms in the industry were receiving for similar products, Nucleon management estimated that the company could negotiate a combined supply contract and royalty agreement with the following terms: Nucleon would receive a $5 million payment upon FDA approval of CRP-1 plus royalties equal to 40% of the partner's gross sales of the product. Nucleon would sell CRP-1 to the partner at cost.[5]

Licensing Out Manufacturing and Marketing Rights at Phase III

A second option at the beginning of Phase III trials would be to license out both the manufacturing and marketing rights to a partner. This option would be similar to that discussed above, except, in this case, the partner would also be responsible for Phase III and commercial manufacturing. Nucleon therefore would not have to invest the $20 million in a commercial plant. Under this option, Nucleon could expect to receive a $7 million payment if and when CRP-1 was approved by the FDA. After that, Nucleon would receive a royalty equivalent to 10% of the partner's gross sales of CRP-1.

Moore recognized that Hurst leaned towards manufacturing CRP-1 in-house. He had said, "I keep asking myself, 'How many times will we get to the plate?' If I thought that this were our only chance, I'd go for the home run and take the risks of manufacturing." For his part, Moore decided to review Nucleon's options another time before making a recommendation.

Exhibit 6 Good Manufacturing Practices (GMPs)

The following are some of the major concepts behind "Good Manufacturing Practices" (GMPs):

- A facility must have an uncluttered fermentation area, precautions for fermentation spills, and surfaces that are easily cleaned.
- Adequate air systems to prevent cross-contamination of the product from other research products or micro-organisms in the facility. Closed system fermenters. Steps must be performed in a controlled environment. (A controlled environment is defined as being adequate to control air pressure, humidity, temperature, microorganisms and particulate matter.) An environmental monitoring system is necessary for all manufacturing areas.
- The water used in the downstream manufacturing steps should be of high quality and, again, there should be a monitoring system in place.
- A trained Quality Assurance department is required to oversee and assure GMP manufacturing and control.
- A documentation system is required for the process or support systems.
- Uni-directional production flow is required.
- Validated processes to demonstrate removal of major contaminants is required.

- Validated cleaning procedures to demonstrate those in place are adequate for multi-use of equipment is required.
- A uni-directional flow of raw material, product and personnel is required with product moving from less clean and controlled areas (fermentation) to very clean areas (formulation and filling). There should be positive air pressure differentials between clean and less clean areas.
- Space should be designated for raw material and final product storage. The area should be designed to allow for separate areas for quarantined, released and rejected material and there should be adequate security.
- Space should be designated for media/reagent preparation with a controlled environment.
- There should be adequate space for glassware washing and autoclaving.
- There should be gowning areas for very clean areas (formulation/filling) and possibly the fermentation area.
- Find out now what other microorganisms are being used in the facility and keep track of any new organisms which may be used in the future.

Notes

1 "Clinical grade" indicates the minimum conditions under which drugs must be produced for use in human clinical trials.
2 For some very serious diseases, Phase I trials were performed on afflicted patients.
3 On the horizon was a hybrid of biotechnology and synthetic chemical techniques that could alter or replace existing process technologies. These hybrid companies used molecular biology techniques to clone and produce small amounts of biologically important proteins. The protein was studied to learn the chemical and physical structure of its therapeutically active site and then, using computer-aided modelling techniques, the active site of the protein could be constructed synthetically.
4 This assumes the company already has a pilot plant with a staff of six.
5 All costs, except depreciation, would be reflected in the transfer price.

Case 3–3: Saatchi & Saatchi (A)*

Pioneers of Globalization in Advertising

Introduction

June 18, 1988 was not a day that Maurice and Charles Saatchi would care to remember. Since the start of Saatchi & Saatchi in 1970, as a small advertising agency with just nine employees, the brothers had never received such a rebuff from either the London City or the press.

It was obvious that their latest plans had not been well received. The convertible preference share issue, launched the previous day, was seen as having a dilutive effect on future potential earnings, and the share price had fallen 12% in a single day, continuing the downward trend that had seen Saatchi shares plummet from 397p in 1986 to 372p.

As the brothers met in Maurice's office, it was clear to them both that this situation required immediate attention in three crucial areas, in order to restore clients' and investors' confidence in the company.

First, the company's vision of a global agency was based on the promise of superior efficiency and service. Yet, trading margins in the communications division were falling, as costs grew faster than revenues. Therefore, ways had to be found to leverage the company's global reach into specific sources of extra customer benefits. Furthermore, necessary changes had to be made in the division's strategy and management systems to ensure that these potential benefits filtered through to the bottom line.

Second, an urgent decision had to be taken for the consulting business, too. Vic Miller, head of the consulting division, firmly believed that the business had potential for contributing significant profits, as long as up-front investments were launched for acquisitions and for hiring and training new personnel. However, the combination of falling trading margins, a heavy debt burden on earlier acquisitions, and a price-earnings ratio, which had dropped from 26 to 7 (less than half that of any smaller competitors), had made these kinds of investments increasingly difficult to finance. Therefore, a clear vision and a credible strategy were crucial, to prevent further erosion in the competitive position of this business, which both brothers felt was central to their ambition of building the "world's greatest service supermarket."

Finally, the company's organization and its management systems also needed closer scrutiny. Was the overall structure appropriate for the strategy it had adopted? Were the right administrative processes in place to manage the company's diverse, dispersed and complex businesses? Was the corporate organization playing the right roles and managing the right tasks? One analyst had recently described the organization as Saatchi's Achilles' heel. It was up to the brothers to make the necessary changes to make it the engine of the company's recovery and renewal.

The Advertising Industry

"When I attempt to tell others of the current state of the advertising agency business, it reminds me of nothing so much as Alice attempting to explain her presence in wonderland: 'I can't explain myself, I'm afraid, sir,' said Alice, 'because I'm not myself, you see.'

Certainly, the agency business is having difficulties explaining itself, because it is not itself, at least not in a way anyone in the business for more than a couple of years would recognize. . . . We have altered not only the nature of the agency business so that for the first time we are perceived, unhappily, as just another business, but the fundamental structure of the business as well."

**C. Peebler, CEO Bozell, Jacobs,
Kenyon, & Eckhardt.**

*This A Case was adapted by Eline Van Poeck, MA and Research Assistant in International Management at K.U. Leuven, with Paul Verdin, Affiliate Professor at large at INSEAD and Chair in Strategy and International Management at Solvay Business School (ULB), on the basis of the earlier Saatchi & Saatchi case (ref. nr. 09/90–120) by Sumantra Ghoshal, Professor at INSEAD and Alice Avis, MBA, INSEAD, 1989. A subsequent B Case reports the further developments of the company from 1988 up to the present date (2002). It is intended to be used as a basis for class discussion rather than to illustrate either effective or ineffective handling of an administrative situation.

This case is dedicated to the memory of Professor Sumantra Ghoshal, a true pioneer of globalization in management.

The factor that most strongly influenced the dramatic transformation of the advertising agency business in the 1980s was what the press often described as the "tidal wave from Britain". Up to the late 1970s, the industry was dominated by a few large American companies, both in terms of market share and creative talent, with Madison Avenue in New York being the undisputed advertising capital of the world.

Saatchi & Saatchi changed this traditional structure of the industry, not only by its own explosive growth trough acquisitions and its creative excellence, but also by the UK imitators it spawned. While in 1978, there was not a single UK holding company among the 20 agency groups worldwide, by 1988, there were four.

Saatchi & Saatchi were the first of these British "new wave" agencies, aiming for continuous earnings growth so as to obtain a high P/E ratio and using the resulting financial muscle to buy market share through aggressive acquisitions. These acquisitions were then leveraged to boost earnings by imposing strong financial controls, introducing new creative products, and motivating management through extremely generous performance-related incentive systems.

The Agency Business

Traditionally, advertising agencies had four functional areas: planning and research, account handling, creative design and media planning and purchase. With the exception of the very small companies, agencies rarely competed on price, although under competitive pressures, this was changing. Historically, creative reputation, individual personalities, planning facilities and resources in terms of an international network and marketing services were the main selection criteria for the clients.

The planning and research function had the responsibility of providing implementation on which the agency would develop an advertising strategy for the client. Quality of the planning department was, therefore, often a key basis for differentiation among the various agencies. While planning expenses were part of the standard fee for regular campaigns, they were paid for separately on a fee basis for new product development projects or consumer behavior analysis. For many agencies, such fee-based remuneration accounted for about a quarter of the total income.

The main task of the media department was to plan and buy media. A company's effectiveness at media purchase was often measured by independent research houses commissioned by the clients. A good media department would save clients as much as 20% on their media expenditure. Effective media buying was partly a function of an agency's clout as large agencies enjoyed some advantages in negotiating with media owners. But it was also a function of

the negotiating skills of the buyer, and relatively smaller agencies like Dorland in the UK often outperformed larger agencies such as Saatchi & Saatchi in media buying.

An agency's costs were mostly related to its personnel. For UK-based agencies, for example, salaries accounted for about 60% of the costs, while office and general administration contributed 36%, and depreciation only 4%. In the US, salaries tended to be higher, and accounted for between 65 and 70% of total costs for agencies of comparable size. As a result, the average profit margins of agencies were lower in the US—about 8% of revenues, compared to about 13% in the UK. Among the various functional areas, the creative design department typically accounted for between 30 to 40% of total personnel costs, while planning and account handling contributed between 20 and 30%, and media planning and buying contributed between 10 and 15%.

Market Trends

The American multinational agencies, which traditionally dominated the market, were not known for their creative brilliance. Their more limited resources, in terms of marketing services and media buying leverage, and the controversial nature of some of their advertising, confined them to a niche or, at best, a ranking below the top ten in most national markets.

The success of the "new wave" agencies in the 1980s could be partly attributed to the high growth of the industry, resulting from a rise in import penetration[1] in North America and Europe, a general increase in customer spending, a rapid concentration in retail power and the subsequent rise of own label products.

During the period 1980–1987, advertising expenditures grew at a real rate of 5.2% per annum. In 1988, the prospects for future growth looked promising, even though the situation varied a great deal from country to country (see Exhibit 1).

The United States, which accounted for about 55% of the market, was expected to be the slowest growth sector. This was a reflection, in part, of the increasing shift of advertising expenditures into below the line and local promotions.

Europe was expected to remain buoyant, benefiting from the increase in competition in preparation for the single market of 1992. The easing of restrictions on television advertising and the development of new media opportunities, as European cable and satellite channels started up, were also expected to boost advertising expenditure.

The Asia-Pacific market was dominated by Japan, the second largest national market after the United States. Western agencies, however, had found this market to be almost unpenetrable. Unlike any other major market, the Japanese advertising industry was completely dominated

Exhibit 1   The Advertising Industry: Market Size and Growth

Market	Expenditures in 1987 ($M)	Real Growth 1980–'87 (%)	Share of GDP (%)	Growth Forecast 1988 (%)	Growth Forecast 1989 (%)
Top ten countries					
US	90,539	4	1.6	7.5	6.1
Japan	21,961	3.5	0.8	12.7	6
UK	9,457	5.8	1.4	15.7	11
W. Germany	8,836	2.5	0.9	4.6	4.5
France	5,926	6.9	0.7	13.8	12.2
Canada	4,562	3.2		7	7.8
Italy	4,171	11	0.6	19.1	14
Spain	3,346	13.4	1.4	23.9	25.9
Australia	2,720	3.9		8.4	10.3
Holland	2,538	2	1.1	0.2	0.7
Total: Top ten	**153,876**	**5.2**			
Rest of the World					
Rest of Europe	8,140				
Rest of South-East Asia	4,398				
Latin America	4,799			10.4	8.3
Africa	1,473			10.4	8.3
Worldwide Total	**172,685**			**10**	**7.6**

by a handful of large and powerful domestic agencies. Not a single Western agency was included in the top ten. Saatchi & Saatchi operated independently in Japan, but ranked 30th, with less than 1% of the total market.

In the Asia-Pacific region, the growth forecast for some of the emerging economies, such as Malaysia and India, looked promising. Little could be predicted with any degree of accuracy with regard to the Latin American region, because of fluctuations in the dollar to which the national economies were highly sensitive, and because of hyperinflation.

Key Competitors

As described earlier, in the late 1980s, the advertising industry was in the midst of a major transformation. This transformation was, in part, a result of the broader trend of consolidation and rationalization among some of the most advertising-intensive businesses in the world. The wave of international acquisitions and mergers in beverages, food, pharmaceuticals and other consumer product industries, and the tendency of the merged companies to retain a single agency on a worldwide basis, had led to the demise of many medium-sized advertising companies to a polarization of the industry into a few mega-agencies and a large number of specialized boutiques.

The restructuring was being driven by the British pack, with first Saatchi and, more recently, WPP at the forefront. But the Americans were also launching a counterattack, as evidenced by the mega-merger of BBDO and DDB Needham in 1986 to form the Omnicom group, and D'Arcy McManus and Masius with Benton and Bowles in 1985. Exhibit 2 lists the major advertising groups and provides some data on their revenues and profitability in 1987. Exhibit 3 shows their ranking in each of the world's ten largest advertising markets.

Dentsu was the largest of the Japanese agencies and enjoyed an unprecedented 29% share of its home market. Despite its size, it had no presence outside Japan, except for its share in HDM, a relatively small international agency, ranked 15th on a worldwide basis, that was jointly owned by Havas Publicis Counseil, a French company, Young and Rubicam, and Dentsu. Unlike the other top ranking agencies, Dentsu had grown organically, fuelled by the stronger growth of its clients. With many Japanese agencies eager to enter Europe before 1992, there was speculation that Dentsu might soon set up a European base.

The Interpublic Group comprised three agency networks: Lintas, McCann-Ericsson Worldwide, which were the 6th and the 8th largest agencies, respectively, and Lowe Marschalk. The agency had excellent international coverage,

Exhibit 2   Top Agency Holding Groups Worldwide 1987

	Ranking		Billings $M	Income $M	Ros %	Nationality
	1983	1987				
Saatchi & Saatchi	8	1	11,360	1,685	14.8	UK
Dentsu	2	2	6,780	N/A	N/A	Japan
Interpublic	1	3	6,620	993	15	US
Omnicom	N/A	4	6,270	896	14.3	US
WPP	N/A	5	5,950	893	15	UK
Ogilvy	6	6	5,040	724	14.4	US
Young & Rubicam	4	7	4,910	736	15	US
Hakuhodo	11	8	2,900	N/A	N/A	Japan
Eurocom	N/A	9	2,760	N/A	N/A	France
D'Arcy Masius B & B	13	10	2,494	371	14	US
Grey	12	11	2,462	369	15	US
Leo Burnett	10	12	2,462	369	15	US
FCB	9	13	2,300	344	15	US
WCRS/Belier	N/A	14	1,630	230	14.1	UK/France
HDM	N/A	15	1,380	204	14.8	US/Japan
Bozell, Jacobs, K&E	N/A	16	1,330	185	13.9	US
LoweHSpink & Bell	N/A	17	1,270	N/A	N/A	UK

N/A: because did not exist in 1983.

Source: Advertising Age.

particularly in developing countries. It had won a number of prized accounts because of its strength. Foreign billing represented 60% of its total revenues, up from 55% in 1986. The group had strong client links and a record of excellent financial performance, but suffered from a reputation of having only mediocre creative talent.

The Omnicom Group was formed in the spring of 1986 through the merger of two US-based agencies— DDB Needham and BBDO—that ranked 4th and 12th, respectively, on a worldwide basis. The merger was largely a response to the British innovation of the US market. Initial performance of the group, however, was

Exhibit 3   Advertising Industry Rankings Worldwide 1987

	US	Japan	UK	W.G.	France	Canada	Italy	Spain	Australia	Holland
Agency										
Dentsu	–	1	–	22*	4*	–	21*	8*	–	19*
Young & Rubicam	1	17*	5	6	8	3	4	15	5	2
Saatchi & Saatchi	2	30	1	9	11	11	8	10	17	7
B&B	5	–	2	7	20	13	20	1	1	17
BBDO	3	–	27	1	21	27	7	5	2	1
Ogilvy & Mather	4	39	6	4	13	–	1	13	6	3
McCann Ericksson	13	9*	11	3	14	1	1	2	8	8
JWT	7	14	3	8	17	2	5	3	12	18
Hakuhodo	–	2	–	37	–	–	–	–	–	–
Lintas	12	–	15	2	7	2	9	4	14	4
Holding Group										
Saatchi & Saatchi	1	N/A	1	3	8	N/A	6	1	3	3
Interpublic	3	–	2	1	5	1	3	2	2	
Omnicom	2	–	13	2	7	–	2	1	1	

*HDM: Dentsu owns 33 $\frac{1}{3}$ %, Y&R owns 33 $\frac{1}{3}$ % + joint venture.

unsatisfactory. In contrast to the 14.3% growth of Saatchi, or to the 20.7% growth reported by Interpublic, Omnicom grew by only 9.2% in 1987. DDB Needham dropped 12.9% in gross income, while BBDO reported only a slight increase of 1.4%.

The group was diversified both geographically and functionally. However, it was weak in some important sectors, particularly in the UK, Canada, France and Japan. Although it offered over 43 types of marketing communications, the companies were small and mainly US-based. The group's objectives were to fill out its areas of regional weakness, and to offer the client a full range of marketing services.

Finally, the more recent developments of WPP, reported toward the end of the case (PC 3–35), could be seen as a wild card in the game.

The Growth of Saatchi & Saatchi: Strategic Foundations

In 1970, Maurice Saatchi quit his job to join his brother, Charles, in founding an advertising agency. Until then, the two brothers had pursued very different careers. Charles left school at 18, and became one of the top copywriters in a leading London agency before leaving to set up his own creative consultancy. Maurice, meanwhile, went to the London School of Economics and then joined the Haymarket publishing group as promotions manager for Campaign, the advertising industry's trade journal.

The agency, a metamorphosis of Charles' creative consultancy, started with £1 million of billings, £25,000 in financial backing, 9 employees, all under 27 and entirely creative, except for Maurice Saatchi, and Tim Bell, an old friend and associate of the two brothers.

From these modest beginnings, by 1986, the agency had grown to be one of the world's largest advertising groups, with billings of £2 billion, spread over 57 countries and 10,000 employees (see Exhibit 4). Behind this almost incredible achievement lay a set of beliefs that the two brothers shared and which they pursued with both courage and vigor throughout the period.

First, they were fully committed to the concept of globalization of markets and, thus, to the vision of a global agency. Second, they believed that size mattered and that big could be beautiful. Third, they believed that careful attention to financial strategy was key to developing and implementing a growth-oriented business strategy. Fourth, they saw advertising as one element of broader management services and believed that clients would reward a company that offered them the facility of one-stop shopping for their diverse needs.

These four beliefs are further explained below.

1. Vision of a Global Agency

Saatchi & Saatchi embraced the concept of globalization fully, and positioned themselves as the champion of global advertising agencies. Such an agency, they claimed, could enjoy a number of clear advantages.

First, because of their global information systems, they could help their clients market their products globally by identifying similar customer segments across national boundaries. Second, they could exploit economies of scale in their own operations such as media buying and production, and pass those savings on to the client. Third, they could have the organizational structure and systems in place to service a global account effectively.

"A powerful force drives the world toward a converging commonality—and that force is technology. Almost everyone everywhere wants all the things they have heard about, seen or experienced via the new technologies. The result is a new commercial reality—the emergence of global markets for standardized consumer products on a previously unimagined scale of magnitude."

Professor T. Levitt, 1985

As evidence of their commitment to this philosophy, the Saatchis put Harvard Professor Levitt on their board and took out large advertisements in leading newspapers such as the Wall Street Journal and the Financial Times, extolling the benefits of global advertising.

Some, however, discounted Saatchi's talk about global information systems and global media discounts.

"It's garbage, and they haven't invested in developing any system for information sharing or superior research facilities. They conduct worldwide studies but that's not an advantage, since all multinational agencies do that," claimed an ex-employee of the company. "It's in their interest to promote the idea of a global media discount, but it's such a small part of media spend that they never give out a figure."

Others raised more fundamental questions about the appropriateness or even feasibility of global advertising. They believed that Saatchi & Saatchi underemphasized the continued importance of national differences. A senior marketing manager in a large British consumer products company pointed out that even in Europe, local campaigns were necessary in most markets to maximize effectiveness of media spend because of differences in media availability and legal restrictions (see Exhibit 5).

"Advertising is about as close as you can get to a cultural thing in business, and country differences in cultural preferences are not about to go away just on the say of some starry-eyed Harvard professor."

Exhibit 4   Saatchi & Saatchi PLC (£ million)

	1971	1972	1973	1974	1975	1976	1977	1978	1979	1980	1981	1982	1983	1984	1985	1986	1987
Turnover (c)	13.7	17.1	21.1	22.2	28.9	35.2	42.6	59.1	71.5	84.7	102.1	258.3	603.2	855.4	1307.4	2087	3954.2
Revenue										13.2	17.1	39.6	101.8	147	301.6	443.9	773.8
Pretax Profit	0.1	0.4	0.6	0.6	0.8	1	1.3	1.9	2.5	3	3.6	5.5	11.2	18.3	40.5	70.1	124.1
Post-tax Profit (d)						0.4	0.5	0.6	0.8	1	1.5	2.6	6	11.4	21.7	37.4	69.6
Goodwill (e)							0.1	0.1	0.1	0.1	0.3	0.5	0.6	1	3.7	14.9	
US GAAP Post-tax Profit						0.4	0.5	0.5	0.6	0.9	1.1	2.1	5.2	9	15	22.5	33.1
EPS adj. for impact a rights issue (87)							2.1	3.2	4.1	5.2	6.7	9.4	13.1	22.2	31.6	38.2	43.9
Current Assets						7.1	9	13.2	14.8	18.8	32.8	92.9	123.7	193.9	336.8	739.8	763.9
Including cash and investments						1.7	2.7	3.6	5.2	6.2	9.7	31.4	26.9	59.7	132.3	189	215.9
Current Liabilities						7	8.2	11.9	13.6	17.3	30.7	86.3	120.1	174.4	266.3	692.3	744.6
Fixed Assets						0.8	0.9	1.1	2.1	2.5	3.6	12	15.8	21.6	32	119.4	133.5
Goodwill						1.8	1.7	1.2	1.3	1.4	6	20.4	25.4	39.2	177.2	402.1	151.5
Long-term Liabilities	0.1				0.2	0.1	-	-	-	0.2	-	-	17.8	38.4	100.3	124	78.6
Capital (e)						2.2	2.5	2.6	2.6	3.1	7.2	34.1	38.2	66.3	249.8	598.1	
Acquisition Cost						0	0	0.3	0.5	0.3	1.7	16.4	11.8	16.1	152.3	443.2	154
Contingent Liabilities (f)						N/A	N/A	2	N/A	N/A	6	16	21	N/A	80	164	61.5
Capital Raised (g)	0.03					0	0	0	0	N/A	3	25.2	0	19.5	174.3	392	
Average Employees	11					507	521	644	744	730	777	1486	3049	3748	6226	9774	15630
Offices	1	1	2		6	6	6	7	8	8	9	66	71		91	150	
Countries	1	1	2	3	4	1	1	1	2	2	2	37	40		54	57	58
Market Rank in Advertising Industry																	
UK	N/A	N/A	26	13	4	4	4	4	2	1	1	1	1	1	1	1	
Europe (incl. UK)	-	-	-	-	-	-	-	-	-	2	1	1	1	1	1	1	
US	-	-	-	-	-	-	-	-	-	-	-	13	7	6	5	1	
World	N/A	N/A	N/A	N/A	N/A	N/A	N/A	N/A	N/A	N/A	N/A	9	8	7	5	1	

(a) Includes Ted Bates and other acquisitions for part of the year only.   (b) Estimate.   (c) Billings and non-advertising fees.   (d) UK accounting, after-tax, minority, exceptional and preference items, but before goodwill.   (e) In 1986, Saatchi & Saatchi wrote off £507.1 million of goodwill against reserves. Included here for comparative purposes only.   (f) Estimate of maximum future ability.   (g) Includes £100 million of 6.3 convertible preferred stock in 1986.

Exhibit 5   Current Regulations on TV Advertising in Europe

Country	TV Households (million)	No. of channels accepting advertising	Total ad. Mins. P/week	Specific Features/Comments	Restrictions
Austria	2.78	2	280	Limits on no. of spots for a brand p/month. Bookings taken in Oct. for the following year.	Tobacco, spirits banned. Beer, wines, pharmaceuticals restricted
Belgium	3.5	3	926	Channels broadcast in Flemish and French in the 2 regions. General spots	Tobacco, alcohol banned. State TV only carries non-commercial
Denmark	2.2	–	–	New advertising financed channel being launched with 70 minutes per week	–
Finland	1.8	3	310	Booking period 6 months ahead	Political parties, religious groups, alcohol, undertakers, slimming drugs, tobacco are banned
France	20.5	6	1194	All channels accept advertising	Alcohol, tobacco, press, cinema, shows and retailers are banned on TV.
Greece	3	2	399	Tow state-owned stations providing national commercial coverage.	Pharmaceutical products and cigarettes are banned.
Ireland	0.92	2	882	National TV broadcast on two channels. 59% of homes receive BBC/TTV from the UK	Cigarettes and spirits are banned.
Italy	18.53	350+	7189	Three state-owned channels. Over 350 commercial channels.	Tobacco is the only ban for independent TV stations.
Netherlands	5.32	2	246	–	Tobacco is banned.
Norway	1.55	–	–	Commercials are not allowed	All TV advertising.
Portugal	2.42	2	608	Both state-run channels funded by advertising.	Tobacco banned. Alcohol allowed after 22:00 hours.
Spain	10.33	2	704	Only two state-run channels offer national coverage although 3 regionals accept advertising.	Tobacco, alcohol banned.
Sweden	3.33	–	–	Commercials are not allowed on TV.	All TV advertising.
Switzerland	2.49	1	150	One state-owned station consisting of 3 regionals serving the major language groups.	Alcohol, medicine, tobacco, religion, politics are banned.
Turkey	6	2	224	Supply still inadequate, bookings made at beginning of the year.	Alcohol, medicine, tobacco, religion, politics are banned.
UK	20.6	3	1354	Three majors of ITV, Channel 4 and TV-AM.	Tobacco, spirits are banned.
W.Germany	25.34	4	451	Demand high, bookings made in Sept. for following year.	Tobacco, prescription drugs are banned.

Source: Advertising Age/James Capel.

2. Big Could Be Beautiful

The structure of the advertising industry had been stable for decades, as a result of both client inertia and the norms and customs of the business. Traditionally, client turnover had been low, and only 2% of accounts moved from one agency to another during any particular year. This was partly due to risk aversion among the major advertisers, but switching costs were also believed to be high because of the investments both the agency and the client had to make to establish close working relationships that were necessary for building a shared understanding of the role of advertising in supporting the client's business. These long-term agency-client relationships were also supported by a set of well-established industry norms. Like accountants, doctors and lawyers, advertising agencies were not expected to solicit business unless invited by the client, or to promote themselves obtrusively. IPA, the industry trade body, was the protector of these norms which were seen as integral to the creative mystique of advertising that made it different form a "mere business."

The Saatchi brothers were convinced from the start that size was an extremely important source of competitive advantage in the business. Economies of scale or cost sharing were part of the benefits. But perhaps the most important advantage of size was not scale, *per se*, or cost sharing, but market power. Volume gave visibility and, thereby, the ability to attract good personnel and clients. Besides, size also gave an agency the flexibility to invest in developing new products, to take risks, and to build highly specialized capabilities.

The brothers realized that the existing rules of the game were stacked against any notion of fast growth of a new agency. Therefore, they decided not to play to those rules. Charles set aside one day a week to promote the agency. This ensured that the name Saatchi & Saatchi was on the front page of Campaign every week. Maurice broke the rule of no solicitation: he began each working day by making 25 cold calls to leading clients of competing agencies. The company also refused to join IPA.

Ultimately, however, the business did not offer a potential of organic growth that would satisfy the ambitious and impatient Saatchis. Acquisitions were the only route to the express lane, and it was primarily in this arena that Saatchi & Saatchi created a new legacy in the advertising industry.

By 1974, the company had made several acquisitions, moving into France, Belgium and Holland, and buying three regional agencies in the UK. With the exception of Notley Advertising and E.G. Dawes, these acquisitions were relatively unsuccessful. However, they boosted the agency and taught the Saatchis a great deal about what to do and what not to do in future takeovers.

The first headline-hitting acquisition of Saatchi & Saatchi came in 1975 with the reverse takeover of Garland-Compton, the 11th largest UK agency, with billings of £17.4 million. It was just what the Saatchis needed to gain first division status so as to be able to attract the risk-averse large consumer product companies that had so far been beyond their reach. It also gave the company a public quotation, which later proved to be the principal tool for future growth. Furthermore, the brothers were paid to receive the benefits: they gained a 35% stake in the merged company and were paid £400,000 by Compton Advertising, who were of the understanding that they were taking over Saatchi & Saatchi, and merely retaining the brothers as local managers over the merged business. Charles and Maurice thought differently. Campaign was briefed and the headline that Friday read, "Saatchi swallows up the Compton group". The two agencies were merged in Garland-Compton's offices, creating the 4th largest UK agency, with billings of £30 million.

Tim Bell was installed as managing director, with the brothers planning the business strategy. Advising the brothers on the Compton deal was a 31-year-old Harvard MBA, Martin Sorrell, who then worked for James Gulliver, head of the food conglomerate, Argyll. Shortly after the deal, he was signed up to join the company, and remained with the Saatchis until 1986, playing a vital role in the success of their acquisitions and in developing investor relations.

Between 1979 and 1985, the company grew by another twentyfold, through both organic growth and a string of acquisitions that ran up to a rate of about one per month during 1985. The most significant of these acquisitions were those of Garrott Dorland Crawford in 1981 and Compton Advertising in the US in 1982. The former gave Saatchi a second strong agency in the UK, and the latter provided direct access to the corporate advertising budgets of the large American multinational companies.

There were many, however, who contested Saatchi's faith in the advantages of size. Large advertisers saw the trend of increasing concentration in the agency business as a threat, and some of them were prepared to counteract by either buying an agency and converting it into in-house production of advertising services, or by switching to smaller agencies. They believed that large institutions were not conducive to carrying out an essentially creative task. They also believed that, by definition, senior management involvement in client service had to decline as an agency grew in size and, as the Chairman of Procter and Gamble pointed out:

"There was no such thing as an agency business other than its service to clients."

3. Focus on Financial Strategy

A third pillar consisted of its financial strategy, which was ultimately masterminded and implemented by Martin Sorrell, its financial director.

Few agencies before Saatchi & Saatchi had tried the acquisition route to growth. The main problem was getting access to capital. Saatchi, however, got access to the capital market when they acquired Garland-Compton, then the only listed agency in the UK. At the time of the acquisition, Garland-Compton had a P/E of 4. By maintaining effective communication, by ensuring good investor relations, and by showing consistently high profitability, Saatchi drove this ratio up to 20. At the core of their outstanding growth lay the strategy of acquiring low P/E companies on the strength of their own high P/E, which, in turn, boosted their earnings per share (EPS) growth and increased the City's confidence in their stock.

To make this strategy work, they developed a particular approach to structuring the financial arrangements of their acquisitions. Payments for acquisitions were made contingent to the owners meeting profit targets over a period of five years after the acquisitions. This financing method allowed Saatchi & Saatchi to boost earnings quickly, as the earnings of the acquired agency were included immediately in the company's financial reports, while only a part of the purchase price was actually paid.

A significant proportion of any agency acquisition was goodwill. In the US, goodwill had to be amortized over a 40-year period, which resulted in dilution of EPS. The treatment of goodwill in the UK, however, allowed a company to write it off against reserves rather than amortizing it. This helped Saatchi, as they could maintain high earnings growth, despite successive acquisitions.

This financial strategy also motivated managers of acquired companies to cut costs with an iron hand to earn their profit-related bonuses. However, it might also have affected essential investments, as described by Victor Muller, the Arthur Anderson executive Saatchi hired to run its consulting division:

> "Investments after the earn-out period typically had some catching up to do."

4. One-Stop Shopping for Management Services

The fourth strategic pillar of Saatchi & Saatchi was their vision of providing one-stop shopping for all the management services a company required. They believed that clients would be increasingly interested in integrated offers, where a number of services such as advertising, public relations, and promotional activities were all coordinated as a package.

Following this belief, Saatchi expanded their portfolio of activities in two stages. First, between 1980 and 1984, they diversified, through both organic development and acquisitions, from advertising to marketing services (including sales promotion, direct marketing, public relations, and sponsorship). Next, following their 1984 acquisition of Hay consultants, they further expanded into the areas of strategy and management information systems, consulting, and executive recruitment and compensation. As described by Maurice Saatchi, the company's ultimate ambition was:

> "To put together a global service-supermarket that would combine Saatchi's advertising skills, McKinsey's consulting capabilities, the accounting expertise of Arthur Andersen, and the financial clout of Goldman Sachs."

Implementing the Strategy: the Saatchi Organization

The Saatchi & Saatchi organization was structured into two main divisions: consulting and communications (see Exhibit 6).

There were two parallel worldwide agencies within the communications division: the flagship agency of Saatchi & Saatchi (which included Compton and DFS) and Backer Spielvogel Bates. The smaller agencies and service companies were also kept separate, and the company deliberately avoided any moves toward rationalization and merger among the various acquired companies despite, for example, owning 11 different advertising agencies in New York alone.

The group headquarters were exceptionally small for the size of operations that reported to it. There were only about 50 people in the headquarters responsible, at the corporate level, for accounting, financing, public relations, and business development. Through luck, good judgment and persuasiveness, the brothers assembled an outstanding team of senior managers in the headquarters organization, all of whom played important roles in shaping the agency, both financially and strategically.

Fundamentally, the organizational systems and management processes in Saatchi & Saatchi were structures with some clear delineation of the roles and tasks of local management in each of the affiliated companies and central management at the headquarters. Furthermore, efforts were under way to superimpose a new set of administrative mechanisms, on top of these local and central management processes, so as to develop a truly worldwide coordination capability.

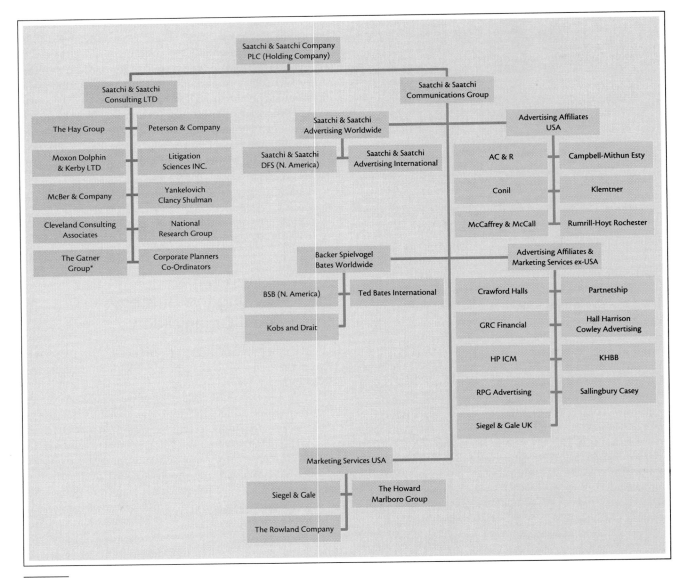

Exhibit 6 Organization Structure

*To be acquired June 20, 1988.

Local Entrepreneurship: Decentralized Responsibilities

The company believed that autonomy was essential for promoting creativity and entrepreneurship in an agency. In the light of this, Saatchi developed a strong organizational philosophy of decentralizing both strategic and operational responsibilities fully to each affiliated agency.

Local management had full responsibility for profit and growth of their unit, and had complete freedom to pursue these objectives in any manner they chose. Such a man-

agement system sat very well with the company's acquisition policy of making payment on a part of the acquisition price, contingent on future performance, on an acquired company and, in fact, was essential to make such a payment system credible to managers (many of whom were also partners) of those companies.

The principle of decentralization was not limited to the relationship between the group headquarters and the various companies, but was extended further down to the relationships among, and even within, each company. For example, there were no systems for cross-referrals among the different companies, nor any incentives for any one company to refer a client to another company within the family. Each company was, in turn, divided into a number of groups, each of which was treated as an independent profit center, and had its own P&L accounts. These groups enjoyed relatively complete operating freedom, and there were no systems in place for information sharing among them. As one manager described:

> *"One can always find some sources of synergy between almost any two groups, and there is an urge to exploit them. But managing those synergies also carries certain costs, much of which are not visible. How does one value the loss of commitment of a key manager, or dilution of the sense of personal responsibility and achievement?"*

From 1987, however, the company was aiming to adopt the idea of "lead countries," those that had developed some specialization in a certain field, and upon whose expertise other countries, on an entirely voluntary basis, could draw.

Global Coordination: Worldwide Account Management

A single manager in the agency that served the headquarters of a multinational client was often designated as the worldwide account director, and carried the responsibility of developing and supporting the client's business for all the services that the agency could provide in any country.

The main tasks of the account director were twofold: to attract the client's business in those countries where they used a different agency, and to coordinate multi-country campaigns. Given the philosophy of decentralization within the Saatchi organization, the role of the account director was that of consultant and coordinator, rather than that of a line manager.

The effectiveness of this role depended on the incumbent's expertise in the client's business and products, and on his or her ability to establish personal credibility among managers in different countries in both Saatchi and the client organizations, by transferring information and acting as a catalyst for the cross-fertilization of ideas.

From 1988 onwards, the global account management system was in a very early stage of implementation, and the jury was out on its effectiveness.

Central Value-Added: Financial Planning and Control

The financial planning and control systems of the company were highly centralized. These systems were rigidly defined, uniform throughout the group, and each company had to adopt them with almost no discretion for any change at the local level. In fact, the financial control function was sepa-

rated from all other operations, and was run directly from the headquarters on a worldwide basis.

Each agency had to forecast its billing three and twelve months ahead, and actual billings were reviewed against these forecasts on a monthly basis. In the event of any negative variances, due to unforeseeable circumstances, the agency was expected to make up for the loss by exploiting some other opportunity.

Costs were monitored on more than 50 different categories, and all variances from budget in either billings or costs were reported to the corporate headquarters as soon as they could be reasonably predicted or, at the latest, by the end of the month. Profitability of each client account was similarly monitored through a system that accounted for all the time spent on the client and full costs, rather than on the basis of a contribution margin. Cash balances of each company were monitored daily and were consolidated on a worldwide basis each day into a single corporate account.

By separating the finance function from the rest of the business, Saatchi & Saatchi were able to design and implement a strong planning and financial control system, which was monitored by account and finance specialists. Some industry observers believed that this financial control system was among the most important benefits that Saatchi brought to an acquired company. In part, this system was also the main source of the company's credibility in the financial markets. As described by an analyst in Goldman Sachs:

> *"One of the problems in covering the agencies as an analyst is that they are run by agency people. They don't run these businesses as businesses should be run. The Saatchis were unique in that."*

New Challenges: The Situation in 1988

> *"We have pushed our luck too hard in the City and Wall Street. Finally, our luck turned against us."*
>
> **A Saatchi employee, who preferred to remain unnamed**

As the Saatchi brothers were among the first to admit, the Saatchi phenomenon was a product of a right set of ideas, applied in the right industry, at the right time, implemented with the right dose of daring and the right quota of luck. Of this success cocktail, by 1988, the last element had perhaps begun to run out.

Perhaps the most visible symbol of the changing fortunes of the company was the departure of Tim Bell and Martin Sorrell. Bell left to join Lowe Howard-Spink, one of the new wave agencies that Saatchi had spawned in the UK. Sorrell, who had left Saatchi & Saatchi to take over WPP, which, thanks to the dramatic and highly visible hostile

Exhibit 7   Share Price
1979–1989

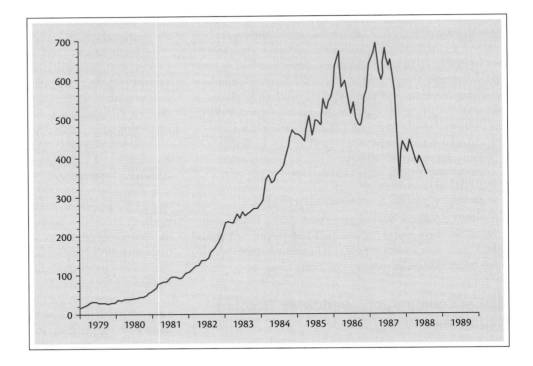

takeover of J. Walter Thompson in 1987, had already become the fourth largest advertising group in the world and was close on the heels of Saatchi for the mantel of global leadership.

WPP had a major presence in all the areas of advertising, marketing services and public relations. In the JWT takeover, it also acquired Hill and Knowlton, the world's largest PR firm. The company, then a loss maker, had since been turned around to make a reasonable profit in 1988. WPP was also perhaps the strongest of the major groups in marketing services, and one of their strategic priorities was to consolidate further this strength by building an extensive international network to support this activity.

The problem caused by the loss of key personnel was compounded by a major move the company made subsequently. In May 1986, the Saatchi brothers bought Ted Bates, the third largest agency worldwide, and one of the most profitable US agencies, for US$450 million, of which they paid US$400 million in cash up front. As against a book value per share of US$390, they paid US$893.5. The financials market's reaction was highly negative (see Exhibit 7). Many analysts criticized the brothers for paying too much, and also for giving up the use of contingent earn-outs.

After this abortive bid, Maurice declared, in the shareholders' meeting in April 1988, that the company's goal was to be scaled back to becoming the leading management services company in the world. The new issue of 6.75% convertible preference shares on June 17, 1988, was a pursuance of this revised strategy. Resorting to what was essentially a debt instrument, eschewing the traditional equity-financing route was itself an acknowledgement on Maurice's part, of the cooling of the company's relationship with the City. The lukewarm reaction to even such a conservative financial approach suggested that the company had to find a way to regain the investors' confidence so as to be able to fund the next phase of their strategic evolution.

Notes

[1]   Imported products typically required higher advertising expenditure to obtain distribution and to build customer franchise.

Case 3–4: Extending the "easy" Business Model

What Should easyGroup Do Next?*

"The only quoted conglomerate I know that works on the stock markets is General Electric. easyGroup is not about unrelated ventures, but about developing a formula for success that can be replicated across seemingly disparate businesses."

—**Stelios Haji-Ioannou**

easyGroup's Planned Entry into the UK Cinema Market

easyGroup was reviewing its plans to open a multiplex in May 2003, under the easyCinema banner to compete head-on against established national operators in the UK like Odeon, Warner Village and UGC Cinema. The group's CEO, serial entrepreneur Stelios Haji-Ioannou, aimed to replicate the success of easyJet, the low-cost airline that he had established in 1995, by creating a similar no-frills concept in the cinema industry. The millionaire businessman's stand was, "Nobody has tried to do this and I am told covert practices abound that prevent cinemas cutting prices. Current prices are far too high—they put people off going to the cinema."

easyGroup believed that it could create a successful cinema exhibition venture by applying the principles that had worked in the low-cost airline business. Firstly, the yield management capabilities that had served them so well in running an airline could be re-deployed in easyCinema. easyJet prices were closely linked to demand and how far in advance tickets were booked: a ticket booked three months in advance would be significantly cheaper than one booked a week before the flight. Likewise, peak-time tickets, like 6pm Friday, would cost more than at a less busy time. While incumbent cinemas in the UK typically operated at 20% capacity, they had never pursued the strategy of offering extremely cheap seats for advance bookings or at off-peak times, or of differentiating price by type or length of film. Several cinema operators

had invested in refurbishing cinemas and upgrading seats in order to attract audiences back. Stelios viewed this as analogous to the business-class on airplanes and questioned whether people would be willing to pay for bigger, more comfortable seats. He believed a cinema operator ". . . should be thinking about squeezing another 30% in there. Why are cinemas charging so much money when they're so empty? It's like what airlines once were." By maximizing both capacity and the extent to which it was utilized, easyGroup hoped to grow cinema admissions well above current rates.

Secondly, the group planned to rely on technology to automate the process of serving customers, thereby reducing labor costs. All bookings would be made through the Internet or from a machine in the foyer, with fares for advance bookings down to 20p. The average cinema had a crew of 20 people. easyGroup's plan was to reduce that number to four primarily comprising security staff and projectionists. The easyCinema concept would dispense with the box-office and ushers. Consumers would purchase tickets on the Internet and print out a unique bar code which would activate an entry turnstile at the cinema.

Thirdly, as in the airline business, the concept would be strictly no-frills with a view to maximizing the number of films screened. The cinema would not show any advertising nor would it support marketing activities or promotional events associated with films. Customers would be allowed to bring in their own food and drink. The group thought that there was no danger of destroying the magic of the cinema-going experience by removing the box-office and the traditional concession stand–on the contrary, "what we're doing is taking away a consumer rip-off. Three quid for popcorn is a rip—off."

Stelios tasked Matthew Lee, part of the six-member New Ventures team, with responsibility for assessing the potential for easyCinema and developing the concept for this new business idea. The core management team comprising Stelios, Nick Manoudakis (Chief Operating Officer),

*This case was written by Yves L. Doz, the Timken Chaired Professor of Global Technology and Innovation at INSEAD, and Anita Balchandani, Senior Consultant at Roland Berger Strategy Consultants. It is intended to be used as a basis for class discussion rather than to illustrate either effective or ineffective handling of an administrative situation.

Exhibit 1	Cinema Revenues and Admissions in the UK, 1997–2001				

	1997	1998	1999	2000	2001
£ million, current RSP[1]	826.5	811.2	841.6	879.5	974.4
£ million, constant 1997 RSP[1]	826.5	784.5	801.9	813.6	883.7
Admissions (million)	138.9	135.2	139.1	143	155.9
Cinema revenues as % of leisure entertainment	1.8	1.7	1.7	1.7	1.8

[1] Retail Selling Price

Source: Euromonitor: Global Market Information Database - UK Market Focus: Cinema; Published October 2002.

Steven Hall (Chief Financial Officer) and the New Ventures Team, would meet in a week's time to discuss whether they should launch easyCinema.

The Market for Cinema in the UK

The cinema industry in the UK was experiencing a revival of sorts. Admissions in 2001 were at the highest level in decades—156 million admissions generated £974 million in ticket sales (Exhibit 1) and were expected to continue to rise at an annual rate of 4% between 2003 and 2010.

One of the factors that had contributed to the steady rise in cinema admissions in the UK since the 1980s was the emergence of the multiplex—the first one in the UK was built in Milton Keynes in 1984 and was an instant success. These venues, with up to 20 screens, comfortable seats, superior picture quality and acoustics and free parking provided a classy alternative to their precursors, the cramped and poorly-furbished one-or-two-screen High Street cinemas often described as "fleapits." Multiplexes also offered consumers a wider choice of films and enabled cinema-going to become a more spontaneous leisure activity. A study by Euromonitor stated that ". . . the majority of the people decide at the last minute to go to the cinema because there is so much choice. Multiplexes are so big that if a film is full there is either another session starting in 40 minutes, or there is something else that they really want to see." Multi-screen cinemas had transformed film-going habits and were credited with luring people out of their homes. In its early years, a multiplex was typically the monopoly supplier to its local catchment area. However, as the number of multiplexes in the country increased (Exhibit 2), competition intensified and it became increasingly common for multiplex operators to compete directly against one another within a locality, giving consumers a wider choice of films and timings to choose from.

From an operational standpoint, multiplexes enabled better use of personnel. Staggered starting times allowed more efficient use of ushers and cleaning staff. Further, UK health and safety laws required that each cinema be manned by one employee per screen to handle emergency situations such as a fire. The multiplex environment enabled cinema operators to employ the mandatory number of employees to manage additional revenue-generating activities such as concession stands and ticket booths.

The Movie Industry

Film production, distribution and exhibition were the fundamental elements of the movie business.

Film Production. Film production was an expensive and very risky business with profitability reliant on the success of a small number of films. In 2001, the cost of making and marketing a Hollywood movie averaged $78.7 million, according to the Motion Picture Association of America. Over $14 billion had been invested in movie productions in the US, the European Union and Japan in 2000, a 12% increase from 1998. With the increase in old and new outlets such as cinemas, DVDs and the Internet, investment was expected to increase even more, according to a media research group in London. The commercial performance of films in most national markets could be best described as a

Exhibit 2	Number of Cinema Sites and Screens in the UK, 1997–2002					

	1997	1998	1999	2000	2001	2002
Sites	747	761	751	754	766	780
Screens	2,383	2,638	2,825	3,017	3,248	3,400

Source: Euromonitor.

heavy-tailed distribution, e.g. the top 20% of films in the UK earned approximately 85% of the revenue. The industry referred to this as "Murphy's Law" or alternatively as "the blockbuster effect".

The making of big-budget films for international distribution had long been dominated by the Hollywood studios: Warner Bros., owned by Time Warner Entertainment; Sony Pictures Entertainment; Disney Studios; Fox Filmed Entertainment, a Fox Entertainment company and VUE owned by Vivendi Universal. The production of a film would begin only when the necessary financial backing had been secured. In most cases this required an assurance that arrangements to distribute the finished product were in place. The Hollywood studios had vertically integrated into the distribution business and were usually able to finance production from their own resources. UK film companies, however, were not large integrated organizations and therefore had to pre-sell film distribution rights to a separate distribution company which contributed to the production budget either in the form of an advance against expected distribution profits or guarantees against which the production company could raise bank finance.

The Hollywood studios accounted for a high proportion of box-office receipts in the UK but there was vigorous competition between them and no one studio dominated. 2001 was a year of big-budget releases. *Harry Potter and the Philosopher's Stone, Lord of the Rings: The Fellowship of the Ring, and Spiderman,* epitomized the shift in film-making towards bigger budget productions.

Distribution. The distribution companies operating in the UK cinema industry were of two types: studio-owned or independent. The top-five distributors—20th Century Fox, UIP, Buena Vista, Warner and Columbia Tristar—were each owned by one or more of the Hollywood studios (Exhibit 3). Their market share fluctuated widely from year to year, reflecting the success of individual films, and their main role was to distribute the films made or acquired by their parent companies. They did not have to bid or pay in advance for the UK distribution rights to those films but acted as the sales and marketing arms of their respective parent companies. Their role was to advise on which films should be released across cinemas in the UK, to develop and execute release and marketing strategies, and to sell exhibition rights to independent cinema operators. In most cases, film release costs, e.g. advertising, promotion and the manufacture of prints, were undertaken by their respective corporate parents. In return the distributors would remit rental receipts to their parents after retaining a proportion of income deemed to be acceptable to the Inland Revenue as a fair reflection of the profits of the UK-based activity.

Independent distributors, on the other hand, did not have access to an assured supply of films. They bid for distribution rights to films made by independent producers and would finance all or part of the production in exchange for the rights to exploit the film. Independent distributors typically specialized in niche, art-house films.

Distributors determined the marketing plans and release strategies on a film-by-film basis taking into account several inter-related factors: type of film; estimated size and composition of potential audience; other films likely to be released around the same time; number of cinemas available and interested in the film; budget available

Exhibit 3   Film Distributors in the UK, 2001

Film distributors	Number of films shown	% of all films	% of box office revenue
20th Century Fox	16	4.2	10.8
UIP	43	11.3	27.7
Buena Vista	31	8.1	21.4
Warner	23	6	6.3
Columbia Tristar	30	7.9	13.3
Total US majors	**143**	**37.4**[1]	**79.5**
Pathé	22	5.8	7.8
FilmFour	16	4.2	0.9
All other independent distributors	201	52.6	11.8
Total	382	100	100

[1] Rounding error

Source: BFI Film and Television Handbook 2002/British Video Association/Screen Finance.

to support the release. Discussions between distributors and cinema exhibitors regarding films that were expected to be popular, would commence up to 12 months before the film was expected to be ready for UK theatrical release. The two parties would agree upon a release date and reserve screens on a provisional basis (a process often referred to as "penciling in"). Distributors targeted exhibitors in three waves: leading exhibitors, followed by specialist multiplex operators, and finally the independent exhibitors. This advance planning enabled distributors to finalize plans for advertising and other promotional activity, expenditure that could be as high as £1 million on the promotion of a major release. Independent distributors, however, were not in a position to plan well in advance because, unlike the integrated distributors, they were not involved with the films that they handled from the outset. Further, they found it more difficult to convince exhibitors to "pencil in" their films before they become available for viewing and consequently had difficulty obtaining the bookings that they desired.

Distribution was essential for a film's financial success, as highlighted by the company that co-produced the film *Trainspotting*. UK box-office takings were just the "shop window" for their product. Investors could recoup their cash from sales to foreign territories, TV stations and, most importantly, from video and DVD rentals. A distributor usually released a film in successive periods to these different channels, beginning with the cinema release and proceeding through to pay-TV, video/DVD rental and sale, and finally free-to-air television. Therefore consumers keen to see new releases had no alternative but to visit the cinema. While cinema represented approximately one quarter

of total revenues (Exhibit 4), it remained highly important because the success of a film in the cinema was viewed as being critical to its success in multiple other markets.

Competition between distributors heightened with the growing importance of advertising and promotional activities which played an increasing role in determining the commercial success of a new release. These included in-cinema marketing (such as "trailers," and point-of-sale promotions), television and radio advertisements, poster advertising and interviews with actors, directors and producers. Music from films was sometimes released simultaneously on CDs and cassettes. Merchandising agreements, such as those with fast-food retailers or consumer product companies, e.g. Coca-Cola's hugely successful campaign as the "drink of choice" with the movie *Bridget Jones's Diary*, and the launch of its special silver packaging at cinema venues.

Exhibition. Cinevan, with its flagship brand, Odeon, was the leading cinema operator in the UK, both in terms of market share and number of screens. Other key operators were UCI, UGC, Warner, National Amusements and Cine-UK (Exhibit 5).

Cinevan, a private equity firm, had purchased Odeon Cinemas in February 2000. It merged the company with ABC Cinemas, which had been acquired from Virgin in 1996. The company, with approximately 3,400 employees, was rebranding its portfolio of 106 sites and 600 screens, under the Odeon banner. Odeon Cinemas had developed a strong proposition as the film-lover's brand, with its slogan "Fanatical About Film." In keeping with these values, it also launched Alternative Odeon, a sub-brand that brought niche,

Exhibit 4	UK Consumer Expenditure on Feature Films by Channel of Distribution (£ mil.), 1986–2000				
	Box office	**Video rental**	**Video Sales**	**DVD Sales**	**Total**
1986	142	284	55	–	481
1987	169	326	110	–	605
1988	193	371	184	–	748
1989	227	416	345	–	988
1990	273	418	374	–	1,065
1991	295	407	440	–	1,142
1992	291	389	506	–	1,186
1993	319	350	643	–	1,312
1994	364	339	698	–	1,401
1995	385	351	789	–	1,525
1996	426	382	803	–	1,611
1997	506	369	858	–	1,733
1998	515	437	940	–	1,892
1999	535	408	882	68	1,893
2000	577	444	1,104	264	2,389

Source: Euromonitor.

Exhibit 5	Market Shares of Cinema Operators in the UK, 2001

Cinema operator	Market share (%)
Cinven (Odeon/ABC)	25
UCI	15
UGC Warner Bros/Village	15
Roadshow	13
Cine-UK National Amusements	10
Showcase	7
Others	15
Total	**100**

Source: Euromonitor: Global Market Information Database–UK Market Focus: Cinema; Published October 2002.

alternative cinema to a targeted customer base. Odeon was also considering other ideas to grow its core cinema business. These included business conference hosting services in cinemas and exhibitions of alternative film content such as Broadway musicals, rock concerts, opera and ballet. In 2002, it showed the World Cup games beamed live from Japan and South Korea. "We will sweat assets going forward," said Richard Segal, CEO of Odeon Cinemas.

In 1984, UCI, an international specialist multiplex operator, pioneered the multiplex in the UK, operating 36 sites with 365 screens. It positioned itself at the leading-edge of technology by offering digital projection and IMAX screens. During the summer of 2002, it launched a website targeted at children. UCI also aimed to capture the premium-segment with initiatives such as "The Gallery," a private balcony where film-goers had access to an exclusive bar, free refreshments and luxurious seats. Both Vivendi and Viacom-owned Paramount had significant stakes in UCI.

UGC Cinemas, owned by Vivendi in conjunction with a private French multiplex operator, had 42 cinemas and was the only exhibitor to invest in customer retention initiatives such as a loyalty card. In July 2002, it launched an initiative to dramatically increase subscriptions to its month-long Unlimited Pass by reducing the price from £19.99 to £12.99 for West End cinemas and £9.99 for all other venues. By November 2002 they had captured 100,000 subscribers.

US-owned Warner Bros and Australian cinema operators Village Roadshow's joint venture, Warner Village, had a portfolio of 36 cinemas including the largest multiplex in the UK—a 30-screen multiplex in Birmingham with six screens dedicated to showing Bollywood films. The company's website, re-launched in February 2002, also included a Bollywood section. In May 2003, Warner Bros sold this chain to SBC International Cinemas, a little-known British exhibitor backed by venture capital

investors, for £250 million. SBC intended to rebrand Warner's properties across the UK under the "Vue" banner over the next six months and planned to appeal to a wider film-going audience.

National Amusements, a subsidiary of a US company which belonged to media and entertainment giant Viacom, operated 19 cinemas under the Showcase brand. These cinemas had more screens than the average multiplex in the UK.

Backed by a consortium of venture capital firms, Cine-UK, with its portfolio of 28 Cine-World cinemas concentrated in small towns and suburban areas, had featured strongly in the Deloitte & Touche Indy 100 list of fast-growing companies and was reported to be up for sale.

Despite the growth in the market, several new cinema ventures had had to exit the market due to the high degree of competition, pressure on profitability and poor capacity utilization. "For the past 10 years there has been a seductive view that you made money by building cinemas. What I hope we are seeing now is a realization that you actually make money by filling them," said an industry expert.

Most industry participants expected consolidation in the market and felt that expansion would be more likely to result from mergers and acquisitions rather than new site development, owing to the difficulty of obtaining sites that fulfilled the space and planning-permission requirements of a multiplex. Further, the cost of building a new cinema was extremely high—a 16 to 18 screen complex could cost up to £15 million—magnified by the fact that operators would compete with each other for the best sites. The industry was at a stage where the cost of entry had "reached prohibitive levels for all but those with the deepest pockets."

The most significant operational cost incurred by a cinema exhibitor was the film rental paid to distributors. There were three main methods of calculating film rentals in the industry:

1. *Nut method,* whereby a monetary figure, the "nut," was agreed for each screen in the exhibitor's portfolio. The nut was intended to represent the screen's weekly operating costs plus an element for profit. However, in practice, the agreed figure was the result of negotiations between the exhibitor and the distributor. The rental fee was the greater of the two sums: 25% of the total box-office takings or 90% of takings above the nut.

2. *Sliding scale method.* Under this approach, the rental paid varied from a minimum of 25% to a maximum of 50% in steps of five percentage points as the takings rose above pre-determined break figures.

3. *Datum scale method.* The rental was 25% of the takings up to a break figure and 75% thereafter, subject to an overall maximum of 50%.

Other methods, such as a flat percentage, were used by a small minority of exhibitors. The exhibitor chose which method of calculation to use but the nut and break figures were agreed with distributors and these had to be negotiated for every film. Usually an exhibitor would agree figures with a leading distributor. If these were satisfactory, the exhibitor sought to persuade other distributors to align to the same method of calculation and terms. Typically, if a film ran well, distributors took the lion's share of the takings. However, if screens were virtually empty, the cinema got a bigger proportion to help it cover its costs. Rental costs varied considerably across what was referred to in the industry as "first-run", "second-run" and "third-run" films. The most expensive first-run films were those screened immediately upon release. After 10 to 14 weeks, an exhibitor could negotiate a lower rental on the film which was then classified as "second-run." Once a movie was released on video some exhibitors—typically small, independent operators—chose to run them as "third-run" releases.

Labor, facility lease expenses, utilities and maintenance were the other key cost elements (Exhibit 6). Labor costs had both a fixed and a variable component. During non-peak periods, a minimum number of staff was required to operate the facility. However, theatre staffing levels were increased to handle attendance volume increases during peak periods (Friday and Saturday evenings), as film-goers typically purchased tickets at the cinema box-office 10 to 15 minutes before the show commenced, except in the case of long-awaited blockbusters. Health and safety laws required movie houses to have a minimum of one staff member per screen to handle emer-gency situations. Lease expenses and associated property taxes were primarily fixed costs. Recent studies suggested that intense competition between operators had increased rents by up to 30%.

The Target Audience

Two broad categories of distinction were used in the industry: mainstream (also referred to as "commercial") and art-house. Mainstream films were those aimed at a wide audience, while art-house films were more special interest in nature. The term art-house, for example, was used to refer to most foreign-language films released in the UK. Films that started out as art-house but attracted a wider audience than expected were referred to as "cross-overs." However, mainstream films generated the majority of box-office receipts and rentals.

National cinema operators historically played mainstream, populist movies, while the smaller, independent venues typically focused on art-house films aimed at the more serious cinema goer. However, over the past few years, larger cinema operators were beginning to realize the benefits of targeting their product to niche customer segments. By bringing art and cult films to appropriate audiences they were able to widen their customer base significantly.

Film-goers in the UK visited the cinema three times a year on average compared with 5.2 times for their US counterparts. 15–24 year olds were the most prolific cinema-goers (Exhibit 7), and were targeted heavily by most cinema operators with special fares, timings and films. Families were another key segment for cinemas, with weekend offers designed around making the movie-going experience more affordable and enjoyable for a family: "We acknowledge that mum and dad don't really want to see Jimmy Neutron for the third time, so why should they have to pay for it?" quoted a multiplex operator in a study by Euromonitor on the market for cinema in the UK. Most cinemas marketed heavily to children—dedicated web-sites with interactive features from forthcoming children's films and giveaways in cinema foyers were standard. Increasingly, cinema houses were also starting to cater to an older audience, typically couples with no kids referred to as "contented couples" by the industry. These movie-goers were willing to pay a premium for a superior experience. For instance, The Electric Cinema, one of the UK's oldest cinemas, had reopened as a cinema with a brasserie, bar and private members-only club. The newly refurbished cinema, boasting leather seating, footstools and tables for food and drink, emphasized comfort, service and quality films.

Exhibit 6   Typical Structure of the Profit & Loss Account of a Cinema Exhibitor in the UK

	%
Box office takings	73%
Concession income	22%
Screen advertising	4%
Other	1%
Total	**100%**
Film rental	27%
Staff costs	21%
Depreciation	9%
Concession cost of sales	8%
Advertising & publicity	3%
Other	19%
Operating profit	13%
Total	**100%**

Source: Industry analysts.

Exhibit 7   Frequency of Cinema Going in the UK

Percentage population	At least once a month	At least twice a year	Once a year or less	Never go to cinema
Male	25	31	24	80
Female	23	40	20	83
ABC1[1]	29	39	20	88
C2DE[1]	19	31	24	74
4-14	31	48	13	92
15-24	50	35	11	96
25-34	29	42	21	92
35+	15	31	27	73

[1] Refers to the hierarchy of socio-economic classes in the UK. This classification spans all dimensions of occupation skill. For example, A represents Professionals, while E represents Unskilled occupations.

Source: The Lifestyle Pocket Book 2002, UK.

Use of New Technology

Research showed that young, avid cinema-goers tend to be heavy users of mobile phones and the Internet. By nature, movies were amenable to content-rich advertising over the web. Most cinema houses had adopted the Internet as a means of reserving seats and purchasing tickets. Some let customers buy tickets using WAP mobile phones. Cinema houses also used mobile messaging services and e-mail to inform customers of special offers.

Pricing Strategies

There was little difference in average prices charged by the leading exhibitors but prices did vary by region. All operators used the simple strategy of varying prices by time of day, day of week, type of seating or customer segment—students, senior citizens and children obtained discounted rates.

The average ticket price in the UK during 2001 was £6.25 which compared with £5.95 in 1997. This represented a 5% increase over the 5-year period. However, prices in London—the highest in the country—were more likely to be in the range of £7 to £8.

The Film Distributors Association (FDA), the main trade association of film distributors in the UK Regulation, of which all major companies and several independent distributors were members, had established a set of Standard Conditions for the licensing and exhibition of films in cinemas in the UK. Under the Standard Conditions, the use of which was widespread in the industry, exhibitors could only charge the admission price for a film that had been agreed upon with the distributor. Consequently, distributors would sometimes refuse permission for price reductions and even take action against unauthorized promotions. Major exhibitors viewed this regulatory provision as being reasonable since a decrease in ticket prices could affect a distributor's rental revenues. The inclusion of this provision in the Standard Conditions had the effect of restricting exhibitors' ability to compete by cutting prices.

easyGroup: 1995 to Present

36-year-old Stelios Haji-Ioannou, son of a Greek shipping tycoon, joined his father's shipping company, Troodos Shipping, in 1988 after graduating in Economics from the London School of Economics and in Shipping Trade and Finance from the City University Business School. In January 1992, he founded his first venture, Stelmar Tankers, a fleet shipping company that was listed on the New York Stock Exchange in March 2001.

easyJet

In 1995, Stelios founded easyJet, Europe's first low-cost, no-frills, point-to-point airline, initially modeled on the successful US-based Southwest Airlines formula: a homogenous fleet, point-to-point services to short haul destinations, rapid turnaround times, high aircraft utilization, and no in-flight meal services. In addition to studying Southwest Airlines, Stelios and his team studied Valuejet, another US-based low-cost carrier, in order to understand why it was unsuccessful. The team regularly traveled to the US, spending time in the headquarters of both corporations to understand the reasons for success and failure in the low-cost airline business. Stelios believed that while they learnt from the low-cost carriers in the US, easyJet essentially "moved ahead of the

Southwest business model" by entirely bypassing travel agents—initially reservations were taken over the telephone and subsequently customers migrated to the Internet for most transactions—deploying a more sophisticated yield management system and pursuing more flexible deployment of planes during the course of the day and from one day to another (unlike Ryanair and other low-cost competitors who dedicated individual planes to specific routes).

The airline started operations with a loan of £5 million from Stelios' father and two leased aircraft operating out of London Luton airport. easyJet's first flight, from London to Glasgow, was priced at £29 one-way. An extensive public relations campaign and compelling advertising slogan—"Fly to Scotland for the price of a pair of jeans"—supported the launch of the service. Passenger figures were encouraging and over the next five years the airline owned and/or leased 18 Boeing 737–300s and covered 27 routes in Europe.

easyJet operated a simple fare structure. All prices were quoted one-way to allow customers the flexibility to choose where and when they would like to fly. Fares were based on supply and demand. The earlier passengers booked, the cheaper the fare would be. The booking system would review bookings daily for all future flights and predict how popular each flight was likely to be. If the percentage of seats sold, i.e., the load factor, was higher than normal, then the price would go up to avoid selling out popular flights months in advance.

In order to offer low fares, easyJet worked towards engineering out costs from its operations (Exhibit 8). £14 per passenger was saved by not offering an in-flight meal, £10 worth of savings per passenger resulted from the use of Luton airport instead of Gatwick. In other countries, however, easyJet operated from major airports, e.g., Charles de Gaulle and Nice in France, while competitors such as Ryanair focused purely on smaller airports, e.g. Beauvais (France). Overall seating capacity was maximized by not offering business-class seating. Travel agents were entirely eliminated because they added 25% to total operating costs—telephone and Internet sales were the primary distribution channels. easyJet also reduced the turnaround time of its aircraft and flew its planes more hours per day—11.5 hours vs. an industry average of 6 hours, and negotiated progressive landing charge agreements with the airports. Cost efficiencies were also captured by operating a "ticketless airline"—passengers required only a confirmation number and passport in order to check-in. Corporate overheads were also kept to a minimum—the airline was based in "easyLand," a bright orange building adjacent to the main taxiway at Luton Airport that reflected the easyJet low-cost ethos.

Despite the emphasis on cost reduction, the airline ensured that passenger safety was not compromised. The fleet comprised only brand new Boeing 737s and experienced pilots were hired who were paid prevailing market rates.

By 1999, the airline had started receiving recognition. easyJet was voted "Best Low Cost Airline" by readers of *Business Traveller* magazine. *Marketing* magazine described the launch of easyJet as "one of the 100 great marketing moments of the 20th century." Given its low-cost focus, the company relied on marketing the brand through PR and sales promotions. Stelios was a skilled PR operator who was able to establish easyJet with minimum of marketing expenditure. He pulled off several publicity stunts such as distributing free easyJet tickets on the launch flight of rival low-cost carrier, Go Airline, while dressed in a bright orange boiler-suit. The company was able to attract an impressive amount of media coverage. Stelios' tongue-in-cheek advertising, positioning easyJet as the David against

Exhibit 8   easyJet—Reengineering the Cost Structure in the Airline Business

Costs borne by all airlines including easyJet	Costs reduced by easyJet	Costs eliminated by easyJet
– Telesales staff	– Advertising	– In-flight catering
– Cabin crew	– Airport and landing fees	– Business class cabin crew
– Pilots	– Aircraft non-utilisation due to delays at congested airports	– Travel agent commission
– Group handling		– Ticketing costs
– Insurance		
– Aircraft ownership cost		
– Air traffic control fees		
– Maintenance		
– Fuel		

Source: Company website.

Exhibit 9	easyJet Passenger Statistics

Year	Annual total ('000)
1995	30
1996	420
1997	1,140
1998	1,880
1999	3,670
2000	5,996
2001	7,664
2002	11,400

Source: Company website.

the airline industry's Goliaths, was highly effective. The company did not retain any advertising agencies—Stelios and his marketing team were the self-styled ad designers of easyJet's campaigns. The company also used its own aircraft as marketing tools to serve as airborne billboards sporting the Internet address, telesales numbers and marketing slogans. A similar marketing approach was to play a useful role in establishing easyJet's subsequent brands.

In 2000, easyJet seat sales over the Internet reached the one million mark (the first ticket was sold online in April 1998). That same year, easyJet went public and was formally admitted to the London Stock Exchange.

In 2002, easyJet's passenger numbers (Exhibit 9) continued to soar. It had a market value of £1.5 billion and, while most full-service airlines were making losses, it posted record profits of £71.6 million (Exhibit 10) and completed the acquisition of Go for £374 million from British Airways. The airline had a strong, stable management team led by Ray Webster, Chief Executive Officer since 1998, who had been with the company since its inception. However, following pressure from shareholders, Stelios stepped down as easyJet chairman and was replaced by Sir Colin Chandler, the former chairman of Vickers Defence Systems. At the time, Stelios said: "I intend to remain a significant shareholder of this company for a very long time," referring to his 21.9% stake, adding, "However, as

Exhibit 10	easyJet Revenue and Profit, Year to end September	

	Revenue (£ mil.)	Protit (£ mil.)
1998	77.0	5.9
1999	139.8	1.3
2000	263.7	22.1
2001	356.9	40.1
2002	552.0	71.6

Source: Company website.

I have made clear on several occasions in the past, I have no other source of income from easyJet other than disposal of shares and as I engage in new ventures, I may need to liquidate some of my stock from time to time." Stelios, his wealth estimated at £500 million, was keen to augment his position as Britain's 26th richest man and to expand the "easy" concept to a range of new businesses.

By 2003, against the backdrop of a weak global economy, easyJet announced its interim results (six months to March 31). Revenues were up 25%, the load factor was at 82.1%, average air fares were down to approximately £37, but losses were at £24 million. Despite this, the company was confident of its ability to succeed in the competitive low-cost carrier market. As a signal of this confidence, shareholders had ratified a move to augment the existing fleet of 65 Boeing aircraft with 102 Airbus A319s.

easyGroup

In 1998, three years after easyJet, Stelios had two assets in place—an airline and a brand. He decided to explore new ventures that would leverage the "easy" brand across new businesses, thus creating easyGroup, a "branded incubator" with a mission to "create long-term capital growth by selecting and incubating substantial, profitable and sustainable businesses that reduce the cost of living and extend the easy brand ("paint the world orange") while maintaining the core brand values."

In addition to the belief that that the "easy" brand could be "stretched," central to easyGroup's philosophy was the belief that, "the Internet and yield management techniques are here to stay" in the words of Nick Manoudakis, COO. All new ventures at easyGroup would be built around these three business fundamentals.

After the public offering of easyJet, the relationship between easyGroup and the airline became that of a brand licensor-licensee. easyGroup licensed the "easy" brand to easyJet, providing the airline with a set of Brand Standards—rules regarding use of the logo, color, and professional standards that the brand was required to adhere to. In the event of a breach of these standards, easyGroup could retract its brand license.

easyInternetcafé

easyGroup's first venture was to establish a chain of Internet cafés based on the application of the same no-frills, low-cost and yield management principles that had worked so well in the airline business. The first branch opened in July 1999 in London near the busy Victoria Station, with approximately 360 PCs over two floors of rented premises. The café had a clean, uncluttered layout, high quality hardware and offered attractive prices.

The business deployed the principles of yield management developed for the airlines to vary prices dynamically based on demand levels. Customers would pay between 50p and £1 for an hour of Internet surfing. To aid yield management, the business deployed a particular "pricing curve" (relationship between occupancy level and price), from a potential set of 10 options. For instance, a steep pricing curve would be used at the Oxford Street store on a day with peak summer tourist traffic. Alternatively, when demand was expected to be low, a soft pricing curve would be used, i.e. rising occupancy levels would trigger small, non-aggressive price increases (Exhibit 11). The business had a Yield Manager whose role it was to monitor store occupancy levels, seasonality and historical demand patterns in order determine the pricing curve to be deployed in each store on a daily basis.

The success of the first opening led to an initial wave of expansion within London. Each store capitalized on a different mix of users but all were in high footfall areas. Demand drivers varied across the stores. Matthew Lynwood, Property Director of the business, remarked, "Tottenham Court Road is more 'techie-land' and very close to the universities. Oxford Street is retail, pure and simple. Victoria has a more backpacking, traveling, touristy profile. Kensington High Street is more upper-class retail with some residents and offices. Then you have the Strand, which is 24-hours and our busiest store overnight."

Over time, however, the business model of the venture evolved considerably. Initially, the cafés housed a "learning zone" with uniformed advisors who would help customers find things online and support the counter from which coffee and snacks were sold. In the second-generation stores, these features were abandoned in favor of a simple, no-frills concept that offered the basic service of Internet access and could be operated with minimal staff. Following this, the group moved away from the "gargantuan" stores and successfully experimented with smaller stores with approximately 100 PCs. In the third phase of expansion, easyInternetcafé began establishing smaller Points of Presence (PoP) within existing fast food establishments–primarily McDonalds, Burger King and Subway. Staff requirements were reduced by introducing computerized vending machines that allowed customers to buy Internet time automatically. As of 2003, easyGroup intended to drive expansion through franchises. Franchisees would take care of store establishment, local marketing and store maintenance, while easy-Internetcafé would run the yield management/pricing system and ensure that franchisees operated under the rules of the "easy" brand license.

The group paid significant attention to international expansion as well—21 Internet cafes were in operation in eight countries within two years. Its Internet café located in New York's Times Square was a symbol of the group's intention to expand into the US. Franchises were to be made available in 15 states across the US and in 10 other countries.

While easyInternetcafé grew considerably (Exhibit 12), it had been a loss-making (Exhibit 13) business since its launch. However, the efforts of the group to improve the cost structure of the business looked promising (Exhibit 14) and

Exhibit 11   Pricing Curves used at easyInternetcafé— Sample

Source: easyInternetcafé.

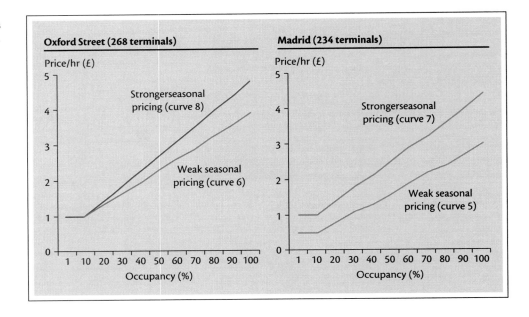

Exhibit 12   easyInternetcafé—Growth Statistics

Fiscal Year (y/e September)	1999	2000	2001	2002	2003 (to 15/4/03)
Number of PCs in use, incl. franchises	358	4,525	8,495	7,469	7,276
Total number of sites	1	11	22	23	28
Legacy stores	1	11	22	21	21
Points of Presence (PoPs)	–	–	–	–	5
Franchises	–	–	–	2	2
Number of international (non-UK) sites	–	5	14	14	16
Legacy stores	–	5	14	12	12
Points of Presence (PoPs)	–	–	–	–	2
Franchises	–	–	–	2	2
Number of customer logons, incl. franchises (mil.)	NA	5.5	16.7	17.8	7.7

Source: easyInternetcafé.

easyInternetcafé was expected to reach cash-flow break-even by mid-2003 and profitability by 2004.

easyCar

easyCar, a car rental service based on similar principles of dynamic pricing, yield management and online booking, was established in April 2000. The first few sites had a rental capacity of 500 cars each. Initially, easyGroup's entire fleet of cars comprised a single model—the Mercedes A-Class—that customers could rent for as little as £10 per day on low-demand days, as opposed to average daily rental charges of £30–40. Launching the business, Stelios said, "The choice of Mercedes reflects the easyGroup brand. easyCar will use brand new Mercedes cars in the same way that easyJet uses brand new Boeing aircraft. We

Exhibit 13   easyInternetcafé Limited—Profit & Loss Account

Date of Accounts	30/09/2002	30/09/2001	30/09/2000	30/09/1999
UK Turnover	3,021,000	10,543,000	6,668,000	
Export Turnover	8,993,000	11,481,000	684,000	
Turnover	**12,014,000**	**22,024,000**	**7,352,000**	**392,000**
Cost of Sales	24,158,000	72,674,000	4,421,000	316,000
Total Expenses				
Gross Profit	**−12,144,000**	**−50,650,000**	**2,931,000**	**76,000**
Depreciation	6,104,000	44,619,000	2,331,000	132,000
Other Expenses	5,817,000	13,640,000	15,696,000	2,178,000
Operating Profit		−64,290,000	−12,765,000	−2,102,000
Other Income	187,000	196,000	525,000	293,000
Interest Payable	3,977,000	3,753,000	1,230,000	17,000
Exceptional Items	9,182,000	0	0	0
Discontinued Operations	0	0	0	0
Pre-Tax Profit	**−12,569,000**	**−67,847,000**	**−13,470,000**	**−1,826,000**
Tax Payable	0	0	0	55,000
Extraordinary Items	0	0	0	0
Dividends Paid	0	0	0	0
Retained Profit	**−12,569,000**	**−67,847,000**	**−13,470,000**	**−1,881,000**

Source: easyInternetcafé.

Exhibit 14 Evolution of Total Cash Costs and Revenues, easyInternetcafé

Source: easyInternetcafé.

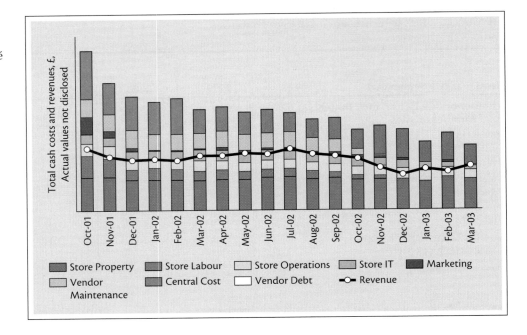

do not compromise on the hardware, we just use innovation to substantially reduce costs. The car hire industry is where the airline industry was five years ago: a cartel feeding off the corporate client. easyCar will provide a choice for consumers who pay out of their own pockets and who will not be ripped off for traveling mid-week."

By May 2003, the car rental business operated from 50 sites across the UK, France, Spain, the Netherlands and Switzerland, with plans to expand that to 80 by the year end. Rental sites were not located directly at airports—seven sites were located close to airports while the rest were located in city centers targeting urban dwellers who would rather rent than own a car. easyGroup refined the operational model of the business in order to pursue innovative cost-saving measures. The average fleet-per-site was reduced because, as Stelios was known for saying, "The skill is never to allow utilization to fall below 90%." easyCar also departed from its policy of procuring cars from a single supplier by creating a competitive market for multiple suppliers. Economies of scale from a uniform fleet were realized only at site level. A particular site rented only one type of vehicle. Cars were no longer rented with full fuel tanks—customers were expected to fuel them—to eliminate the cost of checking and refueling them, thereby enabling quicker re-renting. The policy that cars be returned clean to avoid a £10 cleaning charge was another successful tactic to engineer out labor costs from operations and accelerate turn-around. Customers that picked up and dropped off vehicles at off-peak times benefited from lower prices. Essentially the business had migrated to a pit-stop concept, with car pick-up points situated within a mile of a petrol station. One means to accelerate growth was the establishment of pick-up points in car parks using mobile vans staffed by a single employee. By February 2003, sites had been established in two central London locations—car park owners were guaranteed revenue for 15 to 20 spots in return for permission to operate a car rental site on their premises. The complexity of managing operations at car rental sites had been engineered out by providing a user-friendly, foolproof software that would guide the employee. No transactions were handled on-site as customers would pay at the time of reservation via the Internet.

Yield management also played a critical role in ensuring that utilization rates in the business remained at 85% to 95%. Based on historical demand patterns, seasonality and capacity, the yield manager would vary the pricing curves deployed at site level (Exhibit 15).

The car rental business missed its target of reaching profitability in 2002 (Exhibit 16). However, the group believed that initiatives to reduce labor costs and expand both the size of the fleet and the number of sites (Exhibit 17) would enable it to do so in 2003. It was expected that easyCar would be the second business to go public and the group targeted an Initial Public Offering (IPO) in 2005.

Other Ventures

In November 2000, the group launched easyValue.com, an impartial online price comparison engine, and easy.com, a free web-based e-mail service. A year later, easyMoney, an

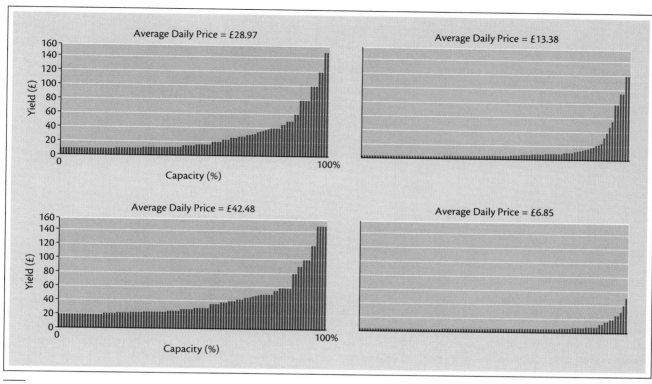

Exhibit 15   easyCar—Illustrative Pricing Curves on Four Days, Location X

Source: easyCar.

Exhibit 16	easyCar (UK) Limited-Profit & Loss Account	
Date of Accounts	**30/09/2001**	**30/09/2000**
UK Turnover	9,430,000	2,007,000
Export Turnover	8,557,000	1,337,000
Turnover	**17,987,000**	**3,344,000**
Cost of Sales	11,019,000	3,273,000
Total Expenses		
Gross Profit	**6,968,000**	**71,000**
Depreciation	3,067,000	494,000
Other Expenses	19,196,000	7,496,000
Operating Profit		−7,425,000
Other Income	181,000	110,000
Interest Payable	1,356,000	163,000
Exceptional Items	−139,000	0
Discontinued Operations	0	0
Pre-Tax Profit	**−13,542,000**	**−7,478,000**
Tax Payable	6,000	17,000
Extraordinary Items	0	0
Dividends Paid	0	0
Retained Profit	**−13,548,000**	**−7,495,000**

Source: easyCar.

online financial services business, was launched. Its first product was a dynamically personalized credit card. It was estimated that Stelios had spent £100 million to expand his easyGroup empire. However, his non-airline businesses had lost £75 million in three years. Funding for all new ventures came from Stelios' personal wealth. In May 2003, all the businesses in operation or being planned, were financed personally by Stelios, with minimal investments from other members of the easyGroup management team.

New Venture Development

easyGroup was constantly in quest of new business opportunities—even visitors to the group website were encouraged to submit business ideas. The group had a New Ventures team comprising six employees tasked with championing and developing new ideas. At any given point in time two to three ideas were in the pipeline.

The company's very nature—described as being "information hungry"– led employees to surf websites and trawl through information about industries (size, growth, etc.) to identify potentially attractive opportunities. These ideas were presented and discussed informally, typically

---

Exhibit 17   easyCar—Growth Statistics

Fiscal Year (y/e September)	2000	2001	2002	2003[1]
Fleet size (Number of cars)	2,358	5,066	6,080	7,552
Total number of UK sites	4	8	10	28
Legacy sites	4	8	9	8
Pit stop	–	–	1	20
Number of international (non-UK) sites	5	7	10	22
Legacy sites	5	7	10	9
Pit stop	–	–	–	13

[1] (to 05/03)

Source: easyCar.

---

through conversation, debate and e-mail exchanges. Most business decisions were made on the basis of data available in the public domain.

Geographic expansion was also high on the group's agenda. The car rental and Internet café businesses were represented in Europe. A team of two was based in the US with a view to spearheading new opportunities in the region as well as growing the existing Internet café operations in the US.

In addition to the planned cinema venture, several new projects were being examined including budget hotels, gyms, budget cruises, bus transportation and home catering. The easyCinema project, however, was the one closest to decision point.

Criteria for New Business Selection

The criteria for new business selection had evolved over time (Exhibit 18). Having learnt from past experience, easyGroup now had a more selective approach to the choice of business that it entered, i.e., understanding ex ante whether capabilities such as yield management could be truly powerful in a particular industry context. "Our eureka moments," said David Rawsthorn, who was involved in conceptualizing the cinema project, "come after days, weeks of being exposed to our principles and to how they apply in an industry." The group sought to operate simple businesses and to explore how it could engineer a complex business into a much simpler one. The "easy" formula essentially required consumer-facing businesses that displayed significant price elasticity, required a high fixed-cost base and low marginal-cost to service additional customers—factors that would enable easyGroup to effectively yield manage. Further, the group believed that

---

Exhibit 18   Criteria for Idea Selection

Industry requirements—The idea proposed must be in an industry that:
- Is consumer facing
- Is a price elastic market with the opportunity to grow the market through lower prices
- Is a perishable commodity, e.g., something that cannot be sold again like a night at a hotel room
- Has incumbents with a high unit cost base
- Has no low-cost competitors in its market

Aligned with "easy" principles—A new venture must:
- Use, fit and build the "easy" brand
- Provide good value to the customer
- Use technology to cut costs and improve quality
- Sell direct to the consumer, e.g., internet sales
- Be a simple offering
- Not play by traditional market rules
- Not be a white-label
- Not bundle products
- Be easy-to-use

Business model requirements—The business model must:
- Have unit cost-savings of the order of 50% compared with the best in the market
- Have zero or very low marginal cost
- Be possible to yield manage the price
- Have the potential to significantly increase utilisation/occupancy rates compared with the industry

Financial requirements—The business must:
- Have the potential for floatation in c.5 years, typically requiring an annual profit of £10 mil. pre-floatation and strong growth potential

Source: Company website.

industries with strong but complacent incumbents were particularly well suited for easyGroup's approach.

Businesses That easyGroup Would Not Consider

Based on the above principles of business selection, the group had developed a common understanding of some of the businesses that they would not enter. With characteristic humor, Stelios cited the example of the funeral business as one of these as funeral spending did not represent discretionary spending and therefore could not be yield managed!

Process of Entering New Businesses

Business models for most new ventures were developed by extracting out complexity from business processes, e.g., easyCar's policy that customers return their cars clean or pay a £10 fine was a way of eliminating significant labor costs incurred in washing cars: "Most car rental companies are a euphemism for car-wash companies," said Stelios. The focus on operational simplicity was facilitated by a conscious "de-skilling" of jobs at car rental sites and by a complete elimination of personnel in the Internet cafés. The newly-launched mobile vans that served as car rental pick-up points, for instance, were one-person operations enabled by a user-friendly computerized software to ensure that all "check-out" process steps were executed at the required service level.

Another approach that easyGroup used to develop its business model was to reverse engineer business operations with the target of arriving at a cost structure that would be half that of its competitors.

The mode of scaling up the business underwent a change from the early days of Stelios' entrepreneurship—from accelerated roll-outs, as characterized by the café and car business, to a phased roll-out. The company decided that, going forward, it would focus on piloting and refining new ideas before replicating them, caution that stemmed from Stelios' "reluctance to be railroaded by expensive mistakes."

Incubation of New Businesses

easyGroup operated with clear guidelines on what the role of the central group should be during the lifetime of a business. The group's involvement over time decreased as a particular business became increasingly self-sufficient and ultimately ready for an IPO. Until the time of an IPO, all businesses were located in the corporate office. After a

business had gone public, it would be physically moved out of the corporate offices and into new facilities of its own.

The corporate office, The Rotunda, based in a converted piano factory in Camden, housed three functions:

- Brand protection, which ensured that encroachments on the "easy" brand were dealt with appropriately and that licensees were complying with brand rules.
- Incubation, which identified, screened, selected and developed new business ideas.
- Services, which supported the organization through functions such as Intellectual Property, Legal, Finance and Human Resources.

The Rotunda was a circular building and the easyGroup office was arranged in a wheel-like formation. Stelios and the core management team sat in open plan spaces in the center while the businesses and corporate functions were crammed along aisles that ran like imaginary spokes. "I like to sit in the middle of everyone else," said Stelios. "It sends a message that, first, you are more accessible, and second, you know what's happening. Luxury doesn't belong at the office, mainly because at some stage you will expect outside investors to invest in your company and these investors should not be funding your lifestyle." The Guardian newspaper described easyGroup's offices as follows: "The place looks as if it is just capable of turning out a student newspaper, but hardly the hub of an empire that now comprises a fistful of easy-branded, orange-hued, cheap 'n' cheerful businesses."

It was in the Rotunda that every evening at 5pm the company would hold a stand-up meeting in which all business units would provide a daily update on their respective Key Performance Indicators (KPI). The objective was to communicate performance figures, highlight strategic developments and address operational concerns. This meeting played an important role in reinforcing the group's ambitions for all its employees and in ensuring that each of the businesses were on track for profitability.

5-year Vision

The group planned to have two public businesses in its portfolio—easyCar and easyInternetcafé—over the next five years. The car rental business targeted an IPO in 2005. During this timeframe, it also planned to have five new start-ups in operation. Stelios aimed to build a cadre of people who would move across new ventures, sharing knowledge and competencies of the "easy" way of doing business.

The group invested in developing its managers. Some of them were about to attend conferences that addressed how franchises could be managed. COO Nick Manoudakis had just returned from the Advanced Management Program at Harvard and had shared his learnings with the entire organization.

easyGroup: Growth Choices

As easyGroup examined the opportunities of launching a no-frills cinema in 2003, another blockbuster year with big budget new releases including *The Matrix Reloaded* and part three of *The Lord of the Rings*, its management team realized that it would face resistance from powerful distributors and incumbent exhibitors who worked in sync with each other. But this would not deter them. easyGroup believed that it would legally challenge the trading practices of these powerful companies, if required, in order to revolutionize the manner in which cinemas were operated. It had successfully targeted industries with strong but "fat, complacent" incumbents in the past. This would be another such opportunity.

The easyGroup team grappled with several questions. How should they roll-out the business? What payment structure for film rentals would be the most viable? Should they build a new cinema or acquire an existing chain? Most important of all was the fundamental question—Was this the right business for easyGroup?

Case 3–5: LEGO (A)*

Abstract -

This case describes the situation facing Kjeld Kirk Kristiansen, CEO of LEGO, in early 1996. It looks at LEGO's product diversification strategy, and the changes going on in the marketplace for children's toys. In particular, it highlights the threat LEGO faces from new competitors such as Nintendo and Sony.

Introduction

As Kjeld Kirk Kristiansen, Chief Executive and grandson of LEGO's founder, reviewed the preliminary financial results for 1996 early one January morning, he wondered what the rest of 1997 would bring. The results for 1996 looked good. LEGO had expanded in a number of directions in the previous 12 months with the opening of the second theme park, the move into watches and the beginning of a move into software; this strategy seemed to by paying off. LEGO was now ranked fifth largest toy manufacturer in the world.

However, there were indications that not all was well. LEGO lost market share in some key markets in 1996, most notably Japan (down 20%). And despite growth of 40% in Eastern Europe, Europe as a whole experienced only modest growth. Consumer sales via toy retailers were slowing; 2% growth for 1996 compared with 4% or more for previous years.

Kjeld, who had been CEO since 1980, was therefore concerned how 1997 would evolve. The global toy market was changing. Over the next 11 months, LEGO would launch the third line of girls' LEGO in almost as many years in an ongoing attempt to appeal to that half of the marketplace. LEGO was also scheduled to trial CD ROM-based building instructions and launch their first LEGO computer game, "LEGO Island." Where should Kjeld focus his energy? Where would future growth come from?

The LEGO Group

Corporate History

LEGO had a long and solid history. Over the previous 40 years, over 400 million children all over the world had played with LEGO. The company was founded in 1932 by Ole Kirk Christiansen in the village of Billund, Denmark. At that time, his firm manufactured stepladders, ironing boards—and wooden toys. Two years later, the company and its products adopted the name LEGO, formed from the Danish words "LEg GOdt" ("play well"). The word "LEGO" was officially registered in Denmark in 1950 and by 1956, Christiansen was beginning to sell abroad with a foreign sales company in Germany. The motto of the firm soon became: "Only the best is good enough."

Growth patterns in the firm had not been consistent. It took 56 years (1932–1978) to reach sales of roughly 134.5 million Euros.[1] In just the next 10 years, however, sales increased fivefold, from 134.5 million Euros in 1978 to approx 672 million Euros in 1988, as LEGO rolled out its successful product formula around the world. The effect of this was that by 1990 LEGO had emerged as one of the top 10 global toy manufacturers and the only European firm on this list. In 1996 LEGO's top markets were Germany, USA, France, Benelux, Great Britain, Japan, Korea, Italy, Austria and Russia.

Through all this, however, LEGO remained a values-based organisation. The core values were: creativity, play, learning and development. "Play" in the LEGO sense was learning. LEGO's purpose was to stimulate children's imagination and creativity in a world without limits—and this became a central theme for all its subsequent product development initiatives. LEGO had three guiding principles: to be a good corporate citizen, to be a global business that respected the interests and culture of local communities and to be a good employer i.e. for the workplace to be

*This case was written by Laura Birkinshaw using public source material about LEGO and the toy industry. March 2002.
© London Business School, March 2002 Sussex Place, Regent's Park, London NW1 4SA, United Kingdom. Used with permission.

healthy and developmental. The corporate culture was built on respect for the customers, the consumers and the employees.

In the 1990's, with LEGO available to kids from Israel to Korea, the sales curve flattened. Kristiansen was struggling to double sales over the next ten years (1988–1998). LEGO was a family owned business and had always been profitable, although full financial details were not disclosed.

Key Financial Data for LEGO(Euros m.)

	1996	1995	1994
Net Sales	1.014	921	768
Operating Result	63	58	63
Profit Margin	6.2	6.3	8.2

LEGO was structured in two divisions: Core Business and New Business. Core Business activities were divided by product lines: PRIMO—toys for babies and toddlers (founded 1995); DUPLO—bricks 8 times larger than traditional LEGO bricks designed for toddlers (founded 1967); SCALA—a flexible doll's house system (to be launched in 1997); LEGO system—the traditional bricks (founded 1955); and TECHNIC—products with very complex technical builds (founded 1977). New Business included four entities: DACTA—educational products, but not CD ROMS (founded 1980); LEGOland theme parks (founded 1968); Licencing (founded 1993); and Media (founded 1996).

At the end of 1995 LEGO had also undergone a transformation in style and structure with the introduction of "Compass Management," the goal of which was a more reactive organisation capable of quicker and better decisions.

Product Development

Production of plastic toys began in 1947 and by 1949, the company was producing over 200 toys including the "Automatic Binding Bricks," a forerunner of the LEGO bricks we know today. The bricks were designed to stimulate creativity in children, allowing them to build and play with their dreams.

Expansion of concepts was relatively slow for the next 20 years and chiefly involved expanding the age range of target children, moving both up and down in years. In 1964, LEGO began packaging bricks in "model sets" that included instructions. Some felt that this compromised the integrity of the brand as it led to more "directed" play.

Production of DUPLO began in 1967 and LEGO opened its first themepark, LEGOland, in Denmark in 1968.

In the 70's LEGO moved to secure both the boys and girls markets by introducing the concept of LEGO figures with the launch of LEGO Family in 1974. 1977 was the birth of LEGO TECHNIC, a range of complicated models targeted at older children.

The early 80's focussed on the younger segment of LEGO's target audience with developments in DUPLO and the introduction of DUPLO Baby with toys like rattles. They also established an educational products division (later known as DACTA) and evolved LEGO TECHNIC to become computer controlled in 1986 to take advantages of new technologies and to maintain the interest of children as they grew older. Also in 1986 LEGO launched a computerised building set for schools, but did not roll it out to the home market as it felt the home market was immature.

Product innovation was a priority within LEGO's Core Business. Every year between 100–300 new LEGO sets were added to the product line, elements and play themes resulting from the hundreds of ideas constantly being worked on in LEGO's four development centres in Japan, Europe and America. Average time for developing a new LEGO product (i.e. a kit) was between 1–5 years. The product lifecycle for kits was also shrinking from 3 to 2 years, perhaps due to themed kits (e.g. Winnie the Pooh).

Changing Consumers and Markets

Against this picture of success, changes in the global toy market and in children's play were threatening traditional toys of all descriptions—including LEGO. The lives of middle-class children in LEGO's traditional markets of Europe and the Americas had changed dramatically in the last 2 decades. A generation ago-with just a few TV channels, no computers, and primitive video games—children grew up in a play economy, in which entertainment was but a small, easily contained part.

Industry analysts argued that children were now growing up in an entertainment economy, saturated with media, in which open-ended, self-guided play was a shrinking part. Children were outgrowing their toys faster and faster in a rush to become "big." Fantasy play was taking on a whole new meaning, thanks to technological innovation. Children who used to play at being firemen by placing pots on their heads and using old garden hoses could now simulate the real fire-fighting experience using software and handheld controls. And why would you even want to be a fire-fighter when you could be a bionic soldier fighting aliens on a mysterious planet using only a TV and a video-game console?

The popularity of these new "play systems" meant that children were spending less time playing with conventional toys and more time playing "outcome-driven" games. Not play for the sake of play, or play for the sake of learning and growing—as LEGO believed—but play for the sake of winning.

New Competitors

Key players in this new market were Nintendo (N64 and GameBoy), Sega, and Sony (Playstation). Nintendo's turnover (2.1 billion Euros) was slightly less than Sega's (2.5 billion Euros), but they looked better placed going forward with their new N64 product. However, not all of this growth in this segment had been profitable. Microsoft was rumoured to be expanding into this market as well over the next few years. The firms that had profited the most from the new type of play were the software companies that created the games to play on these systems.

The growth potential of computer CD ROM games and e-games was hard to estimate. With increasing numbers of children surfing the Internet to find information and entertainment it was unclear what impact this would have on both traditional toys and "game systems." Much of the entertainment available for children on the internet focussed on winning, while many of the CD ROM games traded under the "educational software" label, helping children learn and allowing creativity within controlled parameters e.g. the child could choose which colour to paint Pooh Bear.

The video game market was expected to be worth 23 billion Euros per year by 2000. Between 1990 and 1996 the Video and PC games markets had grown from 538 million Euros to 13 Billion Euros (see Exhibit 1).

In contrast to this, growth in traditional markets over the same period (1990–96) had been much slower with starting figures of 25 billion Euros and final figures of 32 billion Euros. See exhibit 1. Growth in this traditional toy market was expected to reach 64 billion Euros by 2000, but even here, LEGO was under increasing competition.

With the loss of patent protection on its bricks in 1981, competitors like MegaBloks appeared on the scene offering almost identical copies of LEGO. These products were of lower quality, but also of lower price and offered full compatibility with the LEGO system, so children could own a mixture of LEGO and MegaBloks and play with them together.

In addition to this, other creative building products like K'NEX (plastic sticks and joints) offered alternative systems with technical quality approaching LEGO's. KNEX models tended to be larger than LEGO models when completed because of their construction (plastic sticks and joints) and this made KNEX very visually appealing to children—a fact exploited by toyshops and children's open play areas. KNEX was experiencing year on year growth of 35% and now claimed as much as 20% of the construction toy market in some key LEGO countries.

One of LEGO's key competitors, Mattel, was also experiencing strong growth with double-digit growth virtually each year of the 1990's, but Mattel was achieving this in part by pushing down the target age for some of their traditional brands like Barbie to exploit the trend for children to grow up more quickly.

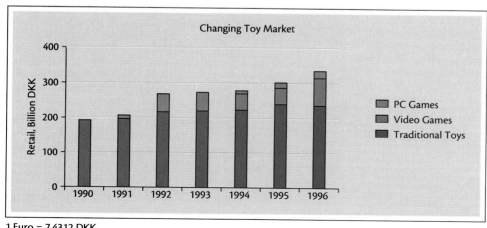

Exhibit 1 Toy Market sales 1990–1996.

1 Euro = 7.4312 DKK

The Challenge

In the early 90's LEGO had made numerous attempts to increase their presence in the girls' market with the Paradisa range in 92, the Belleville range in 94, and Scala in 1997. Research suggested that, in contrast to boys, who liked building for the sake of building, girls preferred to play with the finished product in role- play games and LEGO was struggling to find a product to capture their imagination. LEGO also established a Lifestyle division that entered into licencing agreements, putting the LEGO name on bags, clothing watches etc.

In response to the growth of electronic games, LEGO Media had just been formed (1996) to develop children's software, music, videos, books etc. Part of their aim was to develop multimedia products that allowed children the opportunity to build LEGO models virtually on their computers. LEGO had also been working on a programmable "intelligent brick" concept for almost 15 years. This new product had recently been named MINDSTORMS and was provisionally slated to launch later in 1997. The aim for the MINDSTORMS product was to help children solve complex problems in creative ways using technology.

LEGO still had the same objectives as the early years. LEGO wanted continuous, controlled growth that would secure their financial independence as a family-owned, family-run company. LEGO also considered it very important to "do the right thing" with regards to their employees, the environment and their customers. The objectives for the future had been to increase consumer sales by 10% per year up to the year 2005. It was believed that the driving force behind this growth would be the Core Business, but that New Business would also contribute. The 10-year growth objective envisaged that current turnover would increase almost threefold.

Kristiansen pondered where he should focus, not only for 1997, but beyond. By helping children to learn, LEGO believed they would help build confident, curious and resourceful adults. LEGO wanted to nurture children's curiosity, creativity and imagination. If the market was growing away from these kinds of toys, where was LEGO's place? Was LEGO willing to have slower growth in a bid to stay true to their heritage and do what they believed was right for children? Or should LEGO move with the times and embrace "game systems" in a bid to cross-sell back into traditional products?

Notes

1   For the sake of comparability, all figures are presented in Euros.

Case 3–6: LVMH

Managing the Multi-Brand Conglomerate*

The mission of the LVMH group is to represent the most refined qualities of Western "Art de Vivre" around the world. LVMH must continue to be synonymous with both elegance and creativity. Our products, and the cultural values they embody, blend tradition and innovation, and kindle dream and fantasy.[1]

Abstract

LVMH Moët Hennessy Louis Vuitton, based in France, is one of the world's leading luxury goods companies. It operates in wines, spirits, fashion goods, leather goods, perfumes, cosmetics, watches, jewelry and retailing. The company employs approximately 56,000 employees. Its global distribution network grew from 828 in 1998 to 1,592 stores in 2004. The majority of sales are derived from the Fashion and Leather goods division, with Europe (including France) being the biggest regional contributor. The company is the largest and most widely spread luxury goods company, with a strong brand portfolio and distribution skills. LVMH's "star brands" is a key foundation of the group's strategy. It has built over time one of the strongest brand portfolios in the sector, counting 60 top brands amongst its five divisions and other operations. At the core of the Fashion and Leather business is the Louis Vuitton brand itself. This "star of star brands" is estimated to generate over 80% of earnings in the segment.

The case discusses the following critical challenges for LVMH (a) sustaining its organic growth strategy (b) competition strategy (c) managing multi-brand strategy with star brands (d) managing a decentralized conglomerate (e) leadership and charisma of Bernard Arnault in creating, maintaining and managing a global conglomerate (f) people issues in the luxury industry.

*The case was written by **Ashok Som**, Assistant Professor of Strategy and Management at ESSEC Business School. It is intended to be used as a basis for class discussion rather than to illustrate either effective or ineffective handling of a business situation. The author gratefully acknowledges Lilly Liu, Deepak Yachamaneni, ESSEC MBA Exchange students and Boris Gbahoué, ESSEC MBA student for their research help.
©2004 Ashok Som, ESSEC Business School of France. Used with permission. Reproduction or distribution of this case is strictly prohibited without the prior permission of the author. To obtain reprints of this case, ECCH Reference number 304-274-1, please contact the ECCH at http://www.ecch.cranfield.ac.uk/

Keywords: Managing the global conglomerate, decentralized organization, M&A, synergy, organic growth, competition, multi-branded strategy, star brands, brand management, portfolio management, international management, global operations, luxury goods, France.

Introduction

On March 4, 2004, 54 year old Bernard Arnault stood under his Picasso painting at the LVMH headquarters in Paris and pondered over the future of his fashion empire. He had just announced a 30% rise in net income for 2003, with improved profits for all sectors of the business except watches and jewelry. Margins for the flagship leather goods brand Louis Vuitton topped 45%, due to the increased publicity spending featuring the actress Jennifer Lopez in its latest global ad campaign.

As the chief shareholder in LVMH Moët Hennessy Louis Vuitton, and his ownership stakes in high-profile labels of Christian Dior, Givenchy, Louis Vuitton, Christian Lacroix, Kenzo, Céline, Emilio Pucci, Fendi, Loewe, Donna Karan, and a substantial investment in Marc Jacobs, places much of the future of world fashion in his hands. His properties also include Tag Heuer watches, Moët and Chandon champagne, and a chain of duty-free shops that dot many international airports. The fashion conglomerate's leadership in the luxury sector has been sustained by new product launches, store openings and an increased investment in communications. The group has continued its new launches and initiatives in 2004, including the new leather goods Damier Geant line, the Théda bags, an entire new jewelry line at Louis Vuitton, a new perfume for women at Dior, a new fragrance for men at Guerlain, an array of watch and jewelry creations, and the new Ellipse Cognac from Hennessy.

LVMH has continued to develop its worldwide distribution network. The Louis Vuitton brand, which celebrated its 150th anniversary, opened its largest store in the world in New York. Advancements in markets with significant potential for luxury products, such as Asia, have also bolstered the group's performance. Future focus will be likely on new growth markets and regions such as China, a market with considerable potential for cognac, fashion and perfumes; Russia with promise notably for Sephora, which has already shown promise in several Central and Eastern European countries; India, where Louis Vuitton opened its first store in 2003.

However, the €12 billion fashion and liquor conglomerate controlled by Bernard Arnault is not without worries. Wall Street continues to question whether the company's multi-brand strategy can be sustained. He has to consider the increasing importance of succession as he is approaching the legal retirement age, and would soon need to plan about his successor who could replace him at the helm of his group.

Company Background

History

Established in 1987, LVMH was created by the fusion of two fashion houses: Louis Vuitton, a leather goods specialist founded in 1834 and Moët-Hennessy, a wine and spirits group created in 1971. The luxury group grew through key acquisitions and the development of new products. Under the leadership of Bernard Arnault, the 1990s saw a period of great expansion with the purchase of large stakes in the Company's subsidiaries. In recent years, the luxury group has begun to shed some of its portfolio, with the strategy of focusing on its *"star"* brands, defined by Arnault as *"timeless, modern, fast-growing, and highly profitable"* brands (see Exhibit 1 for a list of the recent acquisitions and divestitures). Observers comment that *"This collection of global brands was the stepping stone for realizing lucrative synergies in the fashion business, which would add to the bottom line."*

With over 56,000 employees and approximately €12 billion in revenues during the fiscal year 2003, the LVMH group operates in 5 primary sectors: Wines and spirits, Fashion and Leather Goods, Perfumes and Cosmetics, Watches and Jewelry, and Selective Retailing. LVMH today controls more than 60 luxury brands across its product lines. The acquisition strategy at LVMH always focused on brands that had strong brand power, resulting in the company to reach leadership positions in almost every segment it served. Each division functions as a Strategic Business Unit with its own General Manager and a top management team. These divisions also manage overseas sales of their respective lines.

Wines & Spirits

The Wines & Spirits contributed to 18% of sales and to 36% of the operating profit in 2003. LVMH, through Hennessy, holds 40% of the cognac market and between 20%–25% of the overall champagne market. In the premium champagne segment, LVMH has a dominant share of 50% built around exclusive brands such as Moët Chandon and Veuve Clicquot. It has also ventured outside the traditional wine belts in France and Italy to acquire high-end wine producers in California and Australia. Given the rising prominence of both California and Australia in the wine business, these moves allowed the company to market a truly global selection of wines and champagnes. However considering the total liquor market, LVMH does not figure in the top 10 due to the absence of its drinks in the 'Popular segment' like beers, whisky and Vodka. However this is in line with LVMH's strategy to focus only on high margin activities. Analysts have suggested spinning off the wines and spirits businesses as a separate unit as they consider it to be non-core to LVMH's fashion image. For example, the sale of Pommery, a profitable champagne brand in 2001 was a strategic move by LVMH. The brand was bought for the vast lands it owned in the Champagne region, as high quality land is limited in this region, LVMH wanted more land to produce more grapes for its Moët and Veuve brands of champagne. When Pommery was purchased its land was also acquired but when it was sold, the land was retained and only the brand was sold.

Fashion & Leather Goods

The Fashion & Leather Goods contributed to 35% of sales and to 60% of the operating profit in 2003 and had an operating margin of 32%. Much of the sales of this division are concentrated in the Asia-Pacific region, particularly Japan which accounts for 33% of the sales. Sales in this segment are directly attributable to the Louis Vuitton brand. This label has grown by leaps and bounds under the leadership of its legendary designer, Mr. Marc Jacobs. Demand for Louis Vuitton products has often exceeded supply, requiring customers to go on a waiting list that often took several months to clear. The Louis Vuitton label, combined with the strength of the LVMH group, has provided opportunities for expanding into new brands and products. Using this as a launching pad, the company engaged in significant brand expansion efforts to reach a wider audience. These efforts were well supported by fashion buyers.

The company has been able to leverage synergies across its fashion brands. For example, its Kenzo production facility has been transformed into a logistics platform for men's ready-to-wear products serving other brands such as Givenchy and Christian Lacroix. Given

Exhibit 1   LVMH Conglomerate at a Glance

Wines & Spirits	Watches & Jewelry	Fashion & Leather	Selective Retailing	Perfumes & Cosmetics
Moët & Chandon*	TAG Heuer*	Louis Vuitton*	DFS*	Parfums Christian Dior*
Dom Pérignon	Ebel*	Loewe*	Miami Cruiseline Services*	Guerlain*
Veuve Clicquot*	Zenith*	Céline*	Sephora*	Parfums Givenchy*
Krug	Christian Dior Watches*	Berluti*	Le Bon Marché*	Kenzo Parfums*
Mercier	Fred*	Kenzo*	La Samaritaine*	Laflachère*
Ruinart	Chaumet*	Givenchy*		Bliss*
Château d'Yquem*	OMAS*	Christian Lacroix*		BeneFit Cosmetics*
Chandon Estates*		Marc Jacobs*		Fresh*
Hennessy*		Fendi*		Make Up For Ever*
Cloudy Bay		StefanoBi		Acqua di Parma*
Cape Mentelle		Emilio Pucci*		Perfumes Loewe*
Newton		Thomas Pink*		
MountAdam		Donna Karan*		

*indicates company status

Acquisitions:
1987   Fashion house Céline
1988   Fashion house Givenchy
1991   Champagne brand Pommery
1993   Fashion house Kenzo
1994   Perfume company Kenzo, cosmetics company Guerlain
1995   Jeweler Fred
1996   Leather goods specialist Loewe
1997   DFS, the luxury goods distribution network
1998   Sephora, the fragrance and cosmetics retail chain
1999:   Champagne producer Krug and the watch manufacturer TAG Heuer, a 34% minority stake in the Italian luxury goods maker, Gucci
2000:   LVMH purchased the US start-up, Urban Decay, and Donna Karan apparel line
2001:   La Samaritaine department store, Acqua di Parma perfumes, a stake in Fendi
2002:   Millennium & Company, prestige wines and alcohol

New business creations:
1987:   Christian Lacroix in 1987
2001:   Newton and MountAdam vineyards
          Marketing De Beers diamond jewelry in a 50–50 joint venture

Divestitures:
2001:   Sale of stake in Gucci to Pinault Printemps Redoute
2002   Pommery champagne brand, Hard Candy and Urban Decay
2003   Canard-Duchene to the Alain Thienot Group
          Final stake of 27.5% in Phillips, de Pury & Luxembourg, an auction house
          Minority stake in Michael Kors, including cosmetics and fragrance licenses
          Marc Jacobs and Kenneth Cole fragrance divisions
          Bliss spa line & Ebel watches

the historically lower profit margins in the ready-to-wear market, synergies resulting in cost savings have boosted profitability. As Muriel Zingraff, Harrods' fashion and beauty director, observed,

What I will say is that we may have more patience with smaller brands if they are owned by a parent company, such as LVMH or the Gucci Group.

Perfumes & Cosmetics

The Perfumes & Cosmetics (P&C) contributed to 18% of sales and to 8% of the operating profit in 2003. This division has an enviable collection of brands such as Christian Dior, Guerlain, Kenzo, and Givenchy. The company has recently acquired popular U.S. brands such as Bliss, Hard Candy, Urban Decay, and Fresh that were geared towards a younger clientele. These acquisitions are an integral part of the drive to internationalize LVMH's perfumes and cosmetics offerings. Europe is the largest market for perfumes perhaps due to the heritage of the brands that the company offered. The P&C division has been able to leverage R&D synergies across brands, while its R&D expenditure is in line with the industry norms, LVMH has been able to generate twice the average growth rate in the industry. It is believed that these R&D skills would help boost sales of the acquired companies. As part of a larger drive to consolidate margins in this division, the company has been integrating R&D, production, distribution, sourcing, and other back-office operations across brands. These moves have been beneficial. For example, integrating the purchasing function across brands has resulted in cost savings in raw materials of 20%. Analysts believe that this division is well positioned to reap the spillover benefits arising from the co-branding strategy under which many of the brands are linked directly to ready-to-wear apparel brands, a unique avenue of differentiation at LVMH.

Watches & Jewelry

The latest portfolio addition at LVMH, Watches & Jewelry, contributed to 4% of sales and to –2% of the operating profit in 2003. In the watches section, the company owned prestigious brands that included Tag Heuer, Ebel, and Zenith, and in jewelry section Fred Joallier and Chaumet. The purchase of the Zenith brand was crucial to LVMH's strategy to expand its watches operations. Most watches have an identical manufacturing process and brands reflect minor differences in quality. According to industry sources, there are only 3 manufacturers in the world from whom all the luxury watchmakers source their products. It is noteworthy that Zenith is the only manufacturer in the world of a certain component used in every watch. LVMH wanted a platform to sell more watches by utilizing its design experience and the production know-how of Zenith. Watches can be one of the most lucrative segments at LVMH with margins as high as 80%.

Unlike its constellation of brands in other divisions, many think that the company does not have quite the same star power in watches and jewelry. Competitors such as Richemont, Hermès, and Bulgari seem to have more recognizable brands and more upscale products in this category. However, tangible synergies appear to be a definite possibility because the division could centralize the manufacturing and utilize Tag Heuer's expertise in retail distribution across all brands. The jewelry business is also extremely competitive due to the presence of leading brands such as Cartier and Van Cleef & Arpels. Despite the Place Vendôme heritage of both Chaumet and Fred Joallier, neither of them are currently profitable.

Selective Retailing

The Selective Retailing contributed to 25% of the sales and to 5% of the operating profit in 2003. The vertical integration strategy of LVMH came to fruition when the selective retailing arm was established. This division manages LVMH investments in Sephora, DFS Galleria, and Miami Cruiseline Services. While this division contributed 26% of company sales in 2002, it had not made a profit in the previous three years. DFS Galleria with 150 duty-free and general merchandise stores is the world's largest travel retailer. Acquired in 1996, this business was a victim of poor timing, since the Asian financial crisis hit soon thereafter. LVMH has since instituted several good management practices, including the execution of a strategy that would reduce DFS' reliance on Asian airports, selective closing of underperforming stores and the creation of DFS Galleria stores in large metropolitan areas. Despite these changes, Japanese travelers are still its most important and loyal customers and any economic development that hurts Japanese travel will invariably find its way to DFS' bottom line. Miami Cruiseline Services (MCS) was acquired in January 2000. It offers retail services on board cruise ships and accounts for 76% of the world's major cruise lines (over 100 ships) as its customers. Conceived as an extension of the DFS concept, Miami Cruiseline focuses primarily (90%) on North American passengers, thus counterbalancing the over-reliance on Japanese tourists. It also manages duty-free operations at the Miami International Airport, the gateway to Latin America, opening possibilities of strengthening LVMH's brands in a region of the world where they are still underrepresented.

In addition to these distribution based assets, LVMH has recently acquired La Samaritaine, the prestigious Paris department store. The company has also entered the retailing end of the made-to-order tailoring business with the acquisition of Thomas Pink, the legendary Mayfair tailoring house that has a worldwide reputation for excellence in shirts. Thomas Pink has retail outlets in the United States as well. LVMH has also taken a minority stake in the 200-year-old U.K. fashion retailer, Asprey & Garrard, that has global aspirations of its own.

Functioning of the Group

LVMH's five product groups are decentralised into production and distribution subsidiaries. Some of the major brands have their own national subsidiaries. Overlaying this, there is a regional structure, with corporate headquarters in Paris, New York, Tokyo, and Amsterdam. The wine and spirits operations of Moët Hennessy have its own headquarters, with main offices in France and regional headquarters in Singapore.

Depending on the geographic region, LVMH has different organizational setups. In France, the hub of LVMH has individual headquarters for every brand, with an LVMH headquarters handling some centralized activities. In contrast, in New York, the central LVMH office houses the LVMH and Givenchy brands, while Dior and Fendi have their own US offices. Tokyo centralizes the human resources function, and each brand operates independently on all aspects of business.

The Group's decentralised organizational structure, helps the Company to foster efficiency, productivity, and creativity. LVMH strives to create a highly motivating and dynamic atmosphere for its employees, emphasizing individual initiative and offers real responsibilities—often early on in one's career. LVMH gives each brand almost complete freedom to pursue its creative vision. However, it does realize synergies through almost 20% discount in advertising by negotiating in bulk for all its brands.

The challenge of this structure is that it requires highly entrepreneurial executive teams in each company within the Group. This entrepreneurial spirit requires a healthy dose of common sense from managers, as well as hard work, pragmatism, efficiency, and the ability to motivate people in the pursuit of ambitious goals.

Bernard Arnault: "The Pope of Fashion"

Dubbed "the Pope of Fashion," Bernard Arnault has spent the past 15 years building LVMH from a small, clothing manufacturer to a conglomerate comprising approximately 50 of the world's most powerful brands. Trained as an engineer at the Ecole Polytechnique in France, Arnault joined his family's construction business where he worked for 13 years, before becoming the president of the company in 1978. In 1984, he left his family business to reorganize a French state-owned holding company, Boussac, which owned Christian Dior. In the late 1980s, Bernard Arnault took control of LVMH. With growing success in his business, Bernard Arnault acquired Givenchy (1988) and Kenzo (1993). Today, through a complex web of partnerships Bernard Arnault owns at least 33 percent of the company's stock.

Bernard Arnault is deeply involved in the creative process, far more than his peers. He believes that in the creative and highly seasonal fashion business, the ability to match effective CEOs with temperamental designers can make the difference between a star and a failure. He believes that *"to have the right DNA in a team is very rare. It's almost like a miracle."* Deemed the *"Billionaire Matchmaker,"* in the past 15 years he has formed close creative bonds with designer John Galliano, whose collections for Christian Dior have been hailed by fashion critics. His selection of Hedi Slimane has done wonders for Dior Homme, and his pairing of Marc Jacobs with Louis Vuitton has been a critical and financial success. His vision of the luxury and fashion industry as he states is:

> 'This link to creativity, it's not far from art, and I like it very much. You must like to be with designers and creators. You have to like an image. That's also a key to success. And at the same time, you must be able to organize a business worldwide.'

Industry Background

> Luxury is not the contrary to poverty,
> but a contrary of Vulgarity
>
> **—Gianni Versace**

> We are in the business of selling dreams. The strength of a brand depends on how many dreams it inspires.
>
> **—Chanel**

The luxury products industry has been estimated to be worth $58 billion, excluding automobiles and travel. The breakdown by sector is shown in Exhibit 2.

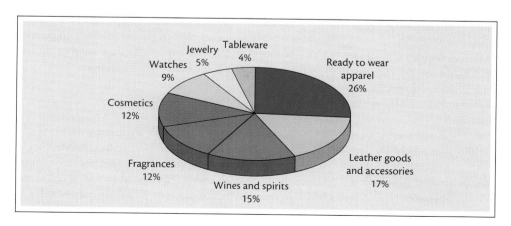

Exhibit 2 Breakdown of Luxury Goods Industry

Source: Merrill Lynch Research.

Exhibit 3   Luxury Market Growth, by Sector

Sectors of the Luxury Products Industry	Annual sales growth, 1998–2002
Home fashions	>10%
Ready to wear	10
Accessories	10
Leather goods	<10
Watches and jewelry	8
Perfume and cosmetics	6
Crystal and silverware	5
Shoes	4

Source: Eurostat.

Major players in the global luxury goods market include: LVMH Moët Hennessey Louis Vuitton, Richemont, Christian Dior, Gucci, Tiffany, Hermes, Swatch, and Bulgari. Traditionally, the luxury sector has been highly fragmented, characterized by a large number of family-owned and medium-sized enterprises. In the past two decades, it has been increasingly dominated by multi-brand luxury conglomerates. Although smaller companies still thrive in this environment by serving niche markets, larger luxury goods companies have acquired or overtaken many of their smaller competitors. (See Exhibit 3 for luxury market growth, by sector.)

Survival of the Multi-Brand Strategy?

LVMH and France's biggest retail-to-luxury group Pinault-Printemps-Redoute (PPR), which controls Gucci, led the consolidation spree in the luxury industry in the late 1990s. More luxury conglomerates have emerged through acquisitions: many separate brands have united under a holding company structure intended to spread best practice and impose commercial and financial discipline. The goal is to allow firms to grow strongly without over-exploiting a particular brand and killing exclusivity.

However, Michael Zaoui, Morgan Stanley's head of mergers and acquisitions in Europe, doubts on the viability of the multi-brand model, citing the slump in luxury M&A activity since 1999. *"It's a hotly debated issue . . . but is the multi-brand model holding up?"* asks Zaoui, whose investment bank has been involved in every Gucci acquisition since 1999 as well as the initial public offerings of Bulgari SpA and Burberry PLC.

According to Zaoui, M&A in luxury goods has slumped to $800 million in 2002 from $10 billion in 1999, and the rate of return on capital employed in the sector has

dropped to 20% in 2001 from 32% in 1997. As companies seek to stretch their brands to target new customers, some 1,400 new luxury goods stores have been opened since 1999: equivalent to strategic investments $4.5 billion. Large advertising budgets are required to attract people to these new stores. According to him, the 10 leading luxury companies spent $1.1 billion on advertising in 2001, equivalent to 8% of sales, compared with 6% of revenue in 1995. *"This expansion trend increases the inflexibility of the cost base . . . it can reduce margins if the growth's not there."*

"Luxury for the Masses"

There has been a systemic change in the luxury products market. In the past decade Gucci sunglasses, Prada handbags, and Louis Vuitton suitcases have become must-have items for many thousands of middle-class buyers. According to the Boston Consulting Group's newly released book, *Trading Up: The Transforming Power of New Luxury,* the trend in the market is toward mass elitism. While traditional luxury brands such as Louis Vuitton, Rolls-Royce and Hermes remain items for the elite, luxury has been democratized for all. According to BCG, "new luxury" could range from a Starbucks frappuccino to a Porsche and can be extended across categories like personal care, homewares and appliances, oral care, toys, restaurants and wines.

Consumers are in a "state of heightened emotionalism" and often address feelings of being overworked, isolated, lonely, worried, and unhappy by shopping for premium-priced products. "New" luxury is the idea that middle-class consumers trade up to premium products because of emotional needs, to give them a sense of indulgence and personal fulfillment. They spend a disproportionate amount of their income on such goods, and trade down in other categories that are perceived to be less important. For example, a consumer may visit a Dior boutique to spend several hundred dollars on a Gucci handbag, and then go to a Wal-Mart or Carrefour to buy cotton socks.

This new middle class market for luxury products creates a wide range of challenges for luxury conglomerates like Gucci and Louis Vuitton, as they have to understand and cater to a different target consumer.

Market Trends

In 2003, the luxury retail market segment was adversely affected by SARS (Severe Acute Respiratory Syndrome) in Asia, the United States led war against Iraq, the strengthening of the Euro and a weak "feel good factor" worldwide. SARS in Asia—which represents 30 percent of the sales in the luxury retail market segment—led to a general decline in travel and spending. Consumers in the United States also spent less in 2003 due to the war in Iraq and a weak economy. According to a study by Cotton Inc., published by *Women's Wear Daily*, consumers put 39 percent of their disposable income into savings and 14 percent to pay down debt in 2003. The strengthening of the Euro has also led to a drop in tourism, which translated into lower sales in the luxury retail segment since a significant portion of luxury retail sales is generated by Japanese tourists. A strong Euro also means equal sales in foreign currencies now appear as less Euro revenues. All of these events contributed to the weak "feel good factor" in 2003.

The luxury sector is cyclical and partially correlated to economic conditions. The luxury retail market segment appears to be rebounding in 2004 after two years of lackluster performance. Mr. Arnault predicted that the coming years will be *"very good for luxury because the world economy is doing well. The U.S. is booming, interest rates are very low and there is a lot of optimism, Japan recovering, and China and the Far East are growing fast."* Consumers dug into their pockets during the 2003/2004 holiday season to purchase more of the finer things in life. This turnaround in the luxury retail market segment ends the slump that plagued the market since the September 11, 2001 terrorist attacks.

However, signs of a turnaround in the luxury retail market are surfacing as consumer confidence improves and spending increases. In addition, performance in the luxury retail market segment is expected to improve throughout 2004. According to Mike Niemira, chief economist for the New York-based International Council of Shopping Centers, *"2004 will be a year of transition. Luxury items are strong and I think they are going to continue to be strong."* Consumer spending in the United States is being propelled by the rebounding stock markets, President Bush's $350 billion tax cut plan, and improving employment rates. Consumer spending in Asia is also recovering after the SARS epidemic.

In the long term, growth opportunities for the luxury retail market remain positive. The luxury retail market is currently driven by Japan, Europe and the United States. However, this market will include other parts of Asia such as China and Eastern Europe in the future as these regions become richer.

Competition

Traditionally, the luxury goods sector has been very fragmented and was dominated by with small and medium size companies which have over the years developed expertise in a particular product. But since the late 1990's-the boom years, the sector has been governed by multi-product and multi-brand conglomerates. Growth by acqui-

sitions has been an important strategy for all the major players in this industry. Conglomerates have been trying to preempt each other in acquiring brands that have managed to survive successfully. This race has changed the dynamics of the industry from being "creativity focused" to more "financially focused." The years since 2000 have seriously dampened spirits as sales stagnated and the conglomerates are paying a heavy price for their acquisition spree.

As the luxury goods industry looks to move beyond the three turbulent years, the independent and family-controlled companies that yielded the spotlight to sprawling conglomerates during the boom years are claiming a measure of vindication. Leaders of several of the world's leading fashion houses said that their strategy of resisting corporate advances had worked. It gave them better control over product direction at a time when consumers are showing signs of weariness with the glitz and hype of some of fashion's biggest names.

"Never be exploited; don't give up control of design,"

says Giorgio Armani, head of the company he owns.

While keeping it in the family may make sense from a brand-development standpoint, it does have limitations, During the past three years, a weak global economy has tested the financial resources of a number of family-owned luxury goods houses. There is also the question of what happens to companies that become associated with the name, charisma and creativity of a larger-than-life founder. While Armani himself has steadfastly resisted the idea of offering shares to the public, he refused to rule out the option of bringing in a big strategic investor, expressing willingness to partner with LVMH or PPR.

Selling to a bigger holding company does not always mean that a formerly privately controlled designer has to compromise on identity. When Phillips-Van Heusen bought Calvin Klein to help the biggest U.S. shirt maker compete against department stores, industry insiders were skeptical that Klein would be able to retain complete design control over his empire. Finances at one of the world's most recognizable brands were dismal. The designer had reportedly been losing up to $25 million a year on its couture collection and millions more on retail operations. Rather than clamping down on Klein's creativity, Phillips spun the label into two new midrange sportswear lines and pledged to cut costs while keeping Klein's 100 designers. Klein continues to play an important role in the image-making of the company. This is an example that shows how designers can funnel their creative energies and coexist with large conglomerates that offer substantial financial support—as both parties have adopted a middle path in the quest for control.

Exhibit 4   Representative Primary Competitors, by Business Unit

Product Sector	LVMH Businesses	Primary Competitors
Fashion and Leather Goods	Louis Vuitton, Loewe, Céline, Berluti, Kenzo, Christian Lacroix, Givenchy, Marc Jacobs, Fendi, StefanoBi, Emilio Pucci, Thomas Pink, Donna Karan	Prada, Versace, Armani, Saint-Laurent, Chanel, Ralph Lauren, MaxMara, Burberry, Ferragamo, Hugo Boss, Gucci, Hermès, Bulgari, Lancel, etc.
Jewelry and Watches	TAG Heuer, Zenith, Dior Watches, FRED, Chaumet, OMAS*	Oméga, Breitling, Vendôme-Cartier, Cartier, Van Cleef & Arpels, Rolex, Baume et Mercier
Perfume and Cosmetics	Parfums Christian Dior, Guerlain, Parfums Givenchy, Kenzo Parfums, Laflachère, BeneFit Cosmetics, Fresh, Make Up For Ever, Acqua di Parma, Perfumes Loewe*	Many brands, including Lancôme, Lanvin et Armani, all brands under L'Oréal, Chanel, Yves Saint-Laurent, Gautier, Calvin Klein, Ralph Lauren, Estée Lauder, Shiseido, Hard Candy*, Bliss*, specialty perfumeries, etc.
Wines and Spirits	Moët & Chandon, Dom Pérignon, Veuve Clicquot, Krug, Mercier, Ruinart, Château d'Yquem, Chandon Estates, Hennessy, Cloudy Bay, Cape Mentelle, Newton, MountAdam	Pommery*, Marne et Champagne, Laurent Perrier, Seagram, Johnny Walker, Smirnoff, Rémy Cointreau, Rémy Martin, Courvoisier, etc.
Distribution	DFS, Le Bon Marché, La Samaritaine, Séphora, sephora.com, Miami Cruiseline Services,	Many stores and retailing franchises

*Indicates former LVMH businesses.

GUCCI-PPR: What After Tom Ford?

Originally a reseller of luggage that was imported from Germany, Gucci took advantage of the economic expansion following World War I. Since then, the company has displayed an innovative streak, improvising leather alternatives. After the Second World War, Gucci began its global expansion strategy with a store in New York in 1953. The company suffered setbacks in the 1970s and 1980s after scandals and murder plots. There was intense fighting within the Gucci family that resulted in poor strategy and dilution of valuable brand equity. In the late 1980s, Investcorp, bought 50% of the company. The revival of Gucci commenced with the appointment of Mr. Domenico De Sole as the CEO. The new CEO hired Mr. Tom Ford, a highly acclaimed designer who revamped Gucci's product designs. The company took firmer control of the brand, its products, and the distribution. Investcorp sold its holdings through an IPO in 1996, making a five-fold return on its original investment. This was followed by a bitter battle for control of Gucci by LVMH and PPR. Finally after poison pill measures taken by the Gucci Management which did

not deter LVMH, PPR raised its offer and took control over the group. The move was welcomed by the Gucci management comprising of Mr. Domenico De Sole and Mr. Tom Ford, who preferred PPR to LVMH for fear of losing their "Creative License" if LVMH took over Gucci..

Gucci started a multibrand model later than LVMH. It acquired Yves Saint Laurent's fragrance and ready-to-wear apparel lines and added the renowned shoemaker, Sergio Rossi, to its umbrella of brands. The multibrand strategy was expected to deliver important synergies. Unfortunately, the benefits were never realized and all YSL pulled down the group's earnings year after year. In the meantime Gucci continued its aggressive ascent choreographed by De Sole and Tom Ford. The brand is strong in North America today and its strategy of portraying Gucci as a youthful and sensuous brand has appealed immensely to the Americans.

After the PPR group acquired a majority control of Gucci, it started "infringing" on the independence enjoyed by the creative duo of De Sole and Tom Ford. It is ironic that the very same group that was supposedly chosen to protect the creative freedom was curtailing it. Tensions with the chairman of PPR group, Pinault, led to both De sole and Tom Ford refusing to renew their 3 year contracts after 2004.

According to analysts, *"The decade old revival of Gucci from almost a dead brand to one of the most promising ones today made Mr. Tom Ford a bigger name than Gucci and PPR would have immense trouble replacing him."* Adding to PPR's woes, in September 2003 a US court started investigations against Pinault for fraud in an unrelated acquisition in the 1990s. These drawbacks indeed have put a question mark on whether Gucci and PPR can continue their growth in future after Tom Ford exits.

A nagging concern for the PPR group is whether Tom Ford is going to be lapped up by the rival LVMH group. Bernard Arnault has been openly critical of Pinault and De Sole but has refrained from saying anything against Tom Ford, since the Gucci episode in 2000. He has recently been quoted by crediting Ford as *"one of the best designers of his time."* These may reflect Arnault's intention to hire Mr. Ford after his exit from Gucci. It could significantly affect the dynamics at LVMH if it can lure Tom Ford to its fold. Sources familiar with the situation feel that Tom Ford is more likely to join a smaller company or launch his own label, than join LVMH. The reason for his quitting is the constraint over his freedom, and given the temperament of Mr. Arnault, Mr. Ford an association with LVMH might not result.

This has created a buzz in the industry as to where Tom Ford is headed and also whom would PPR recruit to replace him. It seems particularly interesting as the new job profile for the position of Head of Gucci is to be a person "out of the Luxury Industry." It remains to be seen if this proves to be a good option to recruit a person from outside the luxury industry for the top position and how a key figure in this industry can make, break or manage a conglomerate.

Managing a Multibrand Conglomerate

Creativity and innovation are synonymous to success in the fashion business. As two analysts recently observed, *"Luxury brands must foster an appreciation and tolerance for creativity that is unconstrained by commercial or production constraints."* In almost all its acquisitions, LVMH had maintained the creative talent as an independent pool without attempting to generate synergies across product lines or brands. Lately though the sourcing is slowly being centralized to gain synergies and cost savings with centralized purchasing mechanism.

Bernard Arnault believes that, *"If you think and act like a typical manager around creative people—with rules, policies, data on customer preferences, and so forth—you will quickly kill their talent."* The company has been decentralized by design and has a very small cadre of managers.

However, industry insiders cite that all is not well with a financial man like Bernard Arnault at the helm. His management style is described as providing "constrained freedom." For example a manager for Céline could recruit a person himself, independent of the central LVMH Human Resources department, but he has to send a copy of the CV of the person he hired so that the head office is kept aware of the new development. Though his managers are given autonomy, they know they are being watched and who has the final word in case of any conflict.

Another concern is the ruthless pursuit towards the bottom line. LVMH believes in "running businesses profitably." Managers are supported as long as they made money over the stipulate minimum. *"You have the freedom as long as you exceed your targets. Once you do not . . . there is no freedom anymore."* The emphasis is on profit and if any division or company did not deliver, it would promptly be sold off. This approach contrasts with the traditional and creative view of "Haute Couture," which though loses money on different set of collections, waits for market to accept its designs, over a period of time.

Managing "Star Brands"

The core pillar of LVMH's current business strategy is "star brands," coupled with innovation and quality. More specifically, Bernard Arnault describes the group's stellar financial performance in 2003 *as "a consequence of the priority placed on internal growth and profitability, the development of brands around the dual goals of innovation and quality, and the conquest of new markets."* (See Exhibit 5 for key financials). According to Bernard Arnault a star brand is one which:

> *timeless, modern, fast-growing, and highly profitable . . . There are fewer than 10 star brands in the luxury world, because it is very hard to balance all four characteristics at once—after all, fast growth is often at odds with high profitability—but that is what makes them stars. If you have a star brand, then basically you can be sure you have mastered a paradox.*

According to him, star brands are born only when a company manages to make products that *"speak to the ages"* but the feel is intensely modern. Such products are designed to sell fast raking in profits for the fashion empire. This is a paradox and he confides that *"mastering the paradox of star brands is very difficult and rare."*

Bernard Arnault has never specified exactly what those 10 "star brands" were, but using his criteria, the following luxury labels could be considered as star brands: Christian Dior, Louis Vuitton, Hermes, Cartier, Giorgio

Exhibit 5   Consolidated Group Performance (in € millions)

	2002	2001	2000	1999	1998	5 Yr. Growth
Total Current Assets	7,168	8,260	8,280	6,887	5,414	32,40%
Total Current Liabilities	6,890	8,017	9,829	8,615	6,328	8,88%
Total Assets	20,658	22,540	21,124	19,671	16,008	29,05%
Total Liabilities	12,864	15,122	14,947	13,194	9,408	36,73%
Total Common Equity	6,022	5,618	4,696	5,400	5,736	4,99%

Income Statement	2002	2001	2000	1999	1998	5 Yr.Growth
Sales	12,693	12,229	11,581	8,547	6,936	83,00%
Cost Of Goods Sold	3,806	3,466	3,821	2,698	2,197	73,25%
Net Income	556	10	705	636	429	29,65%

Source: Thomson Analytics Financial Database.

Armani, Gucci, Chanel and Prada. Of these, LVMH controls just two—Dior and Vuitton, of which he says:

> if you take Vuitton, which has existed for more than 150 years, I think, today, it is also modern. Dior has been there for 50 years, but also I think it is the most hip fashion brand today.

Innovation

Bernard Arnault believes that innovation *"is the ultimate driver, of growth and profitability. Our whole business is based on giving our artists and designers complete freedom to invent without limits."* He has acknowledged their past mistakes, including the rapid expansion of the Sephora beauty and fragrance supermarkets, for which he said LVMH had paid too much. After expanding too quickly in the United States, the Company had to close stores and reposition the unit. In a business based on giving artist and designers the freedom to create without limits, LVHM allows each brand to run itself, headed by a creative director. Only 250 out of the over 56,000 employees are based in the Paris headquarters, the essence of the business is to identify the right creative people to stimulate new and cutting edge ideas, and trusting their instincts.

Quality

In the luxury products business, quality is essential in production as well as in product development. This is also an essential element in LVMH's success strategy. For example, to exercise the utmost control over the quality of its Louis Vuitton "star brand," the company owns manufacturing facilities employing over 4,000 in France, Spain and in the United States, among other countries. While LVMH produces its Louis Vuitton brand in-house, the firm outsources

part of the production of its other fashion labels, such as Céline and Fendi. *"For all of our brands, we manufacture part of the overall production within our facilities to be sure that there is a consistency between what is done by external sub-contractors and what we do,"* explained Jean-Paul Vivier, executive vice president of the LVMH Fashion Group.

Managing People

Human resources and management talent are critical for the luxury conglomerate. When Arnault first began his consolidation, the group was full of problems, and only a few of the companies were profitable. HR Director Concetta Lanciaux confided that his primary concern was to *"have the best managers."* Lanciaux's challenge was particularly difficult because there was a scarcity of executives in luxury goods at the time. Most firms were small, family-owned companies, without graduates or succession planning. LVMH had to recruit and develop talent from different fields. Regarding the mobilization of LVMH's resources Bernard Arnault said:

> In a global context, the progress of LVMH in 2003 will be based above all on the excellence of the fundamentals and its capacity to mobilize its internal resources. We can rely on our traditional strengths, namely the talent of our managers and employees and their determination to make the difference, the appeal of our major brands, the certain values—more than ever in a difficult period, the creativity and excellence of our products and the power of our distribution networks.

> We are continuing to deploy the organic growth strategy[. . .]while still carrying out the sale of non-strategic assets, we will maintain strict management focus, enabling us to reinvest the cost savings achieved in the driving forces of our growth.

LVMH has encouraged and passed on the know-how, skills, the spirit of excellence, and the ethic that conveys, through its creations and products, an exceptional art of living, which is appreciated worldwide. The awakening and education of young people to these values has always constituted an essential part of the Group's goal. LVMH has carried out various original initiatives for young people in France and abroad. It is through these initiatives that primary school children, high school students, art students, young artists and designers, as well as those closer to the Group's new work opportunities such as college and higher education students, can benefit. In 1991, for example, LVMH partnered with Paris-based business school ESSEC to launch the luxury brand marketing LVMH ESSEC chair, funded with FF10 million. Further partnerships have since been launched in Asia as well.

The Company had to hire people with experience in other industries, such as consumer goods, and select people with "good taste." Lanciaux cited engineering and business schools as specific sources of talent. LVMH also instituted strong company-wide induction and training program as well as on-the-job training to introduce the world of luxury to its capable, bright novices to the industry. Lanciaux explained:

With some 40 brands potentially competing against each other in the group, recruitment and everyday business becomes complex. In the case of our group, what builds value and profits is the ability to act in an autonomous way and create new products. The business is built on the number of innovative products that come out every year—20% to 30% of the turnover is based on new products. Therefore our companies' senior executives have to have a large dose of autonomy and creative capacity. People use these as aspirational products, so we need people who manage and dream—and make others dream.

Despite the group's aggressive growth through acquisition, LVMH has tried to treat such moves sensitively, with a vision of integration. Lanciaux commented:

First of all, it was about respecting, identifying and then preserving all of the assets of the Company—not changing everything at once. One of the mistakes that companies in this situation make is that they want to change everything and bring in their own culture. When we buy these brands, we buy them to develop them. To develop the brand, the first thing you need to know is what makes that brand. Very often it's a number of people who are behind it, often invisible. . . . You have to find them, make them visible. This means that we have been able to preserve the integrity of these brands. Our style is not to go in there and replace everybody—never.

Jean-Paul Vivier, executive vice president of the LVMH agrees that the group seeks to foster creativity not just among its design teams but also with professionals throughout the business. He compares the process to mixing the perfect cocktail—LVMH tries to build a work environment that promotes creativity and at the same time adheres to strict business disciplines.

Integration, training and top management seminars designed to support business strategies played an essential role in the professional development of the LVMH Group. Since 2001, it steadily increased the number of training days for all personnel categories within the Group and in centers located in Paris, New York, Hong Kong and Tokyo. The total number of training days in 2001 was 103,585 worldwide. Each of the companies is developing a specific training program that reflects its own vision of excellence and its strategic objectives. At Louis Vuitton, which operates in 44 countries, vendors from all over the world participate in "brand immersion" seminars organized in Asnières, the company's birthplace and communications center. They tour the workshops built in 1859 and the Louis Vuitton travel museum. These sites are filled with the spirit of the company, which has remained constant even as it adapts to changing fashions and trends—a spirit embodied in the skills of the craftsmen, the details, and a unique talent for anticipating, analyzing and meeting the requirements of the contemporary world. In 1999, Hennesy has developed a teaching game called "Strateco" that takes place over two days. It is designed to make all non-managerial employees more aware of economic influences affecting the companies and their operating realities. Another program, "Decompartmentalizing people and their jobs," presents the mission, organization and business of each department in the company's managers and brings together participants from the various departments. Finally, the inter-company seminars offered to all of the Group's managers, focus on topics of mutual interest and are primarily designed to develop or perfect management, communication and leadership skills.

American designer Michael Kors joined LVMH and successfully revived Céline, a dusty brand. However, it didn't seem that anyone at LVMH noticed. During Kors' six and a half year tenure at Céline, the position of chief executive officer turned five times, from Nan Legeai, to Bernard Divisia, Yves Carcelle, Thierry Andretta and, finally, to Jean-Marc Loubier. At the same time, Bernard Arnault attended only two of Kors' fashion shows for Céline. In total, Kors estimated that he spent a total of three hours in Bernard Arnault's company, including the two shows and two "hellos" when he ran into Arnault at the Dior store in Paris. Kors said:

Was I mistreated? No. Was I neglected? Yes. I never felt as though there was a strategy at LVMH as far as pitting the designers against each other or the brands against each other. It's just that I never felt anyone was watching the smaller companies at all, but everybody was spending their time on the two first-born children—Louis Vuitton and Christian Dior. In a way, if you're a nice kid, no one pays attention to you. If you are a bad kid, you get spoiled.

Interesting is the case of Marc Jacobs. In 1997, Marc Jacobs was struggling to keep his namesake brand afloat. Bernard Arnault approached him with an irresistible offer to lend his creative flair to the venerable but stodgy Louis Vuitton label, in return for LVMH underwriting his beleaguered design firm.

Jacobs' designs have helped boost sales and buzz around the $3.8 billion Louis Vuitton brand, which accounts for 60% of LVMH's operating profit. His multicolored Murakami handbag alone drove over $300 million in sales. The 41-year-old designer was also able to develop his own Marc Jacobs label, which soared to about $75 million in sales in 2003, helped by a $50 million investment from LVMH.

However, tensions have arisen between the designer and the Company. Mr. Jacobs believes his ambitions to develop his own brand are being hindered by LVMH. He complains that the French conglomerate hasn't invested enough in the Marc Jacobs business and has locked him out of critical decisions about the operations at his own line. For example, in May 2003, LVMH, while closing its U.S. fragrance division, sold the Marc Jacobs perfume too to Coty Inc. without informing or consulting the designer. None of the proceeds went to Jacobs, instead heading directly to LVMH.

Due to its heavy dependence on creative and modern designs, the departure of key creative personnel would be devastating to Vuitton. Early this year, there was speculation that Jacobs might leave unless LVMH gave more backing to his clothing line. As seen in the example of Tom Ford and Domenico De Sole's departures from luxury rival Gucci, losing its young star designer may spell trouble for the Louis Vuitton brand.

In May, 2004 a spokesman in Paris confirmed that Moët Hennessy Louis Vuitton SA has resolved a yearlong dispute with the New York designer Marc Jacobs artistic director of Loius Vuitton and his business partner Robert Duffy, 49 year old President of Marc Jacobs, by signing them to a new 10-year employment contract and committing to invest in the partners' Marc Jacobs International fashion house. Under the new agreement Marc Jacobs and Robert Duffy received salary raises—and for the first time—stock options. According to Robert Duffy,

Now, Marc and I can achieve our dream of turning Marc Jacobs into a global powerhouse.

Conclusion

Although the Louis Vuitton brand is enormously profitable, none of the other labels rival its level of commercial success. With its current dependence on star designers such as John Galliano and Marc Jacobs, the group's success is highly correlated to the whim of the creative. Given the current internal politics and recent departure of Michael Kors, will consumers remain loyal to the brand or the designer? The bigger questions are, can LVMH oversee so many luxury brands, make them all profitable and maintain the highest standards of creativity? After Bernard Arnault, how to manage this "loose" conglomerate that he has created in the last decade?

Exhibit 6a   Net Sales by Business Group

(EUR million)	2001	(1)	2002	(1)	2003	(1)
Wines & Spirits	2,232	18%	2,266	18%	2,116	18%
Fashion & Leather Goods	3,612	30%	4,207	33%	4,149	35%
Perfumes & Cosmetics	2,231	18%	2,336	18%	2,181	18%
Watches & Jewelry	548	4%	552	4%	503	4%
Selective Retailing	3,493	29%	3,337	26%	3,039	25%
Other businnesses and eliminations	113	1%	− 5	0%	− 25	0%
Total	**12,229**		**12,693**		**11,963**	

(1) As a % of total sales

Source: LVMH 2003 Annual Report.

Exhibit 6b   Income from Operations by Business Group

(EUR million)	2001	(1)	(2)	2002	(1)	(2)	2003	(1)	(2)
Wines & Spirits	676	43%	30%	750	37%	33%	796	36%	38%
Fashion & Leather Goods	1,274	82%	35%	1,280	64%	30%	1,311	60%	32%
Perfumes & Cosmetics	149	10%	7%	161	8%	7%	178	8%	8%
Watches & Jewelry	27	2%	5%	−13	−1%	N/S	−48	−2%	N/S
Selective Retailing	−213	−14%	N/S	20	1%	1%	106	5%	3%
Other businnesses and eliminations	−353	−23%	N/S	−190	−9%	N/S	−161	−7%	N/S
Total	**1,560**			**2,008**			**2,182**		

(1) As a % of total sales   (2) Operating Margin

Source: LVMH 2003 Annual Report.

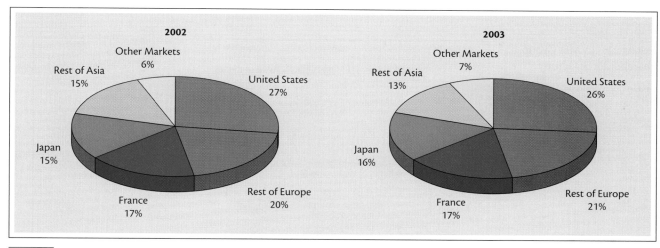

Exhibit 7   Net Sales by Geographic Region.

Source: LVMH 2003 Annual Report.

Exhibit 8   LVMH Global Reach (number of stores in 2003)

North America	344
Latin America	16
France	277
Europe	401
Africa & Middle East	6
Asia	287
Japan	232
Pacific Region	29

Source: LVMH 2003 Annual Report.

Exhibit 9   Benchmarking Louis Vuitton vs. Other Luxury Brands

Brand	2003 Sales (Billions)	Percent Change*	Operating Margin
Louis Vuitton	$3.80b	16%	45.0%
Prada	$1.95b	0.0%	13.0%
Gucci**	$1.85b	−1.0%	27.0%
Hermes	$1.57b	+7.7%	25.4%
Coach	$1.20b	+34.0%	29.9%

*At constant rate of exchange   **Gucci division of Gucci Group

Source: Company reports, *BusinessWeek.*

Exhibit 10 LVMH Stock Performance, 1985 to March 2004

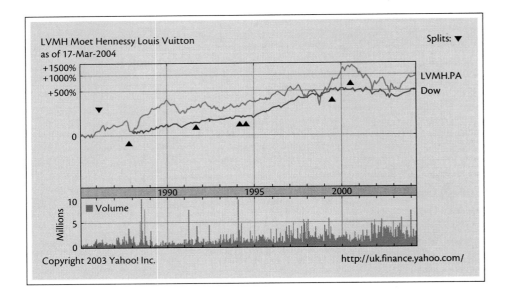

Exhibit 11 LVMH Group Shareholder Structure

Source: Company data, UBS Warburg.

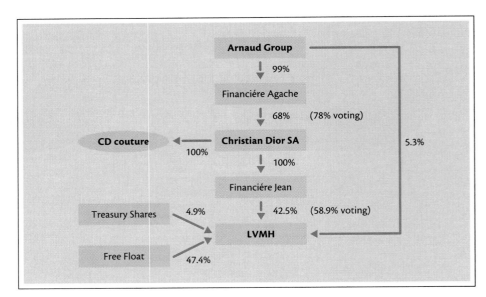

Exhibit 12   The 16 Leadership Factors

Identified by 450 LVMH Group senior executives during LVMH House sessions (October 2001)

Creativity

Comes up with a lot of new and unique ideas; easily makes connections among previously unrelated notions; tends to be seen as original and value-added in brainstorming sessions.

Strategic Agility

Sees ahead clearly; can anticipate future consequences and trends accurately; has broad knowledge and perspective; is future oriented; can articulately paint credible pictures and visions of possibilities and likelihood; can create competitive and breakthrough strategies and plans

Innovation Management

Is good at bringing the creative ideas of others to market; has good judgment about which creative process of others; can facilitate effective brainstorming; can project how potential ideas may play out in the market place.

Managing Vision & Purpose

Communicates a compelling and inspired vision or sense of core purpose; talks beyond today; talks about possibilities; is optimistic; creates mileposts and symbols to rally support behind the vision; makes the vision sharable by everyone; can inspire and motivate entire units or organizations.

Customer Focus

Is dedicated to meeting the expectations and requirements of internal and external customers; gets first-hand customer information and uses it for improvements in products and services; acts with customers in mind; establishes and maintains effective relationships with customers and gains their trust and respect.

Priority Setting

Spends his/her time ant the time of others on what's important; quickly zeros in on the critical few and puts the trivial many aside; can quickly sense what will help or hinder accomplishing a goal; eliminates roadblocks; creates focus.

Building Effective Teams

Blends people into teams when needed; creates strong morale and spirit in his/her team; shares wins and successes; fosters open dialogue; lets people finish and be responsible for their work; defines success in terms of the whole team; creates a feeling of belonging in the team.

Action Oriented

Enjoys working hard; is action oriented and full of energy for the things he/she sees as challenging; not fearful of acting with a minimum of planning; seizes more opportunities than others.

Drive for Results

Can be counted on to exceed goals successfully; is constantly and consistently one of the top performers; very bottom-line oriented; steadfastly pushes self and others for results.

Hiring and Staffing

Has a nose for talent; hires the best people available from inside or outside; is not afraid of selecting strong people; assembles talented staffs.

Motivating Others

Creates a climate in which people want to do their best; can motivate many kinds of direct reports and team or project members; can assess each person's hot button and use it to get the best out of him/her; pushes tasks and decisions down; empowers others; invites input from each person and shares ownership and visibility; makes each individual feel his/her work is important; is someone people like working for and with.

Business Acumen

Knows how businesses work; knowledgeable in current and possible future policies, practices, trends, and information affecting his/her business and organization; knows the competition; is aware of how strategies and tactics work in the market place.

Integrity and Trust

Is widely trusted; is seen as a direct, truthful individual; can present the unvarnished truth in an appropriate and helpful manner; keeps confidences; admit mistakes; doesn't misrepresent him/herself for personal gain.

Learning on the Fly

Learns quickly when facing new problems; a relentless and versatile learner; open to change; analyzes both successes and failures for clues to improvement; experiments and will try anything to find solutions; enjoys the challenge of unfamiliar tasks; quickly grasps the essence and the underlying structure of anything.

Delegation

Clearly and comfortably delegates both routine and important tasks and decisions; broadly shares both responsibility and accountability; tends to trust people to perform; lets direct reports finish their own work.

Assignment Questions

1. What does globalization mean in the luxury industry? What is the international strategy of LVMH? How does it differ from its competitors'?

2. What are the factors influencing companies to seek growth by acquisitions in this industry? How are they managing and integrating these acquisitions? Is this growth sustainable?

3. Does LVMH's structure support its multi-brand strategy and functioning of the group?

4. Comment on the nature of the competition in the luxury industry and the multi-brand strategy.

5. How is LVMH managing its creative talents? Does it differ from its competitors? If yes, how? If not, why not?

6. Comment on the leadership of Bernard Arnault and his management style. How is LVMH "cultivating" leaders for tomorrow?

Notes

[1] www.lvmh.com.

Case 3–7: Swissair and the Qualiflyer Alliance*

The Logic of Qualiflyer

By 1998 it seemed clear that in air travel, "Competition is more between alliance groupings than it is between individual carriers," as Swissair president and CEO Jeffrey Katz observed.[1] The member airlines of multi-carrier alliances now claimed some 53% of global air passenger traffic, and 80% of the profits. SAirGroup (which included Swissair) concluded that carriers that did not belong to a strong alliance were going to fail or be absorbed by larger airlines. Bigger European airlines, notably British Airways, Lufthansa and KLM, were taking the lead in building global alliances.[2]

SAirGroup was hoping that the first European airline network could transform Swissair's current and future situation. Swissair was too big for Switzerland and too small for Europe. In a home market of only 7 million people, Swissair and its subsidiaries Crossair and Balair flew 14 million passengers annually—a far higher number relative to the country's population than other national carriers could claim, and indicative of SAirGroup's high through traffic. But its main hubs—Zurich, Geneva and Basel—even jointly could not handle as much traffic as airports like Heathrow (London), Schiphol (Amsterdam) or Roissy (Paris). More connections to more destinations made these rivals more attractive to the "through" passenger traffic on which Swissair depended. Besides, said Michael Eggenschwiler, Swissair's executive vice president of external relations, "We're suffering today from Switzerland not being part of the EU."[3] Flights to and from EU airports by non-EU airlines were more highly taxed than those of the Union's carriers, and access to European hubs was limited for non-EU carriers. An alliance with Austrian Airlines had added Vienna as a hub, and the acquisition of 49.5% of the Belgian flag carrier Sabena in 1995 brought deep access to Brussels, but these did not add up to a European network.

Swissair also needed to drastically reduce its costs, which were among the highest in Europe. Management wanted nearly 30% reductions in costs by ASK ("available seat kilometers," or seat capacity times distances flown) by 1999, without hurting Swissair's reputation for extremely high-quality service and reliability.[4] The growth of high-yield business on which Swissair depended had reversed with the 1990s recession, as lower-cost airlines and "no frills" start-ups cut prices and yields across the industry. Sharing such costs as ground services, ticketing, lounges and maintenance with alliance partners was an obvious response.

The Founding of the Alliance

In March 1998, Swissair and its partners—the former Belgian flag carrier Sabena, TAP/Air Portugal, Turkish Airlines (THY), France's AOM, Crossair (a regional, mainly short-haul carrier), plus Austrian Airlines and its sister carriers Lauda Air and Tyrolean Airways—announced the founding of the Qualiflyer Group. Katz said that, like Swissair, they were all "quality-orientated smaller airlines looking by being together for strength and a multi-hub European network." Joint marketing and sales operations, lounges and branding were among their first priorities. In 1997, Qualiflyer's members had flown 47.5 million passengers to 294 destinations in 125 countries, and had a collective turnover of $11 billion. That was about 4% of world market share, compared to some 16% for Star Alliance.

Qualiflyer's main hubs included Zurich, Brussels, Vienna, Nice, Istanbul and Lisbon. Swissair said that they were big enough to ensure connections to virtually anywhere, but small enough to offer greatly reduced transit times compared to Heathrow or Roissy. AOM, though small in terms of revenues and destinations, brought access to Orly airport, a second platform for Swissair in Paris. TAP offered privileged access to Portugal, a fast-growing market with otherwise "restricted traffic access, so we can't just fly wherever we want there," noted Katz. Likewise, said Katz, Turkish Airlines was a large carrier with a strong grip on its market, as well as multiple routes into Central and East Asia and the Middle East. Most important, THY and TAP increased the collective home markets of the alliance from 25 to 97 million people.

Qualiflyer remained open to new members and new routes as well. In particular, the alliance would make the group more "attractive to potential partners in the US and Asia," said Swissair executive vice-president and CFO Georges P. Schorderet.[5] Qualiflyer included no US carriers, though Swissair, Austrian Airlines and Sabena had already formed a separate code-sharing[6] alliance called "Atlantic Excellence" with Delta, the US carrier with the highest share of the transatlantic market. Swissair executives made it clear in public presentations that they expected Atlantic Excellence to merge into

*This case was prepared from public domain sources by Dr. Mark Hunter, Senior Research Fellow at INSEAD, under the supervision of Dr. Yves L. Doz, The Timken Chaired Professor of Global Technology and Innovation and Professor of Business Policy. It is intended to be used as a basis for class discussion rather than to illustrate either effective or ineffective handling of an administrative situation.

Qualiflyer.[7] Unfortunately, the lack of "open skies" agreements[8] between the US, Turkey and Portugal made that move impossible at that time. There was also public discussion that American Airlines, a partner with Sabena, might join Qualiflyer. On the Asian side, Singapore Airlines had recently pulled out of the Global Excellence alliance with Swissair and Delta. Swissair, arguing that no single Asian airline could offer sufficient access to the entire region, set up code-sharing alliances with Cathay Pacific, Japan Air Lines and Malaysian. SAirGroup President and CEO Philippe Bruggisser commented that "developing one front while keeping the others going today is the way of the world in the alliance landscape."[9]

Cutting Costs and Widening Markets

Major cost reductions would be possible if Qualiflyer partners used the same airplanes. Said Katz, "We now have a group which can invest in the same concept. So what in the past cost us a dollar might cost us a fraction of that now, especially where it requires a fixed investment or a fixed operation." Swissair planned to buy no fewer than 203 aircraft over the next decade, 80% of them from Airbus and the rest from Boeing and its subsidiary McDonnell-Douglas. It encouraged its allies, starting with Sabena, to invest in mainly Airbus fleets too—by outright purchase or by leasing them from Flightlease, a company owned partly by SAirGroup.[10] However, partners such as THY and Lauda had mainly Boeing fleets, and both THY and TAP earned substantial and growing revenues from maintenance on Boeings. Nonetheless, use of similar aircraft also meant reduced pilot training costs, greater flexibility in pilot schedules, and more efficient maintenance and ground services.

In general, the longer a flight, the more unit costs decline. Thus, said Katz, "In engineering the [Qualiflyer] network, you'll see us push more to longer hauls and to get more utilisation out of the airplanes." That meant harmonizing route schedules and cutting some flights, though at the risk of labor unrest among pilots. Said Katz, "The information flow is improving among labor [unions] in our alliances, just as among other airlines."

Coordinating and combining ground services like catering, cargo, baggage handling and sales offices could further reduce labor, real estate and purchasing costs for the alliance while boosting quality. Swissair pushed for the development of a ground services company to be jointly owned by all Qualiflyer members, and also offered to sell them equity shares in its non-airline subsidiaries. In 1997 these subsidiaries—SAirRelations, SAirServices, and SAirLogistics—set up as separate profit centers,[11] had accounted for 47% of SAirGroup's revenues. (See Exhibit 3, "SAirGroup's Non-Airline Subsidiaries.") SAirServices (aircraft maintenance and ground handling, plus IT for ticketing and reservations) had an EBIT margin of 7%, the best of any division. A sharp exception to its growth was Atraxis, a unit which made airport management software. Atraxis's applications were developed in Switzerland, where airport managers and airlines worked together to build IT infrastructure. Where that wasn't the case, sales lagged, Atraxis managers discovered.[12] At least one Qualiflyer member balked at using Atraxis.

SAirGroup also invested in its partners' non-airline subsidiaries. After THY sold its 40% stake in Havas, the state-owned ground handling company, to a private-sector firm in April 1998, the stake was resold to Swissair. An analyst commented, "It is noteworthy that Swissair indirectly takes part in Turkey's ground handling, airline catering, terminal restaurants, domestic flights and international flights businesses."[13]

Deepening the Alliance Ties

Very quickly, Swissair set about buying minority stakes in seven of the 10 companies that eventually joined Qualiflyer. Besides its 49.5 % stake in Sabena, Swissair soon acquired 49% of AOM, and 10% of Austrian Airlines, which acquired a similar stake in Swissair. (Delta and Swissair had also purchased small stakes in each other's equity.) A SAirGroup spokesman explained: "If we are linked we can collaborate in depth."[14] Another reason, said Swissair's Schorderet, was that "if you want a partner in Europe, it is necessary to take an equity stake—it confirms your commitment." But fears that Swissair sought dominance rather than deeper collaboration and commitment surfaced loudly in Portugal and Turkey, where TAP and THY were nearing privatization. While open to a Swissair bid, the Portuguese state announced it would maintain a blocking "golden share" in TAP. In Turkey, a prominent parliamentary deputy warned that "THY will be absorbed into a corporation dominated by Swissair. This must never be permitted."[15] If Qualiflyer proved a success, however, such protests would surely diminish.

Partner Profiles of the Qualiflyer Alliance

(For comparative basic data, see Exhibit 2, "The Main Qualiflyer Partners at a Glance.")

Swissair, Crossair and Sabena: Growing Past Danger?

SAirGroup's $US7 billion in revenues (including $US3.4 billion for its airline division Swissair alone) represented about two-thirds of the total revenues of the Qualiflyer airlines. Swissair carried nearly 11 million passengers in 1997, with a moderately good seat load factor (the average passenger capacity used on every flight) of 70.5%. The airline had Europe's highest ratings for quality service, and banked on it. While other airlines, including Austrian and Delta, moved to business and economy classes, to gain higher yields

Exhibit 1   Comparing the Qualiflyer, Oneworld and Star Alliances

Alliance (founded)	QUALIFLYER (3/98)	STAR (end 1997)	ONEWORLD (2/99)
Members	Swissair, Austrian, Lauda, Sabena, TAP/Air Portugal, THY, AOM, Crossair, Air Littoral, Tyrolean Airways = 4% global market share.	Lufthansa, United, Air Canada, SAS, Thai Airways, Varig = 16% global market share.	American, BA, Canadian, Cathay Pacific, Qantas = 10% global market share.
Alliance Leader	Members have putative equal status, but Swissair is clear alliance driver and by far the largest member.	All members have equal voting rights, and leadership on some issues is given to smaller members to reinforce commitment.	All members have equal voting rights.
Initial Governance structure	Steering committee under presidents, with reps from mainly larger partners (Swissair, Austrian, Sabena, THY, TAP). Functional working groups are chaired mainly by Swissair.	"Virtual" organization of committees with reps from each partner. Advertising agency serves as alliance marketing dept.	Chief executives decide on strategy. Quickly move to separate, central management. structure.
Codesharing/ joint sales	Yes; "harmonization" of fares "within the respective home markets" is planned. Frequent flyer program harmonization is a priority.	Yes; partners set own fares, and frequent flyer miles are harmonized.	Yes; members launch successive promotions ("passes") for network.
Route linkages	Each partner keeps its national routes. Routes are ceded by subsidiaries within partners.	Members cede certain unprofitable or uncompetitive routes to each other.	Progressive harmonization and rationalization planned.
Alliance branding	Workshop to address "group identity and devices are introduced philosophy" planned for 1999, to be followed by training for managers then staff.	Common branding ("Oneworld benefits") sequentially, after negotiation among members.	Joint branding is key focus from start; intensive training of member staffs.
Cross-ownership	Swissair owns up to 49% of some partners, wishes to buy shares in all partners; Turks and Portuguese pose tough conditions.	No partner can own more than 5% of another.	Tolerated but not required.

Swissair invested in more first-class seats.[16] Meanwhile, to avoid the possibility that competitors with wider reach and resources would absorb or subjugate Swissair, management embarked on a wave of acquisitions, beginning with 49.5 % of the troubled Belgian carrier Sabena in 1995.

Sabena brought Swissair a complementary route network in Africa and access to the major EU hub of Brussels. However, Sabena and its subsidiaries (Sobelair, DAT and City Bird) were notoriously overstaffed, with 11,300 workers for revenues of $US1.94 billion in 1997. The Belgian state held one-third of the capital, which meant that restructuring would encounter potent political obstacles. Swissair also acquired Crossair, a highly profitable regional airline based in Basel-Mulhouse-Freiburg, flying small jets to secondary destina-

tions like Bordeaux and Leipzig, as well as feeder lines to Swissair's main Geneva and Zurich hubs. Swissair hoped to own controlling minority shares in TAP, THY and AOM.

AOM: A New Hub but Shallow Pockets

Founded in 1989 as Air Outre Mer ("Overseas Air"), AOM specialized in carrying passengers between continental France and about a dozen destinations in its sun-kissed overseas departments. By the mid-1990s the company also operated a network in the south of France, flying to Nice, Marseille, Toulouse and Perpignan from its hub at Paris-Orly, as well as to Zurich. Despite high quality ratings and the launch of new business class services, AOM's dependence on vacation flyers and frontal competition with Air France hurt

Exhibit 2   The Main Qualiflyer Partners at a Glance (1997)

	Swissair	Sabena	Austrian	TAP	Turkish
Founded	1931	1923	1957	1945	1933
Hubs	Zurich Basel	Brussels	Vienna	Lisbon	Istanbul
Network	156 cities, 79 countries; EU Access issues	94 cities, 44 countries; Africa and Europe key	67 cities, 51 countries; central/east Europe key	54 cities, 30 countries; Brazil, Angola but no US "open sky"	97 cities, 45 countries; Mid/Far East, No US "open sky"
Subsidiary Airlines	Crossair, Balair	Sobelair, City Bird, DAT (cargo)	Tyrolean, Lauda Air	—	—
Fleet	65 total, 44 Airbus	80 total, 7 Airbus	34 total, 10 Airbus	31 total, 21 Airbus	65 total, 19 Airbus
Passengers	10.8M	6.9M	3.9 M	4.3 M	10.4 M
Workforce	7,335	11,300	4,160	8,307	8,958
Revenues[1]	$7 B (group)	$1.9 B (group)	$1.2 B	$1 B	$1.35 B
Profit	$270 M	($57 M)	$45 M	$48 M	$26 M
Margin	6.2 % (EBIT)	—	2.9 % (EBIT)	—	2 % (Net)

[1] Revenues, profits and margins are for groups.

Alliance (founded)	QUALIFLYER (3/98)	STAR (end 1997)	ONEWORLD (2/99)
Shared ground Facilities and teams	A separate company, Qualiflyer ground services, is created with equal equity from each partner. Group announces that this "will make for job redundancies in certain areas" but denies layoff targets.	Baggage, check-in and other services are provided by members to each other on home-country basis.	Cost pressures induce progressive combining of services among members.
Common fleets	Swissair sees all-Airbus fleet as major advantage; THY, AOM, Lauda, Sabena and Austrian have significant (and recent) investments in Boeings	Not planned.	Not planned.
Common lounges	Most concern is with lounge standards, which vary among members	Open to discussion; but members want to keep lounges as distinctions.	Key focus of alliance promotion and branding.
Common purchasing	Swissair sees this as crucial cost advantage and wishes to accelerate.	Partners place purchasing after branding.	Partners begin with branding but move quickly to purchasing

revenues. Yields were low—about 60% of Swissair's revenue-per-passenger—and the company was also overstaffed, with 2,883 employees compared to 7,335 for Swissair. About half of AOM's 27-plane fleet, and the most recent half, was equipped by Boeing and its subsidiary McDonnell-Douglas. The other half, consisting of older McDonnell-Douglas DC-10s, would have to be renewed soon. Solving any or all of these problems would require new capital.

Austrian Airlines, Lauda Air, Tyrolean: Mediators Between East and West

The Austrian Airlines Group saw itself as the trust-builder in Qualiflyer, promising total commitment to the alliance as well as fierce resistance to "the threat of dominant partners". Even more than Qualiflyer, it considered the Atlantic Excellence group central to long-term strategy. Pride in its product and

Exhibit 3 SAirGroup's
Non-airline Subsidiaries

Sources: Adapted from Crédit
Suisse/First Boston, "SAirGroup,"
10 July 1998.

SAir Services	SAir Relations	SAir Logistics
1997 revenue: $1.2B EBIT margin of 7.0% (17.1% of group) is highest in group.	1997 Revenue: $2.5B (35% of group) Growth rate of 40%	1997 Revenues: $814M (11.6% of group) Low margin (3.5%) but high ROIC (35%, highest in group)
Key Units:	**Key Units:**	**Key Units:**
SR Technics Overhaul/maintenance $700M revenues, margin (EBIT) 6.2%; *52% of business is servicing Swissair*	**Gate Gourmet** Inflight catering $975M revenues, margin 8.9% *#2 worldwide in sector, Present in 84 countries*	**Swisscargo** Sells group freight capacity $619M revenues, 3.0% margin *Tripled sales via Sabena and new plane acquisitions*
Swissport Ground handling $285M revenues, margin 6.5%; *hopes for EU liberalization*	**Nuance** Duty-free retail $1.03B revenues, 5.9% margin *#3 worldwide in sector; In acquisition mode*	**Jacky Maeder** Freight forwarder $190M revenues, 1.4% margin *Leader in Switzerland 16% revenue rise*
atraxis IT solutions $175M revenues, margin 0.8%; *trouble expanding*	**Swissôtel** Hotel operator (17) $260M revenues, 5.9% margin *Revenues rising fast; Present on 4 continents*	**Cargologic** Distribution coordination and tracking services (IT), warehousing Revenue $80M, margin 6.7% *Near completion of highly Automated cargo hub*
aviReal Real estate $122M revenues, 13.7% margin *Serves SAirGroup, Emphasis on cargo hub*	**Railgourmet** RR catering in Europe $119M revenue, 3.9% margin *Margins fall while revenues rise via acquisitions*	

its position as the leading airline in central Europe (with $US1.9 billion in revenues and 3.9 million passengers in 1997) was extremely strong. Through its controlling shares in Lauda and Tyrolean, Austrian Airlines (AUA) possessed low-cost leisure and regional wings. The group owned a fleet of 82 aircraft, about half of which consisted of Airbus planes, with the rest divided among Boeing, McDonnell-Douglas, Fokker and Canadair. AUA planned to replace its American-made planes with Airbuses. Like Swissair, AUA possessed subsidiaries in every aspect of ground and maintenance operations—and like Swissair, its operating costs per ASK were about 20% higher than European competitors like British Airways or Lufthansa. Majority-owned by the state, the airline dominated its home hub of Vienna to an extraordinary degree,[17] with 58% of passenger throughput in 1997. Unlike most European hubs, Vienna was expanding—and meanwhile passenger traffic, cargo and charter revenues were growing steeply as AUA's Eastern Europe flights and destinations multiplied.[18] AUA had collaborated with Swissair since the 1970s on technical flight operations, but integration of reservation and sales systems in the 1990s proved more difficult.

TAP/Air Portugal: The Strain of Growing into Europe

Since 1991, the number of passengers TAP flew had grown by over a third, to 4.3 million, and net assets had doubled since 1993. In 1997 the company showed a profit after 13 years of losses. Maintenance revenues grew by a massive 33.7% from 1996 to 1997, a sign of the confidence other companies placed in TAP. TAP also signed an agreement for the purchase of 18 medium-haul Airbuses—about half its fleet—and prepared to retire its 15 Boeings and "uniformize" its aircraft. However, raising the quality of the product was hard: operating costs shot up nearly 12% from 1996 to 1997, driven by staff costs and supplies and external services. The state-owned company cut its employee base for the fifth straight year, as on-time departures declined to a five-year low of 80%.[19] TAP was preparing to privatize in a program monitored by the European Commission, amid a long and worsening dispute with its 450 pilots over pay and working conditions.

THY/Turkish Airlines: The Long Road to Privatization

THY's passenger total of 10.4 million passengers for 1997 was barely second to Swissair, and its seat load factor of over 80% was impressive—but revenue was only $US1.35 billion, 40% of the sales of the Swiss carrier. Domestic operations dragged down its yield-per-passenger, and were first on the list of assets to be sold off when THY was privatised. Privatization of the state-owned carrier had been promised since 1990 but had never been accomplished, not least because powerful military and political interests had close informal alliances with and interests in THY. The company offered the most important aircraft maintenance services in its region, with 255 licensed engineers specialized in airframes and engines, and particularly experienced in older Airbus A-310s—of which the company owned 14—and Boeing 737s.[20] In October 1997 THY announced it was buying an additional 49 B-737s—26 immediately, with an option on 23 more.

Notes

1   Tom Gill, "A leadership role." *Airline Business*, July 1998. Unless otherwise noted, all quotes of Jeffrey Katz are drawn from this extended interview.

2   See Exhibit 1, "Comparing The Qualiflyer, Oneworld and Star Alliances."

3   Anon., "EU outsider finds playing field uneven; Swissair relies on resourcefulness and creativity to stay competitive." *World Airline News*, 22 May 1998.

4   Op. Cit., Gill.

5   Tom Gill, "Swiss qualify new parteners." *Airline Business*, May 1998.

6   "Code-sharing" was and remains the most common form of airline alliances. It involves sharing flight numbers among two or more carriers, so that each can book the other's flights. This increases the chances that a given flight will appear on a travel agent's or Internaut's screen.

7   See Philippe Brugisser, "The power of SAirGroup alliances." *Schloss Fuschl*, 21 March 1998.

8   The "open skies" era is generally dated from 1992, when the US Dept. of Transportation exempted the KLM-Northwest alliance from antitrust regulations under a treaty with Holland that granted both carriers immunity from prosecution in exchange for access to their domestic hubs. "Open skies" became US government policy, and bilateral treaties were signed with about 50 countries.

9   Pierre Sparaco, "Swissair expands partnership network." *Aviation Week and Space Technology*, 23 August 1999.

10 SAirGroup owned 50% of Flightlease; the other half was held by GATX Capital Corp., a subsidiary of a group with numerous investments in transportation-related companies. By 1999, all of Sabena's aircraft "acquisitions" were done through leasing, principally from Flightlease. See Jo Pearse and Jackie Gallacher, "A touch of Swiss prudence." *Airline Business,* July 1999. Flightlease soon acquired 38-mid and long-range Airbus aircraft at a cost of $5.2 billion, mainly for Swissair and other members of Qualiflyer. See William Hall, "Flightlease order for Airbus Industrie." *Financial Times*, 21 September 1999.

11 Swissair's Qualiflyer partners, notably Austrian Airlines, TAP and THY, had similar operations, but placed them mainly within centralized, functional structures.

12 Such IT is used for tasks like departure control, stand- and gate-allocation, baggage verification and tracing, computerized reservation system revenue accounting, cargo logistics and catering management. See Anon., "Coordination please." *Aviation Week and Space Technology*, 20 October 1997.

13 Auerbach Grayson (analyst's report), "Turkish Airlines," 23 September 1998, p 2.

14 Simon Montlake, "TAP stake is latest step in tightening Qualiflyer." *Air Transport Intelligence*, 1 April 1999.

15 Anon., "THY privatization harmful." *Turkish Daily News*, 18 November 1998 (via Lexis-Nexis).

16 Anon., "Swissair Banks On Improvements." World Airline News, 5 March 1999.

17 AUA's position was so strong that it was able to drive no-frills carrier Virgin Express out of its home market in the mid-1990s.

18 Eastern European destinations went from 8 to 31 from 1989–1997, and weekly flights to the region increased from 43 to 167 from 1992–97. No other European carrier offered as many flights or destinations in the region. Source: Merrill Lynch, "Austria Airlines," 9 October 1998, pp. 18–19.

19 Total employees declined steadily from 10,199 in 1993 to 8,307 in 1997. Annual Report and Financial Statements 1997, "Key Figures" (page numbers blank).

20 In fact, THY possessed a flight simulator for the B-737. See "3rd-Party Maintenance Directory—Turkish Airlines." Flight International, 24 January 1996.

Case 3–8: Ben & Jerry's — Japan*

On an autumn evening in Tokyo in 1997, Perry Odak, Angelo Pezzani, Bruce Bowman and Riv Hight gratefully accepted the hot steaming oshibori towels that their kimono-bedecked waitress quietly offered. After a full day of meetings with Masahiko Iida and his lieutenants at the Seven-Eleven Japan headquarters, the men from Ben & Jerry's welcomed the chance to refresh their hands and faces before turning to the business at hand. It had been just over nine months since Odak had committed to resolving the conundrum of whether to introduce Ben & Jerry's ice cream to the Japan market and, if so, how. The next morning would be their last chance to hammer out the details for a market entry through Seven-Eleven's 7,000 stores in Japan or to give the go-ahead to Ken Yamada, a prospective licensee who would manage the Japan market for Ben & Jerry's. Any delay in reaching a decision would mean missing the summer 1998 ice cream season, but with Japan's economy continuing to contract, perhaps passing on the Japan market would not be a bad idea.

Perry Odak was just entering his eleventh month as CEO of the famous ice cream company named for its off-beat founders. He knew that the Seven-Eleven deal could represent a sudden boost in the company's flagging sales of the past several years. He also knew that a company with the tremendous brand recognition Ben & Jerry's enjoyed needed to approach new market opportunities from a strategic, not an opportunistic, perspective. Since meeting Masahiko Iida, the president of Seven-Eleven Japan just 10 months earlier, Odak was anxious to resolve the question of whether entering the huge Japan market via Seven-Eleven was the right move or not.

*James M. Hagen prepared this case solely to provide material for class discussion. The author does not intend to illustrate either effective or ineffective handling of a managerial situation. The author may have disguised certain names and other identifying information to protect confidentiality.

Ivey Management Services prohibits any form of reproduction, storage or transmittal without its written permission. This material is not covered under authorization from CanCopy or any reproduction rights organization. To order copies or request permission to reproduce materials, contact Ivey Publishing, Ivey Management Services, c/o Richard Ivey School of Business, The University of Western Ontario, London, Ontario, Canada, N6A 3K7; phone (519) 661-3208; fax (519) 661-3882; e-mail cases@ivey.uwo.ca. One time permission to reproduce granted by Ivey Management Services on Jan. 13, 2005.

Copyright © 1999, Ivey Management Services Version: (A) 2001-10-31

Ben & Jerry's Background: 1978 To 1997

1978 to 1994: Growth from Renovated Gas Station to $160 Million in Sales[1]

Brooklyn school mates Ben Cohen and Jerry Greenfield started their ice cream company in a defunct gas station in Burlington, Vermont in 1978, when both were in their mid 20s. The combination of their anti-corporate style, the high fat content of their ice cream, the addition of chunky ingredients and catchy flavor names like "Cherry Garcia" found a following. In addition to selling by the scoop, they began selling pints over the counter and the business grew. With the help of less visible team members, Jeff Furman and Fred (Chico) Lager, the founders took the company public to Vermont stockholders in 1984, later registering with the Securities and Exchange Commission (SEC) for nationwide sale of stock. The company name was Ben & Jerry's Homemade, Inc. and it began trading over the counter with the symbol, BJICA.

Stockholder meetings were outdoor festivals where standard attire included cut-offs and tie dyed T-shirts and where Cohen was liable to call the meeting to order in song. In addition to being a fun company, Cohen and Greenfield determined that it would be a socially responsible company, known for its caring capitalism. Highlighting its community roots, Ben & Jerry's would only buy its cream from Vermont dairies. In the case of one of its early nut flavors, "Rain Forest Crunch," the nuts would be sourced from tribal co-operatives in South American rain forests where nut harvesting would offer a renewable alternative to strip cutting the land for wood products, and where the co-op members would hopefully get an uncommonly large share of the proceeds. As another part of its objective of "caring capitalism," Ben & Jerry's gave 7.5 percent of pretax profits to social causes like Healing Our Mother Earth, which protected community members from local health risks, and Center for Better Living, which assisted the homeless.

The product Cohen and Greenfield were selling was exceptionally rich (at least 12 percent butterfat, compared with about six to 10 percent for most ice creams). It was also very dense, which was achieved by a low overrun (low ratio of air to ice cream in the finished product). This richness and density qualified it as a superpremium ice cream. Häagen-Dazs (founded in New Jersey in 1961) was the only major competitor in the superpremium market. While Häagen-Dazs promoted a sophisticated image, Ben & Jerry's promoted a funky, caring image.

As Ben & Jerry's began to expand distribution throughout the Northeast, it found increasing difficulty obtaining shelf space in supermarkets. Charging Häagen-Dazs with unfairly pressuring distributors to keep Ben & Jerry's off their trucks, Greenfield drove to Minneapolis and gained national press coverage by picketing in front of the headquarters building of food giant Pillsbury which had earlier acquired Häagen-Dazs. His homemade sign read "What is the Doughboy afraid of?", a reference to Pillsbury's mascot and to the company's apparent efforts against the underdog ice cream makers from Vermont. This David versus Goliath campaign earned Ben & Jerry's national publicity and, when combined with some high powered legal action, it gave them freer access to grocery store freezer compartments.

A policy was in place that the highest paid employee would not be paid more than seven times what the lowest paid worker earned. Part of the anti-corporate culture of the company was a policy which allowed each employee to make up his or her own title. The person who might otherwise have been called the public relations manager took the title "the Info Queen." Cohen and Greenfield took turns running the company. Whether despite, or because of, these and other unusual policies, the company continued to grow (see Exhibit 1). In 1985 the company bought a second production plant, this one in nearby Springfield,

Vermont. A third plant was later built in St. Albans, Vermont. By the late 1980s, Ben & Jerry's ice cream had become available in every state of the union.

1994 to 1997: Responding to Fallen Profits

By 1994, sales exceeded $150 million, distribution had extended beyond the U.S. borders and the company had over 600 employees. The future was not encouraging, though, with 1994 actually bringing in a loss. While Ben & Jerry's unquestionably held the second largest market share (at 34 percent compared to Häagen-Dazs' 44 percent) of the American superpremium market, the company had started to lose market share. Net income had also suffered badly since reaching a high in of $7.2 million in 1993 (Exhibit 2). While Cohen was most often the company's CEO, much of the company's growth occurred while Chico Lager was either general manager or CEO between 1982 and 1990. Ben was particularly engaged in efforts to further the cause of social justice by such activities as attending meetings of similarly-minded CEOs from around the world. Board member Chuck Lacy had taken a turn at the helm, but he lacked aspirations for a career as a CEO, just as the company's namesakes did. The slowdown in growth and retreat in market share comprised a threat to the company's survival and to the continuation of its actions and contributions for social responsibility.

The company had never had a professional CEO and it had avoided commercial advertising, relying for publicity on press coverage of its founders' antics and social interest causes. This approach was apparently losing its effectiveness

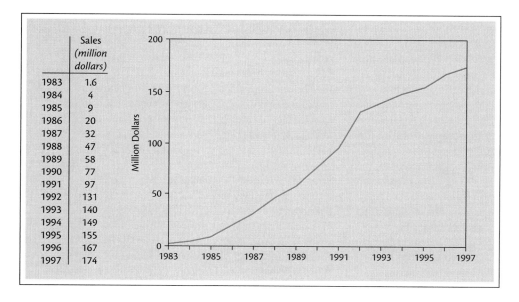

	Sales (million dollars)
1983	1.6
1984	4
1985	9
1986	20
1987	32
1988	47
1989	58
1990	77
1991	97
1992	131
1993	140
1994	149
1995	155
1996	167
1997	174

Exhibit 1   Ben & Jerry's Annual Sales

Source: Ben & Jerry's Annual Reports.

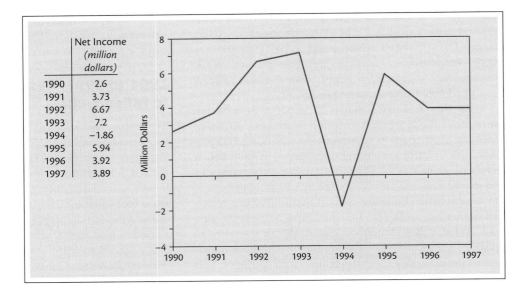

Exhibit 2 Ben & Jerry's
Net Income

Source: Ben & Jerry's Annual
Reports.

	Net Income (million dollars)
1990	2.6
1991	3.73
1992	6.67
1993	7.2
1994	−1.86
1995	5.94
1996	3.92
1997	3.89

and the company could no longer feature an underdog image in its appeals for customer support. Relaxing the rule on executive compensation, the company launched a highly publicized search for a CEO, inviting would-be CEOs to submit a 100-word essay explaining why they would like the job. In 1996, Bob Holland, a former consultant with McKinsey & Co., took the presidency, bringing a small cadre of fellow consultants with him. All of Holland's highly schooled management sensibilities were put to the test as he took over a company that had lacked effective management in recent years, commencing employment for a board of directors that was suspicious of traditional corporate culture. By this time, Cohen, Greenfield and Furman still had considerable influence over the company, controlling about 45 percent of the shares. This permitted them, as a practical matter, to elect all members of the board of directors and thereby effectively control the policies and management of the firm. Holland's relationship with the board didn't work and eighteen months later he was out, the company's decline had not been reversed and morale among the employees was at a low.

While the board was willing to pay a corporate scale salary to its CEO, it was unwilling to let go of the company's tradition of donating 7.5 percent of before tax profits to not-for-profit social causes. A spirit of socially responsible business management would need to continue, as that was still the company's stock in trade as much as the ice cream was. With this, as well as the need to survive, in mind, the board hired Perry Odak at the recommendation of one of its members at a base salary of $300,000, with a start date in January 1997.

While Odak had grown up on a dairy farm in upstate New York, it was not this dairy background that landed him the job as CEO of Ben & Jerry's. His experience at turning around troubled companies was far more important.

Odak was recruited away from a consultancy assignment at U.S. Repeating Arms Company, which he had been instrumental in turning around from its decline into red ink. This followed diverse experiences ranging from senior vice president of worldwide operations of Armour-Dial, Inc. to president of Atari Consumer Products, along with numerous consultancies and entrepreneurial activities that included the start-up team and management of Jovan, a fragrance and cosmetic company. A professional manager who thrived on challenges and abhorred mere maintenance of a company, Odak had entered the business world with a degree in agricultural economics from Cornell University topped with graduate coursework in business.

The Market for Superpremium Ice Cream

Ice cream is noted as far back as the days of Alexander the Great, though it was first commercially manufactured in the United States in 1851. By 1997, almost 10 percent of U.S. milk production went into ice cream, a $3.34 billion market. The ice cream brands that dominated American supermarket freezer cases are given in Exhibit 3 and Exhibit 4. National (as opposed to regional) branding of dairy products, including ice cream, was a recent phenomenon. Dreyer's (owned in part by the Swiss food giant, Nestlé, and branded Edy's on the East Coast) was the biggest brand at 13.9 percent of the U.S. market, in terms of value. The next biggest was Breyer's, a unit of the Dutch-English firm, Unilever, at 12 percent. Blue Bell (from Texas) was fourth biggest at 5.2 percent, and Häagen-Dazs (owned by the U.K. beverage and food company then known as Grand Metropolitan) was at 4.6 percent. Ben & Jerry's came in at

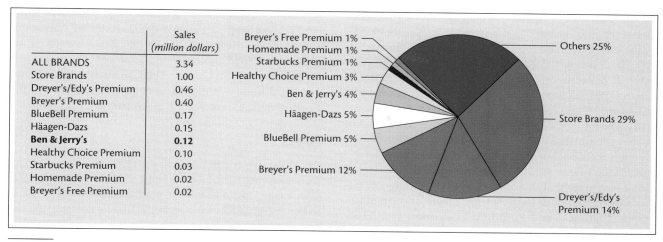

	Sales (million dollars)
ALL BRANDS	3.34
Store Brands	1.00
Dreyer's/Edy's Premium	0.46
Breyer's Premium	0.40
BlueBell Premium	0.17
Häagen-Dazs	0.15
Ben & Jerry's	**0.12**
Healthy Choice Premium	0.10
Starbucks Premium	0.03
Homemade Premium	0.02
Breyer's Free Premium	0.02

Exhibit 3   Top U.S. Ice Cream Brands, 1996 To 1997

Source: Ben & Jerry's.

about 3.6 percent of the market. Healthy Choice Premium ice cream (owned by the agribusiness and consumer food firm ConAgra) was close behind with 3.2 percent. Starbucks (one of Dreyer's brands) had 1.0 percent. The biggest share of the market (some 30.2 percent) came from the retailers' private label products and a number of economy brands (with which Ben & Jerry's did not regard itself to be competing) made up the balance.

There are considerable economies of scale in ice cream production, so despite the advantages of having dispersed production in order to reduce costs of transporting the frozen finished product or the highly perishable cream, milk and egg yolks that are principle raw ingredients, each major manufacturer generally had only a few plants to serve vast markets. Market leader, Häagen-Dazs, had just two plants in the United States, while Ben & Jerry's had three. Even with relatively few plants, Ben & Jerry's was operating at only about half of plant capacity in 1997.

While the Ben & Jerry's brand had the country's fifth highest share of the ice cream market (in terms of value), it still accounted for only a small 3.6 percent of the market. Ben & Jerry's, though, measured its competitive strength not in general ice cream sales (including many store brands and economy ice creams), but rather in sales of super-premium (high fat content) ice cream. The market for this product was much less fragmented, with Häagen-Dazs getting 44 percent and Ben & Jerry's getting 34 percent of the $361 million of supermarket (excluding convenience store and food service) sales measured and monitored by scanner data. If the two companies' frozen yogurts and sorbets were included, their market shares would be 36 percent for Ben & Jerry's and 42 percent for Häagen-Dazs. Both companies specialized in superpremium products, with additional sales being derived from sorbets, frozen yogurts and novelties. Häagen-Dazs had really pioneered the category back in 1961 when Reuben Mattus in New Jersey founded

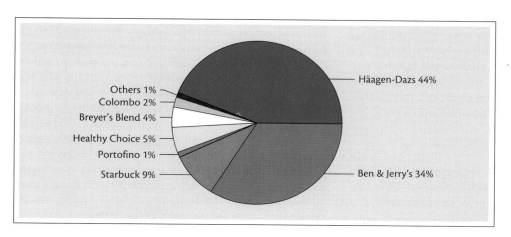

Exhibit 4   Share of Superpremium Ice Cream Brands, U.S. Market

Source: Ben & Jerry's.

the company. The company was later acquired by the giant food company, Pillsbury, which in turn was bought in 1989 by the U.K. liquor and food giant, Grand Metropolitan.

Both Ben & Jerry's and Häagen-Dazs had achieved national distribution, primarily selling their product in supermarkets and convenience stores. Ben & Jerry's had 163 scoop shops, compared to 230 Häagen-Dazs shops. Dairy Queen (with 5,790 shops worldwide) and Baskin Robbins dominated the scoop shop business, though their products were not superpremium. Prices for Ben & Jerry's and Häagen-Dazs would range from $2.89 to $3.15 per pint, often more than twice as expensive as conventional (high overrun/lower butterfat) ice cream and premium brands. Starbucks and Portofino ice creams were other much smaller contenders in the United States with their "premium plus" products, characterized by a butterfat content slightly under that of the superpremium category.

Statistical evidence indicated that ice cream consumption increased with income and education. Starting in the mid 1990s, though, sales growth started to fall off and Ben & Jerry's experienced a decline in profits, even suffering a loss in 1994. Häagen-Dazs and Ben & Jerry's product sales were very widely available across the entire U.S. market and it was clear that future growth would have to come from new products or from new (non-U.S.) markets. More troubling was that Ben & Jerry's was beginning to lose market share in both the total ice cream market and, more importantly, the superpremium market.

Ben & Jerry's International Sales

Ben & Jerry's was intentionally slow to embrace foreign markets. Cohen was opposed to growth for growth's sake, so the company's few adventures overseas were limited to opportunistic arrangements that came along, primarily with friends of the founders. Meanwhile Häagen-Dazs had no such hesitation. By 1997, it was in 28 countries with 850 dipping shops around the world. Its non-U.S. sales were about $700 million, compared to about $400 million of domestic sales. Ben & Jerry's, on the other hand, had foreign sales of just $6 million, with total sales of $174 million. In terms of non-U.S. superpremium ice cream sales, Häagen-Dazs and Ben & Jerry's were still the leading brands, but Häagen-Dazs was trouncing Ben & Jerry's.

Canada

Ben & Jerry's first foreign entry was in Canada in 1986, when the company gave a Canadian firm all Canadian rights for the manufacture and sale of ice cream through a licensing agreement. While about one-third of the product was exported from the United States, high Canadian tariffs (15.5 percent) and particularly quotas (only 347 tons annually) made export impractical. In 1992 Ben & Jerry's repurchased the Canadian license and as of 1997 there were just four scoop shops in Quebec. The Canadian dairy industry remained highly protective even after enactment of the North American Free Trade Agreement.

Israel

Avi Zinger, a friend of Cohen's, was given a license, including manufacturing rights, for the Israel market in 1988. His 1997 sales totalled about $5 million, but the only revenue accruing to Ben & Jerry's Homemade, Inc. would be licensing income and this amount was negligible. To assure quality coming from the plant in Yavne, Israel, Zinger and his staff received training at the Waterbury factory. As of fall 1997, there were 14 Ben & Jerry's scoop shops in Israel, with the shops selling such items as gifts, baked goods and beverages, in addition to the ice cream. Zinger also sold Ben & Jerry's products through supermarkets, hotels, delis and restaurants.

Russia

The company entered into its first foreign joint venture in 1990 by establishing the firm Iceverk in the Russian republic of Karelia, which is Vermont's sister state. This grew out of Cohen's travel to Karelia as part of a sister state delegation in 1988. A goal of the joint venture effort was to promote understanding and communication between the peoples of these two countries. The joint venture agreement specified the following division of ownership shares: Ben & Jerry's—50 percent; the Intercentre cooperative—27 percent; Petro Bank—20 percent; and Pioneer Palace (a facility similar to a YMCA, that provided the location)—three percent. Half of any profits would stay with the Iceverk and the balance would be divided among the partners. Ben & Jerry's contributed equipment and know-how to the venture, while the local partners provided the facilities for the factory and for two scoop shops. After considerable, mostly bureaucratic, delays, the shops opened in July 1992. By 1993, there were three scoop shops and about 100 employees. Iceverk opened several more scoop shops and the venture began to sell pints in supermarkets locally, as well as in Moscow. Ben & Jerry's hired James Flynn to put his University of New Hampshire marketing degree to good use by serving as marketing rep in Moscow. Sales improved as food service customers increasingly bought the product. In 1996, Ben & Jerry's terminated the joint venture, giving its equity and equipment at no cost to its joint venture partners. A retrospective view of that decision is that the company felt that the management time needed to keep the partnership going was too demanding, given the perceived potential. Iceverk no longer uses the Ben & Jerry's name, though it does continue to make ice cream in Petrozavodsk, Karelia's capital.

United Kingdom

In 1994 there was much discussion at Ben & Jerry's headquarters in Burlington about whether the company was ready to strategically (rather than just opportunistically) move into international markets. Susan Renaud recalled the consensus being that no, they were not, but just three months later the company shipped a container of product to Sainsbury, an upscale supermarket chain in the United Kingdom. Cohen had met a Sainsbury executive at a meeting of the Social Venture Network and the executive had encouraged him to ship over some product. This launch was made with no idea of what the pricing would be, nor any knowledge of what kind of packaging and ingredients were acceptable in that market. The company was shipping a 473 ml package, while the standard was 500 ml. With its foot in the door, the company thought it best to try other outlets in England, as well. It tried out one distributor, which had agreed to donate one percent of its Ben & Jerry's turnover to charity. Sales did not materialize and another distributor was tried, this time without the charity constraint. The product had a distinctive market position, with one radio commentator alleged to have said, "If Häagen-Dazs is the ice cream you have after sex, Ben & Jerry's is the ice cream you have instead of sex." By 1997, U.K. sales totalled $4 million.

France

In 1995, the company entered France with great ambivalence. CEO Holland was all for entering the French market and the company sent off a container of product to Auchan, a major retailer Cohen was introduced to through Social Venture Network ties. As global protests grew over French nuclear testing, though, there were discussions in the company about withdrawing from the French market or vocally protesting against the French government. With this internal disagreement concerning the French market, there was no marketing plan, no promotional support and no attempt to address French labelling laws. The company hired a French public relations firm, noted for its alternative media and social mission work, and separately contracted with a sales and distribution company. But there was no plan and nobody from Ben & Jerry's to coordinate the French effort. In 1997, sales in France were just over $1 million.

Benelux

Ben & Jerry's entry into the Benelux market was also without strategic planning. In this case, a wealthy individual who had admired the company's social mission asked to open scoop shops, with partial ownership by the Human Rights Watch. By 1997, there were three scoop shops in Holland. Sales totalled a mere $287,000, but there was the prospect of using the product reputation from the scoop shops to launch supermarket and convenience store sales.

In short, Ben & Jerry's fell into several foreign markets opportunistically, but without the consensus of the board and without the necessary headquarters staff to put together any kind of comprehensive plan. As the company had never developed a conventional marketing plan in the United States, it lacked the managerial skill to put together a marketing campaign for entering the foreign markets.

As a result, by 1997, Ben & Jerry's international sales totalled just three percent of total sales. While the company had nearly caught up with Häagen-Dazs in U.S. market share, Häagen-Dazs was light years ahead in the non-U.S. markets. With declining profits and domestic market share at Ben & Jerry's, it was beginning to seem time to give serious attention to international market opportunities.

Focus on Market Opportunities in Japan

Background on the Market for Superpremium Ice Cream in Japan

In the 1994 to 1996 period when Ben & Jerry's was having its first taste of a hired professional CEO (Bob Holland), it struggled with the prospects of strategically targeting a foreign market and developing a marketing plan for its fledgling overseas operations. In particular, the company made inquiries about opportunities in Japan, the second largest ice cream market in the world, with annual sales of approximately $4.5 billion (Exhibit 5). While the market was big, it was also daunting. Japan was known to have a highly complex distribution system driven by manufacturers, its barriers to foreign products were high and the distance for shipping a frozen product was immense. Ben & Jerry's would be a late entrant, more than 10 years behind Häagen-Dazs in gaining a foothold in the market. In addition, there were at least six Japanese ice cream manufacturers selling a superpremium product. A major Japanese frozen desserts company, Morinaga Seika, had made proposals to Ben & Jerry's on two different occasions in 1995. In both cases the proposals were rejected. In January 1996, Morinaga actually conducted focus groups to evaluate Ben & Jerry's products. It was beginning to seem appropriate to taking a closer look at the Morinaga proposals and other options.

Despite the challenges of entering Japan, that market had several compelling features. It was arguably the most

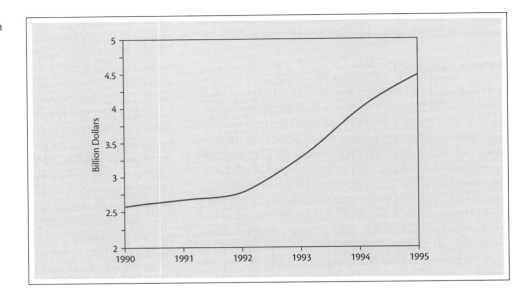

Exhibit 5   Japan Ice Cream
Market Size

Source: Ben & Jerry's.

affluent country in the world, Japanese consumers were known for demanding high quality products with great varieties of styles and flavors (which practically defined Ben & Jerry's) and it seemed that the dietary shift toward more animal products was still underway. By 1994, Japan's 42 kilogram annual per capita consumption of milk was less than half that (103 kg) of the United States, and cheese consumption was about one-tenth that of the United States. Commercial dairy sales had really only taken off after World War II, when school lunch programs were initiated with milk as a regular component. Incomes in Japan increased dramatically from the 1950s to the 1980s so that animal-based food products and home refrigerators were affordable to a large number of people.

Though Häagen-Dazs' financial figures were not published by its parent, Grand Metropolitan, market intelligence suggested that the ice cream maker had Japanese sales of about $300 million, with Japan providing the highest margins of any of its markets. Häagen-Dazs had managed to capture nearly half the superpremium market in Japan. It entered the market as an imported product and later began production in Japan at a plant owned jointly by Häagen-Dazs, Sentry and Takanashi Milk Products. About 25 percent of Häagen-Dazs' sales there appeared to be from scoop shops. In addition to gaining visibility through scoop shops, Häagen-Dazs operated a fleet of ice cream parlor buses, with upper deck cafe tables, at exhibitions and other public gatherings. On the one hand, Häagen-Dazs would be a formidable competitor that would likely guard its market share. On the other hand, there would be no apparent need for Ben & Jerry's to teach the local market about superpremium ice cream. The market seemed to welcome imported ice cream and expectations of

falling tariffs on dairy products suggested new opportunities for ice cream imports from abroad. Häagen-Dazs' flavors were generally the same as U.S. flavors, with some modifications, such as reduced sweetness. While prices were attractive in Japan, about $6 per pint, it was unclear how much of that would go into the pockets of the manufacturer versus various distributors.

In contemplating an entry in the Japan market, it was hard to avoid thinking about the case of Borden Japan. Borden introduced a premium ice cream to the market in 1971 through a joint venture with Meiji Milk. The product was highly successful and Borden was leader of the category. In 1991, the Borden-Meiji alliance came to an end and Borden had extreme difficulty gaining effective distribution. Borden did not follow industry trends toward single serving cups of ice cream and it suffered greatly when distributors started lowering the price of the product, sending the signal to consumers that Borden was an inferior product. After sales had fallen by more than two-thirds in just two years, Borden withdrew from the Japan market. Desserts were uncommon in Japan, leaving ice cream primarily for the snack market. Thus, single serving (about 120 ml) cups became popular, accounting for about 45 percent of sales (Exhibit 6) and ice cream came to be sold increasingly in convenience stores. By 1993, about a quarter of all ice cream sales were in convenience stores, compared to 29 percent in supermarkets (Exhibit 7).

One concern at Ben & Jerry's was its size. With total worldwide sales of just over $150 million, it was very small in comparison to Häagen-Dazs, which had estimated sales of $300 million in Japan alone. At least five Japanese companies already in the superpremium market were larger

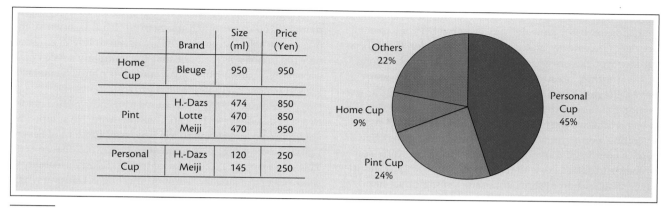

	Brand	Size (ml)	Price (Yen)
Home Cup	Bleuge	950	950
Pint	H.-Dazs	474	850
	Lotte	470	850
	Meiji	470	950
Personal Cup	H.-Dazs	120	250
	Meiji	145	250

Exhibit 6   Japan Superpremium and Premium Sales by Package

Source: Fuji Keizal Co.

than Ben & Jerry's, with leaders Glico, Morinaga, Meiji and Snow Brand all having total ice cream sales three to four times that of Ben & Jerry's and, in each case, ice cream was just part of their product line.

Cohen was not very enthusiastic about the sort of financial or managerial commitment that was apparently required to enter the Japan market and he couldn't see how entering that market fit in with the company's social mission. Others on the board shared his attitude. Two immediate problems were that entering Japan would not be the result of any social mission (the concepts of social mission and corporate charity being very foreign in Japan) and the company's lack of international success suggested that it may already have been spread too thin in too many countries. Jerry Greenfield, however, was interested enough to visit Japan on a market research tour in early 1996. The purpose was to see just how Ben & Jerry's might gain distribution if the company were to enter the Japanese market. Valerie Brown of Ben & Jerry's

fledgling marketing department accompanied Greenfield. Contacts for the visit came primarily from Valerie's classmates at Harvard Business School, from a consulting company and from the Japan External Trade Organization.

Alternative Strategies for a Ben & Jerry's Entry into Japan

In his visit to Japan, Greenfield was willing to consider entry into Japan through such diverse distribution channels as Amway Japan, Domino's Pizza and department stores. One of his meetings was with the Japanese distributor of Dreyer's, the American company with partial ownership by the Swiss food giant Nestle. Dreyer's, not being perceived as a direct competitor, was Ben & Jerry's largest distributor in the United States. Dreyer's had licensed its trademark with a joint venture operation in Japan in 1990. Sales had since fallen and the joint venture seemed to have had difficulty with its

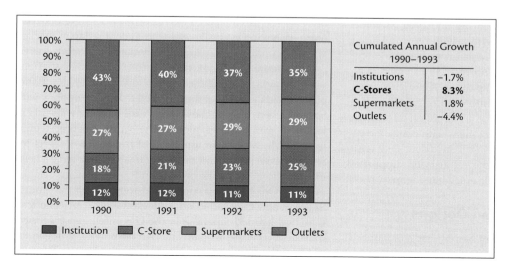

Cumulated Annual Growth 1990–1993	
Institutions	–1.7%
C-Stores	**8.3%**
Supermarkets	1.8%
Outlets	–4.4%

Exhibit 7   Japan Ice Cream Market by Channel

Source: Ice Cream Data Book (Morinaga).

biggest customer, Seven-Eleven Japan. The retailer's demands for just-in-time delivery required Dreyer's to maintain large inventories and the retailer demanded the right to rapidly drop flavors which did not meet sales expectations.

Another meeting was with a high level team of Seven-Eleven executives, including Masahiko Iida, the senior managing director, and Yasayuki Nakanishi, the merchandiser of the Foods Division. Iida expressed interest in selling Ben & Jerry's ice cream, suggesting that Ben & Jerry's could sell directly to Seven-Eleven, avoiding some of the distribution costs that are typical of the usual multi-layer distribution system in Japan. On the other hand, a major American beverage distributor in Japan warned that it would be the kiss of death to enter the market through some kind of exclusive arrangement with a huge convenience store chain like Seven-Eleven. The balance of power would be overwhelmingly in the retailer's favor.

Meiji Milk Products (with $447 million of ice cream sales), in combination with its importer, the giant Mitsubishi Trading Company, expressed interest in distributing Ben & Jerry's products. This team clearly had very strong distribution resources, including an exclusive supply contract for Tokyo Disneyland. One concern was that Meiji already had a superpremium brand called Aya. Despite Meiji's strong interest, though, this option had probably become a long shot on account of earlier protests by Ben & Jerry's leadership of deforestation practices by another division of Mitsubishi.

Other marketing possibilities that had surfaced in 1996 included an arrangement with the advertising agency that had charge of Japan Airlines' in-flight entertainment, as well as a chance to open a scoop shop at a highly visible new retail development about to be built at Tokyo Disneyland. If anything, the many options, focus groups and proposals made the decision about what to do with Japan even more difficult. The fact that the Ben & Jerry's board was divided on whether the company even had any business in a Japan launch discouraged further action. By late 1996, Holland was following up discussions with a well-recommended Japanese-American who was available to oversee marketing and distribution of Ben & Jerry's products in Japan. Ken Yamada, a third generation Japanese American from Hawaii, had obtained the Domino's Pizza franchise for Japan. His compensation would be a margin on all sales in Japan. When Bob Holland's employment with Ben & Jerry's ended later in the year, he was still in discussion with Yamada, but he was still lacking the enthusiastic support of the board of directors for a possible entry into Japan.

A Fresh Look at the Japan Options

Perry Odak assumed leadership of Ben & Jerry's in January 1997, inheriting the file of reports on possible strategies for entering the Japan market. Neither the file nor institutional memory indicated much momentum leading toward any one of the Japan strategies. In being hired, however, Odak had the board's agreement that the company's sales (and especially profits) must grow and that non-U.S. markets were the most likely key to that growth.

In February 1997, Odak added a business-related detour to a scheduled trip to Thailand with his wife. He stopped by Tokyo for a courtesy call to Mr. Iida, the President of Seven-Eleven Japan, a controlling parent company of 7-Eleven U.S.[2] This was to more or less make up for Ben & Jerry's inability to send a CEO to a January "summit" meeting in Dallas at which Mr. Iida and the head of the U.S. 7-Eleven operations had wished to meet face to face with the leaders of its major suppliers. 7-Eleven U.S. was, in fact, Ben & Jerry's biggest retail outlet and Ben & Jerry's was a major supplier to Seven-Eleven.

After about 10 minutes of pleasantries at this introductory meeting at the Seven-Eleven headquarters in Tokyo, Iida asked Odak point blank: "Is there anyone at Ben & Jerry's who can make a marketing decision? We'd like to sell your product, but don't know how to proceed or with whom." Rather taken aback at this surprisingly direct inquiry, Odak replied that he could indeed make a decision and he resolved to sort through the Japan options and get back to Iida in short order.

Back in Burlington, Odak installed Angelo Pezzani as the new international director for Ben & Jerry's Homemade. Odak had known Pezzani since 1982 when they both started work at Atari on the same day. Pezzani's position was then general consul of Atari Consumer Products Worldwide. Going over the options with Pezzani, it appeared that partnering with Yamada was still the strongest option for entering Japan, but the Seven-Eleven option had not yet been well developed for consideration. Yamada represented considerable strength with his Domino's success and with the fact that Domino's already offered ice cream cups as part of its delivery service in Japan. Possible drawbacks were his insistence on having exclusive rights to the entire Japan market, with full control of all branding and marketing efforts there.

Pezzani and Odak decided to continue negotiations with Yamada, keeping that option alive, and to simultaneously let Iida know that they wanted to explore options with Seven-Eleven. They requested an April meeting with Iida in Japan to move things along. The April meeting would include Mr. Nakanishi, the head of frozen ice desserts for Seven-Eleven Japan, and Bruce Bowman, Ben & Jerry's head of operations. To work out ground arrangements for the meeting, Odak and Pezzani needed someone on the ground in Japan and they called on Rivington Hight, an American who had learned Japanese in the U.S. intelligence service, married a Japanese woman and had been living in Japan for much of the past 30 years. No stranger to Odak or Pezzani,

Hight had also worked for Atari in 1982 as president of Atari Japan. Like Odak and Pezzani, he had held a variety of management positions and consultancies in the years since.

The April meeting in Japan was basically intended to lay the framework to begin hashing out the many details that would be involved if Ben & Jerry's were to enter the Japan market through Seven-Eleven. It was a chance for the critical players in each company to get together. Perry brought Pezzani, Bowman and Hight. Arriving at the Ito-Yokado/ Seven-Eleven headquarters building at the foot of Tokyo Tower, the Ben & Jerry's team walked into a lobby full of sample-laden salespeople and manufacturers nervously awaiting their chance to put their products on the shelves of some 7,000 stores. The receptionist quickly identified Odak and company and immediately put VIP pins on their dark lapels, directing them to the VIP elevator that went straight to the executive suite on the 12th floor. A hostess there immediately guided the group across the plush white carpeting to a spacious meeting room, where they were served tea while awaiting Iida and Nakanishi. Odak arrived with more questions than answers, but he was determined that any product Ben & Jerry's might sell in Japan would be manufactured in Vermont, where the company had considerable excess capacity. Also, the costs of labor and raw dairy products were higher in Japan than the United States, so the 23.3 percent tariff and cost of shipping seemed not to be prohibitive. As a result of the Uruguay Round of GATT, the tariff would be reduced to 21 percent in the year 2000. The introductory meeting went well, but they had not yet addressed any of the difficult issues except to establish that it would be possible to export the product from Vermont to Japan.

Wrestling with the Details of the Seven-Eleven Option

Odak, Pezzani and Bowman had a full plate of issues to resolve. The first question was market. Iida had said he was interested in Ben & Jerry's product because it was something new to Japan and particularly unique with its chunks. Seven-Eleven had even tried to get a Japanese company to co-pack a chunky superpremium ice cream, but the Japanese packer was unsuccessful with its production processes. Research supporting a clear market for this novel product in Japan was scant, though it seemed unlikely that Seven-Eleven would commit shelf space to a product it had any doubt about and both Iida and Nakanishi certainly knew their market. A skeptical view of Seven-Eleven's interest in bringing Ben & Jerry's to Japan was that Seven-Eleven's combined U.S. and Japan operations would become so important to Ben & Jerry's (potentially accounting for a substantial portion of its sales) that Seven-Eleven could, in some fashion, control the ice cream

maker. Even if that were not part of Seven-Eleven's motivation, it could be a concern.

While Ben & Jerry's management was leaning toward an entry into Japan, it was not a foregone conclusion. The entry would require a commitment of capital and managerial attention. As the product would be exported from the United States, there would be the risk of negative exchange rate movements that could make exports to Japan no longer feasible, thus making Ben & Jerry's financial picture less predictable. Commodity risk was also a serious concern in that the price of milk could rise in the United States, hurting Ben & Jerry's relative to competitors producing ice cream in Japan.

Assuming that an entry into the Japanese market was desirable, there were a number of apparent options for gaining distribution there, making it necessary to seriously consider the pros and cons of entering by way of Seven-Eleven. The most obvious pro was immediate placement in the freezer compartments of over 7,000 convenience stores in that country. In the early 1990s, the convenience store share of the ice cream market had increased and it appeared that these stores were now accounting for at least 40 percent of superpremium ice cream sales in Japan. Equally positive was the fact that Seven-Eleven had taken advantage of its size and its state-of-the-art logistics systems by buying product directly from suppliers, avoiding the several layers of middlemen that stood between most suppliers and Japanese retailers. These cost savings could make the product more affordable and/or allow a wider margin to protect against such risks as currency fluctuation.

On the negative side, if the product was introduced to the market through a convenience store and it was just one of many brands there, would it be able to build its own brand capital in Japan like Häagen-Dazs had? Would the product essentially become a store brand? Without brand capital it could be difficult to distribute the product beyond the Seven-Eleven chain. An alternative approach of setting up well located scoop shops, along with an effective marketing or publicity campaign, could give the product cache, resulting in consumer pull that could give Ben & Jerry's a price premium, as well as a range of marketing channels. Would committing to one huge retail chain be a case of putting too many eggs in one basket? A falling out between Ben & Jerry's and Seven-Eleven Japan could leave the ice cream maker with nothing in Japan. Even during discussions with Ben & Jerry's, the retailer was known to be terminating its supply agreement with the French ice cream manufacturer Rolland due to allegedly inadequate sales. Presumably Seven-Eleven could similarly cut off Ben & Jerry's at some future date.

While weighing the pros and cons of the business arrangement, there were also production issues which Ben & Jerry's had to consider. Nakanishi insisted the ice cream be packaged only in personal cups (120 ml) and not the 473 ml (one pint) size that Ben & Jerry's currently packed. The main argument for the small cups was that ice cream is seldom consumed as a family dessert in Japan, but rather is consumed as a snack item. A secondary argument was that, for sanitation purposes, customers liked their own individual servings. Cake, for example, was generally served in restaurants with each slice individually wrapped. Nakanishi's insistence was despite the fact that Seven-Eleven stocked Häagen-Dazs and some of its local competitors in both sizes.

Bruce Bowman embraced the challenge of designing a production system that would accommodate small cups that the company had never packed before. It seemed that about $2 million of new equipment would be needed, though it could be installed in the existing buildings. The sizes of some of the chunks would have to be reduced in order for them to not overwhelm the small cups. Besides requiring these known adjustments to production operations, Seven-Eleven might be expected to request other product changes. Japanese buyers were known for being particularly demanding in their specifications.

Ben & Jerry's had long been shipping ice cream to the West Coast and to Europe in freezer containers. Shipments to Japan were feasible, though the Seven-Eleven approach to just-in-time inventory procedures would make delivery reliability especially key and, of course, costs would have to be minimized. Logistics research indicated it would likely take at least three weeks shipping time from the plant in Vermont (the St. Albans plant would be used if the Japan plan were implemented) to the warehouse in Japan. Because of the Japanese label needed in Japan, production would have to carefully meet the orders from Seven-Eleven. The product could not be shifted to another customer, nor could another customer's product be shifted to Japan.

A number of sticky points needed to be resolved. In addition to changing the package size, Seven-Eleven wanted to provide its own design for the package art and the design would definitely not include a photo of Ben and Jerry. Packaging had always been an important part of the Ben & Jerry's product. Funky lettering and the images of Ben and Jerry are part of what made the product unique. If Seven-Eleven were given control over the package art, what would that do to the benefits of developing a global branded product? Would consumers be confused about the placement of the product as they travelled? On the other hand, the carton designs had already been evolving somewhat and maybe a bit more evolution would satisfy Seven-Eleven. In fact, the earlier focus groups by Morinaga brought out the concern that it was too bad the "strange Ben & Jerry's packaging" had to detract from the good ice cream.

Ben & Jerry's sent a number of samples to consider and Nakanishi developed a short list that would be tested (if the deal went forward) in a couple dozen Seven-Eleven stores so that the top five flavors could be identified for the market entry. "Chunky Monkey" was near the top of Nakanishi's list, though the name absolutely had to change, he said. It turned out that only minor ingredient modifications would be needed to reduce the sweetness and to replace "vegetable gum" with "protein solids."

Through numerous communications and several meetings during the summer of 1997, a number of issues were discussed and resolved. For example, Seven-Eleven would acquire only a six-month exclusive right to Ben & Jerry's and even that would be only for the specific flavors being sold to Seven-Eleven. Because of its relatively small size and inability to cover a loss, Ben & Jerry's was asking for sale terms that would transfer title (and all risk) for the product at the plant gate. It also was asking for 12 weeks lead-time on any order to allow for sourcing of ingredients, as well as efficient production scheduling. It appeared that these requests would not be too burdensome for Seven-Eleven. The sensitive issue of price was intentionally left until late in the discussions. Häagen-Dazs was being sold for 250 yen per 120 ml cup and Seven-Eleven wanted to position Ben & Jerry's at a slightly lower price point. This would be problematic for Odak, who had recently increased the domestic price for Ben & Jerry's ice cream in part to support the product's position as equal or superior in quality to Häagen-Dazs.

A concern yet lurking in the boardroom in Burlington, Vermont was what would be the company's social mission in Japan. Since the early 1990s, the company had moved beyond using its profit to fund philanthropy. The new imperative was to make the workplace, community and world a better place through regular day-to-day operations. On the other hand, profits were still needed in order to even have day-to-day operations and a new market (such as Japan) could be the ticket to those profits. In the meantime, no particular social mission had emerged from the summer discussions of entering the Japan market.

The Approaching Deadline for a Summer 1998 Japan Launch

Odak and his staff had made steady progress narrowing and developing their Japan options during the summer of 1997. If they were to enter the Japan market for the summer 1998 season, though, they would have to commit to one plan or another no later than autumn 1997. Two distinct entry options had emerged.

The Yamada option was largely the same as it had been at the beginning of the year. His proposal was to have full control of marketing and sales for Ben & Jerry's in

Japan. He would position the brand, devise and orchestrate the initial launch and take care of marketing and distribution well into the future. He would earn a royalty on all sales in the market. By giving Yamada full control of the Japan market, Ben & Jerry's would have instant expertise in an otherwise unfamiliar market, as well as relief from having to address the many issues involved in putting together an entry strategy and in ongoing market management. Yamada knew frozen foods and he had an entrepreneurial spirit and marketing savvy, evidenced by his success in launching and building up the Domino's pizza chain in Japan. Giving up control of a potentially major market, though, could not be taken lightly. Because Yamada would invest his time in fleshing out and executing a marketing plan only after reaching agreement with Ben & Jerry's, there was no specific plan available for consideration. Even if there were, Yamada would retain the rights to change it. For the near term, however, Yamada would expect to add selected flavors of Ben & Jerry's ice cream cups to the Domino's delivery menu, providing an opportunity to collect market data based on customer response.

The Seven-Eleven option would leave Ben & Jerry's in control of whatever market development it might want to pursue beyond supplying Seven-Eleven in Japan. While Seven-Eleven would provide an instant entry to the market, the company would not be in a position to help Ben & Jerry's develop other distribution channels in Japan. The retailer thought it could sell at least six cups per day at each store, which would be the minimum to justify continuing to stock Ben & Jerry's. Looking at the size of Seven-Eleven's ice cream freezer cases suggested that this would

require approximately 10 percent of Seven-Eleven's cup ice cream sales to be Ben & Jerry's products. Ben & Jerry's was as yet unknown in Japan and it did not have the budget for a marketing campaign there. Sales would have to rely primarily on promotional efforts by Seven-Eleven, but the company was making no specific commitment for such efforts.

Another option was increasingly compelling—that of holding off on any Japan entry. Japan's economy was continuing to languish, with increasing talk that it could be years before recovery. A financial crisis that had commenced with a devaluation of Thailand's currency in July 1997, seemed to be spreading across Asia. If the pending Asia crisis hit an already weakened Japanese economy, the economics of exporting ice cream from Vermont to Japan could become infeasible.

Though the value of the yen had recently fallen to 125 yen to the dollar, Ben & Jerry's could still sell the product at the plant gate at an acceptable profit with room for both shipping expense and satisfactory margins for Seven-Eleven and its franchisees. If the rate went as high as 160 yen to the dollar, then the price in Japan would have to be raised to a level that might seriously cut into demand, especially relative to Häagen-Dazs, which had manufacturing facilities in Japan.

It would be a long evening meal as Odak, Pezzani, Bowman and Hight gave their final thoughts to the decision before them. Not only had Odak promised Iida that he could make a decision, but Yamada needed an answer to his proposal as well. In any event, Ben & Jerry's had to proceed with one plan or another if it was going to have any Japanese sales in its 1998 income statement.

Notes

1 Monetary values are in U.S. dollars unless otherwise noted.
2 A brief explanation of the relationship between the Japan Seven-Eleven organization and the U.S. 7-Eleven organization is in order. 7-Eleven convenience stores originated in Texas in 1927 as a retail concept of Southland Corporation, which had been in the ice business. Southland began using the 7-Eleven banner in the 1950s because the stores would be open from 7 A.M. to 11 P.M. The business grew through company-owned and franchised stores. Southland gave a master franchise for Japan to the Ito Yokado Company, a large supermarket operator there, which in turn established Seven-Eleven Japan to conduct the 7-Eleven business in Japan through company-owned and franchised stores. In the 1980s, Southland was in financial distress and Ito Yokado, along with its subsidiary, Seven-Eleven Japan, bailed out Southland, acquiring a controlling interest in the company. In this light, Odak's dinner with Iida in Japan constituted a sort of executive summit between Ben & Jerry's and its largest customer.

Case 3-9: The Tale of Eloise and Abelard or Tough Love for HP-Compaq*

"Eloise and Abelard", was Carly Fiorina's reply when she had been asked for two code names to be used by lawyers who were secretly preparing the paperwork for the computer industry's biggest ever merger. America's best-known business-woman, who holds a Stanford degree in medieval history, told puzzled advisers that the love letters of Héloïse and Abélard are an important part of French medieval literature.

Carly Fiorina could have had second thoughts about choosing this early twelfth century couple as patrons for her company's secret marriage with Compaq; her heroes had actually been caught in a family feud with no happy ending. At the age of 36, Pierre Abélard was already a scholar of considerable renown, when he fell in love with a brilliant 15-year-old girl of noble origin. Héloïse, who had studied all the arts and spoke Latin as well as ancient Greek, was the niece of Fulbert, priest at Notre Dame of Paris. Abélard offered to become her preceptor and the two managed to hide their affair until Héloïse became pregnant. Her uncle arranged a secret marriage, yet privately prepared a terrible vengeance: two paid thugs assaulted Abélard in his sleep and castrated him. Vilified by Fulbert, Abélard became a monk to continue his scholastic career, while Héloïse was forced to take the veil.

Carly Fiorina could have been the Héloïse of American business. She is young (only 47 in 2001), glamorous, a superb saleswoman, and one of only half a dozen female CEOs of a Fortune 500 company. When she arrived at HP in 1999 after a brilliant career at Lucent Technologies, she embarked on a high-speed program of restructuring. However, she had bad luck, compounded by bad judgment that may reflect either inexperience or her marketing past. After a sparkling first year, she promised a second that would even be better. This unwise pledge cost her credibility and support in the markets. Internally, the early adulation had turned to skepticism, then outright hostility as it became clear that she lacked the magic to maintain HP's sales growth during one of the worst downturns in the history of the technology industry. By early 2001, as the company's stock was hovering at $33 a share, down $25 on the quote that had greeted her arrival at HP, Carly Fiorina called in McKinsey. After weeks of analysis, the consultants could not see much reason for HP to trade above $30. If HP wanted the stock to rally, it had to look out for a partner.

From mid-spring 2001 on, it was clear to Carly Fiorina that there couldn't be a better partner than Compaq. Through July, she skillfully managed to get most of HP's board members on her side. Only Walter Hewlett, the son of one of the company's co-founders, displayed some low-key opposition. Of all the delicate merger issues, the trickiest was the fate of Compaq's CEO Michael Capellas, who personified better than anyone else the Abélard role that was written for his company. Compaq's strongest advocate of the merger, Michael Capellas hoped to become co-CEO of the combined company, but HP's directors wanted him only to run the merger integration for a year, with no clear prospects of anything to follow. He finally settled for a newly created president post, reporting to Carly Fiorina.

On Labor Day, the secret union became official with HP's $25 billion all-stock offer for Compaq. Under the terms of the deal, HP shareholders would own approximately 64 percent and Compaq shareholders 36 percent of the merged company. The two companies estimated cost savings from the merger at $2.5 billion, while admitting revenue attrition of about 5 percent. Carly Fiorina pointed in particular to the $45 billion of combined material purchases that could result in cost savings of 3 to 4 percent.

The day after the announcement, HP's shares plummeted 18 percent, making it the worst first day reception ever of a merger. The next day, the stock continued its slide with a 7 percent loss, while Compaq's stock was down 18 percent over the two days. Together, the happy couple lost about $13 billion in market capitalization in just 48 hours, which essentially eliminated any premium for Compaq shareholders, raising doubts that the merger could proceed.

---

*This case was written by **Dr Stephan Schubert**, Ashridge Management College, United Kingdom. It is intended to be used as the basis for class discussion rather than to illustrate either effective or ineffective handling of a management situation.

The case was compiled from published sources.

Used with permission.

It was as if the patronage from the dark Middle Ages had casted a gloomy light on the high-tech merger. While HP and Compaq staffers were still mulling over the markets tough love treatment for their marriage, terrorists piloted high-jacked airplanes into the Twin Towers and the Pentagon. Only a few weeks later, Carly Fiorina would definitely have been forgiven for cursing her medieval patrons, when Walter Hewlett began to act as if he was playing Fulbert's part. Walter Hewlett was the only member of HP's founding families still on the board of directors, which he had joined in 1987. His initial skepticism towards the proposed merger turned into a family feud as other Hewlett and Packard heirs joined him in his opposition. The family foundations could line up 18 percent of HP shares against the proposed merger, yet the weight of their opposition was considered to be much greater.

For six months, the two sides spent tens of millions of dollars in a bitter proxy battle, during which they swamped shareholders with advertisements, mass mailings, faxes and even phone calls. The contest became increasingly personal when HP's other board members derided Walter Hewlett in a letter to shareholders as "a musician and academic . . . who has never worked at the company or been involved in its management." The company also said that he missed crucial board meetings for playing cello in his old boys' club and for a bicycle race.

While the merger had been on the edge of collapse to the end of 2001, it made a promising start into the new year as competition authorities on the two sides of the Atlantic waved it through without any serious conditions. Then, Compaq shareholders overwhelmingly approved the merger at an extraordinary meeting in March that Michael Capellas called the highlight of his career. The final act of the family drama was staged a few days later at HP's extraordinary meeting, when shareholders voted in favor of the merger with a small margin of 51.4 against 48.6 percent.

The new company was officially launched on April Fool's day in 2002. A few months later, Michael Capellas reportedly shuddered when he was told of Abélard's fate and said: "I'm glad I didn't know." On November 11 of the same year, he resigned from his post as HP President to follow other career opportunities that would soon lead him to the top position at WorldCom.

As his car drove away from HP's Palo Alto headquarters, Michael Capellas reflected on his last 18 months in the Silicon Valley. He remembered the state of the computer industry in 2001, and the arguments that he and Carly Fiorina had pushed to win the merger contest He also recalled their opponents' point of view and the alternative proposals that had been brought up. All his thoughts inevitably led to one question: did he leave a company in good shape for the challenges ahead?

Exhibit 1: Chairman's Letter
[IBM Annual Report 2001, Excerpts]

A massive shift is under way in our industry. You may think I mean the transition to a networked world. After all, IBM was one of the first to recognize this change and the impact it would have. And make no mistake, we are experiencing an explosion of technological innovation that will lead to permanent changes in business, government, education, health care and every other area of human endeavor—as every significant institution, every product and service, as well as billions of people, become permanently "connected."

But that's not the shift I'm talking about. The revolution I'm describing is that customers are finally driving the direction of the information technology industry.

Technologists Talking to Technologists

The first 30 years of this industry's history consisted of the technology inventors inside I/T companies talking to the technology implementers inside businesses and institutions. For most of that era, the applications of the technology were fairly limited—focused on the automation of back-office processes like accounting and payroll, or desktop applications such as word processing and e-mail.

Then, starting in the early 1990s, businesspeople began to understand the importance of information technology to everything they wanted to do. It's gotten to the point where it's almost impossible to distinguish between the business strategy and the I/T strategy of any successful enterprise. Approximately half of the investments that customers make in I/T are now driven by line-of-business managers, not chief information officers. This is a remarkable shift in just five or six years. Not that CIOs have become unimportant. They now sit at the table where technology is translated into business value. And their traditional bailiwick of infrastructure, too, has been transformed by the networked world. But there's no question that business strategy now sets the technology agenda, not the other way around.

Prior to joining IBM, my career as a management consultant and executive took me inside the inner workings of many industries. So I was surprised, on entering this one, to learn that the computer industry had been able to get away with inventing new things and just "throwing them over the wall," leaving customers to figure out how to integrate and apply them. That wasn't easy for those customers, for a lot of reasons. One was the absence of common standards. The industry model was designed around a variety of proprietary architectures (which, to be candid, technology providers were using to control customers). This came as quite a shock to me, since all my prior experience had taught me that you either give the customer what he or she wants, or the customer walks.

Well, guess what? Customers have finally put on their walking shoes. They've made it emphatically clear to this industry that they will no longer cede control to the makers of the technology.

That means customers are demanding integration, and refusing to accept piece parts that aren't designed and delivered to work together. It means they are demanding solutions, not "speeds and feeds." And it means they insist that the technology adapt itself to the needs of their business and help them gain some tangible competitive advantage—to squeeze cost from their supply chains, to create lasting relationships with customers, to empower their key constituencies (internal and external) with tools and knowledge. [. . .]

The New Industry Model: Innovate or Integrate

To survive, you have to do one or the other really well. To lead, you have to do both. The vertical integration of the technology industry in the '60s and '70s had given way by the early 1990s to a dizzying array of "pure play" companies (specialists in PCs, databases, application software and the like). This explosion of entrepreneurial and technical creativity was, on the one hand, a testament to our industry's enduring power. It's a well that will never run dry. Businesses, however, desperately needed someone to help them make sense of this chaos. Hence, the emergence over the past several years of technology integrators—and the rush of traditional professional services companies into e-business consulting.

As I/T moves out of the back office and into the executive suite, value and growth in our industry are driven less than they used to be by technical innovation or product excellence, as necessary as those remain. What matters most today is the ability to integrate technology into the lifeblood of business. The people who help customers apply technology to transform their businesses have increasing influence over everything from architecture and standards to hardware and software choices and partners.

The New Business Model: Services-Led

A lot of people now understand the lead role played by I/T services. However, building up the requisite skill base, not to mention an appropriately sophisticated management system, is nontrivial. You can't buy your way into it, or just

go out and hire a lot of smart people. You need a certain scale and range of disciplines. Also, you can't just layer one kind of expertise on top of another. This isn't just filling up two beakers, one labeled "customer" and the other labeled "technology." It takes years and a lot of knowledge to be able to mix those elements properly.

Plus, services is rapidly expanding and evolving in some surprising ways. It now encompasses not just labor-intensive consulting, but also the utility-like delivery of computing—from applications, to processing, to storage. We see the beginnings of this trend in Web hosting and our own" e-business on demand" offerings, where customers don't buy computers, but acquire computing services over the Net, on a pay-for-use basis. To play here, as well as in the globally booming strategic outsourcing arena, you have to be willing and able to use your balance sheet to support growth.

IBM, of course, had deep experience in I/T services. But in our old business model, it was buried inside a revenue stream dependent on selling hardware. We had to extract our service operations and turn them into a profit center in their own right. That involved a lot of trial and error. But today, IBM Global Services has evolved into the world's largest and most innovative consultancy, systems integrator and strategic outsourcing leader.

The New Computing Model: Infrastructure Plus Ubiquity

It became clear to some of us in the mid-'90s that the PCdriven, client/server computing model had run its course, and was being replaced by network-based, distributed computing. This meant that, on one end of the scale, the workload was moving back to the infrastructure—to industrial-strength servers, storage, databases and transaction-management systems. On the client end, it has spawned a proliferation of network-connected devices of all kinds: PDAs, cell phones, videogame systems, set-top boxes and beyond—to the whole pervasive-computing world of embedded components in everything from house-hold appliances, to medical devices, to cars. And tying it all together was an emerging category of software with a wonderfully descriptive name, which hardly anybody had heard of five years ago—middleware. [. . .]

The New Marketplace Model: An Open Playing Field

A lot of companies—including many of our leading competitors—still don't acknowledge or fully understand that common standards are essential in a networked world, and that no one will ever again control customers through proprietary technology. [. . .]

We know what it's like to be on the wrong side of history. The future won't be kind to those who ignore this lesson.

> *Put these models together, and you see a changed competitive landscape with very new dynamics. There will be a different lineup of winners and losers. And at the head of the pack, we will see the emergence of a new type of enterprise with a whole new type of corporate culture. We've been building such a company for nearly a decade: big but fast; entrepreneurial and disciplined; at once scientific and market-driven; able to create intellectual capital on a worldwide scale, and to deliver it to a customer of one. [. . .]*

Louis V. Gerstener, Jr.
Chairman of the Board

Exhibit 2: The Computer Industry in 2001

There is little doubt that the year will be remembered as *annus horribilis* in the computer industry. By September 2001, total losses already amount to $1.2 billion, while 31,000 jobs have gone. With the Internet bubble deflated and the U.S. economy sliding towards recession, IT budgets of U.S. companies are estimated to grow only by 2.5 percent in 2001. After September 11, the market outlook for 2002 has become even dimmer with a growth forecast of only 1.5 percent. Yet, the Internet bust and the incipient recession of 2001 have only exacerbated longstanding problems, which had been hidden over the previous three years by marked exuberance in corporate IT spending.

Among the fundamental problems, Compaq's CEO Michael Capellas identifies the end of the technology development model that has been predominant in the IT industry over the past two decades. The old way, as he describes it, saw companies develop proprietary technologies and take them to market with high profit margins before repeating the cycle again and again. This old proprietary-based model has given way to a model of "standard building blocks," and consequently, to a commoditization of hardware. In the new model, hardware manufacturers tend to be penalized for being different. Their up-side for developing unique enhance-ments is severely limited because it is easy for competitors to replicate them quickly.

So most of the engineering innovation takes place at Intel and Microsoft, the major providers of the standard building blocks, which tend to concentrate the industry's profits. There is still room for innovation in computer hardware—in high-end servers, where customers demand special features and will pay for them, and in cheap special-purpose devices like handhelds. But increasingly, the innovation will be on top of the standard Wintel platform instead of what were once more sophisticated proprietary systems.

Essentially all of the industry's long-standing problems are at work in the PC segment, which has consequently been the hardest hit. Once a high growth era, the PC business has come to a halt in 2001, which marks the first ever decline in annual PC sales, down 2 percent in the second quarter on the previous year. For the whole year, the decline in PC spending is estimated at 14 percent worldwide, with a drop of 23 percent in the U.S. alone.

While market saturation has not previously been a problem for a product that became obsolete within a year or two of purchase, it is a real problem now as PCs benefit from life expectancies of three to four years. Consumers currently see little reason to upgrade as long as new applications are more restrained by the speed of Internet connections than by PC performance.

A further problem for the PC business is the industry's trend towards commoditization. Assembled from standard components, PCs have become, in essence, interchangeable. Consequently, whoever can build them most cheaply has the advantage. This trend has handed the market leadership to low-cost manufacturer Dell, with a worldwide market share of 13 percent in the second quarter and a share of 25 percent of the North American market. Dell's progress comes at the expense of its main rivals Compaq and HP, whose market shares are declining. Worldwide, Compaq accounts for 11 percent of PC shipments (12 percent in the U.S. market), while HP's share is below 7 percent (U.S.: 10 percent). In 2001, IBM managed to increase slightly its global market share to 6.3 percent.

Another challenge for the PC business is the rise of devices such as handheld computers, personal organizers and Internet-capable mobile telephones. The combined sales of these devices will probably overtake PC sales in 2001. The PC is now just one of many devices through which people gain access to information. One major computer manufacturer has already created an Access division, which includes PCs and other personal devices.

Resisting better than the PC business to the downward trend in corporate IT spending, the enterprise server and network equipment segment is expected to grow at annual rates of 6 to 7 percent through 2004. Compaq dominates the low end of the market with a global share of about 30 percent, followed by Dell (18 percent), IBM (13 percent), and Hewlett Packard (9 percent). Following a full-scale price war late in 2000, Dell has become market leader for standard servers in North America, the largest market, with a share of 32 percent, closely followed by Compaq (30 percent). About one third of the mid and upper range global UNIX market is accounted for by Sun Microsystems, followed by Hewlett Packard (23 percent), IBM (15 percent), and Compaq (7 percent).

The demand for open systems such as those based on UNIX servers has grown in recent years as businesses sought inter-operability and scalability from their computing platforms. However, for systems that are critical to their core business functions, companies historically relied on mainframe computer systems due to their high reliability. Today, there is market demand for open computing systems while maintaining the same level of security, reliability, and performance provided by mainframe computers with better cost efficiency in operations. As in the PC business, the server segment currently experiences a growing trend towards commoditization with standard Wintel platforms having replaced proprietary microprocessors, architecture and operating systems at the low end of the market.

Information has value only if it is accessible instantly, around the clock. As more and more organizations depend on fast, reliable access to online information for airline reservation and telephone billing systems, e-commerce, ATMs, product designs, inventory management, e-mail archives, Web portals, patient records, credit cards, life sciences, global capital markets etc, information storage has emerged as the most strategic information technology. Customers may postpone application and PC upgrades, but they cannot easily control the onrushing wave of new information, or the need to store, move, manage, and access it. Independent market data confirm this trend. According to Gartner Group, storage industry hardware revenues will probably grow 22 percent on an annual basis through 2004. By the end of 2002, total spending on information storage will overtake spending on servers.

In 2001, Direct Attached Storage Systems accounts for about 70 percent of the worldwide disk storage market, while Network Storage Systems represented the remaining part. This relation is expected to be exactly opposite by 2006. EMC was the leader in the network segment with a global market share of about 30 percent.

Also contrasting with the gloom in the PC business are the growth perspectives in digital imaging. According to optimistic forecasts, the currently $18 billion market could grow to $60 billion by 2003.

In the printer industry, the past years have been marked by growth in laser and inkjet devices as a result of the increasing penetration of personal computers and local area networks into home and office markets. In 2001, estimated industry-wide revenue for printer hardware and associated supplies in the 1–50 pages per minute speed category, including monochrome and color laser, inkjet and dot matrix printers, exceeded $40 billion. While the market is mostly flat and even slightly declining in 2001, industry analysts expect modest growth through 2005. Profit margins for printer hardware are negatively affected by competitive pricing pressure, but supplies continue to be a relatively high margin recurring business. The dominant business model for hardware manufacturers is to build an installed base of printers that will generate demand for supplies and services. The laser printer market is dominated by HP, which has an approximate 50 percent market share, followed by Epson and Canon. The same top-tier also dominates the inkjet printer market, which accounts for 76 percent of hardware shipments.

A growing segment of the computer industry are IT services, a global $500 billion market. Yet, after two years of 20 percent annual expansion, the IT services market has been sluggish in 2001 with only incremental growth. IT outsourcing is expected to expand at strong double-digit annual rates over the next years, as corporations continue to abandon non-core activities. In North America, the biggest market, IT outsourcing is estimated to grow from $101 billion in 2001 to $160 billion in 2003.

Growth rates for IT consulting, systems integration, and customized software development will be lower than for outsourcing services, but margins will be higher as no big upfront investments in capacity are required. Today, nearly 40 percent of the $230 billion global software market is represented by middleware, which essentially is e-business enabling software such as data management and transaction processing.

Source: adapted from company and other publicly available information.

Exhibit 3: Hewlett Packard in 2001

If Silicon Valley has an establishment, Hewlett Packard (HP) definitely belongs to it. The company is the archetypal start-up, formed in 1938 by Bill Hewlett and David Packard, who worked in a rented garage building electronic instruments. In the 1970s, the group diversified into computing, but it made its most important breakthrough in printer technology just as the PC revolution was taking off in the 1980s. That enabled HP to claim leadership in the printer market, a position it has never let slip.

From the outset, the company founders privileged a tight set of values such as technology leadership, meritocracy and humane management practices. Over time, these values have given way to a strong corporate culture and an "HP way" of doing things, making HP one of the best companies to work for.

Yet by the mid-1990, the "HP way" had become distorted. The tolerant, people-oriented culture had turned into sclerotic decision-making, as HP managers avoided dissent, while employees enjoyed a system akin to lifelong employment, regardless of performance. In July 1999, Carly Fiorina took over as CEO with the mission to totally reinvent HP according to the original HP way. One of her first decisions has been to spin-off the test and measurement equipment business—a difficult and emotive decision as it meant to cut HP from its historic roots. In late 1999 and early 2000, HP's management briefly looked at acquiring Eastman Kodak in a move that would have radically accelerated HP's push into photography and digital imaging. Having dropped the idea, the company then saw its $18 billion bid for PriceWaterhouseCoopers' consultancy business collapse as HP's stock lost 15 percent over weak quarterly results. A successful takeover would have added 30,000 consulting professionals to HP's 600 in-house staffers, transforming the company into a global player in the IT and management consulting business.

In a recent interview with the Financial Times, Carly Fiorina noted that 36,000 of HP's 88,000 employees worked in business units that are unprofitable. As of October 31, 2001, HP's major business segments included Imaging and Printing Systems, Computing Systems and IT Services.

■ The Imaging and Printing Systems segment provides printer hardware, supplies, imaging products and related professional and consulting services. Printer hardware consists of laser and inkjet printing devices, which include color and monochrome printers for the business and home, multifunction laser devices and wideandlarge-format inkjet printers. Supplies offer laser and inkjet printer cartridges and other related printing media. Imaging products include all-in-one inkjet devices, scanners, digital photography products, personal color copiers and faxes. HP purchases its laser engines and cartridges from outside suppliers.

■ The Computing Systems segment provides commercial PCs, home PCs, workstations, UNIX servers, PC servers, storage and software solutions. In 2001, the PC business accounted for about one fifth of HP's total revenues. HP entirely outsources its PC manufacturing to external contractors. The UNIX server offering ranges from low-end servers to high-end scalable systems such as the Superdome line, all of which currently run on proprietary PA-RISC architecture and UX operating system, but HP is set to migrate its UNIX offering to standard Wintel components. PC servers offer primarily low-end and mid-range products that run on the Windows and Linux operating systems. Storage provides mid-range and high-end array offerings, that accounted in 2001 for 8.7 percent of the global storage market. The software category offers Open-View and other solutions designed to manage large-scale systems and networks. In addition, software includes telecommunications infrastructure solutions and middleware.

■ The IT Services segment provides customer support over the entire IT environment, consulting, outsourcing, technology financing and complementary third-party products delivered with the sales of HP solutions. Consulting provides industry-specific business and IT consulting and system integration services in areas such as financial services, telecommunications and manufacturing, as well as cross-industry expertise in CRM, e-commerce and IT infrastructure. Outsourcing offers a range of IT management services, including transformational infrastructure services, client computing managed services, managed web services and application services to medium and large companies.

The markets for printer hardware and associated supplies are highly competitive, especially with respect to pricing and the introduction of new products and features. HP is the global leader in printing devices with a 45 percent share of worldwide shipments. As prices are continually under pressure, HP's ability to maintain or build market share profitably depends on continuous cost reductions. In addition, low price refill and remanufactured alternatives for HP supplies are available from independent suppliers and, although generally offering lower print quality, may put pressure on the supplies business. HP sees important areas for new growth in digital cameras and photo printers.

The areas in which the Computing Systems segment operates are intensely competitive, characterized by rapid and ongoing technological innovation and price reductions. HP has failed to capitalize on the Internet revolution in order to rebuild its distribution model for PCs. In addition, the company's dependence on retail partners for the distribution of its printers represents a significant risk factor for a rebuilding of its distribution model.

The support and consulting markets have been under significant pressure as customers scrutinize their IT spending in response to the global economic downturn. However, the downturn also has contributed to increased use of outsourcing services as customers attempt to reduce their IT costs and focus their resources on their core businesses. Many of HP's competitors in this segment are able to offer a wide range of services through a global network of service providers, which may be larger than HP's network, and some of its competitors enjoy significant brand recognition.

HP's current business strategy is divided into two approaches. The first is to compete against other narrowly focused companies in the industry in both products and services within the servers, software, storage, services and support, PCs, workstations, personal information appliances, and printers and supplies markets. The second approach the company takes in its strategy is to leverage the depth of its products and services across all of its business segments.

Source: adapted from official company information and other publicly available information.

Hewlett Packard Selected Financial Data (in $ million)

Year ended October 31,	1999	2000	2001
Net Revenue	42,370	48,870	45,226
of which:			
Imaging and Printing Systems	18,550	20,468	19,447
Computing Systems	17,814	20,653	17,771
IT Services	6,255	7,150	7,599
Costs of products sold and services	34,135	35,046	33,474
R&D	2,440	2,634	2,670
Selling, general and administrative	6,522	7,063	7,259
Restructuring charges		102	384
Inventory turnover (times)			
Imaging and Printing Systems	6.6	5.9	5.6
Computing Systems	11.6	12.4	13.3
Total Cost and Expenses	38,682	44,845	43,787
Earnings from operations	3,688	4,025	1,439
of which:			
Imaging and Printing Systems	2,363	2,666	1,987
Computing Systems	988	1,007	−450
IT Services	494	474	342
Net Earnings	3,491	3,697	408
Shares outstanding (in million)	2,018	1,979	1,936

Note: Stock quote at month end (in $): December 1999: 21.75   December 2000: 43.88   December 2001: 33.38   Employees: 88,000

Source: Annual Report. Some data has been reclassified in order to preserve a consistent presentation throughout the case study.

Exhibit 4: Compaq in 2001

"The computer industry has a new giant," declared The Washington Post, while the Chicago Tribune announced the creation of the world's second biggest technology company, "on the heels of IBM." These expansive headlines celebrated in early 1998 the $9.6 billion takeover of Digital Equipment (DEC) by Compaq—then the biggest merger in the history of the computer industry.

With hindsight, the quoted headlines belong to the last days of the computer industry's golden age, a recent past that is already beginning to seem like a distant age for the company. In fact, instead of strengthening the company's competitive position, the blockbuster merger proved to be a total disaster, distracting valuable management resources at a time when the merged company's core business would have needed more attention.

A Texas-based upstart founded in 1981, Compaq was a runaway success, breaking all records for first-year sales. It has been a large company almost from the outset, pioneering the PC business with its IBM clones. Driven by marketing and sales excellence rather than technical brilliance, Compaq thrived as Intel and Microsoft, which were its early-on partners, established industry standards. In the early 1990s, falling profits in the PC business drove the company into the server business, where margins were

higher. In 2001, CEO Michael Capellas appears to be all set on following the example of Lou Gerstner by transforming the computer company into a global service business. Underlining its new ambitions, the company has created Compaq Global Solutions, a marketing organization that works with each of Compaq's business segments and alliance partners to develop complete information technology solutions. Such solutions consist of Compaq products and services from across its business segments and alliance partners' expertise to solve the complex business issues facing Compaq's enterprise customers. In 2001, Compaq's operations are organized within three business segments: Enterprise Computing, Access, and Global Services.

The Enterprise Computing segment consists of three global business units: Industry Standard Servers (ISS), Business Critical Solutions and Enterprise Storage.

■ The ISS unit is using standard components designed and manufactured by third parties that are widely available across the industry. Unit revenue was significantly lower during 2001 as intense price competition and a shift in sales mix to lower-end servers resulted in average selling price declines of 27 percent. Despite declining revenue, Compaq maintained its worldwide market share lead in industry-standard servers and regained its number one position in North America.

- The Business Critical Solutions unit provides NonStop Himalaya and high performance AlphaServer systems or solutions that deliver the highest levels of availability, performance, scale and mana-geability for telecommunications, financial services, high performance technical computing and other business-critical market segments. In 2001, Compaq has been able to maintain its leading position in the fault-tolerant server market. Future revenues are expected to decline, as Compaq will gradually phase out its proprietary Alpha chips in favor of standard Intel architecture. The new server systems will be available in 2004, allowing the business unit to match the performance of new proprietary systems recently introduced by its two main competitors.
- The Enterprise Storage unit provides global storage solutions, including storage area networks, automated backup solutions, network attached storage and a complete suite of SANworks by Compaq storage management solutions. In 2001, Compaq has regained its number one world market position in overall storage with a share of nearly 18 percent. In network storage, the company is one of the leading providers with a global market share of about 20 percent.

The Access segment delivers products and solutions designed to provide home and business users with any-time, anywhere access to information, communication and entertainment.

- For the business customer, the Access segment offers a broad range of innovative computing devices, services and solutions, including desktop, notebook, work-station and thin client products marketed under the Evo, DeskPro, Armanda and other brands, as well as a full line of Compaq branded monitor and networking products.
- For the home user, the Access segment offers Presario branded desktop and notebook Internet PCs and a line of monitors and printers.
- In addition, the Access segment offers an innovative line of personal devices and solutions marketed under the iPAQ brand, targeting the convergence of business and home computing. These include handhelds, as well as home networking products, desktop computers, microportable projectors and Internet access appliances. While sales of the iPAQ Pocket PC have not met expectations yet, the handheld has already won industry awards.

Within the Access segment, the PC business accounts for the major part of sales. In an overall declining PC market, Compaq managed in 2001 to preserve its number two position in the North American market by matching the market leader's aggressive prices.

The Compaq Global Services segment consists of four global business units:

- Customer Support offerings include lifecycle support services, business-critical services and high availability support services for multi-vendor, multi-technology hardware and software products. Lifecycle support services consist of installation, user assistance, maintenance, upgrading, replacement and disposition services available through a product's end of life. In 2001, the Customer Support unit has accounted for 56 percent of revenues in the Global Services segment.
- Systems Integration offerings include end-to-end information systems consulting, technical and application design services, systems integration, Internet and network architecture, project management services and e-business solutions.
- Managed Services offerings include outsourcing and resource management services, as well as business continuity and recovery services.
- Financial Services offerings include customized enterprise financing solutions that encompass computers, networks and technology upgrades, as well as asset management services for large and multinational business customers.

In response to changing industry practices and customer preferences, Compaq's business model is slowly evolving from a distribution model to a direct and auto-replenishment model. Compaq's products and services are sold and delivered primarily directly to large enterprise, government and education accounts, supplemented by dealers, value-added resellers, systems integrators and authorized service providers.

Compaq's products and services are sold and delivered primarily through dealers, consumer retail channels and authorized service providers to medium-sized business and home customers, and increasingly through direct sales and delivery, including via the Internet.

In 2001, Compaq continued to expand its direct product distribution model, principally in North America. At the end of 2001, Compaq was shipping approximately 59 percent of its North America product sales via its direct model. Since direct sales made by Compaq may compete with the sales made by third-party resellers and distributors, these third-party resellers and distributors may elect to use other suppliers that do not directly sell their own products. Therefore, any increase by Compaq of its commitment to direct sales could alienate some of its channel partners, particularly in the European Union where the direct sales model is not widely embraced. As a result, Compaq may lose some of its customers that purchase from third-party resellers or distributors, which in turn could adversely affect Compaq's revenues.

Source: adapted from official company information and other publicly available information.

Compaq Selected Financial Data (in $ million)

Year ended December 31,	1999	2000	2001
Net Revenue	38,447	42,222	33,554
of which:			
Enterprise Computing	12,947	14,253	10,699
Access	18,128	20,624	15,193
Global Services	7,413	7,483	7,789
Costs of products sold and services	29,798	32,417	26,442
R&D	1,660	1,469	1,305
Selling, general and administrative	6,341	6,044	5,328
Inventory turnover (times)	15.5	16.1	18.5
Total Cost and Expenses	7,793	8,930	7,885
Earnings from operations	946	2,642	639
of which:			
Enterprise Computing	674	1,656	163
Access	−437	145	−587
Global Services	998	884	1,062
Earnings before income taxes	934	569	−785
Shares outstanding (in million)	1,693	1,702	1,688

Note: Stock quote at month end (in $):   January 2001: 23.57   November 2001: 10.15   Employees: 78,000

Source: Form 10-K. Some data has been reclassified in order to preserve a consistent presentation throughout the case study.

Exhibit 5: Dell in 2001

Headquartered in Austin, Texas, Dell was founded in 1984 by Michael Dell, the computer industry's longest-tenured chief executive officer, on a simple concept: that by selling computer systems directly to customers, Dell could best understand their needs and efficiently provide the most effective computing solutions to meet those needs. This direct business model is behind Dell's accession to market leadership. It eliminates retailers that add unnecessary time and cost, or can diminish the company's understanding of customer expectations. It allows Dell to build every system to order and offer customers individually configured systems based on industry-standard technology at competitive prices. And it also enables the company to introduce the latest relevant technology much more quickly than competitors with slow-moving, indirect distribution channels, turning over inventory every three days on average.

Dell is enhancing and broadening the fundamental competitive advantages of the direct model by applying the efficiencies of the Internet to its entire business. Dell led commercial migration to the Internet, launching www.dell.com in 1994 and adding e-commerce capability in 1996. The following year, Dell became the first company to record $1 million in online sales. Today, Dell operates one of the highest volume Internet commerce sites in the world, receiving more than one billion page requests per quarter at 80 country sites in 27 languages/dialects and 31 currencies.

Dell is increasingly realizing Internet-associated efficiencies throughout its business, including procurement, customer support and relationship management. At www.dell.com, customers may review, configure and price systems within Dell's entire product line, order systems online, and track orders from manufacturing through shipping. At valuechain.dell.com, Dell shares information with its suppliers on a range of topics, including product quality and inventory. Dell also uses the Internet to deliver industry-leading customer services. For instance, thousands of business and institutional customers worldwide use Dell's Premier Dell.com Web pages to do business with the company online.

From its beginnings in the PC business, Dell has continually expanded into most of the other hardware segments.

■ PowerEdge servers have made Dell the fastest-growing company in the category since their introduction in September 1996. In 2001, Dell has become No. 1 in the U.S. for standard Intel architecture server shipments. Dell servers offer affordable performance, reliability and scalability for all business-critical applications, including e-mail, database and high-performance computing environments.

■ PowerVault and Dell-EMC storage products offer customers a comprehensive range of solutions with exceptional manageability, flexible interoperability and solid performance to protect their vital information today, while offering the scalability to expand when their data requirements grow.

Dell Selected Financial Data (in $ million)

Year ended February 1,	2000	2001	2002
Net Revenue of which:	25,265	31,888	31,168
Desktops	14,654	16,901	16,519
Enterprise	4,295	5,740	5,922
Portables	6,316	9,248	8,727
Inventory turnover (times)	n.a.	59	n.a.
Costs of products sold and services	20,047	25,445	25,661
Earnings from operations	2,457	2,768	2,271
Net Earnings	1,860	2,310	1,780
Shares outstanding (in million)	2,536	2,582	2,602

Note: Stock quote at month end (in $):   December 1999: 51   December 2000: 17.44   December 2001: 27.18   Employees: 39,000

Source: Annual Report. Some data has been reclassified in order to preserve a consistent presentation throughout the case study.

- PowerConnect switches are standard-based network switches that connect computers and servers in small- to medium-sized networks or in the branch offices of larger organizations. PowerConnect offers enterprise-class features and reliability at a fraction of competitors' prices.
- OptiPlex desktops are developed for corporate and institutional customers who demand highly reliable, stable, manageable and easily serviced systems within networked environments. Industry-standard technology contributes to the first-rate dependability and low total cost of ownership of OptiPlex systems.
- Latitude notebooks meet the wide-ranging needs of business and organizations, including powerful performance, portability and flexibility. Commonality of peripheral modules and docking solutions help lower the total cost of ownership. From wireless-ready, highly expandable full-featured models to thin, light ultra-portable models, the Dell Latitude family is designed to meet the changing needs of business.
- Dell Precision workstations deliver the performance to run highly complex applications, such as three-dimensional computer-aided design, digital content creation, software development and financial/economic modeling. Customized to clients' needs with single or dual processors, Dell workstations offer high-performance technology, certified by leading application vendors, in affordable, state-of-the-art desktop and mobile solutions.
- Inspiron notebooks are targeted to customers who require high-performance computer systems at aggressive prices, along with industry-leading service and support. Typical customers are individuals or small-to-medium sized businesses that are looking for optimum performance for their investment.
- Dimension desktops are designed for small businesses and home users requiring fast technology turns and

high-performance computing. The product line commonly features the latest high-performance components on an award-winning platform.
- Dell monitors span entry-level to traditional and flat panel displays.
- Dell delivers a vast array of its own and of third-party peripherals such as cameras, projectors, software, memory, notebook accessories, printers and, from 2002 on, also handhelds.

Dell is the only company that has complete control over sourcing parts, assembling them, and delivering hardware directly to the customer. Its operation is the modern-day equivalent of Henry Ford's River Rouge automobile plant, where raw materials went in one end and cars came out the other—only Dell is global and virtual, with partners ranging from component suppliers to package-delivery firms.

Source: adapted from official company information and other publicly available information.

Exhibit 6: Sun Microsystems in 2001

Although Sun Microsystems (Sun) is often taken for a one of Silicon Valley's hip, young companies, it is in fact the last of the old computer makers. Besides Apple, Sun is the only important firm that has not adopted any part of the Wintel platform. It continues to design its own chips and write its own operating system, an anachronism in today's world. So far, Sun has stayed two steps ahead of the Wintel competition by continually moving upmarket, but that is getting harder to do. In the 20 years of its existence, Sun has been singularly focused on products and services for network computing. Network computing is based on the premise that the power of a single computer can be increased dramatically as it is interconnected with other computer systems for the purposes of communication and sharing of computing power. Sun's product line consists of computer systems and workstations, storage, software and associated services. Its customers use the products and services in a wide range of technical/ scientific and engineering applications to build mission-critical computing systems on which they operate all elements of their businesses.

Sun's products are based on several core technologies including Solaris^{TM} Operating Environment, UltraSPARC? (UltraSPARC Scalable Processor Architecture) microprocessor architecture, and the Java^{TM} programming language. Sun's business strategy is built around its single focus on network computing, the core elements of its strategy include:

- An end-to-end architecture that extends the common Java technology based programming environment from devices as small as smart cards and cell phones to large multi-million dollar servers
- On-going innovation in microprocessor architecture, systems design, and software to help ensure continuing technology leadership and resulting price-performance advantage
- Commitment to open public application programming interfaces
- A large partner community of commercial software developers, system integrators, and resellers to add value to Sun products and services and to extend its reach and expertise
- A direct sales organization for large customer accounts increasingly organized to deliver a single point of contact
- A mission-critical support organization staffed worldwide to help ensure high satisfaction and profitable use of its products

This strategy means that rather than offering the customer the cheapest server or storage array, Sun is focused on providing the combination of software and hardware that will give them the best value including: (1) minimize porting and migration costs when upgrading, and (2) maximize system uptime and availability.

Its leading-edge technologies provide the company with a competitive advantage in the marketplace, enabling it to develop and deliver more valuable systems technology that translates into better long-term profit margins on its products.

Across the company's business areas, the primary competitive differentiators for Sun's products are their price/performance, scalability and reliability.

- The Enterprise Systems Products group provides an integrated family of mid-range and high-end enterprise servers systems for mission critical and high-performance computing environments.

- The Volume Systems Products group provides entry enterprise servers, blade computing (management of a pool of modular, single board servers, as one computing environment, which allows companies to dynamically allocate and re-allocate resources to changing workloads) and workstations with low price point and high computing density for horizontally scalable environments (clusters of smaller servers). The entry servers deliver network computing in a compact package, with a range of options in processing power, form factor and scalability.
- The Processor and Network Products group develops UltraSPARC microprocessors, associated companion ASICS, and leading-edge Network and Cryptographic products and technologies. At the heart of Sun systems, these components deliver world-class performance.
- The Network Storage group directly, and through third party relationships, provides complete storage solutions for an end-to-end IT infrastructure, from the operating system to servers, storage, software, services, and support.
- The Software group designs, develops and brings to market the Solaris Operating Environment, the Java platform and Sun ONE middleware.
- The Sun Services group includes the design, implementation and operation of enterprise and Internet computing environments, systems integration and support, professional services and education.

Sun competes with systems manufacturers and resellers of systems based on the Wintel standard. Some of these firms compete aggressively on price and seek to maintain very low cost structures in order to increase their market share in the enterprise server market. This competition creates increased pressure, including pricing pressure, on Sun's workstation and lower-end server product lines. The company expects this competitive pressure to continue through 2003, with the anticipated releases of new software products from Microsoft and new microprocessors from Intel (64-bit Itanium).

As its business design is based on a competitive advantage and a resulting enhancement of its gross margins from investments in innovative technologies, Sun incurs higher fixed R&D costs as a percentage of revenues than many of its competitors. In addition, as a result of its investments in a significant direct sales force, the company incurs higher fixed selling costs as a percentage of revenue. To the extent that Sun is unable to develop and sell products with attractive gross margins in sufficient volumes, its earnings may therefore be materially adversely affected by its cost structure.

Source: adapted from official company information and other publicly available information.

Sun Microsystems Selected Financial Data (in $ million)

Year ended June 30,	2000	2001	2002
Net Revenue of which:	15,721	18,250	12,496
Computer Systems and Network Storage	12,841	14,196	8,574
Services	2,300	3,235	3,403
Costs of products sold and services	7,549	10,041	7,580
R&D	1,630	2,016	1,832
Selling, general and administrative	4,065	4,445	3,812
Inventory turnover (times)	14.1	9.9	6.7
Earnings from operations	2,393	1,311	−1,248
of which:			
Computer Systems and Network Storage	4,951	4,289	1,230
Services	472	711	896
Earnings before income taxes	2,771	1,548	−1,048
Net Earnings	1,854	927	−587
Shares outstanding (in million)	3,379	3,417	3,242

Note: Stock quote at month end (in $):   December 1999: 38.72   December 2000: 27.87   December 2001: 12.3   Employees: 39,000

Source: Form 10-K. Some data has been reclassified in order to preserve a consistent presentation throughout the case study.

Exhibit 7: IBM in 2001

IBM was making computers before present CEOs at its main rivals were even born. Yet, in the early 1990s, venerable 'Big Blue' had to struggle for survival as it had failed in the 1980s to acknowledge the rising threat of minicomputers to its predominant main-frame business. As IBM found itself increasingly on the wrong side of the market, some angry investors wanted to unlock shareholder wealth by breaking up the company into small 'Baby Blues'. Under the new management of Lou Gerstner, however, IBM was able to stage an impressive comeback by reinventing its business model based on the assumption that the future of the computer industry was not in computers, but in services. The company progessively pulled out of the consumer PC market and sold in 1999 its data network infrastructure and connectivity operations to AT&T. The company used its financial strength to fund an expensive push into IT outsourcing, an industry segment that it pioneered and that it continues to dominate.

The company's business model is relatively straightforward. IBM sells services, hardware and software. These offerings are bolstered by IBM's research and development capabilities. If a customer requires financing, IBM can provide that too. The fundamental strength of this business model is IBM's ability to assemble the optimal mix of these offerings to design tailored solutions for customers and to continue to win in the marketplace.

Organizationally, the company's major operations comprise a Global Services segment; three hardware product segments—Enterprise Systems, Personal and Printing Systems, and Technology; a Software segment; a Global Financing segment; and an Enterprise Investments seg-

ment. The segments are determined based on several factors, including customer base, homogeneity of products, technology and delivery channels.

The Global Services segment is the world's largest IT services provider, supporting computer hardware and software products and providing professional services to help customers of all sizes realize the full value of IT. The segment provides value through three primary lines of business:

- Strategic Outsourcing Services creates business value through long-term strategic partnerships with customers by taking on responsibility for their processes and systems.
- Business Innovation Services provides business/industry consulting and end to end e-business implementation of such offerings as Supply Chain Management, Customer Relationship Management, Enterprise Resource Planning and Business Intelligence.
- Integrated Technology Services offers customers a single IT partner to manage multivendor IT systems' complexity in today's e-business environment including such traditional offerings as Product Support, Business Recovery Services, Site and Connectivity Services, and Systems Management and Networking Services.

Learning Services supports the three primary lines of business and helps customers design, develop and deploy curricula to educate their employees. The Global Services segment is uniquely suited to integrate the full range of the company's and key industry participants' capabilities, including hardware, software, services and research.

The Enterprise Systems segment produces powerful multipurpose computer servers that operate many open-network-based applications simultaneously for multiple users. They perform high-volume transaction processing and serve data to personal systems and other end-user devices. The servers are the engines behind the bulk of electronic business transactions, including e-commerce. The segment also includes system-level product businesses such as the company's disk storage products, tape subsystems and the company's storage area networking products. In network storage, IBM had in 2001 a global market share of about 9 percent.

The Personal and Printing Systems segment produces general-purpose computer systems, advanced function printers, and point-of-sale solutions. Major business units include PCs, Retail Store Solutions, and Printing Systems. Major brands include ThinkPad mobile systems and NetVista.

The Technology segment provides components such as semiconductors and HDDs for use in the company's products and for sale to original equipment manufacturers (OEM). IBM has one of the world's largest and most sophisticated semiconductor design and manufacturing operations. The company continues to receive more U.S. patents each year than any other corporation.

The Software segment delivers operating systems for the company's servers and middleware for IBM and non-IBM platforms. IBM is the leading global provider of middleware, which accounts for 80 percent of the segments net revenue.

The Global Financing segment is the world's largest provider of financing services for IT. The segment provides lease and loan financing that enables the company's customers to acquire complete IT and e-business solutions—hardware, software and services—provided by the company and its business partners. Global Financing, as a reliable source of capital for the distribution channel, also provides the company's business partners with customized commercial financing for inventory, accounts receivable and term loans, helping them manage their cash flow, invest in infrastructure and grow their business. Global Financing also selectively participates in syndicated loan activities.

The Enterprise Investments segment provides industryspecific IT solutions, supporting the Hardware, Software and Global Services segments of the company. The segment develops unique products designed to meet specific marketplace requirements and to complement the company's overall portfolio of products. As IBM's strategy is to outsource the manufacturing of customized systems to third parties, the segment's importance is declining.

Having successfully transformed itself from a mainframe manufacturer into a full-service IT powerhouse, IBM has no peer at the high end of the market. Acknowledging the industry's tendency to common platforms and open standards, the company prepares the future by shifting more and more resources to the development of standard-based high-end solutions. For example, about 1,000 IBM developers, more than at any other software or hardware company are working on the open-source Linux operating system.

Source: adapted from official company information and other publicly available information.

IBM Selected Financial Data (in $ million)

Year ended December 31,	1999	2000	2001
Net Revenue of which:	87,548	88,396	85,866
Global Services	32,130	33,149	34,947
Hardware	37,908	37,745	33,402
(Enterprise Systems)	13,834	14,194	13,743
(Personal and Printing Systems)	15,593	15,098	11,982
Software	12,694	12,641	12,966
Costs of products sold and services	55,994	56,342	54,084
R&D	5,505	5,374	5,290
Selling, general and administrative	16,294	17,535	17,197
Inventory turnover (times)	n.a.	7.9	7.8
Earnings from operations	9,755	9,145	9,295
Earnings before icome taxes	9,971	10,891	10,458
of which:			
Global Services	4,464	4,517	5,161
Hardware	2,058	2,702	1,303
(Enterprise Systems)	1,584	1,922	1,830
(Personal and Printing Systems)	25	101	−153
Software	3,099	2,793	3,168
Net Earnings	7,712	8,093	7,723
Shares outstanding (in million)	1,800	1,743	1,723

Note: Stock quote at month end (in $):   December 1999: 107.22   December 2000: 84.49   December 2001: 120.24   Employees: 320,000

Source: Annual Report. Some data has been reclassified in order to preserve a consistent presentation throughout the case study.

Exhibit 8: EMC in 2001

EMC is a company entirely focused on information storage. More than 70 percent of its sales are derived from cutting-edge network systems that help customers' to reduce their costs through resource consolidation and to manage complexity through a single point of control. Its world class products and skills have made EMC the global leader in the industry it pioneered some twenty years ago. According to a recent survey, IT professionals responsible for purchasing storage ranked the company number one in product innovation, product reliability, after-sale service, service-level guarantees, and interoperability standards. EMC also was deemed overall customer satisfaction leader by a wide margin. As the research director responsible for the survey told *Forbes* magazine, "EMC has the highest ratings we've ever seen—in any customer survey, for any company, ever."

The company's strategy is to constantly devise better, simpler, more cost-effective ways to safeguard, preserve, move, copy, view, analyze, and manage information. To that end, EMC does pioneering work in several areas. By automating more and more of the labor-intensive, error-prone processes involved in managing information, the company works toward the goal of enabling a single person to manage 1,000 terabytes of information by the end of this decade—or 100 times more than can be handled today. Another path breaking project is the development of self-healing storage environments that will guarantee that critical business applications and information are always available to users—100 percent application uptime. By and large, EMC's investment in intelligent storage R&D is several times larger than the amount dedicated by its closest competitor.

In information storage software, EMC has a multi-year lead over its competitors. The company's software revenues grew 75 percent to $1.44 billion during 2000, making EMC one of the largest application software companies in the world. To extend this leading position, EMC intends to invest $750 million in software development 2001 alone, while also leveraging the combined engineering and product capital of the five software companies acquired during 2000.

Source: adapted from official company information.

Exhibit 9: NEC Corporation in 2001

NEC is a leading provider of systems, components, services, and integrated solutions for computing and communications applications. The company was formed in the 1920s as a joint venture between Western Electric Company of the United States and two Japanese individuals. Initially, NEC acted as a sales agent for telephone equipment manufactured by Western Electric, but it soon started production of similar equipment in Japan. As early as in the 1980s, the company adopted a global strategy with 50 foreign subsidiaries and affiliates to conduct its diversified manufacturing and sales operations closer to its customers. Yet in 2001, NEC is still an essentially Japanese-focused company with 73 percent of net sales booked in the domestic market. The company is committed to the development of its technology capability by reinvesting a constant share of its net revenues in R&D (6.3 percent in 1999 and 6.4 percent in 2000).

In April 2000, NEC reorganized its operations by creating three in-house companies, each of which focuses on serving the needs of a particular market and customer base.

EMC Selected Financial Data (in $ million)

Year ended December 31,	1999	2000	2001
Net Revenue of which:	6,716	8,873	7,091
Storage Systems	5,983	7,967	5,916
Services	733	906	1,175
Costs of products sold and services	3,258	3,730	4,247
R&D	573	783	929
Selling, general and administrative	1,436	2,103	2,214
Earnings from operations	1,241	2,257	−698
Earnings before icome taxes	1,357	2,441	−577
Net Earnings	1,011	1,782	−508
Shares outstanding (in million)	2,061	2,164	2,211

Note: Stock quote at month end (in $):   December 1999: 54.62   December 2000: 66.5   December 2001: 13.44

Source: Annual Report. Some data has been reclassified in order to preserve a consistent presentation throughout the case study.

■ IT Solutions delivers highly reliable Internet-related services and other computing solutions to enterprise, government, and individual customers by providing software, hardware, and services necessary to design, integrate, and operate these elements. The products and services of the in-house company include systems integration services, software, Internet-related services, and maintenance and customer support services, as well as PCs, where it is the leading supplier in Japan. It also offers mainframe computers, UNIX and PC servers, workstations, supercomputers, and storage systems. IT Solutions works with HP to develop servers that employ Intel's 64-bit processors, allowing for faster processing speeds. The in-house company also teamed up with Intel to create the Express 5800 series of PC servers and workstations, running a Windows operating system. The combination of de facto open platform components and a Windows operating system results in a low cost fault-tolerant solution.

■ Network Solutions designs and provides wireline network infrastructure, mobile and wireless network infrastructure, and mobile terminals, which enable its customers, primarily network service providers, to build and operate their networks with a high degree of service quality and reliability and in a cost-effective manner. The in-house company's products include optical network systems, switching systems, IP network systems, mobile and wireless network systems, and mobile terminals.

■ Electron Devices is a leading provider of semiconductors, displays, and other electronic components used in computers, communications products, digital consumer electronic products, and automobiles.

The size and number of NEC's competitors vary across its product and service segments. They may have greater financial, personnel, and other resources than NEC has in a particular market or overall. Competitors with greater financial resources may be able to offer lower prices, additional products or services or other incentives that NEC cannot match or offer. These competitors may be in a stronger position to respond quickly to new technologies and may be able to undertake more extensive marketing campaigns. They may also adopt more aggressive pricing policies and make more attractive offers to potential customers, employees, and strategic partners. They may make strategic acquisitions or establish cooperative relationships among themselves or with third parties to increase their ability to gain market share.

Further, some of NEC's competitors are currently selling commercial quantities of products that NEC has not begun to market. By being able to offer these products in commercial quantities before NEC does, its competitors may establish significant market share and positioning that NEC may be unable to overcome once it begins marketing that product.

Source: adapted from official company information.

NEC Selected Financial Data (in $ million)

Year ended March 31,	2000	2001	2002
Net Revenue of which:	44,823	42,934	41,077
IT Solutions	20,395	17,686	17,789
Network Solutions	13,722	14,558	15,759
Electron Devices	10,085	9,753	6,789
Costs of products sold and services	30,220	31,596	31,559
Selling, general and administrative	10,930	9,869	9,961
Earnings from operations	988	1,470	−451
Earnings before income taxes of which:	269	733	−3,712
IT Solutions	754	667	604
Network Solutions	512	660	427
Electron Devices	440	542	−1,192
Net Earnings	90	449	−2,512
Shares outstanding (in million)	1,627	1,853	1,668

Note: Stock (ADR) quote (in $):   1999, full year average: 16.87   2000, 4th quarter average: 20.25   2001, 4th quarter average: 10.95
Employees: 150,000

Source: Form 20-F. The exchange rates used to convert Yen data correspond to the weighted average rate for the relevant 12 months period. Some data has been reclassified in order to preserve a consistent presentation throughout the case study.

Case 3–10: Newell Company: The Rubbermaid Opportunity*[1]

In October 1998, the Board of Directors of the Newell Company was considering a proposed merger with Rubbermaid Incorporated to form a new company, Newell Rubbermaid Inc. The transaction would be accomplished through a tax-free exchange of shares under which Rubbermaid shareholders would receive Newell shares valued at approximately $5.8 billion at a ratio which represented a 49 percent premium on Rubbermaid's current stock price. At the time of the transaction the annual revenues of Newell and Rubbermaid were, respectively, about $3.2 billion and $2.4 billion. If approved, the agreement would mark a quantum step in Newell's growth, but, equally, it would pose a formidable challenge to the company's demonstrated capacity to integrate and strengthen its acquisitions.

Newell: Riding the Acquisition Tiger

In 1998, the Newell Company had revenues of $3.7 billion distributed across three major product groupings: Hardware and Home Furnishings ($1.8 billion), Office Products ($1.0 billion), and Housewares ($.9 billion). Over the past ten years the company had achieved a compound sales growth rate of 13 percent, an earnings per share growth rate of 16 percent and an average annual return on beginning shareholder equity of 21 percent. These results were consistent with Newell's formal goals of achieving earnings per share growth of 15 percent per year and maintaining a return on beginning equity of 20 percent or above. Further financial details on Newell are given in Exhibit 1.

Acquisitions

Acquisitions were the foundation of Newell's growth strategy. Given the relatively slow growth of the product markets in which it chose to operate, Newell's corporate goal for internal growth was only 3 percent to 5 percent per annum—with internal growth being defined as the growth of businesses that Newell had owned for over two years. Actual internal growth in the past five years had averaged about 5 percent per annum. This put a premium on acquisitions if Newell was to meet its aggressive growth targets. Indeed, over $2 billion of its current sales were the result of over 20 acquisitions made since 1990.

Newell's approach to acquisition was both aggressive and disciplined. Its targeted acquisition candidates were generally mature businesses with 'unrealized profit potential' which further passed a number of screening criteria, including having a:

- Strategic fit with existing businesses—which implied product lines that were low in technology, fashion and seasonal content and were sold through mass distribution channels
- Number one or two position in their served markets and established shelf space with major retailers
- Long product life cycle
- Potential to reach Newell's standard of profitability, which included goals for operating margins of 15 percent, and Sales, General and Administrative costs at a maximum of 15 percent

*Professor Joseph N. Fry prepared this case solely to provide material for class discussion. The author does not intend to illustrate either effective or ineffective handling of a managerial situation. The author may have disguised certain names and other identifying information to protect confidentiality.
Ivey Management Services prohibits any form of reproduction, storage or transmittal without its written permission. This material is not covered under authorization from CanCopy or any reproduction rights organization. To order copies or request permission to reproduce materials, contact Ivey Publishing, Ivey Management Services, c/o Richard Ivey School of Business, The University of Western Ontario, London, Ontario, Canada, N6A 3K7; phone (519) 661-3208; fax (519) 661-3882; e-mail cases@ivey.uwo.ca.
Copyright © 2000, Ivey Management Services Version: (A) 2000-06-05 One time permission to reproduce granted by Ivey management Services on Jan. 13, 2005.

Exhibit 1   Selected Financial Information For Newell Company, 1996–1998 ($000)

	To End Q3/98	12/31/97	To End Q3/97	12/31/96
Net sales	**$2,650,263**	**$3,336,233**	**$2,395,037**	**$2,972,839**
Cost of products sold	1,786,640	2,259,551	1,631,253	2,020,116
Selling, general and administrative expenses	404,882	497,739	365,123	461,802
Goodwill amortization and other	40,502	31,882	22,872	23,554
Operating Income	418,239	547,061	375,789	467,367
Interest expense	43,966	76,413	54,363	58,541
Other, non-operating, net	(213,373)*	(14,686)	(12,862)	(19,474)
Profit before tax	587,546	485,334	334,288	428,300
Income taxes	250,740	192,187	132,373	169,258
Net Income	**$336,806**	**$293,147**	**$201,915**	**$259,042**
Current assets	1,767,370	1,433,694		1,148,464
Property, plant and equipment	834,486	711,325		567,880
Trade names, goodwill, other	2,001,862	1,559,594		1,342,086
Total Assets	**4,603,718**	**4,011,314**		**3,058,430**
Current liabilities	1,061,675	714,479		665,884
Long-term debt	912,650	786,793		685,608
Other non-current liabilities	243,862	285,241		206,916
Convertible preferred securities	500,000	500,000		
Shareholders' Equity	1,885,531	1,725,221		1,500,022
Total Liabilities and Shareholders' Equity	**4,603,718**	**4,011,314**		**3,058,430**
Approximate common shares outstanding (000)	173,000	163,300		162,000
Earnings per share (fully diluted)		$1.80		$1.60
Stock Price $High/Low	$54/37	$43/30		$33/25

*Primarily gain from sale of Black & Decker holdings.

Source: Company Financial Reports.

The size of the acquisitions varied. In 1996, Newell made one acquisition for $46 million cash, in 1997, three material acquisitions for $762 million cash and in 1998 to date, four material acquisitions for about $413 million cash. Once acquired, the new companies were integrated into the Newell organization by means of an established process that had come to be called "Newellization."

Newellization

Newellization was the profit improvement and productivity enhancement process employed to bring a newly acquired business up to Newell's high standards of productivity and profit. The Newellization process was pursued through a number of broadly applicable steps, including the:

- Transfer of experienced Newell managers into the acquired company
- Simplification and focusing of the acquired business's strategy and the implementation of Newell's established manufacturing and marketing know-how and programs

- Centralization of key administrative functions including data processing, accounting, EDI, and capital expenditure approval
- Inauguration of Newell's rigorous, multi-measure, divisional operating control system

Newell management claimed that the process of Newellization was usually completed in two or three years.

Continuing Operations

A summary of Newell's product groups and major lines is outlined in Table 1. These products were, for the most part, sold through mass merchandisers. In 1997, Wal-Mart accounted for 15 percent of Newell's sales; the other top ten Newell customers (each with less than 10 percent of Newell sales) were Kmart, Home Depot, Office Depot, Target, J.C. Penney, United Stationers, Hechtinger, Office Max and Lowe's. International sales had increased from 8 percent of total sales in 1992 to an expected 22 percent in 1998 as Newell followed customers and opportunities into Mexico, Europe and the Americas.

Table 1   **Newell Product Lines, 1998**

Housewares	Hardware and Home Furnishings	Office Products
Aluminum Cookware and Bakeware Glassware Hair Accessories	Window Treatments Home Storage Picture frames Hardware	Markers and Writing Products Office Storage

Newell's fundamental competitive strategy, which applied to all of its operations, was to differentiate on the basis of superior service to its mass merchandise customers. For Newell, superior service included industry-leading quick response and on-time, in-full delivery, the ability to implement sophisticated EDI tie-ins with its customers extending to vendor-managed inventories, and the provision of marketing and merchandising programs for product categories that encompassed good, better and best lines.

Organization

Newell centralized certain key administrative functions such as data management (including order-fulfillment-invoice activities), divisional coordination and control, and financial management. Otherwise, the presidents of the company's 18 product divisions were responsible for the full scope of manufacturing, marketing and sales activities for their product lines and for the performance of their businesses.

Divisional coordination and control were facilitated by the fundamental similarities of the Newell businesses. These similarities made it possible for corporate level management to develop a common pool of managers and know-how that could be transferred relatively easily from one division to another. The business similarities also made it possible for corporate management to apply a common set of detailed operating standards and controls across the businesses, and to play a knowledgeable role in reviewing divisional progress and plans. Corporate management held monthly reviews (called brackets meetings) with divisional presidents to track multiple operating and financial measures and to ensure that appropriate attention was given to items that were off budget. As a result, divisional management operated in a goldfish bowl under high pressure, but they were paid very well for meeting their targets.

Outlook

In Newell's view, the company's adherence to a highly focused strategy had established a sustainable competitive advantage for the corporation and this, coupled with abun-

dant acquisition opportunities and internal growth momentum, would support the continuing achievement of its financial goals.

Rubbermaid: A Fallen Icon

Rubbermaid was a well known, and, for several decades, a renowned manufacturer of a wide range of plastic products ranging from children's toys through housewares to commercial items. From 1986 through 1995 Rubbermaid was ranked among the top 10 in *Fortune*'s list of America's most admired companies, including the No. 1 spot in 1993 and 1994. But by March 1998 Rubbermaid had fallen to No. 100. After a wonderful run of growth and profitability, extending as far back as the 1960s, the company had clearly hit a rough patch.

Rubbermaid earned its early reputation by setting aggressive goals for 15 percent growth in revenues and profits and then, by and large, meeting its targets. Under the intense and very personal management of Stanley Gault, an ex-senior executive at General Electric and CEO and chairman of Rubbermaid from 1980 to 1991, the company was pressed to broaden its product line through development and acquisition and to meet demanding operating targets. From propitious beginnings Rubbermaid became an ubiquitous brand and a Wall Street darling — with sales and profits, respectively, at the end of Gault's tenure of $1.7 billion and $162 million.

Rubbermaid's earnings momentum continued into the early years of Gault's successor, Wolfgang Schmidt, but the good times were to be short-lived. In 1994[2] Rubbermaid was hit by a doubling of plastic resin prices. The company's clumsy reactions to this shock revealed a number of accumulating problems. *Fortune* enumerated them in a 1995 article:[3]

- Customer relations: Rubbermaid angered its most important retail buyers with the heavy-handed way it has passed along its ballooning costs. Some are so angry that they have given more shelf space to competitors.
- Operations: Although it excels in creativity, product quality, and merchandising, Rubbermaid is showing

itself to be a laggard in more mundane areas such as modernizing machinery, eliminating unnecessary jobs, and making deliveries on time.

- Competition: It has been slow to recognize that other housewares makers—once a bunch of no-names who peddled junk—have greatly improved over the past half dozen years. The premium prices that Rubbermaid charges over its rivals have grown too large, and customers are turning away.
- Culture: The company's extraordinary financial targets . . . seem unrealistic—and straining to reach them is proving increasingly troublesome. Some of the friction between Rubbermaid and its customers can be traced to Rubbermaid's voracious appetite for growth.

Rubbermaid's profits peaked in 1994 at $228 million. In 1995 sales were up 8 percent but the company took a restructuring charge of $158 million pre-tax and net earnings fell to $60 million. The restructuring charges were taken in anticipation of a two-year program designed to reduce costs, improve operating efficiencies and accelerate growth. In 1997, Rubbermaid reported[4] that the realignment activities were substantially complete and that the company "has or initiated closure of all nine locations slated for closure in the plan, completed the associated reductions, and achieved the estimated annual savings of $50 million anticipated in the 1995 program." Unfortunately, this action did not have a material effect on sales, which remained essentially flat, and operating profits, which dipped somewhat, as detailed in the financial summary given in Exhibit 2. Thus, early in 1998, Rubbermaid announced another restructuring charge, which it estimated would reach at least $200 million pre-tax, to fund a program that would include centralizing global procurement and consolidating manufacturing and distribution worldwide.

Rubbermaid Lines of Business

In 1998, Rubbermaid manufactured and sold over 5,000 products[5] under four key brand names:

Exhibit 2   Selected Financial Information For Rubbermaid, 1995–1998 ($000).

	To End Q3/98	12/31/97	To End Q3/97	12/31/96	12/31/95
Net sales	$1,936,829	$2,399,710	$1,825,416	$2,354,980	$2,344,170
Cost of products sold	1,383,564	1,748,424	1,327,990	1,649,520	1,673,232
Selling, general and administrative expenses	353,805	416,641	314,229	432,063	402,586
Operating Income	199,460	234,645	183,197	273,397	268,352
Interest expense	27,795	35,762	28,463	24,348	10,260
Restructuring Costs	73,740	16,000	16,000		158,000
Other, non-operating, net	(23,749)	(51,032)	(49,729)	4,046	4,457
Income taxes	42,586	91,370	77,717	92,614	35,863
Net Income	$79,088	$142,536	$110,746	$152,398	$59,772
Current assets	952,841	816,204		856,720	
Other assets	445,995	399,716		475,346	
Property, plant and equipment	784,228	707,974		721,914	
Total Assets	2,183,064	1,923,984		2,053,980	
Current liabilities	802,231	567,084		742,841	
Long-term debt	152,556	153,163		154,467	
Other non-current liabilities	171,302	153,385		142,992	
Shareholders' equity	1,056,885	1,050,262		1,013,700	
Total Liabilities and Shareholders' Equity	2,183,064	1,923,984		2,053,980	
Approximate common shares outstanding (000)		149,900		151,000	158,800
Earnings per share (fully diluted)		$0.95		$1.01	$0.38
Stock Price $High/Low		$30/22		$30/22	$34/25

Source: Company Financial Reports.

- Rubbermaid: a wide range of household utility products encompassing five categories (Kitchen, Home Organization, Health Care, Cleaning, and Hardware/Seasonal) and 23 product lines.
- Graco: children's products in six product lines focusing on baby strollers and related items.
- Little Tikes: juvenile products, with 11 product lines focusing on toys and furniture.
- Curver: a European-based home products business with revenues of $180 million, acquired at the beginning of 1998.

Rubbermaid's international sales and operations had been growing in recent years as it followed its customers abroad. The Curver acquisition increased foreign sales, including exports from the U.S., to about 25 percent of total revenues, helping the firm along the path to its goal of 30 percent by 2000.

Rubbermaid Strategy

Rubbermaid's strategy reflected an uneasy balance of not necessarily consistent ambitions. The 15 percent growth goals of the past had disappeared from public statements, but there was no question that the company remained aggressive in its goals and optimistic about its prospects. To achieve its aims Rubbermaid relied on a multi-faceted competitive strategy. It wanted, at once, to be a company with a:

- Strong consumer franchise based on unique product features, quality and rapid innovation, and on brand recognition and aggressive advertising. Rubbermaid had, for example, set a goal that 10 percent of each year's sales should come from new, high value products and it had reduced new product time to market from 20 plus months in the 1980s to six months currently, with a goal of four months by 2000.
- Low-cost sourcing, production, and fulfillment base. The company was in the process, for example, of cutting product variations by 45 percent and consolidating its supplier base from 9,000 to less than 2,000 vendors.
- Reliable and efficient supplier to mass merchandisers. Rubbermaid was moving, for example, to scheduling manufacturing by customer order and to just-in-time service and continuous replenishment of its best selling items.

There was a tension at work behind these aims. In its 1996 Annual Report Rubbermaid noted that its market was at a point of inflection, in which the control of information was shifting from mass marketers to individual consumers. In this context Rubbermaid claimed that it would strike a

new balance in its strategies, to continue to lead in innovation while becoming a low cost producer. Similarly, in its 1997 Annual Report, the company noted that in a squeeze of higher costs and lower retail prices it was making bold moves to become the low-cost producer, while retaining world-class quality and innovation. Finally, another "point of inflection": in his 1997 Letter to Shareholders, Wolfgang Schmidt promised that, "with the initiatives of the past two years and the opportunities ahead, we are at the inflection point from which we can combine our financial strength and innovation capabilities with a more favorable cost climate to generate stronger shareholder returns."

The Outline of a Deal

Newell's appetite for all of Rubbermaid might have been whetted with its $247 million acquisition of Rubbermaid's Office products division in 1977, adding about $160 million of annualized revenues to Newell's developing office products line of business. Whatever the stimulus, talks soon began on a total combination of the two firms.

Negotiations led to a provisional agreement under which Rubbermaid shareholders would receive 0.7883 shares of Newell common stock for each share of Rubbermaid common stock that they owned. Based on Newell's closing price of $49.07 on October 20, 1998 this represented $38.68 per Rubbermaid share or a premium on 49 percent over Rubbermaid's closing price of $25.88. Under this arrangement Newell would issue approximately 118 million shares of common stock to Rubbermaid shareholders and would assume approximately $500 million in net debt. Rubbermaid shareholders would end up holding approximately 40 percent of the combined company. The transaction represented a tax-free exchange of shares and would be accounted for as a pooling of interests.

Newell management forecast[6] that, as soon as the transaction was completed, they would begin the "Newellization" process and improve Rubbermaid's operating efficiencies to achieve 98 percent on-time and line-fill performance and a minimum 15 percent pretax margin. They also expected revenue and operating synergies through the leveraging of Newell Rubbermaid's brands, innovative product development, improved service performance, stronger combined presence in dealing with common customers, broader acquisition opportunities, and an increased ability to serve European markets. They forecast that by 2000 these efforts and opportunities would produce increases over anticipated 1998 results of $300 million to $350 million in operating income for the combined company.

Exhibit 3   Simple Pro Forma Financial Information For Newellrubbermaid, ENDQ3–1998 ($000)

	Newell Q3/97–Q3/98	Rubbermaid Q3/97–Q3/98	Simple Pro Forma NewellRubbermaid Q3/97–Q3/98
Net sales	3,591,459	2,511,123	6,102,582
Cost of products sold	2,414,938	1,803,998	4,218,936
Selling, general and administrative expenses	537,498	456,217	993,715
Goodwill amortization and other	49,512		49,512
Operating Income	589,511	250,908	840,419
Interest expense	66,016	35,094	101,110
Other, non-operating, net	(215,197)*	48,688	(166,509)
Profit before tax	738,692	167,126	905,818
Income taxes	310,554	56,239	366,793
Net Income	428,138	110,887	539,025
Balance Sheet as of End Q3/98			
Current assets	1,767,370	952,841	2,720,211
Property, plant and equipment	834,486	784,228	1,618,714
Trade names, goodwill, other	2,001,862	445,995	2,447,857
Total Assets	4,603,718	2,183,064	6,786,782
Current liabilities	1,061,675	802,231	1,863,906
Long-term debt	912,650	152,556	1,065,206
Other non-current liabilities	243,862	171,302	415,164
Convertible preferred securities	500,000		500,000
Shareholders' Equity	1,885,531	1,056,885	2,942,416
Total Liabilities and Shareholders' Equity	4,603,718	2,183,064	6,786,782
Approximate common shares outstanding (000)	173,000	150,000	291,000
Earnings per share (fully diluted)	$2.47	$0.74	$1.85

*Primarily gain from sale of Black & Decker holdings.

Source: Estimates based on Company Financial Reports.

Notes

[1]   This case has been written on the basis of published sources only. Consequently, the interpretation and perspectives presented in this case are not necessarily those of Newell Company or any of its employees.

[2]   Materials accounted for between 45 and 50 percent of Rubbermaid's net sales.

[3]   Lee Smith, "Rubbermaid Goes Thump," *Fortune*, October 2, 1995.

[4]   Rubbermaid Annual Report, 1997.

[5]   In 1997 Rubbermaid had sold its Office Product business to Newell for a $134 million pretax gain, which it promptly offset by a one-time charge of $ 81 million for asset impairment related to acquisitions.

[6]   Newell Press release, October 21, 1998.

Case 3–11: Cooper Industries' Corporate Strategy (A)*

The business of Cooper is value-added manufacturing.

—Cooper Industries' management philosophy

Manufacturing may not be glamorous, but we know a lot about it.

—Robert Cizik, Chairman, President and CEO

Cooper Industries, a company more than 150 years old, spent most of its history as a small but reputable maker of engines and compressors to propel natural gas through pipelines. In the 1960s, the firm's leaders decided to expand the company to lessen its dependence on the capital expenditures of the cyclical natural gas business. During the next 30 years, the company acquired more than 60 manufacturing companies that dramatically increased the size and scope of Cooper Industries (Exhibits 1 and 2). Through a process that both insiders and outsiders called "Cooperization," the company welded a group of "independent, over-the-hill companies into a highly efficient, profitable, competitive business."[1]

By 1988, the diversified industrial products company derived $4.3 billion in annual revenues from manufacturing 2 million items. Cooper's products ranged from 10¢ fuses to $3 million turbine compressor sets marketed under an array of brand names, the most famous of which was Crescent wrenches. "We decided a long time ago," said Robert Cizik, chairman, president, and CEO, "that if we could do an outstanding job at the unglamorous part by making necessary products of exceptional quality, then we could be successful indeed."[2]

In early 1989, Cooper Industries tested this philosophy when it launched a $21-a-share, $825 million tender offer for Champion Spark Plug. The Cooper bid trumped a $17.50-a-share bid by Dana Corp., a $4.9 billion auto-parts manufacturer. Although Champion had a well-known brand name and worldwide manufacturing facilities, it faced a shrinking market for spark plugs as the auto industry shifted to smaller engines. In response to the declining market, Champion's aggressive attempts to diversify into other automotive product lines had failed, and 1988 profits had fallen to $24 million. At 25 times 1988 EBIT, Cooper's bid was highly risky.

Company History

In 1833, Charles and Elias Cooper built an iron foundry in Mount Vernon, Ohio. C&E Cooper evolved in stride with the Industrial Revolution, making first a steam powered Corliss Engine that generated power for manufacturing plants and then switching by 1900 to produce natural gas compressors, which pumped gas through pipeline networks to customers. By 1920, Cooper was the recognized leader in pipeline compression equipment. However, another company, Bessemer, manufactured the engines that initially extracted the gas from underground wells. The compatibility of these two companies led to a merger that Cooper initiated in 1929.

By the late 1950s, Cooper-Bessemer was still a small company with about $50 million in annual sales. However, it had developed production expertise and had built a reputation for customer service in the natural gas industry. In 1957, the company elected 38-year-old Gene Miller as president. Miller, an engineer, was also only the second president outside the strong chain of Cooper family influence to lead the company.

In 1958, Cooper suffered a cyclical downturn, during which a corporate raider acquired enough Cooper shares to elect two board members. This experience had a profound impact on Miller, convincing him of the need to diversify. Said Miller, "We shouldn't dare limit ourselves to being engine builders, with perhaps a few sidelines to get us over the rough spots. We had to work toward a radical change in our outlook."[3] Miller planned to guide Cooper through a phase of corporate growth that would put the company in a wider range of product markets. Instrumental to Miller's strategy was growth and diversification through acquisitions.

Research Associate Toby Stuart prepared this case under the supervision of Professor David Collis as the basis for class discussion rather than to illustrate either effective or ineffective handling of an administrative situation.

Exhibit 1 Cooper Industries' Acquisitions

Year	Business	Description
1963	Ajax Iron Works	Engines and compressors
1964	Pennsylvania Pump & Compressor Co.	Process compressors
1966	Ken-Tool Manufacturing Co.	Tire changing tools
1967	Lufkin Rule Co.	Measuring tapes and wooden rules
1968	Crescent Niagara Corp.	Wrenches, pliers and screwdrivers
1970	Weller Electric Corp.	Electric soldering tools
1970	Dallas Airmotive, Inc.	Aircraft engine overhaul and service
1971	Howard Industries' Micro Grinder line	Motor-driven hobby tools
1972	Nicholson File Co.	Hand files
1973	Southwest Airmotive Co	Aircraft engine overhaul and service
1973	Xcelite Inc.	Screwdrivers, nutdrivers and pliers
1973	Nordberg Engine & Parts Services	Engine parts and services
1975	Standard Aircraft Equipment, Inc.	Aircraft engine overhaul and service
1976	J. Wiss & Sons Co.	Scissors, shears and snips
1978	Dallas Fixed Base Operations	Aircraft engine overhaul and service
1979	*Gardner-Denver Co.	Petroleum drilling and mining equipment
1980	Pinking Shears Corp. Product Line	Pinking shears
1980	Cannon Manufacturing Corp.	Ball valves
1980	McDonough's Plumb tool line	Hammers, axes and hatchets
1981	*Crouse-Hinds	Electrical distribution products, traffic control equipment, lighting fixtures, and electronic wire and cable
1981	*Kirsch Co.	Drapery, hardware and window coverings
1981	Pfaff & Kendall, and Hilldale Co.	Light poles
1982	Sullair Mining Equipment Corp.	Mining equipment
1982	Escadril Pump Product Line	Hydraulic pumps
1982	Westinghouse's Lighting Products	Lighting fixtures
1982	G.E.'s One-Piece Terminal Board Line	Terminal boards
1984	Risdon Corporation	Specialty wire products
1984	Turner Industries, Inc.	Portable propane torches
1984	Phalo's Computer Cable Line	Electronic cable
1985	*McGraw–Edison Co.	Electrical power distribution equipment, lighting fixtures and auto products
1985	OPI, Inc	Well service pumps
1985	The Breneman Co.	Roller shades
1987	H.K. Porter, Inc.	Bolt cutters
1987	*Joy Petroleum Equipment and Products	Pumps and compressors
1987	Underwriter's Safety Device Division	Fuseholders
1987	Joy Molded Rubber Products	Electrical connectors
1987	*Joy Industrial Compressor Group	Air and gas compressors
1988	Wiltshire File Pty. Ltd.	Hand files
1988	*Beswick Division	Power and electronic fuses
1988	B.C. Richards & Co. Pty.	Valves
1988	Macey Mining Services Pty. Ltd.	Electrical connectors
1988	*RTE Corp.	Electrical power distribution equipment
1988	Enterprise Engine Aftermarket Business	Engine repair parts

*Indicates transaction price in excess of $50 million.

To help him achieve these goals, Miller enlisted a leader with "current ideas" and expertise in finance. In 1961, Miller recruited Robert Cizik from Standard Oil, to join Cooper as executive assistant for corporate development. Cizik, a midwesterner, had earned a degree in accounting and economics from the University of Connecticut. After briefly working as an accountant, he joined the Air Force during the Korean War. He then entered the Harvard Business School and graduated as a Baker Scholar in 1958.

One of the first items on Miller's and Cizik's agenda was to free top managers and corporate board directors from the restraints of daily operations. To this end, Miller

Exhibit 2   Cooper Industries' Divestitures

Year	Business	Description
1971	Lufkin Dial Indicators Line	Measuring instruments
1973	Atkins Saw Product Line	Hand and band saws
1974	Ken–Tool Division	Tire changing tools and equipment
1975	C-B Southern	Compressor packaging
1977	Wiss Garden Tool	Garden Tools
1978	Danco Division	Plastic tool accessories
1981	Rotor Tool Division	Portable air and electric tools
1981	Vanguard Studios	Decorative accessories
1981	Cooper Airmotive	Airmotive engine overhaul and service
1982	Svenska Kirsch AB	Window hardware distributor
1982	Belden Distribution	Electrical products distributor
1982	Arrow–Hart Dano	Electrical coils
1983	EDCON	Seismic services
1983	Traffic Control Products	Traffic lights and systems
1984	Cooper Electronics Division	Electronics production equipment
1984	Arrow–Hart PPS/PNS Switches	Micro switches
1984	Belden Bit–Driver	Data transmission equipment
1984	Worldsbest Industries, Inc.	Infant furniture
1985	Weller Mini-Shop	Motor-driven hobby tools
1985	Bussmann Process Automation Prod. Line	Automated plating systems
1985	Chain Link Fence Business	Vinyl coated link fence
1985	Alex Stuart Design	Office furniture
1985	Carlton Santee	Real estate development
1986	Onan, Inc.	Portable electric generators
1986	Boker Knives Product Line	Pocket knives
1986	Gardner–Denver Company Africa Pty. Ltd.	Mining equipment
1986	Gleason Reel Division	Cable reels
1986	Battery, Inc.	Storage batteries
1986	Clarke	Floor cleaning equipment
1987	McGraw–Edison Service/Controls	Electric motor services/control
1987	Nicholson Sawblade Product Line	Sawblades
1987	SPI Lighting Product Line	Indirect office lighting
1988	Hughes W-K-M Do Brazil	Valve service and repair

and Cizik formally redesigned Cooper's structure. Under the new system, a small, ten-member policy-making management team headed the company, with a number of operating division managers underneath. Each division manager was responsible for his division's operations and profits and reported directly to President Miller. In the 1965 annual report, Miller called it a "relatively simple, yet highly flexible organizational structure."

To fortify the new structure, Miller and Cizik established clear lines of communication between the parent management team and the divisions, and among the divisions themselves. Cizik also established a uniform accounting system that included comprehensive planning and reporting techniques and capital investment procedures for each division.

In 1965, the company changed its name to Cooper Industries and, in 1967, moved its headquarters to Houston. Cooper was ready to make acquisitions, but

would not diversify wildly under the assumption that professional managers can oversee any kind of business, regardless of products, markets, or manufacturing processes. Cizik articulated his opposition to conglomeration, "I believe that to exercise [management control], management must thoroughly understand the company's activities—its production process, products, and markets; the laws that relate to its various activities; and the cultures and customs of the areas in which it operates."[4] Therefore, Cooper's leaders would set limits on the degree of diversification and the timing of their acquisitions. Cooper decided to pursue only companies that exhibited stable earnings, or earnings countercyclical to the oil and gas transmission industry. To ensure consistent earnings, Cooper would focus on products that served basic needs and that were manufactured with mature production technologies. Furthermore, Cooper would seek acquisition candidates that possessed its own strongest assets: it would concentrate on high-quality manufacturing companies preferably with market-leading positions.

Diversification began in 1967 when Cooper acquired the Lufkin Rule Company. Founded in Cleveland, Ohio, in 1869, Lufkin manufactured measuring rules for the lumber industry. By the 1960s, Lufkin was a market leader in measuring tapes and rules and produced premium-quality products used mainly by architects, carpenters, and home "do-it-yourselfers." When Lufkin came up for sale in 1967, Cooper believed the company and its hand tool business offered exactly the right kind of diversification. Virtually everyone recognized and used hand tools; they were also simple products whose designs and technology changed very slowly in an evolutionary fashion. "Few products are lower tech than a hammer," Cizik once explained.[5] Most importantly, with few market fluctuations in their sales, hand tools would help Cooper level its cyclical revenues, which were so closely attached to the natural gas industry.

Lufkin also brought to Cooper its recently appointed president, Bill Rector, who envisioned building the world's best hand-tool manufacturing group. Rector proposed adding a "tool basket" group to Cooper, which would be comprised of selected, high-quality, brand leaders joined under modern management. The hand-tool industry was comprised of hundreds of small companies, many of them a century old and still under the influence of their founding families. Cizik described these businesses as "third generation companies . . . suffering from a lack of capital investment and effective management."[6] The companies, many of them unprofitable, reinvested minimally and their manufacturing operations were high cost. Additionally, most hand-tool producers had extended their product line beyond their original best-selling items to provide something for everybody. In many instances, a company's money-losing hand tools outnumbered the profitable ones. In 1967, Cooper signed Rector on as a corporate vice president and provided him with capital to develop the Tool Group.

With Lufkin in place, Cooper quickly acquired two more hand-tool companies. The first, Crescent Niagara Corporation, was one of the most recognized names in the industry and made the well-known Crescent wrench. In 1968, Cooper acquired the unprofitable Crescent Niagara from a small group that had recently bought the company from its family owners. Two years later, Cooper bought Weller Manufacturing Corporation from family owners hoping to retire. Weller, the world's leading manufacturer of soldering tools, operated throughout North and South America and in Europe and gave Cooper's Tool Group added marketing power.

While retaining their original brand names, the three companies, Lufkin, Crescent, and Weller, were folded into the new Tool Group, headed by Rector. The Tool Group revamped the manufacturing operations of the acquisitions, updating processes and equipment and consolidating plants. In some cases, Cooper completely shut down manufacturing sites in the North and opened new plants in the South. The advantages of moving to the South, explained Cizik, were not solely in lower wages or even in new facilities. The key was to "move into an atmosphere where you're able to train your people from scratch. You're not locked into the practices of 20 years ago. You go to South Carolina, and even with the high cost of training and scrappage and breakage that you may have to take for two or three years, you get to a stage where you have a skilled work force doing things without an eye toward history."[7] While implementing manufacturing changes, Cooper also concentrated production on the most profitable and popular hand tools. Tools selling at low rates and most left-handed items were eliminated. At Lufkin alone, Cooper scaled back 3,500 different measuring rules and tapes to 500. In the more drastic case of the Nicholson Company, a maker of saws, rasps, and files that Cooper acquired in 1972, the product count was streamlined from 30,000 to 3,000. Among the products eliminated was a rasp for scraping burned toast.

By 1970, the Tool Group had set up headquarters in Apex, North Carolina, on the same site where Lufkin had opened a new state-of-the-art manufacturing plant. C. Baker Cunningham, another Harvard Business School graduate who had started at Cooper's corporate planning department in 1970, joined the Tool Group in 1971 as director of finance and introduced a new computer system to manage inventories, sales, shipping, and billing for all tool products. Also at Apex, the Tool Group centralized sales and marketing of all the hand tools. As the Tool Group expanded, it developed a small sales force by retaining only the best people from each acquisition and training them to promote all the products under the Cooper umbrella. After the first three companies had joined the Tool Group (Lufkin, Crescent, and Weller), the size of the combined sales force was smaller than Lufkin's original team. The consolidated force allowed international salespeople in a country where one brand name was particularly popular to use its leverage to sell other tools in the Tool Group (Exhibit 3).

Cooper's early experience with the Tool Group helped further define its diversification program. Cizik, who by 1969 was chief operating officer, felt that Cooper needed an approach to evaluate acquisitions within its manufacturing focus. Division managers would seek "complementary" acquisitions, defined as logical extensions of Cooper's existing products or markets. The corporate staff, meanwhile, would pursue "diversification" acquisitions. Together these acquisitions would fulfill Cooper's basic corporate growth objective (an increase in pre-tax earnings per share at a compound rate of 11%) and would improve the "quality" of earnings by adding stability. At the same time, Cizik emphasized that the process of

Exhibit 3

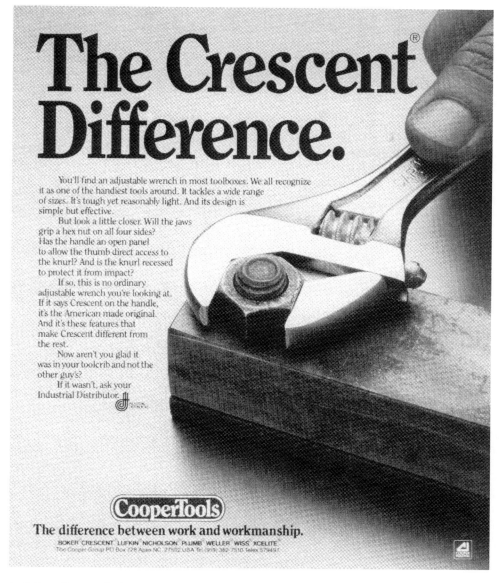

The Crescent® Difference.

You'll find an adjustable wrench in most toolboxes. We all recognize it as one of the handiest tools around. It tackles a wide range of sizes. It's tough yet reasonably light. And its design is simple but effective.

But look a little closer. Will the jaws grip a hex nut on all four sides? Has the handle an open panel to allow the thumb direct access to the knurl? And is the knurl recessed to protect it from impact?

If so, this is no ordinary adjustable wrench you're looking at. If it says Crescent on the handle, it's the American made original. And it's these features that make Crescent different from the rest.

Now aren't you glad it was in your toolcrib and not the other guy's?

If it wasn't, ask your Industrial Distributor.

CooperTools
The difference between work and workmanship.
BOKER CRESCENT LUFKIN NICHOLSON PLUMB WELLER WISS XCELITE
The Cooper Group PO Box 728 Apex NC 27502 USA Tel (919) 362-7510 Telex 579497

building Cooper Industries could involve subtraction as well. "People often think success is measured only by adding, adding, and more adding," said Cizik. "That's extremely important, but you have to keep examining what you have, and you can't be afraid to get rid of the things that have served their useful time."[8] Cooper divested 33 businesses between 1970 and 1988 (Exhibit 2).

Throughout the 1970s, "complementary" development continued in the Tool Group with four more acquisitions (Nicholson File in 1972, Xcelite nut runners in 1973, Wiss scissors in 1976, and Plumb hammers in 1980). The most important, Nicholson, was a file and saw maker based in Providence, Rhode Island, whose main asset was its expansive distribution system of independent hardware whole-

salers and industrial distributors that reached 53,000 retail outlets in 137 countries. Additionally, at Apex, a quasi-R&D group tested new products and designs for all the group's acquired companies and introduced new hand-tool products under its existing brand names during the 1970s. By 1974, all of Cooper's acquisitions had relocated their manufacturing operations to new plants, mostly in the South. Shortly after, Cooper was recognized as the world's largest and most efficient manufacturer of non-powered hand tools. At this time, Cizik decided not to enter the electric power-tool industry in the face of Black & Decker's commanding market share.

Besides the complementary mergers in the Tool Group, Cooper's corporate staff orchestrated an important diversifying acquisition. In 1970, Cooper had quickly followed Lufkin with a second diversification, this time into the aircraft service business. Cooper purchased Dallas Airmotive, a company that repaired and leased jet engines and distributed aircraft parts and supplies. Cooper later supplemented this acquisition with four more air-service companies.

With the "tool basket" well underway and the aircraft service division established, in the early 1970s Cooper's corporate management team turned to the Energy Division and applied some of its hand-tool strategies there. Specifically, Cooper retrenched and concentrated its resources on compression equipment for oil and gas, where it was the industry leader. In 1976, Cooper purchased Superior, a maker of engines and natural gas compressors that filled the gap between Cooper-Bessemer's largest and smallest products. After the Superior deal, Cooper supplied 40% of the horsepower requirements for gas transmission in North America. Concurrently, it stopped producing compressors for petrochemical applications (ethylene, ammonia, nitrogen, oxygen markets, etc.), where Dresser Industries and Carrier dominated the market. This meant reducing the work force at the original Mount Vernon plant from 1,300 to 250. Cizik reasoned that supporting engineering, development, and service for the multiple applications cost too much. "We could probably have gone ahead and invested $100 million over four to five years for the latest technology. But competitors weren't going to be standing still. I thought we could come out of that and still be third or fourth in many of those lines."[9]

In 1975, in the midst of the oil embargo, Cooper elected Robert Cizik as CEO. Cooper's Energy Division benefitted greatly from the increased activity in the United States that persisted into the early 1980s, and its climbing energy income offset falling hand-tool sales during the simultaneous recession. According to Cizik's vision of a multimarket company, "not everything will be clicking at the same time." However, there will be "movement back and forth between businesses as you need them."[10] Correspondingly, Cooper rerouted the flow of capital expenditures to the energy division.

In 1979, Cooper made its biggest move to date, purchasing Dallas-based Gardner-Denver in what then qualified as one of the 10 largest mergers in U.S. history. A company equal in size to Cooper, Gardner-Denver manufactured machinery for petroleum exploration, mining, and general construction. Cizik described the merger, valued at $635 million, as a "complementary move," involving Cooper in natural gas and petroleum exploration for the first time, and thus filling out Cooper's existing Energy Division. By adding Gardner-Denver, Cooper now served a range of needs spanning exploration, production, transmission, distribution, and storage for the oil and natural gas industry, and doubled the number of employees, shareholders, and plants.

Gardner-Denver had grown rapidly in the 1960s and 1970s, but was notorious for its lack of planning and cost controls. For example, it had invested heavily in developing a blasthole drill for mining that turned out to be a "gold plated" white elephant. It was also known as the company that cut prices at just the wrong time, and its sales force, in the words of another industry player, was "looking for nothing but payday and five o'clock."[11]

After the merger, Cizik closed Gardner's Dallas headquarters and moved its corporate functions to Cooper's Houston headquarters. Cooper believed Gardner-Denver's management structure was too centralized and stifled effective decision making at the operational level. Cooper also thought that Gardner's centralized functions were overused. Cizik appraised the situation, "If you try to combine too much under one umbrella, such as consolidating sales into a corporate function, you end up with a lot of people who can't possibly cover such a huge, diverse marketplace, or know much about the plethora of products they're trying to sell."[12] Cooper trimmed Gardner's sales and administrative expenses from the pre-acquisition 16.6% of revenues to Cooper's 11.4% level. It also cut Gardner-Denver's working capital: Cizik was convinced that inventories and receivables were too high. In a review of Gardner-Denver's products, Cizik spoke about "reclaiming" what was useable. Cooper kept product lines capable of healthy development, eliminating others with little potential.

By the late 1970s, Cooper's acquisition guidelines had evolved to include an additional dimension, acquisition by necessity. When Colorado Fuel & Iron (CF&I), a specialty supplier to Lufkin, stopped production of its 1095 steel, Cooper could find only one other source in the world, a German company offering a much more expensive product. Instead, Cooper bought the CF&I equipment and moved the operations to a newly acquired plant, forming Cooper Steel.

In 1981, as Cooper was in the process of absorbing Gardner-Denver, the company engineered its third diversification (following its move into tools and aircraft service) by capitalizing on an unexpected opportunity to acquire Crouse-Hinds. An electrical products company, Crouse-Hinds had been on Cooper's wish list for years. Subject to a hostile takeover attempt, Crouse-Hinds welcomed Cooper as a white knight, and after a prolonged, acrimonious battle, it joined Cooper on friendly terms. Equal in size to the pre-merger Cooper or Gardner-Denver, Crouse-Hinds became the core of Cooper's new electrical and electronic business. It was a worldwide producer of electrical plugs and receptacles, fittings, and industrial lighting, and had just acquired Belden, a well-known manufacturer of electronic wire and cable and electrical cords. Together, Crouse-Hinds and Belden increased Cooper's revenues by 50% and gave the company a foothold in the "path of power"—the transmission, control, and distribution of electrical energy from the generating plant to the end user. Describing the acquisition, Cizik said, "This is a true diversification, compared with what I referred to as a complementary move with Gardner-Denver. In that respect it compares to our acquisitions of Lufkin and Dallas Airmotive, except on a much larger scale."[13]

Throughout the electrical industry, Crouse-Hinds was considered one of the best managed companies. Crouse-Hind's CEO, who had joined the company in 1965, stayed on at the helm after the Cooper acquisition until he retired two years later, and Cooper assigned an experienced, younger Crouse-Hinds executive to succeed him.

Many Wall Street analysts criticized this acquisition for reducing Cooper's exposure to the booming oil and gas business. New criticisms of Cooper's ability to service its increasing debt burden were also voiced in 1981 when Cooper acquired Kirsch, the world's largest manufacturer of drapery hardware. In a similar hostile takeover attempt/white knight situation, Cooper had been forced to move quickly to acquire Kirsch, a company it had been eyeing since the 1970s. In fact, Cooper's board gave first approval to purchase Kirsch on the same day that it had closed the Crouse-Hind's deal. Commenting on the action, one investment banker said, "If Cooper had its choice, it probably would have wanted to finish one deal and then work on the other, but the world doesn't wait for you."[14] Kirsch had a customer base similar to Cooper's and employed many of the same manufacturing processes.

Closing out the busy year of 1981, Cooper sold off its Airmotive Division. Cooper had built its airmotive group into a "decently profitable" unit that it divested at a net profit of $27 million. During the time it was part of Cooper, the unit balanced Cooper's revenue and income stream, but by 1981, Cizik concluded that continued operation of the group conflicted with Cooper's manufacturing-oriented corporate strategy.

Following this period of heavy activity, Cooper repeated its historical pattern of concentrating on digesting recent acquisitions. Said Cizik, "A growing company can outrun its capabilities if it isn't careful to bring up the supply lines. . . . We have to restructure ourselves at a time like this, before we feel comfortable moving out again."[15]

Electricity became Cooper's next target for complementary business-unit development as energy prices slid in the mid-1980s. As one initial skeptic later commented, "I don't know whether Cooper saw the downturn in energy coming, but it eventually proved to be a wise move to diversify and reduce exposure in that area."[16] In 1985, Cooper acquired McGraw-Edison, an electrical company that was put into play by Forstmann Little & Company, a New York firm specializing in leveraged buyouts. Before Forstmann's intentions of a McGraw-Edison buyout were made public, Cizik had approached McGraw's chairman to propose a friendly merger. Cizik, however, was rebuffed; the company was not interested in pursuing a combination. After the Forstmann-McGraw announcement at $59-a-share, Cooper tendered a $65-a-share offer for McGraw-Edison that was eventually accepted.

McGraw-Edison, a leading manufacturer of products for the control and transmission of electrical power, as well as lighting fixtures and fuses, put Cooper at the first stage of electrical power distribution with its transformers, power capacitors and other products. These connected directly, in the "path of power," to the many secondary electrical power distribution products Cooper had acquired through Crouse-Hinds (for example, circuit breakers, receptacles, and plugs). The "path of power" continued to a third level, the point of consumer use in the home or commercial area, where McGraw's recessed, emergency, and track lighting augmented Crouse-Hind's leading position in the indoor and outdoor lighting market.

Following the acquisition, Cooper retained most McGraw senior managers, but began streamlining and consolidating its operations and, in the process, spun off a number of incompatible divisions. Three years later, in 1988, Cooper complemented McGraw's transformer product line with the $324 million acquisition of RTE, a maker of transformers and a supplier of transformer components to Cooper.

At the time of the merger, RTE was fighting a hostile takeover by Mark IV Industries. The company was also suffering from capital constraints resulting from an unsuccessful acquisition program, and Cooper subsequently pumped over $50 million in capital expenditures into the RTE operations. Because of a culture clash with Cooper's "lean and mean" cost structure, many senior managers at RTE left within a year of the acquisition. Cooper consolidated McGraw's and RTE's R&D staffs in one facility and reduced the size of their combined sales force, while also limiting RTE's free-spending habits. In addition, Cooper consolidated computing functions so that RTE's mainframe could be shut down, and eliminated 30 to 40 financial and treasury positions. The RTE restructuring created over $10 million in annual savings for Cooper.

In late 1987, Cooper expanded its existing industrial compressor business with the $140 million purchase of Joy's industrial air and turbo compressor business. After the deal, Cooper eliminated duplicate product lines and suspended manufacture of unprofitable products. It also rationalized manufacturing operations, closing Joy's Indiana plant. Furthermore, Cooper consolidated the two companies' competing distribution channels. The total number of distributors serving the combined company was expected to fall from 160 to 120 over four to five years. However, Cooper would gain leverage with each remaining distributor because it would have a much greater sales volume and a wider product offering.

Exhibit 4   Cooper Industries' Financials ($000s)

	1988	1987	1986	1985	1984
SALES	4,258,275	3,585,785	3,433,296	3,067,169	2,029,915
Cost of sales	2,904,336	2,430,183	2,301,970	2,070,992	1,357,949
Depreciation and amortization	154,650	135,368	127,131	105,815	73,636
Selling and administrative	701,859	622,643	615,943	534,471	368,376
Interest	111,922	86,075	103,080	97,723	20,572
Total costs and expenses	3,872,767	3,274,269	3,148,124	2,809,001	1,820,533
Total operating income	385,508	311,516	285,172	258,168	209,382
Income taxes	161,102	137,705	137,450	123,088	102,518
NET INCOME	224,406	173,811	147,722	135,080	106,864
Long-term debt	1,170,267	884,351	863,615	1,158,310	156,765
Capital expenditures	128,249	100,889	109,497	115,794	68,509
Net plant and equipment	1,115,181	1,016,647	937,741	973,235	685,548
TOTAL ASSETS	4,383,976	3,800,363	3,400,032	3,635,873	1,953,698
SHAREHOLDERS' EQUITY	1,771,712	1,592,912	1,419,946	1,318,001	1,240,143
Number of employees	46,300	43,200	40,200	46,000	30,000
Return on year-end assets	5.1%	4.6%	4.3%	3.7%	5.5%
Return on year-end equity	12.7%	10.9%	10.4%	10.2%	8.6%
Earnings per share	2.20	1.73	1.52	1.39	1.06

[a]Includes gain on the sale of Dallas Airmotive.   [b]Restated to include Crouse–Hinds on a pooling of interest basis.
[c]Includes income from discontinued aircraft service operations.

Cooper's Businesses in the Late 1980s

In 1988, Cooper was a broadly diversified manufacturer of electrical and general industrial products, and energy-related machinery and equipment. U.S.-based Cooper had 1988 revenues of $4.3 billion and over 46,000 employees worldwide, although 85% of sales were in North America. The company operated in 3 distinct business segments with 21 separate profit centers (Exhibits 4, 5, 6, and 7).

Electrical and Electronic. The E&E segment was Cooper's largest in 1988, generating one-half of corporate sales and 57% of operating profits. Cooper had entered this segment with the 1981 purchase of Crouse-Hinds. By 1988, E&E had four sub-segments, each representing quite diverse businesses (Exhibit 7), but all focused on the mature North American market that accounted for over 90% of segment sales.

Cooper competed in power transmission and distribution systems with its McGraw-Edison and RTE operations. About 85%–90% of power system sales were direct to utilities, where the transformers increased and reduced the voltage and channeled the power produced by a generator. Prior to their acquisition by Cooper, McGraw and RTE were roughly tied for third place in the U.S. transformer market, behind GE and Westinghouse. Following the acquisitions, however, Cooper gained a leading market position, despite other consolidations in the industry that reduced the number of major competitors from seven to three. At the consolidated level, the division

used the "Cooper Power Systems" brand name because its competitors were so well-known, but each of the products maintained the McGraw or RTE brand name. Because these products were sold directly, offering a complete product line that met North American standards provided an important competitive advantage. Furthermore, Cooper's reputation for quality products helped garner sales because of the high costs associated with product failure in such vital systems.

Cooper's lighting division was composed of three formerly independent entities: Crouse-Hinds Lighting and McGraw-Edison's Halo and Metalux subsidiaries. In the mid-1980s, Cooper combined the three businesses and rationalized manufacturing facilities, adopting a focused-factory approach that allowed three underutilized plants to be closed. In 1988, Cooper was in the process of eliminating duplicate administrative functions among the companies and developing a unified market identity through consolidating sales representatives and marketing programs. Cooper also began constructing a showroom to display all of its lighting products and to train architects, designers, and lighting distributors in its full product line.

In the broad and highly fragmented lighting fixture market, Cooper was perhaps the most widely spread manufacturer, participating in fluorescent, high-intensity discharge, and incandescent fixtures. In this industry, the top eight firms had a combined 60% market share in 1988, but as the eighth firm represented only 2% of the total, the industry was characterized by a large fringe of small producers. Foreign

1983	1982	1981	1980[a]	1975	1970
1,850,280	2,393,989	2,866,031	2,335,923	478,066	225,651
1,250,359	1,642,279	1,864,738	1,555,022	346,291	164,037
67,909	63,816	56,598	46,282	9,571	4,280
363,101	401,878	429,207	356,749	54,848	29,477
28,460	44,202	56,712	50,320	7,439	3,924
1,709,829	2,152,175	2,407,255	2,008,373	418,149	201,718
140,451	241,814	458,776	327,550	59,917	23,933
69,282	106,679	217,506	156,120	28,783	11,553
71,169	135,135	284,545[b]	185,216	31,134	12,380
175,005	272,888	154,270	301,016	71,030	31,496
86,237	117,650	128,653	115,414	17,817	7,698
683,318	685,067	624,230	532,025	102,843	47,227
1,949,447	2,036,547	2,335,381	2,023,705	369,196	183,926
1,250,649	1,265,646	1,284,899	1,076,407	177,150	100,262
30,000	31,000	39,000	37,000	11,262	8,247
3.7%	6.6%	12.2%	9.2%	8.4%	6.7%
5.7%	10.7%	22.1%	17.2%	17.6%	12.3%
0.64	1.38	2.84	2.02	NA	NA

competition was limited because the large size-to-weight ratio of lighting fixtures made transport costs prohibitive. Distributors and manufacturers tended to develop stable, long-term relationships, and, in 1988, Cooper was looking to the day when it could install paperless ordering and invoicing of all Cooper lighting products. Cooper believed that its service level and premium-priced, market-leading products would attract distributors to offer its full product line exclusively or with only one other manufacturer's products.

In the distribution and control area, Cooper dominated the market with its Construction Materials Division (CMD), the crown-jewel of Crouse-Hinds. CMD manufactured protective electrical equipment for hazardous applications. CMD's reputation was so widespread that its products were often included in engineers' design specifications because of its reputation for superior quality.

Cooper's Belden division produced wire and cable used in the electronics industry. Although the cable business was fundamentally low-tech, Belden participated in the more sophisticated end of the product range. Cooper had invested heavily in upgrading Belden's manufacturing facilities. Sales through distributors comprised 75% of the division's revenues; the remainder came from the OEM market.

Commercial and Industrial. In the commercial and industrial segment Cooper participated in the non-powered hand-tool and window treatment businesses, and in the automotive aftermarket. In the Tool Group, consolidation of acquisitions

was completed and new manufacturing facilities constructed by 1988, and the company held the preeminent market position in most of its tool lines. Cooper's automotive division consisted of Belden's auto-related cable business and Wagner Lighting and Wagner Brakes, acquired with McGraw-Edison. These businesses serviced the automotive aftermarket, where operating through effective distribution networks was the key to accessing the myriad small car-repair outlets. After revamping its production equipment for quick changeovers, Wagner was positioned to take advantage of Cooper's experience in managing distribution-oriented businesses.

Compression, Drilling, and Energy Equipment. The compression and drilling segment had been Cooper's largest in 1981, generating over 50% of revenues and over 60% of operating profit. However, the collapse of the energy industry in the early and mid-1980s caused sales of oil and natural gas equipment to fall precipitously. By 1988, this segment accounted for 21% of Cooper sales and less than 10% of operating income.

The size and breadth of the collapse of the energy industry induced Cooper to take drastic actions. Employment in the compression and drilling segment was reduced by half, as eight plants were closed to control costs and pare down operations. However, Cooper took advantage of the depressed prices in the petroleum industry to make acquisitions that complemented existing product lines. The acquisition of Joy's petroleum equipment business and several smaller mergers increased Cooper's participation in flow control products.

Exhibit 5   Cooper Segment Financials ($000)

Electrical & Electronic	1988	1987	1986	1985	1984	1983	1982	1981	1980*
Revenues	2,077,522	1,736,446	1,699,708	1,425,463	798,310	768,174	798,440	872,127	825,726
Operating Income	307,644	264,657	259,973	225,633	126,166	105,913	90,774	109,397	95,368
Identifiable Assets	1,985,361	1,521,455	1,441,857	1,426,135	435,592	430,218	428,290	449,767	439,060
Group Return on Sales	14.8%	15.2%	15.3%	15.8%	15.8%	13.8%	11.4%	12.5%	11.5%
Group Return on Assets	15.5%	17.4%	18.0%	15.8%	29.0%	24.6%	21.2%	24.3%	21.7%

Commercial & Industrial	1988	1987	1986	1985	1984	1983	1982	1981	1980
Revenues	1,260,121	1,195,829	1,142,372	927,283	586,453	518,162	489,353	540,812	403,577
Operating Income	184,318	171,143	162,675	134,146	98,798	84,581	64,945	92,340	97,518
Identifiable Assets	1,006,904	985,528	990,512	1,020,648	495,310	447,310	446,977	479,986	346,318
Group Return on Sales	14.6%	14.3%	14.2%	14.5%	16.8%	16.3%	13.3%	17.1%	24.2%
Group Return on Assets	18.3%	17.4%	16.4%	13.1%	19.9%	18.9%	14.5%	19.2%	28.2%

Compression & Drilling	1988	1987	1986	1985	1984	1983	1982	1981	1980
Revenues	912,320	642,825	564,647	691,926	642,926	556,001	1,106,836	1,447,970	1,101,206
Operating Income	47,093	(4,529)	(21,865)	11,987	28,266	(4,872)	161,072	341,639	212,442
Identifiable Assets	1,177,758	1,131,090	826,675	937,831	928,850	974,111	1,071,732	1,193,762	1,045,832
Group Return on Sales	5.2%	–0.7%	–3.9%	1.7%	4.4%	–0.9%	14.6%	23.6%	19.3%
Group Return on Assets	4.0%	–0.4%	–2.6%	1.3%	3.0%	–0.5%	15.0%	28.6%	20.3%

*Restated to include Crouse-Hinds on a pooling of interest basis.

Primary competition in this area came from Cameron Iron Works and FMC, while competition for the remaining production and drilling equipment was fragmented.

In the market for natural gas compression equipment, Cooper retained its number one position with the Cooper-Bessemer, Ajax, and Superior product lines. Despite a weak market, the company was optimistic about the prospects for this equipment, as the five competitors consolidated to three.

Corporate Role

Cooper Industries held increasing shareholder value as a central corporate objective. Management had established a

Exhibit 6   Cooper Industries Comparative Stock Price Performance

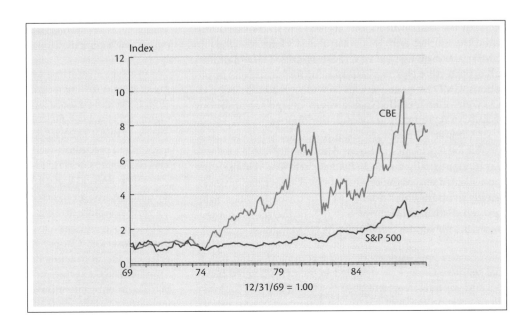

Exhibit 7   Cooper Industries Segment Information

Electrical & Electronic	Primary Products	% of Revenues	Market Position	Distribution Method
Power Systems		15%		Direct Sales
RTE	Transformers		Co-Leader	
McGraw Edison	Dist Switchgear		#1	
Lighting Fixtures		12%		Distributor
Halo	Incandesent		#2 (Tied)	
Metalux	Fluorescent			
Crouse-Hinds	High Intensity			
Electronic Cables		8%		Distributor
Belden	Wire & Cable		#1	
Distribution and Control		14%		Distributor
Crouse-Hinds	Elec. Constr. Mat.		#1	
Arrow-Hart	Dist. Equip		#2	
Bussmann Beswick	Fuses	–	#1	
Subtotal		49%		
Commercial & Industrial				
Automotive Aftermarket		10%		Distributor
Wagner	Brakes		#1	
Headlights			#1 (Aftermarket)	
Tools		14%		Distributor
Campbell/Lufkin	Non-power		#1	
Nicholson/Crescent	Hand Tools			
Window Treatments		6%		Distributor
Kirsch	Drapery Hardware	–	#1	
Subtotal		30%		
Compression & Drilling				
Industrial Compressors		7%		Distributor
Gardner-Denver/Joy	Air-Compressors		#2 (Tied)	
Energy Equipment		13%		Direct Sales
Cooper Energy Services	Gas Compressors		#1	
Gardner-Denver	Drilling Equip		NA	
Demco/WKM	Valves	–	NA	
Subtotal		20%		

Source: Lovett, Mitchell, Webb & Garrison, Inc., September 20, 1989.

long-term earnings-per-share growth rate target of 5% above the rate of inflation and a return on equity objective of 12% on top of inflation, reflecting sustainable targets for a "superior" manufacturing company. Furthermore, Cooper targeted 40% as a desirable debt to total capital ratio and preferred to finance expansion with cash or convertible preferred stock. These goals were to be achieved in part through a strong corporate emphasis on cash flow; Cooper acted on the motto "cash flow is king." In particular, strong cash flow would allow Cooper to aggressively pursue its acquisition program and meet its earnings growth target. During the 1980s, internal growth generated one-half of total corporate growth, with the other 50% arising from acquisitions. Because of Cooper's numerous acquisitions, $1.38 billion of Cooper's total $1.77 billion in stockholders' equity represented goodwill.

A number of guidelines directed Cooper's pursuit of potential acquisitions (Exhibit 8). Cooper sought companies that had stable earnings and had proven manufacturing operations using well-known technologies. Ideally, these products were mature and filled essential needs. Additionally, Cooper looked for companies that served a broad customer base. Finally, Cooper searched for firms with high-quality products that were market leaders with widely recognized brand names. Cooper reviewed about 100 potential acquisitions annually, and signed confidentiality

**Cooper Industries' Acquisition Guidelines
for Diversification.**

- Seek acquisitions that exhibit stable earnings
  or earning patterns that are countercyclical to those
  we already have.
- Acquire products that serve basic and essential needs
  and that are derived from proven technologies,
  thereby contributing to the objective of operating in
  stable markets with predictable growth.
- Acquire manufacturing companies with products that
  are of high quality and that are leaders in their markets.

**Cooper Industries' Guidelines for Acquired
Complementary Products**

- Broaden existing product lines.
- Offer opportunities for enhanced earnings through
  cost management.
- Enhance Cooper's strength in distribution.
- Strengthen a business unit's market position.
- Enjoy widespread brand name recognition.
- Serve a broad customer base.

Source: Cooper Industries Management Philosophy.

agreements to analyze internal documents for roughly one-half of these. While in principle Cooper would divest any business at the right price, it was not transaction-driven and was unlikely to divest the cores of the company. Cooper discouraged management bids on divisional sell-offs.

In 1988, Cooper derived 16% (reaching as high as 20% during the previous decade) of its revenues from overseas operations, although almost all of its manufacturing operations were located in the United States. Each of Cooper's divisions had a global responsibility for its operations. Cizik was a strong advocate of improving manufacturing efficiency in the United States, believing that high volume, a cooperative and involved work force, and technological advantages in the U.S. were adequate to compete with overseas producers. Consequently, he believed that investing outside the U.S. was unnecessary if its sole purpose was to achieve lower manufacturing costs.

With each acquisition, Cooper tailored its structure to suit the new configuration of businesses. Management sought to weld synergistic business units under the responsibility of one individual. Therefore, when new companies were acquired, Cooper typically broke them up and combined the pieces with other Cooper divisions to minimize both product transfers between divisions as well as resources shared among business units. Breaking up newly

acquired businesses also allowed Cooper to closely examine their parts. For example, when Cooper acquired Wagner Brakes with McGraw-Edison, it separated the brake operations from the automotive lighting business so that it could focus on production difficulties. Only after the problems were ameliorated through manufacturing improvements did Cooper consider reconsolidating the division.

Continuing with its original decentralized operating philosophy, Cooper exercised central control over corporate policy but delegated day-to-day operating decisions to the "semi-autonomous" operating units. Each of the three executive vice presidents (EVPs) were entitled to a staff of one assistant and one secretary, and division heads had no formal relationships with each other. In 1988, Cooper maintained a total corporate staff of 317 that occupied four floors of a Houston office building, and had total corporate expenses of $50 million. Politics played a negligible role at the company and decisions were made quickly. Despite Cooper's decentralized operating philosophy, however, Cizik stressed that "Cooper puts a great deal of emphasis on control—control that's achieved by working as an operating company, not a holding company. To us that means that we just don't buy and sell businesses; we're actively involved in running them. Our corporate management team participates in every policy decision made in our organization. But at the same time, day-to-day questions are answered at the operational level, and those operations are also heavily involved in determining their own future direction." [17]

Cooper's three senior vice presidents oversaw administrative, financial, and manufacturing consulting functions that were conducted at the corporate level, and they dealt directly with division managers (Exhibit 9). Each division focused primarily on operations. The CEO was removed from daily operating decisions and concentrated on developing the corporate strategy, appraising management performance, and evaluating potential acquisitions and asset dispositions.

Senior Vice President of Finance. Dewain Cross, senior VP of finance, and his department had responsibility for implementing and monitoring corporate standard accounting and control functions at all the divisions. One member of the corporate finance staff tracked each division in detail and was responsible for understanding its financial reports. Corporate finance also had an internal audit staff and a four person team of manufacturing cost systems experts who were available at the request of division management.

Following acquisitions, Cooper set up reserves to cover anticipated closing costs involved in rationalization. This ensured that division managers incurred no write-offs on their monthly profit and loss statements as they went through the rationalization process. Also, within 30 days after every acquisition, Cooper began to install its own

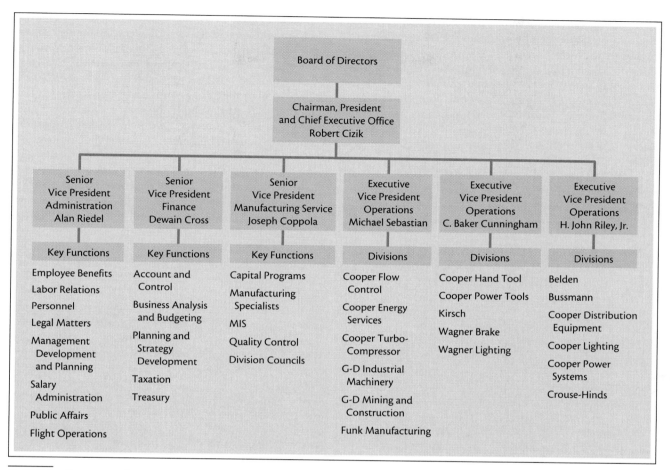

Exhibit 9   Corporate Organizational Structure, 1988.

financial and cost accounting systems on an IBM. As Cross said, "There are only two times to change a business. One is right after you buy it. The second is when it is losing a lot of money. These are the two times when there is the least resistance to change."

All divisions were required to submit Cooper's standard monthly financial report (approximately 150 line items) to corporate headquarters, but they had discretion over how to keep their internal ledgers. Cooper used direct variable cost accounting rather than a full cost absorption system. It also had a large set of internal control guidelines that each division had to follow, such as the number of people required to sign a check above a specified dollar value. Indeed, Cooper's two books of procedures were bigger than its accounting manual.

Because Cooper was extremely cash-conscious, the austerity of Cooper's financial control systems often collided with the systems in place under previous managers. This meant that incumbent managers often left following a

Cooper acquisition because they were unable to adjust to the new culture. Cooper tightly controlled working capital and charged divisions interest for its use, although there were no corporate overhead charges or charges for corporate services to divisions. The finance department had central control over treasury and taxation functions so that all divisions effectively maintained a zero-dollar balance in their accounts.

Cross also set guidelines for developing the business unit strategies that each of the 21 Cooper divisions prepared every 3 years. Cooper's strategic planning approach was bottom-up: Each profit center developed its own plan under the guidance of its EVP, assisted by Cross's corporate planning and development group, comprised of a staff of seven MBAs. Headquarters was, however, actively involved in strategic planning and all plans had to be presented to and accepted by Cizik and the corporate staff, often after many suggestions and improvements. Cooper only occasionally used outside consultants. In any given year, 7 of the 21 divisions prepared a plan, with new acquisitions formulating their first strategic plan in the year following their acquisition. These comprehensive analyses identified the market, projected market demand, presented an industry overview, and identified types of companies viewed to be desirable acquisition candidates. Separate strategies were developed for each major product line within a division. They elucidated the business unit's view of the competitive situation and outlined strategic options and reasons for the strategies chosen.

Cross, along with the appropriate EVP, also reviewed the annual budget for each division. The annual budgeting process enabled the corporate officers and division managers to agree on short-term performance objectives for each division.

Senior Vice President of Administration. Attorney Alan Riedel, Cooper's Sr. VP of administration, was the only director inside Cooper besides Cizik. Riedel had as his foremost responsibilities managing the company's legal affairs and establishing and administering personnel policy and benefits programs. He also handled labor relations, shareholder and public relations, and environmental matters, and oversaw the management development and planning (MD&P) program. Cooper maintained a uniform pay scale based on the Hay System. Base salaries throughout the company were similar for employees of corresponding ranks in different divisions, and all were competitive with industry standards. However, bonuses often reached 20%–40% of base salaries, and were discretionary; division managers had a bonus pool determined by Corporate Administration that could be awarded largely at their and the EVP's discretion. In addition to salary and bonuses, key managers were granted stock options. With each new acquisition, Riedel's office gradually adjusted pay scales at the acquired division up or down until they reached Cooper's targeted level, with the adjustments taking three to five years. Typically, however, these adjustments were small as pay scales in the industries Cooper participated in tended to be homogeneous. Cooper also required all acquisitions to adopt its standard benefits package for medical insurance and pensions, which could lead to dissatisfaction because it was sometimes conservative relative to the benefits package of the premerger company.

Cooper handled labor relations at the corporate level. Half of Cooper's plants were non-union; the company maintained a strong union-avoidance policy. Contract renewal and National Labor Relations Board matters were handled by the labor relations staff. Riedel handled antitrust matters, an area particularly important because of Cooper's active acquisition program.

Management Development & Planning, initiated in 1970, was integral to Cooper's management system. MD&P evaluated organizational effectiveness and individual strengths and weaknesses by focusing on the performance of key managers. Under the program, about 800 division and corporate executives and managers developed qualitative professional development or project-related goals for the forthcoming year. Quantitative goals often reinforced business unit objectives that were established through the annual budgeting and strategic planning processes. At the end of the year, each employee prepared a progress review worksheet that compared achieved to targeted objectives. Additionally, employees in the program were reviewed by their supervisors. For example, as CEO, Cizik met annually with each executive vice president to review his personal progress, the managerial capabilities in his segment, and the detail of necessary future improvements. The objectives for the EVP in the upcoming year, mutually determined at that meeting, became, in Riedel's words, "the road map for action items that are to occur during the year." Similarly, each EVP conducted annual reviews of all of the managers in the division he supervised. While review results were not formally tied to incentive compensation, managers with poor reviews were unlikely to receive substantial bonuses.

Each EVP and Sr. VP fully embraced MD&P, even though it was extremely time consuming. Cizik noted that "everybody hates the MD&P because it is so much work, but when it is done everyone loves it." The program uncovered existing or potential management gaps and identified people worthy of promotion: it was the method that Cooper used to determine management succession. In addition, the program distinguished candidates for interdivisional transfers, which generally occurred at the higher echelons of the organization; 24 such transfers were made in 1988. Cooper preferred to bring in one of its own people as general manager or controller of a new division, and typically had many personnel requirements in the finance and plant manager areas following an acquisition. MD&P developed an internal pool of people in these areas that could be moved around, but a lack of a sufficient number of such people was often the constraint on further acquisitions. Internal transfers were less frequent in the marketing and sales areas where experience was believed to be business specific. Also, MD&P identified managers who would benefit from corporate-developed management training programs, with courses such as "finance for non-financial managers."

Senior Vice President of Manufacturing Services. In 1975, Robert Cizik formed a corporate-level Manufacturing Services Group, chartered to institute manufacturing improvements throughout the company's operating divisions. Cizik felt that "the problem with U.S. manufacturing [was] manufacturing itself." He promoted Joe Coppola, an operating manager with an engineering background, to lead the new manufacturing group.

In 1988, the Manufacturing Services Group consisted of 14 professionals, all with 10 to 15 years of operations experience, and had an operating budget of $1.8 million. Its staff included experts in facilities, automation, and environmental engineering, and in materials management, quality control, and management information systems. The Group had four major objectives: to promote major manufacturing improvements to reach the point of "best value delivered" for the products in each segment; to administer the $200 million 1988 capital expenditure budget; to operate interdivisional councils focused on such aspects of operations as quality control; and, with Riedel's personnel department, to run a manufacturing training program for recent engineering schools graduates. The group also published guides on manufacturing issues for the divisions.

The Manufacturing Services Group used benchmarking and cross-referencing to improve production methods and had a bifurcated strategy for introducing the manufacturing improvements. In the case of new acquisitions, the group simply stepped in and worked with EVPs and their operating managers to improve plant efficiency and to transfer Cooper's manufacturing know-how and processes to the new division. In almost every acquisition, Cooper considered the majority of the plants to require production improvements. In contrast, in keeping with Cooper's philosophy, the group maintained a strict policy of never entering an old Cooper division unless they were invited by division managers. There was, however, no charge for their services. Once requested, the group used a three-tiered approach to implementing improvements, acting as a catalyst for change. The first stage was conceptual: the engineering department, assisted by local personnel, determined the ideal configuration for the factory. The process stage followed, designed to show current employees how the new methods would be more efficient than the old ones. This stage typically involved reconfiguring the machinery in the plant for cell rather than batch production. The process stage was heavily communicative: its primary goal was to inculcate factory workers into the new production process, convincing them of its superior efficiency, and would often take two to three years. The final step was the technological stage, during which the group introduced new machinery and technology into the factory. The group spent about 60% of its time on acquisitions and 40% on existing Cooper divisions.

At all stages of the manufacturing improvement process, the group relied heavily on the participation of local personnel, attempting to give them ownership of the project. The group generally coordinated and directed the three stages, but division employees implemented the changes. Bill Brewer, president of Cooper Power Systems, said of the group, "One of the greatest aspects of Coppola's group is that they are viewed as an extension of our organization. They are constantly called on and are available for concepts and opinions. They have a broader perspective than any one plant can have, and are therefore able to broker success and failure throughout the company."

Coppola's group administered capital expenditures. The capital budget for each division was reached after balancing division requests with available funds and was made consistent with division strategies. Cizik was often involved in the capital budgeting process, making suggestions and amendments to proposals. Corporate headquarters supported all capital and personnel needs that were required to meet division strategies, which often involved sizable investments in newly acquired companies to improve their manufacturing capabilities. Division managers could authorize expenditures up to $100,000; an EVP's approval was needed for expenditures above $100,000; Cizik's signature was required for all projects over $1 million; and the board of directors approved all investments over $5 million.

The Manufacturing Services Group also ran quality, purchasing, traffic, environmental, plant engineering, and technology councils that met four times annually. Each council typically had 12 members, each representing a different operating division, who rotated on an annual basis. For example, in 1984, Cooper established the purchasing council, which soon discovered that some divisions were purchasing steel from the same supplier at different prices. The council then negotiated advantageous prices with various steel companies for all Cooper divisions (Cooper purchased over $100 million of steel annually). In similar instances, the councils allowed managers from different divisions to share information and insights, which helped maximize Cooper's leverage in negotiating with suppliers and vendors.

Finally, the group oversaw a manufacturing training program for entry-level engineering graduates. In 1988, Cooper recruited 16 graduates, primarily from 12 "preferred" Midwestern universities. The two-year program consisted of four intensive six-month job rotations; each participant was required to work in at least three of Cooper's four manufacturing sub-functions, as well as to hold a foreman's job. Program graduates were offered supervisory positions, or assignments leading to supervisory and managerial positions.

Executive Vice President of Operations. Each of Cooper's three EVPs headed a worldwide operating segment. Describing his job, H. John Riley, Jr., EVP of the Electrical and Electronics Division, said "Cizik invests a lot of authority in our hands. Each of us functions in a capacity similar to that of the typical chief operating officer. This is what makes the system work." Cooper's EVPs served four major functions. They handled organizational and administrative matters, including selecting key division managers, conducting personnel reviews under the MD&P program, and prioritizing tasks. They also approved all capital expenditures up to $1 million. Second, they worked with the Sr. VP of Finance and division managers to develop the three-year business unit strategic plans. Likewise, they performed strategic planning and analysis at the segment level: they set the long-term strategies for the business segment, and attempted to balance short-term performance with long-term strategic objectives. Third, EVPs located and analyzed potential acquisitions that complemented their segments. As soon as Cooper engineered a complementary acquisition, the appropriate EVP would spend a considerable amount of time on "Cooperizing" the new operating unit. Welding the acquisition with a Cooper division generally required that he make multiple visits to plants and distribution facilities, overseeing the transition while Cooper installed its management systems and culture. EVPs spent approximately 50% to 60% of their time in the field.

Finally, the EVPs regularly reviewed financial statements, annual budgets, and quarterly forecasts. They received monthly financial statements from each division, which allowed them to roughly compare actual to budgeted performance. EVPs did not focus on any single measure in evaluating a division's performance, but looked at all financial data that would indicate if the strategy was on course, such as sales, profitability, growth, cash flow, and return on assets. These financial data were supplemented with operating data, including order rates, which served as indicators of the level of product demand for the upcoming period, and first-pass line fill, or service-level data, which provided information on the number of orders that could be filled from stock. In many of Cooper's businesses, the ability to immediately fill orders was important for effective distribution, and Cooper maintained first-pass fill targets of 95% to 98% of orders.

Each EVP had a general management background and had risen through a division within his operating segment. For example, Michael Sebastian, EVP of Compression and Drilling, was a group manager at Gardner-Denver and joined Cooper when Gardner was acquired. He rose to the EVP position by 1981. Similarly, Riley joined Crouse-Hinds in 1963, became a division head of Crouse-Hinds in 1972, and then was promoted to EVP of Cooper in 1982. Cunningham rose through the Tool Group to head the Commercial and Industrial Products division.

Except during the Cooperization process, EVPs had a management-by-exception philosophy, seldom intervening in routine division management unless a division suffered prolonged, unsatisfactory performance or violated the boundaries set during the strategic planning process. However, each EVP maintained an ongoing dialogue with his division managers and encouraged them to be up front with problems. Conversations were initiated by either party. In addition to reviews of monthly financial performance, EVPs also advised division managers on resolving particularly difficult operating situations. If unsatisfactory performance continued unattended for a quarter, an EVP would probably request a meeting with division managers to question the methods they had planned to improve the situation. At all times the discussion focused on the steps necessary to comply with the strategy rather than on assigning blame for poor performance. Division managers valued the knowledge, understanding, and support of the EVPs, whom they viewed as extensions of the divisions. Only after extended poor performance would an EVP take direct corrective action.

Chairman, President, and CEO. As chairman, president, and CEO, Robert Cizik developed Cooper's corporate strategy. Initially, his idea that Cooper adopt a manufacturing focus met some resistance. He noted, "I had to argue for five or six years about being a manufacturing company before the others finally accepted it." In 1988, Cizik, Riedel, Cross, and Cunningham had been at Cooper for about 20 years over which time they had developed a team approach, centered on Cizik's strategic vision. At headquarters, Cizik, the three EVPs and the three Sr. VPs had offices near each other and often met informally to apply their collective talents to problems.

Cizik approved all acquisitions and took charge of investor relations. "Cooper" was used as a brand name only on Wall Street, where Cizik closely interacted with investors and analysts. Cizik was approached by many investment bankers and personally reviewed many of Cooper's acquisition candidates. In particular, he focused on diversifying acquisitions. Because Cooper had few decision makers, the company was able to act quickly on acquisitions, opportunistically undertaking purchases, such as the Kirsch and Crouse-Hinds mergers.

At Cooper, each of the three operating segments had little physical interaction with the other two: divisions in different segments rarely supplied each other, and Cooper did not have a transfer pricing policy. However, if a division in the commercial and industrial segment was building a new plant, for example, it would be expected to purchase Cooper lighting products and construction materials. If disputes developed between the divisions about these transactions, Cizik would ask the EVPs of the two operating segments to resolve the conflict.

As CEO, Cizik was not involved in day-to-day operations. His biggest regret was that he no longer had time to visit each plant annually. However, he was always available if a serious problem developed at the operational level, and a telephone conversation with a division manager would bring him up to date on the division's progress. Cizik's involvement with each division became more visionary: his role was to push the frontiers, for example, suggesting to divisions that they expand into Europe. His strategic concepts, such as maintaining "strong brand image," provided focus for divisions. Said Bill Brewer, "Cizik is a very lively participant in the strategy meetings. He makes excellent, directed comments and has a keen sense of the potential of a proposed strategy for success."

Cizik spent an average of twelve days a year on the MD&P process. His participation was essential: he reviewed each EVP and Sr. VP and their organizations and scrutinized the minutes from the divisional MD&P meetings. He also conducted probing, all-day reviews with each EVP and pushed managers to make difficult personnel decisions under MD&P.

Champion

In January, 1989, Champion agreed to a "sweetheart" sale of the company to Dana for $17.50. Dana was a $4.9 billion, Toledo-based manufacturer of power transmission equipment for the automotive original equipment market. At the time of the Dana-Champion announcement, Chinook Partners L.P., a partnership formed by descendants of Champion's founding family, held 35% of Champion's stock. The partnership objected to the proposed Dana merger, referring to it as a deal done at "the Toledo Country Club." According to *Business Week*, three weeks after the Dana bid, Cooper "crashed the party" with a $21-a-share tender offer.

At the time of the takeover battle, Champion principally manufactured spark plugs and windshield wipers and derived most of its revenues from sales to spare-parts distributors (Exhibit 10). In early 1989, it had a brand name that was recognized worldwide and was a market leader in spark plugs and wipers (35% of Champion's sales were overseas).

However, motivated by declines in the spark plug market, Champion had attempted to leverage its internationally recognized brand name by expanding into other automotive product lines. In the most extreme case, the company proposed to penetrate the automotive tool business, although Snap-On, MAC, and Matco had a combined market share of 92%. In addition, Champion began licensing its brand name as well as putting it on bought-in parts. These new ventures required significant management and capital outlays, and after a short period of time, most proved unprofitable.

Champion's capital expenditures from 1975 to 1988 were 2% of sales, and its overall operating margin was 4.7% for 1988. Its U.S. division suffered an operating loss of $6.4 million in 1988, however its Asian-African and European divisions had operating margins of 13.7% and 11.6%, respectively. *Forbes* described Champion as a "bloated auto parts maker" that, according to industry sources, was manufacturing with 1950s technology. The company had swollen corporate overhead expenses that included the operation of its own fleet of jets.

At the time of the tender offer, Cooper was also considering a $700 million bid for Cameron Iron Works, which manufactured petroleum and natural gas-related equipment, including valves and technically advanced forged products. These product lines would complement Cooper's Compression and Drilling segment. However, undertaking both acquisitions was likely to send Cooper's debt to total capitalization ratio to the 55% to 60% range, and Cooper was aware of the risks of attempting both deals. Cizik realized that, in addition to the financial risks, purchasing either or both companies would have profound operational and organizational ramifications for Cooper Industries.

Notes

1   *Wall Street Transcript*, October 15, 1984, pp. 75, 590.
2   *Houston Post*, August 6, 1989, p. D1.
3   David N. Keller, *Cooper Industries 1933–1983* (Ohio University Press, 1983), p. 98.
4   Keller, *Cooper*, p. 244.
5   *Wall Street Transcript*, October 15, 1984, pp. 75, 590.
6   Sam Fletcher, "Cooper industries builds on merits," *The Houston Post*, August 8, 1990, p. D4.
7   James Flanigan, "Bob Cizik: He talks a good game—Plays one, too," *Forbes*, July 8, 1979, pp. 100–104.
8   Keller, *Cooper*, p. 157.
9   Flanigan, *Forbes*.
10 Keller, *Cooper*, p. 211.
11 Flanigan, *Forbes*.
12 Keller, *Cooper*, p. 9.
13 Keller, *Cooper*, p. 314.
14 *Wall Street Transcript*, December 13, 1981.
15 Keller, *Cooper*, p. 339.
16 *Wall Street Transcript*, March 7, 1988, pp. 88, 618.
17 *Wall Street Transcript*, May 31, 1982, pp. 65, 989.

Exhibit 10   Champion Spark Plug Financials ($000)

	Dec 88	Dec 87	Dec 86	Dec 85	Dec 84	Dec 83	Dec 82	Dec 81	Dec 80
SALES	738,000	719,900	883,800	829,400	816,500	764,400	783,700	818,600	799,800
Selling, General, & Administrative Expense	189,600	187,200	213,800	194,200	183,800	178,400	171,900	185,400	190,600
Net Income	23,600	19,100	(17,200)	15,200	27,300	27,000	26,800	30,300	36,900
Earnings Per Share	0.670	0.500	-0.450	0.400	0.710	0.700	0.700	0.790	0.960
Dividends	0.200	0.050	0.200	0.400	0.400	0.400	0.800	0.800	0.800
Total Current Assets	375,800	462,500	436,700	443,300	398,000	387,200	394,000	421,500	428,100
Net Plant, Property & Equip	185,500	177,100	194,800	177,800	163,500	163,900	173,400	178,400	181,300
TOTAL ASSETS	575,600	653,000	647,700	640,800	579,300	571,700	590,900	626,000	636,200
Total Current Liabilities	170,300	202,900	236,100	211,600	165,800	161,000	176,700	183,800	162,900
Long Term Debt	13,900	17,500	23,500	29,700	26,000	22,300	23,300	31,400	41,400
TOTAL EQUITY	349,900	387,400	351,800	368,700	359,400	359,500	361,100	384,300	405,900

Analyzing Cases and Preparing for Class Discussions

This book, properly understood, is really about how to analyze cases. Just reading the book, however, is no more likely to fully develop one's skills as a strategist than reading a book about golf will make one a golfer. Practice in applying the concepts and tools is essential. Cases provide the opportunity for this necessary practice.

Why the Case Method?

The core of many strategic management courses is the case method of instruction. Under the case method, you will study and discuss the real-world challenges and dilemmas that face managers in firms. Cases are typically accounts of situations that a firm or manager has faced at a given point in time. By necessity, cases do not possess the same degree of complexity that a manager faces in the real world, but they do provide a concrete set of facts that suggest challenges and opportunities that real managers have faced. Very few cases have clear answers. The case method encourages you to engage problems directly and propose solutions or strategies in the face of incomplete information. To succeed at the case method, you must develop the capability to analyze and synthesize data that are sometimes ambiguous and conflicting. You must be able to prioritize issues and opportunities and make decisions in the face of ambiguous and incomplete information. Finally, you must be able to persuade others to adopt your point of view.

In an applied field like strategic management the real test of learning is how well you can apply knowledge to real-world situations. Strategic management cases offer you the opportunity to develop judgment and wisdom in applying your conceptual knowledge. By taking the relatively unstructured information in a case and by applying the concepts they have learned, students develop judgment in applying concepts. Alfred North Whitehead discussed the importance of application to knowledge:

> This discussion rejects the doctrine that students should first learn passively, and then, having learned, should apply knowledge. . . . For the very meaning of the things known is wrapped up in their relationship beyond themselves. This unapplied knowledge is knowledge shorn of its meaning.

Alfred North Whitehead (1947). *Essays in Science and Philosophy*. New York: Philosophical Library, Inc. pp. 218–219.

Thus, knowledge is gained as you apply concepts. In the case method, you do not passively absorb wisdom imparted from your instructor, but actively develop it as you wrestle with the real-world situations described in cases.

How to Analyze Cases

Before discussing how to analyze a case, it may be useful to comment on how *not* to prepare a case. We see two common failings in case preparation that often go hand-in-hand. First, students often do not apply conceptual frameworks in a rigorous and systematic manner. Second, many students do not devote sufficient time to reading, analyzing, and discussing a case before class. Many students succumb to the temptation to quickly read a case and quickly latch on to the most visible issues that present themselves. Thus, they come to class prepared to make only a few superficial observations about a case. Often, they entirely miss the deeper issues around why a firm is in the situation that it is in and how it can better its performance. Applying the frameworks systematically may take more time and effort in the beginning, but it will generally lead to deeper insights about the cases and a more profound understanding of the concepts in the chapters. As you gain experience in this systematic approach to analyzing cases, many of you will find that your preparation time will decrease. This appendix offers a framework that will assist you as you analyze cases. The framework is important, but no framework can substitute for hard work. There are no great shortcuts to analyzing cases, and there is no single right method for preparing a case. The following approach, however, may help you develop your ability to analyze cases.

1. **Skim through the case very quickly.** Pay particular attention to the exhibits. The objective in this step is to gain familiarity with the broad facts of the case. What are the apparent challenges or opportunities the company faces? What information is provided? You may find it especially useful to focus on the first and last few paragraphs of the case in this step.

2. **Read the case more carefully and make notes, underline, etc.** What appear to be important facts? The conceptual frameworks in the chapters will be essential in helping you identify what are key facts. Throughout the course, you will want to address central questions such as the following:

   - What is the firm's performance?
   - What is the firm's mission? Strategy? Goals?
   - What are the resources involved in the firm's value chain and how do they compare to competitors on cost and differentiation?
   - Does the firm have a competitive advantage?
   - Are the firm's advantages and disadvantages temporary or sustainable?
   - What is the value of the firm's resources?
   - Are the firm's resources rare?
   - Are the firm's resources costly to imitate?
   - Is the firm organized sufficiently to exploit its resources?

Depending on the case, you may also want to consider other frameworks and questions where appropriate. Each chapter provides concepts and frameworks that you may want to consider. For example:

   - What are the five forces? How do they influence industry opportunities and threats? (Chapter 2)
   - What are the sources of cost differences in an industry? (Chapter 4)
   - What are the bases and potential bases for product differentiation in an industry? (Chapter 5)

Each chapter suggests more specific questions and concepts than those above. You will want to consider these concepts in detail. In some cases, the instructor may offer direction about which concepts to apply to a given case. In other instances, you may be left to use your judgment in choosing which concepts to focus on in analyzing a case.

3. **Define the basic issues.** This is perhaps the most important step and also the stage of analysis that requires the most wisdom and judgment. Cases are rarely like tidy problem sets where the issues or problems are explicitly stated and the tools needed to address those issues are prescribed. Generally, you need to determine what the key issues are. In doing this, it may help for you to begin by asking: What are the fundamental issues in the case? Which concepts matter most in providing insight into those issues? One trap to avoid in defining basic issues is doing what some decision-making scholars label "plunging-in," which is drawing conclusions without first thinking about the crux of the issues involved in a decision.[i] Many students have a tendency to seize the first issues that are prominently mentioned in a case. As an antidote to this trap, you may want to consider a case from the perspective of different conceptual frames.

4. **Develop and elaborate your analysis of the key issues.** As with all of the steps, there is no substitute for painstaking work in this stage. You need to take the key issues you have defined in Step 3, examine the facts that you have noted in Step 2, and assess what are the key facts. What does quantitative analysis reveal? Here it is not just ratio analysis that we are concerned with. Just as body temperature, blood pressure, and pulse rate may reveal something about a person's health but little about the causes of a sickness, ratio analysis typically tells us more about the health of a company than the causes of its performance. You should assemble facts and analysis to support your point of view. Opinions unsupported by factual evidence and analysis are generally not persuasive. This stage of the analysis involves organizing the facts in the case. You will want to develop specific hypotheses about what factors relate to success in a particular setting. Often, you will find it helpful to draw diagrams to clarify your thinking.

5. **Draw conclusions and formulate a set of recommendations.** You may be uncomfortable in drawing conclusions and making recommendations because you do not have complete information. This is an eternal dilemma for managers. Managers who wait for complete information to do something, however, usually act too late. Nevertheless, you should strive to do the most complete analysis that you can under reasonable time constraints. Recommendations should also flow naturally from your analysis. Too often, students formulate their recommendations in an ad hoc way. In formulating recommendations, you should be clear about priorities and the sequence of actions that you recommend.

6. **Prepare for class discussion.** Students who diligently work through the five steps above and rigorously examine a case should be well prepared for class discussion. You may find it helpful to make some notes and bring them to

---

[i]J. E. Russo and P. J. H. Schoemaker (1989). *Decision Traps: The Ten Barriers to Brilliant Decision-Making and How to Overcome Them.* New York: Fireside.

class. Over the years, we have observed that many of the students who are low contributors to class discussions bring few or no notes to class. Once in class, a case discussion usually begins with a provocative question from the instructor. Many instructors will "cold call"—a question directed to a specific student who has not been forewarned. Students who have thoroughly analyzed and discussed the case before coming to class will be much better prepared for these surprise calls. They will also be better prepared to contribute to the analysis, argument, and persuasion that will take place in the class discussion. Discussions can move rapidly. You will hear new insights from fellow students. Preparation helps you to absorb, learn, and contribute to the insights that emerge from class discussion.

Summary

Students who embark in the case method soon learn that analyzing cases is a complex process. Having a clear conceptual approach like the VRIO framework does not eliminate the complexity. This systematic approach, however, does allow the analyst to manage the complexity of real-world business situations. In the end, though, neither cases nor real-world businesses conclude their analyses with tidy solutions that resolve all the uncertainties and ambiguities a business faces. However, the case method coupled with a good theory like the VRIO approach and hard work do make it more likely that you will generate valuable insights into the strategic challenges of firms and develop the strategic skills needed to lead a firm.

Illustration/
Photo Credits

Illustration for part openers by P.J. Loughran
Illustration for boxed features by Gary Hovland

Glossary

above average accounting performance when a firm's accounting performance is greater than the industry average

above normal economic performance when a firm earns above its cost of capital

absorptive capacity the ability of firms to learn

accounting performance a measure of a firm's competitive advantage calculated by using information from its published profit-and-loss and balance sheet statements

accounting ratios numbers taken from a firm's financial statements that are manipulated in ways that describe various aspects of the firm's performance

acquisition when a firm purchases another firm

acquisition premium the difference between the current market price of a target firm's shares and the price a potential acquirer offers to pay for those shares

activity ratios accounting ratios that focus on the level of activity in a firm's business

ad valorem tariffs where a tariff is calculated as a percentage of the market value of an import, regardless of its weight or volume

adverse selection when an alliance partner promises to bring to an alliance certain resources that it either does not control or cannot acquire

agency problems when parties in an agency relationship differ in their decision-making objectives

agency relationship when one party to an exchange delegates decision-making authority to a second party

agent the party to whom the decision-making authority is delegated

architectural competence the ability of a firm to use organizational structure and other organizing mechanisms to facilitate coordination among scientific disciplines to conduct research

auction a mechanism for establishing the price of an asset, in mergers and acquisitions, when multiple firms bid for a single target firm

audit committee sub-group of the board of directors responsible for ensuring the accuracy of accounting and financial statements

average accounting performance when a firm's accounting performance is equal to the industry average

backward vertical integration when a firm incorporates more stages of the value chain within its boundaries and those stages bring it closer to gaining access to raw materials

barriers to entry attributes of an industry's structure that increase the cost of entry

below average accounting performance when a firm's accounting performance is less than the industry average

below normal economic performance when a firm earns less than its cost of capital

board of directors a group of 10 to 15 individuals drawn from a firm's top management and from people outside the firm, whose primary responsibilities are to monitor decisions made in the firm and ensure that they are consistent with the interests of outside equity holders

business angels wealthy individuals who act as outside investors in a typically entrepreneurial firm

business cycle the alternating pattern of prosperity followed by recession followed by prosperity

business strategy a firm's theory of how to gain competitive advantage in a single business or industry

buyers those who purchase a firm's products or services

capabilities a subset of a firm's resources, defined as tangible and intangible assets that enable a firm to take full advantage of other resources it controls

cashing out the compensation paid to an entrepreneur for risk-taking associated with starting a firm

causally ambiguous Where imitating firms do not understand the relationship between the resources and capabilities controlled by a firm and that firm's competitive advantage

centralized hub where each country in which a firm operates is organized as a full profit-and-loss division headed by a division general manager and where strategic and operational decisions are retained at headquarters

chairman of the board the person that presides over the board of directors; may or may not be the same person as a firm's senior executive

chairman of the board (duties of) supervision of the board of directors in its ratifying and monitoring roles

chief executive officer (CEO) the person to whom all functional managers report in a U-form organization; the person to whom all all divisional personal and corporate staff report to in an M-form organization

chief executive officer (CEO) (duties of) strategy formulation and implementation

chief operating officer (COO) (duties of) strategy implementation

closely held firm a firm that has not sold very many of its shares on the public stock market

co-brand Tying the brand of a product to the brand of another firm's or division's product

collusion when two or more firms in an industry coordinate their strategic choices to reduce competition in that industry

compensation policies the ways that firms pay employees

competitive advantage when a firm creates more economic value than rival firms

competitive disadvantage when a firm generates less economic value than rival firms

competitive dynamics how one firm responds to the strategic actions of competing firms

competitive parity when a firm creates the same economic value as rival firms

competitor any firm, group, or individual trying to reduce a firm's competitive advantage

complementary resources and capabilities resources and capabilities that have limited ability to generate competitive advantage in isolation, but in combination with other resources can enable a firm to realize its full potential for competitive advantage

complementor a firm is a complementor when its customers value its products more when they have this other firm's products than when they have a particular firm's products alone

compound tariffs where both market values and the weight or volume are used in calculating a tariff

conduct refers to the strategies that firms in an industry implement

conglomerate merger a merger or acquisition where there are no vertical, horizontal, product extension, or market extension links between the firms

consolidation strategy strategy that reduces the number of firms in an industry by exploiting economies of scale

controlling share when an acquiring firm purchases enough of a target firm's assets to be able to make all the management and strategic decisions in the target firm

coordinated federation where each country in which a firm operates is organized as a full profit-and-loss division headed by a division general manager and where operational decisions are delegated to these divisions or countries, but strategic decisions are retained at headquarters

core competence the collective learning in an organization, especially how to coordinate diverse production skills and integrate multiple streams of technologies

corporate spin-off exists when a large, typically diversified firm divests itself of a business in which it has historically been operating and the divested business operates as an independent entity

corporate staff provides information about a firm's external and internal environments to the firm's senior executive

corporate strategy a firm's theory of how to gain competitive advantage by operating in several businesses simultaneously

cost centers divisions are assigned a budget and manage their operations to that budget

cost leadership business strategy focuses on gaining advantages by reducing costs below those of competitors

cost of capital the rate of return that a firm promises to pay its suppliers of capital to induce them to invest in a firm

cost of debt equals the interest that a firm must pay its debt holders to induce them to lend money to the firm

cost of equity equals the rate of return a firm must promise to its equity holders to induce them to invest in the firm

crown jewel sale where a bidding firm is interested in just a few of the businesses being operated by the target firm, known as its crown jewels, and the target firm sells these businesses

culture the values, beliefs, and norms that guide behavior in a society and in a firm

cumulative abnormal return (CAR) performance that is greater (or less) than what was expected in a short period of time around when an acquisition is announced

current market value the price of each of a firm's shares times the number of shares outstanding

customer-switching costs exist when customers make investments in order to use a firm's particular products or services and when these investments are not useful in using other firms' products

debt capital from banks and bondholders

decentralized federation where each country in which a firm operates is organized as a full profit-and-loss division headed by a division general manager and where strategic and operational decisions are delegated to these country managers

declining industry an industry that has experienced an absolute decline in unit sales over a sustained period of time

deep pockets model a firm that takes advantage of its monopoly power in one business to subsidize several different businesses

demographics the distribution of individuals in a society in terms of age, sex, marital status, income, ethnicity, and other personal attributes that may determine their buying patterns

depression a severe recession that lasts for several years

direct duplication the attempt to imitate other firms by developing resources that have the same strategic effects as the resources controlled by those other firms

diseconomies of scale when a firm's costs begin to rise as a function of that firm's volume of production

distinctive competence a valuable and rare resource or capability

distribution agreements when one firm agrees to distribute the products of others

diversification economies sources of relatedness in a diversified firm

divestment selling a business with which a firm had been operating

division each business that a firm engages in, also called strategic business units (SBUs) or business group

dominant-business firms firms with between 70 percent and 95 percent of their total sales in a single product market

dominant logic a common way of thinking about strategy across different businesses in a diversified firm

economic climate the overall health of the economic systems within which a firm operates

economic measures of competitive advantage measures that compare a firm's level of return to its cost of capital instead of to the average level of return in the industry

economic value the difference between the perceived benefits gained by a customer that purchases a firm's products or services and the full economic cost of these products or services

economic value added (EVA) calculated by subtracting the cost of the capital employed in a division from that division's earnings

economies of scale when the per unit cost of production falls as the volume of production increases

economies of scope exist in a firm when the value of the products or services it sells increases as a function of the number of different businesses in which that firm operates

emerging industries newly created or newly re-created industries formed by technological innovations, change in demand, or the emergence of new customer needs

emergent strategies theories of how to gain competitive advantage in an industry that emerge over time or have been radically reshaped once they are initially implemented

environmental threat any individual, group, or organization outside a firm that seeks to reduce the level of that firm's performance

equity capital from individuals and institutions that purchase a firm's stocks

equity alliance where cooperating firms supplement contracts with equity holdings in alliance partners

escalation of commitment an increased commitment by managers to an incorrect course of action even as its limitations become manifest

event study analysis a way to evaluate the performance effects of acquisitions for bidding firms

executive committee typically consists of the CEO and two or three functional senior managers

explicit collusion exists when firms directly communicate with each other to coordinate their levels of production, their prices, and so forth (illegal in most countries)

external analysis identification and examination of the critical threats and opportunities in a firm's competitive environment

finance committee sub-group of the board of directors that maintains the relationship between the firm and external capital markets

financial resources include all the money, from whatever source, that firms use to conceive and implement strategies

firm-specific human capital investments investments made by employees in a particular firm over time, including understanding the culture, policies, and procedures, and knowing the people to contact to complete a task, that have limited value in other firms

firm-specific investments when the value of stakeholders' investments in a particular form is much greater than the value those same investments would be in other firms

first-mover advantages advantages that come to firms that make important strategic and technological decisions early in the development of an industry

five forces framework identifies the five most common threats faced by firms in their local competitive environments and the conditions under which these threats are more or less likely to be present

flexibility how costly it is for a firm to alter its strategic and organizational decisions

formal management controls include a firm's budgeting and reporting activities that keep people higher up in a firm's organizational chart informed about the actions taken by people lower down in the organizational chart

formal reporting structure a description of who in the organization reports to whom

forward vertical integration when a firm incorporates more stages of the value chain within its boundaries and those stages bring it closer to interacting directly with final customers

fragmented industries industries in which a large number of small or medium-sized firms operate and no small set of firms has dominant market share or creates dominant technologies

free cash flow the amount of cash a firm has to invest after all positive net present-value investments in its ongoing businesses have been funded

friendly acquisitions when the management of a target firm wants the firm to be acquired

functional manager a manager who leads a particular function within a firm, such as manufacturing, marketing, finance, accounting, or sales

functional organizational structure the structure a firm uses to implement business-level strategies it might pursue where each function in the firm reports to the CEO

general environment broad trends in the context within which a firm operates that can have an impact on a firm's strategic choices

generic business strategies another name for business-level strategies, which are cost leadership and product differentiation

geographic market diversification strategy when a firm operates in multiple geographic markets simultaneously

global opportunities opportunities for a firm to optimize production, distribution, and other business functions throughout the world in all the markets in which it operates

golden parachutes incentive compensation paid to senior managers if the firm they manage is acquired

greenmail a maneuver in which a target firm's management purchases any of the target firm's stock owned by a bidder for a price that is greater than its current market value

harvest when firms engage in a long, systematic, phased withdrawal from a declining industry, extracting as much value as possible

hedonic price that part of the price of a product or service that is attributable to a particular characteristic of that product or service

holdup when one firm makes more transaction-specific investments in an exchange than partner firms make and the firm that has not made these investments tries to exploit the firm that has

horizontal merger when a firm acquires a former competitor

hostile takeovers when the management of a target firm does not want the firm to be acquired

human capital resources the training, experience, judgment, intelligence, relationships, and insight of individual managers and workers in a firm

imperfectly imitable resources and capabilities that are more costly for other firms to imitate, compared to firms that already possess them

increasing returns to scale in network industries, the value of a product or service increases as the number of people using these products or services increases

inelastic in supply where the quantity of supply is fixed and does not respond to price increases, such as the total supply of land, which is relatively fixed and cannot be significantly increased in response to higher demand and prices

industry structure attributes of an industry that determines its competitiveness; measured by such factors as the number of competitors in an industry, the heterogeneity of products in an industry, and the cost of entry and exit in an industry

informal management controls include a firm's culture and the willingness of employees to monitor each others' behavior

initial public offering (IPO) when the stock of a privately held firm, or a division of a corporation, is first sold to the general public

institutional owners pension funds, corporations and others that invest other peoples' money in firm equities

intermediate products or services products or services produced in one division that are used as inputs for products or services produced by a second division

internal analysis identification of a firm's organizational strengths and weaknesses and of the resources and capabilities that are likely to be sources of competitive advantage

invented competencies illusory inventions by creative managers to justify poor diversification moves by linking intangible core competencies to completely unrelated businesses

joint venture where cooperating firms create a legally independent firm in which they invest and from which they share any profits that are created

learning curve a concept which formalizes the relationship between cumulative volumes of production and falling per unit costs

leverage ratios accounting ratios that focus on the level of a firm's financial flexibility

licensing agreements where one firm allows others to use its brand name to sell products in return for some fee or percentage of profits

limited corporate diversification when all or most of a firm's business activities fall within a single industry and geographic market

liquidity ratios accounting ratios that focus on the ability of a firm to meet its short-term financial obligations

management control systems include a range of formal and informal mechanisms to ensure that managers are behaving in ways consistent with a firm's strategies

managerial hubris the unrealistic belief held by managers in bidding firms that they can manage the assets of a target firm more efficiently than the target firm's current management

managerial know-how the often-taken-for-granted knowledge and information that are needed to compete in an industry on a day-to-day basis

managerial perquisites activities that do not add economic value to the firm, but directly benefit the managers who make them

market extension merger where firms make acquisitions in new geographical markets

market for corporate control the market that is created when multiple firms actively seek to acquire one or several firms

market leader the firm with the largest market share in an industry

matrix structures where one employee reports to two or more people

mature industries an industry in which, over time, ways of doing business have become widely understood, technologies have diffused through competitors, and the rate of innovation in new products and technologies drops

merger when the assets of two similar-sized firms are combined

M-form an organizational structure for implementing a corporate diversification strategy, where each business a firm engages in is managed through a separate profit-and-loss division

mission a firm's long-term purpose

mission statement written statement defining both what a firm aspires to be in the long run and what it wants to avoid in the meantime

monopolistically competitive industries where there are large numbers of competing firms and low-cost entry and exit, but products in these industries are not homogeneous with respect to cost or product attributes; firms are said to enjoy a "monopoly" in that part of the market they dominate

monopolistic industries industries that consist of only a single firm

moral hazard where partners in an exchange possess high-quality resources and capabilities of significant value to the exchange but fail to make them available to the other partners

multinational opportunities opportunities for a firm to operate simultaneously in several national or regional markets, but where these operations are independent of each other

multipoint competition when two or more diversified firms simultaneously compete in the same multiple markets

mutual forbearance a form of tacit collusion where firms tacitly agree to not compete in one industry in order to avoid competition in a second industry

network industries industries where single technical standards and increasing returns to scale tend to dominate; competition in these industries tends to focus on which of several competing standards will be chosen

new entrants firms that have either recently begun operations in an industry or that threaten to begin operations in an industry soon

niche strategy when a firm reduces its scope of operations and focuses on narrow segments of a declining industry

nominating committee sub-group of the board of directors that nominates new board members

nonequity alliance where cooperating firms agree to work together to develop, manufacture, or sell products or services, but they do not take equity positions in each other or form an independent organizational unit to manage their cooperative efforts

nontariff trade barriers the establishment of product performance standards that cannot be met by imports, the restriction of access to domestic distribution channels, imposition of local purchasing requirements for government purchases, or implementation of a variety of environmental and labor regulations that foreign firms must meet in order to do business in a country

normal economic performance when a firm earns its cost of capital

objectives specific, measurable targets a firm can use to evaluate the extent to which it is realizing its mission

office of the president together, the roles of chairman of the board, CEO, and COO

oligopolies industries characterized by a small number of competing firms, by homogeneous products, and by costly entry and exit

operational economies of scope shared activities and shared core competencies in a diversified firm

operations committee typically meets monthly and usually consists of the CEO and each of the heads of the functional areas included in the firm

opportunism when a firm is unfairly exploited in an exchange

organizational chart a table that summarizes the formal reporting structure within a firm

organizational resources a firm's formal reporting structure; its formal and informal planning, controlling, and coordinating systems; its culture and reputation; and informal relations among groups within a firm and between a firm and those in its environment

pac man defense fending off an acquisition by a firm acquiring the firm or firms bidding for it

path dependence when events early in the evolution of a process have significant effects on subsequent events

pecuniary economies sources of relatedness in market power between bidding and target firms

perfectly competitive industry when there are large numbers of competing firms, the products being sold are homogeneous with respect to cost and product attributes, and entry and exit are very low cost

personnel and compensation committee sub-group of the board of directors that evaluates and compensates the performance of a firm's senior executive and other senior managers

physical resources all the physical technology used in a firm

poison pills a variety of actions that target firm managers can take to make the acquisition of the target prohibitively expensive

policy choices choices firms make about the kinds of products or services they will sell—choices that have an impact on relative cost and product differentiation position

policy of experimentation exists when firms are committed to engage in several related product differentiation efforts simultaneously

predatory pricing setting prices so that they are less than a business's costs

price takers where the price of the products or services a firm sells is determined by market conditions and not by the decisions of firms

principal the party who delegates the decision-making authority

privately held a firm that has stock that is not traded on public stock markets and is not a division of a larger company

processes the activities a firm engages in to design, produce, and sell its products or services

process innovation a firm's effort to refine and improve its current processes

process manufacturing when manufacturing is accomplished in a continuous system; examples include manufacturing in chemical, oil refining, and paper and pulp industries

product differentiation a business strategy whereby firms attempt to gain a competitive advantage by increasing the perceived value of their products or services relative to the perceived value of other firms' products or services

product diversification strategy when a firm operates in multiple industries simultaneously

product extension merger where firms acquire complementary products through their merger and acquisition activities

productive inputs any supplies used by a firm in conducting its business activities, such as labor, capital, land, and raw materials, among other things

product-market diversification strategy when a firm implements both product and geographic market diversification simultaneously

profitability ratios accounting ratios with some measure of profit in the numerator and some measure of firm size or assets in the denominator

profit-and-loss centers where profits and losses are calculated at the level of the division in a firm

proprietary technology secret or patented technology that gives incumbent firms important advantages over potential entrants

Question of Imitability "Do firms without a resource or capability face a cost disadvantage in obtaining or developing it compared to firms that already possess it?"

Question of Organization "Is a firm organized to exploit the full competitive potential of its resources and capabilities?"

Question of Rarity "How many competing firms already possess particular valuable resources and capabilities?"

Question of Value "Does a resource enable a firm to exploit an external opportunity or neutralize an external threat?"

quotas a numerical limit on the number of particular items that are allowed to be imported into a country

real options investments in real assets that create the opportunity for additional investments in the future

recession a period of relatively low prosperity, when demand for goods and services is low and unemployment is high

related-constrained diversification a strategy wherein all the businesses in which a firm operates share a significant number of inputs, product technologies, distribution channels, similar customers, and so forth

related corporate diversification when less than 70 percent of a firm's revenue comes from a single product market and its multiple lines of business are linked

related-linked a strategy wherein the different businesses that a single firm pursues are linked on only a couple of dimensions, or where different sets of businesses are linked along very different dimensions

reputation beliefs customers hold about a firm

Resource-based View (RBV) a model of firm performance that focuses on the resources and capabilities controlled by a firm as sources of competitive advantage

resource heterogeneity implies that for a given business activity, some firms may be more skilled in accomplishing this activity than other firms

resource immobility resources controlled by some firms may not diffuse to other firms

resources the tangible and intangible assets that a firm controls, which it can use to conceive of and implement its strategies

retained earnings capital generated from a firm's ongoing operations and retained by a firm

rivalry the intensity of competition among a firm's direct competitors

seemingly unrelated diversified diversified firms that are exploiting core competencies as an economy of scope, but are not doing so with any shared activities

senior executive the president or CEO of a firm

shakeout period exists when total supply in an industry is reduced by bankruptcies, acquisitions, and business closings

shared activities potential sources of operational economies of scope for diversified firms

shark repellents a variety of relatively minor corporate governance changes that, in principle, are supposed to make it somewhat more difficult to acquire a target firm

single-business firms firms with greater than 95 percent of their total sales in a single product market

"Skunk Works" temporary teams whose creative efforts are intensive and focused

socially complex resorces and capabilities that involve interpersonal, social, or cultural links among individuals

social welfare the overall good of society

specific tariffs where a tariff is calculated as a percentage of the weight or volume of the goods being imported, regardless of their market value

stakeholders all groups and individuals who have an interest in how a firm performs

standstill agreements a contract between a target and a bidding firm wherein the bidding firm agrees not to attempt to take over the target for some period of time

stock grants payments to employees in a firm's stock

stock options where employees are given the right but not the obligation to purchase stock at predetermined prices

strategic alliance   exists whenever two or more independent organizations cooperate in the development, manufacture, or sale of products or services

strategic management process   a sequential set of analyses that can increase the likelihood of a firm's choosing a strategy that generates competitive advantages

strategy   a firm's theory about how to gain competitive advantage

strategy implementation   occurs when a firm adopts organizational policies and practices that are consistent with its strategy

strengths   valuable resources and capabilities

structure-conduct-performance model (S-C-P)   theory which suggests that industry structure determines a firm's conduct which in turn determines its performance

substitutes   products or services that meet approximately the same customer needs but do so in different ways

substitution   developing or acquiring strategically equivalent, but different resources as a competing firm

supermajority voting rules   an example of a shark repellent that specifies that more than 50 percent of the target firm's board of directors must approve a takeover

suppliers   those who make a wide variety of raw materials, labor, and other critical assets available to firms

supply agreements   where one firm agrees to supply others

sustainable distinctive competencies   valuable, rare, and costly to imitate resources or capabilities

sustained competitive advantage   a competitive advantage that lasts for a long period of time; an advantage that is not competed away through strategic imitation

tacit collusion   exists when firms coordinate their production and pricing decisions, not by directly communicating with each other, but by exchanging signals with other firms about their intent to cooperate; special case of tacit cooperation

tacit cooperation   actions a firm takes that have the effect of reducing the level of rivalry in an industry and that do not require firms in an industry to directly communicate or negotiate with each other

tactics   the specific actions a firm takes to implement its strategies

tariffs   taxes levied on goods or services imported into a country

tax haven   a country that charges little or no corporate tax

technical economies   sources of relatedness in marketing, production, and similar activities between bidding and target firms

technological hardware   the machines and other hardware used by firms

technological leadership strategy   when firms make early investments in particular technologies in an industry

technological software   the quality of labor–management relations, an organization's culture, and the quality of managerial controls in a firm

temporary competitive advantage   a competitive advantage that lasts for a short period of time

temporary cross-divisional and cross-functional teams   groups of individuals from different businesses and different functional areas who are brought together to cooperate on a particular new product or service

tender offer   when a bidding firm offers to purchase the shares of a target firm directly by offering a higher than market price for those shares to current shareholders

thinly traded market   a market where there are only a small number of buyers and sellers, where information about opportunities in this market is not widely known, and where interests besides purely maximizing the value of a firm can be important

transaction specific investment   when the value of an investment in its first-best use is much greater than its value in its second-best use; any investment in an exchange that has significantly more value in the current exchange than it does in alternative exchanges

transfer price   the price that one part of a diversified firm charges another part of the firm for intermediate products or services

transnational opportunity   where firms treat their global operations as an integrated network of distributed and interdependent resources and capabilities

transnational structure   where each country in which a firm operates is organized as a full profit-and-loss division headed by a division general manager and where strategic and operational decisions are delegated to operational entities that maximize local responsiveness and international integration

U-form structure   organization where different functional heads report directly to CEO; used to implement business level strategies

uncertainty   when the future value of an exchange cannot be known when investments in that exchange are being made

unfriendly acquisition   when the management of the target firm does not want the firm to be acquired

unrelated corporate diversification   where less than 70 percent of a firm's revenues is generated in a single product market, and when a firm's businesses share few, if any, common attributes

value added as a percentage of sales   measures that percentage of a firm's sales that is generated by activities done within the boundaries of a firm; a measure of vertical integration

value chain   that set of activities that must be accomplished to bring a product or service from raw materials to the point that it can be sold to a final customer

venture capital firms   outside investment funds looking to invest in entrepreneurial ventures

vertical integration   the number of steps in the value chain that a firm accomplishes within its boundaries

vertical merger when a firm vertically integrates, either forward or backward, through its acquisition efforts

visionary firms firms whose mission is central to all they do

VRIO framework four questions that must be asked about a resource or capability to determine its competitive potential

weaknesses resources and capabilities that are not valuable

weighted average cost of capital (WACC) the percentage of a firm's total capital that is debt times the cost of debt plus the percentage of a firm's total capital that is equity times the cost of equity

white knight another bidding firm that agrees to acquire a particular target in place of the original bidding firm

zero-based budgeting where corporate executives create a list of all capital allocation requests from divisions in a firm, rank them from most important to least important, and then fund all the projects the firm can afford, given the amount of capital it has available

Company Index

Name Index

Subject Index